ISAIAH BERLIN

BUILDING

LETTERS 1960–1975

Edited by Henry Hardy and Mark Pottle

Additional research · Brigid Allen, Victoria Benner, James Chappel,
Georgina Edwards, Hugh Eveleigh, Jason Ferrell, Steffen Groß, Nicholas Hall,
Serena Moore, Eleonora Paganini, Teisha Ruggiero, Patrick Wise-Walsh

Archival Research · Michael Hughes

Consultant Russianists · Tatiana Pozdnyakova, Josephine von Zitzewitz

Consultant Hebraist · Norman Solomon

Transcription · Betty Colquhoun, Esther Johnson

[D]reary people occasionally turn up useful facts and contribute to learning in all kinds of ways in which the more imaginative are too impatient
to do.

IB to Dan Davin, 24 April 1968

★

For more information on Isaiah Berlin visit
⟨http://berlin.wolf.ox.ac.uk/⟩

BUILDING

LETTERS 1960–1975

———

ISAIAH BERLIN

Edited by Henry Hardy and Mark Pottle

Chatto & Windus

London

Published by Chatto & Windus 2013

2 4 6 8 10 9 7 5 3 1

First published in Great Britain in 2013 by
Chatto & Windus
Random House, 20 Vauxhall Bridge Road,
LONDON SWIV 2SA
www.vintage-books.co.uk

Addresses for companies within The Random House Group Limited
can be found at: www.randomhouse.co.uk/offices.htm

The Random House Group Limited Reg. No. 954009

A CIP catalogue record for this book
is available from the British Library

ISBN 9780701185763

Designed in the Department of Typography & Graphic Communication,
University of Reading

Typeset by Deltatype Ltd, Birkenhead, Merseyside
Printed and bound in Great Britain by CPI Group (UK) Ltd
CROYDON, CRO 4YY

In memory of Jean Floud

1915–2013

The history of education – as opposed to the theory of it – is one of the most fascinating subjects in the world. The theory of education ... But I must not go on.

IB to Yigal Allon, 7 June 1972

Discretion is a great public virtue, but destructive of personality to a degree, it seems to me.

IB to Hamilton Fish Armstrong, 4 December 1969

Burn this letter at once: even though my letters are not likely to be scrutinised by faithful archivists, it is undesirable to leave libellous documents of this kind about.

IB to Meyer Weisgal, 21 September 1961

[E]verything must be published – small and great, black and white, embarrassing and ennobling [...].

IB to Samuel and Miriam Sambursky, 2 December 1968

CONTENTS

ILLUSTRATIONS

The subject is IB where not otherwise stated

1 The editors will be grateful to be notified of any identifications additional to those on p. xii. For a larger version of this plate see ⟨http://berlin.wolf.ox.ac.uk/studydoorbig.jpg⟩.

SECOND PLATE SECTION

CREDITS

Credits name as many as are known to the editors of the following: photographer
(or scanner)/agent/copyright owner/owner of original

Illustrations in the text (listed by page)

Plates

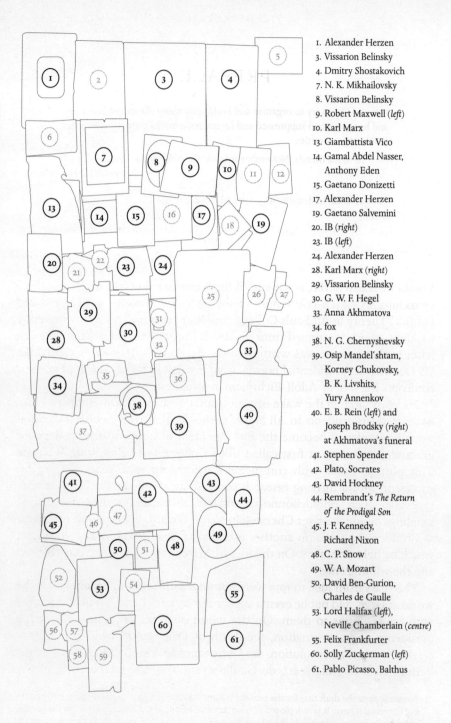

1. Alexander Herzen
3. Vissarion Belinsky
4. Dmitry Shostakovich
7. N. K. Mikhailovsky
8. Vissarion Belinsky
9. Robert Maxwell (*left*)
10. Karl Marx
13. Giambattista Vico
14. Gamal Abdel Nasser,
    Anthony Eden
15. Gaetano Donizetti
17. Alexander Herzen
19. Gaetano Salvemini
20. IB (*right*)
23. IB (*left*)
24. Alexander Herzen
28. Karl Marx (*right*)
29. Vissarion Belinsky
30. G. W. F. Hegel
33. Anna Akhmatova
34. fox
38. N. G. Chernyshevsky
39. Osip Mandel'shtam,
    Korney Chukovsky,
    B. K. Livshits,
    Yury Annenkov
40. E. B. Rein (*left*) and
    Joseph Brodsky (*right*)
    at Akhmatova's funeral
41. Stephen Spender
42. Plato, Socrates
43. David Hockney
44. Rembrandt's *The Return
    of the Prodigal Son*
45. J. F. Kennedy,
    Richard Nixon
48. C. P. Snow
49. W. A. Mozart
50. David Ben-Gurion,
    Charles de Gaulle
53. Lord Halifax (*left*),
    Neville Chamberlain (*centre*)
55. Felix Frankfurter
60. Solly Zuckerman (*left*)
61. Pablo Picasso, Balthus

Heroes and villains on IB's study door: key to Plate 1

PREFACE

I should like to try to organise and build something sometime in my life, and have a certain suppressed and secret desire to do good, to which this would give an outlet.

IB to his friends, November 1953, on the offer of the Wardenship of
Nuffield College

I am as usual in despair: *why* can't I be *concise*? Too late, alas! too old to mend.

To Pat Utechin, 22 August 1974

I

WE LEFT Isaiah Berlin, at the end of the previous volume of his letters, three years into his eleven-year tenure of the Oxford Professorship of Social and Political Theory at All Souls College, and four years into his happy marriage to Aline, which continued until his death thirty-seven years later. The last letter in that volume was written on the day John F. Kennedy accepted the US Democratic presidential nomination; the first letter of this third volume confronts the trial of Adolf Eichmann in Jerusalem.

Six years later, in the wake of notoriously unsuccessful attempts to introduce graduate students to All Souls, Berlin decides to relinquish his professorship in order to become the first President of a new Oxford college for graduate students – at first called Iffley College, but before long Wolfson. This post he holds with conspicuous success for nine years, leaving his successor with a thriving research community, imbued with his own idiosyncratic, open, unhidebound personality, in a distinguished new set of buildings beside the river Cherwell in North Oxford. In his penultimate year as President he takes on another presidency,[1] that of the British Academy, which he held until 1978. On the Ides of March 1975 he retires from Wolfson and the volume ends.

The years from 1960 to 1975 were not uneventful ones in Britain and in the world at large, and public events appear throughout Berlin's letters, together with his reactions to them. On the world stage we encounter Kennedy's presidency and assassination, the death of Dag Hammarskjöld in a plane crash, the Algerian revolution, the Cuban missile crisis (at the start of which Berlin had a ringside seat), de Gaulle's vetoes of UK membership of the

---

1 For some time the draft title for the present volume was *Presiding*, an idea still sufficiently tempting to record it here. It is redeployed as a section title below, as is a discarded title for the second volume, *Professing*. Admittedly the letters from this first period are about almost anything rather than IB's conduct of his chair, but the post was his formal position, his anchor in Oxford, attached to which he wrote as he did.

EEC, Leonid Brezhnev's succession to Nikita Khrushchev in Moscow, the assassination of another Kennedy, the six-day Arab–Israeli war, the crushing of Alexander Dubček's 'Prague Spring', Richard M. Nixon's tenure of and resignation from the US presidency, Yassir Arafat's leadership of the PLO, and the long agony of the Vietnam War. In the UK the sexual revolution is epitomised by the *Lady Chatterley* trial, Macmillan sacks seven members of his cabinet in 'the night of the long knives', Hugh Gaiskell's premature death rocks the Labour Party, John Profumo resigns over his affair with Christine Keeler, the Franks Report ushers reform into Oxford (in the teeth of resistance, especially from All Souls), a South African cricket tour is cancelled because of apartheid, it is revealed that the CIA has been funding *Encounter* magazine (leading to Stephen Spender's resignation as an editor), Britain joins the Common Market, Oxford undergraduate men's colleges begin admitting women, and Margaret Thatcher becomes Tory leader.

Much happens during this period in Berlin's own life too. Now thoroughly established as a public intellectual and a historian of ideas, and despite epic delays and prevarications, he publishes some of his most important work, including a long introductory reply to his critics for the book he regarded as his most important, *Four Essays on Liberty*; major studies of the ideas of Giambattista Vico and J. G. Herder; an attack on the scientific view of history; defences of the discipline of political theory and of the claim that knowledge does not always liberate; and essays on, among other topics, Leo Tolstoy, Chaim Weizmann, L. B. Namier, Alexander Herzen, Giuseppe Verdi, the Russian intelligentsia, Benjamin Disraeli and Karl Marx, Maurice Bowra, Georges Sorel, Niccolò Machiavelli, Ivan Turgenev, Zionist politics in wartime Washington, nationalism, J. L. Austin and Oxford philosophy, Israel's twenty-fifth anniversary, the divorce between the sciences and the humanities, and romanticism. He continues to give talks on the BBC Third Programme (renamed Radio 3 in 1970), and also appears on television and in a documentary film. He is on the board of Covent Garden, and is appointed to the Order of Merit and the Presidency of the Aristotelian Society. He receives ten honorary doctorates. He spends many months in the US on a number of occasions, as a visiting professor at Harvard, CUNY and Princeton, as an assessor for the Harkness Foundation in Pasadena, and to visit friends; he attends conferences in Geneva, Nicosia and Venice, and travels to Israel for music festivals and meetings of the governors of the Hebrew University of Jerusalem; he lectures at Harvard, in Chicago, Kentucky, New York, Princeton, St Andrews, Stanford, Toronto, Venice, Washington, DC (the famous Mellon Lectures on romanticism), and the University of Washington; he spends Italian summers in Portofino and Paraggi (where he and his wife build a house), and holidays at Abano Terme spa and in the Aegean, Barbados, India, Iran, Paris, Nice and Switzerland.

All the time, as always, there is a constant stream of gossip, reflection and commentary, ironic humour and warm personal feeling. He writes about an enormous range of topics to a sometimes dazzling cast of prominent figures in many parts of the world. He explains his ideas and reacts to the people and places he encounters on his travels. The social and intellectual comedy once more finds its perfect observer and narrator, even when serious events are afoot. He displays his own personality in all its inspiring and maddening complexity. If this is not one of the best letter-writers of the twentieth century, we are ready to eat our respective hats.

II

> I stuff all letters into huge sacks and they disappear into my mother's house in Hampstead and I haven't looked at a single one of them since – I once plunged my hand into some past letters, and it was so appalling – I was reminded of so much that was no longer the case – warm friendships now in limbo, past rows, long healed but with a certain capacity for, if not re-opening, at any rate touching on ancient wounds, etc. – that I have never done it again.
>
> IB to Cyril Connolly, 18 May 1972

> [T]he true portrait can only be restored, warts and all, if everything is published in full so that the critics cannot say that unfavourable details have been edited out. As for what kind of image [...] emerges, that is immaterial: even if his old friends are embarrassed by this or that, the truth and history will profit.
>
> To Rinna Samuel, 12 August 1969

The letters included in this volume are a far smaller proportion of those available than before, simply because many more letters have survived from the period it covers. Well under a quarter of the letters that have been transcribed are here, and the transcribed letters are in turn only a smallish portion of the extant corpus. Much of the omitted matter is of the highest quality. This gives the volume a somewhat different character from its predecessors, and it should be stressed that those who seek a full picture of Berlin's correspondence will need to read the letters, and parts of letters, that have been excluded. In due course it is intended to publish much, at any rate, of the missing material in the Isaiah Berlin Virtual Library, ⟨http://berlin.wolf .ox.ac.uk/⟩, the official website of the Isaiah Berlin Literary Trust.

Nevertheless, we hope we have provided a selection that is more than a taster for the whole, and respects the spirit of the second epigraph to this section, even though this cannot be followed literally. Inevitably our personal interests and biases have influenced our choice, but we have tried to include the best material about the most interesting and important topics, as well as the letters that display Berlin's epistolary personality at its most engaging. As before, cuts have been made within letters in order to create space for (extracts from) a wider range of material, but without, we hope, sacrificing clarity or continuity. In other respects, too, our principles of selection have been essentially the same as those explained in *Enlightening*, though more severely enforced because of the greater bulk of available material; also, because the period covered here is more recent, we have felt obliged (and in rare instances compelled) to omit material in deference to the sensitivities of individuals still living. But we have as before not censored passages that might be thought to show the author in an unfavourable light.

The most important change in this volume concerns one particular correspondent. Berlin's widow Aline Berlin, to our delight, has decided to allow us to include our selection from her own letters from Berlin, which was not done in the previous volume. This is an enormous gain, and we are exceedingly grateful to Lady Berlin for her bold generosity. Most of these letters date from Berlin's first lengthy post-marital separation from his wife, as a visiting professor at Harvard in 1962, and they are entirely *sui generis* in their passionate intensity – combined, as always, with plenty of social gossip. They show a crucial side of Berlin not often otherwise on display, and reflect his frequently stated enthusiasm for the 'irrational' institution of marriage. This enthusiasm, it should be added, extended to the new family he acquired through his marriage. His letters to Aline's three sons show him as an affectionate stepfather who took great pains with her children.

As before, the production of this volume has been very much a team effort, and would not have been possible, at any rate before more years had passed, without the team of helpers of various kinds on whom we have had the good fortune to rely. The other Trustees of the Isaiah Berlin Literary Trust, Aline Berlin, Peter Halban, Alan Ryan, Jon Stallworthy and Patricia Williams, have nobly read and commented on draft material and offered support and advice at key moments. Michael Brock, sometime Vice-President and Bursar of Wolfson, has put his unrivalled personal knowledge of the College's history, and of Oxford University more generally, unstintingly at our disposal, and his wife Eleanor has also given us the benefit of her personal memories of early Wolfson, and of IB. We have built on the past work of researchers, transcribers, cataloguers and administrators – principally Brigid Allen, Victoria Benner, James Chappel, Betty Colquhoun, Jason Ferrell, Steffen Groß, Serena Moore, Eleonora Paganini, Teisha Ruggiero and Michael Hughes. In the office Hugh Eveleigh, Patrick Wise-Walsh, Georgina Edwards and Nick Hall have shouldered the burden of tasks often more rewarding in the outcome than in the execution. Esther Johnson has continued to transcribe reams of letters with never a squeak of complaint; Josephine von Zitzewitz and Tatiana Pozdnyakova have withstood a barrage of pedantic enquiries about Russian translation and Russian sources respectively; Nigel Rees has generously helped with elusive quotations; our textual designer Paul Luna has once again put his peerless typographical instincts at our disposal, and our typesetter Peter Boswell of Deltatype has performed the complex task of giving them physical form. Jennifer Holmes kindly saved us from a number of errors, some of them egregious.

We warmly thank our publishers and their freelancers for their forbearance in the face of misbehaviour we are too embarrassed to particularise. We have been most aware of patient help from Becky Hardie, Rowena Skelton-Wallace, Nicky Nevin, Neil Bradford and Kris Potter, but there are no doubt other unsung heroes behind the scenes; Anthony Hippisley read the proofs with a frighteningly eagle eye, especially where matter in Russian is concerned; Vicki Robinson cheerfully made a demanding index in the teeth of a deadline made more fierce by our own delinquencies.

We have been helped on individual points by Karen Abramson, Norma Aubertin-Potter, Shlomo Avineri, Simon Bailey, Joshua L. Cherniss, Richard Davies, Jeremy Drew, Robert Evans, Jean Floud, Simon Green, Samuel Guttenplan, Simon Head, William J. vanden Heuvel, Leofranc Holford-Strevens, Enrique Krauze, David Langslow, Javier Lara Bayón, Kevin Lewis, John Ledingham, Fergus Millar, Peter Oppenheimer, Stephen Plotkin, Beata Polanowska-Sygulska, James Randall, Robert Silvers, Adam Sisman, Karen Syrett, Jennifer Thorp, Clare Woodcock and Cecil Woolf; and by many others, especially archivists, librarians and other institutional officers, too numerous to list here exhaustively, who have often gone well beyond the call of duty in answering our enquiries. Last but not least, Mary Merry has provided the similarly alliteratively named editor with miraculous personal support.

A thankfully small minority of archivists, copyright owners and literary executors are less than helpful, to say the least, and we have had some diverting (in both senses) dealings with unresponsive and/or uncooperative persons in a position, and disposed, to obstruct our search for letters and information. When material in an archive is not made readily available to bona fide researchers, it is difficult (unless there are good reasons for an embargo, as indeed there sometimes are) to understand why it is held there. Discretion draws a veil over the details.

Finally we make so bold as to say that we have made a positive and productive duo, and should like to thank each other for help and support through various vicissitudes whose story must wait to be told till another day, if then.

HENRY HARDY
MARK POTTLE[1]

---

1 Mark Christopher Pottle (b. 1959), historian, teacher and editor; Fellow of Wolfson 1992–9 and from 2011; principal editor of the diaries and letters of Violet Bonham Carter; co-editor of a number of original First World War documents; Research Associate, *Oxford Dictionary of National Biography*, 2000–2. For Henry Hardy see p. 523, note 2.

CONVENTIONS AND ABBREVIATIONS

The format of the names, addresses and dates in the letter-headings has been standardised, and the most common addresses abbreviated as follows:

All Souls	All Souls College, Oxford
CUNY	City University of New York
Hollycroft Avenue	49 Hollycroft Avenue, London NW3
Headington House	Headington House, Old High Street, Headington, Oxford
Paraggi	500 Scalini, Paraggi, Santa Margherita Ligure, Italy
Princeton	Institute for Advanced Study, Princeton University
Wolfson	Wolfson College, Oxford

All Oxford colleges except New College and Exeter College are referred to in the notes without the word 'College' (Christ Church in any case not being known as 'Christ Church College'). 'CCC' and 'Corpus' are both Corpus Christi College and 'Univ.' is University College. All colleges mentioned are in Oxford unless otherwise stated, and Universities are in general referred to without including the word 'University' (so 'Cambridge', 'Columbia', 'Exeter', 'London' etc.), unless the context does not make clear that a university is in question. Information in the form 'Balliol classics 1929–33' indicates that the person concerned was an undergraduate at that Oxford college reading that subject during that period.

Knighthoods are in general indicated by the date and rank of the earliest entitlement to be addressed as 'Sir' (e.g. 'KCMG 1949'), and any subsequent upgrades (e.g. 'KCB 1953, GCMG 1955, GCB 1960') are omitted. Plain 'Kt' means Knight Bachelor, the bottom rung of the ladder of knighthood. Life peers are referred to as such rather than by their longer specific titles (e.g. 'life peer 1976' not 'Baron Bullock of Leafield 1976').

Page references are not introduced with 'p.' or 'pp.' when the context makes it obvious that that is what they are. Cross references of the form '(256/6)' mean 'see page 256, note 6'.

Originals are typed unless said to be in manuscript. The location of these originals is provided as part of the index of correspondents. Where we have used carbon copies (mostly those retained by Berlin's secretaries), this is stated: Berlin often amended top copies, and we should be grateful to be made aware of the whereabouts of top copies of any letters, whether or not included here. Signatures have been added (in square brackets) to letters of which we have seen only carbons.

People and other subjects requiring a gloss are in general footnoted when they are first referred to, but not otherwise. The index will quickly locate this introductory note (its page reference being given in italics) if it is needed to elucidate a later reference. Recipients of letters are referred to by their initials in notes to letters received by them.

We have endeavoured to provide biographical information for all persons whose names appear in the text, except those mentioned very briefly in passing; in the few cases in which the note is not to be found at the first mention of the individual in question, a forward cross reference is given; on occasion we have been unable to identify an individual, but we have not thought it necessary to add a note to that effect.

Listed below are people referred to more than once without a surname (given in the text in square brackets for single surnameless references). The incomplete versions of their names in the left-hand column are not annotated unless they are used for the earliest reference to their bearers; rather, these names can be assumed to refer to the individuals in the right-hand column unless otherwise stated, or the context makes clear that someone else is meant. Many but not all of these individuals, together with other important or frequently mentioned people, are subjects of the entries in the biographical glossary that precedes the indexes. These people are glossed only briefly on their first occurrence, and on that occasion an asterisk before the surname indicates that an entry is to be found in the glossary, thus: 'Isaiah *Berlin'.

Adam	Adam von Trott
Aline	Aline Halban, later Berlin
Arthur	Arthur M. Schlesinger, Jr
Avis	Avis Bohlen
BB	Bernard Berenson
BG/B.G.	David Ben-Gurion
Bob	Robert B. Silvers
Cal	Robert Lowell
Cecilia	Cecilia Dick
Chip	Charles Bohlen
David	David Webster
Diana	Diana Cooper/Hopkinson/Menuhin/Trilling
Douglas	Douglas Jay
DW/D.W.	David Webster
Dwight	Dwight Macdonald
Edmund	Edmund Wilson
Felix	Felix Frankfurter
Freddie	A. J. Ayer
Garrett	Garrett Drogheda
George	George Harewood
Gilbert	Gilbert Ryle
Goronwy	Goronwy Rees
Herbert	H. L. A. Hart
Ida	Ida Samunov
(Sir) Isaac	Sir Isaac Wolfson
Jack	Jack Donaldson

Jacob	Jacob Rothschild
Jenifer	Jenifer Hart
Joe	Joseph Alsop
John	John Sparrow
Kay	Katharine Graham
Leonard	Leonard Wolfson
Mac	McGeorge Bundy
Marietta	Marietta Tree
Marion	Marion Frankfurter
Maurice	Maurice Bowra
Meyer	Meyer Schapiro
Nicolas	Nicolas Nabokov
Nicky	Nicky Mariano
Nin	Nin Ryan
Noel	Noel Annan
Noam	Noam Chomsky
Oliver	Oliver Franks
Peter	Peter Halban
Phil	Philip Graham
Philip(pe)	Philippe Halban
Rai(mund)	Raimund von Hofmannsthal
Renée	Renée Ayer, later Hampshire
Richard	Richard Wollheim
Ronnie	Ronald Tree
Rowland	Rowland Burdon-Muller
Roy	Roy Harrod
Solly	Solly Zuckerman
Stephen	Stephen Spender
Stuart	Stuart Hampshire
Susan Mary	Susan Mary Alsop
Sylvester	Sylvester Gates
Walter	Walter Legge
Wystan	W. H. Auden

A list of other abbreviations follows. For publication details of books listed see ⟨http://berlin.wolf.ox.ac.uk/lists/books/index.html⟩.

⟨ ⟩   enclose (*a*) substantial manuscript additions to typed items made by IB (or by secretaries in carbons), but not most small MS corrections; (*b*) URLs, accessed on 31 October 2012, but subject to change[1]

---

1 The editors will be grateful to be notified of any changes to these URLs, and of other updatings and corrections, all of which will be posted at ⟨http://berlin .wolf.ox.ac.uk/published_works/b/corrections.html⟩ before being incorporated in future impressions. Please write to *henry.hardy@wolfson.ox.ac.uk*.

{ }	encloses matter mistakenly present in manuscript
[?]	uncertain transcription of preceding word, or (if preceded by space) illegible word
[ ]	gap in carbon typescript where typist could not interpret IB's dictation
[…]	text omitted by editors (an ellipsis to the right of a signature indicates an omitted PS)
AC	IB, *Against the Current*
AD [numeral]	Anno Domini ('in the year of the Lord', i.e. the stated number of years after the conventional year of birth of Jesus of Nazareth); numerically equivalent to CE
b.	born
[numeral] BCE	the stated number of years before the Common Era; numerically equivalent to BC (before Christ)
the Berlins	Aline and Isaiah Berlin
BI	*The Book of Isaiah: Personal Impressions of Isaiah Berlin*, ed. Henry Hardy (Woodbridge, 2009)
Bt	Baronet
CC	IB, *Concepts and Categories*
CCC	Corpus Christi College, Oxford
[numeral] CE	the stated number of years after the beginning of the Common Era; numerically equivalent to AD
CIA	Central Intelligence Agency
Co.	(Irish) County
Corpus	Corpus Christi College, Oxford
CTH	IB, *The Crooked Timber of Humanity*
CUNY	The City University of New York
d.	died
DBE	Dame Commander of the Order of the British Empire
DCL	Doctor of Civil Law
Dept	Department
ed.	edition / edited by
eds	editions / edited by (more than one editor)
EEC	European Economic Community ('Common Market')
FBA	Fellow of the British Academy
FIB	IB, *Freedom and Its Betrayal*
FDR	Franklin Delano Roosevelt
FO	Foreign Office (London)
GDR	German Democratic Republic (East Germany)
Hon.	Honorary
HM(G)	Her Majesty('s Government)
HUJ	The Hebrew University of Jerusalem
IB	Isaiah Berlin
[IB p.p.]	signed for IB *per pro.* (by the agency of) a secretary

the IBVL	The Isaiah Berlin Virtual Library, website at ⟨http://berlin.wolf. ox.ac.uk/⟩
IDF	Israel Defense Forces
Jr	Junior
Kt	Knight
L	IB, *Liberty*
L1	The first volume (1928–46) of this edition of IB's letters
L2	The second volume (1946–60) of the same
LMH	Lady Margaret Hall (Oxford undergraduate college)
LRB	*London Review of Books*
LSE	London School of Economics (and Political Science)
MC	Military Cross
Met	New York Metropolitan Opera
MI	Michael Ignatieff, *Isaiah Berlin: A Life* (London, 1998)
MIT	Massachusetts Institute of Technology
MI Tape	recording of interview by Michael Ignatieff (interviews conducted 1988–97)
MP	Member of Parliament
MSB	Oxford, Bodleian Library, MS. Berlin, followed by specific shelfmark and folio(s), e.g. MSB 232/1–3 = MS. Berlin 232, fos 1–3
NATO	North Atlantic Treaty Organization
NY	New York
NYRB	*New York Review of Books*
NYT	*New York Times*
NYU	New York University
ODNB	*Oxford Dictionary of National Biography*
OM	Order of Merit
OUA	Oxford University Archives
PEN	(international association of) Poets, Playwrights, Editors, Essayists and Novelists
PhD	Philosophiae Doctor (Doctor of Philosophy)
PI; PI2	IB, *Personal Impressions*; 2nd ed.
PPE	Philosophy, Politics and Economics (Oxford undergraduate course)
PPS	Parliamentary Private Secretary
PRC	People's Republic of China
PS	postscript/Private Secretary
PSM	IB, *The Proper Study of Mankind*
RAMC	Royal Army Medical Corps
RAFVR	Royal Air Force Volunteer Reserve
repr.	reprinted
ROH	Royal Opera House, Covent Garden, London
RT; RT2	IB, *Russian Thinkers*; 2nd ed.
SEATO/Seato	Southeast Asia Treaty Organization

SM	IB, *The Soviet Mind*
SOE	Special Operations Executive
Sr	Senior
SR	IB, *The Sense of Reality*
SS	Schutzstaffel ('Defence Corps' of the Nazi Party)
SSEES	School of Slavonic and East European Studies (UCL)
[Sub]committee	Opera Subcommittee, ROH
TD	Teachta Dála (Irish MP)
TCE	IB, *Three Critics of the Enlightenment: Vico, Hamann, Herder*
Times	*The Times* (London)
TLS	*The Times Literary Supplement*
trans.	translated by
TV	television
UCL	University College London
UCLA	University of California, Los Angeles
UGC	University Grants Committee
UK	United Kingdom (of Great Britain and Northern Ireland)
UN	United Nations
Univ.	University College, Oxford
US	United States (of America)
USSR	Union of Soviet Socialist Republics
WEA	Workers' Educational Association

PROFESSING

The chair of social and political theory (continued)

1960–1965

I am trying to write lectures, I am reading nothing, and am in a state of total bureaucratic life. It is very depressing to be a professor even here, where there is less bureaucracy than in the USSR or the USA.

IB to Martin Malia, 10 December 1960

But what with lectures to be delivered here, papers to be read, doctorate theses to be examined and all the other appalling routine of professors (which according to Freddie Ayer is three times as heavy at Oxford as in London), I do not wish to mislead you or myself about my likelihood of fulfilling my promise.

IB to Peter Calvocoressi, 13 January 1961

There is an Anglo-Saxon academic world quite different from the Latin one, where all the professors are judged by their intellectual eminence or political views, but *never*, never in terms of relations with students, which hardly exist; they are so remote, impersonal and grand. Perhaps it is because there is so much talk in our universities, especially Oxford and Cambridge, that people publish too little.

IB to Richard Crossman, 6 March 1963

On 23 May 1960 the Prime Minister of Israel, David Ben-Gurion,[1] announced in the Israeli parliament, the Knesset, that Adolf Eichmann,[2] the fugitive Nazi SS officer held primarily responsible for the organisation of the 'final solution', was under arrest in Israel, and would be tried there on a capital charge for crimes against the Jewish people. From the early 1950s Eichmann had lived secretly in Argentina, and it was from there that he was abducted, by Mossad agents, in mid-May 1960, and flown to Israel. The dramatic circumstances of his arrest and arraignment attracted international attention, and the subsequent highly controversial trial was televised by Israel and watched across the world. The broadcast of the proceedings was not only a means of demonstrating their judicial fairness, but also of emphasising their symbolism. At Nuremberg the prosecution case had been built largely upon documentary evidence, but in Jerusalem it would be the testimony of survivors that would convict, in Ben-Gurion's words, 'one of the greatest war criminals'.[3] 'In one sense no trial in history is simpler to understand,' observed The Times. '[...] Yet at the same time few trials raise more complex points – legal, moral and political.'[4]

TO TEDDY KOLLEK[5]

27 July 1960 [*manuscript*]

Portofino [Villa Cipressina, Portofino Mare, Italy]

Dear Teddy,

[...] I see that there is no avoiding a trial. What is its political purpose? to remind the world about the slaughter? it is anxious not to be; it is irritated by efforts to bring up the ghosts of even the recent past: it will stop its ears; to nail down the guilt of the guilty – Germans, British et al? enjoyable but politically unwise for a state: a luxury in which individual Monte Cristos can indulge, but not communities; to remind the Jews that they are one & in a precarious state in the Galuth?[6] they either know or don't know this: & this won't convert anyone. Justice for its own sake? then the victims must not sit

---

1 David *Ben-Gurion (1886–1973), Polish-born Zionist, one of the principal founders of the State of Israel. (Further biographical details for Ben-Gurion, and other prominent figures mentioned in the text – asterisked as above on first mention in the notes – are given in the Select Biographical Glossary.)

2 (Karl) Adolf Eichmann (1906–62), joined SS 1932, Lieutenant-Colonel 1941; became the Gestapo's expert on Jewish affairs, and as chief of sub-section 'IV-B-4' of the Reich Security Main Office (RSHA) 1942–5 directed the assembly, transport and mass murder of *c.*6 million Jews in Nazi-controlled Europe; escaped from American captivity 1946 and later lived in hiding in Argentina; tried in Israel for war crimes, 11 April to 14 August 1961, sentenced to death 15 December 1961, hanged 31 May 1962.

3 'Gestapo's Chief Jew-Baiter Caught after 15 Years: To Be Tried in Israel Court', *Times*, 24 May 1960, 12d.

4 'Eichmann', leader, *Times*, 7 April 1961, 15b.

5 Theodor ('Teddy') *Kollek (1911–2007), director-general of Ben-Gurion's office 1952–64, 'the best disseminator of news in Israel by far' (IB to Norman Bentwich, 18 October 1961).

6 The Jewish diaspora.

in judgement: they can take reprisals: assassinate: punish: but not try. Still I see it *is* to be. If so, is it quite hopeless to hope that after condemnation E[ichmann] will be handed over to someone else – Germans, Argentinians, Egyptians – to do what they like, as an unclean object? – nothing in the world wd make so deep an impression on the world, I am quite sure, as an act by a small and deeply wronged people which refuses to plunge the dagger to the hilt. I suppose it all lies in B[en-]G[urion]'s almighty hand – I know there is boiling public opinion, the victims of the camps, the people with branded limbs etc. etc., still their baffled desire for revenge or even justice can be *braved*. And the moral effect wd be quite *enormous*. Just as an offer of money for transplanting Arabs, in season, i.e. in 1948–9 wd have created many allies in unexpected places, whom today Israel lacks; so something of this kind (I shd be delighted to see the Egyptians welcome Eichmann at the border!) wd stop the mouths of many a critic. Gestures are not without effect even in our world. Still, it is all up to B.G.: if our sanctimonious exhibitionists like Victor Gollancz[1] did not offer to fall on their knees in public to save Eichmann's life! If anything is an argument in favour of capital punishment it is the tone & character of its most vociferous opponents (the argument for Zionism was *always* that) – still I believe fervently that one should (a) spare E & (b) expel him, despite those who agree with me. Public political trials + the people's justice – Christ, Joan of Arc, Charles I, Louis XVI & all those tried by Germans, Russians, Nuremberg etc – only sows doubts about the motives of the executioners. [...]

love

Isaiah   [...]

TO ROWLAND BURDON-MULLER[2]

16 September 1960 [*dictated in August*]

[Villa Cipressina, Portofino Mare, Italy; as from] All Souls

Dear Rowland,

Aline[3] says she has a letter in which you reproach me for not replying to your letter. Your grievance is just but you must not blame me too much: I have had a wretched summer. The Summer Term is in some way[s] my worst: because I do not lecture I feel I ought to give more of my time to undergraduate societies, and as I can never speak impromptu I prepare and prepare papers for them and waste a great deal of time on that and am no good at the end of term, but always collapse into some kind of wretched malady. [...]

Well, at any rate, May was no use, for I had too much work to do, and

1 Victor Gollancz (1893–1967), Kt 1965; publisher and writer; gravitated from liberalism to socialism, embracing pacifism; five weeks earlier he had written to *The Times*: 'I pray that Eichmann may not be hanged.' 22 June 1960, 13e.

2 Rowland *Burdon-Muller (1891–1980), connoisseur of the arts.

3 Aline Elisabeth Yvonne *Berlin (b. 1915), IB's wife.

June entirely eaten up by the appalling task of having to produce an address on the subject of Tolstoy, to be delivered in Venice in honour of the fiftieth anniversary of the death of that great writer. This was a Congress convened by the Fondazioni Cini, a quite respectable establishment on the Isola San Giorgio in Venice, which promotes 'cultural events' – the World Congress of Philosophy met there two years ago, and a great many other world bodies too. The founder of the Foundàtion is, as you may imagine, a Fascist Count,[1] elegant, rich, exceedingly affable, most civilised, good-looking – just appointed Governor of the Vatican City – and one of the most awful men I have ever met. A great 'friend of everybody's', adored by all, I thought a smooth and fascinating scoundrel, although I have no evidence for it – second only to Volpi[2] as a success under the Fascist system. At any rate his son was killed in the war, and in memory of this son he rebuilt – exquisitely too – the old Abbey of St George in the island, just in the Lagoon between Riva dei Schiavoni and the Lido, and there this commemorative occasion occurred. It was peculiar. I felt I could not refuse, as [one of] Tolstoy's charming grandchildren, Signora Albertini[3] – a very nice, gay lady whom I know – begged me to do something about this, and I persuaded David Cecil[4] to participate in it too, and there appeared Dr Serge Tolstoy[5] from Paris, who is the spit image of the young Tolstoy himself, and various other Tolstoys [...].

A large number of persons appeared from various countries. There was a powerful Indian delegation – as boring as Indians always are – because India is the only country which really took Tolstoy seriously. There was a strange American delegation consisting of George Kennan[6] – dear George, after scrapping his original address because he found that the Soviet delegation found it somewhat too political, delivered a long, emotional speech about what a failure Tolstoy was, including a marvellous sentence: 'Tolstoy was tortured by sexual problems all his life: we have solved them by means of our sense of humour.' David Cecil immediately pushed a note across to me saying that he was wildly fascinated by what possible form this could have taken. Nabokov,[7] who was there too – Nicolas, I mean – simultaneously pushed

1 Vittorio Cini (1885–1977), count of Monselice, financier, appointed Minister of Communications by Mussolini, February 1943; interned in Dachau after breaking with Mussolini; his son Giorgio secured his release by bribing his guards; after Giorgio's death in a plane crash in 1949 his father established the Fondazione Giorgio Cini on the Isola di San Giorgio Maggiore in his memory.
2 Giuseppe Volpi (1877–1947), count of Misurata, Italian businessman and politician; Finance Minister under Mussolini 1925–8. He skilfully negotiated concessions in Italy's debts to Britain and America, and in 1932 founded the Venice International Film Festival.
3 Tatiana Mikhailovna ('Tania') Soukhotine-Tolstoi Albertini (1905–96), maternal granddaughter of Tolstoy.
4 David *Cecil (1902–86), English literature don.
5 Sergey ('Serge' in French) Mikhailovich Tolstoy (b. 1922), great-grandson of Tolstoy.
6 George Frost Kennan (1904–2005), US diplomat, Soviet expert, historian; an influential exponent of the policy of containment of the Soviet Union; ambassador to Yugoslavia 1961–3; thereafter based at the Institute for Advanced Study, Princeton.
7 The composer Nicolas *Nabokov (1903–78) had largely organised the event.

a note to me saying this gave him an entirely new view of Mrs Kennan.[1] [...]
Tolstoy detested Venice of course – he never went there, he loathed it as an
obvious city of pleasure, luxury, and in *Anna Karenina*, when the couple elope
to Venice, he is, I think, the only author known to me who successfully resists
the temptation to make one word of description of Venice. [...] America
was also represented by Professor Ernest Simmons,[2] who has written a vast,
though rather vulgar, biography of Tolstoy – who delivered quite a good
speech, and Professor Slonim,[3] who insulted the Soviets, saying that they
treated Tolstoy altogether too much as if he were a member of the Writers'
Union.[4] Quite funny but somewhat tactless.

Now as to the Soviet delegation itself. We did not know if they would be
coming or not, but in the end they sent one. It consisted of the Secretary
of the Writers' Union – a dim hack from Siberia whom nobody had ever
heard of – a loud-voiced critic of no great literary worth, who delivered
several speeches such as might go down in a noisy assembly of party fanatics
somewhere in the 1920s; an old professor who was perfectly genuine but dull
as ditchwater, who explained how difficult it was to check Tolstoy's manuscripts and see to it that the word for morphine was not confused with the
word for chlorine in his illegible manuscripts etc.; and finally a man who
accompanies the Soviet delegations to Italy, one Breitburg,[5] very intelligent,
obviously in a position of fair authority in Russia, and although appearing as
a mere organiser and translator, obviously in some general sense in charge
of the delegation. Mr Breitburg studiously ignored all the obvious fellow-
travellers and friends of the Soviet Union present and made himself perfectly
agreeable to me, and in the end presented me with two bottles of vodka and
two little boxes of caviare. I wondered what I had done to deserve this: was
I regarded as the weakest link in some important chain? It is indeed true that
in England they have no allies among the liberal intelligentsia. There are
a few Communists, of course, but all the old fellow-travellers have been alienated by the many outrages on the part of the Russians, and apart, therefore,
from real petty Communist hacks and Sir Charles Snow,[6] who is an out-and-
out protagonist of a rather shocking sort, they have nobody they can appeal
to. I wonder if this is a method of slow cultivation of people who, while

1 In 1931 George Kennan married Annelise Sørensen (1910–2008), a Norwegian he met while
  studying in Berlin.
2 Ernest Joseph Simmons (1903–72), literary historian; pioneer of Russian studies in the US; his
  weighty *Leo Tolstoy* (Boston, 1946) was reissued in two volumes in NY in 1960.
3 Marc Slonim (1894–1976), author of *The Epic of Russian Literature from Its Origins through Tolstoy*
  (NY, 1950), reviewed by IB in *Partisan Review* 17 (1950), 617–23.
4 The Union of Soviet Writers, founded in 1932 to extend Communist Party control over literature: exclusion from the Union was an effective ban on publication.
5 Semen Moiseevich Breitburg (1899–1970), expert on, and editor of a number of books about,
  Tolstoy.
6 Charles Percy Snow (1905–80), Kt 1957, life peer 1964; writer, scientific administrator, and pundit;
  his novels were popular in the Soviet Union.

not prepared to condone anything, nevertheless, when occasion offers, may vote in favour of continuing relations with them rather than the insulation to which they are at present, entirely through their own fault, subjected. In France and Italy, after all, there are powerful parties of intellectuals on their side. In America any form of pro-Soviet opinion is, I suppose, automatically [a] conspiracy, and people are either secretly and violently for or openly and violently against. At any rate, we all behaved very mildly with regard to one another and the Congress was on the whole a success. Whether the Tolstoy family thought it was adequate to the memory of their great-grandfather I do not know. [...] I then came back to England and, as always happens after pleasure, immediately felt unwell. However, for once stoically ignoring this, I went to the American ball, which was inconceivably dreary,[1] as far as I was concerned, although probably enjoyed by everybody else, and the next day went to Italy, where for about five days I felt quite well, and after that began having a series of chills and flus, which has gone on ever since. [...] Mrs Fleming,[2] who used to be Lady Rothermere, is coming to stay with us on Monday, and Sir Maurice is bound to appear sooner or later from some Greek island or other. But I do not look forward to any of this at all, I must admit to you. For I feel wretchedly low – a condition I have to hide from my mother,[3] who otherwise probably, despite her advanced years, would come flying straight here in order to attend me – and the more people come the more responsible I feel for doing something for them and the less I feel that I can do so. Aline is by nature less sociable than I am in any case. So really this summer is, I think, ungay. On the other hand, my stepchildren are all enjoying it very much. [...]

The last thing socially that we did before I fell properly ill was to go to a nightmare dinner party given by some friends of Aline's here called Belligrandi [...]. Aline found herself next to a Count Murari[4] who explained to her that the only government that is any good today was that of South Africa, where at least some sort of stand is being made on the part of white men against horrible black men, that it was a great pity that the US had given up its leadership of the white world and that Italy had shamefully let down the Germans during the war. I had no idea that these things were being said and only saw Aline smiling uneasily and trying to talk to her other neighbour. But Italy is full of persons with such views, who concealed them carefully enough immediately after the war but are now all coming into the open.

1 Possibly the annual Independence Day dinner and ball held at the Dorchester Hotel on 4 July under the auspices of the American Society in London.
2 Ann Geraldine Mary Fleming (1913–81) née Charteris, society hostess; her second husband (1945) was Esmond Cecil Harmsworth, second Viscount Rothermere (1898–1978), newspaper proprietor; he divorced her in 1951 because of her attachment to Ian Fleming (creator of James Bond), whom she married in 1952.
3 Marie *Berlin (c.1880–1974).
4 General Count Sebastiano Murari della Corte Brà (1879–1945) served in Mussolini's army.

I had the pleasure of cutting Sparrow's[1] greatest friends, the Clarys, in Munich railway station. He stared very hard at me, remembering as he did that he had met me no fewer than three times with, I think, Victor Cunard[2] and Sparrow and poor Momo Marriott[3] in Venice two years ago, and three years ago too, but as he then ventured the sentiment that Mosley,[4] to whose lectures in Venice he went, was absolutely right in all he said, only impossibly idealistic, I saw no reason for not cutting him. Ghastly couple they are. [...] If you have a moment do sit down and write me a letter. I am in a perfect condition for reading a letter from friends. For what I ought to read – Karl Marx[5] and the like for my lectures – simply will not go into my head. Forgive me for this low, low letter – the lowest you have ever received – and do not blame me for my silences. They are not occasioned by anything except sheer physical and at times intellectual exhaustion.

Yours ever

I.B.   [...]

TO JACQUELINE DE PROYART[6]

[Mid September 1960; *carbon*]

[Villa Cipressina, Portofino Mare, Italy]

[Dear Jacqueline,]

[...] I read your manuscript notes for the talk which I am now more bitterly sorry than ever to have missed in Venice, and was moved and exhilarated. I think you are perfectly right. [...] Tolstoy was not, in the Christian sense of the word, religious, not humble, and bared his soul not to God, but to himself, and exposed ruthlessly the pretensions and hypocrisies of his characters and of himself, because he believed that the truth could be obtained here below by a sufficient degree of purity, sincerity, self-examination, illumination, all that was delusive, corrupt etc. In fact he believed the

---

1 John *Sparrow (1906–92), Warden of All Souls 1952–77.
2 Victor Cunard (1898–1960), inter-war foreign correspondent of *The Times*; served in Political Intelligence Dept, FO, 1941–6.
3 Maud Emily Wolff ('Momo') Marriott (1897–1960) née Kahn, daughter of NY banker and philanthropist Otto Hermann Kahn (1867–1934), and sister of 'Nin' Ryan (39/5); she died in October 1960 after a long and painful illness.
4 Oswald Ernald Mosley (1896–1980), sixth baronet; Fascist politician; founder of the anti-Semitic British Union of Fascists 1932; interned during the Second World War as a security risk.
5 Karl Heinrich Marx (1818–83), German political theorist, economist and revolutionary; co-founder of modern communism with Friedrich Engels, his collaborator in the writing of the Communist Manifesto; the subject of a celebrated 1939 biography by IB (485/4); for the genesis of this work, and its reception, see 544–5.
6 Jacqueline, comtesse de Proyart de Baillescourt (b. 1927) né Aymé de La Chevrelière, French Russianist; lecturer, Faculty of Humanities, Poitiers, 1959–87; a friend of Boris Pasternak, she helped bring the Russian original of *Doctor Zhivago* to publication; on nominating committee of Nobel Prize in Literature, 1958 (when Pasternak won). Her talk in Venice was on 'Léon Tolstoï et la vanité' ('Leo Tolstoy and Pride').

precise opposite of what existentialists of every hue – whether irreligious or atheistic – believe: they believe that all efforts to deduce rules for living, all justifications of moral or intellectual or social or political positions from the facts – whether of science or history or transcendental revelation – are foredoomed to failure, since there are no patterns or reasons or purposes in things or facts themselves – to this extent they accept Hume[1] – and it is only a form of weakness, an attempt to find an alibi, to lean against the universe because we are too cowardly or deluded to lean on ourselves – to seek truth outside because we are too terrified to look within ourselves and realise that it is created by ourselves – hence the rejection of all theology and metaphysics, rationalism etc.

All this Tolstoy is opposed to with his entire nature. He believes that the truth about what to do and what there is can be discovered, but only if we remove the scales from our eyes etc., and go through some kind of *askesis*[2] (recommended by Rousseau[3] or whoever it may be). [...] He believed in men as strongly as the most naive optimists of the eighteenth century – 'If only men would do this or that, get rid of this or that incubus, stop this bad practice, that stupid, wicked, unnecessary form of belief or behaviour, return to some ideal point *x*, then death is conquered, truth reigns, men's hearts open, harmony reigns, a solution is easy, simple, at our feet; moral strength, sense of truth, that is all we need to reach the summit and let others do so.'

That is the optimism of which you speak. He thought the summit was attainable and that it was here. This is a far truer analysis of him than the nihilistic, destructive, sceptical, angry, barbarous Tolstoy who kicked everything over and glories in the discomfort of the feeble intelligentsia, liberals, etc. [I hope I] interpret you correctly! And you are also perfectly [right that] psychologically his *angoisse* springs from his sheer vitality, the difficulty of the ascent, the darkness against which alone so passionate a search for light can be explained, and the constant inability not to see the cracks in everything, the blackness. For someone possessed of such appalling undeceiving sharpness of vision, it is not true to say that he was in any sense of the word an

---

1 David Hume (1711–76) né Home, Scottish philosopher and historian; a central figure in the Enlightenment, he had close dealings with, among others, Rousseau; he was regarded as a sceptic. In his *Treatise of Human Nature: Being an Attempt to Introduce the Experimental Method of Reasoning into Moral Subjects* (3 vols., London, 1739–40) he pointed out what is now called 'the is–ought problem' or 'the naturalistic fallacy': it is impossible to derive an 'ought' from an 'is', moral conclusions from empirical premises.

2 'Self-discipline'.

3 Jean Jacques Rousseau (1712–78), Swiss-born French philosopher, believed in the potential goodness of man and the corrupting effect of civilisation. His *Social Contract* (1762) invested sovereignty with the people, envisaging a society based upon liberty, fraternity and equality, ideals that inspired the French Revolution, for the excesses of which he is sometimes blamed by his critics. Rousseau was one of the six subjects chosen by IB for his 1952 lectures for the BBC Third Programme, *Freedom and Its Betrayal: Six Enemies of Human Liberty*, published under that title in 2002.

escapist, for such things have been said, but they are not just. He did try to
escape of course to the Caucasus, to the peasants, to the little children, to
simplicity etc., but he was never deceived, he knew, when it was no good,
that it was no good, and the anxiety came from perception of the truth –
truth on earth – truth of facts – truth presented to a realistic vision – on the
part of a man at once appallingly penetrating and with abnormal powers
of realising what he wanted – and not the despair of someone to whom
the world is genuinely a meaningless succession, something depending upon
rationally unintelligible grace, something which contains no beginning of
an answer to the devouring problems, which have to be either presented as
not soluble here or not soluble by any communicable or rational means [...].

I. What do you think of my hero Herzen?[1] Tolstoy said about him that
he was at once profound and brilliant, a combination scarcely ever found
together. I like the thought of him, fat, small, electric, tumbling down the
stairs to see the sceptical Tolstoy in 1861: the only man who ever completely
captured the formidable Tolstoy at once, so that the great denigrator never
said anything really critical about Herzen – despite all his disapproved society
of ladies and his intolerably liberal views [...].

Yours ever,
[Isaiah Berlin]

TO ROBERT CRAFT[2]

10 October 1960

Headington House

Dear Robert,

I know exactly the kind of quotation you want and cannot think of any
off hand. [...] The only thing which comes to my head is the most hackneyed
of all patriotic Russian quotations, which comes from Pushkin's *Ruslan and
Lyudmila*, very early in it – after describing various Russian mythological
creatures he says 'here is the Russian spirit ... here it smells of Russia'.[3] I wish
I could think of something more apt.

The point is that the whole of Russian literature is absolutely self-preoccupied, from the comedies of the late eighteenth century to *Zhivago* and
beyond. The Germans are pretty self-centred but they are as nothing to the
Russians, whose sole subject is Russia – and this even in the most Western

---

1 Aleksandr Ivanovich Herzen (1812–70), revolutionary socialist thinker and writer; one of IB's
  intellectual heroes because of his defence of personal liberty, and his rejection of extremism and
  justification of violent means in pursuit of utopian ends; his political essays were published as
  S togo berega (*From the Other Shore*, 1850), and his memoirs as *Byloe i dumy* (*My Past and Thoughts*,
  1852–68).
2 Robert Lawson Craft (b. 1923), US conductor and writer, known for his close friendship and
  artistic collaboration with Igor Stravinsky.
3 Line 41 of the poem (1820), in 'Song 1' (strictly 'there' for 'here').

and aesthetically pure novels of Turgenev. This seems so universal and taken for granted – almost unconscious at times – that one very seldom gets any conscious emphasis on the point that Russian artists are the most self-conscious in the world, and that when, for example, national Russian music was created in the 1860s and earlier, this succeeded because it was not artificial chauvinism, but merely the expression of a feeling which was in any case pervasive – the subject of constant debate – at the centre of awareness – and not a provincial admiration – conscious archaism, a deliberate attempt on the part of an isolated group to awaken dormant memories, etc., as it was in a good many other countries. As soon as the Russians feel that 'the Russian spirit is present' they fall into natural and not artificial ecstasies, and the result, though often rhetorical and sometimes tortured, is not exotic or artificial. [...]

Yours,

Isaiah   [...]

TO ROWLAND BURDON-MULLER

11 October 1960

Headington House

Dearest Rowland,

Surely you have received my *enormous* letter dictated in Portofino, signed, sent to you *at least* three weeks ago?[1] If not, this is *very* mysterious. I have been, as Brian and Alfreda [Urquhart][2] might have told you, more or less ill all summer with a hideous infection wrongly diagnosed by the local Italian doctor – not that he could have done much to help [...].

Everyone else seems very well. Sparrow is said to be appearing against *Lady Chatterley* in the case about to be brought against the publishers of that bad book by D. H. Lawrence (I am in favour of publishing it because I am against all censorship; that the book is not a good one, it must be admitted), but this is not true – I think it is merely a rumour started by himself to see how far it would get.[3]

---

1 Letter of 16 September above.

2 Brian Edward Urquhart (b. 1919), later (1986) KCMG; senior member of staff of UN from its inception in 1945, Under-Secretary-General 1974–86; married, 1944, Alfreda Huntington (divorced 1963).

3 Penguin Books' plans to publish an unexpurgated version of D. H. Lawrence's *Lady Chatterley's Lover* in August 1960 led to a landmark trial (20 October to 2 November), which determined in favour of publication on the grounds that it was 'for the public good'. The prosecution called no witnesses, but Evelyn Waugh, for one, disputed the verdict, considering the work 'dull, absurd in places & pretentious': letter to Michael Rubinstein, 21 August 1960, in *Lady Chatterley's Lover*, 50th anniversary edition (London 2010), 345. In a controversial article in *Encounter* (February 1962, 101), John Sparrow also contested the verdict, arguing that the work promoted sodomy, which was illegal.

Dear Stuart[1] is obviously happy in London and about to deliver an inaugural lecture, suitably enough on 'Emotion and Expression', or something of the kind, which sounds more like his own personality than like philosophy. [...]

Have you read Diana Cooper's memoirs?[2] [...] I find them very readable, though there is a cold-hearted quality allied with a kind of enviable sincerity, as when she reports the death of some very dear friend and remarks: 'Very sad.' If she felt no more than this, that is that, and certainly conventional expressions would be nauseating, at the same time one is a little taken aback. Still, Proust has described all that very truthfully and shockingly in the scene where Swann tells the Duke and Duchess of Guermantes that he is stricken with a fatal disease, and they are dressing for dinner and they are very sorry but they have to go on dressing for dinner and they go out to dinner, and his emotions are well analysed.[3] But if you haven't read the volume, I shall certainly send it to you. I haven't read it myself yet, except in extracts in the *Sunday Times*. I do not see Diana now, for she has become very demanding and I cannot sacrifice Aline, my work and everything else to her, as doubtless she would like from all her friends; but I am fond of her and admire her, although when Shaw-Stewart[4] said 'She has no heart, but her brain is in the right place' he was not very far from the truth. Except that this is not quite fair, she is full of sudden affections, and having no notion of what the world is like or what human beings are like, like an ageing actress who puts her foot in everything and gets everything wrong, suffers herself, misplaces her affections, misunderstands the reactions to it etc. That is not quite the behaviour of a heartless, clever person, but of a kind of Ondine,[5] a vulnerable one, placed in a world for which she was ultimately not made and bringing off her existence in it by colossal virtuosity invented to meet an unmeetable situation, if you see what I mean. But I must not go on, the instrument is wilting from my feeble hand, half an hour is as much as I can do of anything

---

1 Stuart Hampshire had recently succeeded A. J. Ayer as Grote Professor of Philosophy, London, and on 25 October 1960 he gave his inaugural lecture on 'Feeling and Expression', published for UCL in 1961 and later included in his collection *Freedom of Mind: And Other Essays* (Princeton, 1971).

2 Lady Diana Cooper (1893–1986) née Manners, actress, society hostess and author, wife of the diplomat and politician (Alfred) Duff Cooper (1890–1954), first Viscount Norwich. IB refers to the third and final volume of her memoirs, *Trumpets from the Steep* (London, 1960): 'When she is at her happiest, Lady Diana Cooper is an engaging self-reporter: at her worst she is a poor little rich girl with a pout' (*Times*, 27 October 1960, 15e).

3 IB particularly admired this scene from *The Guermantes Way*, the third volume (published in two parts: Paris, 1920–1) of Marcel Proust's *À la recherche du temps perdu* (Paris, 1913–27).

4 Patrick Houston Shaw-Stewart (1888–1917), Fellow of All Souls 1910, director of Baring's Bank; one of the most brilliant among Lady Diana Cooper's many pre-war admirers; killed in action in France, 30 December 1917.

5 Also 'Undine', the title of a popular fairy story (Berlin, 1811) by Friedrich Heinrich Karl de la Motte, Baron Fouqué (Friedrich de la Motte Fouqué), in which the eponymous water-sprite gains a soul – and thereafter feels human pain – once she marries a mortal, the knight Huldbrand.

now and I must more or less go back to bed. It is only that I was worried by the non-receipt of my earlier letter. Do write and reassure me.

Yours ever,

Isaiah

TO IRVING SINGER[1]

2 November 1960

Headington House

Dear Irving,

It really has been years and years. [...] What are you doing? What are you writing? You might well ask this question of me too – all I produce is little fragments, an article on history which you may have seen in the new periodical called *History and Theory*;[2] a piece on Tolstoy to appear in *Encounter*; a piece on Vico[3] which has appeared in the obscurest of all places – the bulletin of the Italian Institute in London; a piece on John S. Mill[4] delivered to an even obscurer institution, a harmless though somewhat bogus body called the Council of Christians and Jews, which they will publish as a pamphlet probably in a year or two's time; but nothing big, nothing solid, nothing genuine. I have not yet reached the stage when I can read violent attacks on myself unmoved: there is a piece by your remote colleague Marshall Cohen[5] – who came to Oxford and had tea with me but whose features I do not remember and whom I certainly did not ask a second time (that may be the cause of the trouble – I may have preferred Dreben[6] all too much and all too openly) – which attacks me with extreme violence in the pages of the Scottish *Philosophical Review*.[7] The injury is bad enough; but in addition to

1 Irving Singer (b. 1925), Harvard-educated philosopher; associate professor of philosophy, MIT, 1959–69; professor from 1969.

2 'History and Theory: The Concept of Scientific History', *History and Theory* 1 (1960), 1–31, repr. as 'The Concept of Scientific History' in CC and PSM.

3 Giambattista Vico (1668–1744), Italian philosopher and jurist; 'a profound and original thinker, who, after being overshadowed by his contemporary, Montesquieu, has been re-discovered at regular intervals ever since, but has even more to say to the present age than to his own' (IB to Edmund Gray, 6 September 1966). IB's 'piece on Vico' is 'The Philosophical Ideas of Giambattista Vico', in *Art and Ideas in Eighteenth-Century Italy: Lectures Given at the Italian Institute, 1957–1958* (Rome, 1960), 156–233; repr. in revised form in VH and TCE.

4 John Stuart Mill (1806–1873), philosopher and economist, much admired by IB for his defence of individual freedom and variety; author of *On Liberty* (1859) and *Utilitarianism* (1861). IB's 1959 Robert Waley Cohen Memorial Lecture, *John Stuart Mill and the Ends of Life* (London, 1959), repr. in L, marked the centenary of *On Liberty*.

5 (Stephen) Marshall Cohen (b. 1929), US philosopher; studied at Harvard and Oxford, and taught at Yale and elsewhere before joining the law faculty at the University of Southern California.

6 Burton Spencer Dreben (1927–99), US philosopher; on advice from IB he studied under J. L. Austin when a Fulbright Fellow at Magdalen 1950–1; assistant professor of philosophy, Harvard, 1956–61; professor 1961–73; Dean of the Graduate School of Arts and Sciences 1973–5.

7 Marshall Cohen's highly critical review, 'Berlin and the Liberal Tradition', appeared in the journal of the Scots Philosophical Association and the University Court of St Andrews, *Philosophical Quarterly*, vol. 10 no. 40 (July 1960), 216–27. After some generous encomiums in the opening

a personally offensive article he sent it me with an inscription in ink explain-ing that there was no man he respected more, etc. etc. There is no need to believe in the unity of theory and practice or behaviourism or operational-ism etc. to see that this could not be quite true in view of the vitriolic essay. Still, days have passed and after meditating various powerful answers I have decided that no answer at all is best. [...]

What news is there of me? I am happily married, I have stepchildren, I live in a large house in Headington, I hate being Professor, I hate lecturing, I hate work, I see fewer people than I used to, I tick over, I go to the same place in the summer and the same place in the spring, and on the whole enjoy monotonous routine. I read less, I talk less, there are three large books I must write, and will write if I possibly can, but equally may not: on political theory – the critical turning-point in the eighteenth century when romanticism bursts in; on Belinsky;[1] on Marxism. [...] Who interests you, who excites you, whom do you believe in, whom do you hate? Really there is nothing to say about me, I am much as you left me, only older and weaker. I do not feel in the least professorial. Do you feel like a teacher responsible for the minds and lives of young men? [...]

Do write again.

Yours ever, with much love

Isaiah

The Algerian War of Independence (1954–62) pitted the guerrilla forces of the Algerian Front de Libération Nationale (FLN) against the largely conscript army of the colonial power, France. The ensuing struggle was marked by extreme brutality on both sides, and in November 1960 IB was invited to express his condemnation of it publicly, while explicitly siding with the liberation struggle. That he could not straightforwardly do so foreshadows his later reluctance to join similar initiatives in support of Castro's Cuba and in opposition to the war in Vietnam.

TO IGNAZIO SILONE[2]

3 November 1960 [*carbon*]

Headington House

Dear Mr Silone,

Thank you for your letter of October 28. I was greatly moved by your statement [...]. It is a noble document, and I should be proud and indeed

paragraph Cohen came quickly to his point: 'Not only does Berlin seem to me philosophically inadequate, but he also seems historically provincial' (217).

1 Vissarion Grigor'evich Belinsky (1811–48), radical journalist and literary critic, who believed that literature should be judged in terms of its moral effect and reformative power, and who thus 'transformed the concept of the critic's calling in his native country' (RT2 210). *Ru Thy*

2 Ignazio Silone (1900–78), Italian socialist politician and writer; a founder member of the Italian

eager to sign it, but for one sentence in it, at the end of the third paragraph [...]. What disturbs me is that it calls not merely for condemnation
of the [Algerian] war, and the right to refuse to be conscripted – with which
I agree entirely – but for active help to the FLN. The right of disobedience
you say is an extreme right and to be used only in extreme circumstances.
I agree. The right of passive resistance, of disobedience, yes, of course.
But the right to give positive aid to those who use terrorist methods? The
right to conspiracy? If you grant that, you grant the right to create a situa-
tion in which the State, whether democratic or any other, will disintegrate.
Nevertheless of course the right exists, if the State and government are bad
enough. Violence against the tsarist regime in Russia, against Austrians in
Italy, against Nazis and Fascists, against Franco, against Russia in Eastern
Europe, seem to be justified. Against de Gaulle?[1] Is this morally so clear?
To me it seems that one only has the right to use all weapons against the
State if one has convinced oneself that nothing is worse than the monstrous
order which grinds one down. This is true of Franco, Hitler, Stalin, perhaps
Batista,[2] etc. I cannot get the thought out of my mind that if de Gaulle's
State is made to collapse what will succeed it would not be a virtuous Sixth
Republic of a democratic kind, but the Generals, Soustelle[3] etc., and then
the Communists; or vice versa. Would that be better? Surely, despite the
horrors of the Algerian war, not; but if so, does one wish to proclaim the
right (and do you not really mean the duty?) to collaborate actively with
Algerian terrorists? In short, even though I am not prepared to condemn
it, I do not want to subscribe to a positive call for terrorism (as opposed to
disobedience) even as a weapon against terrorism. I felt that about the Jews
in Palestine (to whose cause I was otherwise enthusiastically devoted) when
they began to assassinate [...].

Yours sincerely,
    [Isaiah Berlin]

Communist Party in 1921; after the Second World War he joined the anti-Communist Congress
of Cultural Freedom, becoming Director of its Italian section.

1 Charles André Joseph Marie de Gaulle (1890–1970), French general and statesman; a veteran of
  the French Army during the First World War, he led the Free French in exile 1940–4; head of
  provisional government 1944–6; returned to power 1 June 1958 at behest of the Fourth Republic,
  as it collapsed over the settlers' revolt in Algeria; President of the Fifth Republic 1959; secured
  a French withdrawal from Algeria 1962; that year he made the presidency an office directly
  elected by the people, which he held until 1969.

2 Fulgencio Batista y Zaldívar (1901–73), brutal and corrupt Cuban dictator; President 1940–4,
  1952–9, but in effective control from 1934. He fled Havana in the early hours of New Year's Day
  1959 as Fidel Castro's revolutionary army closed in on the capital.

3 Jacques Soustelle (1912–90), close wartime ally of de Gaulle who broke with his chief over
  Algerian independence in 1960, and afterwards joined the terrorist OAS; lived in exile from 1961
  until 1968, when he was granted an amnesty.

*The 50th anniversary of Tolstoy's death fell on 20 November 1960. Tolstoy's
granddaughter Tatiana Albertini was invited by the Soviet authorities to the
official celebrations; uncertain whether to accept, she wrote to IB for advice.*

TO TATIANA ALBERTINI

8 November 1960 [*carbon*]

                                                        Headington House

Dearest Tania,

The question you put to me is grave, I have thought and thought about it
and propose to reply in strict business terms. Now then: let us examine the
pros and cons.

1. Pros. You will get the very agreeable treatment accorded to highly honoured guests. You will meet your relations easily, also various writers, actors,
highly placed persons, much more easily and frequently than otherwise. You
will be allowed to go wherever you wish. It will be perfectly safe for people
to see you, they will be eager to meet you and opportunities will be given to
you for relatively private conversations with old friends, relations, 'interesting' persons etc. All this is not to be despised.

2. Cons. You will undoubtedly be put in an embarrassing position at all
those ghastly banquets, terrible toasts, the unspeakable visit to the house
in Moscow and to Yasnaya Polyana.[1] The speeches about Lenin and his
attitude to Tolstoy; Tolstoy the father of the Russian Revolution; Tolstoy
as the champion of the working man, of patriotic armies, of simple good
men like Khrushchev,[2] and the enemy of the corrupt, sophisticated, treacherous, decadent West; all that will be difficult to bear. Worse still will be the
speeches of the Western guests – I do not know who they are, but let us
assume M. Aragon,[3] the Italian equivalents, perhaps our Mr Priestley[4] (who
is capable of anything under those circumstances – Maugham[5] is not going),
our Sir Charles Snow etc. You will certainly be 'used', asked for interviews,
for impressions of the country, and have to invent endless neutral formulae
which while not offending your hosts nevertheless convey as little as possible
and do not ring too false. This will be a ghastly nuisance and morally intoler-

---

1 Tolstoy's country estate and birthplace, some 120 miles south of Moscow. There he wrote *War
  and Peace*, and he is buried in a forest in the grounds.

2 Nikita Sergeevich Khrushchev (1894–1971), Soviet leader; First Secretary, Communist Party,
  1953–64, Prime Minister 1958–64; worked as a metal-fitter before entering politics, and had little
  formal education.

3 Louis Aragon (1897–1982), French writer and poet; joined the Communist Party 1927; thereafter
  devoted himself to writing in support of the Party.

4 J[ohn] B[oynton] Priestley (1894–1984), writer of prodigious range and output. Often dismissed
  as provincial in his homeland, he was popular abroad, and his famous and much-revived play *An
  Inspector Calls* was premiered in Moscow and Leningrad in 1946.

5 (William) Somerset Maugham (1874–1965), writer and playwright, one of the most commer-
  cially successful, if not most critically praised, authors of the twentieth century.

able. All this you know for yourself: and this is, no doubt, what causes you and Serge T[olstoy] to shy away from the idea. There is a further deterrent – that should you refuse to go now they may not be so pleased to give you a visa later, whether as a member of the Red Cross or otherwise. Refusal would entail lack of sympathy: you will have earned a black mark which may be a nuisance later. What then, as your grandfather used to say, must one do?

[...] No, in your case I would not go. I think what one's instincts tell one is to be followed: if one disobeys them – one may be carried away by the immediate excitement and pleasure of the experience, but one is eaten by guilt afterwards, and one expiates it in all kinds of outré and exaggerated fashions. Psychological scars are not to be invited. On the other hand one must certainly not offend the Soviet authorities in order not to forfeit the possibility of getting a visa for the purpose of going as a private, or semi-private, person later. Let me therefore give you this piece of hideously cunning and crafty advice. In your place I should accept, for the moment, with enthusiasm, behave as if preparing for the journey. Do everything towards it. And then at the last moment do precisely what they do – develop diplomatic illness, find some irresistible reason for remaining behind of a sudden catastrophic kind; just like your relations who were not able to come to Venice. Display every sign of distress and grief, and explain that nothing would have suited you better than to go and that you are heart-broken at the sudden cause – whatever it may be – which has operated as an insuperable obstacle. They may see through this or not; but even if they do, what they dislike is an open snub, an open insult; provided you preserve the conventions and behave with courtesy and display an enthusiasm, however hypocritical, you will be forgiven. That is my reading of their official behaviour. Then, I think, they will not refuse you a visa next year when you can go, no doubt more expensively from your own point of view, but in morally far easier circumstances. It will be more difficult to see people than if you were an honoured guest of the Soviet Union, but still you probably will see them if you are open enough about it, even if you make a statement about how splendid it is that 60 million copies of *War and Peace* are being printed, or that Tolstoy should be recognised so beautifully and nobly by his own country – that will be less awful than the unspeakable things which you would have to go through during the official festival. I wish I knew whether I had any judgement or not. This advice may be quite mistaken. This, I think, is how I should behave if I were Tolstoy's grandson: but the suggestion is so eccentric that my imagination does not begin to compass such a possibility. [...]

Yours,

[Isaiah]

In late December 1954 IB was appointed to the board of directors at the Royal Opera House, Covent Garden, and in June 1956 he joined its Opera

Subcommittee, of which he became Chairman late in 1959. The Subcommittee
dealt with repertory, productions and casting, and IB was an active chairman:
he saw it as his role to help the ROH balance 'the rival claims of English singers
and foreign "stars", of international and national styles, of orginal libretti and
English translations, of acknowledged masterpieces, which form the staple of
every Opera House, and relatively rarely staged or new works.'[1] The influence of
the Subcommittee was affected by its relations with David Webster, the General
Administrator of the ROH, and one of the main architects of its post-war
development. IB's opinion of Webster was less than positive, and he believed
that Webster regarded the gentlemen amateurs who advised him with a degree
of disdain. The Subcommittee's other key relationship was with the Musical
Director – for a crucial decade from 1961, Georg Solti ('George' to IB).[2] Solti's
ambition was to make Covent Garden 'quite simply, the best opera house in the
world',[3] and in the opinion of many he succeeded. He was a forceful character,
never in thrall to the Subcommittee, and IB soon complained of 'the de facto
authority of the Webster–Solti dictatorship'.[4] But the lack of democracy implicit
in Solti's style did not obscure for IB his fine qualities as Musical Director, or the
extent of his achievement at the Royal Opera.

TO JOAN SUTHERLAND[5]

11 November 1960 [*carbon*]

Headington House

Dear Miss Sutherland,

This is only to say that your performance in *Sonnambula* on Thursday
3 November, was the most heavenly I have ever heard or hope to hear in
my life. I write this to you not as Chairman of the Opera Subcommittee
of our great organisation, but in a purely personal capacity. I have never in
my life written a fan letter to a singer before, although I have heard a great
deal of opera in my life; to go through a 'musical' experience is a transforming event in one's life: Toscanini's performance of *Falstaff* in Salzburg in
1938 was that;[6] Chaliapin's *Boris* was that;[7] the Beethoven Sonatas played

1 IB to John Tooley, 21 October 1960.
2 22/5.
3 Noel Goodwin, *Independent*, 8 September 1997, 16.
4 IB to Garrett Drogheda, July 1962.
5 Joan Sutherland (1926–2012), Sydney-born operatic soprano, joined the Covent Garden opera
  company in 1952; her glittering career was closely associated with the ROH.
6 Arturo Toscanini (1867–1957), Italian conductor; one of IB's heroes, both for his musical genius
  and for his refusal to conduct under the Fascist regimes. IB misremembers the date of the famous
  Falstaff (Giuseppe Verdi's last opera, 1893), which is likely to have been summer 1937 (Toscanini
  conducted at Salzburg 1934–7).
7 Fedor Ivanovich Shalyapin (Chaliapin) (1873–1938), Russian bass, gave memorable performances
  in the title role of Mussorgsky's *Boris Godunov* at Covent Garden during the 1928–9 season; IB
  recalled hearing him sing that role in Petrograd in 1916.

by Schnabel;[1] and Chopin as played by Rachmaninov[2] and afterwards by
Lipatti.[3] This was the sum until 3 November. Your performance was more
sublime than in *Lucia*[4] and the fact that the London critics did not go mad
with joy and pride merely indicates what is to be thought of them. [...]

Yours sincerely,

[Isaiah Berlin]

TO PEGGY JAY[5]

28 November 1960 [*carbon*]

[Headington House]

Dear Miss Peggy,

[...] I have seen [Peter][6] twice and he was in a somewhat reduced state.
In a sense, of course, not being elected to All Souls is a misfortune that has
happened to many and not broken their spirit – e.g. Herbert,[7] David Cecil,
Trevor-Roper[8] and countless, countless others. Nevertheless I do see that in
this particular case, having been educated to believe in it by his father as
a marvellous establishment, it would be fearfully depressing. I delivered an
immense lecture to him on the Monday after the fatal Saturday, in which
I tried to do precisely what you later suggested – I told him that the blow was
only one to vanity – which although the most painful possible kind of wound
is ultimately the least damaging – that he was extremely able with fellowships offered him at St John's and, if he wanted it, New College, a splendid
place in the Treasury, the world genuinely before him, adored by so many,
about to marry, etc. etc., and that All Souls was tremendously not what it
was cracked up to be, and certainly not what it was in his father's day (and by
God that is true! it is now of a dimness not to be exaggerated), and carried on
on these lines, but I could see that it was having little effect. It was obviously
a terrible blow and he would take some time to recover.

1 Artur Schnabel (1882–1951), Polish-born pianist and composer renowned for his interpretation
of Beethoven's piano sonatas.
2 Sergey Vasil′evich Rachmaninov (1873–1943), Russian composer, conductor and pianist, gave his
last recital in London in March 1939.
3 Dinu Lipatti (1917–50), Romanian pianist and composer, visited England on several occasions
1946–8; died prematurely of Hodgkin's disease; IB had mourned his passing in 'Lament for
Lipatti', *House and Garden* 7 No 3 (March 1952), 91, 98.
4 Sutherland's sensational performance in the title role of *Lucia di Lammermoor* at Covent Garden,
17 February 1959, in a Franco Zeffirelli production, brought her international renown, and she
gave acclaimed debuts as Lucia at the Paris Opera, La Scala and the Met 1960–1.
5 Margaret Christian ('Peggy') Jay (1913–2008) née Garnett, local government politician and
Labour party activist, married, 1933, Douglas Patrick Thomas Jay (1907–96), economist, Fellow
of All Souls 1930–7 and Labour politician (divorced 1972).
6 Peter Jay (b. 1937), writer and broadcaster, son of Peggy and Douglas Jay (previous note);
Assistant Principal, HM Treasury, 1961–64; Principal 1964–67; Economics Editor, *The Times*,
1967–77; Presenter, *Weekend World* (ITV), 1972–7; ambassador to the US 1977–9.
7 H. L. A. *Hart (1907–92), philosopher of law and college head.
8 Hugh *Trevor-Roper (1914–2003), historian and college head.

I am not one of those who think that the clever, fortunate and happy need such punishment to improve them – that is a Calvinist view which I reject with both hands. I have seen him again since your letter – in the line of business – and he seems to be somewhat more cheerful. [...]

Goodness how he reminds me of Douglas – the same very quick mind, the same capacity for nailing an argument, or an opponent, with piercing instruments, to some terrible gibbet, the same lively, dry and devastating intellect. But I must admit to you that he writes a good deal less well than Douglas – don't tell him that for goodness' sake – and that was part of his undoing at All Souls. The general papers, although they had ideas in them, were vast heaps of uncoordinated prose, frightfully chaotic, and not a bit Wykehamist (that I suppose is a good thing); as for his philosophy paper, you must ask Stuart Hampshire.[1] He was the philosophy examiner and Douglas really ought to have a talk with him. Anyway [Peter] really did impress me deeply when I asked him why he didn't want to take a philosophy fellowship. He said he had learnt the techniques, knew how to do things, did them well, but was not interested in the answers sufficiently – moral and political philosophy really did interest him deeply, and logic and the theory of knowledge not. It is remarkable to find in someone of his age sufficient wisdom to realise that one may not want to take a job which one could do beautifully, but was ultimately not what one was interested in – I wish I had known that when I became a don at New College – it took me years to discover that I was not really a philosopher in the proper sense – and the waste and the humiliation and the driving oneself against the grain! I shall go on 'building' [Peter] up so far as I can, I promise you. I like him very much indeed, and shall ask him to a meal at All Souls as soon as the present 'rawness' has passed.

Yours ever,

[Isaiah]

TO DWIGHT MACDONALD[2]

29 November 1960

Headington House

Dear Dwight,

You are, believe me, *profoundly* wrong. Anything you may have seen, heard, judged, had no correspondence in the subjective feelings of the victim. I was, believe me (but you won't, and yet you *must*, for it is the truth) in continuous agony throughout;[3] I always am, during every lecture I have

---

1 Stuart *Hampshire ('Hants') (1914–2004), philosopher.

2 Dwight Macdonald (1906–82), US writer, editor and journalist; gravitated from Depression-era Trotskyite radicalism to fierce Cold War anti-Stalinism; active in the 1960s in opposition to the Vietnam War, and in defence of the right of students to protest.

3 IB had given the 1960 Hermon Ould Memorial Lecture (sponsored by PEN), 'Tolstoy and

ever delivered, even the most hack performance in Oxford, in a field I know well, and on a topic I have often spoken about before. What causes this I do not know: but it is the most appalling nuisance. On this particular occasion I went on leafing through my notes feverishly, in the little room I was left in before I emerged (where I could not exchange those pleasantries with the members of the Committee that I was expected to); when it all began I was thoroughly rattled by observing the old Baron Meyendorff,[1] Vice-President of the Russian Duma in 1908 or thereabouts, in the front row, who, I thought, knew Tolstoy and would certainly see through me as an impostor on the entire subject. I was terrified of going on for too long, and in the middle my notes and pages got muddled. So I went pattering on desperately, while trying to shuffle the pages, and towards the end did finish much sooner than I intended – to the relief and profit of the audience, because I could not find six pages which I had intended to read aloud [...]. The only other person I know who goes through similar states is Dr E. Wind[2] – the best lecturer I ever heard – who literally locks himself up for two days before any lecture and learns the whole thing by heart. Still, if my lectures were as good as his, perhaps it would be worth it. [...]

In a day or two I shall succeed in forgiving you for your most unworthy analysis of my state!

Yours,

Isaiah

TO THE EDITOR OF *THE TIMES LITERARY SUPPLEMENT*

[Published 2 December 1960][3]

All Souls

Sir, –

In the leading article in your last issue, in the course of which you give an account of my Hermon Ould Lecture on Tolstoy, which is, in general, both accurate and generous, you say that Tolstoy wondered whether 'Because a peasant, left to himself, would never appreciate Beethoven or Homer, must the effort to produce great works of art simply cease?'[4] In my lecture I tried [to make], but perhaps did not succeed in making, it clear that Tolstoy believed in the transforming function of works of art as ways of revealing

Enlightenment' (in RT), at Friends' House in Euston on 23 November.

1 Aleksandr Feliksovich Meyendorff (1869–1964), Octobrist, member of the imperial Duma from 1907; left Petrograd for Riga 1918, Riga for England 1919 (aboard a British minelayer); Reader in Russian Institutions and Economics, LSE, 1922–34.

2 Edgar Marcel Wind (1900–71), philosopher and art historian; first Professor of the History of Art at Oxford 1955–67: IB among others had supported the creation of the chair, and Wind's appointment to it.

3 On p. 779, headed 'Tolstoy and the Enlightenment'.

4 [C. M. Woodhouse], 'Tolstoy and Enlightenment', TLS, 25 November 1960, 759.

truth which the sciences could never perform; and specifically contrasts the
Iliad (and the Bible and folksong) as genuine, because popular and universally
intelligible, forms of art, with Mozart, Pushkin etc., whose art is in some
sense false because it sprang from, and appealed to, only civilised (and therefore corrupt) persons (like himself).

Isaiah Berlin

TO GARRETT DROGHEDA[1]

3 December 1960

Headington House

Dear Garrett,

[...] I shall return to the fold in February. And still I beg you do let us look
round for somebody with musical authority of some kind. We really do need
such a one if we are to write off Legge.[2] He has just written me that it has
taken him three years to find out what a hideous Machiavelli I am – this is
all because of my horrible 'betrayal' of Giulini[3] and by implication of him
too – and therefore I feel pessimistic about his further cooperation. I may be
wrong – and he really has been useful in the past: some of our performances
owe more to him than the Administration will acknowledge; his suggestions
and advice are always far better than George [Harewood]'s,[4] indeed the best
of all. I shall make a last desperate effort to lure him back, but am not confident of success. I shall try to see him in January. As a last thing we shall have
to put all our hopes on Solti,[5] and goodness knows how that will work out:
he and the AP[6] are not natural stable mates and the AP knows this well – very
well indeed. The only thing to do (forgive this unsolicited advice!) for you
and me and everybody, is (*a*) not to be irritated, (*b*) not to be over-influenced
by what either the AP or Solti say, but press for what we think right, without,
if possible, taking sides in what will certainly not be a very smooth sort of

1 Garrett Moore (1910–89), 11th Earl of *Drogheda 1957; newspaper proprietor and opera
  manager.
2 (Harry) Walter Legge (1906–79), impresario and record producer; founder of the Philharmonia
  Orchestra, 1945, and one of the driving forces behind the post-war success of the EMI label; in
  IB's eyes a key contributor to the deliberations of the ROH board; 'ruthless in the pursuit of
  his own ends, though these were invariably connected with the art of music' (Peter Martland,
  ODNB).
3 Carlo Maria Giulini (1914–2005), Italian conductor; guest conductor, Covent Garden, 1958–67;
  joint conductor (with Solti) of the Chicago Symphony Orchestra 1969–72; principal conductor,
  Vienna Symphony Orchestra, 1973–6.
4 George Henry Hubert Lascelles (1923–2011), 7th Earl of Harewood, opera administrator;
  founder editor of *Opera* magazine 1950–3; Director, ROH, 1951–3, 1969–72.
5 Georg Solti (1912–97) né György Stern, KBE 1971, Hungarian conductor; Musical Director,
  Covent Garden Opera Company, 1961–71; Music Director, Chicago Symphony Orchestra,
  1969–91; Musical Director, Orchestre de Paris, 1972–5.
6 'The arch-procrastinator', with 'the artful dodger' one of IB's two occasional nicknames for
  David Webster.

passage. If I am wrong, so much the better. I will be able to remember my pathetic words in about a year's time! If I am wrong I shall be ready to give a dinner in honour of Sir David Webster[1] and invite all his dearest friends – and you know how well I love that world!

Yours ever, ⟨with genuine love⟩

Isaiah

TO MORTON WHITE[2]

10 January 1960 [sc. 1961]

Headington House

Dear Morton,

I too am bogged down in the most fearful morass of administrative and intellectual obligations and shall also be brief – reluctantly.

1. Charles Taylor:[3] he is a very nice man, sincere, idealistic, high-minded and attractive. We all (as Meyer Schapiro[4] used to say about you) like him very much indeed: Hampshire, Ayer,[5] Bernard Williams[6] and all. He is fundamentally a reformer and preacher, soaked in French semi-Marxism – Merleau-Ponty,[7] Sartre[8] and the various interpreters of Marx at present flourishing in Paris. He is also a very active member of the *New Left Review*, of nuclear disarmament etc. etc. His ideas are not terribly clear, but he seeks to be intellectually lucid, honest and logical. He is not at all bogus, not dotty, and argument with him is interesting because, although he is not a very close reasoner, he has what is called a position: a genuine philosophy ⟨& Weltanschauung⟩ which is a compound of existentialism and Marxism (with Christian overtones and undertones), not in the sense of John Wild,[9]

---

1 David Lumsden Webster (1903–71), Kt 1960; theatre and opera house administrator; General Administrator, ROH, 1946–70; Governor and General Administrator of the London Opera Centre 1962–71.
2 Morton *White (b. 1917), philosopher, historian of ideas.
3 Charles ('Chuck') *Taylor (b. 1931), Canadian philosopher.
4 Meyer *Schapiro (1904–96), art historian, artist and polymath.
5 Alfred Jules ('Freddie') *Ayer (1910–89), philosopher.
6 Bernard *Williams (1929–2003), philosopher and college head.
7 Maurice Merleau-Ponty (1908–61), French phenomenologist philosopher; Professor of Philosophy, Collège de France, 1952–61; with Sartre, founded and edited the journal *Les Temps modernes*; later broke with Sartre, and abandoned his commitment to Communism, over the Korean War (1950–3).
8 Jean-Paul Charles Aymard Sartre (1905–80), French philosopher, novelist, dramatist and critic, a leading exponent of existentialism; awarded, and rejected, the Nobel Prize in Literature 1964; his *Critique de la raison dialectique* (1960) attempted a synthesis of Marxism and existentialism.
9 John Daniel Wild (1902–72), US philosopher, leading exponent of existentialism and phenomenology; one of the founders in 1962 of the Society for Phenomenology and Existential Philosophy, which was inspired by, inter alia, the works of Sartre and Merleau-Ponty; taught at Harvard 1927–61, Northwestern 1961–3, Yale 1963–9, Florida 1969–72.

but on lines somewhat similar to Hampshire's last book.[1] He does rather like a following: he is an earnest, genuinely noble, concerned sort of man, with shining Quaker eyes, who wishes to persuade one that empiricism is defective, that the social sciences ⟨⟨& epistemology too⟩⟩ cannot do without ⟨quasi-⟩teleological notions, or at any rate concepts of ⟨human⟩ purpose, not allowed for by the drier positivists ⟨& empiricists⟩, and in other respects rep- resents a kind of male version of Iris Murdoch.[2] [...] He is in fact a left-wing ideologue, ⟨with a sound training in logic & philosophy,⟩ of a very pure kind, very unusual in our day and circles. On the other hand I do not think he will please the philosophy department much. At Oxford he got an excellent First in Modern Greats[3] in philosophy, politics and economics equally, and in All Souls irritated the more pompous of my colleagues by totally ignoring the more traditional habits of All Souls and devoting himself to various social and ideological tasks in sublime disregard of conservative susceptibilities. I like him very much indeed: I really do; and I see no harm in his being tried out at Harvard. His bête noire philosophically is Hare of Balliol.[4] And Ryle[5] is pretty suspicious of him, as you may imagine. He is in certain embar- rassed ways an ally of Gellner[6] – perhaps he will join forces with my enemy Marshall Cohen.

The latter's piece about my political views appears to me to be personally offensive and filled with (Jewish, I think) neuroses of a very embarrassing kind: he sent me a copy of his piece, with a scribbled note saying there was no one in the world he admired more than me. The last is what really got my goat and so I did not reply. God knows, I tend to think that anything said against me must be true automatically; his is the only piece which appears to me ⟨perversely⟩ irrelevant to most of what I have to say, genuinely a misun- derstanding or perversion of my views and statements. But I may be biased and mistaken. ⟨At any rate M.C. has now sworn fealty to Gellner, I gather

1 *Thought and Action* (London, 1959). 'Its bold rationalism alone constitutes a new departure in contemporary philosophy and its challenge will be felt for many years to come.' Gershon Weiler, *Philosophical Quarterly* 11 no. 45 (October 1961), 382.

2 (Jean) Iris Murdoch (1919–99), later (1987) DBE; novelist and philosopher; philosophy tutor, St Anne's, 1948–63, Fellow 1948–99; lecturer, Royal College of Art, 1963–7.

3 A name used at the time for PPE, i.e. philosophy, politics and economics. Greats, or Literae Humaniores, the second part of the classics course, comprised philosophy and ancient history

4 Richard Mervyn Hare (1919–2002), Fellow and Tutor in Philosophy, Balliol, 1947–66; White's Professor of Moral Philosophy and Fellow of CCC 1966–83; a prisoner of war working on the Singapore and Burma–Thailand railways 1942–5.

5 Gilbert Ryle (1900–76), Waynflete Professor of Metaphysical Philosophy and Fellow of Magdalen 1945–68; editor of *Mind* in succession to G. E. Moore 1947–71. He was a leading figure in Oxford linguistic philosophy, 'capable of being parodied but impossible to imitate: "Le style, c'est Ryle", J. L. Austin accurately noted' (*Who's Who in the Twentieth Century*, Oxford, 1999); Austin's remark is in his review of Ryle's *The Concept of Mind*, TLS, 7 April 1950, Religious Books Section [sic], xi.

6 Ernest André Gellner (1925–95), social philosopher and (later) anthropologist; Professor of Philosophy, LSE, 1962–84. His *Words and Things* (London, 1959) was a polemical assault on lin- guistic philosophy and its mainly Oxford-based exponents, and Ryle's refusal to publish a review of the book in the journal *Mind* provoked a long correspondence in *The Times*.

from G. – this must be concealed from C[harles Taylor]'s Oxford friends. All marvellously political & sectarian, like Communist squabbles in the 1850ies.⟩ […]

Yours ever,

Isaiah   […]

TO THE EDITOR OF *ENCOUNTER*[1]

21 January 1961 [*carbon; not sent*]

Headington House

[Sir –]

I did not know Bernard Berenson[2] well, but I visited him on half a dozen occasions during the last years of his life. Had I not done so, I might well have accepted the low estimate of his personality made by my friend Meyer Schapiro, if only because of the great respect that I have for Mr Schapiro's opinions. As it is, I consider it mistaken. About Berenson's values and achievement as a historian and critic of art I am not competent to speak. But the total impression of Berenson's character which Mr Schapiro's indignant words convey seems to me profoundly unjust.

Berenson possessed a very powerful intellectual personality, and when he was interested in a subject or in a visitor (he was infinitely sensitive to nuances both of persons and of ideas – about works of art I cannot speak), his conversation was sharp and arresting. His views were original and first-hand, and the ratio of thought to words was uncommonly high, so that one's own mind was made to race. My first impression was that of a polished, mannered and highly self-conscious aesthete; but presently I became aware that I was in the presence of a man of extraordinary breadth and precision of knowledge, of acute ironical and deeply civilised intelligence, but above all of a man who possessed the unique vitality and distinction (if not the creative gifts) of a man of genius. The quality and effect of his conversation is difficult to convey – at any rate I will not attempt to do so. The only persons in my experience in whose talk ideas and images mingled with a similar 'life-enhancing' effect were Pasternak, Keynes and Freud.[3] Mr Schapiro conveys the impres-

---

1 *Encounter* had published Meyer Schapiro's critical essay on Berenson, 'Mr Berenson's Values', in their January issue.
2 Bernard *Berenson (1865–1959), art historian, collector and authority on the Italian Renaissance.
3 IB met Boris Leonidovich Pasternak (1890–1960), the Russian poet, novelist and translator, author of *Doctor Zhivago* (1957), several times during his visit to the Soviet Union in 1945; he arrived at Pasternak's Peredelkino dacha bearing gifts from the poet's sisters, Josephine and Lydia, who lived in Oxford; in 1956 he met him again, and smuggled a copy of the manuscript of *Zhivago* back to England. He came to know and admire the economist John Maynard Keynes (1883–1946) during the latter's visits to Washington during the Second World War; their first meeting, at High Table at King's Cambridge in the 1930s, had not been a success, Keynes being cuttingly dismissive of the philosophical paper (on pleasure) that IB had come to give. IB met the Austrian psychologist Sigmund Freud (1856–1939) only once, in October 1938, not long after Freud's London exile

sion of a personality so deeply flawed that whatever it might once have been it had become hopelessly corrupted into triviality, snobbery, pretence – into a character clever, meretricious, venal and false. I can testify, without fear of contradiction, that when Berenson talked about ideas, books or persons with sympathetic persons the precise opposite was true. Mr Schapiro speaks of his attitude to the Jews. Berenson spoke to me about it often. Like Heine[1] (with whom he felt an affinity) and perhaps Marx (the analogy with St Paul[2] and Spinoza[3] was a very characteristic *jeu d'esprit* and no more), he broke away from his East European Jewish milieu early in life, and was clearly in his youth determined to place the maximum distance between himself and the detested Pale of Settlement;[4] he probably felt at one time that he had succeeded in this, but towards the end of his life this goal seemed to him at once less attainable and less desirable. I do not think that he was embarrassed by his origins: but he had revolted against them, and bitterly attacked them and the national feelings they inspired in others. By the time I came to know him he discussed this difficult – as it seemed to him – relationship freely and openly, nor did the presence of non-Jews deter him in the least. On this entire topic I disagreed with him very sharply (as I suspect that I do, for different reasons, with Mr Schapiro), and said what I thought. He argued courteously, firmly, with great perspicacity and knowledge and a kind of sardonic gaiety; and I see no reason to doubt his sincerity. His point of view was similar to, and in my view as deluded as, that of Pasternak in *Doctor Zhivago*.[5] Mr Schapiro says that the motive of both his conversions was desire for social ease and advancement. I do not believe this, and cannot see how anyone who did not know him intimately can be in a position to judge. He was worldly, pleasure-loving and, unlike his ancestors, in harmony with physical nature. He understood himself and others, and wished to obtain from life all it could give: occasionally he wondered whether, in this remorseless pursuit, he had squandered too many of the gifts he knew himself to possess. I am glad

had begun, and when he was in the advanced stages of cancer: IB left 'feeling that he had spent an hour in the company not of a genius, but of an old Jewish doctor, clever, malicious and wise' (MI 92).

1 Heinrich Heine (1797–1856), German-born poet and influential radical thinker, converted from Judaism to Christianity in 1825.

2 Saul of Tarsus (*c*.5–*c*.67 ce) began as a persecutor of Christians, but after his conversion by a dramatic vision of Jesus of Nazareth he took the name Paul and became a Christian missionary.

3 Baruch (or Benedict) de Spinoza (1632–77), Dutch rationalist philosopher and freethinker born in Amsterdam into a Jewish family which had fled persecution in Spain; his *Tractatus Theologico-Philosophicus* was published in 1670.

4 The region in the western provinces of Imperial Russia, bordering Prussia, Austria-Hungary and the Black Sea, in which Jews were allowed to reside permanently, but beyond which their residence was restricted.

5 When IB visited Pasternak in Moscow in 1945 he became aware that the writer struggled to reconcile his Jewish origins with his Russian identity. When, eleven years later, Pasternak entrusted IB with a manuscript of *Doctor Zhivago*, IB 'went away, read the chapters and immediately knew that Pasternak's crisis of identity had been resolved' (MI 147).

to have known him; apart from the pleasure of friendship, it enlarged my conception of what a man endowed with unusual power of will can do to achieve moral and intellectual independence. Mr Schapiro sees him as a slave to squalid social values. The man I knew, whatever he may have been in earlier years, seemed to me rational, morally untroubled, and free.

[Isaiah Berlin]

TO WALTER LEGGE

28 January 1961 [*carbon*]

[Headington House]

Dear Walter,

I have given up all hope of seeing you. Not for want of trying on my part! I shall do so no more, absorbed as I am in lecturing on Karl Marx to an audience partly sceptical, partly too dense to understand, partly shot through with suspicion about my intentions, partly fanatically hostile in any case – blooded radicals with ladies with bloodshot eyes and horse-tail *chevelures*[1] glaring at me balefully and scribbling notes to be used at my forthcoming execution under the new regime. I shall not escape from all this until March. Shall I at least see you on 15 February, or whenever the Subcommittee meets? I suppose not. You really should have been at the last Subcommittee meeting, at which Solti explained why now he was in love with *Midsummer Night's Dream*, and about his experiences in New York. Meanwhile your own programmes seem wonderful to me. I can only come to London sparingly, as I really am in a frantic state this term, all due to my illness last summer, which has piled too much on my back now, but I long to come to three or four of the events advertised. Would you ask your office to be so very kind and send me tickets? If this is too much bother I can, of course, get them through the normal channels. [...] But you won't answer this letter, you have written me off, I know it well.

Yours,

[Isaiah]

TO ARTHUR LOURIE[2]

3 March 1961 [*carbon*]

[Headington House]

Dear Arthur,

You ask about the Censor of St Catherine's;[3] yes indeed, a very good man. I know him well, he is a vigorous, explosive Yorkshireman, who will certainly

1 i.e. ponytails.
2 Arthur Lourie (1903–78), South-African-born lawyer and Zionist; Israeli ambassador in Canada 1957–60, London 1960–5.
3 Alan *Bullock (1914–2004), historian; founding Master, St Catherine's, 1960–80.

go a long way yet; I do not believe he will stay in Oxford for ever, but will become head of the BBC, or a powerful editor, or occupy some other public post of great importance and influence. So far, so good. Also he has just received £10,000 from Marks and Spencer for his new College and is therefore well disposed towards the Jews, Israel etc. On the other hand, he is the author, as you know, of the biographies of Hitler and Bevin;[1] he is quick-tempered; assumes all Jews to be enemies of his hero Bevin – for reasons which he does not ignore, but about which he argues with some pugnacity and aggressiveness. Now you must judge for yourself whether the inevitable heckling to which he will be exposed for having chosen these two characters for his biographies will or will not irritate him too much. If he can go arm in arm with some congenial companion, say Marcus Sieff,[2] I should say yes, but if he [is] to be taken around by some typical Israeli cultural cicerone, then I should be doubtful. He can only be allowed to go if enough fuss is made of him, if BG is not rude to him etc. But he would like the country and its vigour and its rawness, and is in principle a friend and an ally. So I leave it there.

Yours,

[Isaiah]

TO MICHAEL BROCK[3]

3 March 1961 [carbon]

[Headington House]

Dear Brock,

I write to you at the behest of my colleague, Harold Hanbury,[4] in connection with my request for an amplifier as an aid to lecturing in the South School.[5] The Clerk [of the Schools] kindly provided an instrument, and, imperfect as it is, it was a considerable assistance. Lectures on popular subjects (e.g. Marxism) appear to attract unusually large audiences; and when I found myself moved into the South School, I realised that, added to

1 Ernest Bevin (1881–1951), trade unionist and Labour politician. Bullock's sympathetic *The Life and Times of Ernest Bevin* was published in three volumes (London, 1960–83); the last volume dealt with Bevin's time as Foreign Secretary, 1945–51, when he was faced with the difficult task of reconciling Zionist aspirations with the expectations of Palestinian Arabs; his determination to limit Jewish immigration from post-Holocaust Europe was deemed unforgivable in the eyes of Jews and their supporters.

2 Marcus Joseph Sieff (1913–2001), later (1971) Kt; younger surviving son of Israel Moses (Baron) Sieff (1889–1972, President of Marks and Spencer 1967–71), and grandson of Michael Marks, who founded the firm in Leeds in 1894. Marcus Sieff joined Marks and Spencer in 1935, becoming Joint Managing Director 1967–83 and Chairman 1972–84.

3 Michael *Brock (b. 1920), historian and academic administrator.

4 Harold Greville Hanbury (1898–1993), jurist; Fellow of All Souls and Vinerian Professor of English Law 1949–64.

5 One of the primary lecture theatres in Oxford's grand 19th-century Examination Schools building: MGB was the University's acting (i.e. executive) curator of the building 1960–6.

my other imperfections, the lack of a stentorian voice was going to prove a considerable obstacle to those who sat in the back rows of that acoustically dreadful room. Shout as I might, little apparently was heard among the back rows. I admit that the mechanical drill in the street outside, with which I competed for some forty minutes of my midday lecture, was a new and unexpected handicap; but even without it the difficulties of audibility are very large. After the machine was installed, things went better and my voice sometimes rose to a scream and at others sank to a whisper as the result of the vagaries of the instrument; nevertheless, according to testimony the total result was better. Surely something could be done, as it is in practically every lecture hall in the United States for example, to make shouting unnecessary and reduce the natural inequalities between the lecturers who can roar and those who cannot? Hanbury says I am to write to you as the ultimate fount of wisdom and authority in this matter. I should have thought that some public address system with loudspeakers attached at large and symmetrical distances around the room would make it unnecessary for lecturers to raise their voices above ordinary speaking pitch and strength, and so conduce to that excellence in lectures which has become a topical subject. It is difficult, for some at any rate, to think and bellow at the same time; some subjects automatically attract larger audiences than others; since the *Isis*,[1] fortunately, has said nothing on the subject, we can still afford to act with dignity, as well as efficiency, in this matter and remedy a defect before complaints about it have arisen among the more obstreperous consumers. [...]

Yours ever,

[Isaiah Berlin]

TO ROWLAND BURDON-MULLER

[mid-March 1961, *manuscript*]

University College Hospital, London

Dear, dear Rowland

My little operation on my nose is over.[2] I am reading peacefully: the American doctors are said by my jolly Mr Musgrave here to have left their job on me very botched in 1944 – that is when I allowed the lunatic Mrs J. W. Garrett of Baltimore with whom later I became so bitterly brouillé[3] – to send me to Johns Hopkins hospital, whence all my sinus trouble & trembling eyelids began. [...] My last powerful experience was with the Russian

---

1 Oxford University student magazine founded in 1892, noted for its satirical style.
2 On 10 March 1961 IB underwent minor surgery at University College Hospital, London, to remove a nose polyp; a week later he was recovering at home: 'I had an operation on my nose which did me neither good nor harm. That is the most that can be expected of any operation and so I am quite content' (to Umberto Morra, 5 June 1961).
3 Alice Warder Garrett (1877–1952), wife of John Work Garrett (1872–1942), US ambassador to Italy 1929–33; a renowned Baltimore hostess. We have not discovered why IB became *brouillé* ('at odds') with her.

delegates in Sussex.[1] The idea was that they shd send some people to meet corresponding British journalists, dons, M.P.s etc. for a "free" discussion of coexistence. [...] I didn't join them in the first two days: but I arranged for them all to [go to] the opening night of *Fidelio* – a *splendid* performance [...] conducted *incomparably* by Klemperer,[2] which the Russians apparently *resisted*: why music? why culture? they had come to discuss "coexistence" & this was an irrelevant interruption. However the very firm Quaker who was in charge said that all had been arranged, & firmly took them in hand. Once orders are issued they behave like Prussians or lambs. I went with Aline & Princess Schwarzenberg the Austrian Ambassadress & joined the party at the reception in Cov. Garden. A bunch of thugs they looked & were. In the bus on the way to the country house in which Germans used to be indoctrinated into British democracy[3] – & which is therefore full of German notices which annoyed the Russians – as well as that *Fidelio* was sung in German – in the bus, Mr Surkov[4] began to tell me why Pasternak's mistress had to go to jail for 8 years for receiving money from P.'s royalties abroad.[5] She was described as a filthy whore; a woman engaged on subverting not only the financial but the moral politics of the Soviet State; a liar, a cheat, & an evil influence. I was told that while the English clapped their hands with joy when the blood-stained murderer Hammarskjöld[6] – the enemy of liberty & justice – murdered Lumumba,[7] they cried out with hypocritical horror when a squalid

1 A thirteen-strong Soviet delegation arrived in London on 20 February, at the invitation of the Great Britain–USSR Association, for talks at Wiston House, West Sussex, on coexistence.

2 Otto Klemperer (1885–1973), German-born conductor, recommended by Mahler for his first conducting post; made famous in Britain by his long association with Walter Legge's Philharmonia Orchestra, of which he became Principal Conductor for life in 1959; guest conductor at Covent Garden 1961, 1962, 1963, 1969.

3 Wiston House was the home, from January 1951, of the 'Wilton Park' forum for democracy, established by the British government in January 1946 to prepare German prisoners of war for democratic participation in their post-war government.

4 Aleksey Surkov (1899–1983), Soviet poet and novelist, noted for his patriotic poetry during the Second World War; led the Russian delegation to England, February 1961; as First Secretary of the Union of Soviet Writers, prominent in the campaign against Boris Pasternak, which led to the latter's expulsion from the Union, and his inability to accept the 1958 Nobel Prize in Literature.

5 Olga Vsevolodovna Ivinskaya (1912–95), Russian translator of poetry; muse and mistress of Boris Pasternak, whom she met in 1946 when working as literary editor for the journal *Novyi mir* (*New World*); she was arrested and sent to the Gulag 1949–53, probably because of her association with Pasternak, and after her release, on Stalin's death, moved to the writer's village of Peredelkino, where she worked closely with Pasternak as his literary assistant. In December 1960 she was sentenced to eight years' imprisonment, and her daughter to three, charged with keeping royalties from the sale of *Doctor Zhivago*. Before his death in May 1960, Pasternak had expressed fears about Ivinskaya's fate, and in the West her conviction was seen as a straightforward act of political repression.

6 Dag Hjalmar Agne Carl Hammarskjöld (1905–61), Secretary General, UN, 1953–61, developed the UN's peacekeeping role, and invoked Article 99 of its Charter to initiate preventive diplomacy in the Congo crisis; killed in a plane crash in Northern Rhodesia (now Zambia), 17/18 September 1961, while trying to further diplomatic initiatives there.

7 Patrice Émery Lumumba (1925–61) né Élias Okit'Asombo, Prime Minister, upon independence, of the Republic of Congo (formerly a Belgian colony); leading proponent of pan-Africanism, and of Congolese union; subsequently deposed, and murdered by political rivals in the breakaway

prostitute – who led a man of genius to write his worst book – the worthless
Zhivago – was imprisoned for receiving stolen goods – 100-000 dollars sent by
the pimp Feltrinelli[1] through the spies he filtered into Russia for P's ill gotten
royalties obtained by betraying his country – *then* the great British public
threw up its hands in horror! Did I know with whom I was sympathising?
this woman's husband committed suicide in 1941. Why? because he found
her secret diary: containing no fewer than 74 – 74 he repeated in a voice of
thunder which reverberated down that poor bus – *lovers!* *this* is the strumpet
the British public felt sorry for, Lord Russell wrote about in the *Times* etc.
etc. etc.[2] I cd only riposte by saying that I cd not check or deny their *facts*: the
trial had not been attended by foreign journalists: but that (a) Pasternak was
the second most famous author in the world now, never mind whether justly
or not; anything touching him automatically obtained world wide repercus-
sions; (b) nobody wd *believe* the Russian story, however true: for the motives
for persecution were too great. [...] They cd imprison "evil influences" (it
is now plain to me that they mean to canonise Pasternak, who really *did*
loathe them, on the principle of "if you can't beat 'em, join 'em") as much
as they wished: but the effect in the West cd be very melancholy. They wd
alienate even the left wing intelligentsia, etc etc. So we went at it ding-dong
till we got to Wiston House [...] & dropped to bed exhausted at 2 a.m. – On
the next day we "debated" hammer & tongs. The Russians made nothing
but loud propaganda speeches: they said the *Times* was a fascist sheet – the
poor foreign editor, Iverach Macdonald,[3] a most mild, temperate, if anything
mildly pro-Soviet man, nearly had a fit: they said they didn't read the M.
Guardian because it was a worthless liberal paper, the editor there & then
left the meeting: they complained that the press had not given their speeches
enough space: they read long intolerably dreary statements obviously made
up in Moscow: "our" delegates, particularly the socialists were fearfully
upset: I did not mind: this is mechanical behaviour for them, & after heaping
horrible insults of a personal kind on us, they lunched & dined amiably, as if
nothing were the matter. They feel at *war*: war has certain rules, e.g. sitting
at common tables during truces: but as soon as the truce is over, one shoots
to kill. It is difficult to get [across] to anyone not there, how very unnatural
& inhuman these naturally quite human beings, artificially, under orders,

Katanga Province, 17 January 1961. Lumumba had requested UN protection, and the Soviet
Union held Hammarskjöld personally responsible for his death. Despite Soviet vilification,
Hammarskjöld was posthumously awarded the Nobel Peace Prize in 1961.

1 Giangiacomo Feltrinelli (1926–72), Italian left-wing political activist and publisher – the first to
  publish *Doctor Zhivago* (in an Italian translation in 1957). Ivinskaya was a crucial intermediary in
  Pasternak's dealings with Feltrinelli.
2 Bertrand Arthur William Russell (1872–1970), 3rd Earl Russell, Cambridge philosopher, political
  campaigner and Nobel laureate (in literature); he had expressed his 'deep regret' at the 'savage
  sentences' passed on Ivinskaya and her daughter, which he attributed solely to the fact that 'they
  were friends of Pasternak' ('Bad Habits in Moscow', letter, *Times*, 30 January 1961, 11e).
3 Iverach McDonald [*sic*] (1908–2006), Highlander and Russianist; foreign editor, *The Times*, 1952–65.

become. It is not diplomatic but army training: I prefer the non-dissimulated to the white sepulchres like Surkov or Malik[1] whom I thought of *infinite* nastiness. The new ambassador, Soldatov[2] (appropriately so called) is *much* nicer. I enjoyed it all. I liked their language: I saw, or thought I saw, how and why they behaved as they did & what they wanted & why; & was instructed. I was amused during the visit to the Brighton Pavilion to a civic reception by the Mayor, to see that they *could* not decide if the Pavilion was comical or serious; to laugh or express admiration for this Bokharan-Chinese rococo fantasy:[3] I loved their insistence on a joint Communiqué which neither side desired to subscribe to [...] because otherwise they wd be upbraided in Moscow for incurring expenses & doing "no work" etc. I complained to Surkov that I had just been described in a Soviet publication as "a shameful ignoramus with aspirations to knowledge of 19*th*[-century] Russian culture, expectorating filthy drivel & uttering unoriginal libels against Lenin".[4] He laughed amiably & said that did not matter provided I was not called by the name of a beast e.g. a hyena, like T. S. Eliot, Hammarskjöld, Auden,[5] Gaitskell[6] etc. which *might* be fatal! So we parted. Much love to you, & do write again: your last letter was quite brilliant.

I.B.

TO ANN FLEMING

17 March 1961 [*carbon*]

[Headington House]

Dearest Ann,

Forgive me for not writing with my own hand, but I am feeble after my hideous operation – it was not very painful; what was really fearful was being woken every two hours in order to be given an injection of cortisone, which

---

1 Yakov Aleksandrovich Malik (1906–80), Ukranian-born Soviet diplomat, succeeded Andrey Gromyko as Soviet ambassador in London 1952–60; afterwards Soviet Deputy Foreign Minister and later (1968–72) Soviet ambassador to the UN.

2 Aleksandr Alekseevich Soldatov ('soldat' means 'soldier') (1915–99), Soviet diplomat; succeeded Yakov Malik as ambassador in London 1960–6.

3 The magnificent Royal Pavilion in Brighton was built for the Prince Regent, later George IV, between 1787 and 1823, and is extravagantly oriental in design. 'Bokharan' suggests a fusion of Arabic and oriental styles: the region of Bukhara in Uzbekistan straddles the ancient Silk Road.

4 Viktor Arsen'evich Malinin (1921–99), in a review of Franco Venturi's *Roots of Revolution: A History of the Populist and Socialist Movements in Nineteenth-Century Russia* (London, 1960) in *Novye knigi za rubezhom po obshchestvennym naukam* 1961 no. 1 (January), 40–7 at 46–7, attacked IB for his introduction (later included in RT as 'Russian Populism'). The passage to which IB refers runs: 'this "specialist" is clearly a complete ignoramus when it comes to the history of Russian social thought. He solemnly and with great aplomb pronounces stupid things [...] right down to an unoriginal slander of Leninism.'

5 W[ystan] H[ugh] Auden (1907–73), poet and writer; a close friend, from their undergraduate days, of IB's lifelong friend Stephen Spender.

6 Hugh Todd Naylor Gaitskell (1906–63), Leader of the Labour Party 1955–63; his brand of revisionist socialism, and his willingness to speak up for political prisoners in the Soviet Union, led to his being criticised by the Soviet press.

was afterwards discovered to be unnecessary, being founded on a misinterpretation of something which the surgeon had told Goldman![1] In the end I succeeded with diabolical pleasure in embroiling all the three doctors, the surgeon, the doctor and the anaesthetist, in contradictions with their own advice and each other, so that they ended rather like the Prime Ministers and Dr Verwoerd[2] – total inability to reach a formula, hatred of me (the problem), realisation that I realised that all of what all of them said could not be true, and that the only problem was who was lying how far to cover up what, and general moral chaos. However I am recovering nevertheless: and your delicious present, beautiful both without and within, eggs within eggs in the most exquisite Chinese fashion, did much to expedite my slow recovery. Alas, my poor nose! Have you ever read a story by Gogol about a nose?[3] It is an exquisite surrealist story now set to music by various composers about a man who put some ointment on his nose at night in order to get rid of a pimple and in the morning found a smooth surface where his nose had been, and worries about whether his colleagues at the office will notice, and then emerges into the street and sees his nose in fur coat and exquisite top hat accompanying two beautiful ladies into a carriage. The nose is very gallant and gay and has tremendous adventures which the original owner observes with wonder and envy. This goes on for some days: it is a very good story. My nose remains plebeian and unadventurous.

Sparrow has just rung up to say that he has inflicted a crushing defeat upon Maurice (do not report this! It will do such terrible, terrible damage, worse than South Africa). No doubt we shall hear about the crushing comeback; there is something in what Connolly[4] says about arriving at the Oxford platform at intervals of fifteen years only to hear voices say 'Did you hear what Maurice said about Roy[5] ...?' Or 'Have you heard about the awful row between All Souls and Magdalen?' etc.

Ava[6] has written especially to say that she has received a visit from the

1 Carl Heinz Goldman (1904–92), Leipzig-born Jewish general practitioner; fled Germany in the 1930s, and qualified to practise in Britain in 1935; served with the RAMC during the Second World War, and afterwards became one of London's most fashionable society doctors.

2 The Lancaster House conference of Commonwealth Prime Ministers decided after much wrangling, 15 March 1961, that South Africa would leave the Commonwealth on becoming a republic (on 31 May): at the root of their decision was their opposition to the apartheid policies of the government of Dr Hendrik Frensch Verwoerd (1901–66), Prime Minister of South Africa 1958–66.

3 *The Nose* (1836), one of the St Petersburg stories of Nikolay Vasil'evich Gogol (1809–52), made into an opera with the same title (1930) by Dmitry Shostakovich (1906–75).

4 Cyril Vernon Connolly (1903–74), writer and literary reviewer; from 1950 until his death chief literary critic of the *Sunday Times*; a near contemporary at Oxford of Maurice *Bowra (1898–1971), classicist and Warden of Wadham, and Roy Harrod (next note).

5 (Henry) Roy Forbes Harrod (1900–78), Kt 1959, economist; Student (i.e. fellow) in Modern History and Economics, Christ Church, 1924–67; Nuffield Reader in International Economics 1952–67; official biographer of John Maynard Keynes.

6 Ava Waverley (1896–1974) née Bodley, political hostess, whose second husband was John Anderson (1882–1958), 1st Viscount Waverley 1952. Although she 'took no part in public life',

Queen of Greece,[1] who is a most accomplished philosopher – I am glad
not to be at the luncheon, to which the Greek Ambassador had most kindly
invited me, at which there was obviously to be a parade of intellectuals
before their Majesties of Greece. Light conversation about abstract subjects
with a flirtatious German pseudo-bluestocking, with Maurice roaring on the
right and Noel Annan[2] roaring on the left, is not my idea of a quiet afternoon
for a remote and ineffectual don.

Is there a certain waspishness in my words today? I ascribe it to my physical condition. Soon I shall return to a universal and insufferable benevolence.
When shall we see each other again here? It was so nice last time.

Yours,

[Isaiah]

The victory in 1959 of Fidel Castro's[3] Cuban revolution, which overthrew
the brutal American-backed dictatorship of Fulgencio Batista, was perceived
in Washington as a serious threat to US interests. Castro quickly introduced
radical socialist reforms, indulging in revolutionary rhetoric, and in the opinion
of John F. Kennedy, the Democratic presidential candidate in 1960, Cuba had
become 'Communism's first Caribbean base'.[4] In office Kennedy sought to
dislodge this foothold, and he sanctioned the CIA plot to oust Castro initiated by
his predecessor, Dwight D. Eisenhower. This policy culminated in the disastrous
'Bay of Pigs' invasion of 17–19 April 1961, in which a paramilitary brigade of
CIA-trained Cuban exiles was quickly defeated after landing on the south-west
coast of Cuba. The popular anti-Castro uprising that the invasion was meant
to trigger never happened, and the episode instead advertised to the world the
popularity of the Communist Cuban regime.

Among the international intelligentsia there was considerable support for
Castro, and the British theatre critic Kenneth Tynan[5] was one of the signatories
of a full-page advertisement in the New York Times of 6 April 1960, under
the auspices of the 'Fair Play for Cuba Committee', which complained of an
anti-Castro bias in the Western media; other signatories included Simone de
Beauvoir, Jean-Paul Sartre, Norman Mailer and Truman Capote. But elsewhere

Ava Waverley probably exercised 'more indirect influence than any woman of her generation'
(Times, 24 December 1974, 12e).

1 Princess Frederica of Hanover (1917–81), a distant cousin of both Elizabeth II and Prince Philip,
   Duke of Edinburgh, and consort of King Paul of Greece (1901–64), who reigned 1947–64.
2 Noel *Annan (1916–2000), Provost of King's, Cambridge.
3 Fidel Alejandro Castro Ruz (b. 1926), Cuban revolutionary leader and politician; Prime Minister
   of Cuba 1959–76, President 1976–2008; led the rebellion that toppled the Batista dictatorship;
   from 1961 he aligned Cuba more closely with the Soviet Union, on whose aid the Cuban
   economy was heavily dependent; became an idol of liberation movements worldwide.
4 Speech in Cincinnati, 6 October 1960, The Speeches, Remarks, Press Conferences, and Statements of
   John F. Kennedy, August 1 through November 7 (Washington, 1961), 511. The quotation in the next
   paragraph is on the same page.
5 Kenneth Peacock Tynan (1927–80), journalist, writer, and theatre critic; creator of the wildly
   successful revue Oh! Calcutta! (1969); socialist and supporter of nuclear disarmament.

the anti-democratic aspects of Castro's regime were stressed: 'Castro and his gang', said Senator Kennedy in October 1960, 'have betrayed the ideals of the Cuban revolution and the hopes of the Cuban people.'

TO KENNETH TYNAN

26 April 1961 [*carbon*]

[Headington House]

Dear Mr Tynan,

Thank you for your letter of 21 April. You must forgive me if I do not respond to your invitation to express myself in favour of setting up a Cuban Defence Committee. My reason is this: I have talked to two Cuban Democrats who look on Dr Castro as a bloodstained tyrant: this I do not necessarily accept; but I think the parallel between him and the early Bolsheviks is considerable, and I cannot persuade myself that some of his more repressive acts have any justification. The defence is always that in order to make an omelette one must break eggs: this too is no doubt the justification which would be urged by President Kennedy; if I were a statesman or even a Member of Parliament I should feel obliged to have to make up my mind about which was the necessary evil in terms of omelettes and eggs, and plump; as a private citizen I do not feel obliged to declare myself. [...]

Yours sincerely,

[Isaiah Berlin]

TO KENNETH TYNAN

1 May 1961 [*carbon*]

[Headington House]

Dear Mr Tynan,

You must forgive me for going on with the subject of Cuba. I see from your letter in *The Times* that you believe many good things about Castro.[1] I do not. I think his economic and educational achievements are smaller than has been made out and that his repression started long before any serious danger of invasion or counter-revolution: as indeed happened in 1917–18 in Russia too and for similar ideological reasons. Castro may not be a Communist but I think he cares as little for civil liberties or the fate of individual human beings as Lenin or Trotsky. But even if I am wholly mistaken in this – and perhaps evidence will emerge one day to make this clear either way – this

---

1 Tynan had earlier led a group of sixteen prominent figures in a letter to *The Times*, 18 April, protesting against American involvement in the 'Bay of Pigs' invasion. On 28 April he wrote again, independently, to defend this stance against criticism that Castro was undemocratic and authoritarian: he credited Castro's regime with considerable progress towards social equality, and argued that 'in a state of emergency a government may be forgiven if it has recourse to censorship' (19 April, 13e; 29 April, 9e).

does not make the American part in the invasion either intelligent or right; and if your original letter had confined itself to saying that it was foolish and wrong I should have had no objection to signing, except for a general distaste for round robins, committees with little influence, etc., which perhaps I could have brought myself to have overcome. But I must confess that I did not feel about the Cuban situation that unmistakable feeling of outrage which blows all fine calculations out of the window.

When one has a real sense of horror at thorough wickedness, one should surely go by one's instinct and not hide behind reasoning. The Moscow trials, Munich, Hitler, Mussolini (*pace* Mr A. J. P. Taylor),[1] the Spanish war, the Abyssinian war, Franco, Salazar, Stalin, Budapest, the persecution of homosexuals, Verwoerd, flogging, the *Zhivago* affair and its horrible aftermath (Madame Ivinskaya and her daughter) – these allow of no doubts. But Suez (perhaps because of my pro-Israel feeling – though I do not like to think this true), FLN terrorism in Algiers and in France, Jewish terrorism in Palestine, CND, Eichmann, the Chinese drive to collectivisation – these do not produce this instinctive reaction, at any rate in me. Castro belongs (for me) in this category. The Algerian generals are enemies to all that I believe in, but Castro – the jails and executions which started before the danger of an invasion (I agree that the invasion gave him a true reason as well as an excuse for doing something which he obviously is not temperamentally averse to in any case, [and was] therefore the more unfortunate), the link with Khrushchev – all this does not promise justice or liberty. I am not prepared to throw a stone at Castro's regime. I accept a good deal of what you say with such obvious sincerity and politically (to me) sympathetic feeling as true – the results of Batista and Machado[2] (whom the Americans helped the Cubans to remove) cannot be removed by using only gentle and civilised means. But neither am I ready to defend the regime. In such a state of mind it would certainly be dishonest of me to speak out. Not that it matters whether I do or not – I am beginning to think that you may regard my earlier letter and this one as mere symptoms of self-importance. I sign far too many letters of this type and my name has consequently become of no worth now – if ever it was of any. Still, when asked to sign a protest against Franco's prisons – even though this means to appear on the same page with Thorez[3] and other Communists whose moral right to protest against this sort of thing does not exist (your letter in the *Times* contains some very compromising signatures in this sense)[4] – I sign; I see no alternative; so too in the case of the South

1 A. J. P. *Taylor (1906–90), historian.
2 Gerardo Machado y Morales (1871–1939), President of Cuba 1924–33, changed the constitution in 1928 to allow his re-election, virtually unopposed, and became increasingly despotic; his regime fell after widespread unrest, and contributed to the radicalisation of Cuban politics.
3 Maurice Thorez (1900–64), French Communist Party leader; a loyal Stalinist who influenced the French Party's refusal to endorse Khrushchev's 1956 denunciation of the 'cult of personality'.
4 Kingsley Martin (95/1) and Eric Hobsbawm (378/2), signatories of Tynan's 18 April letter

African cricketers who came to Oxford – I said a boycott was perfectly justified and was involved in bitter controversy with some perfectly nice honourable persons on this issue.[1] Castro seems to belong to quite a different box
– one has to swallow a great many abominable acts and condone and explain
away. Here I feel no moral compulsion. [...]

Yours sincerely,

[Isaiah Berlin]

*In January 1961 de Gaulle's clear victory in a referendum on his Algerian policy
appeared fatally to weaken the resistance to independence of the terrorist OAS
(Organisation de l'armée secrète) and the high-ranking army officers who supported it. But on Saturday 22 April 1961 four retired generals led a coup, seizing
control of the government in Algiers and threatening the Fifth Republic itself.
Although the 'Generals' Putsch' proved short-lived, there is no doubting the
anxiety of the government in Paris, in particular about the loyalty of the army.
In a broadcast early on the Sunday morning, the Prime Minister, Michel Debré,[2]
warned that renegade troops were preparing to parachute into aerodromes near
Paris as a preliminary to seizing power: 'When the sirens sound,' he urged the
people, 'go there, on foot or by car, and try to persuade the troops of their great
error.'[3] That evening de Gaulle made a stirring appeal to the nation to reject the
'odious and stupid adventure' of what he called 'a group of partisan, ambitious and fanatical officers': 'Thus the State is thwarted, the nation defied, our
power degraded, our national prestige abased, our role and our place in Africa
compromised. [...] Frenchwomen, Frenchmen, look at where France is in danger
of going in relation to what she was in the process of becoming. Frenchwomen,
Frenchmen, help me.'[4]*

TO ROWLAND BURDON-MULLER

14 May 1961

Headington House

Dear Rowland,

Forgive me if I do not write you a long letter – you are right this is the
worst of seasons for me, with lectures, undergraduates, committees and
fearful time-eating occupations of various kinds, devouring one's substance

(published 19 April), were conspicuous in their failure to condemn Stalinism.

1 In May 1960 IB was one of the 56 senior members of the University who jointly protested against
the cricket club's decision to play a match against the touring South Africans, arguing that the
fixture would serve only 'to condone the practice of racial discrimination in sport, and to associate the University of Oxford with it in the public mind' (*Times*, 10 May 1960, 7a).

2 Michel Debré (1912–96), Prime Minister of France 1959–62; Minister of Economics and Finance
1966–8, Foreign Affairs 1968–9, Defence 1969–73.

3 *Times*, 24 April 1961, 14a.

4 ibid, 14a, 14c.

from all ends. I have a fearful sense of waste too – nothing that I say seems worth saying, or that I write seems worth writing, nor do I much enjoy the barren controversies in which I am forced to indulge with critics of my works in the pages of such publications as the *Listener*. [...]

As for France and the General's revolt, it was really rather exciting. We arrived there from Italy by a train from Turin – at 10 p.m. loudspeakers kept saying in Turin (this was some four or five days before) that there was no guarantee that the train would arrive in Paris, since it was possible that the French would start a strike at 4 a.m. and that the passengers travelled at their own risk. [...] There was no strike and we reached Paris peacefully. We saw Joe Alsop,[1] who, of course, was deeply depressed and at the same time revelling in the hideous Cuban business [...]. Joe then came to see us on Saturday morning[2] quite early and asked if we did not think the news very bad. We still thought it was Cuba, but when he discovered that we did not know he was only too delighted to tell us the most gruesome details of the General's revolt, predicted they would invade Tunis (and I suppose capture the Queen Mother – a rich prize – then staying with the President of Tunis) and otherwise delighted in painting flesh-creeping, hair-raising pictures. Paris did seem a little nervous that day, but we saw no tanks or militia. We went peacefully to the theatre in the evening to see a Russian play and on the next day saw various old friends, dined with the Rumbolds[3] in the evening. When we came back at about midnight Salem telephoned us at about 12.30 to say that he was sorry to interrupt our sleep but we should doubtless be interested to know that M. Debré made the speech he did about the parachutists being expected within four or five hours – and all good men to go to the airports. We did not think this applied to foreigners. I was going to London anyway on the Golden Arrow on the Monday, as term had started and I was shamefully late for it already, and had stretched my stay in Paris as far as possible – but then I felt deep reluctance to leave, I longed to see what would happen next. Meanwhile Mme Philippe de Rothschild[4] – Pauline Potter to you – had assembled a tremendous dinner party for Monday night in honour of the Alsops, including the entire French cabinet, other than de Gaulle, and all their wives and actresses and the Arons,[5] and other American journalists,

---

1 Joseph Wright ('Joe') *Alsop (1910–89), newspaper columnist and commentator on foreign affairs.
2 22 April.
3 (Horace) Anthony (Claude) Rumbold (1911–83), KCMG 1962, diplomat; British minister in Paris 1960–3; ambassador to Thailand and UK representative on the council of the Southeast Asia Treaty Organization (SEATO) 1965–7; ambassador to Austria 1967–70. His (first) wife was Felicity Ann (1917–84) née Bailey (divorced 1974).
4 Pauline de Rothschild (1908–76) née Potter; born in Paris to wealthy American expatriate parents, she married, 1954, her second husband, Baron Philippe de Rothschild (1902–88); worked for the couturier Schiaparelli in London and Paris, and later designed dresses in her own right; helped her husband translate English (especially Elizabethan) poetry.
5 Raymond Aron (1905–83), leading French sociologist and political philosopher; professor

and the Bruces[1] from London, and Mr von Hofmannsthal[2] etc. etc., to the number of 70 or 80, to which I had already refused to go some weeks before on the ground that I detested this kind of affair in France, where the whole thing is too stiff and formal and boring – while Aline was rather looking forward to going. But at this point she thought that it might perhaps not be very propitious for a large dinner party, and indeed a message shortly arrived saying that those who wished to come could still come, but the dinner party as such had been cancelled. Indeed M. Joxe,[3] who was in Algiers on a dangerous and delicate mission, had not even cancelled! So a little informal party was arranged instead for a mere 30 or 40 – so informal that when some woman appeared in a short evening dress, not realising that it was to be strict day dress, she was informed by her hostess that on no account could she dine in it, and when she begged piteously to be allowed to stay rather than sent back to her flat to change, was told that she could go upstairs and wear one of her hostess's day dresses. Meanwhile Nin Ryan,[4] who had arrived for the Rothschilds' party on Saturday, decided to go straight back home to England on Sunday, asking me nervously all the while whether I thought she was behaving in a craven fashion.

I told Aline that I would rather she came back with me to England with the children, who were staying with their father, since to be divided from England and having to telephone from Oxford all the time, and to be told that the telephone wasn't working, would be rather nerve-racking. She was only too anxious to come, and collecting the children rapidly we found no difficulty in getting train tickets and left France at midday on Monday.

Meanwhile the Ritz Hotel was full of rich persons ordering cars and racing either to the coast or Switzerland, feeling that the trains were no longer reliable; money was difficult to get from the cashier as people had withdrawn large sums; the whole thing was really rather terrible. I felt appalling about having to leave, particularly when the liftman asked me if in fact I was going; what was the use of explaining that I had a lady to examine for a doctorate at crack of dawn on Tuesday morning and a lecture to deliver on Tuesday

of sociology, Sorbonne, 1956–68; a regular contributor to Le Figaro; married, 1933, Suzanne Gauchon (1907–97).

1 David Kirkpatrick Este Bruce (1898–1977), US diplomat, ambassador to UK 1961–9; married, 1945, his second wife, Evangeline (1914–95) née Bell.

2 Raimund von Hofmannsthal (1906–74), American Anglophile and sometime London correspondent of Time, son of the Austrian poet Hugo von Hofmannsthal (1874–1929), librettist of Der Rosenkavalier): 'He was a delightful companion, a generous host, an ideal guest, with a gay and unwounding wit, and understood and valued art and love and human society and personal relations above the values of public life' (IB, Times, 20 April 1974, 20f).

3 Louis Joxe (1901–91), Gaullist minister, responsible for Algerian Affairs 1960–2; credited with negotiating Algerian independence in the Évian Accords of March 1962.

4 Margaret Dorothy ('Nin') Ryan (1901–95) née Kahn, daughter of the banker and philanthropist Otto Kahn, and herself a keen patron of the arts; married, 1928, John Barry Ryan (1900–66); 'She loved the arts (but especially music) [...]; nothing of cultural value was alien to her' (IB, Independent, 10 February 1995, 16).

afternoon, while de Gaulle was falling? We travelled very peacefully in a not very full train – the only frightening thing about the whole affair being the fact that the army was never once mentioned either by de Gaulle in his magnificent speech, or by Debré,[1] or by anyone else; which made it clear that the army was regarded as unreliable. It is very terrifying about France: if de Gaulle was suddenly to go – die, be shot, or be otherwise removed – nobody knows what would follow next. The Communists could very easily stage a coup – nobody else could now – although what their motive would be is obscure, unless ordered to do so from Russia. But every Frenchman one talks to knows that there is no heir – and the rumours that de Gaulle wants to train Léon Noël[2] to succeed him – he is a nice ineffective sort of ambassador as I remember him, not a man of great personality. Meanwhile Arthur Schlesinger[3] visited us here and explained all about Cuba. He claims to be much against it,[4] which I can believe, and was given a bad time by the editorial staff of the *Observer*. The socialists are not outraged: their stake in Kennedy is very considerable and although the shares have dropped they cannot possibly sell them for they have nothing else to invest in; they are not pro-Castros, on the ground that they find it intolerable to admit that decent socialism cannot be practised in Latin America without immediately linking itself with Communism, abolishing free speech, and shooting some innocent people. The Communists are delighted by the whole thing. I am much depressed.

Yours,

Love

    Isaiah

On 12 May 1953 IB had delivered the inaugural Auguste Comte Memorial Trust Lecture at the LSE, choosing as his subject the unsustainability of historical determinism, and as his title 'History as an Alibi'. The lecture was published in a revised form the following year as Historical Inevitability *(London, 1954), and alongside 'The Hedgehog and the Fox' and 'Two Concepts of Liberty' is*

---

1 In fact the army was alluded to in both speeches: de Gaulle had declared 'I forbid every Frenchman, and in the first place every soldier', to execute the orders of the rebels, while Debré had stated that government orders 'have been issued to the [paratroop] units to repel by all means, and I emphasise by all means, this mad attempt' (*Times*, 24 April 1961, 14c, d).

2 Léon Philippe Jules Arthur Noël (1888–1987), French diplomat and politician, ambassador to Poland 1935–40; de Gaulle's President of the Constitutional Council 1959–65.

3 Arthur *Schlesinger, Jr (1917–2007), historian and political adviser.

4 Schlesinger was one of the few advisers in the new administration to speak out against the 'Bay of Pigs' adventure, although he later reproached himself for not speaking out more forcefully during the crucial councils. Instead he sent the President memoranda, and Kennedy, reminded by McGeorge Bundy of the existence of one of these, later observed: 'That will look pretty good when he gets around to writing his book about my administration. Only he better not publish that memorandum while I'm still alive.' Douglas Martin, 'Arthur Schlesinger, Historian of Power, Dies at 89', NYT, 1 March 2007, C14.

*one of IB's best-known works. In the audience at the LSE was E. H. Carr,[1]
with whom IB had sparred in print in the years immediately before, IB criticis-
ing Carr's* The Bolshevik Revolution, 1917–1923[2] *for depicting history 'as
a procession of events ruled by inexorable laws'.[3] 'History as an Alibi' was an
extended statement of this point, and in making it IB alluded both explicitly and
implicitly to Carr's writings. The criticism upset Carr, who counter-attacked
eight years later in his 1961 Trevelyan Lectures at Cambridge, published that
year as the immensely successful* What is History?:

Sir Isaiah Berlin is a deservedly popular and widely-read writer. During the past
five or six years, almost everyone in this country or in the United States who has
written an article about history, or even a serious review of a historical work,
has cocked a knowing snook at Hegel and Marx and determinism, and pointed
out the absurdity of failing to recognise the role of accident in history. It is
perhaps unfair to hold Sir Isaiah responsible for his disciples. Even when he talks
nonsense, he earns our indulgence by talking it in an engaging and attractive
way. The disciples repeat the nonsense, and fail to make it attractive […]. It is
Professor Popper and Sir Isaiah Berlin who between them have flogged this very
dead horse back into a semblance of life; and some patience will be required to
clear up the muddle.[4]

*An edited version of the Carr's lectures was broadcast on the BBC, and appeared
also in the* Listener, *and it was in the correspondence pages of that journal that
IB responded to Carr.*

TO THE EDITOR OF THE *LISTENER*

[Published 18 May 1961]

Oxford

Sir,
    My friend Mr E. H. Carr is to be congratulated on casting off the cloak of
anonymity which he has so often worn when castigating his opponents. Miss
Wedgwood has effectively replied to his charges in the *Listener* of 4 May;[5]
Professor Karl Popper[6] is well able to look after himself; and I should like
to deal only with the charges that Mr Carr has thus far made against me
(hitherto his frequent but uncomplaining victim) in your pages. Mr Carr

1 E. H. *Carr (1892–1982), diplomat and historian.
2 Vol. 1 of his *A History of Soviet Russia* (London, 1950–3).
3 Review, *Sunday Times*, 10 December 1950, 3.
4 E. H. Carr, *What is History?* (London, 1961), 91–3; for the 'dead horse' see also overleaf.
5 *Listener*, 4 May 1961, 788. (Cicely) Veronica Wedgwood (1910–97), DBE 1968, OM 1969, historian; though holding no permanent post Wedgwood lectured extensively and published widely,
   notably on the English Civil War.
6 Karl Raimund Popper (1902–94), Kt 1965; Austrian-born philosopher; Professor of Logic and
   Scientific Method, LSE, 1949–69; author of *The Open Society and Its Enemies* (1945) and *The Poverty
   of Historicism* (1957).

chooses to maintain that, according to me (1) determinism must be false; (2) historians should not look for causes of human action; (3) it is the positive duty of historians to give good and bad marks to the principal personages whose acts they discuss. Mr Carr speaks of this as nonsense and complains that my 'disciples' are responsible for diffusing it. I am most curious to know who these mysterious disciples are, or where they spread their pernicious doctrines. As for the views attributed to me, the last two seem both naive and strange; I know of no one today who asserts either. Certainly, I do not hold any of these opinions. What I have argued is that (*a*) if determinism is true, as it may be, certain disturbing implications follow, which few determinists have seen, and fewer still have tried to face; (*b*) a number of very poor reasons have been advanced in support of determinism (among them some excellent specimens supplied in these lectures by Mr Carr); (*c*) historians who make impersonal forces responsible for what men have done are guilty of a fallacy; those who refrain from all value judgements, even by implication, gratuitously deprive themselves of a normal right of men in free societies; while those who, in a fanatical pursuit of an amoral objectivity, seek to rob the words used by most historians (including Mr Carr) of all trace of the evaluative force (moral or other) which they have in common speech are recommending an impossible remedy for a non-existent disease.

These propositions I have defended in the past and should be prepared to defend again. Since they are not those which Mr Carr ascribes to me, it is (fortunately for me and your readers) unnecessary to repeat my arguments here. Still, it is no bad thing that Mr Carr should have shown us how he deals with one of the deepest and most agonising issues in the history of thought. His prose is always clear, vigorous and agreeable, and liable to no such misunderstanding as my own seems to have occasioned in the mind of Mr Carr. But his short way with the problem of individual freedom and responsibility (the 'dead horse' which, in Mr Carr's horrifying metaphor, Professor Popper and I 'have flogged into life') is a warning to us all of what may happen to those who, no matter how learned or perspicacious, venture into regions too distant from their own.

Mr Carr speaks of his indulgence towards my follies. I am glad to reciprocate by offering him my sympathy as he gropes his way in the difficult, treacherous and unfamiliar field of philosophy of history.

Yours etc.,
Isaiah Berlin

TO HENRIETTA GIRSHMAN[1]

22 May 1961 [*carbon*]

Headington House

Dearest Mrs Hirschmann,

[...] I hear that you have acquired my acquaintance, Mr Eric Leinsdorf,[2] as conductor at Boston – he is a highly competent musician and was obviously a child prodigy in Vienna, his arms shoot out like snakes and every performance is up to the mark. I see no sign of genius: but that perhaps nowadays is almost unobtainable. [...] And he is a very nice man too, much more approachable than I am sure Munch[3] was and as good a conductor as anyone who is now conducting: but my heart is lost to the austere, noble, dedicated and saintly Giulini, who is conducting at Covent Garden at present, and is a conductor freer of intrigues, ambitions and normal weaknesses (this is sometimes very daunting and makes him remote and over-intense) than any musician I have ever met. He conducts Italian opera marvellously, better than anyone now living. Unlike Cantelli,[4] he is not a virtuoso, and a most passionately dedicated, severe and scrupulous musician whom the orchestras love, and has kept himself pure of all the intrigues that surround him in the Scala (which does not realise what a wonderful man they have). At any rate, brought up as I am in the old-fashioned nineteenth-century Russian 'moral' approach of the men of the 1840s and 1860s and 1880s, he is my man. As Musical Director we have coming to us Mr George Solti – a Hungarian – very different from Giulini, exciting, extroverted, vain, brilliant, dynamic, not anxious to conceal his gifts or bow before the gifts of others.[5] No doubt it takes all sorts to make the world; but at present at Covent Garden we have a galaxy of conductors – Klemperer, Solti, Giulini, Kempe[6] – such as no opera house can now boast. My life is divided between my duties in Oxford and thoughts about conductors; Cuba, Laos, the atom bomb, Berlin pass me

1 Henrietta Leopol'dovna Girshman [German 'Hirschmann'] née Leon (1885–1970), widow of Moscow manufacturer, collector and art patron Vladimir Osipovich Girshman (1867–1936) and frequent model for painter Valentin Serov (L2 594/6).

2 Erich Leinsdorf (1912–93) né Landauer, Austrian-born conductor, assistant to Arturo Toscanini and Bruno Walter at the Salzburg Festival 1934–7; moved to US 1937 to conduct for the Met, naturalised American citizen 1942; Music Director, Boston Symphony Orchestra, 1962–9.

3 Charles Munch (1891–1968) née Münch, Alsatian conductor; Music Director, Boston Symphony Orchestra, 1949–62; founded the Orchestre de Paris 1967.

4 Guido Cantelli (1920–56), Italian conductor; killed in an air crash at Orly, Paris, soon after being appointed musical director of La Scala.

5 IB later wrote to Pat Utechin: 'Solti is complaining bitterly about the lack of publicity in England. He is a terrible prima donna, and nothing is ever enough for him. This is part of the general secret of his technique. We have known some other people not altogether unlike that' (10 January 1962).

6 Rudolf Kempe (1910–76), German conductor, enjoyed a fruitful association with Covent Garden, conducting the *Ring* cycle 1955–9; succeeded Thomas Beecham as chief conductor of the Royal Philharmonic 1961–3; artistic director 1964, principal conductor for life 1970.

by. The American Ambassador, Mr Bruce, talked to me about these things and I answered as best I could, but I was thinking of Verdi's *Falstaff* and *Aron and Moses*[1] by Schoenberg. [...]

With much love,

Yours,

[Isaiah]

TO GARRETT DROGHEDA

29 May 1961 [*carbon*]

[Headington House]

Dear Garrett,

1. About Eddy,[2] yes, I think I do feel fairly strongly; I have talked to Jack[3] and one or two others and they on the whole agree. I see no harm in having him and Jimmy[4] continue with us, because they represent a class of musical dilettanti who are otherwise not represented, and as Eddy comes but seldom, he doesn't clutter up the Committee,[5] but I agree that another year or two is right and not perpetuity as a principle. Legge did say he was going to be at the last Committee meeting and I have not upbraided him for not coming, nor do I intend to. If he chooses to ignore us, there is no harm in that. Jack told me that you wanted me to be stern with him. I do not think that that would be advantageous from our point of view, though perhaps enjoyable in itself. [...] We have had a splendid season: there is no need to create hostility and sabotage beyond what is already happening, simply for the sake of tidiness and strictness of administration. Consequently I should leave him alone to stew in his own not fearfully attractive juice. (Please do not put this letter on file! It really would do harm if someone came across it in official Covent Garden literature!) Burn this letter, for I am about to say other things which I do not want recorded.

2. Solti: I do not think that he will eat out of anyone's hand except his own, but in so far as he does eat out of hands, it would be only out of those which

---

1 *Moses und Äron*, known in English as *Moses and Aaron*. IB championed Covent Garden's performance of this work (181–4).

2 Edward Charles ('Eddy') Sackville-West (1901–65), 5th Baron Sackville 1962, music critic and author, for many years a Director of the ROH. 'He is best described as a "dilettante" in the original and splendid sense of the term: that is to say, as a man who, for pure love of them, devoted himself to the arts' (*Times*, 6 July 1965, 14e).

3 John George Stuart ('Jack') Donaldson (1907–98), life peer 1967, farmer; Director, ROH, 1958–74, Sadler's Wells 1963–74; later (1976–9) Minister for the Arts; married, 1935, Frances Lonsdale (1907–94), biographer of Evelyn Waugh and Edward VIII; 'Donaldson cared, not for his own career, but passionately about advancing the interests of the arts' (Tam Dalyell, *Independent*, 10 March 1998, 13).

4 James Frederick Arthur ('Jimmy') Smith (1906–80), music administrator; chairman, Sadler's Wells Opera, 1948–61, Covent Garden Opera 1950–61.

5 sc. the Opera Subcommittee, as opposed to the full ROH board.

he regards as of the highest importance, and these he will rightly judge to belong to yourself and David and not to me, and he is right. I am sure our relations will always be perfectly peaceful, but the bond of genuine affection which is growing between Giulini and myself is not likely to spring up in that rather dry and somewhat treacherous soil. But of course I should like to see him. [...]

    Yours,

      [Isaiah]

TO GARRETT DROGHEDA

   1 June 1961

                                    Headington House

Dear Garrett,

   Thank you very much for your letter. You sound rather more cross than usual: tremendously so, in fact, but do what I will my conscience remains clear. Let me take the points in order:

   1. Change of date for the Opera Subcommittee. I ask for this every year, as the third Wednesday in June coincides with the Encaenia lunch here, and this courtesy has always been granted me. [...] Next time I promise to send you a prepaid telegram and follow this up by extracting a personal assurance from you over the telephone: what more can I do? I am on the other hand extremely sorry that you will not be at the Subcommittee, particularly if Solti is to be there, as it must obviously then be an important meeting. Is it hopeless to expect you? [...]

   2. Jimmie is always yoked to Eddy in my correspondence with you. I am all for his resigning from the board, but really see no reason for dropping him from the Committee, on which he performs unobtrusive but useful functions. Eddy comes seldom (the reason for keeping him rather than otherwise), Jimmie quite assiduously and armed with quite a lot of minor but cumulatively useful information. I wish ⟨Sir T⟩ Armstrong[1] or Denison[2] were half as helpful (once again a case arises for burning this letter I fear! but you will have less compunction about this one than about its predecessor, I feel sure). Now as to Legge, he did indeed not tell me that he was not coming [...]. My advice [...] is to be absolutely correct, neither more nor less, and display neither a grovelling anxiety for his society nor irritated disdain. It is certainly in our interests not to antagonise him, although we need not go very far in avoiding this. You will perceive a certain tendency to pacification,

1 Thomas Henry Wait Armstrong (1898–1994), Kt 1958; Organist, Christ Church, 1933–55; Principal, Royal Academy of Music, 1955–68; Director, ROH, 1958–69.
2 John Law Denison (1911–2006), Music Director, Arts Council of Great Britain, 1948–65; Director, South Bank Concert Halls, 1965–76.

not to say appeasement, in all the above: this unfortunate quality of my character makes me unformidable to DW and indeed to everyone else; and because of this I cannot complain to DW about not being kept in touch with Solti's movements or intentions, for if I do so he will take as much notice of that, as you well know, as of the barking of a very distant dog. You are perfectly right to say that the Chairman of the Opera Committee should know what the Musical Director intends to say before he says it: but if you choose to have one who lives in Oxford and is quite incapable of making himself ⟨fearsome to⟩ the tough and ambitious characters upon whom his information depends, a degree of systematic neglect of that ineffective figure is bound to occur. [...] I shall certainly send a message to Solti inviting him to the Subcommittee – a telegram on the 19th is probably the best method. But I think you will find that, once he is in the saddle, all our powers will be seriously diminished and he will not be at all easy to deal with and his tastes will not really coincide with ours. Still, I think we were right to have him, just as it was right to have Legge in his time. The results during the last two years seem to me to have been remarkable. [...]

As to your more specific points, I shall certainly bring Crespin[1] – she is a very good artist but not a marvellous singer and her parts have to be selected carefully for dignity and splendour rather than vocal importance. [...] As for Di Stefano,[2] I fear that his gay and affable remark to you is not to be taken too seriously – he is continuously dropping out of Scala performances for which he is booked and is a notorious breaker of engagements. Still, of course, we must cling to him as much as possible and you are quite right about Scotto,[3] she would be an excellent Zerlina, for example. As for Tebaldi,[4] she is indeed a problem. Where do you want her? I should much prefer her in *Traviata*, for example, which she sings well, to even Sutherland, but that we are surely not allowed to do. Her parts are now very limited as her voice is extremely precarious, sometimes splendid, sometimes terrible – that is why there is no dependable report on it. [...]

Meanwhile, let me remind you strongly that you have promised to come to the Box on the 5th for *Boris*; that the performance starts at 7 p.m.; that I have secured the little box entirely because of your most welcome promise, and that we could have a jolly altercation about all this during the intervals

---

1 Régine Crespin (1927–2007), French soprano; debut at Mulhouse 1950, at Covent Garden as the Marschallin in *Der Rosenkavalier* 1960; a distinguished concert career was checked by the onset of difficulties in her highest register.

2 Giuseppe Di Stefano (1921–2008), Italian tenor, famed for his 1950s partnership and recordings with Maria Callas; debut at La Scala 1947, at Covent Garden in 1961 as Cavaradossi in *Tosca*.

3 Renata Scotto (b. 1933), Italian soprano, known especially for her interpretations of Puccini and Verdi; debut at La Scala 1954, at Covent Garden 1962; Zerlina is the country girl who escapes the amorous attentions of Don Giovanni in Mozart's opera of the same name.

4 Renata Ersilia Clotilde Tebaldi (1922–2004), Italian soprano chosen by Toscanini for the 1946 re-opening of La Scala, where she sang regularly 1949–54 before joining the Met (1955–73).

[…]. I shall look forward to seeing you on the 5th despite your harsh treatment of me – I wish I were able to do that with David, or Solti, or anybody at all! […]

Yours,

⟨Isaiah⟩

TO JACOB TALMON[1]

8 June 1961 [carbon]

All Souls

My dear Yaakov,

[…] You will be much amused to see – if you look at the Listener at all – that I have been having a long wrangle with E. H. Carr. I had no idea that my criticisms of his views had got under his skin to so deep an extent that he decided to devote practically the entire gist of his Trevelyan lectures in Cambridge to refuting my ideas. I suppose I ought to regard this as an honour: yet his theses seem to me – but I am no doubt biased – divided between truisms which no one would deny and attacks upon views which nobody holds. Still, this may be a little unfair. His last letter in reply to my criticisms was very mollifying. Perhaps one should not conduct public controversies, but this one has been held within the bounds of relative decency. No I did not act as host to BG. I saw him for a moment, but not in Oxford. He is very unaltered and with de Gaulle forms one of the great anachronistic figures of our time.

I am sorry you did not get Bullock to Israel. As for Taylor, his last book is so revolting and his loss of reputation over it, even in the most left-wing circles, is so enormous that you are well off in not securing his services.[2] He now seems to me to think of nothing but how to please Lord Beaverbrook,[3] and although he claims that he does it all for money, he does it partly for fame and partly because he is embittered about not getting his chair, and is therefore determined to cause as much pain and embarrassment as possible to what might be called a respectable opinion, whether right or left. Hence mad paradoxes and favourable reviews from Mosley and all the neo-Nazi papers

1 Jacob/Yaakov Leib Talmon (1916–80), Polish-born Israeli historian specialising in totalitarianism; lecturer, HUJ, 1949–60; Professor of Modern History 1960–80.
2 Taylor's revisionist The Origins of the Second World War (London, 1961) caused controversy by appearing to lessen Hitler's personal responsibility for the war: 'This is a story without heroes; and perhaps even without villains' (17). IB considered it 'a piece of perverse and pernicious nonsense, brilliantly done […] which, [it] seems to me, if followed by the young, as it may well be, for the book is beautifully written, can do incredible moral and political damage' (to Teddy Kollek, 9 May 1961).
3 William Maxwell Aitken (1879–1964), 1st Baron Beaverbrook 1917, newspaper proprietor and politician. Taylor's enthusiastic review of Beaverbrook's 1956 Men and Power, 1917–1918 was 'the start of a close friendship' (D. George Boyce, ODNB); Taylor afterwards became a highly-paid columnist in Beaverbrook's Sunday Express, and Director of the Beaverbrook Library in the Daily Express building.

in Germany. His most devoted followers are hideously embarrassed and the
favourable reviews by Joll[1] and Beloff[2] and Marquand[3] have recoiled upon
their heads somewhat. I think perhaps the reaction against him is too strong
– he is a clever man and a good writer – nevertheless the general behaviour
of most socialists is that he cannot be decently spoken to – that he really has
in some way sold himself in order to get notoriety and avenge himself on the
cautious, the truthful, the scrupulous, the idealistic. [...]

Yours ever,

[Isaiah]   [...]

A reply from E. H. Carr to IB's letter about Carr's What Is History? *appeared
in the Listener on 1 June.*

TO THE EDITOR OF THE *LISTENER*

[Published 15 June 1961]

Oxford

Sir,

My purpose in replying to Mr Carr was to reiterate the position which
I took in the lecture which he so vigorously assailed, not to modify it. If
I have contributed to Mr Carr's bewilderment, this can only be due to my
lack of skill in exposition. Yet what can I do to remedy this condition (which
I am truly sorry to have caused) but once again summarise, as clearly as
I am able, what I think to be true, in contrast with the views that Mr Carr
sincerely, but mistakenly, believes me to hold?

1. My reason for not asserting that determinism must be false is simple –
I did not, and do not, know whether it is false. [...] What I did say, and still
believe, is that the arguments in favour of determinism are not convincing,
let alone conclusive, and that acceptance of it logically entails a far more
drastic revision of some of our commonest convictions and notions than is
usually allowed for. The belief, for instance, that men who acted in a particular way in a particular situation could, within certain limits, have acted differently in this same situation, in a more than merely logical sense of 'could',
seems to me to be one of these.

I argued in my lecture that this assumption underlay the normal thought

---

1 James Bysse Joll (1918–94), Fellow and Tutor in Politics, New College, 1946–50; Fellow, St
Antony's, 1951–67; Stevenson Professor of International History, London, 1967–81. His review is
'The Ride to the Abyss', *Spectator*, 21 April 1961, 561.

2 Max Beloff (1913–99), historian; Gladstone Professor of Government and Public Administration,
Oxford, 1957–74; Fellow of All Souls 1957–74. His review is 'Gathering Storm', *Sunday Telegraph*,
16 April 1961, 6.

3 David Ian Marquand (b. 1934), academic, politician and political commentator, leader-writer for
the *Guardian* 1959–62; Research Fellow, St Antony's, 1962–4; Lecturer in Politics, Sussex, 1964–6;
Labour MP for Ashfield 1966–77. His review is 'The Taylor Doctrine', *New Statesman*, 21 April
1961, 627–8. His father was the Labour MP Hilary Marquand (1901–72).

and language of most men and most historians (including Mr Carr), whereas they do not imply a belief in determinism as described by Mr Carr, but rather the contrary. But this fact, although it may create a presumption against determinism, is not, of course, tantamount to showing that determinism is false, still less that it must necessarily be so; only that if it is, at any rate for practical purposes, a valid hypothesis (as it may be), then much that historians and common men (including Mr Carr) assume or believe will turn out to be false.

I also argued that we cannot really embrace determinism, that is, incorporate it in our thought and action, without far more revolutionary changes in our language and outlook (some among them scarcely imaginable in terms of our ordinary words and ideas) than are dreamt of in Mr Carr's philosophy. On the other hand, Mr Carr is perfectly right in supposing that I believe that the determinist proposition that individual (or indeed any) actions are wholly determined by identifiable causes in time is not compatible with belief in individual responsibility. Mr Carr believes that both these irreconcilable positions are supported by 'common sense and common experience', whereas I think that only the second is what ordinary men assume. It is this paradox that is at the heart of the problem of free will, and, as I have admitted already, I do not know what its solution is. It is this issue that Mr Carr dismisses as a 'dead horse', as many eminent thinkers have tried to do before him. It has, unfortunately, survived them all and may, I fear, survive him too.

2. If Mr Carr supposes that I deny the proposition that 'to understand all is to pardon all' he is, once again, perfectly right. But if he infers from this that historians should not, in my view, use all their powers to understand and explain human action, then he is certainly wrong. It seems to me, to give an example, that the better we understand ourselves, the less liable we may be to forgive ourselves for our own actions. But from this it does not begin to follow that historians should not look for 'social or economic causes of the two world wars' because their discoveries may explain away the moral responsibility of specific individuals; they may or may not. It is the business of historians to understand and to explain; they are mistaken only if they think that to explain is *ipso facto* to justify or to explain away. This truism would not need stating were it not for a tendency on the part of some modern historians, in their understandable reaction against shallow, arrogant or philistine moral judgements (and ignorance or neglect of social and economic causes), to commit themselves to the opposite extreme – the total exoneration of all the actors of history as products of impersonal forces beyond conscious human control.

3. It is one thing to recognise the right of historians to use words which have moral force, and another to order or recommend historians to deliver moral judgements. I can only say again that to attempt to purge the historian's language of all evaluative force is neither desirable nor possible. But it

is a far cry from this to inviting or commanding historians to give marks 'to outstanding figures of the past', of which I am accused. In matters of moral judgement historians seem to me to have the same rights and duties, to face the same difficulties, and to be liable to the same lapses as other writers and other men who seek to tell the truth.

May I therefore, in answer to Mr Carr's three queries, say this:

(a) I know of no conclusive argument for determinism in the sense in which he uses the term. It does not seem to me to follow from this that determinism is either necessarily or in fact false. Whether true or false I do not believe it to be compatible with the common-sense notion of personal responsibility.

(b) Following Marx, I see no reason for denying that men have a limited freedom of individual action, but within conditions that are largely not of their own choosing. Neither in my lecture nor in my letter did I cast any doubt on the existence of social or economic causes for these conditions, whose importance has been gravely underestimated before our time; but I see no compelling reason for supposing that these conditions include necessary and sufficient causes of every individual action.

(c) It is not, in my view, the historian's duty to praise or blame individual historical personages, but he has no less right to do so than anyone else.

These are the conclusions arrived at in my lecture, and both my letters are merely attempts to repeat them. These views may be mistaken, but they are, at any rate, not those attributed to me by Mr Carr. I sincerely hope, therefore, that in his forthcoming book, which I shall read, like all his other works, with eager interest, he will not charge me with views which neither of us holds. I know that he would not do so willingly.

Yours etc.,

Isaiah Berlin

TO TATIANA ALBERTINI

23 June 1961 [carbon]

[Headington House]

[Dear Tania,]

I have so many things to ask you to forgive that I do not know where to begin. First of all for not replying to your letter of two or three months ago […]. However, we have been leading a mad life […] in going to London too often, trying to do too much, enjoying ourselves too little, so that we are now exhausted, flat, longing for peace, rest and the sympathy of friends. Meanwhile, of course, I am making further arrangements of a destructive kind – which can only lead to trouble, exhaustion and innumerable small diseases – such as journeys to India, the United States etc. The fact that one acts freely, but at the same time under compulsion, is a philosophical paradox which I do not propose to solve in this letter. That is my condition, and to some extent Aline's.

[...] We are here until 14 July. On that day I take a train for the hideous and hateful city of Geneva. There, there is to be a Conference called 'Contemporary Reality in the Soviet Mirror', over which, quite insanely, I agreed to preside. This is not at all a good idea. There are to be no Iron Curtain representatives and therefore all the English, American, Italian, French, etc. personages who come will take pleasure in denouncing the distortions, lies and general inadequacies of Soviet writing about contemporary history. This is quite easy to do and will then be reported by the press as simply another move in the Cold War. This is not very desirable. It is perfectly easy to denounce the poor Soviet historians for their shortcomings: but in a way inelegant and unfair. If one wants to attack the State itself, that is another matter. But the unfortunate historians, some of them at least, try and do their best under hideous conditions – they are easy prey, though it would be far more interesting if an objective account were given of what they are doing, why they are doing it, what tendencies their work consciously or unconsciously betrays, what the connection is between the writing of history, politics, social development, attitude to countries abroad, etc. in Russia, without indulging in tempting but gratuitous philippics. I shall urge the Conference to do this but fear that my words will have little weight, and that I shall simply be branded as yet another stimulator of Cold War hysteria. I shall do my best to avoid this, and now realise that it was a mistake to accept the chairmanship of this enterprise. At the same time I feel ashamed of giving it up now, and some of the historians who are coming are old friends, so I feel I shall be letting them down too. More sleepless nights, agony. Self-accusations of weakness, muddle, unnecessary waste. [...] The Leningrad ballet, at present dancing in London, is splendid. The critics – the more aesthetic ones – think it appalling, as I am sure everybody influenced by Diaghilev is bound to do – coarse, realistic, 'populist', and the décor is hideous and the production not much.[1] But the spontaneity, freshness, sincerity, vitality and skill of the dancers are so immense, the men are so strong and catch the ladies who leap upon them so easily and well, instead of crumpling like our more refined men dancers – the acting and the miming are so vivid, passionate and infectious that everything is forgotten – at least by me. Not to be bored by a ballet for two hours is a unique experience, which the English, I think, do not know at all. [...]

[Isaiah]

---

1 The Leningrad-based Kirov Ballet's much-anticipated four-week season had opened at Covent Garden on 19 June: the reviews were mixed, *The Times* discerning political didacticism in its dance – a 'moral earnestness' that ultimately descended into 'dramatic cliché' (20 June 1961, 16b).

TO GEORGE HAREWOOD

26 June 1961 [*carbon*]

[Headington House]

Dear George,

Thank you very much indeed for your letter. It seems to me valuable and important and interesting, and I should like with your permission to circulate it to members of the Subcommittee [...]. Before I come to my comments I should like to say that, as you well know, our liberty of discussion will I hope remain the same, but our liberty of direction will of necessity be curtailed by the existence of a Musical Director.[1] We were always warned of this by David, much as the Israelites were by the prophet Samuel, when they wished to elect unto themselves a king in the form of Saul. Still we, like the Israelites, were not to be deterred. We shall pay for this, whether to our advantage or not remains to be seen.

I agree with much of what you say, but not absolutely everything. To take your letter in your own order. I understand all too well how maddening the casual critical chat of the Subcommittee must have been (and still is) to the administration.[2] If you are engaged in painful and responsible planning of an elaborate mosaic, casual criticisms from not always well-informed and nearly always amateur quarters – even assuming complete bona fides – can obviously be an appalling nuisance. I am not least [sc. the most] innocent in this respect (I shall always remember my tiresome attitude about *The Trojans* and indeed about Sutherland and *Lucia* too – two howlers which are written on my heart – and there may indeed be many others). Nevertheless it seems to me that the advantages of this kind of arrangement outweigh its vices. So long as ultimate responsibility rests not with a single Napoleonic intendant or impresario, but with a body of half or quarter-time amateur dilettanti – as is inevitable in our present arrangements in England in general – anything that makes for complete freedom of discussion is (surely) good, anything which hampers it is bad. This extreme liberalism and laissez-faire I am prepared to defend, without even calling in its most redoubtable champion, Lord Robbins,[3] to assist me. Not only are occasional good ideas born as the result of chitter-chatter of this sort, but the only way in which a body of men gathered from many corners can be made to feel that they are genuinely concerned with the day-to-day operation of the Opera (and if they are not then they will feel a remote advisory body and be no good at all) is by involving them in petty detail. That this is a great bore for the administration I freely

1 Georg Solti, due to take up his new post that autumn.
2 Harewood had recently left the ROH for the Edinburgh Festival.
3 Lionel Charles Robbins (1898–1984), life peer 1959; Professor of Economics, LSE, 1929–61; Director, ROH, 1955–81; chairman, government committee on higher education (167/3), 1961–4; chairman, *Financial Times*, 1961–70; President, British Academy, 1962–7.

concede [...]. I honestly do not think it right, even if it has obviously utilitarian advantages – to tell anyone on the Subcommittee (and particularly the Chairman) to stop fussing about details or making small suggestions. I fully understand your argument and what you say is perfectly rational, but in the circumstances I don't think I agree.

On the other hand, with all the rest that you say I agree warmly and enthusiastically and am very glad that you have said it. I shall do my best to support you in it all. I think it is absolutely true that we do at times forget – at least in less conscious moments – what the proper proportions should be between the claims of the repertory, of revivals, of new works, of our own composers, etc. I do not think that we have in fact sinned much in this respect – I have not gone through our past programmes, but would you say that there was something wildly lopsided in them in the last three years, say? That we have, for example, concentrated too far on repertory and omitted all new works or failed to revive important works of the past at the expense of stock pieces or the *dernier cri*?[1] [...]

[...] I agree entirely with you that to discuss works merely in themselves and then give up because this or that singer is unavailable, or because public response is uncertain, is too much of a hand-to-mouth operation; and yet there is the eternal question of balance between our own singers and visitors versus Solti's plan for creating a full resident company (I cross my fingers and think about Kubelik,[2] who was so certain of being able to do precisely that not more than seven years ago), and this has to be woven into the ideal balance of old and new, bread-and-butter and caviar. But fundamentally, of course, you are quite right. We must plan ahead in the way in which the Metropolitan and Paris do not and the Scala (and I suspect Vienna) do. This alone will give shape, stability, continuity and a compass to our deliberations. Yet the administration will have to put up with, I think, chivvying and harrying on points of detail and reactions to last night's performances and favourite and unfavourite singers and small points about which professionals know all and amateurs know little – for if that is given up, immediacy and liberty are gone, yet I can't deny that I see exactly what you mean. Anyway, it is all on the knees of Solti. Tell me what you would like me to do and I shall do it – whether to circulate your letter (slightly bowdlerised) to the Subcommittee (and/or the board) or only your list, with an introduction either by you or by me embodying your points.

Thank you very much for your letter.

Yours,

[Isaiah]

1 'Latest fashion'.
2 (Jeronym) Rafael Kubelík (1914–96), Czech-born conductor and composer, Georg Solti's predecessor as Musical Director at the ROH 1955–8, where he controversially announced a policy of opera in the vernacular, sung wherever possible by a resident company: 'these were not great years at Covent Garden and when Kubelík left in 1958 his policy of English-language performance was revoked' (*Times*, 22 August 1996, 19a).

⟨P.S. I agree entirely with your point about the leading singers whom it is our duty to bring to London. But then how do we do this, and yet not concern ourselves at all with what works are proper 'vehicles' for them?⟩

Without first securing his permission, IB had showed Harewood's letter to Garrett Drogheda, chairman of the ROH board.

TO GARRETT DROGHEDA

28 June 1961

Headington House

Dear Garrett,

Don't tell George that you have seen his letter to me – please don't. I shall write to him on the lines we discussed and ask him whether he minds an expurgated version being circulated without comments by me. I shall tell him that nothing can be done before September – I have talked to Pavitt[1] about it and he points out that our actual programme is not very different from what was suggested by George. So much the better. I think he is fussing about nothing: that is to say that what is valuable in his suggestions we are already in favour of explicitly, and what we do not approve is in fact not enormously useful. Nevertheless I shall encourage him and tell him how interesting and valuable all his suggestions are, etc. etc., in my best avuncular style.

God be with you,

⟨Isaiah⟩

TO JACK DONALDSON

28 June 1961 [*manuscript*]

Headington House

Dear Jack,

Sorry not to have seen you at the last Board meeting for many reasons. […] I enclose a letter from George, which I have secretly shown to both Garrett and Burnet and sworn them to secrecy about having seen it, as indeed I am swearing you. I propose to show it to nobody else. I also enclose my answer. Burnet thought it slightly tiresome […] in the sense that he is speaking like a Civil Servant about the House of Commons. He really ought to remember on which side he now is. Nothing is more irritating than to be told that one is hampering the administration and making silly amateur suggestions about

---

1 Burnet Pavitt (1908–2002), managing director, Hoffmann–La Roche UK (pharmaceuticals) 1956–71; Director, ROH, 1958–80, and for many years chairman of the Opera Committee: 'Burnet is sometimes too nice to voice the objections that he deeply feels: but when he talks to one in private his opinions seem to me as penetrating and as unbiased as anybody's that I have ever met' (IB quoted by Ian Lowe, *Independent*, 5 September 2002, 18).

everything – no doubt we are, but also sometimes have excellent ideas that greatly improve things, particularly Walter – e.g., we got Kraus[1] into *Tosca* in place of someone else and he was marvellous. If *Moses* comes on this will also be due to us, and the whole Giulini connection would never have been preserved in its present flourishing state by David and George, I promise you. But the real point is that George is no doubt quite right – we ought to keep a schema for three or four years before our eyes, so that when we depart from it, we shall at least know what we are departing from. [...]

Anyway as you will see I have written him a most appealing letter, congratulated him on all his bad ideas with exquisite hypocrisy, which I hope you will condone. Meanwhile, do not have seen his letter and send it back to me – it would be truly terrible if you lost it [...].

Yours,

Isaiah

Do I owe you *money*? Please tell – it is oppressing my Judaico-puritan conscience.

TO JACK DONALDSON

29 June 1961 [*manuscript*]

Brooks's

Dear Jack

Garrett really *is* intolerable. I showed him George's letter which I sent you – & *begged* him *not* to reveal this – of course he told George at once – who is probably furious (justifiably: the letter contained some rough passages) with me for making bad blood gratuitously. I have now written to George, grovelling, & saying I had shown his letter to Garrett & to Burnet, but I cd not *quite* confess I had shown it to you too. So *don't* betray me: as for my reply nobody had seen that but George (& secretly yourself). Well it will all blow over, I suppose. George won't trust me quite so much: doesn't matter. But Garrett! forget the whole thing.

Isaiah

---

1 Otakar Kraus (1909–80), Czech-born British baritone; with Covent Garden company 1951–73, for whom he sang Scarpia in its revival of *Tosca*, December 1960: 'Mr Otakar Kraus's Scarpia was dramatically commanding and musically pleasing save that there was not enough sheer power in the voice to dominate situations such as the mighty and magnificent climax to the first act' (*Times*, 7 December 1960, 15d).

TO E. H. CARR

3 July 1961

Headington House

Dear Ted,

Thank you for your letter. I am, I must admit, relieved that our correspondence in the *Listener* need not continue, for in writing letters to journals,
try as one might, one's words acquire an exaggerated quality, both more
pompous and more self-conscious than one can possibly wish them to be,
which need not occur in private life.

You urge me to write an essay re-stating my position. This would surely be
an insufferable imposition on the public, even if someone agreed to print it. For
I am sadly Bourbon-like, I really have nothing much that I would like to change,
only re-state the whole thing in language perhaps more temperate and clearer,
rather on the lines that I adopted in my rejoinders to you in the *Listener*. [...]

As for moral judgements etc., I genuinely plead that I have been misunderstood. Mill argues that even though we may not like, let us say, addiction
to drink or tobacco, provided it does no harm to other people, we have no
right to prohibit it by law. This, *mutatis mutandis*, is my position about moralising. I think that to pass moral judgements, both implicitly (in the choice of
morally charged words which we cannot entirely avoid) and explicitly (when
something very splendid or very outrageous occurs) is a natural human need in
articulate societies; for human beings, whether they know it or not, 'inevitably'
think in terms of moral values. Obviously, the right to satisfy this need must
not be abused (sorry to be so sententious), but from this it doesn't follow that
it ought to be withdrawn. I know of no historians who do not in fact, either
by commission or by omission, pass moral judgements: after all you yourself
identify some forces or persons as progressive, others as futile or trouble-
somely reactionary [...]. I was really not trying to urge people to moralise, so
much as telling them that they cannot help it in any case, and that it is difficult
to know what would be the case if they could – what a perfectly objective
account of history could be like; whether if you suppressed all evaluation,
any human beings or events in the normal sense of the word would emerge
at all. That is surely not tantamount to urging men on to thunder forth praise
and condemnation? And to condemn the over-moralistic is surely to condemn
them morally (or aesthetically) – that is for boring us, or wasting our time, or
distorting the facts owing to a desire to assert their subjective tastes and prefer-
ences? And in what capacity do we utter these strictures? Surely *as* historians
or at least *as* connoisseurs of history? Still, I will not inflict yet another sermon
upon you, for it is all contained in my original homily.

I wish I thought that I had moved from 1953.[1] As you say, people with

---

1 IB refers to the gestation of *Historical Inevitability* (London, 1954), which inspired Carr's Trevelyan

active minds don't stand still, and it is sad to me to think that I probably have stood perfectly still. But so long as I think so, what can I do but remain silent? So I suppose I shall have to bear your now admittedly over-stern strictures in stoical silence when your book appears. [...]

You will be delighted to know that I have had a postcard from my colleague A. L. Rowse,[1] your Trevelyan predecessor, informing me that in one of the chapters of his book on *The Use of History*, all our problems had long ago been satisfactorily settled and that there was really no need for either your or my remarks on the subject. His postcard ends characteristically with the words 'Ever troubled to read it, any of you?' I haven't and I shan't, nor will you. If he reviews your book anywhere, we shall all be called silly, theorising idiots, who haven't spent long enough in the Public Record Office – this will be far more unjust to you than to me, but my colleague is not overburdened with the sense either of justice or of reality. ⟨Do come and see us – I think we ought to publish a dialogue one day.⟩

Yours ever,

Isaiah

After a five-week stay at Portofino, July–September 1961, IB travelled to Israel (via Rome) to attend the inaugural Israel Festival of classical music in the Roman theatre at Caesarea. He went, as he wrote to Burnet Pavitt, his friend on the ROH board, 'simply because I promised Nicolas Nabokov and one or two other people to do so – Aline at the last moment quailed and will not follow, wisely I am sure. I simply hate the thought of leaving this delicious, lonely (by which I mean tourist-covered, absolutely impassable) shore for the heat and fuss etc., but I think I must go.'[2] In the event it proved to be the first of many joyous visits to the Festival, which grew apace in the years ahead, expanding both its cultural horizons and its geographical reach.

Lectures at Cambridge, January–March 1961; according to Anthony Quinton it was 'a cavalry charge of the intellect – vast, exciting, glitteringly colourful and somewhat disorganised' (TLS, 21 December 1956, 769).

1 Alfred Leslie Rowse (1903–97), historian; Fellow of All Souls 1925–74; Trevelyan Lecturer, Cambridge, 1958; as convinced of his own genius as of others' inability to recognise it – 'I'm a genius, Raymond [Carr], a genius, but everyone says I'm a shit': Maurice Bowra, 'ALR Loquitur', *New Bats in Old Belfries, or Some Loose Tiles*, ed. Henry Hardy and Jennifer Holmes (Oxford, 2005), 155. He complained that Sparrow had read none of his books. ' "Do you know my *Tudor Cornwall*, John?" "No," replied John and gestured to the figure on his right: "Do you know Stuart Hampshire?" ' A. N. Wilson, 'This Trying Time', LRB, 1 October 1998, 27. Rowse was loathed by IB. His *The Use of History* was first published in London in 1946.

2 To Burnet Pavitt, 5 September 1961 (dictated earlier).

TO ALINE BERLIN

4th [September 1961; *manuscript*]

Grand Hôtel de la Ville
Via Sistina, 67–71 (Trinità dei Monti), Roma

Darling Aline,

There is a high wind blowing – sirocco? – I hope the aeroplane will not buffet – I return these 3 volumes – to be taken back to Oxford. I love you very hotly & continuously: I did not go for a walk but sat here, on the balcony & thought about you, us, the children, the house in Paraggi[1] – I am *very* optimistic. We are really much more fortunate than anyone we know – even the Cecils[2] – envy towards us is quite justified. I love, adore you & envy myself.

Isaiah

TO ALINE BERLIN

Thursday Night [7 September 1961; *manuscript*]

Galei Kinneret, Tiberias

Darling Aline,

I love you *very* much. I enjoyed our conversation this morning from Jerusalem […]. Nabokov is suffering from heat, Jacob[3] not: *N.* says you shd *not* come: Jacob says, children will want to *sit* in Jerusalem 10–12th & in Sharon after that: *one* day to Negev, *one* to Tiberias, & *basta*:[4] *this* they *could* stand. But I am a little shaken: why not come in spring? Why not do it *definitely*? Straight from London by air: then back to Rome & to Paraggi for 1–2 days on business & home? more rational. Yesterday we lunched with B.G.: he does not like me a bit: *she* says you are too good for me & have made me much more *human*.[5] They have a nice lively daughter. Our Kollek-provided guide talks about nothing but 1) archaeology 2) the great patriotic war – we don't react enough. Jacob is enjoying himself *greatly* […]. If I am to hear Casals[6] I have to stay till the 18th & then fly home & hide in Oxford from my ma, till the 21st? I am undeniably pleased to be here: even as a tourist surrounded

1 The Berlins were planning to build a house overlooking this bay near Portofino.
2 David Cecil married, 1932, Rachel (1909–82) née MacCarthy, only daughter of the literary critic Desmond MacCarthy: 'Rachel MacCarthy was the perfect match for her husband. […] They were perfectly happy together, drawing their many friends into that happiness, for fifty years' (Rachel Trickett, ODNB).
3 (Nathaniel Charles) Jacob Rothschild (b. 1936), 4th Baron Rothschild 1990; banker and philanthropist; close friend of the Berlins.
4 'Enough'.
5 David Ben-Gurion married (NY, 1917) Paula Monbaz (1892–1968), a fellow Poalei Zion (Socialist Zionist) activist. They had three children, Geula, Amos and Renana.
6 Pau Carles Salvador ('Pablo') Casals i Defilló (1876–1973), Catalan cellist, pianist, conductor and composer, regarded as the greatest cellist of his generation. He lived in voluntary exile after the Spanish Civil War and refused to play in countries – including, for many years, Britain and the US – that he regarded as showing toleration towards the Franco regime.

by 'goyim'[1] – Jacob for this purpose counts as ¾ gentile – I *like* the faces, stones, etc. I feel at home, unnervous, unself conscious, don't mind being bored, exhausted, etc. Nabokov *loves* it: my mother cd not be more wrong: he *loves* Jews, *hates* Arabs, wont go into Jordan, loathed Nazareth & is incredibly sympathetic here. We have not seen Sasha[2] yet for I dread this a little. All that divides me from Stuart & Tess[3] is here: I don't mind the familiarity, chaos, lack of dignity, noise: *nothing* is stiff, German, disapproving: I went to Kollek's house with Jacob (only) & had a sharp argument with officials about Eichmann & didn't mind: they were quite tough & argued almost rudely. Whereas one nasty remark in this week's New Statesman in a review of a Mr Kalb by David Marquand[4] upset me for 3 hours & robbed me of a little sleep, how weak & silly & absurd! But I recovered sooner here, because the atmosphere is *hostile* to introverted self laceration. Please kiss Peter & Philippe for me: they *will* love it. I enclose a suitable card. I'll try to telephone again. Marriage to you is the *only* thing I ever did that I cannot be delighted enough by: I blame myself for *everything* else: for Mrs B.G. is right.

love,

Isaiah

For five months starting on 1 September 1961 Stuart Hampshire was George A. Miller Visiting Professor of Philosophy at the University of Illinois at Urbana–Champaign. Although Renée[5] was with him (they married there), he was far removed from the English cultural milieu that, in IB's eyes, largely defined him, and was in consequence very lonely.

TO STUART HAMPSHIRE

9 October 1961 [*carbon*]

[Headington House]

Dear Stuart,

You may not realise it, but I, too, am an authority on solitude. To begin

---

1 'Goy' (plural 'goyim') is Hebrew and Yiddish for 'gentile'.

2 Alexander Schneider (469/1), 'an old friend and a bit of a podletz ["scoundrel"]' (to Marie Berlin, 24 December 1963).

3 Teresa Georgina ('Tess') Rothschild (1915–96) née Mayor, married (Nathaniel Mayer) Victor Rothschild (1910–90), 3rd Baron Rothschild, in 1946. She was educated at Cambridge, and met her future husband while an intelligence officer at MI5 during the Second World War; her close friendship with Stuart Hampshire also dated from those days.

4 'Wrap-Up', David Marquand's hostile review of Marvin Kalb's *Dragon in the Kremlin*, appeared in the *New Statesman*, 1 September 1961, 277: 'a sillier book on a serious subject I have never read'. The remarks about IB appear to make fun of Kalb rather than of IB: 'In Paris [...] he met Sir Isaiah Berlin ("one of the West's outstanding intellects"). He told Berlin that he was anxious to learn about the Russo-Chinese alliance because he felt that our entire civilisation was being threatened by a powerful, but mysterious, coalition of forces. Sir Isaiah agreed. "Certainly", he said, "the threat is mysterious and powerful".'

5 Renée *Hampshire (1909–80), wife of Stuart Hampshire.

with, I am utterly miserable if alone; but at least I know it, and avoid it now by every possible means. I was never so miserable in my life, quite literally, as on three occasions when I found myself alone: the first was in Munich for four days; the second in New College at the beginning of 1932 when I had been made a lecturer, Maurice was away and I knew not many people in September and October – my hatred for the Fellows of New College helped, I suppose; the third occasion was Harvard in 1949, when I knew scarcely anyone and used to go to bed early because I could not face the long empty evenings. I could not read or eat, and was too ashamed to go to New York or Washington where I had friends. [...] American solitude [...] induces, at least in me, first a sense of extreme gloom and sense of appalling isolation which undermines all endeavour and causes one to feel that one will never see the familiar world again: [...] the reason for never even contemplating the idea of settling in the United States is that such pockets of solitude are built into the very atmosphere itself – human association, in spite of all the warmth and humanity and easiness and lack of strain of certain bits of America, is infinitely more difficult than it is in Europe, and the pauperisation – the process of giving out without taking in – is absolutely remorseless. I think I understand your condition and sympathise. Why ever did you go? [...]

I am going to India on 9 November.[1] I have now refused to do so six times on moral grounds, but have now received a formal letter from the Vice-Chancellor[2] instructing me to go, giving me four weeks' leave of absence, and informing me that this is the highest service that I could render to the University, the country, the world etc. I wish to fly via Moscow and Tashkent, but Aline says the Himalayas are very dangerous. My mother is to hear nothing of it. Thank you, by the way, for telephoning her when you arrived. It was very kind.

Israel was a great success. Nabokov adored it more than any human being has ever adored anything. He kept exclaiming all the time how free he was, how happy he was, how much at home he felt, how he had never felt at home since 1917 to a similar extent, and this communicated itself to his hosts, who reciprocated in kind. Even Jacob was stirred [...]. The most splendid moment was in Ben-Gurion's Summer Court, Sde Boker,[3] where he kept running about in brown shorts in order to exclaim that a group of huts built on the edge of a most stupendous-looking desert crevasse was to become some kind of centre of higher learning, and no doubt mystical studies as well, obviously

---

1 IB had been invited to attend a literary conference in Delhi, part of a year-long celebration in India of the centenary of the birth of the poet and author Rabindranath Tagore (1861–1941).

2 Arthur Lionel Pugh Norrington (1899–1982), Kt 1968; President, Trinity, 1954–70; Vice-Chancellor, Oxford, 1960–2; Warden, Winchester College, 1970–4; a leading reformer in 1960s Oxford.

3 Kibbutz in the northern Negev mountains where Ben-Gurion lived and died; nearby is Midreshet Sde Boker, the educational and research settlement that he inspired: construction on the site, which overlooks the magnificent Zin valley, began in 1962.

to counteract the Weizmann Institute[1] – at this point Isaac Stern,[2] who really is a marvellous violinist and a very nice but not tremendously intelligent man, said to Nabokov 'You know what he reminds me of? He reminds me of Abraham – that's what he reminds me of. He's just like Abraham. Don't you think he's just like Abraham?' It was difficult to keep a straight face. Your old friend Walter Eytan,[3] who was there, was engaged in drafting a telegram to congratulate de Gaulle on his escape and a large conversation occurred at lunch about the precise translation of the Russian phrase meaning 'Life's task', which Ben-Gurion wanted to use and which was too intelligentsia a phrase for Eytan's somewhat Germanic intellect. Nabokov helped vigorously with all this and was in Seventh Heaven. Raimund was also there. His bosom friend was the barman of the King David Hotel. I do not think perhaps that he was quite as pleased with it all as the others. Clayre[4] arrived, looking madder than ever and established himself near Tel Aviv for three days by himself, pleading the need for solitude. He then asked me which kibbutz on the whole gave greatest opportunities for solitude and private life. I tried to explain that the purpose of kibbutzim was not exactly private life and if that is what he wanted it was a very different establishment he needed. However, he walked off with a look of mad joy in his eyes in a northerly direction and has, I think, fetched up at Ginnosar – Gennesareth to you – where I do not think he is particularly happy. I do not know quite what is wrong, but something certainly is. When I would ask him where he was going to spend the evening, he would say 'I am off. I'm going to the Kings Hotel to read T. S. Eliot to a Brazilian girl', and then would come back a quarter of an hour later and report that the Brazilian girl was not there as she had been swiftly removed by her mother, who obviously anticipated the worst. There really is a screw loose somewhere – rattling audibly. The music festival was a great success, particularly Casals, scarcely audible, in the theatre at Caesarea. The only worrying moment was when two Roman soldiers suddenly appeared in togas with broad purple stripes. I had a nightmare vision of some enormous breach of taste – silver trumpets or a Latin speech – and asked Kollek if this could be stopped. However, they turned out to be actors from a brief comic

---

1 Founded in 1934 in Rehovot, west of Jerusalem, by Chaim *Weizmann (1874–1952, first President of Israel),with funding from his close friends Israel Sieff, Simon Marks and Harry Sacher.

2 Isaac Stern (1920–2001), US violinist, regarded as one of the great violinists of the twentieth century; born in Kremenets (now in Ukraine) to Jewish parents, but raised in San Francisco, and made his debut with the city's symphony orchestra 1936; played regularly in Israel.

3 Walter George Eytan (1910–2001) né Ettinghausen, diplomat; Munich-born contemporary of IB at St Paul's and Oxford; first Director-General of Israel's Foreign Ministry 1948–59; Israeli ambassador to France 1959–70.

4 Alasdair Clayre (1935–84), 'philosopher, economist, lyricist, poet, novelist and singer' (*Times*, 13 January 1984, 12); elected to a prize fellowship at All Souls 1959; took his own life. 'With the world at his feet, and a rare armoury of outstanding intellectual and artistic skills at his disposal, […] he was never able to commit himself exclusively to the exploitation of any one of these gifts' (ibid.).

film about Caesarea who had not had time to take off their togas, and were there merely as spectators. You are quite right about the absence of strain. That's what I, and I daresay Nicolas, probably liked best about the whole of that country. 'The assurance of an aristocrat and the boldness of an artist,' said Raimund enviously about Nicolas as he firmly made his way towards the President of Israel[1] at a concert, determined to be introduced to him by me. The President, a simple peasant figure, asked him to visit him on any day at any hour. Nicolas was transported: he thought it very unlike the White House. However, I enjoyed myself immensely: I really do like them all very much.

The golf club[2] – have you seen it? – is richly comical – particularly the gentlemanly figures in short trousers and pipes trying to look like planters, who make very gentlemanly conversation at the bar. It really represents a tremendous repressed desire to return to the womb of the Mandate.[3] It is not widespread, but when it occurs it is pathetic and touching. Maurice, meanwhile, had been in Syria with Elizabeth[4] on his cruise – Elizabeth apparently behaved frightfully, kept demanding better cabins, better lamps, better food, made a fuss about being kept inside a bus for an hour and generally behaved in a tart and, to Maurice, surprising manner. However, he managed to keep her in order, so he claimed, and indeed Elizabeth herself said that he was a wonderful arranger and that although all the other members of the cruise were rather terrible, Maurice adored every one of them and came to life as she had never seen him come to life before. Miss Beecham has spread the rumour that Maurice is deaf: however, Elizabeth and I disproved this by experiment.

Clayre's novel has had maliciously hostile reviews:[5] I daresay because he was unwise enough to let Cape print the fact that he was a Fellow of All Souls on the cover. You have probably seen some of them: especially the one by MacInnes or Naipaul, or one of those men, who said that it was a typical novel of a sensitive young man of 26 if it weren't so much like a caricature of a sensitive novel by a young man of 26. […] My task at present is to persuade Stravinsky[6] to set the first words of the Old Testament to

1 Yitzhak Ben-Zvi (1884–1963), Ukrainian-born Hebrew scholar and Zionist; President of Israel (succeeding Weizmann) 1952–63.

2 The Caesarea Golf and Country Club, officially opened in January 1961, brainchild of the keen golfer James Armand de Rothschild (1878–1957): 'built by Jimmy Rothschild at vast cost – so Scottish, so green, with men in shorts sipping whiskies, mostly from South Africa, like advertisements for Empire Grade tobacco, and tremendous British talk' (IB to unknown recipient, 1 November 1961).

3 The period of British governance in Palestine, 1920–48, under the mandate of the League of Nations from 1923.

4 Presumably the widowed, childless Elizabeth Bowen (468/3) rather than the wife and mother Elizabeth Longford.

5 Alasdair Clayre's only novel, The Window, was published in London by Jonathan Cape in 1961.

6 Igor *Stravinsky (1882–1971), composer.

music in their original Hebrew form (this is my idea and perhaps not a very good one) for the Israel Festival 1963.[1] They are rather worried over there about Stravinsky's alleged anti-Semitism, but there is nothing in that, I have decided.[2] Nabokov is hysterically anxious to stop him from going to Russia [...]. How much capital could they make out of Stravinsky?[3] He is surely too tough and cynical – they could acclaim his coming but his sentiments on world peace would hardly make headlines for them. Why is Nicolas so frantic? It is obviously connected with his own inability to go there. Stephen[4] longs to go to India with me, but they are strangely reluctant to invite him – he must have been there too many times. I shall hate it, I'm sure. But you really would have enjoyed some of our experiences in Israel – the Stern–Istomin–Rose trio is the best in the world by far.[5] They played at Ein Gev, and I have heard nothing like this since Piatigorsky–Schnabel–Flesch in 1929.[6] Their performance in one of the Southern settlements, where one sat on sacks of straw, and a perfectly nice Foreign Minister made an amiable speech calling Nabokov 'a very great composer', also had its point – the enormous moon, the very bright stars – this extreme nearness of the bright blue sky and the terribly bright colours without nuances does induce the notion that Heaven is very near and that powerful, almost [palpable?], presences govern the universe. The passage from Judaea to Galilee really is one from the Old to the New Testament. Nature changes accordingly, and the charm of the Sea of Galilee has very little to do with the style of the Old Testament. But I must curb my transports, for I think they are all too much for Aline altogether. I must start thinking about political philosophy, Oxford, the pupils, and all that. [...]

[Isaiah]

---

1 A task whose eventual upshot was *Abraham and Isaac* (72–3).

2 'Stravinsky's essentially pragmatic attitude to the Nazi regime may repel, but it is not direct evidence of sympathy. Though anti-Semitic, like many Russians of his class, he neither advocated nor supported violent or political measures against Jews [...]. Unlike Wagner, he seems never to have behaved with condescension, or indeed in any noticeably specific way, towards Jewish friends; his frequent and nauseating anti-Semitic remarks come mainly in letters to fellow anti-Semites like Benois, Diaghilev or Reinhart.' Stephen Walsh, *The New Grove Stravinsky* (NY, 2002), 30.

3 Stravinsky visited the Soviet Union in autumn 1962, and according to Robert Craft he was profoundly moved to set foot on Russian soil again; but the visit neither rehabilitated his music in the Soviet Union, nor left him with a hankering for his homeland (ibid. 46).

4 Stephen Harold Spender (1909–95), poet; co-editor of *Encounter* 1953–67; Professor of English, UCL, 1970–7; IB was devotedly attached to Spender, his undergraduate contemporary.

5 In 1960 Stern formed a much lauded trio with the pianist Eugene Istomin (1925–2003) and the cellist Leonard Rose (1918–84).

6 Gregor Piatigorsky (1903–76), Russian-born cellist; Carl Flesch (1873–1944), Hungarian violinist; Artur Schnabel, pianist; the trio performed at the Queen's Hall and the Wigmore Hall in October 1930.

TO AN UNIDENTIFIED CORRESPONDENT

1 November 1961 [*carbon*]

[Headington House]

In bed with influenza, and also cholera, for the injection I have just had has certainly brought on the disease. I feel probably only a little less wretched than you must. But I am resigned to bed and like it. Activity is what I hate. I am content to observe, not interfere, and have all my life been afraid above all of being involved. How I became married is the source of deepest mystery to me, even now. I have lived vicariously for so long that direct life is something very strange and odd. I wish I could rise and come to see you and tell you about my fortnight in Israel with Raimund and Mr Nabokov and Jacob Rothschild – whose secret marriage in a Registry Office to a Catholic lady[1] is a sign of the times (naturally Evelyn Waugh[2] sent dry notes all round regretting the apostasy). The chief attribute of Israel is extreme lack of strain – despite the noise, the vulgarity, the ugliness of the towns, the aggressiveness, the lack of manners, the pushing, jostling, milling, energetic, Victorian population, so earnest, so humourless, so convinced that virtue and vice exist and that work brings salvation in the best Protestant manner – despite all this, the fact that one can talk to anyone from the President to the humblest labourer in exactly the same tone of voice, and that you cannot tell but what the shopkeeper who serves you may have a doctorate of music in Vienna, and the hotel booking clerk comes from a mysterious family in Portugal (mine did; but this is becoming like a chronicle by Raymond Mortimer[3] and nothing could surely be less desirable, at least for me, than that). And now I must go to India. This mysterious lure of the East is something new in my life. I must deliver a speech on Tagore. But what am I to Tagore and Tagore to me? You were quite right to enquire. His poetry in translation is like Mrs Hemans[4] or Ella Wheeler Wilcox.[5] *Gitanjali*![6] Insipid, sentimental trivialities – in English at any rate. And yet, it may be that he is a great Indian poet. [...] I have now written a powerful speech about Tagore and nationalism which I shall deliver with Gladwyn-like[7] aplomb. Aline has made me take out the

1 Jacob Rothschild married Serena Mary Dunn in 1961.

2 Evelyn Arthur St John Waugh (1903–66), novelist; converted to Catholicism 1930.

3 (Charles) Raymond Bell Mortimer (1895–1980), critic; literary reviewer, *Sunday Times*, 1948–52; chief literary reviewer from 1952; his *Channel Packet* (London, 1942) was notable for its travel sketches.

4 Felicia Dorothea Hemans (1793–1835) née Browne, poet; prolific writer of verse, including 'Casabianca' (1826), her memorial to the French boy martyred on *L'Orient* in the Battle of the Nile: 'The boy stood on the burning deck / Whence all but he had fled [...]'.

5 Ella Wheeler Wilcox (1850–1919), American poet: 'Laugh and the world laughs with you; / Weep, and you weep alone' ('Solitude', 1883).

6 *Gitanjali* ('song offerings'), a collection of English translations by Tagore of his Bengali poems, which helped win him the 1913 Nobel Prize in Literature.

7 (Hubert Miles) Gladwyn Jebb (1900–96), 1st Baron Gladwyn 1960, diplomat; UK ambassador to France 1954–60; Deputy Leader of Liberal Party in House of Lords 1965–88: 'the last Liberal

word 'race' whenever it occurred, including 'leave the unequal race', on the ground that 'unequal race' is ambiguous – I meant it in the sense of 'unequal contest', but the Indians may take offence.[1]

[...] Do you know Mr Nehru?[2] I have never met him, but am filled with deep suspicions: surely, he must suffer from some heavy inferiorities obtained at the time of his sojourn in Harrow and Cambridge to behave as he does. From there, Aline and I will go to Persia, which I am sure is a much more exquisite country – I detest Indian art and adore Persian – but again I must avoid Raymond-Mortimer-like transports. [...]

I shall send you a postcard from India. Do you think 'throttled sorrow embottled in my breast' a good line? It is written by my great patron who resides in that country.[3] Three of my pupils in Delhi are to give a reception for me. Tormenting boredom! What does one not do for one's country? I wish you all possible health.

[Isaiah]

TO ALINE BERLIN

Thursday [9 November 1961; *manuscript*]

2 King George's Avenue, New Delhi

[...]

Darling Aline,

The flight was perfectly uneventful. I met *Solti* on the aeroplane & invited him vaguely to lunch with his wife in Oxford in January – on a Sunday inevitably – the first after Peter returns to school – but this is provisional. He was met by a young woman in Zurich I did not remember – who sent you ("Aline") her love – she knew us in Oxford – I had to pretend to have met her – dark, not v. pretty, Swiss? *not* Mrs Solti (I think) – most odd. I sat next to a very sweet Australian business man who turned out to believe in the literal accuracy of the bible – a Goy – *very* pro-Zionist – adored Israel fanatically – *very* shocked that I, a Jew (I admitted this quickly) did not believe that Jeremiah literally predicted all world history. Still, he forgave me. In spite of his piety he gave a good account of a night with a Geisha in Kyoto. Very simple, firm, fanatic: religious & highly sexed. Istanbul airport

---

trumpet' (IB to Rowland Burdon-Muller, 2 April 1974). IB met Jebb when the latter was at the FO during the Second World War, and their friendship dates from this time.

1 IB's lecture, 'Rabindranath Tagore and the Consciousness of Nationality', was delivered on 13 November as part of the Tagore centenary celebrations in Delhi.

2 Jawaharlal Nehru (1889–1964), a Kashmiri Brahmin educated at Harrow School and Trinity, Cambridge; one of the principal leaders of the independence movement in India; first Prime Minister (on independence) and Minister for External Affairs 1947–64.

3 Humayun Zahiruddin Amir-i Kabir (Humayun Kabir) (1898–1969), educationalist, politician, poet, philosopher; Exeter College PPE 1931, and thus IB's Oxford contemporary; his *Poems* (Oxford, 1932) includes 'The Sea', which in turn includes the line 'The throttled sorrow seething in his breast'.

was not amusing: now Teheran airport: the Turkish dolls are better made than the Persian: the Persian boxes were hideous but caviar is about £9. 10 a kilo – quality uncertain. The longest bit is Teheran–Delhi. Rather tedious. But the jet is marvellous: only too much food and drink all the time: but not itself too terrible. I was met by people who must have expected me to look more impressive: (a) secretary of the Delhi Academy (b) *his* secretary: who bowed & touched his forehead all the time. First *strong* taste of Orientalism & Indian touch (except for the Indian air hostess who gets on in Istanbul & has Mrs Ayer-like[1] slits between blouse & skirt) + (c) Mr Scott of the High Commission – a foreign office young man: just like all the others – amiable & serviceable. The Gore-Booths[2] only came back to-day at 3.30 from Bombay. Of course no possibility of sleep: I tried to do so, but slaves – in splendid uniforms & turbans & starched aigrettes[3] instead of feathers, kept marching in & out – I did not dare ask not to be disturbed, I was so fascinated by this absolutely feudal culture. [...]

Nabokov's Congress has organized a reception for me before you come: the British think them rather dim but inoffensive. [...] The emissaries of the Congress have told me how good are the papers of the other delegates – A. Huxley,[4] the Russian, the Egyptian etc. – very nasty of them. [...] I feel very well, a little tired. I miss you dreadfully & am *very* lonely: cd you bring me one thin vest? Or I'll buy one here. I shall read a lot of books on the aeroplanes: I am now a mad devotee of jets: I adore them: I am frightened & pleased at the same time. Queer. The weather *is* warm enough for the Indian touch. I shall wait for the Gore-B's before sending this, so I can tell you about *clothes*. Meanwhile I love you more than you love me: much much much more: & since I think you do rather love me, it is all very satisfactory. I wrote to Philip[pe] from Istanbul & Peter from here.

[...] Tell my mama & yours that I am blissfully happy. I am not. But I am quite content. I broadcast to-morrow. I love you with unnecessary passion. At the age of 52! [...]

Isaiah

---

1 A. J. Ayer married, 1960, his second wife, Alberta Constance ('Dee') Wells (1925–2003) née Chapman, journalist, novelist and broadcaster.

2 Paul Henry Gore-Booth (1909–84), life peer 1969, diplomat; British High Commissioner in India 1960–5; Permanent Under-Secretary of State, FO, 1965–9; Head of HM Diplomatic Service 1968–9; married, 1940, Patricia Mary Ellerton (1921–2012).

3 Plumes used in a headdress, named after the crested egret.

4 Aldous Leonard Huxley (1894–1963), novelist and essayist. Huxley's works were not to IB's taste, but he wrote after his death: 'I really do not think that his mystical rot is all that rot, I think he was stumbling about on the edges of something which in years to come will become more and more interesting' (to Noel Annan, 25 May 1970); Huxley's paper on 'Literature and Modern Life' at the Tagore conference was given on the same day as IB's, 13 November.

TO CHARLES TAYLOR

28 December 1961

[Headington House]

Dear Chuck,

I won't bore you with the long and dreary story of negotiations with the board.[1] When the thing first came up, I had to defend your case against (a) the charge that the title did not correspond with the contents, (b) that it was about psychology and should have been submitted to the psychology board, (c) that the examiners pronounce themselves incompetent to judge its merits although they did in fact judge them quite highly, (d) that the social studies board should have pronounced itself incompetent to appoint examiners, etc. etc.

After a swift tactical look, I decided to plead entirely guilty to (a) and be ferocious and unyielding on (b), (c) and (d). This worked fairly well. The board didn't like to be told that it didn't know what it was doing; it enjoyed my self-inculpation on point (a) and thought the examiner's report somewhat pedantic. What I was terrified of was that they would send it back for some psychologist to look at, which would certainly have produced incalculable results. However, they didn't, and after an ominous wobble and some sinister remarks by Ryle, it was let go on the condition that the title was changed in order not to mislead possible researchers in the Bodleian who might wish to look at it. The rest you know.

When it came up the second time, Ryle objected to the new formulation, but after I said that I entirely agreed with him, Ryle, when the business had been formulated by the implacable Kneale[2] – Ryle's favourite candidate for all Oxford Philosophy professorships, after all – cast up his hands despairingly and gave in.

So this is the end of the long trek. I am very glad: we all know there is nothing in titles and are great egalitarians, nevertheless we also know that not to receive a title one has applied for (as the Warden of All Souls, for instance, failed to obtain the QC) [ ] leads to private neuroses and public difficulties.

I understand well that you wish to live among Canadians: nevertheless your departure is a grave business. The New Left seem to have crumpled themselves into something very inconsiderable. Ralph Samuel[3] and the man

---

1 With Elizabeth Anscombe (370/5), IB had supervised Charles Taylor's doctoral thesis, and in Michaelmas term 1961 he oversaw its final consideration at a meeting of the Board of the Faculty of Social Studies. The eventual title of the thesis was 'Explanation in Social Science', replacing 'Explanation by Purpose and Modern Psychological Theory'. Taylor's book *The Explanation of Behaviour* was published in London in 1964.

2 535/3.

3 Raphael Elkan Samuel (1934–96), British Marxist historian, nephew of Chimen Abramsky; taught at Ruskin 1962–96; like E. P. Thompson, with whom he had much in common, he left the

from the West Indies whose name I cannot remember are not a sufficient set of batteries for the thing to run on: meanwhile I find that I can talk very amiably and profitably to MacIntyre.[1] He is a most stimulating person for me to talk to, as he alone, it seems to me, shares at any rate some of my [ ] interests in Oxford. Certainly no one else does.

I saw with amusement the portrait of me drawn by Stuart H. for the benefit of the *New Yorker* (did you see the article on Oxford philosophy by Mehta?),[2] in which I am represented as a lonely thinker desperately having abandoned formal philosophy, a talker driven desperate by lack of company, and in no sense an Oxford philosopher, or really a philosopher at all. I wonder what you thought of the whole piece.

Meanwhile, I get a series of letters from Birnbaum[3] in search of a job, security etc. – I tried to write a testimonial for him to the London School of Economics where the wicked Glass[4] put him up in the hope that it would get him and MacRae[5] knocked off and be able to appoint Gellner. However, this monstrous plot miscarried. Whatever may be thought of Gellner as a professor of sociology, he certainly won't do, at any rate as yet – MacCrae, of whom I know nothing, seems to have got the job in the teeth of the Party. So much for [ ].

Meanwhile, I have decided that Hamann[6] is the man. He really is a mys-

Communist Party of Great Britain in 1956 over the Soviet invasion of Hungary, thereafter devoting himself to the New Left, 'which sought to free the spirit of socialism from the dark record of Stalinism and also from the pragmatism of social democracy' (*Times*, 11 December 1996, 11a).

1 Alasdair Chalmers MacIntyre (b. 1929), Lecturer in Philosophy, Leeds, 1957–61; Research Fellow, Nuffield, 1961–2; Senior Fellow, Council of Humanities, and Visiting Professor, Princeton, 1962–3; Fellow and Preceptor in Philosophy, Univ., 1963–6; Professor of Sociology, Essex, 1966–70; Professor of History of Ideas, Brandeis, 1970–2; University Professor in Philosophy and Political Science, Boston, 1972–80.

2 Ved Parkash Mehta (b. 1934), Indian writer and journalist (later US citizen), blind from the age of four, educated at Balliol and Harvard. His article for the *New Yorker*, 9 December 1961, 'Onward and Upward with the Arts' (repr. in *Fly and the Fly-Bottle*, London, 1963), was a critique of Oxford philosophy, prompted by the controversy over Ryle's decision not to review Gellner's *Words and Things*.

3 Norman Birnbaum (b. 1926), US sociologist; taught at LSE 1953–9; Fellow of Nuffield 1959–66; on the founding editorial board of *New Left Review* 1960.

4 David Victor Glass (1911–78), sociologist and demographer; Martin White Professor of Sociology, LSE, 1948–78. 'Some found David Glass a hermetic person, introvert and ascetic. Others liked to see him thaw when he talked about books, or about India. [...] He will be remembered at LSE as one of the great men who have given distinction to this unique academic institution' (*Times*, 27 September 1978, 16g).

5 Donald Gunn MacRae (1921–97), Professor of Sociology, LSE, 1961–78, Martin White Professor of Sociology (in succession to David Glass) 1978–87.

6 Johann Georg Hamann (1730–88), German pietist theologian and anti-rationalist philosopher, one of the key forerunners of romanticism: 'The most passionate, consistent, extreme and implacable enemy of the Enlightenment and [...] of all forms of rationalism of his time [...]. His influence, direct and indirect, upon the Romantic revolt against universalism and scientific method in any guise was considerable and perhaps crucial' (TCE, 255); 'a Protestant mystic who disliked the analytical rationalism of the Enlightenment and saw more creative power in feeling, language, and especially poetry, the "mother-tongue of the human race"': M. J. Inwood, 'German Philosophy', *The Oxford Companion to Philosophy* (Oxford, 2008); Inwood's quotation is

terious personality to have sat in Königsberg (Kaliningrad) all by himself – quarrelling with Kant[1] and [ ] for England and France, which he had visited, apparently uninfluenced by any thinkers except pietists and mystics. Then to have made a combination of Hume and fundamentalism – Hume could destroy rationalism and the idea that there are a priori methods of discovering anything – i.e. to make room for faith. If faith in tables, which we cannot prove, why not faith in God? Combining the proposition that language and thought are identical and that therefore God's word must be read in Hebrew or Greek and not in translation, for there is no meaning that can be detached from the words that convey it, only similar meanings which other symbols can convey, similar but not identical – a nominalist and positivist theory of thought and language worthy of our day.[2] Out of this combination grew Herder[3] and the general opposition to intellectualism, general propositions, science, the West, the outer world, proof, abstraction, eternal truths, and other illusions and delusions into which man has 'alienated' himself.

All the constructions of the rationalist philosophers seem to Hamann to be so many lifeless masks by means of which living beings conceal or distort their true features. It is this kind of talk and this kind of attitude which must have occurred in German Switzerland as well, and which I suspect is ultimately responsible for Rousseau's hatred of forms, rules and institutions which have imprisoned and distorted the free spirit of man and misrepresented it to itself – for *The Nephew of Rameau*[4] and the whole early 'alienation' literature. I propose to read some Hamann – it is written in hideous, unreadable German, worse than anybody's – and then write an essay about him as a source of all these good and bad things. It is very difficult not to exaggerate and cast too much back into the past which one discovers at a later date, but I shall do my best.

In the meanwhile, I have written a review of your old tutor, Carr, who has,

---

from *Aesthetica in nuce*, in Johann Georg Hamann, *Sämtliche Werke*, ed. Joseph Nadler (Vienna, 1949–57), ii 197.15.

1 Immanuel Kant (1724–1804), German philosopher, the central and synthesising figure in modern philosophy; born in Königsberg, Prussia, he studied and taught at the University there, becoming Professor of Logic and Metaphysics 1770–96; his concern with metaphysics is often contrasted with David Hume's sceptical empiricism, while his doctrine of the categorical imperative asserted the existence of absolute moral law. It was through Kant's involvement that Hamann, who was also born in Königsberg, found employment as a low-grade civil servant there.

2 Cf. TCE 359–61.

3 Johann Gottfried von Herder (1744–1803), German philosopher, poet, and critic; a founder of German romanticism, influence on Goethe, and dissenter from the Enlightenment, he emphasised the inseparability of thought and language, and according to IB was in large part the originator of populism, expressionism and (cultural and value) pluralism (TCE 176–7).

4 *Le Neveu de Rameau*, short dialogue by Denis Diderot (391 / 4), regarded as his masterpiece; begun c.1760 and first published posthumously in 1804 in a German translation by Goethe; it imagines a confrontation between 'Moi' (Diderot) and 'Lui' (Jean François Rameau, nephew of the composer Jean Philippe Rameau), in which the moral outlook of the former is pitted against the amoral cynicism of the latter, questioning the values of the Enlightenment and of *ancien régime* society.

as you know, published his Trevelyan lectures in book form. Hegel[1] and Marx
are the heroes, Popper and I are the villains, not unexpectedly in this work.
In reviewing it for the *New Statesman*, I had to begin by saying that I had to
declare an interest since I was mentioned less frequently only than Hegel and
Marx, though not as respectfully. You should read it: it is a very lively, brisk,
readable, gay little book, but in spite of the fact that he believes in progress,
purpose, and sacrifices which this generation must make for the next, and
chides Russell for saying there is less liberty in the world today than there
was a hundred years ago – less liberty for whom? Russians, Indians etc.? – in
spite of the natural sympathy which it will to some degree awaken in you,
you will, on the whole, be disappointed – it is over-crude, over-simple, over-
shallow. It takes on philosophical issues with great gaiety and boldness and
does nothing to them at all, because he doesn't understand intellectual issues
or ideas – never has – and as the late Austin[2] would have said, 'He simply
hasn't a philosophical head on his shoulders' – not that he needs one, but if
he will enter these waters he ought to learn to swim.

I had a jolly controversy with him in the pages of the *Listener*, where these
lectures originally appeared, and indignantly disavowed all the idiotic views
attributed to me (such as that historians should stop looking for causes of
behaviour, or that they should constantly label people as good and bad, and
fail in their duty if they stop moralising for a moment – as a caricature of my
views I did find this faintly recognisable – others, I fear, will probably think
it perfectly just and valid criticism). Still, do read it. It is a great caution and
proves that those not philosophically trained don't begin to understand that
queer, perhaps superfluous, but still endlessly fascinating subject.

Meanwhile, I have been to India – they are very enthusiastic and half-
baked and exhausting and Nehru is extraordinary. He knows perfectly well
what he is doing: he knows that he applies a double morality, and is not the
least ashamed of it; he knows that he is travelling with the Africans and the
Asiatics, that Russia is a fellow-traveller, and he thinks on the whole that the
West is out. He would like to go more gently than the Chinese, with less
massacre, and thinks that his 400 million Indians – a large, soft, pacific, inefficient, heavy mass – will as always absorb all the foreign poisons and work out

1 Georg Wilhelm Friedrich Hegel (1770–1831), German philosopher; author of *The Phenomenology
  of Mind* (1807) and *The Science of Logic* (1812–16); made Professor of Philosophy, Berlin, 1818; his
  teleological view of history and dialectical method of reasoning profoundly influenced Marx
  and Engels.
2 John Langshaw Austin (1911–60), White's Professor of Moral Philosophy, Oxford, and Fellow
  of Corpus 1952–60; a close friend of IB's, and one of the great intellectual influences in his
  life; leader of the Oxford school of linguistic philosophy, in opposition to the logical positivism
  of A. J. Ayer: 'the intellectual freshness and force, both of Austin and of Ayer, were such that
  although they were in a state of almost continuous collision – Ayer like an irresistible missile,
  Austin like an immovable obstacle – the result was not stalemate, but the most interesting, free
  and lively discussions of philosophy that I have ever known' (PI2 144).

its own salvation more painlessly, if more chaotically, than the more ruthless and disciplined militarised nations to the East and West of him.

He is tremendously vain, and the fact that the Russians broke through the police cordon at Tashkent[1] and swarmed round him and showed genuine warmth of feeling moved him profoundly, and he has been a friend of the Russians ever since; he similarly adores the Japanese, who showed similar feeling; as for the English, his whole political outlook – the playing by ear, the occasional unscrupulousness, the empiricism, the disdainful reference to Marxism as interesting in the nineteenth century but obviously too crude for us today – all that is very England-derived. He is touchy, he is self-conscious, and like everyone else in the world he wants recognition. There is no doubt that Hegel had the profoundest insight of anyone when he realised [that] what people want more than anything else in the world is to be recognised – whether they are individuals or nations or classes – and that all aggression derives from a wound to that particular craving. When Nehru began speaking of his surprise that some third-rate Indian film had had a wild success in Moscow, where everybody was singing the tunes, his face glowed more than at any other point in our long interview; when the Indians at my conference were told that the Russians esteemed Tagore as one of the greatest poets in the world, that a medal was struck in his honour, and four stamps, and that 60,000 schoolchildren etc., they were far better pleased than by any other single thing which had been said.

The Indians want to be treated as a new exotic culture, whose poets are the best in the world, whose novelists outshine Proust, people who dazzle if they are looked up to, and the whole British connection therefore – and in a sense too much about them is known, they have not been behind a wall like China or Japan or Central Asia, it is a nuisance to them – they would like to start life again.

It is extraordinary to me that anyone should be surprised about Goa[2] (I say, suddenly changing the subject). The thought that Nehru or anyone in Asia believes in rules or principles, even on the ground of expediency, because it is a labour-saving device and likely to produce favourable conditions for development at a lesser price than power politics, must be off his head. Nehru does not seem to me to have the slightest respect for the United Nations, but looks on it as I find myself unconsciously looking at it, as an instrument registering the shifts in the balance of power, and not an entity possessing some kind of deliberative or executive character of its own. Nehru is infinitely sensitive to public opinion, but the public opinion

1 During Nehru's visit to the Soviet Union in September 1961 he was taken to Tashkent to witness the supposedly positive influence of Soviet government in that underdeveloped region.

2 After weeks of heightened tension, Indian military forces ejected the Portuguese from Goa, Daman and Diu, their three colonial enclaves on the west coast of India, 18–19 December 1961. Nehru was subsequently criticised for rejecting UN appeals for the avoidance of military action.

that he recognises is in the first place that of India itself, then Asia, then Africa, then the Iron Curtain countries, and the West hardly at all. Naturally, since America is powerful, it must be kept in with', and he greatly enjoys his encounters with the West – he likes them individually, he is intrigued by them, adores flirting with handsome Western ladies like a Samson who practises brinkmanship with a number of formidable Delilahs, and he loves Western company. Something like Roosevelt[1] – a man who has betrayed his class and has become a popular idol – he delights in his own virtuosity, and has before his eyes constantly the fate of the Kuomintang – an ossified nationalist party which rotted away until it fell before Communism. Hence the extraordinary position of Menon,[2] whom he keeps by his side, not only, I think, because he is tied to him by sentimental bonds, but also in order to prevent himself from selling out or appearing to sell out to comfort, appeasement, respectability, a cosy semi-capitalist regime which, he perfectly realises, means stagnation and ultimately collapse and defeat. At any rate, that is my reading of his complex and peculiar character.

I did talk to students in India, and they were very disarming and very delightful, but not in the end repaying: there is no intellectual bite, no firmness, no toughness at all, and one ends by walking easily and triumphantly through a marsh. There are cynical, clever men at the top, and passive, receptive, gentle, patient people below. If real social justice and rationalisation ever come to India it will be through some spellbinder whom people won't bother to resist and under whose spell they will enjoy falling. Otherwise, caste is still extremely strong, drift, general atmosphere of toleration and compromise. They think they can absorb all the electric shocks of their neighbours and somehow run them into the ground. I wonder.

How are you? Do write to me about yourself. What books are you reading or writing? And will you be publishing about causes and purposes?

Yours ever,

[Isaiah]

During the Venice Biennale in September 1958 IB attended a performance of Stravinsky's opera Oedipus Rex *and his ballet* The Rite of Spring, *conducted by the composer, and was moved to write a fan letter to Stravinsky – 'an*

---

1 Nehru sought 'to set in motion a radical social and economic revolution in a deeply conservative and impoverished society' (*Times*, 28 May 1964, 16a), and the same might be said of the 32nd President of the US, Franklin Delano Roosevelt ('FDR') (1882–1945), who responded to the Great Depression by promising America's poor a 'new deal' that would include public works programmes and social security: in consequence political opponents alleged that he was a traitor to his class.

2 Krishna Menon (1896–1974), Indian Minister of Defence 1957–62: 'his qualities as much as his failings of personality set him apart from the mainstream of Indian political life [...] and made him a peripheral figure, magnified by the communist-hunting demonology of American journalists as much as by the attacks of those in India who turned on Menon when they dared not tackle Nehru' (*Times*, 7 October 1974, 14f).

absurdly pompous document which I regretted immediately',[1] *as he later
confessed to the composer's collaborator and friend, Robert Craft. The letter
nevertheless helped make a friendship, and that December the composer lunched
with the Berlins at Headington House. It was on another such occasion, in
October 1961, that IB suggested the Biblical story of Abraham and Isaac (Genesis
22:1–18) as the theme for a composition that Stravinsky intended to write for the
Israel Festival. Stravinsky's imagination was caught by the rhythmic quality
of the Hebrew text, from which IB read aloud, and at Stravinsky's request IB
supplied a transliteration into phonetic English, which the composer used as his
libretto for the work. What resulted was a 'strangely hermetic masterpiece',*[2]
*a complex twelve-minute cantata for baritone solo and chamber ensemble,
officially commissioned in January 1962, and premiered at the Israel Festival in
August 1964.*

TO ROBERT CRAFT

12 January 1962

Headington House

Dear Bob,

[…] The chief item of news which I hasten to communicate to you is that
the commission for *Abraham and Isaac* is definitely settled – I mean that the
Israel authorities guarantee the sum stipulated (fifteen thousand) and that
I am formally to communicate this fact. I am very glad indeed that this is
so: and fervently hope that no obstacles will arise in the path of what I am
utterly convinced will be a splendid masterpiece. I shall certainly arrange to
be in Israel in the summer of 1963. Or rather not summer, for now the plan
is to have the festival in October, when the weather is far cooler and all the
amenities much more available. I am exceedingly sorry to be unable to be
there this summer, and only hope that all will go well. I wish I could be there
– I feel that I could point out aspects of life and nature, both comical and fascinating, which are not obvious and are easily missed, and that I should have
acted as quite a decent cicerone and mediator and shock-absorber (there are
no serious shocks: but they can be a trifle crude, and a certain amount of jostling, so to speak, can occur, despite or rather because of an excess of good
will), and I hope it will not be too hot for you at the end of August. Jerusalem
is perfectly agreeable in the evenings, but Tel Aviv is stifling, and Caesarea
can be too. I doubt now if Casals will be there at any time: one of the conditions of acceptance is apparently that his Oratorio on the Infant Jesus in
the Manger,[3] which lasts three-and-a-half hours and is not thought a work

---

1 To Robert Craft, 21 September 1958, L2 648. The fan letter is at L2 646–7.
2 Stephen Walsh, 'Stravinsky, Igor, §10: Final Years, 1959–71', *Grove Music Online* and *New Grove
Dictionary of Music and Musicians* (London, 2001), xxiv 554.
3 Casals's oratorio *El pessebre* (*The Manger*), which draws on Catalan folk traditions, was given its
world premiere in Mexico in December 1960.

of unforgettable splendour (these three-and-a-half hours are apparently unforgettable – every minute seems eternal), be performed. This may be too much for the Israelis, both intrinsically and because of the subject [...].

Yours ever,

Isaiah

TO MEYER WEISGAL[1]

15 January 1962 [*carbon*]

[Headington House]

Dear Meyer,

The situation looks much brighter. It will, now, I think, be possible for my family to arrive on about 4th/5th. [...]

As for the climax of the whole thing – the Roman feast, the snow white pillows, the brimming cups, etc. – it would be angelic of you if you could arrange for something which would suit my stepchildren better than the sophisticated company to which you and I are far too used. We have I think discussed it: either a kibbutz of not too big a kind – a Brenner[2] is perhaps too big – or is there not somewhere in the neighbourhood of Rehovot a Youth Aliyah Seder where they would feel more at home among the innocent and still idealistic? That would be better than the ageing voluptuaries by whom you and I are surrounded on such occasions. Also, must I make reservations in some Jerusalem synagogue for the following morning in order to imbue them with the proper feelings? Sir Isaac's[3] synagogue in Jerusalem was the nastiest place I have ever visited and our friend Raimund still keeps a card in his wallet on which are printed the words 'Members of the congregation are requested not to speak during the Service', signed 'The Management', exactly as in the cinema or a hotel. Do you recommend any establishment in Tel Aviv? Or must we return to dear old Yeshurun? I leave it all to you, but remember, like the Kennedys, we are a devout, close-knit, pious, easily shocked family and have to be treated with the respect due to the very old-world and sensitive who cannot take a step without ecclesiastical advice.

Yours ever,

[Isaiah]   [...]

1 Meyer Wolf Weisgal (1894–1977), Polish-born Zionist who lived, from 1905, in the US, where he worked as a journalist, editor, impresario and fund-raiser; Chaim Weizmann's personal representative there 1940–9; Chairman, Executive Council, Weizmann Institute of Science, 1949–66, President 1966–9, Chancellor 1970–7. '[H]is own life [...] is, in the end, an unending sacrifice on the altar of his people, whose past means everything to him, whose faults excite his alternate sympathy and indignation, whose present he contemplates with pride, despair and a strange mixture of fury and love, and upon whose uncertain future his gaze is still intermittently and anxiously directed.' IB, contribution to *Meyer W. Weisgal* (NY, 1964), repr. as 'A Generous Imaginative Idealist' in Edward Victor (ed.), *Meyer Weisgal at Seventy* (London, 1966), 87–9 at 89.
2 Givat Brenner, just south of Rehovot, one of the largest kibbutzim in Israel.
3 Isaac *Wolfson (1897–1991), businesman and philanthropist, eponymous benefactor of Wolfson College.

TO MORTON WHITE

15 January 1962

Headington House

Dear Morton,

I am very sorry to hear that you will be in Princeton at about the time when I am at Harvard – but nevertheless I think we may organise meeting somehow. Perhaps we shall write two books, one each on this topic, as a result of discussion. I still feel passionately interested in the subject, as I am sure you are, and Carr's book[1] merely whetted my appetite. As you will have seen from reading it, it is a little too crude – and although no doubt his sentiments are progressive and his desire to be scientific great, his intellectual equipment for these things is not quite adequate. He has just invited me to dinner with every expression of flattering regard and although this is a little more sincere than the ghastly inscription upon his offprint offered me by Mr Marshall Cohen, nevertheless our relations remain peculiar. I think that he thinks that we tease each other in public in a gay and lively intellectual fashion, but fundamentally are at one against a vast philistine world which we both dislike and despise – this is not quite true; nevertheless I fall into this pattern all too easily and shall probably go and dine with him after all these exchanges. [...]

For the first time in my life I have had a fan mail – a rather embarrassing one – from various persons either sympathising with my maltreatment or denouncing Carr – mostly on the left, curiously enough. For once I have not had hideous embarrassing right-wing supporters, who are the permanent menace of my life and whom I probably do my best to attract without consciously intending to do so. [...]

Carr is not a very nasty man – though he has been wounded by circumstances and has for thought and philosophy the contempt engendered by long years in the Foreign Office and general philistinism of temperament, from which he does suffer. He was acclaimed as one of the greatest thinkers of our age by Deutscher[2] in *The Times Literary Supplement*, although he was warned in rather Delphic terms that his mistaken use of the word 'absolute' and other things of this sort exposed him to a flank attack from Popper

---

1 E. H. Carr, *What is History?* (London, 1962: Macmillan). See also 'What is History?' (an exchange of letters with E. H. Carr), *Listener* 65 (1961), 877, 1048–9; 'Mr Carr's Big Battalions', review of E. H. Carr, *What is History?*, *New Statesman* 63 (1962), 15–16.

2 Isaac Deutscher (1906–67), Polish-born Jewish historian and left-wing commentator, author of highly-regarded biographies of Stalin (Oxford, 1949) and Trotsky (3 vols, Oxford, 1954–63). His determinist approach to history and his positive view of the Soviet achievement – his critics regarded him as an apologist for Stalinism, even if not an unreserved one – put him at odds with IB, and their differences were exacerbated by sharply conflicting approaches to Judaism and Israel. IB regarded him as a perverter, albeit brilliant, of the truth: 'nothing that Carr, Deutscher or C. P. Snow say will make people forget the price that the Russian Revolution exacted. I believe in the *Weltgericht* ['last judgement'], don't you?' (IB to Richard Crossman, 6 March 1963).

and myself.[1] The trouble with his book is that too much of it is marching through open doors: most of the propositions seem to be unexceptionable but neither new nor interesting – in the *New Statesman* I was politer than I felt because I was a victim – you will understand the state of mind in which one writes a review of this kind – what I really longed to say and did not say was that, although very sprightly, vigorous etc., and directed against all kinds of academic dodos, most of the things are not worth saying. Still, this is not, I think, the general view of the historians among the reviewers: most of them feel that he has made a tremendous breakthrough, that he is a brave man bravely facing a splendid future and is marching with great optimistic steps, breasting the current (in my excitement I fear I am mixing metaphors too much) on the right side of the forces of history, welcoming the vast changes which the world is undergoing instead of shrinking from them into pessimism and blindness.

[...] Fundamentally he is one of those people wounded by lack of social recognition at a sensitive moment of his life who has conceived a violent hatred for the entire liberal establishment and will welcome any force which will destroy his hated persecutors, even if it destroys him, too – a kind of Samson complex. It is not worship of power as such, which other weak, neurotic characters have shown, or the worship of beauty by cripples like Goebbels,[2] but a violent desire to be avenged upon a particular society which somehow humiliated him, or in which he wasn't able to fit, by calling in the bears out of the woods like the prophet Elisha, if you remember the story. His big history of the Soviet Union is really an amazing book – excellently organised, full of industry, but systematically ignoring all but official sources, because the defeated cannot be worth listening to, since they belong to a world that has collapsed and their views are perverted by it, while the winners are making our world; and objectivity is that view of the world which their victories create and which we had better adopt if we are not to misunderstand and to perish (these two latter are practically synonymous). It is a very, very, very crude mixture of Hegel and Marx. [...]

Yours,

Isaiah   [...]

---

1 Deutscher's approving review of Carr's *What is History?*, 'Between Past and Future', appeared in the TLS, 17 November 1961, 813.

2 (Paul) Joseph Goebbels (1897–1945), Nazi Minister for Public Enlightenment and Propaganda 1933–45, had a deformed right leg which caused him to walk with a limp.

TO VED MEHTA
  17 January 1962

Headington House

Dear Ved,

You ask me what the reactions of my colleagues are to your piece on Oxford Philosophy. I have spoken to few of them, not, for example, to Hampshire or Hare or Miss Murdoch or Ryle or Strawson,[1] but those to whom I have spoken are in various degrees outraged and indignant. This I will not attempt to conceal from you. And I understand most of them quite well: if one is engaged on a serious and extremely difficult vocation, such as that of philosophy, it is, to say the least, irritating to be represented as believing and saying things that certainly do not exactly correspond to what one is attempting to think out and explain very precisely and painfully. The *New Yorker* is a satirical magazine, and I assume from the start that a satire was intended and not an accurate representation of the truth. In any case, only a serious student of philosophy could attempt to do that. [...]

I remain grateful to you for what you have not said about me, and I think the piece is a genuine success in a Toulouse-Lautrec sort of way, rather like Tolstoy's accounts of German theorising with which he does not sympathise, or Voltaire's (and Russell's) reflections on, say, the schoolmen[2] of the Middle Ages. But I fully understand the feelings of such of my colleagues as must feel about your piece what Christians would feel about Gibbon[3] when they have been caricatured to make the *New Yorker*'s holiday. Still, parody is your right, and its right, and if the victims protest, that is their right too, surely. [...]

Yours sincerely,
  Isaiah   [...]

TO NOEL ANNAN
  18 January 1962

Headington House

Dear Noel,
  Yes, I do see why a controversy between the Warden of All Souls and the

---

1 Peter Frederick Strawson (1919–2006), Kt 1977, Fellow and Praelector in Philosophy, Univ., 1948–68; Waynflete Professor of Metaphysical Philosophy and Fellow of Magdalen 1968–87.
2 Also known as 'scholastics': teachers of philosophy and theology in the 'schools' of medieval Europe, whose systematising Aristotelian logic brought about a great intellectual advance before being stigmatised in the Renaissance as pedantic obscurantism expressed in crabbed and barbarous Latin, and succumbing to the challenge of new approaches.
3 Chapters 15–16 of the first volume of Edward Gibbon's monumental *The History of the Decline and Fall of the Roman Empire* (London, 1776–88) contain a famously negative portrayal of the early Church.

Provost of King's about Lady Chatterley would be unedifying[1] – although might it not prove that sex occupies precisely that position in the public consciousness that, say, religion, evolution, atheism occupied a hundred years before? [...]

Maurice is in splendid form. He has just denounced Sparrow's article to me as not merely trivial and mad but ill-argued and inconclusive, and has written to Sparrow to say how well he thought of it. Sparrow was very touched and thinks he is a nice kind man after all. Am I am capable of being shocked? Yes, I am. If you ask why Tawney[2] had all those honorary degrees and Maurice hasn't, there is every reason. Goodness, but you must burn this letter!

yrs

Isaiah   [...]

TO GARRETT DROGHEDA

29 January 1962

Headington House

Dear Garrett,

A démarche was made to me today by my Oxford colleague, Lord Salter.[3] He said that he and his friends had, on a number of occasions, experienced a feeling of indignation when, unable to obtain tickets for their friends for a performance at Covent Garden, because the house was sold out, they observed the Directors' Box unoccupied. He felt that tax-payers like himself had a right to demand that if they themselves were refused tickets, all available seats should be occupied. He wondered whether he might not air this in the House of Lords by demanding that an enquiry in connection with the new subsidy should be instituted into the most economical way of running the Opera House, etc., etc. He did not see why if, by a certain specified time, those who had a right to the Directors' Box had made it plain that they did not require it, it could not be sold to members of the public. I did my best to assuage his feelings, but he kept coming back to the topic, mentioned the names of persons not known to me who, he maintained, had voiced

---

1 Annan was one of the 36 witnesses called by the defence in the *Lady Chatterley* trial: he averred that 'Although not the greatest of Lawrence's novels, it was a very important one' ('Evidence Ends with 35 Witnesses Not Called', *Times*, 1 November 1960, 6c). For John Sparrow's views see 11/3.

2 Richard Henry Tawney (1880–1962), Professor of Economic History, London, 1931–49, Emeritus 1949–62. At the end of his life Tawney held honorary doctorates from nine universities (Birmingham, Chicago, Glasgow, London, Manchester, Melbourne, Oxford, Paris, Sheffield), Bowra from ten (Aix, Columbia, Dublin, Harvard, Hull, Oxford, Paris, St Andrews, Tehran, Wales).

3 (James) Arthur Salter (1881–1975), KCB 1922, 1st (and last) Baron Salter of Kidlington 1953; civil servant, politician, political theorist; Gladstone Professor of Political Theory and Institutions and Fellow of All Souls 1934–44, Honorary Fellow 1974–5; Independent MP for Oxford University 1937–50; Conservative MP for Ormskirk and government minister 1951–3.

feelings similar to his own, some of whom were in influential positions, the House of Commons and Lords, etc., with whom he had discussed it. I report this for what it is worth: but I wondered whether there was not something in this [...]. I asked Salter on how many occasions he and his friends had observed the Box empty, and he swore that during the last two years it had happened on more than half a dozen occasions. I finally calmed him down – at least I think I did – and said I would get his complaint ventilated in the right quarters.

Yours ever,

[Isaiah]   cc David Webster

PS If it is thought impracticable for members of the Royal Opera staff to occupy the Box when those entitled to it do not want it, I have another suggestion to make. Perhaps waxworks of the Directors, or at any rate the relevant portions of them, could be made (and also of the guests, of either sex, whom they are likely to invite) and an ever-varying selection of these be presented from the Box, in characteristic attitudes?

John Sparrow's long reign as Warden of All Souls began when he defeated A. L. Rowse in a keenly contested election in February 1952. Faced with the prospect of Rowse as Warden, IB had no hesitation in declaring himself 'a hot Sparrovian',[1] but within little more than a decade he had grown deeply disillusioned with his friend's stewardship of the College. After one College dispute in the summer of 1960, in which Sparrow had worsted the philosopher Michael Dummett,[2] publicly mocking him, IB was moved to write a letter of mixed protest and warning:

I wish [...] the College to be great & glorious & widely respected: it cannot be if *you* are not looked up to & corporately worshipped (& not merely admired & feared & liked by x, y, z, individually) that is all. It can easily be done, if you will only not enjoy yourself so richly when opportunity offers at the expense of our monsters. For monsters they are: but ours.[3]

During the early 1960s the fellows of All Souls became increasingly polarised over the issue of reform. Oxford was then beginning to feel the force of the changes affecting post-war higher education, including demands for wider social access and increased emphasis on graduate studies and research. As one of the University's wealthiest and most prestigious colleges, All Souls was ideally equipped to play a leading role in reform, but almost all initiatives were opposed by Sparrow, who drew support from what IB termed 'the troglodytes, or

1 L2 272.
2 96/4.
3 IB to John Sparrow, 27 July 1960.

"Fortress All Souls" party'. This was a small group of older fellows determined to maintain the club-like atmosphere of the College, and who wanted 'as few strangers as possible'. Against them were ranged 'the extreme fauves'[1] – mostly younger dons who wanted All Souls to be more engaged in the University and the challenges before it. IB was bound by personal loyalty to Sparrow, but by temperament and principle to the party of reform. In the spring of 1962 the battle lines were being drawn, and a motion to admit women to All Souls – which had no real hope of success – was an early, symbolic shot across the Warden's bows.

TO CHARLES TAYLOR

23 February 1962 [*carbon*]

[Headington House]

Dear Chuck,

[...] Clayre is back from Israel – he says he liked kibbutz life very much – and I think perhaps he did, although I am astonished that someone so sensitive and devoted to privacy could have stood the racket of it all so well. Have you all been there? You really would like it as I do. I do not believe that either of us is devoted to privacy in the least, and I defend it, like all forms of negative freedom, with a passion which only corresponds to my desire to escape from it in real life.

In All Souls the usual nonsense is going on – we are about to elect two Research Fellows – about that we may not do too badly – the only stuffy candidate, an elderly archaeologist, is I think likely to be rejected by the new vogue of left-wing sentiment against which the Warden struggles with a kind of sardonic cynicism of a man who likes to think of himself as drowning but will sink as many people with him as possible before the final cataclysm; there is also a motion to lift the bar in the constitution which prevents women from being elected – the motives are entirely malicious as there are no suitable women candidates in view, and it is merely designed to give the Warden pain – it will not pass and is known not to be likely to pass, but is meant to be a demonstration of exasperated hostility by the *jeunesse* and for that reason Stuart proposes to vote against it. About myself, I am not sure. My master, J. S. Mill,[2] would after all have been in favour, and I have no objection to the measure as such – on the other hand it will cause acute discomfort to the four or five troglodytes who inhabit All Souls and to whose form of life a masculine society seems indispensable, and also if it passes it will entail women guests, and above all the wives of the fellows in constant attendance;

1 All quotations in this paragraph are from IB to Harry Fisher, 17 February 1964.
2 While briefly Liberal MP for Westminster 1865–8, Mill proposed an amendment to Disraeli's 1867 Suffrage Bill that would have enfranchised women on the same terms as men; though defeated, it was an important landmark on the road towards women's suffrage; two years later he published the seminal *The Subjection of Women* (London, 1869).

the prospect of sitting between Mrs MacCartney and Mrs Hanbury[1] seems a superfluous hair shirt which one sees no reason for inventing. You can see from all this that nothing alters here. [...]

Yours ever,

[Isaiah]

TO ROWLAND BURDON-MULLER

26 February 1962

Headington House

My dear Rowland,

You must forgive me for not having written you for so long, but I have been in a state of appalling busyness, I don't myself know why – I have five committees in London, two of which are quite genuine ones [...].

There is nothing of great note to report: Nureyev, whom you will soon see in the United States, is a splendid and most attractive dancer, denounced by the idiotic London ballet critics – not all of them, but one or two – for reasons which I cannot fathom.[2] Indeed it is difficult to get first-class singers and conductors to come to London because our critics are both violent and uncorrupt: they denounce artists much more harshly than anyone else and as what matters to an artist are the press notices which, if bad, are immediately sent by their enemies to various countries in order to spoil their careers, and no amount of violent applause by the audience, forty curtain calls, etc. will compensate for a bad notice in a well-known journal, three of them have announced that they will never come to London again – one is Schwarzkopf[3] (I feel vaguely relieved: although she is an excellent singer and the wife of my colleague Walter Legge on the board of Covent Garden, I cannot get it out of my head that people have told me that she was the mistress of Joseph Frank,[4] the butcher of Poland during the war, and if this is true it gives one

---

1 Nedella (1899–1989) née Mamarchev, Bulgarian wife of Carlile Alymer Macartney (1895–1978), who was a historian of Hungary and Research Fellow, All Souls, 1936–65; Anna Margaret Geelmuyden Hanbury (1901–80) née Dreyer, wife of Professor Harold Hanbury.

2 Rudolf Khametovich Nureyev (1938–93) made his debut with the Royal Ballet opposite Dame Margot Fonteyn in *Giselle* on 21 February 1962, having sought political asylum in France in June of the previous year, while touring with the Leningrad Kirov. He had been that company's rising star, and had caused a sensation in Paris: '[His] conquest of Covent Garden [...] might have been predictable but could hardly have been more complete' (*Times*, 22 February 1962, 13b).

3 (Olga Maria) Elisabeth Friederike Schwarzkopf (1915–2006), DBE 1992, German soprano; joined Deutsche Oper 1938, and the Nazi Party the following year: 'it was her membership of the Nazi party, her involvement in a number of propaganda films for Josef Goebbels, and her appearance at Paris in 1941 [...] for the German occupying troops that later came to dominate any discussion of this part of her career' (Raymond Holden, ODNB); her Nazi Party membership emerged in 1981; she married the Jewish Walter Legge in 1953.

4 sc. Hans Frank (1900–46), Nazi Governor-General of occupied Poland from November 1939; the seventh defendant to appear in the witness box at the Nuremberg trials, and 'the first to make an outright declaration of guilt' (*Times*, 20 April 1946, 3e); sentenced to death and hanged.

gooseflesh, even at this date); Nilsson[1] (who may, however, come back); and now Siepi,[2] who says that his excellent performance in *Don Giovanni* with splendid and, for me, over-garish décor by Zeffirelli, had not been sufficiently praised or indeed noticed at all.[3] There is nothing to be done about this: the critics are proud, independent and uncorrupt; that they are very bad is simply a misfortune. I do not believe that little cosy luncheon parties by the unattractive David Webster would put them in a better humour. My Chairman, Garrett Drogheda, keeps writing angry notes to proprietors of newspapers who quite properly defend their critics. This goes on boiling round me and adds to the zest of life in a sense. [...]

There is a blizzard outside and Aline begs me to go for a walk – her passion for the open air is very great. She says will you come to the Ritz in Paris? She also says there never was a question of a second bar – only an inconspicuous sitting-down place at the Vendôme end where people may order drinks. She says it will not show.[4] I wonder.

As for politics, you will be glad to think that I appeared on a television programme virtually for the first time in my life together with Mademoiselle Sagan,[5] three other French authors, two actors, etc., all of whom explained why they had signed the manifesto against the Algerian war[6] – one of them said she was ashamed of being French, etc. – and I delivered a peaceful little talk on the nature of the artist and political commitment. The French Embassy were most anxious to stop this particular performance, and I regret to say when they learnt that I was in the programme it appeared to them more respectable than they had thought before. Very depressing for me. Still, if my reactionary reputation can do some good to a radical cause, so much the better. I have also incurred the wrath of the Duke of Devonshire

1 Birgit Nilsson, stage name of Birgit Märta Svensson (1918–2005), Swedish soprano who enjoyed a long association with Bayreuth: and appeared several times at Covent Garden: her performance in the title role of Richard Strauss's *Elektra* at Covent Garden in 1969 was 'talked of with awe' (Peter Waymark, *Times*, 28 September 1970, 4d).

2 Cesare Siepi (1923–2010), Italian bass; a long-standing member of the Metropolitan Opera, where he sang Philip II in *Don Carlos* in Rudolf Bing's first season there; especially praised for his Mozart roles, notably Figaro and Don Giovanni.

3 In one lengthy review of the first night, 9 February, Siepi's Giovanni was singled out for praise, unlike Zeffirelli's 'extremely elaborate sets' ('Mozart Obscured by Romantic Gloom', *Times*, 10 February 1962, 4a). Franco Zeffirelli (b. 1923) né Gianfranco Corsi, later (2004) Hon. KBE; Italian film, theatre and opera director.

4 As one of the directors of Paris's Hôtel Ritz 1948–79 Aline was involved in planning its renovation in 1961.

5 Françoise Sagan, pseudonym of Françoise Quoirez (1935–2004), French novelist who published her first novel, *Bonjour tristesse* (1954), when she was eighteen: 'something of a legend in France, where she is the only writer under 40 years who is mentioned in the same breath as MM Camus and Sartre and Anouilh' ('New Novel by Mlle Sagan', *Times*, 4 September 1957, 13c).

6 An open letter of protest against the Algerian War signed by 121 French intellectuals and public figures, including Françoise Sagan, Jean-Paul Sartre, Francois Truffaut and Pierre Boulez, which became known as the 'Manifesto of the 121'; it was published in France on 6 September 1960 in the magazine *Vérité–liberté*.

by signing a letter against our new immigration Bill which will wound black and yellow men all over the world.[1] So you see your influence is working in my blood like a delayed reaction. Still, by the time I come to Cambridge, Mass., I expect I shall have lapsed into my quietist, unpolitical habits. [...]

Several splendid rows are brewing here, all wonderfully parochial, but then I have always thought that only small worlds were interesting, the events in a large world are so vague, their consequences so difficult to determine, so impersonal, so ramified, that I find it difficult to get them within any kind of focus or perspective – I still feel, when people talk about politics to me, as I did when my father[2] used to do so, respectful, apprehensive, bored, inadequate, remote. The first row is whether Charlie Chaplin is to get an Honorary Degree here or not.[3] I am in favour because I think he is a man of genius, an Englishman, and this is enough. There are, however, those who think that he is a mere clown, that we disgraced ourselves by giving a degree to P. G. Wodehouse,[4] that if we are not prepared to give one to Groucho Marx or the acrobats who perform at the Alhambra, why should we give it to Chaplin? The only thing which is tiresome to me about him are his pompous and bogus pronouncements on ethics and politics which occasionally emanate from him and which are exceedingly pretentious and embarrassing. Still, he is a man of genius and that is that.

The second row is whether women should be admitted to Fellowships of All Souls. You can imagine what John Sparrow feels about that. I think if it is passed – it is most unlikely to be – he will resign. The spectacle of a woman sitting in the Buttery at All Souls would really drive him off his head. Aline thinks that that would be far, far worse than four new bars at the Ritz. She is very anti-feminist and has always been so. [...]

It is, as it always is when I start dictating a letter to you, about 2.30 a.m. and I must stop. Aline is moaning gently next door and I cannot keep her awake any longer. [...]

Yours ever,
Isaiah

1 The Macmillan government's restrictive Commonwealth Immigration Bill, which came into force on 1 July 1962, was widely attacked for treating Commonwealth citizens 'much the same as aliens', and because it would, 'even though incidentally, involve a colour discrimination' ('A Bad Bill', Times, 14 November 1961, 11b).
2 Mendel *Berlin (1884–1953), timber merchant.
3 Charles Spencer ('Charlie') Chaplin (1889–1977), film actor and director; awarded an Hon. D.Litt. by the University of Oxford on 27 June 1962.
4 The decision to award the writer P[elham] G[renville] Wodehouse (1881–1975), creator of the comic characters Bertie Wooster and Jeeves, an Hon. D.Litt. in 1939 had been 'widely regarded as a piece of donnish eccentricity' (Iain Sproat, ODNB).

6 March 1962 [*carbon*]

[Headington House]

Dear Hugh,

Thank you for sending me the piece on Carr.[1] You ask whether it is fair to the old monster – over-generous it seems to me. He is not quite the Macaulay[2] or even the Froude[3] of our days. Surely it is worth adding that his analogy between history and cricket – we record the centuries scored by Jack Hobbs[4] and not the ducks of the others – implies an even vulgarer view of history than Macaulay's, in which all we do is score and sing the victories of the winners like court minstrels, as if history were nothing but a game and its sole values were victories and defeats. And it is also perhaps worth mentioning that he resolutely refuses to look at the evidence of the failures and the martyrs and the minorities, even if only to condemn it, and that this no reputable historian has ever openly done before, not even the Russian Communists [...].

You would greatly oblige me if you did not quite so greatly enjoy yourself at my expense by representing me as a Hector dragged in the dust behind my persecutor's chariot. The top of page 5 is very funny but I do not much like being made fun of openly in public. But worse is page 11 where 'pig stick' is too brutal – that you really must change into something a little less sadistic.

It is a most beautifully written piece and I enjoyed reading it very much. Carr will not mind it. He does not mind criticism much, although mine evidently got underneath his skin, but my relations with him like yours with Alan Taylor persist. In a way I even like him, but do not respect him at all – I suspect that must be your feeling about Alan. Have you been asked to contribute to the Festschrift for the latter?[5] At least Carr is free from that ambition. And you must not say that Carr is a political philosopher, for why is he one? He is a social thinker of some order – but he has no interest in concepts or doctrines as such. You say that your profession of faith only differs from his slightly (although significantly) – it differs by a whole heaven. To see history as an autostrada, ignoring all the by-paths down which the victims

---

1 A draft review of Carr's *What Is History?*: many of IB's comments were included in Trevor-Roper's 'E. H. Carr's Success Story', *Encounter*, May 1962, 69–76.

2 Thomas Babington Macaulay (1800–59), 1st Baron Macaulay 1857, historian, essayist and poet whose enormously successful and influential *The History of England from the Accession of James II* (5 vols., 1849–61) is regarded as a monument to the Whig interpretation of history.

3 James Anthony Froude (1818–94), historian; Regius Professor of Modern History, Oxford, 1892–4; his popular *History of England from the Fall of Wolsey to the Death of Elizabeth* (12 vols, 1856–70), though more diffident in tone, to some extent emulated the success of Macaulay's great work.

4 John Berry ('Jack') Hobbs (1882–1963), Kt 1953, Surrey and England opening batsman, scored 197 centuries in first-class cricket.

5 Martin Gilbert (ed.), *A Century of Conflict, 1850–1950: Essays for A. J. P. Taylor* (London, 1966); after much toing and froing IB contributed 'L. B. Namier: A Personal Impression' (repr. in PI).

have trodden into the swamps (as he does), and as a constant choice between at one time equally possible paths, some which lead forward and some backwards (as you do), presuppose totally different conceptions of what men, choice, freedom, progress, success etc. are. I know that you wish deliberately to understate this: but do not understate it too much! The hungry sheep who read *Encounter* deserve to have the difference between sound and rotting food made clear to them. You understand the nature of history better than any of your contemporaries in England, and I dare say in Europe, and there is no reason for concealing this fact.

　　Yours ever,

　　　[Isaiah]

TO ANDRZEJ WALICKI[1]

13 March 1962 [*carbon*]

[Headington House]

Dear Walicki,

　　[...] I have received Malia's book on Herzen.[2] Have you seen it? If not, I shall send it to you with pleasure. It looks solid, excellently written, and altogether a masterpiece – my friend Prof. George Fischer[3] of Cornell, who has just come back from Moscow, declares that the local savants there recognise it as a worthy and important work and are prepared to withdraw their usual strictures about the West as ignorant, superficial, uninterested in Russian things, philistine, blind, and self-preoccupied. I am delighted that you are working on Slavophils versus Westerners.[4] There is really nothing serious about them in the West – nor really in Russian either: there are learned works which tell one who they are, when they were born, what books they read, what exhibitions they held, [...] but all this, apart from questions of bias and interpretation, is ultimately merely erudite, works of compilation and not of understanding or criticism. And yet, of course, both they and their opponents said things which are original and fascinating and better than corresponding essays in the West. I would much rather read Herzen, or even

1　Andrzej *Walicki (b. 1930), Polish social and political historian.

2　Martin Edward Malia (1924–2004), historian and Soviet specialist; assistant professor of history, University of California, Berkeley, 1958–64, professor 1964–91. His *Alexander Herzen and the Birth of Russian Socialism, 1812–1855* (Cambridge, Mass., and London, 1961) was a reworking of his Harvard dissertation, which had been inspired by his professor there, Michael Karpovich, and also by IB.

3　George Fischer (b. 1923), Associate, Russian Research Center, Harvard, 1947–61; associate professor of history, Brandeis, 1958–60; later taught at Cornell, Columbia and City Universities.

4　There was a fierce debate among intellectuals in 19th-century Russia between the 'Westerners', who advocated closer identification with the cultural values that had underwritten political, social and economic progress in Europe, and the 'Slavophils', who favoured patriotic identification with the uniqueness of Russian culture. Walicki later published *The Slavophile Controversy* (Oxford, 1975), which IB reviewed in the *Slavonic and East European Review* 59 no. 4 (October 1981), 572–86.

Bakunin,[1] today, than Carlyle[2] or Ruskin,[3] who seem absolutely dead. The last person really to be soaked in the writings of these authors – Emerson,[4] Ruskin, Edward Carpenter,[5] and other secular clergymen – was Gandhi, which reminds me that I was in India in November [...] and much enjoyed it. I attended a Congress to celebrate the 100th Anniversary of Tagore. There was no Polish representative, but there were three Russians, a lady who spoke no English but only Bengali – that was very well received by the Indians – and the writer Vsevolod Ivanov,[6] whom I like very much. We saw the Taj Mahal together by moonlight. India is an extraordinary country: full of vitality, appetite for life and learning, teeming with the most extraordinary mixture of ancient religion, superstition, prehistoric rites, holy men on beds of nails, violent paroxysms of self-lacerating ascetics, and nuclear reactors, exceedingly clever and cynical modern economists, highly skilled politicians, etc. My hour and a half with Mr Nehru was very fascinating. I liked him very much and realised that [...] the criticisms of him both in English and American newspapers miss the nature of his problems and the kind of solutions he brings to them. In short, I am for him and against his critics, and so, I dare say, would Chernyshevsky[7] have been, although the populists[8] would,

1 Mikhail Aleksandrovich Bakunin (1814–76), Russian anarchist revolutionary, critical of Marx's authoritarian socialism; offered his alternative to a dictatorship of the proletariat in *Statism and Anarchy* (1873). 'I have never written about [Bakunin] and I suspect that if I did I should be fallen upon [...] by various anarchists, neo-anarchists, dissident Marxists etc. for making out this splendid man, almost the first to enunciate the proposition that we must first clear the ground and then we shall see – that anyone who plans for the aftermath of the revolution is a reactionary – as, if not cynical, at any rate frivolous, and simply in search of strong sensations and with a very powerful desire to blow things up for the sheer hell of it because the world was a suffocating box.' IB to Paul Roazen, 29 October 1970; he had in fact published 'Herzen and Bakunin on Individual Liberty' (repr. in *RT*) in 1955, and made essentially this point.

2 Thomas Carlyle (1795–1881), philosopher, essayist and historian, whose 3-volume *The French Revolution* (London, 1837) informed Dickens's *A Tale of Two Cities* (London, 1859); notwithstanding his immense influence on Victorian contemporaries, 'twentieth-century readers found uncongenial the intricacies and dramatic flourishes of his prose style' (Fred Kaplan, ODNB).

3 John Ruskin (1819–1900), writer, artist, social reformer and philanthropist; first Slade Professor of Fine Art, Oxford, 1870–8, 1883–4; the most important art critic of his era, champion of the Pre-Raphaelites.

4 Ralph Waldo Emerson (1803–82), American essayist, lecturer, poet and philosopher, a key figure in the New England Transcendentalist movement.

5 Edward Carpenter (1844–1929), socialist writer and poet, advocated a range of progressive causes, which he embodied in his overt homosexuality, vegetarianism and sandal-making; influenced Siegfried Sasson, E. M. Forster and D. H. Lawrence, and was considered by Tolstoy 'a worthy heir of Carlyle and Ruskin' (Chushichi Tsuzuki, ODNB).

6 Vsevolod Vyacheslavovich Ivanov (1895–1963), Soviet writer and dramatist, fought with the Red Army in Siberia during the Civil War; his graphic war novel *Armoured Train 14–69* (1922), reworked as a play (1927), achieved a permanent place in the Russian repertory.

7 Nikolay Gavrilovich Chernyshevsky (1828–89), editor, literary critic and revolutionary. His influential novel *What Is To Be Done?* (1863) was written while he awaited sentencing on fabricated charges of subversion, which led to a long exile with hard labour in Siberia: 'far more than Marx's *Capital*, [it] supplied the emotional dynamic that eventually went to make the Russian Revolution' (J. Frank, 'N. G. Chernyshevsky: A Russian Utopia', *Southern Review* 3 (1967), 68).

8 Movement of agrarian socialists in late nineteenth-century Russia, dedicated to the overthrow of the tsarist regime, and regarding the peasantry as the seedbed of national regeneration.

I think, have found themselves more at home among the handsome and aristocratic Brahmins whom I met and the teachers of Sanskrit and the infinitely tranquil life (and poverty) of the rural districts in which the peasants really do have faces of the type so much admired by Herzen.

Talking of whom, I am not doing much about him now, save that I have to write a brief introduction to a new English edition of the autobiography[1] – *My Past and Thoughts* is not a very good translation of even the title, but I cannot do anything about that. The introduction will say nothing, only introduce the English reader to a few facts about his life, and say that the work is a masterpiece – a masterpiece which is gradually more and more pessimistic, I think. By pessimism, I mean that he begins with an ideal vision of the world – utopian or realistic, right or wrong, is not important – but at any rate a vision which entails the possibility of a radical transformation of the existing order and an undervaluing of those iron economic laws or social laws of which Stalin once spoke. Gradually, not so much as a result of 1848, but of personal misfortunes and a deep scepticism of nature and I dare say a general sense of realism which never really forsook him, he begins to pay more and more attention to fixed laws, the relative inflexibility and unchangeability of men, the appalling nature of the task before reformers or revolutionaries, the power of tradition (which he both mocks at and admires in England), the lack of taste for liberty on the part of the masses, the hollowness of the slogans in the name of which they are led to slaughter, the emptiness of even the most radical politician, and the unsympathetic nature of the ideals of the extreme left, the feebleness of the liberals, the repulsiveness of the conservatives, the irreconcilability of civilisation and the awakening of the masses to the gap between 'the intelligentsia and the people', which then becomes such an extraordinary refrain in Russian thought. [...]

Talking of academics, my brilliant colleague, Professor A. J. Ayer, the friend of Adam Schaff,[2] has had an article printed in *Voprosy filosofii* in Moscow, and is indeed going to Moscow in the spring to lecture. He is an unreconstructed logical positivist of the old-fashioned kind who is fighting what seems to me a losing battle against the newer English semi-positivism – fructified by the later works of Wittgenstein,[3] a far wider and more tolerant

1 Herzen's memoirs, *My Past and Thoughts*, trans. Constance Garnett [1861–1946] (London, 1968); IB's introduction repr. in AC and PSM. *by Cur   Proper study in M*

2 Adam Schaff (1913–2006), Polish Marxist philosopher, studied in Moscow 1941–6, returning to the University of Warsaw as the Director of the Institute for Philosophy and Sociology; was considered the main ideologue of Polish Communism during the 1950s, but gravitated towards a more revisionist Marxism during the 1960s, and in 1968 was removed from the Central Committee of the Polish United Worker's Party (the Communist Party of Poland).

3 Ludwig Josef Johann Wittgenstein (1889–1951), Vienna-born British philosopher; studied at Cambridge 1911–13, and was Bertrand Russell's protégé and collaborator; taught at Cambridge from 1930; Professor of Philosophy 1939–48; became a naturalised British citizen 1939; his 'Logisch-Philosophische Abhandlung', *Annalen der Naturphilosophie* 14 (1921), 185–262, trans. by C. K. Ogden and others as *Tractatus Logico-Philosophicus* (London/NY, 1922), inspired the logical

and humane stream than the rigorous followers of Carnap[1] in Vienna and elsewhere in the 1930s. He is an extremely able and charming man and a brilliant lecturer, and I hope you meet him when you are in Moscow – it is well worth it. I do not know whose hands he will be in – his correspondent so far as the 'V.F.' is concerned is one Melvil,[2] apparently a Russian or at any rate a writer in Russian. Freddie Ayer once read and approved of my book on Marx (which has now been translated into French by Gallimard),[3] but is remote from social and political thought, and proposes to have a look at dialectical materialism, which he is hardly likely to like, and if he says anything favourable about it, it will be from natural courtesy rather than conviction. However, he will come back with clear impressions of what he has seen, and they will, I am sure, be interesting. [...]

Do not abandon the Russian thinkers! I realise why you are fascinated by Mickiewicz.[4] It is, I am sure, a far richer, more poetical, more fascinating outlook than the relatively simple-minded Russians, yet you really have a duty to interpret these people to a wider world [...]. It is extraordinary that they do not understand in Moscow that a kind of lucid, scholarly, moderate and above all deeply sympathetic presentation of the views of the major Russian thinkers in the nineteenth century such as you are capable of will redound far more to the glory of their country, and will serve to explain even their present thought and its particular quality far more successfully, not only to the West but to Africa and Asia as well, than the mechanical, unreadable, official stuff that pours out from their own presses, and depresses even the most faithful Communists, the best friends they have abroad. Still, it is difficult to convince bureaucrats of the values and importance of intellectual production – they are suspicious of it as such in all countries, and the Soviet Union is, alas, no exception.

But if you want to see Slavophils and Westerners in action, go to India. There they are battling each other in the most genuine fashion, and if you go to India, do not omit to go to Nepal – a thirteenth-century kingdom only opened to tourists in 1950. The government and parliament are in jail (I mean the democratically elected one), the king governs directly and it is called 'direct democracy' – direct, certainly. Our guide, with real or assumed

positivism of the Vienna circle, and the Cambridge school of analysis between the wars; his posthumously published *Philosophical Investigations*, trans. G. E. M. Anscombe (Oxford, 1953), influenced the analytic philosophy of post-war Oxford.

1 Rudolf Carnap (1891–1970), German empiricist philosopher and logician; a leading member of the Vienna Circle and exponent of logical positivism in the 1930s; later Professor of Philosophy, UCLA, 1954–62.

2 Yuri Konstantinovich Mel'vil' (1912–93), Soviet philosopher whose career lasted from the early Cold War to the end of the Soviet era; a specialist in Western, particularly American, philosophy; Head of Dept of the History of Foreign Philosophy, Moscow State University, 1968–85.

3 Prestigious French publishing house founded in 1911 by Gaston Gallimard (1881–1975).

4 Adam Bernard Mickiewicz (1798–1855), Polish Romantic poet, subject of AW's *The Paris Lectures of Mickiewicz and Russian Slavophilism* (Cambridge, 1968).

naivety, asked us what we thought of the method of direct democracy, and explained that he was himself a freelance journalist who unfortunately had no newspaper to contribute to, for all newspapers had been suppressed. There are five ambassadors – British, American, Russian, Chinese, Indian – the Chinese cannot speak to the American at table, and the whole thing is a kind of cross between Bernard Shaw and vaudeville. The country is marvellously beautiful, it is full of lamas from Tibet, and you will never see medieval life in its purity again. Not even animals are allowed to carry, for some religious reason, and so it is one log one man, two logs two men; 40 per cent are Buddhists, 30 per cent Hindus, the inhabitants are like children awoken from long sleep who look on all tourists and foreigners with large, wide-open eyes, delighted to welcome them, naive, impressionable, responsive, delightful. It will obviously not be long like that: whether India or China will have a greater influence upon it is uncertain. I cannot believe that the present ramshackle despotism will last for ever. […]

Quite a lot of books have appeared on Marxism lately – the burden of all of them is early Marx more important than the late Marx; Marx good, Engels[1] not good; historicism good, positivism not good. I meditate writing a general study of all this now, but heavens, I have too many pupils, too many lectures, and I dare say this is all the fault of temperament and not really circumstances: I really must try and achieve at least one solid work – say a study of Belinsky – and not scatter myself in all these directions all over the place. […]

I hope you are morally and physically well – especially the former, but perhaps even more the latter. Health matters a great deal, for relation between body and mind is not even dialectical, but with so directly causal a nature as sometimes to humiliate one deeply.

Yours,
    Isaiah Berlin   […]

In the autumn of 1961 IB learned of a plan to install a wealthy businessman named Dr George Wise[2] as the President of the Hebrew University of Jerusalem: 'As a piece of pressure tactics by the American governors,' he observed, 'it is fascinating and terrible.'[3] IB was a governor, and opposed Wise's candidature: partly because of the aggressive manner, as he saw it, in which it was advanced,

1 Friedrich Engels (1820–95), German political theorist, longtime friend of his occasional co-author Karl Marx, with whom he was a journalist and agitator in the 1848 revolutions, seeing some active armed service, and exiled in England from 1849. From 1859 he framed Marx's life and work for the socialist public, coining the phrase 'materialist conception of history', and after Marx's death in 1883 he edited Marx's manuscripts for publication, in particular *Capital* vols 2 and 3, and also re-published many of Marx's works with new introductions and notes.

2 George Schneiweis Wise (1986–87), teacher, businessman, philanthropist; chairman of governors, HUJ, 1953–62.

3 To Victor Rothschild, 27 September 1961.

*but also because he felt that appointing to such an important academic office
a candidate whose sole qualification appeared to be his wealth ran counter to
'the whole ethical and intellectual ideal of Israel, which I for one find deeply
attractive, moving and noble'. The underlying issue was that of academic
independence: 'Universities must run themselves, or else they degenerate rapidly;
a few distinguished men from outside, perhaps, but the curse of American
universities is precisely this absence of academic self-government. That is why
only about five of them are as good as the best universities of Europe.'[1]*

*On his return from Israel in September 1961 IB involved himself heavily
in the campaign against Wise, writing to Victor Rothschild on 27 September:
'having just been to Jerusalem, as you know, I feel devotion and zeal in an
unusual degree – it is a change to feel so uncynical about something'. The British
governors proved solidly against Wise, and sought to delay a decision about the
Presidency until spring 1962. On 28 December IB wrote to Teddy Kollek:*

So far as financial pressure is concerned, what made the worst impression here
was [the US governors'] angry message to the effect that if the meeting to
elect the President were postponed from November, they accepted no financial
responsibility for collecting money for the University until May, and all aid
would cease during that period. This was perhaps no worse than the hints we
dropped that, if Wise were elected President, no further money would be col-
lected in England, but at least ours came long after theirs! I see that Americans
probably think that the British Governors are divided into (*a*) pompous, old-
fashioned snobs like Lord Samuel, [Norman] Bentwich[2] and other nineteenth-
century fossils, and (*b*) highbrow academics like Krebs, myself etc., and that
jointly we look down upon these vulgar rich Americans (so we do, of course)
and imagine we are still fighting some kind of Anglo-American war. There is
some truth in this: but also justification. I agree that some bridge will have to be
built between London and New York.

*The crisis came to a head in March 1962 at a heated meeting of the governors
of the University in the King David Hotel in Jerusalem, which IB attended: 'It
was a most distressing affair: everyone behaved as badly as, I thought, they only
behaved in Oxford or Cambridge or Columbia or Harvard.'[3]*

TO ALINE BERLIN

Tuesday [27 March 1962; *manuscript*]

King David Hotel, Jerusalem

Darling Aline

Not at all *dull*. It all began in the aeroplane. [...] I sat next to a Mrs Gimbel,[4]
a Governor, who gave me an innocent but very incriminating account of how

1 To Reb Shneur Zalman, 23 October 1961.   2 277/4.
3 To Eli Ginzberg, 15 October 1962.
4 Elinor Gimbel (1896–1983) née Steiner, then Hess, businesswoman and philanthropist, married
(secondly) Louis S. Gimbel 1927; founder and national president of the Women's Division of the

Dr George Wise, the candidate, "operates". At Lod we had a meeting with Racah[1] *at once*: in the V.I.P. waiting room. Then in the car: I was over-met: by Kollek's representatives *and* by Racah & co. Awkwardness. Next day uninterrupted intrigue, from which I liberated myself by taking up an unfamiliar au dessus de la mêlée attitude & general loftiness. [...] The meetings *boil* with violent feeling: and yesterday, after a series of small scenes, the chairman, the controversial Dr George Wise dramatically resigned, swept out of the room, & went off to the sickbed of his wife's father. The American delegation also left pro tem., & are meeting separately. [...] At the moment of writing I am sitting at a meeting boycotted by the Americans – the newspapers here are full of this – & Elath[2] (whom I dined with last night – *both* are coming to Oxford in May – I fear 1 night may be inevitable) is sending me funny Russian notes. I hope to kill off all the Jerusalem clients – Talmon & Co – Halevys[3] etc. before I go to Rehovot on Friday or Saturday. All but Ida.[4] She is [...] very poor: she protests she wants no money: because she has enough to live on & pay the doctors for her 2 operations, for 1 year. If you *can*, cd you ring up Dickie & ask him whether we need Bank of E. permission to send her say £400. 0. 0 as from May: in 4 3-monthly instalments. My mother *not* to know of this: she insists that *no* money is needed: this is supported by Ida, & is false. Everyone, of course, asks after you, everyone whatever. [...] Mr Ben Gurion is *not* interested in me: a cold message of greeting: but after you come we shall impose ourselves on them in Sde Boker, near Beersheva, on our Southern journey.[5] I do not really mind what he thinks: for the children it will be nice to see the extraordinary establishment in his retreat. And if he snubs me, I do not (much) mind. Mrs B. G. will be all over you. We shall bring her something from Iran. I have decided that I mind non-recognition less than you. The ex-minister of Justice – Felix Rosen(blueth)[6] – who is on tutoyer[7] terms with the Dreyfuses, who has met me at least 6 times asked

American Friends of HUJ; director of Liebman Breweries Inc (which manufactured Rheingold Beer).

1 Giulio Racah (1909–65), Italian physicist, emigrated to Palestine 1939; Professor of Theoretical Physics, HUJ, from 1939, Dean of the Faculty of Science 1946–8, Rector and acting President of the University 1961–5; made important contributions to spectroscopy; the Racah Institute of Physics at HUJ was established in 1970 in his honour.

2 Eliahu Elath (1903–90) né Epstein, journalist and diplomat; Israel's first ambassador to Washington 1948–50; ambassador to UK 1952–9; President of HUJ 1962–7.

3 Relations of IB through the marriage of his mother's sister Ida to Yitzhak Samunov (next note). Yitzhak's sister Rivka (1892–1971) married Eliezer Halevy (1897–1976; and see L1 10/2); their son Efraim (b. 1934) worked for Mossad from 1961 (Director 1998–2002). Thus IB's aunt was married to Efraim's uncle.

4 Ida Samunov (1887–1985) née Volshonok, IB's aunt (a younger sister of Marie Berlin); widowed by the death of her husband Yitzhak Samunov (1886–1950).

5 They did, together with Aline's two younger sons on their first visit to Israel.

6 Pinhas Rosen né Felix Rosenblueth (1887–1978), Berlin-born lawyer, Zionist leader and Israeli politician; co-founder of the Progressive Party 1948; as Minister of Justice for much of the period 1948–61 he laid the foundation of the Israeli legal system.

7 To address as 'tu' rather than 'vous' in French, i.e. to be on familiar terms.

them in my presence what language I spoke, & did not trouble to enquire my name. I was embarrassed but not offended. So there. In spite of my usual happiness here – less than in the Jacob–Nabokov days because of the meetings & the painful tension – I cannot bear to be without you. [...]

I love you I love you I love you. First & last: I sleep badly: & in the interstices I think about you, us, the future more than the past. I really *do* adore you infinitely: *more* than you me, yes yes yes.

Isaiah

TO MARTIN GILBERT[1]

1 May 1962

Headington House

Dear Gilbert,

I wish I could participate in the Festschrift,[2] but I cannot, not at all for the reasons allegedly given by Bullock and the others – but simply because I shall not be able to produce it in time, knowing myself as I do. I am terribly unproductive and terribly ashamed of being so: I bear literary children with the irregularity of some particularly ill-conditioned elephant, and since I must, on pain of eternal disgrace, produce something like five pieces of 'original' writing by the end of next year, I cannot undertake another one, come what may. I am as you know extremely fond of A.J.P.T. and would like to do him honour, despite everything. But no can, no ought. [...] I should be delighted to contribute £10 as a fee for anyone you like to put in my place. I wish I did not know myself so well: the books I have promised to review and have not reviewed stand accusingly on my shelves like so many acts of theft: so do all the broken promises to editors and publishers. You cannot possibly judge me in this respect more harshly than I judge myself.

Yours ever,

Isaiah Berlin

TO SAM BEHRMAN[3]

28 May 1962

Headington House

Dear Sam,

I was terribly moved by your letter. I am really devoted to Felix[4] – nothing more terrible could have happened to a man of his temperament and habits

---

1 Martin John Gilbert (b. 1936), later (1995) Kt; Fellow, Merton, 1962–94; research assistant to Randolph Churchill 1962–7; official biographer of Winston Churchill from 1968.

2 For A. J. P. Taylor: 84/5.

3 110/6.

4 Felix Frankfurter (1882–1965), Vienna-born lawyer and judge; appointed by FDR to US Supreme Court (1939–62); retired from that office 1962 after a stroke. IB first met him as a visiting professor

than to be incapacitated in that particular way. I am sure that what the doctor said was true – the most bitterly ironical comment on the situation I received from Dean Acheson[1] whom I saw in London who reported that Marion[2] had told him that she had taken this particular illness of Felix's much better than previous sicknesses of his. I adore and admire Marion, but there is something marvellously egomaniacal about her, about her whole relationship with Felix and her general view of the world. She reminds me of no one so much as of the late Virginia Woolf,[3] whose genius lay in this direction and whose universe had wonderful content, which nobody has ever succeeded in describing anything like so marvellously as she, even at her worst, but which possessed no windows of any kind.

Do go on letting me know about Felix. I wrote him a long letter from Israel about Eichmann, which I do not suppose he has read. I went to the trial for half an hour or so; everyone was in some sense German – the judges, the lawyers, the policemen were all German Jews. The whole thing was conducted most tidily. The prisoner in the glass box looked steadily down and wrote more or less ceaselessly, occasionally licking his lips; he looked like a small, slightly cancerous rat, not very Nordic but not exactly Jewish either, although this has been said. I hope they do not hang him, but I fear they will. The judges cannot plead extenuating circumstances for him as they have for General Salan[4] (I can well understand and sympathise with de Gaulle's fury about this), but the President could determine on some other punishment or at least commute the death penalty. My feeling is approximately this: the purpose of the trial was not simply the execution of an elementary act of justice: it is clear that if other Nazis are found lurking in Latin America or Iceland or Siam, it is unlikely that a special expedition will be sent to kidnap these, or that even if they found themselves in Israel by some accident or were secured by the Israelis by legal means, a similar trial would be mounted. That everyone is agreed about. If you then ask why, it seems clear that it [is] because the purpose of the trial, as everyone

in Oxford in 1933–4, and 'the Justice' provided IB with important introductions in Washington during the war.

1 Dean Gooderham Acheson (1893–1971), US lawyer and public servant; Secretary of State during the second Truman administration 1949–53; one of the orignators of NATO and the Marshall Aid programme; later a foreign policy adviser to Presidents Kennedy and Johnson.

2 Marion A. Frankfurter (1890–1975) née Denman, married Felix Frankfurter 1919. 'Anti-Marion propaganda is in full swing, but not at all justified. I speak as a witness for her. She is profoundly moved by Felix's condition, weeps disconsolately and is utterly devoted and attached to him, although Acheson and the others will not say so' (IB to Maurice Bowra, 20 January 1963).

3 (Adeline) Virginia Woolf (1882–1941) née Stephen, writer and publisher; for IB's first impressions of her, and hers of him, see L1 68–72.

4 On 23 May 1962 General Raoul Salan (1899–1984), chief of the Organisation armée secrète (OAS), which sought the assassination of de Gaulle as part of a terrorist campaign against Algerian independence, was found guilty on five capital charges at a military tribunal in Paris. He was nevertheless spared the death penalty amid emotional scenes in the courtroom, a majority of the judges having identified extenuating circumstances.

understands, was so to speak educational: to bring home to the world and
to the Jews what had actually happened, the whole hideous, unforgettable
story, etc. Now if the thing were simply elementary justice, one does not
argue that because one has put one murderer to death one lets the others
off because it is not worth impressing the moral upon the public again.
It therefore seems to me clear that the open as well as covert motive for
the trial was in some sense political or educational or historical, but not
mechanically judicial. If this is so, we are permitted to think of the public
consequences of the punishment and not merely about its judicial correct-
ness. It seem to me that if they kill him, people will say 'The Jews have their
victim. Blood for blood, six millions for one, now the deed is done and it
is time they stopped boring the world with endless reminiscences of the
horrors of what had been done to them. They have had their victim, they
have slaughtered him, and now they must stop maddening other people
with the story of their hard times and forget the whole thing.' In a sense,
the killing of Eichmann would be regarded as a symbolic closing of the case.
This is surely not desirable. Still, they are all very bloodthirsty there, their
interest in the outside world is very small, the desire for his death very great,
and so I fear that they will, in fact, hang him. This will do them no good
from any point of view, but advice from outside is not welcome.

I had a good time in Israel this spring, save at the University elections at
which with great difficulty the Governors did somehow manage to avoid
electing the American nominee, a Dr George S. Wise, a very rich paper manufacturer who lives in Mexico, whom I thought a nightmare figure. The British
Governors were a trifle too academic: all fine old Anglo-Saxon aristocracy like
Sir Hans Krebs,[1] Sir Ben Lockspeiser,[2] Sir Isaiah Berlin, Prof. Neuberger[3] and
that sort of thing. But the Americans looked rather like a Jewish Caribbean
cruise: decent, provincial bourgeoisie, as remote from universities, learning,
scholarship, students as, let us say, Yvonne Hamilton, or even further. They
were dreadfully offended at the opposition to their candidate by the rest of
us. A Mrs Gimbel with whom I travelled in the aeroplane informed me that
she was not really Jewish as she was descended from several generations of
freethinkers – she also later informed me that the non-election of Dr Wise
was a second crucifixion of a Jew in Jerusalem since Jesus Christ. Do you
know her? She owns Rheingold beer. She is well worth meeting. She is in
President Kennedy's Committee for something and is a foolish and ill-gotten

---

1 Hans (Adolf) Krebs (1900–81), Kt 1958; studied medicine at the universities of Göttingen,
   Freiburg, Munich and Berlin; left Germany 1933, naturalised British citizen 1939; Nobel Prize in
   Physiology or Medicine 1953; Whitley Professor of Biochemistry and Fellow of Trinity 1954–67.
2 Benjamin ('Ben') Lockspeiser (1891–1990), Kt 1946; London-born Cambridge-educated aero-
   nautical engineer and senior government administrator of Jewish-Polish descent; secretary,
   Committee of Privy Council for Scientific and Industrial Research, 1949–56.
3 Albert Neuberger (1908–96), born in Germany and educated at the University of Würzburg; left
   for London 1933; Professor of Chemical Pathology at St Mary's Hospital 1955–73.

widow with a degree of charmlessness I have seldom seen equalled. Her interest in the University of Jerusalem might just as well have been interest in abstract art or the Kabbalah. No doubt it is desirable that persons like this, in as much as they are rich, should be attracted to good rather than worthless causes; but in the end too many of them, or too much energy on their part, discredits the cause to which they are attached, and diminishing returns, and ultimately negative returns, begin coming in. Do tell me about her – Mrs Elinor Gimbel – for such I believe to be her name – I was fascinated by her conversation: when she informed me that she was a friend of Kingsley Martin,[1] Professor Bernal,[2] and I think C. P. Snow, I began to realise that she must have been a fellow-traveller of the 1930s who switched to Israel as a safer cause at some stage of her life. I suppose the pursuit of causes like suicide and tranquillisers is one of the by-products of prosperity. Little of this is to be observed in Israel: it seems to me the happiest society I have ever seen – the coarser, the more charmless, graceless, noisy, aesthetically blind, etc. the happier. If I were under thirty and in pursuit of pleasure, I should certainly live there and not in the West. As it is, I shall be lecturing to the Slade School tomorrow, to Reading University the day after, to three hundred doctors in Oxford the day after that […].

I notice a certain note of melancholy in your letter and I am in that mood myself. Perhaps, if we meet, two negatives will yield a positive – two blacks, in spite of what they say, do make a white at times, so let us not delay too long. Of course, if either of you or I could look and feel like Stravinsky or my mother at eighty, the urgency would not be so great. But I suspect that this is not for us. So let us make haste.

Yours ever,
⟨with much love
    Isaiah⟩

The failure of the motion to admit women to All Souls in the spring of 1962 had been anticipated even by its promoters, whereas the College's decision not to elect the brilliant mathematical logician Georg Kreisel to a fellowship caused anger and surprise. All Souls was unique among Oxford colleges in not admitting students. Its membership comprised instead several categories of fellow, and the elections to these posts animated the College as few other issues did. A significant minority of All Souls fellows were distinguished men pursuing non-academic

1 (Basil) Kingsley Martin (1897–1969), political journalist; editor, *New Statesman and Nation*, 1931–60, editorial director 1961–2; set out to make that journal 'the flagship weekly of the left' (Adrian Smith, ODNB).
2 John Desmond Bernal (1901–71), physicist and Marxist; Professor of Crystallography, Birkbeck, London, 1963–8, author of *Marx and Science* (London, 1952), and winner of the International Stalin Prize for Strengthening Peace Among Peoples 1953.

*London-based careers. Some of them, in addition to being out of the academic
swim, tended to arrive poorly briefed for College meetings, and consequently
were susceptible to determined lobbying. It was in these circumstances that
Kreisel was rejected by a combination of non-academic outsiders and inner
'troglodytes', solely on the grounds of his supposedly difficult character. That
non-academic criteria weighed so heavily in the process (there was a sense that
xenophobia also played its part) was in IB's eyes highly discreditable to All
Souls, and the episode marked a watershed in his feelings towards the College.*

TO JAMES JOLL

28 May 1962 [*carbon*]

Headington House

Dear James,

It is time that I, in my turn, sent you a bulletin about Oxford. There
is really nothing to report except the customary horrors. The end of last
term was a bit clouded for me by having to take part in three elections,
each of which was agonising, each in its own way. First of all, one at All
Souls at which we elected Mack Smith[1] (O.K.) and Professor M. Mallowan,[2]
husband to Agatha Christie and millionaire, presumably, who does not
need our money, is a professor in the University of London, and wants the
Fellowship for purely prestige purposes, namely to write a catalogue of
his archaeological researches. He is a perfectly respectable scholar, but it is
a waste of money. For the first time, I really did become furious more or less
in public about the fact that not enough votes could be got even to allow
Kreisel,[3] the mathematical logical genius whom Dummett[4] worships, to be
considered for election. He is an unattractive man and there may be reasons
for not electing him, but the objections to him were it seemed to me purely
personal ones. [...] The attack of the massed philistines was disgusting to
behold. I was for the first, and I hope last, time rude to Lord Brand,[5] and
spoke with such violence to John Sparrow that he could hardly believe his

1 Denis Mack Smith (b. 1920), historian of Italy; Fellow of Peterhouse, Cambridge, 1947–62;
  Senior Research Fellow, All Souls, 1962–87.
2 Max Edgar Lucien Mallowan (1904–78), later (1968) Kt, archaeologist; Professor of Western
  Asiatic Archaeology, London, 1947–62; Director, British School of Archaeology in Iraq, 1947–61;
  while in Iraq worked on his monumental *Nimrud and its Remains* (2 vols., London, 1966), which
  he finished when a Fellow at All Souls 1962–76; he married the crime novelist (Dame) Agatha
  Mary Clarissa Christie (1890–1976) in 1930.
3 Georg Kreisel (b. 1923), later (1966) FRS, Austrian-born mathematical logician; sent to England
  before the *Anschluss*, he attended Trinity, Cambridge, and studied under Wittgenstein; Professor
  of Logic and the Foundations of Mathematics, Stanford, 1962–85.
4 Michael Anthony Eardley Dummett (1925–2011), philosopher; expert on Frege, tarot cards and
  electoral reform, campaigner against racism; Fellow of All Souls 1950–79; Wykeham Professor
  of Logic, Oxford, 1979–92.
5 Robert Henry Brand (1878–1963), 1st Baron Brand of Eydon 1946, merchant banker (Lazard) and
  public servant; Fellow of All Souls 1901–32, 1937–63.

ears. The results of the election were clinched by a combination of outside philistines and the inner group of troglodytes who hate all strangers, never invite guests themselves, and loathe those of others, and have generally made All Souls socially repulsive. You can imagine exactly who I mean [...].

The second election was sociology: the Reader. On one side Birnbaum – for whom I have a hankering affection despite all his unfortunate qualities. But he wrote nothing, put into his testimonials the minutest reviews, about which Herbert Hart complained, then Jenifer[1] spread the story that he had done this, was trying to get in on worthless little reviews, then the story was carried to Birnbaum, then he complained that Hart had been indiscreet and disloyal and unacademic, etc. etc. etc. You recognise your old University, I hope? There was also a Pole in, who was intellectually first-rate, but, so we were told, while working with UNESCO in Chile, had denounced his fellow workers as Communist agents and has written letters to the head of every single Latin American Government to say so. This may be exaggerated: at any rate, it produced cold feet even in me. We elected a worthy mediocrity called Wilson from Leeds,[2] and that is that.

The third election was in Jerusalem, where a disgusting paper manufacturer from Mexico in virtue of his wealth tried to make himself President and was kept out after huge loss of blood to make room for dear Elath, not ideal but perfectly worthy and respectable. The chief corpse left in the field was the one worthy candidate, a physicist of worldwide fame called Racah from Florence, a charming Italian of blameless character and excellent intellectual attainments. All this is very embittering – I took a long time to recover from it. I hate being an elector and shall in future decline appointment to these bodies: life is short and I find I take these things too much to heart (I feel I am speaking like Rowse).

The beginning of term was a little better. Our imported Professor Ernst Bloch[3] from Tübingen, who delivered a splendid, fervent, neo-Marxist, revisionist allocution, not at all what is considered philosophy here, rather moving, very confused, splendid in a way, but more like a leading article in *The Times Literary Supplement* than a contribution to knowledge, if you see what I mean. There also arrived a most amusing Russian critic called Chukovsky[4] from

---

1 Jenifer *Hart (1914–2005), historian, wife of H. L. A. Hart, and IB's first lover from 1950.
2 Bryan Ronald Wilson (1926–2004), Reader in Sociology, Oxford, 1962–93; Fellow of All Souls 1963–93.
3 Ernst Bloch (1885–1977), German Marxist philosopher of Jewish descent; returned to GDR from exile in America, 1948, as Professor of Philosophy at Leipzig, but forced into effective retirement after the 1956 Hungarian uprising, which he supported; after construction of Berlin Wall, 1961, remained in West Germany, which he was visiting, and was given honorary chair at Tübingen.
4 Korney Ivanovich Chukovsky (pseudonym of Nikolay Vasil´evich Korneichukov) (1882–1969), author, literary critic, translator, publisher; famous for his children's writing, in prose and verse. He credited Russian children with defying Soviet censorship after children's fantasy was proscribed: 'It was, he believes, the children themselves who won the victory by taking their dolls and nonsense poetry with them into the "illegal underground" ' (*Times*, 21 May 1962, 8e).

Moscow aged 80, to receive an honorary degree, having just got a Lenin prize in the teeth of Communist opposition to him in Russia. Very gay he was. He described Maurice as a man of passionless enthusiasms – saying 'marvellous' about everything without the least spark of feeling or interest. He has been in this country twice before, on the first occasion as a penniless house painter;[1] on the second occasion with Milyukov[2] as part of a Liberal Russian delegation in 1916 to report on the British war effort to Russia, when he stayed with the Duke of Devonshire. A very, very superior man. [...]

We are now expecting Rowland and nobody is panting to come to lunch with him, not even Pears[3] or Stuart or Sparrow. I shall myself not be at all displeased to see him – I like that high continuous sound and view of the world completely different from anyone else's [...]. In fact I find that just as Berenson – if you remember – told us that what he liked best was to see the defeated – a Commander-in-Chief immediately after his defeat, a Prime Minister immediately after his collapse – so I like seeing the last representatives of a culture or a style – Dr Chukovsky, the last representative of the pre-Revolutionary Russian intelligentsia [...] – Nicolas Nabokov who is also the last breath – also Stravinsky in his own way – and various characters in Israel who you can well imagine represent the last of their kind. I went to the Bertrand Russell dinner[4] very much in that spirit.

There are no rows here that I know of. The death of George Paul[5] is an appalling thing, and I still cannot bring myself to write an appropriate note to his widow. [...]

Goodbye for now.

Yours ever,

[Isaiah]

TO MARGARET PAUL[6]

30 May 1962 [*manuscript*]

All Souls

Dear Margaret

When I heard of George's end I could not bear to think of it at all. The news came long after the event: I was abroad & did not hear of it till well

---

1 Chukovsky spent some 2 years in Britain *c.*1903 working as the London correspondent of an Odessa newspaper: it allowed him a valuable immersion in English literary culture.

2 Pavel Nikolaevich Milyukov (1859–1943), Russian liberal politician and historian; a founder of the Constitutional Democratic ('Kadet') party; Foreign Minister in Prince Lvov's 1917 administration; left government May 1917 after the 'Milyukov note', promising the Allies continued Russian support in the war, led to disturbances in Petrograd; received an Hon. LL.D. at Cambridge 1916.

3 David Francis Pears (1921–2009), philosopher; University Lecturer, Oxford, 1950–72, Reader 1972–85; Fellow and Tutor, CCC, 1950–60; Student of Christ Church 1960–88.

4 A dinner to celebrate Russell's 90th birthday (18 May 1962).

5 George Andrew Paul (1912–62), Fellow and Praelector in Philosophy, Univ., 1945–62, Domestic Bursar 1955–62. He died of cold and exposure after capsizing in a dinghy on Coniston Water.

6 Margaret Elizabeth Paul (1917–2002) née Ramsey, then (1952–64) economics tutor, St Hilda's;

into the term from an accidental source. I never knew George well: but I had known him, more or less, since the end of the thirties: I liked & admired him deeply & was frightened of him. Our relations were never wholly easy: in his presence I felt more than usually frivolous, worldly, absurd. I knew that his unsleeping eye detected the tiniest deviations from whatever was genuine and worthy. By nature I like to say too much, to exaggerate, embellish, inflate. This was not possible in his – to me – severe presence. I was convinced at all times that he was right and I wrong: that dry light was best, that his self critical & self punishing style was more than a corrective, that it really did wash away the worthless sand & water from such tiny specks of gold as anyone ever dredged up: except that in his case the nuggets were bigger than most people's – far far bigger than anything I had ever, in my frantic haste, dredged up in any streams I entered. Whenever I saw his figure walk along the High street, I felt great pleasure in the mere fact that so independent a man – so remote from any kind of herd or type – existed at all. I used to be among the chosen few who attended his marvellous lectures on Locke [...]. I shall not forget the first occasion of our meeting: in Cambridge, in the late thirties, when I read a paper on, I think, "Pleasure". I saw on the floor of Braithwaite's[1] room (I believe) the cleverest face I had ever seen. It only spoke a sentence or so & knocked a hideous hole in my edifice. I recognized it for what it was, tore up the paper, & made enquiries about my opponent. The world does not gain by the fact that he is dead & I am alive. I shall not, if you'll forgive me, come to his Memorial Service. Only duty or a relatively remote relationship brings me to such. I am very glad that it is being held. And I beg you not to bother to reply to this in any way.

Yrs ever

Isaiah

TO PETER HALBAN[2]

8 June 1962 [carbon]

[Headington House]

Dear Peter,

Thank you very much indeed for my presents – I love Miss Los Angeles[3] and Fischer-Dieskau.[4] When I see you I shall tell you all about the Lord

---

younger sister of the philosopher Frank Ramsey and the then Archbishop of Canterbury, Michael Ramsey; widow of George Paul (they married 1938 and had four daughters).

1 Richard Bevan Braithwaite (1900–90), Fellow of King's, Cambridge, 1924–90; Sidgwick Lecturer in Moral Science, Cambridge, 1934–53, Knightbridge Professor of Moral Philosophy 1953–67.

2 Peter *Halban (b. 1946), stepson to IB.

3 Victoria de los Ángeles (1923–2005) née Victoria de los Ángeles López García, Barcelona-born Spanish soprano, made her debut at Covent Garden in 1950, at the Metropolitan in 1951, and performed regularly at both houses until 1961.

4 Dietrich Fischer-Dieskau (1925–2012), German baritone, one of the greatest singers of his generation, noted for his rendering of German lieder, particularly Schubert's song cycles; conscripted

Mayor's Banquet: it was splendid beyond our expectations, also we were placed much more highly than we deserve, thus exciting envy and indignation among grander people who sat much lower for no good reason. It does not do to be too favoured.

You are right about Burdon-Muller: he is a queer old gentleman, but very nice as you say. You will remember him with pleasure in fifty years' time; he belongs to a world that is quite dead and gone, and that is always fascinating.

Thank you again,

Yours,

[Isaiah]

TO JOHN SPARROW

Thursday [21 June 1962, *manuscript*]

All Souls

My dear old friend

This mode of address always indicates a crisis: not, I am overjoyed to say, a personal one, only to do with the dear old College: therefore easier to bear. There is, as you might imagine, much feeling about last Saturday's proceedings: among persons one wd not expect to be so affected: the 'neutral' grey middle section: the bold ones, Gibbses,[1] etc. who feel (or say) that the danger of over-stressing the "club" as against the academical aspects of the College is now too great for intellectual decency. The more extreme, young, etc. long to say something violent about that next Saturday, & connect it somehow with the question of "Them" as Bob B[rand] calls them on the ground that the main objection to women is social, & that this type of consideration has not been improperly exaggerated (is this a pleonasm?). I *hate* scenes: they inflict unnecessary wounds: however desirable between old friends they are horrible in public: & I shall do my best to prevent this by persuasion: & try to persuade them to keep the two issues – i.e. academic v. club and women (v. what?) apart: and to think of formulating positive proposals, if they have them, rather than angrily thrash about in the void. Beloff proposed to hold a private meeting of interested Fellows to consider the "situation" – I can honestly tell you that I had *no* idea that anyone besides myself felt it so deeply – but I turn out (to my surprise) to be more of a type & *far* less of

into the German army, he became an American prisoner of war in Italy in 1945; on 30 May 1962 he sang at the premiere of Benjamin Britten's *War Requiem* in the rebuilt Coventry Cathedral, and in 1971 he became the first German musician to perform in the State of Israel.

1 Norman Henry Gibbs (1910–90), Chichele Professor of the History of War and Fellow of All Souls 1953–77. 'Largely to his discreet handling must go the credit for the smooth and successful inauguration in a somewhat conservative college of the radical Visiting Fellowships' programme that All Souls embarked upon in 1966. Gibbs was in charge of the scheme for its first five crucial years. He was no less successful in re-stocking the College cellar after the austerity of the war and early post-war years.' Bryan Wilson, *Independent*, 21 May 1990, 14.

an individual than I had flattered myself that I was. This meeting has now been summoned privately – I found that *my* name was attached to that of the conveners together with Beloff's – I had not authorized this, but did not mind since morally I was wholly committed after those passionate words with which I broke out – again to my own astonishment – to you; as I spoke I listened with a kind of amazement to the sentences I spoke, so uncharacteristic of me, I thought afterwards. I hope at this private assembly to moderate things: to dissuade from silly steps. [...] The passions are running quite high: oddly enough about Kreisel from the Gibbses (literally) et hoc genus omne:[1] I was reproached by Gibbs for not speaking on Kreisel & explaining how superb he was: he (Gibbs) is rather anti-Mack Smith, & very anti-Mallowan. It shocked me too that twelve Fellows did not want Mack Smith *to be considered*: (he only got by with thirty votes in the first vote). Isn't that rather terrible? Beatty got *forty*: the weakest, safest, palest of them all. It does argue a bad state of affairs: I am sure that you agree: if a club, at least a first class club: better a first class research institute than a bad club: but even if you don't think this fair, you'll agree that it is an exaggeration of the truth. This letter calls for no action: & no knowledge: it is what is called "confidential' – I *could* not go to a serious meeting as it were behind your back: some of them may think me your agent or 'stool-pigeon': let them. I wd rather you did not speak of it to anyone: although if faced with having communicated this intelligence to you I shall own to it openly and without embarrassment. I shall take part in no personal conspiracies. Dixi et etc.[2] How are you? wd you like to telephone me? I shall keep nothing from you, if you do, as always.

Yours

With all my love (as we used to say in the thirties – Goronwy's[3] usage I think) and indeed also yours ever

Isaiah   [...]

TO ROBERT CRAFT

25 June 1962

Headington House

Dear Bob,

[...] I think *The Flood*[4] is magnificent and sent you an idiotic account of

---

1 'And all that kind of thing'.

2 'Dixi et salvavi animam meam' ('I have spoken and saved my soul'), the closing words of Karl Marx's *Critique of the Gotha Programme* (1875).

3 (Morgan) Goronwy Rees (1909–79), writer, Principal of University College of Wales, Aberystwyth, 1953–7, forever dogged by his close association with the spy Guy Burgess (after whom he named a dog). It was Rees, a close friend of IB's from undergraduate days, who told IB that he had been elected to All Souls, November 1932 (Rees was a Fellow 1931–46, 1951–4).

4 Craft selected and arranged, from the Book of Genesis, the libretto to Stravinsky's *The Flood*, a 'dance drama' with choreography by George Balanchine, first performed on CBS television in

it from *The Times* which I hope arrived. Here there is much raving about Britten's *Requiem*[1] – critics cannot write because they are too moved to set pen to paper and must allow themselves a week or two to recover from a transforming experience which has determined their entire outlook etc.: I wonder, I wonder. He is a gifted composer no doubt, but there is some-thing wrong in the tone in which these reactions are communicated. Eddy Sackville-West, now Lord Sackville, sat in floods of tears from the beginning to the end; Mr David Drew[2] cannot trust himself to write; the *Times* man thinks that all works should be dated by this central event;[3] will this read as one of the great curiosities of criticism, even less than in a hundred years' time? Your guess is as good as mine, but I have a feeling that we shall guess the same. [...]

Yours,

Isaiah   [...]

TO STEPAN VOLK[4]

9 July [1962; *carbon*]

[Headington House]

Dear Dr Volk,

I am most grateful to you for the three books on Belinsky; one I possess already, but I am sure that one of our libraries will be delighted to have it. I hesitate to burden you with further requests, but if it is not too difficult to get M. Ya. Polyakov, *Vissarion Belinsky: lichnost', idei, epokha,*[5] Moscow, 1960, I should be grateful for it. I am going to Harvard the whole of next term, where the library contains a great deal more material on the Russian nineteenth century than anything to be found in Oxford. However, I shall be engaged on non-Russian topics: a book on critical turning-points in the history of political philosophy and one on some enemies of the Enlightenment with whose views I cannot sympathise but who, like many opponents of what one believes, detect weaknesses in one's own position which it is desirable to note. Hatred lends sharpness to vision as much as love: there is surely a sense in which one can learn more from enemies than from friends. At least, that

America in June 1962; *The Times*'s special correspondent in NY considered it 'disjointed, tiresome and pretentious' (*Times*, 20 June 1962, 15f).

1 Benjamin Britten's *War Requiem*, commissioned to mark the consecration of the new Coventry Cathedral – the original having been destroyed by German bombing in November 1940.

2 David Ernest Drew (b. 1938), ballet dancer; soloist with the Royal Ballet, Covent Garden, 1961; principal 1974.

3 '[T]the work is so superbly proportioned and calculated, so humiliating and disturbing in effect, in fact so tremendous, that every performance it is given ought to be a momentous occasion.' 31 May 1962, 16e.

4 Stepan Stepanovich Volk (1921–93), Soviet historian; member, Leningrad branch, Historical Institute, Soviet Academy of Sciences, 1950–69; foreign correspondent, *Izvestiya*.

5 'His personality, ideas and times'.

is the spirit in which I propose to treat Vico (he was not so much an enemy as a critic of the Enlightenment and said many fantastically original things), Hamann and de Maistre,[1] who really were passionate but gifted irrational-ists.[2] Then, one day, perhaps I shall return to my beloved Belinsky, Herzen etc. A reprint of *Byloe i dumy* in Mrs Garnett's old English translation is to appear here with an Introduction by me as soon as I can complete it. I have not started it yet and it was due two years ago! I must finish my letter, or else this will be delayed further still. Please forgive me.

Yours sincerely,
[Isaiah Berlin]   [...]

TO A. J. AYER
9 July 1962

Headington House

Dear Freddie,

[...] I hear that you were surprised by the attack in *Kommunist*. But this is all a very routine occurrence – I have had more than my share of similar treatment, and it makes no difference to what the next step is, as it depends too little upon one's own opinions and entirely upon changes in the Soviet line. I heard from Frank Roberts,[3] who is just leaving Moscow, that your host Melvil is in a very gloomy state – due, I gather, to having made himself too amiable to you, and not taken into sufficient account that Dee is a journalist. But I am told you have been called by an animal name – say a hyena with a typewriter – past repentance.[4] One brief article on Lenin's *Notebooks on Hegel*, claiming inspiration from them, would restore you to favour instantly, and if you were to say that it was I who opened your eyes to this valuable source of light it would mend my position too. If you don't do this we shall only be called fools for our pains by Sir Charles Snow, and, if you are brave enough to say it, Sir Solly[5] too. Whatever it is that makes such a course

1 Joseph Marie, comte de Maistre (1753–1821), French ultramontane writer who regarded the horrors of the French Revolution as divine judgement on the secularism of the Enlightenment. 'Of all black thinkers he fascinates me most.' IB to George Steiner, 27 December 1966.

2 '[...] all of whom made penetrating criticisms and sometimes outright attacks on the philosophy of the Enlightenment, which, although at times over-violent, contained truths that are perhaps more relevant to our condition today than at the time when these attacks were composed, since the gloomiest prophecies of all three thinkers have been more than adequately verified by the events of the late nineteenth and the twentieth centuries.' IB to Verna Johnson, 30 January 1964.

3 Frank Kenyon Roberts (1907–98), KCMG 1953, diplomat; ambassador to the USSR 1960–2, to the Federal Republic of Germany 1963–8.

4 In August 1948 the Soviet novelist Alexander Fadeev (1901–56), one of the founders of the Union of Soviet Writers, famously censured Western writers: 'If jackals learned to type and hyenas owned a fountain pen, they would probably create the same kind of thing that Henry Miller, Eliot and the other Sartres have written.' *Pravda*, 29 August 1948, 5.

5 Sir Solly Zuckerman (1904–1993), Kt 1956, later (1971) life peer, scientist and public servant; Sands Cox Professor of Anatomy, Birmingham, 1943–68; Professor-at-Large, East Anglia, 1969–74; from

improbable will stand as a wall, believe me, for all future time between you and the Schaffs and Melvils, however moderate, polite, affable etc. etc. etc. Some learnt this early, some late, and some, I suppose, like dear Sebastian Sprott,[1] never learn it at all – strange.

Yours,

Shaya

TO JACK DONALDSON

13 July [1962]

Headington House

Dear Jack,

[…] You may have seen in *The Times* that our worthy musical director announced that Pritchard[2] was to conduct *Moses and Aaron*, and that Brook[3] was to produce.[4] When I saw this I was exceedingly annoyed, for had we not been told that this work would be put in the hands of some person of international reputation? […] And whatever one may think of Pritchard he is not that, yet, nor I think ever will be quite […]. Anyway, I have vented vials of my wrath to poor Garrett, who had already written a very stiff note to Solti, in effect demanding an explanation. A copy of this has reached me, and I then rang up the artful dodger,[5] and he too said, had I been present at the press conference I would have been amazed at what occurred, that he would not occupy my time in giving me full details of that (why not?), but that in fact Pritchard would not be able to do it as his Glyndebourne commitments did not permit that. But that is not the point. I fully see that the Subcommittee must take a back seat, but decencies must be preserved, and anyway this is something to be said to the full board. I see that he [Solti] longed to say something about *Moses and Aaron* to the press conference, but he should have cleared it with somebody, surely? At any rate I do not propose to have a row with him about that and be blamed if he abandons us and goes to Chicago for $50,000 a year. All the same, I am glad that Garrett stuck one of his pins, which your flesh and mine have received so often, into the doubt-

1974 President, British Industrial Biological Research Association; involved in many governmental advisory committees; as trustee of the Wolfson Foundation (1965–87), strongly opposed to IB's application for funding for Wolfson College.

1 Walter John Herbert ('Sebastian') Sprott (1897–1971), sociologist; Professor of Philosophy, Nottingham, 1948–60, of Psychology 1960–4; joined the Bloomsbury set as a friend of Keynes, and was known as 'Sebastian' there and at his alma mater, Cambridge, where 'sprott' became 'a label for fashionable cleverness' (A. H. Halsey, ODNB).

2 John Michael Pritchard (1921–89), later (1983) Kt; conductor, Glyndebourne Festivals, 1952–77; Principal Conductor, Glyndebourne Opera, 1967–77, Musical Director 1969–77; guest conductor, Covent Garden Opera, 1952–77.

3 Peter Stephen Paul Brook (b. 1925), theatre and film director, producer, co-director of the Royal Shakespeare Theatre; Director of Productions, ROH, 1947–50.

4 Georg Solti announced his plans for *Moses and Aaron* at a press conference on Monday 9 July 1962.

5 David Webster (23/1).

less astonished and indignant Solti. Myself, I think that if he cannot conduct it himself we must put it off till the year after. The critics are quite clear (I say this on the basis of conversations with only three of them at the beautiful performance of Berlioz in St Bartholomew the Great) that this is likely to be much the most important work we do in the course of the year, and to entrust it to a routine conductor would not be right. [...]

Yours,

Isaiah

TO CHARLES TAYLOR

14 September 1962 [*carbon*]

[Headington House]

Dear Chuck,

[...] Don't go into Parliament, I say dogmatically, you will be far more effective outside it, surely. You will find yourself with one arm and one leg at least tied to entities marching in directions of which you do not wholly approve, if you do, even if you are a member of the noblest, most radical party, with no prospect of entering any kind of government. There would be no harm if, like John Stuart Mill, you entered Parliament at the height of your powers and influence (which I confidently predict) but not at the beginning. [...]

As for here, you know well that you are leaving your allies in a somewhat de-vitalised state. [...] Perhaps I am being pessimistic, but I think in a sense that what has happened is that ideas have become conventionalised and toothless, and the fighters for them haven't anything to rally round sufficiently. They would be happier if there were a Labour Government in power and they could become a disloyal Fronde inside that: the real issue is genuinely, today, the battle for and against the Common Market. This really has certain epic qualities, inasmuch as it clearly will affect the fate of England in a very decisive manner for a very long time to come. Gaitskell and Macmillan[1] hate each other beyond the call of duty: and Gaitskell is convinced that Macmillan is a mere actor shamming with no sincere conviction behind his theatrical attitudes. This I think is false: he is an actor and no doubt much of what he says is purely 'political', but I think with regard to the Common Market, even if it is purely subjective, he feels the emotions of Peel before the Corn Laws, or Wilson and the League.[2] He knows that he may split the Party and may

---

1 (Maurice) Harold Macmillan (1894–1986), later (1984) 1st Earl of Stockton, publisher and Conservative statesman; Foreign Secretary 1955, Chancellor of the Exchequer 1955–7, Prime Minister 1957–63, Chairman, Macmillan Ltd, 1963–74, President 1974–86; Chancellor, University of Oxford, 1960–86.

2 The decision of Sir Robert Peel (1788–1850), Prime Minister 1834–5, 1841–6, to repeal the Corn Laws protecting British agriculture led to his resignation in 1846, schism in Tory ranks, and a Whig government. The Democrat Woodrow Wilson (1856–1924), 28th President of the

be defeated, and that the whole thing may be reduced to a fearful shambles: but he has a philosophy of history, he is not a shallow empiricist, despite the moustache, the tastes, the Clubs, the slightly false grand manner. I think fundamentally that he is a pessimist and thinks that the barbarians will win in the end. But he thinks that he can build dams against this and hold out for quite a time and the Common Market is one of these. And with luck (and the help of God – in a grim Scotch way he certainly believes: the friendship with Ronnie Knox[1] was not an accident and his present friendlessness if anything adds to his Presbyterianism) a compromise may yet emerge in which not everything that he believes in will go under. This lends a certain dignity to the spectacle, as I think you would also think if you were here. As for socialism in its best forms – a mixture of genuine theoretical conviction and capacity for practical action – it is to be found not in low-tension countries like England and Scandinavia, but in Italy, where the enemy is very fierce and very black […].

As for me, I come to Harvard as Ford Research Professor, with no duties to lecture or to teach – and shall indeed not do these things. Apart from lectures in Yale on 'Three Turning-Points in the History of Political Thought', about which I really must speak to you, and a book to be called *Three Critics of the Enlightenment*, about which I have talked to you too much, I have no immediate tasks in hand – unless there is also the Introduction in which I confute (I hope) all my critics and emerge as a dreary supporter of the *juste milieu*, what can I do if I still believe, unlike you, in the deep truth of that saying of C. I. Lewis that 'the truth when it is discovered will not necessarily prove interesting'?[2]

But do telephone to me at Lowell House, or I shall telephone to you, if you would let me know where, for I long to see you.

Yours ever,

[Isaiah]

US, also suffered political defeat on an issue of principle – American support for a peace settlement in 1918 based on his 'Fourteen Points', including membership of the League of Nations. Campaigning on this platform at the midterm elections in 1918, the Democrats lost control of both houses of Congress.

1 Ronald Arbuthnott Knox (1888–1957), Roman Catholic priest and writer. Ordained as an Anglican priest in 1912, Knox converted to Catholicism in 1917, was ordained in 1919, and was Catholic Chaplain at Oxford 1926–39. He had tutored Macmillan in 1910, an engagement that ended when he refused Mrs Macmillan's request that he avoid religious discussion with her son; they nevertheless became lifelong friends.

2 One of IB's favourite quotations, usually given in (variants of) the form 'There is no a priori reason for thinking that the truth, once discovered, will necessarily prove interesting.' It is a typically Berlinian 'improvement' of this from Lewis's *Mind and the World-Order: Outline of a Theory of Knowledge* (NY, 1929), 339: 'If the truth should be complex and somewhat disillusioning, it would still not be a merit to substitute for it some more dramatic and comforting simplicity.' Clarence Irving Lewis (1883–1964) taught at Harvard 1920–53; Edgar Pierce Professor of Philosophy 1948; a leading figure in the development of analytic philosophy in the US.

TO DAVID WEBSTER

17 September [1962]

Headington House

My dear David,

I am off today to the United States for four months, to Harvard – Boston has no opera worth speaking of, and even the inferior (compared to Covent Garden) delights of the Metropolitan are far away. So I shall have to go through a period of musical austerity, lightened only by the worthy Leinsdorf. But I shall look forward to receiving minutes of the board's and Subcommittee's meetings, which will surely tell me more than those horrible critics. They really do seem to me to be nastier in London than anywhere else [...] – sometimes one sighs for the easier professional morals of the critics of Paris, who seldom stray from the line laid out before them by the authorities they know they have to keep in with: it would be nice to have at least one or two critics like that: but then Anglo-Saxon standards of good and evil prevail and I sternly drive away the thought of all that corruption and log-rolling.

Let me begin this part of my valedictory blessing by saying that I honestly think that we have never – or rather the public has never – had it so good. It seems to me that the partnership between Solti and yourself has worked out marvellously well and has produced noble and memorable results, and that anyone who does not acknowledge that is either deaf or moved by unworthy motives. [...] I know that you must think (I gather that from Tooley's[1] harsh letter to me) that I have over-praised Solti in the draft of the Opera Section's report; it represents my genuine views; it may not be the whole truth about him, but it is certainly nothing but the truth – and it certainly does not say more than the general critical consensus. [...] The greatest glories come to opera houses through a continued partnership of two highly gifted personalities who understand each other: like Toscanini and Gatti-Casazza[2] at the Metropolitan, and indeed before that at the Scala, & Reinhardt–Walter[3] in pre-war Salzburg. Do let us build towards this! By conscious effort – as if it seems to require a modicum – even a lordly dish – of butter on you know who's plate, why not? These are only tentative remarks intended to stimulate

---

1 John Tooley (b. 1924), Kt 1979, Assistant General Administrator, ROH, 1960–70; General Administrator 1970–80.

2 Giulio Gatti-Casazza (1868–1940), Italian impresario; director of La Scala 1898–1908; worked closely with Toscanini, who moved with him to NY when he became director of the Met 1908–35.

3 Max Reinhardt (1873–1943) né Max Goldmann, Austrian actor, theatre director, and impresario; one of the founders of the Salzburg Festival 1920. Declining Goebbels's offer of the status of 'honorary Aryan', he emigrated permanently to the US 1937. Bruno Walter (1876–1962) né Bruno Walter Schlesinger, German-born pianist and conductor, began his long association with the Salzburg Festival in 1925 while Musical Director of the Berlin State Opera; forced to leave Germany for Austria 1933, and Austria for France 1938, he settled in the US 1939, and later conducted at the Met and the NY Philharmonic.

reflection; as I shall not be there to pester and plague you for at least four months, I do not feel too contrite about placing this on your plate. [...]

Yours ever,
    Isaiah

In autumn 1962 IB spent a sabbatical term at Harvard as the Ford Visiting Research Professor, working on the text of what eventually became Three Critics of the Enlightenment: Vico, Hamann, Herder. *He also wrote 'Three Turning-Points in Political Thought', the three Storrs Lectures that he delivered at Yale under the auspices of the Law School: 'these were attended far beyond my expectations and perhaps beyond the merits of the lectures themselves'.*[1] *Although he had no special obligations at Harvard he gave a seminar at the Russian Research Centre, a public lecture under the auspices of the Government Department, and addressed a number of student societies. He also visited (in addition to Yale) Princeton, Columbia, Cornell, Indiana, Illinois and Brown, 'largely for the purpose of meeting scholars in my own field – on all these occasions I cannot deny that I delivered public lectures also, for it seemed indecent to refuse to do so in view of the extreme scarcity of lecturers in the field of the history of ideas'. While at Harvard IB stayed in the familiar surroundings of Lowell House, a homely undergraduate residence that he had originally visited in January 1949. This was his first prolonged absence from Aline since their marriage, and it proved an unwelcome reminder of bachelor days. Although he spent productive hours in Harvard's 'magnificent' Widener Library, and attended glittering society gatherings in Washington and New York, he missed Aline terribly. She joined him in America in the first week of November, and they returned to England together in late January 1963.*

TO ALINE BERLIN

Thursday 20 September 1962 [*manuscript*]

Lowell House G24, Harvard

Darling Aline, dearest Aline,

I am not as miserable as I was, but not tremendously happy either. Best begin chronologically. The flight was perfect. The object trembled a little here & there, as soon as the faintest tremors began, one was told to fasten seat belt. It used to pass after 30–40 seconds. Even I could not mind it. We arrived punctually [...]. I went immediately to the Coop:[2] ordered goods: came back to my room: horror. Small, + regulation Oxford undergraduate bedroom & a shower. No bathroom: shower, w.c., washbasin. I *know* they

---

1 All quotations in this paragraph are from IB to Verna Johnson, 30 January 1964. The lectures were on the Greeks (published as 'The Birth of Greek Individualism' in L), Machiavelli and romanticism. .

2 The Harvard Cooperative Society, a university shop opened by students in 1882; its retail services were later extended to MIT.

cannot afford to give me much for 350 dollars for 4 months. But I suddenly felt terribly depressed. It was worse than 1951 & 1953, & like 1949. Still I am determined to *work*. [...] I have *never* in my life before had such acute & violent longing to be with anyone as I have now with you. It is not just the old "images" though there are plenty of them too haunting me whenever I sit alone in my nice hard wooden chair, good for one's back. I love you to a degree that it is *absurd* to suggest can be discovered in literature, however marvellous, or through the words of others. So late in life! So physical & moral & total in one: it is *grotesque*, with so little time really, to separate even if there [? are?] work & children & this & that: I'll stick this though just to show – god knows whom or why – that I *can* work [...]. Your telegram just arrived. Yes yes I *should* go home: it is *not* an unreasonable suggestion, but I won't. I shd be too ashamed. My room looks nicer: I have bought a kettle, flat stove, 3 tumblers, 3 cups, 3 spoons, scales, a shaver, & an electric shoe-shine box. A pewter water jug I rejected in the end: but I have television, radio, Dictaphone, ½ a secretary (next week). No visitors! I sit, cough (I have 99·2: & shall soon have flu: don't mind: the only problem is how to get *fed*: I think it is soluble) I must stop now: for a moment: the man at the door has asked me to go to a Tutors' meeting. I know none, & shall behave like an elderly Humbert H[umbert][1] – European Prof. much too remote – save for charming smiles – to be easily asked to Thanksgiving. *Nobody* will ask me to that, I swear to you, this year, unless you are here, I shall go on in a moment. I am at the post office. I have the letter cards. I feel they are a kind of con-necting cord. Really too strange! I have constantly lived here: yet this time I feel alone, bereft, cut off, widowed, too awful: I think about nothing except you, the *children,* H. Hart, my mother not at all: *she* is part of the old depar-tures. Of course Nabokov telephoned: then Stern: Stern *furious* because N. had arranged for him & me to dine with Marietta[2] instead of him "who is this lady? *great* friend of yours?" etc. Now Marietta has invited the Sterns[3] too. They accepted eagerly. [...] I really will, I will I will sit here & work & economise on human contacts. If I am gloomy (I suppose I should not mind absence of bath: I do) I shall break myself like a widower or man whose relatives have all perished in an earthquake & who hopes to meet his beloved soon (in Nov.) in heaven. Gombrich[4] & Gilbert[5] called last night. I discour-

---

1 A European who moves to New England to write – after Humbert Humbert, the 37-year-old anti-hero of Vladimir Nabokov's *Lolita* (Paris, 1955).

2 Mary Endicott ('Marietta') Tree (1917–91) née Peabody, US socialite and Democrat political activist; married Desmond FitzGerald 1939; they divorced 1947, whereupon she married, as his second wife, (Arthur) Ronald Lambert Field ('Ronnie') Tree (1897–1976), English gentleman of American descent and independent means, Conservative MP for Harborough 1933–45, PPS to three successive Ministers of Information 1940–3.

3 Isaac Stern had married his second wife, Vera Lindenblit (b. 1927), in 1951 (divorced 1994).

4 Richard Francis Gombrich (b. 1937), Lecturer in Sanskrit and Pali, Oxford, 1965–76; Fellow of Wolfson, 1966–76; son of the art historian Ernst Gombrich (213/3).

5 Felix Gilbert (1905–91), German-born historian; emigrated to US in 1936; taught at Bryn Mawr

aged them. This is like some ghastly Magic Flute test.[1] I shall write again on Friday, tomorrow. When you come I think we boldly stay in the Ritz, & to hell with the Colleges. Are there kitchenettes in the R?

    love
        Isaiah

TO ALINE BERLIN

    1 a.m. [25 September 1962; *manuscript*]

                                                        Lowell House, Harvard

Darling Aline – darling, darling –

I've 'done' New York. [...] Lunch with Sterns & Nicholas, who is much older, feebler, weaker, if he goes on like this he will soon die: I tried to persuade him to "let up". [...] dinner with Marietta, dressed v. voluptuously: there – Adlai Stevenson (frightfully affable to me)[2] Nicholas, his son + wife[3] (very warm enquiries about you) Leonard Bernstein[4] after the tremendous opening of the new Lincoln Center – a long Kennedy talk – A. Schles[inger], late & drunk & obviously miserable & concerned, the Backers[5] (left before dinner – enquired after you) Behrman[6] *not* there (ill) – in spite of terrible fuss – offer of 4 bedrooms, I insisted on returning by jet to Boston to-night – discipline – my purpose in being here etc. unintelligible to them all. There is a crisis about Israel & the new Arab refugee plan at U.N: Mrs Stern anxious to "influence" Stevenson & Schlesinger (who is somehow dealing with it too) at the party: I was dragged into a corner & told it was my "duty" to stay & intrigue. This was not possible anyway & rather squalid somehow. I left obstinately, driven to Idlewild by Stern. Stern *very* kind to me. [...] I have a horror of N.Y. parties: all terribly false, gloomy, pseudo-gay. Too many lions at Marietta's party anyhow, all thinking the other lions bores: Bernstein

---

1946–62; Fellow of the Institute for Advanced Study, Princeton, 1962–75; wrote, inter alia, on the Italian Renaissance.

1 In Mozart's *Die Zauberflöte* Pamina and Tamino must endure magical ordeals to prove their love.

2 Adlai Ewing Stevenson (1900–65), Democratic politician, Governor of Illinois 1949–53, and presidential candidate 1952, 1956; beaten by John F. Kennedy in the race for the Democratic nomination in 1960; the new president appointed him US ambassador to the UN 1961–5; he and Marietta Tree had a long affair.

3 If Nicholas is Nicolas Nabokov, and if this is his wife rather than his daughter-in-law, it is his fourth, Marie-Claire Paulette Joséphine Brot (b. 1921), whom he married in 1953 (divorced 1970). The son would then presumably be theirs, Alexander Nikolaevich Nabokov (b. 1954). But if the wife is his son's, the son is Ivan Nikolaevich Nabokov (b. 1932) and the wife Claude Thérèse née Joxe (b. 1929).

4 Leonard Bernstein (1918–90), American composer, conductor and pianist; Musical Director, NY Philharmonic, 1958–69; composer of the musical *West Side Story* (1957).

5 George Backer (1903–74) and his second wife Evelyn Straus ('Evie') (1905–71) née Weil; a Jewish Democratic politician, a Zionist, and publisher and editor of the *New York Post* 1939–42.

6 Sam(uel) Nathan Behrman (1893–1973), Harvard-educated playwright, screenwriter and author, noted for his Broadway comedies, e.g. *No Time for Comedy* (1940), made into a film starring James Stewart.

v. affable: we all agreed we must meet as often as possible: I have no such intention: I don't think they have either. The general line is that *whoever* is being spoken of – Stephen Spender, Chip, Grahams,[1] etc. are much older & sadder than when last seen. Arthur is *rolling* downhill: I like him very much: with me he is better: I get him on to intellectual topics which he is quite good on, & it is a relief to him, & he feels happier & more dignified in speaking of them. You may be right: perhaps I shd not have left. But now that I am here, I shd grimly go on. I have no luck with secretaries – I frighten them at first interview I think. The one hired for me here, after ordering with me the now useless & costly dictaphones, ran out. God knows what I shall do. I do depend on this so much. I feel tired but peaceful. To-morrow I shall sit in the library & slog away. I love you too much really; all paths wind back to you: the duller the social life – Nin's jour fixe atmosphere was too comically con-ventional – & Marietta's evening was as always flat & exhausted – the more intensely I think about my good fortune in the perfectly real life we lead. None of these people seem to possess real relations with anybody. Their marriages are hollow [...] and one is not conscious of talking to fully func-tioning human beings – everybody is being desperately amusing all the time – like Mr Kurnitz[2] – everything is miserable & in pieces – they are all psycho-analytic gibier.[3] Stuart escaped it by plunging into his nightmare-fantasy *completely* & *never* facing reality at all. It seems so smug & boastful, but I truly believe that we live as they do not – they are, of course, exceptionally rotted out by society, I suppose. When I sat in the jet reading some not v. good but still serious book on literature, I felt so much happier, more interested, than on those sofas with the Arthurs, Mariettas, Stevensons, Bernsteins – those famous important &, I suppose, gifted, interesting, even quite responsible, benevolent "good" people – & the spectacle of poor ravaged Nicholas & his depressed son – honestly Burdon Muller is better! [...] I love you totally, & if I didn't wd have no cause for living. I called my poor mama (from Boston).

 love,
  Isaiah

I cannot go to bed without writing you. But if it is tired, I am sorry. I am morally O.K.

1 Katharine ('Kay') *Graham (1917–2001), newspaper publisher, and her husband Philip Leslie ('Phil') Graham (1915–63), lawyer (former pupil of Felix Frankfurter), journalist, and publisher from 1946 of the *Washington Post*. The manic-depressive drinker Phil Graham took his own life in 1963, and was succeeded at the *Washington Post* by his widow.
2 Harry Kurnitz (1908–68), prolific American screenwriter who wrote (inter alia) comedies for Danny Kaye and mystery stories as 'Marco Page'.
3 'Game birds'.

TO ALINE BERLIN

26 September [1962; *manuscript*]

Lowell House, Harvard

Darling Aline,

I sit surrounded by my electric gadgets: radio, telly, shoe-shiner, teapot, coffee pot, immersion plugs etc. & am subject to homesickness. Last night with Hammonds:[1] a lot of enthusiasm about you: he is *very* shocked at Ch. Chaplin's degree: I disloyally explained how it was all Maurice's doing, but said I favoured it, & we had a peaceful argument. Mrs H[ammond] really hates New England & solid reliability & longs for life & adventure. Mason limps & is very nice. A dull but morally satisfactory evening. [...]

Nobody is interested in me this time. It is rather delicious not [to] be lionized, believe me. But my telephone does not ring, & it is I who have to reflect: shall I see Yakobson,[2] Mrs Pickman,[3] etc. or not? The answer is, not. I feel not at all happy of course on this desert island [...] but neither am [I] acutely miserable. I force myself to work which of course I dislike & between think of nothing but you: before marriage, even in 1955 perhaps, I owned myself much more, wanted to & could give myself to others – now this is totally different, I am on leave, all I have & am is elsewhere, & I perform mechanically here: I don't mind if I am happy or miserable, please or offend, do well or not: it is like a kind of conscription: it has to be done, but there is *no* question of its being one's own activity: it is compulsory & routine & real life is elsewhere. Funny. I used to be where my body was geographically. This division of body & feeling, physical process & real personality is queer. How much more can one love?

Isaiah   [...]

TO ALINE BERLIN

Friday [28 September 1962; *manuscript*]

Lowell House, Harvard

My Darling Aline

Your second letter just received. It is 8.30 a.m. [...] I am listening to WHXR (local equivalent! class. mus. all day). It has been raining + S.W.

1 Mason Hammond (1903–2002), Pope Professor of the Latin Language and Literature, Harvard, 1950–73; he married, 1935, Florence Hobson (1909–99) née Pierson.

2 Roman Osipovich Jakobson (1896–1982), eminent Russian-born philologist and linguist, an original member of the post-revolutionary formalist group of Russian critics and literary historians; settled in US 1941; Professor of Slavic Languages and Literatures, Harvard, 1949–65, and Visiting Institute Professor at MIT 1957–70; IB met, and came to admire, him while in Washington in 1945; awarded an Hon. D.Litt. at Oxford 1981.

3 Hester Marion Pickman (1893–1990) née Chanler, whom IB met at Harvard in 1949: 'very Catholic, very gay, very cultivated, very original – indeed in the county round about there lurk ancient untouched Edwardian originals of great splendour of personality' (L2 95).

winds (everyone here calls it the "old Sou'wester". I suppose Stuart will find that entertaining) for 72 hours solidly. [...] I am intoxicated by the books in the Library. There I sit all day & work: for all I know my telephone may be ringing in L. House, but it is really for the sake of those wonderful rooms in the Widener, *all* books, & materials at one's disposal, that I came. I propose to telephone *this Saturday* only because 6 days without people (in effect: how much do Constables[1] & Hammonds count?) is stoical enough: so when Nin offers Atlantida in N.Y, I don't feel morally obliged to refuse. I prefer her absurd *salon* to Marietta's gloomy chilliness – where the guests are left to fend for themselves & fall into deeper & deeper boredom [...]. Oddly enough, I, who used to *scream* if I had to live one day alone, am inured: Spartan simplicity & solitude are not unbearable. Only your absence. My thoughts are literally filled with you at all non-professional moments, whenever, that is, I am not actually reading or writing. Goodness! to be *so* love-subjugated! [...] Now I must, I suppose, go & buy some galoshes. Oh dear! perhaps it *was* wrong to go. But I cannot think about this now. To work! the driving rain & wind, the lack of interest of everybody else, my avoidance of almost everybody (&, it seems to me, their avoidance of me: wounding to amour propre, but I think I am at once too familiar & too remote – 9 years a long time – perhaps there are other lions): James [Joll]? will he come here? I daresay he may be right. I see all those unmemorable articles on the front page of the Sunday N. Y. Times etc.: & all that music: the Berlins:[2] the New York apartment: Sam Barber[3] & the quiet weeks in the homintern[4] villages just outside N.Y. – To work!

love

Isaiah

I am v. grateful to Peter for his very sympathetic little letter: to which I shall reply v. soon. I love you very very much. And miss you disastrously. Still these things are sent to test us: in what? stupidity?

---

1 William George ('W. G.') Constable (1887–1976), art historian and gallery director; Slade Professor of Fine Art, Cambridge, 1935–37; Curator of Paintings, Boston Museum of Fine Arts, 1938–57; married 1926 Olivia née Roberts (1901–87).

2 Gerald Asher ('Gerry') Berlin (1919–2012), lawyer, musician and music critic, chairman of the board of the Massachusetts Civil Liberties Union 1961–70; married to Miriam ('Mimi') H. Berlin (b. 1926) née Haskell, assistant professor, Russian, European and Middle Eastern History, Wellesley College, 1958–75; not related to IB.

3 Presumably Samuel Barber (1910–81), American composer. His widely recognised *Adagio for Strings*, based on the second movement of his string quartet, op. 11 (1936), was aired by the media at the time of Kennedy's death, but not (as is often stated) played at his funeral.

4 Coined from 'Comintern' by Maurice Bowra to describe a freemasonry of homosexuals, this term has since gained wider currency.

TO ALINE BERLIN

Tuesday [2 October 1962; *manuscript*]

Lowell House, Harvard

Darling Aline,

I was *delighted* to talk to you on Saturday *and* on Monday: in spite of the news about Philippe.[1] By the time you get this, I shall have had a telegram from you. Nothing to worry about, surely? I am in favour of an operation: sooner or later it will have to be done: it is surely the reason for P.'s sudden pains which came on & off: & if he has had his operation, & recovered normally, which is certain, you cd come here with a light heart. I am being very 'sensible' about all this surely? Don't be too anxious: it is nothing to terrify one. I am being reasonable about my life too: I see a minimum of people: I have just refused an invitation from 'Anne' (Leinsdorf)[2] to dine on the eve of Kippur. But I have not given the true reason: it wd embarrass them too much, & represent me as a kind of religious zealot which you surely do not wish me to seem even to them. I am in a state of impassivity: at peace: arrested: in a vacuum, in a thermos. Hence all my thoughts are automatically turned to the real life: how *can* Stuart live here? It is a most unreal life for Europeans! Everyone *here* knows he has accepted Princeton: how he will pine! But he will never admit it. A mistake involving Renée is not officially admissible, like saying that God uttered inaccuracies in the Bible: so he will die, as he has lived, in a dream, in a state of dependence, this most rational, science worshipping, self critical, open eyed man! In a ¼ hour I have to go to meet Willi Brandt of Berlin:[3] for ¾ hour: then back to the Library where I shall read till 10 p.m. – then home & the refrigerator, coffee + Jewish salami & some apples. I am *not* a contented bachelor: no no! I love you passionately & exclusively & think of nobody else. If I can keep at it & work, it will have been worth while. But you will be very bored, I fear! Very. Cambridge is really rather hell: worse than Cambridge, England. Still it fills me with perverse pride that I *can* go on like this. […] I love love love you. No more to say. Next Sunday *I* telephone you, I think, no? good-bye – I long to go home really.

Isaiah

---

1 He needed an operation for appendicitis.
2 Anne Leinsdorf (1917–2012) née Frohnknecht, wife (1939–68) of Erich Leinsdorf.
3 Willy Brandt (1913–92) né Herbert Ernst Kahl Frahm, German statesman; socialist anti-Nazi activist (fled to Norway and assumed name Brandt to avoid capture); Mayor of West Berlin 1957–66; leader of Social Democratic Party of Germany 1964–87; Deputy Chancellor of Federal Republic of Germany 1966–9, Chancellor 1969–74.

TO SUSAN MARY ALSOP[1]

5 October 1962 [*carbon*]

[Lowell House, Harvard]

Dearest Susan Mary,

I shall certainly arrive on Monday the 15th, though by what means Heaven only knows, for I have solemnly promised to spend the weekend in North Haven, Maine, of all places, with my old, old friends, the Aubrey Morgans.[2] And this I must certainly do. I shall then have to travel from Rockland, Maine somehow – at any rate, I propose to arrive sometime in the middle of the afternoon on the 15th, and leave you on the 16th, in my mad, pleasure-seeking life, in order to attend a concert of the Leningrad Philharmonic here in Boston.

[…] Have you ever seen *Le Misanthrope*?[3] It was performed here in excellent translation by Richard Wilbur,[4] and although badly acted, made an indelible impression on me. The hero, who is obviously regarded as absurd by Molière, becomes a romantic hero of the end of the century. At any rate, whenever I see a classical play by some splendid writer – Ibsen or Racine, or the like – it has an effect on me like a glass of wine on someone who has never drunk any alcohol before – I feel: Why is more fuss not made about this? Why are people not speaking about it all the time? Why cannot there be a theatre in which nothing but the three or four hundred great masterpieces – there must be at least that number – are done constantly – (rather like the flood of the p aperbacks of classics which I feel are doing nothing but good) – instead of the dreary stuff that goes on. Allow me to stop these dreary reflections and say that I am sorry that I cannot come for the weekend and that I shall descend upon you with ice from the cold waters that wash the Maine coast clinging to me. And beg for receipt au bout de table nowhere near important persons. Dim, cosy, undemanding, anonymous persons is what I should like for company! I am terrified of the others more now than ten years ago or than when Joe originally asked me to dinner and I remained silent and inhibited throughout and he did not give me up. For that I shall be eternally grateful to him. I remember one story which the horrible C. P.

---

1 Susan Mary Alsop (1918–2004), wife of Joe Alsop. See 631.
2 Aubrey Niel Morgan (1904–85), Welsh-born Deputy Director-General of British Information Services 1942–5, Personal Assistant to UK ambassador in Washington (Sir Oliver Franks) 1948–52; and his wife Constance Cutter Morgan (1913–95), daughter of Dwight Morrow, former US ambassador to Moscow; both wartime colleagues and friends of IB's. Franks recalled of Aubrey Morgan that he 'went out to meet life, believed in causes and fought for them' (*Times*, 25 September 1985, 14).
3 Five-act comedy of manners by Molière – pseudoymn of Jean Baptiste Poquelin (1622–73) – first performed in 1666, and generally regarded as his masterpiece.
4 Richard Purdy Wilbur (b. 1921), Pulitzer Prize winning American poet and literary translator; Professor of English, Wesleyan, 1957–77; noted for his translations of Molière and Racine.

Snow,[1] whom I met only once, told in my presence. 'H. G. Wells[2] and I were after the same woman. A most extraordinary thing, she went off with some totally unknown person!' That is the kind of person I should like to sit next to, but I daresay the mood will pass before I come to your grand, delightful, fascinating dinner, and the dear Bohlens[3] and all.

Yours ever,

[Isaiah]

PS Am I being too tiresome? I rather think so.

TO PETER HALBAN (stepson)

5 October 1962 [carbon]

Lowell House, Harvard

Dear Peter,

Thank you very much indeed for your letter.

Indeed I was most melancholy when I arrived – the room looked so bare and ill-furnished, small and dark; there was no bathroom; I think I had forgotten how sordidly I lived before marriage – I have indeed been spoiled by Headington House during all these years.

The first thing I did was to go to the Harvard Cooperative store where I bought an ingenious electric immersion instrument – the kind of thing that you plug into a hole at one end, and where you put the metal end into a cup at the other end and it heats itself and boils coffee or tea or water inside a glass. As you know I am fascinated by gadgets and I acquired this one as soon as I could. I did everything the instructions told me to do, at which moment the telephone bell rang in my outer room and I ran to answer it. Presently I began to smell a curious smell, to which I paid no attention because I think that my nose is not very sensitive and I never trust it. However, when black clouds began to invade the room I realised that something was up, stopped my telephone conversation, went into the bedroom and discovered my bed a flaming mass with newspapers and books burning merrily, and the blanket, the mattress and the sheets as well, as a result of some accident – the thing inside the cup of water must have dropped out of it and set fire to everything. All I had was a small cup, which I kept pouring on the bed. In the end

1 This may be a slip for C. P. Scott: Snow was 39 years younger than Wells, still alive, and IB had many opportunities to meet him, whereas he seems to have met Scott only once, at his interview for the *Manchester Guardian* in 1932.

2 Herbert George Wells (1866–1946), novelist and social commentator; Wells believed in free love, and dubbed himself a 'Don Juan among the intelligentsia': H. G. Wells, *Experiment in Autobiography: Discoveries and Conclusions of a Very Ordinary Brain (since 1866)* (London, 1934), ii 465.

3 Charles ('Chip') *Bohlen (1904–74), US diplomat and Soviet specialist, and his wife Avis (1912–81) née Thayer.

I extinguished the flames, but the smoke of burned woollen blankets and mattress stuffing is something which I am sure you have no idea of. Black clouds enveloped me, and although I opened the window the smoke refused to go out except very slowly. Into this walked the Master of the House – I was very pleased to see him, but my complaints about the room were no longer very real: I was in a morally somewhat weak position to make them. However, he procured me a new mattress, blanket and everything and I was all right.

I am very glad that you are in the upper school, and am sorry you should have the bother of doing those three things over again, but it is nice to do European history. I am sorry for the jazz; I live opposite neighbours who play nothing but music between 1680 and 1740 – Bach, Vivaldi, etc. – all day; so I am luckier than you. I am glad you loved Portofino, so did I very much indeed this time. Please go on writing.

Yours sincerely,

[Isaiah]

TO ALINE BERLIN

Friday 5 October [1962; *manuscript*]

Lowell House, Harvard

Darling Aline,

Whenever you feel depressed, sit down and write to me *at once*. It will be very good for us both. I am grimly resolved not to go under. [...] I am glad Philippe is to be operated on to-morrow: a relief & nothing really serious. This (next) Sunday we shall speak – these are the happiest moments of my present life. The rest of the "civilized" life here – lunch with mathematicians or philosophers or Russian experts – concerts with Master [Richard] Gombrich singing in Stravinsky's Symphonie de psaumes under Leinsdorf – etc – [...] is not for me (or you). I shall never come to Cambridge Mass again. New York possibly, or Washington but not a cultural centre. This is your influence on me: & very glad of it I am. [...] It is the low tension, the muted quality of life that does not suit me somehow: in Oxford I do not mind it: here it is too conscious, goody-goody-Zurich like. Like Haifa. I think that to keep going I may have to telephone you twice a week: or at least 3 times a fortnight. I feel better (like you) already as a result of having written this. We must not again separate – that is clear. [...] Ask Donaldson please what was the result of my deliberately pro-Solti appeal to the Board. I'd love to know. Bing[1] has asked me to his box *any* night: and lunch also. I shall be

---

1 Rudolf Franz Joseph Bing (1902–97), later (1971) KBE, Austrian-born, naturalised British opera manager; helped found the Edinburgh Festival 1947; General Manager of the Met 1950–72.

appreciative, but careful. These intrigues bore me generally. Behrens is neurotic about his health or really ill: I have not seen him yet. I love you!

    Isaiah

TO ARTHUR SCHLESINGER

    8 October 1962 [*carbon*]

[Lowell House, Harvard]

Dear Arthur,

    […] Thank you for mentioning me to your exalted friend – I do not mean this ironically – I am coming to Washington on the 15th to dine with Joe and Susan Mary – a farewell party for Chip and Avis – at which it is alleged certain uniquely important persons will be present.[1] The idea terrifies me; under Joe's imperious auspices no human contact was ever achieved, but I cannot refuse. I shall spend a peaceful weekend before that somewhere in northern Maine with Aubrey Morgan and his wife and will come as to a slaughter. These things, in the end, do not matter and I do not know why I should feel so nervous, but I always do and [the absence of] this social slavery – this lack of independence – is what I prize so much in Joe or even in Dean Acheson, or Rowland – they may leave havoc behind them but at least they are not perpetually searching for cosiness and sympathetic company and security and dependability […]. And you? I don't believe you suffer from this at all. I believe you belong, despite everything, to the independent and free. Hence, I envy you and Chip and the President. Gaitskell adored him – said he was wonderfully rational and looked forward – perhaps a bit too optimistically – to collaboration. You must not think of leaving Washington. If you really want to know why I believe this strongly, you must have a talk with me.

    Yours,

    Isaiah   […]

TO ALINE BERLIN

    11 October 1962

Lowell House, Harvard

⟨Darling Aline,⟩

    Please supply solutions for the following puzzle: *A* observes *B* in the grip of a terrible bore at a party given at the British Embassy in Washington. He turns to *C* who says to *A*, "Do do something to rescue *B*, otherwise he will want to go home." *A* says, "Oh – we must find a pretty girl. What about

1 The Alsops had invited IB and J. F. Kennedy, among others, to a dinner on 16 October for the Bohlens, who were bound for the Paris Embassy. This would be IB's first meeting with JFK.

D?" To which *C* says, "No, don't do that. *D* is a bloody bore, as *E* has so very rightly said." Who are *A*, *B*, *C*, *D* and *E*? ⟨They are: A = Schlesinger, B = the President, C = Mrs K[ennedy] D = Evangeline B[ruce] E = Isaiah Berlin. Too awful! Untrue & v. nasty & bound to spread.⟩

[...] I dined with the old Schlesingers[1] tonight where Arthur was. He was also very sweet. He reports that Adlai freezes only to two persons in the world – the President of the United States and myself. How strange. I am really very fond of Arthur. He is in a very difficult position, sniped at from all sides and without dignity. His father, who is an exceedingly nice old man, and his mother, who is very sweet, both suffer deeply as a result. His children were there and were perfectly nice. His wife remained in Washington.

You must be reconciled to being called Mrs here, they all say it and say it with the best possible intentions. I really must do something about Master [Richard] Gombrich, who was very kind to me when I first arrived, and I have not seen him yet at all. The real advantage of this life is the Widener Library, which is absolute heaven. Once I am there I no longer feel lonely or unhappy among all those books; there is no library comparable to it in Europe and I think I shall have to come back here and work in it some day without any attachment to Harvard or Lowell House or anything. Everyone asks when you are coming, how they are to meet you, etc. Fortunately my room is not big enough to enable me to give a party, but no doubt Olivia [Constable] would oblige (Heaven forefend).

⟨I *must* go to bed! Tomorrow to the North with the Morgans. To-night with nice kind boring Bostonian *gentry* at the Massachusetts Historical Society. Very U.[2] Perkins is trying to get me made (I think) a guest of the Somerset Club[3] (very restricted, I expect) in which you & I shd *stay*. But we need not. I'm not stopping him. It would be funny to invite Weisgal to dine there. Edm. Wilson[4] is at last *not* on speaking terms with Levin[5] who is *most* affable to me. Wilson is in very "poor shape". But enough! I love you more and more desperately, as if we shall never meet. This will reach you *after* telephone on Sunday. I shd

1 Arthur Meier Schlesinger, Sr (1888–1965), American historian, and his wife, Elizabeth Harriet née Bancroft (1886–1977), parents of IB's friend Arthur Schlesinger, Jr.

2 Upper-class (as opposed to non-U), a distinction introduced by Nancy Mitford in *Noblesse Oblige: An Enquiry into the Identifiable Characteristics of the English Aristocracy* (London/NY, 1956).

3 Elliott Perkins (1901–85) taught history at Harvard 1937–69; Master of Lowell House 1940–63. The Somerset was a choosy old-fashioned Boston social club, founded 1852.

4 Edmund Wilson (1895–1972), New-York born, Princeton-educated literary critic, writer and social commentator; Associate Editor of the *New Republic* 1926–31, and a regular book reviewer for the *New Yorker*; despite a highly unsuccessful visit to Oxford in 1954, during which Wilson disliked almost everything he was shown and everyone he met, IB had deep reverence for him as 'a great critic, and a noble and moving human being' (PI2 181).

5 Harry Tuchman Levin (1912–94), literary critic and author; Irving Babbitt Professor of Comparative Literature, Harvard, 1960–83; cordially disliked by IB. 'My *great* friend Harry Levin met me among the books in the Library. Butter wd not melt in his mouth: they *must* see me etc. [...] I ignored this. Lofty politeness is my note: yes, sometime, not now, we are busy scholars etc.' IB to Aline Berlin, 5 October 1962.

never have been a don. Something gayer wd have suited us both better: or not?
I *long* for –
    Isaiah⟩

*American involvement in the abortive Bay of Pigs invasion in April 1961
confirmed Fidel Castro's suspicions of American intentions, and led to a closer
relationship between Cuba and the USSR. In February 1962 the US announced
an economic embargo of the island. It was against this background that the
Soviet leader Nikita Khrushchev decided in May 1962 to place nuclear missiles in
Cuba, ostensibly to deter any further American-sponsored assault on the island.
Tensions between the superpowers were already high after the construction in
the Soviet zone of Berlin of the Berlin Wall, work on which began in August
1961. At the end of May 1962 Castro agreed to the placement of the Soviet
missiles, and the first shipment is believed to have reached Cuba on 15 September.
On 14 October the missile sites were detected by an American U-2 reconnaissance
plane, and on 16 October McGeorge Bundy[1] set before the President irrefutable
evidence of the imminent threat against the US. The President informed the
American people of this in an address broadcast on radio and television on 22
October, by which time he had already decided on his response: a naval blockade,
or 'quarantine', of Cuba; a request for an emergency meeting of the UN Security
Council; and a personal appeal to Chairman Khrushchev 'to move the world
back from the abyss of destruction', and instead 'join in an historic effort to end
the perilous arms race and to transform the history of man'.[2]*

*   The tone and content of the President's address make clear his unflinch-
ing resolve in the face of unimaginable peril: 'We will not prematurely or
unnecessarily risk the costs of worldwide nuclear war in which even the fruits
of victory would be ashes in our mouth – but neither will we shrink from that
risk at any time it must be faced.' The immediate crisis was resolved when the
USSR agreed, on 28 October, to remove the missiles in return for an American
pledge not to invade Cuba. This face-saving formula could not conceal that
Khrushchev's bluff had been called, and this contributed to his removal from
office two years later. By contrast, it greatly augmented Kennedy's standing.*

*   IB had the opportunity to observe the President and some of his retinue at
a dinner party in Washington on the day Kennedy was told of the missiles in
Cuba – IB was unaware of the impending crisis at the time – and later wrote of
'the first real court that this country has ever had'.[3] Later still he reflected on the
President's behaviour that night:*

---

1 McGeorge ('Mac') *Bundy (1919–96), academic and administrator, at this time national security
    adviser to JFK.
2 'Radio and Television Report to the American People on the Soviet Arms Buildup in Cuba',
    22 October 1962, *John F. Kennedy: Containing the Public Messages, Speeches, and Statements of the
    President* (Washington, 1962–4), ii 807–8.
3 To Gladwyn Gladwyn, 24 January 1963.

He was in a jolly mood, which was very extraordinary, considering that that was the morning on which he had been shown the photographs of the Soviet installations on Cuba. And I must say the sangfroid which he displayed, and the extraordinary capacity for self-control, on a day on which he must have been extraordinarily preoccupied, was one of the most astonishing exhibitions of self-restraint and strength of will which I think I've ever seen.[1]

TO ALINE BERLIN

4 p.m. 17 October 1962 [*manuscript*]

American Airlines to Boston from Washington

My Darling Aline.

I really must sit down & use my solitude to dictate my book (Yale lectures). The week-end with the Morgans in North Haven – a bleak millionaire's island off the Maine Coast, was perfectly agreeable. I read a lot, & talked to my hosts. I like them: he is full of life, & she of repressed sensitiveness: subdued wealth is v. much *her* upbringing. It must be an immensely restricted neighbourhood: with a rough passage by boat from Rockford [...]. Very nicely, prettily built inside: she *has* imagination & taste: I was much impressed. We were taxy-ing in La Guardia, where I have just abandoned Dr J. Cohn,[2] twenty minutes before I had to get into the aeroplane. 38 minutes from Washington to N.Y. 50 minutes from N. Y. But it is beginning to rise: rocking: swaying, wait! I must tell you about the Important Young Man – Napoleon – surrounded by Maréchaux Bohlen, Alsop, Graham; Arthur Schles[inger] is *not* a Marshal: only a Lieut-General. Avis is *very* sweet. Really very very nice. Susan Mary has invited us for the 16*th* Nov – just after my Yale lectures. I accepted rapidly. Susan M. is no good with either the P[resident] or Jacqueline.[3] But no good at all. Joe *admires* them utterly. So do the Grahams & the Bohlens (the Grahams more[)] – Phil is perfect for & with him: rough chaff + energy + wit + neurosis + loyalty: K. reacts to all this with amused & delighted young tycoon – American century – bold handsome young executive chaff etc. *Not* my style at all. (It is bumping: but I don't mind). At first easy conversation with "our "set"["]: Chip & Avis, Kay & Phil, Susan-M. a Mrs somebody [...]. Then the stiffness which always follows the entrance of royalty. No dinner jackets (K. dislikes them). I had a haircut in his honour: too short & I looked absurd. Still: *He* is as you imagine: not noisy, a bit off hand ("How do you do Professor? Doctor? Professor?") rather tense (Joe thought

---

1 Interview with Arthur Schlesinger, Jr, 12 April 1965, ⟨http://www.jfklibrary.org/Asset-Viewer/ Archives/JFKOH-IB-01.aspx⟩, 1; 'On JFK', NYRB, 22 October 1998, 31–7 at 31.

2 Josef Cohn (1904–86), German-born scientist; Chaim Weizmann's personal assistant and US representative for Sieff Institute affairs for many years; Executive Vice-President, European Committee, Weizmann Institute, from 1955.

3 Jacqueline Lee Bouvier Kennedy (1929–94) née Bouvier had married Senator John F. Kennedy in 1953.

him particularly 'relaxed'), quick, smart, no jolly laughter, but some jolly chaff across the table to old friends, including Hervé[1] whom he detests. I was 'oversold' to him by Chip, Joe, Phil. I had no conversation with him alone, but was put down next to him in the men's study after dinner (meal very good.): he eyed me suspiciously, like a man of action faced with a notorious, possibly unintelligible or even ironic intellectual: I was cross examined about Gaitskell a bit, whose speech he disliked of course. He is *not* anxious to please (like Nehru) or to tell stories (like MacM[illan]) or have a serious discussion (like Gaitskell: more like Gaitskell's facetious moods, but interspersed with bits of business. Hervé told what de Gaulle shd do with Sekou Touré;[2] Berlin problem rapidly compared with Cuba;) my friends kept *trying*, too obviously, to draw me in: "now Isaiah knows *all* about this, better than anybody, Mr President: K. wd turn unwillingly to the foreign virtuoso, & vaguely listen. I made short speeches, but no sooner did I *painfully* take off, hating the flights, rather as with Nehru, than Phil or Chip wd interrupt, & K. with relief, would plunge into internal American politics, votes in Pennsylvania, or Mississippi, with little jokes – "*All* governors of N. Y. State were *great*: all geniuses' or "he's the kind of fella that knows the whole world & hates everybody' etc.: I don't think he was as impressed with me as our friends hoped he wd be. The whole idea of my début was appalling. He gave me up fairly early, I thought: & with relief turned me over to his wife saying "you go sit with Jackie. She wants to bring you out, or somep'n.". I said afterwards that I *liked* him. They wd all have been horrified too deeply if I hadn't. He parted affably enough. She is very nice indeed. Not at all like Nabokov's descriptions. Easy, sincere & amusing. Her face began by looking like Colette Clark's,[3] but when she speaks, becomes vivid & animated. His face does not move at all. She talked about Berenson: Nehru: Ayub Khan:[4] & you wd find her amiable & easy. Not common: not like her sister (whom I met for a second at Rai & Liz [von Hofmannsthal's], & who *is* a hollow society mechanism.): she wd be agreeable & well received in any polite society; curiously un-Hollywood. Quite shrewd: not at all happy: not attractive to me: the tremendous silent, sexy look emphasised by Nabokov, not visible to me: *unembarrassing*. I was not "enchanted": but I am sorry for her: she said she had a horror of her future after J. ceased to be President: Boston wd be terrible (it is). And he, J., wd lapse into his family's habits, which were not hers. Oddly frank. I talked to her about Burdon Muller: quite well received. In short I got on better with her than with him – neither can take Susan M. at all [...]. Now to work. It

---

1 Hervé Alphand (1907–94), French ambassador to the US 1956–65.
2 Ahmed Sékou Touré (1922–84), Marxist first President of Guinea 1958–84, who had obtained his country's independence by opposing de Gaulle's plans for continued domination by France of her African territories.
3 Colette Clark (b. 1932), daughter of the art historian Kenneth Clark (177/3).
4 Muhammad Ayub Khan (1907–74), President of Pakistan 1958–69.

was gay, the 16 hours in Washington: Kennedy *is* a leader, strong, oddly cautious, a bit common (how cd he not be with those parents?) but unemotional, terre à terre, tough, quick, independent, ruthless, soulless, gifted, serious, anxious to pick up what he can wherever he can. I wish you cd meet him: I think you wd neither like nor mind him: & he wd like you very well: eye for quality. I love you & miss you dreadfully: I am really terribly lonely. Images are streaming in.

Isaiah

TO ALINE BERLIN

Monday [22 October 1962; *manuscript*]

Lowell House, Harvard

Darling Aline,

My God, but it is dull here. Dull & depressing [...]. To-night after hearing Kennedy's speech at 7 p.m. among undergraduates here – they were silent & depressed – I dined with 4 "Slavic concentrators' very wise, very dull, my first proper contact with *any* students: I "charmed" them, I fear: they immediately offered to drive us to Yale for my first lecture: I cd not refuse: you will not mind that: not Jews funnily enough. Jacob telephoned to-night: I am glad they are here. He does *not* like N.Y.: I do. I love you desperately: I am now in a state of continuous "images" – how will I hold out till the 5*th*? [...] The Leinsdorfs are *bound* to ask us to dinner after dinner; *one* we may have to accept: but you can always "fall ill" & fly off to N.Y.: never never will I (a) part from you again: anyway the children won't need you quite so badly in the future: (b) come to Harvard. I was offered a well paid one-term-a year job by M.I.T. – I seem to be living modestly here, yet almost beyond my means – everything is very expensive. I am tired, frustrated, cannot bring myself to dictate my horrible lectures – chapters of book. I *will*. How fascinating about your "first husband" & Hans.[1] I quite understand. You *are* loved: & you love. This Americans lack: they fall in love; then they get into states: the psychoanalyst gets to work; the sillier & least educated girls in the streets say "do you have a compulsion neurosis about meals? The boy I go with has a guilt complex about penis envy' etc. Poor Stuart! All this for years & the atmosphere in Princeton is very bogus & depressing. She[2] *is* a monster. [...] Kennedy's speech: he *had* to do something, given that what he said was true (as I am sure it is) & missile bases *are* being built in Cuba, probably as a blackmail weapon vis a vis Berlin. The New Statesman & Iris M[urdoch] will *shriek*: how will England take the naval searches: yet I have a feeling that (1) Kennedy believes that by acting now, he will prevent a chain reaction as in the 30ies with Hitler: *that* is his constant idea: that England brought on

1 Hans *Halban (1908–64), nuclear physicist, Aline Berlin's second husband 1943–55.
2 Renée Hampshire, whom IB blamed for the Princeton episode in her husband's career.

the war by weakness & blindness etc. – Cuba is like Hitler & the Rhineland or the like.[1] He may be right: but his words to the Cuban people rang false: he shd not have talked about their lack of freedom etc.[2] (2) he is not too optimistic about avoiding a war in this *decade* (3) he wants to be sane, brave, a leader, to take on a duel with Khrushchev: he is frightened of *erosion*: one must act: one must perform: one must live carefully & dangerously: life is a war, & one must live under a continual shadow of death: very romantic, rather terrifying: I see why Joe & Phil love him so: to them he is Alexander the Great in a plumed helmet ready for the barbarians, who has broken through American tedium & is conscious of history, duels, immortal fame. Ben Gurion is not dissimilar. Nor is de Gaulle. Hemingwayism. An aesthetic, heroic–hellenic view. I am not at home here – in this time. You & Philippe more. I do love you, oh!
        I.

TO MICHEL STRAUSS[3]

    25 October 1962 [*carbon*]

                                                  Lowell House, Harvard

Dear Michel,
    Please do not worry about Iris Murdoch – I did want to read it on the air-plane, but am now doing quite nicely without it. It can wait until I get back to England. I spend my days at Harvard peacefully, mainly at the Widener, and though I keep on saying to myself that I must work from 9 a.m. until 7 p.m. I don't really do that. All my meals, I am afraid, are taken by old acquaintances of various sorts and I am on the whole enjoying myself in spite of the rela-tive discomfort of the room. However, I am now fully electrified which adds to the joys of life. I have a refrigerator, a television set, a telephone, a radio, an electric kettle, an electric pan, an electric coffee pot, an electric shoe shine set, and several other delicious objects; so I live in the new age. [...]
    The old familiar faces are all as old and familiar as before. The charm

1 In his address to the nation on the evening of 22 October 1962 Kennedy observed: 'The 1930s taught us a clear lesson: aggressive conduct, if allowed to go unchecked and unchallenged, ultimately leads to war. This nation is opposed to war.' loc. cit. (120/2), 807. At Harvard the President had written a senior thesis entitled: 'Appeasement at Munich: The Inevitable Result of the Slowness of Conversion of the British Democracy from a Disarmament to a Rearmament Policy' (March 1940), published as the best-selling *Why England Slept* (NY and London, 1940).
2 Without ever mentioning Fidel Castro by name, Kennedy's speech was hard-hitting in its con-demnation of the regime in Cuba, 'that imprisoned island': 'Finally, I want to say a few words to the captive people of Cuba, to whom this speech is being directly carried by special radio facilities. [...] We know that your lives and land are being used as pawns by those who deny your freedom. Many times in the past, the Cuban people have risen to throw out tyrants who destroyed their liberty. And I have no doubt that most Cubans today look forward to the time when they will be truly free.' loc. cit. (120/2), 806, 809.
3 Michel *Strauss (b. 1936), stepson to IB, married Margery Tongway (b. 1932) in 1959.

of the place has to some extent evaporated for me, perhaps because I have not been here for so long and, on the other hand, have been here so often. Also I am oppressed. This is a psychological condition, not deriving from objective conditions, but from my own character, about which your mother rightly complains – that I am not doing enough work, that the lectures will not be finished, that what I do will not be scholarly enough, that there are not enough footnotes, that the whole thing is much too impressionistic, that I ought to be quite different from what, in fact, I am. Still, I expect I shall get over that, too.

There is a tremendous [talk] going on about the elections to the Senate; one of the candidates being my old friend Stuart Hughes.[1] All kinds of eminent Boston Brahmins are putting their names down for him on the grounds that (a) the Republicans are blind and reactionary, (b) the Democrats in Massachusetts are hideously corrupt and, (c) {that} although Stuart Hughes has plenty of faults, he is at any rate civilised, honest, and brave. He will not be elected to the Senate, needless to say, but if he accumulates enough votes to show the strength of opinion it is thought that this might make an ultimate difference. I wonder.[2]

[...] I love the Co-op and always go into it on my way to the Widener and buy some useless object. I have refrained so far from buying shirts with button-down collars for fear of your mother; I shall keep this up. Perkins is trying to make arrangements to get us quarters in the Somerset Club, which is very grand, and I do not think ultimately that it may suit us. On the other hand, it may. It would be very funny to live there, for many reasons which your mother would well understand and you, perhaps, too. I should love to invite Professor Wolfson,[3] or one of the more East European members of the Russian Research Centre of unmistakable appearance, there to dinner, for example. Tonight I went to a dinner of an extremely solemn and pompous body called the Massachusetts Historical Society, of which I'm a member – God knows why – where I listened to an extremely pompous speech by a very nice Bostonian – the solemn and beautiful faces around me really were like an English provincial assembly of the mid-nineteenth century. I like that in America above everything – those gentle grave civilised faces with their simple sense of humour and their courteous and charming manners. This

1 (Henry) Stuart Hughes (1916–99), cultural and intellectual historian; Professor of History, Harvard, 1957–75; Gurney Professor of History and Political Science from 1969; son of a US Solicitor General and grandson of the Republican nominee for President 1916.
2 Hughes contested, as an Independent, the Massachusetts Senate seat vacated by the President: he came third in the poll, won by the President's younger brother, Edward M. Kennedy (Democrat). The Cuban Missile Crisis made Hughes's pro-disarmament stance seem unrealistic, and he gained only a tiny percentage of the vote. The Times remarked that Edward Kennedy was 'as photogenic, youthful and energetic' as Hughes was 'unconventional' (5 November 1962, 11f).
3 Harry Austryn Wolfson (1887–1974), Lithuanian-born scholar of religious history and philosophy, known for his work on the first-century Jewish philosopher Philo and on Spinoza; Nathan Littauer Professor of Hebrew Literature and Philosophy, Harvard, 1925–74.

is only to be found in New England. Tomorrow I set off for Maine with my friends the Aubrey Morgans to an island for three days. Everyone tells me it will be bitterly cold and quite awful, but I'm sure I shall enjoy it, for I think the company is what makes for enjoyment for me, and not nature, which I happily ignore – except when the company is bad and I get colds from it; when the company is good I survive. I have decided that Stuart is quite right and all my diseases are highly psychosomatic. On Burdon-Muller's advice, I have bought a hot-water bottle and several medicines and am going well equipped. Everyone is still going about now in open shirts and khaki trousers and white socks except me, who have a good woolly vest, a thick cardigan and a tweed suit to keep me warm in my central-heated room.

God be with you and Margery, and do write me if there is something I can possibly do for you. Edmund Wilson is no longer on speaking terms with Harry Levin. Harry Levin, who does not like me at all, could not be sweeter to me and has invited me to dinner twice. That is sinister too. [...]

Yours,

[Isaiah]

TO PETER HALBAN

25 October 1962 [*carbon*]

[Lowell House, Harvard]

Dear Peter,

Thank you very much for your last letter. It is a real joy to receive them. I live peacefully and go to the Widener Library every day and read a great many books and make notes and keep on putting off the task of actually writing from day to day in a most cowardly manner. I am sure you realise how nice it is to take notes but how painful it is actually to write. There are plenty of beautiful 'non-commercial' radio stations in Boston which produce classical music at any hour of the day or night, more or less, and this I switch on whenever I am too tired to go on working, and listen very contentedly. There are also some excellent concerts by the Boston Symphony orchestra conducted by our friend Leinsdorf, and I have seen the enormous new Lincoln Centre in New York in which the concert hall has been built but the opera house not yet – the concert hall looks like a very grand airport, as most modern architecture today tends to do.

I should rather like to have my operation[1] in New York, but have made no arrangements for it. There is 'nothing to take out' exactly, only to patch up if you see what I mean. And I think it would be much nicer if my mother wasn't there brooding over me in a worried manner. I wish I didn't worry so

---

1 A hernia operation, which took place at University College Hospital in London in the second half of April 1963.

much myself: worry about not writing books, worry about writing books when I have written them, worry about what people will think, worry about the fact that other people write good books, but that mine are somehow patchwork, etc. etc. etc. I'm sure this is a fault of character and not of the [work] itself. One constantly anticipates failure and one constantly wonders if things are going to come off or not, and as a result of one's worry they come off less than they would if one was more confident and being in the saddle would simply let the horse carry [one]. I envy the self-confident, and the unworried, and the people who really can take holidays and forget themselves instead of having constant nagging thoughts about having this, that and the other to [do]. Answering letters, in fact, is a kind of drug – great relief from real work.

[...] Forgive the emptiness of this letter. It is much easier to write if one isn't obliged to think thoughts and try to put something 'worthwhile' in a letter, but just chat along as best one can. So do do the same.

Yours ever with love,

[Isaiah]

TO PHILIPPE HALBAN[1]

25 October 1962 [carbon]

Lowell House, Harvard

Dearest Philippe,

Thank you very much for your exquisite letter. [...] Indeed, I set my bedroom on fire. Very remarkable it was – I had never set a fire before and this was a most tremendous blaze which I finally managed to put out with endless glassfuls of cold water. If you have never been in a room in which a blanket, sheets, mattress were a wet, smoking, blinding, tear-producing mess, you cannot know what it means. Otherwise my life is perfectly peaceful and I am enjoying myself, quite. I imagine you are enjoying yourself, quite. I probably enjoy operations much more than you do and much look forward to the one in December if it is decided upon. I shall make no decisions until your mother arrives here and gives me her advice. As always I shall be guided by her in everything. Do tell me how it feels to be a boarder: is it strange? Is it tough? Is it odd? Even at Harvard, the Dragon School[2] is known: it seems to have a worldwide fame – I wish I had gone to such a school. I'm sure I should have been a better scholar as a result – I never was much good at Latin and Greek, and worse still at mathematics. So how I managed what I did manage remains a mystery. I used cribs much too much and regret

1 Philippe Halban (b. 1950), stepson to IB.
2 North Oxford preparatory school, founded in 1877 to provide education of a high standard to the children (primarily the sons, to start with) of Oxford dons.

it terribly. On the other hand, I was the most conscientious translator into Latin and Greek and pretty poor it was. I only 'came off' late in life – I hope you come off much earlier than that. Anyway Westminster is better than St. Paul's, and you will, I think, enjoy it more. I've just been to Washington, where I met our old friends the Walkers,[1] the Bohlens (Celestine is now a girl of about twelve, she's forgotten her French but it is hoped that now her father is the Ambassador in Paris she will recover it). Perhaps they will all come to Portofino in the summer; indeed I hope so. Thank you again for your letter, which I enjoyed very much indeed, and I hope all is going well with everything.

Yours, ⟨with much love⟩
    Isaiah

TO NICOLAS NABOKOV

25 October 1962

Lowell House, Harvard

Dearest Nicolas,

[...] Aline is not yet here. I am working in the Widener, am trying not to [live] at all, but do my work. I cannot, alas, go with Liebermann[2] and you in May for I am in Oxford then for the term and cannot possibly detach myself. But you must not run about so much, believe me. Miss Holli and I thought you were not looking at all well and we beg you to moderate your movements. Take a long, long rest and be at peace. Why shorten one's life unduly? Look at Stravinsky – it pays to be heartless, not mind things, think about money, and pleasure, and all one's friends, and live a long and happy life. Let me enjoin this upon you. After Washington and the merry-go-round there, I am particularly impressed with the need for this. There they are engaged in explaining how the others whom we mention are not doing work of real importance at all, but various small tasks, whereas they, of whom we are speaking, are in the centre of things.[3] But it is all very Roman and I felt terribly Greek, not to say Judaean. Now I know exactly what it must have been like to have paid a visit to Rome in, say, the third century AD when the

---

1 John ('Johnny') Walker III (1906–95), American museum curator and writer; studied with Bernard Berenson at I Tatti; Chief Curator, National Gallery of Art, Washington, 1939–56, Director 1956–69; married 1937 (Lady) Margaret Gwendolen Mary ('Margie') née Drummond (1905–87), eldest daughter of (James) Eric Drummond (1876–1951), 16th Earl of Perth; they met in Rome, where her father was British ambassador.

2 Rolf Liebermann (1910–99), Swiss composer and music administrator who worked across genres; Director of the Hamburg Staatsoper from 1959–73; of the Paris Opera 1973–80.

3 A short time later IB wrote to Robert Oppenheimer (251/1) of Joe Alsop's 'compulsively geo-political talk: it makes one feel appallingly small and trivial' (4 December 1962).

barbarians were pressing on the frontiers, and the Pentagon was involved in political action. *Pace, pace, idol mio.*[1]

Yours,

Isaiah

TO MAURICE BOWRA

27 October 1962

Lowell House, Harvard

Dear Maurice,

Let me give you all the news as rapidly as possible. It is all much duller and quieter. The absence of the Jameses has removed a civilised centre of life and there is no replacement for them, nothing remotely similar. Even your old friend, Mrs Kingsley Porter, the murderess, has finally expired. The absence of the Schlesingers is also deeply felt. The gossip about him is continuous. The professors are anxious to explain that his job is a very menial one, that Bundy is much more important (which is no doubt true). They are all very much like marshals around Napoleon there – that's what Arthur does, merely attracts a lot of unfavourable notice – constant attacks upon him occur in the reactionary newspapers as a typical Harvard 'egghead' and the President is thought constantly to explain that he is not under Arthur's influence and uses him for unimportant tasks – but he has sense enough, obviously, not to sack any member of his staff simply because he is under attack – loyalty to one's own men under such circumstances is an obvious minimum requirement of any degree of influence and success. Arthur is not happy, adores Washington and hates it, and does not know whether to stay or go. [...] I saw Joe in full glory and also the President himself who certainly is somebody. Mrs Kennedy is very nice indeed – not at all like her photographs or the stories about her – you would like her very much. She is gay, easy, amiable, candid, cosy and good company and no difficulty at all. He is exceedingly tough, clear and powerful, and certainly wants to be like Alexander the Great. Surrounded by his marshals, he really is a splendid sight. Too political and brutal for me, but a sort of great man or potentially one. His hero is Churchill and [he] does not share the views of his father. He is constantly alert, never lets go, some kind of electric current moves unceasingly within him and he is thinking political thoughts all the time and never relaxes for one single second. Although on the whole his mood of relaxation

1 'Peace, peace, my idol', apparently a slight confusion between two Mozart/da Ponte operas: 'Pace, pace, mio dolce tesoro' ('Peace, peace, my sweet treasure') occurs in *The Marriage of Figaro*; 'idol mio' is from *Così fan tutte*. There are also 'Pace, pace, mio dio' ('Peace, peace, my god': Verdi, *La forza del destino*) and 'Resta in pace, idolo mio' ('Rest in peace, my idol': Cimarosa, *Gli Orazi e i Curiazi*).

takes the form of rough chaff, not quite as bad [as] ordinary White's Club[1] stuff, but something of the kind undoubtedly. He is the American version of the young man who might have been in Oxford in the 1920s, and a friend and protégé of F. E. Smith.[2] He is very unasleep. His entourage is deeply in love with him and there is a kind of Greek situation in that respect. [...]

Yours,

Isaiah   [...]

TO ALINE BERLIN

30 October 1962 [*dictated over several days*]

Lowell House, Harvard

⟨Darling Aline,⟩

I listened to the President's speech[3] surrounded by students in Lowell House. Reception was curious: most of them were stunned, someone started clapping at some particular sentiment of the President, but the rest stopped him, whether because they could not hear what the President was saying owing to the clapping or for some other motive was not clear. My "cleaning" woman asked me whether I thought there would be war and was much relieved to hear from me that there wouldn't. Last night I went to a meeting addressed by Stuart Hughes, frightfully boring speeches by not very competent people, an enormous crowd in the lecture hall and a thousand people turned away outside. People are neither bellicose nor hostile to the administration: the general mood is one of worry. Most people feel that the President "had to do something", but nobody knows if what he did was right, how it would come out – there is neither confidence or lack of confidence in my world. Somewhat like England on the eve of Suez but without the Labour Party.

Last night I dined with Lionel Salem.[4] He is exactly like his parents: thinks the Americans are terrible sheep, follow the President much too meekly, there is no democratic principle at work, not really much to choose between the Soviet and the American system – since they are all naive, stupid, etc., etc., in short he is like a sharp indignant young man from Paris. In his house upstairs there lives a nice, French-Norwegian girl who was present at dinner

1 Exclusive London gentleman's club, known for, among other things, the eccentricities of its betting book; established 1693.
2 Frederick Edwin Smith (1872–1930), 1st Earl of Birkenhead 1922, lawyer and statesman famed for his brilliance, feared for his cutting wit: 'Judge: You are extremely offensive, young man. Smith: As a matter of fact, we both are, and the only difference between us is that I am trying to be, and you can't help it.' [Frederick, Second] Earl of Birkenhead, *Frederick Edwin, Earl of Birkenhead*, vol. 1 (London, 1933), 115.
3 On the Cuban missile crisis, 22 October.
4 Lionel Salem (b. 1937), French chemist and banker; later (1993–9) founder and director of the Centre de vulgarisation de la connaissance, Centre national de la recherche scientifique.

plus a Canadian scientist and two 'concentrators on Soviet affairs' – rather English and very bright and nice. We all went to the Stuart Hughes meeting together and Lionel was terribly contemptuous and indignant about the whole thing. It was most fascinating to watch his reactions, the Englishman's reactions, the Norwegian-French girl's reactions, and the Americans' reactions to the whole thing. I could write a little essay about national characteristics on the strength of it.

[…] I really must sit down and dictate those lectures – if it were not for that my life here would not be so bad, but the oppressive clouds are beginning to collect – you're quite right about my tendency to worry – but it is now too late to mend, alas. I hope to 'break the back of it' by the time you are here.

[…] Last night I dined with the Hammonds, it was clear that he wished me to make a short speech on the political situation, but I managed to wriggle out of that by chaffing them out of it. I only hope that I was polite. I said, 'No, no. I cannot make a short statement. Are you asking me to say a few words?' Everyone laughed, I hope happily. The result was that nobody discussed Cuba and a perfectly pleasant evening was had by all. G. Santillana[1] was there, he expressed a platonic wish to see me sometime, but his wife and I really cannot talk to each other – although I have nothing against her. She is now a great friend of Rowland and so is he! When you come we shall do something about them. Iris Origo[2] will be here two nights this weekend and I shall see her for a moment somewhere after dinner. I hate coming into formal dinner parties at about 9 p.m. as I shall be forced to do. Everyone rises, one is introduced with a most tremendous éclat – and the degree of politeness everywhere can be cut with a knife. Now I have made an engagement for us with the Gilmores[3] as well. It cannot be helped, it cannot be helped! But I am really trying to reduce it to a bare minimum. You will have to come armed with a strong anthropological sense and remember that life is long and all things pass.

Yours, ⟨with love (as one says to *all* Americans)
Isaiah⟩   [...]

⟨I am off to Washington again to-morrow to dine at the W[hite] House

1 Giorgio Diaz de Santillana (1902–74), Professor of the History and Philosophy of Science, MIT, 1954–67. His *The Age of Adventure: The Renaissance Philosophers* (1956) appeared in the same series as IB's *The Age of Enlightenment: The Eighteenth-Century Philosophers* (1956) and Morton White's *The Age of Analysis: Twentieth-Century Philosophers* (1955). Married, 1948, Dorothy Hancock (1904–80) née Tilton; they lived for most of their married life in Beverly, Massachusetts.

2 Iris Margaret Origo (1902–88) née Cutting, writer and biographer, married 1924 Antonio Origo (1892–1976), and lived for much of her life in Tuscany; became a close friend of Bernard Berenson, who had been her mother's lover.

3 Myron Piper Gilmore (1910–78), Renaissance scholar, Professor of History, Harvard, 1954–74, Director, Harvard University Center for Italian Renaissance Studies, Villa I Tatti, Florence, 1964–73; and his English wife Sheila née Dehn (1917–95); they married 1938.

– I cannot *refuse* I suppose – but I fear Devonshires[1] & dolce vita – I *cannot* wait for you! I really find it terribly intolerable!⟩

TO JACQUELINE KENNEDY

10 November 1962 [*manuscript*]

The Ritz-Carlton, Boston

Dear Mrs Kennedy,

Aline and I are very grateful indeed. It was the most memorable evening I have spent in the United States, and (with one exception) anywhere else:[2] I must apologise for talking so much, so rapidly, probably such nonsense: but it is something which, when in seventh heaven, I cannot arrest. But I hope you will forgive me all the same: I shd have exercised more British restraint. I must also confess at once that after vainly trying to preserve the fragment of porcelain with which you rewarded me, I gave it to Marian Schlesinger[3] who asked for it. I found it painful to part with it: but more painful to refuse. I am very glad indeed, not merely on public grounds, but personally, that the heathen gods of old Japan shd in fact not have been able to get the best of so mighty good a man as the President.[4] I shd have liked to serve him very much. I used to feel this about Franklin R., about whom we were ordered, in the British Embassy, to be neutral in thought, word, deed. I was anything but. Perhaps I am a natural hero worshipper, and at-the-feet-sitter: but this is the second occasion only on which I have felt a passionate desire to offer my services, however unwanted, to anyone. After the Alsops' party the other night, after you and the President had left, Phil Graham said to me '*You* be objective; *you* be fair and impartial; *we love* him.' I had no wish to be fair, objective etc: if one undergoes what is called an Experience, one has no wish to remain judicious and calm. But I must not go on and bore you with all this

1 See 323/6. This dinner appears to have been postponed till after Aline's arrival.

2 IB and Aline had been invited, apparently at the First Lady's instigation, to a 'post-missile-crisis' dinner at the White House. The 'one exception' must be IB's meeting with Anna Akhmatova in Leningrad 17 years earlier.

3 Marian Cannon Schlesinger (b. 1912) née Cannon; married, 1940, Arthur Schlesinger Jr (divorced 1970). The 'fragment of porcelain' was from an item IB had broken at the dinner, to the First Lady's evident amusement, and on 20 November she sent him another piece – complete with a mock certificate of authentication – to be donated to the British Museum, or else to the Heathen Gods Division of the Tokyo Archaeological Institute (for which fanciful creation see next note).

4 In the early hours of 2 August 1943 the Japanese destroyer *Amagiri* rammed and sank Lieutenant John F. Kennedy's patrol torpedo-boat PT-109 in Blackett Strait, south of the Solomon Islands. Kennedy was later decorated for leading his crew to safety and arranging their rescue. The adventure was immortalised in the eponymous Jimmy Dean song 'PT-109', which stood high in the US singles charts in 1962, and which Jackie Kennedy sang at the end of the evening described here. The chorus ends: 'The heathen gods of old Japan, yeah, they thought they had the best of a mighty good man.' In her letter of 20 November (previous note) Mrs Kennedy invited IB back to the White House, noting that 'PT-109' had another 11 verses that she and JFK would love to teach him. The song as released offers only another 4.

14.4.62°

flow of uninvited feeling. Monsieur Malraux[1] is a man of genius and entitled to do so: I am not, & [for] me to enlarge on our – to me marvellously delightful & fascinating conversation – as I shd like to – wd be mere impertinence and presumption. May I again say how deeply honoured & truly grateful I am.

ys sincerely,
Isaiah Berlin

TO GARRETT DROGHEDA
29 November 1962

Lowell House, Harvard

Dear Garrett,

I should have written you long ago to acquaint you with the general gossip. Cuba was a most marvellous business: after hearing the President's speech among a lot of Lowell House students, who were rather depressed by the news for about three hours, I recovered rapidly. I went to a number of radical meetings which said exactly the sorts of things that liberals might have said in England – nobody is quite as far to the left here as our more intemperate nuclear disarmers – at least I have come across none – but I survived during the entire week in a state of lunatic optimism – lunatic, I am informed by the persons in Washington best qualified to know, because they said there really was a risk of something terrible happening. My optimism was founded on too little. Nevertheless I do not know why but I have a feeling that the eve of war produces a very different mood everywhere and that one has a kind of preliminary sense of build-up which on this occasion was conspicuously lacking. So instead of wandering about gloomily I went to New York and attended a performance of *Die Meistersinger*, which was exceedingly good – all produced by local talent as far as I could see. And Aline went to hear *Ernani*, which she said was very good indeed, with Leontyne Price[2] and everyone you would expect. Bing admires Solti extravagantly, thinks he is a conductor of genius, does not, I suspect, like him personally very much, but will do much to keep him here, so the tug-of-war may one day start in real earnest. We certainly must not lose him to America. [...] Bing, for what it is worth, is certainly of the opinion, or appeared to be when talking with me, that Callas[3] was through. And if even George says so, surely this must

1 André Malraux (1901–76), French novelist; Bruce Chatwin recalls IB as 'surely for verbal dexterity Malraux's most distinguished rival': *What Am I Doing Here* [sic] (London, 1989), 132.
2 (Mary Violet) Leontyne Price (b. 1927), American soprano; made her debut at Covent Garden 1958, La Scala 1960.
3 Maria Callas (1923–77) née Anna Maria Sofia Cecilia Kalogeropolos, legendary US-born Greek soprano. By the early 1960s Callas's recurrent vocal troubles were causing her gradually to withdraw from the stage: she made her last operatic appearance, as Tosca, at Covent Garden in 1965.

be true? Still this is a painful issue and I do not wish to be a back-seat driver. I saw Stravinsky after his visit to Russia and he is in a state of great exultation – they treated him very well but although he enjoyed it very much and adored his conversation with Mr K. while there and thought that Madame Furteeva,[1] whom I have never met, but whom you know, was a woman of irresistible charm and intelligence – his wife thinks this too – nevertheless he is a very shrewd old fox and taken in by nothing. Mild efforts to stop the performances of *Agon* under Balanchine[2] were made by the Russians, but were foiled: the works were played to apparently madly enthusiastic audiences, somewhat to the chagrin of the authorities. When on the radio Stravinsky was asked what his work in progress was, he explained he was doing a Biblical piece for the State of Israel[3] – this was very badly received. No further questions asked about his future, and a general frost. However he seems to have recovered from that since he was asked to spend a holiday in Yalta or somewhere and obviously intends to go back sometime if his life and strength persist. [...]

The atmosphere here is really very different from that of England. There is a genuine sense of energy, and though the people are troubled, they think almost entirely in terms of this country alone, at least in Washington – what they can do and what the Russians or Chinese can do – the Europeans are regarded, I fear, as more or less dependencies. The British Cabinet is thought to possess Macmillan, a real man – and Home,[4] a real man, who although his views may be disapproved of in enlightened circles (rightly) he is nevertheless regarded as independent, forceful, and ice-cutting. The rest are discounted. Nothing much is known about Heath,[5] McCleod[6] seems temporarily to have disappeared behind a cloud (no pun intended), Rab[7]

1 Ekaterina Alekseevna Furtseva (1910–1974), leading Soviet politician; secretary, Central Committee of the Communist Party, 1956, first female member of the Presidium 1957; Minister of Culture 1960–74.

2 George Balanchine (1904–83) né Georgi Melitinovich Balanchivadze, Russian-born US ballet dancer and choreographer credited with being the primary architect of American classical ballet. While chief choreographer of Diaghilev's Ballets russes he met Stravinsky, beginning a life-long collaboration: his ballet *Agon*, with music by Stravinsky, was first performed in America in 1957.

3 *Abraham and Isaac* (72–3).

4 Alexander Frederick ('Alec') Douglas-Home (1903–95), Conservative politician, succeeded as 14th Earl of Home and Baron Home of the Hirsel 1951, but disclaimed his peerages for life in 1963; Kt 1962; life peer 1974; Foreign Secretary 1960–63, 1970–4; Prime Minister 1963–4.

5 Edward Richard George ('Ted') Heath (1916–2005), Conservative politician; government Chief Whip and Lord Privy Seal with FO responsibilities 1960–3; Secretary of State for Industry and President of the Board of Trade 1963–4; Leader of the Opposition 1965–70; Prime Minister 1970–4; Leader of the Opposition 1974–5.

6 Iain Norman Macleod (1913–70), Conservative politician; Secretary of State for the Colonies 1959–61; Chancellor of the Duchy of Lancaster and Leader of the House of Commons 1961–3; editor, *Spectator*, 1963–5; Chancellor of the Exchequer 1970 (died shortly after taking office); 'his radical initiatives at the Colonial Office had cost him a degree of support not only in the parliamentary party but also out in the constituencies' (David Goldsworthy, ODNB).

7 Richard Austen ('Rab') Butler (1902–82), later life peer (1965) and KG (1971); Conservative politician; Home Secretary 1957–62; Deputy Prime Minister 1962–3; Foreign Secretary 1963–4; Master

is thought to be very soft. They think in terms of personalities almost entirely – which is inevitable in this country where, when you ask people in Washington what they are doing, they do not say 'I am working in the Treasury' or 'I am working in the Department of the Interior', but 'I work for McNamara'[1] or 'I work for McGeorge Bundy' or whoever it may be. Our Ambassador[2] – whom I met for the first time the other day in Washington – is well liked and the Cecil charm worked beautifully everywhere. The Embassy under him is filled with stock figures, I do not know who they are but the general impression is there is nobody there much to talk to. During the war, when conditions were obviously different, this was not so: there were a number of fiery personalities about, each of whom had excellent individual relationships with all kinds of people in the American administration and this made an enormous difference. [...] And if you have a chance of seeing Maudling[3] you might impress upon him the desirability of sending forth agents – I think the Foreign Office and the staffing of the Embassies is pretty hopeless as they stick to their trade union very jealously and closely – who have personality and ideas, even those who go beyond their brief and occasionally get themselves into trouble for going too far and talking too much, rather than cautious, moderate, sensible, dull civil servants. [...] But I must not go on like this – it gets me back to the old days when I used to report during the war – a thing I much enjoyed doing, but [for] which I have neither the materials nor the opportunity now, and this is all nonsense I expect. But there is political champagne in the air and it really is rather exciting. And even Mrs K's encouragement of the arts – though much sniffed at and looked down upon by people not directly associated as so much snobbery and phoniness – gives the whole thing a new air. It is very rare that direct encouragement of 'culture' proceeds from [the White House] and these parties for Nobel Prize winners, composers, or painters is also part of the new pattern. Even Justices of the Supreme Court are gay and gossipy – Lady Pamela[4] would have a wonderful time if she settled here save that Mrs K. does not approve of her much – something to do

of Trinity, Cambridge, 1965–78; beaten by Harold Macmillan in the post-Suez race to succeed Anthony Eden as Prime Minister and Conservative leader.

1 Robert Strange McNamara (1916–2009), US Defense Secretary in the Kennedy and Johnson administrations 1961–8; president of the World Bank 1968–81; remembered as an architect of the Vietnam war who came to regret, and publicly recant, his role in the conflict.

2 (William) David Ormsby-Gore (1918–85), 5th Baron Harlech 1964; UK ambassador in Washington 1961–5; grandson of James Edward Hubert Gascoyne-Cecil (1861–1947), 4th Marquess of Salisbury.

3 Reginald Maudling (1917–79), Conservative politician; President of the Board of Trade 1959–61; Secretary of State for the Colonies 1961–2; Chancellor of the Exchequer 1962–4; Home Secretary 1970–2.

4 Pamela Margaret Elizabeth Berry (1914–82) née Smith, second daughter of F. E. Smith, 1st Earl of Birkenhead; wife of the newspaper proprietor (William) Michael Berry (1911–2001), later (1968) life peer; a famous society hostess and a close friend of IB.

with things said by her or at her instance about her sister Lee,[1] I gather. But I must stop, otherwise I shall become gravely indiscreet and we shall both get into trouble.

Yours ever,

Isaiah   [...]

TO BERTELL OLLMAN[2]

18 December 1962

Lowell House, Harvard

Dear Bertell,

It was very good to hear from you and I am very glad that your thesis is getting on. Plamenatz[3] is a just and severe judge as well as a sympathetic one, and I have infinite confidence in his judgement and capacity to help. So mind you gain his respect. As for me, there is much to tell – the atmosphere in Washington is extraordinary indeed – the change is unbelievably rapid and remarkable, and all the old New Dealers, whom I know, seem dazed by the pace and the direction.[4] [...] But to turn to graver matters: what is to be done about supplementing your finances? Is there anything I can do for you in this country? Tell me whom to approach and I shall do my best to do so. [...] I am having a very good time with Marcuse,[5] a Marxist after my own heart, a most intelligent and delightful man who correctly maintains that E. H. Carr has neither understanding of nor interest in ideas of any kind and should be prevented from writing about them. How could I dislike anyone who thought that? In general it seems to me that I prefer intellectuals, however wrongheaded, to narrow professionals, however sound – what matters is the range of ideas and not consistency or some superficial form of correspondence to the facts – that has, at any rate, been the impact on me of meeting all kinds

---

1 (Caroline) Lee Radziwill (b. 1933) née Bouvier, American socialite; younger sister of Jacqueline Kennedy.

2 Bertell Ollman (b. 1935), Marxist political theorist, IB's student at Oxford (M.Phil. 1963, D.Phil. 1967); taught at University of the West Indies 1963–6, from 1967 at NYU (becoming Professor of Politics); married to Paule Yvonne née Gaudemard (b. 1939).

3 John Petrov Plamenatz (1912–75), Montenegrin-born social and political theorist; elected to a Fellowship at All Souls on the strength of an Oxford doctoral thesis failed by the examiners, in IB's eyes 'perhaps the greatest miscarriage of academic justice known to my generation' (PI2, 148); Fellow of All Souls 1936–51; University Lecturer in Social and Political Theory, Oxford, 1950–67; IB's successor as Chichele Professor of Social and Political Theory 1967–75.

4 Kennedy introduced to Washington 'a new generation of pragmatic young activists who came to be known as the New Frontiersmen' (Richard Holbrooke, ' "The Doves Were Right": Toward the End of His Life, McGeorge Bundy Re-evaluated His Advice to President Johnson', NYT, 28 November 2008, B12), and were dubbed 'action-intellectuals' by the journalist Theodore White in the eponymous article 'The Action-Intellectuals', Life, 9 June 1967, 43–76.

5 Herbert Marcuse (1898–1979), German-born American philosopher, leading figure in the Frankfurt School; his One Dimensional Man (1964) addressed the causes of alienation in advanced technological society, and was much read by the protesting students of the time.

and sorts of people here. Nothing seems to me to argue smallness of mind more surely than addiction to some one small pattern in which the mind can comfortably go to sleep – whom that cap fits I leave you to judge, not Hegel or Marx, at any rate – but some of their disciples ever so much. I must now stop and go to New York for a, believe me, well-deserved holiday (not a lunch or a dinner here passes without being turned into a seminar it seems to me). But tell me what I can do financially – that is what matters, I fear, more than anything else at the moment. If you have an idea let me know at once at this address. Aline and I both send our fondest affection to Paule.

Yours,

[Isaiah]

TO SAM BEHRMAN

8 January 1963

Lowell House, Harvard

Dearest Sam,

Thank you for sending me James Baldwin's piece.[1] To say it was agreeable reading would not be quite right. It is absolutely terrifying. Apart from the rot which appears in it from time to time and the great eruption of personal bile, it is obviously genuine and frightening. When, as a result of genetics, the majority of the population of New York is black, what will things be like? The other day I suddenly had a nightmare vision of all those proud buildings on Park Avenue and 5th Avenue empty of white inhabitants with just coloured ones running along in Chinese blue padded jackets – after the revolution, that is to say. Ghettos always breed violence in the end, it seems to me, and I should be relieved to think that this country will escape it, but I do not feel too sure. When he describes the feelings of a Negro child on learning that it has not got the ordinary rights of an ordinary citizen and this is rammed into the young Negro by everybody as he grows up, I thought I had remembered something of the same sort somewhere else – in the Western provinces of the Russian Empire, for example, on the part of persons not altogether unknown to you and me. Goodness me, it really is disturbing. [...]

Yours, ⟨with much love

Isaiah⟩

1 James Arthur Baldwin (1924–87), American novelist, dramatist and social critic; his powerful 'Letter from a Region in My Mind', an essay on the condition of African-Americans in the US, appeared in the *New Yorker*, 17 November 1962, 59–144; repr. in his *The Fire Next Time* (NY, 1963).

TO VERA WEIZMANN[1]

9 January 1963

Lowell House, Harvard

[...] I heard an account of Dick Crossman's lecture on Dr W[eizmann] in Columbia here.[2] I did not hear it myself, nor have I seen a copy, but from all accounts it is not the kind of thing I should have liked to have listened to. He consistently stresses the aspects of Dr W. that he admired most – his toughness and realism, his dislike for gentiles, opportunism etc. – which he exaggerates violently – he represents Dr W. as a kind of ruthless power-maniac with a tremendous male fist behind a deceptive silk glove, which seems to me to do hideous injustice to his subject. True, he dislikes his opponents even more, but he seems to use him as a battering-ram for the purpose of discrediting the politicians in England and elsewhere whom he wishes to do down – I do not for example believe in the truth of the conversation (can you verify it? I do hope not!) in which Dr W. said to him, 'Are you an anti-Semite?' and he said, 'Of course.' And Dr W. then said, 'Every gentile is. I am glad you are honest about it.' Dr W. may have said the last of these things, but I do not believe the question was ever put. Perhaps I feel these things so strongly partly because the portrait of Dr W. is one that the more intelligent among his enemies wish to impress upon [the] historical imagination of our times; and partly because Dick is so consistently nasty both to me and about me in print and otherwise. I am sure this gives a bias to my judgement – one does not wish bloody-minded persons on the same side as oneself, and if one finds them there it is irritating. [...]

Yours ever, ⟨with much love
    Isaiah⟩

TO VED MEHTA

17 January 1963

New York

Dear Ved,

[...] The story about Namier[3] and me is not quite correct – even though Lady Namier[4] may have told it to you so. What occurred was that Namier came to see me and took away a copy of my book on *Historical Inevitability* – or I may have sent it to him – because I refer to him in it. He did indeed

---

1 Vera *Weizmann (1882–1966) née Chatzman, wife of Chaim Weizmann.

2 Richard *Crossman (1907–74), Labour politician and committed Zionist. His *A Nation Reborn: The Israel of Weizmann, Bevin and Ben-Gurion* was published in London in 1960.

3 Lewis Bernstein Namier (1888–1960) né Ludwik Niemirowski, Kt 1952, historian; Political Secretary of the Jewish Agency for Palestine 1929–31, Professor of Modern History, Manchester, 1931–53. IB published a memoir of him in 1966, repr. in PI.

4 Namier had married (secondly) 1947 Iulia (Julia) Mikhailovna de Beausobre (1893–1977) née Kazarina; her biography *Lewis Namier* was published in NY in 1971.

write to me and say, 'You must indeed be very clever to understand what you say',[1] which amused me greatly. This letter remained in my private possession until E. H. Carr also came to tea, and to him I told this story as an example of Namier's mordant humour. Carr thereupon published it in some Sunday paper or told someone who published it. I did not mind very much, but Namier thought I must be terribly upset and wrote me a long letter explaining that this did not represent his genuine attitude towards me, hoping that I had not taken it amiss, wondering who could have been such a cad as to have given it to a gossip-columnist, etc., etc. I wrote him a letter reassuring him on this score, saying that our friendship and my veneration for him were unimpaired. However, all this really does not matter. I may be thin-skinned, but not quite as thin-skinned as this. I am sure that Lady Namier will write a most distinguished biography of her husband, but I do not think the facts will be quite right, as he himself was not always absolutely scrupulous – sometimes telling one thing, sometimes another – I have several variants of this kind in my memory, but never mind. One day I shall write a sketch of him myself. He was one of the most remarkable men I ever knew. [...] Namier's attitude towards [A. J. P.] Taylor near the end of his life was one of undisguised hostility, so far as conversations with me were concerned. He thought he had betrayed his gifts, and after the fuss about the Regius Professorship, as you know, Taylor broke off relations, which hurt Namier and increased his already highly uncharitable interpretation of Taylor's entire behaviour, both intellectual and personal, in the last five or six years.[2] He, Namier, was in some respects not unlike Karl Marx both in genius and in character. But this is another story and needs qualification. I am not surprised that Butterfield[3] should defend Taylor's book, but I think I know what Namier would have said – the idea that he would have partly approved and partly disapproved is not compatible with anything that he said about Taylor and about the origins of the war to me and to many other people. But never mind, your sources are yours, and your conclusions too. But I think Trevor-Roper is quite right. Taylor would never have published this book if the Master had still been alive. Never! And rightly not. So Namier's death is a tragedy in more than one respect. [...]

Yours ever,

⟨Isaiah Berlin⟩

1 For the detail of this affair, and IB's letter to Namier of 25 May 1956, see L2 530/1, 531.

2 Taylor was appointed to a lectureship at Manchester University in 1930, and there 'came under the influence, which he later denied, of his professor, Lewis Namier'. The latter's support was crucial in securing Taylor's return to Oxford in 1938 as a Fellow of Magdalen; Namier, however, played an undisclosed role in Taylor's failure to be appointed Regius Professor in 1957, an affair that 'remains a subject of uncertain legend, but it did not prevent an embittered man denigrating the university he loved' (A. F. Thompson on Taylor, ODNB).

3 Herbert Butterfield (1900–79), later (1968) Kt; Professor of Modern History, Cambridge, 1944–63, Regius Professor 1963–8, Master of Peterhouse 1955–68. For the book see 47/2.

TO JACK DONALDSON

[18? January] 1963

Lowell House, Harvard

I was just about to write you a long gossipy letter about music, Covent Garden etc. but everything has been knocked out of my head by Hugh Gaitskell's death.[1] I can imagine your distress must be greater than mine, for you have known him far longer and were a real friend to him whereas I merely knew him and liked him. It seems to me a fearful disaster from every point of view. These are the moments when I know, and do not merely believe, that Prof. E. H. Carr and the Marxists are wickedly wrong – that personal factors and chance and luck enter history in the most obvious way and to deny this is fanaticism and evasion and a kind of cowardice. I shall be home soon – call collect.

Isaiah

TO JACK STEPHENSON[2]

[21 January 1963, *carbon*]

[Lowell House, Harvard]

Dear Jack,

Distances are too wide, my life is too scattered. How are you? I understand very well about the weekends with your mother – to whom please give my fondest affection. My mother too is getting no younger and I feel guilt about not living in the same town and leaving her alone for so much of the time – supposing her servant suddenly pegs out in some way, what then? Alone in that house? This worries me in the evenings and at nights, less so during the daytime when I am busy with other things. [...] I am here in order to finish three books ostensibly – it is easier not to finish three books than not to finish one – but everyone is very hospitable, I know this University well since this is virtually the fourth occasion that I have been here and I know the kinds of things to do in order not to finish my books, like giving lectures and talks on the grounds that one must, that it makes a bad impression if one refuses all invitations, etc. The fact is that I overdo it and regret it and exhaust myself, and write articles on philosophy for West African papers which appear in the *Sunday Times*[3] – I'm glad you did not think it too obscure or useless for

---

1 Gaitskell died at the Middlesex Hospital on the evening of Friday 18 January from systemic lupus erythematosus, an autoimmune disease uncommon in men which had run an unusually rapid and aggressive course.

2 John Vere Stephenson (1909–73), a St Paul's School contemporary of IB 1922–8, and lifelong friend; read classics at Jesus, Cambridge, 1928–32; civil servant.

3 'The Purpose of Philosophy', *Insight* (Nigeria) 1 no. 1 (July 1962), 12–15, commissioned by Viscount (Anthony) Head, 1st UK High Commissioner, Nigeria, 1960–3; repr. in the *Sunday Times*, 4 November 1962, 23, 26.

your pupils – and so on and so on. I have not the slightest faith in anything I write myself. It is exactly like money – if you make it yourself it seems a forgery. [...] This is no doubt a most neurotic attitude towards one's work, but certainly absurd objectively speaking. Yet I have felt it all my life. Hence total lack of confidence in anything I do. No doubt psychoanalysts could explain this – perhaps explain it away – perhaps even alter it– but still it is too late for an old dog to learn new tricks. So I suppose I shall remain much as I am. I was much distressed by Gaitskell's death. I knew him and liked him; he was a very intelligent and honourable man. I find it difficult to conceive a government under Mr Brown[1] – still more so under Mr Wilson.[2]

Meanwhile, my love and devotion and belated wishes for a Happy New Year to you and Betty.

Yours,

[Isaiah]

TO GLADWYN GLADWYN

Postmark 24 January 1963 [*carbon*]

Lowell House, Harvard

Carissimo barone,

I shall never attempt to write to you by hand again – the labour is too great, the risks of mis-cyphering too many. I very greatly enjoyed your letter. Let me, before I go any further, say sadly that we cannot go to the isles of Greece this summer – terribly tempting though it is – for we are tied to our solid Italian coast by the exigencies of my stepchildren, whose dates do not fit the cruise, and are determined by their father – the whole thing is alas not unscramblable. I am much upset by Hugh's death. It seems to me to be a great disaster. He was intelligent, honourable, perceptive, and not unimaginative: he really did not suffer from Attlee's xenophobia,[3] was a rational being and combined principle and expediency in what seemed to me an almost ideal way. He was, I think, occasionally wrong, but less so than anyone else in post-war British politics. Public faces seem, on the whole, ter-

---

1 George Alfred Brown (1914–85), later (1970) life peer; Deputy Leader, Labour Party, 1960–70; First Secretary of State and Secretary of State for Economic Affairs 1964–6; Foreign Secretary 1966–8; lost to Harold Wilson the February 1963 leadership contest that followed Gaitskell's death.

2 (James) Harold Wilson (1916–95), became, under Attlee, September 1947, the youngest cabinet minister since Peel; soundly beaten by Gaitskell in a leadership contest in November 1960, he defeated George Brown to become Labour Party Leader in February 1963; Prime Minister 1964–70, 1974–6; Leader of the Opposition 1963–4, 1970–4. Where George Brown had a reputation for volatility and drunkenness, but was considered fundamentally honest and courageous, Wilson was regarded as a brilliant, but untrustworthy, opportunist.

3 Clement Richard Attlee (1883–1967), OM 1951, 1st Earl Attlee 1955, KG 1956, Labour statesman; Deputy Prime Minister 1942–5, Prime Minister 1945–51; Leader of the Opposition 1951–5. IB believed him to be anti-Semitic (568), which may be behind his adverse judgement here.

30.4.74

rible to me: one can admire, be fascinated, approve, be excited by, etc. but for the most part they are, in virtue of being in public life, inhuman in some way: too brassy or too brutal or made of some non-human substance – too coarse and unscrupulous for private relationships, and this seems to me to hold for successful and unsuccessful politicians more or less equally, i.e. both for Churchill and for Crossman. Gaitskell seemed to me to have retained his human properties and to possess a conscience which neither tortured nor hampered him. But I must stop writing an obituary.

From here England seems a very small island indeed – I quite see why – the sense of its being a satellite is not something which even Anglophiles even shy at – the White House really is an extraordinary affair – the first real court that this country has ever had [...].

Yours,

Isaiah

IB's essay 'Does Political Theory Still Exist?', first published in French in 1961, appeared in its original English form in a 1962 collection of essays.[1] According to one reviewer, 'His answer is extremely nuancé but definitely hopeful.'[2] Richard Crossman, in a review in the Manchester Guardian,[3] *was less charitable, both about the collection as a whole and about IB's article. He lamented the fact that most of the contributors – IB included – were 'unable either to commit themselves to a political philosophy or even to theorise about any aspect of politics. [...] Academic political philosophy, like academic economics, has become a mental discipline as sterile as it is strenuous, which sends its student out into the world equipped with ingenious justifications for political inactivity and social disbelief.' As a professor of social and political theory IB could hardly allow such an assault to go unchallenged, especially one by an ex-colleague with ambitions to become a minister in the next Labour government, and known to be 'vigorously and ominously interested in reform of a kind unlikely to be friendly to Oxford and Cambridge'.[4]*

TO RICHARD CROSSMAN

31 January 1963

Headington House

Dear Dick,

I have procured a copy of the *Manchester Guardian* with your review, and although I wish I hadn't ... You are back at your old bone, I see, on which

1 Peter Laslett and W. G. Runciman (eds), *Philosophy, Politics and Society*, 2nd series (Oxford, 1962).
2 [A. H. Hanson], TLS, 3 May 1963, 318.
3 Richard Crossman, 'Opium of the intellectuals', *Guardian*, 21 December 1962, 8.
4 A. H. Halsey, 'The Franks Commission', in Brian Harrison (ed.), *The History of the University of Oxford*, vol. 8, *The Twentieth Century* (Oxford, 1994), 723.

you gnaw and gnaw – the fiddling dons of Oxford, dreary and craven pedants engaged in their petty and destructive tasks while worlds are crashing and great problems are crying out for solution. I doubt whether you are just even to the Enemy in the late 1920s and early 1930s about whom you so furiously circle, but what you say is not true nor just about the authors of this book. [...] The most typical of the present-day political philosophers represented in that book is certainly Williams, who is a passionate socialist, not in addition to, but as part and parcel of, his particular kind of rationalism, which makes him about the most successful teacher of philosophy in London at present – his TV performances and the excitement he imparts to his young people spring directly out of his deep preoccupation with political issues – there is no lack of positive doctrine there, or lack of desire to face contemporary issues, or indeed, of success in doing so. [...]

As for my poor self – my title, which you think characteristically subtle and cautious, was not invented by me, but set me by the French political periodical to whose symposium I contributed it:[1] so for that you must blame all those Hegelians and Marxists in Paris. As for my statement that there is no dominant political treatise in the twentieth century – or whatever it was – I stand by it [...]. Well do I remember a conversation between you and Richard Pares,[2] somewhere in the early 1930s, about whether *Mein Kampf* was a more important work of political theory than someone Richard was standing up for – I think Tawney or Graham Wallas.[3] I think there is no denying that Hitler was more influential in the short run, and, if effects of effects are counted, perhaps in the long run too, but it is not that that counts – what stands up to the ravages of time is intellectual depth and power, not tracts in which the mind is chained to immediate practical purposes, and never rises beyond that. Lenin's only serious work on political theory, *State and Revolution*,[4] half sunk as even that is under the weight of dead polemics, has less relevance to the theory and practice of Communism than any of his or anybody else's Communist works – would you not agree?

I see no harm in teaching people how to see through bad arguments and shabby reasoning and sloppiness and emotion disguised as argument – in fact, others do it much more skilfully and well than I do, for I am perhaps

---

1 'La théorie politique existe-t-elle?', *Revue française de science politique* 11 (1961), 309–37 (English version in CC and PSM). ⟨handwritten note⟩

2 Richard Pares (1902–58), historian; Fellow of All Souls 1921–45, 1954–8; Professor of History, Edinburgh, 1945–54; 'perhaps the most admired and looked up to of the Oxford teachers of his generation' (PI2 122).

3 Graham Wallas (1858–1932), Professor of Political Science, London, 1914–23; socialist, member of the Fabian Society; author of *Human Nature in Politics* (London, 1908) and *The Great Society: A Psychological Analysis* (London, 1914). Tawney's works include *Equality* (London, 1931).

4 V. Il'in (N. Lenin) [sc. Vladimir Il'ich Lenin], *The State and Revolution: The Marxist Doctrine of the State and the Task of the Proletariat in the Revolution* (Petrograd, 1918; English eds, Detroit/Melbourne, 1918), predicted a 'dictatorship of the proletariat' (*passim*) that would supplant the bourgeois State and lead to a new, eventually Stateless, world order.

much too fascinated by the historical evolution of ideas and patterns of thought, and am blamed with some justice for being insufficiently analytic, in trying to inject too much life into the discredited ideas of dead reactionaries and revolutionaries. If scholasticism is what you want to attack, Russia, China and the Church of Rome go in for this far more than our Western universities, which are almost over-scrupulous in trying to get inside the ideas of their opponents, and are despised for it by them. In the early nineteenth century the German metaphysical patriots – Jahn,[1] Arndt[2] and such – complained of the professors for being professorial and scholarly and not arming the young men sufficiently in defence of the German nation and German ideals. And in due course there arose the Treitschkes and the Sybels[3] and the other political professors who thundered away and supplied plenty of ideology for 1871 and 1914. Surely Meinecke's *Die Deutsche Katastrophe*[4] – one of the noblest tracts of our times – is a sufficient answer to those who want professors to plug political programmes and ideologies, however sincere and eloquent? I honestly think that you are trying to revive some very dead old horses, with verve and skill and literary gifts worthy of a better cause.

Myself, I am caught between all fires: you think me a cautious and subtle evader and craven pedant; almost everyone else blames me for intemperate polemics, over-wild generalisations, insufficient caution and dedication to minute analysis, and not enough intellectual neutralism. So I'm damned if I do, and I'm damned if I don't. Still, never mind about me. I wish to convince you that books like the one you reviewed, even if they are not particularly good of their kind, do more good, even politically, than programmatic statements would. [...] I fear I haven't convinced you. Still, you mustn't be so fierce and beat innocent dons about the head so much, just because they remind you of some unattractive ghosts in our common past. I still think your book on Plato[5] admirable, and am pleased to have written that blurb, even though I got panned for that too. If I thought you really thought the

---

1 Friedrich Ludwig Jahn (1778–1852), Prussian educator and nationalist who promoted gymnastics associations as a means of national regeneration after the defeat by Napoleon. Though he was regarded as a liberal reformer in his day, his ideas were appropriated by 19th-century German militarist nationalists.

2 Ernst Moritz Arndt (1769–1860), German prose-writer, poet and nationalist who emphasised the importance of language in defining German nationhood: 'he was infinitely nearer to reality than Fichte or the romanticists and he never descended to the coarseness and vulgarity of Jahn'. Hans Kohn, 'Arndt and the Character of German Nationalism', *American Historical Review* 54 no. 4 (July 1949), 802.

3 Heinrich Gotthard von Treitschke (1834–96), Prussian historian, writer and nationalist; anti-Semitic, anti-British – his insults against the English were applauded in crowded classrooms in the University of Berlin. Heinrich Karl Ludolf von Sybel (1817–95), German historian and politician, founded the historical journal *Historische Zeitschrift* 1859; Treitschke succeeded him as editor.

4 Friedrich Meinecke (1862–1954), German liberal historian, succeeded Treitschke as editor of *Historische Zeitschrift* 1896–1935; his *Die Deutsche Katastrophe: Betrachtungen und Erinnerungen* (Wiesbaden/Zürich, 1946) identified antecedents of Nazism in Prussian militarism.

5 R. H. S. Crossman, *Plato To-day* (London, 1937; 2nd ed., 1959).

thoughts you have expressed in that *Guardian* article, I honestly wouldn't have written this letter – but I believe that it is founded on a profoundly false impression of what is going on. Nothing you say will alter my belief that you don't wish to appear merely as a literary tiger who doesn't care whom he bites provided he slakes his thirst for blood.

No need to answer this, but I wish you would.

Yours,

⟨Isaiah⟩

TO RICHARD CROSSMAN

11 February 1963

Headington House

My dear Dick,

I am most grateful to you for replying to me at such length and with such attention to subjects for which you obviously can't have much time in your very active and busy life. [...]

I suspect that you *do* despise dons too much, particularly when they are minute, technical and professional in subjects which, I suspect you think, are ruined by such treatment, e.g. philosophy, economics, politics, and indeed the entire field of the humanities. It seems to me that what happens is that advance, at least since the Renaissance, was always made by what must have seemed to be abstruse and technical in its own day – Descartes, Leibniz, Kant, Hegel, and even Berkeley[1] and Hume must have seemed so to the best-educated & clearest-headed 'practical politicians'. The revolutions occur by piecemeal advances by 'technicians' of this kind, and then are popularised by the Lockes and Voltaires, the Rousseaus, Carlyles, Laskis etc., who may or may not be original themselves but certainly build on the comparatively abstruse writings of their predecessors or contemporaries [...].

Now as to Dahrendorf.[2] I agree with you rather than with Herbert Hart, who thinks Dahrendorf's article absolutely worthless, and a demonstration of the low standard among sociologists. I don't go so far as you: but it had the same effect on me as on you, namely it gave me a jolt and made me think. And nothing is more important in an essay, or perhaps I too go too far now – at any rate, nothing is better than a sharp jab of this sort unless it is some new, original truth. On re-reading Dahrendorf I now think that he

---

1 George Berkeley (1685–1753), philosopher, Bishop of Cloyne 1734–53; advanced the doctrine of immaterialism, which denies the reality of any external world beyond the mind (an approach often called subjective idealism), in *A Treatise Concerning the Principles of Human Knowledge*, part 1 (Dublin, 1710; no part 2 occurred).

2 Ralf Dahrendorf (1929–2009), later KBE (1982), life peer (1993); German-born sociologist and politician; Professor of Sociology, Tübingen, 1960–6; later Director, LSE (1974–84), Warden of St Antony's (1987–97) and British national (1988). In his review Crossman described Dahrendorf's essay 'On the Origins of Social Inequality' as 'easily the best contribution' to the book (142/1).

has simply repeated in a new and useful form what Pareto[1] has been saying all along about the circulation of elites, namely that there is always an in-group and an out-group, and that inequality is inherent in the very structure of society. Well now, I wonder: what does make some societies more equal than others? The fact, it seems to me, that among the ideas which form the constellation of values by which the society lives, and which is indispensable to its cohesion, must also be the idea of equality itself, that there are no natural inequalities, of birth or hereditary or physical or mental endowment, that one man is, on the whole, as good as another, etc. This may be false; it may be a myth; but provided that it is a central value in a given society, the in-group will never feel safe unless it allays the suspicions of the out-group on this score – and doesn't give the out-group the impression that they, the in-group, regard themselves as in some way specially entitled to govern. Of course, every society has to have somebody who orders and somebody who is ordered: this self-evident truth even Tawney (and, indeed, almost everyone who has written about equality) recognised – except, I suppose, out-and-out anarchists who think there is need neither of a government of persons nor even of the administration of things. But leaving them out, if you look con-cretely at societies which are attempts towards equality, say New Zealand or Australia (leaving out the Aborigines), or Scandinavia or Israel, all of which are obviously more equal than say England, which is a deference society essentially, still – the striking thing there is that the people in charge have to suck up to a very considerable degree to their electors, and govern in such a way that the man in the street is not too suspicious of any ambitions to perpetuate themselves on the part of the elite or any claim of special attributes or superior status on the part of the governing group. If they do suck up in this fashion, this itself does make such in-groups more open, more penetrable, easier to turn out – in fact, makes a democracy. [...]

And now, about Lindsay[2] and Laski.[3] About Lindsay I am prepared to com-promise. His ideas seem to me like huge buses looming out of a vast London fog and then being swallowed again in the darkness. Still, there were these

---

1 Vilfredo Federico Damaso Pareto (1848–1923), Italian economist and sociologist, made a pro-found contribution to methods of economic analysis (cf. the term 'Pareto optimal').

2 Alexander Dunlop Lindsay (1879–1952), 1st Baron Lindsay of Birker 1945; Master of Balliol 1924–49; Principal of University College of North Staffordshire (Keele University 1962) 1949–52; liberal thinker, author of *The Modern Democratic State* (London, 1943); unsuccessful anti-appeasement Independent Progressive candidate for Oxford City in a famous by-election in 1938 after the Munich agreement.

3 Harold Joseph Laski (1893–1950), Graham Wallas Professor of Political Science, LSE, 1926–50; member, executive committee, Labour Party, 1936–49, chairman 1945–6; successively a pluralist, Fabian and, in the 1930s, Marxist thinker: 'It has been widely held that his early books were the most profound and that he subsequently wrote far too much, with polemics displacing serious analysis. [...] Nevertheless, few people have devoted such energy to a sincere attempt to combine liberty, equality and internationalism in theoretical terms and to promote these ideals through teaching and participation in public life' (Michael Newman, ODNB).

giant shapes, and it was derived from T. H. Green[1] and men who certainly had something to say of great importance. I can understand very well why you learnt from him and I would not at all deny that you have a clear mind and in some ways rather intolerant intellectual standards. I knew Lindsay well and was fascinated by him as a politician and was influenced by him as a personality. I think he stood for something: and that his big book on democracy is perhaps unjustly neglected. […]

Laski is another matter. I do think he was a shallow rhetorician who, as Lindsay himself thought, ruined the subject. It isn't only that he was muddled in the sense that Lindsay was, but that if you read him with any problems in mind you will never never find anything approaching a solution. You speak about his thousands of students, or rather of his 'students all over the world who would find your description of him as "waterlogging the subject"[2] a ludicrous libel on a very great teacher'. If they did, they would be wrong. I have indeed met his pupils, in India, in Israel, in America, and in England too, I suppose. According to them, and I believe them, he was a brilliant lecturer, a very kind and dedicated teacher, a devoted teacher who adored his pupils, was very nice to his colleagues, took infinite trouble, excited and fascinated and provoked and dazzled. All that I am prepared to concede. But it seems to me that the proportion of ideas per page, so to speak, in his writings is ludicrously low, with the consequence that, while he had a powerful effect as a sincere socialist agitator – often dishonest but probably most of the time genuinely passionate – his effect upon his disciples was to make them mistake words for thoughts, and words about words for words about things. […] I think that Lindsay was somebody in the tradition which I respect no less than you, but I really think that Laski was its betrayer. Ernest Barker[3] talking in rapid platitudes from the right, Laski talking similar rot from the left – that, more than logical positivism, is what I think caused the whole thing to fold up, as well, no doubt, as external circumstances. You charge me with being too much a member of my generation: try to make young men today read Laski and see what happens. […] No intellectually first-rate person – in whatever walk of life – it seems to me, was shaped and made by Laski, as they were shaped and made by Lindsay, and Tawney, and the Balliol tradition generally, and perhaps by Graham Wallas, and the Fabians as well. Laski seems to me much more like one of those German social-democratic

---

1 Thomas Hill Green (1836–82), liberal Idealist philosopher; White's Professor of Moral Philosophy, Oxford, 1878–82; believed in active citizenship, and stressed the practical utility of philosophy, inculcating in a generation of public figures (e.g. H. H. Asquith) a 'semi-secular ethical progressivism' (H. C. G. Matthew on Asquith, ODNB).

2 In a part of his letter of 31 January not included here.

3 Ernest Barker (1874–1960), Kt 1944, political theorist; Professor of Political Science and Fellow of Peterhouse, Cambridge, 1928–39; a strong advocate of individual liberty; his writings contributed towards a revival of political pluralism in British politics and society in the late twentieth century; a vociferous supporter of Chamberlainite appeasement on the grounds of its 'realism'.

word-spinners who give the Weimar Republic its bad, not its good, name. I did hear him lecture once or twice; the fireworks were terrific and extremely enjoyable to listen to, but at the end of it, if you tried to remember what was said, nothing remained except a sensation of exhilaration. [...]

You are profoundly mistaken if you think that the current tradition of teaching politics in Oxford is to 'make monkeys' out of the great philosophers. Of course I remember the things you refer to. How Locke or Plato were taught in such a way that it became impossible to understand why they had ever acquired any reputation, considering that they uttered fallacies that any first-year undergraduate could easily expose.

You say that you read the book right through – not my piece, I fear. I do not say that it deserved it: but if you had read it to the end you would surely have seen that my whole thesis was that political theory was the succession of great patterns or models which liberated men from previous patterns or models and then in their turn became stereotyped; that they illuminated what other models had obscured but then usually obscured what the others had illuminated; and that people go back to old models when the situation is such that something analogous to the old predicaments and problems recur. The first thing, therefore, in trying to understand a political theory is to grasp where the shoe pinched – what were the social circumstances, what were the questions that were agonising, and why the new model – society organised geometrically, as by Plato, or biologically, as by Aristotle, or atomically, as by the Stoics, or the great metaphors of the social contract or organism or the general will or base and superstructure or whatever it may be – seemed so liberating and illuminating and got such a grip on the imaginations of societies and their teachers: that first, before the muddles and inconsistencies and incoherencies could be attended to. Otherwise of course the whole intellectual history of mankind becomes unintelligible, and with it the function and effect of social or political theories.

[...] I still think you have an allergy to Oxford and all its ways: that you think of it entirely in terms of the worst pedantries of the 1930s and that what he who runs cannot read is not worth reading. If you will only let me, I should like to have a crack at convincing you that you are not altogether fair.

Yours ever,

Isaiah   [...]

TO RICHARD CROSSMAN

6 March 1963 [*typescript heavily corrected in manuscript*]

Headington House

My dear Dick,

If I did not reply to your last letter at once, it was mainly inspired by a desire to spare you; I don't know why this weakened [...].

Why does nobody write a major work on political philosophy? It may be because the main objections to our way of life are not political, and perhaps not even economic, but social: and social philosophy has no academic discipline, no tradition of pure argument; it breeds either (often local and trivial) sociological accumulations of data on the one hand, or huge, vapid American balloons out of Durkheim[1] or Weber[2] on the other; also, there is no major masterpiece because nobody hates our political system quite enough – not really – or feels it threatened enough, *in fact*. If Communism were a greater immediate menace in England, I think it would evoke a proper debate: but nobody is prepared to die for capitalism anywhere in Europe; people are prepared for a modified collectivism; & haggling about how much is not an issue of principle; in America they do not feel threatened enough. Masterpieces, I suspect, are produced in siege conditions – not necessarily in the midst of wars and upheavals, but as in the case of Hume, who felt the terrible tremors in France, and thought the radicals had gone too far and was terrified of the consequences.[3] We seem in a condition of taking Russia for granted and the Cold War for granted and the atom bomb for granted; there is no real ideological warfare tearing out entrails in England today – not as there was in the 1930s and perhaps even the middle 1940s. The 'angry' literature today is about corrupting education – the 'religious' element in all the talk about alienation, in CND, in all the loose Rousseauism–D. H. Lawrenceism [...] is very clear – false cultural values, social disintegration, not about why X should obey Y, or 'Who whom?', which is presumably what politics is about; the complaints are against a psychological malaise, hypocrisy, lack of love, lack of understanding, lack of acceptance, 'alienation', class consciousness and class education, etc., and not oppression of the majority by a wicked or

1 Émile Durkheim (1858–1917), French sociologist, regarded as one of the founders of the modern discipline; the first professor of sociology at the Sorbonne (1913).

2 Max(imilian) Carl Emil Weber (1864–1920), German philosopher and economist, and one of the founders of modern sociology; author of *Die protestantische Ethik und der Geist des Kapitalismus* (1904–5, revised 1920), trans. Talcott Parsons as *The Protestant Ethic and the Spirit of Capitalism* (London/NY, 1930).

3 Hume wrote his *A Treatise of Human Nature* (London, 1739–40) in La Flèche in France, but it is not clear what IB would mean by 'the terrible tremors in France' if this is the work he has in mind, since the French Revolution was still 50 years in the future. Edmund Burke's *Reflections on the Revolution in France* (London, 1790) would make more sense, though IB's remarks would then be an understatement.

deluded minority, corrupt bureaucracies, some groups of rascals – Dawson[1] and Chamberlain,[2] as it were, or Attlee and Bevan,[3] or Gaitskell and Brown – who must be turned out. However sociological the approach, however anti-aesthetic, it is not a cry for justice or political and economic equality or participation in government or nationalism and anti-nationalism; it is not utilitarian or anti-utilitarian, for or against individual values and liberties; but much more like Christian Socialism – a plea for a spiritually integrated society and the destruction of barriers, and a plea for some sort of peaceful, gentle, little-England-ish rational social order based on psychological and sociological information and hypotheses. This is not political at all, or if that is too strong, it has much more to do with juvenile delinquency or the collapse of faith in God or parents, or the social order, than with anything that Marx or Lenin, let alone Mill, or even you and I are, or used to be, interested in. This is an essentially anti-political mood, and it is worldwide – one finds it in Russia and Germany as much as here, and certainly it is prevalent in America, and I suspect elsewhere as well. No demand, no supply: it seems to me that this is a better explanation than wicked, fiddling logical positivists: or rather that we are a by-product of the same *Zeitgeist*.

But that they have their own share of blame to bear, I don't deny.

Yours,

Isaiah   [...]

TO STEVEN LUKES[4]

4 April 1963

Headington House

Dear Lukes,

Thank you for the article,[5] about which I shall [say] something in a moment. I should love to discuss it with you – unfortunately, I leave for France on Sunday and return on the 14th only to go to hospital for an operation [...].

---

1 (George) Geoffrey Dawson (1874–1944) né Robinson; Fellow of All Souls 1898–1906, 1911–44; Editor, *The Times*, 1912–19, 1923–41; regarded by Bob Boothby in the late 1930s as 'the Secretary General of the Establishment, the fervent advocate of appeasement': Robert Rhodes James, *Bob Boothby: A Portrait* (London, 1991), 175.

2 (Arthur) Neville Chamberlain (1869–1940), Chancellor of the Exchequer 1923–4, 1931–7; Minister of Health 1924–9; Prime Minister 1937–40; the champion, though by no means the sole architect, of the discredited policy of appeasement, whose apotheosis was his triumphal return from the Munich Conference, September 1938, at which it was agreed, in Czechoslovakia's absence, that Nazi Germany should annexe the Czechs' Sudetenland.

3 Aneurin ('Nye') Bevan (1897–1960), South Wales miner and miners' leader; Minister of Health in Attlee's post-war government 1945–51; Minister of Labour and National Service 1951; the driving force behind the creation of the National Health Service in 1948.

4 Steven Michael Lukes (b. 1941), political and social theorist; graduate student, Nuffield, 1962–4, Research Fellow 1964–6; Fellow of Balliol 1966–88, University Lecturer in Politics 1967–88.

5 Graeme Duncan and Steven Lukes, 'The New Democracy', *Political Studies* 11 no. 2 (1963), 156–77. A footnote (176/4) was added in the published text in response to IB's objections.

I am in sincere agreement with the tenor of the entire piece – particularly with the polemic against the proposition that because certain samples of voters demonstrate apathy, ignorance etc. this is (a) an incurable and (b) a desirable state of affairs. The whole notion of consensus is suspect, it seems to me; it smacks too much of the arguments for tacit social contracts which take apathy and 'alienated' attitudes on the part of the public towards the government – like that, say, of peasants in most countries at most times, or of most non-Nazi Germans under Hitler – as equivalent to consent, and is in fact the basis of most of the specious conservative argumentation, from Burke onwards, against the active participation by individuals in the running of their own society – leaving things to specialists, elites, professionals etc. which goes with the notion of politics as either too important or too dishonourable (or both) for the average decent individual. There is much to say about all this – it all began with the Stoics etc., but about that we can talk later.

In the meanwhile, you ask whether I am annoyed about the quotation from my lecture. I am. You place me in the company of persons who represent apathy as a *sine qua non* of peaceful government, and that of anti-democrats in general. It is true that by negative liberty I do mean freedom from interference, but (a) I do not think that this must be defended at all costs against other values, such as justice, welfare and the development of all kinds of social faculties and attributes which all vigorous societies must possess – at most I only defend a minimum area which must not be invaded, and seek to establish that these other equally important values, in favour of which liberty should on occasions be pushed aside, should not themselves be called liberty, else there is intellectual confusion and wickedness in action; (b) that the desire to be determined by oneself and not external forces is basic, and it is only its perversion that has led to totalitarian consequences – in your version, I am in the company of those who warn against it as such, as likely to lead to the subversion of liberalism; (c) there is nothing that I have ever written that militates against democracy – i.e. the desire for the maximum possible participation by individuals in their common life – even Constant,[1] from whom I certainly derive, thinks that democracy is the only safeguard for any degree of individual liberty, even though some democracies have crushed it more than some enlightened despotisms. So I think it is grossly unfair to put me in this company, and misrepresents my position thoroughly. Hence I should be obliged if you would leave me out altogether.

[...] I neither say nor believe that only where the electorate is reasonably apathetic can individual liberty survive or good government flourish. The

---

1 (Henri-)Benjamin Constant (de Rebecque) (1767–1830), Swiss-born liberal political thinker, active in French politics under Napoleon, and later the Bourbons; his advocacy of individual freedom against the potential tyranny of the group made him strongly critical of the ideas of his compatriot, Rousseau.

most vigorous egalitarian societies today, say Denmark or Israel or New Zealand, do not conspicuously crush individual liberties or democratic action; yet it looks in your text as though I am likely to maintain the opposite. I therefore demand justice! [...]

So let me (*a*) enter my protest, and (*b*) encourage you to visit me in hospital or make a date with me in Oxford in early May.

Yours sincerely,

Isaiah Berlin

TO ANNA KALLIN[1]

[Early April 1963, *manuscript*]

Headington House

Dearest Нюта![2]

Я не умею писать по русски: ни слов ни чувств. Есть как будто что сказать а слова и даже буквы не идут: может быть потому что я пересталъ мыслить по русски еще ребенком – и поэтому только 'детское' умею выражать на этом языке. Простите мне [sc. меня] – я перейду на неуютный, неличный неинтимный английский язык.[3] I know, I know that you were expecting it for years, and yet when it happens it is not as one expects it, and much worse, and nothing is ever the same. It was so when my father died, and I dread the moment when I am left without my mother, dread it exceedingly. In a way I think that your mother[4] was terribly fortunate: to be uprooted from one's native soil is awful enough: but it is tolerable only if a link remains and no matter how much you quarrelled and made up this very process was a timeless Russian proceeding and preserved continuity and saved your mother (and perhaps you also) from total Entfremdung.[5] My poor mama really is alone: I come to see her & quarrel too, but not enough: I feel guilt, but know no remedy. Solitude i.e. not having enough people who understand what we say, is a fate to which we, выходцы из вост[очной] Европы,[6] have to accustom ourselves – & never shall. So was your mother very tired when she died? I hope so. It is worse when persons full of desire to go on living – in violent fear of death, die. 91 is a marvellous age: & it is the living whom one loves and feels for. Of dear! All words are like sticks when one tries to say *anything* – nothing, nothing emerges – I only want to

1 Anna ('Niouta') *Kallin (1896–1984), IB's BBC Third Programme radio producer.
2 'Nyuta' (diminutive: Anna > Ania > Aniouta > Nyuta/Niouta).
3 'I can't write in Russian: neither words nor feelings. There are things that I want to say, but the words and even the letters won't come: maybe this is because I stopped thinking in Russian when I was still a child – so I can only express "childish" things in that language. Forgive me – I'll change to the comfortable, impersonal, non-intimate English language.'
4 Ida Kallin (1871/2–1963), wife of Samuel Kallin (1871/2–1941).
5 'Alienation'.
6 'East European expatriates'.

say that I was terribly moved by the fact that you wrote as you did [...]. вот и все, совсем недостаточно и выходитъ сухо и все о себе а остальное так и остается недосказанным и никогда вероятно сказано не будет. А пока нужно routine продолжать и быть молодцом и держаться во всю: а зачем – не ясно. Вот толко какой то еврейский атавизм – дисциплина – живем у чужих[1] – no concessions – no yielding – carry on etc.

I feel this *very* strongly: a member of an imaginary army, which keeps being decimated & destroyed, but keeps marching to an unknown but obligatory goal – Kafka[2] etc. But I must not go on. This is only to wish you marvellously well: if you are in a *possible* mood come to the director's Box on Saturday night – only my mother Aline Michel [Strauss] Stuart & I – you need wear nothing (Don Carlos)

Fondest love

Шая[3]

TO JACK DONALDSON

29 May 1963

Headington House

Dear Jack,

I enclose a cutting from the *Sunday Express* of an article[4] by my sadly fallen colleague A. J. P. Taylor, who, as Lord Robbins informed us at the board, was universally despised, which is unlikely to give you pleasure. I had some rather insincere condolences from John Denison, while Burnet Pavitt was genuinely shocked by what he thought the horrible nastiness of the author. Garrett has complained to Max Aitken (a lot of good that will do) and called it a day. Taylor has indeed become a sort of delighting dog in Lord Beaverbrook's pack, prepared to snap and bite at any unarmed passer-by – this is merely part of the general anti-culture campaign which the *Evening Standard* has conducted for years. Taylor, ever since he failed to get professorships, glories in his prostitution – he is not a very wicked man by nature, but is now a pathetic mountebank, I fear. What is less agreeable is that David Webster not only adored the piece but did not at all mind telling me so: how can you like a man who does that? [...]

1 'That's all, nowhere near enough, and it comes out all dry and only about myself, and the rest will remain not fully expressed, and will probably never be said. Meanwhile one has to continue with the routine and be brave and hold on like hell: but it is not clear why. This is just some sort of Jewish atavism – discipline – we live among strangers.'

2 Franz Kafka (1883–1924), German-speaking Prague-born Jewish novelist whose works deal with the isolation and alienation of the individual and the oppressive nightmare of existence.

3 'Shaya', affectionate family diminutive of 'Isaiah', also used by friends of IB's earlier years.

4 In 'Why Must You Pay for the Culture Snobs?', *Sunday Express*, 26 May 1963, 16, Taylor drew attention to the wealth and influence of the board of governors at the ROH, among them 'Sir Isaiah Berlin, CBE, well-known socialite, who is also Professor of Social and Political Theory at Oxford University – a cultural, though not a very tuneful subject', arguing: 'Covent Garden gets its subsidy because of its standing in High Society, not because of its artistic value.'

In the meanwhile, I have an uneasy feeling that if the Beaverbrook press and the left wing of the Socialists get together on the subject of having a swipe at upper-class culture, Third Programme,[1] Covent Garden and that kind of thing, damage could ensue. That we shall not really protect ourselves adequately against that by appointing a nice, gentle, serious, really worthy person like Bernard Williams, although of course we ought to do it in fact. And that we ought to have something more powerful to protect us: (a) an honest-to-God composer – if not Britten, because he doesn't want to come, then Tippett;[2] if not Tippett, then Lennox Berkeley.[3] It does not matter if they are positively useful or not – there is a limit to which [sc. how far] we can eliminate professional musicians from our midst. And Solti needs some control. Moreover, I myself would be in favour of admitting Lord Boothby.[4] He will madden everyone, but if we lose Walter, he would be far more loyal in a way, even though naughty, and would, if requested to do so, defend us powerfully and successfully in every medium known to man; give much better than he got; and altogether do for us what Brendan Bracken[5] did for the Ministry of Information, which, because people were frightened of being mocked publicly by him, got far less attacked in the House of Commons when he took over than at any previous time.

[…] I have now arrived at the considered conclusion that he [David] is in fact not a nice man, does not wish us well, is not interested in opera, but merely carries on the business as competently as he can because that's the kind of man he is; that he likes competence and likes his own position, but that he really likes none of us and on the whole thinks Bagrit[6] is worth the lot because there is no nonsense about aesthetics and one can talk on a jolly business basis. Believe me, I do not exaggerate.[7] I know one can soften him and talk to him in a jolly

1 BBC radio's third national network (after the Home Service and the Light Programme), which began broadcasting in September 1946 and was later (1970) absorbed into the new Radio 3; it was unashamedly highbrow in content, and claimed a tiny listenership.
2 Michael Kemp Tippett (1905–98), later (1966) Kt, English composer, known especially for his oratorio *A Child of Our Time* (1944).
3 Lennox Randall Francis Berkeley (1903–89), later (1974) Kt, English composer; Professor of Composition at the Royal Academy of Music 1946–68; close friend of Benjamin Britten.
4 Robert John Graham ('Bob') Boothby (1900–86), KBE 1953, life peer 1958, Conservative politician; briefly a minister in Churchill's wartime government before being forced to resign over a financial impropriety. President of the Anglo-Israel Association 1962–75. His television and radio appearances on current affairs programmes had made him a household name: '[he] has led a none too dignified personal life, but has seldom been wrong about a political issue' (IB to Teddy Kollek, 14 April 1970).
5 Brendan Bracken (1901–58), 1st Viscount Bracken 1952, Conservative politician; Churchill's wartime 'brash, tough, cynical, political "fixer"'; his appointment as Minister of Information (1941–5) 'raised eyebrows – and turned out to be a master-stroke' (Jason Tomes, ODNB).
6 Leon Bagrit (1902–79), Kt 1962; Deputy Chairman, Elliot-Automation Ltd, 1957–62; Chairman 1963–73; Director, Technology Investments Ltd, from 1963; Director, ROH, 1962–70; Founder, Friends of Covent Garden, 1962, Chairman 1962–9.
7 IB wrote to Garrett Drogheda, 12 February 1964, about Webster's reaction to the news that he [IB] was resigning from the ROH board: 'I have just told D.W. about my departure – not even

manner on a good-fellow basis, and I have done it myself in the past, but there really is something tiresome about a man with whom you can get on provided you keep off opera, casting, policy etc., while as soon as these subjects are mentioned he grows sulky, bored, resentful etc. I do not say that we should have got on better with someone like Bing, but there must be competent managers like Mr Bean[1] who can do the business side while retaining a very high ratio of human niceness, decency and idealism.

Do let me know as soon as you get back, and I shall report the latest developments on the front.

Yours,

Isaiah

In the second half of 1961 John Profumo,[2] Secretary of State for War, had a brief affair with Christine Keeler,[3] a glamorous young model and showgirl, who was also involved with Evgeny Ivanov, the Soviet naval attaché in London.[4] Ivanov and Keeler were both friends of Stephen Ward,[5] a society osteopath whose clients included Viscount Astor;[6] it was at a party at Astor's Cliveden estate that Profumo had first encountered Keeler, swimming naked in the pool. In December 1961, having been warned off any association with Ward and his circle by the cabinet secretary, Profumo ended his relationship with Keeler. But her embarrassing disclosures about their affair induced him to mislead the Prime Minister's aides about its true nature, and then, in an act of political suicide, to deny categorically in the House of Commons, on 22 March 1963, that there had ever been any impropriety. Direct evidence to the contrary mounted, as journalists and politicians probed the Ivanov link, and the possibility that national security had been compromised. It had not, but Profumo's private indiscretion

---

a tear – what a dry-eyed crocodile! *How* he despises us all (including Jack who insists on loving him)! all except Bagrit – possibly – whom he thinks vaguely formidable.'

1 Thomas Ernest Bean (1900–83), Assistant Circulation Manager, *Manchester Guardian*, 1928–44; General Manager, Hallé Concerts Society, Manchester, 1944–51, Royal Festival Hall, London, 1951–65; secretary, London Orchestral Concert Board, 1965–71.

2 John Dennis ('Jack') Profumo (1915–2006), 5th Baron of the Kingdom of Italy; Conservative MP 1940–5, 1950–63, Secretary of State for War 1960–3 (resigned 4 June 1963); his public rehabilitation was sealed with a CBE in 1975 in recognition of his services to charity.

3 Christine Margaret Keeler (b. 1942), dancer, model and escort; the subject of an iconic 1960s image, shot by Lewis Morley, which depicts her sitting naked on a strategically placed Arne Jacobsenesque 'ant chair'.

4 Evgeny Mikhailovich Ivanov (1926–94), assistant naval attaché and intelligence officer at the Soviet embassy in London 1960–3.

5 Stephen Thomas Ward (1912–63), osteopath and artist. Among his society clients was William Waldorf ('Bill') Astor, 3rd Viscount Astor (next note), who leased him a cottage in the grounds of Cliveden for a peppercorn rent. From 1959 Ward lived intermittently, but not intimately, with Christine Keeler; after Profumo's disgrace Ward was made a scapegoat, and was found guilty at the Old Bailey on charges of pimping; he took a fatal overdose on the morning of the last day of his trial.

6 William Waldorf ('Bill') Astor (1907–66), 3rd Viscount Astor 1952; Conservative MP for East Fulham 1935–45; for Wycombe, Bucks, 1951–2.

had now become a public lie. With his wife's encouragement he determined to make a clean breast of it, and on 4 June 1963 admitted in a letter of resignation to the Prime Minister that he had deliberately misled his colleagues and Parliament.

   The Profumo scandal came at a time of increasing permissiveness in society – the Lady Chatterley case was fresh in the memory – and led to a national debate on standards of morality in public life. There was a sense of changing eras, epitomised by the ageing Harold Macmillan, who was completely wrong-footed by the scandal, and appeared to be losing his grip on power. That October he resigned.

TO ROWLAND BURDON-MULLER

20 June 1963

Headington House

Dear Rowland,

   […] I am in no better position to tell you about the Profumo case than anybody else. I do not really know anything extra. Lord Hailsham[1] spent the weekend at All Souls and gave a fairly coherent account of the chronological situation, which was more or less revealed by the Prime Minister's speech in the House of Commons the other day, so I won't go over that. The extraordinary thing, I suppose, is Profumo's marvellous boldness in lying – to sue for libel when one knows that one has acted in a discoverably culpable way takes some nerve. Oddly enough, nobody has complained about his dago origins: some say the family comes from Sicily, others Sardinia, others Trieste. His father was a K.C., his grandfather certainly Italian, his mother English and very wealthy.[2] His brother-in-law, Lord Balfour of Inchrye, wrote quite a brave letter to The Times[3] – he is one of Lord Beaverbrook's minions, which is why, perhaps, the Daily Express didn't go after Profumo as much as it might have done – saying what a good man he was, how kind to his family, how good to his constituents, how loyal to his Prime Minister, how excellent a War Secretary, how devoted to the army, and saying that so proud and

---

1 Quintin McGarel Hogg (1907–2001), 2nd Viscount Hailsham 1950 (peerage disclaimed 1963; life peer 1970); Fellow of All Souls 1931–8, 1961–2001; barrister and Conservative politician; held numerous ministerial posts under Eden and Macmillan; later (1970–4, 1979–87) Lord Chancellor.
2 Profumo's paternal heritage was Sardinian; his family's considerable wealth derived from his grandfather, a founder of the Provident Life Association.
3 Harold Harington Balfour (1897–1988), 1st Baron Balfour of Inchrye 1945, John Profumo's brother-in-law, journalist, businessman and Conservative politician; wrote to The Times as a parliamentary colleague of Lord Hailsham, following the latter's infamous television interview on 13 June 1963, in which he declared that 'A great party is not to be brought down because of a scandal by a woman of easy virtue and a proved liar' ('"Cannot Imagine a Greater Blow to Public Morality": Lord Hailsham Speaks Out', 14 June 1963, 9a). Balfour argued that such condemnation should have been tempered by Christian charity, as well as by an appreciation of Profumo's virtues: 'Lord Hailsham had no mercy' (17 June 1963, 13d).

powerful a Christian as Lord Hailsham should really find some elements of Christian charity in his attitude towards his fallen colleague. [...]

Macmillan's position was a truly difficult one: he had slipped over Galbraith, who had obviously behaved indiscreetly but not improperly, and did not want to be accused again of persecuting his Ministers.[1] He is fundamentally an extremely decent man, who believes in personal liberty and shies away from the subject of sex and the like with extreme horror – "when I was young, we put women on a pedestal", he once said to me, and I daresay that is his attitude still. So when Profumo assured him that there was nothing in the charges against him, it was difficult for him to go on probing – nothing can demoralise a cabinet so much as a Prime Minister who distrusts the word of his colleagues and probes their private lives, apparently gratuitously, upon information lodged by dubious members of the underworld. Moreover, it was difficult for Macmillan to rise in the House of Commons and make a thunderous proclamation of the sanctity of family life and the importance of private morality, when in fact his own had been in so queer a condition – he himself had always behaved honourably, and was a victim, as you well know, of the unprincipled if affable and delightful Lord B;[2] and although he behaved beautifully throughout his life, with both courage and honour, great wounds have been inflicted upon him personally, as you know, and this inhibits him from striking the kind of moral stance that *The Times* would have liked from him. The *Times* leading articles were rivers of cant and hypocritical preaching – so was a spate of letters they released.[3] Sparrow wrote a good letter to *The Times*,[4] condemning Profumo but complaining about the nauseating Victorian rubbish which most of the tweedy ladies in the Cotswolds contributed to *The Times* and which that paper eagerly printed.

1 Thomas Galloway Dunlop ('Tam') Galbraith (1917–82), later (1982) KBE, a junior minister in Macmillan's government, had resigned on 8 November 1962 after one of his direct subordinates, John Vassall, a homosexual Admiralty clerk to whom he had written personal, but not incriminating, letters, was imprisoned for spying. Galbraith was later exonerated, and Macmillan criticised for having accepted his resignation while believing him to be 'the victim of a campaign of innuendo' (*Times*, 9 November 1962, 12a).

2 In 1929 Boothby began an affair with Macmillan's wife, Lady Dorothy Evelyn née Cavendish (1900–66), which continued intermittently until her death, and may have resulted in the birth a daughter, Sarah Macmillan; in political circles the affair was commonly known, and impeded Boothby's career; but Macmillan stoically reconciled himself to the arrangement, and remained on ostensibly friendly terms with his wife's lover.

3 The leader of 11 June 1963 – 'It *is* a moral issue' – was followed on 13 June by an approving letters page: e.g. 'Your leading article on moral standards is a sign of hope, at least, to people grown increasingly dismayed by the tawdry standards of our day' (Hilda M. Stowell, 13 June 1963, 13g).

4 Sparrow dismissed the notion that 'a lapse on the part of a Minister indicates widespread corruption': 'The unhappy incident has made an impression on the British public which needs no reinforcement from any Puritanical crusade in Parliament or the press' (one of several letters collectively entitled 'It *Is* a Moral Issue: Power of the Electorate to Voice Its Opinion', 13 June 1963, 13e).

All this is due to my friend the Editor,[1] who is an old-fashioned Liberal who sees himself as the Savonarola[2] of our corrupt society. I wish he didn't. [...]

Four nights ago we dined at Buckingham Palace to meet the President of India.[3] It was a magnificent spectacle: Lord Cobbold, the Lord Chamberlain,[4] with his staff, looked peculiar enough, but the marvellous gold objects on their red velvet cushions under floodlight in the Banqueting Chamber – Jacobean and Stuart objects, so far as I could see – looked very handsome. So did the gold plate off which we dined. The meal itself was like a College meal, neither good nor bad, but the flowers – roses, petunias, etc. gushing from the golden bowls – it was the most magnificent thing I ever saw. I daresay all this was put on specially for the Indians because they like Oriental splendour. At any rate, it was most enjoyable, and in some respects comical. Poor Macmillan looked very worn out and sat on a sofa beside me. I described it all to Lord Brand, who to my astonishment had never been in Buckingham Palace and longed to go – this just means he wasn't on any list.

Mason Hammond arrives soon and will doubtless express his shock over our moral condition – I shall have to defend it. Ronnie and Marietta are here, and coming to see us on Friday. In every country house in England nothing but the Profumo case is discussed, and it seems to me everywhere else too. Never has there been a subject which has given so much pleasure to so many [...].

And now for the purification of our national life! There are a number of members of the cabinet, not to speak of MPs, who will have to liquidate all kinds of compromising associations, I suspect. Otherwise, the last weeks really have had a flavour of Rasputin and the last days of the old regime.[5] In general, I suppose it is fair to say that what with the Duchess of Argyle's hideous incontinences, the Galbraith, Vassall, Fletcher-Cooke[6] etc. scandals,

1 William John Haley (1901–87), KCMG 1946; Director-General of the BBC 1944–52; editor of *The Times* 1952–66. Haley had written the *Times* leader of 11 June (157/3), which became a 'historic indictment of the Macmillan government (whom he considered a 'bunch of thugs'). [...] His moral outlook shaped his attitude to government policies' (Siân Nicholas, ODNB).

2 Girolamo Savonarola (1452–98), Dominican monk and religious reformer; led a puritanical campaign against worldly corruption, which included 'bonfires of the vanities'; briefly controlled Florence 1494–5, before being declared a heretic by the Pope; he was publicly hanged in the Piazza della Signoria and his body burned.

3 Sarvepalli Radhakrishnan (1888–1975), Kt 1931, philosopher and public servant; Spalding Professor of Eastern Religions and Ethics, and Fellow of All Souls 1936–52; Vice-President of India 1952–62; President 1962–7. He was at this time on a State visit to Britain, during which he was invested with honorary membership of the Order of Merit by the Queen.

4 Cameron Fromanteel Cobbold (1904–87), 1st Baron Cobbold 1960, GCVO 1963; Governor, Bank of England, 1949–61; Lord Chamberlain of HM Household 1963–71.

5 IB is referring to the fall of the Romanov dynasty in Russia in 1917, and the corrosive influence at court of the monk and mystic Grigory Efimovich Rasputin (c.1869–1916).

6 Charles (Fletcher) Fletcher-Cooke (1914–2001), later (1981) Kt; Conservative MP for Darwen, Lancs, 1951–83; Joint Parliamentary Under-Secretary of State, Home Office, 1961–3; resigned amid prurient speculation about his relationship with a young man apprehended by the police for speeding in his (Fletcher-Cooke's) car.

Bishops proclaiming that *Lady Chatterley's Lover* is required reading for Christians, etc. etc., sick comedians, and a kind of association of left-wing thought and louche lives, something of a Weimar type really is upon us. Perhaps all this will do no harm. But I feel that a generation really is passing from the stage – Macmillan at Buckingham Palace assured me that he would take no honours; 'It is delightful for me as a poor crofter's grandson to give people Knighthoods of the Garter and that sort of thing, but to take them is no fun at all,' he said; 'I shall not sit about the House of Commons giving unwanted advice or loll about the House of Lords doing the same – no, no, I go back to publishing.' We shall see. I like him and respect him and don't wish him to be excessively unhappy. He has behaved very well on the whole, and I am sorry for the condition he is in. [...]

⟨yrs with *much* love⟩
    Isaiah

TO ROWLAND BURDON-MULLER ⚹

19 July 1963

Headington House

My dear Rowland,

I am still reeling under the impact of your great philippic, the most thunderous denunciation of our time I have had the pleasure of reading for a long while. I think I must answer your points one by one, for otherwise you will think me an ally of the squalor which you so eloquently denounce. [...]

1. It strikes you that I am more critical of Haley and Miss Keeler than I am of Lord Astor and of Profumo. I am. Profumo has been punished. What did he do? He had an affair with a prostitute; he was told to keep off the osteopath because he was a security risk – whereupon he dropped him. He continued with Miss Keeler because he was obviously infatuated, told her no secrets so far as we know, and merely deceived his wife,[1] lied to his government and to Parliament. Nobody in their senses wishes to exonerate him on these charges. His chief crime is of course not to have had an affair – I cannot remember who it was, whether Gladstone or someone else, who said he had only known two Prime Ministers in his life who were not adulterers; if you consider what Lloyd George[2] was doing [...] Profumo is almost angelic by comparison. I met Profumo once or twice and did not like him, but his worst

1 Profumo married, 1954, the stage and film actress (Babette Louisa) Valerie Havelock-Allan (1917–98) née Hobson; when Profumo confided to her his indiscretion with Keeler she advised him publicly to confess this, which he did; she afterwards stood by him.
2 David Lloyd George (1863–1945), 1st Earl Lloyd George 1945, Liberal statesman; Prime Minister 1916–22. Depicted in the biography written by his son Richard, *Lloyd George* (London, 1960), 'as an oversexed philanderer' (in the words of Kenneth O. Morgan, ODNB), he had affairs with the wives of three Liberal MPs, and maintained a separate household with his secretary-mistress Frances Stevenson.

crime was of course to have gambled on getting away with his lie when
what he was gambling was the credit of the government [...]. At any rate,
The Times's horror of the level to which our national life has sunk because
a cabinet minister went off with a tart – when the Editor knows very well
what the private lives of some of our ministers over the last fifty or sixty
years [have been] – does strike me as hypocrisy and cant.[1] [...]

I have really nothing against Miss Keeler herself except the extremely nauseating quality of the prose style of her memoirs,[2] of which I read about five
lines – but even that I am willing to withdraw. Prose style is not everything.

2. [...] It was a very common occurrence in the eighteenth century,
and only slightly less common in the nineteenth, for dignified persons to
meet ladies of easy virtue in the company of English peers; the traffic in
girls under sixteen in France and England of the eighteenth century really
was something disgusting, and the one point on which I agree with you is
complaining of a system in which the rich can exploit the poor in this way.
But if we press this to its logical culmination, that of course means that we
must abolish the society in which some people are conspicuously richer than
others, and this may indeed be right; so long as some are much richer than
others, prostitution will continue and no amount of attempts to conceal it
– in the way in which elegant persons keep beautiful mistresses and do not
advertise this fact – will in the end prevent scandals from breaking out. This
points to a straight Communist moral, and all I would say against that is that
perhaps the price which we paid for the abolition of prostitution would in
this case be too high, for it would destroy a great many things in our culture
– as it conspicuously has in Russia – which we prize, and one must weigh one
thing against another when one embarks on violent reforms or revolutions.
But I could not agree with you more in regretting a society in which money
buys sexual pleasures and prostitution is regarded as a normal thing. I do not
myself believe in either *noblesse oblige* or *richesse oblige* – this is too inegali-
tarian a formula. Of course cabinet ministers and grand persons in general
should behave carefully for fear of jeopardising the institutions in which they
believe and which they symbolise. And Profumo behaved abominably. But
I do not, unlike *The Times*, believe it to be a moral question, but a social and
political one. My instinct is the opposite: I detest irregularity; I detest sexual
looseness so much that I cannot bear to enter a night-club – even the most

---

1 Richard Crossman wrote that Profumo's crime was 'to be caught in the act of doing what scores
  of [his] colleagues did unscathed. In British politics evasion is nine points of innocence'; the case
  exposed 'the peculiar loyalties, hypocrisies, lies and evasions which oil the wheels of our political
  system. [...] I still feel outraged at the fate meted out to poor Profumo when X and Y, who failed
  to sack Burgess and Maclean, got their peerages.' 'Pleading from the Grave', *New Statesman*, 25
  February 1972, 242.

2 The *News of the World* paid Keeler £23,000 for her 'confessions', an act condemned by the Press
  Council: 'By thus exploiting vice and sex for commercial reward the *News of the World* has done
  a disservice both to public welfare and to the press' (*Times*, 7 October 1963, 7f).

respectable kind of one – and flee from the slightest touch of Bohemia, let alone tarnish. But I cannot defend this; this is simply a personal thing and I do not wish to deprive people of freedom of behaviour simply because it upsets and offends me. With John Stuart Mill, I believe on the whole that behaviour which does not directly frustrate other people should be condoned even if it is disgusting; that is to say, it should not be punished, although of course one has the right to say what one likes about it. [...]

You complain that there is no distinguished behaviour any more. I understand very well what you mean. That, I think, is part of the price of the greater equality which despite inequalities of wealth is undoubtedly growing in all our societies. There was more distinguished behaviour in Tsarist Russia than in the Soviet Union – not, perhaps, a higher social or private morality, but certainly more *tenue*.[1] There was more *tenue* under Louis XVI and Louis XV than under Napoleon, under whom peasants were less oppressed, innocent blood was shed less often, horrors of injustice and brutality were far less frequent. I do not say that one is necessarily the price of the other, but it does seem historically as if social justice carries with it destruction of aristocratic principles and, with them, of aristocratic manners. Nothing is more attractive than persons of aristocratic upbringing and texture with radical ideas destructive of the values of their own class – we have all known such people. But to the extent to which they are successful, the next generation, though they may live in a more equitable universe, certainly lose the aristocratic texture, which is itself the fruit of acute and agonising inequalities, accepted usually without murmur both by oppressors and victims, by lords and peasants.

You say that it is in the worst of taste for Profumo to have gone with the Queen Mother to the races immediately after lying to the House. So it was. But of course, what he was trying to do was to brazen it out and get away with it, and if he had done – and he might easily have done so but for the mysterious behaviour of the osteopath, who may or may not be bent on blackmail – the proprieties would have been preserved, none of this would have come to light, a few cronies would have giggled about it in the purlieus of the City or Parliament, and you would have had little cause for general complaint. So all we can say about that is that he had bad luck. That he behaved badly there is no doubt, but that many who have behaved badly – Palmerston,[2] Lloyd George, Mr Asquith,[3] and others nearer home – have not

1 'Good manners'.

2 Henry John Temple (1784–1865), 3rd Viscount Palmerston, British Whig statesman, Foreign Secretary 1830–4, 1835–41, 1846–51; Prime Minister 1855–8, 1859–65. Nicknamed 'Cupid', Palmerston was a 'considerable womaniser [...]. Proud of his virility, he recorded sexual successes and failures in his pocket diaries, methodical in this as in other matters' (David Steele, ODNB).

3 Herbert Henry Asquith (1852–1928), 1st Earl of Oxford and Asquith 1925, Liberal statesman, Prime Minister 1908–16. Asquith's reputation was for intemperance and not infidelity; but he

been publicly disgraced is due to skill and luck, not to a superior morality on their part.

As for Lord Denning, he is enjoying himself reading the Duchess of Argyll case.[1] No! Of course Profumo behaved badly, of course Astor's tastes are depraved. But there are many worse vices not similarly denounced by *The Times* – cruelty, treachery, cowardice, poverty, or rather, insufficient indignation about it. I see perfectly why the French believe in *la hypocrisie anglaise*.

I go to Israel on the 25th and to Italy on 5 August, as always. Dear me! I fear that my last letter irritated you almost as much as my pro-Israeli sentiments – dare I add that that poor little country – for poor it undoubtedly is, even you cannot deny that it is both poor and small – does not at least drop blister-causing bombs on native villages as Lord Kinross's friends seem to be doing. Still, I must not go on teasing you about our differences. Lord Astor will, I think, have to seek a house for himself in France – the storm, after all, is not quite as bad as it was in the case of Wilde,[2] and poor Macmillan, who as you say has been a good Prime Minister, is very civilised – for all that Lady Violet Bonham Carter,[3] who has hated him since Suez, calls him now, or has called him in a letter to me, an 'acrobatic barnacle' – will leave the scene and go sorrowing into exile and publishing books again, I suppose. We have just come back from staying a weekend with the Wyndhams – Peter Quennell,[4] Fred Warner,[5] the Prime Minister and Lady Dorothy Macmillan and Lady Bridgeman[6] were there; Aline is very reluctant to leave her home,

enjoyed the company of intelligent and attractive young women, and formed an *amitié amoureuse* with Venetia Stanley (later Montagu), a close friend of his daughter Violet. Asquith's letters to Venetia Stanley came into the possession of Lord Beaverbrook, and were made available to Roy Jenkins in the writing of his biography *Asquith* (London, 1964).

1 Among the salacious details revealed in the 1963 divorce case brought by Ian Douglas Campbell, 11th Duke of Argyll (1903–73), against his wife (Ethel) Margaret née Whigham (1912–93), on the grounds of her adultery, was the existence of a photograph of the Duchess fellating an unidentified male companion. There were rumours that the man in question was a government minister, and Lord (Alfred Thompson) Denning (1899–1999), life peer 1957, who conducted the government inquiry into the Profumo affair, was obliged to investigate.

2 Oscar Fingal O'Flahertie Wills Wilde (1854–1900), writer; convicted of gross indecency in 1895 for his relations with male prostitutes, and sentenced to two years with hard labour; after his release from Reading gaol in 1897 he lived in self-imposed exile on the Continent, based in Paris, and died there in 1900.

3 (Helen) Violet Bonham Carter (1887–1969) née Asquith, DBE 1953, later (1964) life peer; only daughter of H. H. Asquith and his first wife, Helen Melland; a leading Liberal Party activist and public figure. IB wrote to Dollie de Rothschild after VBC's death in February 1969: 'I really am terribly sorry that Violet is no more. I actually liked her as well as admired her and was amused by her, and by all her marvellous, fearless, sometimes heartless, sometimes noble public gestures. She really does date back to a grander age – Winston – Sir Thomas Beecham – indeed Jimmy [James de Rothschild] himself' (5 March 1969).

4 Peter Courtney Quennell (1905–93), later (1992) Kt, editor, *History Today*, 1951–79.

5 Frederick Archibald ('Fred') Warner (1918–95), later (1972) KCMG, diplomat. His early career was temporarily blighted by his friendship with Guy Burgess. Ambassador and Deputy Permanent UK Representative to UN 1969–72; ambassador to Japan 1972–5.

6 Mary Kathleen Bridgeman (1905–81) née Lane-Fox; wife of Robert Clive Bridgeman (1896–1982), 2nd Viscount Bridgeman.

but enjoyed the twenty-four [hours] that we spent. We arrived mid-Saturday and left mid-Sunday; not a word was said about any scandals; the Prime Minister talked blandly and I must say well about Tolstoy and Dickens and Balliol and history and the Western world; he is something of an old actor but there is also something very decent and intelligent about him, and his successor, whoever he is, will not be as good.

That Philby should drop on his head as well is almost too much.[1] I had always assumed that he was the Third Man, from the moment of the escape of Burgess[2] and Maclean,[3] because although I had never met him or seen him I knew him to be such an intimate friend of theirs and to occupy so delicate a position that it seemed scarcely possible that he was not, but I suppose it took them all this time to pin it down. The whole thing, I admit, reminds me of the end of the Weimar Republic: then, too, there were property deals and scandals, pimps and left-wing tarts and negroes and transvestism and awful night-clubs and a taste for violence in the streets [...].

In my own way, I am just as addicted to the past as you are and just as horrified by the present – dear Stuart is always asking me whether there is not something sinister and suspicious about the fact that I dwell on the world before 1914 with such devotion and dislike contemporary phenomena so much. But I priggishly fight against it and try and not judge too much, although not too successfully. There is always something ludicrous about the older generation that wrings its hands at the misdeeds of the younger ones. Still, no less true remark was ever made than that to understand was to forgive – the more I understand myself, for example, the less I find to forgive. So why extend this charity to others? [...]

Yours, with much love

Isaiah

⟨P. S. Your second Profumo-philippic arrived today. *Why* do you suppose that I know Profumo? I met him on public occasions twice and do not know him in any real sense – we should have been unlikely to stop & talk if we met in the street. I do not feel in the least close to the situation: nor is there any

1 The spy Harold Adrian Russell ('Kim') Philby (1912–88) escaped to Russia at the end of January 1963, after having been confronted with evidence of his guilt by British intelligence services earlier that month; in fleeing to Moscow he followed in the tracks of Donald Maclean and Guy Burgess, spies who had defected in May 1951. There had long been speculation in the American press that Philby was the so-called 'third man' in their spy ring, although as late as November 1955 Macmillan, then Foreign Secretary, had cleared Philby's name in the House of Commons, even though MI5 were by then persuaded of his treachery.

2 Guy Francis de Moncy Burgess (1911–63), spy; joined the British secret service in 1938 and subsequently secured Kim Philby's entry into MI6; Goronwy Rees's account of 'the filthy squalor of Burgess's domestic life' in his book *A Chapter of Accidents* (London, 1972) was considered by Richard Crossman 'the best thing in the book' (*New Statesman*, 25 February 1972, 242).

3 Donald Duart Maclean (1913–83), diplomat and spy; a Cambridge associate of the traitors Anthony Blunt, Guy Burgess and Kim Philby, and a wartime colleague of IB at the British Embassy in Washington.

reason, except the gossip of unreliable Hungarian journalists to think that P. took Miss K. into his wife's bedroom. P's sole real offence – & it is real – was to have put his own career before that of his public responsibilities. Parnell & Dilke are not parallel cases,[1] but Lloyd George certainly is, & so is Palmerston whose private morals were very loose indeed – as for the 18th century, not comparable. No: our young people are, if anything, puritanical: they are severe on – against *dolce vita*: & sexual freedom etc. is one of their forms of protest against the elegant vices of their Regency parents. They do not drink, they are critical about marriage: they are such as Wells or Shaw would like them: very earnest, squalid, charmless the nuclear marchers: severe, promiscuous and disapproving: not louche in the usual sense: sexually loose on principle rather than by inclination. Of course drugs, pimps, procurers, snobs, Soviet agents etc. is very unattractive: but compared to racial riots & concentration camps a small price to pay for a free society. I detest it, if anything, more than you: but no gracious living is possible without it. I.B.⟩

TO BERNARD WILLIAMS

13 September [1963]

All Souls

Dear Bernard,

[...] I have had very depressing letters from Stuart; his *noumenal* freedom does not seem to compensate him for lack of it in more familiar spheres. The thought of emigration is obviously to him exceedingly painful – and I imagine that Mrs H. cannot bear to be questioned about anything, least of all by American officials about her past. Hegel says somewhere (this is always a good beginning of any continental essay on anything now) that philosophy represents the mirror image of a society, etc.[2] – certainly in the case of our admirable and gifted and anything but shallow friend the preoccupation with decision, will, freedom, autonomy, self-determination is the mirror image of something – and the fantasies, inhibitions, repressions and the violent though imaginative abnormalities of Mrs H. lie much deeper in the realm of the irrational than any of the more obvious prejudices and

1 The Irish Nationalist leader Charles Stewart Parnell (1846–91) was infamously ruined politically after his adultery with Mrs Katharine ('Kitty') O'Shea (1845–1921) was revealed in the divorce courts in 1890; they married the following year. The promising ministerial career of the Liberal Charles Wentworth Dilke (1843–1911), 2nd Bt, was also derailed by a divorce case – although in this instance it is almost certain that Dilke was falsely named as the co-respondent; he later returned to politics, but never to high office.

2 Probably a reference to this passage: 'Philosophy is by its nature something esoteric [...]; it is only philosophy because it is directly opposed to the intellect, and thus still more to common sense, by which we mean the local and temporary limitations of a breed of men; in relation to this the world of philosophy is in and for itself an inverted world.' Introduction (1802, with Friedrich Schelling) to the *Critical Journal of Philosophy*: Georg Wilhelm Friedrich Hegel, *Sämtliche Werke*, ed. Hermann Glockner (Stuttgart, 1927–51), i 185.

superstitions which, I daresay rightly, shock him in people in general and his friends in particular. He is right about my depression about my piece – it is the Presidential Address to the Aristotelian Society[1] and the depression is proportionate to the degree to which it falls short of such an occasion. I only hope there is no discussion of it afterwards, for if there is, anybody could drive a coach and four through almost anything that I say. The subject lies near my intellectual heart (what a dreadful expression) but the nearer it is the more blurred become both the ideas and the words by which I seek to express what I think – some awful Heisenbergian effect[2] seems to occur whereby [the more] obvious the point the more crucial it seems to make it, the more confused the means, the less successful the effort; whereas the remoter the point, the less deeply concerned with it one is oneself, the better one's perspective, the clearer and more elegant the instruments – that, too, is a subject worth somebody's investigation. [...]

Yours,

[IB p.p.]   [...]

TO SHIELA SOKOLOV GRANT[3]

7 November 1963

Headington House

Dear Shiela,

Very well, I subside, as often, as always, and return to my old, delighted loyalties and affections. I still see no reason for even a tiny nail, let alone a hammer, for I replied to your letter as soon as I physically could. [...]

Meanwhile, a handsome volume has arrived with a beautiful acknowledgement to you as an eminent writer, and to Dr Lampert,[4] and a most vicious attack upon me, upon Martin Malia, who has written much the best

1 'From Hope and Fear Set Free', Proceedings of the Aristotelian Society 64 (1963–4), 1–30; repr. in CC and PSM.

2 Werner Karl Heisenberg (1901–76), German theoretical physicist; Professor and Director of Max Planck Institute for Physics, Göttingen, 1946–58; awarded the 1932 Nobel Prize in Physics for his contribution to the creation of quantum mechanics. His uncertainty principle (1927) states that there is a trade-off in the accuracy with which certain pairs of physical properties can be determined, so that, for instance, greater accuracy in measuring a particle's position entails less accuracy in measuring its momentum. IB applies this in the sense in which the act of observation affects what is being observed.

3 Shiela Sokolov Grant (1913–2004) née Grant Duff, author and journalist. Her friendship with IB dated from her undergraduate days (LMH PPE 1931–4). Foreign correspondent in Germany and Czechoslovakia in 1930s; became strongly pro-Czech, her book Europe and the Czechs (Harmondsworth, 1938) contributing to the growing disillusionment with appeasement; married 1942 Noel Francis Newsome (1906–76), creator and wartime Director of BBC European Service; after their 1952 divorce she married (also 1952) Micheal Sokolov (1923–98), a Russian and an officer in the RNVR (who changed his name to Sokolov Grant before the marriage).

4 Eugene ('Genia') Lampert (1914–2004), Russian studies scholar; of a White Russian émigré family, he studied in Germany and France, arrived in England 1939 and settled; created a course in Russian studies at Keele University 1965, Professor 1968–76.

book on Herzen that has ever been written, and on other wicked Western persons;[1] written, moreover, by a man[2] to whom no one even in Moscow much wishes to speak, as he was apparently guilty of sending at least ten innocent intellectuals to torture and to death – so Soviet visitors have told me here, so it must be all right to talk about it. So you are not in altogether good company: [...] but your visa to Moscow is, I should say, ensured – though if you come with me, which I should like very much, it may be that you will be greeted as if you were arm in arm with a Fascist dragon. I should rather enjoy that, and so I daresay would you. I have had a rather tormented letter from Lampert about the unfortunate contrast between him (white) and me (black), which is due, he suspects, to the fact that he had not sufficiently impressed his Soviet hosts that his own book with its essay on Herzen had been dedicated to me, was inspired by me, etc. etc. – under pressure I fear he denied me, or at least did not affirm what he might – not very culpable in the circumstances, for one is always anxious to please, and if one is accused of over-friendship with the enemy, one is liable, in amiable and troubled character, to shuffle and compromise: but later it troubles one's conscience and makes one very guilty in relations with the person so disowned. I propose to take a magnanimous attitude about this and say that I understand everything and that he must not blame himself.

I saw Douglas two nights ago and he was very funny; he said 'To think that a year ago the Socialist party was led by an absolutely honest upright man and the Conservative party by a shabby, contemptible old crook; and now, it does seem as if the opposite ...'. He ought to have stopped at 'and

1 The book is Yu. G. Oksman [168/4] (ed.), *Problemy izucheniya Gertsena* [*Problems in the Study of Herzen*] (Moscow, 1963), and the 'vicious attack' Ya. E. El'sberg, 'Ideinaya bor'ba vokrug naslediya Gertsena b nashe vremya' ['The ideological battle over Herzen's legacy to our age']. El'sberg attacks (437–45) IB's treatment of Herzen in his 1956 introduction to Herzen's *From the Other Shore*, defending the orthodox Soviet view, which takes its cue from Lenin's pronouncements on the subject. This defence is bound up with the Cold War polemics about the opposing political systems under which El'sberg and Berlin were writing. El'sberg welcomes the appearance of an English translation of *From the Other Shore* but is critical both of Berlin's interpretation of the work and of Berlin's relative lack of attention to other things that Herzen wrote. He claims that Martin Malia has made much the more important contribution to scholarship on Herzen.

2 In response to an enquiry from Henry Hardy, IB explained (letter of 25 October 1993): 'El'sberg [né Shapirshtein; 1901–76] was a secretary to Kamenev, an original Bolshevik revolutionary who was duly executed by Stalin. Naturally this made the secretary's position difficult: he was sent to Siberia and had to work his passage back. He had been a member of the Academy, was undoubtedly a well-read and clever man, but as he had betrayed so many people to the secret police during the 1930s they didn't want to re-admit him; in fact they expelled him: under pressure from Khrushchev they did re-admit him. He made a violent attack on me, for obvious reasons, if only to show his utter loyalty to the official views on Herzen, Belinsky etc. – Dr Lampert, who may still be alive, was very sovietisant, and I think possibly in with him, and he used to come back to England from the Soviet Union and tell me with bated breath that the scholars thought I was a very sinister influence because of my misinterpretation of the nineteenth-century revolutionaries. However, I did meet a Soviet scholar in the Bodleian – a very nice Shakespeare expert, in the company of a philosopher called Asmus – two perfectly decent men: I complained to them about these attacks on me, and one of them said, "This does you nothing but the greatest honour", implying, though he didn't quite say, that my opponent was a scoundrel – which indeed he was.'

now' and I could have filled in the rest. He obviously loves Home much more than Wilson; and who should blame him? Cricket, insularity, the Eton–Winchester match, are deeper roots in Douglas than collective ownership and the Kaldor/Balogh world.[1] It would indeed be ironical if Wedgwood Benn, through insisting on pushing this bill through,[2] made it possible for un-used-up British peers to ride up and down the country and capture its inhabitants by that upper-class charm and beau-monde breeziness, which it is well known that nobody in England can resist [...] and [they] are hypnotised into voting for these delightful, candid, blue-eyed, fair-haired young champions of all that is most English against the cunning and soiled politicians. But I do not think that this will quite happen; but enough of it will to confuse the issue and frighten the old Labour fixers. It is an interesting spectacle. The Liberals are saying that the removal of Macmillan has in itself had so tonic an effect on the country as to seem like a post-election state: they do not need a new election, 'the new man must be allowed to get into his stride and be given a chance, people are no longer bored and tired with the old gang just because this new figure has emerged'. I wonder. But it is all very fascinating to watch; education is by far the deepest issue: not knowledge, or training, but status, class, accent. If the Conservatives went really bald-headedly for the Robbins Report, they would, I think, just get in. But I expect they won't.

Do answer.

Yours,

　　Isaiah

On 23 October the Robbins Committee published its wide-ranging report on higher education in Britain,[3] calling for a rapid and sustained increase in the number of students at university, and emphasising the development of post-graduate studies in the sciences. It thus acknowledged the needs of industry in the technological age, while also recognising demands for greater social equality. In this latter respect the report was critical of Oxbridge: Robbins recommended greater meritocracy in the admissions procedures of the ancient

---

1 Both were Hungarian-born economists who acted as advisers to the Labour government of Harold Wilson. Nicholas (né Miklós) Kaldor (1908-86), later (1974) life peer; naturalised British 1934; Fellow of King's College, Cambridge, from 1949; Reader in Economics, University of Cambridge, 1952–65, Professor 1966–75; special adviser to the Chancellor of the Exchequer 1964–8, 1974–6. Thomas Balogh (1905–85), life peer 1968; Fellow of Balliol 1945–73; Reader in Economics, Oxford, 1960–73; Leverhulme Fellow, Oxford, 1973–6. As economic adviser to the Labour Party Balogh worked closely with Harold Wilson in the run up to the 1964 General election, and after the Labour victory worked in the Cabinet Office 1964–70.

2 In November 1960 Anthony Neil Wedgwood ('Tony') Benn (b. 1925), Labour member for Bristol South East, having succeeded to his father Lord Stansgate's peerage, was disqualified from his seat in the Commons. His campaign to allow peers to renounce their titles resulted in the 1963 Peerage Act, which allowed him to resume his Commons career; he held cabinet rank in the Wilson and Callaghan governments.

3 *Higher Education: Report of the Committee Appointed by the Prime Minister under the Chairmanship of Lord Robbins*, 1961–63 (London, 1963).

universities, as well as improved efficiency and openness in their administration.
Oxford responded quickly, and on 18 March 1964 Oliver Franks[1] was appointed
chairman of a University committee charged with a thorough internal review.
The Franks Commission, as it came to be known, was the most famous of
a number of internal reviews conducted by the University in the 1960s. There
was a determination in enlightened quarters to take Oxford forward, and in this
endeavour IB was well equipped to play a role. To the educational reformer he
epitomized 'old college tradition – mahogany and silver, and nuts and wine',[2]
but the considerable time that he had spent since the war at US universities,
notably Princeton and Harvard, had made him acutely aware of Oxford's need
to change.

TO GENIA LAMPERT

7 November [1963]

Headington House

Dear Genia,

Thank you very much for leaving me the book. If I had known it was
El´sberg I shouldn't have worried; after all, even the cautious and tactful
Chukovsky told us when he was here that El´sberg had been expelled from
the Writer's Union for sending no fewer than ten persons to torture and
death quite deliberately and on false evidence. According to my inform-
ants, quoted admittedly by Malia, no decent person has anything to do with
him in Moscow. This is confirmed by Jakobson. And the article really is old
Stalinist clap-trap. [...]

I read the article somewhat rapidly and do not mind the abuse of myself
as a shameless and ignorant publicist at all. This was, as Simmons[3] told me,
very much to be expected. But what was it that you find intelligent in it?
That Herzen was a revolutionary all his life is in a sense of course true, and
I have nowhere denied it. But the proposition that *Letters to an Old Comrade*
are in some way an approach to a Marxist position – because of references
to workers and so on – is an old Stalinist cliché, of which, so Malia says, all
the true scholars, and in particular Oksman,[4] are terribly ashamed. [...] The
Soviet commentators have not, so far as I know, made a single illuminating

1 Oliver *Franks (1905–92), philosopher and public servant.
2 To McGeorge Bundy, 18 May 1966.
3 John Simon Gabriel Simmons (1915–2005), librarian-lecturer in charge of Slavonic books,
  Oxford, 1949–69; Reader in Russian and Slavonic Bibliography 1969–70; Librarian and Senior
  Research Fellow, All Souls, 1970–82; played a key role in building the bibliographical base of
  Slavonic studies in Oxford. Author of the invaluable *Russian Bibliography: Libraries and Archives*
  (Twickenham, 1973).
4 Yulian Grigor´evich Oksman (1895–1970), Russian literary critic; studied at the Universities
  of Bonn, Heidelberg and Petrograd; worked as a government official and academic; he was
  denounced, and imprisoned in the Gulag 1937–46; resumed his academic career on release, and
  from 1958 forged links with Western Slavists, notably Gleb Struve, assisting him in his publication

observation about Herzen's ideas – as opposed to bibliography etc. I once asked Chukóvsky why not: he made it very, very plain, in words, that he himself adored Herzen and liked Belinsky (he cannot read Chernyshevsky) but could not write about them because the truth is not permitted and he does not wish to indulge in mechanical phraseology – that is why he confines himself to the fourth- and fifth-rate radicals, about whom he can say, on the whole, what he pleases and point morals too. But do tell me what you find in El´sberg that is positively intelligent. He speaks of Herzen's 'understanding of the people' or some such phrase, something which Herzen neither possessed nor claimed to possess, indeed, openly said that the reactionaries possessed in higher measure than he and his friends. What anticipations of the present regime are there in my hero's writings?

Yours,

Isaiah

TO GENIA LAMPERT

19 November 1963

Headington House

Dear Genia,

Let us go on, then, for I am enjoying this very much; but I shall be brief, for I think we really must meet and talk.

[…] I fear that El´sberg is crawling, or attempting to crawl, back to favour over my poor dead body – I could wish for a worthier assassin. He contrasted you with me because you were recommended to him as a well-wisher, as opposed to me, an ill-wisher: these things are pretty crude in the Soviet Union, as you know, and it is a mistake to think otherwise. If you were to utter a single sharply critical word about some political scholar, say about the attempt to suppress Herzen's unfriendliness to Marx and Marxism (more to Marx than Marxism), you too would fall out of favour. […]

Now as to Herzen's attitude to the bourgeoisie, you cannot, can you, complain of my attitude about this – I emphasise and over-emphasise in everything I have written about Herzen his hatred for the bourgeoisie – even El´sberg comments on this […]. But I do not think that Herzen's anti-bourgeois attitude brings him closer to the official political morality – Soviet Communism – which in all the respects that are relevant practised precisely what he detested in the bourgeoisie – and what in *Letters to an Old Comrade* he predicted would happen if the revolution was made too soon, that is to say, if the new building was made out of the 'stones of the old prison-house'.[1] What is so marvellous about Herzen is the terrible and devastating

of works on the poets of the 'Silver Age'; he published anonymously in the West, was discovered, officially proscribed, and expelled from the Union of Soviet Writers in October 1964.

1 Apparently a 'quotation' from Herzen's *From the Other Shore*: 'The fatal error [of the French

insight into social psychology in general – without very much understanding, I think, of specific groups of human beings, specific groups of French workers, Russian peasants, etc., whom I don't think he did understand all that well – that enabled him to say that if the revolution was made too soon then the revolutionaries, bred as they are themselves in certain bourgeois habits, would reproduce these things under the guise of revolution, as indeed has happened in Russia, where the culture, as cannot be denied, is petit bourgeois to a degree. [...]

As for Malia's remark to Oksman,[1] I find that terribly difficult to believe. Perhaps he said it in order to make Oksman feel better – I have never heard of a single case of anyone writing about the nineteenth century (and not many about the twentieth) feeling that they must 'load their colours' or utter a few anti-Communist slogans in order to get by. I have no wish to defend American idiocies, McCarthyism, etc., as you may imagine, but I know Malia intimately and he has never said to me that he wrote down a single line to placate anyone – and indeed, with all his left-wing views, it was he who was perpetually trying to stop me from suggesting that Herzen towards the end of his life came even a millimetre closer to the Marxist point of view, saying that this was totally false (I believe him to be right, and myself to have been over-influenced by Soviet critics) and that it was a piece of Marxist claptrap which Oksman and all his friends begged him not to be taken in by. Who is telling the truth here? Do not, in your perfectly intelligible anti-bourgeois feeling, let yourself be persuaded about America in the way that cold warriors are persuaded about Soviet scholars. There is absolutely no pressure, even of the mildest kind, upon persons writing about Russian history in America. To maintain that Herzen was a violent revolutionary, Communist, full anticipator of Lenin, and that therein lies his chief glory, would not get any American professor into trouble politically, though it would (and quite properly) intellectually. You do not quite believe me. You speak of experiences of your own. Please tell me about them.

As for Communism and baby-eating: what, of course, people object to is not Communism but baby-eating as such, whoever may be eating the babies. And plenty of babies have been eaten in Russia, rather more than elsewhere, if you exclude the Germans. Baby for baby, do you really maintain that more have been devoured in America? Or babies of better quality? Or that those who devoured them licked their chops more cynically or more

radicals in 1848] is [...] to have tried to free others before they were themselves liberated [...]. They want, without altering the walls [of the prison], to give them a new function, as if a plan for a jail could be used for a free existence.' A. I. Gertsen, *Sobranie sochinenii v tridtsati tomakh* (Moscow, 1954–66), vi 51; Alexander Herzen, *From the Other Shore*, trans. Moura Budberg, and *The Russian People and Socialism*, trans. Richard Wollheim, with an introduction by IB (London, 1956), 57.

1 According to Lampert, Malia had told Oksman that, in order to get published, he (Malia) had had to toe the orthodox American anti-Communist line.

brutally? America is a troubled and in many ways coarse, in parts brutal, society, and many Senators and businessmen and whoever are no doubt swine; but it is even now impossible to make a career in America by sheer cynicism and opportunism, as it seems to be possible in Russia – somewhere on the way one would be exposed, and there are decent and human figures strewn all over the path – the thing is confused and messy, and the better for that, whereas in Russia the mess was eliminated a long time ago, and what remains is personal decency, it seems to me, in personal relations, cut off terribly from public faces and public attitudes. [...]

You think there is no more collective nonsense in Russia than there is in the West. I do not agree. The Russians I have met know – are conscious of – the fact that public pronouncements and the conformist declarations of their colleagues are genuine gibberish, and that gibberish-utterers are more cynical and more vicious, it seems to me, than their opposite numbers in the West, who are more confused, more deluded, less classifiable, less publicly rewarded. After all, someone like Blackett,[1] who has defied official opinion for years and has carried on the most warm relations with the Soviet Union, gets an honorary degree at Oxford; an opportunist and a cheap-jack like Snow[2] gets elected to something at St Andrews; there is no wave of denunciation of their wickedness blared forth from any official trumpets, although if this happened to Snow I should mind only the fact that it made him look like an honest man and a martyr; when Miss Mitford is accused of undermining the American way of life by exposing the morticians,[3] this is a comic, not a tragic, event, whereas in Russia ... Shall we ever be able to agree about this? Perhaps not.

As for the baseless abuse of me, why should you atone for it? John Simmons, rightly I think, says that I must expect to be so treated, that anyone must who incautiously tells the truth or what he takes to be true. [...]

Yours,

Isaiah   [...]

Early in the afternoon of 22 November 1963 John F. Kennedy was shot and fatally wounded as his motorcade drove through the streets of Dallas, Texas, where he had gone to help heal divisions between the State's Democrats. The suspected assassin, Lee Harvey Oswald, a twenty-four-year-old ex-marine, was taken into

1 Patrick Maynard Stuart Blackett (1897–1974), physicist and government adviser; awarded an Hon. D.Sc. by Oxford 1963; subsequently OM 1967 and life peer 1969.
2 C. P. Snow was elected Rector of St Andrews by the student body – the traditional electorate – in 1961, and held the post for the customary 3-year term.
3 Jessica Lucy (Freeman)-Mitford (1917–96), writer, journalist and self-avowed Communist, the fifth-born of the 6 Mitford sisters. She spent much of her life in California, and, with her second husband, the lawyer Bob Treuhaft, 'wrote a macabre and satirical exposé of the funeral business, *The American Way of Death* (1963), which became a best-seller and established her as a witty and effective critic of her adopted society' (Anne Chisholm, ODNB).

custody by the Dallas police, but on his way to be questioned two days later was
himself shot dead by a local nightclub owner, Jack Ruby.

IB heard the news of the President's death at the University of Sussex, as he
arrived to deliver a lecture on Machiavelli.

I dined with my hosts and was walking towards the lecture hall when someone
said to me, 'Isn't this terrible?' I thought, idiotically, he meant that it was
a terrible thing to have to go in to lecture, since he knew, as all my friends do,
the agonies I suffer before talking in public, whatever the occasion. I therefore
said, 'Yes, I do feel awful, but I suppose I must go through with it.' A few yards
later someone else said to me, 'This is appalling news.' I realised something had
happened, and was told that President Kennedy had been assassinated. I found
it impossible to continue walking – the last time on which this had happened
to me (in an even greater degree) was when I read about the death of President
Roosevelt in 1945 […]. I did not feel so violently when I heard of the death of
Kennedy, but he too, with all his obvious faults, was a liberator and a hero, on
the right side on all the public issues that mattered. I begged to be allowed an
interval of a quarter of an hour or so before beginning my lecture. This was
granted. I drank two glasses of cold water, came to and delivered my lecture in
a perfectly normal manner.[1]

Conspiracy theories soon began to circulate about the events in Dallas, and
IB wrote to Pat Utechin[2] on Christmas Eve, 1963: 'America is very guilty about
the Kennedy assassination. They do not blame communists, plotters etc: oddly
enough the national paranoia has taken the far nobler form of guilt about what
can be wrong with their own condition which makes such crimes possible.
General self-abasement à la Russ. intelligentsia. Not a witch hunt, even tho'
there may be a witch.'

TO ARTHUR SCHLESINGER

28 November [1963]

Headington House

Dear Arthur,

1963 is a most terrible year. At the beginning Gaitskell, in the middle
Pope John XXIII,[3] and now this greatest of all disasters. I do not wish to
exaggerate: perhaps it is not at all similar to what men may have felt when
Alexander the Great died; but the suddenness and the sense of something of
exceptional hope for a large number of people suddenly cut off in mid-air
is, I think, unique in our lifetime – it is as if Roosevelt [had] been murdered

---

1 In Sandra Martin and Roger Hall (eds), *Where Were You? Memorable Events of the Twentieth Century*
   (Toronto etc., 1981), 206–7.
2 Patricia ('Pat') *Utechin (1927–2008), private secretary to IB.
3 Angelo Giuseppe Roncalli (1881–1963), Pope John XXIII 1958–63; died 3 June 1963. Aged 77 when
   elected, he was expected to be a 'caretaker'; instead he proved a dynamic reformer, promoting
   'internal reform and external conciliation' (*Times*, 4 June 1963, 13a); 'Few pontificates have so
   captured the imagination of the world' (ibid., 11b).

in 1935, with Hitler and Mussolini and everybody else still about and a lot of Chamberlains and Daladiers[1] knocking about too. I was told it five minutes before addressing the students of the University of Sussex, as I was told about Hugh Gaitskell ten minutes before addressing the Harvard Law Club. This seems a very egoistic note to strike suddenly, but its very personal, even its objective, significance seeps into one's blood, particularly if one has to fight it off for an hour, like grappling with a nightmare or trying to hit out at the coils of some frightful Laocoon stranglehold. Still, I suppose we must let the dead, etc., but I cannot – I think constantly about the past. Lady Pamela is already eagerly re-furbishing her memories of President Johnson, and there is naturally much speculation about the fate of Dean, Adlai, Averell[2] etc. etc. – which I do too, but with a fearful sense of shame.

[...] I was asked to go on the BBC and say something about Kennedy together with others, but didn't because I can't bear public expressions of grief – Denis Brogan[3] did very well – and I indignantly refused the request of the *Observer* for anecdotes about Hickory Hill.[4]

I mustn't go on; do ring up, there is nobody we wish to see more than you. Love to Marian – come to *N.Y.*

Yours,
   Isaiah

TO BERTELL OLLMAN

3 December [1963]

All Souls

Dear Bertell,

[...] Here we are somewhat stunned by the news of Kennedy's death – I do not doubt you do not take it all as being what it appears – although I wish I could formulate some hypothesis that was at all plausible. I really admired Kennedy very much indeed – all the talk about how he represented youth and vigour and enterprise and action is not empty; it is really very rare for heads of States not to be predictable, and literally nobody, so far as I could see, in Washington would undertake to prophesy what the President would do in this or that juncture, and this I regarded as immensely to his credit – a kind of self-assertion of individual control, what certain persons like to

---

1 i.e. appeasers. Édouard Daladier (1884–1970), Prime Minister of France 1933, 1934, 1938–40, was a signatory (without illusions), with Neville Chamberlain, Hitler and Mussolini, of the Munich Agreement of September 1938.

2 (William) Averell Harriman (1891–1986), veteran US diplomat and Democratic politician; appointed ambassador at large by Kennedy 1961; Assistant Secretary for Far Eastern Affairs 1961–3; Under-Secretary of State for Political Affairs 1963–5; ambassador at large 1965–9.

3 Denis William Brogan (1900–74), Kt 1963, specialist on American history; Professor of Political Science, Cambridge, 1939–68.

4 The Virginia home of, first, Senator John F. Kennedy, and then, from 1957, his brother Robert and his large family.

call liberty – the not being dominated by other persons or circumstances to the limits possible in a given situation – of which he seemed to me a far richer and fuller example than anyone now in charge of things in England. Saint-Simon,[1] and after him Hegel, as you know, said that in order to do great things one must be *passionné*[2] – that he had in full measure. When he fixed his round, slightly protrusive eyes upon one and asked questions to which he expected answers, and would not take evasions or vagueness for answers, that was very impressive; he had an immense desire to squeeze life like an orange and win something from it – not let anything pass, not drift, not take for granted; all conversations were designed either for pleasure or for profit – either to extend his knowledge or to be amused, but never simply to drift along as most people's conversations do. I thought that he was humanly a little stiff, and not the kind of life I should like to lead myself nor character-istics I should like my friends to possess, but in a leader of a State probably excellent and admirable. Anyway, let that be. I am sure the circumstances of his assassination will be discussed, like the Dreyfus case,[3] for ever, and all kinds of people, even if some very convincing account is finally produced, will believe that it was not quite like that, or not like that at all, but some-thing altogether different that really happened. The trauma upon American consciousness will, I should say, be considerable, though what its effects will be I simply do not know, and I do not know who does [...].

Yours,
    Isaiah   [...]

In 1963 Robert Craft published Dialogues and a Diary, *one of a series of works chronicling his lifelong association with Stravinsky. The volume included several passages about IB, among them a vignette of an October 1961 encounter with Stravinsky and the poet Robert Graves, during which Craft observed the latter listening 'enviously' as Stravinsky and IB conversed in Russian. Elsewhere Craft noted that 'an ironical gaiety' underlay everything that IB said, but in furnish-ing his readers with a particular example of this he unsettled IB, eliciting a strong letter in protest.*

May 15 [1962]. *Paris. Isaiah Berlin to discuss 'Abraham and Isaac' with I[gor] S[travinsky]. He has a habit of concluding his sentences with an upset belied by*

1 Claude-Henri de Rouvroy, comte de Saint-Simon (1760–1825), French utopian social theorist, regarded as one of the originators of socialism and of social science.
2 When dying Saint-Simon is reported to have told his patron, the French banker and social reformer (Benjamin) Olinde Rodrigues (1795–1851): 'Remember that to do anything great you must be impassioned.' 'Notices historiques I: Saint-Simon', in *Oeuvres de Saint-Simon et d'Enfantin* (Paris, 1865–78), i 121. In the first of his *Lectures on the Philosophy of History* (1832) Hegel wrote: 'Nothing great in the world has been accomplished without passion.' op. cit. (164/2) xi 52.
3 Alfred Dreyfus (1859–1935), a Jewish captain in the French Army, was falsely convicted of treason in December 1894; the affair revealed deep and enduring divisions in French society, which was polarised by anti-Semitism.

the string of preceding adjectives. Thus, X. is 'intelligent, charming, capable, and a complete crook'. Isaiah claims that his favorite piece of English music is *On Hearing the First Cuckold of Spring*, and, talking about the group of American composers – Piston, Schuman, Barber etc. – he says that their pieces are 'like *New Yorker* short stories: you don't actually have to read them'.[1]

TO ROBERT CRAFT

26 December 1963 [*carbon*]

[Carlyle Hotel, New York]

Dear Robert:

I was and am appalled and upset by your references to me on p. 203 of *Dialogues and a Diary*. There are other misrepresentations of me in this book, but the entry on p. 203, headed 'France, May 15, 1962' seems designed to bring me into open ridicule and contempt. Let me add that while not a single statement in this entry is accurate, most of it is absolutely untrue. In particular, the attribution to me of the caricature of 'Cuckold of Spring' (I had never seen or heard this odious little joke until I saw it in your pages) humiliated me very deeply.

Can you undertake to instruct your Publishers – Doubledays – to delete the entry for 15 May 1962, *in its entirety*, from any reissues of the book, and guarantee that it will not be reproduced in any form outside the USA?

If not, I shall have to instruct my solicitor to take appropriate measures regarding Doubledays.

I wish I knew what made you do all this; for I have surely never done you any harm.

Yours sincerely,

[Isaiah]

At the beginning of December 1963 IB travelled to Pasadena, California, as a member of the Appointments Committee of the Harkness Foundation, to visit Commonwealth Fellows at American universities on the Pacific coast; Aline joined him in America soon afterwards, and they spent Christmas and New Year 1964 on the East Coast.

TO KAY GRAHAM

5 January 1964 [*manuscript*]

Carlyle Hotel

Dear Kay

It was marvellous & delightful – Washington – the Chip/Joe row took one back, along a very familiar series of boxes, to the dim, happy past – all

1 Igor Stravinsky and Robert Craft, *Dialogues and a Diary* (NY, 1963), 178; 38; 203, first entry under section heading 'France' (entry excised from the edition published in London in 1968).

the rows – Prich[1] – Phil[2] – Chip & Joe like Mutt & Jeff[3] – Maclean[4] &c & c. & c., which terrible as it may have seemed at the time, is now an indelible and precious, delightful, ingredient of the soil of which the past is made, & on which I dwell continually. Thank you very much indeed: very very much: the opening dinner & the Brandon close[5] were very fine – but your dinner was what, I cannot deny, I looked forward to: I love New York: it is to me like a huge toy shop filled with delights – all play, no work, wonderful buildings, eccentric people (bare-kneed kilted bearded men in velour hats & elegant gloves: followed by 2 Buddhists in robes staring at a machine shop window etc.) & I love it, & Washington is where our youth is rooted – I was never really young, & younger in my e[arly] thirties than I was in my twenties, & I fell in love there [...] & every time I enter Georgetown I see with bemused eyes. I shd have been appalled & gloomy if you had not been there: the only thing I regret is not to have had a chance of a long, indiscreet, dangerous conversation, more candid than I can possibly have with anyone else there [...]. So it wd be a *good* thing if you came to Europe – Portofino or Oxford – & Aline wd be very pleased, she assumes that she bothers people by coming, & is deeply touched by her welcome in Washington. [...]

much love

Isaiah

TO HAMISH HAMILTON[6]

14 January [1964]

Headington House

Dear Jamie,

You will by this time, I suspect, have heard from Iris Origo about my plaintive letter to her about her quotations from BB in her introduction to the Diaries. An Italian graduate student in Berkeley, Cal., suddenly brought the *Atlantic Monthly* to my bedroom, and there I read it, fascinated, admiring, until I came to the passage dealing with myself, when I felt a hideous sinking of the spirits. If I am told that I am unduly sensitive, I cannot possibly

---

1 Ed(ward) Fretwell Prichard, Jr ('Prich') (1915–84), US lawyer who worked for FDR during the war; IB shared a house with him in Washington in summer 1943; his hopes of a political career were ruined after he was convicted in 1949 of ballot-stuffing during a senatorial election in Kentucky; he rebuilt his public reputation through public works, notably the advocacy of higher education.

2 IB and Phil Graham had had a 'terrible row' in March 1952 that led to a period of estrangement, followed by an 'official' reconciliation (L2 516).

3 The eponymous knockabout characters in a famous US cartoon strip, drawn by H. C. ('Bud') Fisher from 1907.

4 For IB's wartime row with the spy Donald Maclean see 524, L1 532.

5 Presumably the dinner hosted at the end of IB's Washington visit by (Oscar) Henry Brandon (1916–93) né Brandeis, the *Sunday Times* correspondent in Washington 1949–83.

6 Hamish ('Jamie') Hamilton (1900–88), publisher.

disagree; but you will say that you knew that already, and if you say that I shall not disagree either.[1]

No doubt things read differently to oneself when they are about oneself than they do to other people. The spectacle of Namier, myself and Mr Horovitz[2] regaling the aged humanist with humorous Yiddish anecdotes drawn from our rich (but hitherto mysteriously concealed) ghetto experiences is a truly strange one. I do not for a moment believe that Namier ever remotely – or could have – titillated the Old Boy in this fashion. About the late Mr Horovitz, I cannot tell, perhaps he did. No doubt Sam Behrman did precisely this (indeed, I think he told me that he did, and this may be the source of the confusion). If I knew Yiddish, had a turn for such entertainment and could do jolly party turns of this sort (like, say, Victor Gollancz), I should have been delighted to do it & boast of it, too, but it seems to me to distort what occurred in the most peculiar fashion. It is, as I told Iris, as if she had been represented as telling salty Yankee tales or K. Clark[3] as going back to fundamentals, casting away the cloak of polite culture and going back to braw Scotch stories, told in the vernacular, in the manner of Harry Lauder.[4] If (can you imagine it?) K. Clark had any talent for this, and did it to amuse his friends, perhaps he would not mind this being reported either. However, there is nothing to be done. BB did write this down as if it had really happened; and Nicky[5] selected it as throwing some sort of light upon his tastes (as indeed it does; and also about his failing grasp of reality). The text is sacred and must not be tampered with, and little as I relish the thought of being represented in this ludicrous way, I should not wish anything to be done to alter what has been written by an interesting and remarkable, if not exactly benevolent, old teller of tales. I did, of course, talk to him about the Jews, virtually whenever we met – or rather, he talked about them to me: but never in a manner to suggest nostalgia for what he describes as 'mother's cooking', always in a portentous, tragic fashion, and I did once write him a serious letter from Naples describing the embarkation of a ship proceeding to Israel on which I sailed, and the contrasting behaviour of the Israelis and the American Jews who travelled on it, a letter

1 On New Year's Eve, 1963, IB had written to Pat Utechin: 'I am making a hideous fuss about remarks about me in the latest Stravinsky & Berenson books: so you see, all is normal.'

2 Bela Horovitz (1898–1955), Hungarian born founder, in Vienna in 1923, of the art publisher Phaidon; convinced Ernst Gombrich to write for that firm his hugely successful *The Story of Art* (London, 1950).

3 Kenneth Mackenzie ('K') Clark (1903–83), later (1969) life peer, OM 1976, art historian; Slade Professor of Fine Art, Oxford, 1946–50, 1961–2; first Chairman of the Independent Television Authority 1954–7; his famous television series *Civilisation* was broadcast by the BBC 1969; Clark had worked closely with Berenson at I Tatti 1925–7.

4 Henry ('Harry') Lauder (1870–1950), Kt 1919, Scottish miner turned music-hall singer: 'while not inventing the stage Scotsman, [he] did much to construct and reinforce certain notions of Scottish identity' (Dave Russell, ODNB); his stage turns included 'Stop your tickling, Jock' (1905).

5 Elizabetta ('Nicky') Mariano (1887–1968), employed by Berenson as his librarian and secretary in 1919. She became his mistress and an integral part of his life and work at I Tatti.

which Nicky said he liked and which had no sly humour or cosy familiarity or ghetto memories about it.[1] In the next passage, where he conducts that most embarrassing comparison of himself with me, I can strictly complain of nothing: it is not true that we came from similar circumstances. I was brought up until aged nine in the most conventionally middle-class, bourgeois fashion imaginable – in a hideous stone house in the very German city of Riga, and later Petrograd, with a dreary governess and the severest possible middle-class values: and was afterwards transplanted bodily to London, NW3 – nothing to boast of, but evidently not very similar to BB's childhood.[2] But since he chose to believe that we were culturally identical twins, let that be so. Iris, when she wrote to me, spoke about his 'puzzled jealousy' of me – a strange thing if true. Jealousy of what? Puzzled by what? But let that pass. It is only that I do not want these passages repeated in the introduction, where they are pinpointed and therefore attention is drawn to them particularly, when in fact they convey a factually false impression. But diarists are entitled to their subjective feelings, and even to their falsehoods, and that is why I cannot possibly ask for any change in the text – that must, as I said, be sacred and stand (I suppose). But do let it be left out in the introduction. That is really all.

Oh dear – I wish that instead of wanting things set right I was merely delighted to have been mentioned at all by so fascinating a man, and yet the spirit and not merely the flesh is weak: when Meyer Schapiro wrote his denunciation of BB I nearly rushed into print with a letter passionately defending him,[3] and not like Ben Nicolson,[4] half defending him (or a quarter), and only did not publish it because in the end I did not wish to hurt the feelings of Meyer, to whom I am devoted. And now that I have seen what BB says about me, my four-square stand is diminished: to one square at the most, or perhaps to none. Isn't it terrible that personal relationships play so large a part? Bloomsbury made so much of this, I am not sure it was not too much, and prefer to be made of granite, impartial, just, unfeeling. [...]

Yours,

Isaiah   [...]

---

1 Letter of 11 April 1958, L2 617–21.
2 Berenson's father, an impoverished Lithuanian Jew, emigrated to Boston in 1874, followed by his young family in 1875.
3 Letter of 21 January 1961, 25–7 above.
4 (Lionel) Ben(edict) Nicolson (1914–78), son of Harold Nicolson and Vita Sackville-West, and a close friend of IB from Oxford in the 1930s; art historian; editor, *The Burlington Magazine*, 1947–78.

TO MARTIN GILBERT

22 January [1964]

Headington House

Dear Gilbert,

I am pretty immovable, yes. Taylor insulted me publicly, so much that even the editor of the paper sent some sort of oblique apologies to me for what even he thought was a little too caddish. Whatever my feelings about Taylor are, therefore, why should I publicly celebrate him? That seems to me too Christian an attitude – humility is a virtue that can be overdone. I therefore do not propose, in my present state of mind, to do this, and cannot quite understand why you should either: Taylor's latest views about Jews and intermarriage are worthy of Wells or Joad[1] at their worst – even Muggeridge[2] would have shrunk a little before giving this kind of advice in a painful situation. I feel that Taylor was once a friend – but that friend is dead. Why don't you telephone to me, and have a meal, and talk about this – I should much like it.

Yours sincerely,
    Isaiah Berlin

TO HAMISH HAMILTON

22 January [1964]

Headington House

Dear Jamie,

I *have* bad luck. And now a letter from Nicky to answer as well, in which she blames herself for allowing the word 'ghetto' to occur. But *this* is not at all what I mind; the fact that I don't come from one, even in BB's sense, does not make such origins mindable – if I did feel this, even for a moment, I should be *much* too ashamed to confess it, even to myself. So now I must write her a letter in turn, explaining why I had not written to her originally, that I should have been delighted to come from a ghetto, etc. etc. What a bore, what a nuisance. The odd but clear explanation given in Nicky's letter is in fact that the old boy knew perfectly well that what he was saying was not true – there, and presumably elsewhere. But that we did not need telling. BB knew very well what integrity was, but it was not among his many gifts. Still, I shall not spit upon his grave, and have just refused to review the book for the *Spectator* on these grounds. I wonder what Raymond Mortimer, e.g., will

1 Cyril Edwin Mitchinson Joad (1891–1953), Head of Philosophy, Birkbeck College, London, 1930–53, and a well-known populariser of philosophy on the BBC programme *The Brains Trust* in its radio incarnation. His best-known catch-phrase was 'It all depends what you mean by ...'.
2 (Thomas) Malcolm Muggeridge (1903–90), journalist and broadcaster; editor, *Punch*, 1953–7; enormously successful through his outspoken television appearances.

make of it in the *Sunday Times*. BB once told me that he despised Raymond more deeply than any Englishman he had ever known, then said, 'No. There are other people in Gloomsbury who were more *mesquin*:[1] Clive Bell,[2] for instance.' I defended them, but feebly. He probably said this of all of us, at one time or another. But Nicky has been tactful & kind to the major- ity – whether he [Berenson] meant this I do not know: it emerges nowhere (I hope) in print, and you must certainly not repeat it to him [Mortimer], or anyone. But in view of what Raymond is bound to say, I could not bear not to tell you – what games he played, what strange, elaborate nets he wove, what an interesting man, alternately attracted and repelled by himself, with a hate–love attitude towards all but persons he felt totally superior to. But there, enough. Let the book have its proper fate.

    Yours,

      Isaiah

TO GARRETT DROGHEDA

    27 January [1964]

Headington House

Dear Garrett,

    The more I think of it, the more terrible the idea of Ustinov[3] as producer of *The Magic Flute* grows to be in my mind. I ought, I suppose, to have been more outspoken about that at the Subcommittee [...]. Ustinov has a broad, un-grown-up, schoolboy humour, and *L'Heure espagnole* was very taste- less and coarse, with hideous vulgarities; so, indeed, were parts of *Gianni Schicchi*[4] – the décor of the latter was excellent, so was the conducting and the singing, but the movements of the actors and leerings were, I thought, overdone and embarrassing – this was even more so in the Ravel. One can, of course, take the view of *The Magic Flute* which George seemed to – that it is all dominated by the horse-play of Papageno; without going so far as the opposite extreme – Toscanini's sublime conception of the love music and everything to do with the temple and the sun – or Klemperer's noble

---

1 'Petty, mean-spirited'.

2 (Arthur) Clive Heward Bell (1881–1964), art critic and writer; married, 1907, the painter Vanessa née Stephen (1879–1961), elder sister of Virginia Woolf. In 1920 the Bloomsbury trio of Vanessa Bell, John Maynard Keynes and the painter Duncan James Corrowr Grant (1885–1978) visited I Tatti; Bell took 'a deep dislike to Berenson's manner' and was 'invariably wrapped in sulky silence' throughout the visit: this no doubt confirmed Berenson's opinion of 'Gloomsbury'. Ernest Samuels, *Bernard Berenson* (Cambridge, Mass., 1987), 273–4.

3 Peter Alexander Ustinov (1921–2004), actor, dramatist, film director; directed operas at Covent Garden, Hamburg, Paris, the Edinburgh Festival etc.

4 The conclusion of Georg Solti's first year as Musical Director at Covent Garden was marked by a triple bill consisting of Schoenberg's *Erwartung* and two comic operas, Ravel's *L'Heure espagnole* and Puccini's *Gianni Schicchi*: according to *The Times*, Peter Ustinov 'made a remarkable debut' as the operatic producer of this programme, 'resourceful, stylish, and always sensitive to the interaction of music and drama' (18 June 1962, 5a).

beauty and gravity – I infinitely prefer these to what the opposite might easily become – high jinks – the geniuses of Geraint Evans[1] and Ustinov combined – and music-hall stuff, with sentimentality in the serious scenes substituted for classical beauty. So if you have any influence with Solti, do stop him from approaching Ustinov too early. I shall send no copies of this letter to anyone, but shall beg you to ask Solti to hold his hand, at least, while we think of other ideas, and perhaps ask people tomorrow whether they have some. To ruin *The Magic Flute* is almost unavoidable, yet we might think of a way out if we try hard enough. [...] Ustinov is what is called 'amusing' – to offer him *The Magic Flute* is like offering *A Midsummer Night's Dream* to Glock for the sake of Puck, and it would come out at best like Rossini, more likely like Offenbach, most likely of all like vaudeville.[2] [...]

Yours,

[IB p.p.]

In June 1961, within a few months of taking over at Covent Garden, Georg Solti announced that he intended to stage the English premiere of Schoenberg's dramatic oratorio Moses and Aaron. *The work had been staged only twice before, in Zurich in 1957 and in Berlin in 1959, and it was an ambitious undertaking for any company. It was slow to materialise at Covent Garden. In a July 1963 review of Solti's first two years in charge, the music critic of* The Times *observed that some of the Musical Director's 'best plans' had been 'thwarted or postponed',[3] a production of Schoenberg's opera among them. IB did not know the opera, but saw it as a flagship work that was vital to the development and international reputation of the ROH, and in February 1964, sensing that Solti's commitment to it was flagging, and egged on by Garrett Drogheda, he wrote him a strong letter of encouragement. Soon afterwards it was announced that* Moses and Aaron *would be included in the 1964–5 season, with Solti himself at the rostrum. It would be staged on a grand scale, with a huge cast, memorable designs by John Bury, and bold production from Peter Hall.[4] There were nearly*

---

1 Geraint Llewellyn Evans (1922–92), later (1969) Kt; principal baritone, ROH, 1948–84; of his 60 or so principal parts 'many of the most successful, such as Mozart's Figaro, Papageno and Leporello [...] or Verdi's Falstaff, were comic; his genius was for comedy, in the widest sense of the word' (Cliff Morgan, *Independent*, 21 September 1992, 11).

2 Covent Garden's next production of *The Magic Flute*, in July 1966, was produced by Peter Hall; it was favourably received, if not favourably remembered by Hall himself (see interview with Barbara Isenberg, *Los Angeles Times*, 24 January 1993, *Calendar*, 60 and 89 at 89).

3 *Times*, 26 July 1963, 16e–g. IB doubted Solti's enthusiasm for the work as early as 1962, writing to Drogheda on 19 July: 'Burnet thinks that Solti may never allow us to do this work at all, since he is not interested in it for himself'; and on 6 February 1964 Drogheda wrote to IB with confirmation: '[Solti] does not now wish us to do Moses. [...] He has decided that it is not a great masterpiece.'

4 Peter Reginald Frederick Hall (b. 1930), later (1977) Kt; theatre, film and opera director; founded Royal Shakespeare Company as a permanent ensemble 1960; Managing Director at Stratford-on-Avon and Aldwych Theatre, London, 1960–8; Associate Director 1968–73; Director, National Theatre, 1973–88; a plan for him to work alongside Colin Davis at the ROH, as a joint director of productions, did not materialise.

two months of rehearsals for just six performances. Before the first night (28 June 1965) Solti described the endeavour as 'the most difficult, and the most reward-ing, task of my life', adding: 'If we have all done our job properly, it should be an unforgettable experience.'[1] *This it proved to be. By common consent the pro-duction was 'not only a major vindication of the work, but also one of the Royal Opera's greatest post-war successes'.*[2] *It also enjoyed a succès de scandale with the depiction of an orgy 'complete with dozens of naked "virgins" disporting themselves around the golden calf. Solti, in the pit, complained that from his vantage point he was the one person in the house who could never see them.'*[3] *Soon after the first night IB wrote: 'With all his faults, the Musical Director has proved of terrific value to us; he really has transformed both the reality and the image of Covent Garden.'*[4]

TO GEORG SOLTI

10 February [1964; *carbon*]

Headington House

Dear George,

First, let me condole with you once again about the events of last Friday.[5] *Force majeure* not even all our prayers, let alone an insurance company, will insure against; I thought everyone's behaviour was heroic and that we have absolutely no reason for any self-criticism or self-condemnation in this par-ticular case. The first scene was a great triumph and if Evans can emerge through the tunnel he may yet impose a new image of *Rigoletto* on our con-sciousness; he has the artistic resources – whether his voice can be made to do this is another question – it must for him be a most dreadful blow in his career. No baritone, I am sure, wants to remain Papageno, Leporello, even Falstaff, Iago, Figaro only. In the end I suppose it is a matter of training and discipline, which we haven't yet established in this country. But I must not go on about this, when you know and understand so much more about it than I do. Anyway, I feel absolutely convinced that out of the marvellous ingre-dients of our *Rigoletto* a great and magnificent structure can yet be erected under your powerful and inspired hand. And I am sure you believe it too.

What I really wanted to raise was *Moses and Aaron* again. We did have a few words about it in your room in the Opera House but that was not an

1 *Times*, 7 June 1965, 4f–g.
2 Stephen Follows s.v. Solti, ODNB.
3 ibid.   Sub v   see under
4 To Garrett Drogheda, 5 July 1965.
5 Covent Garden's 1964 production of *Rigoletto* – which IB thought 'literally the most enjoyable opera in the world' (to Bernard Williams, 25 January 1964) – was dogged by misfortune. Geraint Evans, singing the title role for the first time in his career, fell ill, delaying the opening night. On the new date he gamely took the stage, though still not fully recovered. His voice failed him, and he apologised personally at the end of the performance.

evening appropriate to this, and I apologise for even bringing it up then. I see that with a new work, so controversial and discussed, which makes equally big demands – enormous ones, in fact – not only on the performers but on the audience too – (why should they respond to it more readily than they ever have in the history of music to the genuinely revolutionary and original?) one has to be absolutely convinced of the value of the work to make so much effort, sacrifice so much of oneself, physically, emotionally, and in the case of the Opera House itself, financially. Our original motive for promising to do it still seems to me valid: it is, so far as I can judge (not that my views can claim to have the slightest aesthetic weight), a noble, austere, uncompromising work of major dimensions, artistically and historically important. I do not accept what Sir Thomas Armstrong said at our Opera Subcommittee meeting – that from the point of view of prestige we had missed the moment, that had we done it three or four years ago it would have been a world event, whereas now it will not make an impact. Of course it has to be prepared for, very differently from the way in which *Khovanshchina* or *Katerina Ismailova*[1] were offered by us: critics from abroad have to be invited; articles in the press, both musical and general, stimulated; lectures on Schoenberg and this opera in particular arranged, both for the Friends of Covent Garden and the BBC and perhaps at one or two universities as well. All these things I think the 'Schoenbergians' would be prepared to help with – they are as near to a fanatical musical sect as we have in these days – as the Wagnerians or the Brahmsians were before them; and their help should on no account be scorned. In short, I think that the 'right mood' for the work could probably be, by perfectly legitimate and honourable means, created. Moreover, since it is not the kind of work that would enter the repertory, even in the sense perhaps that *Wozzek*[2] has, it would be a pity if our performances disappeared into oblivion or became mere respectful memories. I am sure that records could be made of so authoritative a kind that these performances and these records would become the classical exposition of Schoenberg at his most ambitious and profound. In this sense, I do not see why the impact should not be cumulative and great. If this were done, you would surely and deservedly become a great opener of gates: no first-class performance of this work, so far as I know, has been performed in a great opera house [...]. If Schoenberg even begins to be what his most passionate followers claim for him, there is surely a case for so permanent and conspicuous a service to music as the identification of Covent Garden and yourself

1 *Khovanshchina*, an unfinished opera by Mussorgsky, orchestrated by Shostakovich, was premiered at the Kirov in Leningrad on 25 November 1960, and at Covent Garden on 18 June 1963 (IB contributed a 'Historical Note' to the programmme). *Katerina Ismailova*, the revised 1963 version of Shostakovich's 1934 opera *Lady Macbeth of the Mtsensk District*, was first staged at Covent Garden on 2 December 1963.
2 Alban Berg's three-act opera, in German, first performed at Covent Garden on 22 January 1952.

with a magnificent exposition of this new chapter in the history of opera. I know of no musical development of similar *bahnbrechend* importance; no matter how excellent our performances of e.g. Britten are – and you have served that composer nobly and memorably, as he knows and everyone knows – historians of music will not accord him the same crucial importance, it seems to me. I may of course be mistaken about this, but this is how it looks at present: Poulenc, Shostakovich, Prokofiev, come below this. Stravinsky belongs, like them, to an earlier chapter.

For these reasons, and quite apart from what we are to say to the public if we suddenly drop *Moses*, I would urge you most urgently to reconsider this question [...]. This, of course, is not to be considered if the work is genuinely not good enough, or even if you do not feel drawn towards it or simply do not like it. If that is so, there is nothing to be done: for certainly nobody else could do it – it would be foolish even to consider the possibility and we must then take our punishment like men. But I still have a feeling which will not leave me, that unless we go boldly forward and perform modern masterpieces – even if our main concern is still to establish a solid classical repertory – we shall stand still or retrogress; and that Britten, Shostakovich, even Henze, are not quite enough to ensure this, although of course Britten in particular is a very proper object of special devotion for us. No doubt *Moses* would involve us in quite a heavy financial loss; but perhaps with recordings and the BBC this could to some degree be defrayed. [...]

Please forgive me: I did not think you would mind this great outpouring about a matter on which I feel strongly; I believe that other members of the board also have views: but I don't wish to speak for them, nor can I: of course in the end it is your decision and yours alone.

[Isaiah]

TO TEDDY KOLLEK

21 February [1964]

Headington House

Dear Teddy,

Forgive me for these tourist requests, but to whom else can I turn? The situation is this. [...] My mother has had a cataract on both eyes diagnosed by Michaelson[1] (my mother is terribly secretive and does not want any facts about herself known: most unreasonable, but persons over eighty years of age must be humoured, even when they are not one's own mother), and I have urged her to be operated on in the Hadassah Hospital by that excellent man. The operation occurs, I think, on Tuesday next (remember you

1 Isaac Claude Michaelson (1903–82), Edinburgh-born ophthalmologist; specialist in ophthalmology, Territorial Army, Middle East, 1939–46; emigrated to Israel 1948; Director, Dept of Ophthalmology, Hadassah University Hospital, Jerusalem, 1954–73.

know nothing), and of course my mother does not want me to come out; nor, indeed, could I, for various ghastly reasons. Meanwhile Aline proposes to pay her a surprise visit […]. Hence the request for a room at the King David for two nights. She proposes to go to the Hadassah on the Friday afternoon, Sabbath or no Sabbath, and also on the Saturday; and if you could have a meal with her on Friday evening or Saturday she would be extremely pleased. My mother is to know nothing of this until Aline actually arrives, when she will no doubt send a telephone message. She leaves Israel at crack of dawn on Sunday morning.

Do not on any account think of going to meet her at Lod – that is really unnecessary and would embarrass her as a terrible sacrifice of your time and energy, which should of course, as is well known, be devoted entirely to thoughts about music festivals and nothing else at all. But if you could communicate with her in the King David that would be kind – and if you could ask the hotel to send her a car to meet her at the airport, and if the driver could be supplied with a handful of Israeli currency, that would be most useful. Let me once again beg your forgiveness for all this dislocation. […]

Yours ever,

Isaiah   […]

TO MARIE BERLIN

3 March [1964]

Headington House

Dearest Ma,

Since you cannot read my letters at the moment, I shall not make this too personal and intimate, but simply report that Aline is back in excellent health, having enjoyed her visit to Jerusalem very much indeed. Particularly she enjoyed her day with you. […]

I realise that you are longing for the *Evening Standard*, so I think I had better order it for you. I am putting in the latest sheet of financial news, which I know fascinates you like a kind of game. I had the pleasure of travelling with Mr Bloom[1] in the train from London, who enquired most tenderly about you, and so of course did Mrs Greenberg, who had no idea that you were in hospital and was much relieved when I told her that you were all right: she spent about a quarter of an hour on the telephone praising every aspect of your character while I applauded these sentiments.

I am also delighted to hear that you have grown two years younger than you originally were owing to your father's peculiar political arithmetic – that is very satisfactory, and you can regard yourself now as living in 1962. As you can see, I am talking nonsense for want of something concrete to say.

---

1 Mr Bloom and Mrs Greenberg were presumably Hampstead friends of Marie Berlin.

Now about plans – always an agreeable thing to talk about: my assumption is that you will be well enough to come back by yourself on the 25th and that I shall meet you at London Airport when you arrive. Of course, I could come over and fetch you, but not, unfortunately, before the 27th, as I have a television appointment with Professor Ayer and Mr J. B. Priestley to talk about some idiotic subject on the BBC:[1] it would be difficult to cancel that except under conditions of extreme urgency. I know that you will say that you don't need anyone, that you can go perfectly well by yourself, etc. etc., and I know this to be true. [...]

I can find nothing to worry about – if there is something do tell me and I shall start worrying at once. I was really terribly relieved when Aline came back and gave me all this news. Of course I knew that it was all right ever since Professor Michaelson was so kind as to send me his messages, but given your own determined desire not to worry me and always to conceal your ailments and minimise all these things and say that there is no necessity for me to come and everything is perfectly all right, etc. etc., I am naturally suspicious, and had to send a trusted agent of my own. But Aline brought back an exceedingly good report and now my mind is set at rest [...]. I have absolutely no more to tell you at the moment – *comme à la guerre* – like soldiers at the war say 'hoping this finds you as it leaves me',

With much love,
    Isaiah

The reforming energy in All Souls evident in the doomed motion to admit women in Spring 1962 found a more acceptable cause a year later with the publication of the Harrison Report.[2] This emanated from a university subcommittee chaired by Robin Harrison,[3] soon to become Warden of Merton. Harrison investigated the status of the 250 or so holders of university posts to which no college fellowship was attached – the so-called 'non-dons'. Harrison urged that more college fellowships be made available to them, sentiments that resonated strongly with the reformers in All Souls, where a college version of the Harrison Committee was convened to consider the issue. It deliberated for much of 1963 with the best of intentions, but with very modest results: eventually just three new fellows were admitted to the college. The exercise nevertheless invigorated reform there.

Harrison made clear that he regarded Merton's ancient endowments 'not as a reason for safeguarding privilege but as a resource for promoting educational

---

1 IB and Ayer appeared in the inaugural *Conversations for Tomorrow*, presented by J. B. Priestley; the programme was recorded on 26 March, and transmitted on the evening of 25 April, days after the launch of BBC2 (on 20 April). The recording survives, and a transcript is available in the IBVL at ⟨http://berlin.wolf.ox.ac.uk/lists/nachlass/conversa.pdf⟩.
2 *Report on the Closer Integration of University Teaching and Research within the College System* (Oxford, 1962).
3 (Alick) Robin Walsham Harrison (1900–69), Warden of Merton College, at which he had been an undergraduate, and later (1950–63) Fellow and Tutor in Ancient History.

advances', and he advocated wealth redistribution between the colleges.[1] *All*
Souls could not ignore this proposal, and in the spring of 1964 plans were drawn
up to spend some of its excess revenue – which had grown to an embarrassing
size since the late 1950s – on additional research fellowships, and on a new build-
ing in College to accommodate them.

Once again IB found himself siding with the 'young fauves' against the
'troglodytes', and this had serious implications for his long friendship with John
Sparrow. After a key vote in March he wrote to Bernard Williams:

I am in the mood for feeling guilt about everything, particularly about having
assisted in a vote at All Souls – which would have pleased you – whereby the
Warden scored 5 votes and the rest of the College 35, so that he is now speaking
of resigning. Everyone is apologising all round and wounds are being unsuccessfully staunched. When I see you I shall tell you the whole terrible tale: for once,
justice was on the side of the crushing majority (as you might guess).[2]

The vote left Sparrow isolated, and IB likened him to a Douglas Fairbanks hero,
fending off the rapier thrusts of multiple assailants. What he did not anticipate
is that, like the Fairbanks hero, Sparrow would elude his attackers and ulti-
mately defeat them.

TO JOHN SPARROW

14 March 1964 [*manuscript*]

Headington House

My dear old friend,
    I too am distressed. Not, of course, about the College's views, which seem
to me right. But about voting & speaking on the opposite side from you.
I mind this *much* more than, I am sure, you even now think. I have enough
public conscience not to vote for what I think against the College's interests,
or abstain. But only just enough: & I wish I hadn't [...]. I didn't & don't like
Kreisel: but I thought the attitude of the majority of the College was such
that to my own astonishment I felt suddenly totally "alienated" from the
College & its affairs. I decided it had too little respect for the intellect: &
found the Stoic maxims about how not to mind what others think or do
were suddenly true of me. I attended meetings of committees & the College
& did not care a bit what they did. [...] Stuart (alone I believe) noticed this
queer snapping of bonds in my feeling about the College (forgive this egocentric pompousness) and said he too was glad to be gone: but he is not,
whereas I am, deeply institutional in my loyalties. But I felt bland & detached
& thought about Romanticism. What, funnily enough, revived my loyalties

1 *Times*, 19 May 1969, 10h.
2 To Bernard Williams, 13 March 1964.

was talks with Crossman: his desire to humiliate and tread down the Oxford which you deeply & I with modifications but also deeply love & believe in.

My feeling for All Souls revived. It will never be quite what it was: never of Manciple-like single mindedness. But it awoke again. I thought that it must either [*sic*?] go forward vigorously: if it stood fairly still, it would wither & be defeated from outside – Crossman & Maurice & Nuffield & all our ill wishers. The Harrison Committee took this view: you alone dissented & written communications were called for: I had *no* intention of writing anything: I have never in my life before circulated anything to the College (I believe) & have *never* lobbied save once, when I passionately wished you to be Warden. But when Beloff's letter arrived, it seemed to me ill argued & mistaken: I sat down & wrote a rejoinder: it was too long & badly written: I thought: all the College needs is the Harrison documents reduced to a few clear heads: plus the argument against Beloff: this will at least crystallize discussion & help to avert those nightmarish chaotic endless mornings. I never thought, of course, that there was such unanimity, or I should not have bothered: it was there, I am sure, before the Fisher–Berlin[1] document: that only summarised the views of the great majority of the Harrison Committee. I thought Fisher was a better draughtsman than I: I am sure he is: but I took care to say to you, more than once, what I believed: & to Bill Deakin[2] & James Joll too, very explicitly: I wish to spring no surprises. And I did no "lobbying" (although there is nothing wicked about that). Fisher drafted the summarised Harrison + anti-Beloff: it seemed to convince even Beloff. Was I morally at fault in any way? disloyal? secretive? I cannot see it. I thought (& think) your position too extreme: but you are too proud and too contemptuous (rightly I daresay) of the majority of our colleagues, & too aesthetically fastidious to seek untidy compromises or "explore" their minds or "sound out" views. A. H. Smith[3] lost cause after cause in New College: but he was not wholly human: & did not seem to mind or remember or care: only the rejection of his application for D.Litt seriously wounded him. But you mind greatly: like a Renaissance prince full of virtue & a sense of honour. You *are* all this: not a professional politician, like Churchill not like Roosevelt: imaginative, unbending, disdainful; with, ultimately far greater devotion to personal relationships than for public aspects of anything: naturally aristocratic, and liable to pay the price of this: you cannot *bear* the common & even the slightly cheap. I remember the *present* Lord Salisbury[4] when he

---

1 Henry ('Harry') *Fisher, then Fellow and Estates Bursar of All Souls, later (1975–85) IB's successor as President of Wolfson.

2 260/2.

3 Alic Halford Smith (1883–1958), philosopher; Acting Warden (on the death of H. A. L. Fisher), New College, 1940–4; Warden 1944–58; Vice-Chancellor, Oxford, 1954–7.

4 Robert Arthur James ('Bobbety') Gascoyne-Cecil, Viscount Cranborne (1893–1972), 5th Marquess of Salisbury 1947; Unionist MP, South Dorset, 1929–41. In February 1938 Cranborne resigned with his chief, Anthony Eden (then Foreign Secretary), in protest at Chamberlain's conduct of

watched even his more intransigent seeming colleagues – Duff Cooper[1] for example – calling on Chamberlain in 1939 to get jobs – 'like earthworms" he said "they *do* crawl in' while he watched them, not prepared to make any concession to a man he disapproved of and, I suppose, despised. Of course you hate the very thought of intrigue: I don't hate it so deeply, though I don't take part in it: I did not intrigue with, say, Fisher any more than you with Beloff: I encouraged him to formulate a position I could support, but openly; as soon as I had his draft, I emended it & sent it to you at once: & did not collect other names. You spoke of a 'stab in the back': I know it was not meant altogether seriously – I did not conceal anything – but I was wounded all the same: you knew my views – they were the orthodox Harrison Committee ones – still perhaps you did half or three quarters think me 'disloyal' in some way. But I truly thought (& think) it unwise for the College to stop growing on a substantial scale: we argued about this in the committee: did I do something morally wrong, even inelegant? I do not feel it: if you think so, tell me, I beg you: I love, admire, respect you deeply: I am delighted to have an opportunity for saying it: I would vote for you as Warden, as anything almost, again, now, or, I think, at any time: we each have unattractive allies, that, I suppose, is inevitable: but I am not anxious to play a prominent part in College politics: you cannot avoid it: it is only when issues of principle emerge that I find I cannot retreat. Perhaps we should have talked about this more, both the substance and the methods, and the drift of opinion in the College (about the last I genuinely knew nothing) but I did not think you were anxious to do this. We disagree: that must occasionally happen: but if you think I behaved improperly in some way & aren't saying so, then I should find that far more painful than *any* public issue: I would – & I mean this *absolutely* – resign my fellowship & go to St. Antony's or Nuffield (what else could I do?) than live in the thought that I was under some real cloud in your breast: that would make me utterly wretched. I care for personal relationships (intimacy) more than for the good of the College: but surely it is 'all right' to disagree? even in public? as I did so deeply (over Buxton) with David Cecil (to whom I was closer then than now)[2] or with Stuart over a million issues (he wrote me

foreign policy; he returned to office under Churchill as Paymaster General 1940; Leader of the House of Lords 1942–5, 1951–7; Secretary of State for Commonwealth Relations 1952; Lord President of the Council 1952–7.

1 In October 1938 Duff Cooper, First Lord of the Admiralty, resigned over Munich. After the outbreak of war Chamberlain broadened his government, admitting both Churchill and Eden, but not Duff Cooper. On 21 September 1939 the latter met the Prime Minister, ostensibly to discuss his plans for visiting the United States: 'I had thought that he would have said one word of regret at not having been able to offer me a post in the government and perhaps would have suggested that he might be able to later. It would not have meant anything but would have been civil. He said nothing of the kind.' John Julius Norwich (ed.), *The Duff Cooper Diaries 1915–1951* (London, 2005), 278.

2 For IB's disagreement with David Cecil over the appointment of John Buxton see 635.

a *bitterly* offensive letter over my public praise of Diana Cooper) or any other intimate friend? When Maurice, a day or two ago, attacked me for our examination Fellowships ('every one knows how you elect *them*[']) or not advertising research Fellowships ("its got round the university") I defended 'our' position with acrimony – till he seemed to climb down – even though I think he may be right about the public relations aspects of the latter. [...]

I value our lifelong friendship more than I can say (this cliché is literally true: whatever *can* be said, lacks depth: is finite: nothing that is fundamental & ultimate is, by definition, embraceable in words however finely chosen, however authentic & personal and true), it is one of the rocks on which my life, & I think Aline's life too, is based. Any crack in that, any thought of it is insupportable to me. Still, if there *is* a crack, do say so. I know that one does not like to face reality much; at least I don't: but doubt is worse. I have fewer roots in environment than a native Englishman – but by nature I *am* rooted, not rootless and cosmopolitan (though you have sometimes thought me that, I suspect): I have lived my life in Oxford: & since the war my life has been intertwined with some, if not all, branches of yours: this is a profession of love and faith, & if it embarrasses you – (like Mrs D[alloway][1] why will comic things break in on the most deeply felt experiences? They always do with me. I cannot be solemn: only serious) I cannot help it. There.

    Yours
      Isaiah

TO ALAN PRYCE-JONES[2]
16 March 1964

                                      Headington House
Dear Alan,

[...] You must be very kind to Sparrow: he has just sustained a severe defeat in All Souls with a vote of thirty-five of his colleagues against him with three supporters, of whom I, I must admit, was not one – deserted by all his supporters, he stood there proud and, I must add, in the eyes of some certainly, rather bloody, but certainly unbowed. He speaks of resigning. I do not think this will happen, and indeed hope it will not. The more that can be made of him in New York the better, I am sure. Know nothing of this: but remarks about the imperfect wisdom of fellows of All Souls and their lack of judgement will at the moment not be ill received.

---

1 The eponymous heroine of Virginia Woolf's *Mrs Dalloway* (London, 1925).
2 Alan Payan Pryce-Jones (1908–2000), writer and critic; editor, *The Times Literary Supplement*, 1948–59; he left England in 1960 for America, and worked as a book critic for, among other publications, the *New York Herald Tribune*.

I hope we shall see you in April in New York.
Much love,
   Isaiah

*The Berlins spent the week of 15–23 April in the US: IB lectured on Herder at
Johns Hopkins in Baltimore, and they also visited Washington and New York.*

TO NOEL ANNAN

1 May 1964

Headington House

Dear Noel,

How much I enjoyed receiving your letter! Reading it, I mean. I too grazed
on the edges of the same meadows. I am not sure how I should react to your
tremendous intellectual evenings – perhaps favourably. Trilling[1] embarrasses
me because of his cautious, Anglophile thin skin and anxiety to please. My
friend Morton White in Harvard is somewhat the same – the same half-
obtrusive half-hidden Jewish origins, same thin skin, same neuroses, same
love for people whom he suspects may not appreciate him at his full value;
but him I know intimately and am wholly cosy with, whereas Trilling makes
me feel uneasy at the moment. [...]

I met Bob Silvers[2] for the first time in New York, at Marietta Tree's house,
with the Lowells.[3] I like him and them very much indeed. Robert Lowell
is very distinguished – the slowness of utterance and extreme purity, the
innocence and civilised qualities, quite apart from the poetical ones, are very
fine; but then everyone likes him, so this is not exceptional. Silvers I got on
with; and he got on with me. There, too, was an ex-graduate student from
Oxford called Wahl,[4] the biographer of de Gaulle; a young man somewhat
on the make, I suppose, but intelligent and very nice to me, and I fall for that
in any case, and really ask for nothing better, particularly when abroad. So
I spent a happy evening, gossiping with Silvers about all our common friends
– cosiness and gaiety he possesses, and anyone who has both these properties
wins my heart at once and sometimes for ever: I see why he and Richard

1 Lionel Trilling (1905–75), US literary critic and essayist, taught English at Columbia, where he
   had been an undergraduate, from 1932, Professor 1948–74; George Eastman Visiting Professor,
   Oxford, 1964–5; Visiting Professor, All Souls, 1971–2; author of *The Liberal Imagination* (1950),
   which made him 'a model of the intellectual in Cold War America' (Louis Menand, 'Regrets
   Only: Lionel Trilling and His Discontents', *New Yorker*, 29 September 2008, 89–90).
2 Robert B. ('Bob') *Silvers (b. 1929), co-editor, NYRB.
3 Robert Traill Spence ('Cal') Lowell (1917–77), the highly regarded US poet, and his second wife,
   the writer Elizabeth Hardwick (1916–2007), married in 1949.
4 (Anthony) Nicholas Maria Wahl (1928–96), assistant professor of government and tutor in
   history and literature, Harvard, 1958–64; associate professor of politics, Princeton, 1964–77,
   professor 1977–8. Wahl knew and admired de Gaulle, and was supremely well qualified to write
   a biography of him, but it never materialised.

Wollheim[1] seem so well suited to each other. Dwight and Mary[2] are a different matter and there is no need to discuss them here and now. I thought her article in defence of Miss Arendt[3] was a bit too tough; I wish to go on being friends with her, so I have done and said nothing in a craven way that you can sympathise with, I think, though there were some genuinely horrible things in that which make one glimpse what it is that those who hate her hate her for; and Dwight, with all his brightness and independence, is in some part of him a great big foolish hobbledehoy [...]: it is an endearing quality but maddening too. Anyway, I enjoy meeting him very much too, and always have, except in 1940 when I first met him and he thought that I was so frivolous as to be characteristic of his image of England, which in his opinion deserved to lose the war if everybody was as unserious as Guy Burgess and I. You can imagine what our conversation was like in July–August 1940. [...]

I missed you at the Royal Academy Dinner the other night: it is wonderful to see such members of the Establishment there as Antony,[4] Bill Coldstream,[5] Freddie Ashton[6] – some relaxed and happy to wander among the Cabinet Ministers as patrons of the arts, others slightly embarrassed and

1 Richard Arthur Wollheim (1923–2003), Reader in Philosophy, UCL, 1960–63; Grote Professor of Philosophy of Mind and Logic, London, 1963–82; IB regarded his socialism as of 'the Weimar Republic type [...] – Bohemian, free, demanding moral, sexual, social freedom etc., in fact *Kulturbolschewismus*' (to Umberto Morra, 5 July 1961).

2 Mary Therese McCarthy (1912–89), novelist, critic and social commentator. Her defence of Hannah Arendt's *Eichmann in Jerusalem: A Report on the Banality of Evil* (London, 1963), 'The Hue and Cry', appeared in *Partisan Review* 31 no. 1 (Winter 1964), 82–94: IB thought it 'a poor and unworthy piece – Mary's love for Hannah Arendt is obviously beyond analysis' (to Teddy Kollek, 21 February 1964). McCarthy's friendship with Arendt generated an extensive correspondence published as *Between Friends: The Correspondence of Hannah Arendt and Mary McCarthy, 1949–1975*, ed. Carol Brightman (London, 1995); she married, 1938, the writer and literary critic Edmund Wilson; they were divorced in 1946.

3 Hannah Arendt (1906–75), German-born Jewish philosopher and political theorist; studied under Martin Heidegger; left Germany for France after being interrogated by the Gestapo, and France for US after being interned; in NY she became part of the intellectual scene that clustered around *Partisan Review*. IB had a deep and visceral aversion to her works and character: 'The Eichmann book I have not read; but I must own to you that I have no respect for her; the earlier books seem to me metaphysical free association of some kind – [...] the one on the human condition, much admired by all kinds of distinguished people, seemed to me founded on refutably false historical propositions, "not true, not new and not amusing", as Trotsky once said about a speech by Stalin. Still, this may be unfair and spring from some deep personal prejudice, for when I met her in 1942 her fanatical Jewish nationalism – which has now turned into its opposite – was, I remember, too much for me' (to Bernard Crick, 4 November 1963). The remark of Trotsky's IB is thinking of may be from Trotsky's posthumous biography of Stalin, in which he describes Stalin's writings as 'dry, flabby and false' ('sukhi, vyaly i fal´shivy'): *Stalin: An Appraisal of the Man and his Influence*, ed. and trans. Charles Malamuth (ready for press 1941, but publication postponed until after the war), 2nd ed. (NY and London, 1946), 260.

4 Probably Anthony (*sic*) Frederick Blunt (1907–83), KCVO 1956, later (1979) annulled after his exposure as a Russian spy (one of the cell that included Burgess, Philby and Maclean); art historian; Surveyor of the King's Pictures 1945–52; of the Queen's Pictures 1952–72; Adviser for the Queen's Pictures and Drawings 1972–8; Director of the Courtauld Institute of Art 1947–74.

5 William Menzies Coldstream (1908–87), Kt 1956; Slade Professor of Fine Art, UCL, 1949–75.

6 Frederick William Mallandaine Ashton (1904–88), Kt 1962, later (1977) OM, Principal Choreographer to the Royal Ballet (so named 1956) 1933–70, Director 1963–70.

defiant and wondering whether their integrity is compromised by appearing in such a place at all.

I adored Johns Hopkins: small, not too self-conscious, with some quite clever men to talk to, perfectly civilised, not in a state of open, cut-throat intellectual competition, all men's hands against all men, a kind of Hobbesian state of nature, like Harvard; not a self-conscious, snobbish, agreeable but genuinely reactionary establishment like Princeton, with its Charley's Aunt, spa atmosphere; not stuffy, like Yale – my God, Yale was stuffy when I was there, although I was very well treated; but like Cornell, and even Brown, peacefully pursuing perfectly reputable intellectual ends, with perfectly adequate standards all round, and students tortured neither by ambition nor, so far as I could see, social or racial ulcers of various sorts. I delivered a talk in Princeton to some specially selected seminar, amidst the shyness of the President, the gloom cast by dear George Kennan, the self-conscious presence of Stuart (Mrs H. now describes herself as a non-friend who has known me since birth, and is prepared, I think, to make up). Next year I have to deliver the Mellon Lectures[1] and Woodbridge Lectures[2] – I really do feel that we have become absolutely venal Greeks, going to Rome at every possible opportunity: the general assumption, according to Stuart, is that Englishmen come to America purely to make money or its equivalent; not true, perhaps, but sufficiently near the truth to be embarrassing; nor do I think I am altogether wrong in supposing that the intellectual drawing-power of England for Americans has somewhat diminished: those who like it, like it because it is gentle, civilised, etc., not because there is something specific to learn [...].

Alan Taylor solemnly informed me at a meeting of the British Academy that in his forthcoming volume of the Oxford History of England – Twentieth Century – he will proclaim that far the greatest influence philosophically was Freddie Ayer and to some degree his disciple Ryle; some kind words will be spoken about Russell; otherwise nobody – a footnote on Wittgenstein, no mention of Austin.[3] I am sure he is capable of doing it too: one really must not get annoyed at such things, and yet I am frightened by the degree to which it is historians who really do make a picture of the age [...].

Meanwhile, I propose to press graduate students on All Souls. Is that a good idea? I really do not see why not. The home of the old humanities

1 IB's six Mellon Lectures, delivered under the title 'Sources of Romantic Thought' at the National Gallery of Art in Washington, DC, between 14 March and 18 April 1965 (213–16).
2 'Two Enemies of the Enlightenment' (Johann Georg Hamann and Joseph de Maistre), four lectures delivered at Columbia University, 25–8 October 1965. The 2nd and 3rd lectures survive as recordings, and transcripts appear in the IBVL: see ⟨http://berlin.wolf.ox.ac.uk/lists/nachlass/⟩.
3 Taylor must have been teasing: of the five philosophers named here only Bertrand Russell is mentioned in his history, and then not in relation to philosophy, a subject Taylor deliberately avoided: 'Some omissions are excused only by ignorance. [...] I do not understand the internal combustion engine [...]. Nor could I have made much sense of modern philosophy. At any rate, I chose the subjects which seemed most urgent, most interesting, and with which I was most competent to deal.' A. J. P. Taylor, English History, 1914–1945 (Oxford, 1965), vi.

– that's all right – plus some studentships for graduate students as well –
why not? A belated St Antony's or Nuffield, but with more emphasis towards
history, literature, *Geisteswissenschaften*[1] in general. [...]

Yours,

  Isaiah

*In June, with reformers in the ascendant at All Souls, the College formally
adopted motions to elect more research fellows, and to erect a building in part
of the Warden's garden (within sight of his lodgings) to house them. The latter
proposal was naturally particularly objectionable to John Sparrow, and he gave
notice of his intention to oppose it. He also perversely proposed the admission
of graduate students, apparently in the hope of deflecting attention from the
schemes already agreed. To his chagrin this idea gathered momentum, and
became central to the reformist platform. Two options presented themselves:
either the College could admit a number of graduate students in the manner of
Nuffield (social sciences) or St Antony's (international relations), or it could go
into alliance with another college that already had graduates. The difficulties
involved in acting alone were considerable, and IB preferred association with
what he called 'a running business'.[2] Corpus was one possible partner, but the
more exciting prospect was a union with St Antony's. IB believed that this had
the power to transform the College, as he later explained to his colleague Harry
Fisher:*

I don't reject the other plan – only I think it very much a second best when
an opportunity of becoming the dominant research institution in the United
Kingdom – which it needs and has at present not got – is open. What has really
altered the opposition is the existence of St Antony's and Nuffield: which with
much more limited resources than ours have always made a much bigger impact
and do more for the university, and probably for learning. [...] It seems to me
that either we must transform ourselves or go into partnership with a smaller
firm which is livelier, and take them over, as it were – swallow them whole. The
most acute personal problem which arises of course, is who shall be Warden?
I do not like facing this at all.[3]

1 The humanities, as opposed to *Naturwissenschaften*, the natural sciences.
2 To Harry Fisher, 30 December 1964.
3 ibid.

TO MARY MCCARTHY

7 August 1964 ⟨no longer! 25*th* is more like it.⟩

⟨As from⟩ Headington House
⟨In fact, Argentina,[1] Paraggi & the rest of it⟩

Dearest Mary,

News has reached me from New York that the review of Miss Arendt on Eichmann that appeared in the TLS[2] was written by none other than Stuart Hampshire and myself! As I have heard it at this distance – I am writing this in Italy – Portofino – you will surely have heard it in New York. The author of this remarkable piece of intelligence is said to be Mr Lionel Abel,[3] whom I am not conscious of ever having met. The light of natural reason will suggest to you that this may not be entirely accurate. In fact, of course, there is not a word of truth in it. Neither Stuart nor I have anything whatever to do with the review, which was commissioned without the benefit of our aid. I cannot deny that I do know who the author is: and, under the oath usual in such circumstances, have never, never divulged who it is, under pain of the most dreadful consequences. Still, if you were to guess correctly I should confirm it. The only clue I can give you is that it is someone totally remote from the whole situation, not a Jew ⟨& v. remote from Jews⟩, not someone particularly interested in the subject, not someone you have ever known, an odd choice for the TLS to have made, a very uncharacteristically imaginative one: that you should resent his references to yourself I can well understand and warmly sympathise with. I hate my detractors with a bitter hatred, particularly when they make out that they are not really detracting. I haven't forgiven a man called Marshall Cohen[4] for writing an offensive personal attack on me, full of venom and personal spite – black sentiments of all kinds – and sending me the piece with a note saying that he did not hope that I would agree, but that I was to rest assured that he admired me, etc. etc. To hell with insults in public and apologies in private, as someone inelegantly once said to someone else in New York (I will tell you the story one day). As for the book itself – I am glad that I told you my view of Miss Arendt before this one

1 Albergo Argentina, a Paraggi *pensione*, now the Hotel Argentina.
2 [John Sparrow], 'Judges in Israel: The Case of Adolf Eichmann', TLS, 30 April 1964, 365–8.
3 Lionel Abel (1910–2001), playwright and essayist, Professor of English, State University of NY at Buffalo, 1967–79.
4 IB wrote to Patrick Gardiner, 19 April 1971: 'I have had a letter from Marshall Cohen proposing an armistice and more, on the grounds of a statute of limitations and his acute discomfort about the fact that whenever I come into a room I don't appear to notice him in it and look straight through him to the opposite wall – a practice I have now enjoyed doing for a very great many years and absolutely hate to relinquish. I suppose I shall have to behave in a queenly manner and be magnanimous, but I am sorry to lose my one authentic enemy, at least the only one I ever met. My other enemy, Professor Orsini of Wisconsin, who thinks me an ignoramus and a charlatan, I have never met. I have no doubt he's a learned, charming and most distinguished man, whereas those who think well of one's work are poor sad half-wits, whom one has taken in all too easily.'

had ever been thought of, otherwise you might have suspected a tiny bit of bias. As it is – although I have not read the book properly, it seems to me one of her clearer, better argued, more incisive works – not the dark, Teutonic, cloud of irrelevancy and free association that the other works seemed to me to be [...]. I cannot help thinking that her attitude to Zionists, and to some extent Jews, is somewhat like Koestler's[1] towards Communists – there is something there which will go on punishing her & us for ever: whether it is right to do it in public quite so much (you think it noble, unswerving quest for truth: I cannot help seeing it as an act of self-flagellation) is the question. Still, do not let us go on about Miss A. People quarrelled about Max Nordau,[2] so famous, so forgotten, just as much about Koestler, Deutscher etc. Miss A. and Mr K. are about as memorable. [...]

I am due to lecture in Washington in the spring, March and April, on a subject of which I know little and over which I shall get into trouble, and I am altogether in a sad way intellectually, though not otherwise. I cannot help feeling pleased about Beaverbrook's death[3] – the general line about him is that he was wicked but irresistibly charming, gay, delightful: I stayed a night under his roof and dined with him once – during the war – and found him dreary, charmless, frightfully boring, revolting in every way, particularly because of the bad jokes, pointless coarseness, unattractive bleakness and emptiness, and the nauseating atmosphere of toadyism and masochistic familiars who liked to be trampled on and grovel, by which he was surrounded. [...] I am in a state of excessive indignation about everything, from which I deduce old age and hardening of the arteries. Why does the fact that the *New Statesman* calls *The Cherry Orchard* a Marxist play annoy me so much? Why does Conor Cruise O'Brien?[4] Why does the mere thought of Teilhard de Chardin[5] infuriate me? He is a good man, kind, learned, perfectly harmless. Why do I know in advance that Koestler's new book will irritate me beyond words? Why do I think that Pasternak, just because he was the last nineteenth-century author, was morally a man whose shoes these others

1 Arthur Koestler (1905–83), Hungarian-born British novelist and journalist; his youthful interest in Zionism was later replaced by an interest in Communism, which in due course gave way to science, and later still to parapsychology.
2 Max Nordau (1849–1923), né Max Simon Südfeld, Hungarian-born physician, writer and Zionist, author of the 1890s cult book *Degeneration* (London, 1895), originally *Die Entartung* (Berlin, 1892).
3 Lord Beaverbrook had died at Cherkley Court, his Surrey home, on 9 June.
4 Conor Cruise O'Brien (1917–2008), Irish diplomat, politician and author; resigned from UN and Irish diplomatic service December 1961; Vice-Chancellor, University of Ghana, 1962–5; Albert Schweitzer Professor of Humanities, NYU, 1965–9; TD (Labour) Dublin North-East 1969–77.
5 (Marie Joseph) Pierre Teilhard de Chardin (1881–1955), French Jesuit and palaeontologist, sought to reconcile evolutionary theory with Christian teaching. His works, unacceptable to the Vatican, were published posthumously, notably *Le Phénomène humain* (1938–40) (Paris, 1955), trans. Bernard Wall as *The Phenomenon of Man* (London, 1959). 'Teilhard de Chardin / Wrote *The Phenomenon of Man* / Which surely you must know / Is as far as we should go.' Arnold Mallinson, 'The Piltdown Skull', in *Under the Blue Hood: A Hotchpotch 1923–1985*, ed. Henry Hardy (Oxford 1986), 217.

are not fit to *lick* (to use a Russian expression)? Nobody must ever send me a book for review. I don't like this century and everything that is typical of it, the hollow virtuosity, Alexandrianism,[1] rope tricks. I devoured Leonard Woolf's autobiography[2] with the most intense admiration and pleasure, and cannot, for all my personal affection, read a line of either Nabokov. *Etwas* ist Los.[3] Before this mood of self-pity goes too far I must stop. Do write.

Yours,

    Isaiah

⟨P.S. I've read this through, & it is an *idiotic* letter: Do forgive me: but I cannot write a new one: & I don't deserve an answer. Still …

Did you see the marvellous photograph of Stephen, Wystan, Christopher I. in the *Observer*? Do you think Shelley, Byron, Keats wd have looked like this? Why has C. Isherwood fizzled out?[4] In my (& his) youth he was clearly the best prose writer of his time in English. If Auden is (a) a genius (b) *can* be fearfully boring, does this mean that Plato & Shakespeare & Dante might have been so too? Gouty, Doughty & Shopkeeper:[5] you see how dotty I am. All this is induced by having *had* to compose an éloge to A. Huxley.⟩[6]

On Sunday 23 August 1964 IB attended the world premiere of Stravinsky's sacred cantata Abraham and Isaac *in Jerusalem. Stravinsky dedicated the work 'to the people of the new State of Israel', and although the performance itself was met with 'tepid applause', his appearance on stage to take his bow 'drew a prolonged ovation'.[7] Stravinsky greeted the audience by saying 'Shalom' – by his own admission, the only word of Hebrew he knew. Robert Craft conducted the premiere in Jerusalem, and also a later concert at Caesarea, which IB was unable to attend.*

---

1 In the elaborate and highly ornamentated style of the Greek poets of the Alexandrian school in the Hellenistic age (*c*.323–31 BCE).
2 Leonard Sidney Woolf (1880–1969), author and publisher; married Virginia Stephen 1912; dedicatee of IB's *Vico and Herder*. His five volumes of autobiography – *Sowing* (1960), *Growing* (1961), *Beginning Again* (1964), *Downhill All the Way* (1967), *The Journey not the Arrival Matters* (1969) – give first-hand insight into Bloomsbury and its most famous member; the third volume, covering 1911–18, to which IB here perhaps refers, won the 1965 W. H. Smith Literary Award; the early volumes are one source of inspiration for the titles of the present edition of IB's letters.
3 '*Something* is going on.'
4 Christopher (William Bradshaw) Isherwood (1904–86), English novelist and playwright, perhaps best known for his 1930s novels *Mr Norris Changes Trains* (1935) and *Goodbye to Berlin* (1939). He nevertheless published throughout his life, and afterwards, and his 1964 novel *A Single Man* 'came to be widely regarded as [his] masterpiece' (Peter Parker, ODNB).
5 'Gouty, Doughty and Shopkeeper, as the late Mr Joyce referred to the three great classical poets of. Europe.' (to Christopher Sykes, 23 February 1969). In *Finnegans Wake* (London, 1939), 539, Joyce refers to 'that primed favourite continental poet, Daunty, Gouty and Shopkeeper, AG'.
6 Aldous Huxley had died at his home in Los Angeles on 22 November 1963; the *éloge* in question is IB's contribution to Julian Huxley (ed.), *Aldous Huxley* (London, 1965).
7 *Times*, 25 August 1964, 5b.

Autograph manuscript page from Stravinsky's Abraham and Isaac,
dedicated to the librettist

TO ALINE BERLIN

19 July [sc. August] 1964 [*manuscript*]

King David Hotel, Jerusalem

Darling Aline,

The journey was without incident: I began to miss you more or less in Rapallo: I was in a carriage by myself – which I like best – tiny, 3 seats, the important priests left since the alternative was huis clos with his acolyte and me – I don't mind wheels – but fall into solitude, self pity & terrible Sehnsucht-love:[1] worse than any German. I tried to read, succeeded, but then failed again. […]. Arrived peacefully – not much noise or disorder in the El-Al – "they" are

---

1 'Sehnsucht' means 'yearning', 'wistful longing'.

gradually acquiring manners – behave a bit like Cypriots let me say – & was met with honour by Propes[1] & Gaby Cohen,[2] who immediately inquired about you, the children etc. Very nice. It was *there* that I learnt that the *first* Stravinsky evening is on *Sunday* – Propes said he had cabled me, but I have no telegram […]. If I had known, I cd have *left* a day later etc. – I am still simmering a little about this. Stravinsky arrives to-morrow, Thursday: do I, or do I not, accompany Kollek to the airport? I think may be not. If I have *nothing* to do … may be it will be comical: the arrival, the honour etc. Mrs S. is suffering from a nervous *tic* in the face: I shall enjoy that, I fear. Craft, the tic, the whole thing *may* be funny. I am seeing "nobody" here. Elath: tea (quite enough) – our Italian friend Segre[3] has become a "Professor": nothing has been said about Ben Gurion: I won't *offer* to go & see him, but I have a feeling I shall not leave without. I am to lunch with Yigal Al[l]on[4] to-day: after that freedom! books, peace, rest: they are all gone, all, it is a great relief: Talmon, Scholem,[5] Sambursky[6] (after all in Oxford for a whole *year*) Weisgal, Mrs W[eizmann], Lady Samuel,[7] *this* is the time to come. Now I must be off to see my poor aunt. Kollek *v* pleased with his pig & *unpainted* alabaster which he wisely chose. I got Gaby C[ohen] a ½ bot. of brandy. My maid "Katie" is *Indian* – same accent & manner as Mrs Gubby: *delightful*. I think Stuart thinks about humanité – mankind en gros – very right & proper – like Voltaire & Marx, while I cannot help thinking of them en détail: let him make the law & govern, while I rescue the victims of his regulations: he can be Lenin, I will be Gorky;[8] he will be thanked by millions, I will be

1 (Aaron) Zvi Propes (1904–78), born in Jelgava (now in Latvia), founder in 1961 of the Israel Festival, an annual international cultural event. His Polish-born wife's name was Mar(i)a (b. 1905/6).

2 Gavriel ('Gaby') Cohen (b. 1928), historian; member of the Palmach (note 4 below) 1948; professor, Tel Aviv, 1976, dean of the school of history 1983–6; Labour member of the Knesset 1965–9.

3 Vittorio Segre (b. 1922) became Dan Avni on joining the British Army in Palestine in 1941; Dan Segre was his preferred name in 2010 (email to Henry Hardy, 16 September 2010); Israeli Foreign Ministry 1949–67; Senior Research Fellow, Middle Eastern Studies, St Antony's, 1967–9; Professor of International Relations, Haifa, 1972–86; later Reuben Hecht Professor of Zionism.

4 Yigal Allon (1918–80) né Peikowitz in Kfar Tavor, Palestine; a field commander in the Haganah, the underground military organisation of the Jewish community in Palestine (the Yishuv). The Haganah was founded in 1920, and became the core of the post-independence Israel Defense Forces (IDF). Later Allon was one of the founders of the Palmach (Plugot Mahats, 'strike force'), the elite force established by the Haganah in May 1941; Commander-in-Chief of the Palmach 1945–8, and later a general in the IDF; a leading figure in the Ahdut HaAvoda–Poalei Zion workers' party; Minister of Labour 1961–7; Deputy Prime Minister 1968–74; interim Prime Minister February–March 1969; Minister of Foreign Affairs 1974–7; architect of the Allon Plan, formulated directly after the Six-Day War, which outlined a territorial compromise as the basis for Israeli–Arab coexistence.

5 Gershom Gerhard Scholem (1897–1982), professor of Jewish mysticism and cabbala at HUJ, began his career as Gerhard Scholem, a mathematician, in Germany.

6 Samuel Sambursky (1900–90), German-born Israeli scientist and historian; first Director of the Research Council of Israel 1949–56; Dean of the Faculty of Science of the HUJ 1957–9; from 1959 Professor of History and Philosophy of Science.

7 Hadassah Goor (1896–1986), wife of Edwin Herbert Samuel (1898–1978), 2nd Viscount Samuel.

8 Maksim Gorky (pseudonym of Aleksei Maksimovich Peshkov) (1868–1936), Russian writer, playwright and Marxist of independent outlook. He used his paper *Novaya zhizn'* (*New Life*) to

complained to & of by hundreds. So we shall divide the world. [...] Meanwhile I think of you *continuously*: the delicious warmth does not make up: You wd adore it here with me now: no people: no duties: marvellous view from corner room. I love you – I am *not* free – don't wish to be – nor do you.

Isaiah

TO ANDRZEJ WALICKI

7 September [1964]

[Paraggi; as from] Headington House

Dear Walicki,

[...] I have been in Italy for about three months trying to work; I have dictated about 100,000 words of odds and ends – Herder, Hamann, something in honour of the First International, even, which I am to deliver in Stanford[1] – Malia is expected here (Italy) any day now – he is passing on his way from Nice to somewhere else – we shall certainly speak of you with great affection and I hope your ears will burn – is there any book that I can send you? Nothing, so far as I know, has appeared on nineteenth-century ideas that is of the least interest: you don't really, do you, want Koestler's book on how men of genius conceived their original ideas?[2] He has spent years and years on this, but it seems to me from the reviews to be an autodidactic work of amateur psychology, a huge collection of evidence but something of a mouse from all these mighty mountains. Still, I may be unjust. The Togliatti[3] funeral here has been a tremendous affair, with almost a million people in Rome: he was obviously a most interesting and remarkable man. I have just read a violent onslaught by Deutscher in the *Espresso*, which is solely dictated by personal considerations of some sort, and represents Togliatti as an obedient instrument in Stalin's hands, without an analysis of what enabled him to create the biggest Communist Party in Western Europe. I think that on the whole, Deutscher is the least objective and factually least reliable writer among serious writers on politics to be found today: under the cover of dis-

criticise Lenin's dictatorial methods after the 1917 Revolution, but was silenced by the censor on Lenin's orders. He later lived abroad, returning to the Soviet Union in 1928, and becoming first president of the Union of Soviet Writers (1934) and a proponent of socialist realism.

1 IB made a lightning visit to Stanford in the first week of October to deliver a lecture at the invitation of the Hoover Institution: his lecture was later published as 'Marxism and the International in the Nineteenth Century' in SR: 'I have to fly for 24 hrs to Stanford (Hoover library) on Oct 4/5 & then literally *back* & broken & into bed. It is *madness* which otherwise only musicians seem liable to' (to Robert Craft, 25 July 1964). *Sense of Reality*

2 Arthur Koestler, *The Sleepwalkers: A History of Man's Changing Vision of the Universe* (London, 1959), 'a book that grips the attention from the first page to the last' (Ivor Bulmer-Thomas, TLS, 30 January 1959, 55).

3 Palmiro Togliatti (1893–1964), General Secretary of the Italian Communist Party 1927–64. On his return to Italy from exile in the Soviet Union in March 1944 he participated in the national governments of 1944–7, afterwards leading his party towards constitutional engagement in Italian politics. He died in Yalta on Friday 21 August, and his funeral in Rome the following Tuesday dominated the capital.

passionate objectivity he hurls poisoned darts into both the left and the right, all except his own tiny faction of Trotskyists and semi-Trotskyists; and has, consequently, one of the least deserved reputations in the world for objectivity, solidity, good judgement. But he has his value as a pamphleteer – as a historian, thinker ...

    Yours ⟨very sincerely⟩

    Isaiah Berlin   [...]

TO NICOLAS NABOKOV

    7 September [1964]

Headington House

Dearest Nicolas,

    Jerusalem! I arrived two days before – having been deceived by Propes about the dates of the concert and so could only attend one performance. I met the cortège at the airport: it was an unbelievable spectacle: Kollek, Propes, Mrs Propes[1] with a fairly thin bunch of flowers, Tsur,[2] also with a bunch of flowers and a typed-out speech in his hand, on the 'apron' of the great airfield of Lydda. Enter the El-Al Boeing – out of which emerged the diminutive figure of our friend, on a very hot day, brilliant sunshine, in a towel, followed by Vera Arturovna.[3] He rushed into my embrace (and I kissed him with sincere emotion, he was slightly unshaven), after which Mr Tsur and Mrs Propes deposited their flowers in the ample bosom of Mrs S., who wilted under them until I took the burden off her and looked exceedingly silly myself. After a few words were spoken, Tsur, in a beautiful, high baritone read out the words of welcome (the Minister who was supposed to be present could not make it). They slowly moved off towards the car. At this point the Children's Orchestra struck up on a neighbouring balcony – goodness knows what they were playing, but the Stravinskys fortunately realised that this was in their honour, and that the red carpet (literally) was also in their honour, and waved graciously. The car then very slowly moved off, leaving me with two bunches of flowers listening to Tsur's very long but quite jolly stories. Then it was discovered that of the fourteen pieces of luggage which Kollek and I were to bring to Jerusalem (the Propeses, particularly Mrs Propes, left as adjutants in the Stravinskys' car – Mrs Propes as the lady-in-waiting is superb), thirteen were present but one was missing. Craft, by the way, emerged last – the ironical smile upon his lips was the only genuine reaction seen on the airfield that afternoon, more or less. Despite everything, I like talking to Craft – he is very intelligent and has an acute

---

1 199/1.

2 Jacob Tsur (1906–90) né Tchernowitz in Vilnius, Lithuania; Israeli diplomat (ambassador to France 1953–9) and Zionist leader; president of the Israel Festival 1964.

3 Vera Arturovna Stravinsky, Igor Stravinsky's wife (641).

sense of the ridiculous, and despite his crimes against me, he possesses a trembling human soul, buried somewhere within all those neuroses, which occasionally struggles out in a touching though embarrassing fashion. The piece of luggage missing, naturally, was thought to contain all the scores, Mrs S's furs, jewels etc. Frantic calls to Paris, general *perepolokh*[1] until we all arrived in Jerusalem and it was discovered that nothing was missing as they had thirteen pieces of luggage in any case and not fourteen. He was very tired indeed. Rehearsals begin immediately. What do you think of the new piece? To me, it is a kind of cuneiform – perhaps it is very good. *Threni* I had *dirges* no difficulty with. At any rate, they were very satisfied with the orchestra, which [sc. who] were alleged to be able to understand it all; the poor baritone just sang isolated notes with no idea of why and what. [...]

Igor Fedorovich [Stravinsky] was in an excellent mood throughout; he drank unbelievable quantities of Irish whiskey, which he prefers to Scotch, and was in a bland, peaceful, amiable frame of mind. Sometimes he wondered if he was in Jerusalem or Constantinople; otherwise his mind did not wander. Mrs S. lay in bed with neuralgia, occasionally came down and chatted amicably to all. Mrs Propes, as lady-in-waiting, surpassed herself. Tsur's addresses of welcome at the airport, at the concert, etc., were exactly like good René Clair farce – pompous, funny, disarming, lengthy and delicious. The best moment was when he produced Stravinsky at a press conference in the King David Hotel and explained that Abraham had been preparing to sacrifice Isaac on the site of the King David Hotel itself, with appropriate jokes added. Professor Nelson Glueck,[2] whom I brought, could hardly contain himself for indignation, as he knows the precise spot on Sinai where this event occurred. Stravinsky was asked whether he approved of the fact that Wagner is not allowed to be played in Israel: 'In not playing Wagner, you are avoiding many very disagreeable sounds,' he said, and continued; '*Parsifal* is the most terrible bore; as for *The Ring*, it is a harmonic work; I am interested in counterpoint.' Craft felt it incumbent upon him to explain that *Tristan* was, after all, the beginning of the kind of music that Stravinsky was nowadays writing. Stravinsky grudgingly agreed that *Tristan* was an exception – but the rest of Wagner was loathsome mush, the Israelis were perfectly right to forbid it. That gave great pleasure. He also graciously mentioned my part in the 'libretto', which produced a crop of local journalists around me: I denied all, but doubtless something terrible will appear sooner or later in *Newsweek* and elsewhere which will make me suffer, which Stravinsky will not mind at all.

The whole thing, on the whole, was a triumph in the sense that he felt

1 'Panic'.
2 Nelson Glueck (1900–71), US-born archaeologist; ordained rabbi by the Hebrew Union College in Cincinnati, of which he was President 1947–71; as Director of the American School of Oriental Research in Jerusalem 1932–3, 1936–40, 1943–7 he conducted important excavations east and south-east of the Jordan; he appeared on the cover of *Time* magazine 13 December 1963.

well, that the hall in Jerusalem was very full, that everyone got up when he entered, that the Prime Minister and the cabinet were present – as well as the American Ambassador[1] – a very nice man but a *toosha*[2] – a mass of kindly flesh. You should have seen the expression on the face of the Minister of Education when the first notes of *Abraham and Isaac* were sounded. He [Stravinsky] conducted *Im* [sc. *Vom*] *Himmel hoch* and the *Symphony of Psalms*; Craft a capriccio for piano and strings and *Abraham and Isaac*. […]

You were talked about the whole time: by Propes, by Teddy, by the Stravinskys, by Tsur, by me – in all stages of production. Your absence was genuinely and sincerely regretted. And you would have enjoyed it. The comical moments were many. The mere appearance of this rough assembly, with a few absurd looking German Gelehrte sticking out from amongst a rough forest of white and blue shirts and mops of rough white hair – like the editors of the *Reader's Digest* – the whole 'frontier' public: enter this extremely delicately constructed little porcelain figure, very slowly limping along towards the podium, pale, refined and sophisticated, with no suspicion of any 'narodnik'[3] quality, in an audience soaked in it; with a lot of bewildered persons who had no idea what the sounds were meant to convey or whether they were meant to be anything at all, applauding the compliment to themselves, and then, after he said 'Shalom' loudly, applauding still more madly: it was touching, ridiculous and very sweet, and you would have enjoyed it very much indeed.

The new President of Israel[4] is as accessible as the old, and speaks Russian with much the same accent – so, now, does the Prime Minister (Ben-Gurion didn't). […]

How are you? I hear that you are not too well: the Stravinskys were very much concerned about your health, as you about theirs. Don't do too much! It really doesn't matter about the precise details even of your great Festival! Ask yourself, I beg you, for the sake of what is it that you are wearing yourself out so rapidly? Why should you not live a little more easily under a little less strain, with a little more *douceur de vivre*, a little more conversation with me? Will you telephone me from Berlin in Oxford after 13 September – and will you live quietly until then? I know that my words are in vain, that I am writing on water. Oh, you should have been there in the restaurant, the new *Regence* underground restaurant in the King David, when I had to approach the Hungarian pianist who is head of the little jazz band that performs there and tell him that if he wanted to render a service to music could he wait for twenty minutes or so until Mr Stravinsky finished his meal – he took it very

1 Walworth Barbour (1908–82), US ambassador to Israel 1961–73.
2 'Hulk'.
3 'Populist'.
4 Shneur Zalman Shazar (1889–1974), Israel's Russian-born first Minister of Education 1949–51 and third President 1963–73, succeeding Weizmann's successor Yitzhak Ben-Zvi.

well – Stravinsky then handed me drunken sheets with scrawls of note-like entities on it, meant to be half tango, half waltz, signed Igor Manteuffel: the Hungarian band leader, though he asked for an autograph, was not fully aware of Stravinsky's full size, but said to me 'Here I am; I was in a concentration camp for two years; I have lived in some terrible holes; here I am talking to Mr Kollek, a most important man; if I were talking to anybody else – say, you – in what other country is this possible? Why, when President Ben-Zvi was on a boat, and I was playing on it, and I wanted to take a photograph, he would not let me do it until he had examined my camera to see if it was OK; and Mr Ben-Gurion asked me whether I was happy; in what other country? in what other country?' *Pourvu que ça dure.*[1] I wonder. Mrs S. longs to see Arab Jerusalem, but did not make much fuss about that. I shall always bear with me the image of I.F.'s molten condition, liquid, vague, totally happy, tipsy – very different from anything in New York – he was much happier in Jerusalem, I thought – perhaps he is all right in Hollywood. And Craft talked touchingly about how nice and human Stephen was, and how inhuman Auden and how awful Miss Arendt.

Do telephone me.

Yours,

Isaiah   [...]

TO ROWLAND BURDON-MULLER

7 September 1964

                                                              Headington House

Dearest Rowland,

First let me thank you most deeply for your two splendid letters on Goldwater.[2] A more magnificent document, at once noble and entertaining, penetrating and crushing, I have not read. [...] I do not, myself, believe that the danger that Goldwater will be elected is great. I am not quite so sure that he might not have defeated Kennedy; I do not see how he can defeat Johnson. What is disquieting, of course, is that he could gather quite so much support; and even if he does not get in, someone else, backed by the same forces, might easily acquire a huge following in, say, four or five years' time. I wonder, however, whether Goldwater followers are not simply the old 20 percent – quite enough too – who were isolationists during the war, did not want to go to Europe but to Japan towards the end of it, supported McCarthy

1 'Let's hope it lasts', the (apocryphal) words of Napoleon Bonaparte's mother Laetitia (1750–1836) on his becoming Emperor in 1804.

2 Barry Morris Goldwater (1909–98), born in Phoenix, Arizona, Republican Senator for his home State 1953–65, 1969–87; Republican Presidential candidate 1964; advocate of a strongly conservative agenda. He was resoundingly defeated by Lyndon Johnson in 1964, but bequeathed a new republicanism that underpinned the presidencies of Richard Nixon, and later Ronald Reagan and George Bush, Sr.

and McCarran,[1] and are in fact the old combination of Southern 'Bourbons', Texas industrialists, Catholic bigots, Fascists, lunatics, political neurotics, embittered ex-Communists, unsuccessful power-seekers of all kinds, as well as rich men and reactionaries, in whom America has never been poor [...]. This is the optimistic view. The pessimistic view is that Goldwater, because he is obviously not like Hitler – that is, not a nasty maniacal figure, but a jolly, all-American boy brimming with bonhomie, physical benevolence, exceedingly simple, crude, spontaneous and intelligible – just because he is not like McCarthy and is the American dream come true – nothing to do with the horrible Anglo-Saxon East-coast plutocrats and cookie-pushers, the cold, handsome, European-style gentlemen who have run American politics hitherto, but represents the pushing, bustling, enterprising, class-conscious, open frontier society of Texas and Arizona, and the racial mixture of blood in his veins which is the new, vigorous, anti-European America – the revolt of the socially low-born and oppressed – that {because} for these reasons he is far more dangerous than a real Fascist maniac would have been. I think he is dangerous, and I think that his policies are confused and abominable [...]. Yet I do not believe for a moment that this is the moment when they will become manifest.

[...] I have a feeling that in the end it is Kennedy and his splendid administration that has conjured up these devils. It was Kennedy who communicated to the whole nation the electric desire for leadership, for adventure, for intense living. There is no need to find in this a streak of Fascism, but something of the *arditi* – the pre-Fascist Italian mentality which d'Annunzio[2] represented in a perverted form – was certainly present. And having aroused these particular spirits among Americans, having whipped them up into a romantic frame of mind, where men of destiny – Bonapartism – great Napoleonic adventures – were in the air, above all, no passive acceptance of events or drifting or comfortable living, but constant encounters with destiny, hard choices, etc. were placed before them – having done all this, he created the atmosphere in which someone like Goldwater is likely to have more success than the average run-of-the-mill politician, in whom I, perhaps rather cynically, believe. My view is that only those people can govern great nations who

1 Both men were of Irish descent, US Senators and fiercely anti-Communist. Joseph Raymond McCarthy (1908–1957), Republican senator from Wisconsin 1947–57, used his Chairmanship of the Senate's Permanent Subcommittee on Investigations to expose 'un-American activities' in government and in public life generally; his witch-hunt was eventually discredited, and demagogic 'McCarthyism' came to represent the excesses of the Cold War. Patrick Anthony McCarran (1876–1954), Democratic senator from Nevada 1933–54; Chairman of the Senate Internal Security Subcommittee and chief sponsor of the 1950 Internal Security Act, which embodied domestic anti-Communist paranoia.
2 Gabriele d'Annunzio (1863–1938), Italian poet, dramatist and politician; served with great distinction during the First World War, and was an ultra-nationalist political leader afterwards, drawing on the *arditi* – the Italian elite shock-troops (the word means 'daring' or 'bold') – for support; inspired the early Fascist movement.

love power – who enjoy it; if they do not (like Stevenson), they are no good. Roosevelt, Truman,[1] Eisenhower,[2] all did: Roosevelt and Truman were excellent, Eisenhower I detest – it is his face, I think, that upsets me most. The mixture of vanity and stupidity and lack of principle – as evinced now and as evinced before in his attitude towards Marshall,[3] and his shaking hands with McCarthy – is revolting: in a way, I preferred Taft,[4] who was an honest, dry, narrow man. Still, I suppose he would have led America to the same sort of disaster as Neville Chamberlain led England to, and he much resembled him. My favourite President remains Truman, despite your strictures on the Truman Doctrine,[5] which I well remember, but about which I think I somewhat disagreed with you. Nor do I mind Johnson all that much; the vulgarity, the commonness, the lack of nobility are terrible; still, he was brave when courage was needed, in the 1939–40 period, when to be a New Dealer from Texas was not all that easy, and when he gave support to Roosevelt of a very unconditional kind against all kinds of local conservatives, and got scolded for it. I have a feeling that there is some kind of early idealism still lurking somewhere, and that from time to time he calls upon it, like a kind of remote reserve which he can revive at will (and also suppress at will, I fear), and that he wants to go down to history as a great, liberal, reforming friend of the people – not something I at all object to. I wish I could like either of our contenders for power – Sir Alec or Mr Wilson – half as much. [...]

   Much love
   Isaiah   [...]

1 Harry S. Truman (1884–1972; the 'S.' doesn't stand for anything), Democratic statesman; Vice-President 1945, becoming the 33rd President of the US 1945–53 on the death of FDR in April; defined America's response to the Cold War with the Truman Doctrine (1947; note 5 below), the Marshall Plan (1948), the Berlin Airlift (1948–9), NATO (1949), and US involvement in the Korean War (1950).

2 Dwight David ('Ike') Eisenhower (1890–1969), Supreme Commander, Allied Expeditionary Forces in Western Europe, 1943–5; of NATO 1950–2; Republican 34th President of the US 1953–61; pressurised Britain to pull its forces out of Suez in 1956, thus ending the covertly co-ordinated Anglo-French/Israeli military operation there.

3 George Catlett Marshall (1880–1959), five-star General, US Secretary of State 1947–9; Defense Secretary 1950–1; initiated the 'European Recovery Program' or 'Marshall Plan' (1948–51). Marshall was a victim of baseless 'un-American' allegations by Joseph McCarthy: campaigning in Wisconsin during the 1952 presidential race, Eisenhower struck from his speech – on the advice of aides – a passage defending Marshall, his wartime colleague; when this omission was discovered, and revealed in the national press, Eisenhower's stock fell appreciably; and while he privately disapproved of McCarthy, he failed to deploy the moral authority of the presidency against him.

4 Robert Alphonso Taft (1889–1953), lawyer, Republican Senator from Ohio 1939–53, was defeated by Eisenhower in a bitter contest to secure the Republican nomination in 1952, the last of his three unsuccessful attempts.

5 Cardinal element in US post-war foreign policy, enunciated by President Truman on 12 March 1947 in response to the Communist threat to Greece and Turkey, and seen by the Soviet Union as a *casus belli* in the Cold War. It asserted that the US would 'support free peoples who are resisting attempted subjugation by armed minorities or by outside pressures': 'Recommendation for Assistance to Greece and Turkey', repr. as 'Special Message to the Congress on Greece and Turkey: The Truman Doctrine' in *Public Papers of the Presidents of the United States: Harry S. Truman* [...] 1947 (Washington, 1963), 176–80, quotation at 178–9.

TO MEYER SCHAPIRO

17 November 1964

All Souls

Dear Meyer,

I want to put one question to you – if you have no time you must not answer it – perhaps a bibliography would be sufficient. What, I ask myself – and you – happened socially, demographically, economically in the eighteenth century to have produced the extraordinary spate of young men, particularly in Germany in the 1770s and 1780s, who were poor, 'pale and fevered', consumptive – who joined professions only to leave them, owed money, gambled madly, believed in their stars, wandered from city to city, defied their parents, and in earlier phases are called *Sturm und Drang* and later are called Romantics? If you read the lives of Schleiermacher,[1] the Schlegels,[2] Wackenroder,[3] Novalis[4] and his brother Erasmus,[5] Tieck,[6] Steffens,[7] etc., you are struck by the extraordinary similarity of these chaotic young men: their revolt against parents, contempt for all forms of tidiness, order and reason, poverty, debt, inability to manage their own lives, clumsiness and inexperience in society, awkwardness with women, passionate masculine friendships (Wackenroder, writing to Tieck, speaks in marvellously innocent homosexual terms), and despite the marriages to all these Dorotheas and Carolines and Rachels and Hannah Arendts of every kind, the constant decrying of women even by the happily married Schelling[8] and declaration that only men have the capacity for infinity, true unhappiness, sacrifice etc.

1 Friedrich Ernst-Daniel Schleiermacher (1768–1834), German Protestant theologian and pioneering exponent of hermeneutics; influenced by the Romantics, notably Friedrich von Schlegel.

2 August Wilhelm von Schlegel (1767–1845), German Romantic poet, critic, and gifted translator, notably of Shakespeare's plays. Friedrich von Schlegel (1772–1829), philosopher, poet and critic, brother of August Wilhelm; central to the German Romantic movement, and founder of its early periodical the *Athenaeum*.

3 Wilhelm Heinrich Wackenroder (1773–98), German Romantic writer who did much to extend Romantic interest in painting and music, particularly through his close friendship with Ludwig Tieck, who ensured posthumous publication of an extended edition of his *Outpourings of an Art-Loving Friar* (1797).

4 Pseudonym of the German Romantic poet and philosopher Friedrich von Hardenberg (1772–1801), proponent of 'magical idealism' (the theory that the natural world can be transformed by the power of the imagination), whose only completed collection of poems, *Hymnen an die Nacht* (Berlin, 1800), was a poetic response to the deaths in the same year of his first love and fiancée (Christiane Wilhelmine) Sophie von Kühn (1782–97) and his brother Erasmus.

5 Erasmus von Hardenberg (1774–97), the favourite brother of Novalis.

6 (Johann) Ludwig Tieck (1773–1853), German Romantic poet and dramatist; a promoter of Shakespeare's plays in Germany; he completed, with his daughter Dorothea, the work of translation begun by A. W. Schlegel.

7 Henrik Steffens (1773–1845), Norwegian-born philosopher and physicist; studied in Copenhagen, Kiel, Jena and Berlin, and was an important conduit between German and Danish romanticism; appointed to a professorship at Berlin University 1832; his efforts to reconcile science, philosophy and religion were influential on, among others, his friends Friedrich Schelling and Friedrich Schleiermacher.

8 Friedrich Wilhelm Joseph (von) Schelling (1775–1854), German philosopher, one of the principal

Also why should there suddenly in the 1770s and 1780s be such a spreading of every kind of seer, clairvoyance, Cagliostros,[1] women with stigmata,
mesmerism, hypnotism, Bible societies, mystical trances, expectation of
miracles and also mad gambling, state lotteries, general unhinging from both
rationalism and Enlightenment and tradition and conservatism?[2] This is even
noticeable in Germany, where the Industrial Revolution was feeblest. What
can I read about this? Surely you who know everything will tell me? I know
of no book on the eighteenth century which gives the proper economic or
social or sociological explanation of this pretty drastic and catastrophic transformation of society, which seems to have got going in a big way in the 1770s
and reached a climax in the 1790s and early years of the nineteenth century.
Halbwachs[3] gives statistics of Prussian suicides but that's about the only clue
I have and is a consequence and not a cause. You cannot disapprove of this
thoroughly Marxist approach on my part – it indicates, as you see, winds of
change before which even I seem to be bending. Dr Wind seems unable to
help me – a short bibliography would be marvellous.

Warmest greetings,

Yours,

Isaiah

TO ROWLAND BURDON-MULLER

31 December 1964

Headington House

Dear Rowland,

A Merry Christmas. A very happy New Year. Your exquisite Pasternak
Tolstoy,[4] which is obviously both vividly realistic and filled with hero-
worshipping romanticism of a somewhat German sort, is at present looking
down upon me from a bookshelf immediately opposite me as I write; it
is rather formidable, and makes all one's acts, both in life and in 'work',
seem trivial and vain. That of course is the effect of Tolstoy's face in old

---

proponents of German romanticism; a Tübingen contemporary of Hegel, and collaborator of
Fichte; he married, 1803, Karoline née Michaelis, then Böhmer (1763–1809), the divorced wife of
August Schlegel, her second husband.

1 Alessandro, Conte di Cagliostro (1743–95), probably an alias for the charlatan Giuseppe Balsamo,
a professed alchemist and magician who operated in late 18th-century Parisian society.

2 Cf. 14 December 1964 to Morton White: 'Why should the second half of the eighteenth century
suddenly be filled with waves of irrationalism, women with stigmata, somnambulists, peasants
in fields suddenly prophesying, Freemasons and Rosicrucians, and a tremendous retreat of all
those triumphant rationalists of the 1740s and '50s – all ending in a huge outburst of German
romanticism?'

3 Maurice Halbwachs (1877–1945), French sociologist influenced by Durkheim; author of Les
Causes du suicide (Paris, 1930).

4 Leonid Osipovich Pasternak (1862–1945), Odessa-born Russian Impressionist, father of Boris
Pasternak, painted portraits of his friend Tolstoy and of other famous contemporaries, notably
Gorky, Rilke, Chaliapin, Rachmaninov, Einstein and Lenin.

age, when one does not know whether the expression conveys a frown or a smile beyond all those ferocious eyebrows, beard, on the whole terrifying expression. [...] The philosopher Wittgenstein once said that in order to give worthy presents to people, what one needed was not money but time. This is very true. I look at this fascinating and moving drawing – all the more pleasing for being slightly sentimental – every day, and it has entered the texture of my life. Thank you very much indeed.

Meanwhile, the world moves on (alas). Would I rather that it stopped? I am not sure. No, on the whole let things march forward, even though this brings all kinds of disagreeable prospects nearer – such as my lectures in Washington, about which I tremble and shiver and shake.[1] I ought never to have accepted them – the subject, the place, the whole thing is unsuitable, and I am caught, and all my serious work is stopped. But never mind. Forward! Things are seldom either as good or as bad as they seem (profound truth, gleaned from deep experience, that I offer you!). You were so stern with me for failing to dread Goldwater sufficiently – but there, I was not altogether mistaken, despite all those 25 million votes, in a nation of such size, rather smaller than might have been feared [...]. Our situation here is far more worrying:[2] it is a very bad thing that a party of the left should fumble and stumble in this inexperienced fashion: the chief things that are wrong seem to be that the new advisers of the government don't know their way about Whitehall, and when things look menacing do not quite know what buttons to press, which Treasury officials do what, who to go to in the Bank of England, etc. – they know these things, but some of them become confused and panic, I suspect, so that they shy about in a way that the Conservatives, with all their faults, do not, who, like drunken but experienced old skippers, bring the boat into some sort of port, though perhaps not the right one – whereas these people know perfectly well the port they are aiming at – I sympathise entirely with their ends – but are much more liable to reefs, squalls and the ramming of other ships. All the domestic purposes of the Labour Party seem to me perfectly good – there are three fields, however, in which their behaviour is and will continue to be worrying:

1. Europe[3] – apart from the rights and wrongs of particular policies, there is a great deal of xenophobia, Little Englandism, desire to be left alone by horrible foreigners, preserve our Welfare State and decent democracy against huge cigar-smoking Common Marketeers from Milan and the

---

1 For these (Mellon) lectures see 313–16.
2 After the General Election on 15 October the Labour Party (under Harold Wilson) had taken office for the first time since 1951, with an overall majority of only 6 seats.
3 Britain's membership of the EEC had become a key issue in domestic politics since the Macmillan government's application to join in 1961 – an application opposed by the Labour Party under Gaitskell, and vetoed by President de Gaulle in January 1963. Harold Wilson, prime minister in October 1964, had opposed Macmillan's 1961 application largely on party political grounds, but made two bids of his own to join Europe in the years that followed.

Rhineland. I sympathise with all this but it is highly unrealistic: there really is a great deal of inefficiency and economy of effort in England – not among the workers particularly, but among the bosses. The Late Lord Marks,[1] who really was a very enlightened shopkeeper, complained bitterly for years to me about his absolute inability to stimulate manufacturers into manufacturing the kind of objects that people wanted to buy, their total lack of enterprise, flexibility, imagination, or the desire to do or be anything at all except make their regular incomes, play golf. If you can imagine a huge collection of Eisenhowers crossed with Winthrop Aldriches[2] sitting about in British industry, you will get the picture. Anything which can needle these people into realising that they are in extreme economic peril, and their country with them, is good. How far the Labour Government will succeed in penetrating their hives is not clear; but entrance into Europe really would have upheaved this situation and injected jets of fresh water into these stagnant pools: at a price of dislocation, which could have been cushioned by a genuinely welfare-minded and tough left-wing government. The combination of the Labour Party and entrance into Europe would have been right. For historical and moral reasons, though, this seems unlikely.

2. Education: A great deal needs to be done, obviously (I cannot tell you in what an upheaval Oxford is, particularly All Souls, as between the zealous reformers – such as me – and immovable rocks of tradition, such as John Sparrow), but again, if an over-violent expansion of universities is commanded before the schools are reformed, and many more schoolmasters produced, and better conditions introduced into overcrowded, under-staffed, ill-built schools, we really shall get a hideous collapse of standards in the humanities at least – this will in due course be remedied, but at a far vaster price than needs to be paid.

3. As a dependency of this, the arts: the tendency on the part of any Labour Government to say that we can do as well as any foreigner – British singers, British players, British painters, British folk song, skiffle groups, arts and crafts, as against all this expensive, snobbish, highbrow nonsense – such as expensive opera, Callas, and foreign conductors and the rest – could do a lot of damage to what is at present the greatest flowering of the expensive arts in England – opera, films, plays by 'foreign' playwrights, etc. It is a strange thing that, for instance on the Covent Garden Opera board, on which I sit, it being clear that it would be a good thing to have a body less obviously weighted towards the City and Conservatism, it is literally impossible to find prominent persons with socialist views who could be considered as having anything to say about opera – there are about two, and they are both Labour

1 Simon Marks (1888–1964), Kt 1944, life peer 1961, retailer and business innovator; Chairman, Marks and Spencer Ltd, 1916–64.
2 Winthrop Williams Aldrich (1885–1974), US lawyer and banker, liberal Republican; ambassador to UK 1953–7.

Ministers and therefore cannot be had. Queer. One would have thought that there would be prominent socialist intellectuals with a taste – and more than a taste, knowledge of music. For a year now they have been searched for: even dear Stuart cannot suggest names. Talking of him, I wonder how long it will be before we recover him: for I cannot believe, despite all his assurances, that Princeton is to be his home for so very long. I have never in my life known a more patriotic Englishman – without any nationalism – so wedded to the soil of his ancestors.

And talking of dons, I hope you are being regaled by the splendid debate on the Warren report[1] in the *Sunday Times*. Did you read Trevor-Roper's article? Sparrow's answer? I have no doubt that Trevor-Roper, who never sallies into the field unless he is heavily armed against any possible attack, will deliver some fearful blows next Sunday – he has been attacked on two fronts, by Sparrow in the *Sunday Times* and by the *Observer*, which detests him anyway – why he did this is not clear to me, except that I am sure he believes in the truth of all that he says, and says it very pointedly and elegantly and formidably, as always. He sees himself, I think, as the Colonel Piquart[2] – the only man who detected the mass of lies by which Dreyfus's innocence had been concealed – of the day, and is determined to make justice prevail. I wonder how happy he and Lady Alexandra[3] are in Los Angeles, where they are ensconced at present. He sees himself as a scourge of absolute justice, visiting the wicked and the feeble, and bringing them before the bar of reason. Yet I cannot myself believe that the facts were very different from what the Warren Report declares – from the fact that it suits all parties, the right, the left etc., it does not follow that what it says is false: unless one is obsessed by the view that all history is a succession of conspiracies, and that what one must ask for always is 'Who is behind it?', 'Who is to blame?' – did the Freemasons really cause the French Revolution? did the Jesuits poison Cimarosa? did the Jews cause 1914, 1939 and everything else? and are the Communists really poisoning the American people by fluoridising water? For Trevor-Roper the world really is full of figures of light and darkness, plotting and counter-plotting against each other, crafty long-term intriguers ruthlessly crawling and creeping towards their horrible goals and blocked by the few Sherlock Holmeses, here and there, who alone can stop

1 The Report of the Warren Commission, the official US government enquiry into the assassination of President Kennedy, was published on 27 September 1964. Its conclusion, that Lee Harvey Oswald had acted alone, has never been universally accepted, and doubts about its procedures began to be aired at the time: see, for example, the *Times* leader of 26 September 1966, 'The Shots Are Still Heard' (9a–b).

2 Lieutenant-Colonel Georges Picquart (1854–1914), chief of French military intelligence, played the key role in exposing the miscarriage of justice at the heart of the Dreyfus affair (174/3); he was subsequently forced out of the army by anti-Dreyfusard elements, in a gross perpetuation of the original injustice that he had uncovered; with Dreyfus's eventual exoneration he was reinstated, and became Minister of War under Georges Clemenceau 1906-9.

3 383/1.

the fearful Moriartys. I do not believe that the world is quite as free from such influences as people who don't believe in them at all would like to say, but I think that Hugh Trevor-Roper's mind really is perhaps too filled with angels and demons, and that for all his passionate addiction to the Enlightenment – which is genuine – his rationality and his genuine desire to get at the truth (far more serious than that of most historians), his mind is nevertheless infected by the very demonology of the medieval enemy whom he is trying to destroy. But I may be doing him an injustice – my intellectual respect for him is really very great and – what is far rarer – I actually like him.

What more can I tell you? Lady Avon[1] is giving a ball which we shall not attend (no grown-ups asked, so far as I can see, except a few committed dancers) – this is to help her get through the winter, which is otherwise too grim for her. Sparrow is fighting a battle to prevent change at All Souls like one of those old Douglas Fairbanks heroes on a table with a flashing rapier holding off seventeen potential assassins: it is a magnificent spectacle, but I fear will not save him. [...]

Yours ever, with much love

Isaiah   [...]

TO BERTELL OLLMAN

9 January [1965]

Headington House

Dear Bert,

I was very glad to get your letter. I fully see, of course, that since you are sure that you are clearing away a lot of misunderstanding and rectifying a distorted image and doing justice, your introduction, for purely psychological – if no other – reasons, had to be what it was – lengthy, mounting to a climax, and indignant, at least in the beginning. Very well: but let me once again press this avuncular advice upon you, even at the risk of having it hurled back in my face: a thesis should not [be] a burning indictment, although a book can, and if you feel that the truth has been obscured or trampled underfoot, obviously should be. [...] You are a vehement, eloquent, passionate writer – a Polish cavalryman galloping bounding across fearful obstacles – there are a great many gnarled tree-trunks and beds of long-dried streams in which the hooves of your horse might easily slip. Do be careful, look before and after, imagine your examiners defending positions incompatible with your own – dry, suspicious and not necessarily at all sympathetic! I am not saying this to discourage you, of course, but the opposite: at this moment, justice to yourself rather than justice to Marx is paramount, though there is nothing incompatible between them. So: you say that my remarks might cause you

1 Clarissa Anne Spencer-Churchill (b. 1920), Countess of Avon, niece of Winston Churchill, married Anthony Eden (from 1961 1st Earl of Avon) in 1952.

to double or triple your introduction: do do that if it is necessary – and then condense after the whole work has been done and you can perform a retrospective surgical operation for the sake of the general proportions of the thesis (a book, I say again, is another matter). I feel like Polonius, advising not Hamlet but Cyrano de Bergerac.[1] [...] I shall be in England till the end of June more or less, after that in Italy I suspect. So tell me your plans. Please give our love again to your wife and yourself – another image, not Polonius and Cyrano, occurs to me: it is like the elder Marx writing to Karl *begging* him not to upset the powers that be. True, the younger Marx disobeyed, but remember too (genius apart), he never completed any major work – all his works, even the longest, are fragments of one enormous lifelong exposition – all, that is, except his thesis, which is a model of lucidity and convention!

Yours,

Isaiah   [...]

In September 1960 IB was invited by the National Gallery of Art in Washington, DC, to give the 1965 A. W. Mellon Lectures in the Fine Arts, one of the greatest accolades that could be bestowed upon an academic in this field. He formally accepted the commission in December 1960, his only stipulation being that he be freed from the obligation to submit a written copy of each lecture in advance: 'The reason for this is that I find that lectures read from a typescript sound dead and unconvincing even to the lecturer himself; and therefore prefer to lecture from notes.'[2] Previous lecturers included IB's compatriots Kenneth Clark (1953) and Ernst Gombrich[3] (1956), renowned art historians whose lectures not only succeeded brilliantly but also resulted in important books: Clark's The Nude: a Study of Ideal Art *(London, 1956) and Gombrich's* Art and Illusion: a Study in the Psychology of Pictorial Representation *(London and New York, 1960).*

In accepting the commission IB sketched out his preliminary ideas about the overarching theme of the series:

The lectures themselves will be concerned with the roots of romanticism, i.e. the common root of the Romantic revolution in the arts, politics, philosophy and human behaviour in general, which seems to me the greatest single break with the past in the modern age – greater than Marxism or any of the industrial revolutions; at least, if not greater in transforming social behaviour, deeper

---

1 Polonius in fact advises his son Laertes in Shakespeare's play *Hamlet*: 'Give thy thoughts no tongue / Nor any unproportioned thought his act' (1. 3. 59–60). (Savinien) Cyrano de Bergerac (1619–55) was a French soldier, satirist and violent controversialist. IB's point is that Ollman suffered not from Hamlet-like self-doubt but rather from the dangers of irrepressible elan.

2 To Huntington Cairns, 19 December 1960.

3 Ernst Hans Josef Gombrich (1909–2001), later (1972) Kt, art historian; Director of the Warburg Institute and Professor of the History of the Classical Tradition, London, 1959–76.

and further-reaching in its transformation of social, moral and political ideals, habits, concepts, language.[1]

He viewed the delivery of the lectures, and their likely reception, with the greatest apprehension, and more than once lamented ever having taken them on. In the event they proved to be the most celebrated lectures of his entire career. They were delivered under the title 'Sources of Romantic Thought' at the National Gallery of Art, weekly for six weeks, beginning on Sunday 14 March 1965 – a 'prodigious exercise in prepared extemporisation before a huge audience'.[2]

Writing to Arthur Schlesinger in September 1964, IB predicted that after he had delivered the lectures he would return to Oxford and 'then worry about how bad they were and how little relation they bear to the as yet unwritten book which I will not have delivered on time. All this is surely normal, truly ghastly as it really is for someone like me, who was clearly intended for a much jollier and idler life (I say proudly).'[3] He ran true to form, and the planned study of romanticism never appeared, while the lectures themselves were published only posthumously.[4] Had it not been for the foresight of the BBC, those who did not attend would never have had access to the lectures, which were recorded as they were delivered, and broadcast on the Third Programme in August and September 1966.

4.29 Quattro liriche di Antonio Machado..................*Dallapiccola* sung by MARY THOMAS (soprano) with THE COMPOSER at the piano
4.37 Five Songs, for baritone and eight instruments.....*Dallapiccola*
† sung by JOHN NOBLE (baritone) with members of the VIRTUOSO ENSEMBLE
4.49 Three Japanese Lyrics *Reginald Smith Brindle*
† sung by JOSEPHINE NENDICK (soprano) with SUSAN BRADSHAW (piano) ERIC ALLEN (marimba and vibraphone) JAMES HOLLAND (percussion) Conducted by THE COMPOSER

4.58 ENGLISH SONG
Song-cycle: Love blows as the wind blows (W. E. Henley) *George Butterworth*
5.10 Three Rivers (settings of poems by his wife, Jacqueline Laidlaw)................*Philip Cannon*
5.21 Song-cycle: On Wenlock Edge (A. E. Housman) *Vaughan Williams*
† sung by JOHN MITCHINSON ENGLISH STRING QUARTET with JAMES LOCKHART (piano)

5.45 JAZZ TODAY
The best of present-day jazz on records
Introduced by CHARLES FOX

SIX LECTURES BY
Sir Isaiah Berlin

THIRD
7.55

CHICHELE Professor of Social and Political Theory, Fellow of All Souls, Professor Berlin has recently been appointed Master of Wolfson College, where about two-thirds of the student body will be scientists. This is the appointment of a very special philosopher.

Those who have heard Professor Berlin's previous broadcasts will agree with an assessment in *The Sunday Times* that he 'combines vast erudition with irrepressible gaiety' and that he shows 'that it is possible to preserve within a scrupulous academic framework the wit and high courtesy of private conversation.' And of his delivery: 'he uses his voice like a great cellist persuading an unwilling audience to listen to unaccompanied sonatas.'

The overall title of these six lectures, *Some Sources of Romanticism*, suggests again that there are no conventional boundaries to Professor Berlin's erudition or to his enthusiasm for fresh woods. In these lectures Sir Isaiah demonstrates that the advent of Romanticism was the first moment in the history of the West when there was a kind of tyranny of Art over Life. He demonstrates further that the interest of Romanticism is not simply a historical one; that a great many concepts of the present day—nationalism, existentialism, democracy, totalitarianism—are still affected by Romanticism. He examines how the ideas of Rousseau, Kant, Schiller, and others paved the way for the Romantic movement, but he finds its primary sources in the Pietist movement of late seventeenth- and early eighteenth-century Germany.   HELEN RAPP

Helen Rapp's announcement of IB's Mellon Lectures, Radio Times, 4 August 1966, 40

1 To J. Carter Brown (Assistant Director, National Gallery of Art), 16 November 1964.
2 MI 244. *Ignahtff*
3 To Arthur Schlesinger, 23 September 1964.
4 *The Roots of Romanticism*, ed. Henry Hardy (London and Princeton, 1999).

After the series had ended, IB's BBC producer Helen Rapp wrote to reassure him that it had been enthusiastically received:

Just a note to tell you that your lectures were, as I always knew they would be, a great success with absolutely everybody, and although you did hope there would be no reviews, the BBC Critics in fact insisted on talking about them – something I could not stop and quite honestly did not want to stop. I enclose a script of their discussion which I am sure will disprove your point that Radio critics disapprove of 'highbrow subjects'.[1]

'The Critics' was a 45-minute weekly panel discussion broadcast on the Home Service, and on Sunday 11 September, on the eve of the broadcast of the final lecture, its members gave their reactions to 'Some Sources of Romantic Thought' (as the BBC entitled the lectures), with special reference to the fifth lecture, 'Unbridled Romanticism':

ERIC RHODE[2] [...] What's new for me here is that, brought up in this country, I do know that English romanticism has been influenced by German thinkers, but it's taken Berlin with his cosmopolitan grasp of the field to show me how important these thinkers are to an understanding of the movement. And what he's shown in this series of lectures, broadly speaking, is that in the middle-eighteenth century certain German thinkers of, as he calls it, humble origins reacted against the aristocratic enlightened thinkers, and gradually through this reaction a new model of the world emerged. Briefly, the enlightenment thinkers had seen the world as being like a jigsaw puzzle which could be put together. The world contained a series of facts which could be dug out. Now the new model that emerged was radically different in that the world was seen as a dark and terrible flux. [...] man had to, out of this dark and terrible flux, in order to exist, create through his will various values, various ideologies – and [...] to be willing to die for his ideologies or these various values. This is, I take it, the main point of these lectures. And Berlin then draws out of this the fact that various extreme and unpleasant ideologies have emerged, but also a new kind of tolerance. [...]

ROBERT ROBINSON[3] [...] One felt one was in the presence of a magus – a most comprehensive intellect, but a magus as well. And I think it was marvellously absorbing, even in spite of the delivery, which was so staccato and curious – rather like a straight man in a music hall. But that's by the way. The notions in this particular lecture, the fifth lecture, that he poured out, such as the self becoming aware of itself through contact with the not-self – that's to say the world – he had derived these notions from the original philosophers. But I wonder if they have ever been expressed by the original philosophers as clearly and as convincingly as this man did it. And I think the real value of this lecture,

1 Helen Rapp to IB, 16 September 1966.
2 Eric Rhode (b. 1934), British writer, broadcaster, and critic; later a practitioner of, and author on, psychoanalysis.
3 Robert Henry Robinson (1927–2011), broadcaster and writer, later well known for presenting the BBC TV show *Call My Bluff* and Radio 4's *Brain of Britain* and *Stop the Week*.

and the whole series of lectures, is that he showed these notions to underpin,
to lie right underneath, like so much clay, present-day notions of art and culture
and philosophy and psychology.

DAVID SYLVESTER[1] I learnt more about my own time from that lecture than
I've learnt from any statement or summary of that kind of length before. It
was an extraordinary illumination. These lectures are not going to be published
for some time – if ever – knowing how difficult Berlin finds it to go into print.
I hope the BBC will repeat them at the earliest possible moment.[2]

TO ISAAC STERN

[c.9 February 1965; *carbon*]

[Headington House]

Dear Isaac,

I really do hasten (no *sic*) to reply to your letter of 17 January. I am in
a fearful state – my lectures for Washington are totally unprepared and they
will be a flop: I do not so much mind (save that I do) that, but then there is
a book to come and to carve out a worthy book out of unworthy lectures,
with the guilt and shame of their effect hanging over one, is an unalluring
prospect. Nevertheless, of course we must see each other as soon as I arrive
in the United States, no matter what condition I am in. I come just the day
before my first lecture, which is on Sunday the 16th [sc. 14th], and then start
wailing like our ancestors, covering my head with ashes and wishing I were
dead. [...]

The *Histoire*[3] sounds marvellous: I heard a very inferior performance of it
in the Festival Hall once and conceived not a very high opinion of it, about
which I am sure I am wrong, for it is surely a great classical piece which marks
a stage, etc., and it is just my stupidity. That is what Toscanini said to the late
Shotzinoff[4] when the latter complained that although he liked Beethoven
well enough in general, he could not quite 'get' the *Mass* in D – 'maybe you
are stupid', said Toscanini: I expect to feel this about *Moses and Aaron*. [...]

Meanwhile the Hebrew University is giving fearful trouble: there is a war
to the knife in Tel Aviv between the slighted Dr Wise, who has now acquired

1 (Anthony) David Bernard Sylvester (1924–2001), writer, broadcaster, critic and art curator; 'in
  his prime, the country's most influential critic of modern art' with a position 'not unlike that of
  Roger Fry a half century or so before' (*Times*, 20 June 2001, 19a).
2 The lectures were repeated by the BBC in October–November 1967 and in June–July 1989 (not to
  mention airings elsewhere), and can now be heard (by prior appointment) at the British Library's
  Sound Archive in London, or at the National Gallery of Art in Washington. The last lecture is
  also available in the IBVL at ⟨http://berlin.wolf.ox.ac.uk/lists/broadcasts/roots32.mp3⟩.
3 *L'Histoire du soldat: lue, jouée et dansée* (*The Soldier's Tale: To Be Read, Played and Danced*), a work
  in two parts by Stravinsky, libretto by Charles-Ferdinand Ramuz; premiered in Lausanne 1918.
4 Samuel Chotzinoff (1889–1964), Russian-born American pianist and critic; author of *Toscanini:
  An Intimate Portrait* (NY, 1956).

the University of Tel Aviv and has mounted an Assyrian campaign against the poor Judeans. I have to attend endless committees about that too; not to speak of procuring money for indigent Israeli scholars who wish to come to Oxford – they pine and pine until they come, and then they find the dons here cold and inhospitable and terrible trauma[s] are inflicted upon them and their lives are reduced to ashes. Oh dear, how sad this letter is becoming. The telephone has just rung and Aline has informed me that the new Macmillan–Prokofiev *Romeo and Juliet* at Covent Garden was an almost indecent success: the clapping for Nureyev and Fonteyn[1] lasted for forty minutes; the thing has become a kind of highbrow Beatle affair, and the hysteria has reached an incredible pitch.[2] Also we have done a splendid *Arabella*, with Fischer-Dieskau – it is all excellent, the critics are raving, Covent Garden has reached quite a genuine height, etc. etc., and yet all the music is tainted for me by a touch of *kitsch*: one performance of *Fidelio* by Toscanini, or *Falstaff*, also by Toscanini, or *Don Carlos* by Giulini, or *Don Giovanni* with Franz Schalk[3] – and all these things shiver into nothing, and the ignoble tastes of our most famous and most gifted conductors is a strange and disturbing symptom of our times. Giulini alone remains pure and noble, but he stops early in the twentieth century, as if all great art were faintly antiquarian. Is this too pessimistic? Perhaps it is. [...]

[Isaiah]

On 11 February representatives of All Souls gave evidence before the University's internal enquiry, the Franks Commission. Although the College had been discussing reform for two years it had very little to show for this. A modest contribution to a joint scheme, promoted by Robin Harrison, to create a common fund to assist in the foundation of two new 'graduate societies' planned by the University was passed in September 1964. But this initiative left the portals of All Souls undisturbed, and Franks sought some more tangible sign that the College would live up to its communal obligations. That it was not doing so was apparent to all: it had great wealth yet spent an insufficient proportion of this on academic activities. It was fortunate, then – or Machiavellian? – that on 30 January, less than a fortnight before its appearance before Franks, the College adopted by a large majority a resolution 'to incorporate graduate students, in one way or another, in our College body without delay'.[4] Sparrow later candidly

1 Margot Fonteyn de Arias (1919–91), née Margaret ('Peggy') Hookham, DBE 1956; guest artist with the Royal Ballet from 1959, having previously been principal; later (1979) awarded the title prima ballerina assoluta.
2 The premiere of Kenneth MacMillan's *Romeo and Juliet* at Covent Garden on 9 February 1965, with Nureyev and Fonteyn in the title roles, attracted 43 curtain calls. To some observers, though, the 'exquisitely youthful' pairing of Christopher Gable and Lynn Seymour, a week later, was 'certainly the superior' (*Times*, 18 February 1965, 16a).
3 Franz Schalk (1863–1931), Austrian conductor, co-founder of the Salzburg Festival.
4 College meeting of 30 January 1965. The voting was 31 for, 15 against, with two abstentions: see David Caute, 'Crisis in All Souls: A Case History in Reform', *Encounter*, March 1966, 3–15 at 10.

admitted that the College's treatment at the hands of Franks 'would have been very different'[1] had that decision not been taken. Delay, however, was his most potent weapon: he simply regarded this vote as non-binding, and took no steps to execute it. IB wrote to a colleague in frustration that May:

As for the poor old college there seems to be a real difference of view between those who fundamentally want to do as little as possible and wonder with how little they can get away – of whom the Warden is the leader – and those who are genuinely anxious to use the existing resources for the College to create something new and useful […]. Goodness me – but it really is difficult to proceed with a chairman who is so passionate a partisan.[2]

TO GARRETT DROGHEDA

16 February [1965]

Headington House

Dear Garrett,

I agree with you wholly, without qualifications. Of course Solti has the faults that we know, not only personally but musically too – but all you say is incontrovertible. Certainly Colin Davis[3] is the best English conductor; but that, I am afraid, is not saying enough; Beecham[4] and Hamilton Harty[5] are no more – there never was in our lifetime anyone approaching them of English descent to touch the first-class continental conductors, let alone the great ones. […] Colin Davis can conduct Berlioz wonderfully, and Stravinsky well: Mozart, Verdi, Wagner, Strauss – perhaps one day. It is lucky to have him in England, in case one day we have to fall back on him should Solti go and we be unable to secure another like him – he is, of course, better than all the other English conductors, Pritchard cannot really hold a candle even to him – but to exchange Solti for him is like exchanging champagne for Muscatel (the other English conductors are cider), we must not even think of it: despite all the trouble he gives, all his egotism, etc., all his (for me) inability to conduct Mozart properly, even Verdi not always nobly and beautifully enough, he is a first-class conductor of world scale and prestige – all the critics recognise this, and the public does too – and in German and central European opera he is incomparable, and even in works not congenial to his gifts he is brilliant

1 ibid.
2 To Roger Makins, 18 May 1965.
3 Colin Rex Davis (1927–2013), later (1980) Kt; Conductor, Sadler's Wells, 1959; Principal Conductor 1960–5; Musical Director 1961–5; Chief Conductor, BBC Symphony Orchestra, 1967–71, Chief Guest Conductor 1971–5; Musical Director, ROH, 1971–86; Principal Guest Conductor, Boston Symphony Orchestra, 1972–84.
4 Thomas Beecham (1879–1961) Kt 1916, 2nd Bt 1916; conductor, composer and operatic impresario; founder of the London Philharmonic Orchestra 1932, of the Royal Philharmonic 1947.
5 (Herbert) Hamilton Harty (1880–1941), Kt 1925; Irish composer and conductor; Permanent Conductor, Hallé Orchestra, Manchester, 1920–33.

and attention-compelling. The fact that David probably has trouble with him is the fate of every impresario and opera manager, and we must not above all do what the Scala did in losing Giulini. [...]

What Benjamin Britten said is absolutely correct: *Midsummer Night's Dream* and *Billy Budd* would have sagged without him, and *we* would have been rapped by the critics, endlessly, tiresomely and damagingly, for not having done Britten justice, not doing enough for English music, and so would have become a cockshy for the present government, while at the moment, owing to the prowess of our Hungarian conductor, we are felt to be something of an asset. Why I am taking this inordinate length simply to say 'yes', I cannot think: just ⟨lack of time for brevity⟩

Yours,
    Isaiah

TO KAY GRAHAM[1]

5 March 1965 [*manuscript*]

All Souls

Dear Kay,

I was very sorry not to dine with Pam[2] – but I can't always get away with impunity: & at present I am working like a black (if this is still a permitted phrase) on these damned lectures, of which I have even the sketch of only *one*. God knows what will happen to the rest. I am glad to think I shall soon see you. And, I suppose, 'the others' too. Including Marion? I had a vivid account of her from Sylvester Gates[3] who went to Washington – nobly – more nobly than I – to see her immediately after. I am *terribly* sorry the Judge is dead.[4] He did transform a whole chunk of my life: without him I shd never have got my job or met anybody in America: & it totally altered & lifted my life more or less forever. Also I liked him – & especially his well known defects – very much: & I liked liking what others were irritated by: whenever I saw Arthur Goodhart[5]

---

1 The next letter was sent in two versions, manuscript and typescript, which do not entirely coincide. The manuscript version (dated 5 March) is used here, with two additions from the typed version (dated 8 March), which opens: 'I have decided to dictate this and send a manuscript as well, just to show good will, devotion, intimacy etc. But what is the use of this if it remains totally illegible as, on second thoughts, it obviously is? So here is the valuable autograph plus the official version.'

2 Pamela Berry was a frequent visitor to the US.

3 Sylvester Govett Gates (1901–72), barrister and banker; Gates had been a pupil of Felix Frankfurter's at Harvard when a Commonwealth Fund Fellow there 1925–7. His lifelong friendship with IB began in the 1930s; at IB's request he served on the Trust created to manage the affairs of Wolfson College (301–3).

4 Felix Frankfurter had died on 22 February.

5 Arthur Lehman Goodhart (1891–1978), Hon. KBE 1948; American-born jurist who spent most of his working life in Britain, but retained his US citizenship; Professor of Jurisprudence, Oxford, 1931–51; Master, Univ., 1951–63; Trustee, Wolfson Foundation, 1958–71.

embarrassed or Walter Lippmann[1] wince or Marion push in a pin, I felt loyal,
superior & pleased, if you see what I mean. He really was an exceptionally
nice & good man, & a credit to the human race & was an antidote to my
ambivalent anti-semitism (which understood Phil's occasional explosions on
this topic all too well:) he behaved very well when it was too common not
to do so: & when he would (in worldly terms) have got further by being
more dignified, judicious, "wise" & quite deliberately chose to be sincere &
truthful. But all this I ought to write to *Marion*: only I *won't*. My lectures get
me down. So do two letters from kind friends – one a Spaniard in the White
House, another in the State Dep. (decent ex-pupils) who say that an irritat-
ingly flippant article in the W. Post[2] appeared about me – one says "nastily
flippant", the other going on about the dreary Irving Berlin story, & asserting that I have an "impediment of speech" & am no good at lectures (true
enough!) & describing me in very socialistic terms: one of my correspondents says that nothing like this appeared about Sir K. Clark or Prof. Gombrich
– my predecessors – & offer (*slightly* crocodilish) sympathy. Oh dear! I *wish*
I did not mind so much: outright hostility is preferable to being described
as an entertainer: may be the writers exaggerate: but they don't know each
other & *both* profess indignation. Do you think you cd persuade your staff to
lay off me? it would be *such* a relief!

   I lead such an unpublic existence now – so out of all the worlds – that
I feel I don't deserve this pillory. I know I am not really – by serious standards
– much good: but am I ~~so grotesque? such a figure of fun~~? I so utterly like
Cecil Beaton? Igor Cassini?[3] Groucho Marx?[4] I have at last begun to enjoy
long deserved obscurity in England: especially in Oxford: I looked forward
to Washington, I suppose: I think in terms of private relationships. I must
stop this maundering. It is no fault of yours: but I shd be pleased if you are
sympathetic: & agree that journalists *are* invaders of privacy, not quite like
human beings, engaged in causing humiliation in public to non-public faces.
Or will you defend them through thick & thin? Or only through thin? [...]

   I wish I cd be idle all day & read newspapers: I adore gossip about the
others: when *I* am mentioned I die. You must be *particularly* sensitive, understanding, attentive, please.

   love,
      Isaiah

1 Walter Lippmann (1889–1974), US journalist and essayist; widely syndicated and influential columnist for the *New York Herald Tribune* 1931–67, and winner of a Pulitzer Prize 1962.
2 In her column (28 February 1965, F7) Maxine Cheshire describes IB as 'of Baltic origins and bur-
dened with a slight speech impediment'.
3 Igor Cassini (1915–2002) né Igor Cassini Loiewski in Sevastopol, poison-pen American gossip columnist, the second incarnation (1945–63) of 'Cholly Knickerbocker', the widely syndicated gossip
column in the *New York Journal American*. Martha Gellhorn described his mouth as 'like a hog's
ass in fly-time': *The Letters of Martha Gellhorn*, ed. Caroline Moorehead (London, 2006), 122.
4 Names (missing in MS version) supplied from typed version.

PS I gather that the University of West Kansas has decided to cancel an invitation to me to become an instructor, in view of my now notorious speech impediment: it is no use my telling them that others complain that there is not impediment enough. Consequently I propose to sue the *Washington Post* for heavy damages.[1]

TO ARTHUR SCHLESINGER

5 March 1965 [*postcard*]

Headington House

Rigorous seclusion in the Sheraton Park Hotel as from the 13th: horrors of unprepared lectures; gloom, self-contempt, dislike of public exposure, total lack of interest in Vietnam – I would rather have a leg sawn off with[out] an anaesthetic than deliver these lectures: why the sustained masochism of my life?

Isaiah

TO GARRETT DROGHEDA

9 March [1965]

Headington House

Dear Garrett,

I hope you are enjoying China. I envy you enormously. I have no doubt that Baba M.[2] is a most entrancing and valuable companion – you need not repeat the second attribute to her. I have longed all my life long to see China, and probably never shall. Just as before the war I expressed the greatest lack of interest in the United States and then my life was totally transformed by going there.

You will have heard by now that Solti has agreed to do *Moses* and so has Vilar,[3] so we are launched. Whither, time alone will show. If Solti himself is involved in this I feel that things will not be left undone, although David's enthusiasm for the work will, I suppose, be correspondingly lowered. We have to watch this situation with some care, at least, you and Burnet will [...]. I know that you will constantly be reminding me about my 'moral' responsibility for this, but I shall then remind you in turn that were it not for your insistence that I should write to Solti, and your constant – I do not deny, disinterested and admirable – egging on, I should not have gone out on this gigantic limb.

1 PS added in typed version.
2 Lady Alexandra Naldera ('Baba') Metcalfe (1904–95) née Curzon; younger daughter of George Curzon, 1st Marquess (1921) and Viceroy of India; a society figure.
3 Jean Vilar (1912–71), French actor and director; founded, 1947, the Festival d'Avignon, and restored and re-energised the Théâtre national populaire; *Moses and Aaron* was produced by Peter Hall, not by Vilar as originally advertised.

The most important thing, I am sure, is now to enlist the sympathy and help of outside bodies, i.e. the BBC, European radio stations and various organs of publicity.[1] I think that you should give a lunch for the leading critics – when arrangements have got on a bit – and work them up, each critic, I suppose, sitting next to not another critic but a fanatical *Moses* addict – Hans Keller,[2] Glock[3] and other Schoenbergians should be there, as well as David, Solti etc. If that goes well, we shall have a lot of sympathy to lean on – the main purpose of such a lunch would be not just to advertise our virtue in doing the thing, but discussing the work in general and stressing our appalling difficulties and asking for advice and help – nothing flatters critics so much as that approach, instead of a recital of how well we are doing and how well we mean to do.

I don't really feel happy about Chagall[4] as a decorator and designer. George Harewood will for once I think be very helpful and ought to be galvanised a bit to herald our cause: I wrote to him about *Moses* and had a very affable response. The responsibility for the whole thing, let me repeat, is entirely yours: I am sure it will be a glorious success and Sir T. Armstrong will be chosen to present you with an illuminated address.

Yours, ⟨with love⟩

Isaiah

TO MORTON WHITE

18 March 1965 [*manuscript postcard*]

Sheraton Hotel, Washington, DC

How are you? I shall telephone you as soon as I feel less terrified (after 25 yrs?) of my own prospective lectures in the Nat. Gallery: the first one went off "all right": but that was a dishonourable apéritif – worthy of Marshall Cohen – full of well received jokes & jabs – a thoroughly smart job. Now for the substance. I feel like G. E. Moore[5] – *your* story I think – (Mrs Moore:

1 There was considerable coverage in the press before the first night on 28 June, and in mid-June Solti, the producer Peter Hall and the designer John Bury all spoke at a lecture evening on the opera at the ROH.
2 Hans Heinrich Keller (1919–85), Vienna-born violinist, broadcaster and writer on music, highly original in his approach, joined the BBC at the suggestion of William Glock, and was with the music division 1959–79; championed the works of Britten and Schoenberg.
3 William (Frederick) Glock (1908–2000), later (1970) Kt, pianist and critic; Controller of Music, BBC, 1959–72; Director, ROH, 1968–73.
4 Marc Chagall (1887–1985), Russian-born French painter and graphic artist, influenced by Russian folk art and contemporary avant-garde; his public commissions include the two large murals in the Lincoln Centre in NY (1966); he did not work on the ROH's 1965 *Moses and Aaron*.
5 George Edward Moore (1873–1958), philosopher; an important influence on the Cambridge Apostles, of which he was a member, and the Bloomsbury Group, of which he was not; Professor of Philosophy and Fellow of Trinity, Cambridge, 1925–39; appointed to the Order of Merit 1951; he married, 1916, Dorothy Mildred Ely (1892–1977).

"I am sure they will like your paper, dear". "If they do, they will be *wrong*".)
So on Monday I'll call you. Or you me as Lenin wd say.

Isaiah

TO PAT UTECHIN

25 March 1965

Washington, DC

Dear Pat,

The agony continues. One lecture is done, indeed two are. About the first there was a glowing review by a legal luminary and clarinet player comparing me to Mozart playing in one of his concerti. So I cannot complain although the review was somehow highly embarrassing as well. But do not let us go on about me – you will learn all about that when I come back, in a fluster, as usual, about the Royal Academy.[1] Now as to business [...].

You will not be altogether surprised to hear that at this moment I am in bed with the flu, sinusitis, etc. – none of this, of course, must reach my mother's ears – and although I shall deliver my next (3rd) lecture on Sunday, I am forced to cancel all the accepted invitations here, New York, etc., with fearful resultant chaos. I am quite comfortable, but all those lectures in February in Oxford have finally told. I really ought to *retire*. I cannot conceive what would happen if I were in bed now in Oxford and flooding you and everybody else with superfluous and unnecessary work! So count yourself lucky for the moment. Please keep me posted about what is happening, e.g. who was elected at All Souls, which Warden Sparrow has signally failed me to tell [sc. to tell me]. You might perhaps ring up Max [Beloff], and ask him whether the number of our colleagues has in fact grown, and if so by how many, plus names.

Yours ever,

Isaiah   [...]

TO PAT UTECHIN

Tuesday 20 April 1965 [*manuscript*]

Carlyle Hotel

Dear Pat,

The lectures, thank God, are over: Very peculiar it all was: very: I mean at the last one, last Sunday, after I left the platform, all these pompous Washington persons + assorted students from God knows where, stood up & produced a kind of Khrushchev style ovation: I felt more ashamed than pleased: my lectures must have been *very* rhetorical to have produced *that*

---

1 IB was due to speak at the annual dinner of the Royal Academy of Arts, at Burlington, London, on 28 April (the subject of his 2 May letter to Garrett Drogheda, below).

effect: however there is no doubt that in a vulgar sense of the word they were what is called 'a success" – though I, of course, hated every minute & felt an acute sense of prostitution. All v. pathological I daresay. [...]

Yours
    Isaiah

TO GARRETT DROGHEDA

2 May 1965

Headington House

Dear Garrett,

Thank you for your most, most heart-warming letter. I am glad that ordeal is over. I do not believe Olivier[1] or Callas can go through such agonies as I did. Oddly enough, I have no power of reproductive memory: I could never learn verse at school[2] – the thought of having to do what in those days was called 'repetition' darkened my schooldays. Of course it was not impromptu: I wrote out some words in the aeroplane coming back from America – they were typed – I looked at them once, twice, three times – thought of reading them aloud – rejected this notion – made notes on a single sheet of paper – lost them – realised I could not look at my typescript during dinner because it was too long – scribbled what I could on another bit of paper – and then threw myself in at the deep end, with a sense of shame and despair: despair at being able to do justice to the occasion; shame at being such a victim of vanity as ever to have accepted this invitation. Apparently all the listeners of the BBC Home Service that evening heard me saying 'Was that all right? My God, I'm glad it's over', and I suppose also Frank Longford's[3] soothing words, as well as a mooing sound, which might have meant anything, from the lips of the Archbishop of York,[4] my other neighbour.[5] But if you thought it was all right, I am very pleased. [...]

Yours,
    Isaiah

1 Laurence Kerr Olivier (1907–89), Kt 1947, later life peer (1970) and OM (1981); actor; one of the foremost interpreters of Shakespeare of his generation; Director, National Theatre, 1962–73, Associate Director 1973–4.

2 In the early 1970s IB recited the opening of Milton's *Lycidas* without prior notice in the common room of Wolfson College at 60 Banbury Road, when this title was proposed for the College magazine (etymologically the name means 'wolf's son'); his ability to learn verse was evidently better than he admitted.

3 Francis Aungier ('Frank') Pakenham (1905–2001), 7th Earl of Longford 1961; politician, writer, philanthropist and campaigner against the 'permissive society'; (Labour) Leader of the Lords 1964–8, Secretary of State for the Colonies 1965–6, Lord Privy Seal 1966–8.

4 (Frederick) Donald Coggan (1909–2000), Archbishop of York 1961–74, of Canterbury 1974–80.

5 As was customary the speeches at the Royal Academy's annual dinner were broadcast on the BBC Home Service – on this occasion at 9.00 p.m. on the night of the dinner itself, 28 April. IB replied to a toast to the guests by Sir Charles Wheeler, and proposed a toast to the Academy.

TO AN UNIDENTIFIED CORRESPONDENT[1]

[11/12 May] 1965

Headington House

⟨Dear Dick⟩,

This is only to say how grateful I am for kind treatment. We both enjoyed ourselves a very great deal, and I only hope we weren't too much of a nuisance – I think I shall always love Washington beyond all other cities, for every possible reason, and shall always wish to go back there as a kind of Mecca. I cannot believe that anyone has ever had equally fervent feelings for it before – I have experienced scarcely any chagrin there, only pleasure. May I come and see you again in the autumn, when I am at Princeton?

⟨Tomorrow we have to go to the opening of the Kennedy memorial – nobody knows what to wear – is it a Garden Party? a Memorial Service? a Race meeting? grey top hats? trilbies? no hats? The Queen's presence, does it determine appearances? or Mrs Kennedy's – in the same direction? And so on – we shall see

yrs
    Isaiah B.⟩

On 14 May 1965 the British memorial to President John F. Kennedy at Runnymede was unveiled by the Queen. The ceremony was attended by the President's family, led by his widow, Jacqueline Kennedy, while Harold Macmillan, Prime Minister during Kennedy's presidency, gave an address on behalf of the Trustees of the Memorial, of which IB was one. The memorial stands in three acres of land beside the Thames, given by the people of Great Britain to the US, and chosen for its association with Magna Carta, the memorial to which stands nearby. In a personal message issued on the eve of the ceremony Jacqueline Kennedy reflected: 'My husband loved history and what you have done today in his honour would please him more than my words can express. [...] In a sense he returns today to the tradition from which he sprang.'[2]

TO JACQUELINE KENNEDY

14 May 1965 [*manuscript*]

Headington House

Dear Mrs Kennedy,

I cannot say how deeply disappointed we are – Aline and I – not to have seen you; save on that strange & moving afternoon at Runnymede, when in front of the stand – I felt promoted beyond my station – there appeared in

1 Since this letter is in the files of the National Gallery of Art in Washington, where IB delivered his Mellon Lectures (213–16), it may have been written to a then member of staff there.
2 *Times*, 15 May 1965, 7a.

a prettily painted booth (like a décor of a ballet impresario) there appeared
before us some of the most celebrated and important and decorative persons
in the world, and each said his piece with feeling and great and proper solemnity, & then sat down like performers in a sacred rite. I felt immensely moved
– but that was a thing in itself. It did not, alas, compensate us for not being
able to show you our exhilarating city. David Harlech[1] had, indeed, made it
plain that this was scarcely to be thought of: our "arrangement" was built
on sand: that, naturally enough, what with London and Derbyshire and an
overlong 'schedule', neither you nor the Senator (from N.Y.) could possibly
dream of the journey to Oxford. I understand this all too well. And it is very
sad indeed that we could not, in the end, accept Evangeline Bruce's very
kind summons to dinner: I am, for better & for worse, a don: I *have* to talk to
undergraduates that evening: I have a lifelong *appalling* & hideous crushing
sense of academic duty: I feel I *must* try to be a good, conscientious professor,
do what is right, fulfil promises, live laborious days, not fall into too much
(worldly) temptation: & anyway human relationships seldom flourish at
large dinner parties, no matter how gay and brilliant (particularly not then).
So I shall do what dons do, & talk to my undergraduates. But it *is* frustrating
and there is something incredibly melancholy about hope deferred. I did so
enjoy (& so did Aline) the call you allowed us to make in New York. But what
I still remain *eternally* grateful for was your courtesy & kindness to me at the
first evening at the Alsops two years ago. I shall never forget it.[2]

Goodness me! I remember that whole evening – the day on which the
Cuban photographs had first been shown to the President (I recorded it
all dutifully on a tape provided by Arthur Schlesinger) – I was, as you may
imagine, in what is called "a state". The President was very nice to me, but
I still continued in a state of nerves, terror, admiration, excitement, sense
of anxiety, terror again. This was *not* made easier by the fact that I saw Chip
Bohlen – saw rather than heard, like a lip reader – say to Phil Graham, something like "do you think he made out all right?" – then a dubious head-shake
from Phil "didn't think he did too well' – like a début by a new singer, an
entertainer, a prospective bridegroom for all the world! I realised I – my
conduct under fire – was being discussed. Then I was placed beside you (I do
hope you will forgive these elderly reminiscences – if you have got so far) &
all was light. As Oscar Wilde said of Robbie Ross, when the latter came to
greet him when he walked out of Reading gaol & took off his hat – doffed
it – to him: "men have go[ne] to heaven for less".[3] You performed a great act
of emancipation.

Oxford is exceedingly beautiful at this very moment: it is not yet quite

---

1 Lord Harlech chaired the Kennedy Memorial Trust.

2 122.

3 Robert Baldwin ('Robbie') Ross (1869–1918), journalist and gallery owner, intimate and steadfast
  friend of Oscar Wilde. The incident to which IB here refers actually occurred in 1895, early in

HEADINGTON HOUSE
HEADINGTON, OXFORD
TEL. 61005

14. 5. 65

Dear Mrs Kennedy,

I cannot say how deeply disappointed we are — Alice & I — not to have seen you just now on her stage & moving afternoon in Runnymede, when it from the start — I felt poor to beyond my station — there appeared in a pretty painted book (there a view of a fuller impression) there appeared declaration of persons in the town, & each said his piece but feeling & gave a proper solemnity, & then sat down like so & persons in a varied rite. I felt immensely moved — but there was a king in itself. It did not, alas, compensate us for not being able to see you our exhausting city. David Harlech too, I say, made it plain how this too seems to be thought of: our "amateur" is built on sad:

In her reply to IB's letter Jacqueline Kennedy explained that it had been torn in pieces by her 5-year-old nephew Anthony Radziwill, but rescued by her family aide John Joseph ('Muggsy') O'Leary

Wilde's term in Reading gaol, when Ross waited in a corridor of the bankruptcy court in Carey Street (at which Wilde was obliged to appear), so that he could raise his hat to him.

dark: there is a great feast going on in my College at All Souls on this very evening: sounds of revelry (and noisy argument) can be heard in the room in which I am writing: nothing is more agreeable than private thoughts recorded in a public or semi-public place. Our house is filled with, & surrounded with various flowers: it is all terribly good for the nerves: there are few visitors for once, & you would find it – would have found it – I think, peaceful and delightful. But you cannot be everywhere: I must contain my soul in patience. We shall be in the U.S. in the autumn & then we shall go, I hope, to the East. Perhaps you will be free for an afternoon again – we both send you our devoted greetings.

Yours sincerely,
Isaiah Berlin

TO E. A. ROSE[1]

14 May 1965 [*carbon*]

[Headington House]

Dear Mr Rose,

I have just come again upon your letter to Messrs Behr and Ross,[2] to which they replied. You sent me a copy of this letter. I could not follow your reasoning, and therefore decided to make no explicit reply. On second thoughts, it seems to me that my acquiescence might have seemed consent, and I have therefore decided to answer you.

There is no country whose policies were beyond reproach in the 1930s, nor, I daresay, at any other time in recorded human history. I have no wish to defend the foreign policy of the British Government in the 1930s, nor the Palestine policy in the later 1930s or the 1940s, before, during and after the war; there were plenty of protests and condemnations of these policies at the time, with some of which I was associated. But no matter how disastrous these policies were, and however marred by occasional callousness, they sprang from perfectly intelligible motives such as any normal nation governed by fallible human beings could be expected to be swayed by; and in this respect were wholly unlike the behaviour of the totalitarian powers. However this may be, it does not alter the fact that in offering asylum to refugees this country has a better record than most others, perhaps than any

1 Ernest Albert Rose (1879–1976) né Rosenheim; engineer, lieutenant-colonel (retired; war service in Europe 1914–19) and motoring enthusiast.
2 The Jewish refugees Werner Meyer Behr (1902–76), financial consultant, and Victor Ross (b. 1919) né Victor Theodor Karl Rosenfeld, journalist and publisher, were co-chairmen of the charitable Thank-Offering to Britain Fund, a charitable initiative begun by the Association of Jewish Refugees in 1963, and later explicitly linked to the 25th anniversary of the refugees' flight from Germany and Austria in 1938–9. The fund appealed to its members to 'Give now what you would have paid then for the visa which you got for free': Omri Behr, 'From Berlin to London: Werner M. Behr OBE', *AJR Journal* 11 no. 1 (January 2011), 5. The fund supported lectures and academic research under the auspices of the British Academy.

other; the brief – and perhaps unnecessary – panic in 1940 was very soon over, and did incomparably less damage than the behaviour of other belligerent or even neutral countries at this period. As for the millions slaughtered by the Germans, you surely know as well as I do that a great many of these could not bring themselves to believe – as, indeed, who could? – that if they stayed put they were doomed; this applies to members of our own families in north-eastern Europe, who could perfectly well have emigrated, had they wished to do so, but who refused to budge because, save for pressing reasons, human beings are attached to their homes and do not wish to believe the worst; no doubt many more could have been saved if immigration policies of the majority of free countries had been different from what they were; but it seems to me unjust and uncharitable – to use no stronger terms – to wish to suppress feelings of natural gratitude to a country and a community which enabled men to save their lives, their liberties and their prospect of happiness – especially when most other countries signally failed to do so – because they did not display a real virtue and altruism which few communities in recorded history have ever shown, or, so long as human nature remains what it is, could conceivably be expected to show. For these reasons, I wholly reject your argument and sincerely hope that very few feel as you do.

Yours sincerely,

[Isaiah Berlin]

TO E. A. ROSE

25 May 1965 [*carbon*]

All Souls

Dear Mr Rose,

Thank you for your letter of 20 May. I fear we must indeed agree to differ. There is one simple question that I should like to put to you: if someone had rescued you when you were drowning, would you decline to thank him on the ground that he could not or would not rescue others in the same plight? I see that you might not wish to be treated as a privileged case, and might actually prefer to drown with others rather than be saved alone; but this is not the issue. Would you in fact decline to thank your rescuer, provided that you did call for help and that he did give it to you, even though he had absolutely no interest in doing so save the desire to respond to your call? If, having been rescued and having lived to construct a new life for yourself in the land of your rescuer, you then said, 'I owe you my life and the opportunity of liberty and the pursuit of happiness, but my debt to you is fully cancelled by your failure to do as much for others', then indeed there is no common ground between us.

Yours sincerely,

[Isaiah Berlin]

TO KORNEY CHUKOVSKY

1 July [sc. August] 1965 [*editorial translation of Russian manuscript*]

[As from] All Souls

[Dear Korney Ivanovich,

I am writing to you from blissful Italy [...]. Anna Andreevna [Akhmatova][1] visited us – I don't know how she felt in England – in London the British Council chose a bad hotel for her: and in Oxford she stayed at the same – good old – Randolph. We did all we could ... And the impression she made on all of us was enormous. She found Bowra to be a genius of a translator – in a dignified and stern way and justly she condemned Georgy Ivanov[2] and Mayakovsky[3] for their lies and gossiping, and also various American publishers for their various underhand dealings in relation to her. Well there you are. And she told me off because I have translated Turgenev – her attitude to Turgenev is similar, more or less, to Dostoevsky's. And meanwhile the publisher has asked me to write a 'new' preface to the new translation of *War and Peace* – there is no other book in the world which would be less in need of a preface, especially of a preface written by me – am I a man of letters? or a Tolstoy scholar? And you, according to the rumours in the Italian newspapers, have published a preface to the Leningrad edition of Pasternak – he, it is true, really needs an introduction [...]. Also Voznesensky[4] has visited us – I didn't see him in Oxford – but in London I listened to him and heard: there is something in him – but does one really have to make such a din and be such a rallying orator? Perhaps this is one of the *ricorsi*[5] of 'old man Vico', as Herzen used to call him – where we have fallen again into the Homeric era, and 'Bards' and poetasters and bayans[6] and a whole crowd of epics

1 Anna Akhmatova (1889–1966), pseudonym of the Russian poet Anna Andreevna Gorenko, made famous before the Revolution, when she was associated with the Acmeist movement, but ostracised afterwards for failing to conform to Soviet literary orthodoxy, remaining unpublished 1923–40. A brief period of rehabilitation during the war years was reversed soon afterwards, partly at least as a result of her meetings with IB in November 1945 and January 1946. Towards the end of her life there was some relaxation in official displeasure, and she was permitted to travel abroad to accept marks of international recognition: in 1964 she was the first recipient of Italy's Etna–Taormina prize, and on 5 June 1965 she received an Hon. D.Litt. from Oxford (in the company of Siegfried Sassoon, who was similarly honoured), as a result of a proposal by IB.

2 Georgy Vladimirovich Ivanov (1894–1958), Russian poet associated with the Acmeists and, after his departure to the West, with the literature of the émigré movement.

3 Vladimir Vladimirovich Mayakovsky (1893–1930), Russian poet and playwright who combined futurism with fervent support for the anti-Tsarist cause; *The Times* announced his death in April 1930 as 'Suicide of Bolshevist "Court Poet"' (15 April 1930, 15c).

4 Andrey Andreevich Voznesensky (1933–2010), Soviet poet and writer; emblematic of the new wave of Soviet poets who flourished during the greater artistic freedom of the Khrushchev era. *The Times*, referring to a poetry reading that he gave in Moscow in November 1962, dubbed him the 'Russian Poet Who Can Pack a Stadium' (31 December 1962, 9c). He arrived in Britain at the end of May 1965 for a two-week visit which included a poetry reading at St Antony's, 2 June.

5 Vico advanced a theory of cyclical historical change, whose phases he called *corsi e ricorsi* ('occurrences and recurrences').

6 Russian epic poet-singers.

inflame every heart and especially everyone's nerves. There was loud noise and Stravinsky was played, and the ungifted English translators shouted and old ladies applauded vigorously – and yet he is (possibly) a poet: in Oxford all the Soviet scholars were enraptured by him, and just scholars as well – Obolensky[1] etc. And as to me … there is real blood boiling in his vessels, very electrifying – and he is no fool at all – and he is an admirer of yours – and all that – and yet, and yet … anyway he has a greater gift than Tarsis.[2]

Do come! they have come to love you so much here.

Yours,

Isaiah Berlin]

TO SHIRLEY ANGLESEY[3]

[Early August 1965, *manuscript*]

Pensione Argentina, Paraggi

Dearest Shirley

Excellent! meraviglioso. […] Choose a fine day: telephone us or send us a message – it is some distance from our squalid sleeping quarters or filthy beach that we love so, to the telephone which is in the middle of a kitchen with women cooking, washing, darting, & above all, & continuously screaming. Still one *can* communicate. If you specify the train's arrival at Sta Margherita (or Rapallo if *very* special train) you will be fetched by Aline: it is all within (my: I walk like mad) walking distance. Don't overestimate the beach: it is humble & failed to please Diana C. on a notorious occasion which I can describe to you and/or Henry at will: but we have a boat of sorts. And a house being built: 400 steps on foot: uphill: no mule or ass as yet: 'worth the grind' as old fashioned English guide books used to say. So tell us when: we shall roll out a modest carpet. […]

Much love

Isaiah

---

1 (Prince) Dmitry Dmitrievich Obolensky (1918–2001), later (1984) Kt, Russian-born historian; Professor of Russian and Balkan History, Oxford, 1961–85, Student of Christ Church 1950–85.

2 Valery Yakovlevich Tarsis (1906–83), Russian writer, literary critic and translator. He was critical of the Soviet regime, and was imprisoned in a psychiatric hospital 1962–3 for sending his work abroad to be published; he later recounted this experience in the novel *Ward 7*, published in English in 1965 (London and Glasgow), in Russian in 1966 (Frankfurt).

3 (Elizabeth) Shirley Vaughan Paget (b. 1924) née Morgan, Marchioness of Anglesey, later (1983) DBE, writer; in 1949 she had assisted IB with his translation of Turgenev's *First Love*, first published with Alex Brown's translation of *Rudin* (London, 1950).

TO JOHN SPARROW

7 August 1965 [*manuscript*]

Pensione Argentina, Paraggi

Dear John,

[...] I wish you could tell me whether or not to go to Venice on the 6*th* or so to take part in a Settecento Conference[1] – the trouble of writing a paper in *haste* – to have it translated into Italian – the enormous waste of time at *all* conferences – the premia on vanity, self importance, exhibitionism, brilliance in "intervention" – the equal shame arising from having spoken and having not spoken – appalling polyglot conversations (I don't know what's come over this pen – as Lady Halifax[2] said in the course of a correspondence concerned with the question of whether or not my remarks to Freddy Birkenhead did or did not convey my true attitude to my late colleague, friend, and master) in the course of which *nothing* of interest is conveyed & all sides pretend to understand & appreciate what are to them often unintelligible syllables, and so on. This agonizing question I shall evidently have to decide for myself. Shall you be – who says that? – in Venice on Sept 6–8 or so? it wd influence my choice – pray don't make foolish jokes about which way – but how could you.

Yours,

Isaiah

P. S. Of course if you *are* there & I cannot come, you'll think ....etc.

TO EDWARD BRIDGES[3]

[August] 1965 [*typed transcript of lost manuscript original*]

As from Paraggi

Dear Edward,

Thank you very much for your message about Oliver: I know – at least when I left England a month ago I thought I knew – what was in his mind: he wanted All Souls to drop graduate students (if we were not to have 200 or some vast number) and provide research facilities – à la Princeton – for scholars in or outside Oxford for limited periods. The idea was inserted in his mind by his colleague, the very active Editor of the Oxford Magazine,

---

1 The Conference took place in September; IB did not attend.
2 Dorothy Augusta Wood (1885–1976) née Onslow, Countess of Halifax; she married, 1909, Edward Frederick Lindley Wood (1881–1959), 3rd Viscount Halifax 1934, 1st Earl of Halifax 1944, under whom IB worked in Washington when Halifax was UK ambassador there 1941–6.
3 Edward Bridges (1892–1969), KCB 1939, 1st Baron Bridges 1957, civil servant, veteran of the First World War, MC 1917; Permanent Secretary, HM Treasury, 1945–56; Fellow of All Souls 1920–7, 1954–68.

1 Heroes and villains: IB's study door, Headington House
(for a key to some of the persons shown see p. xii)

2 Pablo Casals and Isaac Stern play in Caesarea, September 1961
(front row: 1 Teddy Kollek, 4 Arnold Goodman, 10 IB, just above Casals's bow):
'The music festival was a great success, particularly Casals, scarcely audible, in the theatre
at Caesarea' (to Stuart Hampshire, 9 October 1961)

3 With David Ben-Gurion and Aline, Sde Boker, April 1962: 'Mr Ben Gurion is *not*
interested in me: a cold message of greeting: but after you come we shall impose
ourselves on them in Sde Boker' (to Aline Berlin, 27 March 1962)

4 On Paraggi beach, early 1960s: 'this delicious, lonely (by which I mean tourist-covered, absolutely impassable) shore' (to Burnet Pavitt, 5 September 1961)

5 Stuart Hampshire at Paraggi, 1960s: 'No more English Englishman has ever been created' (to Maurice Bowra, 18 November 1965)

6 John F. Kennedy and
'Chip' Bohlen, 16 April 1963:
'I must tell you about the
Important Young Man –
Napoleon – surrounded by
Maréchaux Bohlen, Alsop,
Graham' (to Aline Berlin,
17 October 1962)

7, 8 Joe Alsop and Arthur Schlesinger (AS in 1963), who fell out in 1967 over Vietnam: 'This is,
alas, the end of a beautiful friendship' (to Rowland Burdon-Muller, 26 January 1967)

9 (*left*) Rowland Burdon-Muller, 'the last witness of his age' (to Mary McCarthy, 7 August 1964), 1964; 10 (*right*) Garrett Drogheda, August 1968: 'Garrett really is intolerable. I showed him George's letter which I sent you – & *begged* him not to reveal this – of course he told George at once' (to Jack Donaldson, 29 June 1961)

11 With André Malraux (*left*) and François Bédarida, director of the Maison française (*right*), for Malraux's honorary DCL, All Souls, Saturday 18 November 1967; Aline in pale coat

12 (*left*) Anna Akhmatova at her dacha in Komarovo, September 1964; 13 (*right*) The only photograph of Anna Akhmatova and IB together: June 1965, Radcliffe Square, Oxford (Dmitry Obolensky, AA, IB and Anna Kaminskaya, granddaughter of Nikolay Punin, Akhmatova's third husband)

14 Kenneth Wheare and McGeorge Bundy, 28 June 1966, at a press conference to announce the creation of Wolfson: 'It – the entire operation – Iffley–Wolfson – is about to be completed: I feel dazed & terrified & wish I had not started it all' (to Joe Alsop, 24 June 1966)

15, 16 Cecilia Dick and Frank Jessup, founder fellows of Iffley College,
and central figures in the establishment (in both senses) of Wolfson College

17 John Sparrow in
the Codrington
Library, All Souls:
'John is far superior
to everyone there,
and that is what
ensures its present
decadence'
(to Sylvester Gates,
25 July 1966)

18 IB presents
Edith Wolfson
to the Queen at
the ceremony for
the laying of
the foundation
stone, Wolfson
2 May 1968;
Isaac Wolfson
and Aline
look on

19 At Headington House, 1968

20 Visiting the neighbours: with Robert
Maxwell, Headington Hill Hall, July 1969

21 With Stuart
Hampshire and
Nicolas Nabokov
on the lawn
at Headington House,
1969 (*photo by
Dominique Nabokov*)

John Vaisey,[1] an "educational" economist and a great pal of Crosland.[2] I do not think this an intrinsically bad idea: the need exists: there is no reason why dons who have to finish a book should always go from Nottingham or Oriel or wherever to America where they do get both money and free time: it *would* put us back into an active academic swim: but perhaps we've gone too far along the graduate road to swap horses: if we build a building we could use it for many purposes: some for graduates: some for research scholars in whatever proportions the situation calls for, depending, as it were, on immediate needs.

When (I think) Rohan Butler[3] and I originally put up the scheme to subsidize scholars from other colleges and universities, Roger Makins[4] persuaded me that we should never be allowed to get away with dispensing such bounty by ourselves: even with a committee to which outside "appointees" could be co-opted. Now I am not so sure. At any rate I shall not be there to vote for I shall be in Princeton till January. Let us build *rapidly*! Not bother for whom precisely we are building: *not* be put off by pseudo-patriotic considerations of building shortages etc.: and hold our horses about graduates for say a year or so. But advertise our intention clearly and loudly *before* the Franks Report is out:[5] and keep in touch with Oliver who, I am *sure*, longs to be informally and even continuously consulted, privately, and unofficially. But if it is to be graduates, let us go forth! anything but needless hovering and caution.

Yours ever,

Isaiah

Glyndebourne: *Werther*! My God! pure goo: and of very inferior quality.[6]

TO ALINE BERLIN

16 September 1965 [*manuscript*]

Ritz Hotel, London

Darling Aline,

I love you as deeply as at any moment – as deeply as during the darkest

---

1 John Ernest Vaizey (1929–84), later (1976) life peer, economist; Fellow and Tutor, Worcester, 1962–6; Professor of Economics, Brunel, 1966–82.
2 (Charles) Anthony Raven Crosland (1918–77), Labour politician, held cabinet office under Wilson and Callaghan; Secretary of State for Education and Science 1965–7.
3 Rohan D'Olier Butler (1917–96), historian and civil servant; Fellow of All Souls 1938–84.
4 Roger Mellor Makins (1904–96), KCMG 1949, 1st Baron Sherfield 1964; Fellow of All Souls 1925–39, 1957–96; British ambassador to the US 1953–6; Joint Permanent Secretary of the Treasury 1956–9; Chairman, UK Atomic Energy Authority, 1960–4.
5 The report of Oliver Franks's Commission of Inquiry was nervously awaited by the University, particularly All Souls: it appeared in May 1966.
6 This judgement can be confirmed by the first-named editor, who attended a rehearsal of this production of Massenet's opera as a schoolboy.

days of 1954[1] – & cannot live without you & mind the 4 days to come *acutely*!
I am myself astonished at the force & blotting out of *everything* else by this
overwhelming feeling.

    I.

*IB took sabbatical leave from Oxford for the whole of Michaelmas Term 1965
in order to visit Princeton at the invitation of their Council of Humanities. He
arrived in America on 17 September, Aline joining him shortly afterwards, and
they returned to England in the second week of January 1966, having spent the
New Year in Barbados. At Princeton, IB made profitable use of the university
library: 'Material here is infinitely more accessible than in Oxford or London,
and there is actually more of it, terrible but true!'[2]*

TO ROBERT CRAFT

17 September 1965 [*manuscript*]

                                  The Carlyle, New York

Dear Bob,

    The Memorandum[3] is this: you did the Sacre *beautifully* on the 14*th*: and
the nasty remarks of the *Times* critic[4] (which I hope you took no notice of:
Giulini *genuinely* – I admire him for it – does not read notices, & lives in his
music and ignores them all: his fame is smaller than say Solti's & Karajan's:[5]
but his life and work are of far greater worth: & justice in the end will be
done him) – I don't know who he is: Mann? Noble?[6] but if Mann, it is no different from other rubbish – & vulgar rubbish – that he writes: I don't know
what these people failed at: Legge is a failed conductor: Martin Cooper[7]
a failed minor composer: *don't* regard all this: your labours for, with, about

1 IB's relationship with Aline, then married to the physicist Hans Halban, began in 1954, causing
  much emotional turmoil (L2 444 ff.).
2 To Herbert Nicholas, 28 October 1965.
3 The letter was written on paper headed 'Memorandum', and bearing the arms and address of the
  famous Carlyle Hotel in NY's Upper East Side.
4 In a concert of Stravinsky's music given at the Royal Festival Hall on 14 September, which
  was partly televised, Craft conducted *Le sacre du printemps*, and the European premiere of the
  Variations in Memory of Aldous Huxley, and Stravinsky himself conducted *Fireworks* and *The
  Firebird*. Stravinsky's conducting was praised by the music critic of *The Times*, in marked contrast
  to that of Craft, whose '*Rite of Spring* is best forgotten: it was tentative, insecure, and woefully
  dull, accompanied by a television lighting rehearsal of the most disturbing and inept nature
  imaginable' (15 September 1965, 14a).
5 Herbert von Karajan (1908–89), Austrian conductor; Music Director, Berlin State Opera, 1939–45,
  Berlin Philharmonic Orchestra 1955–89; his membership of the Nazi Party in the 1930s checked
  the progress of his career after the Second World War.
6 William Somervell ('Bill') Mann (1924–89), chief music critic, *The Times*, 1960–82; (John) Jeremy
  Noble (b. 1930), music critic, *The Times*, 1960–3.
7 Martin Du Pré Cooper (1910–86), Music Editor, *Daily Telegraph*, 1954–76; notwithstanding his
  comments to Craft, IB had great respect for Cooper's musical understanding, particularly his
  ability to connect a composition to its broader cultural base; their friendship began with a chance
  meeting at the Holywell Music Room in Oxford in 1930/31.

the immortal figure whom you now know better than anyone, assures you a place not merely in heaven (on which I am a poor authority) but on earth too. And *I* say this to you – who have suffered one minor irritation at your hands[1] – but who will always remain your friend and disinterested admirer: I say this to you not just to staunch what *must* – for you are a great *minder* I am sure, as I am, & cannot flick these things off as one should & the great heartless geniuses (& non-geniuses – Milhaud[2] for example) do: I am afraid you will always wince: but if you didn't you would not be capable of entering into, interpreting, understanding at all: & the pachydermatous aren't all that happy. [...]

But the real purpose of this note is to say what the famous Spooner[3] (you know about Spoonerisms?) said to a friend of mine in 1921: "Mr Harrod, you must not think you aren't the man you once used to think you were". To hell with them all: your prowess & deep musical understanding are not matters of doubt & have *prestige mondial*.[4] [...]

yrs
    Isaiah

TO DAVID ASTOR[5]

28 September 1965

Princeton

I wish I could do what you asked me to do – namely to review the two Kennedy books.[6] I am fascinated by the figure of Kennedy although I am made uneasy by what I do not want to call Fascist, but at any rate rather frightening qualities in him which excited and even delighted me when I met him, but also kept on disturbing me afterwards. [...] I have too much to do here now: and cannot get through my work as it is: of course, if there were unlimited time and I could do it next year – but that is plainly impracticable. Also I know Arthur Schlesinger a little too well [...] and so I feel the

---

1 See 174–5. *'Cuckold of spring'*.

2 Darius Milhaud (1892–1974), French composer who experimented with polytonality and was influenced by jazz; one of the group of composers inspired by Cocteau's manifesto *Le Coq et l'arlequin: notes autour de la musique* (Paris, 1918) and known as Les Six.

3 William Archibald Spooner (1844–1930), clergyman and College head, Warden of New College 1903–24, is famous because his name was given to the verbal slip known as a 'spoonerism', in which the initial letters of two words (typically) are transposed. The neatest examples are 'evidently student inventions': 'You have tasted a whole worm'; 'Who has not nourished in his bosom a half-warmed fish?'; 'Our Lord is a shoving leopard' (Alan Ryan, ODNB).

4 'World renown'.

5 (Francis) David Langhorne Astor (1912–2001), third of five children of Waldorf Astor, 2nd Viscount Astor, and Nancy née Langhorne; editor, *Observer*, 1948–75. IB knew Astor from his undergraduate days at Balliol in the early 1930s, and they had mutual friends, including Adam von Trott (345 / 1).

6 One of these was Arthur Schlesinger's memoir *A Thousand Days: John F. Kennedy in the White House* (Boston, 1965), which won him a (second) Pulitzer Prize in 1966.

embarrassment one always feels in reviewing books by friends, which I find ties one hand and foot and makes the whole thing agonisingly self-conscious.

[…] Perhaps Joe Alsop – of all people – is the man to do it for you. He is a good writer (at present, I daresay, he is in Vietnam and otherwise occupied) but he adored Kennedy, and Kennedy liked him, and he would do justice to all the aspects, both to the Napoleonic quality – the ambition, the energy, the fear of failure and passionate romantic view of success, the intelligence, complete unafraidness of ideas, the capacity to excite and use intellectuals – and at the same time, though I daresay Joe may not wish to bring this out, the vulgarity, the rich millionaire's swimming-pool aspect, the flirtation with one pretty girl after another, the conventionality, the touch of philistinism; or if not he, perhaps Galbraith[1] would do it – you would get worthy pieces, something to remember, from either of these. I did meet him, I was fascinated by him, and as you can see from the last two or three lines of my letter, I should have liked to say something about him – his quality of respect for civilized and humane qualities and the drive for power, which was there in Napoleon too, after a fashion. ⟨& of course the 'impact' – the difference he made to America & the world – *this* absolutely transforming comet –⟩ But I cannot, I cannot. Do forgive me. Perhaps there will be an anniversary when I could do this for you, but not in the next month or so.

Yours ever,

Isaiah

On 6 November, with IB at Princeton, All Souls voted 35 to 22 not to admit graduate students, directly contradicting its statement of intent to the Franks Commission in February. An alternative scheme to admit visiting fellows, which had been proposed earlier by Bryan Wilson, the leading opponent of the graduates scheme, was later adopted instead, and sixteen were in residence in 1966–7. In its own way this initiative proved a success, but it left 'the ancient anatomy [...] essentially undisturbed',[2] a profound and bitter disappointment to those who had entertained hopes of 'genuine, long-term reform, a change in structure and outlook'.[3] IB never ceased wishing for transformative change at All Souls, but at the College meeting on 6 November, from which he was absent, he appeared directly to oppose it. Bryan Wilson read from a letter in which IB made clear that he favoured the visiting fellows scheme. Having once been an influential supporter of graduates, IB's apparent change of tack left his erstwhile allies deeply disappointed. His difficulty was that, given the Warden's obstructive

---

1 John Kenneth Galbraith (1908–2006), prolific, celebrated Canadian-born American economist; author of *The Affluent Society* (London/Boston, 1958); an adviser to President Kennedy, and his ambassador to India, 1961–3, Galbraith recounted his experience of the Kennedy years in his memoir *Ambassador's Journal* (London/Boston, 1969).

2 A. H. Halsey, op. cit. (142/4), 736.

3 Caute, op. cit. (217/4), 12.

behaviour, and the endless discussions that ensued, he was prepared to back any reform that seemed likely to succeed: as he wrote to Edward Bridges in August, 'if it is to be graduates, let us go forth! anything but needless hovering and caution'.

During the spring and summer of 1965 he came to the conclusion that the union with St Antony's, which he most favoured, was dead: 'neither side is really keen on it, and with [the] bride poverty-stricken and unwilling and the bridegroom rich and timid, no happy marriage could be expected. So let that be that.'[1] The alternative of a graduate scheme run by All Souls on its own did not attract him, because he felt that the 30 or so graduates who would be admitted would be far too few to make a real difference, a view apparently confirmed by Franks. In these circumstances, and given that he knew that Franks himself favoured a visiting fellowship scheme, IB tried, from America, to extricate himself from old alliances while simultaneously entering into a new one. The situation was further complicated at the eleventh hour by the news that the St Antony's scheme might not be dead after all. The epistolary results read like a comedy of errors, in which the porters at All Souls became the hapless scapegoats: all could have been avoided had letters not lain hidden in the College lodge … Whatever the truth of this may have been, IB's position that autumn was a confused one, as he freely admitted. As he wrote to Bryan Wilson early in September: 'I feel a certain cowardly relief at being absent from the "crucial" meeting, since I am not quite sure where in fact I stand: I am temperamentally liable to compromises.'[2]

TO HARRY FISHER

8 October 1965

Princeton

Dear Harry,

I have a letter from Wilson enclosing his memorandum about the future of the College, telling me that it has wide support and begging me to add my name to the signatories. As I shall not be in Oxford to vote or speak at the 'crucial'(?) meeting, I hesitate to do so. I am *rather* attracted by it. I have been away, as you know, for some time and out of things, so I do not know what has been happening; but my position is roughly this: I am still an unregenerate supporter of the St Antony's scheme; that alone, it still seems to me, would have produced an impressive complex of researchers and graduate students and would have been able to attract outside money if this was needed. But this is obviously dead, so I must regard myself in this respect as an (intellectual) widower.

1 To Roger Makins, 18 May 1965.
2 To Bryan Wilson, 7 September 1965.

Our own graduate scheme, with or without Corpus, seems to me a second best – I don't think we shall do it very well, but neither will it be too bad. It is certainly better than (*a*) simply expanding the number of our permanent research fellows; (*b*) doing nothing at all; (*c*) giving money to other places and persons like a Fund, to be spent by them wherever they are, in no special connection with us. But Wilson's scheme (which I originally propounded in one of the earliest of Harrison Committees) does attract me. Nowhere in England can scholars who have work in hand and want to finish it and need library facilities and a certain amount of leisure to do this – except in London with money supplied by the British Academy ⟨(or odd bodies)⟩ (certainly not much) or grants from their own universities (who are seldom in a position to give much). A rotating procession of scholars mainly from *outside* Oxford, but from England, i.e. supported only to some degree by those universities and not in need of, say, more than facilities plus an extra £1,000 to £2,000 a year maximum, would be immensely useful and popular. It should of course extend to within Oxford as well. It might not do more to keep us in touch with Oxford, but it would transform our relations with the learned world, and go a very long way toward answering questions – at present not really very easy to answer – about our purpose and desirability as an institution. [...]

My main objection to the graduate scheme at present is that it is not big enough to make enough difference – it is very well for Nuffield to feel happier with a relatively small number of graduates, but they live in the place. Ours wouldn't, and I cannot help feeling – as I always have – that we must not cut too miserable a figure beside the other rich colleges. [...]

Isaiah   [...]

TO HARRY FISHER

10 November 1965

Princeton

Dear Harry,

Thank you very much indeed for your telegram and letter. [...] I hope the College has decided one way or the other and that the case will not be further reopened. I agree that more operations will kill the patient; more opening up of the body to inspect its [sc. the] exact position of its organs, etc. We must, as the late President Kennedy said about America, get the College moving. Standing still is death, and movement, even if in an uncertain direction, is preferable. This I take to be [y]our view, and if so I agree with it. [...]

I shall be back in January and if you then want me to talk to the Warden – if it will still be necessary – I shall, with great reluctance, for I hate talking until 3.00 a.m. in words spoken in fury (not by me, I add priggishly), etc., etc. But if it is necessary, I will, for I suppose few people do talk to him, and isolation is one of his misfortunes. Goodness but All Souls is detested by English academics in the United States! It is the natural hatred of all the alienated and dispossessed – a kind of Bastille against which the mob will turn as the opening of the revolt of the slaves and of the underdogs. I defend the College. The Americans are much amused.

    Yours,

      Isaiah   [...]

⟨P. P. S. My wife is back, (this letter was dictated 6 days ago) & says she heard that the College voted against the graduates [...]. If you did write me a line about what happened I shd be very grateful. But you may be too busy or not in the mood: one thing is clear: we *must build* swiftly [...]. I share entirely your feelings for if we do little, Franks will rightly try to abolish us. IB.⟩

INGATHERING[1]

A brief history of Iffley College

1965–1966

If any of thine be driven out unto the outmost parts of heaven, from thence will the Lord thy God gather thee, and from thence will he fetch thee.

Deuteronomy 30:4

The wish of the fellows, which emerged rapidly, clearly, and forcefully, was that Isaiah Berlin, Fellow of All Souls and Chichele Professor of Social and Political Theory, should be the College's first President.

Frank Jessup[2]

[Y]ou are at the height of your creative powers with, now, an enormous capital stock of learning to make use of in works of original scholarship; and I can't bear to think of you wasting your time and gifts administrating, being chairman of boring committees and so on and so on.

Marcus Dick to IB, 27 December 1965

The effect of living next door to the Hampshires has had a catastrophic effect on Isaiah. He is insane to want to be head of one of the new alleged colleges. They are no more than luncheon clubs formed from the scrubbiest scrubs to be found in Oxford, all with deep resentments and hatreds, which they will certainly turn on to their head as soon as they have one. Mrs H is to blame. She infuses good doings all round her, and the more unsuitable they are the better. Isaiah thinks he can raise money for them but he can't, anyhow he needs at least £3,000,000. He hopes to combine it with several other jobs, but if it is anything, it is a whole-time job in itself, and a pretty awful one at that. I have cabled, written and talked to him about it, but he is being unusually obstinate. I hope the sceptical air of Oxford will cure him when he gets back. It all derives from his conviction that nobody in England is interested in his subject. This may, alas, be true but it won't be remedied by a lot of disgruntled chemists and geographers.

Maurice Bowra to Joseph Alsop, 1 January 1966

---

1 'The ingathering of the exiles' refers to the promised return of Diaspora Jews to Israel, and calls to mind the admission of 'entitled' non-dons of Oxford to Iffley College (185–6, 241–3).

2 *Wolfson College, Oxford: A Short History*, with revisions by Stuart McKerrow and Jane Potter (Oxford, 1999) [revised ed. of Jessup's *Wolfson College, Oxford: The Early Years* (Oxford, 1979)], 9.

In the first half of the twentieth century Oxford could lay claim to be one of the world's leading universities on the basis of its undergraduate teaching in the humanities alone. After 1945 this would no longer be the case. Throughout the developed world higher education was transformed by the rapid growth of science and technology, and the associated emphasis on research and graduate studies. It was a reality grasped by successive British governments: 'The Second World War was a watershed: it marked the onset of a period of more than thirty years in which public support of scientific research at British universities was recognised as a major priority of the government and indispensable to Britain's survival as a great power.'[1] Henceforth, if Oxford was to maintain its world standing, its traditional strengths would have to be paralleled, and even outstripped, by postgraduate work in the sciences. Government funding of Oxford science increased rapidly from 1945: but how would Oxford's ancient collegiate structure respond?

By the mid-1960s the issue could no longer be ignored. The growth of the sciences at Oxford after the war occurred within university departments, not in the colleges. The colleges were primarily devoted to undergraduate teaching, and it was not in their economic interest to give fellowships to academics, however worthy or eminent, who worked in subject areas that very few, if any, of their undergraduates were reading. While the numbers of undergraduates in the mainstream science subjects were always substantial, in the smaller subjects they were insignificant: in 1962 there were 124 finalists in physics, but only 9 in metallurgy, 10 in agriculture, 11 in forestry and 14 in geology. (Compare the figures for the humanities: for example, there were 243 finalists in PPE and 321 in modern history.) Those working in the smaller science subjects therefore very rarely secured a full college fellowship, and were informally known as the 'non-dons'. Although they undeniably made an important contribution to the university they enjoyed what a former Vice-Chancellor, Sir Arthur Norrington, called 'half-membership'.

The 'non-dons' were not exclusively scientists: many were to be found in the social sciences, archaeology, oriental studies etc. But most worked in the science area just to the north of the city – a hinterland of the dispossessed. By the early 1960s there were signs that its inhabitants were becoming discontented to the point of militancy, and in November 1961 the microbiologist W. E. ('Kits') van Heyningen[2] chaired a large meeting of non-dons that called for action. Partly as a result of this, three university enquiries were convened in

---

1 J. G. Darwin, 'A World University', in *The History of the University of Oxford*, vol. 8 (142/4), 625.
2 William Edward ('Kits') van Heyningen (1911–89), senior research officer, Sir William Dunn School of Pathology, Oxford, 1947–66; Reader in Bacterial Chemistry 1966–79; Founding Master of St Cross 1965–79.

quick succession (Harrison, 1963; Norrington, 1963; Norrington, 1964), which did much to define and quantify the problem.

But the University's response was also driven by external factors. Taxpayers were funding the growth of Oxford science, yet the colleges closed their doors to its practitioners. It was an obvious injustice, rooted in the historic divide, cultural and intellectual, between the arts and the sciences at Oxford. In the late nineteenth century this neglect of the sciences might have been accepted, and even celebrated, but not in the 1960s, and particularly not during an era of Labour ascendancy. The point was made in January 1964 by Richard Crossman, who became a cabinet minister in the Labour government elected that October. In an article on the Robbins Report he lambasted Oxford and Cambridge for their exclusivity:

> Millions of taxpayers' funds [...] have been given them for the purpose of building up new faculties in the universities. But very often this aim has been quietly sabotaged by denying to these university teachers the college rights without which Oxbridge life is poor indeed. At Oxford today 55 per cent and at Cambridge 45 per cent of university teachers are excluded from the self-perpetuating oligarchy of the senior common room.[1]

To men like Maurice Bowra and John Sparrow, each Warden of an ancient college, each steeped in the glories of Oxford's humanities, each a doyen of the senior common room, the non-dons were 'scrubs' – defined by the OED as 'insignificant or contemptible' people. The term betrays a social and intellectual prejudice to which IB was not immune. He too occasionally alluded to the 'scrubs'; but there was a profound difference between his attitude and that of his conservative colleagues, as would be proved by events. Bowra himself was not unmoved by the plight of the non-dons, writing to Felix Frankfurter on 1 February 1963 that they

> have indeed a case – their wives complain of social inferiority, they don't get free meals, they lack status. But it is hard to take them all in. Some are no good, others are bright but impossible, most of them do subjects which are more or less useless to colleges, every one of them living in means an undergraduate living out, and of course they will talk their heads off at College meetings, with the happy knowledge that they have really no responsibility to see that things are properly run.[2]

'The right solution', Bowra observed, 'is to gather all of them that can read and write (some can't) into a graduate college and to turn over a large wad of graduates to them.' This idea, cloaked in more decorous language, was the central conclusion of the 1963 Norrington subcommittee, which in

---

1 Richard Crossman, 'Apartheid in Education', *Observer*, 26 January 1964, 10.
2 Library of Congress, Washington, DC, Felix Frankfurter MSS, quoted in Brian Harrison, 'Government and Administration', in *The History of the University of Oxford*, vol. 8 (142/4), 736.

its report to Congregation[1] proposed the creation of two new graduate societies. That report was approved on 25 February 1964, and Norrington was given the chair of a committee that spent a year working out the details. On 12 March 1965 it was formally announced that two new graduate societies, St Cross College and Iffley College, were to be founded. Each would have a fellowship open to women as well as men, and numbering not more than seventy; and to each would be assigned 'a certain number of postgraduate students' – rather ominously, the precise figure was left vague. The university also decreed that those with five years' service, but no fellowship – i.e. the non-dons – would be entitled to one,[2] and it was anticipated that these new fellows would form the governing bodies of St Cross and Iffley Colleges. This was a partial solution to what became known as the 'entitlement' problem – how to accommodate within the collegiate structure those university members currently outside it.

On 9 August 1965 Kits van Heyningen was named as the first master of St Cross. One of his first acts was to approach IB privately with a view to his becoming the head of Iffley College. Van Heyningen proposed that they would work in tandem: any funds that either raised would be divided equally between their two colleges, which would rise together. IB declined the offer. Iffley would be a college in name only: there would be too many fellows, too few students, and too little sense of academic community. 'A college,' he later noted, 'in order to live, has to have younger people in it.'[3]

Iffley and St Cross were born of the University's desire to turn the non-dons quickly into dons, and IB regarded them, as originally conceived, less as colleges than as waste-paper baskets into which the 'scrubs' were to be thrown. Neither college truly addressed the need for more graduates which had been a principal conclusion of the Robbins Report. In written evidence to the Franks Commission Robbins himself observed: 'I am sure that if we are to make our proper contribution to the intellectual leadership of the world, we must take graduate studies far more seriously than we have done in the past.'[4] This was an opinion that IB wholeheartedly endorsed, and which he understood much better in the light of his recent experience at All Souls. There, a golden opportunity to create 'the largest graduate and research institution not only in Oxford but in the United Kingdom' had been squandered.[5] The union with St Antony's had not been consummated, but IB had glimpsed the potential. In a memorandum written in the summer of 1966 he identified the failure of either of the proposed graduate colleges to

1 The decision-making assembly of senior members of the University.
2 Their rights were enshrined in the entitlement statute carried on 1 March 1965: *Oxford University Gazette* 95 (1 June 1965), 1256.
3 Interview with Raymond Hoffenberg, n.d.
4 The Franks Report (293 / 1), i 48, para. 94.
5 To Harry Fisher, 30 December 1964.

deal adequately with the problem of graduate numbers: 'St Cross, because of lack of funds and accommodation, is at present in no position to help more than a tiny number of graduate students. The same is the present condition of Iffley, which, if it is to do its job, needs substantial transformation and, indeed, re-creation.'[1]

On 30 September 1965 the University Gazette published lists of the first official fellows of St Cross and Iffley, and when the newly appointed fellows of the latter college first met they still had no head. The mathematician Charles Coulson[2] declined the honour in mid-October because he wanted a house, which was not on offer, and by 4 November the Iffley fellows had decided to approach IB (then at Princeton), effectively for the second time.[3] The details were conveyed to him by Aline, who had dined with Cecilia Dick, one of the new Iffley fellows, before leaving for America; official notification came in a telephone call and a letter from the Vice-Chancellor, Kenneth Wheare.[4] Ostensibly this was the same offer that IB had already turned down. This time, however, the invitation came from the Iffley fellows themselves, and there was no question of being harnessed to St Cross. As their head, IB would be free to act independently.

IB was then in the process of rearranging the mosaic of his academic life. He yearned for more contact with like-minded academics, who could be found on the East Coast of America, but not in Oxford, or indeed anywhere in England. Spells in America invigorated him, although he had absolutely no desire to emigrate. The possibility of a visiting professorship at CUNY, which would pay handsomely by British standards, had encouraged him to contemplate resigning his Chichele chair in favour of an itinerant life as a senior research fellow, with a base in Oxford and regular visits to the US. That this might mean leaving All Souls came as a blessing, and one (as he might have put it) that did not come heavily disguised. The Iffley offer could be made to fit perfectly into this complicated pattern.

Bowra, Sparrow and other Oxbridge friends wrote urging IB to decline. What they did not see – and who could? – was that he would accept the Iffley offer only if he could transform it. Instead of a top-heavy college-cum-social club for scientists, with a small number of graduates, a new type of Oxford college, but one that mirrored, indeed inverted, the traditional model. Instead of undergraduates, graduates; instead of dominance by the humanities, dominance by the sciences; but, as in the traditional undergraduate college,

1 IB, 'Plan and Reasons for the New Graduate College at Oxford', late June / early July 1966.
2 Charles Alfred Coulson (1910–74), theoretical chemist; Rouse Ball Professor of Mathematics, Oxford, 1952–72, Professor of Theoretical Chemistry 1972–4; Fellow of Wadham 1952–74.
3 Extant correspondence may not reveal the whole story, or its timing, but IB's close friendship with Cecilia Dick (248/3) was probably crucial to his being asked to reconsider taking Iffley on.
4 Kenneth Clinton Wheare (1907–79), later (1966) Kt, Australian-born constitutional expert; Rhodes Scholar at Oriel 1929–32; Fellow of All Souls 1944–57, 1973–9; Rector, Exeter College, 1956–72; Vice-Chancellor, Oxford, 1964–6; Chancellor, Liverpool, 1972–9.

a wide range of disciplines. At Wolfson's opening ceremony in November 1974, IB recalled the thinking behind this approach:

> As St Antony's is to modern political studies, as Nuffield to the social sciences, so must we be to the natural sciences. But to coop scientists up, to insulate them from the humanities, seemed wrong. They didn't want it themselves. Academic variety alone keeps us from the excesses of inbreeding, from tedium, from the sense of isolation that this often causes. A community must on no account be too monochrome: this can be a very suffocating atmosphere. Our graduates, like our fellows, must be drawn from both the arts and the sciences.[1]

And the student body must also be large, as in the traditional college: Iffley would be big, with up to 300 graduates.

As reinterpreted by IB, the Iffley offer now scored high on every count: it would give him a purposeful – even prestigious – base in Oxford that would allow him to take regular sabbaticals in America; it would give him the perfect alibi for leaving All Souls; it would enable him to succeed where All Souls had so conspicuously failed, by creating a large and diverse graduate community in Oxford; and in doing so, he would satisfy a desire deep within him to perform some service for Oxford, and for England, which he believed had given so much to him. Everything depended on whether or not he could raise sufficient funds to realise his scheme without scrimping (to which he was resolutely opposed), and it was on this basis that he conditionally accepted the Iffley offer.

The stars were in near perfect alignment for this quest. IB was aware that McGeorge Bundy, whom he knew well, had recently become director of the Ford Foundation, one of the few charitable trusts capable of operating on the scale needed. Through Joe Alsop, next to whom Aline sat at a dinner at this juncture, IB was able to take soundings on whether Bundy might be interested, and a meeting was arranged at which IB described the pre-history of Iffley College:

> And then I told him the story, and I said I didn't know very much about it, but I realised that there were a number of people, among them quite eminent scientists, to whom no fellowships had been given […]. And then he said something which then became a ploy which I used in general propaganda, which was entirely his invention. He said 'A lot of scientists are coming here; there's a brain drain going on. We don't really want it to increase; we don't want to denude England of scientific talent, because, from the point of view of Europe and resistance to the Soviet Union' – which of course was closest to his heart at that time – 'we don't want England to be weakened. And therefore if you think that this could keep scientists in England who otherwise might come here, there is a case for it.' The

---

1 *Lycidas* (Wolfson's then magazine) 3 (1974–5), 4.

Lyc anthropy
of cours.

idea had never occurred to me. However, I thought it was certainly a very good propaganda point. And there was some truth in it too, and I said, 'As a matter of fact, most of these people, I suspect – I don't know – are scientists, and inevitably, if this comes into being, it will be largely scientific, and maybe even become a base for scientists in the way in which St Antony's is for modern political studies and Nuffield is for social studies.' That's how I conceived it.[1]

Bundy was prepared to back the plan to the tune of £1.5 million, but only so long as IB could find matching funds in Britain. This proved to be the most difficult task of all. The one institution capable of meeting his needs was the Wolfson Foundation, but its founder, Sir Isaac Wolfson, and his son Leonard[2] were heavily reliant for advice on this matter on a key trustee, Sir Solly Zuckerman, who proved determinedly opposed to IB's plans. Zuckerman had close connections with the Labour government of the day, which displayed a marked anti-Oxbridge ideological bias, evident not least in the writings of the former Oxonian Richard Crossman. The winds of change were blowing against ancient privilege – and further gilding the glory of Oxford would be a difficult policy to argue for. But helping the University to change tack, and to realise its potential in a new direction – this was a powerful idea, one in which IB passionately believed, and which he was prepared to champion.

*

TO CECILIA DICK[3]

12 November 1965 [*carbon*]

[Princeton]

Dear Cecilia,

Aline is back and has brought mysterious rumours of the search for a head of Iffley. I have no idea what the plans are or whether there is any money at all, i.e. graduates – without whom the College must surely remain no more than a centre for dons whose only purpose is each other's society. Have the University or other colleges assigned any funds to it at all?

But my real purpose is to urge the claims of Stuart [...]. Is there any chance of this? I am writing you, as you will surely have guessed, behind his back; Maurice, I know, thinks him no good at business, but he is, as so often, wholly mistaken about this. He thinks the same about me and this is not quite true either. If there is a reasonable chance of Stuart's being considered, do, if you

---

1 Interview with Raymond Hoffenberg.

2 Leonard *Wolfson (1927–2010), businessman, philanthropist, benefactor of Wolfson College.

3 Cecilia Rachel Dick (1927–95) née Buxton; Lecturer in Modern History, LMH, 1950–1, 1953–87; University Lecturer 1957–87; Fellow of Iffley 1965–6; Fellow and Domestic Bursar, Wolfson, 1966–94. She married, 1952 (divorced 1968), IB's friend Marcus William Dick (1920–71), Professor of Philosophy, East Anglia, 1963–71.

agree, press his claims. [...] But if there were a job to do, and no one else could be found, I should at least like to be told so – but please rule me out if anyone else who you and others think adequate, and especially Stuart, would come – I do not believe I should be more than adequate at best, although the thought of a new and unencumbered collection of serious persons does tempt me, I admit. There now, that is really all. The real purpose of this letter is to ask you to put Stuart's name into the hat. I think it would work beautifully. I think the Vice-Chancellor[1] might think so too. I shall be back in January, not at all looking forward to the bloodstrewn battlefield of poor old All Souls, which seems to be bent on self-extinction. But perhaps this is too pessimistic.

I hope you and your children are well. We are having a swell time.
Yours,
    [Isaiah]

TO JOHN SPARROW

12 November 1965 [*carbon*]

[Princeton]

Personal

My dear old friend,

Aline brought the news of the College decision[2] and oddly enough I felt surprised and upset. [...] My feeling is this: we can only save ourselves if we get going rapidly, almost precipitately, at once. We need not two or three striking names – window dressing that [is] not helpful to us – but clear public evidence of making ourselves useful: i.e. of offering facilities to academics who want to finish their work and need a year or two in libraries [...]. Franks is right, in supposing that a rich college, if it wants to do something like this strongly enough, can do it and then always beg, borrow or steal enough money out of some other fund to defray expenses if they are not absurdly large. The thing which I feel most strongly is that we must make a bold public move of some kind if we are not to attract too much hostility and opposition from everyone, against which we are not morally in a mood to defend ourselves with too much righteous energy. This bold move must consist of giving out more than we think, in our careful moments, we can do [...]. It is a strange thing – in Canada, where I have been, and the East Coast of the US, universities contain exiled English professors filled with bitter hatred of All Souls – and this communicates itself to American colleagues. Some public humiliation of the college would be very popular. But we can avert it, it seems to me, by announcing a bold programme. Not guided by

1 Kenneth Wheare.
2 Of 6 November (236–7).

too much common-sense control or moderation or careful consideration of what funds will supply how much. [...]

I still feel panic-stricken; I still feel the College is in danger of deep inner malaise and extreme unpopularity without.

Forgive these melancholy reflections. I am terribly sorry now not to have been there to vote, although I could not have been, compatibly with the minimum obligations here. [...]

Yours,

[Isaiah]

TO MAURICE BOWRA

18 November 1965

[As from] Headington House

Dear Maurice,

[...] Princeton is really rather nice. Very like a spa. Very gentlemanly indeed, full of enormous tall blond Anglo-Saxon young men who cannot rouse themselves to any revolutionary activity. Foreign agitators – MacIntyre of Univ., Chuck Taylor of All Souls and Montreal, and Professor Stuart Hampshire – are trying to needle them into some kind of protests against United States policy everywhere; but while Harvard produces hundreds of signatures to documents of protest, Princeton cannot raise more than thirty or forty. That is very typical. I have been put into the History Department by Stuart – a very eccentric act – since he does not think I quite fit into the Philosophy or Political Theory one. I have accepted this fate with extreme good will. The historians are very nice. Stone[1] is a totally transformed man – gone is the bitter, foolish, waspish, exasperated protester of Oxford days – he is now contented, happy, integrated – even fatter, with a perpetual smile of happiness flitting around those handsome, Jacobin features. His attitude to England is extremely ambivalent, as is that of most English emigrants. I have no intention of joining the brain drain. There is a kind of resentment about Oxford on the part of those who have been in it – Englishmen, I mean – which occasionally communicates itself to those Americans who have not; on the other hand the Americans who have been to Oxford are most loyal and affectionate. [...]

You will naturally wish to hear about our neighbours.[2] Our relations are unnaturally good. Both plainly long to come back to England. Ever since

---

1 Lawrence Stone (1919–99), Fellow of Wadham 1950–63; Member of the Institute for Advanced Study, Princeton, 1960–1, Dodge Professor of History 1963–90. In the US, 'freed from the Oxford infighting, [he] flourished'; and in 1965 he published 'the book which made his reputation', *The Crisis of the Aristocracy, 1558–1641* (Oxford, 1965) (Michael Thompson, *Guardian*, 5 July 1999, 18).

2 'We live cheek by jowl with the Hampshires (my jowl, Mrs H's cheek, with Aline and Stuart hovering like angels above us – that is the fantastic image which I wish to convey): this is odd but not disagreeable.' To Herbert Nicholas, 28 October 1965.

Dr Robert Oppenheimer[1] of the Institute observed that he had never seen Stuart so happy as he is here, I realised that this was the opposite of the truth. He longs to come back, and when Hare was appointed to his chair in Oxford, although he did not himself apply, it was another door shut. Nor will All Souls be so very ready to take him back as a research fellow in view of their sudden turnabout and decision to spend their money on institute-like associates – at least I gather so. I am not sorry not to have been at that day-long College meeting – God knows what they all said, and why they all decided as they did; in principle there is perhaps something to be said for making All Souls make room for all kinds of scholars from the provinces and Oxford and Cambridge colleges who want to finish their work, and want a year or two of leisure and facilities; perhaps All Souls can do this better than simply to have forty or fifty graduate students, which would not be much of a drop in the bucket and after whom they would not look particularly well. But from Sparrow I gather that what they want is some brilliant persons, and not many of them, and not have to pay for them; this is, I think, impossible and fatal; the whole point of All Souls is it has some money – perhaps not as much as some people suppose, but at any rate some – this money it must spend on needy scholars; the needy scholars need not be first-rate if they are good, reliable, honourable men working in provincial universities on decent pieces of work, and simply want a year or two in which to go on with their work; to be able to afford them facilities would be a greater service than to look for striking and marvellous persons – who anyway don't exist – to put in the shop window. At least this is my view, and I have so written to John. [...]

I did go to Washington for one evening and stayed with Joe, and met at dinner the McNamaras, who were charming, Mac Bundy, who I think is getting out of government, according to newspapers, to be head of the Ford Foundation, who is unnaturally lively, and rather nervous, I thought, Stephen Spender, and some unknowns. The conversation with Stephen and McCone,[2] the ex-head of the CIA and a frightful Catholic reactionary, about Negroes was funny and awful. Joe is quite mad on the subject of a Vietnam war, and wants to go on fighting and fighting – it gives him infinite satisfaction. My suggestion that as soon as an honourable stalemate is reached some arrangement could be made whereby fewer persons there were killed was exceedingly ill-received. He thirsts for blood, and looks upon the brave American troops in Vietnam – who doubtless are extremely courageous and splendid – more or less as certain persons in France looked upon the para-

---

1 (Julius) Robert Oppenheimer (1904–67), US theoretical physicist; as Director of Los Alamos Scientific Laboratory 1943–5 he oversaw the Manhattan Project, which made the first atomic bomb; Director and Professor of Physics, Institute for Advanced Study, Princeton, 1947–66.

2 John Alex McCone (1902–91), Republican politician, Chairman of the Atomic Energy Commission 1958–61; Director of the CIA 1961–5; promoted non-weapons use of nuclear power and an end to testing of nuclear weapons; resigned in April 1965 over disagreements with President Johnson's Vietnam policy.

troopers in Algiers. Peace in Vietnam really would bring sorrow to his heart. Yet I am very devoted to him and to his wife; my suggestion that McNamara was really a very nice man, and at the first opportunity really would like to conclude anything that looked like an honourable armistice without loss of face, was exceedingly ill-received. Victory to the end or nothing. [...]

To return to private affairs: Mrs H. could not be more affable. There aren't quite enough private delinquents to look after: a Jewish logician, Kripke,[1] for whom she would cook Kosher food at 2 and 3 a.m., is now at Harvard and does not come quite so frequently; the backward children in Trenton, NJ, are looked after by professional psychologists and sociologists without hearts, therefore much spare affection is spent upon a stray dog, who belongs to others, but who is fed regularly because the others don't feed him enough. The result is that it is now inflated like a balloon and is giving trouble. There is some hope that my neighbour Prof. Alonzo Church[2] will go mad, because he works in a soundproof and airproof room at night and sleeps by day, and has been heard muttering to himself lately – that would certainly produce something to do. Towards myself the attitude is more than friendly: peace has been declared with a vengeance. They both long to come home: could he not be made head of Iffley College? He really is a better administrator than you think: he was a perfectly good bursar at All Souls, and she would be quite good at looking after all those scientists' wives and their lunatic children; If he is impossible, what about me? If I could get some money out of Mac Bundy with your help for Iffley would that not be a good thing? I again long to leave All Souls which I think is going to be very painful and uncomfortable. [...] But whatever happens, even if All Souls is quite right to reject the graduate idea and go in for being Princeton – which may be right – indeed if I were asked at the beginning I think I should have said so myself, having originally invented the idea (I confess) – so long as John is there, there will be too much strife, too many feelings trampled on, much misery and indignation, so could I not get out? Is it too late to apply for Iffley? If not, do tell me. Not that I shall necessarily do it – but it would be very nice to know – except that I don't wish to do it across Stuart's body – if there is any chance for him then I certainly wouldn't do it. The idea of presiding over Cecilia, Dr Schenk[3]

---

1 Saul Aaron Kripke (b. 1940), brilliant Jewish-American logician and philosopher of language; Harvard mathematics undergraduate 1958–62; held academic positions at Harvard 1962–8, at Rockefeller 1968–76, and later (1976–98) at Princeton (as McCosh Professor of Philosophy).

2 Alonzo Church (1903–95), US logician and mathematician; taught at Princeton from 1929, as professor of mathematics and philosophy from 1961; professor of philosophy and mathematics, UCLA, 1967–90.

3 Hans Georg Artur Viktor Schenk (1912–79), Prague-born historian, left Czechoslovakia shortly before the German invasion in March 1939 and settled in Oxford, where he was appointed University Lecturer in European Economic and Social History 1949; Fellow, Iffley, 1965–6, Wolfson 1966–79 (Dean of Degrees 1968–79); IB wrote the preface to his *The Mind of the European Romantics: An Essay in Cultural History* (London, 1966), repr. in POI as 'The Essence of European Romanticism'.   *Power of Ideas*

and Mendelssohn[1] does not daunt me at all [...]. I cannot apply for it, but if they should approach me I would certainly not turn it down out of hand. I should value your advice most deeply of course.

The rule of Johnson is really very peculiar: the more cunning he is, and the more Machiavellian, the more it is liked: it is assumed that all politics are dirty and he is the best player of that particular game, therefore the more he deceives, the more he cheats, the more heads he cuts off, the cruder his tactics, the more delighted they are, the tougher they feel him to be – more of a leader, a shrewd old operator. He is not expected to be noble, handsome, generous, brave, benevolent, wise – only efficient, ruthless, competent, patriotic. I dare say the feelings about Wilson are much the same. Wilson is much respected here; no other member of the British Government is. Stewart[2] is thought feeble, Callaghan[3] lightweight, Healey[4] vain, and scoring small points but losing big ones, and also filled with ungovernable political biases and passions, and Gaitskell much lamented on all sides. But nowhere is Heath admired. In general we seem to have been written off. [...]

What about A. J. P. Taylor's new book?[5] Stuart does not think that psychoanalysis has done him enough good. I have written an essay in his honour for a Festschrift to be presented to him – an absurd undertaking – but I longed to write an essay on Namier whom he hates more than anyone else in the world and put it into the Festschrift for him. I do not think this would be an altogether absurd move – do you? I have asked him about it, and he is not very pleased, but cannot say no.

The Negro problem is genuinely appalling here: I make myself dreadfully unpopular by saying that even if full rights are granted them, jobs given, total social equality ensured – difficult as this is – this will not solve their problems so long as they continue to look black and have crinkly hair. And that any chemist who invented a substance that would bleach them and un-crinkle their hair would help a great deal more than a lot of good, decent liberals. This is exceedingly ill-received everywhere. I cannot help applying

---

1 Kurt Alfred Georg Mendelssohn (1906–80), German-born British medical physicist; left Germany March 1933 and began work at the Clarendon Laboratory, Oxford, at the invitation of Professor F. A. Lindemann (Lord Cherwell, 281/3); Reader in Physics 1955–73; Fellow, Wolfson, 1966–71, Professorial Fellow 1971–3.

2 Robert Michael Maitland Stewart (1906–90), later (1979) life peer; Secretary of State for Education and Science 1964–5, for Foreign Affairs 1965–6; First Secretary of State 1966–8; Secretary of State for Economic Affairs 1966–7, for Foreign and Commonwealth Affairs 1968–70.

3 Leonard James Callaghan (1912–2005), later KG and life peer (both 1987); Chancellor of the Exchequer 1964–7; Home Secretary 1967–70; Secretary of State for Foreign and Commonwealth Affairs 1974–6; Prime Minister 1976–9; member of Shadow Cabinet 1961–4, 1970–4.

4 Denis Winston Healey (b. 1917), later (1992) life peer; Secretary of State for Defence 1964–70; Chancellor of the Exchequer 1974–9; member of the Shadow Cabinet 1959–64, 1970–4.

5 *English History, 1914–1945* (Oxford, 1965), the concluding, 15th, volume of the Oxford History of England; described by *The Times* as 'outstanding though highly controversial' (30 December 1965, 11a).

Zionist criteria to this situation too – when recently there was a meeting in New York at which 600 professors appeared who called themselves socialists, and were anything from mild liberals to members of the Party, and a Negro leader jumped up and said, 'You will not take away this movement from us. It is ours and we don't want any whites mixed up with it', this was quite a new turn: the idea of not wanting even Communists, or any white helpers, not merely not those who patronise, but even those who are prepared to collaborate, because this is a black movement, revolutionary in character, intended to upset white society and not to come to its aid, even in the most high-minded way, is something new and rather sinister. This is not true, of course, of the majority of Negroes, but the mere fact that it should exist will certainly in due course produce exceedingly powerful consequences. I do not feel that any of us will be alive to see it, but I am sorry for white races in about the year 2100. I feel rather like Joe: doomed is what we are, we shall soon be eating grass (if that); however in the meantime Princeton is anxiously trying to acquire at least 5 per cent of Negroes and is not succeeding even in that. The dangers of New York are very genuine – one cannot go to the subway in the evening, and crime is enormous. […]

Yours,

[IB p.p. Baillie Knapheis][1]

TO KENNETH WHEARE

19 November 1965

Princeton

Dear Ken,

First let me thank you very much for your encouraging words on the telephone this afternoon. It may have seemed to you that I was, if anything, somewhat precipitate in saying that I was strongly inclined to accept your and Iffley's invitation without even coming home for consultations, or 'casing the joint'. I have, as you know, been thinking of ways in which I could be of help – I feel far from sure that I have made much of my chair – and yet I am conscious of a deep debt to the University which has always treated me exceedingly well – I know of no one whom it has treated more considerately – ever since I became a member of it; and this seems to me an opportunity for which I am exceedingly grateful, and by which I feel both genuinely honoured, and made, with reason, nervous. I have always believed strongly in graduate studies; and while All Souls College may in the end be right in supposing that it is not the best institution for it, this does not diminish my

1 Baillie Knapheis (b. 1941) née Klass, personal secretary to IB 1965–7; former wife of Brian Knapheis (Baruch Knei-Paz), married Christopher Tolkien (b. 1924) 1967.

personal desire to do something to help, if I possibly can, in whatever capacity in the University. [...]

I realise that more money – a good deal more – would be needed to make a go of Iffley if it is to be able to afford to build accommodation and offer facilities to graduate students, without whom, it seems to me, a college of this kind must remain no more than a happy association – at best – of university teachers – morally admirable, but unlikely to contribute intellectually or socially to the needs of the University, which seem to me greater at the moment in the graduate fields. I do not know what sort of money-getter I am; it seems to me that I am a poor and inefficient mendicant [...]. I suppose I could get down on my knees to the Wolfson Foundation. If all my efforts prove unavailing, as well they may, or if Iffley is disappointed in me (as they may be), I suppose our association could be terminated at the end of a trial period of two or three years. I do not suggest this as a formal prospect: but I do not suppose they want to be committed too deeply any more than I do. I have no excessive confidence in my own powers; they may well over-estimate me and I do not want them to feel I have been planted on them without the possibility of change. [...]

Yours ever,
    Isaiah Berlin

TO BRYAN WILSON
    23 November 1965

                                                                Princeton

Dear Bryan,
    Thank you very much for your letter. The result did not really astonish me. What worries me more is that we shall start on too modest a scale and that it shall all run into sands. Surely if we are to save ourselves we must begin with a gesture – inviting 10 to 12 Associates, even if our facilities are inadequate – and not striking names at all, but worthy scholars with work on hand in Oxford, Cambridge, other British universities. Never mind about abroad for the moment. When there is a building, they can be accommodated better, but even now some would like to come. Perhaps we could do what the Princeton Institute does (Woodward[1] knows all about this). Some are recommended by resident professors, some are thought of by other scholars who write Oppenheimer, some think of themselves, and a selection is duly made. Anything that commits us heavily at once would be good. Anything that does not would be bad.

I realise now that my second letter said that I did not object to being cited

---

1 (Ernest) Llewellyn Woodward (1890–1971), Kt 1952; fellow, All Souls, 1919–44, 1962–71; Professor of Modern History, Oxford, 1947–51; professor, Institute for Advanced Study, Princeton, 1951–6.

on the side of your scheme. But now you will have received a letter that lay
neglected beneath a heap of rubbish in the All Souls Lodge. I sent it post
haste by my wife to reach you before the crucial meeting to say that I had
heard from my 'allies' and that in the circumstances I did not wish to participate, however vicariously, in the debate because I had been shaken by my
correspondents. However, I imagine that you did not get this letter in time,
so my old allies will suspect me of duplicity. It is in no way your fault, of
course, nor anyone's, except our idiot porters – if only I had trusted the post.
Never mind, let the past bury its dead. The future alone is interesting.

I am glad there was no bitterness during the debate. I am sure there was
plenty afterwards. I shall be back in mid-January. I am sure we will all need
to fasten our seatbelts during the next two terms when the Franks storms
blow up.

Thank you very much indeed again for your friendly, very informing, very
interesting and very nice letter.

Yours ever,

Isaiah

TO HARRY FISHER

25 November 1965

Princeton

Dear Harry,

I am most terribly sorry to bore you with a matter which by now concerns only myself and my own sorrows. In my last letter to you I expressed
surprise and dismay at the fact that Wilson should have quoted a letter of
mine supporting his scheme. I have just had news to the effect that the letter
which I sent off via my wife in order to get there before the meeting, begging
him on no account to commit me to his policies, saying that as a result of
information which I have received I now realise that St Antony's etc. were on
the map again and I much preferred that to his scheme – only got to him two
or three days ago, as for some unaccountable reason they lingered in the All
Souls Lodge for days and days and days (together with other letters), owing
apparently to the idiocy of one of the porters, for by now Wilson will have
received this letter, but the horse has bolted and there is nothing to be done.

But I now realise why he might very honestly have thought that I was
more in support of his scheme than I actually was – the effect of your letter
was to produce my – as I thought – urgent letter aligning myself either on
the other side, or at any rate in some neutral and non-existent position. I am
so sorry about this – I do not suppose that anything was altered by this, but it
does at least explain to you what might have seemed a very peculiar ambiva-
lence of behaviour to others. I do not suppose I shall ever catch up with that.
[...] But I thought I would write to you all the same, because otherwise you

might reasonably have been very puzzled by my behaviour and thought that your letter had had no effect upon me. On the contrary, it had a decisive effect: the obstacle was of a purely technical character – perhaps the Lodge at All Souls needs a drastic reform as much as other parts of the College, and will not, of course, get it.

I feel distressed about the whole thing, and have written to the Warden to say so – not that that does any good. After that I shall stop talking about my own 'position' and hold my peace. I shall be back in mid-January. Other undelivered letters sent by the same method – I still cannot understand why they weren't forwarded – have led to similar complications in other quarters, unconnected with the College. I am spending my time now in trying to explain the mysterious nature of the All Souls messenger service. As for the future of the College, that is another matter. I propose – in part at least as a result of all this – to take some drastic decisions with regard to my own occupation in Oxford, but about that I shall let you know, if I may, when I see you.

Yours,

Isaiah

PS What *can* you have thought of me? I did not conceive that what happened actually happened, and could not understand how Wilson could have behaved like that. Now I fully understand.   *Bryan*

TO KENNETH WHEARE

25 November 1965

Princeton

Dear Ken,

I have to report – I suppose clandestinely, as he may not wish it known – a telegram from Sir Maurice saying he has *very grave* misgivings about Iffley and me, and is certain that I shall be *utterly miserable* there ⟨the wire has no italics: but the text is pretty strong⟩. I am to await his letter. Nevertheless, as is my habit, probably I will telephone him. […] I do not know why Maurice worded his message so violently. It shook me a bit, but if only he thinks this, and if there is no objective basis for it, it will make no difference. ⟨I expect John Sparrow will be sharpening knives too. No matter.⟩[1]

In effect, what I am asking you to do is (*a*) to tell me how things really are, and above all your personal view – how much you are for and how much

1 IB wrote to Marcus Dick, 22 December 1965, that Sparrow was behaving 'as though I think that I have the drive and personality of Bullock, the paternalism of [John] Bam[borough, Principal of Linacre], the push of Van Heyningen, the cunning and practical ability of [Norman] Chester [Warden of Nuffield], etc. Very amusing, very funny, and all malicious. I see that he is enjoying himself greatly. That he should think me mad does not surprise me. No man ever had less public spirit.'

you are against – this I really promise not to divulge for I fully do understand what it would mean; and (b) to keep the situation in solution until my arrival. ⟨Let us say that, shaken as I inevitably am, I am 60–40 in favour.⟩

Thank you very much for all this.

Yours ever,

Isaiah

⟨P. S. The thing that really bothers me is: can there be graduates without *lots* more money? If I cannot collect it, will it be a College in a real sense, ever? or only a hostel or a country club, or "centre" – & if so *am* I the man? I'll discuss all this gladly on return. But if 1) my biennial absences for 1 term 2) delay till Mid-Jan are unacceptable, then so be it: & I shall accept the withdrawal of my name with, perhaps, some relief. I don't see how I *can* even ¾ commit myself: only 60/40: please tell Iffley that. This much damage Maurice *has* done. If you even ½ agree with his very black diagnosis, I shd be grateful if you cd tell me: I wish he had not put his oar in so brutally: I've no doubt he is stirred, subjectively at least, by the most devoted & altruistic & paternal/ avuncular motives!⟩

TO MAURICE BOWRA

3 December 1965

Princeton

Dear Maurice,

I am deeply grateful to you for your letters and telegram. Do not for a moment suppose that I misunderstood your motives at any level – I realise that at first you thought that my decision had something dramatic and enter-prising and creditable about it, but that later you thought that the job was so awful that I had not grasped what it was, and, given my temperament, habits and outlook, could not but make a total failure of it. And from this you wished to save me, with the purest good will in the world, a considerable penetration into what I am and can do. All that you say is extremely wise and relevant and I have taken it to heart and my ardour has correspondingly cooled. But let me explain my situation.

[…] I am not at all bored with being professor – nor are the duties arduous, nor do I find them back-breaking, nor irritating in any way. That is not the point; that is not the case. I could go on quite peacefully, being professor until the age of 67, lecturing away, sitting on committees (which I enjoy!) and looking after graduate students, which I like doing very much. What then is wrong? Fundamentally only one thing: that my chief interest is not in social and political theory as it ought to be conceived – telling people what is justice, what is the right to burn draft cards in the United States, under what circumstances one should die, and in what circumstances kill, etc. – but in the history of ideas, about which I have been writing and propose to go on writing (one book thank God is almost finished, it needs about another four weeks' work).[1] In this subject there is in England no interest whatever, and there never has been. [...] Consequently I find myself totally isolated, with nobody to talk to about Vico, Herder, eighteenth-century Germans, nineteenth-century Germans and Russians, or even Renaissance sources. Who can I talk to about this? Who are the experts? Or even the knowledge-able amateurs? Gombrich, Wind, Warburg in general[2] and not much of that. Whereas whenever I come to America there are at least a dozen persons superior to me in learning, and very clever and interesting persons both imported and native, from whom I can literally learn – which is what I adore doing. A year ago I was offered something called the Albert Schweitzer Chair in the City University of New York[3] [...]. I have not the slightest intention of leaving England for any purposes whatsoever. I wish to remain in Oxford at all costs: it is my home and I am tied to it by a thousand ties, and abroad is abroad, and not the same thing at all; quite apart from moral and political considerations. [...] In the end, they said would I come for at least one term out of their four or our six. They then promised to pay me sums which col-lectively would amount to a little less than I now get as a professor at Oxford, but not much less. I said that I might think about that, but that of course would entail my having to resign my chair, as I entirely agreed with the Oxford principle that professors must sit in their universities for three terms out of three, and not five terms out of six – whole time or nothing. They were very surprised, but accepted this. Nobody in America understands why one cannot get away for one term out of two years, because they are about and travelling all the time. This in part is why the graduates don't get too well looked after here, save in rich universities where there is a profusion of professors, like Harvard, Berkeley, Princeton, Yale, etc. [...] What attracted me about the arrangement was not vacating my chair – which as I say is perfectly comfortable – but the need to go and talk to people interested in the history of ideas in any place in which they can be found in any quantity, speaking languages which I understand, i.e. New York and its vicinity.

1 Wildly optimistic as ever. The book was published as *Vico and Herder: Two Studies in the History of Ideas* in 1976: for the story of its complex vicissitudes see the editor's preface to TCE. *3 Cn hs q*

2 i.e. the Warburg Institute of the University of London, of which Ernst Gombrich was then the Director (1959–76), and Edgar Wind a former Deputy Director (1934–42); the Institute is prin-cipally concerned with cultural history, art history and the history of ideas, particularly in the Renaissance.

3 In 1965, as part of a State-wide initiative to raise standards of learning, ten chairs were created in the higher education institutions of NY, five to be designated 'Albert Einstein Chair in Science', and five 'Albert Schweitzer Chair' – the latter in honour of the German theologian, musician, medical missionary and Nobel laureate Albert Schweitzer (1875–1965), OM, who had died on 4 September of that year. IB was offered the Albert Schweitzer chair at CUNY, but declined, since this was a full-time post; he was offered instead, and accepted, the visiting post of Professor of Humanities (1966–71). The Schweitzer chair went to Arthur Schlesinger, who held it with distinction 1966–94.   *19 17- 07*

It was then that Iffley came along. It is perfectly true that I had thought about this before – rejected it – on the ground that without money and without graduates the College does not seem genuine to me; and when you asked me whether I wished to apply for it I said I didn't and that of course holds. But if they want me, the matter seems altered: my reason for being inclined to accept – and I certainly haven't accepted yet – only said that if my conditions were granted I should be strongly inclined to do so – are these: (1) I should like to do something concrete for the University. It has always treated me well, and I should like to repay. There is some ancient deposit of social conscience which has been stimulated into life by the extreme lack of it, as it seems to me, at All Souls. (2) A new beginning is always attractive and exciting. (3) It seems to sit well – and then if the City University of New York pays for me, I should not need to take money from Iffley and at the same time be able to get away to talk to the historians of ideas at fixed intervals for say three to four months every two years. (4) This is a more real job than a research fellow of anywhere, less ambivalent. I realise of course how much time it will take – for one has to spend a lot of time with these people – that it means sitting in an office, with a lot of dreary bureaucratic work. None of this frightens me. What does terrify me is the prospect of collecting money. I do not know that I shall be any good at that. [...] I realise the absolute truth of all you say: that the fellows are among the insulted and oppressed, and fiercely embittered by their past lives, and very dull, and their wives probably worse. That one will have to be apostolic to a degree, and salve their wounds with all kinds of balms, and that one will be criticised for what one does and doesn't do all the time, and that they will gang up against one constantly, led by Jessup[1] and Cecilia. That even though they graciously grant permission to me to go away to New York at fixed intervals, they will in the end resent it and complain that I didn't spend enough time among them; that one will have to commute from Headington to Iffley every morning, be there on the dot, say, of 9.30, sit in an office with a secretary till lunch and deal with papers, and then go off on these awful money-hunting missions to the UGC, to America etc. like poor Bill Deakin,[2] and the rest of them. I'm sure that people think I can simply go to [Isaac] Wolfson and touch him for a million, and call the college Wolfson College, and that will be that. Nothing is further from the truth; people are trying to do that with the old boy all the time, but all he really thinks about now is, I am sure, some huge temple in memory of his father in Jerusalem, or something of that kind. My only real hope, Lord

1 Frank William Jessup (1909–90), Director, Dept for External Studies, Oxford, 1952–76; Fellow, Iffley, 1965–6, Wolfson 1966–80 (Librarian 1974–90); author of *Wolfson College, Oxford: The Early Years* (241/2).

2 (Frederick) William Dampier ('Bill') Deakin (1913–2005), DSO 1943, later (1975) Kt, historian, and research assistant/literary collaborator of Winston Churchill; founding Warden of St Antony's 1950–68, in which role he was obliged to seek funds for an expanding institution – he claimed to dislike this task, but discharged it assiduously. Intimate friend of Aline Berlin.

Marks, is dead. The rest are not a very attractive lot, and not particularly fond of me. [...].

Anyway, I shall not decide anything until I come back. And I shall come to see you as soon as I return. I think that Wheare understands my position clearly, and that undue hopes and fears will not occur. I am convinced that everyone I ask – and I haven't asked anyone but yourself (and I wrote to John only) – will advise against, because I am thought of as a garrulous dilettante, and no kind of administrator, and tremendously unsolid [...].

Meanwhile let me say again that I am deeply moved by your letter and telegram, and so far from holding it against you, I think it a most genuine token of a lifelong friendship.

Yours,

Isaiah

PS Oddly enough Aline is rather in favour of Iffley and promises to adapt herself. Believe me, it is not desire for escape. I don't mind being professor and I can take All Souls despite everything. Thank you again.

TO KENNETH WHEARE

13 December 1965

Princeton

Personal

Dear Ken,

[...] There is a thin, ⟨it is growing denser: 3 telegrams to-day denouncing my "madness" from respected colleagues! It is as if I was about to join The Party: or the R. C. Church: but the tones are even more urgent. Dear me! And you won't pronounce.⟩ but entirely uniform, stream of negative advice trickling through to me on this subject. A half-a-dozen good men think it is sheer lunacy, although they put it differently. I have taken your telegram to heart and am 'standing firm' – although your letter says nothing in answer to my central and least discreet enquiry – about your own personal and private views on this matter. Perhaps you will tell me when we meet. Division of opinion among my friends is natural enough – and I must make up my own mind and not be launched off into the unknown by some vague, generally favourable breeze: nevertheless the unanimity of the no-sayers is rather daunting. Is it really so lunatic a prospect?

Yours ever,

Isaiah

TO HELEN GARDNER[1]

21 December 1965 [carbon]

[Princeton]

Dear Helen,

[...] I wish I weren't so afraid as I now am that most subjects are better taught in good American universities than they are even in Oxford. We may preserve supremacy in ancient history, classics, medieval English history, and hold our own (just) in philosophy – I honestly do not know about English, and perhaps we are all right in some branches of natural science – but in the rest, i.e. modern history, the Slav world, the East, non-English literatures, the arts, it really is immensely better here. You will not emigrate, neither will I, for personal reasons – because we are what we are and can only live on the soil that we do – and moral and social and political reasons as well; but if I were a young man, swayed mainly by intellectual considerations, I should think twice before settling down in a British university today. The future would not seem very safe to me. It cannot be the function only of money. It is a combination here of the emigration from Europe in the 1930s and 1950s and 1960s plus the terror induced by the Sputnik[2] and the enormous leap forward of State universities and the like. I am particularly affected – I take an interest in the history of ideas – not so much as a subject to teach, but intrinsically – and to whom can I speak about this in our country? Whereas here the market is teeming, as it is in Germany, France, Italy, even the Soviet Union. [...]

Yours,

[Isaiah]

TO JOHN SPARROW

21 December 1965

Princeton

Dear John,

[...] My thoughts about Iffley astonish me greatly – I have not received your promised letter – but perhaps the spoken word is better. My 'lunacy' continues – Maurice attributes all this to well-known derangement of feeling that comes upon those who stay away from home too long. But still I have not gone so far as some: when the Institute here offered me a job – honourable but beyond my powers, it is true – I did have the sense to persuade them not to discuss it. ⟨my thoughts are crystallized: if I can get enough money

1 Helen Louise Gardner (1908–86), later (1967) DBE; Fellow and Tutor in English Literature, St Hilda's, 1942–66; Reader in Renaissance English Literature 1954–66; Merton Professor of English Literature and Fellow of LMH 1966–75.

2 Generic name for a series of Soviet satellites ('sputnik' is Russian for 'satellite'), the first of which, *Sputnik 1*, was launched on 4 October 1957.

at once – to avoid Bill D.'s begging bowl – I shall consider Iffley. If not, not. Don't write to the millionaires warning them against me, in my own interest. [...]⟩ [...]

Yours,

Isaiah

TO LEONARD WOLFSON

22 December 1965 [*carbon*]

[Princeton]

Dear Leonard,

Why has the day only twelve or sixteen or twenty-four hours? Why cannot one do three or four things at the same time? Why should I, an academic, have such a desire to do so many things, see so many persons, be in so many places? I really must discipline myself and remember life is short, the work is long, the master of the house impatient, the slaves idle, etc., as it says in our prayers.

But the immediate purpose of this letter is to ask you whether I could see you in London (I assume you are too busy to come to Oxford) about something near my heart and directly connected with me personally (I will give no further hint of it, but you may or may not guess as there has been too much gossip about this already) sometime in January after I come back. [...]

I am buoyed up by all kinds of hopes and assailed by all kinds of fears. I seem to have reached some kind of curious change of life, and am about to launch on unexplored seas. Or perhaps not. In any case, I will tell you when I see you. I hope you are well. I send you the compliments of the season.

Yours,

Isaiah

TO SAMUEL SAMBURSKY

27 January 1966

Headington House

Dear Shmuel,

[...] I feel a strong sense of moral obligation to accept [Iffley] if I can get some trifling sum, say £2 million, to run it; if I cannot get this, then how could I begin anything? And if I do, will this annoy the heads of St Antony's, St Catherine's, Linacre, Nuffield, and most of all All Souls, where terrible palace revolutions and counter-revolutions have been succeeding each other with bewildering rapidity, and which is about to be attacked in *Encounter* by David Caute,[1] a fellow who has just resigned [...]? So you see the pass at

1 (John) David Caute (b. 1936), historian and novelist, Fellow of All Souls 1959–65, resigned over the College's failure to admit graduate students; visiting professor, NY and Columbia, 1966–7;

which we have arrived. You are a beneficiary of a counter-revolution;[1] I am mildly disposed in favour of it if it goes far enough. I cannot feel those terrible passions which seem to scorch the hearts and entrails of my colleagues. The College seems demoralised, but no doubt by the time you come it will have recovered. Someone will have to be found to administer the scheme under which you come. My candidate is Hampshire, but there is so much general poison at the moment running through the veins of All Souls in all directions that no one can be elected to anything till things settle down, and the Warden is not the man to see to that – he does not soothe the savage hearts of his fellows: he prods them into life and exacerbates their feelings. There is low gossip for you in plenty! [...]

There is a great deal to tell you – I will save it up for when we meet. Everybody in Oxford is sitting writing long personal letters to Lord Franks. Is it possible, or am I mistaken in the impious, cynical suggestion that they all take themselves a little too seriously? Perish the thought! Let me say nothing against civic responsibility, yet the result is absolutely absurd.

Yours,
    Isaiah

TO LEONARD WOLFSON

3 February 1966

[Headington House]

Dear Leonard,

I enclose a ⟨fairly⟩ brief memorandum, because I have a feeling that what cannot be said fairly briefly need not be said at all. (But you must allow for my natural exuberance, which I cannot always wholly repress.) Whatever the outcome, I much enjoyed our lunch, and hope we may meet again soon to talk about things in general, which we clearly both enjoy.

Yours ever,
    Isaiah

Reader in Social and Political Theory, Brunel, 1967–70; his *Isaac and Isaiah: The Covert Punishment of a Cold War Heretic* (London and New Haven, 2013) examines the fraught relationship between IB and Isaac Deutscher against the background of the Cold War. In his *Encounter* article (217/4) Caute reserved special censure for the Warden, whom he considered 'profoundly wedded to the past' (15): 'To the preservation of the status quo Mr Sparrow has brought not only a lawyer's experience of manoeuvre but also a profound grasp of the fourth dimension of defence, delay. The climate of frustration, logic-chopping, "thinking again" (i.e. reconsidering a decision already made by the College) and depressing inertia in which All Souls business is often conducted could doubtless be conveyed only by a novelist' (7). If IB privately endorsed much of Caute's critique, even of Sparrow, he considered his article ill judged.

1 Sambursky planned to visit All Souls under the visiting fellows scheme favoured at the College meeting of 6 November 1965 (236–7), which represented a 'counter-revolution' to the much-discussed graduate scheme.

PS 1. I have said nothing in this about being head of ⟨the College⟩ myself, but I would of course be ready to do so if the funds were guaranteed by, say, April, and not otherwise. I have told my potential colleagues that.

2. Nothing can be done about religion. English Universities will not accept Catholic or Methodist colleges, and even Anglican ones are beginning to be looked on as slightly anomalous. This College would be tied to no one religion. On the other hand, if the donor wanted it, special links could be created with, for example, Israel, via Rehovot, or places for graduate students or researchers etc. Besse[1] asked for Frenchmen to be invited to St Antony's; there are scarcely any now, because they do not come; the College would reserve places for them if they did.

3. Do take me off my tenterhook soon. I feel that it is slightly absurd, at my age, to wonder about my 'future'. Whichever way you decide, do not let this agony last too long!

I dined with Franks on the day I lunched with you. He was terribly enthusiastic, and said he would do anything to help. Nobody is allowed to refuse his recommendations!

TO LEONARD WOLFSON

4 March 1966 [*carbon*]

[Headington House]

Dear Leonard,

I dined with Solly solo Wednesday. I thought I was going to meet Cockcroft[2] and Dodds,[3] but Solly said he had not remembered to ask them – perhaps it was all a misunderstanding. At any rate, we had what was probably a jollier meal. You will have had my memorandum – Solly produced no objections to it, and only spoke of alternative means – these, no doubt, are always with us.

Is there anything further you would like me to do, or must I compose my soul in peace? I do not find that prospect unattractive, save that I must decide so soon. Anyway, I suppose I must start writing to America now. I cannot tell if Solly was or was not impressed by the fact that I now have all the Oxford eminences, the Vice-Chancellor, Oliver Franks, and the heads of science departments, who are all very enthusiastic indeed [...], there is not a dissenting voice, and they are prepared to sign a round robin if necessary, explaining why they think such a College would make a crucial difference to science in

---

1 St Antony's was founded in 1950 as a postgraduate college, with a £1.5 million donation from the French merchant and benefactor Antonin Besse (1877–1951), Hon. KBE 1951; one-third of its students were to be French nationals, an aspiration never realised.

2 John Douglas Cockcroft (1897–1967), Kt 1948, OM 1957, Director of Atomic Energy Research Establishment, Ministry of Supply, Harwell, 1946–58; shared the Nobel Prize in physics 1951; Master of Churchill, Cambridge, 1959–67; Trustee of the Wolfson Foundation 1959–67.

3 (Edward) Charles Dodds (1899–1973), Kt 1954; Courtauld Professor of Biochemistry, London, and Director, Courtauld Institute of Biochemistry at Middlesex Hospital, 1927–65; President, Royal College of Physicians, 1962–6; Trustee, Wolfson Foundation, 1965–71.

Oxford; and certainly not science alone. I too must have someone to talk to –
though they seem to me, both as human beings and intellectually, if anything
superior to my own world. Do not let this go too far.

    Yours,

      Isaiah   [...]

TO MCGEORGE BUNDY

   7 March 1966 [*typescript draft corrected in manuscript*]

                                        Headington House

Dear Mac,

   [...] I have sent the memorandum to the Wolfson Foundation, containing
the plan. The memorandum is fourteen pages long; I have spared you my
most eloquent moments, and enclose a drier version which contains all the
brass tacks – the entire substance of the thing. I cannot find anyone here to
be critical of the scheme, even in points of minor detail – only critical of me,
for being so rash as to believe myself capable of managing the enterprise.
About that I would rather volunteer no views; they may be right, but I (still)
feel convinced and enthusiastic. The only relevant facts are these:

   [...] The Oxford administration is solidly in favour – so are all the major
scientists and heads of all the scientific departments – I have not asked the
others, apart from Oliver Franks (who has spent hours on it, and beautifully emended all my cruder formulations), but I can answer for my own
'humanistic' colleagues. The most helpful and energetic of all has been Lord
Florey,[1] who is, as you probably know, a Nobel Prize winning Australian, who
invented penicillin, and is a very shrewd, intelligent, nice man, who has just
ceased to be President of the Royal Society, a major statesman of the sciences
in England. [...] And I have of course spoken to my old friend, the left-wing,
dreamy but charming Nobel Prize winning Professor Dorothy Hodgkin,[2]
Royal Society Professor of Crystallography, who is very keen indeed. And
so it goes. All these say that they welcome nothing so much as a chance of
sending their ablest research postgraduates and postdoctoral colleagues to
such a college, and would eagerly involve themselves in conferences, meetings, and invitations to colleagues in industry and other scientific establishments, and in the US and Europe, to come and discuss and cooperate with
various schemes.

   I have never met scientists as a body before, and so far from being narrow,

---

1 Howard Walter Florey (1898–1968), Kt 1944, life peer 1965, OM 1965; Australian Rhodes Scholar;
    shared Nobel Prize in Physiology or Medicine 1945 for his work on penicillin; Professor of
    Pathology, Oxford, 1935–62; President of the Royal Society 1960–5; Provost of Queen's 1962–8;
    Chancellor of the Australian National University 1965–8; Trustee of Wolfson 1967–8.

2 Dorothy Mary Crowfoot Hodgkin (1910–94), OM 1965, chemist and crystallographer, awarded
    the Nobel Prize in Chemistry 1964; Fellow, Somerville, 1936–77; Royal Society Wolfson Research
    Professor 1960–77; Fellow, Wolfson, 1977–82; Chancellor, Bristol, 1970–88.

or dull, or outside the world, they seem to be a wonderful body of men, upon whom I look with almost mystical admiration, and in whose society I feel unaccountably happy. Nor do I believe that this will wear off on my part (I do not know about theirs). [...]

Now as to even more concrete details. Supposing the Wolfsons establish a building: could you provide for the rest? i.e. the equivalent of about £2 million, or a little more? And if the Wolfsons, as the price of their support, were to want to call the college 'Wolfson College', which I suspect would be a demand by the old boy, would you still be prepared to do this? Or would you prefer to do the whole thing yourself? [...] I ought to add at this point what I have said before, that Oliver himself is extremely favourable to the whole thing, and keeps egging me on, to the best of his ability, and hinting at bits of his report (at present under lock and key with policemen guarding it at the press) in order to encourage me to go forward. I do not know if you want him to write to you – if you do, he would, I believe, be glad to do so.

The awful thing is that I cannot keep the fellows of Iffley and the University waiting too long – I must be fair to them – and therefore I have to have the answer in principle by mid-April or so. The Wolfsons know this, and are calling some kind of special meeting on the subject, so my question is hypothetical. Supposing they do their bit, how would you react? [...] I am terrified of the prospect, and at the same time committed to the idea of doing it. If it *is* possible to build something new, unusual, large and to do with what is surely *the* major development of our century – the great scientific breakthrough – then it would surely be craven to evade it.

Finally let me say again that, however things turn out, I will always be eternally grateful to you – you will always have a huge fund in my private, inner bank – I only wish you would spend it somehow, i.e. call on me for something, sometime. I am grateful to Joe – he is attacked on all sides, as you may imagine – but without fully agreeing with his views, especially the more thunderous ones; I spend my time defending him, and enjoy doing it. I really love him, with all his warts; it is marvellous to have friends, and wonderful not to be so old that one can no longer do anything much. On this absurdly romantic note, let me end.

Yours ever,

[Isaiah]   [...]

TO ARTHUR GOODHART

7 March 1966 [*carbon*]

Headington House

Dear Arthur,

[...] Leonard Wolfson is quite taken with the idea – at least that is my impression, but Solly is proving a fearful nuisance, as you anticipated. When

I knock down his objections (I have now had to have dinner with him three times!) he mutters about alternative objectives, e.g. Manchester, Birmingham etc., but I do not think that Sir Isaac really wants to be commemorated there, all that much. I am in touch with Bundy, but that is a dead secret. The ideal is £1½ million from Wolfson plus £2 million from Ford. If you do see Wyzanski[1] or any other Ford Trustee, you might whisper to them how bold and original the scheme is, and how necessary for the development of graduate studies in England, especially scientific, and more especially technological, i.e. applied – that the Government is really very poor, and is thinking about provincial universities for party political reasons or social prejudice of the intelligible kind,[2] but that the plant is here, so are the most distinguished professors, and Oxford is likely to have to supply teachers and researchers for years to come, whatever may be happening in the provinces. That if England sinks – as it surely will if we do not train graduates, especially in the sciences – this will not be good for Europe, and that if the College is set up, it will absorb quite a lot of European students (that is Florey's good idea), which will promote European cooperation in a very practical fashion. I genuinely believe in this; and Ford should believe in this too. Certainly Bundy does. Will Ford give any money? Will they mind the College being Wolfson College, which I am sure Isaac will want? If they do mind, will they give the whole sum? Negotiations with Bundy are dreadfully secret – no officials know of this – he is in his first year; like a chancellor he will, I think, be allowed to nominate his own honorary degrees – in this case, he will be given leeway with tens of millions, surely? That is what I lean my hopes on, but I do not think they will give him any money unless some is forthcoming from England. They will say if this matter of technologists etc. is so crucial, why does not the Government do more? Why not indeed? [...]

The sum mentioned in the memorandum is £3½ million: this could I suppose be scaled down to £3 million, but scarcely below that. It sounds an awful lot; unless it is found quickly, the hideous prospect of going around the Foundations with a huge wooden begging-bowl, à la Bill Deakin, faces me. For that I am not prepared. I am at present, as you may imagine, frightened acutely, (a) of failure, (b) of success. Do come and hold my hand. I really need this. How are you? When will you be back? Will you be flying over specially? Can I intercept you before you go to the Wolfson meeting?

    Yours,

      Isaiah

---

1 Charles Edward Wyzanski, Jr (1906–86), appointed Federal Judge by FDR 1941; Chief Judge, Federal District Court, Massachusetts, 1965–71; governing body, Ford Foundation, 1952–76.

2 In compiling his 1963 report on higher education, Lord Robbins had 'continually warned that resource-priorities over the next twenty-five years would have to lie with the newer civic and provincial universities': Jose Harris, 'The Arts and Social Sciences, 1939–1970', in *The History of the University of Oxford*, vol. 8 (142/4), 226.

TO JOSEPH ALSOP

13 March 1966 [*manuscript*]

Headington House

Dear Joe

[…] I have been Wolfsoning. If Wolfson produces the building & Mac the endowment, I shall be fatally committed. I am still thought pretty mad (though less so) but burn with faith. I have written a piece off for Mac: by now perhaps they have decided one way or another: life with Mr Wolfson – he is a compulsive talker about money & business (his own) will *not* be easy: Aline will scarcely be able to take being shown off as a captive princess to his business friends: she is muttering terribly: with my masochistic desire (late in life) to offer myself on an altar, I could perhaps *just* take those *terrible* feasts of Trimalchio: Petronius got it absolutely & horribly right:[1] Mr W. may be a genius & have a generous nature: but he is a noisy, vain, self-centred tycoon: a trifle coarse: not, you might think, quite one of us: still if it must be … Of course I'd rather be supported by Ford *entirely*: dignity wd not be sacrificed: it wd be undemeaning (W. *is* demeaning). I expect it is too late or unsuitable for you gently to intervene again by way of wondering what is happening: still, if you could … My opponent on the W. Foundation is Bill Walton's[2] friend Solly Zuckerman: not a good person. […] Maurice is deaf, kind, devoted, like a half extinct half erupting volcano: one never knows at whom & how strongly the fire & lava will burst out: Are you coming? When?

Love, fondest love from me & Aline to you both. We miss you enormously: your friendship in every way & sense is *infinitely* precious to me (& her).

Bless you,

Isaiah   […]

TO LEONARD WOLFSON

14 March 1966

[Headington House]

Dear Leonard,

I was delighted to see you at dinner, which I greatly enjoyed, even though you plunged me in gloom. Do you really think that June – when all the other

---

1 Gaius Petronius Arbiter (*c.*27 BCE–66 CE), Roman writer, author of the only partly extant *Satyricon*, a satirical text in Latin prose, interspersed with verse, of the Neronian period; the principal narrative in book 15 describes the excesses at an ostentatious dinner given by Trimalchio, a vulgar, snobbish and ignorant nouveau-riche freedman.

2 William Turner ('Bill') Walton (1902–83), Kt 1951, later (1967) OM, composer. Walton wrote, at Zuckerman's behest, a *Roaring Fanfare* for the inauguration of the new lion terraces at London Zoo, June 1976 (Zuckerman was then Secretary to the Zoological Society of London): the score was dedicated 'To Solly Z., that Lion of Lions'.

rival schemes jostle for recognition – will be more propitious to our plans than a special meeting?

I saw Sir John Cockroft in Cambridge – he was charming to me, and showed me round his college, which I duly admired – I did not try to nobble him about Oxford, for, after all, he knows the content of the memorandum, and I did not wish to appear over-anxious about accepting all those burdens and responsibilities – the scheme is important for the future of graduate studies in England, especially in science, and that he appreciates – and not for my particular future. I cannot demean myself too much by begging for support for something that stands on its own merits, and promises me little but sweat, even if not blood, and I hope not tears; I have the deepest faith in Wolfson College, but it seems to me that I have done all that I can at this stage. If there are complications about personalities, at which you lightly hinted, there is nothing, surely, that I can do about that. But I do long to know where I am, and I leave the matter in your hands: I am sure that you will do whatever is right, and not let my suspense continue too long. [...]

Yours,
Isaiah

TO RAIMUND VON HOFMANNSTAHL

16 March 1966 [*carbon*]

[Headington House]

Dear Raimund,

I enclose a secret copy of a document I dispatched to an American Foundation – and one paragraph of an earlier version which I revised, for fear that the American Foundation might say, 'If it is as bad as that why does not the British Government do something urgent and big? Because it does not, perhaps your account is exaggerated.' It is impossible to convey in America the full degree of prejudice against Oxford and Cambridge in the present Labour Government – equality is a noble ideal – and in its interests Oxford and Cambridge require reform – but when the desire for social justice takes resentful and emotional forms, it leads to repression and gratuitous damage, rather than reform. I cannot say this to Americans, because it would be washing too much linen in public, but it is, as you know, the truth. If you wish to make use of this, it would be marvellous, but do tell me what you are doing because I do not want to cross wires prematurely. I leave for Italy on Saturday, and shall telephone to you on Friday. [...]

Yours,
[IB p.p. Baillie Knapheis]

TO BERNARD CRICK[1]

29 March 1966

As from All Souls

Dear Crick,

Thank you for sending me the texts.[2] My chief difficulty is simply that I agree with you more than (you think that) you agree with me: not only as against the obvious common enemy (the suppressors of differences in favour of a final solution), but as against fanatical individualists – anti-planners, laissez-fairists, Hayekites[3] and even Proudhonists[4] (who hate the State, and believe in the sacredness of small property as a guarantee of morality), and so on; and that, not only because such persons elevate uninterference into a supreme goal, and disregard the claims of security, justice, equality and simple humanity, like the real bogey-liberals of the nineteenth century, [...] who see totalitarian monsters in the mildest, most desperately needed social reform, New Deal and socialist; but also because such people do not realise that some liberties menace other liberties; that, as you say, some liberties perish *without* social planning; that laws – even though Bentham *is* right, and laws do curtail liberty always – are indispensable if men are to enjoy even a minimum of such liberties (or liberty) as all non-monists demand. Sorry about this monstrous sentence: but perhaps it is not really involved or obscure. I, too, have voted for socialists with a clear conscience: and shall do so now.

Our chief difference, and there *is* one, is that you want to identify liberty (or freedom: is there such a nuance as you suggest? maybe) with action; I, with the opportunity for it – to take it or leave it. Obviously no action without liberty – in politics or whatever – but no liberty without action? At least political activity, participation in the pursuit of common goals – why? I am ready to condemn societies in which there is a tendency to escape, in

---

1 Bernard Crick (1929–2008), later (2002) Kt; political theorist; taught at LSE, becoming senior lecturer 1957–65; Professor of Political Theory and Institutions, Sheffield, 1965–71; Professor of Politics, London (Birkbeck), 1971–84.

2 Crick had sent IB a copy of his 1966 inaugural lecture at Sheffield, 'Freedom as Politics', published as a pamphlet in the same year by the University, and repr. in Crick's *Political Theory and Practice* (London, 1973), 35–62. The lecture was inspired by, and took issue with, IB's *Two Concepts of Liberty* (Oxford, 1958), and included a humorous verse summary of Crick's argument, reproduced as an appendix to the published article – except when the latter was included in Peter Laslett and W. G. Runciman (eds), *Philosophy, Politics and Society: Third Series* (Oxford, 1967), 194–214 – and to the present volume (603–5). The reference to 'texts' may show that Crick sent (type?)scripts of lecture and appendix as separate items.

3 Friedrich August von Hayek (1899–1992), Austrian-born British economist, Nobel laureate 1974. His advocacy of the free market and his strong opposition to Keynesian economics were central to neo-conservative thinking in the late twentieth century.

4 Pierre-Joseph Proudhon (1809–65), French socialist-anarchist. His much quoted dictum 'Property is theft' was his answer to the question posed in the title of his seminal pamphlet *Qu'est-ce que la propriété?* [*What Is Property?*] (Paris, 1840).

which horror of 'the coldest of all cold monsters' (Nietzsche, is it?),[1] the
State – pursuit of privacy, aestheticism, irritated superior neurotic or fastidious 'noli me tangere' – is endemic. Men are diminished thereby, obstacles to
expression of personality created. But societies in which this is forbidden, or
strongly discouraged (Australian fines on non-voters), do ignore Constant's
plea for *some* room in which I can stand on my head and crow like a cock if
I feel so inclined.[2] They do deny a right: perhaps they increase liberty somewhere else thereby. I doubt it historically: certainly they decrease inactivity
and stimulate public spirit, participation, *civisme*, concern for one another,
etc. – but freedom? If I *have* opportunities, if doors *are* open to me to be
active in many ways and I know I could if I wished, or even if I did not wish,
and I simply choose to sit still, why am I politically not *free*? I, you, such men
may wither; such societies may decline. There may [be] (and I should agree
that there *are*) reasons for working against the multiplication of such lonely
lives and ivory towers and caves, and it may *lead* to loss of vitality, 'dehuman-
isation', to anomie, and so to being fully prey to despots or nonsense. But
why is the freedom to sit still and be gloomy not a freedom? Deplorable, but
still a freedom? At least politically? (Psychologically is another sense of the
word: and confusion results from identifying neuroses with literal slavery or
oppression, surely.)

You charge my 'negative liberty' with being such isolation or loneliness.
Unjustly. (This *is* a genuine misunderstanding of my text.) I specifically
discuss the Stoic–Kantian attempt to identify freedom with contraction of
the vulnerable surface, and a sour grapes attitude to public life: if I cannot
have what I crave for, then I'll suppress the craving and be 'free' or 'liberated'
from the heteronomous, enslaving passion.[3] And I do say (I haven't my text
here, alas) that this logically leads to saying that the most complete liberty is
death, like Miss Arendt's freedom to commit suicide[4] – you can't oppress or
enslave the non-existent![5] [...] The extent of 'negative' liberty for me – surely

1 Friedrich Wilhelm Nietzsche (1844–1900), German philosopher and philologist, radical critic
   of Christianity, and of the moral and philosophical basis of Western culture and society; the
   quotation is from *Thus Spake Zarathustra* (1883–5), part 1, 'The New Idol': 'The State is called
   the coldest of all cold monsters. Coldly it also tells lies; and this lie creeps from its mouth: "I, the
   State, am the people."'
2 Constant, *Principes de politique* (1815), chapter 1, 'De la souveraineté du peuple': *Écrits politiques*,
   ed. Marcel Gauchet ([Paris], 1997), 318 (the examples are IB's).
3 'The doctrine that maintains that what I cannot have I must teach myself not to desire, that
   a desire eliminated, or successfully resisted, is as good as a desire satisfied, is a sublime, but,
   it seems to me, unmistakable, form of the doctrine of sour grapes: what I cannot be sure of,
   I cannot truly want.' L 186. For the Stoics see L 182, 186; for Kant, L 182/1, 183, 184/2.
4 In *The Burden of Our Time* (NY, 1951), 410, Hannah Arendt refers to suicide as the 'last and apparently still indestructible guarantee' of freedom, and elsewhere she alludes to the Greek/Roman
   association of suicide with noble courage, and its obverse – that the failure to commit suicide
   denotes cowardice and slavishness: *The Human Condition* (Chicago, 1958), 36/30.
5 'The logical culmination of the process of destroying everything through which I can possibly
   be wounded is suicide.' L 186.

I *say* this[1] – depends on how many doors are genuinely open to me, the 'size' of the doors, and the vistas they reveal, and *not* on contracting myself into the least space, building walls round myself, and insulating myself from other men. [...] The wider the opportunities for activity – social, political etc. – the greater the freedom of a man, a group etc. But you want to identify [freedom] not with the openness of the doors, but with the actual march through them. Why? To march is good: to sit still, be self-absorbed, choose cork-lined rooms, abdicate is against the deepest interests of men as such. Your or my or Marx's or Mill's view of man's nature may entail this; but why is such perverse behaviour *unfree*? 'Get out of your corner, stop brooding and realise your personality!' 'And if I don't?' 'Then I'll jolly well educate (get at?) you and bring it out, no matter what you want!' 'So you will force me to be free?' [...]

So much for our genuine differences. They seem small to me; but you may think them crucial; for if you think that I think that a man is politically undeprived if not interfered with, I don't – I only think he is politically free even if inactive; but in a sorry state. 'The law has been abrogated. You are *free* to vote against the rascals, to deny God, to join the Communist Party, to say on the radio that Marx was a foxy old humbug.' 'I am not interested. I am an aesthete.' 'Slave!' Is this a parody of what you mean? If so, I *have* misunderstood you, as you have me.

[...] If Kant's society is a freer society (as it is), it is so because more doors to men have been swung open. Human beings can enter into more fertile and 'fulfilling' relationships with one another. Whether they in fact do so depends on their characters and wishes; their love of life and each other; their being animated by generous ideals. But these are not freedoms, but active *powers*: freedom (or liberty) is the condition for activity. I think that what you call freedom (a free spirit; a liberal outlook; liberal-handed) I prefer to call power. You want to say, 'How free they are! How mobile, active they are, how richly their gifts are realised and scattered', whereas I wish to say, 'How free! How untrammelled! How uninhibited – whithersoever they wish to move, they can; nothing can stop them!' Freedom for you *is* the living of the life; for me it's its condition. As a decent standard of living *makes possible* freedom, so freedom makes possible the desirable political activity (or, I fear, inactivity: of course freedom alone is not enough; unless there are positive social ends to pursue, political freedom to pursue them is not much use – is that all you are saying?). Why is this revoltingly trivial? For I *do* say it. *What* has this to do with isolation and loneliness? Demand for open doors is not the same as a pathetic plea to be left alone. The cap does not seem to me to fit at all. If you feel like being harsh, by all means (I believe in freedom, including

---

1 See L 177/1.

freedom to abuse); but since you do not wish to misrepresent, hearken unto my words. [...]

'Freedom is doing something with it.' Forgive my 'verbalism': with *what*? I too am not for sitting pretty. I am all for *exercise* of rights, Mill's bold, creative, independent man (you are right: I should *not* have said that his idea of liberty has little to do with his positive ideals, any more than – if I am to be vain for a moment – mine is unconnected with my ideals) – but why are creativity, self-realisation etc. *liberty*? Those who fight and die for liberty die to remove a yoke, to break down walls, to remove something horrible – they don't die to create, only to let in air, light – to make *possible* creation. We are back again at the old point, on which Hamann once said, 'I gnaw and gnaw and will gnaw myself to death.'[1] [...]

You quote my encomium to negative liberty,[2] but you omit to go on, and so your reader will suppose that I am praising the revolting triviality of having no obstacles to my silly, sweet will. This, too, is real misunderstanding. If he read on, he would see that the point there (I seem to remember – no text alas!) is the incompatibility of some ultimate values and ends with one another: and the (logically as well as practically) inevitable suppression of most of these in a society dedicated to positive liberty: this is very different from the beauties of 'mere' non-interference, though doing down the latter is the first step to the anti-political society you abhor too. First you align me with the sceptical Tory Hume, then you say that I do not allow even for what the sceptical Whig Tocqueville wanted[3] – when, mind you, I do myself speak of demands for what is often called freedom or liberty – e.g. by newly liberated peoples – which does not neatly fit either into negative or positive liberty; and only wonder if it is useful to call *this* – liberty, if confusion is to be avoided. [...]

So on some things we genuinely disagree, I think: e.g. freedom as the opportunity vs. freedom the activity. I do not think the gap is huge, but it is there; even though the gap between either of us and those who (like Crossman or the younger Marquand in the *Guardian*) say 'politics is about power', or the real freedom-haters, is much vaster. On others you *do* misrepresent me: my free men are not self-isolated, lonely exiles and hermits, fleeing from the all-devouring monster State. They just need and get elbowroom, and now and then ask themselves which of several open avenues to

---

1 'Reason is language, *logos*. On this marrowbone I gnaw, and shall gnaw myself to death on it.' Johann Georg Hamann, *Briefwechsel*, ed. Walther Ziesemer and Arthur Henkel (Wiesbaden and Frankfurt, 1955–79), v 177.18. See TCE 250, 323.

2 'The "negative" liberty that they strive to realise seems to me a truer and more humane ideal than the goals of those who seek in the great, disciplined, authoritarian structures the ideal of "positive" self-mastery by classes, or peoples, or the whole of mankind': *Two Concepts* (271/2), 56.

3 A reference to active citizenship, which Constant called 'the liberty of the ancients', and, connected to this, a conception of human beings as the deliberate makers of their own history. See *Political Theory and Practice* (271/2), 57–8.

walk, but normally they participate in the *polis* fully. And they vote to suppress the freedom of enemies of freedom, but with a qualm or two. This I wish to induce in you. Remember Acton[1] and forgive this wordy piece. I can only say that Butterfield was much more upset at my few words about him;[2] and never spoke to me again.

Yours most sincerely,

Isaiah Berlin   [...]

TO THE EDITOR OF *THE TIMES LITERARY SUPPLEMENT*[3]

15 April 1966 [*Aline Berlin's manuscript, corrected by IB*]

All Souls

Sir, – While reading your issue of 7 April with much interest and agreement, I was astonished to see that, in your leading article, you charge me with holding that 'common sense and good judgement' are all that is needed 'to understand the workings of human beings'. I do not know why you should wish to attribute this ridiculous view to me. My views on history have at times been misinterpreted in your pages, but never to this degree: if it were no more than a passing gibe I should not have felt justified in writing; but it goes well beyond this, for it is a complete misrepresentation.

In the article to which you presumably refer (in the first issue of *History and Theory*), I dealt with the logic of historical explanation. In it I maintained (*a*) that all explanation involves some reference to logical 'models'; (*b*) that the analogy between the models used in most natural sciences and those of history had been exaggerated by positivist thinkers, since (*c*) the more specialised the type of history – the more aspects of life it deliberately excludes (e.g. economic history, the history of technology, the history of architecture, and the like) – the more its central concepts, such as what counts as evidence, proof, validity, truth etc., will resemble those of the natural sciences. The less

---

1 John Emerich Edward Dalberg-Acton (1834–1902), 1st Baron Acton 1869, historian and moralist; Regius Professor of Modern History, Cambridge, 1895–1902, during which time he laid the basis of the 12-volume *Cambridge Modern History* – none of his planned chapters in which, characteristically, was ever completed. Acton also planned to write a history of liberty, but produced only a mass of notes.

2 At L 137/1 (on L 138) IB speaks of 'a fatal internal contradiction in the views of those who believe in the historical conditioning of historians and yet protest against moralising by them, whether they do so contemptuously like E. H. Carr, or sorrowfully like Herbert Butterfield'. IB wrote to Noel Annan, 15 October 1953: 'The only people who could reasonably be annoyed are apologetic, of the Butterfield kind (he has written me a ten page letter [16 May 1953] – [a] sweetly phrased protest at what I think of his views)'; and to Morton White, 22 March 1954: 'And now I must sit down [...] and see what I can do about placating Butterfield, who is under the impression that I have denigrated him wildly'. In his reply to Butterfield (10 April 1954) IB wrote: 'regarding the main issues I think that you are right – that we do start from positions which are not in the end reconcilable at all. You do believe that it is arrogant and ignorant and dangerous to condemn, denounce and fight campaigns on moral issues. I, on the whole, do not.'

3 Published as 'New Ways in History', TLS, 21 April 1966, 347.

specialised a historical narrative is, the more levels of experience it seeks to describe, incorporate, integrate and account for, the more the concepts with which it operates will resemble those of ordinary, non-scientific thought; and I gave logical reasons for this thesis. I went on to say that history needs whatever it can obtain from any source or method of empirical knowledge. It follows that as archaeology and epigraphy and philology have altered historical writing in the past, so anthropology, psychology, sociology can alter, and are altering, it at present: nor is there any assignable limit to the influence upon history of disciplines yet undreamt of. But to say that scientific knowledge (recondite or not) is indispensable to historians is very different from saying that history can itself become a natural science. The work of integrating the data provided by the sciences into a credible account of past human experience has not (at any rate as yet) proved reducible to a method governed by a set of principles or laws (or models). It is such reduction that the early positivists, Comte,[1] Buckle,[2] perhaps Engels (never Marx) demanded; and this ideal has been held up to historians by some among their modern philosophical successors. The new history would be to the old as post-Newtonian astronomy and mechanics were to medieval or Babylonian accumulation and rule of thumb; it would abandon painstaking description and piecemeal analysis, and turn into a branch of law-governed predictive sociology. This I did venture to describe as 'a chimera' – a misconceived conjunction of ill-fitting elements.

Of course, whatever can be quantified – statistically analysed – should be. What computers can do, they should be made to do. If Professor Aydelotte[3] can throw light on Victorian parliaments by using IBM machines, he adds to knowledge. When Mr Finley[4] speaks of the transformation wrought in ancient history by sociological methods, I can only register enthusiastic agreement: sociology is probably at its best in union with history, law, politics, classical scholarship – more fruitful than when it seeks to discover universal social laws. But it is a far cry from this to the vision of the total quantification of history; and so long as this is the case, common sense, depth of historical insight, the synthesising power of the imagination will be

---

1 (Isidore Marie) Auguste François Xavier Comte (1798–1857), French positivist philosopher and sociologist who believed that human society progressed through three stages of development – theological, metaphysical and 'positive', i.e. scientific.

2 Henry Thomas Buckle (1821–62), historian; author of the two-volume *History of Civilization in England* (London, 1857, 1861): 'Many critics in his own day and later thought of Buckle as the English disciple of Comte, but, as Mill declared, Buckle agreed with the founder of positivism on little other than the basic notions of the regularity of human behaviour and the historical progress of civilisation from superstition to science' (Thomas William Heyck, ODNB).

3 William Osgood Aydelotte (1910–96), US historian noted for incorporating statistical methods into his research, taught at Iowa 1947–78.

4 Moses I. (né Isaac) Finley (1912–86) né Finkelstein, later (1979) Kt, American-born left-wing ancient historian and sociologist who emigrated to Britain during the McCarthy era; British subject 1962; Fellow, Jesus, Cambridge, 1957–76, Master, Darwin, 1976–82.

more obviously necessary (but of course not sufficient: although you seem to think that I confuse the two) for historians, no matter how open to scientific influence, than for chemists. Chemists doubtless need these gifts too, but their students can go at least some little way by the application of the relevant rules. Historians – at least 'generalists' – cannot get even so far: this much Vico and Hegel, Weber and Dilthey[1] (and, by his practice, Marx) have taught us. This is what your article (unlike the contributors to your issue and the historians they approve of) seems reluctant to accept.

All this is no doubt a mere philosophers' quarrel, and of little concern to working historians. Still, since it has been mentioned, one may as well get it right. I have no serious grievance; the standards of polemical journalism are not, and cannot be, those of learned journals. I write only to repudiate an absurd charge, and to set the record straight.

Yours truly,

I. Berlin

TO JOSEPH ALSOP

20 April 1966

Headington House

Dearest Joe,

Never shall you have another manuscript letter from me if I can help it – I see. I feel as if I had completely lost the use of my hand as a writing instrument, the beginning, no doubt, of general atrophy and mechanisation, to which I am resigned.

Meanwhile, I have been through quite a lot in my own quiet way. First a delicious week in Italy; then five days in Israel, attending to the affairs of the miserable University,[2] which lives, like everyone else in Israel, on huge deficits which they feel sure somebody sooner or later from the United States will cover. The contrast between the academic delegations of England and America are very extraordinary: we are a respectable body, led by the eminent Law Lord, Lord Cohen,[3] the great Nobel Prize-winner Sir Hans Krebs, the idealistic do-gooder Professor Norman Bentwich,[4] a couple more professors, myself – a staid, high-minded, soft-spoken, somewhat academic, rather timid delegation; facing us on the other side of the table, a red-faced

---

1 Wilhelm Dilthey (1833–1911), German philosopher, literary critic and historian; influential in the development of the social sciences and of hermeneutics.

2 sc. the HUJ.

3 Lionel Leonard Cohen (1888–1973), Kt 1943, life peer 1951, Lord of Appeal in Ordinary 1951–60; did much voluntary work on behalf of the HUJ, and the Lionel Cohen Foundation was established there in his honour.

4 Norman de Mattos Bentwich (1883–1971), British colonial official and moderate Zionist; Professor of International Relations, HUJ, 1932–51. In retirement he worked on behalf of the University, which for him symbolised the modern Jewish renaissance.

collection of tycoons, the head of Emerson Radio, a couple of men from California, some pretty aggressive Zionist ladies, who might *just* have known Mrs Roosevelt, and one miserable, captive, ninth-rate professor. No meeting-ground. They look on us as stuffy British academics, penniless, thin-blooded, unintelligible, the kind of men you cannot tell a jolly story in front of; we look on them as coarse, plutocratic vulgarians, remote from all intellectual issues, anxious for nothing but publicity of the most loathsome kind, anxious to degrade the standards of the University to their own horrible glory. So you can see, the meetings were somewhat tense: the Israelis uneasily flapped between us, anxious to please both sides, looking for intellectual certificates from us, and dough from fountain blue [*sic*]. At the end of all this I went to see Herod's Palace at Masada,[1] caught flu, flew back, went to bed with heavy pneumonia. Should I have stopped Mac from coming? No! The Bowra in me came foremost. I arose from my bed of sickness, and went to lunch with Leonard Wolfson, Sir John Cockcroft, Professor Solly Zuckerman, Mac, Shepard Stone,[2] and Dill's[3] old assistant, General Sir Harold Redman,[4] who is secretary to the Wolfson Foundation. You would have enjoyed the scene.

1919–96 Mac was absolutely marvellous. He spoke with great dignity, force, sincerity, and a kind of noble eloquence which I had never heard from him before. [...] Quite apart from his benevolent interest in my Oxford affairs, his character emerged in such exquisite form that I am now his devoted and dedicated slave. I like him very much indeed, and I think he likes me, now, which was not always the case.[5] Perhaps all he needed – as everyone always does – is moral reassurance, and genuine admiration, which I gave him (I hope he

1 Palace built by Herod the Great in the first century BCE at the north end of the fortress of Masada, a huge, iconic outcrop of rock on the south-west shore of the Dead Sea, the last stronghold of Jewish resistance in the Zealots' revolt against the Romans, AD 66–73; the breaching of the fortress by the Romans after a two-year siege prompted mass suicide among the defenders.

2 Shepard Stone (1908–90), Director of International Affairs, Ford Foundation, 1952–67; President of the International Association For Cultural Freedom 1967–74; Berlin Director of the Aspen Institute for Humanistic Studies 1974–88. Stone had a PhD in history from Berlin (1933), and while at the Ford Foundation directed programmes that encouraged scholarly and intellectual association between America and Europe.

3 John Greer Dill (1881–1944), KCB 1937; served in Boer War and First World War; Field Marshal 1941; Head of the British Joint Staff Mission, Washington, 1941–4.

4 Harold Redman (1899–1986), KCB 1953, veteran of the First and Second World Wars; Lieutenant General 1952, Vice-Chief of Imperial General Staff 1952–5; Governor and Commander-in-Chief, Gibraltar, 1955–8; Director and Secretary, Wolfson Foundation, 1958–67.

5 In 'Goodbye to Berlin', a review of MI repr. in *Unacknowledged Legislation: Writers in the Public Sphere* (London, 2002), 169, Christopher Hitchens quotes 'his character [...] always the case', and also, from the next paragraph but one, 'I have never admired anyone so much, so intensely, for so long as I did him during those four hours' (placing the latter quotation before the former and running the two together either side of an ellipsis). He implies that these quotations show that IB supported Bundy's views on Vietnam, without indicating that the passages from which the quotations are taken are entirely about the negotiations over the funding of Wolfson. As a writer claiming the moral high ground, Hitchens should have eschewed this intellectual sleight of hand. He could have argued his case without it, though he would have had difficulty with IB's publicly stated opposition to the war (310–11, 601–2).

noticed). We have got somewhere, though not perhaps as far as I'd hoped. Sir Isaac was not there; Leonard Wolfson is quite anxious for the scheme; the Ford position is that they back British contributions pound for pound, but will not advance any themselves – which seems to me quite proper. But will the Wolfsons do it?

Solly was like the villain of the piece: violently hostile to the scheme, pathologically opposed to Oxford and Cambridge, not very keen on me. [...] We must contain ourselves now in patience until, I suppose, June, when all the Wolfsons meet. Solly will do his best to wreck the scheme. What I am afraid of is that other schemes will then be advanced as alternatives [...], and there will be no argument about any of these except my scheme, which Solly will declaim against passionately, pulling out all his stops, with no Mac to pull him up, on his facts or his arguments; and controversial things are seldom backed by Foundations. Well – I live in hopes. There is little more that I can do. If the Wolfsons don't come through, or don't give enough, the scheme is dead as far as I am concerned. If they do, it all marches forward with big strides, and you will be the original begetter of it all, unless that be Aline, who I think spoke to you.

But do convey to Mac what I wasn't able to do sufficiently in front of Shepard Stone, because it would have seemed so like sucking up of the most awful kind – that I have never admired anyone so much, so intensely, for so long as I did him during those four hours or so that we were together. He and his Mr Stone came to dinner with us here, with Maurice, Oliver Franks and Bill Deakin, and of course Ann Fleming [ ]. Ann Fleming was splendid. She was fascinated by Franks, whom she rightly compared to Lord Halifax:[1] wherever Maurice moved, Franks moved away from; they get on in theory but not in practice. Maurice worries me: he claims to have been ill on his Hellenic cruise, and then had a heart attack in the airport – not violent, but definite. He feels ill, and ought to rest and doesn't, and has knocked off smoking, but drinks too much brandy. I think he somehow wants to conk out, but also doesn't, wants to preserve his life, and is too impatient to do so. However, he may recover from all this. He was marvellous with Mac, of course, and explained – after having opposed the Iffley scheme for some weeks – that he was its original champion, and that he had done more for graduate students than any man in Oxford; upon his Atlas-like shoulders he bore the burden of progress against a ghastly front of dough-faced reactionaries he has had to contend with all his life; and in every respect, delivered a splendid and eloquent oration, little connected with the facts, magnificent in its own unique way as an exercise in creative imagination, if not in accu-

---

1 As ambassador in Washington 1941–6 Halifax was the signatory of IB's FO reports from there 1942–6. IB's cordial relations with his chief, who was known for aloofness, were doubtless assisted by Oxford connections: Halifax was elected Chancellor of the University 1933, and an Honorary Fellow, All Souls, 1934.

rate description of reality. Everyone flirted with everyone, even Lady Franks thawed visibly,[1] and a happy time was had by all. If it all comes off, a large commemorative bust of Isaac Wolfson on one side and you on the other, dos-à-dos, will have to be placed in the vestibule of St Isaac's College, just on the way into the mosque-church-temple-synagogue, which we shall doubtless be stimulated to set up to satisfy all interests. [...]

We look forward greatly to Susan Mary's coming. You cannot be drawn from Vietnam, doubtless. I wonder if the Catholics there would have been to the taste of the late Evelyn Waugh. He died, as everyone pointed out, in the most holy manner, on Easter Sunday morning, after Church,[2] but he was dreadfully miserable all the same, and his death has affected Maurice very sharply. The obituaries of him seemed to me no good at all. He was a man of genius, mad, disagreeable, pseudo-romantic, and in continuous agony of spirit, and deserves better than the rather conventional pieces about what a good friend he was, and how rich his sense of humour. The uneasy piece by Muggeridge, the uninteresting piece by Christopher Sykes[3] were not worthy of him. I did not like him, although our relations were courteous; he seemed to me the best writer of the English language at the time of his death; perhaps Connolly will write something about him that will be worth reading. I wonder what Graham Greene[4] will say – he must say something: they had a curious love–hate relationship, as you can imagine. [...]

    Yours, with *much* love
        Isaiah

TO MCGEORGE BUNDY

    28 April 1966 [*carbon*]

                                                        Headington House
Dear Mac,
    [...] Your letter to Solly is a masterpiece, though I doubt whether it will make much difference. His motives still seem to me more obviously

1 In 1931 Oliver Franks married Barbara Mary Tanner (1907–87), 'a formidable Quaker wife made of very hard stone' (to Phil Graham, late January / early February 1948).
2 Easter fell on 10 April: Waugh died at his home, Combe Florey, near Taunton, Somerset.
3 Christopher Hugh Sykes (1907–86), writer and traveller; Deputy Controller, BBC Third Programme, 1948, Features Dept 1949–68; biographer of Adam von Trott, 1968 (345/1); authorised biographer of Waugh, his lifelong friend, 1975.
4 (Henry) Graham Greene (1904–91), later (1986) OM; novelist; like Waugh, a convert to Catholicism; they had been contemporaries at Oxford, but became friends only later in life. After Waugh's death Greene wrote: 'We were deeply divided politically, we were divided even in our conception of the same Church, and there were times when certain popular journalists tried to push us into what the Indonesians call a confrontation, but Evelyn Waugh had an unshakable loyalty to his friends, even if he may have detested their opinions and sometimes their actions. One could never depend on him for an easy approval or a warm weak complaisance, but when one felt the need of him he was always there' (*Times*, 15 April 1966, 15c).

irrational than most of our own reasons; I tried afterwards to summarise in my own mind what his official objections were – and beyond the proposition that science withers in Oxford – which in view of such characters as Florey and Hinshelwood,[1] Wilkinson[2] and Dorothy Hodgkin, is obvious nonsense – I could not think of a single concrete point, true or false. When he said that the late Lord Cherwell[3] understood Oxford and therefore never tried to create a scientific centre here, that was the very opposite of the truth: he found the Clarendon Laboratory a shambles, and left – hateful man as he was – a flourishing structure of first-class physicists behind him.[4] And so on. But he keeps shaking the confidence of poor Leonard W., who seeks reassurance from everyone: he now proposes to go to the Minister of Education, Tony Crosland. I was much relieved to see in one of your documents that he approved the scheme. [...]

I shall, of course, send you the details of what Oxford University has financially provided, as soon as I get the Registrar to set it forth in exact detail. There is at present a visitation of the University Grants Committee here, and they are all nervous and preoccupied. I do not believe we shall get anything from the UGC – we shall apply, of course, but once they hear of the sums involved, they will not wish to add to them. I do not exactly blame them, but it is a typically short-sighted policy all the same. Industry in Britain may do something towards special studentships; otherwise I cannot say that I hope for much more here. I wish I could. The contempt for learning of the British rich is old and deep and traditional by now; I am trying to persuade Maurice in his Romanes Lecture at Oxford, the central event of our oratorical year, to denounce this, and let fly, bar no holds, and let the lecture proceed in his postprandial style, rather than the unnaturally moderate style of his published works. I feel like nothing so much as a small European nation called upon to produce an account of its own resources and future by the stern George Kennan, and Will Clayton[5] in 1947, in Paris at the Marshall Plan Conference

---

1 Cyril Norman Hinshelwood (1897–1967), Kt 1948, OM 1960; Dr Lee's Professor of Chemistry, Oxford, 1937–64; shared Nobel Prize in Chemistry 1956; Senior Research Fellow, Imperial College, London, 1964–7.

2 Denys Haigh Wilkinson (b. 1922), later (1974) Kt; Professor of Nuclear Physics, Oxford, 1957–9, Professor of Experimental Physics 1959–76, head of Dept of Nuclear Physics 1962–76; Student, Christ Church, 1957–76.

3 Frederick Alexander Lindemann (1886–1957), 1st Baron Cherwell 1941, physicist, scientific adviser to the government; Dr Lee's Professor of Experimental Philosophy (i.e. Physics), Oxford, and Fellow of Wadham 1919–56; Reader in Experimental Philosophy and Student of Christ Church 1921–57; personal assistant to Winston Churchill from 1939. 'Long before [Lindemann] retired, the new Clarendon [Laboratory] which he had persuaded the university to build was one of the foremost physics departments in Britain' (Robert Blake, ODNB).

4 One such was Kurt Mendelssohn, a future fellow of the College that IB was trying to build: Mendelssohn left Germany soon after the Nazis came to power, and at Lindemann's invitation joined the Clarendon Laboratory, where he 'directed a thriving independent research group and contributed greatly to the establishment of the reputation of the Clarendon as an important centre of low-temperature and solid-state physics research' (Times, 19 September 1980, 17f).

5 William Lockhart Clayton (1880–1966), American cotton magnate and administrator; appointed

⟨⟨I was one of the agents between the two worlds, then, as now⟩⟩ And yet
a great deal of good flowed from that. This is what, it seems to me, you are
doing in relation to the danger of creeping paralysis which might otherwise
come upon us. Solly's position is rather like that of Molotov.[1] May he suffer
the same fate: after all, Molotov is alive and well, only not listened to much
these days. I may be wholly mistaken, but I have a feeling, based on nothing
much, that Solly's days with HMG are counted also. I sincerely hope that the
firmness and lucidity of that admirable document you addressed to Leonard
Wolfson will put some backbone where it is much needed.

I shall not bore you by again speaking of my admiration and my gratitude. ⟨Unlike Lord Moran, I shall consult you about my memoirs.⟩[2]

Yours ever,

Isaiah   [...]

TO LEONARD WOLFSON

29 April 1966 [*carbon*]

[Headington House]

Dear Leonard,

[...] I hope you did not mind my probably illegible, gloomy prognosti-
cations about the Minister of Education. I may be quite wrong about this
– I know Crosland, though not well, and have always respected his objectivity and integrity on public issues. He tends to be 'difficult' mostly on
private ones; so I think I may be quite wrong in suspecting him of undue
Oxfordophobia. I shall be much interested to know what he says. McGeorge
Bundy and Shepard Stone saw him, I think, when they were in London, a day
or two after our luncheon, but whether they mentioned these things to him,
I have no idea. I have had a most encouraging letter from Bundy, re-stating
all that he said to us at lunch, saying that he had authority to go up to £2

Assistant Secretary of Commerce by FDR during Second World War; Under-Secretary of State
for Economic Affairs 1946–7; worked for a time afterwards as unpaid adviser to General Marshall,
Secretary of State, and was one of the architects of the post-war Marshall Plan, and the General
Agreement on Tariffs and Trade (GATT).

1 Vyacheslav Mikhailovich Molotov (1890–1986), Soviet politician and diplomat, Prime Minister
1930–41, Foreign Minister 1939–49 (his signature appears on IB's diplomatic pass for entry into
the USSR in 1945), 1953–6; co-signatory of the August 1939 Nazi–Soviet pact; a staunch Stalinist,
he was demoted from office by Khrushchev, expelled from the Party in 1962, but readmitted in
1984; according to Churchill he had 'a smile like a Siberian winter' (Richard Owen, 'Unrepentant
Molotov Forgiven at 94', *Times*, 7 July 1984, 5f).

2 Charles McMoran Wilson (1882–1977), Kt 1938, 1st Baron Moran 1943, physician; Dean, St Mary's
Hospital Medical School, 1920–45. Moran was widely criticised for his memoir *Winston Churchill:
The Struggle for Survival, 1940–1965* (London, 1966), which chronicled his time as Churchill's personal physician; Moran argued, in his defence, that he had told Churchill of his intention to write
the book, but Randolph Churchill, in a letter to *The Times*, made plain that it had been published
against the wishes of the Churchill family (*Times*, 26 April 1966, 13d).

million without further reference to his Trustees, and expressing passionate confidence in the plan. He says that if the thing came off it would be the biggest grant the Ford Foundation has ever made towards anything in Europe; that this would naturally cause surprise and perhaps jealousy among other potential clients, but that he was prepared to face that. Conversely, if the thing did not come off, the offer would be withdrawn, and the funds not spent on anything in England, so that nobody was to think that if Wolfson College did not get it, somebody else in England would. All this he made clear to us at the lunch, I think. He makes his offer conditional upon my accepting the job, which of course touches and flatters me, but terrifies me too a little. Still, I am not going to look back now: I know that every time there is a hitch, or I make a mistake (and how can one avoid this? infallibility is not in our power) Solly will say 'I told you so'. This I cannot help and will not think of.

So on this note of high hope, I end.

Yours ever,

Isaiah

PS I enclose an interesting letter by Lord Robbins from *The Times* that you may not have noticed.[1] It is interesting because Robbins was accused by *The Times* of bias against Oxford and Cambridge in his famous report, and a desire to dilute standards by spreading the academic butter too thin among too many universities, etc. He is indeed a very public-spirited man – I know him well and admire him very much; I have worked with him on committees, really love him and respect him – but he does not let his democratic tendency – or the kind of feeling that even London has towards those proud towers of Oxford and Cambridge – run away with him. He himself [likes?] to say that in education peaks are inevitable, that talent attracts talent, there must be top institutions towards which the dimmer ones are bound to feel envy and resentment and hostility, and that this must not be taken into account in formulating policy. If even he says this, what real case is there for not wanting to help the best to remain so – to preserve standards without which there must be a general decline? Is this too subjective on my part? Do I fail to see some huge beam in my own eye? Possibly. I am anxious to explain that this scheme does not represent some sort of formal advance in my own life.

---

1 In its leader 'The Cost of a University' on 25 April 1966 *The Times* had charged Lord Robbins with advocating an 'equalitarian approach' to higher education that would prevent Britain from competing with the 'Harvards and Berkeleys'. In his reply Robbins quoted from his 1963 *Report on Higher Education* to show that he had been misrepresented: 'talent should attract talent [...]. Moreover, such concentrations are not only probable but also desirable.' Robbins opposed not academic elitism but rather the 'freezing' of institutions into established hierarchies; [...] there should be recognition and encouragement of excellence wherever it exists and wherever it appears'. 25 April 1966, 11b; 'The Cost of a University', letter, 26 April, 13e; op. cit. (167/3), chapter 2, 9, para. 37.

I shall, as you know, derive no income from it – I propose to take no salary, even though my successor will have to – and academically it does not represent a promotion for me. Why then do I believe in it? There is in it for me, after all, if not blood, certainly sweat and, I expect, plenty of tears. I do not think I deceive myself when I say that my only motive is that I think it a job very well worth doing for Oxford and for England, and that it is creditable to everybody concerned. I cannot deny that Bundy's extraordinary enthusiasm – which I had not anticipated, for I had no idea what had transpired between him and his Trustees – was immensely encouraging, and the turning-point in Ford policy and in the destinies of Oxford – but I really must not go on. You tell me I am a salesman. Believe me, I have never promoted any cause in the past, and do not, to tell you the truth, ever wish to have to do it again. In this case I do feel committed. [...]

TO MCGEORGE BUNDY

9 May 1966 [carbon]

[Headington House]

Dear Mac,

[...] On the 17th, Sir Isaac and his son will come here to case the joint, and will meet, at their request, Oliver Franks, the Vice-Chancellor and Florey. [...]

I get the impression from Leonard Wolfson, whom you really have fired and stiffened, that he wants satisfaction on two points, one of which is, I think, impossible, and the other tricky:

1. As he mentioned at our lunch, he wants the University to guarantee that it will itself continue an adequate endowment in the event of inflation or some other cause undermining your contribution. Quite apart from the unlikelihood of such a contingency, in any conditions in which Western institutions in general could go on, the University cannot do this. A College is a College; if it becomes poor, it contracts its activities. All a college can do is live within its means, and this of course, Wolfson College can promise. But this is not a matter for you to think about, fortunately, and the Wolfsons will have to have that out with the Oxford authorities.

2. They do not want adverse comments or publicity from Government or educational circles. Consequently, although this was communicated to me in hideous secrecy, to which I must also commit you, General Redman went to see Crosland. I have a feeling that this was in some way stimulated by Solly, or at least apprehension about him, who in his turn must have primed Crosland or someone in his department. All these suspicions may be unfounded, but they seem highly plausible to me. Crosland, without positively condemning the scheme, said, as I would have expected, that the poor were more deserving than the rich, that Manchester Institute of Technology and Strathclyde University deserved bounty more than Oxford and Cambridge,

that it was a pity that the great American foundations knew about Oxford and Cambridge characters like Bill Deakin, myself etc., and were inclined to favour them at the expense of the deserving poor in the underprivileged academic world, etc., but of course it was for the Wolfson Trustees to decide what they wished to do, etc. He said that he had had a long conversation with yourself on the subject, and these apparently were the fruits of his reflections about that.

I have, of course, no idea how your conversation with him went, but I got the impression from your communication to the Wolfsons that he seemed to you to approve of your and, by implication, the Wolfsons' bounty. Redman said in his secret memorandum to the Wolfsons that he had argued with Crosland, and in the end got him to retreat. I am not at all surprised that he should take this line: as a socialist Minister of Education he is no doubt committed to an egalitarian line – fatal as this is in all intellectual enterprises – and he referred Redman to the UGC. I have no notion what Wolfenden[1] will say, but I should like to find some means of conveying to him that if the Wolfsons do not do this at Oxford, it is highly unlikely that they will support Strathclyde: it is far more likely to go to a concert hall in Glasgow, Israel etc. At any rate I see that the Wolfsons would like public approval from some respected quarter: they need not doubt about reactions from Oxford; Franks, Florey and five or six other celebrated and trusted figures will certainly not be reluctant to voice their approval: but if they want the Government to do it, they may run into some difficulty: I shall do my best to help them, but how far that will go I do not know. My impression of Crosland – whom I do not know well, but do know – is that in matters affecting Oxford he does suffer from a good deal of inverted snobbery, and is anxious to appear not to favour it in any way: he does not suffer from a positive antipathy to it, like Crossman, but there is a touch of love–hate all the same, which can work out very oddly, and is certainly not the kind of rational line that, say, Gaitskell, would have taken. I think the Prime Minister would be much saner and more constructive in all this, unless of course our old friend, whose surname so deeply belies his nature,[2] gets at him too. So the duel is on, and I feel faced with Professor Moriarty.

I dine with Victor Rothschild[3] and Mr Loudon[4] on the 16th. I hate being

1 John Frederick Wolfenden (1906–85), Kt 1956, later (1974) life peer; Vice-Chancellor, Reading, 1950–63; Chairman, UGC, 1963–8; chairman of the committee that recommended, in the eponymous 'Wolfenden Report' of 1957, the decriminalisation of consensual private adult male homosexual acts; Director and Principal Librarian, British Museum, 1969–73.
2 'Zucker' is German for 'sugar'.
3 (Nathaniel Mayer) Victor Rothschild (1910–90), 3rd Baron Rothschild 1937, later (1975) GBE, zoologist; Assistant Director of Research, Dept of Zoology, Cambridge, 1950–70; Director General and First Permanent Under-Secretary, Central Policy Review Staff, Cabinet Office, 1971–4.
4 John Hugo Loudon (1905–96), Hon. KBE 1960, oil executive; President, Royal Dutch Petroleum Co., 1952–65, Chairman 1965–76; Trustee, Ford Foundation, 1966–75.

driven to the position occupied by Trevor-Roper (and indeed Robbins too, despite his alleged pro-redbrick and anti-Oxford/Cambridge sentiments – he is nevertheless a perfectly rational man), of supposing that socialist governments are moved by envy, malice, spite etc. and all manner of uncharitableness. I can think of a great many socialists who are not: but you know the characters involved as well as I, and the present conjuncture is not all that simple. That is what I meant by saying that Wolfson's second demand is somewhat tricky, i.e. the desire to extract public support from government circles. It seems mad that any government in financial difficulties should wish to look a gift horse in the mouth. If they merely looked it would not matter much; perhaps I am going through a brief phase of groundless apprehension affected by Leonard W's own constitutional nervousness. Of course there may be critical remarks in the *New Statesman*, and the like. That would not matter in the least. I think I must simply try and pump some courage into the Wolfsons, and tell them that none of these things will mean anything in five years' time.

By the time the lunch on the 17th occurs, the Franks Report will be out, and I should think a full blaze of publicity will surround it. My poor college will be attacked, and I shall be avoiding journalists anxious to extract a statement twistable into a jolly headline. Do not believe a word you see in the British press! That is the only advice I can give you. *The Times* is less bad than the others, but now that it has modernised itself, it too is on the way of the NYT.

Yours ever,

Isaiah

TO OLIVER FRANKS

9 May 1966 [*carbon*]

[Headington House]

Dear Oliver,

Here is another secret document. As you will perceive, my fears about the Minister's reactions were well founded. What he said to Redman is very different, evidently, from what he must have said to Bundy. I do not quite know why the Wolfsons thought it necessary to go to him, but I suppose Solly put them up to it, and him up to them. At any rate, this is the way my suspicious mind sees it. I see that Crosland would have to take the line that the poor deserve the money more than the rich, but the remarks about the kind of persons Bundy would be likely to know, etc., argue a rather more personal strain of feeling, which does not seem to me to do him much moral credit. I do not think there is anything I can do about that, and I do not propose to try. But I see that [the] Wolfsons need reassuring: your views will surely do that, and the fact that, if need arises, and if their announcement is made at some period when your own report is not being hotly debated, you would perhaps be prepared to defend their and Ford's decision. And I should think that would be true of Florey, and other scientists in Oxford. But I feel that they need private or public reassurance, or both, from eminent persons outside Oxford: I doubt if any socialists will do this. Whatever their real views, the fashion is for egalitarianism, even in intellectual matters – where it can well be fatal – and in this respect we are rather like Covent Garden, but, if anything, more of an Aunt Sally, inasmuch as we are not socially quite so 'national'. [...]

Yours,

[Isaiah]

TO MCGEORGE BUNDY

18 May 1966 [*carbon*]

[Headington House]

Dear Mac,

[...] Crosland was, I think, a trifle irritated at favour shown to Oxford, perhaps to even so crusty a representative of old college tradition – mahogany and silver, and nuts and wine – as myself. But he consulted a Labour Alderman on the City Council here, called Pickstock,[1] who I think is his adviser on such matters, as he is an official of the Delegacy of Extra-Mural Studies, and is presumably free from any suspicion of Conservative bias, or corruption by college life, a crumbling old establishment. Pickstock, who knew nothing at all about this – had never heard of any such plan – thought it a splendid idea for such a college to be established at Oxford; and then wrote to Crosland after their conversation, saying that of course if the college were to be a seat of privilege and wealth like All Souls, he would not be in favour of it, but from what he understood of the scheme, it was in line with the most ardent socialist aspirations. I do not say that, by the time he came to write this letter, he had not had a conversation with Mr Frank Jessup, his chief, who happens to be a Fellow of Iffley College – all this, however, was done without any knowledge on my part. I have never met Alderman Pickstock, but I think he is a very sound man. The fact that he is going to be Mayor of Oxford in a year or two will do no harm either from the point of view of future conflicts about building problems, etc., which are bound to arise (if all goes well).[2] The problem now is how to effect [sc. communicate] the content

1 Francis (Frank) Vincent Pickstock (1910–85), miner's son and railwayman; won a WEA scholarship to Queen's, where he read PPE 1934–7; after demobilisation (as a Major), joined Oxford's Extramural Delegacy, retiring 1978; Fellow of Linacre 1966–78; Lord Mayor of Oxford 1967–8.

2 Pickstock was 'a great wrangler and schemer in these complicated local dealings between the grand incompatibilities of Oxford University, the extramural board, local education authorities, the WEA, the trades unions, and goodness knows what else': Fred Inglis, *Raymond Williams* (London 1995), 133.

of the Crosland–Pickstock correspondence to the Wolfsons. This, I suppose, I ought to make it my business to accomplish. So much on the local front.

Yesterday we went to dine with Victor and Tess Rothschild and met the Loudons – I have no idea what he thought. He is such a courteous, elegant, superior man, a friend of St Antony's with Gene Black[1] and Bill Harcourt,[2] I imagine – but we had a brief, but as far as I was concerned very satisfactory, conversation, and I promised to keep him abreast of developments [...]. His main point was the undesirability of an excessive brain-drain to the US and the consequent weakening of Europe, and he seems to be quite right about that.

No sooner did we depart from them than after a brief night's rest, I rushed down to Oxford to give lunch to Sir Isaac and Leonard Wolfson, accompanied by General Redman – I invited to meet them Oliver, Florey and Kenneth Wheare. Oliver was very fine. He explained that the Franks Report emphasised that the future of Oxford lay with (a) colleges; (b) science; (c) graduates; and that the creation of this college was wholly in line with all that he and his colleagues thought, and that the University of Oxford was more likely to adopt most of its [the Report's] recommendations (which is true). [...]

I do not know how much of all this was taken in by Isaac Wolfson, but Leonard certainly took it in. Isaac was exceedingly amusing, offered Franks all kinds of jobs in his firm, and enjoyed himself enormously. We all then went to see the site, which fascinated Wolfson senior, they had tea with Bullock, and drove off to London in high fettle. [...]

You will be having some visitors in New York shortly. [...] Solly is coming, and will certainly seek to see you. I suppose indirectly this is my fault, that if I had not started the whole business ... He probably feels that he made a fool of himself in front of you, and will seek to obliterate this impression. But I cannot help thinking of him as Professor Moriarty, bitterly determined to do his worst. He is in a highly irritated and uncertain mood, because of his own condition of suspended bureaucratic animation in the government set-up.

What is more important is that Sir Isaac Wolfson will be staying at the Pierre Hotel in New York, from 27 May till (I think) 7 June, and wishes 'to take you to dinner'. You must surely see him: you will have a hilarious time: the mixture of Scot and Jew, the strenuous Calvinist Jewish trader, is in a kind of way irresistible. I really think he wants this College now: he has a reputation of promising things to people, and then suddenly slipping the carpet out from under them, saying that Leonard, or the trustees, or somebody is to

---

1 Eugene Robert ('Gene') Black, Sr (1898–1992), banker; President of the World Bank 1949–63; Chairman of the Brookings Institution 1962–8.
2 William Edward Harcourt (1908–79), 2nd Viscount Harcourt 1922, KCMG 1957; Managing Director, Morgan Grenfell & Co. Ltd, 1931–68, Chairman 1968–73; Honorary Fellow, St Antony's, 1963–79.

blame for the last-minute debacle. But in this case it might just not happen, because of the overwhelming attraction of association with the greatest foundation in the world.

[…] Do send a message to Sir Isaac at the Pierre, which is absolutely the right setting for him. The exchanges between him and the Oxford dons were something I shall never forget. On the whole, both sides emerged with credit.

Yours,
Isaiah

TO BERNARD WILLIAMS

21 May 1966 [*manuscript*]

All Souls

Dear Bernard

A letter from the M[inister] of E[ducation] & Sc[ience] has been received by the Wolfsons withdrawing his reservations unreservedly: if this is your or Shirley's[1] doing – & even if it isn't & you've said nothing – thank you *very* much. A bientot.

yrs
Isaiah

TO BERNARD WILLIAMS

13 June 1966

Headington House

Dear Bernard,

Just to continue the saga – forgive me – but I feel you ought to know the whole story.

Last Tuesday, the Minister of Education and Science called on me, and he behaved with the greatest sweetness and enlightenment. He began by saying that he wished to express his regret at having received General Redman's suggestions so coolly – it was an emotional reaction, which I would well understand, in favour of egalitarianism – but on reflection it was clear that it would be a good thing for the future, not only of Oxford, but of graduate studies and science in England, in general, and he had consequently written the letter he had written. We then had a general discussion of the subject, in which he appeared most ready and willing to accept what I cannot help feeling is the proper, enlightened view.

1 Shirley Vivian Teresa Williams (b. 1930) née Brittain, later (1993) life peer, Labour politician; PPS, Minister of Health, 1964–6; Parliamentary Secretary, Ministry of Labour, 1966–7; Minister of State, Education and Science, 1967–9, Home Office 1969–70; Shadow Cabinet 1970–4; Secretary of State for Prices and Consumer Protection 1974–6; later (1981) one of the founders of the Social Democratic Party (SDP); first wife of Bernard Williams (1955; divorced 1974).

I could not resist vaguely asking him about the AUT[1] – he said he did not remember precisely what he had said, but perhaps he had spoken of the capriciousness of donors, perhaps it would be a good thing if the publicity that attended a grant of this vast sum of money to Oxford – if it came off – would draw attention to the irregular and unsystematic way in which such gifts were given. I begged him not to use this particular gift as the basis of underlining the unaccountability of private donations, without at least expressing approval for this particular instance of such unsystematic generosity. This he promised to do, and he said that if the publicity we got was too unfavourable, he was prepared to make a statement saying that he at any rate had been consulted, and approved. I could not really ask for more. It is only fair – as the expression goes – to tell you that the story so far ends happily, and that the inconsistency of his public utterances and private assurances must be ascribed to some genuine deep division in his own mind, which he has, to a degree, at any rate, allowed rational considerations to overcome. Anyway, I thought he behaved very well indeed, and my faith in ultimate human reason – never very strong – was correspondingly reinforced. That you will be pleased to hear about all this I have no doubt.

Thank you very much for the offprints. I shall scan them very closely.

Yours,

Isaiah

TO LEONARD WOLFSON

18 June 1966 [carbon]

All Souls

Dear Leonard,

I should like to have a talk with you if I may before the fateful day. I shall telephone your secretary on Monday morning, when I shall be in London, to see whether you could see me: I feel that I ought to make my position clear to you. My chief fear is under-endowment, the dangers of which Cockcroft impressed very wisely and forcibly on me. If the College is to be called after your name the prospect of ever raising money for endowment from other sources is clearly not great; nor, as you know, am I prepared to go round hat in hand as other colleges are at present obliged to do; nor would you like it

---

1 Soon after Crosland had withdrawn his opposition to the Wolfson plan, in late May 1966, IB was disconcerted to hear that he had alluded to it in strongly negative terms at a meeting of the Association of University Teachers (AUT). According to Michael Brock, who had been present, Crosland had referred obliquely to a large impending grant 'from private sources to a well-known British university', and had lamented that such largesse only entrenched the undesirable inequality that was inherent in the system: 'as one thinks of these things one is bound to wonder whether this can be at all good for higher education in this country – whether such gifts are socially desirable, or intellectually useful' (IB to Bernard Williams, 31 May 1966, summarising Brock's account).

if I did. Anyway, I should like to have half an hour's talk with you again and/
or Sir Isaac, if that is desirable. It would not be right for me to offer to do
something in conditions that made it impracticable, but do not think that
I do not understand your difficulties. [...]

Yours ever,

[Isaiah]

TO NOEL ANNAN

22 June 1966

Headington House

Dear Noel,

[...] I do not know what the Wolfsons will do – I fear that they will either
put the matter off and leave Ford in the lurch or offer me just not enough
money to cover the endowment, something awful, then I shan't know
what to do and what to say. If they say would you rather have a million and
a quarter or nothing, I shall be forced to say nothing, since I cannot take
this College on with an insufficient endowment and go through torments of
a Bill Deakin-like kind, but then the University of Oxford will rend me limb
from limb. [...]

Yours,

Isaiah

⟨P. S. Stop press: the Wolfsons *have* given 1½ million – at present – hideous
secret – & wd like to say somewhere that they have consulted eminent
persons – Franks, Robbins, Florey, yourself etc: Balogh carried a v. private
message of approval from the All Highest. Do you *mind* being mentioned:
if so, tell Gen. Redman. Myself I feel dazed weak, unreal & terrified of the
Press Conference. God! *why* did I begin.⟩

TO JOSEPH ALSOP

24 June 1966 [*manuscript*]

Headington House

Dear Joe

It – the entire operation – Iffley–Wolfson – is about to be completed: I feel
dazed & terrified & wish I had not started it all, or indeed existed at all: after
the Editor of the Times[1] (to whom I said something of this) told me "to
embark on a thing of this kind at your age is *very* gallant!" I feel 97 yrs old
& defeatist. Still, fear of failure is a terrible incentive & *may* carry Aline &
me through. And of course I am madly exhilarated too: and wish to put it

1 William Haley.

on record that no man ever had a nicer, nobler, more loyal or more effective friend than yourself. You are a very *good* man. (Remember that.) Without you *nothing* wd have moved: Wolfsons made it plain that *they* would not have moved without Ford: & Mac wd scarcely have *heard* of it – I shd *never* have had the temerity to approach him – you well know that – without your inter-mediation: never. Your task is not done: you must advise me about architects: policy: everything: when we meet (when? in Sept–Oct in U.S. – or before?) I shall tell you about the fantastic diplomacy (to give it a polite title) that preceded it all here: the relations with Ministers: Educational Authorities: opponents: millionaires: etc. But it is *your* triumph & probably my funeral.

Isaiah

PRESIDING

The genesis of Wolfson College

1966–1975

The best of his essays deserve to last. [...] But it could well be that his longest lasting achievement will prove to be something quite different, namely Wolfson College [...]. Throughout as many future centuries as it lasts, everyone who studies there, or teaches there, or carries out research there, or writes books there, will owe a personal debt to Isaiah.

Bryan Magee, 'Isaiah As I Knew Him', in BI*₁₉₁₄*

Postgraduate studies must have parity of esteem with undergraduate studies: to give reality to this view involves large changes. But though the University should take the lead in these, college co-operation will be essential since, in the collegiate university, those who are not fully brought into college life inevitably suffer.

The Franks Report[1]

[A]cademic administration obviously taxes not only energy and will but imagination and creative capacity to a high degree – those who think it merely a matter of concentration and relatively easy direction of energy [that] could just as well be used for higher purposes are indulging in a form of sour grapes and sneering at what they cannot do. This is a well-known academic vice.

IB to Norman Chester, Warden of Nuffield, 13 July 1966

---

1 University of Oxford, *Report of Commission of Inquiry* (Oxford, 1966), i 125 (para. 280).

> For which of you, intending to build a tower, sitteth not down first, and
> counteth the cost, whether he have sufficient to finish it? Lest haply, after
> he hath laid the foundation, and is not able to finish it, all that behold it
> begin to mock him, saying, 'This man began to build, and was not able
> to finish.'
>
> Luke 14:28–30

> Who should build Wolfson College in Linton Road, Oxford? Is there
> a single British architect who could be regarded as a genuine master?
> What American architects (among whom there are unquestionably
> masters) would you fancy? Or a Finn? Or a Dutchman, or a Japanese? We
> have about ten days in which to decide, and then the avalanche will come
> down; the reviews will denounce us, either for doing something obvious,
> or for not doing it.
>
> IB to Gorley Putt, 26 May 1967

Once the Wolfson Foundation had decided to match the Ford Foundation's
grant, IB's plans for establishing a large graduate college in Oxford advanced
rapidly. On 27 June 1966 the University's Hebdomadal Council declared
its support, and on 26 July a specially convened meeting of Congregation
promulgated a five-part decree that put all the major elements in place.
The University accepted with 'deep and warm gratitude' the two grants
in question;[1] with the approval of Ford, it named the new college after its
British benefactor; it incorporated Iffley College, which now ceased to exist,
in Wolfson College; it allocated to the new college, subject to planning permission, the beautiful nine-acre north Oxford site of Cherwell, the former
home of the Haldane family; and it appointed IB President. It was entirely
apt that Sir Arthur Norrington, who had done so much to lay the ground-
work for the expansion of graduate studies in Oxford, should introduce the
decree in Congregation, and in so doing he praised IB's special contribution:
'It is due to his enthusiasm and confidence, and to his very high reputation
here and in the United States, that these grants have been offered to us.'[2]

IB was determined to accept the headship of Wolfson only after the grants
involved had definitely been offered and accepted. This was a strategic move,
designed to give him more leverage over the grant-giving bodies – in particular the Wolfson Foundation, which he felt was the more likely of the two to
set conditions on its gift. From the very beginning he sought to keep both the
University and the donors at arm's length, and he strengthened the College's

1 The Wolfson Foundation promised £1½ million to meet the costs of building, furnishing and
  equipping the college; and the Ford Foundation $4½ million (£1.62 million) for its endowment
  – that is, the cost of staff salaries, fellowships, common table etc.
2 'Speech for Congregation on 26 July 1966 (Wolfson College Decree)', fo. 1 (OUA UR 6/WF/2,
  file 1), quoted in 'Wolfson College Begins with £3m. Benefaction', *Times*, 27 July 1966, 12f.

independence during its formative years by creating a Trust to manage its affairs. It was initially chaired by the Nobelist pioneer of penicillin, Sir Howard Florey. 'Since its whole point is to prevent too much interference by University committees,' IB observed, 'they are naturally suspicious of it.' But it was designed also to keep the Wolfsons in check, and IB welcomed Leonard Wolfson's participation in it precisely because he was likely to be 'much tamer inside than outside such a body'. Leonard of course knew that he was a captive member, and to some extent enjoyed the dynamics of the situation: IB wrote to him in June 1967 about the need to ratify the College's choice of architect: 'as for the Trust, we are in your hands (don't smile – it is true)'.[1]

For practically a decade, until his retirement in March 1975, IB involved himself in every detail of the new College. He worked conscientiously to see through what he had begun, but in September 1966, shortly after taking up the reins, decamped to New York to spend a sabbatical as visiting professor at CUNY. Just before leaving, he wrote to his Oxford colleague John Simmons: 'My first act on assuming office is to run away from it. You will, I fear, regard this as typical.' Doubtless there were those who did. When the news about Wolfson had first been leaked to the press a short note appeared in the *Observer* to the effect that, in agreeing to be head of Iffley, IB had 'laid down stringent conditions about how much time off he must have for his own work'.[2] IB did indeed negotiate with the Iffley fellows the regular sabbaticals that were essential to his studies, but it was an arrangement that they welcomed, not least because it gave them more involvement in the running of the College; and, crucially, it also relieved them of the responsibility of meeting a principal's wages – while at Wolfson IB waived his salary, taking only modest expenses for travel and entertainment.

The main reason why he could contemplate lengthy periods away from Wolfson was the quality of his deputy. Writing about progress on 28 July 1966, two days after the College officially came into being, the University Registrar noted: 'But perhaps the most encouraging development is that Berlin has secured as Bursar of Wolfson College Mr Michael Brock, who is the Senior Tutor of Corpus Christi and incidentally a member of the Hebdomadal Council. Brock is a man of great experience in academic matters, very energetic, and possessed of enormous common sense.'[3] His knowledge of the University and the City Council proved invaluable, and he was immensely popular both with the fellows and with the graduate students who later joined them. The creation of Wolfson thus became a collaborative effort between IB, Michael Brock, the fellowship and (from 1968) the first students, and an intense camaraderie developed between them, fostered

1 To Leonard Wolfson, 5 June 1967.
2 *Observer*, 12 December 1965, 40c.
3 Folliott Sandford to Harold Redman, 28 July 1966.

by the cramped conditions in which they lived while waiting for their new college to be built.

The College's first temporary home was an attractive mid-nineteenth-century Italianate house, 15 Banbury Road, not far from the Cherwell site, but in June 1968 Wolfson moved up the road to the roomier surroundings of nos 47 (offices) and 60 (common room facilities). By then the fellowship had grown from 36 to 54, and the first graduate students – 24 in all – arrived that autumn. The College's determination to admit graduates early, and thus fulfil its principal *raison d'être*, placed it under enormous pressure, particularly when the opening of the new buildings was delayed. It was hoped that these would be ready to move into in the autumn of 1973, but that summer Michael Brock wrote: 'Our situation for next term is pretty grim. We are laying our hands on all the temporary accommodation we can find so as to house our freshmen from overseas, and their families.'[1] The causes of the multiple delays were manifold – shortages of materials, of labour, bad weather, problems with the design (notably the flat roofs) – and in October 1973 IB wrote to McGeorge Bundy: 'As a College, we are doing quite well – morale is high, as it always is in England under conditions of enforced collective suffering – our finest hour is going on a little too long, but it still remains moderately fine.'[2]

Wolfson was constructed during a period of deteriorating industrial relations and rising inflation, and the final sum paid by the Wolfson Foundation for its building was in the region of £2.6 million, a 70 per cent increase on the sum originally promised. Had these facts been anticipated in 1966 the venture might not have begun. But Leonard Wolfson did not flinch, and proved the 'very faithful friend' that IB needed. He met the increased costs, and insisted on not cutting the quality of materials, in the spite of the reservations of one of his Trustees, IB's Moriarty, Solly Zuckerman.

The finished building was adjudged an architectural and aesthetic success. In their search for the right architect, representatives of the College building committee covered almost four thousand miles in Britain alone, and went as far afield as Helsinki and New York, looking at finished buildings, before alighting on the British firm of Powell & Moya. According to the architectural authority Nikolaus Pevsner,[3] Powell & Moya were 'first class architects, the best of all academic architects, with suitable buildings to their credit',[4] but apparently to be discounted for this very reason – an example of the strange logic that seemed to IB to rule the field. Construction began at the Cherwell site in 1969, and the buildings were officially opened by Oxford's Chancellor,

---

1 Michael Brock to Leonard Wolfson, 25 July 1973.
2 Letter of 26 October 1973.
3 Nikolaus Bernhard Leon Pevsner (1902–83), later (1969) Kt; German-born architectural historian, and authoritative editor of the multi-volume county-based *The Buildings of England* (1951–74); taught at Birkbeck College, London, 1942–69.
4 Wolfson College Archives, CM.59.67: 'The Search for an Architect'.

Harold Macmillan, on 12 November 1974. As befitted IB's conception of the College, they combined the traditional with the innovatory: there were three quadrangles – the typical feature of an undergraduate college – but also 20 family houses with playing areas for children, and a crèche donated by Aline Berlin. No other Oxford college of this era catered for families in this way. Other notable departures from the norm were the single common room with no high table – a reflection of the egalitarian ethos of the fellowship – and student representation on the governing body and College committees.

Not long after the buildings were inhabited IB retired. It was always his intention to leave once the College was properly launched, and he left a thriving institution that fulfilled many of his hopes for it. In the academic year of his departure there were 294 graduate students, 180 (61 per cent) in the sciences, 73 in the arts (25 per cent), 41 in the social sciences (14 per cent). The ratio of women to men was almost 30:70, low by the standards of a later era, but remarkable in a period when all the undergraduate colleges (and, of course, All Souls) were single-sex.[1] Wolfson was the largest graduate institution in Oxford, and, speaking shortly before the announcement of the Wolfson–Ford funding, in June 1966, Alan Bullock had commented: 'Coming so soon after the Franks Report, this is a great vote of confidence in Oxford. The Franks Report strongly urged Oxford to develop graduate studies, and Wolfson College will be a powerful addition to Oxford's strength on exactly the right side. I know of no one else who could have launched so bold a project with a greater chance of success than Sir Isaiah.'[2]

IB's achievement in bringing together major British and American funding was indeed remarkable, and Wolfson was revolutionary in execution, as in conception. By 1966 the need for an increase in graduate studies in Oxford, particularly in the sciences, was widely recognised. And yet very few, Franks included, could explain exactly how this increase was to be effected. Franks urged that 'within a reasonable time, the graduate colleges should each have not fewer than 100 postgraduate students',[3] while the new foundations of Iffley and St Cross were to make 'major provision for postgraduates'.[4] But neither college was given the site, or the resources, to make this happen, while the overall increases that Franks desiderated were to be realised through 'the collective wisdom of the colleges' – an optimistic prescription, given that it was a failure of collective wisdom that had necessitated his Commission in the first place.

Money was obviously crucial, but not the only factor in solving the problem. It was also a question of ambition and outlook. Michael Brock

---

1 Hebdomadal Council, 'Annual Report of the Trustees of Wolfson College, 1 October 1974 [to] 30 September 1975'. OUA, HC 1/1/282, 325.
2 'New Graduate College to be Endowed at Oxford', *Times*, 27 June 1966, 12e–f.
3 Franks Report (293/1), i 125, para. 280.
4 ibid., para. 277.

remembered this era as one in which the prevailing ethos in Oxford, as far as reform was concerned, was distinctly unambitious: even the reformers themselves thought in terms of what was the least that could be done – to salve consciences, to stem the flow of external criticism. But IB asked what was the most that could be done, and then, with the help of his many friends, he set about trying to do it. In this way he breathed new life into collegiate Oxford – one of the central goals of the Franks Report. In creating a different model – that of the large, multi-disciplined, co-educational, family-oriented graduate college – IB further challenged the older colleges to change their attitudes to postgraduate studies, building on the pioneering achievements of Nuffield and St Antony's. Henceforth the undergraduate colleges would have to take greater care in their provision for graduates, or else lose their best students to a graduate college when they elected to pursue a higher degree. It had taken IB – something of an outsider – to break the mould; and yet, when his work at Wolfson was done, he returned to what was still, despite everything, his spiritual home – All Souls, almost the antithesis of what he had created.

*

TO KENNETH WHEARE

26 June 1966 [*typed transcript of missing manuscript original*]

Rewley House, Wellington Square, Oxford

Dear Ken,

Forgive my hideously late telephone call to-night – product of a meeting with (still) Iffley College. It seems to me of the *first* importance that in answering the Wolfsons, the University say that while it accepts the 'active participation' of the Trust[1] in 'the design, construction etc. of the building of the college' the final decision in *all* matters concerned with the college rests with Oxford (University, Trust, college or whoever). I cannot exaggerate – I really cannot – what W. is capable of, to judge by (others') past experience: this must be in black and white, capable of unambiguous interpretation by a lawyer: otherwise they could reject our architect, stop the flow of funds, litigate etc. – Isaac is very, very tough. Of importance, but not the first, is [...] the idea of the Trust: it will help the college in its first fumbling steps [...]

Of less importance: that it is Iffley that invited the University to call us Wolfson (not the Wolfsons: the college feel strongly about this). Of no importance, that I be elevated to the Presidency: (not Mastership, Principality etc.). Have a nice meeting.

Yours,

Isaiah   [...]

---

1 sc. the Trustees of the Wolfson Foundation.

TO CHRISTOPHER HILL[1]

4 July 1966 [*carbon*]

[Headington House]

Dear Christopher,

Condolences are more in order, alas. But thank you very much all the same. Expropriation? With an income smaller than that of Brasenose and 350 graduates and such to feed? For shame! Unworthy spirit of Newcastle! From you, a leader of the Brahmins, to me, one of the leaders of the untouchables! We shall show the ancient citadels of privilege yet where true equality lies.

Yours ever,

[Isaiah]

TO SHEPARD STONE

13 July 1966 [drafted 4 July, *carbon*]

[Headington House]

Dear Shep,

[...] Mac dominated the press conferences to everyone's advantage. I merely went off to a little private torture by various radio experts and had the dubious pleasure of hearing my own incoherent words at 7.15 a.m. after a sleepless night in the Albany.[2] On the whole it must be said that the Press has let us off very lightly. I think Sir Isaac feels he has not been patted on the back quite enough – not really at all – but on the other hand, there has been no criticism worth thinking of. [...]

At present I am anxiously searching for a kind of general manager of the College[3] and am battling against the University's desire to increase the numbers of my flock in undesirable ways.[4] I shall threaten them, if need be, with resignation: I resign, there is a huge scandal, the money flows back, the Arabian Nights story takes place – the Caliph is turned into a charcoal-burner again and sits among his ashes, and the Ford and Wolfson Foundations are a distant dream. I somehow do not think that this will in fact occur, but it would be useful to hold up this horrid prospect before some of my col-

---

1 (John Edward) Christopher Hill (1912–2003), historian; Fellow and Tutor, Balliol, 1938–65; Master 1965–78; former Communist Party member, and undogmatic Marxist historian of 17th-century England.

2 18th-century residential complex between Piccadilly and Burlington Gardens, London W1, one of the most fashionable of addresses in the capital. The Berlins lived there from 1963, successively in sets A10, D6 and K2.

3 The letter is dated on the day that Michael Brock was appointed to this post, but an earlier draft survives, dated 4 July, which explains the apparent anachronism here. Brock took up office in January 1967 but was 'closely associated with all developments' from this date onwards (Folliott Sandford to Harold Redman, 28 July 1966).

4 Wolfson was obliged to admit fellows under the University's 'entitlement' statute (245/2); IB fought a long running battle to keep the size of the fellowship within reasonable limits.

leagues, who do not perceive the difference between a graduate college and a waste paper basket. But the general manager is not easy to find: dons are unpractical, retiring civil servants are heavy and pompous; college-builders are difficult to find. [...]

Yours,

[Isaiah]

TO SYLVESTER GATES *219/3*

25 July 1966

[As from Headington House]

Dear Sylvester,

[...] I am dictating this from Italy, whither I have escaped from the extraordinary ups and downs of my activities in the last month. When we meet, I should like to tell you about the plots and counter-plots with which the whole story is interspersed. I am now thoroughly frightened [...].

Now: John[1] will have told you of my plans – at least of the request which I want to address to you. You will ask, what is this Trust? First, the motive for it: it seems to me that I have to contend with two major organisations, both of which can be difficult to deal with: the University; and the Wolfsons. There are others, e.g. the Ministry, the City Council and other bodies, which have to give building permission, etc. And, of course, the Ford Foundation, which, but for whose immediate favour, the whole thing would not have got off to a start at all. However, Bundy and Ford are honourable and gentlemanly and do not constitute a problem themselves. The Wolfsons, of course, do. Not that they have so far expressed any sinister or embarrassing intentions, but given the personalities of Sir Isaac and his son Leonard, and the fact that they wish to be 'actively associated' in the physical design, building and equipment of the College towards which they have contributed, or will contribute, £1½ million – the relation with them is bound to be somewhat delicate. They have no particular plans, they do not want to force an architect upon us (Lasdun[2] is the one they in fact use), but they would like the thing to be built fairly quickly to the greater glory of Sir Isaac, who reaches his seventieth birthday next year, and would like to lay a foundation stone more or less then. Leonard, who is a neurotic and impatient young man – far less popular than his ebullient and far tougher father – is not altogether easy to deal with:

1 John Galway Foster (1904–82), KBE 1964, lawyer; Fellow of All Souls 1924–82; Conservative MP for Northwich, Cheshire, 1945–74; Trustee, Wolfson College, 1967–81, Honorary Fellow 1981: 'very good with the Wolfsons; he has a certain rude candour which breaks through a good deal of inevitable pompousness, and on public issues, although crude and naive, is very honest and public-spirited. The kind of lawyer that may be needed' (from an omitted part of this letter).

2 Denys Louis Lasdun (1914–2001), later (1976) Kt, British architect, widely employed after the war; his works include the not universally admired National Theatre on the South Bank of the Thames in London (1967–76).

I rather like him – most people do not. He is sharp, shrewd, clever, neurotic, crushed by an impossible father, but ultimately well-intentioned. His sense of inferiority comes not so much from a complex but from genuine lack of education, and from a 'mean appearance', as Joshua Reynolds explained in the case of someone's representation of [King] David,[1] and altogether I can tell you a good deal about him that would be of a certain interest. Anyway, we have to deal with him – the Wolfsons of course offer their costing experts, and probably experts in obtaining materials, building etc. etc., and, naturally, interior furnishings, etc., which might be of considerable genuine use. At the same time, one must not get into their hands. That is one factor.

The University offers a quite different set of dangers – apart from general pedantry, inefficiency, complexity, and a certain amount of natural envy and jealousy, which all universities breed in different degrees, there is the huge and peculiar problem of this particular College, which was originally founded to be a refuge for non-fellows, and constitutionally must still continue to be so, although I have made it as clear as I could that if they insist on their full pound of flesh – i.e. on stuffing the College with various stray dogs, of whom I have accepted 36 – not all of whom are inferior (some of whom are quite distinguished and most of whom are very nice) – the College will founder, and, with it, compromise the University and lead to some kind of fuss and total deprivation of benefactions from outraged external bodies. This is only an extreme case: my powers of blackmail are not very great: in both these cases, a Trust, simply because it is composed of prominent and actually impressive persons, can exercise a far greater influence on both these bodies than my Fellows and I could by ourselves. The alternative to a Trust [...] is a mixed committee of Wolfson College and the University – which would not be very impressive vis-à-vis the University – and not much impress the Wolfsons. Whereas, if we have a Trust composed of distinguished persons, and including Leonard Wolfson as one of the Trustees, it would frankly overawe Leonard, who would be much tamer inside than outside such a body, and could, if need be, be easily outvoted by it, though I do not think the contingency would arise – in fact, I am sure it would not – and {which} would be a far more powerful bulwark vis-à-vis the University. [...]

Maurice, who was originally against the whole thing, has now completely come round – he believes in alliance with the fait accompli. John genuinely cannot understand my motives; and feels vaguely affronted; which I think I should too in his position. I shall never say so in public, and I may deny it in some cases in private, but I have got a slight sense of nightmare at All Souls. It has death-watch beetle boring away at it at present – it may take a long

---

1 Joshua Reynolds (1723–92), portrait and historical painter, art theorist. He considered Bernini's *David* to have 'a very mean expression', the sculptor having striven for a lifelike pose, but mistaking 'accident for universality' in his conception: *A Discourse, Delivered to the Students of the Royal Academy, on the Distribution of the Prizes, December 10, 1771* (London, 1872), 9.

time to sink, but under the present regime it cannot possibly fail to do so. John is far superior to everyone there, and that is what ensures its present decadence; he is deeply uninterested (disinterested as Americans say) in anything to do with Oxford, except questions like parking of cars, preservation of buildings, and general opposition to change. There is surely something wrong in a College which, having found itself too rich for its normal purposes, now, without any change in these purposes, complains that it is far too poor. But I will not go on about that. I wish him and it very well, and I shall be genuinely sorry to leave it; I have sentimental feelings about having been there more or less, off and on, since 1932, and having to abandon my room, and a view out of the window which I can almost not bear to live without.[1] [...] It might become a dreary mausoleum – but for God's sake do not quote me saying that: it would hurt John's feelings far too much. He wanted me to make a public statement about how devoted I was to the College, and how sorry to leave, in case it was thought that I thought that I was leaving some sort of sinking ship. This is not why I am leaving: but the ship is not in a very good state of repair, nor has it the least sense of direction.

Do write and tell me that if the Trust is set up, you would not be averse to joining it. [...] I ask this as a favour. You mustn't refuse. [...]

Yours,

[Isaiah]

On 4 July David Shapiro[2] had written to Anthony Crosland, Secretary of State for Education and Science (with copies to IB, Shirley Williams and David Marquand), a letter that was perhaps the most strongly worded written attack on the Wolfson College project that IB received. Given the seriousness of the 'onslaught', and the strength and thoroughness of IB's reply, it is worth reproducing the letter in full.

Dear Tony,

I hope that you are issuing a writ for libel against Paul Johnson[3] and the *New Statesman*. He reports you as 'after initial doubts ... now enthusiastic'[4] about Wolfson College.

I cannot believe that this is true. Wolfson College, as you surely appreciate,

---

1 IB had a view of Radcliffe Square, which he regarded as the most beautiful public space in Europe, from his room in the south Hawksmoor Tower in the Great Quadrangle at All Souls.

2 David Michael Shapiro (b. 1934), New College classics 1954–7; met IB in his first term as one of four freshmen allowed to attend a seminar given by IB and E. H. Carr on 'Some Precursors of the Russian Revolution since 1830'; Henry Fellow, Harvard, modern Russian history, 1959–60; graduate student in modern Russian history, Nuffield, 1963–5; Senior Lecturer in Government, Essex, 1965–8; HM Treasury, 1968–72; Reader in Government, Brunel, 1972–88. Shapiro was originally to be the editor of RT (contract dated 1968), a role later taken over by Henry Hardy and Aileen Kelly.

3 Paul Bede Johnson (b. 1928), editorial staff, *New Statesman*, 1955–65, Editor 1965–70.

4 'London Diary', *New Statesman*, 1 July 1966 , 8: 'Tony Crosland, after initial doubts, is now enthusiastic, and so is the PM.'

represents an olde worlde tea shoppe with snob brass attachments allegedly
desired by natural scientists. There is no evidence that Oxford natural scientists
are left out in the cold by existing colleges. If graduate natural scientists envy
the facilities of Nuffield College, the appropriate course would be to improve
facilities actually in the laboratories and also to construct some utility flats for
married couples.

You will realise, of course, that this worthless project has had a precedent
that points to the ultimate futility of the present scheme. St Catherine's College
was allegedly to do wonders for the standing of Oxford natural scientists. Has
it? The merit of the architecture is arguable; intellectually it has turned a fourth-
rate institution into a second-rate institution.

Do you realise that you are presiding over an educational system that is
threatening to become increasingly meritocratic? Your proposed tampering
with the Public Schools can only have that effect. By starving both redbrick and
the new universities of funds you are widening the gap between Oxbridge and
other universities which cannot appeal so successfully to the social snobbery of
both Wolfson and Bundy.

You may treat this as a bill of accusation. If the Soviet authorities give
me a visa, I am off to Moscow and Leningrad for two and a half months on
Monday 11 July. Consider your defence and let me invite you to deliver it on
Sunday 2 October, at lunchtime. I will undertake to supply oysters while we
drink sadly to socialism's past future.

TO DAVID SHAPIRO

29 July 1966 ⟨Dictated *weeks* ago: but lost by the typist⟩

[As from Headington House]

Dear David,

Thank you for the copy of the letter you sent to Tony Crosland. It is, as
you say, a libel. It is compounded of ignorance and prejudice (I refer only to
the stuff about Wolfson College – the rest is another matter): more prejudice
than ignorance, for you know that what is planned is very different from
what you so bitterly attack. You also know (since I have told you, and you
have no reason to disbelieve me – when have I ever deceived you in the past in
any matter?) that what is planned is not amenities for science dons, a fake 'ye
olde' college, and quaint tradition to take in visiting Americans. You know
as well as I do that the agitation for equal rights among the non-fellows in
Oxford had a perfectly intelligible and proper social justification [...]. You
know that not enough was or is being done for graduates, especially in the
sciences. [...] Graduates, postdoctoral men come to Oxford because there
are many distinguished scientists here. That they are here and not elsewhere
is not a fact to deplore, though it may be one to envy. The equipment is
here, the resources are here, and the continuous possibility of invention and
discovery (and without that, teaching declines) is only possible where there
are relatively large departments, so that the dropping out of the four brilliant

men engaged upon a given piece of research – one by death, one by emigration, two because they go off the boil, is not ruinous. The UGC takes the line
that their main support must go towards the new universities. I do not blame
them for this: it seems a perfectly reasonable piece of public policy. If this
is so, then where are Oxford and Cambridge to find support? – and they do
need it, as the sciences, both natural and even others, are expensive, and the
mere taxation of colleges, or rationalisation of their lives in the bleakest sort
of way, will not yield enough.

All this you know. Very well then: for half the University – the 'humane'
portion – to form the effective population of Colleges, [...] while the scientists live in blocks of flats, and go to labs, and live lives largely separated from
their fellows, is undesirable. Arbitrary inequality is an abominable thing. If
we are to have more graduates, because the standard of teaching in Oxford
is still extremely high, and therefore, if they come, they are likely to fructify
the rest of the country; if many of them are to be scientists and technologists
(I do not speak of utilitarian motives, though these are weighty enough), and
scientific advance is the greatest single splendour of our century (historians
of the future will praise this, not our progress in the arts, which is decent but
modest); then it is time that this University awoke to its responsibilities, and
what is sauce for the arts goose is sauce for the science gander.

It is partly a matter of status. Those who are treated as inferiors will
either remain dim, or be embittered, or both. (Why should I say something
so obvious to you? But you force me to, since you ruthlessly and recklessly
ignore all this, and talk about olde shoppes, etc., which is absolute nonsense.)
And the question of equality of status is a paramount issue in our country
in general. You sneer at St Catherine's for rising from fourth-class status to
second-class. Why is this worse than a similar movement on the part of some
redbrick university or a department in it? Why is it wrong to obtain Ford
money to right the balance of science studies in Oxford? And you know very
well that to create a centre in which scientists can meet, conferences can be
held, visiting professors can stay, scientists can live is something totally new
in Oxford, or anywhere in England. Why is it wicked to try and save people
from the second-rate status at present obtaining in that world – material,
not intellectual squalor? Why is this unjust, absurd, 'worthless'? Egalitarian
policy – of a blind kind – means that because A cannot have something, B
must not have it either, and the loaf must be divided neatly in two, even
though only a whole loaf can make a critical difference in some circumstances. This is what every intelligent socialist – as you well know, better
than I – has condemned, from Marx and his followers to Lenin. In Russia this
inequality has merely been driven to violent lengths, so no orchestras are
any good except in Moscow, no universities are much good except two, etc.
etc. This is excessive; but a proliferation of third-rate orchestras would *not*
be right either?

Still, the UGC is right not to pursue this policy, because the number of mouths to feed is great, and they must all be fed. So Oxford and Cambridge must take a back seat as far as government grants are concerned, so long as the condition of the other universities is what it is – the really unfortunate ones, as also you know, are the redbricks, and not your kind. You speak of snobbery. Snobbery is not going to occur at Wolfson College. We do not intend to ape the older institutions, as, with embarrassing uniforms and caps and gowns and wands, the new universities seem to do. Some think it fun and rather gay, but I am more depressed by this than you seem to be – at least as a symptom. If Bundy wants to support a scientific programme in Oxford, and does not wish to do so at Colchester, because he has been persuaded by scientific persons that there cannot be more than so many large departments in England in its present financial condition, and that it is upon these that progress ultimately depends (I accept this argument, and everyone I have asked agrees about it), why is this a crime? There can be research without education – at least widespread education – but there cannot be education without research. Therefore, hideous as this may be to contemplate, Oxford and Cambridge and London, and perhaps Manchester in some respects, and Sheffield and Bristol, are indispensable. For these reasons, I am sure that the Minister of Education and Science will take no notice of the contents of your letter, if, as I am sure is the case, he has the interests of his country at heart. I expect I speak with a certain degree of Oxford bias, because I think that it is so important that this University should not go downhill, and private grants are the only way of preventing this at present. If there is bias in what I say, it is multiplied a hundredfold in your intemperate, ludicrous outburst. I do not believe that you really believe all that you said. Only that you think that you ought to believe it. I shall not be there on 2 October, because I shall be in New York, because nobody here takes an interest in my subject. Is this unreasonable too? Or nonsensical? I shall not circulate my letter to the Minister of Education, Shirley Williams and the rest. They are not only honourable, but intelligent, people, who will, if they love you, forgive your piece of emotional rhetoric. I am not going to say this to anyone but you, because it would sound patronising and horrible, and if people followed your advice, it would do great harm to the material and intellectual progress of England. My point of view may be parochial, but yours ...

Anyway, do not let us go on arguing about his. I have always liked you, and always believed in your talents and sense of social justice, and this distresses me; indeed I find it almost unbearable – the tone, even more than the contents, of your onslaught. I do beseech you to consider that you may be mistaken. Deeply mistaken.

Yours,
    Isaiah

⟨I love you still – even though you deserve all the just strictures on the to me unknown Mr Saville in the N[ew] S[tatesman] & N[ation] [...] made by both Hampshire & Lukes. Still you *do* know the difference between justice & injustice: & if you come to dine at poor old Wolfson (in disguise if your letter is discovered) you'll not prate of port drinking scientists: yes, indeed, all my violent irritation with your looney уравниловка[1] does not diminish my personal &, I see, unalterable feeling (I don't dislike Carr either – & he has said some deeply wounding & false things about me in public: & people *have* tried to make me hate him) [...].⟩
    I.B

TO PHILIP JOHNSON[2]
    4 August 1966

Paraggi

Dear Philip Johnson,
    I replied to your letter by sending a telegram to the Hilton Hotel in Athens, but you had already left. ⟨Johnny Walker⟩, who came to lunch that day, is my witness.
    I ⟨very much⟩ want to talk to you about Wolfson College: nine to twelve acres of lush land and a stream at the bottom; hung over with fearful difficulties about building licences, opposition to 'foreign' architects; colleges are democracies in deed as well as word, and my colleagues are most jealous of their rights.
    It would be marvellous if you came and cased the joint. I shall be in Italy until 10 September, then in England until about 20 September, when I come to New York, if only to evade my responsibilities. You speak of 17 September – if you could advance this by about *two* days, it would be a convenience; but if you cannot, 18 September would be fine. ⟨We could have lunch & take an appropriate walk.⟩ Could you let me know about this here? I too feel happy and proud that you should be thinking about this.
    Yours gratefully,
        Isaiah Berlin

---

1 'Egalitarianism'.
2 Philip Cortelyou Johnson (1906–2005), US architect, and arbiter of architectural styles; his NY designs include the overall plan of the Lincoln Center and the NY State Theater there (1964) He was one of the major names considered by the Building Committee of Wolfson College in its search for an architect: 'I have had a letter from Philip Johnson from the United States asking to be allowed to discuss this. He is a great man of a kind, of course, but I feel slightly nervous about him. However, as he is coming to England anyway on 17 September, I see no harm in letting him case the joint on 18 or 19 September, before I leave. Nobody will be committing himself in any way. I have ordered a huge costly volume called *Philip Johnson* produced by Thames and Hudson, celebrating his works' (to Frank Jessup, 3 August 1966).

TO LIONEL ROBBINS

18 August 1966 [*carbon*]

[As from Headington House]

Dear [Lionel],

[...] Next year is hopeless. I have two – to be published – lectures already to deliver in 1968. It seems absurd to commit oneself for so long ahead, but if 1969 were all right, I think I could make a kind of moral commitment, not quite a promise (the breach of which would condemn me as not a man of my word). [...] In the meanwhile, here I sit with my mountain of gold, brooding about an architect. I wish English architects were better. If a foreign one is invited to build Wolfson College, what fearful obloquy will be heaped again upon my poor old head. And yet, I suppose, one must think about absolute values, posterity etc.

The best architect seems to me to be a Japanese[1] but he may be difficult to get hold of. The English ones are somewhat inadequate. Talking of inadequacy, I feel thoroughly ashamed of having just appeared at a congress of musicologists in Venice, to whom I actually talked about Verdi.[2] The congress was devoted to his works, and so deeply flattered was I to be invited at all that I actually spoke before this learned body of men, most of whom knew exactly what theme in Bellini's *La straniera* affected which particular accompaniment to the third cavatina in the third act of *Stiffelio*, before Verdi had managed to transform it into the better-known *Aroldo*, etc. Fortunately, not one word that I said was understood – probably would not have been even if they understood English, but they did not. Everyone else spoke in flawless Italian. But after this I feel such a terrible charlatan that it is far better that I should not address any public assembly on any topic for a while. [...]

Yours ever,

[Isaiah]

TO MORTON WHITE

19 August 1966

[As from] Headington House

Dear Morton,

The Wolfson situation daunts me, dazes me, crushes me, and in general upsets me. I have no idea what next, and there are fearful difficulties in store not connected with building alone, which I will tell you about as soon as we meet. [...] I shall weep on your waistcoat about Wolfson, you may [be] sure. I now think it an act of lunacy, but it cannot be helped; there is no turning back.

1 Kenzo Tange (315/2).
2 'The "Naivety" of Verdi', later published in the *Hudson Review* 21 (1968), 138–47 (with a dedication to W. H. Auden), and in *Atti del I congresso internazionale di studi verdiani 1966* (Parma 1969), 27–35; repr. in AC.

I am glad that you are working on the freedom of the will – it seems to me the most ancient and the most real of all problems, towards the solution of which nothing has been done by anyone much, which remains as intelligible to almost anybody of average intelligence, as unsolved, insoluble, clear, and in no need of special techniques – indeed more so than any other question whatever. [...]

If you do come to CUNY it would be delightful, and very gay, and we shall relive our youth; so do come. You and I and Arthur – I feel we are all there, stuck together in some curious middle-of-the-road patch of territory – no clear answers about Vietnam, about Berkeley U., about any of the questions upon which it is so easy and delightful to have clear black or white positions, doomed to be condemned by both sides, accused of vices which we half acknowledge because of general scepticism and doubt about our position, or positions in general, and not because we think them just or fair – it is time that someone wrote a historical account of all the doubters and occupiers of middle positions, persons who did not see why the Egyptians had to be drowned in the Red Sea, and doubted the justice of all those hideous punishments dealt out to unsatisfactory characters in the Bible; people who thought that Socrates went much too far, agreed with Gallio, Lucian, Erasmus, Montaigne etc., and thought poorly of Spinoza, Pascal, Ryle, [...] Freddie Ayer, Wagner, and even Meyer, and were not ashamed of not having what is called a position, not signing round-robins, and of not appearing among the marchers in the van of obvious progress.[1] Not that I wish to defend these people – I would rather march in the van, etc. – still, if I was really brave – ...

Yours,
    Isaiah

TO ELIE KEDOURIE[2]

6 September 1966 [carbon]

As from Headington House

Dear Kedourie,

    [...] Thank you for your review on Halifax[3] which I read with great

---

1 *Mutatis mutandis*, this passage calls to mind the speech in defence of adjutants of all stripes by the deputy theatre critic, Moon, in Tom Stoppard's *The Real Inspector Hound* (London, 1968), 11: 'Sometimes I dream of revolution, a bloody coup d'état by the second rank – troupes of actors slaughtered by their understudies, magicians sawn in half by indefatigably smiling glamour girls, cricket teams wiped out by marauding bands of twelfth men – [...] an army of assistants and deputies, the seconds-in-command, the runners-up, the right-hand men [...] – stand-ins of the world stand up!'

2 Elie Kedourie (formerly Eliahou Abdallah Khedhouri) (1926–92), historian and political scientist; taught at LSE 1953–90; Professor of Politics, London, 1965–90: 'he is as you know an upper-class, Baghdad Jew, who lost his status, possessions etc., as the result of the persecution largely induced by Zionism. [...] I rather like him because of the enemies he makes' (to Jacob Talmon, August 1960).

3 Frederick Winston Furneaux Smith, [2nd] Earl of Birkenhead, *Halifax: The Life of Lord Halifax* (London, 1965).

amusement and pleasure. I think that nothing that you say is false, but that the general effect is perhaps a little too harsh. I think that he had a view of life that was not either superficial or cowardly, but exceedingly pessimistic – he thought that the future was always darker than the present or the past, that there was no need to hurry towards it, for it would come inevitably in any case, and that therefore to use a motor on one's boat was self-destructive, and if little bits of weed such as Czechoslovakia came along, you gently pushed them out of the way, instead of tangling yourself up with them, and risking the capsizing of your boat to no purpose. He believed in great fixities: the Church of England, the Church of Rome, America, Russia, India, and the fact that it was impossible to resist these entities without losing more than you gained; so that his policy of 'appeasement', not only versus Germany but versus America and India as well, for which he was so bitterly attacked by Churchill and Salisbury, sprang not from cowardice, but from this gloomy view of life. The view that he knew little about Europe, and did not really believe that Hitler was as awful as all that, is, I think, not true, or not very true, in spite of all the things which are said to that effect, by Rowse and others. He was very reactionary, and very feudal, and very idle, and very pleasure-loving, and very ecclesiastical, but he was extremely intelligent, imaginative, and far from shallow or blind. When he went shooting with Göring, I think he knew what he was doing, and of course was encouraged to do so by Eden,[1] which he never failed, maliciously, to point out. In general you give a perfectly just account of him as a man who tried to flick off everything that might be a nuisance, but, and this may be the biographer's fault to some degree, his extreme cleverness, quickness, and the very sophisticated and elaborate materials of which he was constructed – the stuff about his simplicity which people talk about seems to me rot – does not quite come through. However, on the whole you are much more right than wrong, and he was a disastrous political figure, even in India to some extent. [...]

Yours ever,

[IB p.p. Baillie Knapheis]

In June 1937 an international group of a dozen writers and poets, including W. H. Auden and Pablo Neruda, circulated a questionnaire to their British counterparts asking which side they supported in the Spanish Civil War. The results, published as Authors Take Sides on the Spanish War *(London, 1937), showed overwhelming support for the Republican cause, only five of the 147*

---

1 (Robert) Anthony Eden (1897–1977), 1st Earl of Avon 1961; Secretary of State for Foreign Affairs 1935–8, 1940–45, 1951–5; Deputy Prime Minister 1951–5; Prime Minister 1955–7. In November 1937 Halifax accepted an invitation from Reichsmarschall Hermann Göring (1893–1946) to shoot foxes in Pomerania; Eden later used this visit, which had obvious diplomatic overtones, as an example of how Chamberlain bypassed the FO in pursuit of his policy of appeasement, but Halifax made clear after the war that Eden too had wanted him to accept the invitation.

respondents (among them Evelyn Waugh) siding with General Franco. Thirty years later this initiative was the inspiration for Cecil Woolf and John Bagguley to publish Authors Take Sides on Vietnam, to which IB contributed: 'I am still quite clear about what I felt in the middle 1930s – I was wholly pro Spanish Republican, and remain so still. I wish I could be equally clear about Vietnam.' While he could not join the majority of the more than 160 respondents in their outright condemnation of the war, IB made clear that he did not support it:

After these perplexities and qualifications, which remain with me, let me add this: Apart from the small group who appear to share my doubts, I cannot help finding myself far closer to those who wish the war stopped at any price than to their adversaries. If I had to choose between the two extremes, I have no doubt which I should choose.[1]

TO BRIAN URQUHART

7 September 1966 [carbon]

Headington House [dictated in Paraggi]

Dear Brian,

[...] I have received a questionnaire from a man called Cecil Woolf,[2] who I think must be the brother of Leonard Woolf, only perhaps a little older, say in the early nineties – who says that an interesting questionnaire was sent out at the time of the Spanish Civil War to various persons, and quotes the replies about it from various writers, etc., and would it not be nice to have a similar questionnaire about the Vietnam War. I wish I knew what to reply – nor do I think that I am really a very proper person to ask. Of course I think that the Americans ought not to have gone in; ought not to be there; ought to get out if they can; but I cannot get over a certain nervousness, and more than that, about the fact that if they did so, now – quite apart from prestige and all that – there would be a massacre of their friends or alleged friends, and massacres are more horrible when they are political, even when it is indiscriminate bombing of innocent women and children – at least to me. And if there was a caving in of various South-East countries, simply in order to get on to the Communist bandwagon, it could be unpleasantly reminiscent of the behaviour of central European countries vis-à-vis the Germans in the 1930s, quite independently of one's view of the regimes themselves (about which I do not mind: if they wish to go Communist, let them, of course; nothing is more frightful than an anti-Communist crusade, or if not nothing, little). It really seems a very feeble thing to say, and I really do not know what

1 Cecil Woolf and John Bagguley (eds), *Authors Take Sides on Vietnam: Two Questions on the War in Vietnam Answered by the Authors of Several Nations* (New York, 1967), 20–1. The full text of IB's response is included as an appendix, 'Taking Sides on Vietnam', 601–2 below.

2 Cecil Woolf (b. 1927, so not yet 40), then and now proprietor of Cecil Woolf Publishers (founded 1960) and bibliographer, nephew of Leonard and Virginia Woolf.

I think. Like U Thant,[1] I too am Hamlet-like about this, but fortunately it does not matter what I think, and I can keep it dark, at least while sitting on these hills in Italy, where it is raining quite steadily. Stuart has arrived, which is a great pleasure, and Stephen Spender is expected. So we are not without our civilizing influences. [...]

Love from Aline and me,

[Isaiah]

TO VERA WEIZMANN

22 September [1966; *carbon*]

Headington House

Dear Mrs Weizmann,

I was delighted to see you looking so well and in altogether so excellent a frame of mind; and I much enjoyed our conversation about Bob Boothby. But when I went away, and again the next morning, I found myself somewhat troubled about the topic on which Stein[2] had written you, and that for the following reason. I have not read Bob Boothby's original statement, nor followed any details of the controversy which developed – either Leon Simon's[3] letter or any rejoinder, or indeed anything at all. All I know comes from yourself plus a vague memory of something in some newspaper about the fact that Erskine Childers[4] and his friends now use your name and authority as additional evidence for their charges of bad will on the part of Zionists in general and Dr Weizmann in particular. My feeling is this. If I understand the matter aright – and I am not sure that I do – what Bob Boothby said was that Dr Weizmann had talked to him at quite an early stage – I do not know when – about (*a*) a fully independent Jewish State as his political aim, and (*b*) the need to remove Arabs from it, presumably by peaceful means. I have no notion, of course, of what was in Dr Weizmann's mind before I came to know him myself, which, as you know, occurred in 1938. But after that, while he, like the entire Zionist movement, was obviously not

1 U Thant (1909–74), Burmese Secretary General to UN (in succession to Dag Hammarskjöld) 1961–71; avowedly obsessed with ending the Vietnam war.

2 Leonard Jacques Stein (1887–1973), barrister; educated at St Paul's and Balliol; the first professing Jew to be elected President of the Oxford Union (1910); became political secretary of the World Zionist Organisation on demobilisation 1920; thereafter worked closely with Chaim Weizmann, and in 1963 became consulting editor for the English edition of *The Letters and Papers of Chaim Weizmann* (London, 1968–80), co-editing vol. 1 (1885–1902) of the letters, and editing vol. 7 (1914–17) himself.

3 Leon Simon (1881–1965), Kt 1944; Director of Telegraphs and Telephones, GPO, 1931–5, of Savings 1935–44; a Zionist and supporter of Chaim Weizmann, he emigrated to Israel on retirement; chairman of the executive council of the HUJ 1946–9, of the board of governors 1949–50; President, Israel Post Office Bank, 1950–3.

4 Erskine Barton Childers (1929–96), writer and BBC correspondent, member of the UN Secretariat 1967–89; a champion of the Palestinian cause, and author of *Common Sense about the Arab World* (London, 1960).

inimical to the idea of a Jewish State, he was (that is my impression) ready to accept something less than that, e.g. dominion status within the British Commonwealth, or perhaps even a federal scheme which would reserve full internal self-government to the Jews within their own area. He accepted the Biltmore Resolution[1] during the war, of course, but I should not say that he was one of its most active proponents. When events developed as they did, and it became clear that the British government, not only in 1939 but in 1944/5, was prepared to leave the Jews to the mercies of the then Arab majority of Palestine, his own views naturally altered; and in the event he was, of course, an enthusiastic proponent of the State. But that was the result of events; and not a fixed idea which guided him in the 1920s and 1930s, as it did, for example, the revisionists and others; he seemed to differ from them not merely in the question of means but also of (at any rate immediate) ends of policy. About all this, of course, you must know far, far more than I; I can only judge as I do on the basis of public documents and my own impressions after 1938.

So far as the Arabs are concerned, I never knew him to say in public, nor say in private to me or to anyone I knew after 1938 (or to anyone at all, so far as my personal knowledge is concerned), that he wanted the Arabs removed. The question of exchange of populations was occasionally mooted, and no doubt like all Zionists he would have preferred a situation in which Palestine was ready for Jewish occupation without a native Arab population – that was bound to constitute a source, to put it at its lowest, of friction. But that seemed utopian. If it was indeed true that he spoke of removing Arabs, this would contradict his publicly adopted position throughout his political life as the head of the Zionist organisation. If Bob were right – and I have no means of knowing directly whether or not he is right – this would render Dr Weizmann's position at best ambivalent; and it would make it difficult to rebut the charges of those of his opponents, and anti-Zionists in general, who have wished and wish to accuse him and the movement in general of profound hypocrisy in this respect – of offering to live in peace with the Arabs in public, while privately meditating the possibility of getting rid of them. This attitude seems to me inconsistent with everything that I knew and believed about him, but this, alas, is not sufficient to render it invalid. If there are facts to prove it, then the truth must be faced, and his biographers (and I still do not abandon hopes of writing an extended piece about him one day)[2] will have to say of him, as of other great men, that in the interests of political ends he compromised his integrity and is guilty of duplicity, with which his enemies have been and are only too glad to charge him. Naturally

---

1 Manifesto (commonly called 'the Biltmore program') agreed at a meeting of American Zionists, Biltmore Hotel, NY, May 1942; it stated that restrictions on Jewish immigration to Palestine should be lifted, and a 'Jewish Commonwealth' established there.

2 He never did, though two of his earlier pieces on Weizmann were reasonably 'extended'.

I do not at all wish to believe this to be true: and should be immensely glad and relieved if you could set my mind at rest on this matter. But if what Bob said was correct, then this disagreeable truth cannot be denied. [...]

I wish I could honestly say that what I was chiefly concerned about was the historical truth; I must admit that it is the reputation of Dr Weizmann which lies nearer my heart. Forced to the conclusion that he played fast and loose with this central issue in the future of the Jewish State, I shall accept it; but do I have to? If you tell me I must, I will. [...]

With much love and devotion, as always,

Yours ever,

[Isaiah]

IB spent the autumn of 1966 in New York, fulfilling his obligations as Professor of Humanities at City University, staying at the Blackstone Hotel. He arrived in America at the end of September and returned to England in the middle of January 1967; Aline accompanied him, but she spent a week in Oxford in November. They spent New Year at the Barbados home of their friend Ronnie Tree.

TO NOEL ANNAN

11 November 1966

CUNY

Dear Noel,

[...] First of all, thank you very much for your goodness of heart in writing to me about Namier[1] – you must know that for someone to take up a pen and write to someone else, no matter how great a friend, simply to say how much they liked his piece, is a rare virtue, and one for which one certainly earns a place in heaven. I wrote the piece on Namier because I thought that sooner or later these anecdotes had to be set down; besides which I was fascinated by that extraordinary, and not very nice, but magnificent man – I do not know if it is right to call him a man of genius: streaks of genius he most undoubtedly possessed. Also there is a certain irony in contributing the piece to Taylor's anthology[2] – rather like denouncing Comte in a lecture devoted to his memory;[3] but I must have more natural malice than I give myself credit for – at any rate it was enjoyable. But I have had a most indignant letter from Ted Carr saying that he had *not* leaked that funny private letter to the *Daily Express*, and so I shall have to write a letter of apology to *Encounter*, and an erratum slip in the book to come. I do not wish to hurt his feelings: no

1 i.e. IB's article (84/5) on Namier.
2 sc. Festschrift.
3 Which IB did in *Historical Inevitability* (40), where he charges Comte with, inter alia, a 'naive craving for unity and symmetry at the expense of experience'.

matter how sharp our public tiffs, and how much, whether consciously or not, he wishes to do me down from time to time, I bear him friendly feelings and like him as a man, and always have – unlike Deutscher, whom I detest as a nasty human being, quite independently of his views. His views are, after all, not all that different from those, say, of C. C. O'Brien, with whom I have just been to Cornell, together with Stuart and Northrop Frye.[1] O'Brien really is a tremendous demagogue, and the more he pitches into America, and the more he denounces, and the more bitter jokes he makes, the more he has them rolling in the aisles, the more they love it. The Americans are, I think, the only people who adore being denounced. This has been so from Dickens onwards. National pride and conceit, and national masochism, blend in odd proportions. I rather like O'Brien – I do not exactly believe what he says and I think he is a kind of Irish swashbuckler, a pub fighter, a brawler, red-faced, formidable, clever, brilliant, but inhuman – in the sense that he looks at one from a purely political angle and not exactly as a human being. [...]

Yours, with much love

Isaiah   [...]

TO MICHAEL BROCK

18 November 1966

CUNY

Dear Michael,

Thank you very much for your letter of 8 November, and the copies of this to my wife which I shall pass on faithfully. [...]

I had a lunch with Tange[2] three days ago, and he promised to come to Oxford at the end of January or at the beginning of February. I have also had a letter from Pevsner saying that the choice of Tange would be a national disaster, tragedy etc., and that the man is Eames[3] – wild shot, he says, but a genius. I have made enquiries about Eames. He is principally known as a furniture designer – the designs are of a conventionality difficult to exaggerate, and are to be seen in every multiple store in New York. All who know him say that he would not dream of building a building; but what he has built proved terrible (except for his own little house), and he is a very sensible man really, and sticks to his commercial last. I don't know whether any of this is true – I expect both sides exaggerate wildly. But we are in a curious universe

---

1 (Herman) Northrop Frye (1912–91), Canadian, one of the foremost literary theorists of his day; ordained as a priest 1936; joined the English faculty of Victoria College 1939; University Professor at its parent body, the University of Toronto, 1967–91.

2 Kenzo Tange (1913–2005), Japanese architect; designed the Hiroshima Peace Center and Memorial Park (1949–56).

3 Charles Eames (1907–78), US designer, film-maker and architect; with his wife Ray (1912–88), an innovator in furniture design, using a modular approach, and materials – such as moulded plywood and glass-reinforced plastic – that became more generally available after 1945.

filled with hatred and fanaticism. In the old days there were two schools: the
Bauhaus, all of whose admirers loved one another, and the Corinthian Pillar
school, all of whom in their turn loved one another and that was that, and
you could choose. Now everybody hates everyone and there are no accepted
values. Except that Tange is acclaimed by everyone other than Pevsner. He
speaks of Powell & Moya.[1] ⟨his last letter says that St. Cat's is "perfect" and
'a very great masterpiece' & 'a haven of heavenly peace!' So.⟩ We may indeed
have to end up with something like that, except that the Smithsons[2] seem
rather better – but not without at least a preliminary struggle for someone of
world prestige, surely. The head of the National Gallery in Washington has
just come back from Japan, and he and his wife raved about Tange. So does
really everyone who has been there and has seen his buildings. He may be no
good to us – his buildings may be too monumental – I see that it may all be
idle, and we shall have to end up with someone else. I am fully prepared for
that. Nevertheless we must not be put off by Pevsner, who according to local
experts is a tremendous authority on the history of the subject, but possesses
no taste and no interest in what is going on now, or at least no discrimination
about it. But that I would not know. But I now feel sure that we must not
make anyone our exclusive adviser, and ask everyone. […]

Yours,
Isaiah

TO PHILIPPE HALBAN

30 November 1966 [*carbon*]

CUNY

Dear Philip,

I wonder how much you will like New York this time. In the afternoons
the streets are so crowded as almost not to be walked in – as I watch from
my skyscraper where my office is on the 16th floor above a Woolworth, I am
always swept off my feet by the surging masses. Some people hate this; I on
the contrary rather like it.

Your mother, you will not be surprised to hear, rather complains of the
hectic nature of our social life whereby we are out to dinner almost every
night. Nevertheless there are certain points at which I dig in. For instance
there was a grand party given at the Plaza Hotel last night (given by Mr

---

1 Firm of British architects founded in 1946, whose practice was built on public commissions,
  notably housing, hospitals and educational buildings. Philip Arnold Joseph Powell (1921–2003),
  later (1975) Kt, and (John) Hidalgo ('Jacko') Moya (1920–94), met at the Architectural Association
  School of Architecture before the war. Their other work in Oxford included the accommodation block at Brasenose (1960–1), the Blue Boar Quad and the Picture Gallery at Christ Church
  (1965–8), and the Magpie Lane Annexe, Corpus (1968–9).
2 Peter Denham Smithson (1923–2003) and Alison Margaret Smithson (1928–93) née Gill, architects; married 1949; originators and exponents of the New Brutalist style of post-war architecture.

Truman Capote[1] in honour of Mrs Kay Graham, a very old friend of mine), to which anyone who was anyone was invited, at which men had to wear white masks and women black or the other way about, I cannot remember which. Your mother acquired an extremely handsome mask for this purpose. Quite a number of professors and intellectuals were invited, such as, for instance, the Trillings,[2] who went with the greatest enthusiasm. However this was too much for me: whether shyness or vanity or desperate clinging to academic dignity or what[ever] intervened, but having gone to a dinner for it at the last moment I refused to go. I stood with the crowd outside the Plaza and watched all the notables go in – it was a marvellous spectacle and it was all reported most handsomely in this morning's press – somehow I feel embarrassed and ashamed to attend such gatherings – some ancient radicalism must still be coursing through my veins.

Your mother went and much enjoyed it – though she came home relatively early. Today she naturally has a headache. Nevertheless ruthlessly we go out to dinner with a Russian lady for whose sake, we are told, the famous Russian poet Mayakovsky committed suicide in 1930 – a startling political event, sensational in its day.

Dinner is 'bothersome', which I find simply terrible. All social engagements naturally have been stopped by the time you come so that the evenings may be spent in religious peace. Peter seems all right. Of course he has nightmares about getting insufficient grades in his examination, but I think this is probably not well founded. He seems quite happy and Princeton suits him well.

As for me I am not doing enough serious work. I do my duty, I dictate letters, for there are so many telephone calls, so many people appear to wish to see me on business of an academic kind, and life is so electric, that I have not done a quarter of the work that I proposed to myself. I must really settle down and do something solid. I was fearfully annoyed, as you may well imagine, by the enormous interview with Mr Brandon,[3] which appeared in the *Sunday Times* – he swore solemnly that it would not appear in the newspaper, only in his book. But then broke the engagement, although

1 Truman Capote (1924–84) né Truman Streckfus Persons, American writer; author of the novella *Breakfast at Tiffany's* (NY, 1958) and the extraordinarily successful *In Cold Blood: A True Account of a Multiple Murder and Its Consequences* (NY, 1965); in 1966 he hosted 'the party of the decade or even of the century. Five hundred of the rich, the intelligent, or the merely famous, attended his masked ball at the Plaza Hotel in New York' (*Times*, 27 August 1984, 10g). The women wore white masks, the men black.

2 Diana Trilling (1905–96) née Rubin, married, 1929, the literary critic Lionel Trilling, and pursued in her own right a notable career as a literary critic, author and cultural commentator. Known for her sometimes controversial and outspoken views, she was a contributor to the left-leaning literary press, e.g. *Partisan Review*, as well as mainstream magazines such as *Vogue*.

3 The interview was published as 'A Philosopher Looks at the Future' in *Conversations with Henry Brandon* (London 1966), but it also appeared – contrary to IB's expectations – in Brandon's paper, the *Sunday Times*, as 'My Hopes and Fears', 6 November 1966, 41–2.

he pretends he did not know anything about it.[1] For the Washington correspondent of the *Sunday Times* not to know what his newspaper was going
to contain, and that from his own pen, does not seem a very likely story to
me. So he rings us twice a day. I am always out. By now he has gathered
that I am not that pleased that he is trying to oil up to me. I am adamant.
I have [had] altogether too much publicity of late in England: first the *Sunday
Times* interview; the review of the book in honour of A. J. P. Taylor, in which
I wrote an article which all the reviewers seem to mention fairly favourably;
Maurice's memoirs in the *Sunday Times* would give me pride of place;[2] and
so on and so forth. I really do hate being mentioned in the newspapers, which
pay sums of money, not to me. Nobody here quite understands this state of
mind, or if they do they pretend they don't. I am sure you agree: at the same
time, Wolfson College is quite pleased by all this mention of itself. They keep
sending me short memoranda urging me to get more money for them.

Ford pretends it is broke and cannot pay much to anybody. Nothing to
say – *rien à dire comme à la gare*[3] – this can all be talked about then.

The Trillings are sending their child to Harvard, although fundamentally they really wanted to send him to Princeton, but he rather longs to
go to Columbia or somewhere in New York, and so they compromised on
Harvard. We have not seen them much. They did their duty by asking us
early once and now relations are remote.

[...] Your mother is hurrying me off for once. Hope you are feeling swell.
We are hunky-dory ourselves.

Yours ⟨with love from
    Isaiah⟩

TO GARRETT DROGHEDA

2 December 1966

CUNY

Dear Garrett,

I feel the time has come for a report on the Met[4] (and I shall send a copy
of it to Burnet). Have you seen it? The building, I mean? The whole thing is

---

1 If IB had specifically banned newspaper use, Brandon ought to have informed the publishers
(André Deutsch) of this. Did he? There is no evidence in the many letters on this topic that this
key question was ever directly asked by IB at the time.
2 C. M. Bowra, *Memories: 1898–1939* (London, 1966).
3 'Nothing to say, as at the railway station'; on one of four occasions known to us when he uses the
phrase IB substitutes 'guerre' ('war') for 'gare': to Marie Berlin, 3 March 1964 (185). The origin of
the saying and its original form are unclear: perhaps a family phrase?
4 In 1966 the Met moved from its historic location on 39th Street to become part of the prestigious Lincoln Center for the Performing Arts, between West 62nd and 65th. It reopened on 16
September, in a building designed by Wallace K. Harrison, with a nine-production season – too
many, as its General Manager, Rudolf Bing, later admitted: *5,000 Nights at the Opera* (London,
1972), 236.

an architectural – I will not say disaster – but disappointment, both to those who believe in the most bleak modern architecture (which is meant to attack the observer and force him into the consciousness of the ferocious forces abroad to break through his philistine crust – this is a conception behind the architecture of Messrs Rudolph[1] and Breuer),[2] and to those who really like Corinthian pillars and sweetness and elegance. It is neither one thing nor the other, and much regretted by many persons; and very feebly defended by Nin.

Mr Bing never has had any taste of any kind, so there is nothing surprising about that. However the outside of the Opera House – the Chagalls[3] which are to be seen, when lighted up, by the crowds streaming in from the Plaza ⟨etc. is not too bad.⟩ What cannot be defended is the auditorium – the gold on gold and the jewels on the gold are of a vulgarity which has to be seen to be believed – nor can it be forgotten, for it haunts the imagination. Desmond[4] was relatively kind about it in his notice, because he was softened and softened by charming persons here; and therefore – I dare say quite rightly, for why should one hurt feelings in public? – pulled his punches.

Loew's Opera House is an appropriate name for it inside, just as the joke about Cecil B. de Zeffirelli is perfectly appropriate.[5] The opening night, with its *very* inferior opera, was a near disaster, which nobody wants to defend. Music, décor and everything except Miss Price was detested by all (apparently).[6]

But what depresses one is Bing's deep and genuine lack of taste (this letter is becoming hideously libellous and indiscreet and although it must be read by Burnet and you, I should ask you both not to give it any further circulation and to destroy it).

Let me come to individual items. *Traviata*: quite decent sets – except for the last act, which was hideous and ludicrous – by Cecil B. Very badly conducted

---

1 Paul Marvin Rudolph (1918–97), US architect, designer of the monumental, brutalist Yale Art and Architecture Building (1963).

2 Marcel Lajos Breuer (1902–81), Hungarian-born US modernist architect, designer of the brutalist Whitney Museum of American Art, NY (1963–6).

3 Two large murals by Chagall, *The Triumph of Music* and *The Sources of Music*, visible from the Lincoln Center plaza (but covered when direct sunlight would fade them), adorn the lobby of the Met.

4 Desmond Christopher Shawe-Taylor (1907–95), music critic and journalist; chief music critic, *Sunday Times*, 1958–83.

5 Loews Theatres [sic] was a US theatre chain established by the NY-born Jewish businessman Marcus Loew (1870–1927) in 1904. It began as a nickelodeon enterprise, but evolved into luxury 'movie palaces': five of the grandest of these were built in NY 1929–30, the so-called 'wonder theaters', one definition of which was that they 'must be absolutely hideous' (Christopher Gray, 'The Kings is Dead! Long Live the Kings!', NYT, 11 March 2007, J6). The comic comparison between Franco Zeffirelli and the legendary Hollywood film producer and director Cecil B[lount] DeMille (1881–1959) plays on the extravagance and opulence of their productions.

6 The Met reopened with the premiere of Samuel Barber's *Antony and Cleopatra*: the opera was considered a disaster, despite a fine performance from Leontyne Price as Cleopatra.

indeed by Prêtre[1] – badly produced and frightfully boring and cold. It is the only performance of this work which did not make me swallow huge lumps in the throat (and worse) in the last act. The part was very badly sung by Miss Moffo,[2] who, although she has quite a good voice, has not a spark of feeling, acted badly, and let down the whole thing abominably. The only agreeable voice was Mr Merrill's,[3] who acts badly but sang the baritone part as it ought to be sung, very delicious and very creamy. Awful as some of our *Traviatas* have been, they have never sunk to this level, I do assure you. Cecil B. was not asked to bow at the end, whereas the producer (Lunt)[4] was, and that led to a lot of trouble too. Everybody warmly congratulated everybody on it, but I assure you that it was absolutely no good.

Next in order of non-excellence comes *Gioconda*. This work, which shows one what conventional music can be which has not a spark of inspiration of any kind, despite the pretty ballet music, was beautifully decorated by Montrésor.[5] The Venetian décor was excellent. Bing naturally said that it set operatic design back by twenty years since it was so old-fashioned. It was delightful: and I am sure he [Montrésor] will do very well for us: Tebaldi sang marvellously well – she spoke back in excellent voice and we ought to employ her, whatever Callas may say. It was a pity she was wasted in this pompous work of unending length, which was like a caricature of Italian opera, and funny in that way; but with no possible value in any other. Why they do it is a mystery. Even Nin cannot explain it, except that it has always been in the repertoire. Again, nothing for us to emulate.

Then *Elektra*. I am not as you know a great fan of Strauss. It seems to me quite well done: Schippers[6] is a second-rate conductor (lacking strength and inner fire and authority, but with plenty of métier, somehow always uninteresting and soft; something rather like our Mr Pritchard, but half a class below him) – conducted it very decently. Of course Nilsson sung marvellously. The décor was all right, except that Orestes,[7] a respectable American singer whose name I cannot remember, was too naked and looked frightfully embarrassed about this and moved in a kind of stiffly genteel manner, like a middle-aged bank vice-president whose trousers had accidentally fallen off, and who is trying

1 Georges Prêtre (b. 1924), French conductor; ROH debut 1961; Music Director, Paris Opera, 1966–71.

2 Anna Moffo (1932–2006), American soprano, played Violetta in the 1966 production of Verdi's *La Traviata*, having made her debut at the Met in this role in November 1959.

3 Robert Merrill (1917–2004), American baritone; made his debut at the Met in December 1945, and sang many of the leading roles in a long career there; ROH debut 1967.

4 Alfred Davis Lunt (1893–1977), US actor and director, who formed a famous theatrical partnership with his wife (1922) Lynn Fontanne (1887–1983).

5 Beni Montresor (1926–2001), Italian opera and film director, set designer and children's book illustrator.

6 Thomas Schippers (1930–77), American conductor; Met debut 1955; conducted at the premiere of Barber's *Antony and Cleopatra*.

7 William Dooley (b. 1932), American baritone; Met debut 1964 as Evgeny Onegin; sang Orest (the German form of Orestes) in the 1966 production of *Elektra*.

to preserve his dignity despite this unfortunate accident – but Nilsson carried the whole thing off splendidly, and Resnik[1] as Clytemnestra was the worthy old trooper she is, and all went off perfectly well. Moving it cannot be called. Raimund,[2] who was present, thought poorly of it. So again nothing to envy.

The really splendid performance was that of *Frau ohne Schatten*.[3] That really was marvellous. The conductor was Böhm,[4] and all the singers, Walter Berry[5] and the other people from Vienna, were magnificent. The conductor knew what the work was about, the décor looked expensive, as it should, the lighting was excellent, and except for the end, which had a touch of Radio City[6] about it and was exceedingly vulgar, the whole thing was beyond ⟨praise (esp. scenes between Maler & Malerin). Of course Solti is as good a conductor as Böhm, but whom have we got to sing it? Seems absurd that these works should vie with each other at such close intervals. ⟨It is a magnificent work: I absolutely hate it. But it speaks to Mittel-European souls, words music & all, as Puccini to Neapolitans.⟩

I see that if one likes Strauss one might easily become excited about this. I wasn't but that is neither here nor there. What the Metropolitan does best, I think, is Central European music conducted by appropriate Viennese conductors. What it does worst is Italian, no matter how good the singers. Lavishness, vulgarity, huge display, sensational climaxes – virtuosity is what they are best at. All that Visconti[7] and Giulini stand for they are no good at. Zeffirelli has shot his bolt here, I think, and ought to retire from opera altogether for a bit to recover his reputation. ⟨I shall be back in the 3ᵈ week of Jan, & rush to Berlioz etc. at once: I saw Derry[8] last night: he was in excellent form. We have *nothing* to learn from the Met.⟩

Yours,

Isaiah

---

1 Regina Resnik (b. 1922), American (mezzo-)soprano and opera director; sang at the Met 1944–74 (debut in *Il trovatore* as Leonora); directed a production of *Elektra* in Venice 1971.

2 Raimund von Hofmannsthal's father, Hugo, had written the libretto for this opera by Richard Strauss.

3 The Met's 1966 production of Richard Strauss's *Die Frau ohne Schatten* (*The Woman without a Shadow*, 1919) was its first, and the surprise success of the season.

4 Karl Böhm (1894–1981), Austrian conductor, specialist in the music of Richard Strauss; Covent Garden debut 1936, the Met 1957; conducted regularly at the Salzburg Festival and Bayreuth.

5 Walter Berry (1929–2000), Austrian bass-baritone; Vienna Opera debut 1950; appeared regularly at the Salzburg Festival from 1953; sang Barak in *Die Frau ohne Schatten*, reprising this role for his Covent Garden debut in 1976.

6 The huge 6,000-seat Radio City Music Hall in NY opened as a vaudeville house in 1932, and was later the venue for musical extravaganzas, ice shows etc.

7 Luchino Visconti (1906–76), Conte di Modrone, innovatory Italian film and theatre director, whose films include *Death in Venice* (1971); first directed opera at La Scala 1954; debut at Covent Garden with a memorable *Don Carlos* in 1958; followed this success with several more productions in the 1960s.

8 Presumably Garrett Drogheda's son Henry Dermot Ponsonby ('Derry') Moore (b. 1937), photographer.

TO ROWLAND BURDON-MULLER

26 January 1967

[Headington House]

Dearest Rowland,

Thank you very much for sending me the cutting from the *Boston Globe*.[1] This is, alas, the end of a beautiful friendship, for I cannot conceive that Arthur would ever speak to Joe again. Indeed, by the next post, Arthur himself sent me the same article, with an even more glaring and hostile headline, from some other newspaper. So that is that.

Meanwhile, we keep having letters in *The Times* by pro- and anti-Vietnam dignitaries, something like 1,200 signatures from various British Universities, in which Oxford is poorly represented, but, following that, a powerful letter from three heads of Cambridge Colleges, and a milder one from Sir Maurice Bowra and his colleagues.[2]

I cannot be said to be exactly at peace here – I lecture, attend to the affairs of Wolfson College, and try to frustrate the wicked and knavish tricks of ill-wishers, but I must say that despite everything, despite having to go to the Courtauld Institute in London and lecture there, to what is called a select audience (hundreds of students, and Lady Pamela Berry, Anthony Blunt, Prof. Gombrich and the Little Fellow),[3] I do feel more at peace here than even on the most peaceful days in New York. And the idea of emigrating to the United States, which I must say has never seriously crossed my mind, crosses it even less now. And dear Stuart seems happy to be back – he never really should have left us, and I imagine that he will return to Princeton despite everything, with the most sinking feelings. [...]

Much love,

Yours,

Isaiah

---

1 Joseph Alsop, 'Schlesinger Book Silly', *Boston Globe*, 16 January 1967, 11, which begins 'An extremely clever man, Arthur Schlesinger, Jr, has just published an extremely silly book about Vietnam.' The book is *The Bitter Heritage: Vietnam and American Democracy, 1941–1966* (London, 1967).

2 The anti-war letter of Ruth Cohen (Principal of Newnham), Edmund R. Leach (Provost of King's), and Joseph Needham (Master of Gonville and Caius) asked sardonically whether 'we should surrender not only our conscience but our judgement to the President of the United States'; that of Bowra and seven Oxford colleagues expressed 'respect and good will for the GI in the jungle without endorsing the policy that keeps him there' (25 January 1967, 11c).

3 (Harold) John Golding (1929–2012), Lecturer in the History of Art, Courtauld Institute, London, 1962–77, Reader 1977–81; Slade Professor of Fine Art, Cambridge, 1976–7. Golding was the life partner of James Joll, and had been a pupil, later a colleague, of Anthony Blunt at the Courtauld.

TO ARTHUR SCHLESINGER

31 January 1967

Headington House

Dear Arthur

How horrible of Joe. It was bound to come sooner or later, and will certainly make no difference to *your* reputation, although it may make some to his. There are two Americas involved here, I feel, not merely two temperaments. He knows which side I am on. (I was mocked for this in front of Mac Bundy, and did not retreat.)

You would have enjoyed the scene with Bobby Kennedy[1] here very much indeed. We were all summoned to lunch at the Union, viz., the Union officials; the Master of Pembroke (McCallum);[2] Maurice Shock,[3] a don from University College; Sir Kenneth Wheare (because the President of the Union is at his College); the President of the Union's parents (at once embarrassing and admirable as a move on the President's part; his name is Cohen[4] ‹very Central Park West›); Senator Kennedy's friends summoned by Mr vanden Heuvel:[5] Maurice Bowra, Bill Deakin, Bullock and myself. Bullock did not turn up. We were lined up in the Union, waiting as for royalty. Enter the Senator, who shook hands formally all round, saw me, greeted me with special affability, said breezily, 'I saw David the other day. He sent you greetings.' I said, 'Oh thank you. Where did you see him?' 'At Moucher's.'[6] All this was not frightfully well received by my colleagues, who always had suspected that I moved in some social world not wholly identical with theirs, and looks were directed at me, not unlike those which you must sometimes get from similar persons at Harvard, say. His performance at the Union was splendid. He was asked questions, which

1　Robert Francis ('Bobby') Kennedy (1925–68), younger brother of John F. Kennedy, whose presidential campaign he managed; appointed Attorney General by him (served 1961–4); elected senator from NY 1964; gave his first speech in Britain at a crowded meeting of the Oxford Union Society, 29 January 1967, and afterwards took questions on, inter alia, American policy on Vietnam; assassinated 1968.

2　Ronald Buchanan McCallum (1898–1973), historian; Fellow of Pembroke 1925–55, Master 1955–67; Principal of St Catharine's, Cumberland Lodge, Windsor Great Park, 1967–71.

3　Maurice Shock (b. 1926), later (1988) Kt; Fellow and Praelector in Politics, Univ., 1956–77; later (1987–94) Rector of Lincoln.

4　Ronald Mourad Cohen (b. 1945), later (2001) Kt, Egyptian-born of Sephardic descent; his parents Michel Mourad Cohen (1913–97) and Sonia Sophie née Douek fled Egypt after Suez; Exeter PPE 1964–7; President, Oxford Union Society, Hilary Term 1967; later founder and chairman (1972–2005) of Apax Partners Holdings Ltd.

5　William Jacobus vanden Heuvel (b. 1930), assistant to Robert F. Kennedy, senior partner in the law firm Stroock & Stroock & Lavan; later (1977–81) US ambassador at the UN.

6　Mary Alice ('Moucher') (1895–1988) née Gascoyne-Cecil, Dowager Duchess of Devonshire 1950; married 1917 Edward William Spencer Cavendish (1895–1950), 10th Duke of Devonshire 1938; Mistress of the Robes to HM The Queen 1953–66; Chancellor, Exeter, 1956–70. Lady Mary was the sister of IB's close friend David Cecil, and mother-in-law of Bobby Kennedy's deceased elder sister Kathleen Agnes ('Kick') Kennedy (1920–48), who had married, May 1944, her elder son, William John Robert Cavendish (1917–44), Marquess of Hartington.

he answered with consummate skill – I have decided that he has *physical* charm of an incredible kind, and that all the world loves a schoolboy, and that this, in some inspired fashion, is how he seems ‹to all his student audiences›. In spite of barracking by a lot of Vietniks, he received an ovation, as you may have seen in the *New Statesman*, simply because, although he gave nothing away, his idealism about youth etc. was obviously genuine, and of such a kind as nobody of his age here could have enunciated without self-consciousness and embarrassment, but which with him is perfectly straightforward and disarming. Everybody liked him very much. […]

You saw the review, I hope, in the *Sunday Telegraph* or *Times*, which regretted that Bertrand Russell followed so far below you intellectually – I must lecture on Tolstoy tomorrow, and cannot now continue with this letter. I suppose that Tolstoy, towards the end of his life, was thought of much as Russell is now – ‹marvellously self confident aristocrat› a genius in his own proper sphere, but cranky and silly on social and political issues, though so proud, and so eminent, as not to be ‹assailable› whatever he said, and a kind of sacred monster of a unique kind, with mysterious charismatic properties, not solely derived from his own field of achievement. Then, after he dies, nobody else will be left of this particular type, and nineteenth-century prophets will become a purely historical category. With this deep historical reflection, I leave you in order to read the piece on contemporary history which you kindly sent me. Thank you very much indeed.

Yours,

Isaiah   […]

TO AVA WAVERLEY

24 February 1967 [*manuscript*]

11 Herschel Road, Cambridge

Dearest Ava,

Alas: on March 8 I shall be lunching with the Vice-Chancellor of Leicester University: in Leicester. For am I not bound to look at all modern academic buildings in England, praised extravagantly by our architects, commended in the press, awarded prizes for their beauty, originality, appropriateness, conduciveness to study and contemplation, and, as a rule, of an aggressive bleakness and hideousness which few other modern buildings – in America, France, Finland, Brazil, wherever modern buildings are – can match? Why is it that we have not one architect of first class distinction – only men of second rate order, of various degrees? Do you admire Coventry Cathedral? the Royal College of Physicians in Regents Park? the new *Times* Building (& do you know Mr Rees-Mogg?[1] I shd be *deeply* interested in your view of

---

1 William Rees-Mogg (1928–2012), later Kt (1981) and life peer (1988), City Editor, *Sunday Times*, 1960–1, Political and Economic Editor 1961–3, Deputy Editor 1964–7; Editor, *The Times*, 1967–81.

him. What is thought in Oxford I know) the universities of Sussex, Essex, East Anglia, Warwick, York, etc. etc? To all of which my colleagues and I, in some comical vehicle, will be bound during the next 10 days or so, like the journeys of the Pickwick Club: up & down the land we go, entertained by Vice-Chancellors and Bursars, wearily trudging from building to building, with mechanical praise on our lips for the brutal looking curves of concrete stained by rain in great ugly streaks, for the tiny bed sitting rooms designed to punish their inhabitants by the University Grants Committee: admiring the freedom with which sexes, colours, ages mix in some: & admiring equally the rigid walls between these same groups imposed in others. I must stop. This is like a piece of pseudo-Nicolson[1] prose written to be published. I am sorry. But *that* is where I shall be on the 8*th* March & for weeks & weeks & weeks.

    love

      Isaiah

On 19 May U Thant, Secretary General of the UN, announced the withdrawal of the UN Emergency Force from the Egypt–Israel frontier, the likely outcome being that control of the Tiran Strait, giving access to the Gulf of Aqaba, and thus to the southern Israeli port of Eilat, would revert to Egypt. On the same day religious leaders in Egypt were instructed by their government to preach holy war as the country reinforced its 117-mile border with Israel. On 22 May Egypt closed the Tiran Strait to Israeli shipping, which amounted to a naval blockade. The Soviet Union sent Cairo a message of support, while Arab States began mobilising in support of Egypt. Speaking at an air-force base in Sinai on 22 May, President Nasser[2] declared: 'We are now face to face with Israel, and if they want to try their luck without Britain and France, we await them. [...] If Israel wants to threaten us with war they are welcome.'[3]

    The Johnson administration meanwhile condemned the blockade as illegal, and a threat to peace, and covertly gave assurances of support to Israel, which contemplated the options of either a pre-emptive strike against encirclement, or awaiting UN intervention. Since it was a UN withdrawal that had prompted the crisis in the first place, the prospects from that quarter were not promising, and on the morning of 5 June Israeli planes destroyed the Egyptian air force on the ground, and attacked airfields in Syria, Iraq and Jordan. Within 48 hours Israeli paratroops had secured the east bank of the Suez Canal, and after six days its forces had taken eastern Jerusalem, the whole of the West Bank, and

1 Harold George Nicolson (1886–1968), diplomat, politician and author, husband of Vita Sackville-West; his *Diaries and Letters*, edited by his son Nigel, were published in three volumes (London, 1966–8).

2 Gamal Abdel Nasser (1918–70), Army officer, founding member of the Free Officers' movement that deposed King Farouk 1952; Prime Minister of Egypt 1954–6, President 1956–70; nationalised the Suez Canal Company July 1956, precipitating the Suez Crisis.

3 *Times*, 23 May 1967, 1a–c.

the Golan Heights. The late possibility of a Soviet intervention in support of the
Arab States was overridden by a Presidential order directing the American Sixth
Fleet towards the Syrian Coast, and the ceasefire of 10 June left Israel in posses-
sion of its gains. IB was in London in May 1967 and 'felt desperately anxious
about the survival of the State of Israel'.[1]

TO STEPHEN SPENDER

30 May 1967 [*carbon*]

[Headington House]

Dear Stephen,

I am entirely preoccupied by thoughts of the Middle East; they depress
me, as you may imagine – extremely. What I hate most in a way, even more
than the prospect of what looks like a possible war in various stages, is the
sort of remark that Lord Caradon[2] makes at the United Nations when he
says, 'Fortunately the remarks of the Prime Minister of Egypt are a little
more moderate today than they were yesterday, and upon this we may base
hopes for a peaceful settlement, etc. etc.' That is exactly what used to be said
about Hitler in 1935–36–37 etc. And when the British papers come out and
say 'Naturally the present conflict is very dangerous, but it cannot be settled
unless deeper issues are examined [and a] general settlement is attempted,
from which the natural grievances of the Arabs spring', this is precisely like
the kind of remark that was made about the re-occupation of the Rhineland
in 1936 – which was founded I suppose on guilt about Versailles (which
I never felt), and in this case, guilt about Suez. [...] The Israelis are told to
be calm, moderate, not move, not precipitate the world into war because of
some legal grievance, however legitimate, [...] terribly like the Czechs about
whom Boase[3] once remarked, 'If only those bloody Czechs ceased to exist
we might have a little peace in the world' – except that not merely Boase
but almost everybody feels it about the Israelis – they are like a foundling
which the nations just didn't have heart enough to strangle when it was born,
although the Arabs tried; and which grows to nobody's advantage, whose
interests coincide with nobody's, whose disappearance would create a great
sigh of relief, mixed with a certain amount of gradually vanishing guilt. It
was the condition of a good many little countries in central Europe in the
1930s, but unique to that poor country now. The Americans at least have the
excuse that they are expected to act in a way they cannot be blamed for thinking twice about, whatever they may do in the end; but the British one never

1 *Where Were You?* (172/1), 227.
2 Hugh Mackintosh Foot (1907–90), KCMG 1951, life peer 1964, diplomat; Minister of State for
   Foreign and Commonwealth Affairs and Permanent UK Representative at the UN 1964–70.
3 Thomas Sherrer Ross ('Tom') Boase (1898–1974), art historian of whom IB and others did not
   have a high opinion; President, Magdalen, 1947–68; Vice-Chancellor, Oxford, 1958–60.

expects to act in any situation any longer – they have opted out of all activity as such, into a kind of Scandinavian isolation which would be admirable if it was adopted consciously and openly – they are particularly mealy-mouthed at this moment, it seems to me. However, Stuart would no doubt call all this nationalism, and since Freddie and Dee have signed some sort of pro-Israel resolution, preserves strict neutrality. I love and admire him deeply, as you know, but in political issues he appears to me to behave somewhat like Sartre: the benefits of all the doubts go to the side with which he wishes to identify himself, but which feels no identity with him. [...]

Meanwhile, I am in fearful agony about which architect to choose to build the College. I see myself choosing some very safe and un-enterprising figure and being rightly condemned for it, but all the unsafe enterprising figures seem to be no good for one reason or another. It is rather like preferring Graham Greene or Angus Wilson[1] to say Ginsberg[2] or *The Naked Lunch*.[3] I pass through New York on my way to Brandeis on 9 June. Will you by any chance be there? I stay at the Carlyle Hotel – do let me know.

Now I return to my gloomy thoughts about Palestine. If there really is a flare-up and the Jews are defeated or exterminated there, that will be the end of their whole story; they will remain as a gloomy little sect – the majority will melt into their surroundings, more or less successfully, and a small proud core will remain like Hungarian Protestants, *memento mori*, a skeleton at the feast.[4] Why the poor things cannot be protected, their frontiers guaranteed, their expansion prevented but their extermination discouraged, I cannot understand. It is I think that they are madly unpopular and an eyesore to everyone – Israel has not really mended matters but merely institutionalised them. On this bleak note, let me end.

Yours,

[Isaiah]

---

1 Angus Frank Johnstone Wilson (1913–91), later (1980) Kt; novelist and biographer; 'a lively figure in the 1950s literary revolution', he was, by the early 1960s, 'probably Britain's most distinguished novelist' (Malcolm Bradbury, ODNB).

2 Allen Ginsberg (1926–97), American poet of the beat generation, author of *Howl, and Other Poems* (San Francisco, 1956); correspondence between Ginsberg and William Burroughs appears, with other writings, in their *The Yage Letters* (San Francisco, 1963).

3 Autobiographical novel (Paris, 1959; NY, 1962) by William Seward Burroughs (1914–97), based upon notes written during a period of heroin addiction; the narrative is deliberately surreal, and, according to Mary McCarthy, in a review that appeared in the first issue of the NYRB, 'disgusting and sometimes tiresome, often in the same places' ('Déjeuner sur l'herbe', NYRB, 1 February 1963, 4).

4 IB's comment better fits the Polish Protestants than their Hungarian counterparts: the latter were increasingly discriminated against in the 17th century, but remained a significant minority, and benefited from a greater degree of toleration at the end of the 18th century to flourish again as a national movement in the 19th. Polish Protestantism by contrast declined to the skeletal proportions of modern times.

TO LEONARD WOLFSON
5 June 1967

Headington House

Dear Leonard,

This is in case I do not get you by telephone this weekend. The news from the Middle East is such that it obscures everything. We are suddenly in 1940 all over again – Eden was quite right – he apparently made a marvellous speech in the House of Lords.[1] Still one must go on living: this is only to tell you that after much gestation, to-ing and fro-ing, journeys to Finland and elsewhere, we, i.e. the College, have settled on a British architect – we knew this would give you much satisfaction, and this was not an inconsiderable factor, believe me, in determining the choice, in that, quite apart from gratitude and proper respect, we contemplate working closely with you on all this. The name is Powell & Moya. I cannot officially do anything until this is passed through the building committee, then the full Trust, and after that through the two similar committees of the Hebdomadal Council.[2] I do not believe that the last two bodies will be obstructive; as for the Trust, we are in your hands (don't smile – it is true); they are very sensitive and successful architects, and the only thing wrong with them is that they are at the top of the tree, and are turning away orders – the University of Essex, the Taylorian in Oxford, Leicester University, etc. etc., but it is plain that if they agree to do this – as they will – they will put themselves into it, for they know all too well that on a College in Oxford their ultimate reputation will be based far more than on any other building they are likely to produce in England [...] – our chief difficulty, as you will learn when you come down for the Trust, is of course lack of money too, but I will not frighten you now – that is for later. [...] The College was almost unanimous, i.e. there was one dissenter, who was not against them, but wanted plans etc. submitted from three or so architects, which would have involved 9 months' more delay and the expenditure of £15,000.

Now I must write to Philip Johnson, Bunschaft[3] and Co., and not very easy this is going to be.

Yours,
Isaiah

1 'I will be frank; I do not feel myself in the time of ten years ago, but very much in the 'thirties [...] and if we were to try to do as we did in the 'thirties in respect of Czechoslovakia, at the expense of Israel, we should deserve all we got.' Anthony Eden, Earl of Avon, debate on the Middle East, 1 June 1967, Hansard, HL (series 5) vol. 283, cols. 80–1.
2 The executive committee of the University of Oxford, dating from the Oxford University Act of 1854; from 2000 subsumed within the University Council.
3 Gordon Bunshaft (1909–90), American architect; joined Skidmore, Owings & Merrill 1937, partner 1949; made his reputation with the Lever House plate-glass and aluminium skyscraper in NY 1950–2.

TO PHILIP JOHNSON

7 June 1967 [*carbon*]

[Headington House]

Dear Philip,

You were perfectly right, only too right, I say with gloomy exultation – exultation in human mediocrity, rather like de Maistre. In the end, as you correctly predicted, the English won, slowly, persistently, and by attrition. There were some objective factors which could be regarded as not irrelevant – the fact that we are less rich than we thought we should be; that the buildings have to go up quickly, and with as little expense as is compatible with not having low-priced University Grants Commission [sc. Committee] prefabs – that grim, ever-growing chain of barracks that our modern universities are slowly becoming.

My colleagues rejected Lasdun, Stirling, Sandy Wilson, and insisted on an English architect, backed, as you may imagine, by strong and persistent advice from the RIBA, all the architectural journalists, etc. etc. If I were building a house for myself, or even a theatre, an opera house, a gallery, I think I should have withstood this onslaught. But since this was a college, and had to pass the scrutiny of seven committees, each of which made it clear that it would place the most enormous obstacles in the path of a foreign architect, after the rows which accompanied the rise of St Catherine's – rows which you will agree with me were scarcely worth it – I cravenly yielded. There was certainly nothing else to do: we are half a million short of our minimum requirements; we have to borrow in any case; the Wolfsons demand an English architect, and you were perfectly right in supposing that a single front would be presented, a closed shop in effect declared. If we had unlimited resources, or at least as much money as even St Catherine's had five or six years ago, if the Ford Foundation were not so frightened of being dragged into this as a form of American pressure – which one can understand – if taste, imagination, courage could be made to prevail over the great craving for mediocrity and philistinism by which this country is consumed, things might have been otherwise. But things are what they are, and the consequences will be what they will be, as Bishop Butler once said, so why should we seek to be deceived?[1]

I write this letter to you in sorrow but, I must add, perhaps shamefully, not in anger. The decision has been made, and I feel like Blum[2] after Munich, 'shame and relief'. I only hope the consequences will not be the same.

1 'Things and Actions are what they are, and the Consequences of them will be what they will be: Why then should we desire to be deceived?' Joseph Butler, *Fifteen Sermons Preached at the Rolls Chapel* (London, 1726), sermon 7, 136 (§ 16).

2 Léon Blum (1872–1950), Prime Minister of France 1936–7, March–April 1938, and December 1946–January 1947, the first Jew and socialist to hold that post; pragmatically supported Daladier over the Munich Agreement, September 1938, while professing himself unhappy with the methods by which it had been achieved. He wrote that he was 'divided between a cowardly relief and shame' (*Le Populaire*, 20 September 1938; cited in *The Times*, 21 September 1938, 10b).

And to see you soon in New York, or wherever, and discuss everything in the world, except Oxford and architecture. Please do not let all this go any further; I have been indiscreet enough as it is. My colleagues loved you: but Safety First prevailed. That way lies Baldwin, appeasement, *l'ennemi du bien*.[1]

Yours,

[Isaiah]

TO KENNETH CLARK

7 June 1967 [*carbon*]

[Headington House]

Dear K,

After vast discussions, journeys, visitings, letters and everything that accompanies decisions by committees and colleges governed by the purest principles of democracy, we abandoned our ambition of inviting eminent foreign architects; if only for financial reasons, for, like all institutions of our kind, we found in the end that we had half a million pounds less than we need […]. After all these marches and counter-marches, we finally decided upon Messrs Powell & Moya, whose picture gallery in Christ Church really is a first-class conception and building – at least so it seemed to us who are not gifted with much visual sense. I hope you do not think that too tame. Some of our architectural advisers pressed upon us the claims of younger, untried architects – no doubt it is in principle better to employ men who have not reached the top of their tree, but there was no evidence of genius there, only of lack of opportunity; the risk of becoming a guinea pig simply to demonstrate that their performance fell far short of their promise seemed too dangerous to most of us. And Powell & Moya were virtually the only architects of their calibre not broken by UGC requirements, which seemed to have clipped for good and all the wings of most English architects.

Thank you very much for bothering to answer my first enquiry. When the contours of the building finally emerge, I do hope you will come and look at it and say what you think. You will not, I am sure, blame us for not taking Jacobsen.[2] He may be a man of genius but in his building I feel stifled and behind prison bars.

Yours ever,

[Isaiah]

1 'The enemy of the good'. Stanley Baldwin (1867–1947), 1st Earl of Bewdley 1937; Conservative politician, Prime Minister 1923–4, 1924–9, 1935–7; closely identified with the policy of appeasement; 'Safety First' and 'Trust Baldwin' were the unadventurous slogans of the Conservatives at the 1929 election, which returned a Labour government.

2 Arne Emil Jacobsen (1902–71), Danish architect and furniture designer; his 'Ant' chair was influenced by the plywood mouldings of Charles and Ray Eames; the severity and highly schematic nature of his designs for St Catherine's College (1959) aroused controversy, but the original buildings are now among the few erected in Oxford after 1945 to be Grade I listed (1993); Jacobsen was awarded an Hon. D.Litt. by Oxford 1961.

TO PHILIP TOYNBEE[1]

7 June 1967

Headington House

Dear Philip,

The quick victory looks as if it might happen and I entirely agree about the magnanimity. I think, however, that they are not likely to behave with wisdom or complete generosity; I only hope they will. It is reasonable of them to want guarantees of their security, but the temptation to straighten out the Jordan 'hump', even to keep Jerusalem, may be very strong, although I hope not. This is certainly the moment for some large financial compensation to the Arabs, even if they cannot afford it; they could at least offer to raise a loan. If the Arabs hurled this back in their face, that will be that; but they ought at least to offer. I do tell them that from time to time; so far it has not met with much of a response; but your instincts are as usual quite right. What irritates me somewhat, and even, I suppose, them, is that, say, *The Times*, after withdrawing the hem of its garment during their mortal danger, then preaches to them and tells them not to be brutal, cynical, unwise etc. in the hour of victory. All this advice is doubtless quite valid, but it comes ill from those who averted their faces during the crisis ⟨the *unction* is unattractive⟩; and the illusion that the British and the Arabs would be great friends if it were not for the Jews in Israel is a myth which dies very hard. Arabs simply don't want white men about in their countries, and the Russians, for these purposes, are not white, but grey. The Arabs' attitude in this matter seems perfectly comprehensible to me; I could never blame them for resenting having the Jews in their midst, but the attitudes of the British and Americans, who still half assume that the Arabs would like slightly deferential relations to them, is surely a pathetic, and on the whole discreditable, illusion. [...]

Yours, ⟨with much love⟩

Isaiah

On 11 June IB received the honorary degree of Doctor of Laws from Brandeis University, Massachusetts: he travelled there via New York on 9 June, returning to London two days later.

---

1 (Theodore) Philip Toynbee (1916–81), son of the historian Arnold Toynbee; writer and critic; foreign correspondent of the *Observer*, and a member of its editorial staff 1950–81. His *Friends Apart: A Memoir of Esmond Romilly and Jasper Ridley in the Thirties* (London, 1954) contains memories of the young IB.

TO JOSEPH ALSOP

11 June 1967 [*manuscript*]

'President Special' [PA 100 en route to London]

Dearest Joe,

I have just paid a lightning visit to N.Y–Boston. Naturally the first thing I did was to ring you – no response. But I ran into Stew[art Alsop] at La Guardia while on my way to Boston & he reported on the Rockefeller Party: so that explains it. I heard two speeches: one by Averill [sc. Averell], exploring the wisdom & triumphs of American policy: his remarks about Russia were, as usual, intelligent, true & *well* worth listening to: the other by Prof. Ambassador Reischauer:[1] about the errors & shortcoming of U.S. policy, mainly in Asia. Both seemed v. good: & totally incompatible: if Averill was right, Reischauer was wrong: & vice versa. I was convinced by both. I have no critical judgment: I just like interesting ideas: not the one, clear, permanent truth. Terrible. I am filled with self contempt. But of course *everybody* talked about the Arabs, Israel etc: I was very scared: so, I must say, was the nice gentle little Israeli cultural attaché who called on me by previously long arranged appointment on the Sunday preceding the battle. On the following Thursday I dined with Phil Kaiser[2] in London & met there Hamilton,[3] the super-editor of the *Times*, Sunday Times etc. "I expect I am the only pro-Arab here" he said (he loves Nasser) & was. I suppose the Israelis have so far saved Seato, Nato, etc.: quite apart from the more moving and marvellous aspects of what they did & suffered: how Felix wd have lived through & loved it! how irritated the Dept. of State, the Foreign Office & all foreign offices outside Israel must be: I am moved too by the fact that the French Left, even Sartre, shd have demonstrated pro-Israel feeling: in contrast to high sophisticated New York Jewish intellectuals, very few, I must say, who are more worried about any demonstration of hateful nationalism than the more obviously David/Goliath, Maccabean aspects of the feat. Watching U.N. on television is a kind of drug: the fisticuffs between, say, the Syrian & the U.S. representatives is a queer, undignified, ungrown up squabble between a nasty clever schoolboy & an embarrassed teacher who has to – & anyway does not know how not to – pull his punches. The Israelis did, I am sure, wonder whether

---

1 Edwin Oldfather Reischauer (1910–90), Japanese-born and Japanese-speaking US academic and diplomat; Professor of Far Eastern History and Director of the Harvard–Yenching Institute 1956–61; ambassador to Japan 1961–6.

2 Philip Mayer Kaiser (1913–2007), Balliol PPE 1936–9 (Rhodes Scholar), US diplomat; American Minister to the Court of St James (i.e. deputy *chef de mission*) 1964–9.

3 (Charles) Denis Hamilton (1918–88), later (1976) Kt; editorial director of Kemsley (later Thomson) Newspapers 1950–67; editor, *Sunday Times*, 1961–7; Editor-in-Chief, Times Newspapers Ltd, 1967–81. IB sat next to Hamilton and, feeling 'irrepressibly exhilarated' by the news from Israel, said to him 'It shows that there is a God in Heaven after all', to which Hamilton replied 'I suppose I am the only pro-Arab here.' The Berlins remained late at the dinner 'and on our way back to our flat, walked on air'. *Where Were You?* (172/1), 227.

they *would* be exterminated: historical consciousness (of which the Jews have had too much) is created by such moments: & in the end something permanent, ideas or art, will be produced by it. [...] A novel cd be constructed out of the differing American reactions: and McGeorge [Bundy]? He is perhaps the man for it all:* genuinely rational & free, it seems to me, from prejudice & dark emotions – as free as Wilson & Gaitskell, with a rare capacity for objective political assessment: do you agree? I shall be *very* glad to see you & Susan Mary in Paraggi: & so will Aline.

   love
     Isaiah

I take malicious pleasure in hearing the weighty 'neither anti-Jew nor anti-Arab: after all Nasser's[1] fall may be very dangerous: don't let's be hasty' stuff of such as Frank Giles.[2] I prefer dear Marietta's instinctive heart in the right place reactions: nothing is more absurd than the calm judiciousness of the pompous & powerless.

* but who do *I* deal with now about Wolfson Coll? We *have* chosen the architect. Ha.

TO PHILIP TOYNBEE

   27 June 1967

Headington House

Dear Philip,

   [...] I was in America for two days recently, and there saw left-wing Jewish sociologists plainly identifying themselves with the fighting men of Israel, and in a state of personal euphoria. So they did with the Abraham Lincoln Brigade,[3] so did Deutscher with Trotsky on his white horse and uniform, so did Asians of various sorts when the Japanese became victors in 1905 – it is not an attractive phenomenon, but inevitable in the case of slaves and liberated slaves. It is rather like Mr Shinwell in Parliament who feels 'Our boys have done well.'[4] I sympathise with the feelings of a man who wrote a letter to a newspaper recently saying that he was irritated by his Gentile friends clapping him on the back and saying, 'Well done!' Some professor

1 *The Times* of 10 June 1967 carried the news, under a large headline, that 'Nasser Offers to Resign' after Egypt's humiliating defeat in the Six-Day War; he stepped down only briefly.
2 Frank Thomas Robertson Giles (b. 1919), Foreign Editor, *Sunday Times*, 1961–77.
3 US volunteers fighting for the Republican cause in the Spanish Civil War.
4 Emanuel ('Manny') Shinwell (1884–1986), later (1970) life peer, former Labour cabinet minister, member for Easington, Durham, 1950–70; of Polish-Jewish origin. He had a reputation for pugnacity, and in the debate on the Middle East, 7 June 1967, avowed: 'I am not afraid of the Arabs and Nasserites. I am not afraid of anyone. I take sides, and I am on the side of the State of Israel' (*Parliamentary Papers*, Commons, vol. 747, col. 1071).

in Glasgow tried to do this to me. I turned to stone. Perhaps wrongly but inevitably.

Yours,

Isaiah

TO BAILLIE KNAPHEIS

6 July 1967 [*manuscript*]

Paraggi

Dear Baillie,

Thank you very much for your letter. All is not well here: Aline collapsed: (don't alarm Miss Townshend[1] *too* much) & at first it was thought to be a *heart* attack: then not a heart *attack*, but some sort of coronary disturbance: such I think it was: but due, according to the local specialists, to some sort of 'vaso-mechanical' or circulatory disorder: leading to palpitations, faintness, total weakness etc. After 2 days in a nursing home she demanded to be carried to the house: now she is, thank God, back in a nursing home looked after by some very nice nuns, called *Casa Azzurra* in Rapallo, much better, no longer convinced (as was not absurd, not totally absurd to suppose) that she would never rise again. My own feelings I will not attempt to describe. Anyway it is all much more cheerful now, save that she must rest here for at least another 10–12 days (I privately think longer) while Sir M. Bowra is ruthlessly arriving for his pasta & gin. Peter returns from Yugoslavia on the 8th or 9th & I shall cope a little better. And now to business […].

love

Isaiah

TO PHILIP TOYNBEE

17 July 1967

[As from] Headington House

Dear Philip,

[…] Serene objectivity irritates those who have faced the danger of extermination. When [the Israelis] were in dire danger – at least most of them certainly [thought] that they were, and so did you and I – nobody came to their aid. […] This feeling that they are friendless is certainly a factor in their situation, just as the feeling of monstrous injustice perpetrated against them is at the heart of every Arab attitude. What then can be done? Either they must confront each other, or the powers must force them into some kind of agreement – the latter has not come out very well, but could very well

---

1 Violet Frances Victoria Townshend (1894–1985), IB's typist for several years after his marriage; she later undertook secretarial work for Aline also.

be the solution. Any help from outsiders or peace plans drawn up by well-wishers won't help, especially as they will always contain a certain element of didactic, paternalistic, well-meaning advice to an over-vehement, difficult child. I shall never forget a conversation I had in Jerusalem at the time of the Eichmann trial, when someone whose identity I have completely forgotten said, a propos of all the letters from Archbishops with which they were inundated, calling upon Jews to remember their great spiritual past and the marvellous contribution they have made to religious understanding, to rise above thoughts of mere vengeance, and do something splendid and noble and generous, 'We do not want to be worse than other people, but why are we always expected to behave better than anyone else?'[1] I see that what this man meant was that Israelis are regarded as being on probation. As soon as they do something of which someone even faintly disapproves, the onlookers say 'Aha! He's at it again!' This is no doubt what irritates them and makes all outside advice automatically repellent. How are the Jews and Arabs ever to meet? I simply don't know. [...]

That the Jews have committed faults is not in doubt: they have never had a real Arab policy, and if they said something magnanimous about a refugee problem, and if they explained that they had no territorial ambitions beyond security, no expansionist aims of any kind, it would be better and not untrue, at least so far as the vast majority of Israelis are concerned. Meanwhile there are, as you may well imagine, left-wing Jews, not necessarily Communists, who expect ideal socialist behaviour from the Jews and normal behaviour from the other side. In a sense I understand them: they begin from deep faith in socialist or communist solutions; and think that nationalism is not what it really is – a pathological condition of wounded national consciousness – but a mad excrescence due to 'capitalism' etc. in one of its disguised forms. But they see Arab and African advance as ultimately a march towards lifting the poor towards greater equality, and the Jews as subjectively progressive,

---

1 These remarks are reminiscent, *mutatis mutandis*, of a passage on terrorism that IB drafted in 1946 at the request of Chaim Weizmann, for inclusion in Weizmann's 'Presidential Statement' to the 22nd Zionist Congress in Basle in December of that year. It was incorporated into the address with minimal changes: 'It is futile to invoke the national struggles of other nations as examples for ourselves. Not only are the circumstances different, but our purposes, too, are unique. Each people must apply its own standards to its conduct, and we are left with the task of weighing our actions in the scales of Jewish tradition. Nor must our judgement be dazzled by the glare of self-conscious heroism. Masada, for all its heroism, was a disaster in our history. It is not our purpose or our right to plunge to destruction in order to bequeath a legend of martyrdom to posterity. Zionism was to mark the end of our glorious deaths and the beginning of a new path leading to life. Against the "heroics" of suicidal violence I urge the courage of endurance, the heroism of superhuman restraint. I admit that it requires stronger character, more virile nerves, than are needed for acts of violence. Whether they can rise to that genuine courage, above the moral degradation of terrorism, is the challenge which history issues to our youth.' Barnet Litvinoff (ed.), *The Letters and Papers of Chaim Weizmann*, Series B, vol. 2 (Jerusalem, 1984), ii 629–41 at 636–7. Weizmann sent the revised text to Meyer Weisgal, commenting: 'Isaiah's paragraph about terrorism has some punch, hasn't it?' (letter of 18 November 1946).

but objectively an obstacle. This is a kind of schematisation which seems terrible to me [...]. It is really this in Marxism that has always maddened me – the bogus pattern and the shifting of moral responsibility on to it, and the division into good victims who must be helped (say fellaheen)[1] and the bad victims (say refugees from concentration camps) who must be jettisoned. Every organised religion has some element of this in it. But I am beginning to talk like Bertrand Russell or Freddie and must stop. But do let us meet.

   Yours, ⟨with much love⟩
      Isaiah

TO MEYER SCHAPIRO

20 July 1967

[As from] Headington House

Dear Meyer,

   [...] As for the Middle East, of course I agree. The presence of Begin[2] ⟨& Stern[3] terrorists too: I can't believe that killing Englishmen is so greatly superior to killing Arabs;⟩ is a nightmare, but I honestly do not believe, although this may be mere optimism, that there is anyone of weight in Israel today who wishes to expand from the Euphrates to the Nile.[4] [...] But what is fascinating is that, according to accounts of persons who have just arrived from there, the entire Russian and Polish intelligentsias are passionately favourable to Israel; the more their governments denounce it, the more they feel them to be a kind of collective Daniel and Sinyavsky.[5] The opposite phenomenon is to be found in the United States and partly in England,

---

1 Arab peasants.
2 Menachem Begin (1913–92), Belarusian-born Zionist; commander, 1943–8, of the Irgun (Irgun Ts'vai L'umi: National Military Organization), the right-wing Zionist military force founded in Palestine in the early 1930s by extremist elements within the Haganah, and which employed terrorist methods against British and Arab targets; Begin founded and led the Herut (Freedom) Party after Independence 1948; leader of the Opposition in the Knesset until the 1967 Six-Day War, when he joined a National Unity government; leader of right-wing Likud bloc 1973.
3 The 'Stern Gang', name given by the British to the Zionist paramilitary terror group led by Avraham Stern (1907–42), 'Fighters for the Freedom of Israel' (known by its Hebrew acronym, Lehi); formed in 1940, when Stern and others left the Irgun, Lehi was dedicated to attacking the British Mandatory authority.
4 A possibly unconscious echo of I. F. Stone's article 'Holy War', NYRB, 3 August 1967, 6–14, which IB had just read (338–9): Stone wrote of 'the right-wing Zionists who dream of a greater Israel from the Nile to the Euphrates (as promised in Genesis) with complete indifference to the fate of the Arab inhabitants' (8).
5 Yuly Markovich Daniel (1925–88) and Andrey Donatovich Sinyavsky (1925–97), Russian writers arrested by the Soviet authorities in September 1965 for allegedly disseminating anti-Soviet propaganda by having their fiction published under pseudonyms abroad. They were tried and found guilty in February 1966, and sentenced to five and seven years respectively in hard labour camps. The case became a cause célèbre in the West, where it was taken to mark an end to the era of Khrushchev's liberalisation, and seen as 'a stern reminder that the Communist Party still expects writers to [...] uphold the Communist standards of behaviour' ('Writers Silenced', Times, 15 February 1966, 11b).

where the governments are not so hostile, but part of the intelligentsia is suspicious, and leans over backwards and sideways etc. Of course Dayan[1] is a possibly dangerous figure, but nothing like as suspect as corresponding potential Führers elsewhere, or do you think this is pure chauvinism in me? I cannot deny that the attitude of those who think that the progress made by the Arabs as symbolised by Nasser etc. is placed in jeopardy by Israel, which should therefore be swept out of the way – that it is simply unfortunate that this half-bourgeois, half-socialist State should have got itself entangled with the decrepit and reactionary West, and will therefore have to be got rid of in one way or another, if the colonial peoples are to attain to the next historical stage of their social self-realisation – this, which is a kind of big battalions realism, is detestable to me. It is one thing to complain of specific short-comings – chauvinism, disregard for Arabs' rights and feelings, fanaticism of various sorts, etc., which is of course perfectly justified; and another to evaluate a country or a people in terms of some great historic pattern and then to form one's views in terms of the answer to the question: on which side of the historical process does a given community or race fall [...]? This plus a certain amount of self-suspicion, self-criticism and even self-hatred (in the manner of Miss Arendt) is what I think left-wing Jewish intellectuals may be tempted by – just as there is an equally unattractive attitude represented by militant strutting on the part of Zionist zealots, proud of the achievements of 'our boys'. Sambursky and his wife assure me that there is no puffing out of chests, no self-congratulatory vainglory, no shouting or beating of drums or clashing of cymbals in Israel, and I believe them – I have no evidence to the contrary. Sambursky is very upset by the cold-hearted reaction of the fellows of Oxford Colleges who withdraw the hems of their garments and look the other way when a human community is faced with extermination. I find nothing surprising in this, for the wounds from which these Gentile withdrawers are suffering are many and intelligible. Yet when I read of the Dutch or the Swiss who sacrificed a certain percentage of their daily income to make good the damage, and help with the defence of so remote a country, I do not remain unmoved. ⟨This is written from Italy. Here opinion on the left, apart from the majority of the Communists, is almost too fervently pro-Israel. The Israelis are identified with *the resistance*, Arabs with their old Fascist allies. This may be unfair, but not unintelligible.⟩ Despite urgent calls I have refused to go there because it seems to me a little vulgar to visit that country just at present. I am afraid of triumphal marches and meetings on Mount Scopus.[2] I am told that I am wrong. I do not know what you think.

1 Moshe Dayan (1915–81), Israeli general and politician; rose to prominence during the 1948 War of Independence; Chief of Staff, IDF, 1953–8; led the invasion of the Sinai Peninsula 1956; Minister of Defense during the Six-Day War; resigned 1974 over the IDF's lack of preparedness at the outbreak of the 1973 Yom Kippur War.
2 The northern part of the Mount of Olives, within the municipal boundaries of today's Jerusalem,

I think that there must be some rational, sane point at which one can take up one's stand without falling foul of what Bob Silvers regards as, e.g., Stuart's excessive sympathy for embattled Israelis.

'You and I, we alone are wise, we look before and after ...'. I won't go on with the quotation. It will be very nice to see you in the summer, but tell me what to do about your lodgement. ⟨Love to Lillian⟩

Yours,

Isaiah

⟨P.S. I've just read I. F. Stone[1] in the N. Y. Review on the Middle East. It is an intelligent & troubled piece [...]. Stone's chief fault seems to me to consist in his assumption that the problem is only one of refugees: the Jews, as such, don't need a country in which their status is not a problem: that if e.g. the U.S. had absorbed all the European refugees (millions if need be) that wd have been more satisfactory than displacing the Arabs; in short he believes in the possibility of mass assimilation – say as of Italians or Greeks in America:[2] I shd be in favour of this if it were possible: sheer survival of 'Jewish values' can be bought at too high a price: it may be defeatist to wish to melt, but perhaps immoral to condemn one's descendants to the continuance of an agonized self consciousness & the generation of endless Laskis, Arendts, Max Lerners,[3] Sulzbergers,[4] R. Arons & other casualties & sad examples of false consciousness. But the question doesn't seem to me to arise: assimilation on a sufficient scale is not on: the evaporation rate is, as Namier saw, too slow: the patient will die before he recovers with this medicine. Hence: those who long to belong & be a national community, must not be denounced because their life creates problems with Arabs (who have certainly suffered

---

and a UN-protected Jewish enclave in Jordanian-controlled territory after the 1948 War of Independence; victory in the 1967 Six-Day War brought it within Israel, a fact of great symbolic significance as well as strategic advantage. On 9 June Leonard Bernstein conducted at a famous concert there, organised by Teddy Kollek in aid of a Jewish–Arab youth foundation, and attended by Levi Eshkol, Prime Minister of Israel, Zalman Shazar, President, and Ben-Gurion.

1 Isidor Feinstein ('Izzy') Stone (1907–89), journalist; Washington editor of the *Nation* magazine during the Second World War; from 1953, with his wife's assistance, published from home a four-page newsletter, *I. F. Stone's Weekly*, which quickly gained national renown for independent-minded – if left-leaning – investigative journalism.

2 Stone focuses on the question of refugees, but by no means presents this as the problem in its entirety, while his thoughts on assimilation and Israel are more complex than IB allows. Stone wrote: 'It must also be recognised, despite Zionist ideology, that the periods of greatest Jewish creative accomplishment have been associated with pluralistic civilisations in their time of expansion and tolerance: [...] the greatness of the Prophets lay in their overcoming of ethnocentricity. [...] But Jewry can no more turn its back on Israel than Israel on Jewry. The ideal solution would allow the Jews to make their contributions as citizens in the diverse societies and nations which are their homes while Israel finds acceptance as a Jewish State in a renascent Arab civilisation.' op. cit. (336/4), 11.

3 Maxwell Alan ('Max') Lerner (1902–92), Russian-born Jewish US journalist, editor and academic; syndicated columnist, *New York Post*, 1949–92; Professor of American Civilization, Brandeis, 1949–73.

4 Arthur Hays Sulzberger (1891–1968), publisher of the NYT 1935–61; a practising Jew.

an injustice: so have the East Germans, Sudeten, inhabitants of Czernowitz: & Montenegrins: the question is, wd some other solution not have involved greater injustice & much more misery to many more persons? it is bad to accept imperfect solutions smugly, & not count the cost: but is it not worse to reject them out of fear of facing public opinion, reality etc? as communists, the Council of Judaism, & Mr Stone do?) & problems for American Jews who don't wish to be a minority (that's all right) & deny that they are (that's not all right) & hate everything which brings this melancholy fact home. What *new* approach does Stone advocate? stoppage of immigration from say U.S.S.R. even if the Russians let the Jews go? the reduction of the Jews to a formidable, feared, & potentially persecuted minority in an Arab state? He doesn't know what he wants: he merely hates Jewish Jingoes. So do I. But this is not enough: a Zollverein with Jordan & Lebanon *is* possible: but the ferocious exposure of Israeli vices won't help with it – oh dear –⟩

TO PHILIP POWELL AND HIDALGO MOYA

21 September 1967 ⟨– written before the meeting at Universal House⟩

[Headington House]

Dear Mr Powell and Mr Moya,

I feel that in an excessively English fashion, I forbore to say at any point either yesterday or when you came to tea how very gifted and fascinating I genuinely thought the design of the College to be and how marvellous that you should have been able to produce it so swiftly. The conception of the relationships of various social groups seems to me perfect; so is the relationship of the quads; the islands are a splendid invention and the economy of the space quite masterly. On all this I really should like to congratulate you most warmly and I feel sure that all the colleagues who you met yesterday felt this too. They did not actually reproach me for not voicing their sentiments but would have done so if I had not run away so immediately. The only point on which I (and they) still feel reservations is your sense of the need to preserve so much for development by a future generation. I really do not think that we need be too scrupulous about that – the future must always be left to look after itself, and in any case will. I do not think we shall be blamed for spreading ourselves too widely even if we did cover the high ground to the south-east. And I still feel that the most exquisite of all views in that site is the bend of river and that one could perhaps try something which would enable this to be freely seen from the 'public' rooms and from wherever possible. [...]

Let me once again say that the main purpose of this letter is not to advance my particular quirk, but to say with great emphasis that you have indeed fully and more than fully justified the confidence which we have given you. I really do look forward to months of happy and fruitful collaboration in

which you imagine and realise, while we niggle and hesitate, question and in the end, I am sure, almost inevitably surrender – ⟨though not on everything.⟩
    Yours very sincerely,
        [Isaiah Berlin]

The show trial of the Soviet writers Yuly Daniel and Andrey Sinyavsky in 1966 reverberated in the West for a considerable time afterwards, and dominated the discussions of the Council of the Great Britain–USSR Association in November–December 1967. The Association had been established in 1959 to promote non-political cultural contact between Great Britain and the USSR, and IB was a member of its Council, though never closely involved in its affairs. At a meeting on 29 November 1967, at which IB was present, Violet Bonham Carter, a member of the Executive Committee, urged that the Association bring direct pressure to bear on the Soviet authorities over the Daniel/Sinyavsky trial. Her confrontational approach did not reflect the feeling of the meeting, and as a compromise Fitzroy Maclean,[1] Chairman of the Council, was delegated to seek a meeting with the Soviet ambassador at which he could privately register the Association's protest. This, however, did not satisfy Lady Violet, who eventually resigned over the issue. IB's hesitation to endorse her approach reflected not so much a lack of courage as a heightened awareness of the possibly dire consequences of his actions for the very dissenters that he sought to help. He was haunted by the memory of the bleak conditions in which the poet Anna Akhmatova had lived when he saw her in Leningrad in 1945–6, and also by the realisation that these conditions were almost certainly made worse as a result of his visit.

TO VIOLET BONHAM CARTER

7 December 1967

                                                                    Headington House
Dearest Violet,
    [...] We have two aims in view, (*a*) not to let a shameful incident pass without raising our voice, (*b*) not to make [worse] the position of the two victims – and of the *four* victims who are about to be sentenced in the trial connected with the same 'offence' next week which has been announced.[2] Are these aims incompatible? I have the following experience in the matter.

1 Fitzroy Hew Royle Maclean (1911–96), 1st Baronet 1957, diplomat, soldier, MP, writer, politician; widely thought to have been one of the inspirations for Ian Fleming's James Bond; British Embassy, Moscow, 1937–9; at this point Conservative MP for Bute and North Ayrshire (1959–74); chairman, executive board, Great Britain–USSR Association, 1959–70, later (1977–87) President; 'one of the hardest boiled, toughest specialists on the Soviet Union known to me, regarded by them as a dangerous but intelligent antagonist' (from an omitted part of the following letter).
2 The trial in Moscow of three young Russian writers – Yuri Galanskov, Aleksey Dobrovol'sky and Vera Laskova – accused of publishing the underground literary magazine *Phoenix-66*, and

After my return from the Soviet Union in 1946, I did a certain amount {of}, if not of protest, of critical comment on the appalling conditions of individual persons in the Soviet Union. I learnt to my horror shortly afterwards that one of [sc. among] the direct victims of this were (a) some of my Russian relations, who were in due course arrested, grilled, one of them[1] was exiled to Siberia; where he was not actually killed, but where his health was sufficiently undermined for him to die very shortly afterwards in squalid conditions; (b) the persecution of the famous poetess Akhmatova, a poet of genius and a most distinguished and wonderful woman, with whom I made great friends, and who hinted something about this when I spoke to her on the telephone in Moscow in 1956, and then, when she came and was given a degree at Oxford two years ago, told me the whole horrifying story about the direct effect of an innocent visit by me to her, in the course of which nothing was said about politics; she corroborated in grisly detail the fate of my relations, in which, owing to our warm friendship, she took particular interest, and which she, as it were, investigated. She has written exceedingly moving poems about all this ⟨beautiful as they are, they hardly compensate for the facts out of which they grew⟩. She is now dead, but it cannot be referred to for fear of further reprisals. This is somewhat different from what happened under the Nazis – where I know of no cases of specific persecution as a result of critical comment by friends or relations abroad, although this may, of course, have happened. As a result of knowing all this by about 1948, I submitted to blackmail: in the sense that I sign no letters of protest about Soviet action with my personal name because it became quite plain that the result of this might be torture and death to individual persons [...]; and this is not something which I could take on my conscience – it was clear that the suffering risked was far, far greater than any conceivable value which the addition of my name to a letter, a protest etc. could conceivably have from any point of view. I therefore have ⟨had acutely personal⟩ experience in this matter which I did not want to voice at that meeting, because I could not be sure of who was present. [...] My responsibility for the disgrace of Akhmatova and her sufferings, and the unenviable fate of my two relations, still lies heavy upon my conscience, although I could not have known that a mere meeting with me in 1945 would have had that result. Although I tried to argue that it cannot have been a *mere* meeting with me that produced it, Akhmatova was quite clear that it *was*, and produced tragically conclusive evidence. My own personal silences followed.

This, of course, is not the same thing as a formal act by the Association

---

of a fourth, Aleksandr Ginsburg, who compiled a dissident report on the Daniel–Sinyavsky trial, was expected to open in Moscow on Monday 11 December 1967.

1 Leo Berlin, IB's uncle, Professor of Dietetics, Moscow, who died in 1955 of a heart attack on a Moscow street on seeing the man who had tortured him in a Siberian prison-camp (L2 357/2). Could this be Pasternak's source for the manner of Yuri's death in *Doctor Zhivago*?

and the Council. If we make our protest public will the Russians dissolve the organisation? They may. The flood of protests which have reached them on the subject of Sinyavsky and Daniel evidently made no difference to the fate of these unfortunate men, and merely made Sholokhov,[1] the unworthy winner of a Nobel Prize, demand heavier punishment for them, presumably just to show us. I do not think that the Soviet Union values cultural relations with us much, and at the moment they do not fear us, and while toughness by Americans or even French, whose temporary alliance they value, might have an effect, they pretty well discount us at the moment so far as realpolitik is concerned. At any rate that is my impression. It may be worth putting an end to the Association over this, for what purposes does it really serve from our point of view? I suspect simply as an agency for acting as guides and hosts to a number of Soviet intellectuals, the majority of whom are innocent and decent, if perhaps weak enough to be at least outwardly conformist. When one meets these people one realises that their joy in escaping across the frontier and coming to look at the West is so touching and so great that it is well worth promoting. The hopes of serious cultural relations – except in the region of the sciences and perhaps philology and those sorts of subjects – is not very real. Do we want to jeopardise such exchanges as occur under our patronage for the sake of salving our consciences and telling the truth? Perhaps we do, but that, I think, is the way to put the issues – but I see that some of our members might very well feel otherwise. All the same, the issue has to be faced. The Soviet Union will surely continue to commit crimes of this kind, and crises of conscience of this sort will face us from time to time, even if we pick out only the most horrible cases. All the same, we can't do *nothing*. I should have thought that the best thing to do would be to instruct Fitzroy to warn our opposite number – Surkov – and the Soviet Ambassador[2] too, that the Council feels that it cannot remain silent, and that unless there is some prospect of the alleviation of these victims during this the 'Human Rights' Year there is no telling what we shall do. When we have learnt the reaction to this démarche we can make up our mind what next. [...]

Love

Isaiah

---

1 Mikhail Aleksandrovich Sholokhov (1905–84), Russian writer; born and died in Veshenskaya beside the river Don; awarded the Nobel Prize in Literature 1965, primarily for his epic novel *Tikhii Don* (*The Quiet Don*, 1928–40), which became the most widely read work of Soviet fiction; a politically active member of the Communist Party and from 1939 vice-president of the Union of Soviet Writers.

2 Mikhail Nikolaevich Smirnovsky (b. 1921), Soviet diplomat, regarded as an expert on the US; head of the American Section of the Foreign Ministry in Moscow, then Soviet ambassador to UK 1966–73.

The Berlins spent the last week of 1967 in Jerusalem, returning to England in the second week of January 1968.

TO JENIFER AND HERBERT HART

New Year's Day 1968 [*manuscript postcard*]

Jerusalem

Jerusalem is now incredibly grand & beautiful – no longer a kind of Swiss Cottage + Brandeis U[niversity]. Victor [Rothschild] has just been here & loves it because he *is* treated like a Pasha: Gaza is probably terrible: but the mood is not blown out with egocentric chauvinism, rather they are gloomy about the lack of favour which their minimum needs find in all foreign offices – & wish to know why, if they behave with self sacrificing humanity, generosity etc., their chances of survival & acceptance [don't] increase. They are right to think the Arabs will accept *nothing* at their hands: it seems to them that this holds of all others too. I don't know *what* to say to this.

I.B.

TO MCGEORGE BUNDY

16 January 1968 [*carbon*]

Wolfson

Dear Mac,

May 2nd is the Day. We are all agog. Her Majesty and the Duke of Edinburgh arrive, take luncheon in their railway car (mixed relief and disappointment), those in the Town Hall – City – must on no account be offended. Then a brief visit to Somerville (the Queen wishes to see a women's college), then to us, 3.20? p.m. – a marquee is erected, she is slowly led up in the most dignified manner possible by myself, an old hand at such ceremonies (I have never in my life taken part in any such thing and shake and shiver in every limb), and introduced to persons in rising order of importance, culminating in the Chancellor. After she has performed her appointed function, all those tremendous cars will roll away to Christ Church, where other Powell & Moya buildings are to be unveiled; there, perhaps in the neighbouring college of Oriel, also a royal foundation, a square meal is finally to be given her, the lords and ladies in waiting and the Lord Lieutenant and the equerries. And so the cortège will slowly roll away and the stone will have been well and truly laid.

But to be serious for a moment: if it were possible for you or any representative of the Ford Foundation to be present that would be a great source of satisfaction to the College and to me […]. After luncheon is the crucial hour. Thursday 2 May is the day. […]

Yours,

[Isaiah]

TO ROWLAND BURDON-MULLER

17 January 1968

Headington House

Dearest Rowland,

This is just a brief note to correct a misapprehension on your part. You are profoundly mistaken if you think that my views on Vietnam (which I see are shared by Mrs. Trilling) have anything to do with my friendship with anyone: I am not particularly a friend of either Bundy,[1] although I have happy business evenings with one of them, and it makes me dreadfully ashamed if the motives that you attribute to me were ones by which I was in fact moved. I said what I said because I believed it: it may have been mistaken, although I believe it all still, including Domino, which I am practically alone in holding, except for, it seems, all Australian parties.[2] I do indeed think that massacres are worse or at least as bad as wars and that there is a moral case for not leaving people to be exterminated, however nasty they may be, and however wicked one's motive in joining them in the first place – that is what we did in the case of a good many Czechs and it is not a particularly proud moment in British political history. I know that you disagree with me about this and quite see that there is another very powerful side to the case, for I myself am much agonised about it, as indeed the article[3] conveyed; it is far easier – as I said in it – to plump for one side or the other and feel happy and among allies. I cannot do that. But do not let us controvert the issue: about it we shall, I suspect, not agree. But I do not want you to think my views have anything to do with not wishing to hurt somebody's feelings or, worse still, with friendship with x or y for pure or other impure motives; it is indeed a misreading of everything that I believe myself to be – better that you should think me a fool or heartless or a bloodthirsty hawk than a temporiser, as you appear to.

There!

⟨How are you? don't, I beg you misunderstand this cri de coeur. How are you? how is your health? & why will you not return to England & will you come to N.Y. in late February to see me when I am in the horrible ungentlemanly Blackstone[4] again?

much love,

Isaiah⟩

1 McGeorge Bundy and his elder brother William Putnam Bundy (1917–2000), also a proponent of the Vietnam War, and a foreign policy adviser to Presidents Kennedy and Johnson.
2 Domino theory, a guiding principle of US policy during the Cold War, held that if one country fell to Communism its neighbours would follow, and was used to justify US intervention in Vietnam. According to an American official in Saigon in 1966, speaking to the *Times* correspondent Richard Harris: 'Fundamentally we are fighting this war to stop a Chinese attack on Australia' (14 February 1968, 11e).
3 310–11, 601–2.
4 NY Hotel at 50 East 58th Street, IB's preferred address in NY during the period 1966–70: 'We used to stay at the Blackstone Hotel, which in a frightfully derelict and run-down way had a certain

In 1968 three books were published about the charismatic German Rhodes Scholar Adam von Trott,[1] who was executed for his role in the July 1944 plot to assassinate Hitler.[2] IB had known von Trott well at Oxford, and the authors of two of the books in question, Diana Hopkinson and Christopher Sykes, had consulted him. IB was initially captivated by von Trott, but ultimately considered him 'a man of very ambivalent character who was one of Hitler's victims and a martyr, but who was responsible for a lot of intellectual and spiritual legerdemain, not altogether conscious on his part'.[3] Their friendship never fully recovered from a letter that von Trott wrote to the Manchester Guardian[4] *in February 1934, in which he effectively dismissed the reports of the paper's special correspondent in Germany, F. A. Voigt,[5] about the prevalence of anti-Semitism there. Von Trott wrote of the strict judicial impartiality of the German courts within his purview in Hessen, an area that Voigt depicted as 'notorious for persecution'. According to von Trott 'there was most emphatically no discrimination against Jews' in the courtroom; nor, he implied, was there officially sanctioned violence in the streets: 'Again and again I have spoken to active Storm Troopers who feel themselves pledged to the race doctrine of their leaders but would never consider themselves justified to execute it with methods of violence.' Voigt responded to von Trott's claims with incredulity, observing that the physical beatings of Jews in Hessen were 'known to everyone [...] who has eyes to see and ears to hear. If Mr Adam von Trott is blind and deaf to them, he will be at least equally blind and deaf to the less obvious "legal" victimisation of the Jews.' Von Trott's gruesome execution made his memory especially poignant to his Oxford friends, including his admirer Diana Hopkinson, whose autobiography* The Incense-Tree *was in part an elegy to him.*

cosmopolitan cosiness, but in the end it became too much for Aline (I can put up with almost anything, or so I think I daresay quite falsely): the walls peeled, the bathroom leaked and even the concierge – a charming Count Vorontsov-Dashkov – began to look too seedy, although he is a man of considerable sweetness and charm. So we are about to move to a hotel whose name plunges me into embarrassment – it is called the Ritz Towers' (IB to Elizabeth Sifton, 29 June 1970). Roman Illarionovich Vorontsov-Dashkov (1901–93), born in Tsarskoe Selo, the summer residence of the Russian Imperial family, near St Petersburg, grew up in France but settled in New York.

1 (Friedrich) Adam von Trott zu Solz (1909–44) studied law in Germany before going up to Balliol in 1931 as one of the first German Rhodes Scholars since the First World War. He recoiled at the news that Hitler had become Chancellor in 1933, but returned to Germany that year. In June 1940 he entered the information service of the German FO. For his involvement in the July plot he was executed by being hanged from a beam by piano wire on 26 August. Uniquely for a German national, he is commemorated on the Second World War memorial plaque outside Balliol College chapel.

2 The books are: Diana Hopkinson, *The Incense-Tree* (London, 1968); Christopher Sykes, *Troubled Loyalty: A Biography of Adam von Trott zu Solz* (London, 1968); and Christabel Bielenberg, *The Past is Myself: The Experiences of an English Woman in Wartime Germany* (London, 1968).

3 To Aubrey Eban, 31 October 1961.

4 Von Trott's letter appeared under the headline 'The Nazi Rule In Hessen: Anti-Semitism Denied' in the *Manchester Guardian*, 21 February 1934, 18; Voigt's short reply directly follows.

· 5 Frederick Augustus Voigt (1892–1957), British journalist of German descent, Berlin correspondent of the *Manchester Guardian* 1920–33; one of the first foreign correspondents to warn of the dangers of Nazism, which he regarded as a threat to all European civilisation; his great moral and physical courage belied his frail appearance, and he was vehemently anti-totalitarian.

TO DIANA HOPKINSON[1]

16 April 1968 [*manuscript*]

Headington House

Dear Diana

Thank you for that fearful extract:[2] I suppose that *all* bits of one's remote past – & perhaps less remote too – appal one. I can scarcely come across a letter from the past by someone else without feeling upset: because so much has changed & one has forgotten all that seemed most central & crucial once. I admit that *this* particular letter is not quite so terrible. Still: it seems to me *madly* pompous, affected, silly, artificial & makes me go hot all over – was I really *so* self conscious, so unnatural, did I really ring so false? I feel distressed all over again. If you really want to print it, I won't stop you or (I mean) try to persuade you not to – though I wd rather you told the story in your own (more genuine) words: won't you? If you insist on putting it in – *your* book: & you must be free, let me beg you only to amend it slightly as indicated by me in pencil: it makes the letter a *little* less monstrous (perhaps): oh but I do feel ashamed! it is a tiny thing, I know, but it is lik[e hear]ing one's voice for the first time, reproduced: now I know (I say to myself) why all those people think one false, empty, silly, embarrassing. Embarrassed I painfully am. But there. Do eliminate the *worst*, as requested, dear Diana! As for Adam: I too hope C. Sykes won't get him too wrong.[3] All the people who knew Keynes well were horrified by Roy Harrod's Court portrait:[4] Christopher S. is an honest, nice & sensitive man: he will do his best: & to read proofs with the writer there is *not* ideal. Still: if you think something isn't right, do tell him so. And don't let him speculate on whether Adam was (a) or (b) or (c) etc: let him make up his mind: declare firmly that Adam was thus & thus & not otherwise: & *not* go on about who does & who does not agree with this: otherwise it turns into a book not on Adam but on his reflection in all our minds: which is all right in a fancy film like *Roshamon*,[5]

---

1 Diana Mary Hopkinson (1912–2007) née Hubback, LMH 1931–2, a friend of IB's from her under-graduate days, when she had been romantically involved with Adam von Trott; trained and worked as a copywriter, and worked with refugee children 1936–40; married David Hopkinson 1939.

2 From a letter to her written in November 1933 (printed in its original form at L1 73–5) after he had inadvertently purloined from her home, and then lost, a matchbox in a silver frame. The falsified version appeared in her autobiography, *The Incense-Tree* (345), 121.

3 A reference to the then forthcoming book by Christopher Sykes (345/2).

4 R. F. Harrod, *The Life of John Maynard Keynes* (London, 1951).

5 sc. *Rashomon* (1950), film by the acclaimed Japanese director Akira Kurosawa, in which the appar-ent murder of a samurai and the rape of his wife by the bandit Tajomaru are seen through the contradictory accounts of the three principals and a sole witness: the film explores multiple perceptions of reality and the elusive nature of truth.

but not a biography. Penny plain! that is the ideal. I go back to the extract from my idiotic letter! Ninepence coloured![1] Awful!

    love

       Isaiah

On 2 May the Queen laid the foundation stone of Wolfson College in its pastoral setting beside the River Cherwell. Present, as well as the members of the College and their numerous guests, were children belonging to the fledgling College and from the nearby schools, an 'unrestrainedly appreciative company'. It was a particularly happy day, that 'augured well for the College's future'.[2] IB's speech was one of the few for which he was heard to adopt, in his friend Arnold Goodman's words, 'a style of dignified, deliberate solemnity. [...] He was asked to address the assembly in less than a hundred words, to speak slowly, and to use the microphone with the utmost care. He complied, with results which were admirable and somewhat startling. A bemused friend asked me, on leaving the ground: "Was that really Isaiah speaking?"'[3]

TO CHRISTOPHER SYKES

II May 1968 [*manuscript*]

                           As from Headington House

Dear Christopher,

    Is it true, as they tell me, that you propose to publish a letter from me to A[dam] von Trott in your forthcoming biography?[4] If this is so (or even if not: how can I be sure?) I am plunged into a state of anxiety & apprehension. I have no recollection of what I may have written: the thought that *any* letter of mine wd ever be published to the world never (so naive was I – am I) entered my head – please put me out of my suspended condition & tell me whether this *is* so: & if it is, may I see the text & context? My words are poor things, I truly believe, but, I suppose, mine own. If this is a canard, please forgive me. New York – the student riots – the slowly mounting mass of black anger – is terrifying. Don't publish *this*, will you – by the time you get this I shall be (I hope) in Oxford.

    yrs

       Isaiah

1 In the 'toy theatre' popular in Britain in the first half of the nineteenth century, the stage was replicated in miniature, with tiny detailed images of the characters of popular plays affixed to cardboard mounts: these images were sold in sets, 'a penny plain and twopence coloured' – the former black and white, the latter vividly coloured.

2 Frank Jessup, op. cit. (241/2), 1999 ed., 18.

3 Arnold Goodman, 'IB at 80', contribution to 'Isaiah Berlin: The World and Wolfson – Two Appreciations', *Oxford Magazine* no. 48 (Trinity Term 1989, Eighth Week), 6.

4 Excerpts from IB's letters to Adam von Trott of 26 October 1933 and late July 1934 (L1 62–3, 90–1) were quoted in Sykes's biography, 100, 110–11.

TO CHRISTOPHER SYKES

24 May 1968

Wolfson

Dear Christopher,

[...] I read through the whole of the MS that you sent me – 'waded' with the greatest possible enjoyment in these rich waters – but was duly horrified, as you half-supposed I might be, by the two quotations from my letters. The second letter I dimly remember, the first I have no memory of at all. Are there more letters from me in your possession? The thought that anything I ever wrote privately would ever be printed at all, and more particularly while I was alive, never occurred to me in my life. This is not, I fear, modesty, but unrealism – but the possibility came to me as a violent shock. I would, of course, rather not be quoted at all, indeed not mentioned, but if this is not possible, then I must, at least, attempt to achieve a minimum degree of self-protection. [...]

Now for the [...] letter about the 'Trott row'. There was indeed a breach with me in 1934 as a result of the letter in the *Manchester Guardian*. I vaguely remember the letter itself, which was written to confute F. A. Voigt, who at that time was writing some very true and very brave dispatches from Germany. Isn't that right? I thought, and those who suspected Greuelpropaganda[1] equally thought, that the letter could only be taken as implying that the persecution of Jews etc. had been exaggerated in the *MG*, which would be the only point of writing it. As we all assumed Adam to be what he seemed, a troubled German patriot and not someone playing a complicated political game (which may have been heroic and right, but which was certainly complicated and certainly concealed from our eyes) the letter moved us ⟨– i.e. me & my Oxford friends who knew T.⟩ – to indignation – I can't quite remember who 'we' were; but I know that Shiela G[rant] D[uff], and more particularly Diana, defended Adam, and ascribed my feelings to the fact that, given my origins etc., I would naturally be particularly sensitive to this issue. I cannot clearly remember what happened after this – I think that Adam was told by David A[stor] that I was making critical remarks about him, and according to Adam charged me with 'disloyalty'. Adam then wrote and reported this and begged me not to dissolve our friendship, and entered into a long defence of his acts, ending (so far as I can remember, but I am not sure) with an expression of great regret for having written as he did, even though his ⟨sole⟩ motive was not to weaken his own position in Germany at that time, etc. At any rate, I remember being moved by the letter, which seemed written from the heart. It was, as you rightly surmised, an olive branch, and an apologia. I wish I could lay my hands on it. At any rate, I wrote him the letter which you have (I should dearly like to see a copy of it, out of pure

---

1 Propaganda consisting of (exaggerated) accounts of atrocities (German 'Greuel').

nervous curiosity). Are the strictures about his treatment of Diana better left un-quoted? I suppose it would hurt her feelings to represent him as having treated her as badly as he certainly did, although she may not have felt that. But, as you see, I did forgive him, although I thought that David A. in particular had been very tiresome, and had made particularly bad blood; & that all those girls – Shiela GD, Diana, Maire Lynd[1] etc. – who ⟨loved him &⟩ defended him so violently, were moved by emotions *very* remote from moral or political judgement. All this irritated me fearfully, but his own letter was full of such affection and gaiety and charm (which, as you know, he used marvellously and, in the best sense of the word, quite shamelessly – he was a colossal flirt and tremendous wangler – those who distrusted him did so for this reason) that I was completely melted and probably went too far in my reply. Hence my outburst. You are very sweet and understanding about that and I am very grateful and I do not mind the quotations. They show me to be a gullible ass – still I would rather be that than over-suspicious, which would have been wiser. Hence my letter of introduction to Felix Frankfurter (in, was it, 1936?) and my friendly feelings towards Adam until the summer of 1939, the last time that I saw him, when, although his anti-Nazi views were not in doubt, his talk was *too* ambiguous. This shook me, but did not lead to real doubts until the reports of what he said in England in 1939, not only in Cliveden,[2] but in Oxford and afterwards in America, reached me. I was duly attacked ⟨by Americans⟩ for befriending and helping a dubious personality.

This is really all that I have to report. [...] As for David A., grasp of reality is not the Astors' strongest suit. In this case he seems to be hopelessly blinded by love and worship.[3] I had a letter from Diana, who takes a much calmer and reputable and favourable view of your book. Crossman will review it in the *Observer* and will delight in the 'dialectical' contradictions of Adam's behaviour, I am sure. This will cast more light on the reviewer than on the subject, so, as you say, a splendid time will be had by all.

[...] I repeat, I would *much* rather be left out of this altogether, but if you feel that this would be an offence against the truth, and want to discuss Adam's assurances to me in 1934 about the misinterpretation of his MG letter, then by all means let us talk about this. You say that universities are places for rows. This is true, but in this case it was surely much more than

---

1 Maire Lynd (1912–90), Home Student, Oxford, 1930–4, reading classics; pupil, close friend and holiday companion of IB; reader for William Heinemann publishers; married Jack Gaster (1907–2007) 1938.
2 Grand Italianate mansion overlooking the Thames near Taplow in Buckinghamshire, belonging to Waldorf, 2nd Viscount Astor, and his wife, Nancy (David Astor's parents). It was used by them to entertain a group of politicians and public figures in the 1930s – friends who shared a commitment to appeasement, and whose supposed influence on government policy was exposed in the press as the baleful workings of 'the Cliveden set'.
3 David Astor, who commissioned Christopher Sykes's biography, devoted himself to exonerating von Trott, his Balliol contemporary and close friend, from any imputation of pro-Nazi sympathies or of duplicity in his dealings with his English friends.

a typical flare-up between dons. The political issue was genuine – similar tensions were going on about Communism. Those were not storms in academic teacups, either: ⟨(they led quite a lot of people to very fateful conduct, alas, on the whole.)⟩

Yours ever,

    Isaiah

TO MCGEORGE BUNDY

  31 May 1968 [*carbon*]

[Headington House]

Dear Mac,

By the time you get this I shall have arrived in New York, against all advice, to attend a Commencement at Columbia, which surely should have been postponed.[1] The cause is not my avidity for an honorary degree, so much as embarrassment at the thought that the only motive for staying away is the fear of embarrassment. I propose to come armed with a water-pistol, and if any militant student approaches me I shall rise up against him and say that the dons have turned, the worms fight back, and douse him. La Grande Peur, which is supposed to have seized everybody in 1791, or whenever it was, seems to be nothing compared to the terror of all professors before the slightest sign of student dissatisfaction. Why cannot the professors build barricades of their own? [...]

Yours,

    [Isaiah]

Shortly after midnight on 5 June 1968 Senator Robert Kennedy was shot and fatally wounded in Los Angeles, having just won the California primary in his bid to secure the Democratic Party presidential nomination; he died in the early hours of the following day, 6 June. The assassin, Sirhan Sirhan, was a strongly anti-Zionist Palestinian, apparently motivated by Kennedy's support for Israel, although this was never a central policy in his platform; Kennedy campaigned instead on opposition to the war in Vietnam, and advocacy of the rights of the underprivileged. After his death parallels were inevitably drawn with the assassination two months earlier of the civil rights leader Dr Martin Luther King, Jr, and also with the assassination of his brother, President John F. Kennedy, in November 1963, and there was considerable comment in the press, on both sides of the Atlantic, about the rising levels of violence in society, and in particular of gun violence in the US. The entertainer Sammy Davis, Jr, a friend of the Kennedy family, said after hearing the news in London: 'If America really cares, if they want to stop killing of its leaders – whether they be religious leaders, civil

---

1 In April Columbia University had been racked by student protests, ending with a violent police operation to clear occupied buildings.

rights leaders, or presidential leaders or senators – they've got to do something about it. Take the guns away. Take the guns out of the hands of the idiots, whether they be black or white. Take them away.'[1]

TO ARTHUR SCHLESINGER

6 June 1909 [sc. 1968; *manuscript*]

As from Headington House; in fact, *Quantas* [sc. Qantas; en route to London]
Dear Arthur
I beg you to forgive me for being so inadequate yesterday.[2] There were all kinds of things I wished to say, but offices are not good places for private life […]. All I really wish to say […] is: you now feel terribly low, first because your friend, whom you loved, is dead; and a world which he might have begun to build won't exist: the mixture of courage, radical action, energy, good sense, un-extremism, which could have pulled America & the Left out of the mess and swamp in which we are, won't occur. At least the way out (in the long run I am not pessimistic; and the new world won't be to our taste anyway) will be much slower and costlier. […] Why don't you seek a temporary vacuum; in Oxford, for a little while, just come & stay and do nothing if you like, & read & walk a little, & consider what it is best to do, personally & politically against Nixon[3] on the one hand and Marcuse[4] on the other; opinion is very malleable at the moment surely […]. Or if you must carry on with what is left of the Kennedy forces, come & see us a little later in Italy in July–August – our schedule is patchy but it can be achieved. Don't I beg you sink into understandable bitterness and despair; I am not saying this (forgive me for moralising) from a distance; to my own astonishment I cannot myself hold back my tears in this place in which I am sitting; I really cannot *bear* this Hobbesian world in which no one is safe from maniacs and all forms of life

1 *Times*, 7 June 1968, 5g.
2 IB had been at CUNY the previous day, 5 June, where Schlesinger held the Albert Schweitzer chair of humanities, and had heard his friend deliver an impassioned commencement speech on the subject of 'America 1968: The Politics of Violence' (*Harper's Magazine*, August, 1968, 19–24). When Schlesinger spoke, Robert Kennedy's life still hung in the balance: by the next day, when IB wrote, he was dead.
3 Richard Milhous Nixon (1913–94), Republican 37th President of the US 1969–74; Eisenhower's Vice-President 1953–61; defeated by Kennedy for the presidency 1960, but elected in 1968, and re-elected in 1972; resigned office (the first President ever to do so) after Congress began impeachment proceedings, in response to his involvement in the June 1972 break-in to the Democratic National Committee headquarters at the Watergate offices in Washington, DC.
4 Schlesinger's commencement address included a damning indictment of Herbert Marcuse and the New Left, of which Marcuse was a leading ideologue, for encouraging a belief in the political utility of violence. Schlesinger noted, with irony, that the ultimate winners in any general recourse to violence 'will not be the idealists of the left but the brutalists of the right' (ibid. 23). IB's own considered views on Marcuse were less positive than his remarks to Bertell Ollman (136) would suggest: 'He seems to me to be a frivolous figure, amusing, quite intelligent, somewhat glib, agreeable to talk to, but in the end a café talker like those "free" radicals with whom Marx associated before he went to Cologne and Paris' (to Gershom Scholem, 18 February 1972).

tremble on the verge of collapse; I long for some bourgeois stability; some protection against the turning of all private, inner, disinterested activity into screams and shouts and public issues; the conversion of all that matters most, personal relations, inner life, into sociological and psychological problems – even by sober decent moderates […] – depresses me fearfully. But I see you are in for dark days; if you think it any help come to see us.

Love

Isaiah

TO MCGEORGE BUNDY

17 June 1968

Wolfson

Dear Mac,

Thank you very much for your letter of 4 June. Its contents are most welcome. To hold the Ford shares for at least two years would suit us very well. We shall probably hold them for longer, in fact. I see that your letter was written on the very day on which I went through my peculiar ordeal at Columbia – all in desperate search for a doctorate which I was unable to achieve by my own efforts […].

It was all dreadfully expunged by the news of the next day. I heard Arthur make a commencement address at his and my university and saw him later – his life seemed to me (I hope temporarily) totally in pieces. I only hope that the great wave of self-incrimination, which is natural enough, won't lead to the emergence of some terrible father figure, who will promise to set everything right. The effect in England was very violent indeed, and provoked scarcely any criticism of the United States, but genuine fellow-feeling. There is really no doubt about the special relationship, for proclaiming which I was once publicly denounced by the late Lord Beaverbrook. ⟨I often wondered whether it was genuine. Funnily enough, it is.⟩

If you are coming to England towards the end of this month, do communicate, although if you do not I shall not hold it against you, but I do see that over-developed countries have moral and social problems, as well as economic ones, which no one ever predicted. Rather like the Roman Empire at the beginning of the fourth century AD – but there: I don't propose to try to emulate either Joe or Prof. Toynbee[1] – if I had to choose between them, I would still rather be the former. And so, I am sure, would you.

Yours ever,

⟨Isaiah (earned M.A.)⟩

1 Arnold Joseph Toynbee (1889–1975), historian; Director of Studies, Royal Institute of International Affairs, and Professor of International History (becoming Research Professor), London, 1925–55. His cyclical view of history, set forth especially in his 12-volume *A Study of History* (London, 1934–61), was a regular target of IB's critcism.

TO YEHUDI MENUHIN

18 June 1968

Wolfson

Dearest Cousin,[1]

I am not surprised by the letter which you have kindly forwarded to me. I, too, have had messages from S. F. Vogel,[2] and have shamefully ducked all his requests. I do not know what one owes to one's ancestors: I have warm feelings towards these now so strange-looking men, but when I went to New York some years ago and visited the 'Centre', presided over by our cousin Menachem M.,[3] I went in heavy disguise and preserved my anonymity for fear of being discovered. I had had some correspondence with the present leader's father when I was a schoolboy, but this left no profound impression upon me, I fear. I see absolutely no reason why you should (you surely have no kind of obligation to) play like David[4] before them, especially gratis. You could send them a message if you wished, and so, perhaps, could I, and it would be delightful to send a joint message, but that's about it. Holy men they may be, but barbarous to some extent also: and despite the patronage of my own patron, Saint Isaac, I propose to keep away – there is an element of persistency and highly developed modern advertising technique about these people, which, although it may be condoned, given they have to struggle in our unattractive world, one need not gratuitously associate oneself with. That is my feeling. But you have a kinder heart – and if you yield I shall feel guilt, but still remain personally obdurate. No, no; you have absolutely no duty to exhaust yourself for them. A kind letter would be quite enough. I saw you the other night on a television programme presided over by Robert Morley,[5] with David Cecil and Tariq Ali.[6] What a frivolous man Tariq is. Still,

---

1 Yehudi Menuhin (1916–99), later (1993) life peer; British violinist of American birth and Russian-Jewish descent, and IB's fourth cousin; the first Jewish artist to play in Berlin (under Furtwängler) after the fall of the Nazis; he was a child prodigy, but from the late 1940s concentrated increasingly on conducting and teaching.

2 (Shraga) Faivish Vogel (b. 1936), rabbi, Executive Director of the UK Lubavitch Foundation in London 1960–2008; known as 'the face of Hasidism' in the UK.

3 Menachem Mendel Schneerson (1902–94), leader of the Lubavitcher Jews in NY, one of the most devout sects of Hasidic Judaism, and a distant cousin of IB's; Mendel Berlin, IB's father, cherished his family's link to the 18th-century founder of the Lubavitcher, Rabbi Schneur Zalman, but IB regarded their modern incarnation as 'alarming fanatics', any mention of whom 'would cause his face to tighten into a rare and uncharacteristic expression of dislike' (MI 15).

4 'And it came to pass, when the evil spirit from God was upon Saul, that David took an harp, and played with his hand: so Saul was refreshed, and was well, and the evil spirit departed from him.' 1 Samuel 16:23.

5 Robert Adolf Wilton Morley (1908–92), actor and playwright, had a prolific stage and film career; he had presented the TV show *Sunday Night People* on 9 June, to which IB may here refer?

6 Tariq Ali (b. 1943), writer and left-wing political activist; editor, *Black Dwarf*, 1968–70, *Red Mole* 1970–3.

he compared favourably with Nancy Mitford,[1] who seemed to me nauseating. You alone remained serene and uncontaminated by it all. [...]

Yours, ⟨with love⟩

Isaiah

TO JEAN FLOUD[2]

5 July 1968 [*manuscript*]

Wolfson

Dear Jean:

[...] I did vote for giving S.[3] the money: although Herbert said he could not see, given my stated view, why I did. Lionel Robbins started off by saying that to him Mosley was the incarnation of evil: that if he entered a room, he, Lionel, wd leave it at once. Sayers[4] did not say this: but cast doubts on the importance of the subject. Wheare (chairman) said nothing. Herbert spoke eloquently to the effect that a true and competent account of Fascism was a service not only to the truth but to those who wished to understand & avoid the evils in question. The two chief promoters of the fund were there. One remained silent but voted with the other who spoke forcibly in favour of S. (who in the interview said he *would* write about antisemitism, Lord Nuffield's[5] contributions to the movement, etc.) on the ground that the victims cd only gain by a careful analysis: a warning that even able, interesting, sincere men etc. cd cause such disasters & become so vicious. After this I did, plucking up all my tiny stock of courage, I did say that it *was* embarrassing that Mosley *would* emerge in a better light than that in which we liked to think of him: that there was a problem: Lionel said he was impressed by

1 Nancy (Freeman-)Mitford (1904–73), daughter (eldest of the seven children) of 2nd Baron Redesdale; novelist; married (1933, separated 1939) Peter Murray Rennell Rodd (1904–68); author of *The Pursuit of Love* (London, 1945), *Love in a Cold Climate* (London, 1949), *Noblesse Oblige* (London and NY, 1956) and other best-sellers.

2 Jean *Floud (1915–2013), sociologist and college head.   *biog'r'n Keynes? (2 vols)*

3 Robert Jacob Alexander Skidelsky (b. 1939), later (1991) life peer; historian; Research Fellow, Nuffield, 1965–8, British Academy 1968–70; associate professor of history, Johns Hopkins, 1970–6. Skidelsky had applied for financial assistance from the Thank-Offering to Britain Fund in order to pursue his biographical research into the life of the British Fascist leader Oswald Mosley. The fund's origins (228/2) made Skidelsky's choice of research topic a sensitive one, and caused serious problems when his biography of Mosley was published in 1975. The Fund was administered by the British Academy, and IB was one of its patrons with Lionel Robbins, Ernst Chain and Hans Krebs. JF argued strongly against Skidelsky's application, but never raised the issue with him directly, and their close friendship remained undisturbed.

4 Richard Sidney Sayers (1908–89), Cassel Professor of Economics, London, 1947–68.

5 William Richard Morris (1877–1963), 1st Viscount Nuffield 1938; pioneer British motor manufacturer, Chairman of Morris Motors Ltd 1919–52; a major philanthropist, founder of Nuffield College, Oxford; in 1930, during the Depression, he was persuaded by Oswald Mosley to give substantial financial support to help found Mosley's New Party, in the belief that it would reinvigorate the economy and society; but as Mosley's Fascism became plainer, Morris withdrew his backing.

Herbert's cogent arguments, & wd not oppose; Sayers too: I voted in favour because – given the donors' views – I could not see how we cd defend refusing S. given that we thought (a) that he was good enough (b) that the dangers of fascism in England were not such that the truth shd be suppressed pro tem: (c) that where the case is dubious, it was best to lean towards no censorship. But I remained guilt ridden (not difficult for me) & attacked Herbert with some acerbity when we had lunch in a Wimpy later. If you had been there & spoken as you wrote, you wd have won I think, even against dear (*dear?*) Herbert. Stuart & Wollheim think we cd not but have done as we did. [...]

    I.   [...]

TO JEAN FLOUD

7 July 1968 [*manuscript*]

[Postmark Oxford]

Dear J.

[...] I am about to write to Herbert officially about senior/junior Oxford rapport:[1] nothing about discipline: but something about listening to under-graduate criticism of curricula: and about the reasonableness of their resist-ance to the idea that they should be treated as recruits for technological forces: Trotsky's labour battalions: the Left is deeply divided on this: the ideal of fully developed human beings seems vaguely classical, reactionary, Tory to some: or rather it is theoretically accepted but only after the terrible wars are over: when the enemy has been routed: after the corridor of the dictatorship of the good: when, we all know, it will be too late. [...] How does one *show* that this is naive & it all costs seas of blood not followed by the reign of universal love? This is what the miserable centrists, the contemptible moderates, the crytpo-reactionary sceptical intellectuals have always agonized over. Popper, Hayek, are too dogmatic & too conceited & removed from the actual lives of the people they are prescribing for: & blind, complacent, & scholastic. Chomsky[2] is too irresponsibly utopian. Whom shd one follow? I long for leaders: I am a natural hero worshipper: I long for a flag: I should readily suppress truth, sign petitions supported by specious reasoning, attack old friends, behave like

1 In 1968 Herbert Hart chaired the University's Committee on Relations with Junior Members, a subject largely overlooked in the Franks Report of 1966, but which had become acutely import-ant in the interim. Hart's report, published 1969 and duly implemented, proposed reform of the disciplinary system, and ways of involving students more in the running of the university; it contributed to the quelling of student protests that had, for the most part, already run their course. IB believed strongly that student opinion should be consulted more often, and listened to with greater attention. He did write to Hart, but not until 10 October.

2 (Avram) Noam Chomsky (b. 1928), influential US linguist, philosopher, pioneer in psycholin-guistics, and astringent political commentator; joined the faculty of MIT in 1955, and has taught there ever since; John Locke Lecturer at Oxford 1969; a consistent and active left-wing critic of US foreign policy, adamantly opposed to the Vietnam War.

a partisan, if I found a cause or a leader I wholly believed in: perhaps I can only say this so confidently because I know I shall not find such a one: no feet to sit at [...].

    I.

TO JEAN FLOUD

    20 July 1968 [*manuscript*]

[Oxford?]

[...] Mexico.[1] I was *very* terrified of it: I went there only once in 1944[2] & stayed with a rich American family[3] (I was poorish then: but, you must forgive me for this awful truth, I felt no difference: I adjust too easily: & I've never been seriously poor: never literally anxious about the future: only prey to general self contempt – never self pity – not fear of concrete Elend[4] – although I suppose I feared the Nazis in 1940) and I was depressed. Those frescoes drenched with blood – blood everywhere – in Cuernavaca and Mexico City too: first a Rivera[5] fresco of Aztecs slaughtering human sacrifices: then Spaniards slaughtering Aztecs: then persons being killed in what undergraduates like to call C18: then Spaniards being slaughtered in the Mexican revolution in early C19:[6] then the blood which flowed at the time of good old Juarez, then Madero, Zapata etc:[7] finally a big fresco of a guerilla, & at his feet a farmer with his throat cut with a scythe (I think) & saying Tierra e Libertad.[8] And all those motionless Indians staring at the sky unblinking,

1 JF (on sabbatical leave 1968–9) was lecturing at the Colegio de México in Mexico City in the summer of 1968.
2 In fact 1945 (L1 535–6).
3 The Dwight Morrows (L1 336/3, 523/1).
4 'Misery'.
5 Diego María de la Concepción Juan Nepomuceno Estanislao de la Rivera y Barrientos Acosta y Rodríguez (Diego Rivera) (1886–1957), Mexican painter, and the central figure in the Mexican muralist movement; married (twice) to the painter Frida Kahlo (1907–54). Rivera's monumental and didactic public works, such as those at the National Palace, Mexico City (1929–35), and the Palace of Cortés, Cuernavaca (1929–30), present a narrative of Mexican history that intertwines pre-Columbian themes with revolutionary socialist imagery. IB's memory of these striking murals is, however, notably hazy at the distance of 24 years: for example, even where the subject matter is violent, they cannot be said to be 'drenched in blood'.
6 sc. the Mexican War of Independence (1810–21), fought with eventual success against the Spanish colonial authorities.
7 Benito Pablo Juárez (1806–72), President of Mexico 1858–62, 1867–72, and a leader of the resistance to the French Mexican expedition of 1861–7; he died in office, his country consumed by civil strife. Francisco Indalecio Madero (1873–1913), Mexican revolutionary, and President 1911–13; murdered during a military coup. Emiliano Zapata (1879–1919), influential and revered Mexican revolutionary; supported Madero's successful 1910 coup against the dictatorship of Porfirio Díaz (1830–1915), but after Madero's failure to implement promised land redistribution waged a guerrilla war in pursuit of 'land and liberty'; killed in an ambush by government forces.
8 'Land and Liberty', a populist slogan of the Mexican Revolution (1910–c.1920). The motto appears twice in Rivera's famous staircase mural at the National Palace, but the image described by IB is in fact a conflation of three, perhaps four, of its scenes.

still & fanatical, looking at the sun: too rigid & inhuman. Mexico City full of tourists, the Chapaultepec Conference,[1] & fuss & triviality: & the Reforma Hotel, but the countryside remote, alien, & D. H. Lawrency.[2] Not for me: not for the jolly Jewish singleton, the friend of chattering Russian intellectuals: not even for the privileged British 1st Secretary, as I was, with rebates on everything & treated with exquisite courtesy by the diplomatic colony, offered great glasses of *jugo*:[3] more blood! Suitable for Trotsky[4] or [Alasdair] M[a]cIntyre or ferocious rebels. Not good for soft shelled Liberales like me. Still I did enjoy hot tequila etc. but the sight of a sword swallower & fire eater with a painted face: I saw what the gay, horrible middle ages might have been in Europe & why bookish persons left the world & locked themselves in monasteries. I read the newspapers about the poor Czechs:[5] even Tariq Ali *says, if* the Russians use force in Czechoslovakia, he will actually lead "a large scale" demonstration to the Soviet Embassy. Much good *that* will do [...]

Yrs

I.   [...]

IB was closely involved in every aspect of the emerging Wolfson College, including its physical design. The architects Powell & Moya used the setting by the river Cherwell to create a small harbour, on either side of which the two main accommodation blocks were to be built. The layout reminded IB of the harbour at Portofino, which he knew and loved, except that there, on one side, the buildings opened on to the sea in a curve, whereas in the original plan for Wolfson both sides would be straight, a scheme later modified when the southerly one was given a 'crank'. Although he claimed to have no feeling for natural beauty ('People are my landscape'),[6] IB instinctively baulked at so rigid a shape in so sinuous a setting, and during summer 1968 he peppered Powell with postcards from (and of) Portofino, hoping to persuade him and Moya to change their plan.

---

1 The Inter-American Conference on the Problems of War and Peace met at the castle of Chapultepec (sic) in Mexico City from 21 February to 8 March 1945, concluding with the signing by 20 American countries of the Act of Chapultepec, which committed the signatories to joint action against aggression towards any American State – a major advance in Pan-American solidarity.

2 The novelist D[avid] H[erbert] Lawrence (1885–1930) visited Mexico in 1923, and settled there briefly 1924–5, writing *The Plumed Serpent* (London, 1926), which explores the overwhelming effect on a European widow of the elemental power of Mexico's Aztec past.

3 'Juice'.

4 Assassinated on 21 August 1940 while exiled in Mexico (where until his last year he had lived with Rivera and Kahlo, with whom he had an affair).

5 During July 1968 speculation grew in the Western press that the Soviet Union would use force to stifle the reformist government of Alexander Dubček (1921–92), elected First Secretary of the Czechoslovak Communist Party in January 1968. Dubček's reforms – the so-called Prague Spring – were seen as a threat not just in Moscow but also in Warsaw and Berlin: the future stability of the Warsaw Pact was at stake, a point not properly grasped by Dubček.

6 359/2.

They eventually gave way gracefully, and with humour (though Moya was less convinced than Powell), afterwards referring to the block in question as 'the Berlin Wall'.

TO PHILIP POWELL

   1 August 1968 [*postcard*]

                                                                    Oxford

I continue to persecute you. The colours [of the postcard] are hideous: but you'll have no difficulty in abstracting your vision & Moya's from them. The shape tells its own tale, surely? Can it be that the sylvan scene of "Cherwell", where everything curls & curves, & the trees, branches, grass, stream, each pursues its irregular complex lines & fantastic patterns – is it here that recti-linear rigours are most suitable? Let me persuade you to some gentle inclina-tion to [a] shape less stiff!
   I.B.

TO JEAN FLOUD

   16 August 1968 [*manuscript*]

                                                                    Paraggi

[...] Sir M. Bowra.[1] He gets what he gets by *extorting* it from life (or his friends). He imposed himself on us: I can take almost anything: & owe him a good deal anyhow: Aline wept with frustration when he shouted, inter-rupted, ruined meals, insisted on concentrating on (to her) meaningless pre-war Oxford trivia (which I like, of course) & could not be got off them. He eats as much as he can: his greed is terrific: & he drinks what he can get: omnivorously & indiscriminately: & grows dark purple: he goes up our hill & down it: slips, falls, takes what Evelyn Waugh called "arsers" – all this can be called intolerable exploitation or great & splendid gallantry, according to one's values: it is both I suppose: he is determined to end the last phase at a gallop, whoever is pushed about & trampled *en route*: spirit: appetite: courage: egoism: ruthlessness: like a *condottiere* at the wrong time & place, & on an absurdly petty scale: when I remember his earlier years: how parents trembled at the thought that their sons were being corrupted violently by this Byronic, satanic, brilliant destroyer: & how now he is a pathetic old porpoise, fat, resentful, suspicious, getting what he can by pitiful efforts – unable to secure invitations, admired only by his colleagues & perhaps distant school-masters and smaller U.S. universities – a kind of Churchill unrealized – a Dr

---

   1 Then a house guest of the Berlins at Paraggi.

Johnson without the moral weight & the marvellous gifts & the unimpeachable integrity – goodness! [...]

Yours

I.

TO MARIETTA TREE

16 August 1968 [*manuscript*]

Paraggi

Dearest Marietta,

What heavenly days! someone once asked the German poet Wolfskehl[1] (not a writer of the first or second water; an obscure-ish aesthete who, being a Jew, turned Zionist in New Zealand whither he escaped from Hitler & where he died. But no matter: like a bad encyclopaedia I am always trying to pepper people with a mass of trivial & obscure small facts which merely clutter up the memory gratuitously). Anyway: when this man was asked what kind of scenery he most admired, he said "people are my landscape".[2] It is so with me. I don't mind about real landscape: if the human beings near me are sympathetic all is well; if not, nothing is; no compensation is possible; one unsympathetic person & all is ruined: it is very tiresome to mind so much & socially inconvenient. Imagine then; the company of old beloved friends: whom I truly do adore: plus the perfectly sympathetic & friendly Mrs Bradford (?); in a marvellous villa, in Florence where everything is endlessly re-visitable, re-seeable, never boring, never flat, or too familiar or monotonous or uniform: with *delicious* food, a car (which does make a distinct difference) and again affection, gaiety, sweetness & amusement and (above all – morally sympathetic company) & what *can* one ask for? The weather I really do *not* mind about: Aline does, Ronnie does, most people do, but I do not: only the human landscape matters – just as changeable, precarious, enslaves one just as much: but in this case, perfect. I am trying to convey that I was very happy: so, as far as intimate knowledge goes, are Aline & Stuart (whom Sir M. Bowra obstinately calls Stew) – just arrived in time to dine with Sir M: he seemed subdued but not miserable: the degree of his deafness is a function of how much he eats & drinks: last night he ate enormously, drank copiously, & could not hear a single word anybody (not

---

1 Karl Wolfskehl (1869–1948), poet; born into a patrician Jewish family in Darmstadt; left Germany for Switzerland on the day of the Reichstag fire, 27 February 1933, and in 1938 fled Italy after witnessing the rise of anti-Semitism there; chose New Zealand as his final destination because of its extreme distance from Europe.

2 'Menschen sind meine Landschaft', cited by Alfred Schuler, *Fragmente und Vorträge aus dem Nachlass* (Leipzig, 1940), 51. Schuler 'fulminated against the shallowness of soulless men ignorant of nature and its life-forces, an ignorance epitomised, he thought, in the Jewish poet Karl Wolfskehl blaspheming: "People are my landscape"'. G. L. Mosse, 'The Mystical Origins of National Socialism', in Michael R. Marrus (ed.), *The Origins of the Holocaust* (*The Nazi Holocaust*, vol. 2) (Westport/London, 1989), 47.

merely I) said to him: *and* looked dreadfully purple. Perhaps this *is* the best way to gallop through the last phase: I'd rather decline gently. [...] Again & again thank you: idyllic it was: Pace e Gioia as the hero of the Barber of Seville says more than once.[1]

My love to you –
Isaiah   [...]

TO PHILIP POWELL

17 August 1968 [*manuscript postcard*]

Portofino

The green lawn is marvellous – Portofino is *much* improved by it: but even without it, it is *much* more beautiful, especially because of its exquisite curve, than Cassis, or indeed any French mediterranean harbour city – do, *do* persist in letting your gifts solve this problem! think, *think* of the admiration & gratitude of posterity, long after the problem of graduates' wives and covered garages & pre-helicopter lives have grown obsolete. [...]

I.B.

TO ANNA KALLIN

1 October 1968

Headington House

Dearest N,

[...] I feel depressed by the rapid growth of barbarism – I daresay every generation has – among our young men: the revolutionaries of my day had some respect for knowledge and intelligence, and tried to learn from the 'enemy' in order to use the weapons – whatever they may have been, philosophy or history or mathematics or technology – for their own ends. This generation is complacently ignorant, uses mechanical formulae to dispose of anything that may be difficult or complicated, hates history on the whole, wishes to throw off the past (which I can understand if it is a return to a still older past) – the future cannot be returned to or used, it is only a hollow word! The old nihilists at least thought they respected science – the new ones confuse crudity and sincerity, and when culture is mentioned their hands really do automatically reach for a paving-stone. But I must not go on with this lamentation: it sounds like some decayed liberal from Turgenev, or some horrified old baronet in *The Times*. [...]

I enclose another copy.[2] All this is surely a commonplace to Germans. It is

---

1 'Peace and joy': tediously repeated by Count Almaviva (disguised as the singing teacher 'Don Alonso') at the beginning of Act 2 of Rossini's *Il barbiere di Siviglia* (*The Barber of Seville*).

2 Of his 'The "Naivety" of Verdi' (308/2), which applies Schiller's distinction between the naive and the sentimental to the composer.

only the English who have never heard of Schiller[1] etc. So Salome is shocked.[2] I cannot believe that her husband would have been. What would the late Deutscher have said? Could he have brought himself to condemn Castro in this connection, for example?[3] I really feel depressed for the first time, not by the thought of general decadence, but by the prospect of having to live with Nixon on one side and Brezhnev[4] on the other. We have never lived at a time when there was literally nobody to look up to before. But I must stop. It is all very well for Martin [Malia] and his Church (which cannot be said to be behaving too impressively either), but what are you and I to do?

Yours,

Isaiah

TO MORTON WHITE

15 October 1968

Headington House

Dear Morton,

[...] The dons are on tenterhooks waiting for the next undergraduate outburst. The principal purpose of the real rebels is, of course, not to extort concessions from the University, but to learn the true technique of revolutionary struggle by provoking resistance and fighting; there is a committee headed by Herbert Hart which is supposed to produce rational schemes for the reform of the University – the conservatives maintain that the undergraduates (they hate the word 'students') are largely passive and don't desire any change. I daresay as far as Oxford is concerned [this] is probably pretty true; the liberals and radicals maintain that whether the undergraduates are passive or not, there are many cases for reform (this is what I believe, although I am probably classified as a reactionary). There is a wonderful piece in our radical journal, *New Left Review*, in which the real counter-revolutionaries and reactionaries, who have stopped British progress towards proper revolutionary ideals, are listed as mainly 'white' expatriates beginning with Namier, Wittgenstein (who is regarded as a major political conservative and counter-revolutionary

---

1 (Johann Christoph) Friedrich von Schiller (1759–1805), German philosopher, dramatist and poet; influenced by Kant, he was specially concerned with the nature and value of aesthetic experience, and became a major figure in the Enlightenment in Germany.

2 By the Soviet suppression of the Prague Spring. Salome Halpern (1888–1982), wife of Alexander Yakovlevich Halpern (c.1879–1956), Russian-born lawyer who frequented left-wing Russian émigré circles in New York during the Second World war, when IB met him; after the war the Halperns lived in London, where Anna Kallin was their lodger.

3 At the height of the Czech crisis Fidel Castro unequivocally aligned Cuba with the Soviet invasion: 'The Czech regime was marching toward capitalism, inexorably toward imperialism' (*Times*, 24 August 1968, 1e).

4 Leonid Il'ich Brezhnev (1906–82), General Secretary of the Communist Party of the USSR 1966–82; his period in office was marked by an intensification of the persecution of dissidents in the USSR, and by the Soviet invasion of Czechoslovakia in 1968, which he ordered.

and obscurantist), Popper, Gombrich, myself, aided and abetted by Moore, Austin and other monsters, with only Gellner and Deutscher as children of the light – I daresay those Dead Sea Scrolls were equally reliable, historical documents. [...]

Yours ever,
Isaiah

TO ELIZABETH HARDWICK

6 November 1968

Wolfson

Dear Elizabeth

Thank you for your wholly delightful letter – gloomy though our political prospects are, I see that this can offer material for deathless satire. We both long to see you and Cal.[1] Aline may have to go and visit her mother again, but I shall sit here until the stint begins in mid-February, and back to CUNY, Arthur and the bearded students – who are now, in point of fact, swarming through Oxford, attacking All Souls, putting up obscene graffiti on the walls, some of which are genuinely funny – I daren't dictate one of them, but may add it in manuscript later.

[...] The students are turning everything topsy-turvy, though not in Columbia style. Indeed the Americans who have come here from Chicago or Berkeley or Columbia look with natural contempt upon the local situation – the grievances are not grievances, the outrages are not outrages, student activity [is] a miserable, tame affair compared with what can really happen, the police not a patch on the Chicago cops – they will not have anything to do with these feeble amateurs – they are very disdainful.

The Professorship of Poetry this year, as a result of the idiocy of the last election, has become a total shambles.[2] The students, who have no votes, want Yevtushenko[3] – the only thing wrong with him is that he knows no English, is a bad poet, and has not replied, nor is he expected to; the

---

1 Hardwick and her husband, the poet Robert 'Cal' Lowell, were due in Oxford, where Lowell had a visiting fellowship at All Souls for the academic year 1969–70.

2 In the previous election (1966) for the Oxford Professorship of Poetry ('that combination of indirect Byzantine politics and the Grand National'), Robert Lowell had been defeated by Edmund Blunden after 'an abrasive campaign'; the vote was 477 to 241 (*Times*, 18 July 1968, 3c). The 1968 election was triggered by Blunden's resignation on grounds of ill health, and in the early stages Lowell was considered a possible candidate. In the event he chose not to run in what proved to be a crowded field of eleven.

3 Evgeny Aleksandrovich Yevtushenko (b. 1933), Soviet writer and poet, came to prominence as an outspoken young poet during the Khrushchev years; he accepted his nomination in 1968 and was the overwhelming favourite among the undergraduates; controversy nevertheless surrounded his alleged support for the imprisonment of the dissident writers Yuly Daniel and Andrey Sinyavsky by the Soviet government.

respectable candidate is Roy Fuller,[1] who, as you know, is a decent poet, a nice quiet solicitor – quite blameless, very dull as a human being, and an even duller lecturer (I am told); the dons' candidate is Miss Enid Starkie,[2] a clear, warm-hearted, frightfully boring elderly Irish lady, who has written lots of books about French poets, with not one single idea remotely discernible among all those arid wastes of terribly academic and conventional prose. Her rooms are furnished like her dream of a Chinese brothel, she longs for the wild and the forbidden – is a sweet, uninteresting, garrulous academic lady underneath, and not very far underneath either. Then there are four or five hippies, beatniks, madmen etc., so it does not really matter what happens. Still, it is all really quite nice: after the failure of the great demonstration in London last Sunday,[3] everybody congratulated everybody else – the police said how well the demonstrators behaved, the demonstrators agreed with the police, the press said England was wonderful, and oddly enough there is some truth in this. There is no real desire for violence, and the most frenzied efforts failed to generate it. Be prepared for a quiet time: it really is rather dull here: nobody much entertains anybody else. George Kennan wished to escape lionisation: ultimately he was annoyed at its complete absence. Nobody minds about anybody much. ⟨Oxford relationships – especially social intercourse is remote & calm &⟩ what the Trillings will tell you will not, you will discover, be quite right. He is blinded by (a still continuing) anglomania – she by extravagant hypotheses about the inner lives of us all. It really was wonderful being observed by them, and hearing Diana's highly articulate theories about who we were and how we stood in relation to each other. After all Henry James and T. S. Eliot also, to some extent deliberately, got it wrong; you will *not* be taken in by it ⟨– I promise you. And will get much pleasure & amusement from it all (I hope & believe).

    our love

      Isaiah.

No, I cannot add the graffito: I'll tell you by word of mouth: I daren't put it down, you'll see why when I tell you. 6.11.68: is it really to be Nixon?[4] how shall we bear it?⟩

1 Roy Broadbent Fuller (1912–91), solicitor, poet and author; Professor of Poetry, Oxford, 1968–73; Queen's Gold Medal for Poetry 1970.

2 Enid Mary Starkie (1897–1970), French scholar; Fellow of Somerville 1934–65; Reader in French Literature, Oxford, 1945–65; resigned her readership after being diagnosed with lung cancer; Starkie introduced 'campaigning and competition' to the professorial election in 1951 and had become 'almost the official bard-maker' (*Times*, 18 July 1968, 3c), after managing the successive campaigns of Day Lewis, Auden, Graves and Blunden; stood twice herself, unsuccessfully.

3 In fact the 'Sunday before last', 27 October: around 25,000 joined the demonstration against the Vietnam war organized by Tariq Ali (among others), half the number anticipated by organisers and police, and a quarter of Ali's claimed 100,000 ('Police Win the Day against Militant Few in March', *Times*, 28 October, 1a–c).

4 The outcome of the US Presidential election was still in the balance: at noon on 6 November (local time) Hubert Humphrey, Democratic candidate, conceded victory to Richard Nixon.

By the winter of 1968 the cost of the new Wolfson College buildings was already rising significantly beyond the initial estimates, and IB was obliged to mobilise his board of Trustees behind the first of a number of applications for an increase in funding from the Wolfson Foundation. As a matter of course he kept McGeorge Bundy, his ally on the Ford Foundation, abreast of developments.

TO MCGEORGE BUNDY

25 November 1968 [*carbon*]

[Headington House]

Dear Mac,

[...] In the meanwhile we have, as you know, applied to [the Wolfsons] for an additional grant of £106,000 to cover the cost of the freeholds in the neighbourhood of the College, which the Trustees encouraged us to acquire, mainly as a base for future expansion [...]; and for an extra 10 per cent on the total building costs, i.e. £150,000, which is what the architects' figures look like now (as was not altogether unexpected). Mr Leonard encouraged us to both these courses, and supposed we should run into some trouble at his Board from one Trustee and one only. I really need not mention that dread name again.[1] From all accounts blood flowed freely. However, Mr Leonard, aided and abetted by the loyal Bullock, won the day.

I have yet to receive an account from Alan Bullock of how our Professor Moriarty was once again worsted; he displayed his usual anti-Oxford fury; declared that he would never have accepted the original arrangement, if it had not been made clear to him that no more money would go to Oxford on any possible excuse; he was told that this corresponded to no historical fact: that no such promise was demanded or made [...]. The battle raged on all through the livelong morning; but in the end, after many corpses were left in the field, Sir Charles Dodds left dead, Mr Justice Scarman[2] limping away, we were rung up by the faithful brigadier[3] and told that all was well. So far so good – £¼ million to the good. We really should have been in desperate straits if this had not come forth – Leonard is really a very faithful friend – how much he enjoys these bloody encounters with one of his own trustees I do not know. In a moment of candour he did say to me that he did not think his judgement in choosing his colleagues was always infallible, but on later occasions he very properly took this back. The zoologist will certainly never abandon him, if he can help it – the Wolfson fund is the only source of power in his hands, and power is a commodity to the acquisition and the use

1 Solly Zuckerman, the 'zoologist' mentioned below.
2 Leslie George Scarman (1911–2004), Kt 1961; High Court judge 1961–73; Lord Justice of Appeal 1973–7; Trustee, Wolfson Foundation, 1968–79.
3 Probably (Arundell) Rea Leakey (1915–99), soldier, retired as Major General 1968; director and secretary, Wolfson Foundation, 1968–80. But just possibly Harold Redman, unofficially.

of which he has dedicated his entire life. Naturally, he asked about whether arrangements had been made for a matching grant by the Ford Foundation. I do not know what Leonard said to that – I certainly do not propose to raise it with you now, or at any foreseeable future date. But Leonard might. I enjoy begging for funds no more than did poor Bill Deakin, whom it drove into a kind of decline. At the moment we can go forward.

The University has said nothing about our putative obligations about absorbing more and more fellows. I hope we shall get by. There is the committee on immigration policy, and the absorptive powers of colleges. We have made it plain that we shall play our part, and a little more than our part, but not much more. This has, so far, not been challenged by anyone. Our present chief concern is (a) to acquire the Chair of Genetics ⟨alas, no good, defeated.⟩, which seems to me an exceedingly live subject and (b) to create a fellow–graduate democracy, which may frighten some of the older colleges, but which, in our case, seems to be perfectly feasible. I do not believe that putting graduates on committees or even the Governing Body is at all fatal. If done early enough and peacefully enough, and without the kind of violence which, at present, seems to be surrounding All Souls, it can become an accepted form of life, and make not much difference to the actual decisions reached; while giving intense moral satisfaction to our graduates, who being for the most part scientists, are very sensible and unextreme. Our only Jacobin is a kind of sociologist (it is so everywhere) and provided he does not actually meet either Mr Leonard or Sir Isaac, I think we can carry him safely, and even gladly.

Some very funny graffiti has appeared on the walls of Oxford colleges: one of the funnier is 'Kropotkin[1] is alive and working in Balliol, which is more than can be said for Lord Balogh'. Another is 'None of us can spell'. I will not go on wasting your time.

Until February.

Yours ever,

[Isaiah]

TO SAMUEL AND MIRIAM SAMBURSKY

2 December 1968

Headington House

Carissimi!

This is only to announce the glad tidings that Aline and I propose to come to the Holy City on 22 or 23 December – I have a meeting at Rehovot on 26th, 27th, 28th to consider the policy about publishing the Weizmann

1 Prince Petr Alekseevich Kropotkin (1842–1921), Russian aristocrat and anarchist; jailed for sedition 1874, but escaped into exile 1876, and lived mostly in Britain thereafter; critical of the centralising elements of Marxist theory.

papers[1] – there is quite a fuss about volume 1, which seems to me very well edited, because it contains so many trivial and uninteresting letters which some people [believe] do damage to his reputation – some old friends of his feel that this is not the man they knew and feel embarrassed and chagrined. I, as you may imagine, am faithful to the behests of the great Namier and the great Webster[2] and feel that everything must be published – small and great, black and white, embarrassing and ennobling; except for the kind of letters that might hurt the feelings of the living, at which [point] there then has to be an appropriate footnote saying that certain letters have been left out, giving reasons, saying that they are in the archives and may be consulted by a few bona fide scholars and will be published, it is hoped, in thirty years' time or whenever it may be. I expect to encounter considerable opposition from both those who genuinely believe that there ought to be selection and that political damage or some kind of distorting arises from indiscriminate publication, and from those who, having themselves been barred from writing his biography, have all kinds of grudges against the Institution. So doubtless, as always on such occasions, we shall have a lively time. [...]

Yours,

Isaiah

TO KAY HALLE[3]

9 December 1968

Headington House

Dear Kay,

I wish I could write something about Randolph,[4] but I really cannot. I knew him, I liked him, I admired his military virtues – he was less adapted to peacetime life – but I haven't enough to say about him, and you have plenty of brilliant and interesting writers already on your list. The only anecdote I can offer you is this: when I met him in Washington in 1946 just

1 *The Letters and Papers of Chaim Weizmann* were published in 25 volumes (London, 1968–80): the first to appear was the first volume of letters (1885–1902), edited by Leonard Stein with Gedalia Yogev.

2 Charles Kingsley Webster (1886–1961), KCMG 1946, historian; Director, British Library of Information, NY, 1941–2; Professor of International History, LSE, 1932–53; President of the British Academy 1950–4.

3 Katherine Murphy ('Kay') Halle (1904–97), daughter of Samuel H. Halle, co-founder of Halle's department store chain; journalist, author, Washington socialite, friend of the Kennedy and Churchill families; she campaigned for FDR and JFK, and was an influential member of the latter's Inaugural Committee (1961).

4 Randolph Frederick Edward Spencer Churchill (1911–68), journalist and Conservative politician, only son of Winston Churchill; he died on 6 June 1968 at the age of 57. IB's contribution is 'Randolph', in Kay Halle (ed.), *Randolph Churchill, The Young Unpretender: Essays by His Friends* (London, 1971), 278–9: 'Randolph, if not altogether house-trained, seemed to me altogether free from fear, almost too fearless, if it is possible to be so, both morally and physically. He was liable to suit the action to the word more or less instinctively, which led to consequences which were, at times, counter-productive' (278).

before his father's Fulton speech,[1] he had just been seeing Spruille Braden,[2] then returned as American Ambassador at the State Department. They had evidently had some disagreement, and Braden physically threw him out of his office after Randolph had, apparently, struck him. He, Randolph, was conducted back to the British Embassy in a state of some disarray. I was the first person he met in the corridor of the Chancery. I asked him what he had been doing. He said, 'I called on a Mr Braden in the Department of State. He attacked my country. I struck him. Whenever anyone speaks against my country, I always strike them, don't you?'

His views were sometimes those of a somewhat backward undergraduate, but he was fearless, truthful, loyal, simple and at times wildly entertaining. There was something arrested about him, profoundly unhappy, and his violence, lack of control, were often profoundly pathetic, disarming, and capable of inspiring affection. There was at once something deranged and disturbing and also very sweet about his expression; ⟨he was very affectionate. None of this for publication, surely!⟩

Yours ever, with much love –

Isaiah   [...]

IB spent the spring of 1969 at CUNY, arriving in mid-February and returning to England in the second week of May. He lectured at Harvard, Williams College, Massachusetts, and the University of North Carolina. Aline's mother died in New York at the end of March, while they were there.

TO JACOB HERZOG[3]

18 February 1969

New York

Dear Yaakov,

The first thing that I heard on my arrival here is that my friend Robert Lowell, the great poet, has received an invitation to visit Israel and is bound there at the end of the week. I wonder who conceived this idea. He is a man of genius, and a very moody and peculiar one who, of course, said some queer and hostile things at that same unfortunate meeting with the New York intelligentsia. I saw Elie Wiesel[4] yesterday, and he expressed extreme

1 Churchill gave his famous 'Iron Curtain' speech on receiving an honorary degree at Westminster College, Fulton, Missouri, on 5 March 1946.

2 Spruille Braden (1894–1978), businessman and diplomat, noted for his advocacy of interventionist policies in South American countries; US ambassador to Argentina 1945; Assistant Secretary of State for Western Hemisphere Affairs 1945–7.

3 Jacob/Yaakov/Yaacov Herzog (1921–72), Dublin-born Israeli diplomat; son of an Ashkenazi Chief Rabbi of Ireland, and later Israel, and younger brother of Chaim (1918–97), sixth President of Israel 1983–93; ambassador to Canada 1960–3; Director General of the Prime Minister's Office 1965–72. See also L1 693.

4 Eliezer ('Elie') Wiesel (b. 1928), Romanian-born US writer, academic and human rights

concern about this odd move. ⟨so did the two Columbia professors I told about this. It is a *grotesque* move if unprepared [sc. if not prepared] *very* carefully.⟩ This must have been done by the Cultural Attaché in Washington, operating in a wholly mechanical manner, I should say. However, he *is* going, and I shall certainly dine with him before he does so, and have a talk – but, as you must know, he goes off his head periodically in winter, and although he is a wonderfully clever, fascinating, touching, distinguished and in every way remarkable man – who started life as a top Boston aristocrat, was converted to Rome, and deconverted – he was in jail during the last war for anti-war activities, and is the hero of the anti-Vietnam movement now, so the usual mechanical treatment which is accorded to such visitors by the Foreign Office will produce appalling results. Do not think I exaggerate, for I am not exaggerating. Can you do anything to stop the Foreign Office from attaching some mechanical young woman to him who will din the glories of the country into his ears patriotically, sincerely and disastrously? ⟨It nearly turned the Donaldsons into anti-Semites. They were liberated just in time. The King David Hotel (no, I am not joking alas) have driven them quite mad.⟩

The people for Lowell to meet are (*a*) poets, e.g. Gouri,[1] and, more particularly, people who are deeply troubled about the relations with the Arabs, about the future of the country, doubters and unorthodox persons, above all not propagandists and government officials of any kind at all. He is, no doubt, going to have a desire to escape into all kinds of bohemian environments, as [well as] expecting to be treated as the distinguished man that he is: he should therefore meet a minister or two, but not officials of the Foreign Office, least of all the Foreign Minister[2] or Yadin,[3] or *any* of the other persons who go down well with the average British MP. I should recommend that Amos Elon[4] of Ha'aretz be put in touch with him, and invite him to meet some of the sensitive and troubled youth. Secondly, there would be no harm in his meeting Ephraim Broido[5] in Jerusalem, whom he would quite like, but

---

campaigner; a survivor of Auschwitz and Buchenwald; awarded the Nobel Peace Prize 1986.

1 Haim Gouri (b. 1923), Tel-Aviv-born poet and writer; known for his coverage of the Eichmann trial 1961.

2 Abba Eban (1915–2002), né Aubrey Solomon; Cape Town-born Israeli diplomat and politician; an excellent linguist, he lectured in Arabic at Queen's College, Cambridge, where he had been an undergraduate 1938–40; Deputy Prime Minister 1963–6; Foreign Minister 1966–74: 'often a lone dove in the Labour Party where he argued for withdrawal from the occupied territories' (*Times*, 18 November 2002, 29).

3 Yigael Yadin (1917–84) né Sukenik, prominent Israeli soldier, archaeologist and politician; joined the Haganah 1933, Chief of Operations 1947–8; Chief of Staff, IDF, 1949–52; clashed with Ben-Gurion, and in retirement pursued a distinguished career as an archaeologist; later a politician, co-founding the Democratic Movement for Change 1976.

4 Amos Sternbach Elon (1926–2009), Austrian-born Israeli writer, for many years Ha'aretz correspondent on European and American affairs, and a regular contributor to the NYRB.

5 Ephraim Broido (1912–94), Israeli writer, and translator of Shakespeare.

only quite. (Keep him off patriotic chauffeurs, Pearlman,[1] even Teddy – he's a really very odd man indeed, and to invite him out of the blue seems to me lunacy, but there.) Thirdly, I think he ought to meet some rather sophisticated army commanders interested in archaeology, as it were. I am sure he would do beautifully with soldiers and football players and men of action in general. ⟨he shd spend time in an army camp & talk to the boys, freely. Also in some sweet, left wing Kibbutz likely to be a thorn in the government's flesh. I see I've said this already in the text! It shows how distraught I feel.⟩ Among Ministers he ought, I suppose, to meet Allon, and, I think, Aranne.[2] He responds to imaginative people [...] [H]e must meet Scholem and his friends, and in general anyone with spiritually attractive, highly individual quality. A short meeting with the Prime Minister[3] may make him feel he has met someone, and if he meets the President the latter should be encouraged to tell him Hasidic tales, rather than day-to-day political details which he won't listen to. What he really needs is a left-wing kibbutz, or an army camp for a week, talking freely to simple boys and their commanders. He will probably want to go to a prison and talk to Fatah prisoners – to let him do so and to prevent him would probably be about equally fatal.

I honestly do not want to set up as an authority on this, but do you think you could tactfully insert into the head of whoever is the cultural operator that when choosing obvious left-wing intellectuals they might have a word with me ⟨or at least Sidney Morgenbesser[4] of Columbia, or George Backer⟩ on the subject? I hope it all goes well. I shall no doubt be here when he comes back, and I anticipate, if not the worst, certainly not the best – and remember that his most intimate friend in New York is Miss Arendt, whose view on Eichmann etc. he shares entirely. Poets and soldiers – these are far and away the best kinds of persons for him, and a mad painter or two [...].

Yours,

Isaiah

⟨P.S. I've just lunched with 3 more members of the local intelligentsia: they

---

1 Moshe Pearlman (1911–86) né Morris Perlman, British-born Israeli writer of Polish descent; a student of Harold Laski at the LSE, he was Israeli military spokesman 1948–52; in retirement he devoted himself to literary work.
2 Zalman Aran (1899–1970), Russian-born Israeli Minister of Education and Culture.
3 Then Levi Eshkol (1895–1969), creator of the Israel Labour Party, and the successor to Ben-Gurion as Prime Minister, from 1963 until his death on 26 February 1969, 8 days after the date of this letter; he was succeeded by his deputy, Yigal Allon, who held office for an interim term, followed from 17 March by Golda Meir. Eshkol had held together an unlikely coalition in Israel, and the international community watched anxiously to see how his successor would approach the unresolved territorial issues arising from Israel's victory in the Six-Day War: 'In choosing a new Prime Minister, Israel will also have to choose a new policy, if only by implication' ('Chairman of Genius', *Times* leader, 27 February 1969, 9a).
4 Sidney Morgenbesser (1921–2004), John Dewey Professor of Philosophy, Columbia, 1975–99; much prized by IB for his warmth and famous wit.

too professed to be amazed by this move: I promised Mr Aranne to do "something" about what worried him (& you & me). If Robert Lowell – Cal to his friends – short for Caligula – comes back as he will if taken around by our official guides, my task is impossible. We shall have had it. Don't tell people about my views – it will make things worse if they are self conscious. Evelyn Waugh is nothing to this. Still it may yet be all right.)

IB was never reconciled to Stuart Hampshire's decision to move to the US in 1963, which he attributed largely to the malign influence of Hampshire's wife Renée. From autumn 1965 he looked for practical ways to secure his friend's return, and, when the Cambridge chair in philosophy held by John Wisdom fell vacant in 1968, he lobbied, unsuccessfully, on Hampshire's behalf. IB was always prepared to argue in support of appointments of which he approved, and he believed that Hampshire, in addition to being a first-rate philosopher, was an especially positive influence on young students, as had been evidenced while he was at Princeton. Against a background of student unrest, this was a quality to be valued, but there were deeper emotional reasons why IB wanted Hampshire's return. As he had written to Maurice Bowra on 18 November 1965: 'A life would be saved. No more English Englishman has ever been created.'

TO BERNARD WILLIAMS

19 February 1969

CUNY

Dear Bernard,

I ought to have rung you up before I left for New York to tell you of a disagreeable evening I had at Corpus when Ryle was dining with G. Owen,[1] whose other guest was Nelson Goodman.[2] The only point was that Ryle wanted to know who I thought ought to succeed to Wisdom's[3] Chair in Cambridge. Before I volunteered anything, he informed us all that in his view it ought to be Geach[4] – that he, Gilbert, was an elector – that if Geach went, this would draw Anscombe[5] there automatically – that Cambridge would thus get two for the price of one, and that this was what was wanted; that

---

1 Gwilym Ellis Lane ('Gwil') Owen (1922–82), Professor of Ancient Philosophy, Oxford, 1963–6; Victor S. Thomas Professor of Philosophy and the Classics, Harvard, 1966–73; Laurence Professor of Ancient Philosophy and Fellow of King's, Cambridge, 1973–82.

2 Henry Nelson Goodman (1906–98), professor of philosophy, Pennsylvania, 1951–64, Harvard 1968–77.

3 (Arthur) John Terence Dibben Wisdom (1904–93), Fellow of Trinity, Cambridge, 1935–93, and Professor of Philosophy 1952–68; Distinguished Professor of Philosophy, Oregon, 1968–72.

4 Peter Thomas Geach (b. 1916), Professor of Logic, Leeds, 1966–81; married Elizabeth Anscombe (next note) 1941; both were converts to Catholicism. Geach's style has been called 'deliberately outrageous' (Jenny Teichman, 'Henry James among the Philosophers', NYT *Book Review*, 10 February 1991, 24).

5 (Gertrude) Elizabeth Margaret Anscombe (1919–2001), philosopher; Research Fellow, Somerville, 1946–64, Fellow 1964–70; Professor of Philosophy and Fellow of New Hall, Cambridge, 1970–86;

there had never been a good Cambridge school of philosophy – just because Moore and Russell had made their local habitation there, it did not follow that Cambridge had philosophers, or a philosophy school.

When I remonstrated and said that I thought that Geach was a little too mad, and that so much work could not be put on your blameless shoulders, he said that he knew perfectly well that I would suggest Stuart – that all my life I had helped him into jobs which he did not deserve, e.g. the Bursarship at All Souls, and afterwards London – that he had shot his bolt, that it had never been much of a bolt anyway – that he was perfectly useless as a philosopher and had always been so, and more frightful nonsense of the same distressing, and indeed enraging, order. I did not let this pass altogether peacefully, but then Owen intervened and said that no doubt you'd be in favour of Stuart inasmuch as you felt uneasy about having preceded him to your own Chair,[1] at which Gilbert duly said that this was the worst of reasons, that his mind was made up. Other awkward words followed which I will not bother you with, in the course of which I did not behave in a wholly cowardly manner. He calmed down slightly and wondered whether Pears would not be far better than anyone so far mentioned, and so on. However, I am merely warning you that since he is your colleague you will find that he will behave badly on this issue, and should be resisted. The only point on which he is likely to be sound is the merits of R. Bambrough,[2] about which he has no doubts. I for my part, despite the fact that Stuart is about to buy a house at Princeton, do not really doubt that if offered this particular chair he would probably accept it. And yet, of course, one cannot be altogether certain. But if Gilbert gets away with it, it will be disgrace abounding, and the ruin of a life, and I should have thought a genuine loss to Cambridge. There is no doubt that Stuart has made a mess of his life, or at least has had it made for him – but to punish him for this does seem to me quite wicked and foolish. It is all due, I'm afraid, to Gilbert's fantastic vanity, and the fact that Stuart, quite apart from his review in *Mind*,[3] did not [pay], or was not thought to have tried to have paid, sufficient honour to the master. [...]

Yours ever,
Isaiah

fiercely loyal disciple, literary executor, translator and editor of Ludwig Wittgenstein, one of whose favourite pupils she had been at Cambridge.

1 Bernard Williams had been appointed Knightbridge Professor of Philosophy at Cambridge in 1967, when not yet 40; IB had discreetly canvassed on behalf of the much more senior, and exiled, Stuart Hampshire; while not formally applying for the post, Hampshire appears to have wished to be considered (IB to Herbert Hart, 21 December 1965).

2 (John) Renford Bambrough (1926–99), philosopher; Fellow, St John's, Cambridge, 1950–99, University Lecturer 1957–91.

3 Of Ryle's principal work *The Concept of Mind* (London, 1949), in *Mind* 59 (1950), 237–55. Ryle was extremely put out by Hampshire's criticisms, and BW always supposed that this was the main source of the opinion Hampshire and IB shared, that Ryle was exceptionally vain, which was not BW's impression of him (personal communication).

TO JEAN FLOUD

   28 February 1969 [*manuscript*]

The Hanover Inn, Dartmouth College, New Hampshire

As from CUNY

Dearest Jean

   [...] I was to have delivered a lecture at Harvard: but it was totally cut
off by snow: no cars, planes, trains. Lecture postponed: marvellous relief:
a day gained, anxiety deferred. Then to Williams College, Williamstown,
W. Massachusetts. Sweet. Poor lecture by me, courteously received; next
morning at 10 a.m. meeting with such graduates as might wish to discuss
implications of Tolstoy's views on this & that. No graduates turned up.
Hideous embarrassment on the part of the presiding Prof.: excuses & explan-
ations about morning classes etc: I *could* not say that I was positively jubilant
– it seemed to me to underline my own estimate of the quality of my "performance" the night before – followed by inexcusable frivolity on my part +
malicious gossip when the post-lecture seminar of the younger profs tried to
draw me on E. H. Carr & my feelings about his onslaughts on me – still, the
dreadful humiliation of my hosts was so patent, that I explained that I was
often found unrewarding by students, that fashion had passed me by etc. &
other things like this which my vanity prevents me from altogether believing
– nor are the facts quite so grim – but which I enjoy saying with deep false
humility. In fact I *was* relieved: & went to see the *marvellous* Clark collection
of paintings[1] – *wonderful* Renoirs, Degases, Monets, a beautiful Rembrandt &
a very good Memling(ck?)[2] – really splendid – & so to Hanover New Hants.
I am only reporting all this because I thought it funny: & (I add priggishly)
good for me. Here in Dartmouth, a rather grander collection of profs: rather
impressive: same lecture, improved by shame & remorse about the earlier
version, & no ordeal by graduates. The country even to someone as blind
to visual things as I am, is, under snow, with all those very thin birches &
beaches [*sic*] melting like the all but transparent strings of some vast instrument into the sharp blue & white horizon, the country, I say, returning to
the substantive, is very beautiful indeed. So are all those 18th century New
England houses & churches & College halls – it is scarcely conceivable that
the same country has bred this *and* the Middle Western Babbitts[3] *and* the
Jewish neurotics of New York & California. "Everyone" is reading Philip
Roth's 'Portnoy's Complaint'.[4] (Portnoy is the word for tailor in Russian.

---

1 The Sterling and Francine Clark Art Institute in Williamstown.

2 Hans Memling/Memlinc(k) (*c.*1430–94), Flemish painter.

3 The realtor George F. Babbitt is the eponymous hero of Sinclair Lewis's satire on middle-class
   American life, *Babbitt* (NY, 1922).

4 Of this novel (NY/London, 1969) by Roth (373/2) Richard Jones of *The Times* wrote: 'The book
   has been hailed in America as a masterpiece of absurd humour, but seen from here [... it] is,
   on reflection, about as funny as a cry for help' ('Punch and Judy', *Times*, 19 April 1969, 22e). IB

But the N.Y. R of Books doesn't know this, on the whole). The lives of children brought up by Jewish East European mothers near the Brooklyn & Bronx kitchen sinks must by now be [the] best documented slices of life in the entire Western world. Enough! surely! when, oh when will the Puerto Rican period of American writing begin? You will now accuse me of fanatical antisemitism or Lichtheimism[1] but I cannot take more of the Bellow–Kazin–Malamuth–Roth[2] 'regional' culture: it is too claustrophobic, sticky, hideously self indulgent: it wallows too happily in the Yiddish slough – the mixture of jolly Yiddish idiom, psycho-analysis, obscenity, self pity, & the humour & wit & uneasy jokes of a tormented slave culture is (to put it briefly as H. James wd say) overdone. It arouses a certain kind of nausea: the autobiographical & "pouring out" aspects slop over & drown the minimum of discipline & transformation into some kind of artistic structure which the raw material requires. It stays too raw. And justifies Israel, Zionism etc. which was invented precisely to stop all this: it is all a Jewish version of the most shaming sort of negro spirituals sung with grimaces by show coons: at least *this* is not known in Tel Aviv […]. I am uneasy about poor old Israel: will Nixon + de Gaulle + Brezhnev do it in or try to? It is *such* a nuisance to them all: just like the intolerable perpetually crying & showing off anti-heroes of the disgusting & gifted novels referred to above. […]

Yours

I.

TO LEONARD WOLFSON

6 March 1969 [*carbon*]

[CUNY]

Dear Leonard,

I enclose these two books which you may find of some interest. Eric

wrote to Stuart Hampshire: 'There is something to be said for David Pryce-Jones's observation that Roth could have written a masterpiece, but decided instead to write a best-seller' (28 March 1969).

1 George Lichtheim (1912–73), German-born writer, historian, and theorist of socialism and Marxism. A friend of JF, he was one of the *métèques* (resident aliens: see 538/2) for consorting with whom IB teased her, calling her 'Notre Dame des métèques' ('Our Lady of the Immigrants').

2 Saul Bellow (1915–2005), Canadian-born US novelist of Russian-Jewish descent. In the opening pages of his bestselling novel *Herzog* (NY, 1964) the hero, a Jewish academic called Moses Herzog is undergoing a crisis of self-confidence, and struggling unsuccessfully to deliver a course of adult-education lectures in a NY night school on 'The Roots of Romanticism', IB's original title for his 1966 Mellon Lectures in Washington, DC, which he therefore changed to the less resonant 'Sources of Romantic Thought' (the original title was restored when the lectures were published in 1999). Alfred Kazin (1915–98), Brooklyn-born writer and literary critic, of Russian-Jewish descent; his autobiographical *Starting Out in the Thirties* was published in Boston, Mass., in 1965. Bernard Malamud (1914–86), Brooklyn-born US novelist and short-story writer, of Russian-Jewish descent, whose novel *The Fixer* (NY, 1966) won the Pulitzer Prize for fiction 1967. Philip Milton Roth (b. 1933), Newark-born US novelist and short-story writer, of Galician-Jewish descent.

Goldman[1] is a very shrewd professor who left Johnson before the end of his reign, and both the Johnson loyalists and the disloyalists look on him with disfavour. The first because he abandoned the ship before it foundered, and thus is regarded as one of the causes of its foundering, and the second because he did not get off early enough. He was rather a late rat, and this embarrasses the earlier ones. It seems to me an exceedingly shrewd analysis, and nearer the truth than most, and offers the historians a good many difficult problems of assessing that strange, now deeply hated man, who apart from Vietnam did many good and useful things (it seems to me), although I am not allowed to say so in either public or private here at present, without upsetting too many people in the room. [...]

Nixon's last speech was a marvellously competent performance.[2] He is like a very nervous man on a very thin tightrope, watched by an enormous and not entirely sympathetic crowd, who with immense and conscious effort and much sweat accomplishes the journey across the chasm. This country longs to be cooled down – not for them now those splendid speeches of Kennedy's about making the country move, or Johnson's speeches about the great society – all they want is to disentangle themselves out of their awkward predicaments, have a little peace, get on with normal business, do something to avoid hearing the frenzied shrieks of Negroes, students etc. They long for the empty years of Eisenhower, but they will not get them. Nevertheless, Nixon, if anyone, will manage to create some sort of détente and calm them down, if only by directing attention to foreign affairs, in which they have no fundamental interest, and which they think an interesting game and away from domestic discontents, which grow by mounting awareness of them.

Yours,

[Isaiah]   [...]

TO BERNARD WILLIAMS

7 March 1969

CUNY

Dear Bernard,

[...] I have a feeling in general that the time has come for a certain amount of honest nobbling if something terrible is to be averted – Kneale will I fear

---

1 Eric Frederick Goldman (1915–89), US historian; special adviser to President Johnson 1963–6; first Rollins Professor of History, Princeton, 1962–85; his bestselling *The Tragedy of Lyndon Johnson* (NY, 1969), part White House memoir, part general history, was widely syndicated in the international press.

2 Nixon held a long press conference on the evening of 4 March, after his triumphal return from a diplomatic tour of European capitals, in which he dealt confidently with the major topics of the day, including the war in Vietnam: 'This cool, statesmanlike approach was evident throughout the 60-minute conference. Both the performance and substance were impressive' (Louis Heren, 'Nixon Warns Hanoi to Stop Attacks During Talks', *Times*, 6 March 1969, 6a).

follow Gilbert's lead – at least he may – whatever errors he commits will be honestly arrived at, which may make them no better, but I do not think that he is very suggestible. On the other hand von Wright and Strawson should I'm sure be spoken to by you – the second only to be warned of Gilbert's intolerable line. Of course you are right – of the two, Elizabeth [Anscombe] is clearly superior – I do not myself believe in Geach's great intellectual gifts – only in a ferocious, narrow path, which many schoolmen must have had whose memories have very rightly perished, but I cannot divorce myself from the feeling that if you get her, you will get him, and that together they will wreak a great deal of havoc – stimulate, excite, and wound, bully, destroy – do rather less good than, say, Leavis.[1] But I do see that if Stuart is for some reason impossible, then it must lie between her and David Pears. […] I do not envy you your task, and yet I think there is a life to be saved there. I see no other prospect for our poor old friend, and staying here, despite the fact that he occasionally develops a kind of false euphoria on the subject, stimulated I daresay by the maddening (even to him now, I think) zigzags of his wife, is a genuinely gloomy prospect; despite being a culture hero, he longs for home, and this nostalgia will eat him and eat him as the months go by, and the pathetic happiness with which he returns to England is too much altogether. There now, I have done what I swore I would not do – transfer my anxieties to you (as if you did not feel them already) when I have no responsibility for action and you have at any rate some. Apart from contradicting what Gilbert is likely to say, and getting other people to contradict it also on the grounds of superior intelligence about what our friend is doing, one ought, I suppose, to stress the genuine effect upon the students – that of his mere presence as a force leading to respect for the intellect, and also something that you share – a sensitiveness to what the boys are genuinely troubled about intellectually and morally, the total absence of which characterises Gilbert and most of your electors. […]

I will not go on to you about the Philosophy Department of CUNY. A great, unbreakable generalisation that professors seldom welcome the presence of persons conspicuously cleverer than themselves has led to the often stated proposition by the philosophers that their department is excellent and scarcely in need of improvement. I need not tell you how far this is from any possible true assessment of the facts. A certain clipped utterance and tenseness when the work of local philosophers of greater merit is so much as mentioned characterises the main person responsible for this state of affairs.[2] But I feel happily alienated from the fortunes of this department, to which I theoretically belong, and have ceased giving unwelcome

---

1 F[rank] R[aymond] Leavis (1895–1978), editor of the quarterly review *Scrutiny* 1932–53; Fellow, Downing, Cambridge, 1936–62, University Reader in English 1959–62; 'the most controversial literary critic of his time' (*Times*, 18 April 1978, 18f) – or, one might add, of any time.
2 Efforts to identify the person referred to have thus far proved unsuccessful.

advice, which seems to have worried them, as it turns out unnecessarily, in the past. [...]

The row between the Jews and the Negroes here is very distressing. I cannot help feeling that the ultimate root of this is the fact, not so much of Jewish landlords in Brooklyn, or the fact that Negroes enjoy sharing fashionable prejudices with the ruling class (though there is something in both these things), but that the Jews are hopelessly people of the Book – tend to judge people in terms of intellectual power – and therefore, whether they know it or not, look down upon these coloured dunderheads as numbskulls – what Austin used to call chuckle-headed – and at best try to help them in the most earnest and patronising fashion as the *New York Review of Books* does, etc., and that if one is a physically well-developed, lively and, still more, violent and indignant Negro, there is nobody one would resent so much as clever, bookish, Jewish liberals who have suppressed their contempt and offer help largely from their own dissatisfaction with their own neurotic, subjected state. Mad though it may seem to you now, I sincerely believe that, if the State of Israel survives at all, the ultimate relations between the Jews and the Arabs (though some of the same factors obtain there for precisely the same reasons also) will become more tolerable, and indeed quite 'natural', whereas the incurable state of affairs revealed by Messrs Bellow, Malamud, Roth etc. will go on festering. Never can the lives of any section of any section of[1] mankind have been better documented than that of the Jewish lower-middle class – the first post-ghetto ghetto generation. [...] You really are fortunate not to be here at this moment.

Do send me your lecture. To criticise nonsense is more Kantian and honourable to the rebs,[2] as they are called here, than to treat them as cases. I remember my long conversations with Arthur Calder-Marshall,[3] of all people, about the Nazis in the 1930s – when he was urging me to realise that these were psychologically stricken cases, and that all Hitler's utterances must be treated gently and seriously, and he must be brought to his senses by kindness and understanding on the part of us all. The attitude of people like E. M. Forster towards Russia in the 1930s, that despite everything there was much hope there, that what they were doing was evil but in order that good might come of it,[4] and that even if this was wrong it was something deserving of sympathy, is precisely the state of mind, it seems to me, of people so unconvinced of the value of their own activities as to convey this insecurity to the students, who, if not rightly, at any rate understandably, revolt against

1 *sic* – perhaps deliberately?
2 Student rebels.
3 Arthur Calder-Marshall (1908–1992), author; St Paul's contemporary of IB; Hertford classics 1927–30.
4 'I am not a Communist, though perhaps I might be one if I was a younger and a braver man, for in Communism I can see hope. It does many things which I think evil, but I know that it intends good.' E. M. Forster, 'Liberty in England' (1935), in *Abinger Harvest* (London, 1936), 63.

it and ask for something more solid than self-doubting and pathetic timid steps towards their own confused longings. I cannot help it: I still think that one should talk to everybody in the same tone of voice, and say what one thinks for no better reason than that one thinks it, and not adopt a special sympathetic attitude towards the poor students because they're weak in the head, and one must produce a kind of bedside manner for them. Nothing that I hate more than the view of the world as an enormous hospital in which everybody is either a patient or a nurse or doctor, or all these things at once. [...]

And now I suppose I must go and hear Trevor-Roper lecture on Hitler; my own university – a few doors away. I dined with Edmund Wilson last night – he was not altogether sober – he growled that Trevor-Roper and Taylor were only a couple of British phonies. I put up a mild defence. Wilson's case was, through enormous hiccups, that Taylor said things which he knew not to be true, while Trevor-Roper ran away from the duty of telling us about the seventeenth century properly, instead engaging in obscure polemics for the sake of money and fame – arrogance, prejudice – Tolstoy, Wilson, Dodds, even Leavis, I suppose – anything is better than intellectual flexibility – log-rolling, corruption, getting in with individuals and movements, something which not merely breeds error and causes pain – anything might do that – but destroys the very weapons with which argument can be conducted, and reduces everything into a ghastly mess. For this reason I have always said to myself that I preferred Jesuits to muddled men of good will. At least one knows what one is fighting for and against, and the weapons are kept sharp. The most ghastly pedantry is preferable to low-grade incoherent patter and steamy rhetoric. [...]

Yours,

Isaiah

In 1963 J. S. Fulton,[1] Vice-Chancellor of the University of Sussex, had written to IB (a member of the University's Academic Advisory Board 1963–6) asking for his view on the proposed appointment, supported by the University, of Isaac Deutscher to a Chair in Soviet Studies. IB replied as follows:

Dear John,

Your letter puts me in a cruel dilemma. The candidate of whom you speak is the only man whose presence in the same academic community as myself I should find morally intolerable. How much of this is founded on objective judgement of his academic and intellectual activities, and how much on personal feeling, I find it difficult to say. I feel it is very wrong to leave matters like this: and I certainly have no wish to oppose anything that Asa Briggs,[2]

1 John Scott Fulton (1902–86), Kt 1964, life peer 1966; Vice-Chancellor, Sussex, 1959–67.
2 Asa Briggs (b. 1921), later (1976) life peer; Professor of History, Sussex, 1961–76, Dean, School of

Corbett[1] and the others want – nor would I dream of doing so, even if I had a right to do so, which I doubt. But I think there is a limit below which lack of scruple must not go in the case of academic teachers. If you would like to know my views in greater detail, I should be ready to communicate them in conversation – I would rather not put them down on paper. The man in question is the only one about whom I have any such feeling – there is literally no one [else], so far as I know, to whom I would wish to urge such objections – and of course I do not think that political opinions, especially left-wing ones, should be any barrier to academic employment by your or any university in England at the present moment. I should have supported the claims of Wright Mills, say, or Hobsbawm,[2] vigorously.

    Yours sincerely,
      [Isaiah][3]

IB's letter clearly disconcerted Fulton, who planned to send Martin Wight, the originator of the proposal to appoint Deutscher, to discuss the matter with IB, before meeting IB himself. In the meantime the scheme would be put on hold.[4] In the letter that follows IB says he met Wight (but not Fulton), and gives an account of what he said to him, but no other record of their discussions has emerged. Six years later an article appeared in Black Dwarf[5] *which accused IB of having scotched Deutscher's candidacy, as indeed he seems effectively to have done. IB hotly denied the charge. Had he by this time forgotten that he had written to Fulton in these terms? Did he later modify his position during his conversation with Wight, as he indicates in the letter below?*

TO JEAN FLOUD

18 March 1969

                               CUNY

[...] Diana is still boiling away about the insufficient recognition of her article about Columbia,[6] and is having some kind of obscure and complicated row with Lowell – he wrote a letter to *Commentary*, which appears hostile, but

Social Studies, 1961–5, Pro-Vice-Chancellor 1961–7, Vice-Chancellor 1967–76; Provost, Worcester, 1976–91; Chancellor, Open University, 1978–94.
1 John Patrick Corbett (1916–99), Professor of Philosophy, Sussex, 1961–72, Bradford 1972–6.
2 Eric John Ernest Hobsbawm (1917–2012), Marxist historian; Reader in History, London (Birkbeck), 1959–70, Professor of Economic and Social History 1970–82; a Cambridge Apostle (he was at King's) and long-standing member of the Communist Party of Great Britain; declined to resign, as others did, after the Soviet suppression of the Hungarian uprising in 1956.
3 Letter of 4 March 1963, in response to Fulton's of 28 February 1963.
4 John Fulton to IB, 7 March 1963.
5 'In Defence of Perry Anderson', in 'Dwarf Diary', *Black Dwarf*, 14 February 1969, [12]. The piece by Anderson in question is 'Components of the National Culture', *New Left Review* no. 50 (July–August 1968), 3–57; repr. in Alexander Cockburn and Robin Blackburn (eds), *Student Power* (Harmondsworth, 1969), 214–86.
6 Diana Trilling's article on the student unrest at Columbia, her husand's university, 'On the Steps of the Low Memorial Library: Liberalism and the Revolution of the Young', appeared in *Commentary* 46 no. 5 (November 1968), 29–55.

which is totally unintelligible to me – Greek, you might say – which seems to have given deep offence to Diana, who replied to it at vast and all too intelligible length. She has invited us to dine with Mailer,[1] who, now it appears, cannot come, which is a great relief to me, for I do not think that I should get on all that well with him – I went to one of those evenings at the Theater for Ideas,[2] and more rubbish was talked than anywhere I have ever been, to the apparent satisfaction of the ladies present, who nodded their heads in a vigorous, mindless, idiotic sort of way. Dickens and Dostoevsky would have their own ways – and Tolstoy too – of describing such assemblies. Turgenev might be a little kinder. Meanwhile I have had a letter from Williams College, from the Dean of Students or some such person, who said, 'In the course of your lecture on Tolstoy you caused us to laugh a good many times. Are we to assume that apart from his novels you consider that Tolstoy's views were laughable?' I shall have to answer this letter rather carefully. One really must not allow the faintest note of irony to creep in when talking to a genuinely earnest and truth-seeking audience, I suppose. Very careful one has to be.

Bob Silvers is as delightful as ever, and sends you his fondest love. That brings me to a subject I must broach. Some kind friend has sent me a photostatic copy of a piece in *Black Dwarf*, which you have probably seen, which alleges that I have accused Perry Anderson[3] of anti-Semitism, and that you (described as my acolyte – I hope that makes your blood boil with real fury – it should – I am not sure that you are not part of my 'cohorts' as well, whoever they may be) are responsible for spreading this 'drivel'. He [sc. the author] then gives a very, very distorted version of what was supposedly a confidential matter, namely, the consultation by Sussex University with myself as a potential elector to a job which in fact was never filled, on the subject of the late Deutscher – what in fact I said to Prof. Wight[4] – the only person I saw on the subject – was that I did not think that he was a suitable Professor of Russian History, unless there was somebody else there also professing it, not quite so fanatical, to be able to give at least two sides of the

---

1 Norman Kingsley Mailer (1923–2007), US novelist; his *The Armies Of The Night: History as a Novel, the Novel as History* (NY, 1968) won the Pulitzer Prize for general non-fiction in 1969; a 'Towering Writer with a Matching Ego', an 'all-purpose feuder and short-fused brawler, who with the slightest provocation would happily engage in head-butting, arm-wrestling and random punch-throwing' (Charles McGrath, NYT, 10 November 2007, 1, 31).

2 Artistic initiative begun in NY City in November 1961 by the dancer and choreographer Shirley Broughton (b. *c.*1923), who envisaged 'a place where theatrical ideas could be presented free of the economic demands and creative restrictions of the Broadway machine' (Michael C. D. Macdonald, *New York Magazine*, 19 May 1969, 46). From 1966 the Theater presented 'discussion shows', among the most memorable being that of 30 April 1971, when Norman Mailer debated women's liberation with Diana Trilling and the feminists Jill Johnston, Jacqueline Ceballos and Germaine Greer.

3 (Francis Rory) Peregrine ('Perry') Anderson (b. 1938), British Marxist intellectual, editor of the radical *New Left Review* 1962–82, 2000–3; founded New Left Books 1970.

4 Robert James Martin Wight (1913–72), Professor of Modern History, Sussex, 1961–72, Dean of the School of European Studies 1961–9.

case, that I should almost welcome his presence in a University like Oxford
or Cambridge, where [there would be] some debate on the subject, and at
least more than one point of view obtained – but that if Sussex University
wanted him to hold the job, quite apart from what other electors might do,
I should certainly not oppose it, and would not vote against him, and would
not resign from the board or make any fuss, and go along with their wishes
because I believed that universities should have the people they want, and
that the Committee on their intellectual standards, on which I was supposed
to sit, ought in any case to be disbanded.

What happened after that was that Fulton consulted David Astor, who
had of course been a very intimate friend of Deutscher, who said that indeed
he was very fond of Deutscher, and respected him very much, but that he
had become a furious propagandist, with no regard whatever for academic
values – this is not the point of view which I put forward (but I did not find
it difficult to believe) and after that the matter was dropped. I knew there
was some rumour among the students [...] that I had somehow vetoed
Deutscher, but this is perfectly false. It may have been weak of me not to
decide to oppose him if I really felt that he was unsuitable. In fact I did tell
them that they could do exactly as they wished and not reckon with my
opinion in this matter, since I thought that universities should be permitted
to make their own mistakes, especially new ones.

So the account in *Black Dwarf* is untrue and the remark attributed to me
about 'No Marxist ought to be a Professor of Russian history' is perfectly
apocryphal[1] and obviously absurd and not a view I could conceivably hold.
Still, what I really want to know is how did all this happen? Is it the product
of your taking up cudgels on my behalf with your extremists? Have you been
hopelessly compromised as a progressive figure? The only thing that worries
me is if I become a butt of the lunatics like Sparrow and Beloff, this would
not be good for my College – quite apart from my acute hatred of public
fisticuffs of a personal kind where no principles are really involved, merely,
'I hate what you say and are', 'I hate you for hating what I am and say' etc.
I do think in general that false and damaging allegations ought to be formally
denounced – that even though one cannot catch up with absurd libels, one
should set the record straight if one can, but *Black Dwarf* would not print any
letter of mine, nor do I wish to write to them.

Perhaps it does not matter. I was, as is my wont, rather depressed about
this for six or seven hours. I shall ask dear Bob what he thinks, but apart from
that I suppose I had better do nothing and be lofty and regard the journal
and its contributors as beneath contempt, which, I suppose, in this instance
they certainly are. But if you are still in touch with these people[2] you might

1 *Black Dwarf*'s actual words are 'You can't have a Marxist teaching Russian history.'
2 JF was never in touch with them: a misunderstanding by IB.

tell them that what *Black Dwarf* said about the Deutscher episode is a straight lie,[1] i.e. that even though I might be expected not to be sympathetic to Deutscher's views and personality, my position about him has always been clear: I disliked him personally, read his books with some admiration, was not prepared to vote against him for any post, and would have voted for him for e.g. a fellowship at All Souls or Nuffield or St Antony's. [...] Nor did I think that Anderson's piece was particularly anti-Semitic so much as old-fashioned xenophobic – wicked foreigners subverting British national tradition – the fact that most of the corrupters were Jews is a historical fact and the result of obvious causes, but it is really the attribution of national decay to wicked émigrés, whoever they are, that reminds one so powerfully of every nationalist extremist from de Maistre to the anti-Dreyfusards and McCarthy, who also was careful not to be anti-Semitic, and had his own pet Jews like Anderson. It does infuriate me that I should be put in a category of persons who as soon as they are attacked themselves set up the cry of anti-Semitism. The vulgarity of it is intolerable. There now, having said all these things I feel some relief. [...]

Yours ever,

Isaiah   [...]

TO MAURICE BOWRA

2 April 1969

CUNY

Dear Maurice,

It is all much as you would think it to be. Columbia is in a mess – the professors wonder when their next class is going to be disturbed, and if so what will they do – can they just walk out? Is there some other safer university, or is this both cowardly and inexpedient? The administration is trying to appease, but nobody knows whether this will lead to sharper revolt or, on the contrary, will allay the passions. The streets of New York are full of Christs – what used to be called in France 'un jeune homme avec une [b]elle tête d'un Christ'[2] – their beards vary in size and colour – there are hundreds of them, all wild, all bearded, all very mad, Jews and Gentiles, Negroes and whites – I imagine Rome in the very last years must have looked a little like this. Nixon is treading very warily. Again no one knows whether this will lead to some tremendous *razzia*[3] at the end, or not. Joe is predicting victory in Vietnam very, very soon now [...]. Our friend Arthur Schlesinger is under heavy attack from right and left, as has often occurred in the past – his chief enemy being the saintly

---

1 'It was Berlin who was responsible for Deutscher being refused a university post at Sussex' – almost certainly more true than false. Does IB dissemble or forget?
2 'A young man with a beautiful Christlike head'.
3 'Raid'.

Noam Chomsky of MIT, who is delivering the Locke Lectures in Oxford next term, and who has accused him of being a treasonable intellectual who tells lies about Cuba, and has sold himself to the terrible administration; Arthur, in his turn, has reviewed his political essays and convicted him of at least one heavy misquotation about Truman. The Century Club[1] is on the whole behind Arthur; the boys and girls enormously pro-Chomsky. I propose to invite Chomsky to deliver a Wolfson College lecture on 'The Intellectual and Post-Industrial Society', which may attract a good many listeners – but I think it is time that we had a talk on this from a noble, if somewhat over-idealistic and unpracticable, prophet, whose work in the philosophy of language is of outstanding distinction, even though it has not gained the favour of Ryle. He is very serious indeed, but morally most impressive. I fear that Sparrow would not like him much. Fortunately he is at St Catherine's, where Bullock will be proud of having a world-famous man. I get on well with him – like Charles Taylor he has what is called a spiritual presence, even though he is much cleverer. Charles Taylor was here and complained bitterly about the barbarian turmoil in Montreal. The old Marxists have had some fearful birds come home to roost. The young men do not like them at all, or indeed anything to do with books and reasoning, and want an enormous kibbutz. Lowell has been to the Holy Land, and although it was anticipated that he would incline towards the Arabs on general left-wing grounds, he appears to have adored the Jews. [...] Meanwhile my poor mother-in-law is gathered to her ancestors, having expired, after a very agonising fortnight, at the age of 87, at the Carlyle Hotel.[2] Life has consequently, as you may imagine, not been easy for anyone. We buried her yesterday – the funeral was very proper and marred by no exhibitions of sentimentality or bad taste. Aline is all right. She longs to go home, but does not know if she can leave me. Lord Snow is here, but his reputation is fortunately much diminished, and although he has talked for hours on various television networks, praising the late President Eisenhower, whose funeral is also occurring today, he has become a somewhat despised figure, although still capable of earning quite a lot of money locally. I wonder if Truman will get an equally good send-off – I fear not. I cannot bring myself to admire Ike, who seems to me to have been very vain and very stupid, and although free from certain obvious vices such as crookedness, or blood-lust, or vindictiveness, also free from most virtues.

At this very moment her mother's will is being read aloud to Aline and her brother – a ceremony to which, although I was invited, I decided on grounds of good taste and disinterestedness to refrain from attending. No

---

1 Manhattan gentleman's club founded in the 19th century, formally 'The Century Association'; admitted women 1989.
2 Baroness Yvonne Fanny de Gunzbourg (1882–1969) née Deutsch de la Meurthe, widow of Baron Pierre de Gunzbourg, and daughter of Émile Michel Deutsch de la Meurthe, industrialist, died on 28 March 1969.

improvement in our financial condition is expected – if anything a slight decline, since a source of gifts enabling us to live abroad in the style to which at any rate some members of my family are accustomed has now, alas, disappeared. I do not know how this will affect the house in Italy, but it will.

Apart from the *New York Review of Books*, which thinks that all English writers are very good indeed, England and English writers and professors are at something of a discount here compared to the piping days of Harvard, 1950. My university I think will soon be dismantled owing to the bankruptcy of the City of New York, so how long I shall be allowed to come back here I simply do not know. I have had a message from David Cecil asking me to try and procure him an invitation to lecture here, but fashion has somewhat turned away from polite letters – Trevor-Roper, on the other hand, has been around – Lady Alexandra[1] is exactly like a mad English aristocratic lady in American fiction – absent-minded, distraught, with an imaginary coronet wobbling about on her thin well-born neck, and constantly puzzled and bewildered by everything that is going on. He, on the other hand, did not do quite as brilliantly while staying in Washington as his hosts expected: he would either do a lengthy turn on something or other – Tynan, or Gibbon, or whatever it might be – or fall into a glassy silence and stare in front of him, apparently unable either to hear or to speak. This was much complained of by Joe etc. Lady Alexandra complained that at universities where he was feasted, she was relegated to some faculty wife, was not allowed to come to any of the meals, and had to spend her time reading books in draughty living rooms, while the faculty wife, at the end of her tether, prepared chicken à la king for her. He delivered a lecture in Princeton presided over by some minor figure, while Lawrence Stone came in after the lecture began, sat at the back, left before it was finished, and was seen in a corner of the campus refuting the views which the lecturer had expressed. No contact occurred between them of any sort or kind. Roper's lecture on Hitler was quite good. He defended him as a political genius and drew a contrast between his nationalism and Bismarck's lack of it. The victims were E. H. Carr and Taylor. His lecture on the influence of the Romantics on the writing of history, i.e. Scott, was less interesting, though quite elegant. Plumb[2] has also been about. At the Century Club today I encountered at least five well-known English club men. I think in the course of time they will wear out their welcome. [...]

Isaiah   [...]

---

1 Lady Alexandra Henrietta Louisa Trevor-Roper (1907–97) née Haig, eldest daughter of Field-Marshal Earl Haig (1861–1928) and his wife the Hon. Dorothy Maud Vivian Haig (d. 1939); she married, first, 1941, Rear Admiral Clarence Dinsmore Howard-Johnston (1903–96), director of anti-submarine warfare at the Admiralty during the Second World War, with whom she had three children; in 1953 she began an affair with Hugh Trevor-Roper, and, after an acrimonious divorce, married him in October 1954.

2 John (Harold) Plumb (1911–2001), Fellow of Christ's, Cambridge, from 1946; Reader in Modern English History, Cambridge, 1962–5, Professor 1966–74.

⟨not April 23 [1969].⟩

CUNY

Dearest N,

I enclose a letter to Mrs Deutscher, whom you know and whom at one time you wished me to meet. Deutscher wanted me to write an Introduction to his *The UnJewish Jew*, but for obvious reasons I thought better not.[1] I did not like him at all, as you know, and thought his views in some way were horrifying, but what the *Black Dwarf* says is vilely false and outrageous and maddening. It all begins with an article in *New Left Review*, which I am sure you haven't read, in which Perry Anderson says that native British culture was stifled by a lot of white émigrés from abroad, such as Popper, Gombrich, Wittgenstein and myself – birthplaces and dates of birth are given, which is a kind of inverted elders of Zion – except that I never said that to anybody – certainly I never accused him of anti-Semitism. But then the *Black Dwarf*, which I gather is a grotesque and nasty little journal, frivolously produced by Tariq Ali etc., had a horrid and very libellous little paragraph which accused me (*a*) of accusing Perry Anderson of anti-Semitism – I think the article might indeed make one think that he was one, but I certainly never said this to anyone (let alone in public), but that need not concern you; but also (*b*) that as Deutscher was a Jew, that I had stopped his appointment at Brighton – Perry Anderson had praised Deutscher – that my charge was baseless, and indeed with my kind of record I ought to think twice before accusing other people of such monstrous offences. I do not propose to do anything about this, because obviously to tangle with them would be counter-productive – they would pervert every word one said etc. – but I don't want Mrs Deutscher to think that I put a fatal obstacle in her husband's glorious career, hence I enclose a draft of what I propose to write to her (I think I had better get someone at Brighton, e.g. Martin Wight, to corroborate that such indeed was the case – he is an honest man and will certainly do so, because I think I have told the story quite accurately). If he does, then may I send this letter to her, and could you in your kindness communicate with her and tell her that I am not a monster – that I had no wish to do her husband harm, and indeed refrained from doing so, and of course I did not like his view of me, or his views in general, particularly about the Jews, but that I am really not as detestable as all that, and that what *Black Dwarf* says is a howling falsehood? According to you she is a nice woman, and to cause her this kind of pain, or let her labour under this kind of misapprehension, would distress me very much indeed. Could you do this? Indeed, if it is not totally impractical,

---

1 Isaac Deutscher, *The Non-Jewish Jew and Other Essays* (London, 1968); the introduction was written by Deutscher's wife Tamara (385/2).⟶

I should be glad to meet her after I come back and say all this to her myself if she will let me. I did think Deutscher pretty awful, as you know, but I bent over backwards – perhaps unnecessarily – on the few occasions in which I was concerned in anything that concerned him. I have to admit that I did once suggest that he might *not* be an ideal person for writing the life of Dr Weizmann, which had been suggested to me in Palestine. Apart from that I do not think I offered any obstruction to his career. ⟨Боже мой: как все гадко и скучно!⟩[1] [...]

    Yours,

      Isaiah

TO TAMARA DEUTSCHER[2]

    22 April 1969

                                              CUNY

Dear Mrs Deutscher,

    A fortnight or so ago I received a cutting from a recent issue of a periodical called the *Black Dwarf* (which I gather to be the organ of Tariq Ali and his political associates), in which it was anonymously stated that I had (in private) called an article by Mr Perry Anderson in the *New Left Review* (in which he traced my views to my origins) anti-Semitic, and said that I was scarcely in a position to accuse others of this since I had successfully blocked the appointment of the late Isaac Deutscher to a chair in Russian history at the University of Sussex on the ground that 'A Marxist should not be a Professor of Russian History.'

    I need scarcely say that all these statements are false. And although the fact that they should have been made seems to me scandalous, I do not, despite feeling great irritation, propose to controvert them in public, as the *Black Dwarf* has been described to me by various left-wing socialists to whom I have spoken here as the kind of publication that would take little notice of the fact that the statements ascribed to me were, in fact, never made by me either in public or in private. I did not accuse Mr Anderson of anti-Semitism: I do not know whether he is an anti-Semite or not, nor do I care. What concerns me far more is the libel about my behaviour with regard to the late Mr Deutscher. The facts, which are confidential, and which therefore I do not intend to publish, are to the best of my recollection these:

    At a time when I belonged to a committee responsible for reporting on

---

1 'My God: how vile and tedious it all is!'

2 Tamara Deutscher (1913–90) née Lebenhaft, Polish-born journalist, writer and editor; married Isaac Deutscher 1947: 'She was instrumental in his decision in 1946 to forsake journalism and turn himself into a contemporary historian. In this endeavour she acted as his intellectual partner, joint researcher, critic and typist' (John McIlroy, ODNB); she also assisted E. H. Carr with his multi-volume *A History of Soviet Russia* (London, 1950–78), and edited for publication his *The Comintern and the Spanish Civil War* (London, 1984).

academic standards of the then newly created Sussex University, and there-fore liable to be made an elector to chairs (though not to other posts) in fields concerning which I might be thought to have some knowledge, I was asked whether I thought it a good idea to create a chair in Soviet studies for Mr Deutscher. My view, which I communicated verbally to Professor Martin Wight, was that Mr Deutscher's remarkable gifts would benefit the University most if he were not called on to create a field of studies but to invigorate an existing discipline: that I should, for example, be wholeheartedly in favour of the appointment if, say, one other expert were in the department to look after aspects of the field which Mr Deutscher did not regard as central or relevant to what interested him most. I explained that, so far as I was personally con-cerned, I should have been perfectly ready to support his candidature in any institution which possessed a department, or at least one or two teachers, in this field, e.g. at Oxford or Cambridge, or for a research fellowship anywhere at all; but that, although I did not think Mr Deutscher ideally qualified for the Sussex job, I might well be mistaken: if the University's own people wished to appoint him, I should, if I were an elector, certainly not vote against him, or resist his election in any way, if only on the ground that universities ought to be absolutely free to do what they thought it right to do, whether outsid-ers like myself thought it wise or not; that at any rate this is how I would act in this particular instance. I made it absolutely plain that I should not lift a finger to obstruct your late husband's appointment, whatever my misgiv-ings, nor ventilate my views on the subject to anyone, if the University in fact wished to give Mr Deutscher the post in question.

I feel sure that Professor Wight, and indeed the Vice-Chancellor at the time, Lord Fulton, will bear this out if you ask them. I do not know what happened after this. I gather that others closer to your husband than I (indeed I hardly knew him at all, for we met but twice) were consulted, and that, in the event, no post in this subject was created. But I know nothing of the circumstances; the only point I wish to make is that if the University had wished to appoint Mr Deutscher to be Professor of Soviet Studies, they could have done so in the knowledge that no opposition to this would come from me. Consequently, the statement in the *Black Dwarf* is wholly groundless.

As for the proposition attributed to me by the *Black Dwarf* that 'No Marxist should be Professor of Russian History' – this is a monstrosity of which no one who knows me could (I should hope) believe me to be guilty. Your husband disapproved of my views, if anything, more strongly than I did of his; nevertheless it would have been a betrayal of every intellectual value in which I believe if I had allowed this to sway my judgement consciously in judging his fitness for an academic post. Indeed, when someone, some time after the Sussex episode, asked me whether I would be prepared to support him for a research post at one of the Oxford colleges, I said that I would be glad to do so – that he would bring an element of passionate concern, however wrong-headed I might think it to be, that Oxford could certainly do with. However, nothing came of this, and I heard no more. I write all this since I think that you may have heard this rumour and have been upset by it; and to clear my own record in the face of a baseless calumny. It will probably pursue me whatever I do or say. You must forgive me for imposing upon your time in this fashion: but I feel sure that you will agree it is always desirable to state the truth; and that no decent person could remain unmoved by a false charge of unjust behaviour towards another man, especially if he were brilliant, courageous, gifted, and had in all probability suffered a good deal for his political convictions.

Yours sincerely,
    Isaiah Berlin

Tamara Deutscher replied on 13 May, raising – but not answering – the question why Sussex had an abrupt change of heart. IB's response (2 June) assumes not that she was implicating him, though she surely was, but that she suspected the University Council of blocking the appointment; and he insisted again that, if the University had wished to appoint, he would not have objected, even though he thought it the wrong decision, and had felt bound to say so when asked. He claimed not to know why the decision was made, but the Vice-Chancellor 'must have asked the advice of other persons also'. He defended his narrative vigorously: he was resolved not take proceedings against Black Dwarf, 'but if a serious publication made such allegations, I should have no hesitation. I have checked my facts with Professor Wight and have no doubt that Lord Fulton would corroborate them. [...] I should be grateful if you would let me know whether there is something in this account which you find puzzling or implausible or misleading or false.' He took her non-committal reply (8 June) to indicate that there was not. Wishful thinking on his part, no doubt: but then, as he noted in his letter of 12 June, his motive in writing to her 'was self-exoneration'.

TO ANNA KALLIN

23 April 1969

New York

Dearest N,

[...] My own dear University here seems to be occupied by black militants, but apparently nothing that is happening here, including the fearful goings-on at Harvard from which I have just returned, and the posse of twenty black men with huge rifles at Cornell, photographed by the [*New York*] *Times*, and looking really rather terrible,[1] but nothing of all this begins to equal what is

---

1 The widely-circulated photograph, taken by the Associated Press photographer Steve Starr, of armed members of the Afro-American Society emerging from their occupation of the Student

going on in Japan,[1] where it is all presumably not caused by the Vietnam war, nor by Negro problems, nor by the pollution of the cities, nor by anything but *khandra* and *toska*,[2] which I believe to be the root causes of it all, frivolous as this may sound – of course 'deeper' analysis of these phenomena is possible. There is no doubt that our number is up, and I am glad to be as old as I am.[3] My fellow feeling with poor Herzen was always tremendous, but it has now reached a point of lunatic self-identification. [...] Yes, I have read *Werther*.[4] I do not think the youths today could read it – not obscene enough, nothing about masturbation etc., not 'relevant', only a sense of despair, which is the last thing, alas, that they feel – on the contrary they agitate happily. They are not miserable at all. The people who are miserable are all your old friends from Weimar, to whom students are simply storm-troopers, and who walk about with huge sticks to protect themselves against the 'barbarians'. So Kristeller[5] at Columbia (do you know him?), so all the Viennese economists at Harvard, so, I suspect Wittkower[6] etc. They are ferociously right-wing. The left are more to be found among the *nedouchi[v]shiisya*[7] students and the teachers of not deeply rigorous subjects such as Eng. lit., 'social studies', theologians etc. [...]

Do make it all right for me with Mrs Deutscher – I am told here that I really could bring a libel suit against *Black Dwarf* and get quite a lot of money, but I shall not. I have now verified the text with Mr Wight at Brighton, who consulted me about Deutscher, and he declares it to be accurate and true. I do not know Mrs Deutscher's address, but shall send another copy – *na avos*'[8] – to the Oxford Press. This is causing me genuine distress.

    Yours ever,

    Isaiah

Union Building, Willard Straight Hall, on the campus of Cornell University, 19 April 1969, appeared in the NYT, 21 April 1969, 1.

1 On 2 March 1969, during widespread student unrest in Japan, 230 people were injured in a battle between police and protestors at the University of Kyoto.

2 Russian terms for melancholy.

3 IB also uses the last 10 words at the end of his 1991 interview with Nathan Gardels on nationalism, when he contemplates the death of culture that would be occasioned by the eradication of cultural differences. 'Two Concepts of Nationalism', NYRB, 21 November 1991, 19–23.

4 Goethe's *The Sorrows of Young Werther* (1774): forlorn in his love for Charlotte, and prey to a morbid sentimentality (often called 'Wertherism' after this story), Werther takes his own life.

5 Paul Oskar Kristeller (1905–99), Berlin-born philosopher and authority on Renaissance thought, fled Nazi Europe, arriving in US and joining Columbia University 1939: associate professor 1948; professor 1956; Woodbridge Professor 1968–73 (Emeritus 1973–99).

6 Rudolf Wittkower (1901–71), Berlin-born art historian and expert on Italian baroque, left Nazi Germany for Britain; staff member at the Warburg Institute 1934–56; Professor of Fine Arts, Columbia, 1956–69; Slade Professor of Fine Art, Cambridge, 1970–1; Institute for Advanced Study, Princeton, 1971.

7 'Who hasn't finished studying'.

8 'On the off chance'.

TO ROBERT SILVERS

30 May 1969 [*carbon*]

[Headington House]

Dear Bob,

I am delighted that you have recovered and long to tell you all about Chomsky here. The reception is by no means uncritical although masses of students come. To his lecture on 'The Intellectual and Post-Industrial Society' eighteen hundred persons came in Oxford – I presided as competently as I could. It was very like an exposition of the middle 1930s, full of charm, lucidity, acrid ironies and with the most over-simplified kind of Marxism I ever heard on such an occasion. He really does think that United States foreign policy is entirely dictated by business interests – stated in a sophisticated form this could perhaps be made not too unplausible; in the form in which he gives it, it is exactly like one of the Gollancz Left Book Club pamphlets:[1] his voice, his manner, his charm, his singularly irresistible personality hallows it all. I am about to have a long conversation with him about the Middle East. His views I am sure will be noble, simple and tranquil, like Winckelmann's[2] conception of classical art – but not related to verifiable empirical facts. I love him more than ever, and spend time with him, but his grasp of empirical reality is not very strong. I beg you not to pass this on, but when he solemnly informed us at dinner that the reason for the [re]call of George Kennan by Dulles[3] was that he was too friendly to the Soviet Union – when in fact he had to return because he said that [the] Soviet regime was worse or as bad as the Nazis, at the airport in Berlin, as you recollect (a fact which he seems absolutely astonished to hear) – this seemed to be not altogether untypical. Still I thought his lecture was splendid. Mrs Floud did not; she liked him personally but thought that the content of his remarks reminded her of the crudest and most simplified form of Marxism, which she had once followed and had reacted against in due course. And indeed there is a curious mixture of subtlety and sophistication about theoretical matters, great moral charm and authority, extreme unrealism, dogmatic assurance (the philosophers here refuse to accept his doctrine, either linguistic or philosophical), sense of mission, purity of soul and almost a hatred of empirical reality. If he had stuck to the proposition that intellectuals should always tell the truth, never play being politicians, never temporise or compromise, however utopian or unrealistic their ideas, that would be much better. As it is the boys love

1 Publishing venture begun by Victor Gollancz in 1936 to counter the rise of Fascism: among its cheaply produced editions was George Orwell's *The Road to Wigan Pier* (London, 1937).
2 Johann Joachim Winckelmann (1717–68), German archaeologist and art historian, a pioneering figure in the development of art history as a discipline, and in the understanding of Greek and Roman art.
3 John Foster Dulles (1888–1959), lawyer and Republican statesman, Secretary of State under Eisenhower 1953–9, a strong advocate of the nuclear deterrent in the Cold War.

it – at least the radical ones – and everybody over twenty-seven is highly
sceptical. [...]

Yours ever,

TO PHILIP TOYNBEE

4 June 1969

Wolfson

Dear Philip,

I am just back from America, and remember with pleasure that you
wanted us to come and stay with you. June is no good because of a vast
accumulation of undone business – I cannot begin to convey to you how odd
it is for me to be in the position I am in, doing what I am doing [...].

[...] How very characteristically sweet of you to want to remember our
original meeting. You say it was in Jeremy [Hutchinson]'s rooms when Eliot
spoke – in Beaumont Street?[1] I remember the occasion, I really do: first
the reading of his poetry in a lugubrious voice in, I think, Rhodes House;
then answers to questions [during] which he advised people not to become
poets; then the conversation in Jeremy's rooms in which he wanted to talk
about frivolous subjects, and he talked about the German poet himself [sic]
– Wilhelm Busch[2] – a small gathering and Jeremy and Ben [Nicolson] were
much impressed by the fact that Eliot talked to me quite affably, which was
somehow unexpected. My nostalgia increases too. Yet, could you bear to go
back into the 1930s? If a lamp were rubbed and you suddenly found yourself
in 1935 again? Could you? Even if it were promised that you would not foresee
the future any better than you could have foreseen it at the time – would you
really like to relive your undergraduate days, the party on the river, Miss
Sinclair, Christ Church, Abe Lazarus[3] and all?

Yours, with love,

Isaiah

1 In 1934 the poet, critic and publisher T[homas] S[tearns] Eliot (1888–1965) attended a gathering
  of the Florentine Club, a highbrow undergraduate discussion group, at the Beaumont Street lodgings shared by Stuart Hampshire, who helped to run the club, and Jeremy Nicolas Hutchinson
  (b. 1915), then a PPE undergraduate at Magdalen (1933–6), later a barrister and (1978) life peer,
  3rd husband (1940–66) of Dame Peggy Ashcroft, and 2nd husband (1966–2006) of June Osborn.
2 IB's ability to converse with Eliot about the German satirical poet and illustrator Wilhelm Busch
  (1832–1908) surprised those gathered, not least Hampshire, who felt 'caricaturally English' by
  comparison (MI 90, quoting Hampshire).
3 Abraham Lazarus (1911–67), nom de guerre 'Bill Firestone', charismatic Communist Party member
  active in town politics in Oxford in the 1930s who in 1934–5 led the popular protest against the
  'Cutteslowe walls' (1934–59), built to separate a council estate from private housing in north
  Oxford: 'with flaming red hair and startlingly blue eyes, his ringing voice could be heard, without
  the aid of a microphone, from one end of St Giles' to the other'. Olive Gibbs, 'Our Olive': The
  Autobiography of Olive Gibbs (Oxford, 1989), 92.

TO DOROTHEA HEAD[1]

11 June 1969

Headington House

Dearest Dot,

[...] You can imagine the condition of the cockles of my heart on receiving your undeserved but tremendously welcome letter. I wish I could believe one tenth part of what you say about my little collection of pieces.[2] I have been tremendously attacked for two of them, not just by anarchists or postgraduates but sober professors stimulated to enraged comments – from right and left blows have rained upon me; Catholics and Communists, analytical philosophers and metaphysicians, the *Spectator* and professional journals – all but the mildest of mild liberals have united to smite me hip and thigh. I shake like an aspen leaf, but I cannot retreat. Hence the republication of these essays. I do not think that your young postgraduates[3] will find my pieces enlightening – I hope they will, but I do not somehow think so in the present climate of opinion. Nothing is less popular today than to say that there is no millennium, that values collide, that there is no final solution, that one can only gain one value at the expense of another, that whatever one chooses entails the sacrifice of something else – or that it is at any rate often so. This is regarded as either false or cynical or both, but the opposite belief is what, it seems to me, has cost us so much frightful suffering and blood in the past. I view it with a certain measure of scepticism, not too much, but with a kind of tolerant sense of what costs what, what can only be obtained at a price too high in human lives or feelings – the kind of belief held by, say, Erasmus,[4] Diderot,[5] my hero Herzen (have you read the autobiography, now published in four huge volumes; the most marvellous autobiography

---

1 Dorothea Louise Head (1907–87) née Ashley-Cooper, daughter of the 9th Earl of Shaftesbury, married, 1935, Anthony Head, 1st Viscount Head; a talented amateur portrait painter, herself painted by Augustus John c.1930.

2 *Four Essays on Liberty* (London and NY, 1969), now incorporated in L. IB regarded *Four Essays* as his most important book, distilling as it does his central ideas on the nature and importance of political liberty, especially its 'negative' variant, the freedom of not being interfered with by other people. The eponymous four essays, which follow a long introduction replying to some of IB's many critics, are 'Political Ideas in the Twentieth Century' (1950), 'Historical Inevitability' (1954), 'Two Concepts of Liberty' (1958) and 'John Stuart Mill and the Ends of Life' (1959). The third essay in particular has stimulated an enormous secondary literature which continues to grow to this day. An account of the book's tortuous genesis is given in L.

3 DH's classmates at her local College of Further Education, where, well in to her 60s, she took a diploma in politics.

4 Desiderius Erasmus (c.1467–1536), Dutch humanist scholar and reformer, one of the greatest figures of the Renaissance; published in 1516 an edition of the Greek New Testament with an influential parallel Latin translation; lectured on theology and Greek at Cambridge 1511–14; his complex satirical work *Moriae encomium* (*Praise of Folly*, 1509) was completed in England, in the household of his close friend Thomas More.

5 Denis Diderot (1713–84), French philosopher, and, with Voltaire, the leading figure of the Enlightenment in France; an early freethinking champion of secular, scientific modernity.

produced by the entire nineteenth century and indeed by almost any other period?) and not many others; nor is there any other attitude that makes life tolerable at all. [...]

Having finally reached the age of 60, although I feel responsible for the past and in some degree for the present, I no longer feel much responsibility for the future – let the young do what they can with it, [it is] not for my generation to be too harsh or even ironical about that. I do not mind things quite as much as I used to, but still quite a lot, and when I find myself pilloried by, say, the *New Left Review* and libelled by the *Black Dwarf* (if it weren't the kind of periodical it is, I suppose I could actually sue them for the libellous thing they said about me) I cannot bring myself to feel too indignant. I think these young men live in a far more horrible world than any that I ever went through even in the awful 1930s. We had a lot of very solid hopes and a lot of black enemies, personal and political – Fascism really was utterly hateful, so was Stalinism, nor was there much doubt that in a Europe dominated by Hitler and Mussolini, Franco and Mr Chamberlain, Daladier and Stalin, one really could think of things in terms of black and white – in those days only Roosevelt appeared to be a point of light, since he alone was not frightened of the future, and actually believed that ideas mattered, and that cleverness, ingenuity, brilliance were not qualities to be feared or disparaged, and that only those ideals were worth trying to implement which a lot of the poor and the destitute and the miserable were prepared to turn out and vote for. I do not believe that this is the situation today. I have a feeling that the Gods of yesterday have failed the young, that just as the Soviet Union can no longer be believed in with that utter and guileless faith which so many found so easy to hold in the 1930s, so the Welfare State, prosperity, security, increasing efficiency etc. do not attract those young who feel the need to sacrifice themselves for some worthy ideal, if possible in company with other likeminded persons, and that they are desperately searching for some form of self-expression which will cause them to swim against some sort of stream and not simply drift in a harmless way, too comfortably, with it. Hence all this dashing about, and this terrible sense of ennui which I think ultimately is the cause of all the discontent, no matter what the specific difference between countries – Vietnam, Negroes etc. We feared something: war, economic collapse, totalitarianism. But ennui is worse. It is what the French called *le spleen anglais*[1] in the eighteenth century. Lack of concrete prospects induces this inexorably. However I must not go on so.

Yours ever,

[Isaiah]

---

1 'English depression'.

TO MCGEORGE BUNDY

12 June 1969 [*carbon*]

[Wolfson]

Dear Mac,

[...] The Wolfson College Trustees would be *extremely* honoured and pleased if you would like to attend their meeting at 10.30 a.m. in London at Universal House (you have been there before) on the selfsame day – Friday 18th. There are quite serious issues to settle about building etc. They really would be very happy indeed if you could possibly come – even if you did not stay for the entire proceedings, which seldom last for more than one hour to one hour and a half (Leonard's impatience has its virtues). As Leonard seems somewhat critical of the particular stocks purchased for us out of his money by Messrs Little[1] and Oppenheimer[2] – our advisers – we decided to let *him* do all the investing of the money provided by his Foundation; in the secret hope that if the portfolio chosen by him does not do too brilliantly, he will feel some moral obligation to restore some of it somehow, if his building is not to suffer. You observe the not very deeply concealed cunning of this move, and so, indeed, does he; this is what makes it all above board and all right. It is somehow unlikely that he will come before the Trustees and say that he has had bad luck with his investments and consequently the College will not, after all, have the shape and quality that the Trustees have decided upon. For similar reasons, we intend to extend the Trust, if everyone allows us to, until the final bills are in, for if the Trust is not in existence, the College itself will be liable: this is a terrible prospect, far better surely that the Trustees (including 'Mr Leonard') should be? I have now revealed all our secret thoughts and warmly invite you to come on Friday morning [...].

Yours ever,

[Isaiah]

TO CHIMEN ABRAMSKY[3]

13 June 1969

Wolfson

Dear Chimen,

[...] As for E. H. Carr: he is coming to tea with me quite soon. I am sure he will not be touched by anything I say. I feel that one of his weapons, which I envy him, is being encased in a kind of shell which makes him pretty

1 Ian Malcolm David Little (1918–2012), much-travelled economist; Fellow, Nuffield, 1952–76; Professor of Economics of Underdeveloped Countries, Oxford, 1971–6.

2 Peter Morris Oppenheimer (b. 1938), economist; Bank for International Settlements, Basle, 1961–4; Research Fellow, Nuffield, 1964–7; Student of Christ Church 1967–2008; University Lecturer in Economics 1967–2000.

3 Chimen *Abramsky (1916–2010), historian, bibliographer and book collector.

impervious to what the liberal bourgeois critics say, because he understands their motives and discounts them accordingly, whereas he is on the rising escalator, marching with the new world, and has nothing to fear. I reject this entire conception, but I envy him his fanatic's paradise.

Surely rational philosophers assume that choice is free in time and place and [sc. in?] some transcendent sphere, whatever Kant may have said.[1] Certainly freedom of choice applies equally to rulers and ruled, tyrants and oppressed, executioner and victim, but it is limited by a thousand factors (it is with believing this that I am not credited by my blinder critics), hemmed in not only by obvious obstacles, but of course also by ignorance, passion, pressures – emotional, social, physical etc. etc. – in varying degrees; and still voluntary martyrdom does exist; heroism is not an empty term; we do admire heroic sacrifice quite differently from the way in which we admire beauty or power. Why should a born slave or serf not be able to choose? His horizons may be narrower, but moments must occur, even in his life, in which he has to choose between one purpose and another, one value and another. In the first essay printed in that book of mine[2] I tried to make the point that Fascists and Communists in the twentieth century, instead of making it possible for people to rationally consider and answer questions of an agonising kind, try to shape them in such a way that they lose all desire to ask the questions themselves; so the questions, as it were, are washed away. Marcuse and other people now bring the same charge against liberal bourgeois society – Fascists and Communists operate through terrorism or crude mass indoctrination (and do not succeed on the whole: the Germans, the Russians and the Chinese, although I do not know about the Chinese, are not, in fact, the kind of perfect conditioned Fascists, Communists etc. that the system intended), while liberal democracies do so through the corruption of industrial goods, bread and circuses. There is no doubt some truth in this: the range of choice can be narrowed artificially by men and by circumstances: even I, liberal as I am, say that to speak of political freedom to an Iraqi peasant is to mock him; yet there are provinces where even he is free, and it is this that real determinism surely denies. [...]

Certainly I am influenced by Kant in supposing that awareness of the possibility of choice, however narrow, is one of the things that distinguishes men from animals; that while computers may be substitutes for thought, they cannot be substitutes for a capacity for conceiving purposes, or action in its true sense. [...]

Yours,

　　Isaiah

　　　　　　　　　　　　　　　　　　　　　　　　　　　　　　　　　　[...]

<hr/>

1 Abramsky had asked, 'Do philosophers understand freedom of choice above time, place and space, or are they like historians to be restricted to a given time, a definite country and epoch in history, i.e. to have a relativist, rather than an absolute approach?' IB's response seems not quite to engage with the question as posed.

2 'Political Ideas in the Twentieth Century' (391/2).

TO JEAN FLOUD

26 [July 1969? postmark 6 August 1969; *manuscript*]

[Paraggi]

[...] Arnaldo M.[1] was marvellous: his piece on Jacob Bernays[2] (I won't, of course, insult you by even hinting who *he* was – besides being uncle to Frau S. Freud – but Sparrow, mentioned sweetly but ironically by A.M., *cd* tell you) is not only beautifully written & vastly learned but deeply moving: I told him so: he blushed a little – beneath his semi-tan – he came clothed in flannel bags & a black black alpaca jacket like a pre-1914 Gelehrter, but was pleased (end of sentence: O.K. grammatical). He now hates Richard Wollheim for despising learning as evidenced by the commune into which he converted the philosophy dept of University College: his novel[3] was final evidence of something shameless, exhibitionistic, no part of the world of feeling, learning, civilized relationships. He talked endlessly about his own Jewish upbringing & quoted Hebrew: I felt moved & flattered. He is really, I do believe, the last voice of 19th century scholarship & European enlightenment, with its narrow moral vision & vast intellectual horizons, and noble values and occasional academic pettiness. I admire him very much & feel at home with him: he is not racked by frustrations & jealousies & envies, at least such as wd upset me: last night I saw Ezra Pound.[4] Silent, gloomy, nasty, very handsome, like a man of genius, spoke only twice in a gruff, doom laden voice: once when he identified Grishkin in T. S. Eliot's poem – the one who promises pneumatic bliss[5] – as some Russian ballerina:[6] I corrected his pronunciation & regretted it instantly: the worst of taste! the second time: when his mistress

---

1 Arnaldo Dante Momigliano (1908–87), later (1974) Hon. KBE, peerless ancient historian, was born near Cuneo in Italy into a prominent Jewish intellectual family; both of his parents died in concentration camps during the Second World War. He emigrated to Britain as an academic refugee in March 1939 and was Professor of Ancient History, London (UCL), 1951–75. He had lunched with the Berlins in Paraggi the previous day.

2 Momigliano's short study of the eponymous German philologist Jacob Bernays (1824–81) was published that year (Amsterdam/London, 1969).

3 Wollheim's only novel, *A Family Romance* [a Freudian term] (London, 1969), takes the form of the diary of an academic who sets about poisoning his wife.

4 Ezra Weston Loomis Pound (1885–1972), Idaho-born poet and critic, a leader of the Imagist movement, and champion of writers such as Eliot and Joyce, lived in Italy from 1924, and developed pro-Mussolini and anti-Semitic sentiments; broadcast Fascist propaganda over Rome radio during Second World War; was returned to US to face charge of treason, but considered unfit to stand trial, and confined to a mental institution 1946–58; returned to Italy on his release. 'Have you met, talking of men of genius, Ezra Pound? I found myself in Rapallo at dinner with him. He uttered not *one* single word. I do not know the timbre of his voice. He looked very handsome & distinguished. Is his position in literature like Schoenberg's in music? a vast & crucial influence on men of genius, but himself (perhaps) *not* one?' IB to Mary McCarthy, 7 August 1964.

5 'Whispers of Immortality', in *Poems* (NY, 1920). The fifth stanza runs: 'Grishkin is nice: her Russian eye / Is underlined for emphasis; / Uncorseted, her friendly bust / Gives promise of pneumatic bliss.'

6 Serafima Astaf'eva (1876–1934), Russian ballerina and dance teacher, ran a London ballet school whose pupils included Alicia Markova and Margot Fonteyn; Pound introduced her to Eliot.

said "Well, Ezra: shall we go home?" He said "We shall never get there" &
left. Complained he cd not understand a word I said: I was nervous & self
conscious & gabbled more than usual. He is a genuinely un-nice man – apart
from his fascism & madness & depressed manic collapse – but somehow
magnificent. Again, a lost voice. The record of his reading of his obscene
Cantos[1] is marvellous. And I? You want to know? I have decided that this
endless search, for the sake of one miserable article,[2] into Vico's sources [...] –
which I enjoy terribly – is sheer escape from thinking, which is both painfully
difficult for me & involves me in controversies which I hate even more. The
joys of minute endless scholarship – footnotes of footnotes, is tremendous.
And despite affable letters about my reactionary political views from my
fellow fossilized liberals, I am no thinker: & the desire at once for huge gen-
eralizations about Kulturgeschichte[3] *and* minute reference to obscure Italian
editors – is some sort of playing at true learning which, though I believe in it,
& enjoy it, is not the genuine article. It gives me an opportunity of criticizing
both those whose culture is shallow or narrow or enslaved by clichés and
party labels, *and* of detecting pseudo-learning in the pretentious: so I can
thunder against (say) Deutscher *and* his opposite, Miss Arendt: complain that
Oxford thinkers are parochial *and* that Marcuse's friends are charlatans or ½
charlatans: but what cold comfort is that! I *long* for & always have for the feet
of a genuine master: in Cambridge I shd, I expect, have bowed to Moore &
Wittgenstein: in Berlin in 1900 to Max Weber and Wilamowitz:[4] in Paris to
nobody since Michelet:[5] not those worthy men with small *barbiches*,[6] dedicated but excessively dry Durkheim & Lévy Bruhl[7] like moderate defenders
of la solidarité française: in Russia – ah: luxuriant beards – some eloquent
morally good professor despised by the German cultural philistine Marxists.
But I must not go on. It is a fearful thing to be aware that one is really not
much & not mind much either – & care for nothing but human beings & personal relationships – not like Bloomsbury which somehow reduced even that
to doctrine – but in some untidy, ephemeral, casual way:[8] & feel no shame

---

1 Pound devoted a large part of his life to the *Cantos*, a long, esoteric, kaleidoscopic body of poetry
   conceived as early as 1913, but never completed; they are considered to have greatly influenced
   the development of modern poetry.
2 IB's 'Sulla teoria del Vico circa la conoscenza storica', *Lettere italiane* 17 (1965), 420–31, was included
   in revised form as 'Vico's Theory of Knowledge and its Sources' in VH and TCE.
3 'Cultural history'.
4 Ulrich von Wilamowitz-Moellendorff (1848–1931), one of the foremost Greek scholars of his
   day; Professor of Greek, Berlin, 1897–1921; Hon D.Litt., Oxford, 1908.
5 Jules Michelet (1798–1874), French historian, keeper of the National Historical Archives 1831–52;
   author of the 17-volume *Histoire de France* (Paris, 1833–67); Vico enthusiast.
6 'Goatees'.
7 Lucien Lévy-Bruhl (1857–1939), French philosopher and anthropologist known for his work on
   the mentality of 'primitive' peoples.
8 As an undergraduate IB had read G. E. Moore's *Principia Ethica* (Cambridge, 1903) and found
   himself 'on an open, sunlit plain': 'The writing was marvellously clear, the arguments seemed
   to me totally convincing, the ideals noble and attractive – I felt transported. Reading it was the

about not having contributed one immortal brick to some eternal structure of the human spirit. Lack of ambition? Fecklessness? Frivolity? perhaps. But I am such. There. It is a shameful thing ever to go on so about oneself (the English school education teaches one). [...]

– a signature? why?

~~Isaiah~~

TO HAMILTON FISH ARMSTRONG[1]

19 August 1969 [*manuscript card*]

As from Headington House

Alas! Vladimir Ilyich is no good to me. I shall never write about him: it is not easy to say why: mainly because I *cannot* read him. I remember that Chip B. used to go to bed night after night with a volume of V.I.'s writings tucked under his arm: but I *cannot* drive myself through those terrible arid steppes, vast, monotonous, repetitive, inhumanly tedious. Yes, he was a great man: a more successful Robespierre or Cromwell (Cromwell was more sympathetic) but I cannot begin to get "inside" him: & without that, a mere appraisal of doctrines, achievements, prophecies, what actually occurred, etc. remains dead for me: I really only take an interest in ideas as part of someone's actual outlook & temperament: & V.I.'s is opaque to me. [...]

Isaiah   [...]

TO SYLVESTER GATES

30 August 1969 [*manuscript*]

Paraggi

Dear Sylvester,

I ought to have written days and days ago: but in spite of the theoretical leisure, visitors arrive, one is hustled to the beach, to the hills, to the Post Office. Brock writes daily, there is a grave Leonard / Ian Little crisis – ultimata are in the air – everything on the Leonard front is crackling with menace – shares – interior decoration – how fortunate we were to sell our Pergamon holdings 24 hours before dealings in these commodities were forbidden – & this fills the days: but we *have* had news of you regularly: from Anne: from John: from the hospital [...]. Our summer, I regret to tell you, has been

---

most profound philosophical experience I had yet had. Three or four years later, I came to the conclusion that its thesis was completely mistaken, and I believe this still: personal relationships and the contemplation of beauty are not the principal ends of human life': 'England's Mistaken Moralist', *The Times Higher Education Supplement*, 15 October 1993, 20.

1 Hamilton Fish Armstrong (1893–1973), editor of *Foreign Affairs* 1928–72, the magazine of the US Council on Foreign Relations; IB had a great regard for 'Ham' Armstrong, and found it difficult to refuse his not infrequent requests for copy for *Foreign Affairs* – in this case an article on Lenin.

positively *made* by the absence of the Old Boy:[1] I mean our old friend, you know who (I daren't say the name: but you won't leave this letter about? He may call to visit: gaga as he is, he sees & hears what one does not want him to): every day this freedom, this marvellous freedom from the pathetic, oppressive, demanding, guilt inducing, conversation killing, embarrassing, gross, maddening, at once touching and violently repellent, paranoiac, deaf, blind, thick skinned, easily offended presence is a source of relief and almost joy. How disloyal: how awful. [...] I am reading Heine on Philosophy & Religion in Germany:[2] very funny & good: he thinks Kant is responsible for causing German philosophers to write in hideous gobbledegook – that he invented a terrible terminology out of respect for *science* – wants philosophy not to be light, clear, elegant & therefore trivial – that was for the French – but weighty, attention compelling, in a formal attire – grand, pompous, imposing: & generated the loathsome jargon which Germans mistake for depth. I see why Heine is still hated in Germany: too nasty & too funny. He says that Kant killed God & Robespierre killed the King: but in a quiet, methodical way: & that it is these quiet persons whom one should fear. [...] Aline sends you her warmest love –

Isaiah

TO P. E. TREMENHEERE[3]

13 November 1969 [*carbon*]

[Wolfson]

Dear Mr Tremenheere,

Thank you for your letter of 28 October. You say that you find it hard to understand why my name was included among those who protested against the association of Oxford University with the [rugby] football match with the Springboks.[4] You then quite reasonably compare the persecution practised in the Soviet Union with that of South Africa, and ask me about the Bolshoi Ballet etc. There are two things that I should like to say about that:

    1. Because one cannot protest against everything – if only because that

---

1 Maurice Bowra – whose visit to Paraggi the previous year IB had found particularly taxing.

2 Heinrich Heine, *Zur Geschichte der Religion und Philosophie in Deutschland* (first published in French in 1834). The passages IB goes on to refer to may be found near the beginning of part 3: see the English translation by John Snodgrass, *Religion and Philosophy in Germany: A Fragment* (London/ Boston, 1882), 106–11.

3 Patrick Edward Tremenheere (1912–77), tea-planter in Ceylon until 1954; member of the UN Association of Great Britain.

4 By 1969 the sporting boycott of apartheid South Africa had gathered considerable momentum, and IB was one of five heads of Oxford Colleges who jointly protested against any association of the University with the rugby match against the Springboks to be held at Iffley Road on 5 November. The likelihood of serious demonstrations eventually forced the relocation of the match to Twickenham, where it was played 'under siege conditions'. 'Springbok Storm Fizzles Out', *Times*, 6 November 1969, 1d.

reduces the impact of one's protest – this is no reason for not protesting about anything. One protests if one thinks that one's protest may have some effect: it is clear that to boycott the Soviet Union does not in fact have any effect by now – but if an occasion arises when one thinks, rightly or wrongly, that it may affect opinion, e.g. after the invasion of Czechoslovakia, it is reasonable to suppose that a gesture helps: and for this reason an official reception to some Soviet philosophers at Oxford following the Czech invasion was in fact cancelled here, and my opinion on this was not equivocal. I believe that opinion in and about South African policies have not become as 'jelled' as they have become about the worst policies in the Soviet Union, and for that reason a gesture, a protest, is worth making. Certainly I do not believe in boycotting all social or artistic events, on principle, involving citizens of countries whose policies one is opposed to: only in gestures when these seem worth making.

2. There is something peculiarly horrifying about racial discrimination, because, unlike repression of opinion, those who are victimised by it have no means of avoiding it. I do not of course mean that persecution of dissidents in matters of opinion is, save in exceptional cases, commendable or even excusable – only that those who do it can suppose themselves to be improving the minds of the victims by applying repressive measures to them, as was so often done by the Churches; I do not think that this reason, absurd as it is in the vast majority of cases, can even subjectively be present in the minds of those who discriminate on racial grounds. If degrees of evil can be discriminated at all, racial persecution seems to me a degree worse than other forms of unjust repression.

These are my reasons. That, I suspect, is why South Africa invites more criticism than the USSR in England today: if it persists in its own course, this too will die down, I fear.

Yours sincerely,

[IB p.p.]

TO HAMILTON FISH ARMSTRONG

4 December 1969

Headington House

Dear Ham,

Thank you ever so much for your letter of 18 November. I am always pleased to see the envelope which indicates that a letter from you is within. This is exactly like [being in] a room – say, before dinner at a friend's house, without knowing who else has been invited, and knowing precisely what one's feelings are by the fact that one's spirits either leap or sink at the sight of each person as he or she enters the room. Your envelopes make my heart leap distinctly, although I know the contents are likely to bring my shortcomings home to me in one way or another: 'The Intellectual in Politics' is certainly a good subject […], but it is no good – I hate to say it – to me. No good, because it needs rather more intimate knowledge of what the effect upon the government machine is, whether in America or in England, than I possess, or really ever possessed. I remember what I thought about this in Washington during the war – how different from the institutional impersonality of English bureaucratic activity was the enormously personalised atmosphere of Washington in which people did not so much work in departments as 'for' Harry Hopkins[1] or Don Nelson[2] or whoever it might be – but all that was over, for me, when I left British government service, i.e. by about 1946/7, and I have not known what has happened since, except from hearsay and the newspapers, which really do not give one enough – one needs to have one's nose pressed very close to the windowpane to see what goes on within. In England I never did know it. I have no notion what real difference the dons whom e.g. the Labour Government has conscripted into its service have made, especially in economic departments, which are a sealed book to me. So if I did write it would be too impressionistic, too ignorant, I should tear it up in justified indignation and would not really like to begin. As for Russia, that is even darker. I do not mean politically, but more impenetrable from without. I do not know whether one can really speak of 'public opinion' in that country at all. […]

All this is fearfully negative, I am afraid, and you must forgive me, but if I am not to be candid with you, with whom am I to be candid? And in any case candour is a wonderful liberty and I should hate to give it up for almost anything – I did not join the Foreign Office, because I thought that too big an ox would be put on one's tongue,[3] and if one wasn't allowed to talk, one would cease to think in the long run, which is what happens to most diplomats, it seems to me. (Do not I beg you ask me to write about *that*, the decay of men through systematic discretion. Discretion is a great public virtue, but destructive of personality to a degree, it seems to me. However this is not exactly a subject for *Foreign Affairs*.) […]

Meanwhile fondest love to Christa[4] and my usual apologies, which are none the less deep and heartfelt for not being unique.

Yours ever,

Isaiah

1 Harry Lloyd Hopkins (1890–1946), NY social worker turned New Deal relief administrator, and FDR's closest political confidant; appointed head of the Lend-Lease programme (L1 367/2) 1941, and the President's personal emissary on critical missions to Churchill and Stalin that year.
2 Donald Marr Nelson (1888–1959), US business executive employed by FDR from 1940 in the procurement of materials necessary to Britain's war effort; Chairman of the US War Production Board 1942–4.
3 Aeschylus, *Agamemnon*, 36–7: 'About the rest I say nothing: a huge ox has stepped on my tongue.'
4 Christa von Tippelskirch (b. 1917), Ham Armstrong's third wife; they married in 1951.

TO JOEL HURSTFIELD[1]

5 December 1969 [carbon]

[Headington House]

Dear Professor Hurstfield,

[...] The substance of your letter is, of course, something that goes to the heart of the matter. On the one hand we wish to say that men are responsible, and therefore that some sense must be attached to the notion of choice – we want to say not only that I am free in the sense that I should not have acted in a particular manner if I had not chosen to do so, but also that I need not have chosen as I chose; [...] otherwise no matter how deeply my character, dispositions etc. enter into my action, so that I am not a mere plaything of external forces – which eliminates fatalism – yet, if my character is itself pre-determined, there is a clear sense in which I could not help acting as I did, since I am what I am, things are what they are, my character is what it is etc. – and this seems to be as rigorous a determinism as any other and robs the notion of 'I could have chosen differently' of all apparent meaning [...]. Clearly you and I, in correctly [sc. are correct in] supposing that, say, Carr's notion of the inexorable autostrada down which we all drive with no possibility of turning right or left won't do as a conception not merely of the behaviour of human beings in history – what men do and suffer – but as a conception of human relationships, human nature, the human being as such. What then are we to do? It seems to me clear that, on present evidence, you believe, and I believe, that when you took up your pen to write to me you need not in fact have done so; no matter what your intentions, character, desire to say certain things etc. might be, you could have decided to postpone your letter or not write it at all [...]. If this is not so then the whole complex of such notions as devotion to principle against overwhelming temptation, particular merit attaching to resistance against overwhelming odds clearly perceived, heroic virtue, heroic vice etc. must melt away before the notion that people cannot help acting as they do – if they are made of heroic stuff they act bravely, if of feeble material, weakly, treacherously etc. One can pat heroism on the head as one would a strong and intrepid horse which carried one through dangerous territory. Beauty, courage, capacity for solving problems may be socially admired and their possessors congratulated, but like everything else in the universe, they cannot help being what they are and the idea of acclaiming the fact they chose rightly rather than wrongly becomes a mere registration of what we take them to be, since if they are what we take them to be they could not have acted in a manner different from that in which they did act. I do not believe this – I think it could be true, but if so our vocabulary and thoughts and attitudes would have to be radically altered;

---

1 Joel Hurstfield (1911–80), Astor Professor of English History, UCL, 1962–79.

but I cannot accept that there is anything like enough evidence for any such belief, except by extrapolation from nature – and analogy is not the most powerful of logical weapons.

But if I do not believe this, what do I believe? I cannot state this clearly: only that I do know what I mean when I say that a man can choose between a minimum of two alternatives: to act or not to act in a given manner. I freely concede – it would be irrational not to do so – that the range of possibilities depends upon circumstances, character etc., and has in the past sometimes been regarded as being wider than in fact it could possibly have been – hence men were praised or blamed when they in fact had no choice and the praise or blame did not apply. Still, no matter how narrowly the possibilities are delimited, how small the range of action may be, two alternatives seem always to be available: to do X or not to do it, at least in a sufficient number of situations to justify the notion of choice as a reality. This is what deter-minists profess not to understand – and the reason for it is, I think, quite honourable: they think of the world in terms of a causal model – and then quite rightly maintain that, if you simply eliminate a particular ascribed cause from a particular sequence, all you are left with is a gap in the causal series and that this is mere chance or randomness and not the freedom we are seeking to explain. This, of course, is so: that is why in my last despairing paragraph I say that a genius is needed to offer us a new model which will not simply be causality minus causality [...]. Nobody in two thousand years has yet thought of the right model, but I do not despair. In the meanwhile I do not myself see enormous difficulties in supposing that causality does not govern all events, even though it is right to look for causes if what we are looking for is scientific explanation of what occurs: nevertheless when (I think it was) Wittgenstein[1] said that [...] if you say 'I did X because of Y', and mean by Y a cause, you commit yourself to the proposition that, if the same situation recurs identically, Y will again cause X – this is what is called uniformity, regularity etc.; whereas, if you say 'I did X because of Y', and by Y you mean not a cause but a reason – 'because X seemed to me the best means to Z' – I do not imply that next time I think of Z as one of the ends I might wish to promote, I cannot help doing X. I might or might not. Causes necessitate by definition, reasons do not [...].

May I say again that I am truly grateful to you for your letter – not only for its contents, but for the mere fact that you should have taken the trouble to say it all and say it as you did. My point, to reiterate it again, is that when you say 'Caesar crossed the Rubicon' or 'Hurstfield wrote a letter to Berlin', and someone asks 'Why?', one can say 'Because Caesar wanted to capture Rome' or 'Hurstfield wanted to discuss an issue with Berlin.' The next question,

---

1 It was, in various places: see e.g. Ludwig Wittgenstein, *Preliminary Studies for the 'Philosophical Investigations': Generally Known as the Blue and Brown Books* (Oxford, 1958), 14–15.

'Given that Caesar, Hurstfield etc. wanted this, and circumstances were what they were, does it follow that what they did was causally determined?' The answer to this is 'No'. Caesar could have remained on the Gallic shore, Hurstfield could have gone for a walk or played a game of chess, and this does not entail that the desire to cross the Rubicon or write the letter was stronger because in fact it was implemented. It was implemented because it was implemented, because Caesar, Hurstfield etc. so chose. Still, this needs a new model which I certainly have no capacity for providing. I can only hope that a great man will be found who will extricate the fly from the fly-bottle, as Wittgenstein used to put it.[1]

Yours ever,

Isaiah Berlin   [...]

TO NOAM CHOMSKY

18 December 1969

Headington House

Dear Noam,

Thank you very much for sending me the copy of your letter to *Encounter*.[2] [...] If they do not print your letter you must publish it elsewhere of course. As for Israel, you are quite right: Bob is coming to Israel with me, as you know, towards the end of the month. I wonder what he will think of it all. I propose to let him meet Amos Oz[3] and like-minded persons here – the Israeli intellectuals you speak of are perfectly sane, in spite of the fact that the attacks on Israel in the *Times* and elsewhere seem to me and to them grossly unfair.[4] Particularly one by an old friend of mine called Edward Hodgkin[5] – whom I have known for thirty years and who is a perfectly honest and decent person, but an intimate friend of Moussa Alami[6] and other high-born

1 'What is your aim in philosophy? – To show the fly the way out of the fly-bottle.' Ludwig Wittgenstein, *Philosophical Investigations* (Oxford, 1953), 1. 309.

2 A response to a hostile review of his *American Power and the New Mandarins* (NY/London, 1969) in the August 1969 issue of *Encounter*; Chomsky dealt with the factual points raised by the reviewer, but dismissed the rest as 'mere diatribe' (*Encounter*, December 1969, 93).

3 Amos Oz (b. 1939) né Klausner, Jerusalem-born Israeli writer, prominent in the Israeli Peace movement since 1967; his collection of stories *Where the Jackals Howl*, about the lives of ordinary Israelis in a 1950s kibbutz, was published in Tel-Aviv in 1965; fought as a reservist in the Six-Day War and Yom Kippur War; Visiting Fellow, St Cross, 1969–70.

4 Among the headlines recently appearing in *The Times* were 'Arab Village Blown Up in Retaliation' and 'Israel's Endless War against Insurgency'. Articles by Patrick Brogan, 27 October 1969, 1d; 18 November, 8a.

5 Edward Christian Hodgkin (1913–2006), foreign editor of *The Times*, and author of *The Arabs* (London, 1966); on returning from a visit to the West Bank, Hodgkin filed a special report that, without specifically mentioning the Nazis, drew a comparison between the atmosphere on the West Bank and in Gaza in 1969 with that 'in occupied France at the beginning of 1942'. He also averred that 'The Israelis are at least as determined as are the Russians in Czechoslovakia to crush all opposition' ('Grim Reports of Repression in Israel-Occupied Lands', 28 October 1969, 11e).

6 Musa Alami (1897–1984), Cambridge-educated Palestinian nationalist and philanthropist,

Palestinian Arabs, and who was horrified by the depression and the indignation he met among his old Arab friends on the West Bank, and reported all
that they told him about Israeli misdeeds, without, I think, much scrutiny.
I do not suppose you saw the article in question, which appeared as a turn-
over in *The Times* – I wrote him to say that I could not dispute his facts, for
I had no first-hand evidence, but that the tone of hatred which emerged from
the comparison of the Israeli occupants with Nazis in France or Russians
in Czechoslovakia seemed to me disreputable, and that it would have been
more elegant to compare the rough stuff which doubtless goes on in the
West Bank with, say, the bombing of Iraqi villages by British planes in the
1930s or the reciprocal atrocities in the Balkans in, say, 1912 etc.[1] He professed
to be much upset and I think was, oddly enough, since, despite my views,
we are genuine old friends. But there certainly has been a campaign against
Israel here on the part of the 'quality' press, i.e. the *Sunday Times* and *The
Times*, and this is something new. A great deal of money is being spent by
oil-producing Arabs for advertising and for publicity. This is all relatively new
and rather disturbing. The Jewish reaction, unlike, I suspect, New York, is
privately very bitter but publicly subdued. There is no doubt that the British
government, for largely economic reasons, has turned pro-Arab: justice and
moral feeling play very little part in this. It is a minor kind of realpolitik.

I ought to have written to you months ago about your piece for [ ] (the one
to be published by Mouton). I read it with the greatest care and respect, as
you may know. I do not myself believe that the bi-national ideal begins to be
practicable today [...]. I do not believe that there ever was a point after 1918
when the real symbiosis between Jews and Arabs could have been secured;
I do not mean this to exonerate the Zionists from the very proper charge of
having no clear Arab policy at all – for that they are clearly to blame – but it
seems to me that there just was not enough common historical and cultural
stuff, so to speak, upon which anything lasting could be built; even the Turks
and Greeks in Cyprus have more that they historically share. Frontiers are
another matter. But I profoundly disagree with you about partition in 1936:
I think that if partition had gone through then – as it could have done[2] – the
present situation would have been avoided and the State of Israel would have

---

established, and struggled to maintain, a camp for Palestinian refugee orphans in the Jordan
Valley under the auspices of the Arab Development Society; his efforts, made difficult by the
Arab–Israeli wars, found supporters in both the US and Europe.

1 During the exercise of its mandate in Mesopotamia, principally 1922–5 (i.e. not in the 1930s, as
IB suggests), the British used air power as a cost-effective alternative to the army in the suppression of local uprisings; air policing facilitated control without occupation, but also involved the
fledgling RAF in the bombing of civilian targets. *The Times* observed of the two Balkan Wars of
1912–13: 'It is impossible to admit that any of the combatants have had a clean record in regard
to atrocities' (*Times*, 9 December 1913, 7d).

2 The July 1937 report of the Royal Commission of Inquiry to Palestine (the 'Peel Commission')
recommended partition for the first time, with a permanent enclave from Jaffa to Jerusalem
under British control; Arabs mostly rejected the plan, while Jewish opinion was divided.

been accepted, however reluctantly, by its neighbours, as a permanent ingredient of the Middle East; by now there might have been some thought or consideration of general co-operation, which, of course I agree, is ultimately the only hope.

Nor do I agree that what was done was a terrible injustice towards the Arabs. That it was unjust I do not disagree at all; but not to have done it – to have left the Jews to stew – I forbear from the well-known pun – would have been at least equally wicked. I think that it was Weizmann who said that all we can work towards is the solution that embodies the least degree of injustice – that seems to me the general criterion for situations in which values collide; if rights are to be insisted upon, no solution will be discoverable, for such rights clash, and whichever side wins completely wins so at the cost of ruthless suppression of the other.

Of course I would not maintain that driving the Arabs from their homes, even distances of fifty or a hundred miles, or treating them as security risks, or looking down upon them, or behaving as if they did not exist, or looking on intermarriage with them as disgraceful etc., is, however intelligible in terms of our education and two thousand years of conditioning, either just or decent: it is neither. The question is whether it could have been wholly eliminated, if even the minimum of what alone could have ended the homelessness of the Jews was to be secured; and here I think you underplay gravely what the Jewish Risorgimento, as Segre called it, really sprang from.[1] It seems to me that it was not just a desire for more spacious conditions in which the potentialities of Eastern European Jews would find a freer mode of realisation than Vienna or some Polish village. There was also a real national feeling, that is, a desire to cease living the false lives that the assimilationists were undoubtedly guilty of, and a strong desire to belong to some peaceful and democratic establishment. Yet the chief point of these pioneers was not that the new Judaea would be more just or socially progressive than other societies (as I think you think), but that it was their own, that in it they would have to bother less about what they looked like to others than in the Diaspora. Of course most among them were convinced that social justice would prevail, and be more scrupulously realised than in the corrupt states of the West – all movements that embody values (that one can respect) start with the most idealistic, not to say utopian, conception of what they can achieve; nevertheless, their justification does not lie in these maximal programmes, but in the fact that they wish to right an intolerable wrong, and staunch a wound that destroys the life of those who are afflicted with it. The fact that, in this case, this could only be done at a price – the price

---

1 Segre wrote specifically about the 'political, psychological, economic, and cultural characteristics' of the Italian-Jewish community: see Dan V. Segre, 'The Emancipation of Jews in Italy', in *Paths of Emancipation: Jews, States, and Citizenship*, ed. Pierre Birnbaum and Ira Katznelson (Princeton, 1995), 208.

partly borne by the Arabs – was a deterrent to the most sensitive, and very honourably so; nevertheless the question is whether something was feasible, whether some wrong was not inevitable, which is always the case where there is a collision of values. More happiness, more justice, more freedom (for Jews), the raising of the fallen, healing of the sick could be secured by this – but at the price of some undoubted wrong to the Arabs (which need not perhaps have been as great as it is, but would have been quite large in any case). The question arises whether the misery and the wrong would not have been far greater if these same persons had been allowed to rot in Eastern Europe, or had been transported to, say, Latin America or even the United States, where they would duly have had to face (if they swarmed in in huge numbers – how else?) discomfort, hostility, persecution, at least in the short and middle run; in the long run we are, I am afraid, as Keynes once said, all dead.

So I look upon the whole thing as not simply a fait accompli, which we might as well start from as a basis, and not enquire into the justice of, but as the least bad thing that could have been done, the least unjust, less unjust than the massacres that followed Pakistan, less unjust than what is happening in Biafra or the Sudan (where a fantastic slaughter is going on and nothing said). After all, the situation is that the Jews, at worst, despise and are irked by the presence of the Arab natives of the country, and falsely deny the existence of Palestinian Arab nationalism (somewhat like the attitude of their grand-parents to the muzhiks),[1] while the Arabs literally want to exterminate them, which may perhaps not be surprising; but is a different feeling in kind. The community is in danger of ultimate extermination, if not today, then the day after tomorrow; if they wonder, as well they may, whether the Soviet Union will not, in some localised war, crush them without much intervention from anywhere else (and without the use of atomic weapons), can they be too severely blamed if they did not wish to yield any advantage they possess save against some guarantee of security, however illusory? Yet nobody wants to give it to them; and that for no ideal motives, but largely for fear of loss of revenue, or, in the case of the Russians, of a base for anti-capitalist activity – if you wish to put the most pro-Russian interpretation upon it.

And so we can go on talking; but I shall introduce Bob to Oz and two other Israeli philosophers at Oxford who share his views – one of them belongs to some kind of revolutionary organisation of Israeli students which nevertheless does not favour bi-nationalism, is anti-Stalinist–Brezhnevist and is ultimately, and very decently, patriotic, without being nationalist. It is patriots of this sort who I think cannot swallow the view that Israel even 'objectively' forms the tip of some kind of imperialist spearhead: nor the possibility of a joint State with Arabs today or tomorrow. The only people

---

1 Russian peasants.

who really believe in that at present, it seems to me, are the small group of Matzpen,[1] of whom Oz and his friends say that not more than twenty-five exist in all, and these are Maoists of (they say) a very lunatic kind.

I realise that *Ha'aretz* must have libelled you grossly. I would not worry about that much, but I shall certainly take it up with them if I can; but I am sure that what really enrages you are American Zionists. But you must not take it out on the Israelis. *Ha'aretz* is wildly mistaken in taking it out on you, just as the savage attacks upon Israel by writers in the *New Left Review* in England are equally horrible. These people blindly support the most blood-thirsty elements among the Arab terrorists, and have not gone far beyond analysis of the sense of wrong of which Arab terrorism is a natural, but nevertheless a pathological, manifestation. Of course, to be occupiers and oppressors must have a corrupting effect on the Israelis: but, oddly enough, they, or at least many of them, know this; they do not either speak or think in the cynical and monstrous manner of Soviet Commissars or Greek Colonels. I believe that they would like to be rid of this situation, and would accept any decent offer by the powers. I do not believe that the Soviet Union is prepared for it, since they would lose too many Arab clients, too much opportunity of resisting America. And I do believe that, in some global package deal, the Israelis may be very badly treated, in which case they may behave in some desperate manner, of a Samsonic kind, which I do not like to speculate about.

I am terribly sorry about Bar-Hillel.[2] I hope to be able to tell you more when I come back. He is a decent, honourable, one-track man, inflexible and touching at the same time, a terrible Yekke[3] and a pure-hearted, indignant rationalist: *I like him very much*. I shall be in New York, I hope, towards the end of March, beginning of April. Do let us meet and go on with this.

Yours ever,

Isaiah

---

1 The Israeli Socialist Organization, commonly known by the Hebrew name of its monthly journal, *Matzpen* (*Compass*). Established in 1962 by former members of the Israeli Communist Party, it advocated the 'de-Zionisation' of Israel, which would become an integrated socialist State within a unified Middle East. Though numerically small, Matzpen grew in size after the Six-Day War, drawing on support from both Jewish and Arab left-wing groups in its opposition to the continued occupation of the conquered territories.

2 Yehoshua Bar-Hillel (1915–75) né Oscar Westreich, Austrian-born Israeli logician, philosopher and linguist, influenced by Rudolf Carnap, and later by Noam Chomsky; fought with the Haganah (199/4) during the 1948 War of Independence. After studying in the US he was based in Jerusalem, from 1961, and was Professor of Logic and the Philosophy of Science, HUJ; he suffered bouts of poor health at about this time, which may explain IB's expression of concern.

3 The Yiddish 'Yekke' is a pejorative nickname for German-Jewish immigrants to Israel, implying extreme formality, punctuality and politeness.

TO ARNALDO MOMIGLIANO

9 January 1970

Headington House

Dear Arnaldo,

[...] I have no idea what Bob Silvers thinks of Israel: he certainly was not over-impressed by the three-and-a-half-hours' tea party with the Prime Minister,[1] which we also attended, in which she rose in all her might, like the intransigent old lady that she is, rebutted all suggestions, refused to yield an inch on anything, flashed her eyes and displayed the embattled ferocity of some old immigrant woman at the old Ellis Island – a Neapolitan mother surrounded by her family viewing everyone and everything with suspicion, knowing that everyone wanted to be at her, with plenty of character, but not much anxiety to be accommodating to anyone. You would have enjoyed the occasion more than Bob did. He told me afterwards that he kept saying to himself 'I must not let Isaiah down' – nor did he. He was very reasonable, but got nowhere. He saw a lot of hawks and doves, Arabs and Jews, felt annexation in the air, but I think left less unsympathetic and certainly less ignorant than when he came, but all that remains to be seen. I wish them all extremely well, but they do not make it easy to help or even support them. I wonder what Jean [Floud] will think of it all in May when she, I think, is going. Their sense of total solitude and the desperate *Faremo da se*[2] atmosphere have their own force – yet there are some Frankels[3] there too.

Yours,

Isaiah   [...]

TO GARRETT DROGHEDA

13 January 1970

Wolfson

Dear Garrett,

Thank you for your letter of 26 December that I have only just read on return, hideously crippled by arthritis and old age which caused me to travel in a wheelchair in Genoa and Heathrow. [...]

And now to your valued text: mainly just and true, in part hideously

1 Golda Meir (1898–1978) née Goldie Mabovich in Ukraine; her parents emigrated to the US in 1907, and she from the US to Palestine (with her husband) in 1921; a leading figure in the Mapai Party and the Jewish Agency during the 1930s; Israeli Foreign Minister 1956–66; Prime Minister 1969–74; resigned April 1974 after criticism of Israel's unpreparedness for the Yom Kippur War.

2 sc. 'Faremo da soli' ('We shall act alone').

3 Probably a reference to William Frankel (1917–2008), barrister and influential editor of the *Jewish Chronicle*, the world's oldest Jewish weekly newspaper, 1958–77. The point is unclear: maybe that Frankel was critical of Anglo-Jewish establishment views, including those on Israel, in which case IB is saying there are similar nonconformists in Israel too.

unfair and unreasonably cross. 1. About *Onegin*. To want to get it into the rep is obviously right. Moreover, I am prepared to concede that there must be more than one way of conducting a work (see remarks on *Pelléas* below) – hence perhaps Solti's style, however worrying to me (brought up as I was to consider it a meltingly lyrical, irresistibly charming work, to do with country houses in the nineteenth century in backward but attractive countries, like Russia and Ireland, remote from the neuroses of central Europe), may be acceptable. All the same, whatever my reactions, it may be that he will produce a marvellous performance in his own, undoubtedly very effective, style. Not only do I hope to be proved wrong (as you do), but I am prepared to bring myself to the point of actually expecting this, and applauding the non-realisation of my fears […].[1]

And now to your hideously unfair charges, I mean about *Pelléas*.[2] I do *not* propose to give as good (bad) as I get. It is, of course, one of the most marvellous performances of anything that anyone can have heard in the twentieth century. I am not shaken by the fact that all the eminent critics, Heyworth[3] (whom I find perverse and tiresome), Desmond [Shawe-Taylor] (whom I greatly respect), Martin Cooper etc. said in effect, 'What a splendid performance, but ...'; and went on with 'where is the mystery, the Celtic twilight, the inexpressible yearning, etc. in this lucid, firm, over-definite performance?' They seem to me simply victims of their own particular conception of the work, which cannot be unique. One could have said the same about Toscanini's performances of Wagner – where everything which other conductors made twopence-coloured came out penny-plain, and the soup that Wagnerians adore came out as extremely distinct spaghetti, marvellous strand by strand. I loved it – it sounded almost like Beethoven – but the real Wagneromaniacs felt uncomfortable with it. I personally think Debussy would have been delighted […].

You ask me what I think 'all right' about Covent Garden! You know perfectly well that the business of committees such as ours is to goad the enterprise on to greater and greater heights. No doubt praise where praise is due is right and it is ungenerous and can be wicked to refuse it: but the danger of complacency is far greater than that of excessive self-criticism – let the critics praise, let the public flock, let the artists express delight, let the Friends of Covent Garden display passionate loyalty, but the board and the committees must go on nagging and nibbling if they really do see something to nag and

1 Covent Garden's February 1971 production of Tchaikovsky's *Eugene Onegin*, conducted by Solti in his farewell season as Musical Director of the Royal Opera, was very favourably reviewed by the music critic of *The Times*, William Mann: 'An Opera to Make Addicts', 15 February 1971, 10c.

2 A new production of Debussy's opera *Pelléas et Mélisande*, conducted by Pierre Boulez, was given at Covent Garden on 1 December 1969: it had been absent from the repertoire there for over two decades.

3 Peter Lawrence Frederick Heyworth (1921–91), chief music critic, *Observer*, 1955–87; strongly devoted to the German tradition, he was the author of an important biographical study of Otto Klemperer.

nibble at, and not be accused of carping and destructive criticism if they do. [...] What is right about Covent Garden is that

(*a*) There are now very few really bad performances.

(*b*) {That} we achieve heights, from time to time, that no other opera house, on the whole, can out-climb: the original *Don Carlos* comes first, of course, and after that come such peaks as the original Sutherland *Lucia*; *Cav* and *Pag*; *Frau ohne Schatten*; an excellent *Ring*, which I have sat through one and a half times with mounting admiration, if not pleasure; a matchless, *splendid Tosca* with Callas, a good *Trovatore*, *Otello*, *Parsifal*, *Fidelio*, *Grimes*; a splendid *Wozzeck*; a very good *Billy Budd*, and a sensational *Moses and Aaron*, which, like *Carlos*, was a world event of the first significance, and so recognised by everybody; and if Zeffirelli is not good at Mozart (nor is Solti, although *Cosi* was perfectly all right), and if some of the modern works were a bit tedious, this is the price we have to pay, and no opera house can possibly live without such as Shostakovich, Tippett, Poulenc, although I suppose that *L'Heure espagnole* (combining the worst shortcomings of Solti and Peter Ustinov) was about as low as ever we sank – lower, it seems to me, than even the notorious *Forza*.[1] We have absolutely nothing to be ashamed of; indeed, the reputation of Covent Garden has shot up, as well you know, since those difficult and ill-attended, rightly attacked, early over-patriotic days. I think the brio *has* now slightly gone out of our general condition, partly I think because of our very success. The board is full of attractive and gifted people, all of whom are fond of one another, like the staff and the opera house, and the administration, and we are all very happy and are doing perfectly well, save that an occasional injection of a caddish voice or two – Walter Legge did us no end of good, I may say – helps. What is chiefly wrong is that the administration (I really mean David) are insufficiently prepared to be self-critical or accept the, no doubt, sometimes idiotic but sometimes valid opinions of members of the board when they are not satisfied. D. tends to sulk about this; but we ought to be the first to point to flaws – the feeling that it is caddish or unjust to harass a sorely tried and very worthy body of workers who are doing their best is in the best British tradition, but not good for art. [...] Criticism ought to be encouraged and elicited; knocked down by those who disagree, but not inhibited: whereas I have the feeling that some of the most just, and with most to say, are at times too nice to voice the objections that they deeply feel. More of value is said in private; this is in part inevitable, and natural, but more should be said forcibly at the meetings. Your tendency, if I may say this with the deepest respect, is at times a certain impatience of criticism in virtue of your acute sense of personal responsibility

---

1 The Royal Opera's September 1962 production of Verdi's *La forza del destino*, with a number of imported singers and a consequent hike in ticket prices, was poorly received by the audience, and at her curtain call the soprano, Floriana Cavalli, met with 'a volley of booing and hissing and cat-calls': Harold Rosenthal, 'Opera House Manners' (letter), *Times*, 2 October 1962, 13d; cf. reply by P. H. Frankel, 4 October, 9f.

for the whole thing; one of mine is a narrowness of taste and an excessive passion for the beauty of the human voice at the expense of acting, décor, the personality of singers, human frailty, money etc. We could go through all of the board in this way; but, on the whole, they should be encouraged to gadfly-like rather than punkah-like activity. If the critics are reasonably satisfied and the public does not abandon us, we tend to call it a day. The balance between being purveyors and critical amateurs is hard to draw; nevertheless I think that a little more ferocity is occasionally called for. And although I admit I am an unabashed canary fancier, I have a feeling that our new management are a little too contemptuous of that; the search for 'relevance' in an art form which has not proved very amenable to this kind of treatment makes me a trifle nervous. Still, we are all aged men, and it may be that Peter Hall and Colin Davis are right. Certainly I believe strongly that they must be given a free run without chivvying from us. [...]

(c) On the credit side, and very heavily, we must place the fact that there is very little intrigue, that artists are not exposed to the horrors of [La] Scala or even New York, and that the general atmosphere is decent, friendly and absolutely O.K. so far as I know. Conductors and singers love Covent Garden. Even Callas does.

(d) On the credit side also is the fact that the British company and the singers we have trained have risen far beyond the hopes of 'realists' of even fifteen years ago. [...]

(e) On the debit side we must place the fact that we don't search for singers with sufficient zeal: Joan Ingpen[1] does her best, a good best, but David's reluctance to establish foreign links (due largely, I suspect, to lack of languages), George's natural tendency to seek advice only from certain quarters and ignore [that] of others, etc. lead to the fact that we don't find out about marvellous new young singers in Italy or Peru or Sweden as early as we might – Glyndebourne seems to me, in that respect, sometimes to do much better, I do not know how, but it does. [...]

(f) The real point is that Covent Garden has become an absolutely central part of London and, indeed, British culture, as much as, and, I think, rather more than, the National Theatre, and in that sense is quite unique; which it hasn't been since before the war. It is as intrinsic and traditional and national as the BBC, and that would not have happened without – as you very well know and do not need me to tell you, although I do so with the greatest pleasure – your administration. There now, you have my response. Long may you flourish.

Yours ever,

Isaiah

---

1 Joan Mary Eileen Ingpen (1916–2007) née Williams, musicians' agent and opera administrator; Solti's Controller of Opera Planning, ROH, 1962–71; credited with launching Pavarotti's career by engaging him to replace the ailing Giuseppe di Stefano in *La Bohème* in 1963.

TO GERSHOM SCHOCKEN[1]

21 January 1970

                                                        Wolfson

Dear Mr Schocken,

Thank you very much for your very interesting letter of January 6. If I gave you the impression that Heine was an assimilationist, then I gravely misled you. I know that Heine took an interest in 'the Jewish cultural revival', that he was not disposed to dilute Judaism into some vague ethical affair which would bring Judaism closer to enlightened Protestantism like Riesser,[2] and would have had nothing but contempt for 'German citizens of the Mosaic faith'. All that is clear to me. On the other hand it does seem to me that despite his constant references to the Jews, his mockery of Christianity from time to time, the remark about the silver spoons, dissertations about baptism, the sad poems about the fact that nobody would ever say Kaddish[3] for him, his fear of German nationalism, his attitude nevertheless was an extremely tormented one. He had no policy about the Jews: he neither wished to ignore and 'liquidate' them, in a sense, like his friend Marx, nor yet to represent Christianity simply as a fulfilment of Judaism, like Disraeli,[4] and today our new bishop Hugh Montefiore,[5] who, although an Anglican bishop, keeps repeating that he is a Jew and that he never left the Jewish religion, merely fulfilled it in Christianity. The works in which he pours contempt upon the Jews are just as characteristic of him as those in which he laments Jewish persecution – 'Hund mit hündischen Gedanken'[6] is just as typical as [Der] Rabbi von Bacherach.[7] My point about him was that he was tortured about the whole thing, and tortured because he was preoccupied with the Germans as a topic, because he was fascinated and repelled by them at the

---

1 Gershom Gustav Schocken (1912–90), German-born Israeli journalist, writer and politician; emigrated to Palestine 1933; editor of Ha'aretz (the paper owned by his father from 1937) 1939–90; Progressive Party member of the Knesset 1955–9.

2 Gabriel Riesser (1806–63), German politician and lawyer, pioneer of Jewish emancipation in Germany. He argued that German Jews were not a people apart but a religious denomination, and should therefore be treated as the equals of German Protestants and Catholics.

3 The 'Mourner's Prayer', recited every day for the first eleven months after the death of a Jew, usually by the son of the deceased.

4 Benjamin Disraeli (1804–81), 1st Earl of Beaconsfield 1876, Conservative statesman, Prime Minister 1868 and 1874–80. Disraeli's father, the writer Isaac D'Israeli (1766–1848), was raised a practising Jew, but had his five children christened in the Anglican faith, partly for social advantage; for the adult Disraeli, however, the Christian Church was, as Aubrey St Lys puts it in one of his novels, 'completed Judaism': Sybil, or The Two Nations (London, 1845), i 256.

5 Hugh William Montefiore (1920–2005), son of Sephardi Jews, converted to Christianity in his teens; Bishop Suffragan of Kingston-upon-Thames 1970–8, Bishop of Birmingham 1978–87. Cf. IB's essay 'Benjamin Disraeli, Karl Marx, and the Search for Identity', Transactions of the Jewish Historical Society of England 22 (1968–9) (London, 1970); repr. in AC. ⁿ𝑔 Current

6 'A dog with a dog's ideas', the first line of the fifth stanza of Heine's poem 'Prinzessin Sabbat', in Romanzero (1851), 206.

7 Heine's unfinished historical novel Der Rabbi von Bacherach appeared in 1840.

same time, because all his life he in a sense wrote about nothing else but the German Middle Ages, horrors of German Nationalism, the beauties of the German countryside, on what it was to be a German, and had a painfully self-conscious attitude towards this problem, which led him to the kind of coarse mockery, both of Germans and of Jews, which never extended to the French or the pagan world which he so passionately celebrated at one period of his life. I do not think that I agree that he took pride in his Jewish origins. He was deeply affected by being a Jew, he thought about it painfully and all his life he did not grovel, but he did seem to me to suffer from a certain degree of Jewish self-hatred which he 'took out' so to speak, both on the Jews and on their persecutors. In short he wasn't able to come to terms with his ambivalent position. I do not believe that he would have been a Zionist today – for a short while perhaps, but after that, like Koestler or Miss Arendt or the rest of his unworthy progeny (I do not begin to compare them to him, either as human beings or as writers), he would have reverted to some kind of 'post-Zionist' universalism, or at any rate something which would have exhibited his loathing and contempt for the bourgeois Zionism of New York or Tel-Aviv. […]. I think he was a casualty; of a far more sensitive and far more honest kind than Marx, who never did succeed in healing himself as Hess did,[1] but one who continued to lacerate himself and others, and made his deep neurosis, directly connected with the fact that he could not find his place in the world – he was neither a German nor a non-German, neither a Jew nor a non-Jew in the full sense of these words – into material for magnificent poetry and magnificent prose, but also a great deal of this *espièglerie*[2] – grimaces, unworthy clowning – which embarrasses one still. […]

Yours sincerely,
  [Isaiah Berlin]

TO ROBERT SILVERS

2 February 1970 [*carbon*]

[Wolfson]

Dear Bob,

The Wadham agony continues.[3] The fact that the *New Statesman* today should have said something about how Freddie's withdrawal plunged

---

1 Moses Hess (1812–75), German-Jewish writer and socialist. Hess argued for the assimilation of Jews in the majority culture during the early part of his life, but later advocated the creation of a Jewish commonwealth in Palestine, and is regarded as an early communist Zionist; in this sense, in IB's eyes, he succeeded in 'healing himself'.

2 'Buffoonery'.

3 Wadham College was in the throes of appointing a new Warden in succession to Maurice Bowra, due to retire in August. Stuart Hampshire was a contender for the post, but the College had a long tradition of electing from within its ranks, and A. J. 'Freddie' Ayer, an honorary fellow since 1957, had been widely tipped to succeed Bowra. IB was unduly pessimistic about Hampshire's chances, perhaps because he so wished for his success.

them all into chaos and how Prof. Hampshire is waiting in the wings will not improve matters.[1] I have an awful feeling that, in the end, the Left will vote against Stuart and this will seal his fate. For them he is a Bloomsbury intellectual, too well dressed, too *soigné*, too refined altogether – the Right and the Old, which is much the same, will think that he will be too bored with the details of administration, which is far from true, in fact. I hope to God he gets it. I pray for this daily and hourly but do not feel optimistic. He has done better than Freddie – what mild pleasure this bleak reflection gives him I do not know, but it is insufficient.

I have read Bar-Hillel now and it is a pathetic and touching document. I understand his feelings quite well and still his positive proposals are not related to any possible reality, any more than Noam's. For example: he wants to limit immigration in order not to frighten the Arabs. Why? Everyone knows that in normal times immigration will proceed at the present pretty low rate; but if there is a pogrom in South Africa or the Argentine – let alone Russia – then, of course, these people will want to immigrate much as the French Jews want to at present – not the old families but those who have filtered in during the 1930s and 1950s. Are they to be stopped? If the frontiers are to be established, this should surely be enough. Nobody in their senses supposes that 11 million Jews can immigrate: if Zionism means that it is the duty of every Jew to go to Israel, then it is, of course, idiotic – even I have denounced this at no less an establishment than Isaac Stern's Foundation in New York in the presence of Sidney [Morgenbesser] and some exceedingly fanatical Zionists without being contradicted. [...] I do not believe that there are propagandists who foam at the mouth in the Messianic manner and speak of the ingathering of all the Jews into a mighty kingdom spreading over Jordan, Syria, Egypt etc. from the Euphrates and the Nile. I think he is tilting at an enormous windmill, poor man, but if he has this image before him then I do not wonder that he strikes out at it. He is, in a sense, perfectly right in saying that Zionism and the movement has achieved its goal and should be declared fulfilled and obsolete – all that is properly left is natural sentiment and desire to help, etc., as in America for Ireland of the 1920s, only more so [...].

On the other hand, as far as rights of the dispossessed Arab natives are concerned, he pushed principle beyond reason. It is not a happy thing to be a minority. No doubt this shouldn't be so and everyone should be very nice to everyone else and minorities should not have to claim rights, which should be accorded to them freely, generously etc., but we know that minorities

---

1 In his 'London Diary' column in the *New Statesman* (30 January 1970, 143), Anthony Howard observed that the Wadham process 'seems to be taking an interminable time'; the withdrawal of A. J. Ayer, 'the most-fancied candidate', had left the field 'totally clouded and confused, though Professor Stuart Hampshire (now of Princeton) is said still to be visible as a late-runner on the outside rails'.

suffer in some degree everywhere. Hence to increase the number of Arabs in Israel, by whatever means, seems to me to ask for misery for both sides. Ideally, of course, bi-nationalism would be splendid, but we know that this is not to be for, at any rate, half a century, while wounds heal. The wrongs of the refugees have to be weighed against the right (and even more the desirability) of making Israel a viable community. Hence, the laying down of any principle – that everyone born in what is now Israel's territory should be allowed to come back; or that they should not be allowed to come back; or that all Jews have a right to come back in whatever numbers; or that only those whose mothers pass the religious test etc. should be allowed to come back; or any other generalisation whatever – seems to me likely to cut across actual concrete needs and situations and to draw blood unnecessarily. [...] The old leadership – e.g. the lady for whom you naturally care so little[1] – will see their people as surrounded by implacable enemies who will do nothing for them, are suspicious of everyone, want all their kinsfolk in every country to stand up and be counted, and devote themselves to one task and one only: the up-building of the State of Israel against all other claims, principles, ideals – the old, eschatological pioneers whose analogues are old Marxists, Trotskyites, Maoists etc. etc. All that will pass; and the possibly sometimes far less attractive, but politically and even morally saner, sabras[2] and other un-inflamed characters, equidistant from Begin and Deutscher (who are very similar to each other in some ways; they were brought up under very similar conditions and with very similar ideals), will, if they are allowed to survive at all, come to terms with the Arabs. Bar-Hillel's appeal to the great powers to impose a solution is German again. He is obviously a very decent, upright man but the imposition of any kind of rectilinear schema upon that tangled growth would be a terrible vivisection. [...]

In the meanwhile, I suffer for Stuart: an unnecessary number of wounds – as if some number were necessary – have been inflicted upon him lately and by his own country, too. There is, perhaps, something in being a cosmopolitan after all.

Yours ever,
[Isaiah]

TO STEPHEN SPENDER

5 February 1970

Wolfson

Dearest Stephen,
A very good day today. Firstly, the news that Stuart will have been elected

1 Golda Meir.
2 Hebrew term applied to Jews born in Israel.

Warden of Wadham. I have just written an extremely pessimistic letter
to Bob Silvers saying that I am depressed at the thought that this will not
happen, that Stuart has been treated too badly in his own country, that it
really is awful about all the chairs he has failed to get, etc., but this is a far,
far better thing than anything which has happened in the past and will make
a large difference to Aline's and my life and, indeed, I think, to yours and to
other people as well. So that is a splendid piece of news. All the young voted
for him, all the old against him, and there is a mixed brood of enthusiasm
and exaltation on the one hand and fury on the other among the fellows.[1]
Maurice, as you may imagine, is making the most of this, and is very funny
on the subject. I have no doubt that Stuart will come back with relief and
will never leave this island for long again, as is right. I love the idea of that
old wainscoting as a suitable place in which to hide Black Panthers[2] – a lot
of this will happen around the lodgings. There will be all kinds of drop-outs,
hippies and mysterious middle-aged ladies of no fixed abode entertained at
genteel tea parties with the bewildered wives of the fellows of Wadham and
graduates from Wolfson College. We shall all be taken in hand, and perhaps
a very good thing.

Tonight Natasha[3] is coming to dine at our house with Boulez:[4] that is
very nice, too. Boulez will be here at any moment; I shall accompany him
in a gown to his lecture and he will be introduced by a graduate student,
conspicuously without a gown as a kind of demonstration of the new spirit.
I have no wish to identify myself with the 'nouvelle vague'[5] – I should hate
a life without forms, although I hate the forms on the whole. [...] In spite of
my clinging to my gown, I am moving steadily to the left in a reluctant sort
of way and preparing myself to welcome Conor Cruise O'Brien, who is to
lecture on Fanon,[6] and some other Africans – or rather propagandists for

---

1 Wadham was then the most radical and left-leaning of the older colleges at Oxford, and
  Hampshire's unequivocal support for the admission of women undergraduates proved decisive
  in his favour, being regarded by the younger dons especially as a touchstone for generally progressive views.
2 Members of the militant Black Panther party, formed in California in 1966 to fight for the rights
  of African-Americans; the political aims of the Panthers featured in the broad spectrum of
  student unrest that affected US campuses in the 1960s; Hampshire, while at Princeton, engaged
  positively with this counter-culture, and helped defuse conflict that might otherwise have led to
  bloodshed.
3 Natasha Spender (1919–2010) née Litvin, concert pianist, married Stephen Spender (his second
  wife) in 1941.
4 Pierre Boulez (b. 1925), innovative French composer and conductor, influenced by Schoenberg,
  Stravinsky and Messiaen; among his many posts, he was Chief Conductor of the BBC Symphony
  Orchestra 1971–5, of the NY Philharmonic 1971–7.
5 'New wave': term coined by Françoise Giroud, editor of L'Express, to describe the nascent youth
  culture of the late 1950s and early 1960s.
6 Frantz Fanon (1925–61), Martinique-born French psychiatrist, activist and writer, and widely
  influential anti-colonial revolutionary theorist; controversially argued for the necessity of violence in liberation struggles.

African radicalism – which is giving considerable pain to Sparrow, Trevor-Roper and other old allies. Forward from liberalism![1]

Yours,

Isaiah   [...]

TO ROBERT SILVERS

19 March 1970 [*carbon*]

[Wolfson]

Dear Bob,

[...] Very briefly, I am in favour of rigorously demarcated frontiers, beyond which Israel will not be able to expand, to allay Arab fears. But not of controlled immigration because the moral basis of the state is *not* an asylum for refugees (who, as such, cannot claim a State), but the strange survival of a scattered community, which has mysteriously preserved national attributes, which survive but in a diseased form and breed terrible Steiner–Arendt fantasies[2] without a territorial base, and develop normally only if they are given it: as seems to have been shown in practice. My favourite Hess compares this to those grains of wheat found in Egyptian tombs which, when replanted after 3,000 years, bloomed. It may, in a sense, be a great bore that this has happened, but it has. This being so one cannot ask a sovereign State to promise to limit its immigration; even though in fact, as you say, this makes no difference. There is a certain minimum of face which cannot be lost without inflicting too much collective humiliation. The Arabs of all people understand this excessively well. Internal chauvinism is another matter. I wish I thought that it is only a function of being beleaguered: even if it is, it will grow, which is a very bad prospect. Elon's words in the *New York Review* seem to be perfectly right[3] – what I do not believe is that the Arab States would have allowed this gradual trickling back, although to offer it would no doubt have been excellent for the record. Compensation should, of course, have been offered, and has been offered, but in so low a voice that nobody heard – this is what I said to Golda when you

1 The title of Stephen Spender's 1937 anti-Soviet political tract, *Forward from Liberalism*, published in London by Victor Gollancz's Left Book Club.

2 (Francis) George Steiner (b. 1929), Paris-born US writer and academic; Fellow, Churchill, Cambridge, since 1961, Extraordinary Fellow since 1969; Professor of English and Comparative Literature at the University of Geneva 1974–94. Steiner and Arendt were prominent among IB's intellectual bêtes noires. 'Steiner is what is meant by alienation – if ever there was a "rootless cosmopolitan" [...] it is he' (to Anna Kallin, 23 April 1969). For the history of the phrase quoted by IB, originally used to refer to Soviet Jews, see SM 104/1. *Sov mind*

3 In a review article written after the Six-Day War Elon observed: 'Should there be a Jewish State? [...] During the past decade this argument has become irrelevant and certainly impractical, and today it has become largely obsolete. Immigration to Israel has come to a standstill. Two-and-one-half million Israelis are now a nation, cohesive and resourceful, whatever the argument over Zionism. For Israelis, the issue is not one of theory, but one of physical survival, of individuals as well as of a community. There is no other place to go, as there was for the French community in Algeria' (NYRB, 1 August 1968, 14–20 at 14–15).

were there, and she made Eban say it again, but it was again said in somewhat muffled accents. [...] Do you think that I over-estimate the pressure put on the refugees by their leaders, by agents of Arab States, etc.? I do not think so. The fact that they are used as political pawns does not make their condition less pitiable, or monstrous, and absolve Israel from their duty to offer to do something of a major kind for them. Israel's major blunder, both moral and political, was, of course, after the Six-Day War, not to come out with some tremendously magnanimous proposal, whereby they declared themselves prepared to take back some reasonable numbers of refugees and offered to raise an enormous sum of money – far more than they could possibly afford – something that would put them to genuine financial risk and strain the very existence of the State, [if?] they are not to repatriate them in the empty parts of the Fertile Crescent. I do not doubt both these proposals would have been flung back in their faces by the Arabs, who, by this time were, I think in a totally exasperated and somewhat lunatic state – still, the offer would have been made and could have been repeated over and over again, and perhaps might, in some form, have been accepted. This certainly would have eased the situation, morally, not only politically: what I do not believe in is that any large influx of Arabs into Israel could have ended in anything but the most terrible political indigestion, to put it at its lowest. That Jews cannot and should not govern Arabs seems to me absolutely plain. I do not believe in a peaceful symbiosis even under the most liberal idealistic administration, entirely consisting of Bar-Hillels and Lewontins.[1] In the long run all kinds of things are possible, but it is in the short run that people suffer and die. Hence my general belief in partition, and distrust of artificially created multinational and multiracial states, however right they are in principle. This I am prepared to argue and argue. Of course the problem of Arabs in Palestine is something that the Jews have shut their eyes to in a very ostrich-like manner from the beginning. Maybe they can defend this, and of course the people who tried to preach a bi-national State, the decent old professors, [Norman] Bentwich etc., plus one or two people in the left-wing *kibbutzim*, were protesting against something very wrong and fatal, but there was something pathetic and remote about these people and their position – more like nice old anarchists, shaking their fists against the existence of the police and the army, and forbidding any violence against them, when obviously what had to be done was some radical transformation – the very partition scheme which Noam thinks so wicked, and indeed the United Nations resolutions of 1948[2] which precipitated bloodshed which British policy

1 Richard Charles ('Dick') Lewontin (b. 1929), evolutionary biologist and social commentator, has argued against the validity of the concept of race.
2 UN Security Council resolutions early in 1948 called for an end to violence in Palestine, and implementation of the General Assembly's Resolution 181 (II) of 29 November 1947 (to which IB must here refer). This resolution proposed a plan for the partition of Palestine: it was accepted by the Jewish but not the Arab side, and the failure of either the British or the UN to enforce it

had rendered unavoidable, it seems to me. If at this stage the frontiers of the United Nations Jewish Palestine had been guaranteed by the powers which were then on reasonably good terms with each other, if the United Nations then had sent troops against the advancing Arab armies as they did in Korea, the whole military growth of Israel need not have occurred, and the country could, I think, then have been neutralised and made into an Austria. Once it was clear that military adventures were to be tolerated in that part of the world, the Jews felt abandoned, looked for allies, went to Suez, took the West Bank, and did everything that people do who think that one false step on their part may lead to their total extinction. [That they] were morally obliged to recognise that they were responsible for the creation of refugees, and owed these people restitution, is clear, whether they fled of their own accord or were pushed over the border or whatever happened. Politically I do not think it would have done them the slightest good. The desire to remove them, if need be by extermination on the part of Arabs – from the highest to the lowest, with the exception of the few *politiques*,[1] Tunis, or Egypt, or Lebanon, or Morocco, was already at its height by the end of the 1930s. That is why I think that the plight of the refugees and the fate of the West Bank Arabs are human problems of the first order, which the Israelis are both morally wrong and unwise to try and push under the carpet. What makes me pessimistic is the thought that even if they behaved with utter virtue their general prospects would not have been improved – no kind of gestures or even concrete acts will begin to melt the hatred of so many. When they say that it is the existence of the refugees that has created this, this, alas, is not true, plausible as it sounds. It exacerbated it, it gave it a focus, it created a heroic terrorist mentality, but the Arabs I talked to in Amman in 1934 – and certainly the Palestinian Arabs and even the Lebanese I met in 1947 – were bubbling with hatred. I am still in favour of the Israelis evacuating the West Bank, or at any rate saying that they are prepared to do so on certain conditions; as for the creation of a Palestinian Arab political entity now in the bosom of Israel – that seems to me a pure Manchukuo,[2] a puppet State which Fatah will either sabotage or take over, and whose existence will be regarded as merely a piece of Israeli trickery any decent Arab was bound to reject with indignation. Am I mistaken? Is there really something that Israel can do today which will ensure both a degree of peace and the whole problem of survival? I wish I thought so.

Yours,

[Isaiah]   [...]

---

contributed to the outbreak of hostilities that followed the termination of the British mandate at midnight on 14 May 1948.

1 'Politicians'.

2 The puppet State maintained in Manchuria 1932–45 in order to legitimate Japanese military conquest and colonial exploitation of that region.

IB spent the last week of March and the first week of April 1970 in America with
Aline. They stayed at the Blackstone Hotel in New York; shortly after arriving
IB left for Columbus, Ohio, to attend a major Slavic Conference; he also gave
a lecture at Ann Arbor, Michigan. In New York he attended a conference on
liberalism at CUNY, and with Aline visited Stuart and Renée Hampshire in
Princeton.

TO ANDRZEJ WALICKI

25 March 1970 [*dictated several days earlier*]

[As from] Headington House

Cherissime Ami,

[...] I have still to read your book to the end, and your article on the
Slavophils too, but on Sunday I have to go for a fortnight to the United
States – where I shall talk about Russian historicism in Michigan, and deliver
a speech at the 'banquet' of the American Association for the Advancement
of Slavic Studies on the old, trite, endlessly chewed subject of commitment.
The theses I shall present are familiar enough: (*a*) that the entire forest caught
fire because of the falling of Saint-Simonian seeds in Russian soil at a particularly sensitive and responsive moment – nothing was really said by Belinsky
or Herzen that was not said as clearly by Leroux,[1] George Sand[2] etc., but
the tone, the conviction, the style and, of course, the effect were different,
with the result that the boomerang effect[3] occurred: first these unconsid-
ered seeds moulder in the West; when they fall upon rich Russian soil [they]
spring into tremendous luxuriance and – to change the metaphor – strike at
the West and transform it in turn. This seems to have happened over and
over again, and is a peculiar form of East–West relationship – it is too much
to honour it by calling it dialectic – without which the cultural history of all
of us loses a great deal.

Then I propose to defend the memories of the [sc. my] heroes, Belinsky,
Herzen, Turgenev, Tolstoy, against the charges made against them of
leading to certain undesirable developments in the attitude towards the arts,
the responsibility for which I propose to fix upon more positivistic thinkers; and stress the fact that in the thought of the 'revolutionary democrats'
there was an unresolved struggle between artistic and social motifs, that
Turgenev says both things, the same as Belinsky, in almost the same year
[...]. Turgenev enjoyed these contradictions rather more than poor Belinsky
did. His fate – that of a liberal between the twin pressures of radicals on his

1 Pierre Henri Leroux (1797–1871), French philosopher and literary critic, an important influence
on George Sand (a lifelong friend).
2 George Sand (1804–76), pseudonym of the French Romantic novelist (Amantine) Aurore Lucile
Dupin, baronne Dudevant.
3 IB's own term. See 'Artistic Commitment: A Russian Legacy', a later version of the talk referred
to here, in SR, at 195–6, 216.
Sense of Reality

left and aesthetic unpolitical writers on his right – seems to me the paradigm
of a great many situations since. There is a kind of line from Erasmus to
Montaigne, perhaps Montesquieu, Constant, Tocqueville, J. S. Mill, all in
search of a doctrine, all suspicious of it, all prey to all kinds of melancholies
which, you rightly pointed out, Turgenev derived from Schopenhauer, all
unable to face the proposition that out of the crooked timber of humanity no straight thing was ever made – that belongs to Kant[1] – and yet all
unable to face the contradictory of that either. This is what 'Hamlet and Don
Quixote'[2] is all about, I suppose, and the proposition that Belinsky overcame
this and triumphantly bore the banner of a more resolute, clear-cut, radical
future does not seem to me valid. However, why should I bore you with
all this, or indeed with my doubts about what to deliver a lecture about in
Oxford in the autumn? – there is a kind of pompous public lecture called the
Romanes Lecture which is usually delivered by some prominent outsider and
which, for some reason, I have to deliver this year, contrary to all custom,
I daresay because they haven't been able to find anyone during the last three
or four years in the outside world; a kind of philosophical statesman who
used to exist – Gladstone, Haldane, Balfour[3] – is not to be found these days;
even pseudo-examples of it are very rare, and so I have to do it. Should I talk
about the origins of cultural history? It seems to start in a lawyer's quarrel in
the sixteenth century in France and then gradually to transform itself into
Vico, Herder, Hegel, Burckhardt etc. Or should I talk about the awful fate
of liberals in difficult times, of people who, in Turgenev's phrase, 'cannot
simplify themselves',[4] even though peasant workers, circumstance, history,
the dialectic, the future, the Spirit, the means of production all demand it
and require it? Perhaps the latter will be a little too much *pro domo*[5] – and
since I am not a poet or a novelist I have no obligation to bare my soul in
public to make an Oxford holiday. [...]

Oxford is unaltered save for a certain amount of student rebellion, which

1 Immanuel Kant, 'Idee zu einer allgemeinen Geschichte in weltbürgerlicher Absicht' ('Idea for
a Universal History with a Cosmopolitan Purpose', 1784), *Kant's gesammelte Schriften* (Berlin,
1900–), viii 23.22. One of IB's favourite quotations, which gave CTH its title.

2 See *Hamlet and Don Quixote: An Essay* [1860], trans. Robert Nichols (London, 1930).

3 William Ewart Gladstone (1809–98), Liberal statesman and author; he gave the inaugural
Romanes Lecture, 'An Academic Sketch', in 1892. Richard Burdon Haldane (1856–1928), Viscount
Haldane 1911, Liberal, and later Labour, Lord Chancellor; educationalist and philosopher; co-
translator with John Kemp of Schopenhauer's *The World as Will and Idea* (London, 1883). Arthur
James Balfour ('AJB') (1848–1930), 1st Earl of Balfour, Conservative and Unionist statesman,
philosopher; Romanes Lecturer, 1909 ('Criticism and Beauty').

4 This was the topic IB settled on for his 1970 Romanes Lecture, delivered in Oxford on 12
November, and published as *Fathers and Children: Turgenev and the Liberal Predicament* (Oxford,
1972), repr. in RT. In Turgenev's novel *Virgin Soil* (1877), chapter 37, the hero, Aleksey Dmitrievich
Nezhdanov, writes in a letter to his children, 'I could not simplify myself': I. S. Turgenev, *Polnoe
sobranie sochinenii i pisem* (Moscow/Leningrad, 1960–8), *Sochineniya* xii 288. See also RT2 335,
341.

5 'For (my own) home', i.e. from a local perspective, for the benefit of my own circle.

goes up and down sporadically, more or less in tune with the weather, and which absolutely outraged a Soviet historian in Nuffield, who said to me that the position of the ultra-Conservatives seemed to him the only reasonable one in these circumstances. I was inclined to agree. Nevertheless, I have Turgenev-like qualms – the local Bazarovs,[1] inferior as they are, probably do represent some kind of worrying future, but then I say to myself that I am sixty, this is not my world. I did my best in the one that I did live in, and they must cope with it themselves – my juniors, those vigorous men of fifty and forty who are the main targets of student attack. As for me, I knew the *douceur de la vie*[2] of the late 1920s, the last period of genuine genius in the only fields that I have any understanding of – literature, music, the exploration of personal relationships – and now, as Herzen said, *ruit nox*.[3] More for us, despite everything, I suspect, than for you. On this melancholy sentiment I will close, after wishing you every possible happiness, with the fervent hope that we may see each other again as soon as possible. Have you any plans for visiting the West? Have you heard from Malia? – he is an even worse correspondent than I am, but do not suspect him of any change of feeling towards you. He is devoted to you, and I even more so, but *pereklikat´sya*[4] is indispensable, and I humbly beat the ground with my head concerning my frequent failures to practise what I preach.

Yours,

[IB p.p.]   [...]

TO A. Z. PROPES

15 April 1970 [*carbon*]

[Headington House]

Honoured Herr Direktor!

If you insist on writing to me during a postal strike in the United States to an address already abandoned by me, if only for a short while, how can you expect a concrete and satisfying reply? [...] I am in bed with a sore throat sent on me by our ancient God, doubtless as a punishment for failing to respond to your letter – our God, whatever may be said of other ones, operates according to rules which may correspond to regional or national requirements, but do[es] not allow for journeys to the Western hemisphere. Anyway, I hope to come to the Festival, though when and where and how

---

1 Evgeny Bazarov is the self-proclaimed nihilist hero of Turgenev's novel *Fathers and Sons* (1862), who rejects all forms of traditional authority.
2 'Sweetness of life'.
3 'Night falls.' Possibly a reference to a tragic chapter in Herzen's *My Past and Thoughts* entitled 'Oceano nox', a quotation from Vergil's *Aeneid* 2. 250, 'ruit oceano nox', 'night falls over the sea': *Sobranie sochinenii* (169/1, on 170), x 372.
4 'Communication'.

remains to be seen, and the hope is not a promise and even a promise is not a guarantee. So, as usual, everything vacillates and anything may happen. You ask for a message:[1] I am sure you do not need one from me: who am I to speak with authority about music? To make a pronouncement on the subject will merely expose me to contempt and ridicule. All I can tell you is this:

> Unmusical cultures exist, but however powerful their impact in other ways, they are characterised by a degree of inhumanity due to lack of an entire dimension of human sensibility, for which there is no substitute or compensation. Fortunately this cannot be said of Israel, which has been shaped by a tradition into which music was woven from the earliest beginnings: from Jubal,[2] the youngest genius born to Jewish parents, there was never a period of Jewish history without characteristic musical expression. I am happy to salute the tenth Israel Festival, which represents the noblest flowering of this tradition in our time. It would be invidious to cite the names of individual musicians: they are 'all masters, all skilled, all able to read [i.e. interpret] the [musical] Torah'.[3] It may be confidently asserted that so long as Jews, and in particular the State of Israel, exists, music and its performance will not perish from the earth.

Yours ever,
  [Isaiah Berlin]

TO STEPHEN SPENDER

16 April 1970 [*carbon*]

[Headington House]

Dearest Stephen,

Thank you very much for sending me back that pathetic screed. I did indeed write out my heartfelt cry for bread twice, in my own exquisite hand, of which you must have received one copy, and now I am dashed by the bald announcement that this company, which alone can tend to my needs, refuses to send things abroad and can only supply them within the confines of the continent of the United States. This is terrible news. May I throw myself on your mercy and beg you, as they suggest, or seem to do, to receive the 'consignment' at Storrs[4] and then not indeed to bring it home to me – I cannot burden you, even though you may be going by boat – but simply to lug it along to a post office and have it sent off as is, by sea mail, goods, or whatever it is, with a huge label saying 'Bread Stix desperately

---

1 sc. a message of support for the 1970 Israel Festival, of which Propes was the Director.
2 'The father of all such as handle the harp and organ', Genesis 4:21.
3 IB applies to musicians a phrase from the Passover Haggadah. The original context is: 'Even if we were all masters, all skilled, all able to read the Torah, we should still be obliged to discuss the exodus from Egypt.'
4 Where Spender was based at the time, at the University of Connecticut.

needed by [ ] oldster' to Headington? Would you please do this? I return the relevant documents. [...]

I did attend Freddie's lecture in my turn, arriving late and standing up throughout in order to attract attention and leaving early to indicate that he had gone on too long: that is all I could do to indicate that I was a conscript listener. I know everything is much worse and Nixon does indeed look like the wolf in *Red Riding Hood*. You must remember that in the story he does not in the end eat her, but that more or less the opposite happens. I am having flu, which of course I enjoy, with backache and all kinds of complications – but anything to stay in bed and not face the world. I am the worst evader and avoider of reality that I know – and all my talk about the sacredness of choice and liberty! – you did not hear my heroic performance before the ferocious radicals in the basement in New York: it was rather like Turgenev's passionate description of Bazarov or Lawrence's of carnal passion – psychological explanation is all too easy, alas – it is Bread Stix that I really crave for.

Yours ever,
[Isaiah]

TO ROBERT SILVERS

29 May 1970 [*carbon*]

[Wolfson College]

Dear Bob,

I feel that some kind of report is owing to you by this time. [...] Sir Maurice telephoned to me, saying, 'Bad news. Mrs Stone, wife of Lawrence Stone, told Stuart that he was not wanted in Wadham and spread stories about the hostile reception that is waiting for him.' Absolute nonsense. We are all most eager. The only person who is hostile is Stone's friend Pat Thompson,[1] who is mad, enraged, determined to make trouble. I hope Stuart believes none of this. I have told Thompson what I think of him. He made a scene, etc. [...] One man can do a lot of harm and inflict a lot of wounds, and this, I fear, may happen. However, in the end, Stuart's beauty of character will (I know this to be an incontrovertible truth) quell opposition. Still, it was not entirely without a certain mild maliciousness – I will not say pleasure, but interest – that Sir Maurice communicated this horrid intelligence to me. It is, on the whole, best that you not know it, otherwise it will be thought a kind of spreading story; Stuart will think there is more in this than meets the eye; Renée will think that there is a campaign, etc., none of which is true. But it is as I thought about Stone – happy in Princeton he may be, and it may not be his fault so much as his awful wife's, but a certain envy grips all academics

---

1 Arthur Frederick ('Pat') Thompson (1920–2009), Fellow and Tutor in History, Wadham, 1947–87.

22 Ann Fleming and Maurice Bowra, Paraggi, 1969: 'Ann Fleming, whom Maurice *adored* to his dying day, who may not have adored him, though she gave him much pleasure, and who talks about him […] with a kind of disinterested, very un-malicious penetration. She is surprisingly good on him' (to Noel Annan, 31 August 1973)

23 In Paraggi, 1969: 'I ought to have written days and days ago: but in spite of the theoretical leisure, visitors arrive, one is hustled to the beach, to the hills, to the Post Office' (to Sylvester Gates, 30 August 1969)

24 In his study at Headington House, 1971

25 Jean Floud, Nuffield, 1971

26 Bernard Williams, early 1970s

27 Aline and Wolfson-graduate-students at the Isis boathouses, Torpids, March 1972

28 Walking in Paraggi, 1972

29 In Paraggi, 1972

30 Nicolas Nabokov and W. H. Auden at Headington
House, February 1973: 'As for Wystan [...] I gather
that he is coming to Christ Church, but thinks that he
should have been more warmly welcomed'
(to Ursula Niebuhr, 21 January 1972)

31 IB's mother Marie in old age: 'my debt to her is gigantic as you know too well: all the Herderian beliefs are
founded on the rich & firm tradition in which I was
brought up' (to Stuart Hampshire, 23 February 1974)

32 Wolfson dining hall under construction, January 1972: 'When will it all be ready? The architects say that [...] there is no answer to this question' (to McGeorge Bundy, 26 October 1973)

33 At the 'topping out' of the new Wolfson buildings, 15 December 1972

34 Portofino harbour: one of several postcards sent by IB to Philip Powell in summer 1968 in the hope of persuading him to curve (*see below*) one of the planned accommodation blocks of Wolfson College

35 Wolfson from the east, showing the curve in the accommodation block (*left*) suggested by the shape of Portofino harbour

36 The new Wolfson buildings from the bridge over the Cherwell, 1974

37, 38 By the river Isis, with Eleanor (hidden) and Michael Brock (*left*), and with Aline (*right*), supporting the College during Eights Week, summer 1974

39 Michael Brock (*looking on*), Harold Macmillan's chauffeur, IB and Macmillan at the opening of the new Wolfson buildings, 12 November 1974

40 With Isaac Wolfson and Harold Macmillan after IB's speech at the opening of the new Wolfson College buildings, 12 November 1974: 'a unique moment of triumph never to be repeated in the history of the College, no matter how long its life – which we hope will be many centuries' – from IB's speech, *Lycidas* 3 (1974–5), 4

41 Derek Hill's official portrait for Wolfson College, 1975: 'Derek Hill [...] has kindly painted me for my College and produced a most flattering version under the guise of some relaxed quasi-Irish country figure: I cannot ask for a better disguise for posterity' (to Shiela Sokolov Grant, 13 March 1973)

at a certain stage of their life, particularly those who, having failed in a given place, observe others succeeding in what they regard as their own particular preserve. None of this is news.

Secondly, Cal: I think all is well. He began by rather disliking Sparrow, and still dislikes All Souls, the dinner jackets on Saturdays, the fact that it is all too much like school, too much silly formality and general nonsense. But I am sure he is right in taking the job at Essex which will only occupy him two days a week, otherwise he can live peacefully in London, which is surely the best thing for him now. He would have gone to absolute pieces in New York, I am sure. His lecture to the audience in Oxford under my almost non-existent auspices was a wild success – about 700 persons came, more than for Chomsky, fewer only than, I think, to Boulez: he was not displeased; he read his verse, answered questions. I said that he literally needed no introduction and simply said he is Mr Robert Lowell. I meant this as a compliment. However, I saw that Cal was perhaps not entirely pleased: he made a slight reference to the fact that usually one can start off by making play of the chairman's remarks in introducing the speaker, but in this case it was, alas, literally impossible to do so. From this I detected a certain minute degree of disappointment. So I woke up to my obligations and in closing the lecture paid him appropriate compliments. Well received. After that he went to a party at our house, at which he met all kinds of revolutionary students, which I think he enjoyed. [...]

In my next instalment I will discuss Noam, and the new committee for Arab–Jewish understanding. It is thoroughly to be approved of and seems to me a grave mistake. Now I must see my next visitor, in fact my next three visitors, who are sweltering in my poor secretary's room next door.

Yours ever,

[Isaiah]

TO NICOLAS NABOKOV

25 June 1970

Headington House

Cher Nicolovius,[1]

All the refugees are coming home. Stuart and Sooprooga[2] (how little this appellation suits her!) are back in this country and the fellows of Wadham are awaiting nervously the arrival of this fabulous pair – although no one knows anything by direct inspection – about them strange and terrifying stories are circulating everywhere. My job is to reassure them and tell them that it will

---

1 Perhaps an allusion to (Matthias) Friedrich Nicolovius (1768–1836), Königsberg bookseller and publisher (of, among others, Hamann, Jacobi and Kant). But other Nicolovii are possible, if indeed IB has a particular one in mind.
2 'Supruga' is Russian for 'wife'.

all be all right, and that the eccentricities have been much exaggerated. But can you imagine them presiding over large conventional assemblages? Stuart, yes – but X? One dares not pronounce the name for fear of consequences, as is always done in the case of sacred symbols in the pagan world. Stephen is also back. We called in on them in the middle of our elections when they and Stuart and Wollheim and the rest were sitting in the depths of depression. I am naturally cock-a-hoop about the refutation of the pollsters[1] – anything that upsets careful predictions, the general assumption that vast impersonal forces are guiding our faltering footsteps in directions unknown to us but known only to American scientists, pleases me immensely. There is no limit to my pleasure in the unforeseen and fortuitous – this is what Stuart etc. regard as my hideously reactionary views – but they really spring from the heart of the Russian intelligentsia, like everything else that I believe, and are the core of the great disputes which raged in the 1880s and '90s between the Marxists and the anti-Marxists, and which had real significance to Russia alone, and after that only in my own breast. Lowell is also behaving in a *not* very disciplined fashion – he'll be staying in England for another two years – how much this will please Elizabeth I do not know – I anticipate explosions from time to time and the general intrusion of what might be called the disruptive elements of the New York bohemia in our tranquil milieu. Lowell is sure to go off with somebody sooner or later, and cause general disruption and pain, and then at the same time remain touching, sympathetic and far more gifted than the others. I am fascinated by the relationship between him and Auden. They do not like each other at all: and yet refer to each other in cautious, mildly admiring but nevertheless extremely guarded terms – rather like Tolstoy and Dostoevsky – in general there is a thesis to be written about the interrelationships of writers of the same period and place which appeal to the same public, feel it a duty to be in certain relations with each other, but nevertheless develop some kind of complicated and awkward nexus which they attempt to disguise in all kinds of ways – this certainly happened with, for example, Stendhal and Balzac,[2] Flaubert and Merimée,[3] etc. I must stop – I'm being hurried off by my well-disciplined family, which does not allow

---

1 At the General Election on 18 June 1970 the Conservative Party was returned with an overall majority of 30: only one of the 5 major opinion polls had predicted a Conservative victory. Labour's early showing in the polls had encouraged the Prime Minister, Harold Wilson, to call a June election, but this plan misfired badly, and the 'blatant inaccuracy' of the polls 'turned the calling of an election into a form of Gallup roulette' (Peter Blaker MP, quoted in *The Times*, 3 July 1970, 3c).

2 The French novelists Stendhal (1783–1842), pseudonym of Marie Henri Beyle, and Honoré de Balzac (1799–1850) have been linked 'from their own day to the present. [...] Both are commonly taken by literary historians as the precursors of nineteenth-century realism': Joseph Frank, 'Balzac and Stendhal', *Sewanee Review* 56 (1948), 126.

3 Gustave Flaubert (1821–80), French novelist, whose first published work was *Madame Bovary: moeurs de province* (Paris, 1857), and Prosper Mérimée (1803–70), French novelist, playwright and short-story writer, whose *Carmen* (1845) (Paris, 1846) inspired Bizet's opera.

me to finish this letter. This will be perfectly familiar to you. I must however end abruptly, in extreme frustration, with tears running down my cheeks, dove-pecked as I am [...].

Yours ever,

I.

когда же? где же? в Европе? в бедном Иерусалиме (как все это кончится? *большим* кровопролитием? в котором «наши» евреи будут бороться с Арабскими «гьерильясами»? *ненавижу* [*illegible epithet*] бородатых еврейских «революционеров»! Selbst-hass ужасная вещь – авто-анти-семитизм! Предпочитаю трусливых *либералов*.)[1]

TO MCGEORGE BUNDY

8 July 1970

Wolfson

Dear Mac,

The entire world appears to be in financial straits, and we are no exception. St Antony's declares that it is tottering on the brink of bankruptcy; I think that in a vague way they look hopefully to us as an emergent country to prop up an older economy: and we have indeed made an arrangement with them whereby their new and magnificent dining hall[2] will accommodate the overflow of our students during our interregnum between limited numbers in tight accommodation, and the final emergence of the Wolfsonianum to its full glory. Our building is naturally already in some arrears – about two or three months late – and Mr Leonard paid us a visit today in order to obtain a confrontation with the contractors, who are of his own choosing. The contractors assured him that all would be ready on time, and we have no alternative but to believe that. What cannot be altered had best be put out of mind. [...]

But our chief trouble is financial: we have not lost more than others, but we have lost as much; and as the Ford shares could not be sold until the end of this month in accordance with the arrangement that your Foundation required, and since, as well you know, their value has steeply declined, our academic programme does not look too bright. Where can we economise? Given that the building will be what it is, it would, on financial grounds alone, be difficult, if not impossible, to cut down on the number of resident graduates if we are to leave rooms empty and unused; nor is it possible to charge

---

1 'But when? But where? In Europe? In poor Jerusalem? (How is this going to end? In a *huge* blood-bath? In which "our" Jews will fight against the Arab "guerrillas"? *I can't stand* [*illegible epithet*] bearded Jewish "revolutionaries"! Self-hatred is a terrible thing – auto-anti-Semitism! I prefer the cowardly *liberals*.)'

2 Known to members of Wolfson under this regime as Tony's Diner.

full economic prices either for rooms or meals if we are to retain any kind
of competitive position vis-à-vis other Oxford colleges, who are also building
buildings for graduates [...]. Given all this, we cannot cut either on numbers,
quality or any real degree of subsidisation of their lives; therefore the only
things that we can economise on are such 'luxuries' as visiting fellows, visiting professors, and indeed everything that makes life worth living. We would
be extremely reluctant to do this for obvious reasons [...]; and the awkward
question now arises, given that one of the causes of this situation is the
decline in the value of our investment, more particularly our Ford shares,
can we decently ask you whether you could conceivably do anything to help
us in 1972/3, when this need will become acute (it is not acute now)? You
may very reasonably say that if the Ford shares had doubled in value you
would not be asking us to hand back our profits, and there is no answer to
this in terms of logical symmetry. Nor would I – or the Trustees of Wolfson
College, who have urged me to write to you – expect you to say anything at
all definite at this stage, for how could you possibly? [...] I could, of course, if
this was wanted, spell out in exact financial detail how our income is likely to
be spent, what portion of it must go towards the graduates, the staff, equipment, rates, university contribution, food, overheads etc., and what is likely
to be left for academic purposes – research, distinguished visitors etc. (this
residue is really frighteningly small at the moment – I daren't think about it,
and lie awake, not indeed through the entire night, but say through an hour
or so every second day, brooding about this). [...]

Meanwhile there are bright aspects of our situation also: the fellows are
more distinguished than I ever thought they would be; the graduates appear
happy; in the recent political upheavals, small though they are by American
standards, our forty graduates, so far as internal life of the College is concerned, remained harmonious and at peace with themselves and with the
fellows. [...] We have an excellent entry of graduates from Oxford – I never
thought there would be so many from here as opposed to other universities,
tempted by what they regard as an unstuffy atmosphere – from all kinds of
apparently distinguished colleges (not, I fear, excluding Wadham, the Warden
of which is retiring amid much glory), which will in due course lead to, I will
not say friction, but slightly displeased glances from colleges which do not
see why they should lose some of their most promising undergraduates to us
instead of keeping them as graduates of their own. Considering that we are
not at all grand and we merely huddle in two houses in the Banbury Road, all
this is, in a way, rather surprising: or perhaps not, perhaps it is the very fact
of our amiable egalitarianism that attracts some among the abler scientists
and abler arts students as well. Our best propagandists are our own students
– the letters we receive simply begin with assuring us that it is as a result of
the 'delicious meals (sic!) and jolly company' which they have encountered
at Wolfson that their thoughts have turned towards us. We still virtually

pay nobody anything to speak of: the atmosphere is extremely friendly and agreeable, and if we do as well as this when we rise from the mud and noise of the field at the end of Linton Road, we shall, you might say, be all right. Financial thoughts fill me with gloom, social facts with joy. Thus do I oscillate in a schizophrenic way. We are not unlike the State of Israel: beset with dangers, but inwardly fairly secure and optimistic, and a very great deal less obstinate, less short-sighted and unreasonable.

There now, *Dixi et salvavi animam meam.*[1] I'd love to hear from you whatever your views.

Yours,
  Isaiah

TO MICHAEL BROCK

[Received on or before 12 August 1970, *manuscript*]

Grand Hotel Royal Orologio, Abano Terme[2]

Dear Michael,

[…] 1. Boddington[3] & Miss Goldf.[4] & the furnishing of the President's rooms (*not* the "Presidential *suite*' or I resign forthwith) – Aline is willing to furnish *all 3*: study, coffee room, dining room: the money cd come from the A. B. Trust & be paid to the College: the objects so purchased being its property from the start, save for what I bring in of my own: e.g. my present sofa & armchairs to which I am for historical reasons attached & so on. So *that* can come off Miss G's budget, which *must* ease things somewhat.

2. Bundy's letter. In your covering letter you state my real interests quite accurately of course, but I am not sure that this is the right doctrine for Mr L[eonard]. Bundy is obviously trying to say that Mr L. must not bully me into fund raising activities […] & that my letter to him, all too obviously stimulated by Mr L., is a symptom of his liability to make me commit infra dig acts which he Bundy severely disapproves of & wishes to rescue me from (& feels I shd not have perpetrated) – all this I know him to feel. I don't mind in the least about what Bundy feels about the "abuse" of myself: but it is quite a good pin to drive into Mr L.: he will *not* want to feel that Bundy views him as a bullying driver & me as a feeble donkey spurred on by Wolfson pricks & Ford carrots. Hence (& because the facts too also justify it) it is as well

1 101/2.
2 Where mud was used for health cures.
3 Paul Boddington (1913–98), Buildings Officer, Wolfson, 1967–80, Supernumerary Fellow 1970–80; 'a broad back on which so many burdens have fallen and who has borne them so well': IB, speech at the official opening of Wolfson College, Oxford, 12 November 1974, *Lycidas* 3 (1975), 6.
4 Elizabeth Goldfinger (b. 1936), furniture and interior designer; daughter of the Hungarian architect Ernö Goldfinger. She had recently been engaged by Wolfson in a consultancy role, to assist in the internal design of the College.

to stress how *difficult* it will be to get *any* outside grant for a college called *Wolfson*.

[...] meanwhile here I groan with my arthritis & sciatica alternately – when I have the one I lose the other – in old Formal Logic (Old Corpus 1928) this was called rebutting the horns of a dilemma: I lie on a board, am covered with sticky, dark grey mud, hot, dubiously therapeutic, v. mediaeval, & think about my lack of (a) ideas (b) material for Romanes which has become a nightmare (by the time you & Eleanor[1] come at 10 p.m. on Sept 1, I shall be in a state of lunacy about this & unable to participate in the common table), then I am rinsed, pummelled, & hurled into a radioactive pool whence I am supposed to leap refreshed & radiant (lit.) but in fact slink off to bed & read the Corriere della Sera[2] with a dictionary. This is my brutish life: by the time you come – & Aline & I really look forward to this with the greatest enthusiasm – I may have recovered human semblance. But be surprised by nothing. 61 is a dangerous age.

Yours ever

Isaiah   [...]

TO JEAN FLOUD

11 August 1970 [*manuscript*]

Grand Hotel Royal Orologio, Abano Terme

Dear J.

Here we are. The luxe of this establishment is *very* moderate: rather like the hotels my parents used to frequent in the early twenties: before my mother's sense of financial panic overcame her & we descended to 2 ème & 3 ème categorie in the late twenties. After that I broke away & lived the well known pseudo-bohemian but genuinely cheap life of the Gasthofs & *pensions* in Italy (*not* trattorias, ever). So this is faintly nostalgic: like Herbert's memories of his father's affluence before his crash.[3] Aline likes it, because although below her parents' standards, the culture is the same one & one can speculate about the identities of fellow guests: so do *they* about one: our neighbours – West Side N. Y. Jews very obviously – acc. to Peter [Halban] who overheard them (he is here for one night) – decided that we were American *wasps* – although my identity was a trifle puzzling: Sicilian *origins*, but assimilated evidently. Maurice went off without fuss: he was, I must say, incomparably easier than 2 years ago when he was very apoplectic & in an acuter state of paranoia. "It was a success from *my* point of view" were his last words: I am

---

1 MGB's wife (633).

2 One of Italy's oldest daily newspapers, published in Milan.

3 Herbert Hart's father, Simeón Hart (1871–1953), was a master tailor and furrier in Harrogate. When his business collapsed in 1921 he moved his son from Cheltenham College to Bradford Grammar School. The change suited Herbert, who thrived, and by the time that he went up to Oxford his father's fortunes had revived.

ready to settle for that. The mud is laid – moulded on one – like plaster of Paris: first legs disappear, then arms; one lies on a bed of it anyway: it is hot & comforting & does no good at all, I am sure. Nor does the massage: But the tedium of life here surely will, if only Aline can stand it, but with piscines & golf perhaps she could survive.

[…] I keep reading more by & about Turgenev: I am beginning to know him quite well – (no good for Romanes & Oxford!) is he more like Stephen Spender – always getting into false positions & enjoying explaining how he got into them & anxious to please everybody but above all the very censorious young? & yet devastatingly ironical? or like D. Cecil, unable to like nasty introspective non-U. writers & knowing well & exactly whom his book will please, whom not, & why, & openly preferring gentlemen – or like me, endlessly talking & talking & earning the disapproval of the serious, the grim, the world's workers? or the truly vain like Tolstoy?

yrs

   I.

TO NICOLAS NABOKOV

12 September 1970

[As from] Headington House

Carissimo,

Do certainly come to Abano next year with me. The mud is delicious. The ladies who swim slowly but resolutely in the heated indoor swimming pool (in 'radioactive' water) are less delicious, but would delight you also. Particularly the American millionairesses who would remind you of much. One very ancient Palm Beach playboy – well over eighty – remembers association with Aline many, many years ago. Mrs Milstein (wife) and Mrs Stern (mother) do not seem at all friendly to each other, but Mrs Stern is nicer: surrounded by Mrs Mizroch from Petersburg, who teaches the piano in, I think, Florence or Paris or both, and other ladies of a similar sort, [they] have formed a little Russian colony in the hotel Buja[1] (air-conditioned) which I used to visit. Meanwhile I was beset by the task of writing a lecture about poor Turgenev – the most ferociously attacked of all Russian authors. Every novel after *On the Eve* was attacked with *violence* by both sides. He spent his entire time in apologising to everybody and explaining to the right why he was slightly left-wing and to the left why he was not quite right-wing, and was constantly accused of grovelling (*kuvyrkaniya*) at the feet of the young by Katkov,[2] and

---

1 Now the Hotel Terme Bristol Buja.

2 Mikhail Nikiforovich Katkov (1818–87), conservative Russian writer, editor and journalist; edited Turgenev's work; associate of Belinsky, Herzen and Bakunin. He changed from a liberal-minded Anglophile into an influential nationalist and supporter of the reactionary policies of Tsar Alexander III. Cf. RT2 321–2 etc.

of grovelling at the feet of the Emperor by the New Left Russian periodicals of the 1860s (Belinsky and Herzen are the Old Left). The present agony of liberal professors was anticipated by the hideous malaise of the Russian liberals from 1860 onwards, with precisely the same symptoms of sympathy for the young, horror at their methods, embarrassment in all directions, blows from above, below, side, in front, behind (that is how Turgenev describes it). This occurred endlessly for years and years and decades and decades – Tolstoy and Dostoevsky were too formidable and independent to be so treated, but poor Turgenev was really rather like Stepanushka[1] – (also like you & me) in his anxiety not to be abandoned by the young and terror of constant evidence of being connected in some unaware fashion with agents of the reaction à la CIA. The letters disowning any connection with Herzen, Lavrov[2] etc. at various dates; and the letters disowning *any* connection with the horrible generals of the gendarmerie and the loathsome minions of the Tsar, read pathetically now, but sympathetically too. About this I intend to deliver a lecture which will certainly be regarded as self-reflective and *pro domo*,[3] but not in fact be so at all (there I am, just like my hero, starting to disown ...) Certainly we must go to the Holy Land together next December, come what may. [...]

Isaiah   [...]

TO JEAN FLOUD

18 September 1970[4]

[As from] Wolfson

Dear Jean,
    About Machiavelli.[5] I see that I have failed to convince you. Let me try

1 Apparently a nickname used by IB and NN for Stephen Spender, who resigned as an editor of *Encounter* in 1967 when it emerged that the magazine was covertly funded by the CIA, without Spender's knowledge. IB too was unaware of the CIA's role. The unsatisfactorily sourced and pejoratively worded allegations made by Frances Stonor Saunders in her *Who Paid the Piper? The CIA and the Cultural Cold War* (London, 1999), that IB knew of the CIA funding before it became public knowledge (at which point he strenuously objected to its secrecy, though not to its existence) is at variance, prima facie, with a considerable body of evidence in IB's papers and those of William Hayter, Michael Josselson, Melvin Lasky, Nicolas Nabokov and Stephen Spender. If she is wrong, the recollections of Laurence de Neufville that she reports are also erroneous. Her note also attributes to Robert Bruce Lockhart the belief that IB worked for the Political Warfare Executive (misnamed 'Psychological' in the note) in Washington during the war: this (mistaken) belief was in fact inserted by the editor of Bruce Lockhart's diaries, Kenneth Young: see *The Diaries of Sir Robert Bruce Lockhart*, vol. 2 (London, 1973), 733.
2 Petr Lavrov (1823–1900) née Petr Lavrovich Mirtov, Russian philosopher, sociologist and socialist revolutionary; a member of the populist Land and Liberty movement.
3 421/5.
4 From a tape recorded in Paraggi on 8 September after JF's departure.
5 During JF's stay at Paraggi earlier that summer Machiavelli – on whom IB was finishing the paper eventually published as 'The Originality of Machiavelli' (repr. in AC and PSM) – had been

again. The usual view (and, I add intolerably, yours) is that Machiavelli was writing how to create durable States – that he spelt out what he regarded as the only efficient method of doing so and that, in the course of this, he simply left out moral considerations, i.e. that he did not mind whether the courses he recommended were moral or immoral since he was not interested in the subject. The fact that they offended against Christian and generally current European morality may have been clear to him, or it may not, but if it was, he did not bother to say so. It was as if he were interested in building pyramids for pharaohs and pointed out that in order to do so half a million slaves might have to be used up. Was this humane, shocking etc.? This was not the question he put to himself and did not answer. What the implications are for morality is for others to draw, none of his business.

This is what I disagree with so strongly. Machiavelli makes it plain in the *Discourses* (less clearly in *The Prince*, but pretty clearly there, too) that the men he admires and wishes the Italians to become like are the citizens of republican Rome, or Periclean Athens, or at least Imperial Rome under the 'good' emperors. And he wants men who will recreate these conditions – wants them, not merely tells you how to generate them, or what they should be like. His talk of corruption makes quite plain what his morality is and [that] he has one. You do not want to call it morality because you associate this term with rules of a Hebraic, Kantian kind – so do I, but Trotsky, who talked about 'Kantian-liberal-Quaker-vegetarian nonsense',[1] meant just this, and thought that for a Marxist, for example, there weren't any such rules. All there was was the ideal society and the kind of human beings whom the society would generate, or who were necessary for the purpose of creating this society, so that everything was judged in terms of its making for or against, promoting or retarding, consciously or unconsciously, individually or collectively, the development of this kind of exfoliation of human reason, potentialities etc., or whatever the Marxist ideal may be: and this was called Marxist morality, quite correctly, it seems to me.

It is in this sense that Machiavelli was a moralist, i.e. he had an ideal of what men should be like in his head, but he did not relate this to some universally acceptable standard – say natural law, which men as such cannot get away from, or some notion of 'the normal human being' who is violated by cruelty or exploitation, or enforced ignorance, or the like [...].

The argument between us is, I think, whether Machiavelli can be said to be compounding, or at least conveying, a moral ideal at all, and I think you

---

discussed. Arnaldo Momigliano also contributed to the discussion: his visit to Paraggi 'was especially agreeable, accompanied as he was by a string basket containing books in seven languages which he thought might be of interest to me' (IB to Robert Silvers, 23 September 1970).

1 In *Terrorizm i kommunizm* (Petersburg [sic], 1920), 61 – p. 63 in the English translation *The Defence of Terrorism* (London, 1920) – Trotsky writes: 'As for us, we were never concerned with Kantian-priestly, vegetarian-Quaker chatter about "the sanctity of human life".'

have reservations about supposing, say, Aristotelian morality – not that of rules, but that of kinds of human beings whom it is desirable to generate, and who can only be generated, say, in cities of not more than 10,000 citizens – is a morality at all, because I think that morality for you is a system of 'do's' and 'don't's', as I suspect it is for me and for most people we know, if not for, let us say, Nietzsche, who was certainly a moralist, what else? Nor for Marx, who would not have bound his spell on so many if he weren't one, whatever he may have thought that he was. Neither sociology nor economics are going to send people to their deaths or to kill others unless they have a very powerful moral component, i.e. hold out an ideal life in the name of which, etc.

But all these people believed that they had found the answers to the question how one should live and what one should do, which excluded any other answers as being false, and their premisses and methods are fairly clear. Machiavelli differed from them in that, although his methods and his premisses are clear enough, he is not concerned to maintain that a rational man must believe what he believes and must act as he recommends (although he is extremely anxious that he should); but if this rational man chooses to listen to Christian preachers he dooms himself to impotence politically, and if he chooses to do that, Machiavelli has nothing to say to him.

If you read the last chapter of the *Prince*, which is the most passionate prayer for a saviour of Italy, or if you consider his fury and contempt for bunglers and fumblers, his lamentations about the perpetual possibility of decadence and corruption, his view that only the strongest medicines can possibly cure people of the backsliding and downward slope to which they are, alas, constantly addicted – strong men with ruthless methods can just keep them from it: Caesar Borgia might just do it – you will surely agree that he is not interested simply in what makes States function well, but mainly in how one could get back to the glories of Rome or Athens, because only in such a framework can men develop what he regards as the most desirable, the most glorious, the best kind of life, although Christians evidently do not agree, and if so, down with them, they obstruct what he wants to see done. Telling people that if what he regards as the ultimate repository of values – the *patria* – is in danger, then nothing is noble or ignoble, good or bad, any method is allowed. Men will forget ordinary values and throw in everything they have to save the only thing worth living for – citizenship of the city. What is this if not moral exhortation of the most passionate kind? You can call it political morality, if you like, but there is for him no other, in fact he thinks that morals are, so to speak, a branch of politics, exactly as Aristotle did. There is no non-political morality, at least none that he is interested in (he knows there is one, of course, the Christian one). Why is this not an intensely moral position? To enunciate that, tell people that what they have been taught for ages is not compatible with the only thing that is worth achieving, a glorious pagan State, and that common morality is not compatible with the only life worth leading for a fully developed man – my God! That is what people choose not to look at, even at the present, because people like to think that all good things can somehow be combined by skill, by good fortune, if not in this life, somewhere else, and this is what, if what Machiavelli says is true, cannot be so.

There now, have I convinced you? I expect not.

Yours,

[IB p.p. G. Hylton-Potts]

TO ROBERT SILVERS

6 November 1970 [*carbon*]

Headington House

Dear Bob,

[...] The Middle East! Are we doomed to live under that shadow for the rest of our natural lives? Would you have preferred not to be oppressed by uncontrollable situations – at least uncontrollable by oneself and one's friends? I should. I cannot remember any such period in my own life – from 1932 onwards I have looked on newspapers with apprehension – the happiest period was 1942–5, awful to say. I understand perfectly what is so attractive about living in a community engaged on a painful but victorious march in some universally accepted direction. But I am ashamed of that, and the prospect of that now is so small that this is a very abstract sort of proposition. I expect Chomsky feels he is on a rising wave, perhaps even Mary McCarthy does; Edmund and I do not. And you? Despite all the setbacks do you feel that you are marching uphill with the forces of freedom and reason? Marching? Not struggling not to be left back? I expect you do really. I do not know of anyone as free from the ultimate sense of the forces of history driving one along in some desired direction as, alas, I am myself. Terrible to be an atheist among so many believers!

Yours,

[Isaiah]

On 12 November IB gave the annual public lecture of the University, the Romanes Lecture, in the Sheldonian Theatre at Oxford, taking as his semi-autobiographical theme Turgenev and the 'liberal predicament'. The lecture was a long time in gestation and proved to be one of IB's most memorable. He had written to Noel Annan in May:

I have to deliver a Romanes lecture this year (after making sure that Maurice did it first, of course, otherwise you can imagine what wd have been said)

& propose to deal with Turgenev as a man who got many more kicks than ha'pence for walking a causeway between Scylla (Dostoevsky & the squires he liked best) & Charybdis (bearded students & London & Paris revolutionaries he admired & was privately & reasonably liked by) all his life: & never never caving in (which he knew he wd have found easier & for which fewer wd have blamed him than for his fence walking).[1]

He meant to deal principally with Turgenev's 'controversial position in his own lifetime, but also to some degree the relevance of the liberal dilemma in which he was involved for our own times. [...] The lecture will be delivered [...] to an audience consisting of heaven knows who: it is open to the public and may be very small indeed'.[2]

TO ROY HARROD

17 November 1970

Headington House

Dear Roy,

[...] Thank you very much for your heart-warming words – both for what you wrote and for the act of writing itself which was very generous and very, if I may say so, characteristic of the goodness of your nature.

I, too, love Turgenev. About art he said very different things to different people – Maupassant[3] reports him as saying that the notion of moral or political intent in a novel is as absurd as attributing this to a symphony or a painting. On the other hand, he did say things like 'this is not the time for mere literature – for birds twittering on trees. The times are too grave' etc. and when Tolstoy invited him to take part in a periodical to be devoted to pure literature, avoiding politics, he refused. 'I know that politics are a filthy swamp. But there is dirt and dust in the streets too, yet we cannot after all do without towns.'[4] In fact he said different things to different persons. I think your interpretation is perfectly correct; I think that Turgenev simply believed in telling the truth, as he saw it, whether or not this included moral or political elements – he had no doctrinaire view – he detested all theories and 'absolutes' as he called them, particularly metaphysical or religious ones (this got him into trouble with Tolstoy) – and if he conveyed his own moral or political attitudes by transforming his readers' outlook by his art he was contented. He was indeed a great artist. The Russian government feared him and on his last visit to Russia they saw to it that he did not linger for too long.

1 To Noel Annan, 13 May 1970.
2 To J. Amos, 14 October 1970.
3 Guy de Maupassant (1850–93), French novelist and short-story writer.
4 These passages are from letters to Tolstoy of 29 January and 7 April 1858 (old style). I. S. Turgenev, *Polnoe sobranie sochinenii i pisem* (Moscow/Leningrad, 1960–8), *Pis'ma*, iii 188, 210. For more exact translations see RT2 307.

He claimed to have little imagination – everything that he wrote was in some sense taken from life. Unless he began with some situation which he had actually observed and then transformed it into a work of art he could not get going at all – hence he could not write historical novels and every single story he ever composed, so he claimed, had its roots in a specific episode which he had either experienced or had described to him – never imagined. [...]

I shall certainly read your Chichele Lectures[1] as soon as they are out and hope to send you a copy of my lecture if it ever appears.

How very, very nice of you to write. I really was deeply touched.

Yours ever

Isaiah   [...]

TO ANNA KALLIN

17 November 1970

Headington House

Dearest N,

Alas that I could not even see you, but I was in such an awful state all day – you know how it takes me – and I could not face anyone until it was all over. What you say is absolutely true and most penetrating as always – when I really have something that I want to say it can only occur in the Russian context. The rest is probably all rather *konstruiert*.[2] I shall certainly send you copies of my lecture as soon as they appear, if ever they do. I think it is going to be broadcast sometime in February when, thank God, I shall not be here. I was in terrible agony throughout as always, I much prefer the microphone! And I made one awful mistake. Why did I say that Dobrolyubov[3] talked about 'system', a word then reproduced in Weimar and today in America – meaning the hateful system which revolutionaries must get outside of before they can strike it down? He didn't. He talked about 'sreda'[4] in precisely the sense in which we are all so terribly familiar with this word – I am not sure that he did not begin the fashion – the word 'system' I think did occur on the page, meaning a philosophical doctrine. Anyway, first I make a mistake and then I build more theory on it. How typical. How awful. Moreover the whole passage about the 'box' did not appear in the *Sovremennik* – the censor eliminated it – and only in the restored text which Chernyshevsky edited later long after Dobrolyubov's death – all this for you who at least knows what I am talking about – who else did? Not even Obolensky all that much.

---

1 Harrod's 1970 Chichele Lectures, delivered under the auspices of All Souls, were published the following year as *Sociology, Morals and Mystery* (London, 1971).
2 'Contrived'.
3 Nikolay Aleksandrovich Dobrolyubov (1836–61), Russian literary critic, perhaps second only to Belinsky in terms of influence among the radical intelligentsia; a contributor to the liberal journal *Sovremennik* (*The Contemporary*), and from 1857 chief critic.
4 'Milieu'.

The only head I saw in the entire assembly – and that only when I walked in – was that of Katkov.[1] I did not report the episode where Turgenev refused to shake hands with him[2] publicly during the Pushkin festivities – the only time he was ever rude to any Russian or any friend in public so far as I know – nor the fact that he called his gout 'katkovka'.[3] It would, I think, have been a little cruel. [...]

Yours, ⟨with love⟩
  Isaiah

TO OWEN CHADWICK[4]

27 November 1970 [carbon]

[Wolfson]

Dear Chadwick,

Alas, I know practically as little about Sir Isaac's actual interests in the arts and sciences as you do, but I suspect this is because there is not very much to know. I once had to write something about this myself for a remote publication[5] – I had to resort to general reflections on the fact that the aristocracy in England did very little for learning in the nineteenth and twentieth centuries and that this was left to merchant princes of various sorts, such as – I could not think of any prominent nineteenth-century ones, save towards the end of the century, and after a brief scamper over Joe Chamberlain at Birmingham, the Brothertons at Leeds, the Willses at Bristol, Boot at Nottingham, and finally Nuffield at Oxford, I came to the object of my attention – my benefactor.

Something can be said about the tradition of learning among even the poorest Jews in Russia and Eastern Europe generally, whence Solomon Wolfson – Isaac's father – came, and the fact that the thoughts of rich men of this particular type of origin turn instinctively towards the support of learning, whereas the thoughts of other rich men turn in very different directions, etc. But I fear I am doing very little to help you. Isaac is, of course, fanatically religious – a fundamentalist of a very simple kind so far as Judaism is concerned – and although I suspect he is not very erudite about either the theological or the historical aspects of the Jewish religion, his piety towards his father's memory, and his passionate conviction that discipline is what matters, have made him as powerful a supporter of his own historical

---

1 George Katkov (1903–85), Russian-born Fellow of St Antony's and University Lecturer in Soviet Institutions and Economics 1959–71. See also L2 71/6.

2 i.e. Mikhail Katkov, George Katkov's great-uncle (431/2).

3 'Katkovitis'. Letter to Mikhail Matveevich Stasyulevich, 23 May 1877, in I. S. Turgenev, Polnoe sobranie sochinenii i pisem (Moscow/Leningrad, 1960–8), Pis'ma, xii/1 160.

4 (William) Owen Chadwick (b. 1916), later KBE (1982), OM (1983); Master, Selwyn, Cambridge, 1956–83; Dixie Professor of Ecclesiastical History, Cambridge, 1958–68, Regius Professor of Modern History 1968–83.

5 'A Great Benefactor' [Isaac Wolfson], Rehovot [journal of the Weizmann Institute of Science and Yad Chaim Weizmann], Summer 1968, 18–21.

religion as – among men of wealth and influence – the Jews of this country have ever had.

I have a feeling – though this can surely detract rather than add to material for your speech – that he is like a mediaeval merchant who by building churches and monasteries, and subsidising paternosters and Ave Marias, feels that his relations with Heaven are solidly established, which liberates him for all kinds of purposes on Earth. This is precisely the kind of man he seems to me to be – jolly, energetic, gay, imaginative, with inexhaustible energy, affable, generous, addicted to religious observance like some Arab Sheikh – Ibn Saud,[1] say – and similarly engaged upon petty, ferocious forays in the world of big business. He rises early in the morning, devotes a good deal of time to prayer, and is then in his office, I suspect, before any of his staff. The Jewish holidays are observed with rigorous attention, and he demands the same from his family – knowing well that they must find it something of a nuisance, from time to time – but discipline is all. It is his son Leonard who is a passionate autodidact and reads Gibbon and Namier and Macaulay and Wheeler-Bennett,[2] and anything that anyone seriously recommends him, and has a genuine respect [for] and some understanding of what education, learning, the intellectual life in general are.

I fear that I have failed you: if you think of Isaac as identical with his Foundation, I am sure you cannot go far wrong. I shall come and listen to you with the greatest anticipation and pleasure.

Yours sincerely,

[Isaiah Berlin]

TO JAKOB HUIZINGA[3]

16 December 1970 [*carbon*]

[Wolfson]

Dear Mr Huizinga,

Of course I should have returned your typescript days and days ago – I read it with the greatest pleasure and amusement. I agree with what it is to the extent of about 65 per cent – if I could speak to you again perhaps this would rise, though of what possible importance is my agreement or disagreement? I think the only real ground for disagreement is this: you

---

1 Ibn Saud (*c.*1880–1953), first king of Saudi Arabia (1932–53), largely responsible for realising that country's huge potential oil wealth.

2 John Wheeler Wheeler-Bennett (1902–75), historian, official biographer of George VI; British government service, NY, 1939–45; Fellow, St Antony's, 1950–7; Historical Adviser, Royal Archives, from 1959.

3 Jakob Herman ('Jimmy') Huizinga (1908–94), distinguished London-based Dutch journalist and writer; worked with the Dutch information service in NY during the Second World War; biographer of Paul Henri Spaak.

think that Osborne's[1] explosive vulgarity and horrible slaps in the face of public taste are merely what they are – namely the expression of his own unattractive and ill-bred personality: I think that to a high degree they are precisely that – nevertheless the dialogue – at least as heard from the stage – I have not read his plays and do not intend to do so – is extremely skilfully contrived – the attention even of the most reluctant members of the audience (such as myself) is undoubtedly held – and I think there is considerable talent, if not of the highest order, in that; moreover, I do think that it probably does express the mood, though in a highly exaggerated and caricature fashion – but perhaps that is necessary in order to get through the 'crust' or 'cake' of custom if it is to penetrate at all – of the young men – not those of today, but those of yesterday – who had obtained much of what their fathers wanted for them – money, security, education, status etc., but nevertheless felt unhappy, 'alienated', i.e. not at home in our society, and could not think of the reason and became neurotic, disturbed, ill-tempered and, on the whole, anti-political (not like the young at the moment), with a fearful hatred of all slogans, all formulae, all ideals, everything that both right and left had formulated, and possessed by a general desire to pull down the whole thing and emerge into some kind of other world whose lineaments they could not even conceive. This is the mood of angry romanticism which you will find at other moments of human history, though not perhaps expressed with such coarseness or violence – e.g. in Germany towards the end of the eighteenth and beginning of the nineteenth century, and indeed even in France during certain moments, and among those poets and writers in Russia in, say, 1920 whose moods predate the 1917 Revolution, when it was fashionable to regard Pushkin as rubbish, Shakespeare as worthless, the whole ghastly load of bourgeois sensibility, and feudal sensibility too, as a hideous incubus upon the consciousness of 'real men' – an attitude which all the fathers of Russian Communism found odious and irresponsible. The more violent and fanatical they were politically, e.g. Lenin, the more conformist and conventional in their literary and artistic tastes – it was known as *Kulturbolschewismus*, and was condemned fiercely by the Russian revolutionaries, although much cultivated in Berlin, Hamburg etc., and had a good deal to do with the early moods of people like Auden, Isherwood etc. But I must not start a lecture on contemporary literature, consciousness etc., where I have no possible competence – thank you very much indeed for sending me your piece and I return it with gratitude.

Yours sincerely,

[Isaiah Berlin]

---

1 John James Osborne (1929–94), dramatist and actor. The English Stage Company's production of his play *Look Back in Anger* (1956) transformed post-war British theatre: its stark treatment of the mundane tedium of working-class life epitomised a new genre of 'kitchen-sink drama', while Osborne himself was regarded as the spokesman for a generation of 'angry young men'.

TO GABY COHEN

4 January 1971 [*carbon*]

[Headington House]

Dear Gaby,

[…] I am very sorry indeed not to be able to come to Israel this month – that I shall, alas, not be able to come, so far as I can see now, until this time next year: […] the news from the Middle East, as seen at this end, does not seem too encouraging – the ferocity of the Russians is not altogether easy to explain[1] – these things always have something to do with internal stresses and strains and not simply considerations of foreign policy; I assume therefore that discontent is more rife than correspondents report, although it will not shake the foundations of the State any more than it did at this time a hundred years ago. I am glad I am not a Russian historian, I mean a historian of Russia: it is too gloomy to have to write about a State in which the government is, with very rare intervals, always oppressive, cynical, cruel and opposed to every human end that either its citizens or anyone else regards as worth living for, and sometimes dying for – the only persons upon whom one can dwell with any degree of satisfaction are in bitter opposition to the State or at best indifferent to it – this is a record exceeded in no other country, I suspect, not even Spain or Turkey, which after all was very nice to its minorities. And this is a government which, despite everything, still engages the feelings, the affections, in some sense a kind of loyalty on the part of some people in Israel, which would come gushing forth, I suspect, if it showed the faintest sign of favour or even absence of disfavour! Can one talk of human emancipation when the ex-slaves still think fondly of the lash? […]

Yours,

[Isaiah]

TO PAUL GORE-BOOTH

6 January 1971 [*carbon*]

[Headington House]

Dear Paul,

I see with interest mingled with apprehension that the date of public access to Foreign Office documents is slowly and inexorably moving forward. Naturally my thoughts have veered towards certain of the telegrams and dispatches issued by the Ambassador (and sometimes others) from Washington

1 In a speech on 21 December 1970 the Soviet Prime Minister, Aleksey Kosygin, pledged Soviet support for the Arabs in their 'just struggle' against Israel. His speech came after high-level discussions in Moscow with an Egyptian delegation, the first such meeting to take place since the funeral of Nasser on 1 October: 'Now that we are here together with our Arab friends we can say with all certainty that the Israeli aggressors and those behind them will never reach the aims of their expansionist policy in the Middle East' (*Times*, 22 December 1970, 1e).

to London after 1942. I need not expatiate on the nature of their contents, which you will surely remember, although I probably, naturally enough, remember them more vividly. There was nothing particularly secret in them, as a rule, nor can I claim that the bulk of their contents necessarily proceeded from myself even in the first instance. It was in theory, and sometimes in practice, the product of collective intelligence. What worries me is that there is so much reflection on public personalities in the United States in the bulk of these writings, and some of it in pretty candid and sometimes positively ironical language, that if it were published, it would probably cause embarrassment and wounded feelings not only to friends and admirers and [the] posterity of persons mentioned, but in some cases, and I daresay quite numerous ones, to still surviving personages – Achesons, Harrimans and the like, not to speak of smaller fry. No doubt some of this material could be sequestered and not shown to historians and journalists, but that is always a difficult business, and I do not think that any security considerations could possibly come in to most of the material in question. On the other hand, I do not fancy entrance to America being barred to me for ever on the grounds of *lèse-Amerique*. I wondered therefore whether it might not be a good idea to allow some of this to be gone over and selected and published by serious and wholly qualified historians who would not be tempted merely by the more amusing bits of ephemeral gossip, of which the telegrams, necessarily, to some degree consisted.[1] [...]

Yours ever,

[Isaiah]

TO NICHOLAS HENDERSON[2]

8 February 1971 [*carbon*]

[Wolfson]

Dear Nicko,

You will, perhaps, by this time have had the letter from John Sparrow about Walicki. I had a genuinely heart-rending letter in which he did not spell anything out, but explained that he would love to come back to All Souls, or

1 A selection of the official documents was later published as *Washington Despatches 1941–45: Weekly Political Reports from the British Embassy* (London, 1981), edited by H. G. Nicholas (453/2), who had been IB's main contact in the Ministry of Information in London during the war: they proved reassuringly dull, one reviewer commenting that they veered 'from matters of local American concern (labour troubles etc.) to generalities so general one can only yawn one's way through' (LRB, 5 November 1981, 16–17). IB wrote the introduction, repr. in L1. Much less dull were the indiscreet 'bootleg' addenda to the official record, which IB sent to friends, chiefly Nicholas. Incompletely edited transcripts of the correspondence with Nicholas may be read at ⟨http://berlin.wolf.ox.ac.uk/published_works/f/lnicholas.pdf⟩.

2 (John) Nicholas Henderson (1919–2009), later (1972) KCMG; diplomat and author; PS to Foreign Secretary 1963–5; Minister in Madrid 1965–9; ambassador to Poland 1969–72, to Federal Republic of Germany 1972–5.

anywhere in Oxford, towards the end of this or the beginning of next year. I can imagine his state of mind very well indeed and am most anxious to help him.

If my College had any money to spend on anyone (at present we pay no one), I would willingly invite him to Wolfson; but since he needs money to live on, All Souls alone, where he has been before, can help him. However, I have told them that I am prepared to produce £500 from an educational trust towards their expenses, and this ought to soften their hearts. John Sparrow is perfectly well disposed towards Walicki, whom he likes; I am, as you now, devoted to him; but there are cynics in All Souls who say that if he is as genuinely miserable as his letter (suitable extracts translated into English and sent to the Committee) to me implies, why does he not want to come immediately, why only in October, or January 1972? The answer quite plainly is that he has duties, that he is not in personal danger, that these things take time bureaucratically, etc. etc. Anyway, the attitude of two or three of my ex-colleagues in All Souls on this matter is contemptible – the obstacles (not very formidable) which they put up are probably due as much to fear of some kind of ramp [which] the mere thought of the Warden of All Souls inspires in them as anything else. But the thought that, if not the physical security, at any rate the opportunity to live and breathe on the part of this worthy man, so easily secured at All Souls, which is, after all, not exactly poor, should depend on the whims, the local intrigues, of some very inferior persons maddens me.

You will have a letter from John in which he will ask you for information[1] [...]. I don't need to beg you to convey what it must be like for an honest and enlightened, and morally sensitive, man, engaged on a politically sensitive subject in any Polish university, to be there now. [...]

My love,
    [Isaiah]

I had better not have written you this letter: it contains so much bitter feeling about intolerable, if not named, characters. It seems a terrible thing to say, but perhaps your father[2] did well to die when he did: he would have been driven beyond the limits of even his great patience by those monsters. I sound like Rowse. It must be infectious.

IB spent from mid-February to early May 1971 in America, returning to England for the second week of April to visit his mother; Aline did not accompany him

---

1 IB clearly hoped that as Britain's ambassador to Poland Henderson would be able to further Walicki's case.
2 Hubert Douglas Henderson (1890–1952), Kt 1942, economist; Fellow of All Souls from 1934, Warden 1951–2, his tenure cut short by his death from coronary thrombosis.

for the second half of his stay. He visited Seattle (21–6 February), Vancouver (26 February to 3 March), Washington, Kansas, and Charleston, South Carolina.

TO JOHN WHEELER-BENNETT

19 February 1971 [*carbon*]

New York

Dearest John,

[...] The postal strike was absolutely splendid so far as I was concerned[1] – a heavenly period of freedom from letters from eccentric Indian graduates demanding immediate admission to Wolfson College, elderly American war protestors without degrees demanding the same, and other peculiar figures – as well as gloomy reports of delays in building, bankruptcy of various graduates already in situ, etc. etc. What can I tell you about events in our country? Things are not rising to a revolutionary crisis, so far as I can see. The postal workers are not really very pleased about the strike which their leaders have had to organise if they were to avoid the charge of doing less for their men than, say, the dockers have done for theirs,[2] which obviously endangered their position in the Union. Since nobody is actually starving or exploited, the majority seem to feel that they are merely losing money and are torn between short-term and long-term self-interest. The Common Market is a very big issue. Mr Powell[3] is quite successfully appealing to the Unions, who are likely to be his strongest supporters against wogs and Europeans, who are about equally hated – he assures the Unions that wage-demands if satisfied would have no effect on inflation, which pleases the Unions and drives the Treasury up a tree. I am fanatical about Europe simply because I think that we shall otherwise sink into political insignificance, economic straits and hideous provincialism, which is beginning already. Entering Europe will dislocate things in the short run and cause some misery, but staying out of it will ultimately turn us into Portugal or, at best, Sweden, which would be very sad. All the opponents, although ostensibly concerned about economic facts, standard of living, etc., are in fact possessed by fear and contempt for

1 An official strike by the Union of Post Office Workers lasted from 19 January to 8 March 1971; it was the longest national stoppage since the end of the war and the third major public sector strike that winter. The postal workers sought a 13 per cent pay increase, but opted to return to work without any increase on the 8 per cent offered.

2 A national dock strike had taken place from 16 July to 3 August 1970: the dockers settled for an increase of roughly 7 per cent.

3 (John) Enoch Powell (1912–98), Conservative MP for Wolverhampton SW, 1950–74; Minister of Health 1960–3. Powell was sacked from the Shadow Cabinet on 21 April 1968 for making what his leader, Edward Heath, judged a 'racialist' and potentially inflammatory speech (*Times*, 22 April 1968, 1b) against immigration in Birmingham (the so-called 'rivers of blood' speech). Free from front-bench responsibility, Powell became a trenchant critic of government policy; while not objecting in principle to the idea of European free trade he opposed Britain's accession to the EEC. He was later (1974–83) Ulster Unionist MP for Down South.

foreigners – England is far more isolationist than ever America was and this is a nervous condition preceding decline, inevitably it seems to me. I don't believe that there will be a spring election, and I agree with you that the country is not ready to enter Europe, but neither was it ready for war against Hitler. It should have been, but the price is always much higher if one waits for slow processes. [...]

Yours,

[Isaiah]

TO JEAN FLOUD

15 March 1971 [*manuscript*]

CUNY

Dearest Jean,

[...] New York is unaltered: I am terribly unobservant, so this may be disregarded: but *I* see no great change: The Trillings are also tremendously unaltered: Diana goes screeching on about the iniquities of the Left: Lionel sits there in a thin silvery light, smiling sadly at the irrationality and insensitiveness of friends, colleagues, mankind: how far superior is Edmund Wilson (do you know him? the last great man there is: a natural hero worshipper, I do worship him, pot belly bleary old eyes & all: beautiful, cool, infinitely sensitive quasi-Russian wife[1] of a distinction which reminds me of Mrs Woolf & makes Aline nervous) – Wilson who has been reading Solzhenitsyn[2] & Madame Mandelstamm[3] – & has now decided that the Russians are too horrible – nothing but torture, squalor, total failure of everybody, people *constantly* slipping into hideous horrible morasses for good & all – Russians are *all* sado-masochists, he has decided – and liars & bloodstained brutes or bleeding victims – too hurt, too black, too nauseating, he cannot go on with it at all – he who has written better on them than almost anyone. 'Tell me" he said 'tell me, was I, in your view too polite to Lenin in *The Finland Station?*"[4]

---

1 Elena Mumm Thornton Wilson (1906–79) née Helene-Marthe Mumm von Schwarzenstein, Edmund Wilson's fourth (and last) wife. They married in 1946; she was descended from Prussian aristocracy on her father's side, and from Russian nobility on her mother's.

2 Aleksandr Isaevich Solzhenitsyn (1918–2008), Russian novelist. *One Day in the Life of Ivan Denisovich*, which drew on his experience of eight years in the gulag, was published in 1962 during the era of Khrushchev's liberalisation, but in 1969 Solzhenitsyn was expelled from the Union of Soviet Writers, and the next year prevented from travelling to Stockholm to receive the Nobel Prize in Literature. He was arrested and exiled in 1974 in response to the publication abroad of *The Gulag Archipelago* (Russian language edition, Paris, late December 1973; first English translation London, 1974), but eventually returned to Russia in 1994.

3 Nadezhda Yakovlevna Mandel´shtam (1899–1980), Russian writer, widow of the Acmeist poet Osip Emil´evich Mandel´shtam (1891–1938), who died en route to a Siberian labour camp; Nadezhda's memoirs (1970, 1972), trans. Max Hayward as *Hope Against Hope* and *Hope Abandoned* (London, 1971, 1974), depicted, respectively, her husband's persecution and death, and her experience of widowhood, all set against a backdrop of Stalinist repression and cultural degradation.

4 *To the Finland Station* (1940), a study in the evolution of European socialism and revolution from

I did tell him in the past that Lenin was a cold monster, whereas he used to say that L. was very kind to party members & helped comrades sweetly & effectively: "Yes", I said 'you were." 'I'll change *all* that in the next edition" he said: like obituary writers who, having learnt more about their "subjects" – send to *The Times* for their texts & blacken them a bit, while "the subject" peacefully browses somewhere in Pembroke. Dr Pidduck of Corpus[1] used to do that. I have just returned from Seattle (fresh & quite gay) & Vancouver (heavily British & beautiful) & Kansas (where I defended Herbert against a Prof. who thought his report[2] much too *patronizing* about students – as if these latter weren't *just* as capable of intellectual & social judgment as the dreary limited profs – I defended H. with spirit – astonished at my own pugnacity – if you think of me as mild & conciliatory, you must speak to those at the U. of Kansas, ha!) & to return to the original sentence, am now back. Oh Miss Himmelweit![3] such trouble she is giving! & the Carmel college-trained Mr Chanan![4] Oh the Jews! Alles die Juden![5] If only they wd be silent for *just* a half hour or so – instead of raising their arms & asking me (at Seattle): "how do you feel, Professor, about the world revolution now in progress and its fully justified desire to destroy the present government of the United States?" What cd I say (feebly) "I haven't thought about this in connection with *Kant* (subject of my lecture) but I do see that it is a question which might [...] occupy one's mind". – Oh dear! I *love* being away from affairs – but am also conscious, as you never, *never* are, of being an itinerant comedian moving from one one-night-stand to another: not *like* a comedian but literally one. [...]

    Yours

      Isaiah

Michelet to Marx and Engels; it concludes with character studies of Trotsky and Lenin.

1 Frederick Bernard Pidduck (1885–1952), mathematician, Fellow of CCC 1921–50. 'He was a man of high principles, with rigid and unrelenting standards [...], and both colleagues and pupils had to live up to these if they were not to forfeit his regard' (*Times*, 2 July 1952, 8e).

2 Herbert Hart's 1969 report on staff–student relations at Oxford (355 / 1).

3 Susan Felicity Himmelweit (b. 1948), economist; Wolfson graduate student in maths 1969–74. 'It so happened that several of the leaders of the student revolution of the late 1960s were in Wolfson. The Berlins solved one impending outrage – the plan to empty a bag of soot over the head of some statesman at the Union – by inviting them all to a party. George Smith recalls seeing Isaiah at 60 Banbury Road in an armchair surrounded by students on the floor, the classical scene.' Michael Argyle, 'Isaiah Berlin and the Creation of Wolfson College', a slightly revised text of a speech given at the College's Foundation Dinner on 20 June 1998, *College Record 1997–98*.

4 Michael Asher Chanan (b. 1946), documentary film-maker, writer and teacher; Wolfson graduate student in philosophy 1968–74, when he worked with IB, while also writing music criticism and making films on contemporary music for the BBC. 'I was hardly a model philosophy student, but bonded with Isaiah through our shared love of music': ⟨www.mchanan.com/who-me/⟩. Carmel College in Oxfordshire was a principally Jewish co-educational boarding school, founded in 1948 (closed 1997), where Chanan spent three years before attending Kilburn Grammar School.

5 'All the Jews!'

TO BERNARD WALL[1]

13 April 1971 [carbon]

[CUNY; as from] Wolfson

Dear Bernard,

I entirely sympathise with you about the Latin Liturgy,[2] but I do think that it would perhaps not be in the best of taste for me to appeal to the Pope on this topic; in fact, I think, if not the kiss of death it would certainly weaken the position. But, my God, similar things happen in other faiths – abandonment of Hebrew, Greek etc. I feel the same – and so far as Hebrew in the Synagogue is concerned, if there were a real threat to that I should be in the streets tomorrow.

Yours,

[Isaiah]

TO ALEXANDER GERSCHENKRON[3]

21 April 1971 [carbon]

New York

Drazhaishiy![4]

This is only to warn you that I propose to telephone to you one of these days in order to enquire after your health and general well-being, and views on the *massimi problemi* of our day. All I know is that you have printed a chapter which leaves our friend, E. H. Carr, sprawling on the ground[5] – so Alexander Erlich[6] informs me – he also informs me that the attention

1 Bernard Wall (1908–74), author, translator, and (with his wife, Barbara) Catholic activist and commentator; wrote a regular column in the *Catholic Herald*; closely involved, 1967–73, in the movement to reinstate the traditional Latin Mass.

2 In order to encourage greater lay participation in its rites the Roman Catholic Church granted permissions, from the mid-1960s, for the celebration of most of the mass in the vernacular; this resulted in the widespread displacement of Latin, and among the many signatories to a July 1971 appeal to the Vatican to preserve the traditional Latin mass were Vladimir Ashkenazy, Maurice Bowra, Agatha Christie, Graham Greene, Joan Sutherland and Yehudi Menuhin (*Times*, 6 July 1971, 5a–b).

3 Alexander Gerschenkron (1901–78), economic historian; taught at Harvard from 1948, first Walter S. Barker Professor of Economics 1956–75. His father, Henryk, a Bund political activist, was executed by the Soviet secret police in 1941.

4 'Dearest'.

5 Gerschenkron's treatment of industrialisation in 19th-century Europe had been severely criticised by E. H. Carr in a 1967 essay, and in May 1968, in one of Gerschenkron's Ellen McArthur Lectures at Cambridge, Carr, in the eyes of one reviewer, was 'justly repaid in kind and with interest due', 'roasted alive – or thrown in the dustbin of (economic) history, if you prefer': John P. McKay, *Journal of Modern History* 43 (1971), 134. Carr's attack, 'Some Random Reflections on Soviet Industrialisation', is in C. H. Feinstein (ed.), *Socialism, Capitalism and Economic Growth: Essays Presented to Maurice Dobb* (Cambridge, 1967), and Gerschenkron's rebuttal is in *Europe in the Russian Mirror: Four Lectures in Economic History* (Cambridge, 1971).

6 Alexander Erlich (1912–85), Russian-born economist of the Soviet Union, of Jewish descent; taught at Columbia from 1955, associate professor 1959–66, professor of economics 1966–81.

you have given to his utterances does him too much honour, and that you use powerful weapons of war to blow a very small and unworthy ship out of the water. However, I have not read this, and the fact that you should have done this gives me, naturally, the liveliest satisfaction. The notion of 'serve him right' is based on the retributive theory of punishment, which is indeed the only theory that gives the notion of punishment any significance (surely?). If we are to follow Baroness Wootton[1] and other modern thinkers and the whole purpose of punishment is to deter, reform, educate (these were defences used by the Inquisition), the notion of poetic justice, and to some degree of justice in general, becomes vacuous. So I applaud your act not only on personal, but on the loftiest universal, grounds, à la Hegel. But do ring me up at the above number, or, alternatively, I shall do the same to you. I feel unhappy if I do not know that you are well and 'doing your thing'. My warmest regards to your wife.

Yours sincerely,
Isaiah
[...]

TO ARTHUR SCHLESINGER

22 April 1971 [*no salutation or signature*]

CUNY

Thank you very much for sending me Yost's piece.[2] It is a perfectly decent statement, but too official to be of the slightest use. If the Jews and Arabs were all members of the Century Club, they would listen to such homilies and profit by them. He shows, alas, no sense whatever of what really moves either Arabs or Jews (at least so far as I can tell). [...] What Yost says about the fact that territory never gave security is, alas, not true, and a mere cliché, as indeed most of his article is – well-meant, sincere, decent, careful as all his clichés are. The Russians certainly secured themselves from attack from Germans and Scandinavians in the North by acquiring Baltic ports; Italy stopped being invaded when she occupied her Northern frontiers, Alpine passes etc.; it is inconceivable that Israel could have won the Six-Day War if she did not possess anything in the Negev etc. However, I am no strategist and all this may be nonsense, but I do not believe in the general proposition that security flows only from agreements ⟨dishonest if the UN is too well followed⟩. I am all in favour of having mixed American–Russian etc. forces all over the place, and generally not leaving the Jews and Arabs to glare at each

1 Barbara Frances Wootton (1897–1988) née Adam, life peer 1958, economist and social scientist. As a member of the Penal Advisory Council 1966–79 she led a subcommittee whose report, September 1970, recommended non-/semi-custodial alternatives to prison sentences.

2 Charles Woodruff Yost (1907–81), US diplomat and writer; served in Foreign Service intermittently 1930–71; nominated as the permanent US Representative to the UN 1969, and was an adviser to Nixon and Kissinger on the Middle East; resigned 1971 to concentrate on writing and teaching.

other. Also I wish the Israelis to get out of as large a portion of the West Bank as they possibly can, and not govern all those Arabs – under a million, but still a great many – who at present live there. […] I cannot help feeling that words cost less than territory – nothing that Sadat[1] says need be remembered by his successors, whereas a frontier is a frontier even in these days. However, I am rightly suspected of excessive doveishness by the Israelis I come across (very few now), but even I would not recommend them to accept the Yost plan unless they are ready for suicide for reasons of pure courtesy – just not to be such a fearful bore to everybody, which they have been, are being, are likely to be increasingly in our lifetime. In short, I do not feel optimistic – but the chance of a major war as the result of a confrontation in the Middle East I regard as extremely improbable, and – again I may be hopelessly wrong – U Thant's dire warnings have on me the effect that Leonid Andreev's somewhat hysterical writings had on Tolstoy, 'He is screaming, but I am not frightened.'[2] I just do not believe that major wars occur when both sides are as determined as they are at present not to have one. If it really began to look menacing the Arabs and Jews would start behaving very differently, as the poor Czechs did, the example of whose fate – denounced as they were as oppressors of the Sudeten Germans – obviously does not leave the Israeli memory. […] I suspect Mr Yost would have been for Munich, as William Hayter[3] was, for the most sane, rational and high-minded motives. Yet in principle the German – or Austrian – claim to the Sudetenland was certainly no worse than that of the Arabs to Palestine. My feeling is very simple: if Dayan, Sadat's tough officers, and someone from here – even Nixon himself – could come to any arrangement, it would stick. Otherwise I doubt it.

TO MIRIAM GROSS[4]

4 May 1971

CUNY

Dear Miriam,

Thank you very much for suggesting that I review Nadezhda Mandelstam.[5]

1 Anwar El Sadat (1918–81), Vice-President of Egypt 1964–6, 1969–70, President 1970–81 in succession to Nasser; led Egypt into the Yom Kippur War, 1973, but later sought peace with Israel, and shared 1978 Nobel Peace Prize with Menachem Begin; assassinated by Islamic fundamentalists.

2 Leonid Nikolaevich Andreev (1871–1919), Russian expressionist writer, dramatist and amateur photographer; his plays dwelt on the desolation of the period between the revolutions of 1905 and 1917; after the October Revolution he emigrated to Finland, where he died. The remark attributed to Tolstoy appears in various forms, not including IB's: most commonly 'He tries to scare me, but I am not frightened.'

3 William Goodenough Hayter (1906–95), KCMG 1953, diplomat, UK ambassador to USSR 1953–7; Warden of New College 1958–76.

4 Miriam Marianna Gross (Lady Owen) (b. 1938) née May; married, 1965, John Gross (divorced 1988), 1993 (Sir) Geoffrey Owen; literary editor and freelance journalist; deputy literary editor, Observer, 1969–81.

5 Hope against Hope (445/3).

I wish I could: but apart from not having time to do this marvellous book justice, I really haven't the resources: it harrowed me frightfully. I thought it was one of the most noble, disciplined, superior, and devastating books I had ever read – more depressing in its quiet way than Solzhenitsyn – but if I said what I thought it would embarrass me: I hate baring my soul in public, and in this case nothing less would do – it cannot be reviewed simply, like another such book. It conveyed all the horror that I felt when I was in Russia, both in 1945 and 1956. I used to ask myself what I would do if I suddenly turned out to be a Soviet citizen, as I might very well have been, and it was clear that in that event I should blow my brains out: I should not wish to survive. All this was brought home in the most fearful way by this exceedingly formidable book. [...]

    Yours ever,

      Isaiah

On 13 May Sir Michael Adeane, the Queen's Private Secretary, wrote inviting IB to accept the Order of Merit. This honour, in the sole personal gift of the Sovereign, was founded by Edward VII to be given to 'such persons, subjects of Our Crown, as may have rendered exceptionally meritorious services in Our Crown Services, or towards the advancement of the Arts, Learning, Literature and Science, or such other exceptional service as We see fit to recognise'.[1] After agonising for a few days IB accepted on 18 May. Adeane informed him that the news would be announced from the Palace on the evening of Thursday 27 May, for the newspapers the following morning: 'This will allow you to take avoiding action if you feel that this is really necessary. On the other hand it will not prevent you from receiving the congratulations of your friends, among whom, I hope, I may be allowed to include myself.'[2] IB was genuinely in a quandary about whether or not to accept, a reflection of his habitual lack of self-confidence: 'Hence neurotic spin on my part – shd I refuse? Would that be worse still? etc. etc. etc. Of course I snapped out of this in due course: but I depressed poor Aline quite a lot in the process: instead of mad joy, mad soul searching & embarrassment.'[3]

TO DAVID CECIL

    2 June 1971 [*carbon*]

                                              [Wolfson]

Dear David,

    [...] Thank you very much for your telegram. I wish I could tell you what

1 Stanley Martin, *The Order of Merit: One Hundred Years of Matchless Honour* (London, 2007), 566 (the Statutes are not officially published in full).
2 Letter of 24 May 1971.
3 To Jack Donaldson, 4 June 1971.

I feel, but I am in a somewhat confused state. When the letter arrived from the Palace, my first feeling was one of embarrassment thickening into positive gloom; on the one hand the overestimate of my deserts seemed to me so absurd, I thought that if I accepted it the whole thing would be too incongruous, and there would be too much just indignation, quite apart from the dark emotions which such things inevitably stir in academic and other hearts; on the other hand this was, of course, the most vast compliment ever paid to me, or likely to be paid to me in my life. If I took a view of myself, as it were, from outside and asked myself: do I really begin to belong to the class that included Gilbert Murray,[1] Russell, G. E. Moore (I was partly involved in his getting it), Rutherford[2] and the rest? – the answer was very plain. I felt like Groucho Marx: 'I wouldn't want to join the kind of club that would want to make me a member.' What had I done? No big book. Only a series of pamphlets – if someone like G. N. Clark[3] was given it, I would think it rather dull, but not inappropriate. Could I begin comparing myself with, for example, yourself (I mean this in no spirit of flattery), who has written so much and so well and occupied a position altogether – and properly – superior to mine? Or even K. Clark for his general public prominence and identification, as it were, with bringing culture to the people? Either Clark, it seemed to me, is more suitable; or some terrific scientist: surely one must either have committed an act of genius – either by way of a scientific discovery or some transformation of the whole direction of a subject – or have created a work of art or genius; or at least, if it was not a question of a knockout blow, have scored adequately on points and created a general pattern of work and influence (like Miss Nightingale)[4] which raised one to the required eminence. I remember how indignant I was when Solly got it because I thought that it inflated the currency – would I not feel this about myself, if I could contemplate myself from outside? Were these merely neurotic feelings? I was sure that they were not. So I telephoned Aline and told her that a terrible thing had happened. 'What?' she asked. 'I have been offered an honour.' 'What, the top thing? A peerage?' 'No. Much worse. I would refuse a peerage without

1 (George) Gilbert Aimé Murray (1866–1957), classical scholar and liberal internationalist; Regius Professor of Greek, Oxford, 1908–36; a prominent figure in the League of Nations, 'seen even in his lifetime as a kind of secular saint' (Christopher Stray, ODNB); OM 1941.

2 Ernest Rutherford (1871–1937), Kt 1914, 1st Baron Rutherford of Nelson and Cambridge 1931, born in New Zealand, scientist regarded as the founder of nuclear physics; Langworthy Professor and Director, Physics Laboratories, Manchester, 1907–19; Cavendish Professor of Experimental Physics and Director, Cavendish Laboratory, Cambridge, 1919–37; Nobel Prize in Chemistry 1908, OM 1925.

3 George Norman Clark (1890–1979), Kt 1953, historian; Chichele Professor of Economic History and Fellow of All Souls 1931–43; Regius Professor of Modern History and Fellow of Trinity, Cambridge, 1943–7; Provost of Oriel 1947–57; Fellow of All Souls 1961–75.

4 Florence Nightingale (1820–1910), reformer of nursing organisation and Army Medical Services; led a private nursing expedition to the Crimean War in 1854, and at the army hospital at Scutari oversaw a dramatic improvement in the standards of care; an iconic figure in Victorian Britain, she was appointed to the OM 1907.

the slightest hesitation if only on the ground that I do not wish ever to be obliged to make a speech in the House of Lords, or be pressed by people who thought it my moral duty to speak on this or that issue – no, no. Much, much worse.' 'What?' 'The OM,' I said, apparently with a kind of moan of despair. At the same time, of course, I felt tremendously exhilarated, as if I was about to be transformed from a charcoal-burner into some sort of caliph. I wondered who was responsible for advising the Queen. Wheeler-Bennett, I decided, and I think I am probably right. Then I went home and Aline and I got ourselves into a state of real gloom. My God, I thought, what will Maurice say? – his heart was really set on it. Will he finally have a stroke, and will I be the cause of his demise, if I accept it? Would Rowse insult me in public? I really would be unable to bear it; even Miss Wedgwood's OM – and he is devoted to her – appeared to him thoroughly unworthy and unde-served.[1] He really might have a terrible outburst. This at least compelled me along a line of comical reflections. (Maurice, as it turned out, took it all quite well. 'Do you think', he said, 'that they are saying at St John's "The best piece of news since Blake's peerage"?[2] Or "That will put Bowra in his place"?') So I went brooding on, unable to say yes or no, and in this horrid condition some days passed, indeed four or five days, during which I could not make up my mind. Would I make myself ridiculous by accepting it? That is really what bothered me, I suppose. Would people be too indignant? If I thought they were wrong to be so, then I was quite prepared to be priggish and say to hell with them – but would I share their feeling, and if so was it really all right to accept? [...] The only person I talked to was John Sparrow, who was very sympathetic, and finally, when I expounded all the arguments against taking it on the ground that I should myself be somewhat indignant if someone like myself received it and I were a spectator watching from outside, said 'Well, if you feel like that about it, then perhaps I should refuse.' At this point I realised that I had no wish to do so, and went home and wrote a polite letter of acceptance.

Meanwhile, the Palace had waited for some eight days and had sent secret messages to my secretaries asking whether any reply to Adeane's[3] letter had been sent, and begging them not to let me know that any such enquiries were on foot. Once I had replied and discovered when it was to be pub-

---

1 Veronica Wedgwood was appointed OM in 1969, only the third woman thus honoured (after Florence Nightingale in 1907 and Dorothy Hodgkin in 1965). A. L. Rowse had taught Wedgwood at Oxford, and considered her an outstanding pupil, but believed that the honour that went to her should have gone to him: 'She has my OM' (Donald Adamson, 'A. L. Rowse: An Appreciation', *International Literary Quarterly* no. 6, February 2009, ⟨http://interlitq.org/issue6/donald_adamson/job.php⟩). Wedgwood's dedicated public service included work on behalf of the National Gallery and Victoria and Albert Museum.

2 Robert Norman William Blake (1916–2003), later (1971) life peer; historian, biographer of Disraeli; Student and Tutor in Politics, Christ Church, 1947–68; Provost, Queen's, 1968–87.

3 Michael Edward Adeane (1910–84), KCVO 1951, later (1972) life peer; PS to the Queen and Keeper of HM's Archives 1953–72; Extra Equerry to the Queen from 1972.

lished, I arranged to flee the country, as I thought the press would be too embarrassing and would try and collect anecdotes, etc. But all this proved mere vanity, and apart from one foolish story in the *Sunday Times* – funny, though not true, certainly funny enough to be published – nothing except a very inaccurate account in *The Times* appeared.[1] Aline felt that we were exactly like criminals who had committed a fearful offence which they knew would be discovered on a given day, and couldn't possibly stay to face the music. I do not regard myself as abnormally neurotic, but in this particular situation, silence does seem to me to entail at least a *prima facie* case of mild disapproval (like William Hayter, who, on meeting Aline in the street, said he had not written because he simply did not know what to say!). I expect I shall get used to it all and it is, of course, marvellous. I am very proud and pleased, and I am being given a party by my College at which somebody will make a speech and I will answer, and everything will be as it should be, and a lot of good feeling (I hope) will pour forth.

Nevertheless, I can't be altogether wrong, can I, in feeling that either the standards in everything are declining, as I expect they are, or that I have been wildly over-rewarded? I expect it is all due to a hideous lack of self-confidence which nothing will cure. I apologise for having poured all this out before you, but to whom else could I possibly write? And yet I longed to write to someone and say how very unlike what most people must imagine my feelings to be they actually were, and not at all Tolstoyan about this. I do not think that honours are nonsense; that pleasure in them is contemptible vanity; that everything which marks out and divides men is a source of envy and therefore should be abolished. I believe the contrary of all this: that the more variety, badges, hopes fulfilled and frustrated, emulation (provided that I do not have to take part in the competition), the gayer, the more aesthetically delightful, the more variety, and oddity, and eccentricity, and ups and downs, and unexpected turns and twists, the more defiance of all the box-like forms of life, the rules and regularities, and nervousness about overstepping the mark, and fear of attracting notice. In fact, funnily enough, what in his grotesque lunatic way Rowse is in favour of and Wykehamists are against. Yet my beliefs are obviously quite different from the way in which I in fact react and behave. But I won't go on with this tedious auto-psychoanalysis.

This is only to say that I really am grateful to you for your letter – it restores confidence, it really does bring me back to myself, and I can walk the streets a little more firmly without fear of looking absurdly inflated to my friends and colleagues and neighbours. The funniest letter of all came from Herbert Nicholas[2] in a donnish parody of a letter from the loyal tenantry congratulat-

---

1 IB was described as 'President of Wolfson College and Chichele Professor of Social and Political Theory' (28 May 1971, 1e), but he had resigned the latter post at the end of the academic year 1966–7.

2 Herbert George Nicholas (1911–98), Nuffield Reader in the Comparative Study of Institutions,

ing the squire; the most unexpected from an old New College charwoman who rambled on mainly about the disorder in Sir Christopher Cox's[1] room and his peculiar goings-on. What is still oddest of all is the extreme embarrassment of those who really don't know what to say to one's face and hide behind all kinds of masks of irony and banter, beginning to say something and then interrupting themselves and pretending they really want to talk about something else, etc. etc.

Maurice was very much like his old self. 'Anything from Trevor-Roper?' 'No.' 'No, nor did I. Anything from Goodhart?' 'Yes.' 'Oh. I didn't get anything from him; that's very unusual. What about the Cabinet. Anybody?' Etc. So I end on a note of familiarity and cosiness.

Do let us meet again. I still feel discombobulated. Do you find this strange, foolish, idiotic? If you do, you are right.

Yours ever,

[Isaiah]

TO FRED RIDLEY[2]

21 June 1971

Wolfson

Dear Professor Ridley,

I have just been sent a copy of Mr Arblaster's[3] blast against me – for I was out of the country when the relevant issue of *Political Studies* appeared and had not seen it. I suspect that you normally do not print letters or rejoinders, and if this is your principle I do not wish to ask you to break it for my benefit. On the other hand, the piece is so offensive and contains so little substance, and is so nastily personal in tone, that perhaps it would be wrong of me to pass over it in silence, as I should be strongly inclined to do. I remember Mr

Oxford, 1956–69; Rhodes Professor of American History and Institutions 1969–78; Fellow of New College 1951–78.

1 Christopher William Machell Cox (1899–1982), KCMG 1950; ancient historian and educationalist; Fellow of New College 1926–70; an adviser to successive government ministries dealing with overseas education and development 1940–70; IB felt great warmth towards Cox, a long-standing Oxford friend.

2 Frederick Fernand Ridley (b. 1928), Professor of Political Theory and Institutions, Liverpool, 1965–95; editor, *Political Studies*, 1969–75.

3 Anthony Edmund Arblaster (b. 1937), previously a journalist on the staff of *Tribune*, taught politics from 1970 at Sheffield, where he later (1989–2000) became Reader in Politics. He is the author of *The Rise and Decline of Western Liberalism* (Oxford, 1984) and *Viva la libertà! Politics in Opera* (London, 1992). His notorious attack on IB, 'Vision and Revision: A Note on the Text of Isaiah Berlin's *Four Essays on Liberty*', *Political Studies* 19 no. 1 (1971), 81–6, implies that IB was disingenuous when he stated in his introduction to the book that he had not made substantive alterations to the texts of the component essays. In particular he mocks IB's alterations in his lists of names: 'In the earlier version the list [which in the later version begins "From Zeno to Spinoza, from the Gnostics to Leibniz, from Thomas Hobbes to Lenin and Freud"] began with "From Plato to Lucretius", continued with the Gnostics and Leibniz, but had Thomas Aquinas, instead of Thomas Hobbes, almost as if it had to be Thomas somebody.'

Arblaster as an undergraduate here, and his performance seems to be wholly in keeping with his known character and ambitions, although I am naturally sorry that you should have allowed your excellent periodical (I thought the last two issues particularly interesting because of the proportion of political theory) to forward them. I ought to add that I have no wish to enter into controversy with Mr Arblaster, as he does not seem to me worthy of any decent person's steel – and if the publication of my rejoinder (which need not take the form of a letter, if you prefer that) stimulates him to a reply which you will in turn think it right to publish, I will not for my part reply to that.

I leave the matter in your hands.

Yours sincerely,

Isaiah Berlin

TO THE EDITOR OF *POLITICAL STUDIES*

21 June 1971 [*typescript draft corrected by hand*]

Wolfson

A short rejoinder to Mr Arblaster

Sir,

I should never have dreamt of commenting on Mr Arblaster's reflections (in your March issue) about the changes of view or emphasis in *Four Essays on Liberty*; but he goes further and casts doubts on my integrity, and this I cannot pass by in silence. There is a point, as someone once remarked, at which forbearance ceases to be a virtue. I fail to see why my explicit and exact statement at the beginning of the Introduction to my book, that I have made no radical changes, while those that I have introduced are due to my wish to remove errors and obscurities in the earlier version, should not be regarded as a sufficient explanation for every one of the revisions so painstakingly collated by Mr Arblaster. I do not, of course, dispute anyone's right to question, however harshly, my interpretations of Hobbes or Mill or Freud (I may remark that Mr Arblaster's attempt to correct me on Spinoza rests on a complete blunder on his part: Spinoza has no doctrine of the will), or for that matter Engels or Lenin (why should Mr Arblaster assume me to suppose that knowledge to a Marxist means theory divorced from practice?). But Mr Arblaster has no right, without adducing evidence, to impute to me disreputable motives, and what amounts to an unscrupulous and random use of historical references. This seems to me an objectionable insinuation and particularly out of place in a scholarly or intellectually serious journal.

Yours sincerely,

Isaiah Berlin

TO ROWLAND BURDON-MULLER

22 June 1971

Wolfson

Dearest Rowland,

Thank you very much for your very kind letter. Naturally when I received the letter about the Order of Merit I was immediately plunged into gloom. To begin with, any form of public prominence depresses me; secondly, it was so clear to me that my 'merit' had been wildly overestimated that it seemed to me that what is so clear to myself must surely be clear to everyone else [...]. Believe me, it is not modesty, either true or false that is speaking, but a flat perception of the facts.

I am sorry that you should have to leave your flat in Boston, but I see that it cannot be avoided. Will you enjoy life in Switzerland? It is a nice, quiet part of the world and comfortable and civilised, and central, and you will be able to make comparatively short journeys without any great *bousculades*,[1] and anyway you will be nearer us, and be able to come here [...].

What more can I tell you? We shall be going to the Encaenia[2] lunch at which there is a march of old friends – Auden, Anthony Blunt, Steven Runciman,[3] who are getting honorary degrees here; perhaps they will set off Heath and various officials to whom these things go semi-automatically. What about the Common Market? Have you views on that? I think it is uncommonly brave of Roy Jenkins[4] to come out for it as he has done; Wilson will surely lose face – having come out in favour of it in the past, the manoeuvre by which he now pretends that the terms are not sufficiently good, or at any rate that he must scrutinise them very closely before declaring that we cannot possibly go in, when in fact the terms are, if anything, slightly better than those which the Labour Government was perfectly prepared to accept in the past when de Gaulle stamped on it all, will show him to be the opportunist that he clearly is. All politicians are, but some of them have the skill to avoid the appearance of it. Wilson curiously enough – it is a kind of simplicity and naivety in the end – has not managed to do this. America and England are in the same trough – nobody wants anybody as leader – neither the present

---

1 'Stampedes'.

2 The summer ceremony at which honorary Oxford degrees are awarded and benefactors commemorated: from the Greek for 'dedication festival'. That year's ceremony was held on Wednesday 23 June; among the honorands was the Prime Minister, Edward Heath.

3 James Cochran Stevenson ('Steven') Runciman (1903–2000), Kt 1958, historian; author of a celebrated three-volume *History of the Crusades* (London, 1951–4); of independent means, he held no tenured academic post after 1945, but lectured widely; awarded an Honorary D.Litt. at Oxford 1971.

4 Roy Harris Jenkins (1920–2003), later life peer (1987) and OM (1993); biographer and Labour and Social Democrat politician; Minister of Aviation 1964–5, Home Secretary 1965–7, Chancellor of the Exchequer 1967–70, Home Secretary 1974–6; later President of the European Commission (1977–81) and Chancellor, Oxford (1987–2003).

ones nor anyone in sight. It is a melancholy spectacle and I cannot conceive what will emerge out of it all. The loss of confidence in America is an absolutely startling fact to me – the fact that no purple-faced men can now get up at commencements and deliver the old Republican addresses on clean-limbed young men with faith in God and their family, out to make their way in the world and serve society, etc. – cannot do it not merely because of fear of being barracked but because they have themselves lost inner confidence and such addresses sound a little silly to them – this is a new and startling fact which could not have been foretold even as little as ten years ago. On this melancholy note I end my letter of gratitude.

Yours ever,

Isaiah   [...]

TO A. J. AYER

20 July 1971 [*dictated 12 July*]

[Paraggi]

Dear Freddie,

Thank you for your letter about the Common Market. I qualify on all grounds – I don't support the present Government, I am entirely in favour of entering the Common Market, but I have signed two manifestos already on this subject – one sent to me by Lord Gladwyn, the other by someone else whose name I cannot recollect – and do not think I can go on signing such documents, for fear of making myself ridiculous, nor do I think that it will make the faintest difference to Wilson, as he knows what intellectuals feel and could not care less, I think.

I was inexpressibly shocked about Maurice, too.[1] He was coming to stay with us here. When the telegram arrived I suddenly realised what an enormous gap it would leave in my life, who had known Maurice for almost all of my adult life. I am sure the same is true of you and others. I have got to deliver an *éloge* at St Mary's on Saturday, and am returning for the purpose, but I shall not do it very well, but having been ordered to do it I could not very well decline. Kenneth Clark, I expect, would have done it better. He died fairly suddenly, I gather, after about an hour of pain – I imagine he would have wished it this way: swift, tidy, over quickly. He seems to me to have been a tremendous liberator in our youth – he certainly made a difference to me. You, I think, were freer than I was already then, and still are, and did not need quite so many conventions and inhibitions broken through. He talked about death for so many years that nothing would be more terrible

1 Bowra had died in Wadham on 4 July 1971; he was buried in the nearby churchyard of St Cross. IB learned of his death while in Jerusalem, but returned to Oxford (from Paraggi) especially to deliver the address (included in PI) at Bowra's memorial service on 17 July, held in the University Church of St Mary's.

than a long illness and terror at the end of it, for him. So it might have been much, much worse.

On second thoughts why shouldn't I sign endless numbers of manifestos about the Common Market? – and I have sent off the letter to George Weidenfeld[1] anyway.

Yours,

[Isaiah]

TO ROWLAND BURDON-MULLER

19 July 1971

Paraggi (as from Wolfson College)

Dearest Rowland,

I enjoyed your last letter very much indeed. I am very sorry that you should have to embark on this piece of *déménagement*[2] in the hot summer (I pay no attention to your age – you are marvellously well preserved – if I were as well when I am 70 as you are now, I should really not complain). I realise, of course, that America is not for the old, but Europe is; and the idea of the Swiss hotel is excellent and we shall see more of you, and this will be a source of great pleasure. One does not see people simply because they live too far away, and too many things clutter one's life, one does not choose wisely, one allows events, and persons, and things to dictate one's conduct rather than determine them oneself – at least this is the truth about me and I expect Aline, too. You have always carved your own path in a very enviable and admirable manner.

What you say about Maurice Bowra is perfectly true. I really am deeply upset. He did a very great deal for me when I was very young – he was the most talked-about person in Oxford, parents trembled about the wicked influence he might have on their children, although he was always very positive and a major-key sort of figure, and all that shouting staccato utterance and special style which affected people like Connolly and Evelyn Waugh, and all of us so much, was due to a fearful inner insecurity. When one came to know him he was a very sweet and touching man, and genuinely life-giving and warm-hearted, but he must have been wounded early in his youth, and the rest of his life was emotionally with the poachers, even when he officially crossed over to the gamekeepers, and that is what made him ultimately a friend and an ally – he never did join the pompous establishment, the majority. He was for what he called the 'immoral front' – all the minorities

---

1 (Arthur) George Weidenfeld (b. 1919), Kt 1969, later (1976) life peer, publisher; born in Vienna, emigrated to Britain 1938 at the time of the Anschluss; co-founded, with Nigel Nicolson, the publishing firm Weidenfeld & Nicolson; Chairman from 1948; published and gave its famous title to IB's *The Hedgehog and the Fox* 1953.

2 '(Household) removal'. RB-M, in his 80th year, was planning a move to Lausanne in 1972.

who were disapproved of by the stolid 'silent majority'. On Vietnam he felt as strongly as you, although he was very unpolitical. Still, he was for the workers in the General Strike of 1926, defiantly anti-Fascist and anti-Nazi always, and signed too many letters to the press protesting against every form of oppression, and repression. Some people mocked him for this, and talked about having letter-signer's bursitis, etc. I found it sometimes a little comical, but always honourable, brave and right. Anyway, that stream is now dry and I really lament. I shall miss him fearfully.

You speak of not being too closely bound to material possessions. All very well, but as one grows older surely one does become attached to objects, rooms, familiar landmarks, as one's mobility grows more restricted? You mustn't go too Buddhist – my poor friend Elliott Felkin[1] preached this doctrine, and wished to detach himself completely from love of objects. Don't give away the things you are really attached to – surround yourself with familiar things, don't transform your life more than you need, even in the Swiss hotel. [...]

Do write us again. Aline and I have just been to Jerusalem for a week, but I daren't tell you about that. On that subject you have made up your mind, as I have on the Soviet Union.

Yours ever,
Isaiah

TO GLEB STRUVE[2]

19 July 1971

Wolfson

⟨Дорогой Глеб Петрович!⟩[3]

[...] Thank you very much for your letter. I am glad that a third volume of Akhmatova is being prepared by you. Your services to the 'post-Silver' age are unique and will never be forgotten.[4] It is a pleasure to testify to this. Now, about the actual questions you ask. [...]

I wish I could remember what letter by Punin[5] to AA it is that you are

1 (Arthur) Elliott Felkin (1892–1968) served on the Secretariat of the League of Nations 1923–38, and was Secretary 1938–53 to the Permanent Central Opium Board, which pioneered international narcotics control; he retired to St Jacques de Grasse in the Alpes-Maritimes.

2 Gleb Petrovich Struve (1898–1985), Russian-born Balliol-educated literary historian, translator, poet and critic; Professor of Slavic Languages and Literatures, Berkeley, 1947–67.

3 'Dear Gleb Petrovich!'

4 The first two decades of the 20th century are often called the 'Silver Age' of Russian poetry. Struve prepared new editions of the works of poets such as Anna Akhmatova, Osip Mandel'shtam, Boris Pasternak and Nikolay Zabolotsky, encouraging renewed interest in them in the Soviet Union as well as in the West. In his edition of Akhmatova's work he identified, partly on Akhmatova's authority, the passages inspired by IB's visits to her in 1945–6. See also PI2 253–4. 2nd ed.

5 Nikolay Nikolaevich Punin (1888–1953), Akhmatova's common-law (third) husband 1926–38, one of the most widely read Russian art critics during the 1920s, supported the Russian avant-garde, and opposed State-sponsored socialist realism; died in a Siberian prison camp 1953.

speaking of.[1] I have no doubt that you are right, and that Miss Haight[2] did send me the copy of which you speak, but I have no recollection of it. [...]

You are quite right in supposing that I never met Boris Anrep,[3] nor, so far as I know, had I ever set eyes on him. [...] It is, however, the case, that when I visited her in 1945, AA showed me a ring – I wish I could describe it to you, but my visual memory is very feeble, but there certainly was something black about it, perhaps it had a black stone set in it, which she described as a gift to her from Boris Anrep, and she did say that in a sense he was her last link with the world outside Russia, in the sense that he was, chronologically, the last of those who went abroad and stayed there whom she had seen in Russia, among her intimate friends. [...]

On p. 3, you state that I called on AA in Leningrad during the war (or immediately after its end). In fact, this occurred (I think) in November 1945, i.e. quite definitely after the end of the war. As to whether I am or am not in any way alluded to in the *Poem without a Hero*,[4] I do not know; I do not wish to volunteer anything; the 'cigar', the reference to mirrors (reflected also in one of the poems in *Cinque* which quite definitely refers to my visit to her), the reference to *pogibel*'[5] – I am sure she connected my visit with her disgrace in 1946, etc. – does seem to point to me to some degree. But I feel sure that no unambiguous references can or should be identified in this way: there is a fusion of personalities, of symbolic references, of poetical transfiguration, whatever incidents may have been the mere occasion for the process of poetical creation; and therefore, even if my visit and, most of all of course, her conception of it does enter into these lines, this should not be stated as a definite fact, but only as a possible element in the experience which lay at the heart of the poem. [...] The fact that I was probably the first foreigner to visit her after more than a quarter of a century did affect her greatly, and in this way I earned an undeserved immortality in her verse. But that is all.

Yours sincerely,
Isaiah Berlin

PS [...] I have a terrible, perhaps exaggerated, but very deep and acute and lifelong, horror of the publication of private 'facts', however innocuous – and beg you to protect me in this respect, so far as you possibly can. [...] If

---

1 Letter of 14 April 1942 from Nikolay Punin to Anna Akhmatova, published in N. Punin, *Mir svetel lyubov'yu: dnevniki, pis'ma* [*The World is Bright with Love: Diaries, Letters*], ed. L. Zykov (Moscow, 2000), 354–6.

2 Amanda Chase Haight (1939–89), author of *Anna Akhmatova and Marina Tsvetayeva* (London/NY, 1972) and the biographical *Anna Akhmatova: A Poetic Pilgrimage* (Oxford, 1976).

3 Boris Vasil'evich Anrep (1883–1969), Russian-born mosaicist and painter who worked principally in England, specialising in mosaic pavements. He created the floor of the octagonal Gallery II in Tate Britain (1923), on the theme of William Blake's 'Proverbs of Hell', and the eclectic series in the National Gallery (1926–52) which includes a portrait of Akhmatova as Compassion.

4 505/3.

5 'Perdition'.

you could send me a copy of the Punin letter of which AA left the text to be sent to B. Anrep and myself, I should be grateful.

TO OSBERT LANCASTER[1]

2 August 1971 [*manuscript*]

Paraggi

Dear Osbert,

I was *tremendously* pleased to get your letter. I sweated blood when I was told that I was to pronounce the discourse: it really was terrifying mounting up all those winding steps before that particular congregation: I did try to find an *alibi*: wd not Sparrow, I begged, do it much better? He knew Maurice longer, was probably more intimate, in his day, than anyone; or K. Clark? or Rylands?[2] or Roy? I am very grateful to you for saying that I was right to stress Maurice's goodness & life affirming qualities: when you think how the *senes severiores*[3] trembled at the mere mention of that corrupter of youth! Balliol! Lindsay! David Astor! Sumner![4] Blind & foolish, inhibited & inhibiting; while Maurice opened doors & windows – But all I really have to say is that I think it is no less good & kind & generous of *you*, to write me, who was in a stew from start to finish. I cannot get used to the fact that the great voice will sound in my telephone, in the middle of a pompous meeting with dons of all colours & sizes, booming 'I have a piece of *news*. No, it will *not* keep. Sparrow has written an appalling letter to one of my boys ...' no more. Things will never be the same, at least for me, nor I expect for you, quite. Thank you very much. And my love to Anne:[5] she saw Maurice's golden qualities very clearly & early. It *was* nice of you to write.

yrs
Isaiah

1 Osbert Lancaster (1908–86), later (1975) Kt, cartoonist, theatre designer, social satirist, commentator on architecture; best-known for his 'pocket cartoons' in the *Daily Express*, which he joined in 1939; according to George Malcolm Thomson, the paper's chief leader-writer, 'The annoying thing at the *Express* was, not only was he the only one who could draw, he could also *write* better than anyone in the building' (Bevis Hillier, ODNB); at Oxford (admitted to Lincoln, 1926) with Betjeman, Auden, Spender and Day Lewis.
2 George Humphrey Wolferstan ('Dadie') Rylands (1902–99), literary scholar, theatre director and actor; Fellow of King's, Cambridge, 1927–99, University Lecturer in English Literature 1935–62.
3 'Rather stern old men'. Catullus 5. 2 ('senum severiorum').
4 (Benedict) Humphrey Sumner (1893–1951), Fellow and Tutor in History, Balliol, 1925–44; Professor of History, Edinburgh, 1944–5; Warden of All Souls 1945–51; 'a character of religious simplicity, attuned by early home discipline to "the good life"' (*Times*, 26 April 1951, 6d).
5 Osbert Lancaster married (secondly, 1967) the journalist and author Anne Eleanor Scott-James (1913–2009).

TO NOEL ANNAN

21 September 1971

Wolfson

Dear Noel,

I, too, was absolutely delighted to see you in Padua – I love Sylvester, but he was in a melancholy state. The whole thing was a great change for me as well as a pure and direct pleasure. You must know that I always love seeing you in whatever circumstances, and for whatever length of time and wherever one may be. One always knows about one's own feelings when someone suddenly comes through the door, whether one's spirits leap or descend; they sometimes even descend even when one likes and respects people, but they never leap when one does not. The screen in the Buttery at All Souls used to be a marvellous instrument for measuring one's true feelings about those who suddenly popped their heads round it – it registered at once.

Now, about South Africa. I was once asked to go and didn't for reasons which you could well understand, and was duly beaten on the head for this by the Lord Redcliffe-Maud[1] on more or less Birley[2] principles. My belief is this: if one is very tough and does not mind treading on toes and goes about laying about one as, say, A. J. P. Taylor or Jack Haldane,[3] or other relatively insensitive people can, then there is a case for going. You then tell them a lot of home truths and do not mind whom it annoys, irritates, compromises etc., and this certainly does good, keeps lines open, encourages the liberals, and the rest of it. If, however, one is liable, as I am, as Turgenev was, as I suspect you are, to mind frightfully about hurting people's feelings, if one enters into too many aspects of the situation, sees too many sides of the question, understands only too well the painful and ambivalent position in which some very decent people are placed, etc., then one does little good.

1 John Primatt Redcliffe Redcliffe-Maud (1906–82), KCB 1946, life peer 1967; UK ambassador to South Africa 1961–3; Master of Univ. 1963–76. 'Wholly out of sympathy with the South African government's apartheid policies, Maud remained scrupulously correct in his behaviour and pronouncements, without compromising his integrity or betraying his convictions' (Robert Armstrong, ODNB).

2 Robert Birley (1903–82), KCMG 1967; Head Master, Charterhouse, 1935–47, Eton College 1949–63; Visiting Professor of Education, Witwatersrand, 1964–7; Professor of Social Science and Humanities, City, London, 1967–71. Birley used his Visiting Professorship at Witwatersrand to encourage and foster traditions of liberal democracy that he believed essential to the future of a South Africa freed from apartheid, which he equated with Nazism and abhorred equally.

3 John Burdon Sanderson ('Jack') Haldane (1892–1964), geneticist and populariser of science ('I wish I had the voice of Homer / To sing of rectal carcinoma': 'Cancer's a Funny Thing', New Statesman, 21 February 1964, 298), Professor of Biometry, London, 1937–57; left England for India 1957, becoming an Indian citizen 1961; Head of Genetics and Biometry Laboratory, Government of Orissa (now Odisha), 1962–4; 'so extraordinarily fresh – so alive, so willing to consider – and sometimes devastatingly to smash down – contributions to discussion from any quarter' (Times, 2 December 1964, 13a).

The liberals there know perfectly well that there are plenty of people here who understand them, sympathise with them, condemn apartheid, and the rest of it. After all, when one is a guest of an institution, one feels a certain restraint upon the degree of one's comments on it: once one does that, one concedes too much to it and becomes an honoured guest, and if one is at all eminent or well known, or has a reputation for enlightenment, one tends to rub a tiny bit of the curse off the system. Hence I think I reject the Birley–Maud proposition – and believe in boycotts in cases where it really can affect the system, i.e. vis-à-vis relatively weak powers. It obviously doesn't work against China or the Soviet Union, or even America: it could work against Greece or Portugal, at least somewhat, by affecting the general mood towards them which such countries cannot afford not to mind (the same is true of Israel and Arab countries, etc.), and tough and totally fanatical though the South Africans may be, a steady stream of disapproval, complaint, boycotts, not going to perform to white audiences, and the rest of it, has some chance of wearing down something there – all this on the assumption that you are not likely simply to crash through all this and say what you think and I think in a manner which I should find it quite impossible to do if I went – if you can do it, then I should say yes, perhaps you should go, awful as it would be; if you cannot, I see no possible advantage to the party of light and progress. Voltaire did no good to the subjects of Frederick the Great by going there, nor Diderot by visiting Catherine, nor Professors Toynbee, Barker etc. by their reflections on the shortcomings of the Nazi regime, nor Jouvenel,[1] or again Toynbee,[2] by their calls on Hitler. On the contrary, the proposition that above all one must seek to understand seems to me untrue: when one has understood enough, or what one thinks to be enough, one can take up an attitude and stick to it: there is no need to connect. At any rate, this is what I think – I wonder what, e.g., Stuart would say. If I were in your position, I should give in to my inclinations. In such matters instinct is best.

Yours, with love

Isaiah   [...]

---

1 Bertrand de Jouvenel des Ursins (1903–87), French philosopher and political economist of Jewish descent. He favoured a Franco-German rapprochement, and in February 1936 was granted an interview with Hitler for the *Paris-Midi*; he was not alone in this period in believing Hitler's lies about his intentions, and in thus allowing himself to be used, albeit unwittingly, as a propagandist for German foreign policy.

2 Arnold Toynbee had met Hitler in February 1936 while visiting Berlin to address the Academy of German Law on the theme of 'Peaceful Revision': as this title suggests, Toynbee believed that honourable compromise was possible between Britain and Nazi Germany, and, moreover, that Hitler sought this; on his return he conveyed this view to the Prime Minister and Foreign Secretary in a confidential memorandum.

TO ARTHUR SCHLESINGER

21 September 1971

Headington House

Dear Arthur,

I read your last letter with mixed feelings of pleasure and terror.[1] I knew about Stewart[2] and about Tommy Thompson[3] too. But your narrow shave I had not heard – narrow escapes leave one trembling all the same. And I sympathise with Alexandra[4] – when there was an alarm (fortunately false) about Aline twice as a result of a tumour on the breast I cannot believe that my terrors were less than hers and the intermediate days when one awaits the diagnosis are unspeakable. The fact that death is our common lot does not seem to make the slightest difference. I read Stewart's article in *Newsweek*[5] – I know it was vastly admired by all our friends as well as, I expect, the public, and I have no doubt that he behaved marvellously – whatever else may be said about some of the Alsops, [they] are a truly Roman family, all of them, about the last one left. But I do not know why, I was faintly embarrassed by the fact that he chose to use his predicament to write an article, however genuine and moved by a desire to tell the truth, give comfort, etc. I do not believe that one ought to turn oneself inside out for the benefit of the public, no matter how great the benefit. Baudelaire said that all poets did and writers in general: so this was the inevitable form of prostitution:[6] still, there is a difference in turning one's experience into a work of art and so creating something that lives its own life out of it, and direct transposition of intimate feelings into a public medium. But perhaps this is a tiresome squeamishness. [...]

As for Nixon I do not believe that his basic hatred of Communism – which

1 Schlesinger had recently had a malignant lesion removed from his chest: it was spotted by chance by a surgeon friend, with whom he went swimming, and who 'rather diffidently' urged him to 'have that thing removed right away' (AS to IB, 2 September 1971).

2 Stewart Johonnot Oliver Alsop (1914–74), younger brother of Joseph Alsop, and from 1945 co-author with him of the widely syndicated 'Matter of Fact' current affairs column in the *New York Herald Tribune*; from 1958 he worked alone, contributing regularly to the *Saturday Evening Post* and, from 1968 until his death, writing a weekly column for *Newsweek*; he was diagnosed with leukaemia in 1971 and his gallant struggle with the disease is recorded in *Stay of Execution: A Sort of Memoir* (London, 1974).

3 Llewellyn E. ('Tommy') Thompson (1904–72), US diplomat, specialist in Russian affairs, ambassador to the Soviet Union 1957–62, 1966–9; 'not so well known as George Kennan or Chip Bohlen because of personal modesty but undoubtedly he was the more successful diplomat' (*Times*, 8 February 1972, 14g); died of cancer 6 February 1972.

4 In 1971 Schlesinger married his second wife, Alexandra Temple Allan (b. 1936) née Emmet, and the following year their only child, a son (the journalist and political commentator Robert Emmet Kennedy Schlesinger), was born.

5 Stewart Alsop's article 'Taming the Beast' described his personal struggle against cancer, setting this in the broader context of society's battle with 'the beast' (*Newsweek*, 6 September 1971, 2).

6 Charles Pierre Baudelaire (1821–67), French poet, critic, essayist and translator (notably of Edgar Allan Poe). In 'Fusées', the first part of his 'Journaux intimes', in *Oeuvres posthumes et correspondances inédites* (Paris, 1897–8), 71, he writes 'Qu'est-ce qu'est l'art? Prostitution.'

I still regard as the only disinterested strand in his character – has appeared even weakened. Flirtation with China no more argues abandonment of ultimate objectives than the Russo-German pact on the part of Stalin. Lenin, after all, would have approved of this kind of thing. It is called 'plunging a dagger far in the enemy's back' and it has certainly discomfited Communist parties of all stripes [and] produced pleasing disarray among them.[1] Of course Chip and Averell don't like it much: Chip is a consistent hawk; Averell believes, I suspect, in accommodation with the Russians as the primary objective. Do you? I remain an unashamed hand-to-mouth pragmatist – one plays the game according to change in circumstances as well as one can and does one's best to catch up with changes in the rules: this, of course, unless one's emotions are engaged: I cannot deny that the forcible imposition of the Soviet system (or the Chinese) on a reluctant people or the destruction of Israel (I do not take Arab talk about extermination as mere demagogy and shouting in the bazaars) would fill me with genuine despair.

Meanwhile we are in the throes of arguments about the Common Market. It is not quite as bad as the abdication or Munich or Suez – families are not torn apart – nevertheless a good deal of heat is generated. Roy Jenkins appeared with Marietta in our house in Italy for a couple of nights – I wish I thought he could become Prime Minister one day.[2] He is not an opportunist, it seems to me, and proceeds from principles by means of cool rational argument, but he hasn't got Gaitskell's occasional steeliness, which was there, despite all appearances. His biggest single drawback politically is, of course, the high favour with which he is regarded by the Tories: that really is what does him in – even more than the country houses, the clubs etc., for which he has an astonishing passion. Really somebody with a passion for genealogy! Accurate knowledge of how many viceroys of India were made marquesses and how many were not; who obtained what steps in the peerage when, why, how. Yet his sense of social justice is acute, and his brain, I would think, incapable of being addled. He is by far the best man on either side – better than Healey, who may be abler and more resolute, but is too arrogant, to too many, and has no basis [in] any section of any party. Still, either of those two would guarantee intelligence and decency, whereas Callaghan not. How is Kay (the thought of Heath brings her to mind)? I really must write to her and ask her when she may be coming to England, and I should like to ask you the same – so far as I am concerned, personal relations are still everything – I once tried to say this to Dick Crossman; I have never seen so bewildered

1 In July 1971 President Nixon accepted a Chinese invitation to visit Beijing (which took place in February 1972), leading to speculation that the US would back the PRC's bid for a seat on the UN Security Council as well as the General Assembly: on 16 September the President announced Washington's support for this step, while reaffirming US commitment to Taiwan; Moscow and Hanoi both reacted unfavourably to the prospect of US–China rapprochement.
2 Jenkins was Deputy Leader of the Labour Party 1970–2; he was later first Leader (1982–3) of the Social Democratic Party, which he co-founded.

a look on anyone's face. His diaries will certainly contribute to the gaiety of nations, but [if] any historian looks on them as primary material he will need a severe course in psychohistory.[1] [...]

Yours ever,

Isaiah

TO GLEB STRUVE

24 September 1971

Wolfson

Dear Gleb Petrovich,

[...] I found Punin's letter absolutely fascinating, of course. My memory is becoming very decayed: I have no recollection of seeing it before. I do not want to infer from this that Amanda never gave it to me, but I read it with fascination as an entirely fresh document – I cannot quite believe that not the faintest bell would be rung in my head if I had seen it before. But let that go. I am glad to have seen it. I wonder, too, why AA wished me to see it; I wonder, but not very much, for I think I understand that too – and I understand why Boris Anrep was astonished that my name should be added to his in this connection. I have a notion that AA saw life in terms of isolated events of great significance connected with, symbolised by, incarnated in, meetings with particular individuals who played a part, and were perhaps transformed, in her imaginative experience. Punin wrote her a farewell letter which obviously moved her deeply, as well it might, and there is a sense in which she was saying goodbye both to Anrep and to me, although I do not doubt that our respective relations to her were profoundly different. As for the black ring, I daresay I may have made a muddle about this – she did speak to me of it and perhaps told me that she had given it to Anrep, and not *vice versa*.

As for your commentary (I am much intrigued about the passage that you have left out because it deals with a still living person), as you know she never did see Anrep in Paris – at least I think not – because he was very ill and thought that he had changed physically and perhaps mentally to a degree which made him reluctant to present himself to his old friend; and she too was acutely self-conscious about her appearance – she was, indeed, sadly swollen, as you remember – and did not wish to see him more or less for the same reasons as those which made him unwilling to meet her. I never knew Anrep, as you know, but I imagine he was a person not without great pride and *amour propre*; she, too, romanticised herself immensely, as even her

---

1 Crossman's posthumously published *The Diaries of a Cabinet Minister* (3 vols; London, 1975–7) promised an exposé of the inner workings of the Wilson government, and their publication was delayed by the Cabinet Office on grounds of cabinet confidentiality; this generated a furore of public and press comment, and in October 1975 Lord Chief Justice Widgery decided not to uphold restraining injunctions.

poetry makes evident. In these circumstances every meeting was significant, appearances played an enormous part, every relationship, no matter how intimate and how profound, was also elaborate and shot through with literary feeling. All this seems to me to explain the situation between them well enough, if I am right about all this. I fully understand why Anrep should have not understood why I, too, should have had to be shown Punin's letter, but I understand it well enough, believe me, even though my relationship to AA was, I feel sure, very different from that of Anrep (at least according to AA's account of it to me), and not at all of the kind which Boris Pasternak with uncharacteristic lack of delicacy supposed it to be, at least if accounts of his sisters on this matter are to be trusted. But enough of that: I certainly intend to throw no light upon the 'mystery and motives' which Punin [sc. Anrep] says 'remain obscure' to him. [...]

Akhmatova was never my 'guest' in Oxford. She was told not to stay in any private house – at least so she informed me – and stayed, as you know, at the Randolph Hotel, although she did come to our house and dined with us and the Obolenskys, but this is a very small point. As for her 'misfortunes', you are right: I certainly supposed my visit had done her little good, although Zhirmunsky,[1] on his visit to Oxford, denied, when I asked him, any particularly disagreeable consequences for her as a result of it. But she certainly believed this and wished to believe it, and it became part of her image of herself. [...]

Yours ever,
Isaiah Berlin

TO BERNARD WILLIAMS

13 October [1971]

Headington House

Dear Bernard,

I see what you mean. I cannot bring myself to write Stuart's life, even though I may well not be alive to see it in print, for I have macabre sensations about that. I dashed off Herbert Hart's life with comparative facility, and that of Wheeler-Bennett without batting an eyelid: but I know Stuart a little too well, and to put it all in a *Times*-y style, or any style, is more than I can do except under the most extreme moral pressure, which I don't, fortunately for myself, perceive.[2] If you don't want to do it – for which I can understand the reasons – then I think perhaps we could recommend that

---

1 Viktor Maksimovich Zhirmunsky (1891–1971), Russian literary scholar and philologist, editor of Akhmatova's poems – *Stikhotvoreniya i poemy* (Leningrad, 1976). He was awarded an Honorary D.Litt. at Oxford in 1966.

2 Nevertheless he did draft an obituary of Hampshire for *The Times*, used in part in the published version.

professional necrologist J[ohn] S[parrow], who would enjoy doing it but (having caught a glimpse of what he is writing about me)[1] would produce a portrait that neither you nor I will easily recognise – if alive to read it. But still, perhaps it doesn't matter – *The Times* – what will its worth be – to future generations? [...]

I am much intrigued to see what will happen as a result of the symbiosis between you and the new Principal[2] – I shall not embarrass you by giving a detailed account of my stay in Salzburg with Elizabeth Bowen,[3] Stuart and her in 1937 or so. As for the relative harmony between the moral characters and the official convictions of those with whom one is supposed to co-operate – that is personally painful and philosophically not unimportant: why do people leave e.g. Communism? What shocked them? Not the intellectual errors but the moral categories of their colleagues. I have just delivered a rousing lecture on this at Stanford University. I am not sure that it went down at all well. I should love to talk to you about this. It is what deters me from politics – Gaitskell was the only politician I ever met who did not seem to me too brutal in other respects, and in many respects too hateful: this is what is called an irresponsible attitude – I wish I knew how to shake it off.

Yours,

Isaiah   [...]

TO ALAN BULLOCK

26 October 1971 [*carbon*]

[Wolfson]

[Dear Alan,]

Let me assure you that I have not the faintest reservation about either 'occasion'. The difficulty is of quite a different order. On 5 November I am supposed to go to a concert given by Isaac Stern in London: he is a great friend of mine and I swore solemnly that I would not miss this occasion, but would see him and perhaps sup with him afterwards; on 18 November, I was invited by Humphrey Waldock[4] to some kind of banquet at Gray's Inn – white tie and all – which I should not think will be terribly thrilling, but

---

1 Sparrow had drafted IB's *Times* obituary, and had shown his text to IB, but the published version was written by Stuart Hampshire.

2 Elizabeth Leila Millicent ('Sally') Chilver (b. 1914) née Graves, civil servant and academic; Principal of Bedford, London, 1964–71, of LMH 1971–9.

3 Elizabeth Dorothea Cole Bowen (1899–1973), novelist, one of IB's closest friends from before the war, widowed in 1952. She lectured and taught in the US in a heroic attempt to keep her ancestral home, Bowen's Court, Co. Cork. She was forced to sell in 1959 to a farmer who promptly demolished it – 'a clean end', as she stoically remarked: *Bowen's Court* (1942), 2nd ed. (London, 1964), 459.

4 (Claud) Humphrey Meredith Waldock (1904–81), Kt 1961; Chichele Professor of Public International Law and Fellow of All Souls 1947–72; Judge of the International Court of Justice 1973–9.

I did promise to do this about two months ago simply because I was invited and was pleased to be invited, and I really do not think that I can get out of this now with any honour left. Waldock must be the head of the Benchers of that institution, and the guest lists and everything else are prepared with enormous pomp and care long beforehand, at least I think so. I hate to refuse both your invitations, I really do [...]. Perhaps I could cut the Stern concert with some hideous excuse (I cannot do this to Waldock). How long can you give me? Perhaps your secretary could telephone in a day or two? Apologies, apologies, apologies.

[Isaiah]

TO ISAAC STERN

26 October 1971 [*carbon*]

[Wolfson]

Dear Isaac,

I have no idea where you are, nor would your agents reveal a thing, quite rightly no doubt, but tiresome all the same, and an obstacle to intimacy. I solemnly applied for tickets for the 30th of this month when you swore (I assure you, on the telephone from Corsica) that you would be playing only to receive weeks and weeks and weeks later a dry little card informing me that no such concert was anticipated. To my horror I learnt that you were playing on 5 November when I had committed myself – again weeks and indeed months ago – to dine with the Vice-Chancellor of this University, an engagement I cannot possibly get out of on the grounds that I wished to hear a concert, no matter by how noble a genius and how close a friend. [...] Is 5 November your only engagement here? Why could you not play at midnight like Sasha Schneider and his gang?[1] It is a far more mystical hour and predisposes to *Innigkeit*[2] far more than 8 p.m. when people are either uncomfortably digesting their over-hurriedly consumed dinner, or reflecting about how soon and where they will obtain their next meal. Believe me, late-night concerts would be a marvellous thing, and if people say that they are too exhausted, or bored, by this time, they are not, believe me, either worthy of listening to music or human beings with whom it is worth having any dealings at all. *À bas la bourgeoisie!* The daughter of my dear friend and colleague, Sir William Hayter, is about to publish her autobiography – she is a violently left-wing revolutionary girl – as *Hayter of the Bourgeoisie*.[3] How

---

1 (Abraham) Alexander ('Sasha') Schneider (1908–93) né Abram Sznejder, Russian-Jewish-born violinist and conductor, settled in US 1938; 2nd violinist, Budapest Quartet, 1932–44, 1955–67 (when disbanded); founded Brandenburg Players 1972. With Isaac Stern and the contralto Maureen Forrester, Schneider often gave benefit concerts at the Israel Festival, the trio becoming known there as 'The Stern Gang' (cf. 336/3).

2 'Intimacy'.

3 Teresa Hayter (b. 1940), LMH history 1958–61, postgraduate economics 1968–70, daughter of Sir

can I convey either to parents or children the proposition that a joke title is not entirely appropriate to what will be a humourlessly intense and tremendously silly book? Why indeed should I try to convey this? Let the book and its author meet their proper fate. On this furious note, I end this letter, the entire purpose of which was to express anguish, regret, a mild reproof, and a passionate desire to see you as soon as possible.

Yours,

[Isaiah]

TO JACK DONALDSON

28 October 1971

Headington House

Dear Jack,

[...] Have I told you about my lunch with the High Master, Governors etc. of St Paul's?[1] It was absolute hell. I intend to forward your postcard to me, with orders to return, to at least the High Master,[2] who is both discreet and impressionable (I hope). The smooth silken hypocrisy of both the Headmaster of St Paul's preparatory school[3] and the President of the Old Pauline Club (Colonel Sir Louis Gluckstein),[4] who entirely approve of the quota, was genuinely nauseating: more so than any specific propositions that they advanced. I came in a rather feeble mood, anxious for appeasement and compromise; but no, I found myself burning all boats and bridges (in a most unfamiliar condition of intransigence), and seemed a real troublemaker bent on blood: not a character in which I recognise myself. What a miserable crew! I went away frightfully depressed, having argued forcibly

---

William Hayter, then Warden of New College, and his wife Iris; graduate of Oxford; author of the fierily radical *Hayter of the Bourgeoisie* (London, 1971), in which she observes that 'The function of Oxford education is to train people to service and perpetuate capitalism' (7).

1 IB fiercely opposed the imposition by St Paul's School of a formal quota on non-Christian admissions, which, because of the numbers applying, was likely to fall hardest on children from Jewish families; he sought an interview with the relevant authorities, and, after meeting them, determined to resign from the Old Pauline Club (of which he was a Vice-President) as soon as the new restrictions were published in the school prospectus: he duly resigned in April 1972 (letter of 13 April to Sir Louis Gluckstein).

2 Thomas Edward Brodie Howarth (1914–88), Second Master, Winchester, 1952–62; High Master, St Paul's, 1962–73; Fellow and Senior Tutor, Magdalene, Cambridge, 1973–80.

3 Henry John Gurney Collis (1913–94), Headmaster of Colet Court (the preparatory school of St Paul's) 1957–73.

4 Louis Halle Gluckstein (1897–1979), Kt 1953; Director, British Transport Hotels Ltd, 1963–78; a scholar at St Paul's, Gluckstein was formerly President of the Old Pauline Club (1966–9), a post held at the time of IB's letter by his successor Sir Charles (Reginald) Wheeler (1904–75); he served, and was mentioned in dispatches, in both World Wars, retiring with the honorary rank of Colonel in 1948.

but very badly. I was put into a dock: predicate only. I think I *shall* have to resign loudly. [...]

Yours ever,

Isaiah

TO OMAR HALIQ[1]

25 November 1971 [*carbon*]

[Wolfson]

Dear Dr Haliq,

I was glad and interested to receive your letter. Let me answer your questions in the order in which you put them.

[...] As you know, Hess's Zionism – although it was not called that – was not aggressively nationalistic in any way. He did regard the Jews as a nation and agreed with you and me that land is essential for nationhood. Hess, I ought to explain, was not a rabbi – Marx occasionally called him that in a mocking manner to indicate Hess's incurable attachment to his people (from which Marx managed to detach himself completely) and, perhaps, as an ironical reference to his religious temperament and moral outlook, neither of which Marx, as you may imagine, cared for. Whatever his views, Hess, although descended from a religious family, was not a conforming member of the Jewish or any other religion.

You naturally ask what Hess thought about the fate of the Palestinian Arabs. I imagine that at the time at which he wrote – the 1860s – there was no Palestinian nationality. The Arabs were a subject people governed by Turks and occupied large territories of which Palestine was one of the least populated compared to Egypt or even Syria, at least in the fertile crescent. I have no doubt that if the question of the future of the Arab inhabitants of Palestine had been brought to his notice, he would have abhorred the idea of conquest, and assumed, as a good many people did, that although the Jews were entitled to a country of their own, and although their sense of nationhood was inextricably bound up with memories and symbols of Jerusalem and Palestine, they could therefore, in Hess's somewhat Hegelian vision, only obtain normal realisation in the land to which they had remained attached in so astonishing a manner for so many centuries, and would have assumed that some peaceable arrangement with the Arab natives of the country could have been arrived at either through a bi-national or multi-national State, or voluntary exchanges of population with generous compensation to those displaced, always provided they had voluntarily agreed to it, or something of this kind. No doubt this was impracticable: in the age of

1 Omar Kamil Haliq (1921–2009), born a Palestinian in Haifa, educated in Jerusalem, Rome, London and NY; Counsellor for Research, permanent Saudi Arabian mission to the UN, Geneva, from 1949.

growing nationalism, mild, rational and peaceful solutions were in general growing less likely. Nevertheless, I think this is what he might have hoped for, unlike his hero Marx, to whom he remained loyal until the end, who regarded nationhood in general as a by-product of economic structures of capitalist society – at least in modern days – and would have regarded the whole problem of nationality, whether this or that population was entitled to this or that piece of land, as a piece of bourgeois nonsense. After all, he approved of the annexation of Danish territory by the Prussians, and Engels thought that it was as well that the Czechs be absorbed in a higher German culture – there is a good deal of contempt for, and desire to abolish, tiresome small nationalities which blocked the way to centralised progress. All this was not part of Hess's outlook, and it is one of the main differences between him and orthodox Marxism. I think he would have been very distressed, as you must be and I certainly am, by the present situation. I think that he would have agreed with those who say that solutions are impossible where there is a genuine collision of genuine rights – and that all one wants to promote is a situation entailing the least degree of injustice. What this is there might be disagreement about – but if the principle is accepted, murderous clashes can surely be avoided. At least that is my feeling.

I was much taken aback by the fact that you wondered whether I could even hesitate to reply to your enquiry, because you are a Palestinian Arab. I am not a barbarian, and to have reacted as you supposed I might would have been barbarous and odious. And let me assure you that there are a great many people who think as I do (I mean hold the kind of opinions that you can easily recognise in my essay on Moses Hess)[1] and who would be equally offended if it were suggested that they harboured ill will against Palestinian Arabs who were compelled to leave their country by recent events. You really must not think this: if ever you come to England and wish to come and see me, I should of course welcome you. If even the sharpest collisions of rights – let alone opinions – were to lead to indelible hatreds, humanity would deserve to perish from the face of the earth – or if not humanity, at any rate those who deliberately nurse hatreds in their breasts. I fear that I am now talking in a Hess-like manner, and I only hope you will not disapprove of me as strongly as Marx did of poor idealistic Hess.

Yours sincerely,

[Isaiah Berlin]

---

1 *The Life and Opinions of Moses Hess*, IB's December 1957 Lucien Wolf Memorial Lecture (Cambridge, 1959), held under the auspices of the Jewish Historical Society of England; repr. in AC. Ag Current

TO URSULA NIEBUHR[1]

21 January 1972

Wolfson

Dear Ursula,

How very, very nice to receive your letter. I am glad you enjoyed coming to Oxford, and you must certainly come back. As for Wystan, I wish I knew where to write to him – do tell me, for I gather that he is coming to Christ Church, but thinks that he should have been more warmly welcomed (for God's sake, don't tell him that I told you this). He obviously sees himself as E. M. Forster at King's; in fact he was admitted most grudgingly, I gather, and your host at Christ Church, who thought me 'a walking Sermon on the Mount', which I still enjoy greatly – what does it mean? – is acutely nervous of the whole situation.[2] However, if he comes to live here, he will certainly make Christ Church more famous than it deserves, and it will all be a great success, and I should like to write and tell him how very pleased I, at any rate, am by this news. Have you any idea where he is? Is he in New York? Is that where I write him? I could no doubt find out locally, but I would love to hear from you. [...]

Can you conceive me going to a Zionist Congress? Really! I have never been to a single one, and I hope never to go; anything more pointless or exhausting is difficult to conceive. As for Weisgal, do read his book,[3] it is amusing and it is irritating, frightfully vulgar, heart-warming, maddening, egocentric, full of spite against those he doesn't like, excessive compliments for those he does, inaccurate, but, in the end, an expression of a genuine, disarming, ubiquitous, benevolent fixer – as Beazley[4] said to a don in Christ Church who asked him if he was fattening up the goose which Mrs Beazley

---

1 Ursula Mary Niebuhr (1907–97) née Keppel-Compton, English-born NY theologian, wife 1931 of the American theologian Karl Paul Reinhold Niebuhr (1892–1971); founder of the Dept of Religion, Barnard College, Columbia, 1946, and professor 1946–65.

2 In 1969 Auden hinted that he would like to return to Christ Church, where he had been an undergraduate, in the manner in which E. M. Forster had returned to King's, Cambridge. Forster was made an Honorary Fellow of King's in 1946, and from 1953 resided there permanently, even having his old supervisor's room: 'here he became a familiar and much-loved figure, a symbol of the civilised, liberal values that he had always held so dear' (Nicola Beauman, ODNB). Auden, however, who was given an honorary studentship by Christ Church in 1972, discovered an Oxford 'noisier and more crowded' than it had once been, while 'the dons who welcomed him found that he was no longer the brilliant conversationalist they remembered' (Edward Mendelson, ODNB). He also 'scandalised the sanctimonious diners at High Table in Christ Church by asking when they started masturbating or whether they peed in their bathroom sinks': Peter Conrad, *Imagining America* (NY, 1980), 215.

3 Meyer Weisgal, *Meyer Weisgal ... So Far: An Autobiography* (London, 1971), covers the history of modern Zionism from the Balfour Declaration of 1917 to Independence in 1948.

4 John Davidson Beazley (1885–1970), Kt 1949; Professor of Classical Archaeology and Art at Oxford 1925–56; he married, 1919, Marie H. Ezra (c.1882–1967) née Blumenfield; in the early years of marriage they kept a goose at Christ Church, which Marie Beazley used to walk in Tom Quad.

used to lead on a string, for Christmas: 'The goose is *dead*. Many worse men are still alive.' I look forward to the book you are sending me, and I look forward to seeing you.

[...] Wystan's salon in Christ Church should be worth attending. How welcome I shall be there is not absolutely clear to me – I shall rely upon you to find out. A charming poem in memory of Maurice Bowra and Seferis[1] has been written by the Poet Laureate, Day Lewis,[2] who is, I am afraid, dying. He is a terrible sight to see – poor man. When are you coming? Where is Wystan? Where is he?

Love
    Isaiah

TO BERNARD WILLIAMS

21 January 1972 [*manuscript*]

Headington House

Dear Bernard,

Yes, of course I did hear something.[3] Not a word from Stuart who swallows & does not regurgitate: by temperament & wartime training he has become a coffer of undisclosed secrets, some of which have long become public property: I envy him his capacity for importing without export: like the State of Israel he depends on the good will of allies & supporters who expect no return in kind. I did hear about it, however from, I think, Noel; whom, unlike some (do), I hold in real affection and, indeed, respect: he seemed very genuinely concerned and reported it without any temptation to be amusing, very sympathetically. First let me tell you how deeply touched I am by the fact that you wrote: and second, that I am not without experience of causing pain and distress (to the late Dr Halban for example, *and* his children – but also to others, do not ask me whom) as the price of my own happiness. In my case this particular experience occurred so late in my life that I could scarcely bring myself to believe that it was I who was involved in a classical predicament: I, who had firmly (and, as it turned out now, with a horrible priggish lack of moral & emotional sensibility or generosity) condemned imbroglios of this kind: & behaved with the morality of my uncles

---

1 George Seferis, pseudonym of Giorgios Stylianou Seferiades (1900–71), Greek poet, critic and diplomat; Greek ambassador to UK 1957–61; Nobel Prize in Literature 1963; Seferis was a strong opponent of the military dictatorship in Greece, and both IB and Cecil Day Lewis were among the supporters of a memorial fund to be used to aid the families and dependants of political prisoners in Greece.

2 Cecil Day Lewis (1904–72), poet and, as Nicholas Blake, novelist; Poet Laureate 1968–72; he died on 22 May. The poem in question is 'Hellene, Philhellene' in *Cornhill Magazine* no. 1070 (winter 1971/72), 99–100: it celebrates a triangular friendship – Bowra had been Day Lewis's tutor at Wadham, and they were reunited for the last time with their friend Seferis in Rome in 1968.

3 About BW's decision to leave his wife Shirley for Patricia Skinner, wife of Quentin Skinner.

and aunts: what the poetess Akhmatova said Tolstoy did with Anna, Tolstoy who knew far better & yielded to an abominable moralizing habit. I suspect it was (& perhaps still is) worse for you than for me: not only because I was "free", but because you have a far more philosophical head than I, & think lucidly, & cannot evade conclusions, however unpalatable, which follow from premisses, and feel the need for articulate justification, & don't cheat, as others we know, half unconsciously, do […] which makes things easier not only for them, but for everybody else, but which you cannot & won't do: I moved in a mist: & my interest in anti-rationalism is probably to do with that. But worse still is to falsify – or try to falsify – one's actual emotions, in the interests of peace, or comfort or even justice: ἔρως ἀνίκατε'etc: I did not think of this at Paphos: but [if] I had, it wd have justified Humean isolated plurality of ends – & not your & Stuart's rationalist unitarianism. The ends conflict: whichever you choose, you sustain (& inflict) loss & pain:[1] the effort to think it through & reconcile apparent conflict, & higher syntheses, and Aufhebung,[2] and rising above, and ultimate harmony and das ewig weibliche[3] which schwebt uns hinauf[4] – towards lofty views and the final reconciliation of everything with everything & the marriage of heaven & hell, knowledge & virtue & happiness – all that is nothing but a grand evasion of the fact that conflict is what it is & there is *no* way of avoiding it altogether *and* facing what we know to be 'The case". You must surely have suffered much guilt & agony. Not avoidable, I say dogmatically, save at the cost of some other guilt & agony, *or* lies, self deception, & patter. I see that there *is* a problem for Shirley who will not want to marry again (she *is* a believer, I suppose): & for your daughter: children always want to be loyal to both parents: but you will manage this better than others: I had the same problem: the death of my predecessor did ease matters enormously. I assume & hope that you intend to marry as soon as you are free to do so: I am as much pro-marriage now as I used to be uninterested in my monastic days. She is very very nice, as well as beautiful, Patricia. I was delighted to make her acquaintance: I cannot begin to say how well I wish you both: my view is that you have nothing to worry about, really: no matter how

1 Paphos, on the south-west coast of Cyprus (visited by IB 8–17 September 1971 for a conference in Nicosia), is renowned as the birthplace of Aphrodite, goddess of sexual desire and love, believed to have been born of the sea-foam just off shore. She is invoked by the chorus in Sophocles' *Antigone*, 781–800. IB quotes the first two words of the opening phrase: '"Ἔρως ἀνίκατε μάχαν' ('Erōs anikate makhan'), 'O Love unconquerable in battle'. For IB each emotion (e.g. desire, personified as Eros or Aphrodite) is distinct, and cannot be translated into the terms of another. This is a specific case of his view that values, ends, are irreducibly plural, and can come into irresolvable conflict, as, in *Antigone*, do divine and civic law.

2 'Repeal': 'Aufhebung' is a technical Hegelian term for the idea of something (often a conflict) being simultaneously raised to a higher level and abolished. (heßen)

3 The closing lines (12,110–11) of Goethe's *Faust*, part 2, run 'Das Ewig-Weibliche / Zieht uns hinan' ('the eternal feminine draws us upward').

4 'Floats above us': IB has misremembered the final line.

٩ ᵘˢ μρ ? (v.t.??)

difficult the reconstruction of the abandoned spouses' (terrible word) lives
may be – & your involvement in *that* – you *will* be happy. That is for sure.
And it will be very nice & gay for your friends too. Wounds, in this case, *will*
heal: scars are not vitally important. There is something to be said against
totally unscarred lives, too. […]

yrs
Isaiah

TO VITTORE BRANCA[1]

25 January 1972 [*carbon*]

[Wolfson]

Dear Professor Branca,

I am delighted to hear from you, whatever the occasion. Alas, I am not
able to come to Venice on 9–11 April as I have to be here, and I regret this very
much. I must also add that Dostoevsky is not a subject which I can comfortably pursue: great genius as he is, I feel allergic to him: when I read him it is
like an obsessive nightmare during which I feel there is nothing else in the
world save what he describes – but I am anxious to awake from it at the same
time. One of the Russian critics once said he examines the world through
a kind of magnifying glass which does not merely enlarge the objects seen,
but, by accumulating light, actually scorches them and so distorts them by
burning them somewhat. I think this is true: but this is not quite enough for
a thesis. So with the greatest regret I must, alas, decline. If only you wanted
to discuss Turgenev … and Russian criticism in the nineteenth century – but
one cannot have everything.

With cordial good wishes,
Yours sincerely,
[Isaiah Berlin]

TO ROBERT SILVERS

9 February 1972 [*carbon*]

[Wolfson]

Dear Bob,

We were terribly sorry not to see you on your journey and hope against
hope we shall see you when you are in Europe again – we go to India on 5
March and then to Persia, coming back for 23 March when I must attend my
aged mother and hold the Seder service with her – tête-a-tête I suspect, as she

1 Vittore Branca (1913–2004), Italianist scholar, translator, and expert on Boccaccio; Secretary
  General of the Fondazione Giorgio Cini, on the Isola San Giorgio Maggiore, Venice, 1953–88.

is now somewhat frail. I have a good deal of fellow-feeling about this with dear Sidney, who has written a side-splitting letter on his jury service in New York, in the course of which his efforts to convict the jury of simony etc., get the judge convicted, etc. led to complications.

I am glad you went to Coppet – a charming house. One can see that conversations of a human kind could have occurred there, since the drawing room is reasonably small – Madame de Stael[1] must have been a very good hostess, in spite of her insatiable appetite for almost anything, and her unattractive appearance.

The meetings of A. W. Schlegel and Constant.[2] You are quite right to think that he [Constant] was an extremely intelligent man. Nobody takes any real interest in his views now and a very bad book was written on him by Harold Nicolson,[3] who vaguely identified himself with him as a kind of combination of man of letters and distinguished political failure – but he *is* the original liberal, in some ways more interesting than Tocqueville, and felt about the French Revolution much as I feel about the Russian. I asked Eric Hobsbawm the other day whether he did not think that his party, of which he is still a loyal member – or perhaps disloyal member, but a member – was not on the whole responsible for a great deal more pain than happiness, and shed too much blood with very little to show for it, comparatively speaking, if one was to reckon these things in terms of human beings and not of inexorable cosmic forces, before which we can only bow our heads respectfully, as Franco Venturi[4] does, as elemental events beyond our comprehension. Surprisingly enough, he agreed, but what this is worth I simply do not know. I enjoyed my meeting with him very much. He is a very suitable friend for Richard, and a very suitable acquaintance for me. [...]

The Palestinian in Oxford – I have mislaid his name – answered with great dignity and point to the madly hysterical letter by Uri somebody which set my teeth sharply on edge[5] – the tone and the contents were not those of someone capable of existing in a tolerable society with anyone, despite the

---

1 (Anne Louise) Germaine de Staël (1766–1817) née Necker, prolific French writer, daughter of a *salonnière* mother and Swiss banker father. Her Paris salon, and Coppet, the family estate near Geneva, attracted major figures of the age; she was a powerful personality and political intriguer, scandalous in private life and indiscreet in public, causing Talleyrand to remark: 'It seems that Madame de Staël has written a novel [*Delphine*] in which both she and I are introduced disguised as women' (quoted by Anthony Powell, 'The Paradox of Constant', TLS, 1 July 1949: 428; untraced to a primary source).

2 August Wilhelm von Schlegel and Benjamin Constant were both intimates of Madame de Staël, Constant involved in a long affair with her, complicated by money.

3 *Benjamin Constant* (London, 1949).

4 Franco Venturi (1914–94), Italian historian and Enlightenment scholar; Professor of History, Turin, 1958–84; lived 1947–9 in the Soviet Union, where he researched his famous *Il populismo russo* (Turin, 1952); IB contributed the introduction to the English translation, *Roots of Revolution: A History of the Populist and Socialist Movements in Nineteenth Century Russia* (London, 1960).

5 Uri Davis and Atallah Mansour, 'An Exchange on Israel and the Palestinians', NYRB, 10 February 1972.

Chomsky-ite sentiments – he would drive any sane person mad in no time. He reminds me of the episode in 1913 when the *Sacre du printemps* was first done. You remember there is a moment at which one of the maidens about to be sacrificed shivers, shakes, quivers and quakes to a particularly insistent and marvellous rhythm: at this point voices were heard in the audience, where 'Un docteur!' was several times repeated in rising tones; someone else cried 'Un dentiste! Vite!' This is roughly what I feel about your correspondent. Also, I have just had a flattering letter from A. J. P. Taylor, and therefore ought to report to you that I thought his piece about the spies was grotesque;[1] Stuart says that every statement was very, very false and easily refutable by anyone, and if the piece had not been so palpably nonsensical, beneath all possible standards, Trevor-Roper could probably be able to reply, but even he would, I think, not deign to do it. This ends my usual budget of criticisms – the rest was excellent. [...]

Tomorrow I go to Cambridge, where I suppose I shall visit E. H. Carr and his worthy wife. Also Bernard Williams, now established with Mrs Skinner; the Shadow Home Secretary is eating her poor Catholic heart out somewhere; she is a nice girl and able and could be the first female Prime Minister of England, but this will not improve her position. I do not know exactly what has happened there, but it is sad and Bernard is oppressed by guilt. [...] I am ashamed to say I have appeared in a private film about Oxford philosophy with Freddie Ayer, Stuart, David Pears (described by the *Observer* as perhaps the greatest living philosopher – I propose to call him GLP in the future, his children do so already), Iris Murdoch, Strawson, etc. etc. I did get Herbert Hart into it as well, but the brothers Chanan,[2] two enterprising Jewish boys who promoted it, found his words too academic and dull and are trying to eliminate him. I am engaged in a bitter fight to keep him in, as I was responsible for persuading him into taking part in the film, which I suspect – I have not seen it, since I had a cold on the night it was shown to various commercial persons – is really rather terrible. It will all go to cassettes I suspect. [...]

Yours,

[Isaiah]

---

1 'Through the Keyhole', NYRB, 10 February 1972, 14–18, in which Taylor reviewed, in his characteristically combative style, four recently published books about espionage during the Second World War: 'When spies discover something, it can usually be found in the newspapers as well. [...] To anyone tempted to engage in espionage I commend Taylor's Law (now universally accepted by experts): the Foreign Office knows no secrets. Its rider, too, is noteworthy: the Kremlin is also not richly endowed with them. As for the State Department, it is not even worth postulating a principle. The State Department learns its own secrets only when it reads them in a newspaper.'

2 In 1972 Michael and Noel Aaron Chanan (b. 1939) produced six one-hour films on Oxford philosophy collectively entitled *Logic Lane*, from the title of the first film – so called after the cobbled lane off High Street running through Univ. to Merton Street. Herbert Hart was not in fact filmed.

TO G. S. ROUSSEAU[1]

14 February 1972 [carbon]

[Wolfson]

Dear Dr Rousseau,

[...] I read your piece on Namier[2] with great pleasure. The Namier I knew seems to be quite different from the Namier described by his widow: nor is this surprising: she conceived it as her duty to lead him back to Christ – when I met him, he was a ferocious anti-clerical who had no use for clergymen, rabbis, priests or anyone else – that, indeed, is the Namier of the 1920s and 1930s and [the] greater portion of the 1940s – the post-conversion Namier is clearly a spiritually different figure. I feel sure that her portrait of him is what he would have wished it to be – and, indeed, is inspired by his account of himself to her. To me he looked altogether different: a great man and a great intellectual innovator, but the particular ways in which he made his name and with which he impressed his contemporaries (and events) most deeply – as a transformer of the writing of history and as the most distinguished of all the Zionist intellectuals then alive – scarcely appear in her pages. As for the first, she cannot, of course, be criticised – she says herself she is no specialist and leaves this to his fellow historians. The second I think she avoids because she is in profound non-sympathy with all this aspect of his life: even when I met them in Israel together, when he was engaged on a kind of pastoral tour of that country and was looked after by Talmon, she was plainly uncomfortable and felt profound distaste for the general quality of the Jewish establishment, which profoundly moved him – indeed to tears which I witnessed – but from which she averted her gaze in a perfectly intelligible but, for the purposes of a biography of his evolution, a somewhat inhibitive fashion. But let that be. He will live by his works more than by his personality, the memory of which will gradually fade. [...]

Yours sincerely,

[Isaiah Berlin]

TO ROBERT SILVERS

15 February 1972 [carbon]

[Headington House]

Dear Bob,

[...] I am still waiting for Stuart's article on Rawls[3] – I feel it will be like

---

1 George Sebastian Rousseau (b. 1941), cultural historian; instructor, then assistant professor, Harvard, 1966–8; assistant professor of English, UCLA, 1968–9, associate professor 1969–76, professor 1976–94.

2 G. S. Rousseau, 'Namier on Namier', *Studies in Burke and His Time* 8 (Fall 1971), 2016–41.

3 John Bordley Rawls (1921–2002), Professor of Philosophy, MIT, 1960–2; joined philosophy department of Harvard 1962, becoming John Cowles Professor of Philosophy 1975–9. Stuart

something by Leonard Woolf on Moore – one noble critic about an austere and noble thinker – the sort of thing that makes Crossman violently irritated. Talking of Crossman, he has just sent me some chapters from his diary, which he tells me I must keep under lock and key as they are so terribly security-relevant – I have not read a word of it yet, but shall. It is bound to be amusing, bound to be readable, bound to be interesting, indeed. I am not sure what it is he wants my judgement on, but feel vaguely flattered despite all my inhibitions on the subject.

Goronwy Rees's book on himself and Burgess has been widely reviewed, on the whole more favourably than might have been anticipated:[1] Hugh Trevor-Roper was wholly taken in by Goronwy's account of himself as a poor Welsh boy, unable for a time to get on terms with a languid British aristocracy – I was contemporary with him here and this is not quite what happened: Goronwy's father was a perfectly well set up clergyman in Wales and he had no more difficulty in assimilating to Oxford than, say, Simon[2] in an earlier generation, or indeed Herbert Hart, or the hundreds and hundreds of bright boys who did not come from public schools, but were assimilated into the Oxford texture without the slightest effort or difficulty – the ones who revolted were usually guilt-ridden public schoolboys like Auden or Stephen.

[…] I gather that I am mentioned in Mme Mandelstam's second volume,[3] which Hayward is translating now, in connection with Akhmatova's troubles. I tremble to think of what she says. I expect it will be the truth.

Yours,

[Isaiah]   […]

TO THE EDITOR OF WORLDVIEW

23 February 1972 [carbon][4]

[Wolfson]

Sir,

I should be glad to believe with Mr James Reston[5] that God is not mocked,

Hampshire reviewed his seminal work, *A Theory of Justice* (Harvard, 1971), in a special supplement to the NRYB (24 February 1972, 34–9); written during the Vietnam war, the book is credited with rejuvenating the study of political philosophy; Rawls emphasised individual rights as against the utilitarian tradition of the common good.

1 Goronwy Rees, *A Chapter of Accidents* (London, 1972). 'The Boswellising of Burgess could not have been better or more sympathetically done' (A. P. Ryan, *Times*, 10 February 1972, 12e).

2 John Allsebrook Simon (1873–1954), 1st Viscount Simon 1940, barrister and Liberal politician, son of a Congregationalist minister. Simon won a scholarship (1891) to Wadham, took a first in Greats and was President of the Oxford Union; Fellow of All Souls 1897–1954.

3 *Hope Abandoned* (445/3). IB is mentioned at 357–8, where it is erroneously stated that he sent some Oxford students to see Zoshchenko in 1954; he does not appear (except in an added obituary of the author) in the previous volume, *Hope against Hope* (ibid.).

4 Published (not in letter form, and omitting 'in the end' in the first sentence) as one of four contributions to 'The Judgements of History: A Symposium', under the title 'History as We Would Like It', *Worldview* 15 no. 7 (July 1972), 16. Reston's contribution is entitled 'Not by Power Alone'.

5 James Barrett ('Scotty') Reston (1909–95), Scottish-born Pulitzer Prize winning newspaperman

and that the crimes of statesmen and of peoples in the end obtain their just due at the hands of history. But I find it difficult to divorce myself from the thought that, at any rate in the long run, it is the conquerors and the big battalions that determine the verdicts (despite some shining exceptions) of historians. Over a century and a half ago, Immanuel Kant wrote 'If those revolts which gave Switzerland, the Netherlands, and Great Britain their constitutions, and which are now praised as so felicitous, had failed, historians would see in the execution of their originators the deserved punishment of major criminals.'[1] [...] Alexander, Scipio, Julius Caesar, Charlemagne won their wars; our history books would have been very different if they had not – not merely because events, the course of human history itself, would have been different, but because the judgements of the world upon them are part and parcel of this course, and would have been very unlike the conventional wisdom that would have resulted from their failures. Could anyone doubt what 'the verdict of history', of every journalist and schoolmaster and the vast majority of educated men, would have been if Napoleon had successfully invaded Russia and England, and established his laws in his entire empire for any length of time? If Hitler, or even the Kaiser,[2] had won their wars? There is a story, perhaps apocryphal, of a Belgian who, after his country had been invaded in 1914, and resistance cruelly oppressed by the German armies, asked a German officer whether he was not afraid of the judgement of history. 'No,' the officer is alleged to have replied, 'for we shall write the histories.' Victors are seldom judged: the defeated, the minorities, the persecuted sometimes leave memorials of themselves in the light of which later generations modify conquerors' accounts of their successes. But this does not happen often: the Romans won, but the writings of the Jews are there to testify against them; Europeans exploited and humiliated the Chinese, but there are Chinese writings to shame their descendants, whose own histories used to record little or nothing of this. There is more hope at present that this will not automatically prevail, because the enormities of our own century have been such as to provoke indignation within the ranks of the conquerors themselves. This is new, but it offers hope for greater justice in terms of those deeply held human values that have not altered all that much in the course of centuries. Yet the price that we, in this century, have had to pay for this more universal awakening of the moral conscience has been appalling. It is, I think, this sense of outrage which Mr Reston has in mind; and although I am somewhat sceptical of its efficacy, I share his attitude:

and author; chief Washington correspondent, NYT, 1953–64, Associate Editor 1964–8.

1 'On the Common Saying: "That may be true in theory, but it won't work in practice"' (1793), *Kant's gesammelte Schriften* (Berlin, 1900–), viii 301.

2 Wilhelm II (1859–1941) of Prussia, né Prince Friedrich Wilhelm Albert Viktor, Emperor of Germany and King of Prussia 1888–1918; abdicated 9 November 1918 and fled into exile in the Netherlands, where he died despite Allied attempts to extradite him to stand trial 'for a supreme offence against international morality and the sanctity of treaties' (*Times*, 7 July 1919, 13f).

I should like this doctrine to be true, even though history does not afford too much evidence for it.

Yours faithfully,

[Isaiah Berlin]

Sir Isaiah Berlin OM, CBE, FBA

On 5 March the Berlins flew to India, where IB was to deliver the first Humayun Kabir Memorial Lecture at the invitation of the Indian Council for Cultural Relations. A week later they flew to Iran, and were the guests of HM Ambassador in Tehran, Sir Peter Ramsbotham: 'Shell is ubiquitous here. So are the Russians. Interesting. Israel tactfully unmentioned, but business is plainly done busily under all kinds of tables.'[1] They also visited Persepolis, Isfahan and Shiraz, before returning to England on 22 March, earlier than they would have liked, to attend the ceremony in Oxford the next day at which Leonard Wolfson was given an Honorary DCL: 'All the client kings must attend the feast for the Emperor's son, and there is no doubt that reluctantly I shall have to fly back all the way from Tehran to be present at this inevitably rather dreary occasion.'[2]

TO CHRISTOPHER MACANN

11 April 1972 [*carbon*]

[Wolfson]

Dear Christopher,

Thank you very much for your long and interesting letter – I know Norman Brown[3] well, of course – I taught him many years ago when he was a scholar at Balliol (did you know that he was?) and have continued to be a friend of his ever since. I think, if pressed, he will acknowledge our unbroken and most friendly relationship. He regards me as a man who, despite stumbling on all kinds of genuine sources of hidden gold – Hamann, Vico, the thinkers who really are revealing and boldly original and break through the crust of accepted convention and destroy straitjackets – in spite of this, has failed to learn from them and go on my terrible, middle-of-the-road, conventional way, blinkered, myopic, as one who has seen the light, but failed to acknowledge it, worse in a way than those who dwell in darkness. However, I am very fond of him and wish you to give him my fondest regards.

[…] All that you say about America seems to me perfectly true – I have just

---

1 To Dollie de Rothschild, 14 March 1972.

2 To John Roberts, 23 February 1972.

3 Norman Oliver Brown (1913–2002), US philosopher and historian; taught at Wesleyan University, Connecticut, 1946–62, and later Rochester and California (Santa Cruz); read Greats at Oxford, where IB was his tutor. He applied Freudian thinking to the history of Western civilisation, with a focus on erotic love, and his works were popular with the 1960s counter-culture.

published an essay on Georges Sorel,[1] which the *Times Literary Supplement* printed in its very last issue of 1971. I would send you a copy if I had one to hand – Sorel seems to me to have put his finger in a rather terrifying way on most of the things which are destroying us at present; a man who praised both Lenin and Mussolini at the same time and in almost the same breath is obviously a peculiar figure in the history of thought: he was not a nice man and he said a number of horrifying things, and, had he been alive today, would have led some appallingly destructive movement with far greater success than the late Hegelians, like Lukacs[2] and Marcuse, since his anti-intellectualism liberated him for genuine subversive operations against the, to him hateful, liberal bourgeois culture – he really wanted to go back to Homer and the natural life, or at any rate some kind of passionate activity not trammelled by caution, self-criticism, rationalisations, timidity and liberal values. But I must not go on so.

Do let me know about the progress of your books.

Yours ever,

[Isaiah]

TO LOUIS GLUCKSTEIN

13 April 1972 [*carbon*]

[Wolfson]

Dear Sir Louis,

You will remember that about a year ago, as a result of receiving a letter from an Old Pauline parent about the numerical quota imposed on non-Christian entrance candidates by the School, I wrote a letter to my colleague Professor Max Beloff in which I tried to convey my sense of surprise, and indeed of shock, that the school should have adopted this, in my view, morally unacceptable principle as part of its official policy. When after the luncheon at Mercers' Hall, some months later, to which I had kindly been invited by Mr Winckworth,[3] and at which you were present together with Professor Beloff, the High Master of the School, the Head Master of the Junior School,

---

1 'Georges Sorel', Creighton Lecture, TLS, 31 December 1971, 1617–22; repr. in expanded form in Chimen Abramsky (ed.), *Essays in Honour of E. H. Carr* (London, 1974), and in AC.

2 György Lukács (1885–1971) né György Bernát Löwinger, Hungarian philosopher, literary critic, and sometime government minister, one of the most influential Marxist thinkers of the twentieth century. His seminal work, *Geschichte und Klassenbewußtsein* (Berlin, 1923), was published in English as *History and Class Consciousness: Studies in Marxist Dialectics* (London/Cambridge, Mass., 1971). 'I am in an ambivalent condition about Lukacs: he is obviously a highly gifted man, says some brilliant things and writes a great deal of rot, some of it ordinary Hegelian patter, some of it terrible, official, orthodox, Stalinist stuff. At the same time, he did inaugurate a new kind of approach to the application of Marxism outside economics which only a man possessed of some degree of genius could achieve' (IB to Ronald Sanders, 21 April 1972).

3 John Peter Winckworth (1908–86), solicitor and author; Master of the Mercers' Company for 1961.

and, I believe, the Clerk of the Company, this matter was fully discussed, the arguments advanced by most of those present in defence of inclusion of this formula, whether in the Admission Form or in the Prospectus, appeared to me wholly unconvincing. I will not reiterate the argument in my original letter to Professor Beloff, which, I understand, has been circulated to those most directly concerned. I will confine myself to saying that if an expression causes liberal-minded persons, whatever their religious convictions, to wince or, at the very least, feel moral discomfort and embarrassment, there must be something profoundly wrong with its contents. I do not wish to offer an opinion on the Governors' religious policy as such: but where such a policy runs along the lines of a notorious prejudice, about the long and terrible history of which I do not need to remind you, its adoption seems to me indefensible.

Professor Beloff has allowed me to see the new, revised, formula. It seems to me to differ from its predecessor only in its length. I fail to see why the quota of 'some one seventh' for non-Christians should be regarded as an improvement on the former wording of '85 per cent of Christians', which states the policy in balder and less elaborate form: the substance is unaltered. We did, to the best of my recollection, discuss modifications of the formula which, in my opinion, would have removed most of its offensive aspects. I conclude that these were finally rejected by the Governors. If I am correct in this assumption, I must inform you, as President of the Old Pauline Club, that I hereby resign from that body. I naturally feel deeply reluctant to sever an association which has lasted for more than forty years. But it is clear to me that the spirit of the school which I knew as a boy has in the relevant respect radically changed or disappeared. I do not believe in gestures unless they are absolutely inescapable, and find it painful to resign both from membership of the Club and the office in it which, as I wrote at the time, I felt deeply honoured to be accorded. However, I see no alternative. You will, I feel sure, appreciate my inability to continue as a member of an association which acquiesces in a principle that seems to me morally intolerable. May I request you to convey both my resignation, and the reasons for it, to the members of the Committee of the Old Pauline Club, and to anyone else to whom an explanation is due.

When I originally said that I might feel it necessary to act in this way, you were kind enough to express the hope that I might reconsider this decision. I should like to assure you, and members of the Committee, that I have indeed done so, but find that I cannot, without dishonour, act otherwise.

Yours sincerely,

[Isaiah Berlin]

TO NICHOLAS JACOBS[1]

14 April 1972 [carbon]

[Wolfson]

Dear Mr Jacobs,

Thank you very much indeed for sending the Blumenberg.[2] Indeed, I have the German text, but I am very glad to have the English translation, prefaced as it is by a strong antidote to Blumenberg's most deeply held views. I did indeed know him; he was a charming, modest, very learned man, the last man on earth, I suspect, to be able freely to read Marx's handwriting. He had been taught to do this by Ryazanov[3] personally. I begged him to tell me what he thought were the major defects of my own old book:[4] I pressed him to do this on more than one occasion. He thought that I had not paid sufficient attention to Marx's behaviour to his wife, had not mentioned the illegitimate son (when I wrote my book I did not, of course, know about this),[5] did not dwell sufficiently on the defects of his character. He told me that of all the English socialists he knew, Cole[6] hated Marx the most: thought that despite his genius he had not transformed socialism for the better (strong words!); was responsible for everything that was anti-human, oppressive and fanatical about the movement, etc: that he, Blumenberg, could not agree with this, but respected Cole for these feelings; as for myself, again, he thought my economic section was the weakest (which is surely true, though other things may be weak also), and that I exaggerated Marx's debt to Hegel, who was responsible for muddle and confusion in Marx's head as much as for the bold

1 Nicholas Michael Jacobs (b. 1939), translator, director of the publishers Libris (specialists in German literature) 1991–2010.

2 Werner Blumenberg (1900–65), German historian; an active socialist and founder of the anti-Nazi resistance movement Sozialistische Front in Hanover 1933; fled to Amsterdam (where he died) to escape arrest August 1936; head of German department of the International Institute of Social History 1945–65; author of *Karl Marx in Selbstzeugnissen und Bilddokumenten* (Reinbek bei Hamburg, 1962), trans. as *Karl Marx: An Illustrated Biography* (London, 1972).

3 David Ryazanov (1870–1938) né David Borisovich Gol'dendakh; Ukrainian-born Marxist theorist, scholar and revolutionary; dedicated himself to collecting and publishing the works of Marx and Engels, founding the Soviet Marx–Engels Institute 1921; a victim of Stalin's purges, he was executed on 21 January 1938.

4 *Karl Marx: His Life and Environment* (London, 1939), never yet out of print. A second edition was published in 1948, a third in 1963, a fourth in 1978, and a fifth (edited by Henry Hardy) in 2013.

5 Helene ('Lenchen') Demuth (1820–90), the Marxes' lifelong family servant, gave birth in London to an illegitimate child, Frederick Lewis ('Freddy') Demuth (1851–1929), who became a manual worker in London. In 1962 there surfaced in an archive in Amsterdam a typewritten copy of a letter apparently written in 1898 by Louise Freyburger, Engels's last housekeeper; it claimed that on his deathbed Engels had revealed to Eleanor, Marx's daughter, that her father was also the father of Lenchen's child. While plausible and accepted by some scholars and biographers, there is little other evidence to support the story. Louise Freyburger died in 1950. IB had added a footnote on Freddy Demuth in the 4th edition of the book (Oxford, 1978).

6 (George) Douglas Howard Cole (1889–1959), socialist, political theorist, historian; Chichele Professor of Social and Political Theory, Oxford (IB's immediate predecessor), and Fellow of All Souls 1944–57; Research Fellow, Nuffield, 1957–9.

architectural qualities. Beyond that I could not get him to go: his praise may have been modesty and politeness: I suspect this. [...]

Yours sincerely,

[Isaiah Berlin]

TO OMAR HALIQ

17 April 1972 [*carbon*]

[Wolfson]

Dear Professor Haliq,

Thank you very much for your interesting and indeed moving letter of 3 March, which I have only just seen on my return from Iran. I must admit that none of it is strictly unfamiliar to me, but you put it in a very vivid personal fashion that makes me wish to answer you with equal sincerity.

My Zionist sympathies do not blind me to the fact that the immigrants must often have behaved in the tactless, totally insensitive fashion towards the Arab inhabitants you describe, which must have caused pain and distress and hostility; or [that] the fact that such qualities are not confined to them is relevant, but does not exonerate them. You are perfectly right in supposing that Zionism had no component of violence in its beginnings, or indeed until it acquired an explicitly political dimension: it was an idealistic nationalism of a Mazzinian[1] type, closely allied to religious belief, and violence occurred, it seems to me, only as a response to unexpected obstacles. The fact that Deir Yassin[2] or Kibbiya[3] were, in the last resort, not unconnected with memories of not only the European extermination by Germans, Poles, Balts etc., but riots in Jaffa, killings in Hebron and Safed and elsewhere,[4] serves to explain, though not, of course, to justify, such a 'backlash' – two blacks, whatever the precise degree or extent of blackness, do not make any kind of white. But historically, no doubt this was a product of appalling frustration on the part of the Jews, just as the opposite was the result of an equal bewilderment and frustration on the part of the Arabs.

1 Giuseppe Mazzini (1805–72), Italian nationalist leader, republican, democrat, spent most of his life in exile, and while in Marseilles founded, 1831, the Young Italy (*Giovine Italia*) patriotic movement; one of the driving forces behind the Risorgimento, he continued to campaign for a republic after Italy's unification as a monarchy in 1861.

2 Site of the massacre on 9 April 1948 of up to 254 Arab civilians by Irgun and Stern Gang terrorists, among them the future Prime Minister of Israel Menachem Begin; the killings contributed to the flight of Arabs from Palestine.

3 Jordanian village targeted in a revenge attack by an elite unit of the IDF, October 1953; a large number of homes were destroyed in the raid and 69 villagers – men, women and children – killed.

4 Jews were targeted by Arabs during rioting in Jaffa in early May 1921, and they accounted for around half of the almost 90 people who were killed. In late August 1929 attacks on Jews in Hebron and Safed left many dead: almost seventy were killed in the Hebron massacre, evidence of sectarian tensions that were deeply troubling to the Mandatory authority.

The Jews' motive for coming was simple; they did not wish to be a minority everywhere, for their history was one long martyrology. No sooner were they settled in one corner of a foreign land than the possibility and, ultimately, reality of persecution began to manifest itself and they were set to wandering once again. Consequently they wished to be a majority somewhere and not a perpetually exposed minority with a choice between martyrdom and humiliating submission and a degraded existence everywhere. They were told that a corner of the great Arab territories would, in fact, be given them for what was vaguely defined as a 'national home'. Nobody really knew what this meant. But there is no doubt that the British officials, from the very beginning, trained as they were in Africa and India to be careful of native susceptibilities, and moved by the general plight of the Arab population and what they could not help regarding as the injustice of imposing the immigration of – as you, I'm sure correctly, described it – a wholly foreign population upon them, plainly sympathised with the Arabs and, with a few exceptions, 'dragged their feet' in carrying out what was officially the policy of the Colonial Office as defended in Parliament. I cannot tell you the history of the Mandatory period – I am neither competent, nor is this the place, and you know it better, I expect, than I do – but it is plain that, faced with Arab hostility on the one hand, and the openly unsympathetic attitude of the British officials on the other, the Jews were exasperated. They came from countries in which they had been persecuted. They had been promised liberty, development, autonomy; they found suspicion and obstruction. Some of them certainly felt trapped, and thought that sooner or later they would be abandoned by the West to their enemies among the Arabs, who would exterminate them even as the Europeans had so often done, and as Haj Amin darkly hinted from the mid-1930s onwards might be their fate. The rest I need not tell you: the revolt against them bred aggression on their part, and in any case they came with illusory hopes which were too quickly dispelled. Would they have come if they had known how many Arab inhabitants there were and how unwelcome they were likely to be? I do not know. I think that faced with ferocious and unjust persecution, at any rate east of the Elbe, which the West did little to stop, knowing that wherever they went as homeless refugees they would be bitterly unwelcome, they took refuge not only in the promises of the Balfour declaration,[1] but in a messianic hope

1 The Balfour Declaration, drawn up by Arthur James Balfour when Foreign Secretary, and sent to Lord (Walter) Rothschild as a letter dated 2 November 1917, was a formal statement of the British government's sympathy with Jewish Zionist aspirations: 'His Majesty's Government view with favour the establishment in Palestine of a national home for the Jewish people, and will use their best endeavours to facilitate the achievement of this object, it being clearly understood that nothing shall be done which may prejudice the civil and religious rights of existing non-Jewish communities in Palestine, or the rights and political status enjoyed by Jews in any other country.' *Zionist Review* 1 no. 7 (November 1917), 102; 'Palestine for the Jews', *Times*, 9 November 1917, 7e. The Declaration underwrote British support for Jewish immigration and State-building during the inter-war years.

of salvation, which even in the case of the non-religious has seeped into their souls because their education was inextricably penetrated by the Bible, by daily prayers, everything that bound them spiritually with the ancient names that were the only source of such self-respect and pride as they still possessed – and without which they could not have faced life at all; their nostalgia was continuous for almost two thousand years, and appalling. But of course the injustice to the Arabs was real, and to deny it would be blindness or hypocrisy; but enough Jews have been made to feel aliens by the peoples among whom they lived to render the injustice to them too acute. I do not speak of rights: nor of what human beings would be if they were gentler and kinder and more careful not to misunderstand or ignore or trample on each other. The world [being] as it was, whatever course had been taken, grave injustice must have followed: the only question could be, which was worse? How does one measure that? The Jews were naturally biased in one direction, and the Arabs, equally naturally, in the other. The British officials did not know what to do. They hoped against hope that somehow the situation would solve itself. In 1936 they tried to suppress the Arab revolt against Jewish immigration; in 1938 they tried to suppress Zionist hopes. Democracies are helpless against terrorism: this may be a terrible fact, but it is true; the British tried to yield to the Arab rioters in 1929 and 1931, got into a mess, and did finally leave the country – the result, alas, in part, of Jewish terrorism. It filled me at any rate with a sense of horror which I cannot think about even now without some sense of shame.

None of this, you are quite right in supposing, is to be found in the writings of the fathers of the Zionist movement, any more than you will find it in Herder, who inspired German nationalism (though violence makes its way into the writings of German nationalists as early as the first decades of the nineteenth century); nor will you find it in Mazzini on Italians, or, I expect, in the relevant writings of the Arab awakening. These things come not as a result of doctrine (save, perhaps, in the case of the Germans) but of circumstances, human weakness, stupidity, destructive tendencies and extreme reluctance to face painful realities. All one can do is promote a situation in which there is least injustice, least suffering, least humiliation, least misery and squalor. If one starts at that end one can arrive at, at any rate, tentative solutions: if one does not, and speaks of rights and pride and national honour and absolute justice, then blood will flow and the end will be worse than the beginning. At any rate that is what I believe: it is not a very fashionable or inspiring thing to say. The miseries of the twentieth century are really the worst since prehistoric times: and yet nobody of importance seems to draw any kind of empirical lesson as opposed to huge generalisations of a metaphysical kind. I won't bore you any longer – it is only that I wish to convey to you that I fully understand your letter, sympathise with it deeply, and have tried to answer your questions – inadequately,

I expect. For this I hope you will forgive me, and come to visit me if you are ever here.

    Yours sincerely

      [Isaiah Berlin]   [...]

TO MISS J. NIXON

    21 April 1972 [*carbon*]

                                       [Wolfson]

Dear Miss Nixon,

    In answer to your letter of 4 April about the trial and death of Socrates, I do not know, of course, what the three-page excerpt that you have read contains. But the principal reason for reading Plato's *Apology*,[1] which is about the trial of Socrates, and his *Phaedo*,[2] which is about his death, is that – so far as we know – Socrates was the first man who believed that one could discover the truth both about what there is in the world, and about what one should do and how one should live, by using one's reason and following the conclusions of reasoning wherever it led. He defended this view publicly and maintained that one was allowed to criticise views held by others, no matter how much power or authority the people who held these views might possess, or how much they, or people in general, might be irritated by such criticism; he did not think that it was enough simply to deny or attack views one did not like, but believed in arguing against them by rational means which any normal person could do for himself and could check the correctness of when other people did it. In short, he believed that unswerving pursuit of the truth by rational methods was always justified, and helped to destroy ignorance, prejudice and nonsense in people's heads, which he regarded as responsible for mistakes, for unhappiness, for wickedness – that, and not breaking rules for which no reason could be given. His public criticisms annoyed people so much (they were in an irritated state of mind in any case, because they had just lost a war, with terrible consequences) that they decided to kill him. All science and all knowledge subsequently is based upon his principles, and, what is more, on the example of his courage in following out the consequences of what he discovered to be true, no matter who minded or however unpopular he made himself.

    Yours sincerely,

      [Isaiah Berlin]

1 Plato's version of Socrates' defence, at his trial in Athens in 399 BCE, against the charge of impiety. Socrates was found guilty and sentenced to death.
2 Plato's account of Socrates' last hours, during which he discussed the nature of death and immortality with his friends before accepting the cup of hemlock that would kill him; Phaedo, the narrator, is one of Socrates' most devoted pupils.

TO CHIMEN ABRAMSKY

25 April 1972

Headington House

Dear Chimen,

[…] As for Stravinsky, of course he was a Russian composer; and a pupil of Korsakov;[1] all artists begin as pupils of some master and in some inherited style; nevertheless, Stravinsky always treated the 'Slav' harmonies and rhythms with a certain degree of irony. He came to maturity at a time when the whole *mir isskustva*[2] were in sharp revolt against anything to do with populist, humanitarian, socially conscious, morally earnest and committed art: there is no painter he hated more than Repin:[3] and he once said to me that Mussorgsky's[4] style was appropriate to the canaille ('dlya khamy').[5] All this was grossly unfair. Mussorgsky was a great original genius; but although Stravinsky pottered with his work, and even wrote an end to one of his operas, he was profoundly out of sympathy with it. He thought Balakirev,[6] the founder of the group, a terrible bore – not as bad as Berlioz, but almost. The entire group round Diaghilev, and afterwards their disciples in Paris led by Cocteau[7] etc., were profoundly anti-political aesthetes, who hated above all revolutions, demagoguery, the rising of the masses in the quest of justice and humanity, etc. The Sitwells,[8] though less gifted, were like this in England; at any rate, some of them some of the time. The cosmopolitanism of the early Soviet art was, after all, intended as a protest against con-

1 Nikolay Andreevich Rimsky-Korsakov (1844–1908), Russian composer and conductor, made famous by his brilliant orchestral work *Scheherazade* (1888). His influence on Stravinsky, his most celebrated pupil, is particularly evident in *The Firebird*.

2 'World of art': title adopted by the informal association of Russian avant-garde artists formed in St Petersburg in 1898, and given to the journal they published 1899–1904 (of which Diaghilev was the editor).

3 Il'ya Efimovich Repin (1844–1930), Ukrainian-born painter and sculptor, the leading artist in the Russian Realist movement of the late 19th century.

4 Modest Petrovich Mussorgsky (1839–81), Russian composer whose works include the opera *Boris Godunov* (1874), the piano suite *Pictures at an Exhibition* (1874) and *Songs and Dances of Death* (1875–7). His compositions were posthumously reworked by Rimsky-Korsakov and others, but most modern productions return to his original scores.

5 sc. 'dlya khama/khamov', 'for (a) boor(s)'.

6 Mily Alekseevich Balakirev (1837–1910), Russian composer, pianist and conductor passionately interested in the cause of Russian national music. He became, from 1861, the central figure in the group of young Russian composers known as 'the Five' – the others being Cui, Borodin, Mussorgsky and Rimsky-Korsakov.

7 Jean Maurice Eugène Clément Cocteau (1889–1963), French writer, artist and film-maker; a leader of the French avant-garde and associate of, among others, Diaghilev and Stravinsky.

8 The Sitwells were a literary family comprising the siblings (Francis) Osbert Sacheverell Sitwell (1892–1969), 5th Baronet, writer; Sacheverell Sitwell (1897–1988), 6th Baronet, writer; and Edith Louisa Sitwell (1887–1964), DBE 1954, poet and biographer: '[they] produced almost 200 volumes of poetry, fiction, biography, music, art and literary criticism, giving expression to their own kind of modernism, an amalgam of cubism, futurism and dadaism best described as "Sitwellism" ' (G. A. Cevasco, ODNB). They were the remarkable children of a remarkable father – George Reresby Sitwell (1860–1943), 4th Baronet, antiquary and original.

ventional bourgeois taste. Stravinsky may have disliked philistinism, but the idea of defiance of socially unacceptable regimes, mockery founded upon a serious moral revolt against social inequality, the consumer society, etc. was repellent to him. His Orthodox religion, his love of everything ecclesiastical, his purely aesthetic and hedonistic reactions, his contempt for what he called *Stasovshchina*,[1] amounted to a highly conservative traditionalist but anti-populist position, and dislike of the employment of art for any non-artistic purpose, e.g. national or socialist or ethical ends. Hence his loathing of all socialists, Communists, liberals etc. his acute art-for-art's-sake outlook – which made him look on Lenin and the Russian Revolution as nothing but brutality, barbarism and hatred of beauty. He loathed Dostoevsky, did not altogether like Tolstoy, and loved Chekhov, Pushkin, Evelyn Waugh, T. S. Eliot, the Catholic and the Orthodox liturgies – how could he have liked the 'national' school in Russia or corresponding phenomena in Europe? He loathed Wagner for much the same reasons. I could go on writing to you like this for ever, for it is an endlessly interesting subject – he was the greatest genius I ever knew well – he knew he was immortal, and was happy in the thought.

But despite the journey to Russia – where he was moved by the sights and smells and sounds of his youth and early manhood – he remained implacable about the regime: he became an American patriot, voted for the Republican Party with enthusiasm; he remained an Orthodox believer because it was the religion of his father and his childhood and he remained comforted and happy in it – there was no touch of conscious nationalism in this.

Yours,
Isaiah

TO ANGUS WILSON
27 April 1972 [*carbon*]

[Wolfson]

Dear Angus,
What can I possibly tell you about Freddie? His book *Language, Truth and Logic*, published in, I think, 1935 or 1936,[2] created a great philosophical sensation and acted as a manifesto, provoked violent opposition, made happy converts and liberated a large number of people from what they came to regard as metaphysical delusions or prisons. He has never had a comparable success since, but that need not be said. There were a lot of jokes made in 1939/40 about ARP, or Ayer-Raid Precautions, allegedly being constructed

---

1 'Stasovitis', referring to the autocratic critic Vladimir Vasil'evich Stasov (1824–1906).
2 A. J. Ayer's *Language, Truth and Logic* (London, 1936).

by the older conservative philosophers.[1] When he was in the army – in the Welsh Guards – he was able to read a book and at the same time absorb the contents of a lecture to which he was supposedly listening, since he was able to reproduce it afterwards to the admiration and wonder of his fellow officers. His second book had the Guards' Depot as its address, uncommon in the history of philosophy. He was a great opponent of Austin, and once observed about that redoubtable figure, 'Austin is like a greyhound; he doesn't want to run himself, so he bites the other greyhounds, so that they can't run either.' However, if you use that story, he will know it comes from me, so perhaps better not. The truth about Freddie is that he is somewhat like Max Beerbohm,[2] to whom someone once said, 'I don't like praise being laid on with a trowel, and all said to one's face', to which Max said, 'Oh, don't you? I am not so particular.' The only other epigram by him I can think of is his description of existentialism as 'dramatised tautologies' on a particular philosophical occasion. Oh dear, I am so sorry, I cannot think of any more. I am very glad he is to get this degree[3] – he has not been fairly treated by British Universities, given his fame and his extreme desire for official recognition.

Yours ever,

[Isaiah]

TO DIANA TRILLING

18 May 1972

Headington House

Dearest Diana,

I should have written to you weeks ago about the women's colleges. I have no influence with them myself – they ought to be pleased and proud, privileged and grateful to have you – it is more than they deserve, I do assure you – given the average of the sort of conversations that I overhear on the infrequent occasions when I am asked to dine there […]. If only I had a college to offer you myself with any kind of amenities, I would gladly do it – e.g. if you came a year later, in 1973, I would welcome you with open arms in worthy surroundings (at least, I hope they will be). Anyway, I will let you know as soon as I hear.

Meanwhile I have been listening to a broadcast about my friend Maurice Bowra in which a number of sharp and intelligent and sympathetic things were said by various people – Day Lewis, Hampshire, Betjeman[4] etc. –

1 Air Raid Precautions (ARP) were part of Britain's civil defence during the Second World War.
2 (Henry) Max(imilian) Beerbohm (1872–1956), Kt 1939, caricaturist, writer and critic; a brilliant stylist in any medium, dubbed 'the incomparable' by George Bernard Shaw; his only completed novel was the sparkling *Zuleika Dobson, or, An Oxford Love Story* (London, 1911).
3 An Hon. D.Litt. at East Anglia (1972), where Wilson was Professor of English Literature 1966–78.
4 John Betjeman (1906–84), Kt 1969; immensely popular poet and broadcaster, and defender of threatened (and often unfashionable) architectural treasures; appointed Poet Laureate 1972;

but some extraordinary statements too, e.g. by Noel Annan, to the effect that Maurice was a great reformer who invented the Franks Commission, which totally altered everything here, unlike ghastly reactionary Cambridge, a slough of despond which is rapidly receding backwards – or words to that effect. Maurice was certainly in favour of all the forces of life and progress, but actually had nothing at all to do with the Franks Commission, and did not, as far as I know, institute any radical reforms, although [he] encouraged everyone in all directions. Lord Clark asserted that while England was culturally under the domination of Cambridge and Bloomsbury in the 1920s, Maurice stopped all that, and in the 1930s made Oxford the leading intellectual influence in the country. A very extravagant assertion: Keynes, Virginia Woolf, Forster, Leonard Woolf etc. went on [in] the 1930s exactly as in the 1920s; and while Maurice certainly helped to give Oxford the reputation of a brilliant, glittering, rather cynical establishment, with a great deal of dash, epigrams etc., his influence on English intellectual life was nil. He was a marvellous man, and shaped us all, and liked people to have ideas, and was in favour of a generous flow of wit, and against every kind of narrowness and death, but an intellectual influence is precisely what he was not. Still, there was K. Clark asserting all this, and it will now enter the consciousness, not very deeply perhaps, of hundreds of thousands. History is not, after all, a trustworthy affair.

⟨with much love

yrs⟩

    Isaiah   [...]

TO DIANA TRILLING

    9 June 1972

                                                    Headington House

Dearest Diana,

    [...] I do not think New College will allow any women until later – they first voted for the statute allowing them to have women: then the question arose of whether they were to have them immediately, like the four colleges which really are going to have female undergraduates (whether fellows or not is not quite clear); this, owing to the absence of somebody and the feeble behaviour of someone else, failed to achieve the necessary two-thirds majority, despite warm advocacy by Hayter, which may, indeed, have been somewhat counter-productive. They have acquired the right, but have not voted to implement the right.[1] Typical Oxford situation. Meanwhile Balliol

---

left Oxford without gaining a degree, but found there the friendship, and encouragement, of Maurice Bowra.

1 From the mid-1960s Oxford took its first faltering steps towards dismantling the gender bar imposed by the undergraduate colleges, and in 1974 five of them (Brasenose, Hertford, Jesus, St

and Corpus want to have women fellows but not yet, at any rate, women undergraduates. And so it goes on. I doubt if there is much hope there. No good making you a member of my High Table – there ain't no High Table to speak of, only squalid temporary arrangements which you would not enjoy much. Would St Antony's be better than nothing? But I propose to go on without a fuss and see what can be done about these tremulous women's colleges – I have only spoken to about two, and both profess enthusiasm – whether this will be carried into practice is another question. You could write to Hayter and ask him exactly what the position is, not so much at New College but elsewhere, for he knows about this much more than I, having been involved in the fracas – whereas I, in my still semi-non-existent college, can look loftily upon these squabbles in the underdeveloped, old Oxford world, whence we have emerged into the light of new progressive day.

   [...] Goronwy's book is well worth talking about: you did not guess who wrote the *TLS* review? Only one person, it seems to me, could have quoted that fearful remark by the late Sir Maurice,[1] which I never heard (and which, perhaps a little irritatedly, he would never have uttered in front of me) – only one person – an old friend of yours – who occupies an eminent position in the University of London – in short, Noel. Surely the sociological approach, Oxford v. Cambridge, etc., should have given it to you? Goronwy thinks it is very hostile to him though not to the book. Did you read Crossman's review in the *New Statesman*? Far nastier; it contained some truth, but plainly out to kill.[2] Everyone agrees that it is exceedingly well written. This is not my view: fascinating to read, if only for personal reasons, and I cannot unravel these from others, but I thought it less well written than his other really excellently written books. We must of course speak about this, so do come swiftly. Love to Lionel – we both long to see you both for a long pre-Italian gossip.

Catherine's and Wadham) admitted women undergraduates; a decade later they were all mixed except St Hilda's, which did not admit men until 2008. New College voted to admit women as early as June 1964, but when, in June 1965, there was an attempt to put this principle into practice, by means of a specific alteration of the College's statutes (replacing the sentence 'The College shall be a College for men only and no woman shall be admitted as a member thereof' with 'Both men and women may be members of the College': minutes of governing body, 17 June 1965, SGM2 332), the necessary two-thirds majority was not achieved. After this setback the College welcomed its first woman fellow in 1974, and its first cohort of women students (undergraduates and graduates) in 1979.

1   Bowra is said to have complained that Burgess had 'shit in his finger-nails and cock-cheese behind the ears': [Noel Annan], 'Burgess: Scamp into Scoundrel', review of Goronwy Rees, *A Chapter of Accidents*, TLS, 11 February 1972, 141–2 at 142 col. 2.

2   Crossman argued that the 'obsession' that Rees evidently still felt for Burgess destroyed the objectivity of his account, which is 'less an exposure of the FO spy ring than an elaborate apologia for Mr Rees's failure to denounce Burgess when there was still time. [...] As a picture of Guy Burgess *A Chapter of Accidents* is a brilliant success: as an explanation of the author's behaviour before and after the crisis it is a broken-backed failure.' *New Statesman*, 25 February 1972, 242–3.

⟨yrs
    Isaiah

Stop Press: St. Hilda's College, *have* to-day made you a member of their Common Room – Hurrah!
    I.B.⟩

TO LEONARD WOLFSON

    9 June 1972 [*carbon*]

[Wolfson]

[Dear Leonard,]
    Your father's and your suggestion that we ought, like every other college in the British Isles, to have a crest was very favourably received by the College, young and old. A college is a college and all the attributes of a college go with it. And symbols are not unimportant in the lives of men. I suspect that John Foster, with his gay utilitarianism, may mock at this somewhat – but then he does not see the need for colleges at all and sees no reason why all undergraduates should not feed and live (more economically) in one huge centre. Symbolism means nothing to this jolly opponent of all traditional and historical nonsense. But I do not agree. Nor do, I am glad to say, my most irreverent colleagues at Wolfson College, even at the cost of being pronounced irrational by John. So I do plead for the crest and for the addition of this tiny sum to the bill. What the College would like is to be allowed to use your family Arms, 'differenced' as demanded by the Heralds. They hope that this will be received as a compliment, which they sincerely mean, to your family, and you will surely not want to deprive them of this expression of their real feeling, even if it adds £400 to the building fund. Would you consider the possibility of engraving these arms over the College portals? In for a penny, in for a pound! And particularly before the pound becomes equal to the penny under the next government but two (?). I am not writing separately to your father, but I know that this interprets his wishes as expressed to me. Forward into the past!
    [Isaiah]

TO HAMILTON FISH ARMSTRONG

    13 June 1972

Wolfson

Dear Ham,
    I am the most broken of broken reeds. True, I have all kinds of extenuating circumstances: the main one is exceedingly sad. Old as I am, I have a mother, not surprisingly older still. She is in her ninety-third year, has had a kind of

stroke, and is now in what doctors rather frigidly call the 'pre-terminal stage'. In short, she recognises only me, Aline, the doctor and one of the nurses. It may not be a matter of days, but it is of weeks, and I keep having to go up to London in case I can give her some comfort before the end. This distracts me utterly – I cannot get anything written or said in a coherent fashion. But I also have to confess that I have absolutely nothing to say: and to write without having something to say is something that even I, who do not, as you know, exactly tend to run out of words, cannot bring myself to do. [...] Is there something I could do to save the situation and fill the pages that you must have reserved for me? Is there anyone in England you would like me to persuade to produce something? – I would go on my knees to anyone you designate, whether I know him, or her, or not, to do what you ask. Please tell me and put me out of my agony, or, on the contrary, leave me in it as I deserve to be left. This is one of the most humiliating (and humiliated) letters I have ever had to write. Do forgive me.

    Yours ever, ⟨in sorrow (genuine) & contrition (painful)⟩
      Isaiah

PS Love to Christa, if after this she can bear it!

TO HAMILTON FISH ARMSTRONG
  19 June 1972
                                    Headington House
Dear Ham,

I am still oppressed by guilt about being unable to fulfil your request – similarly about being unable to write a proper piece on Edmund Wilson for the *New York Review of Books*, which I feel absolutely incapable of doing[1] – it is all very well Immanuel Kant saying 'ought implies can'[2] – even if one cannot, one still feels shame and hideous self-accusatory feelings.

All I was going to write for you was how nobody in the nineteenth century or before (obviously) ever predicted that nationalism would be the strongest single force sweeping the world in the twentieth century. Other things were predicted – the military/industrial complex, the rise of Russia and America, German aggression, the revolt of the poor, the socialist revolution, enormous scientific and technological transformations, etc., etc. – but not that no movement, unless arm in arm with nationalism, had any chance of success in this moment of history. But how much could one spin this out? [...]

Meanwhile this reminds me that a graduate student here dealing with

---

1 He didn't (Wilson had died on 12 June). Fifteen years later he wrote 'Edmund Wilson at Oxford', repr. in PI2.

2 i.e. one cannot be blamed for not doing something of which one is incapable – a view espoused (not in IB's words) by Kant.

Anglo-American relations suddenly quoted to me one of my own dispatches, of which I remembered not one word. It all seemed to be very strange, and some of it plainly idiotic. I do not suppose I need to be ashamed of errors and mis-predictions, or of general attitudes which I must have displayed, but there are jaunty, not to say critical, personal remarks about various person-alities – especially Zionists who used to come to see me (e.g. our friend Dr Nahum Goldmann),[1] some of which this man showed me – I hope to God that the individuals of whom I make fun – probably wholly unjustifiably – do not ever get to hear of this, otherwise I really shall be in the soup! I think it is a little irresponsible for the Foreign Office to have opened all these person-alia, trivial in character but potentially offensive to some of those named (I do not, for example, much like the description of my reportage by Mr Eden, who scribbled slightly offensive minutes)[2] – oh dear, life must go on, I suppose, but thirty-year-old casual remarks coming home to roost …

Yours ever,
Isaiah

TO ELENA WILSON

19 June 1972 [*manuscript*]

Headington House

Dear Elena,

I have written you four or five letters, all useless [...]. What *can* I say? I abso-lutely adored Edmund as you know: and felt more reverence for him – (I am a hero worshipper any how: *he* pointed this out to me in a characteristic-ally brusque but affectionate fashion) than for any living man. I felt Russian emotions in his presence: love, acute interest in every word, a sense of pride about knowing him at all and surprise and extreme pleasure at the fact that he liked me at all: deep devotion, fear that I might say something idiotic or trivial or vulgar, & at the same [time] assurance (rightly or wrongly) that he would forgive it; I was also profoundly *moved* by his entire personality, by his vulnerability, his innocence about other people, his – despite all that ter-ribilità[3] – faith in friends and perception in them, sometimes too generous, of all kinds of marvellous virtues and qualities: I really was – as the phrase goes – proud to live on the same earth with him [...]. I won't tell you that

---

1 Nahum Goldmann (1895–1982), Lithuanian-born, German-educated Zionist, based in NY during the Second World War; a leading figure in the establishment in 1936 of the World Jewish Congress, of which he was President 1953–77; President also of the World Zionist Congress 1956–68.

2 IB's Washington dispatches were enthusiastically read by Churchill, who commented in a note to Eden on 27 January 1944: 'The summaries are certainly well written. I have a feeling that they make the most of everything and present a somewhat perfervid picture of American affairs.' Eden comments the next day: 'I agree. There is perhaps a too generous Oriental flavour.' National Archives, FO 371/38537.   *v ardent*

3 'Awesome power'.

he was the greatest critic in any language at the time of his death – he was, no doubt, but what right have I to go on about that? Bob Silvers wanted me to write a piece about him for his journal, but I could not: I cannot set up as a literary specialist, and it wd have been impertinent. [...] There was something about him that was much *older* than the vie littéraire of the twenties and thirties – he would have been far more at home with the robust English writers – Wells, Chesterton, Arnold Bennett, Kipling, Shaw, etc. whom Henry James used to dine with – who talked not about style or aesthetic experience or technique, but about people, mistresses, money, life in general in a very masculine fashion: hence his distaste for the prissy, protected, over-sensitive English literary colony in the 1940ies – he preferred the old bearded *raconteur* and rogue, Compton Mackenzie (who is 95 or so now).[1] I must not go on. His epitaph shd be that he was quelqu'un and had something to say: always: & never spoke unless to say something. All this quite apart from his human properties and deeply touching nature.

What can one say? Nothing. I apologize. Please forgive me. [...] I shall never cease to mourn Edmund for the rest of my days.

yrs with much love
    Isaiah   [...]

TO ROBERT WOKLER[2]

10 July 1972

Wolfson

Dear Robby,

Do not fuss. Rest in peace. You must know that you have absolutely *no* official or *unofficial* status in the matter, and your advice cannot possibly be sought on who is to examine you – and mine only marginally. Do not think about this again. [...] There is *no* question of private communications to these examiners, or special *bonnes bouches* held out to them in the way of a particularly fascinating or intriguing thesis, etc., and this, I am sure, is perfectly right both in principle and practice. I have no doubt that if you were thought to be having ideas about who should and should not examine you, someone might, in the interests of keeping the rules and academic

1 (Edward Montague Anthony) Compton Mackenzie (1883–1972), Kt 1952, novelist, was in fact 88. He came to prominence in Edwardian England with *Carnival* (London, 1912) and *Sinister Street* (2 vols, London, 1913–14) – F. Scott Fitzgerald acknowledged the influence of the latter. Among his later works was the comedy *Whisky Galore* (London, 1947), memorably adapted for film by Ealing Studios (1948).

2 Robert Lucien Wokler (1942–2006), French-born historian of political thought who specialised in Rousseau and the Enlightenment; his Oxford doctoral thesis on Rousseau's social thought (Nuffield, 1976) was supervised by IB, and John Plamenatz was his college adviser; he taught at several universities, including Manchester 1971–98. His *Rousseau* (Oxford, 1995, Past Masters series) is dedicated to the memory of IB, who frequently wrote unavailing references for him as he searched for a job that suited him.

discipline, and purity of conduct, try and disqualify you altogether. So, for God's sake, *don't* have ideas about that. *Don't* worry, and don't think about anything except the thesis, and calm your nerves, and hope and trust that justice will be done without whispering in her ear to compensate her for that bandage over her eyes. You really are more eaten with angst than almost anyone I know, and usually – though there are plenty of real reasons for this, no doubt – without serious cause; just a mass of basic apprehension seeking to settle upon some appropriate object for worry. For such a state I take a small valium pill – or half a one – and read articles in some encyclopedia, one by one in alphabetical order, until my sense of reality is restored. This was a treatment recommended to me by Aldous Huxley, and in my case it works beautifully. I hope it will in yours.

Yours ever,
    Isaiah

TO KAY GRAHAM
17 July 1972

Headington House

Dearest Kay,

After this unheard-of, enormous silence of over a year, it is surely time that we met or at any rate communicated. It is terribly late – long past 2 a.m. – and I am too old, ga-ga, exhausted to be able to say anything of the slightest interest – but as I am going to Italy tomorrow I cannot bear not to write to you. [...]

Do tell me what your plans for the summer are. Aline and I will probably be in Princeton as from about 6 January for about three months or so – at least, I shall be there for that length of time – whether Aline will be able to bear it remains questionable. By this time the World Cup will have been won and lost, for that is what the Presidential election is from the point of view of the world in general: I must say that, if Henry Kissinger[1] really manages to detach China and Russia from North Vietnam to any degree – by whatever means, by American economic aid to Russia and concessions of this or that kind to China – his name will enter the history books; it will be the biggest coup since Bismarck[2] or the Russo-German pact.[3] As it is, he will

1 Henry Alfred Kissinger (b. 1923), German-born US diplomat; Secretary of State 1973–7; an architect of the 1972 Strategic Arms Limitation Treaty, the US rapprochement with China, and the US withdrawl from Vietnam, for which he shared the 1973 Nobel Peace Prize; but also complicit in the secret bombing of Cambodia by US forces during the Vietnam War.
2 Otto Eduard Leopold von Bismarck (1815–98), Duke of Lauenburg, Prussian statesman, Chancellor of the German Empire 1871–90; used victory against France (1870–1) to unite the principalities of Germany.
3 The German–Soviet Treaty of Non-Aggression, 23 August 1939, joined apparently implacable enemies in a marriage of convenience that enabled them to attack and partition Poland, and, with their respective spheres of influence agreed, turn their attention elsewhere. The agreeement

rate a footnote, though a fairly lengthy one. Whom will you elect? I wish I felt enthusiasm about either candidate – I expect McGovern[1] is splendid but I cannot get up any enthusiasm for him – I am not quite sure why – any more than I could, in my day, for Stevenson; Arthur's article in the *Evening Standard* here, explaining that so far from being an isolationist his policies are practically the replica of Eisenhower's, was, though put with fervour and bitterness against wicked British journalists who roused his fury, not altogether convincing; he also wrote a sharp letter to me enclosing various cuttings about the misdeeds of Ambassador Rabin[2] – and ordered me to order the Israel Government to muzzle him. I had some difficulty in persuading him that I did not have the Israel Government in my pocket and could scarcely be expected to send them orders to restrain the indiscreet fellow, or at least to tell him to stop praising Nixon. I am glad they have had a child – it is difficult to imagine what it will look like, given Arthur's genes and Alexandra's – how soon do children acquire recognisable, i.e. semi-permanent, faces? Does one have to wait for three or four years? As a combination of features, no more contrasting ones could well be conceived – I am relieved on the whole that this question cannot be asked of Aline and me. What a strange subject to have suddenly embarked on – I must not pursue it any further; it is only because the hour is so very late that my thoughts are wandering and I am beginning to write total nonsense.

I must stop. This is really only a letter intending to elicit from you a sign of life, and to send you my lifelong and boundless affection.

Yours,

⟨with fondest love

Isaiah

I realize what *may* be the cause of your long silence but I *hope* it is not that.[3] If it is, it is all the more desirable that we resume our old, unique, delightful friendship – not that a single cloud has ever hovered over it, I am happy to say. I don't wish to meet anyone new: old friendship is worth more than anything at all – don't you think?⟩

was negotiated by Molotov and his German counterpart, (Ulrich F. W.) Joachim von Ribbentrop (1893–1946), Hitler's Foreign Minister 1938–45; the 'Nazi–Soviet Pact' was Ribbentrop's greatest coup, establishing him above Bismarck in Hitler's eyes, but thereafter he lost influence; he was tried at Nuremberg, sentenced to death, and hanged.

1 George Stanley McGovern (1922–2012), US politician; Democratic Senator from South Dakota 1963–81; favoured civil rights, action against poverty (at home and abroad), the women's movement, etc.; as Democratic Presidential candidate in 1972 he lost every state to Nixon except Massachusetts, the most liberal.

2 Yitzhak Rabin (1922–95), Jerusalem-born Israeli general and statesman; ambassador to Washington 1968–73; succeeded Golda Meir as Prime Minister 1974–7 (and returned to that office 1992–5); a commander in the Palmach (199/4) during the Zionist revolt against the Mandate; prominent as Chief of Staff during the Six-Day War.

3 Cause undiscovered.

TO JEAN FLOUD

26 August 1972 [*manuscript*]

Grand Hotel Royal Orologio, Abano Terme

Dear J.

What an (physically – but what, it used to be said, is that to the blind &
deaf like me? Thank God I shall not have even a brief biographer – else the
evidence, in friends' casual references – Stephen Spender's, Philip Toynbee's
books – makes me out a monster without senses: no sensibilities beyond
a chatterbox brain) after this fine egocentric opening, I resume: what a marvellous summer: routine in Italy much more set than when you were here
save for 2 days when Bob Silvers arrived (alone: without his lady: who developed or said she developed, a chill. So would I, in her place, if I had the
courage) when there was what Aline calls talk talk talk. Then dear Abano.
Like Bad Homburg in 1910, I think: that's what draws me here: the strang-
est thing – cutting into the beautifully rigid régime (nostalgie de la boue[1]
said Lord Annan with genuine wit, I thought) was meeting an old Russian
landowner – a figure out of *any* Russian 19 century novel, but particularly
Turgenev – whom I recognised by his accent when he enquired, at the swimming pool, whether I had done with the stationary bicycle? He talked in
polite, old fashioned French: "vous avez un accent leger russe" said I boldly.
After that Mr Djanshieff persuaded Aline & me to go to a service in Venice
for Diaghilev & Stravinsky combined: "it sounds terrible" he said "to put
it like that: about a memorial service – religious ... solemn ... but it may
be *amusing*'. It was. I'll tell you when I see you. Composed of Lifar[2] & all
Stravinsky's bitterest enemies and libellers. On the Isola San Michele [...].

Yours ever

Isaiah   [...]

TO HAMILTON FISH ARMSTRONG

28 August 1972 [*manuscript*]

Paraggi

Dear Ham,

Thank you for your sweet forbearance. I think a good deal less well of my
piece than you do – & I am correspondingly encouraged and grateful. Alas,
I only received your proofs *to-day* (the Italian posts are *appalling* & special
delivery means, as I expect you know, *nothing*). I have corrected the proofs
– I cd not send them by the week-end which is over – the past not even the
gods themselves can alter, said Euripides – but I hasten to send them off now,

---

1 'Longing for degradation'. Annan's pun fixes on its literal meaning, 'yearning for mud' – IB was
staying at the Venetian spa resort of Abano Terme, famous for its mud treatments.
2 Sergey Mikhailovich (Serge) Lifar (1905–86), controversial Kiev-born ballet dancer, choreographer
and director; principal dancer, Ballets russes, 1925; ballet master, Paris Opera, 1930–44, 1947–58.

airmail, *espresso* etc. etc – but I am pessimistic about the speed of delivery. [...] I'll do my desperate best. Italians are bound to garble an English cable, especially one of monster size: but if you tell me to cable, I will. You must imagine me in a small Italian post office, at the head of a queue of mothers sending messages to their daughters, nieces to aunts, minor crooks to their accomplices, filing my 1000 word message. But I'll do it, & then get lynched by the queue. It will be appallingly expensive: will you subtract it from my fee? or what? Anyway, what you will command, I'll do.

love

Isaiah

TO OLIVER GATES[1]

1 November 1972 [*manuscript*]

As from Headington House

Dear Oliver,

John telephoned last night and said that Sylvester had been taken ill again. A minute ago Aline telephoned me here and told me that he had died.[2] [...] I was, as you know, deeply devoted to him. We first met forty years ago – in All Souls, I should think, with John Sparrow, and then with Felix; I remember the immediate admiration I felt, & that I wondered whether I should be allowed to meet him again. We did, quite soon after, and I grew more and more aware of how fastidious, how civilized and intellectually and morally, & above all, aesthetically rigorous he was, and when we made friends, how much pride I felt in the fact that a man of such marvellous quality shd put up with me who was made of such loose texture, such a bad scholar, so undiscriminating in so many ways. This I went on feeling for the rest of my life: his friendship remained a source not only of intense pleasure but of pride: it made me think better of myself, better, I daresay, than I deserved, it propped me up in moments of self doubt and self reproach – it was an especial pleasure to describe him to others – it was almost a kind of vanity to indicate to them how high and firm one's own standards could be. He did me countless favours: not least taking on the dreary & thankless task of presiding over my College Trust [...]. I really only want to say that I loved him deeply, shall miss him terribly, so will Aline with whom he had a personal relationship independent of mine – & that I hope you will not grieve too long – & don't, on any account, reply to this.

Yours,

Isaiah

1 Oliver Gates (b. 1937), son of Sylvester Gates and his second wife Pauline née Newton; businessman, DuPont, 1960–7; partner, L. Messel & Co, stockbrokers, 1967–87; later (1987–2010) a financial adviser. In 1940 Felix Frankfurter invited Sylvester Gates's children to stay at his home for the duration of the war: they stayed until 1942.

2 Sylvester Gates died on 1 November, aged 71.

In Tehran in March 1972 IB learned of the death of his friend Jacob Herzog,
who had been Israeli ambassador to Canada and adviser to four Israeli Prime
Ministers. On receipt of the news he wrote to Dollie de Rothschild:[1] 'I sent you
a wire just out of excess of sadness: I really liked him personally very much
indeed: he was a very devoted, sensitive, sympathetic friend to me, quite apart
from his unique (& I think) unparalleled service to Israel: he was sensible,
self-effacing, shrewd, utterly devoted & patriotic without being nationalistic
(v. rare phenomenon)'.[2] In October IB delivered the inaugural Yaacov Herzog
Memorial Lecture in Jerusalem, choosing as his theme 'Zionist Politics in
Wartime Washington: A Fragment of Personal Reminiscence'.[3] The lecture
was published in Hebrew translation, in instalments, between 3 and 11 October
in Ha'aretz (described by I. F. Stone as 'Israel's best and most objective daily
paper').[4] There followed a bitter controversy in the paper between IB and the
Israeli publicist and politician Nathan Yellin-Mor[5] over what had been known
about the Holocaust in wartime Washington, and, crucially, what more could
have been done to avert the tragedy. The first of Yellin-Mor's three articles (18–20
October) was entitled 'The Assignment – To Silence the Outcry: Isaiah Berlin
Confesses His Errors after Waiting 30 Years'. IB was unsure how best to respond
to the ferocity of Yellin-Mor's assault, and in the first half of November he sent
the editor of Ha'aretz, Gershom Schocken, two versions of a letter of reply,
the second (and shorter) of which, enclosed with his letter of 13 November, was
published on 17 November.

TO THE EDITOR OF *HA'ARETZ*

[6 November 1972; *carbon*]

[Headington House]

Sir,

　Mr Yellin-Mor's articles published in your issues of October 18–20 on the
subject of my Herzog Memorial Lecture have only now reached me. His
account and interpretation of the situation which I attempted to describe
are so remote from mine (and I believe from reality) that I see no possibility
of serious argument between us. The difference between our values, values
that inevitably colour our perceptions of the past, is too great. As for Mr

---

1 Dorothy Mathilde ('Dollie') de Rothschild (1895–1988) née Pinto, wife of James Armand de
　Rothschild; like her husband, a philanthropist and Zionist; IB was devoted to her, and gave
　unsparing advice on her many philanthropic commitments.
2 Letter of 14 March 1972.
3 Jerusalem, 1972; repr. as an appendix to L1 (663–93).
4 op. cit. (336/4); no instalment appeared on Saturday 7 October.
5 Nathan Yellin-Mor (1913–80) né Nathan Friedman-Yellin; born in Grodno, Poland; formerly
　a Revisionist Zionist, and one of the leaders of the Stern Gang terror group, he became a left-
　wing pacifist, advocating Israeli withdrawl from the West Bank.

Yellin-Mor's ⟨gratuitous⟩ personal reflections about myself, I do not intend to follow his example and speculate about his own motives.

But I owe it to your readers to correct some of Mr Yellin-Mor's graver misstatements of fact, at least in so far as they grossly misinterpret my own statements and convictions, and this is the sole purpose of my letter. He declares that I 'believed that the barrier between us and the British never existed'. My comments on the unhappy relationship between the Yishuv and the British administration, culminating in the White Paper, refute this.[1] In connection with American reactions to the implementation of the White Paper, he declares that I 'not only saw no need for a great outcry, but undertook to prevent it (in America) and choke it if there were signs that it was about to burst' (18 October). And again, that I was 'quite prepared to cause the dismantling of the tool of Jewish pressure on the United States so that it did not influence the administration, which might have exercised pressure on the British Government' and 'viewed all legitimate pressure as lies and libels'. The first is a more monstrous charge than the second, but both are totally false. In 1941, when I was a British Information Officer in New York, Jewish, particularly Zionist, opinion in America was, as I pointed out, overwhelmingly pro-British – even after Russia came into the war. My task was to induce the Jewish press to publish information about the British war effort – and this it did with unwavering enthusiasm. In 1942 I was transferred to Washington, with the sole task of reporting American opinion to London. I was not instructed or expected to influence anyone towards anything. At no point did I, or was I in a position to attempt to, curb even the most extreme Zionist propaganda. I shared Weizmann's view that some of it was in fact counterproductive, but I understood only too well the bitterness from which it sprang, and had neither the means nor the wish even to try to stem it. Zionists of all persuasions who met me at the time knew of my feelings, particularly with regard to the formation of a Jewish Army under British or Allied auspices, an ambition which I personally shared, even though Mr Yellin-Mor says that I 'viewed the agitation in favour of it as an embarrassing nuisance' and, worse than that, that I 'thought and hoped that in the final analysis five million Jews would hardly be able to influence American policy'. I made it clear in my lecture that while this view was held in British official circles, it was known that I did not hold it, and while I made it clear that I underestimated the ultimate force of American Jewish opinion, to say that I hoped that it would prove as weak as I feared it might prove is

1 Notwithstanding the Balfour Declaration, relations between the Jewish community in Palestine and the British Mandatory authority were at best chequered; in July 1937 the Peel Commission outlined a plan for the partition of Palestine and a two-State solution, but the May 1939 White Paper reversed this, restricting the sale of land to Jews, and further Jewish immigration, and prefiguring a single independent State in which Arabs, by virtue of numbers, would be the controlling constituency.

a loathsome allegation, as groundless as the assertion that it was I, and not the Foreign Office, that viewed Jewish pressure as consisting of 'lies and libels' (19 October) or that I 'did not share in the hope of the abolition of the White Paper'. I hoped for a Jewish State, though perhaps not that which Mr Yellin-Mor desired; and if I did not in 1943 expect the abrogation of the White Paper, this, as I stated, was due to the fact that I did not then know of the views of the Cabinet Palestine Committee, which inclined towards partition (20 October). I did not draw the contrast between the Palestine administration and the British Government attributed to me (19 October). I merely asserted, quite correctly, that decent British officials in London, some of them unfavourable to the White Paper, were all but stung into a counter-offensive by what they regarded as unjust slander and denigration of the British Government by American Zionists.

I could continue. But perhaps the above examples sufficiently illustrate your contributor's methods and credibility.

Yours truly,
   [Isaiah Berlin]

TO GLEB STRUVE

6 November 1972

Headington House

Dear Gleb Petrovich,

[...] If you are in correspondence with Madame Mandelstam I have a favour to ask of you: I do not wish to write to her myself, since I do not know her and in any case do not know where to write to. But if you are writing about something else, you could perhaps add that her statement in the second volume of the Memoirs, that it was I who 'organised' squads of students from Oxford to 'rescue' victims of Zhdanov[1] and Stalin, is without any foundation whatever.[2] It is possible that one or two people who tried to see Akhmatova or others mentioned my name, since I had no doubt talked in 1946 about the writers I had met in the autumn and winter of 1945 – that is the only possible fire beneath this smoke and I should like her to know the truth. I was sufficiently aware of the precarious condition of the kind of writers who were not prepared to save themselves by servile behaviour not to embarrass them, to say the least, by sending people to see them. As for her reflections about Akhmatova's references to me in the *Poema bez geroya*[3] and

---

1 Andrey Aleksandrovich Zhdanov (1896–1948), Soviet politician and cultural inquisitor; First Secretary of the Leningrad Party 1934–48, and head of the city's defences during the siege of 1941–4. As Central Committee Secretary for Ideology 1944–8 he led a brutal campaign to eliminate all Western cultural and scientific influence in Soviet society. He died suddenly in August 1948, and Stalin later accused a group of Jewish doctors of his murder.

2 480/3.

3 *Poem without a Hero*, Akhmatova's longest work, widely regarded as her masterpiece. She began

the 'fatal' part that my visit played in Akhmatova's life, that was made very clear to me by Anna Andreevna herself when she came to Oxford and when we both met her and does not correspond with what Madame Mandelstam reports. But *that* I do not particularly wish to be pointed out to her – A.A. romanticised everything, as you know, and was liable to tragic interpretations; there is no doubt that my visit did add to the cup of her sufferings. But the entire book is so terribly bitter against virtually everyone that I cannot complain if I do not escape. [...]

Yours ⟨with Ваш – с теплым приветом,⟩[1]

Isaiah Berlin

TO SAMUEL SAMBURSKY

13 November 1972

Headington House

Dear Shmuel,

[...] You mention my Herzog lecture. I did read Yellin-Mor's articles, which of course irritated me – I contemplated an extensive refutation of all his misstatements of fact – he is entitled to these odious views, but that is another matter – but I do not want to enter into any relations with him, not even, as Froude once said about the Regius Professor of History in Oxford, Freeman[2] – 'not even those of hostility'. So I may write a short letter to Schocken, which he may or may not publish, rebutting the worst and most odious only of the charges.[3] The purpose of the lecture was, of course, to show how apparently intelligent and well-thought-out premises upon which policies are founded can be blown up by history – that mistaken prognoses sometimes lead to sensible conduct, and how obsessed dervishes like Ben-Gurion sometimes have a deeper insight into events than splendidly gifted but sane and rational men like Weizmann. The only thing I mind being accused of is callousness in face of the Holocaust. I wish I could remember what we knew in those years. My impression is that it was not reported in 1942–4 in such a manner as to make an impact on American opinion, either

---

it in Leningrad in 1940 and continued to work on it until 1962, weaving IB's 1945–6 visits into the text. IB called it 'a kind of final memorial to her life as a poet, to the past of the city' (PI2 237).

1 'Yours – with warm regards'.

2 Edward Augustus Freeman (1823–92), historian of the Norman Conquest, Froude's predecessor as Regius Professor 1884–92. Freeman was aggressively opinionated, and took particular exception to Froude, whose scholarly reputation he sought to destroy through anonymous reviews in the *Saturday Review* spanning two decades. Freeman was known to be the author of these attacks, and in 1879 Froude wrote a dignified reply, ending: 'Here, so far as there is any personal controversy between myself and Mr Freeman, the matter must end. [...] I shall not be a party in any further controversy with him.' J. A. Froude, 'A Few Words on Mr Freeman', *Nineteenth Century* 5 no. 26 (April 1879), 618–37 at 367. Froude attracted much bigger audiences to his professorial lectures than Freeman did.

3 IB means the shorter replacement (see 509) for the letter he had already sent (503–5).

Jewish or gentile.[1] I may be wrong, but that is what I remember: of course, Eden's speech in the House of Commons and the fact that the Commons rose for a minute's silence in memory of the slaughtered Jews in the Baltic and Poland – I think late in 1944 – occurred,[2] although at the time when I composed my lecture I did not remember even that; somebody reminded me of it later, and then I did remember it. But, for whatever reason, news dribbled through about deportations; one assumed, of course, that horrors were going on, but there was no beating of drums, no terrifying, catastrophic news which would produce a real, heard-of reaction. Peter Bergson and his friends,[3] Revisionists,[4] Irgunists[5] etc., did organise marches, advertisements etc., but they were all regarded by the moderate Zionists as sensationalists, people who did more harm than good by infuriating Roosevelt and the American officials, and making Zionist pressure for ultimate objectives – the state, the abrogation of the White Paper, etc. – more difficult. I do not know why news which must, after all, have been in the hands of the Zionist leaders in America was never made really public; why this should have been left to people whose reputations made their credibility too low. At any rate, if there had been a great perturbation among the Jews about this, I should, of course,

1 IB's retrospective impression appears to be confirmed by the contemporaneous press summaries that he sent from Washington from 1942 to 1944. These devote very little attention to newspaper reports of the unfolding Holocaust: see H. G. Nicholas, *Washington Despatches* (442/1), where there is one such reference at 240. But a survey of two large-circulation newspapers, to which IB would certainly have had access, the *Washington Post* and the London *Times* (in May 1943 IB asked his parents to take out a subscription to the latter paper, and have it sent to him in Washington), suggests that while Allied newspaper reporting of the Holocaust was much less extensive than might be expected by a modern reader, a clear and accurate outline of what was occurring in Nazi occupied Europe was emerging by the winter of 1942 (see further 510/1).

2 In the House of Commons on 17 December 1942 Anthony Eden, Foreign Secretary, read an international declaration, to be made public at the same hour in Washington and Moscow, condemning the Nazis' 'bestial policy of cold-blooded extermination' of Jews in Europe: 'the German authorities [...] are now carrying into effect Hitler's oft repeated intention to exterminate the Jewish people in Europe. [...] The number of victims of these bloody cruelties is reckoned in many hundreds of thousands of entirely innocent men, women and children.' At the suggestion of William Cluse, Labour member for Islington South, the whole House rose and stood in silence at the end of the debate with heads bowed (*Parliamentary Debates*, House of Commons, 17 December 1942, col. 2083; 'Nazi Crimes against the Jews', *Times*, 18 December 1942, 8b).

3 Hillel Kook (1915–2001), founder member of Irgun. Under the pseudonym Peter Bergson he became a spokesman for Revisionist Zionism in the US during the Second World War; from 1942 the 'Bergson Group' increasingly worked to publicise the extreme plight of Jews in Nazi-controlled Europe, but its methods stimulated opposition from US Zionists and Jewish groups.

4 As defined by one of its founders and leading exponents, Vladimir Jabotinsky (1880–1940), Revisionist Zionism meant the Mandatory authority becoming a 'colonisation regime' that would oversee mass immigration of Jews to Palestine; their settlement on lands both east and west of the Jordan; and the creation of all of the apparatus necessary to statehood. Revisionists were right-wing and expansionist, rejecting the gradualism and moderation of the Weizmann approach. V. Jabotinsky, 'Jews in Palestine: Revisionists and the Mandate' (letter), *Times*, 6 September 1929, 8b.

5 Supporters of Irgun (336/2), the right-wing Zionist military force active in Palestine from the 1930s; the group was behind the bomb attack on the King David Hotel on 22 July 1946, in which over 90 people of various nationalities were killed, and many injured.

have reported it simply as part of my duties in reporting press reactions and the general movement of opinion. But I do not believe that anything more happened than bits and pieces from here and there, isolated horror stories, no cumulative, dramatic reports. Even about Joel Brand[1] I learned after the war, from books and articles. But let that be. I realised, of course, that all this stir of feelings would arise among people whose memories are bound up with what happened at that time, and young men who have been brought up on accounts of the past, partly true and partly false. But I thought it just worthwhile recording these things, if only as an exercise in how different facts look from different vantage-points, even in so life-and-death a history as this. What did you think yourself? Schocken told me that *Ha'aretz* did publish appalling stories about the extermination from the end of 1942 onwards, with black borders and all – none of this got through to me in my ivory tower in Washington. I could only report, as a Zionist British official, what I knew and felt and did. But enough of this. […]

I suppose Leonard W. was right not to publish the anti-Semitic outpourings of her Vita Sackville-West years;[2] one day it will all appear, no doubt, and lead to further controversy; like the topic of Ezra Pound's and T. S. Eliot's anti-Semitism, which keeps popping up now and then – their friends defend them as if it was not plain that in fact they did have these views, and what is needed is explanation, not apology.

Yours ever,
Isaiah

TO GERSHOM SCHOCKEN

13 November 1972 [*carbon*]

[Headington House]

Dear Mr Schocken,

Thank you for your letter of 5 November. By this time you will have received a letter from me, enclosed with which was a letter to you as Editor of *Ha'aretz* for publication. Since I have no desire to re-open this polemic, which appears to have died down, it would, perhaps, be best to publish nothing at

---

1 Joel Brand (1906–64), Hungarian Jew and Zionist, leading member of the Jewish Aid and Rescue Committee in Hungary. In May 1944 Adolf Eichmann used him to propose a deal to the Allies in which Hungarian Jews would be exchanged for military supplies and basic provisions – the so-called 'blood for goods' deal; Britain and the US considered this a Nazi ruse to begin peace negotiations designed to split the Allies, while the Soviets refused outright to consider it. Brand and others, though, believed that it was an opportunity missed. The proposal was reported in *The Times* under the headline 'A Monstrous "Offer"': 'The British Government know what value to set on any German or German-sponsored offer. They know that there can be no security for the Jews or the other oppressed peoples of Europe until victory is won' (20 July 1944, 2).
2 i.e. the late 1920s, when Virginia Woolf was romantically involved with the writer Victoria Mary ('Vita') Sackville-West (1892–1962). *A Writer's Diary: Being Extracts from the Diary of Virginia Woolf* (London, 1953), edited by her husband Leonard Woolf, omitted such passages.

all; or, alternatively, a shorter letter, which I enclose with this one. Which of these courses is best adopted I leave to you: naturally I wish to refute the more offensive charges, that have no basis in fact, made by Mr Yellin-Mor; but if this is likely to provoke further controversy, I would rather not: not [so much] because of the nature of the case itself as because of my reluctance to enter into any kind of relationship, even that of controversy, with so unbalanced and irresponsible a person. I do not know him, and only saw him on British television once: I thought him brutally fanatical and a little mad: his interviewer also appeared rather frightened of him. You speak of him as an excellent publicist and an interesting man. So were Mussolini and Rochefort[1] and Maurras[2] – yet they did a good deal of damage to their societies and no perceptible good. All this quite apart from Yellin-Mor's opinions, which one can probably agree or disagree with, and which may be interesting or well argued – it is his personality that repels me.

Livne[3] is, of course, another matter: I know him and he is a born protester, congenitally against the government, whatever it may be, a discontented but perfectly human individual, unlike what I take Yellin-Mor to be. I do not mind his indignation at the space you gave me, for which I must again thank you – it was a courtesy on your part for which I shall always be grateful: I do resent his charge of callousness about the Holocaust. On this point I feel that you half agree with my detractors, and this surprises me, and I wonder why you should feel this. I believe that I had made it clear in my lecture that while indignation with the White Paper became a permanent element in almost every group of American Jews during the war, [and] the British Palestine immigration policy was condemned by virtually all of them with varying degrees of grief or indignation, the actual news of the extermination of the Jews in Europe did not make the kind of impact upon them that it would have done had it been brought home to them by press and radio. *Ha'aretz* did not penetrate to opinion-forming circles in America, Jewish or gentile: news of deportations trickled through, for example to my wife and her friends from Paris, but I do not recollect that the full horror ever struck the American public, even the Jews, until quite late.

[...] all I remember (but my memory, of course, is very imperfect) is that Eden told the House of Commons about the murder of Jews in the Baltic countries and Poland, and that the House of Commons observed a minute's

---

1 Victor-Henri Rochefort, marquis de Rochefort-Luçay (1830–1913), French politician, journalist and polemicist, who gravitated with age from the far left to the far right, becoming a prominent anti-Dreyfusard during the late 1890s (174/3).

2 Charles (Marie Photius) Maurras (1868–1952), ultra-right-wing French political theorist and author; prominent in the Action française political movement founded in 1899, and a contributor of anti-Semitic writings to its daily, *L'Action française*; accused of being a collaborationist, he was sentenced to life imprisonment after the liberation.

3 Eliezer Livneh (1902–75) né Liebenstein, Polish-born Zionist activist and journalist; a Haganah and Mapai propagandist during the Second World War, later a Mapai Knesset member.

silence for the dead; this must have been reported in the American press. There were, no doubt, items of news about concentration camps and the like, but nothing, as far as I remember, about the gas chambers – or at any rate, nothing capable of arousing mass protests, whether by Jews or by people in general, against unheard-of horrors.[1] I do not know why this was so: later I learned that there were plans to bomb the railways leading to the camps, and that it was alleged that the Russians refused the right of refuelling to the planes, that for one reason or another efforts to get the RAF to do this failed. But all this is *post factum*. [...]

I do not know what the Americans, or indeed the British, could have done to save the Jews – perhaps Goldmann and others are right and not enough was done. But nobody talked to me about this at the time, none of the Zionists in America nor my visitors from Israel – evidently it was not in the forefront of political attention. So I must still adhere to my view that an attempt to force the American or British governments into some action which they were not willing to undertake would not have succeeded (unless there is evidence about which I know nothing), but might have precipitated a collision during the war which would certainly have alienated the American government, at great cost to Zionist aspirations after the war. But all this I do not wish to repeat again – it was all very clear in my lecture. What did happen, of course, was that extremist Zionist propaganda was responsible for a very determined effort on the part of both the State Department and the Foreign Office to get a joint statement signed by the President and the Prime Minister designed to suppress all Zionist propaganda. The full story of that remains to be told – it was prevented by eminent Jews in Washington,[2] and any Jew involved in this

---

1 In both the *Washington Post* and *The Times* there were reports, 1943–5, of the Nazis' use of the gas chambers, and although they were not numerous they were explicit. On 8 July 1944, for example, *The Times* carried a report under the headline 'Hungarian Jews' Fate: Murder in Gas Chambers'. It concludes: 'When the Germans, in the second half of 1942, started their extermination of Polish Jewry the gas chambers at Oswiecim [Auschwitz] could not cope with all the victims, so two more death camps were erected – Tremblinka [sc. Treblinka] and Rawa Ruska, near Lwow. In these three camps more than 2,000,000 Polish Jews have been murdered since 1939' (3c). The essentials of the Holocaust had been disclosed by *The Times* as early as November–December 1942 in a series of graphic news reports, which gave context to the Allies' joint declaration of 17 December (507/2): 'Nazi War on Jews: Annihilation Commission in Poland' (24 November 1942, 3e); 'Nazi War on Jews: Deliberate Plan For Extermination' (4 December 1942, 3a); 'Terror Against Jews: European Pogrom' (7 December 1942, 3e). The last paragraphs of the latter report are headed 'Final Solution': 'In all parts of Europe the Germans are calling meetings, or issuing orders, to bring about what they call "the final solution of the Jewish problem". All such evidence comes from the enemy himself, as he proclaims the details of his plan.'

2 The proposed joint British–American declaration against Zionist aspirations, due to be made by FDR and Churchill in the summer of 1943, was torpedoed by clandestine Zionist machinations initiated by IB. The planned statement arose from Allied concern that support for a Jewish homeland would be detrimental to the war effort in the Middle East. It was IB who informed the Zionist newspaper-publisher George Backer (one of the 'persons still alive') of rumours of the declaration, and Backer then lobbied Henry Morgenthau, Jr (1891–1967), Secretary of the Treasury 1934–45 (with Backer, one of the 'eminent Jews'), who in turn pressed Roosevelt to drop the statement; and by early August 1943 it was dead. IB successfully concealed his role in the affair

story emerges with credit. I cannot tell the full story even now, for it would compromise persons still alive, a poor reward for their good behaviour. One day I may tell you in confidence about what occurred, and you will then see how baseless the Yellin-Mor/Livne view of the whole thing is. But I cannot write to you about it now, even at the price of unjust accusations. So let that be.

I still wonder what it is that makes you say that things looked to me so very different from the way in which they looked, or look, to you and others in Israel, then or now. You are a busy man, and I do not want to put unnecessary burdens on you; but I should be grateful if you would let me know why you think there is anything to the case of my detractors. Even if Weizmann's tactics were based on what turned out to be a false, or partially false, prognosis, what possible harm can they be thought to have done at the time? I am inclined to defend his tactics as having done the Jews and Zionism nothing but good, above all in averting a split between Zionism and the American administration of Roosevelt, which would have carried on into the Truman regime. The fact that Zionism seemed at least reasonable and morally decent and politically serious and attractive to Truman is due to the avoidance of violent tactics at an earlier stage, when in any case, so far as I at any rate can see, they could not have produced good results or saved a single Jewish life. I may be wrong, but if so it needs more than Yellin-Mor's articles to convince me.

Yours sincerely,

[Isaiah Berlin]   [...]

TO JAKOB HUIZINGA

21 November 1972 [carbon]

[Wolfson]

Dear Mr Huizinga,

I am sorry to have kept your typescript[1] for so long, but I did not want to return it to you before I had actually read it – and as my life is almost as disordered, in some ways, as that of Rousseau – though, I hope, not for the same causes or [with] the same devastating consequences – I took longer over it than was reasonable, and only hope that this will not cause you any inconvenience.

I have always found Rousseau unsympathetic. He is a marvellous touchstone for something – it is not clear what – in that people never fail to react to his writings or his personality, either with admiration and, in some cases,

---

from his superiors in the Foreign Office, revealing it to his biographer only shortly before he died. See MI 117–18.

1 Presumably an early draft of Huizinga's *The Making of a Saint: The Tragi-Comedy of Jean-Jacques Rousseau* (London, 1976).

a degree of self-identification, or repulsion or even revulsion; never with indifference. This, in itself, is proof of a unique quality: of the touching of live issues, still alive today. It is always proof of some depth of insight when a nerve touched so long ago still quivers: when Popper is positively angry with Plato, or Butterfield still horrified by Machiavelli, or a whole row of French writers from Madame de Staël onwards write about Rousseau with enthusiasm or real hostility, and the debate continues as it is still doing today – this is a sign of some eternal, or at any rate long-lived, problem common to all men, or at least our own civilisation. Your indictment in this portrait [of a] paranoiac, egocentric, violently unbalanced, often manic victim of all kinds of (to me unattractive) fantasies precisely coincides with my own prejudices. I should be as nervous, and, indeed, frightened, of meeting Rousseau if I had lived in the eighteenth century as I should be of Carlyle or Wagner, or D. H. Lawrence or all the other 'angry' prophets who thundered at mankind after theological sermons had somewhat gone out of fashion.

I enjoyed your piece very much – it is a remorseless vignette of this ghastly man whose hysterical appeals for pity and understanding are, to me at least, as unmoving as his monstrous behaviour is unattractive. But apart from his literary genius, and his appalling insights as a thinker, which I do not think can be denied, even by his worst enemies – Grimm[1] and Helvétius[2] and even at times Diderot (whom I find irresistibly attractive) seem at times shallow by comparison – apart from all this, he obviously said things, and said them in a fashion which, for the first time, touched chords, and brought into the open feelings and self-images which have, no doubt, in some sense always been there, but which no one had articulated so vividly and passionately. The literature of the nineteenth century, in a sense – the Romantic movement itself – is, I will not say inconceivable, but would surely have taken a different form without this major act of self-revelation, even if what he says about himself is often perverted, false, vain to the point of insanity, romanticised, self-dramatised, to be taken as a collection of symptoms, and not dependable descriptions of states of mind, conscious or unconscious.

I will not burden you with well-known truisms about what Kant genuinely owed to him, e.g. the notion that in morals – as opposed to, say, [the] sciences, or other fields of knowledge – there are not experts, but all men are equally aware and knowledgeable; the notion of civilisation as a prison, which Blake and Tolstoy and Lawrence all find so profoundly sympathetic, however much you and I would disagree, the sermons against conformity, the *Utopias* about natural man that the young today believe so passionately – all this cannot, alas, be dismissed as wild gibberish, [the] disordered raving

---

1 Friedrich Melchior, Baron von Grimm (1723–1807), Bavarian-born man of letters and diplomat.
2 Claude Adrien Helvétius (1715–71), French philosopher and educator, one of the originators of the *Encyclopédie*; his *De l'esprit* (1758) influenced Jeremy Bentham and the development of Utilitarianism. The first subject of FIB.

Freedom & its betrayal

of a mad and self-wounded egomaniac: it obviously represents a permanent kind of revolt against tidiness, order, establishment, the schoolroom, the hierarchy, pastors and masters; something that breaks out in other forms at other times, especially when the forms become too rigid, the society too ossified, mechanical, unresponsive.

Nevertheless, to swim against the stream, as you are doing, is a brave and timely thing to do – the only thing I should fear about the publication of this piece is that you will be accused of ignoring too much of what had moved generations of readers, not only in the *Nouvelle Héloïse*,[1] but in the *Confessions*,[2] which, for all their obvious self-lacerating megalomania, sober and sceptical critics often found it impossible to put down. This is not merely literary talent – there is a quality there of revelation, and a touching of concealed inner psychological centres, which is equally true of Pascal, Dostoevsky, Nietzsche, and which, perhaps, only the abnormalities these men suffered from, which made them personally so impossible (I do not know about Pascal – perhaps he was charming), makes them capable of seeing. But I admire your single-minded desire to tear away masks and debunk – whether in the case of Marx or Rousseau. I enjoyed reading this piece, and for this reason took so long. Thank you very much for sending it to me.

Yours sincerely,

[Isaiah Berlin]

TO JACOB TALMON

21 November 1972 [*carbon*]

[Wolfson]

Dear Yaakov,

[…] Now as to the main issue between me and Yellin-Mor. You are quite right – I did not perhaps sufficiently discount what the reaction of my audience, both those who listened to me and those who read the articles, would be. But I did consult one or two people about the lecture, although, perhaps, rather too late. As you know, I always work to a deadline: I am quite incapable of producing things tidily, quietly, coolly, in a leisurely manner, with time to spare: I can only work under pressure, at the last moment, with the printer's devil practically champing at the door (this Victorian metaphor really does describe my methods of work). When I arrived in Jerusalem I did show my piece to Arthur Lourie and Gaby Cohen and, indeed, Abe Harman[3]

---

1 *Julie, ou la nouvelle Héloïse* (1761), hugely successful epistolary novel by Rousseau in which the story of a passionate love affair throws a critical light on the mores of the age, while pointing to a moral of reconciliation and regeneration.

2 What Rousseau described in its opening words as an unprecedented enterprise in self-revelation was written in exile 1764–70, and published posthumously; it is regarded as the founding text of literary autobiography.

3 (Leslie) Avraham ('Abe') Harman (1914–92), London-born Oxford-educated Israeli diplomat and

himself, and I daresay Cherrick[1] may have read it too. None of them seemed to object to anything in it, or warned me against fearful pitfalls or minefields that might suddenly blow up in my face. So I proceeded. I realised that the reading of the Foreign Office documents was bound to produce a discussion of this topic, and thought it wise therefore to say my piece, and then think no more about it: if it is attacked – *dixi et salvavi animam meam* – and again *quod scripsi, scripsi*.[2] This is the only attitude that I can possibly take up. But of course you are quite right: brought up as they were to suppose that everything was the work of their own hands, that foreign powers had nothing to do with it, that the British were always in some sense the enemies and persecutors, that Americans were friends in need, but during the war scarcely existent at all, that everything that was achieved was achieved by the Palmach and so on,[3] my words must have grated very harshly upon some people's consciousness. [...] Unless one takes up a bold and clear position of a somewhat extreme kind which is supported constantly by easily intelligible rhetoric in particular; if one takes up the kind of middle position that I cannot help, temperamentally, always finding myself in, which depends on qualifications, and qualifications of qualifications, and gives no satisfaction to passionate adherents of any point of view, but is bound to be shot at [by] more impassioned believers – that I cannot help: the kind of sceptical liberalism which characterises me, and the more militant liberalism that characterises you, is bound to produce two fronts always, as always in a crossfire of some kind. One can only comfort oneself with the thought produced by Bishop Wilberforce[4] who said, 'I am always in hot water, but my hands are always clean.' So be it. [...]

Yours ever,

[Isaiah Berlin]

university administrator; ambassador to Washington 1959–68; president of the HUJ 1968–83. See also L2 Plate 41.

1 Bernard Cherrick (1914–88), Dublin-born Israeli university administrator; from 1947 head of the public and media relations unit of the HUJ, from 1968 a Vice-President.

2 Pontius Pilate's reply to the chief priests when they complained of the title that he had written and attached to the cross on which Jesus was to be crucified, 'Jesus of Nazareth the King of the Jews': 'Then said the chief priests of the Jews to Pilate, Write not, The King of the Jews; but that he said, I am King of the Jews. Pilate answered, What I have written I have written' (John 19:21–2). Cf. TCE 252.

3 i.e. by force of arms: the Palmach (199/4) co-operated with the British to defend Palestine from Axis invasion; once this threat had passed, however, the British attempted, unsuccessfully, to close down their operations, which were directed henceforth to the creation of the State of Israel, in defiance of British Mandatory authority.

4 Samuel Wilberforce (1805–73), bishop of Oxford and of Winchester, nicknamed 'Soapy Sam' by Disraeli because of his unctuous manner, though according to a biographer Wilberforce responded to a lady who asked him why he was so known by saying, 'Because, Madam, I am always in hot water, and always come out of it with clean hands': George William Daniell, *Bishop Wilberforce* (London, 1891), 214. He was a vehement critic of Charles Darwin's theories on evolution, and sparred ingloriously on this subject with Thomas Henry Huxley in their famous exchange at the University Museum, Oxford, 30 June 1860.

TO GERSHOM SCHOCKEN

   II December 1972 [*carbon*]

[Headington House]

Dear Mr Schocken,

Thank you very much indeed for your very interesting letter and the enclosures. While I have no doubt that *Ha'aretz* did publish news of atrocities behind the Nazi lines, I still cannot find anyone – outside Israel, that is, or rather, outside Palestine as it was at the time – who claims to have known from public sources, such as newspapers or the radio, or from the kind of talk that went on in government departments outside intelligence circles (about which I knew and still know virtually nothing), that the mass extermination of the Jews was in progress. I know that people like Livne complain that, while facts were from time to time published in, say, *Ha'aretz*, the proportion of space occupied by them in relation to other day-to-day events, internal arguments about this or that, was far too small, and that therefore far too little attention was paid to these matters. If this was so in Palestine, how much more in England and America? Speaking for myself, I can only say that the Zionist leaders I saw did not speak to me of these things, and that this applies not only to Weizmann, who dutifully took part in mass meetings to denounce the atrocities in general terms, but to Ben-Gurion, Sharett,[1] Goldmann, even such Revisionists as I saw, who pressed for a Jewish Army, or the abrogation of the White Paper, or more violent propaganda against the British pro-Arabism, but not specific measures for the rescue of the European Jews (I heard later about plans for bombing trains and death camps, but it was not prominent at the time in the press or conversation) as an end in itself unconnected with the general aims of Zionist political policy. Still, I may be wrong, and if so I would be grateful if you would tell me about this. The items that appeared in newspapers in America were much too scattered, the news had dribbled in over too long a period; it was not concentrated enough by the journalists to produce a single overwhelming impression.

There are two aspects to this issue – (*a*) why did I not say more about the extermination of the Jews in the context of wartime Zionist politics in America?, and (*b*) why was more in fact not done by Jewish leaders in America? Did Jews or Zionists do all that they could have done while the Holocaust was occurring?

I can say something about the first, much less about the second. It is, of course, difficult to recapture what one knew or thought or felt thirty years ago; but I think I am not mistaken in asserting that, whatever may have been

---

1 Moshe Sharett (1894–1965) né Shertok, Ukrainian-born Zionist and Israeli statesman; director of the Political Dept of the Jewish Agency 1933–48; Foreign Minister of Israel 1948–56, Prime Minister 1954–5.

known to intelligence departments of the Allied governments, or to the
governments themselves, or to individuals, or to Zionist or Jewish leaders
at various moments of the war, i.e. before the Allied troops reached the
camps, the ordinary newspaper-reader or radio-listener, and the ordinary
government official with no special sources of information about what was
going on behind the Nazi lines, knew very little about the extermination.
I do not mean to minimise this: of course we all assumed that Jews caught
behind the Nazi lines were in mortal danger and that torture or death was
inflicted on them – upon how many, in what ways, where, that was not at
all clear. That the White Paper doomed innocent men to death was believed
by most Jews, and this, of course, I do speak about in my lecture, very
emphatically; but otherwise, what did we, ordinary individuals or officials,
know? In 1942 it was, I think, James de Rothschild[1] who made a speech in the
House of Commons, after which the House stood for a moment's silence
in memory of Jewish martyrs, I think in the Baltic States but I do not now
remember exactly what was said;[2] meetings occurred in New York addressed
by Weizmann, La Guardia[3] etc. to denounce Nazi atrocities; possibly there
were such meetings elsewhere, in London, or other American cities also;
I do remember that Harold Beeley,[4] of all people, talked to me in I suppose
1944 (I think 1942 was too early, but I am not sure) about Siegelboim,[5] who
had escaped from Warsaw and described the resistance of the Warsaw
Ghetto and committed suicide because too little attention had been paid
to his words and horrors went on unchecked – but this certainly made no
impact on the general American press or radio; and Beeley talked about it
because Siegelboim was so ferociously anti-Zionist, and accused (according
to Beeley) Zionist leaders of being more concerned about Palestine and the

1 James Armand Edmond de Rothschild (1878–1957), one of the leaders of the Jewish community
  in Britain, strongly Zionist; born in Paris, he took British citizenship after the First World War, in
  which he served with the British Army; Liberal MP for the Isle of Ely 1929–45.
2 The scene in the House of Commons to which IB here refers is that of 17 December 1942 (507/2):
  Rothschild's expression of thanks, on behalf of Jews in Britain and throughout the Empire, for
  Eden's 'eloquent and just denunciation' of Nazi atrocities, met with 'sympathetic cheers', but it
  was at the instigation of William Cluse that the House rose.
3 Fiorello Henry La Guardia (1882–1947), US Republican politician of Jewish-Italian descent;
  famed as Mayor of NY 1933–45 for his integrity and advocacy of public against vested interests;
  worked closely with FDR's Democratic administration before and during the Second World War.
4 Harold Beeley (1909–2001), KCMG 1961, academic and diplomat; FO 1946–69; Lecturer in
  History, Queen Mary College, London, 1969–75. In 1946 Beeley had departmental responsibility for Palestine, and he became Ernest Bevin's closest adviser, sharing his Foreign Secretary's
  pro-Palestinian outlook, and also the obloquy that this incurred among Zionists as the Mandate
  unravelled.
5 Szmul Zygielbojm (1895–1943), Polish trade unionist and Bund party politician; represented
  Jewish workers on Warsaw City Council 1927–33; involved in the defence of Warsaw 1939; later
  escaped to the West and devoted himself to the defence of Polish-Jewish interests. He took his
  own life in London, 12 May 1943, in protest at what he regarded as the inaction of the Allies
  over the annihilation of Polish Jewry: 'He had long championed the cause of the Jews in Poland,
  urging that the United Nations should take reprisals against Germany as a last means of saving
  his co-religionists from complete extermination' (Times, 19 May 1943, 3g).

future than about the trapped Jews of Europe. I do not know who believed Siegelboim, but if they did they did not make their views widely known [...]. My general point is that while no doubt columns in the *New York Times* may have reported rumours of Jewish extermination, or about the bitterness and indignation expressed by Jewish leaders at specially convened meetings, this was relatively unprominent in relation to other news and there never was a single climactic moment in which a violent impact was made by some account of unimaginable horror on a fantastic scale, which is what the Holocaust in fact turned out to be. For this reason, if you look at the speeches and other public pronouncements by Zionist or Jewish leaders, I do not believe (though I am subject to correction since I only speak from a very vague memory) that much about this will be found in e.g. Ben-Gurion's speeches, less, probably, than in Weizmann's; that the burden of even the most passionate and ferocious attacks on British policy by Revisionist or Irgun speakers and propagandists was denunciation of the White Paper as such, or of British imperialism or pro-Arabism or anti-Semitism, etc., as part of agitation for a full Zionist programme of a Jewish State, etc., and not concerned with plans, whether realistic or utopian, for the immediate rescue of the victims of Nazism as an end in itself, which is precisely what Siegelboim was so bitter about, and what made Beeley so fascinated with him.

I have spoken about this, by now, with contemporaries of mine who went through the war in London or New York or Washington, Jews and non-Jews; and the general consensus of Englishmen, Americans, Zionist officials, Jewish communal workers is that they knew very little about what was going on in Nazi-occupied territory: that the agitation of people like Peter Bergson and his friends in America, because they were thought to be sensation-mongers and irresponsible and held violent political views, was discounted, and given little of what is nowadays known as 'credibility', and condemned them with various degrees of sincerity as counter-productive in irritating American government officials, who were otherwise considered to be sympathetic but who reacted adversely to assaults by those whose credentials were regarded as doubtful and whose methods extravagant. No doubt there was a tremendous reluctance to believe the worst: people put away such thoughts from their heads so far as they could: but my point is that items of the kind which, say, *Ha'aretz* and also Jewish organs elsewhere from time to time publicised, reporting massacres and mounting repression, were not frequent enough or concentrated enough not to be somewhat obscured by the vast bulk of other war news. Indeed, I remember that when the Soviet Anti-Fascist Committee [...] arrived in New York the papers were full of that; the emphasis was on the heroic resistance of the Jews in Poland, Russia etc., and not at all on their losses. There was nothing like Lidice[1] to

1 Village of 503 inhabitants just north-west of Prague, razed to the ground by the Nazis in

highlight the full horror of what in fact was happening. That is why, when the camps were reached and the truth was known, the effect was so enormous, so appalling, so overwhelming. My point is, to reiterate it again, that in the inpouring of news and information which conditioned Zionist activities, reactions of British or American officials, and so on, the actual facts of the destruction of the Jews played a minor part – almost incredible to us now, with our hindsight – simply because they were neither precise enough nor given enough tragic emphasis, not highlighted enough. If it had excited the Jews of America more than it did, this would have been reflected in what the newspapers, or the official reporters of the various British agencies, or American journalists, were writing. Whether the governments knew more than the public and deliberately concealed it – whether there was censorship by governments or even by Jewish leaders – I have no idea. Perhaps there was. I am merely trying to recapture what the awareness was at the time.

As for the second point, whether more could have been done, that is something I did not speak about because it was not an issue that was raised in the Anglo-American–Zionist discussions in Washington at the time, even though it might be said that it should have been. I confined myself to the agenda, as it were, of the points at issue, of conflict, of turning-points in the actual tactics and strategy of the Zionists, their allies and their opponents. I gather from such Israelis as I have spoken to that neither the Holocaust nor the resistance to it were prominent issues in Palestine either (but this I can only take on hearsay evidence). The only proposal that I ever heard about, and that after the war, was that of bombing the trains carrying the doomed victims, and the camps' crematoria themselves. I have no idea how strongly this was advocated or why it was not done: I can only say that it was not an issue that attracted enough public controversy or passion in any government circle in Washington that I knew of, to become a serious issue. This is a dreadful fact in itself. But I confined myself to discussing what in fact came up, rather than what should have or might have done so. [...]

One last word on the Holocaust: if the critics are right, there was a kind of conspiracy of silence about it on the part of the Zionist leaders. But this is not really credible. There was a relative degree of silence, indeed, but this was due to lack of imagination and perhaps incredulity about the bits that

---

retaliation for the assassination on (27 May 1942, died 4 June) by Free Czech agents of Reinhard Heydrich (1904–42), SS Obergruppenführer, Deputy Reichsprotektor of Bohemia and Moravia, and one of the architects of the Final Solution. The devastation began on 10 June 1942: Lidice's male inhabitants were shot, its women mostly sent to Ravensbrück, and its children either poisoned with gas or abducted under the Lebensborn programme. The Nazis filmed the atrocity and used Prague radio to broadcast their intentions: The Times duly reported this ('A Czech Village Wiped Out: Barbarous Vengeance for Heydrich', 11 June 1942, 4c), and Lidice quickly became synonymous with Nazi terror.

did appear, such as the testimony of Siegelboim. This is a far more plausible explanation of what occurred than the deliberate minimisation of events, suppression of what should have produced a shriek of indignation, as part of a deliberate policy of feeble persuasion as opposed to vehement resistance to the Allied policies. There was appalling bitterness and indignation in 1945–6. That was the effect of the facts that were revealed: the contrast between 1943, say, and 1945 cannot be explained otherwise, it seems to me. Perhaps you do not agree: in which case I should be grateful if you would let me know, when you have a little leisure – I do not wish to burden you with an endless discussion, painful and important as this topic is.

Yours sincerely,

[Isaiah Berlin]

TO KYRIL FITZLYON[1]

9 January 1973

Headington House

Dear Kyril,

Thank you very much for your letter of 23 December. At any rate, you do not take the very low view of my piece on Turgenev expressed by the anonymous reviewer in the *TLS*,[2] who condemned it root and branch with insults, gibes, worse than any that even poor Turgenev received for his novel. I shall have to answer him about the more absurd of his accusations: I hate doing so, as I think on the whole that authors should take nasty reviews with a stiff upper lip and just grin and bear it. But this is a little too much. [...]

Now, as to 'liberal, Western values' among the Russians in the nineteenth century. It is true that Herzen was disgusted by the bourgeois values of the West, and that even before 1848, for it is usually dated from the failure of those revolutions (mistakenly). Even he, before 1847, and certainly moderates

---

1 Kyril FitzLyon (b. 1910) né Kyril Zinovieff; assumed name FitzLyon after emigrating from his native St Petersburg, where his grandfather had been governor; took British citizenship and joined FO; later an acclaimed translator of Russian literature into English.

2 The anonymous reviewer was in fact Richard Harry Freeborn (b. 1926), Professor of Russian Literature, SSEES, UCL, 1967–88, and his review 'The Liberal Dilemma' appeared in the TLS on 22 December 1972, 1553. Freeborn argued that in his 'propensity for sweeping generalisation [...] Sir Isaiah, though seeming to offer a universal diagnosis, makes the issues appear both over-simple and alarmingly parochial'. More seriously, he stated that IB had 'done less than justice to his own standards of intellectual responsibility in dealing with the Russian texts which he claims to have translated himself. Unacknowledged omissions and misrepresentations of the original are conspicuous in the opening paragraph from Belinsky, the text of *Fathers and Children* is rearranged to suit Sir Isaiah's thesis, and there are factual errors concerning the models of Bazarov and the state of present scholarship on the novel.'

like Granovsky[1] or Stankevich,[2] Botkin,[3] Annenkov,[4] and the liberal historians, just to choose a random selection, were very 'West' oriented; and all
those schoolmasters, young doctors and engineers and agronomists and
the rest, to whom Belinsky's publications were directed and about whom
Aksakov[5] speaks as fervent disciples of Belinsky, impenetrable to Slavophil
propaganda – all these people from the 1850s to those of Chekhov's plays
rhapsodised about Western civilisation, progress, science, civil liberties,
everything that the Kadets, and indeed the right-wing SRs and SDs believed
in before the First World War.[6] Belinsky is a peculiar case, because he was
tossed about from one violent conviction to another, but even he, from the
early 1840s till his death, surely believed in a Western model, whether 'socialist' in some vague sense or, towards the end of his life, a capitalist one. He
was always immoderate – the guillotine was never far away – the task was to
destroy the enemies of progress conceived in some Western sense, although
the contents of this concept varied wildly from one period to another. Do let
us discuss it some day, as you say – there is still nothing authoritative on this
splendid subject.

    Yours ever,
    Isaiah

TO GERSHOM SCHOCKEN

    11 January 1973 [*carbon*]

                            [Wolfson]

Dear Mr Schocken,
    Thank you very much for your letter of 3 January, which has just arrived

---

1 Timofey Nikolaevich Granovsky (1813–55), Russian historian, studied in Berlin, was influenced
  by Ranke and Hegel, and became a strong Westerniser, disseminating his beliefs in his lectures at
  Moscow University, admired by, among others, Alexander Herzen.

2 Nikolay Vladimirovich Stankevich (1813–40), Russian philosopher and poet whose ideas on the
  role of the intelligentsia in furthering the cause of the Enlightenment in Russia were influential
  on, among others, Belinsky, Bakunin and Herzen.

3 Vasily Petrovich Botkin (1812–69), Russian essayist, critic and translator, a moderate liberal in his
  younger days. He was an associate of Stankevich and the Westernisers.

4 Pavel Vasil'evich Annenkov (1813–87), Russian literary critic, friend of Westernisers such as
  Botkin, Belinsky, Herzen and Turgenev. His memoir *A Remarkable Decade* (1880), a record of the
  flowering of culture in Russia during the 1840s, gave its title to IB's 1954 Northcliffe Lectures,
  broadcast by the BBC and included in RT.

5 Sergey Timofeevich Aksakov (1791–1859), Russian novelist whose literary reputation was established late in life with the semi-autobiographical *A Family Chronicle* (1846–1856) and *Childhood
  Years of Bagrov-Grandson* (1858), which detail the life of the Russian nobility; his sons Konstantin
  and Ivan were both prominent Slavophils.

6 'Kadets' was the acronymic name given to supporters of the liberal Constitutional Democratic
  Party, founded in Moscow in October 1905; the party drew its support from professionals, and
  numbered many of the nobility in its ranks; the Socialist-Revolutionary Party (SRs) played an
  important role in the February Revolution in 1917, but afterwards fragmented, and the Social
  Democratic Labour Party (SDs) later divided into Bolshevik and Menshevik factions.

here. It was kind of you to reply so succinctly and clearly – but I think that I genuinely disagree with something in your historical analysis of the situation in America during the War.

I do not think that the American Jews could have acted in 1940/1/2 or 1943 or even 1944, as they acted in 1947 or 1948 – they could not even, in my view, have so acted in 1945. Partly because, as you say, they worshipped Roosevelt – not without reason. He did do a great deal for all the American minorities; he was, in some sense, the champion of a new world in which they believed, rightly, they would be treated more justly. The New Deal was not a mirage. On the specifically refugee-Palestine question he was, I now believe, more cynical than anyone believed or knew, at the time. But I do not believe that BG thought that the American Jews could, in fact, have succeeded in bringing the kind of pressure upon him that Silver[1] was working for; when he told me that the American Jews were only one of two sources of strength, he meant it in terms of money, immigration, general enthusiasm and thought – but he never deluded himself about how much they could do in Washington; in this respect, he and Weizmann were not in disagreement, in my view.

As for Peter Bergson, I doubt if, had he concentrated entirely on trying to rescue the Jews in Europe, even this could have achieved much: I think that in 1944/5 the Jews of Hungary and Rumania *could* have been rescued, because the Allies were winning, and these countries were very bulliable; and if the Allies had chosen to bully them, or chosen to allow talk to occur with Fascist leaders, even if they did not mean, in fact, to supply them with trucks etc., a great deal of saving of life could have been achieved – and for not doing this, of course, they are terribly blameworthy. No doubt they were afraid of Russian suspicion of dealing with the enemy: the Russians were acutely sensitive about this; the reactions of the Allies, both governments and officials, were predictable and not mere wickedness, though one can be horrified by the consequences. I do not believe, however, that Jewish pressure alone could have made them do it. This is, I suspect, where we historically disagree. All these are pure might-have-beens, and neither of us can prove our position.

All that you say about the German Jews is, of course, true: there was a genuine fear of increasing anti-Semitism. A great united shriek by the Jewish community of America might have achieved an impact on general opinion – but for this, information would have had to be filtered through sources which they entirely trusted: the Jewish Agency, Stephen Wise[2] etc. would not have been quite enough: *this* the American government, and the

_____

1 Abba Hillel Silver (1893–1963), Lithuanian-born US rabbi and Jewish leader; employed his remarkable powers of oratory to garner significant support in America for the Zionist cause, and was one of its principal spokesmen at the UN in 1947 during its important deliberations on Palestine.

2 Stephen Samuel Wise (1874–1949), Hungarian-born US rabbi, Zionist and social reformer whose Zionist activities spanned fifty years, during which he clashed with many, including Weizmann, 'until in the end the Jewish world was in a sense divided between these two powerful

Allied governments generally, evidently aborted. I am far from exonerating the governments from blame, but I just do not believe that the Jews could have done more than simply have salved their consciences by shouting, and shaking their fists, and doing everything possible, as Siegelboim tried to do in England. What I do not believe is that this cry of anguish would have been practically effective. But this may be simply a part of my general analysis of what the American Jewish situation was like, and about that I may, of course, be mistaken. However, I will not continue to bore you with all this now, and apologize for going on and on. Do let us talk about it.

I wish you would come to England, and we could have a talk.

Yours sincerely,

[Isaiah Berlin]

TO ARTHUR CROOK[1]

15 January 1973

Headington House

Dear AC,

First, let me thank you for your very kind and sympathetic and heart-warming letter. I must, however, say that your reviewer has managed to disguise the admiration which you wrote that he reported to you, very successfully indeed. His identity is no secret to me – I must admit that my sentence about 'Professor Freeborn's standard work on Turgenev' – it is nothing of the kind – was a deliberate trap, which worked only too well: I hope your readers will forgive me for having misled them to that degree. The appalling pseudo-joviality of the beginning of the rejoinder to my letter is, I fear, the result of a conflict of emotions in the breast of one of the most fearful phenomena there are – a resentful professor.[2] I well remember that when he was at Oxford he told his audiences that ideas were not his forte – that all the stuff about German metaphysics, Hegel etc. involved in Russian social and political ideas in the nineteenth century was a closed book to him, that ideas were no part of literature, etc. This is the most respectable part of the explanation of his outburst. You speak of a conflict of opinions: but it is, of course, not this that I minded, but the malevolent tone and the total lack of argument. Whenever anyone criticises me, I take it for granted that they

protagonists – Dr Weizmann taking Palestine and Zionism, and the Jewish international activites being annexed by Wise' (obituary of Wise, *Times*, 21 April 1949, 6d).

1 Arthur Charles William Crook (1912–2005), Editor, TLS, 1959–74.

2 IB responded to the review (519/2) in a published letter, 'Fathers and Children', TLS, 12 January 1973, 40. He objected strongly to criticisms that he felt amounted to 'imputations of dishonesty and of culpable ignorance'. Freeborn was shown the letter by the TLS and replied in the same issue: 'I am glad of the vigorous and ample rebuttal of my criticisms which Sir Isaiah offers in his letter. This kind of response to a review keeps the reviewer on his toes and at least reassures him that someone has read what he has written. I would like to take this opportunity of wishing Sir Isaiah the utmost vigour of mind and heart in the New Year.'

must be right – that I have indeed committed all the faults attributed to me, and probably many more: I was, as I said in my last letter to you, vaguely uneasy about the terrible blast which I had done my best to provoke. But, in the event, the Prof. turns out to be a very paper tiger. [...] I was rung up by Lionel Trilling (whom also I had to dissuade from taking up arms on my behalf), who asked me who the reviewer was – the reviewer of *his* last book was much annoyed at not being thanked, since his identity must surely have been clear to Trilling – I said virtuously that I did not know – Trilling asked me if I thought he was a little off his head – he thought it the queerest thing he had ever seen, and the most embarrassing, in any serious journal. So I am sure that it cannot simply be written down as a straightforward difference of opinion between two writers: you must forgive me if I beg you to be a little careful before you employ Prof. Freeborn again on any work involving dealing with ideas – something is amiss in his mind. [...]

Sorry to go on at such length. And I apologise again for introducing one misleading statement, designed entirely to verify the identity of the reviewer, unexpectedly successfully. I do hate having enemies: I wish I knew how I antagonised the Prof. – I fear that it is by the mere fact of existence – he will have to put up with that for a little longer, I fear.

Meanwhile, I forebear to send you a letter with a lot of quotations about *free born* Englishmen from the *Areopagitica*,[1] which the Warden of All Souls is inciting me to do. Do tell the Prof. that I propose to be magnanimous and not expose him as he deserves!

Yours sincerely,
Isaiah Berlin

TO HENRY HARDY[2]

18 January 1973 [*carbon*]

[Wolfson]

Dear Hardy,

I realise that it is no easy task to plough through Poole,[3] who, from your account, appears to be a terrible intellectual name-dropper. I know what it is to read a book where ideas appear like huge buses in a London fog – they

---

1 *Areopagitica: A Speech of Mr John Milton for the Liberty of Unlicenc'd Printing, to the Parlament of England* (London, 1644), his passionate appeal for freedom from censorship.

2 Henry Robert Dugdale Hardy (b. 1949), editor, publisher and occasional author; CCC classics 1967–9, psychology and philosophy 1969–71; teacher, Shrewsbury School, 1971–2; philosophy graduate student (not IB's pupil), Wolfson, 1972–6 (B.Phil. 1974, D.Phil. 1976); later editor, Oxford University Press (1977–90), then Fellow, Wolfson; IB's editor from 1974, literary trustee from 1996. 'Not for nothing is he the grandson of a famous headmaster' (H. H. Hardy): IB, *obiter dictum*.

3 Roger Poole (1939–2003), literary theorist; Lecturer, then Senior Lecturer, in English Literature, Nottingham, 1969–89. IB had asked HH to read Poole's *Towards Deep Subjectivity* (1972) and give him his view of it.

don't occur any more – a vast shape looming at one which one almost sees the shape of before it disappears into the fog; sometimes I used to feel that about Whitehead[1] – one used to look in despair on all that thick foliage or that frightful darkness, but then, suddenly, he would come out of the wood into a clearing, and those ideas seemed the more valuable because relief was so great at understanding something – it is like liking very long books because of the sheer labour spent in reading them. […]

I gather from what you say about the book that, in general, Poole is against dry factual pellets – against positivism and exactness and verification, and so on. Despite my respect for, and fascination with, romanticism, and my deep and lifelong anti-positivism, I do not wish to discredit rationalism in the least. My feeling is that what the reason can do, it should; what quantitative methods can do, they should do; what science can establish (and that is a very, very great deal), it should; only the imperialism – the belief that they can answer all questions, or that questions that they cannot answer are not questions, the belief in final solutions, in all-embracing monism – that is false. The view of the participant in a process is different from the view of an observer, even though there is a certain sense in which the 'facts' are the same, or can be. Hence Vico etc. […]

I wish you would come and talk to me about these matters sometime; if the price of that is having to read Poole, I will read Poole, but do tell me if I really have to do that. If you feel inclined to come and talk about these subjects, I should be certainly willing, and, indeed, grateful, so do let me know. […]

Yours sincerely,
[Isaiah Berlin]

TO NICHOLAS JACOBS

19 January 1973

Headington House

Dear Mr Jacobs,

Thank you very much for your letter and book – I am afraid that, because I was out of the country, I did not come across it until today, and hasten to thank you.

First, about Chernyshevsky: I can assure you there is no caricature and no self-irony – he was an entirely humourless man, and what he really wanted to do was to produce a portrait of a 'pure' hero, not given to the self-doubtings of Bazarov towards the end of the novel – and there is an account in one of the memoirs about Turgenev – not necessarily too reliable – which

---

1 Alfred North Whitehead (1861–1947), mathematician and philosopher; Bertrand Russell's mathematics tutor at Trinity College, Cambridge, and his collaborator on *Principia Mathematica* (3 vols, Cambridge, 1910–13); Professor of Philosophy, Harvard, 1924–37.

suggests that one of the originals of Bazarov is identical with the original for Chernyshevsky's hero.[1] Turgenev was, as I remember it, asked if this was in fact the same man – there is an oblique reference to someone who was arrested and sent to Siberia – and replied absently that it might have been so. The whole story is told by a lady on whose memory we have no particular reason to rely or not to rely, and certainly Turgenev, like Tolstoy, did not care for Chernyshevsky. Turgenev had been on good terms with him once, and Chernyshevsky admired Turgenev vastly to begin with, but they fell out, as was inevitable, and in the end Turgenev more or less took up Tolstoy's position – Tolstoy looked on him with disdain and spoke of him as a man who 'stank of bedbugs' – it was, in the end, Chernyshevsky's rigid and intense narrowness of vision, and his absence of aesthetic feeling – at least as it was understood by Tolstoy, Turgenev and their friends – that caused this profound antipathy. And there was a social gap also. I must confess that I find the utmost difficulty in reading Chernyshevsky – unlike Venturi, who not only admires him but positively enjoys reading him, I think – but he was a very serious observer of the Russian scene, apart from his commitments and heroic life – although there was also something profoundly naive and simplistic about him – which emerges in this terribly – to me – moving and absurd novel, particularly in the story of his last years, when he was sitting in his bed in his native city, with his lean, Don-Quixote-like legs outside the bed, in slippers, and saying to the socialist lady who interviewed him that he thought the best thing that could be done would be to translate a French encyclopedia, mainly about fauna and flora, into Russian, because that would do much to enlighten the people. The fact that he could not marry his wife – with whom he lived so unhappily and who was so nasty about him – without first making sure that all their political and social views absolutely coincided – he spent a sleepless night when he had certain doubts about one of her opinions, and was relieved only in the morning when she assured him that it was all OK – all this contributes to the portrait of this immensely industrious, immensely well organised, utterly serious, dedicated man, whom Marx admired, not without reason – but who, at the same time, was, as a human being, at once noble and idealistic and phenomenally boring. [...]

Yours sincerely,

Isaiah Berlin   [...]

---

1 The best-known character in Chernyshevsky's seminal novel *What Is To Be Done?* (1863), written in response to Turgenev's *Fathers and Sons* (1862), is the puritanical revolutionary and ascetic Rakhmetov.

TO SHIELA SOKOLOV GRANT

19 January 1973

Headington House

Dearest Shiela,

I brush aside your tiny pinprick – that is nothing new[1] – and wish to know if anything will bring you to our parts in the foreseeable future – and whether, if so, you would like a bed – when? Aline and I will be in New York for about three weeks in the middle of February, but I do not suppose you will be leaving Ireland just then – it must be less horrible there than here – you are indeed right, what could possibly bring us to Ireland by nature – the old chatelaine of Bowen's Court is slowly dying[2] (I mean, faster than you or I), and this is melancholy in itself – I did go to Dublin to deliver a lecture at Trinity College, under the most peculiar, touching, pre-modern, rather marvellous conditions – and saw there my old friend Myles Dillon,[3] but he too is dead now – I suppose the time has come when one watches the pages of the *Times* to see the continuous demise of one's contemporaries – there are those who see this with pride and a sense of survival and indeed outliving others – I do not have any such sentiments – you are not of an age yet when this could possibly affect you, but one day, one day … Anyway, will you be coming here? It is just possible that we shall be in Wexford next autumn, but not until then. In the meanwhile do let me know. Your reproaches are undeserved, and well you know it; but they do draw a reply, and a very good thing too.

Yours ever,
Isaiah

TO ARTHUR SCHLESINGER

23 January 1973

Wolfson

Dear Arthur,

Thank you for your kind words about Romanes – I have had a very severe letter from Gerschenkron, who thinks I am comparing conditions in nineteenth-century Russia and its opponents with American layabouts at Harvard who have nothing to complain of and are just disturbed morons – this does not seem to be quite just. He does not spell this out – but his letter is written more in sorrow than in anger, but I have obviously touched him to

---

1 IB's lifelong friendship with Shiela Sokolov Grant was punctuated by cordial mutual recrimination, fed by what she once described as the tidal ebb and flow of his affection (L1 232/4).

2 Their old friend Elizabeth Bowen, who died just a few weeks later, on 22 February.

3 Myles Dillon (1900–72), Irish historian and philologist, Director of the School of Celtic Studies, Dublin Institute for Advanced Studies, 1960–8, had died on 18 June 1972.

the quick. I am sure he thinks it vaguely insulting to Russian literature and all we stand for. But I am glad you like it. Diana Trilling who also likes it, thinks it is all about her. So does Auden. All this is very enjoyable. [...]

Yours ever,

Isaiah

TO ALEXANDER GERSCHENKRON

24 January 1973 [*carbon*]

[Headington House]

Carissimo!

I have just received your letter about my lecture [...]. I have no need to be told what you genuinely feel: only your affection for me, which, as you know, I reciprocate most warmly, your fear of hurting my unprotected feelings, causes you to pull your punches and only hint at what you regard as a piece of misconceived analogy, sentimental, unworthy, myopic, absurd, and an insult to Turgenev and the past. [...] At any moment now you will be writing to me as Herzen used to write to Turgenev, to the old Magdalen, white-haired and liable to unworthy compromises and appeasements.[1] But believe me, you are mistaken. You think that there can be no comparison between the real horrors of tsarist Russia in the nineteenth century, which bred the avenging Bazarovs, and our world in the West, with its pathetically underbred, underdeveloped, pseudo-revolutionaries – absurd human casualties battening on their parents, miserable *nedorosl's*,[2] who need, at worst, sexual education or psychiatric treatment, or perhaps just a sharp slap from some exasperated adult. That there are vast differences I do not, of course, deny; and I am convinced, even if I did not say it, that the basic cause of unrest is ennui, and therefore afflicts mainly the affluent. Yet this does not go far enough: why this boredom? Because there are not enough altars of a genuine kind on which the idealistic fringe of the young, who once upon a time could, at least in England, go to the colonies, which they saw (whatever happened to them afterwards) as a sacred duty towards the natives; or join the Communist Party to help the unemployed and the hunger-marchers and take away the money from the rich and give it to the poor; or go to war against Hitler; or join the Peace Corps; or otherwise suffer for a cause worthy of being suffered for. With avenues towards this blocked – poverty is no longer bitter or widespread enough, in England or America, to be a fresh, sharp incentive – what are they to do? Nevertheless, you judge too much by the long-haired louts, the disturbed and the barbarous generation which is now mercifully passing away. Believe me, these are but the scum thrown up

1 For Herzen's description of Turgenev as a 'white-haired Magdalen of the male sex' (*Sobranie sochinenii* [169/1, on 170] xviii 35) see RT2 336/4.

2 'Young ignoramuses'.

by a deeper and more important phenomenon. The Marxo-utilitarian world, the Saint-Simonian world, will not last. But I shall not suddenly fall into a mood of prophecy. I am clear enough which side I am on in the wars which are going on at present, even though occasionally I feel ashamed of our side when it goes too far. But there is what de Gaulle called a 'mutation' going on – there is a feeling of inadequacy on the part of us pillars of Western culture, peace, reason, discipline, freedom, art. Of course the young you speak of care nothing for art or even personal relations – Herzen's two absolutes – but then, I never said they did. I do not wish to fall into deeper disfavour with you than, given my belief that something larger is occurring than you allow for, is absolutely inevitable; and shall therefore accept correction. Since the piece is to be printed in the *New York Review of Books*[1] you will have the opportunity of saving me, as you love me, from what must appear to you to be superficial and sentimental errors, some kind of pseudo-liberal *beliberda*,[2] into which you clearly judge me to have fallen, in addition to a totally fallacious parallel between Russia's past and our present, the nightmare of that black autocracy and the repulsive but passing bubble blown up by love-in-seeking students, who care nothing for privacy or truth or knowledge or whatever is valuable in art or science. All this I am prepared to argue with you, and at length. I admit that I perpetrate a Marxist banality with my cliché in the opening of section III[3] – this I shall amend a little – but only a little. For although I grant that turning-points are sometimes caused by smaller or more mysterious or less predictable causes than any generalising historian has ever suggested – nobody believes this more strongly than I – yet the Marxist formula is illuminating too, certainly so far as the nineteenth century was concerned, which is the one period that he seems to me to have understood.

I am deeply touched by the fact that you should have been so careful in not wishing to abrade my feelings – that you should have written so carefully, and with such courtesy, when you felt that my thesis was really rather rubbish [...].

Yours ever,

[Isaiah]

---

1 18 October 1973, 39–44, 1 November 1973, 22–9, 15 November 1973, 9–11.

2 'Gibberish'.

3 In the first edition of the lecture this section opens: 'Critical turning-points in history are reached when a form of life and its institutions cramp and obstruct the most vigorous productive forces alive in a society – economic, social, artistic, intellectual – and it is worn out in resisting them' (50); this was changed in the 1973 reprint to 'Critical turning-points in history tend to occur, we are told, when a form of life and its institutions are increasingly felt to cramp and obstruct the most vigorous productive forces alive in a society – economic or social, artistic or intellectual – and it has not enough strength to resist them' (RT2 342).

In February 1973 IB spent just short of a fortnight at the Institute for Advanced Study, Princeton; early in January his mother's ill health had led him to cancel plans for a three-month stay.

TO SHIELA SOKOLOV GRANT

13 March 1973

Headington House

Dearest Shiela,

I am in bed with flu at the moment, and so have some enforced leisure, otherwise I would allow your tiny pinpricks (not uncharacteristic, if one thinks of the last forty years or so) to sink in more slowly and, as usual, have their stimulating effect. Since I have a firm intention of staying with Herbert and thingamajig in Cornwall,[1] perhaps only for a few days owing to the very Spartan conditions prevailing, Aline and I might contemplate with positive pleasure the prospect of staying in your notoriously far less austere establishment. But if we do come to Wexford, we have promised to stay with Another – Derek Hill,[2] who has kindly painted me for my College and produced a most flattering version under the guise of some relaxed quasi-Irish country figure: I cannot ask for a better disguise for posterity.

As for Elizabeth, nobody knows whether she knew that she was dying. She had put thoughts of Ireland out of her head, it seems, until the very end, when she expressed the wish to be buried next to Alan[3] at Kildorrery and no memorial service anywhere – all this very much in character. I saw her in hospital a fortnight or so before she died; she looked ghostly and corpse-like; her vocal chords had gone and it was difficult to understand her whispers; she was reading what she liked best, a story by some young woman writer. I pattered away nervously, and told her stories which she probably did not in the least wish to hear, and felt embarrassed and *de trop*. Charles Ritchie[4] was

1 Herbert and Jenifer Hart (SSG's Oxford contemporary and lifelong friend) frequently entertained at Lamledra, Gorran Haven, on the south coast of Cornwall: the house was JH's childhood home, which she co-inherited with her sister Mariella from their parents. For the reference to Jenifer as 'thing[a]majig' see L2 59/1.

2 (Arthur) Derek Hill (1916–2000), portrait and landscape painter; born in Hampshire, he settled in Co. Donegal, at St Columb's Rectory near the village of Churchill.

3 Alan Charles Cameron (1893–1952), educationalist, married Elizabeth Bowen in 1923; Secretary to the Central Council for School Broadcasting 1935–45; a First World War MC, Cameron possessed a 'solid frame and military bearing', and was perceived by some as a blimpish figure; but he was also remembered as 'a brave and lovable' man, devoted to his wife, long passages of whose prose he could recite by heart (obituary, *Times*, 4 September 1952, 6e; Deirdre Toomey on Elizabeth Bowen, ODNB).

4 Charles Stewart Almon Ritchie (1906–95), Canadian diplomat and diarist; ambassador to Washington 1962–6; to the North Atlantic Council 1966–7; Canadian High Commissioner to the UK 1967–71. Ritchie began an affair with Elizabeth Bowen – whose marriage was unconsummated – during the Second World War, when he was based mostly in London; their friendship lasted until her death.

somewhere not far off – he was the person she most cared for during the last decades, and I felt that she looked on me benevolently, and indeed affectionately, but wished me to go rather sooner than I went. From her, I went to my 93-year-old mother, who is none too well herself, so I had a somewhat melancholy day before flying to America to lecture and go to bed with more flu. Too many people have died in one year – Sylvester Gates, Leslie Hartley,[1] Oliver Woods,[2] Lord Salisbury and Judy Montagu.[3] Hartley meant very little to me, the others did in varying measure. Since none of them were very young when they died it makes me feel that it is later than I think. Goronwy called yesterday with Margie,[4] who is said to be far from well, but I was not well enough to see him. I must say, this is a good gloomy letter, but you have only yourself to blame for evoking all these graveyard thoughts. I have suddenly become aware of the extreme importance of the most unlikely marriages: Elizabeth, for example, never recovered from Alan's death: he was, you remember, a sensationally boring man, almost unbelievably so, but she could not buy a pair of shoes without him and was never the same after his death more than twenty years ago.[5] The same applies to Diana Cooper; and nearer home, to my mother and my mother-in-law. Though not to the widows of Oxford dons, I suddenly observe, some of whom, on the contrary, are enormously liberated by the deaths of their most distinguished husbands – reflections on this are going to lead me in a gratuitously malicious direction – we might talk about this sometime, but not another word on paper. On this jollier note, I end.

⟨yours ever & ever
    Isaiah

Aline says she'd love to visit you in Ireland: I *have* warned her about your grim style of life and deep apprehensions about our well being. She did not react significantly.⟩

---

1 Leslie Poles Hartley (1895–1972), novelist and essayist; author of *The Go-Between* (1953), adapted by Harold Pinter as the screenplay for a celebrated film (1970); for many years President of the English section of PEN.

2 Oliver Frederick John Bradley Woods (1911–72), on staff of *The Times* 1935–70 (except 1939–45), becoming Chief Assistant to Editor-in-Chief of Times Newspapers 1967–70; an undergraduate Oxford contemporary of IB.

3 Judith Venetia ('Judy') Montagu (1923–72), a well-loved society figure, 'Almost deliberately indiscreet' (obituary, *Times*, 14 November 1972, 16f); she was the daughter of the Liberal cabinet minister Edwin Samuel Montagu (1879–1924) and his wife (Beatrice) Venetia (1887–1948) née Stanley, though it has been suggested that her natural father was Eric Ednam, 3rd Earl of Dudley; she married Milton Gendel in 1962.

4 Margaret (Margie) Ewing (1921–76) née Morris, who married Goronwy Rees in 1940; both died of cancer, he on 12 December 1979, shortly after reviewing AC fulsomely for *Encounter* (October 1979, 23–5).

5 Elizabeth Bowen had written to IB after her husband's death that she had never before known what it was to mourn: he had been 'my father and mother [...]. I now have [...] "no next of kin"' (letter of 8 October 1952).

TO ROBERT JOYCE[1]

26 April 1973 [carbon]

Wolfson

Dear Bob,

I am most grateful for your letter, which warmed the cockles of my heart when they most needed warming. Of course, one should take a grand line about anonymous detractors, and say 'They say – what say they? Let them say',[2] but, nevertheless, one does mind, particularly when the attack is so personal and so scurrilous, and leads to excited talk about who it can be and what is the motive, etc. [...]

You are quite right: the sceptical and liberal and all those who see more than one side of a case, and seek to avoid passionate commitment to causes that do not seem to them to deserve it, are bound to madden the committed and the resentful on all sides, and, like Turgenev himself, become reluctant Saint Sebastians if they find themselves anywhere near the battlefield. This cannot be helped: deflection of arrows is too undignified if one has any concern for truth or justice, or even ⟨for⟩ reason and decent human relationships – the first victims, when polarization and the division of everything into black and white bursts out. At the risk of uttering a terrible platitude, I must say that there is a time to speak out and a time to keep one's peace. I think that I have more or less known which side I was on when sharp issues came up, even if I was not always brave enough to say so – even when the side one was on, and remained on (in my case England, America, the demo-plutocracies, Israel, etc.), did things one was ashamed of. One can be ashamed of one's side, but one does not desert it, particularly under fire – it has to behave quite abominably before one cuts links, and when that is, is for oneself, and for oneself only, to decide. In that respect, I feel sure that this is true of yourself and of the great majority of those whom we like and admire and associate with. I remember having a row about this very issue with Donald Maclean when he was at the Embassy in Washington towards the end of the war, after which our relations deteriorated – I only met him in Washington in, I think, 1943, and the breach was never healed. I should have guessed then that he belonged to some fanatical dispensation, but was too stupid to realise it. I am not comfortable with extremists; this may or may not be a fault, but it is so.

I noticed with distress that a man after my, and I feel sure, your heart died yesterday: I mean Ham Armstrong, whom I liked and admired very much. He seemed to me a very noble character; a man of the purest integrity, genuine, unpompous, with a very clear head and very human heart, who

---

1 Robert Prather Joyce (1903–84), US diplomat and intelligence officer 1928–62; friend of Joseph Alsop; no doubt known to IB in Washington; wrote to IB, 13 April 1973, lamenting the anonymous attack on IB's Romanes Lecture in the TLS (519/2).

2 Motto of the (Scottish) Earls Marischal.

belonged to the best years of the nineteenth century; not for nothing was his father a consul in Rome in the days of Pio Nono.[1] There is, though one is not allowed to say it, something in birth and descent and personal distinction and being – I scarcely dare utter the word – a gentleman. He was ever so much an old-fashioned gentlemanly person, and suffered for it in all sorts of ways, not least in his two unfortunate marriages (though neither of his two first wives was or is odious in any way), but Christa made him happy, I think. The London *Times* gave him a very brief, dry, inadequate obituary, so I up and wrote them a letter which was not very adequate either, still, a bit better than theirs [...].[2] He really was a wonderfully nice man and led a very honourable life and was a moral asset to America which, at the moment (forgive me, but you know my feeling about America), needs this badly, as we do here. I asked myself the other day who in England, if some appalling outrage occurred, some hideous injustice, could thunder against it and be listened to with universal respect, as Gilbert Murray (who was, in fact, not very brave) or, in his heyday, the late Lord Salisbury, or R. H. Tawney would have been, or, in America, Elihu Root[3] or Stimson[4] or Holmes[5] or Learned Hand.[6] And now? Does every generation of old men feel this? But I honestly cannot think of a name. Ham Armstrong belonged to this small category. I did not say this to *The Times* because it would have sounded too sermonising. [...]

Yours ever,

[Isaiah]　　　　　　　　　　　　　　　　　　　　　　　　　　[...]

TO MAX HAYWARD[7]

27 April 1973

　　　　　　　　　　　　　　　　　　　　　　　　　　　　Wolfson

Dear Max,

Thank you very much for your letter about Mrs Mandel´stam. I have not

1 'Pius the Ninth': Giovanni Maria Mastai-Ferretti (1792–1878), Pope Pius IX 1846–78.
2 IB's appreciation appeared soon after Armstrong's death on 24 April: 'his utter lack of pomp and solemnity, his spontaneity, candour, humanity and eager interest in people and ideas melted resistance on the part of those, particularly the suspicious young, who began by thinking of him as a pillar of the American "establishment"'. 28 April 1973, 16f.
3 Elihu Root (1845–1937), US lawyer, Republican politician, diplomat; won the Nobel Peace Prize in 1912 for, among other things, promoting understanding between North and South America.
4 Henry Lewis Stimson (1867–1950), US lawyer and Republican statesman, served five presidents, including (despite his party affiliation) FDR; Secretary of War 1940–5.
5 Oliver Wendell Holmes, Jr (1841–1935), US jurist, Associate Justice of the Supreme Court 1902–32; seriously wounded three times fighting for the Union during the American Civil War; the author of elegantly phrased legal opinions on topics such as the latitude of free speech.
6 (Billings) Learned Hand (1872–1961), US jurist, judge of the Court of Appeals, 2nd Circuit Court, 1924–51; a respected commentator on constitutional liberties, notably freedom of speech and judicial restraint.
7 (Harry) Maxwell ('Max') Hayward (1924–79), Russian scholar and translator; Fellow, St Antony's, 1956–79; widely acknowledged as the leading authority in the West on 20th-century Russian

read volume 2 with the attention it deserves because it lowers me, as did volume 1. I fall into gloom at the end of every fourth sentence, and find it difficult to extricate myself – I go on, but painfully, as in a nightmare.

[...] About my role as 'The Guest from the Future' I have nothing to say: Mrs Mandelstam's conjecture about this is as good as anyone else's and probably better. It is rather like occurring in someone's dream or being the accidental occasion of some great flight of the imagination – a passive part for which the person in question is mere 'raw material' as it were, something in the experience of the writer for which that something cannot be thought accountable; in my case an accidental possibility of surviving beyond my deserts. [...]

Yours,
Isaiah

TO FRANK HARDIE[1]

2 May 1973 [*carbon*]

[Wolfson]

Dear Frank,

Thank you very much for your letter about my fragment on Austin.[2] Your feelings in 1923 about the suspiciousness of clarity were fully shared by the late Dr Weizmann, who used to denounce Moore for his 'clarity' – which seemed to him about as profound as a very shallow limpid stream which left out everything that was worth investigating, or even thinking about. You suspect that I exaggerate (I am liable to do this, I cannot deny) the 'sweeping anti-metaphysical empiricism'. This does not, however, merely mean logical positivism – the full blast of Carnap–Ayer–Wisdom of 1936 vintage – but the general denial of anything that professed to give information about the world as a result of pure thought – in a sense in which, say, Ross[3] has certainly thought that one made discoveries about the universe as a result of pure reflection – and this included at the time most of the bright young men – [...] all the Hampshires and N. O. Browns, and Graham-Harrisons,[4]

literature, and the translator of (among others) Anna Akhmatova, Nadezhda Mandel'shtam, Boris Pasternak and Alexander Solzhenitsyn.

1 William Francis Ross ('Frank') Hardie (1902–90), Fellow and Tutor in Philosophy, CCC, 1926–50, President 1950–69; IB's philosophy tutor at CCC, and a profound influence on his literary style, as well as his intellectual approach: 'extremely clever, modest, sharp – one couldn't get away with a single piece of rhetoric, however harmless, without explaining exactly what one meant, very clearly. Extremely deflationary; all the same, just and kind' (MI Tape 5).

2 'Austin and the Early Beginnings of Oxford Philosophy', in Isaiah Berlin and others, *Essays on J. L. Austin* (Oxford, 1973); repr. in PI.

3 (William) David Ross (1877–1971), KBE 1938, philosopher; Provost of Oriel 1929–47; edited (with J. A. Smith) a major series of translations of Aristotle, on whom he was the leading British authority of his day.

4 Francis Laurence Theodore Graham-Harrison (1914–2001), Magdalen classics 1933–7; joined Home Office 1938; Assistant Under-Secretary of State 1957–63.

and certainly, in those days, Austin himself, who for two or three years could be regarded as a positive disciple of Ayer, whatever his personal opinion or sympathies might be like; and, indeed, he admitted it subsequently, when it was (I have to admit it) safe to say so. My grounds for alleging Prichard[1] was distressed by *Language, Truth and Logic* is that when he and Ayer appeared at the Philosophical Society, he looked on Ayer with such loathing that when Ayer addressed himself to him, he refused to reply directly, and would say to some third party – say, to me, or even to Joseph[2] (who was prepared to cross swords with Ayer, and in a way rather admired the rapier thrusts) – 'Tell him that x, y, z etc.', as if he could not bring himself to address himself to the horrid heretic directly. He was appallingly rude, and so was Joseph. Joachim[3] did not come to these assemblies much, as you know, but I used to go to lunch with him now and then, and he spoke with bitter passion about this wicked man and his wicked influence – Ayer, I mean. I did say that, to Joachim, Prichard and Joseph were 'argy-bargy' while to them he was a dispenser of mere 'talky-talky', which does indicate a certain failure to connect. But they were certainly united in common hostility to what they regarded as a species of philosophical nihilism, far worse probably than even the enormities of Russell.

You speak of J. A. Smith.[4] Yes, of course, on Aristotle he no doubt did influence Joachim profoundly: but by the time of which I speak – the middle 1930s – he was a hardly perceptible figure. None of my contemporaries, or even people slightly older than myself, certainly none of my juniors, ever referred to him as a source of ideas about anything. This may have been unjust, but it was certainly the case. In the first flush of empirical excitement everything that faintly savoured of the a priori or 'necessary connections' was driven out of every door and window – the only voices listened to were those of the Cambridge positivists, plus Miss Stebbing's[5] London circle that

1 Harold Arthur Prichard (1871–1947), White's Professor of Moral Philosophy and Fellow, CCC, 1928–37. As severe on himself as he was on others, Prichard was a formidable controversialist; like his colleagues H. W. B. Joseph and Harold Joachim, he was 'scandalised' by the 'passionate iconoclasm' of A. J. Ayer's *Language, Truth and Logic*, as well as by the youthful self-assurance of its author. ODNB: Richard Wollheim on Ayer (whence the quotations); David Ross on Prichard.

2 Horace William Brindley ('Jobags') Joseph (1867–1943), philosopher, Fellow of New College 1891–1943; he embodied, 'more than any man of his time, the essential characteristics of "Greats" Philosophy: a philosophy firmly rooted in the teachings of Plato and Aristotle' (*Oxford Magazine*, 2 December 1943, 98).

3 Harold Henry Joachim (1868–1938), Wykeham Professor of Logic and Fellow of New College 1919–35: 'A philosopher whose ultimate convictions are still unstable has the advantage that the way is still open for unexpected views and for sudden and brilliant paradoxes. With Joachim this could not be' (obituary, *Times*, 2 August 1938, 12b).

4 John Alexander Smith (1863–1939), Waynflete Professor of Metaphysical Philosophy 1910–36; senior editor of the Oxford series of translations of Aristotle. 'It is said that from 1891 onwards hardly a single work on philosophy was written in Oxford without an acknowledgement of Smith's assistance, yet there is no book that bears his own name' (obituary, *Times*, 20 December 1939, 11d).

5 (Lizzie) Susan Stebbing (1885–1943), Professor of Philosophy, Bedford College for Women,

met at Christmas time. At meetings of the Aristotelian Society, Ewing[1] alone waved his little flag in honour of the old verities and dared refer to Ross, or even Joseph and Dawes Hicks.[2] Kneale[3] was allowed to mention Stout,[4] and Broad's[5] name was just permitted. This duly rubbed off on the Oxford *fauves*. At least, that is my memory. But you may well be right, I may have generalised from too narrow a base, and a lot may have been going on unknown to me; but I only tried to convey the atmosphere of those meetings, and how the world looked to them rather than the 'dead right' view of reality which Prichard suspected that Locke had held. All I remember is that when I asked Prichard what he thought of Charles Morris's book on Idealistic logic, he said, 'There is a lot of activity in it', and about Joseph's book on ethics[6] he said, 'I wish he hadn't written it.'

Yours ever,

[Isaiah]

On 3 June an Honorary Doctorate was conferred on IB at the University of Tel Aviv; among the other honorands was the composer, conductor and pianist, Leonard Bernstein.

London, 1933–43, the first woman to hold a philosophy chair in Britain, strongly influenced at Cambridge by G. E. Moore. Her approach 'anticipated the sensible, debunking generation of philosophers who came back, especially to Oxford, after the Second World War, and amazingly reflected their mood and their no-nonsense style' (Mary Warnock, ODNB).

1 Alfred Cyril Ewing (1899–1973), Lecturer in Moral Science, Cambridge, 1931–54, Reader in Philosophy 1954–66. Ewing's imperviousness to Wittgenstein, who became the dominant force in English philosophy, made him 'unfashionable and relatively uninfluential', yet his criticisms 'of many fashionable philosophical theories were relevant and acute and were expressed with force and clarity' (obituary, *Times*, 16 May 1973, 21h).

2 George Dawes Hicks (1862–1941), Professor of Philosophy, UCL, 1904–28.

3 William Calvert Kneale (1906–90), Lecturer in Philosophy, Exeter College, 1932, Fellow 1933–60; White's Professor of Moral Philosophy and Fellow, CCC, 1960–6; among the 'more open-minded of the older philosophers' he 'regarded Ayer's impact on Oxford philosophy as salutary' (Richard Wollheim on A. J. Ayer, ODNB).

4 George Frederick Stout (1860–1944), Professor of Logic and Metaphysics, St Andrews, 1903–36; Editor of *Mind* 1891–1920; an authority on psychology, Stout 'was perhaps the most direct continuator in contemporary philosophy of the psychological speculations of Locke, Berkeley and Hume' (*Times*, 19 August 1944, 7f).

5 Charlie Dunbar Broad (1887–1971), Knightbridge Professor of Philosophy, Cambridge, 1933–53; influenced by Russell, Moore and G. F. Stout, among others, his tenure of the Knightbridge chair was overshadowed by the return to Cambridge in 1929 of Wittgenstein, whose voguishness he resented, and who 'soon stole any fire Broad may have had' (Anthony Quinton, ODNB).

6 *Some Problems in Ethics* (Oxford, 1931), in which Joseph took issue with Prichard's account of the nature of 'right' and 'good' in the latter's 1928 Oxford inaugural lecture *Duty and Interest*. '[O]ne of Mr Joseph's principal aims is to show that Mr Prichard's theory of these matters is absurd – although, of course, the kind of absurdity that is worth writing a book about': John Laird, *Mind* 40 (1931), 381–5 at 382.

TO ROWLAND BURDON-MULLER

11 June 1973

Headington House

Dear Rowland,

[...] I am glad to hear that you are so well. Aline gave a very good report of you. I have, as you know, just visited Israel on a very short trip, and there I had to deliver a speech to Tel Aviv University, which was the last thing that I wished to do, or do at all well. I know that you think that I am peculiarly sensitive on the entire subject of that unfortunate country, and touch upon [it] even in the conversations with the far more temperate Aline with the greatest caution and with an enormously long pair of tongs – however, it is a harmless story that I am about to tell you. There was an enormously long ceremony, in which we sat in the open in a rather handsome university campus, while 250 MA degrees were slowly being dispensed to the sound of thin clapping from the audience. The next item on the programme was a speech by the President, by persons who received Honorary Degrees, and finally by the Minister of Finance. After the MAs had been conferred, and deep boredom had descended upon the assembly, a body of persons with placards appeared, who were plainly going to 'disrupt' the proceedings: this was the junior staff of the university, complaining of low salaries. I asked the Dean, who was sitting next to me, what was happening; he explained that he had spoken to these people and had not been able to dissuade them from making a protest, but had secured from them a promise that they would do so very gently and sweetly, without undue violence or excessive bad manners. So they marched round and round with huge posters, and the Minister of Finance, realising that the whole thing was aimed at himself, decided to get his speech over and not sit there as a target for the protestors for the extra hour-and-a-half or so which we were condemned to sit through ourselves. He began a fine traditional speech about academic standards. The protesters, as soon as he mentioned these standards, said through megaphones 'No bread, no standards', or words to that effect, and whenever he referred to intellectual quality, said 'No salaries, no quality.' It gradually became cumulatively quite funny, and even the pompous persons sitting round me began to giggle slightly. At this point, the Minister of Finance realised that something had to be done: so he changed the entire tenor of his speech, and, addressing the protestors, said, 'I have an enormous car outside given to me in my capacity as Minister of Finance. I propose to wind up this speech, which is already unconscionably long, and proceed to Jerusalem about my business. If five or six of you wish to get into the car with me and discuss your grievances, I have no doubt that they can be redressed. Kindly stop all this childishness, appoint a delegation, pile into the car with me, and off we go to Jerusalem.' At which there was a burst of applause, much laughter, the demonstration ceased, six stalwart persons entered his undoubtedly rather large car, and the disruption was over. I thought, a bit crude perhaps, but not uncivilised. And so we proceeded to our normal business. I thought you might like to hear of this new variation upon student disturbances. [...]

Brian [Urquhart] appeared here, and spoke about the United Nations with that peculiar mixture of sincerity, despair, seriousness, humour, self-deprecating modesty, realism and profound pessimism which I am sure qualifies all the utterances of serious people about that unhappy organisation.

What more have I to tell you? Nothing much – I have announced to my colleagues that I am about to retire, in a year or two at the most, and begged them with tears in my eyes not to insist upon all kinds of measures likely to make this new and quite handsome college grubbier than it need be until I have been safely buried in the ground – after that, they can do what they wish. Sometimes this Victorian gush works and sometimes it doesn't, and so we tick over. It is sad about the fearful row at the Princeton Institute – I don't know if Aline told you about that – quite interesting in a way, and very violent indeed. There is nothing so terrible as a truly enraged academic – no quarter given and implacable, life-long war and hatred. On this fine bellicose note I end, with renewed thanks for your exquisite present, which is as beautiful as it is useful. I am very sorry not to have seen you for so long.

Yours ever,
    Isaiah

TO YEHUDI MENUHIN

2 July 1973 [*carbon*]

[Wolfson]

Dear Yehudi,

That meeting at the French Embassy was much too brief. We arrived late, having had to go to a banquet of the Master Carpenters – and so I was dressed in all my finery, and when people did not fail to comment on the fact that I was so plainly overdressed, I would reply, 'I cannot help it – a certain vulgarity of personality – a certain exhibitionism – will out', and, let me tell you, some people thought that I meant this perfectly seriously, and Lord Trevelyan[1] was much taken aback, and said to somebody else, when he thought that I was not listening, that he had not previously thought of me in these terms, but one sometimes has to revise one's views. I was very pleased by this. I wish you would let me know about your summer arrangements – perhaps we could meet quietly, somewhere, sometime and not always at the

---

1 Humphrey Trevelyan (1905–85), KCMG 1955, life peer 1968, diplomat; ambassador to Iraq 1958–61; Deputy Under-Secretary of State, FO, 1962; ambassador to USSR 1962–5.

grandest possible assemblies to which our noble descent naturally entitles us to be invited – I really should be grateful. [...]

Fondest love to Diana, and I wish we could meet.

Yours,

[Isaiah]

TO DOUGLAS VILLIERS[1]

11 July 1973

[Headington House]

[Dear Mr Villiers,]

[...] Arthur Koestler does not do justice to my argument. It is not, to use his words, 'that unreason, however irritating or maddening, must be tolerated', or that Jews or anyone else 'have a right to be guided by irrational emotion'. My thesis was and is that to demand social and ideological homogeneity, to wish to get rid of minorities because they are tiresome or behave 'foolishly or inconsistently or vulgarly' (these are indeed my words), is illiberal and coercive and neither rational nor humane. This is the position that, in very different forms, I attributed to Plato, to T. S. Eliot and to Arthur Koestler: it forms the heart of that 'integralist' nationalism in Europe in the last century and a half, and now almost everywhere, which tells men to assimilate to the prevailing ethos inwardly, not merely in outward observance of the prevailing laws and customs; or else get out, or, at best, acquiesce in the treatment accorded to not very desirable outsiders, what Charles Maurras and his followers used to call *métèques*.[2] The notion that differences should not (or cannot) be tolerated, and should therefore be ironed out, and so obliterated, is what, in my view, distinguishes barbarian from civilised societies.

Mr Koestler, if I interpret him rightly, thinks that the mere existence of unassimilated minorities, especially those which are unclear about the nature of their identity, is bound to cause friction, and that it is therefore rational for them, in their own interests as well as those of the majority, to see to it that at any rate their grandchildren come to form part of that majority; whereas I hold the view that this is neither desirable, since variety is not an evil but a good, and the disappearance of any peaceful human species with a rich past is a gratuitous loss to mankind; and moreover, however feasible for individuals, evidently not practicable for the mass. Even if we do not revert again to the terrible fate of the German Jews, the experience of Jews in the Soviet

1 Douglas Villiers (b. 1936), photographer and author; editor of *Next Year in Jerusalem: Jews in the Twentieth Century* (NY and London, 1976), whence this text is taken. The letter (a response to Arthur Koestler, 'The Vital Choice', ibid., 98–105), appears at 106.

2 In the Greek city-States 'metics' were foreigners who enjoyed some of the privileges of citizens of the *polis*, but had no political rights; the late 19th-century French usage carried a pejorative connotation, and Charles Maurras's nationalistic Action française identified 'métèques', with Jews, Protestants and Freemasons, as 'the enemy within'.

Union – the grandchildren, in many cases, of men and women who believed in and practised assimilation with enthusiastic fervour – seems to indicate that the process does not work on the (pathetically) hoped-for scale: the grandparents may force themselves to eat sour grapes, but the teeth of the grandchildren are set on edge. I do not, of course, expect my admired friend Arthur Koestler to accept this view: nor, I feel sure, does he expect me to accept his. But whereas I think we are none the poorer for such differences, he probably thinks that this, too, is a symptom of a lack of serious respect for logic and the belief in the final solubility by a collective act of radical choice, of important social problems. On this, too, we must continue to disagree: I shall continue to tolerate and, indeed, respect his view, even if he does not consent to tolerate mine. [...]

[Yours sincerely,
    Isaiah Berlin]

H. L. A. Hart, R. M. Hare, Stuart Hampshire, A. J. Ayer, by Mark Boxer

TO BERNARD WILLIAMS

18 July 1973

Headington House

Dear Bernard,

Thank you very much for 'The Self':[1] it reached me at the very moment at which I was about to leave for Italy, and it shall accompany me wherever

---

1 *Problems of the Self: Philosophical Papers, 1956–1972* (Cambridge, 1973), Bernard Williams's first collection of essays.

I move. I need hardly say that I am a fan, not to say addict, of your style and content both. Thank you also for your address.

As for the *New Statesman*, the piece[1] was apparently written by Francis Hope,[2] and seemed to me almost below the level of Jilly Cooper,[3] a kind of self-confident, pathetic effort at liveliness, sub-Gellner, no good at all. Stuart, whose piety towards the *New Statesman* in some way survives everything, was particularly shocked that I should have been described as Warden of Nuffield: 'Really, the *New Statesman* must have copy-readers? Sub-editors? This is illiteracy! This is beneath all contempt!' I thought poor Freddie, too, had been badly treated by the cartoonist, Mark Boxer.[4] As for the nasty things about Stuart, you and me, I expect no other: we are none of us defeated enough not to provoke the spleen, and knock off chips from the shoulders, of those who are. That last remark has the rare merit of sounding like Rowse and yet containing truth.

Much love to you both, I leave in literally three minutes' time.

[IB p.p. Pat Utechin]

TO LIDIYA CHUKOVSKAYA[5]

25 July 1973 [*editorial translation of Russian manuscript*]

Headington House

[Dear Lidiya Korneevna,

[...] what you sent me is very very interesting: and I am terribly grate-ful: I have read both the 1908 article about Tolstoy[6] and the letters[7] at least

1 'The Clever Men of Oxford', *New Statesman*, 6 July 1973, 8–11 at 10.

2 Francis Hope (1938–74), New College history 1957–60, elected a Fellow of All Souls 1960; after-wards worked for *Encounter* and the *New Statesman*; Paris correspondent of the *Observer* at the time of his death in the Paris plane crash of 3 March 1974, in which all 345 of those on board were killed.

3 Jilly Cooper (b. 1937), columnist, *Sunday Times*, 1969–82, writing of her experiences as a young working wife; author of *How to Stay Married* (London, 1969) and *How to Survive from Nine to Five* (London, 1970).

4 (Charles) Mark (Edward) Boxer (1931–88), cartoonist (as 'Marc') and magazine editor; first editor, *Sunday Times Magazine*, 1962–5; Assistant Editor, *Sunday Times*, 1966–79; Cartoonist of the Year 1972. In the previously unpublished drawing of IB printed on 541 'Lots of extremely intelligent, unintelligable [*sic*] talk' is shown issuing from IB's mouth.

5 Lidiya Korneevna Chukovskaya (1907–96), Russian writer and poet, daughter of the children's writer Korney Chukovsky and wife of the scientist Matvey Bronstein (1906–38), who was a victim of Stalin's Great Purge; lifelong friend of Anna Akhmatova; her defence of the Nobel laureate Andrey Sakharov from criticism led to her expulsion from the Union of Soviet Writers, January 1974. 'She was a woman of immense courage and unswerving integrity who never uttered a sen-tence in which she did not fully believe. Her conflicts with authority were inevitable but she met them with a kind of fearless stoicism to which there are few parallels in the Soviet Union as it used to be'. (IB, *Guardian*, 9 February 1996, 13).

6 'Tolstoi kak khudozhestvennyi genii' ['Tolstoy as an Artistic Genius'], *Niva* 1908 no. 9, cols 75–104; repr. in *Yunost'* 1971 no. 9, 87–94.

7 'Pis'ma K. Chukovskogo raznykh let' ['Letters of K. Chukovsky from various years'], with introduction and commentary by L. Krysin, *Voprosy literatury* 1972 no. 1, 152–82.

IB by Mark Boxer

twice – with the greatest pleasure (as indeed almost everything which your father published). The article on Tolstoy – despite the rapturous tone (which I myself find most 'attractive') I personally consider one of the best pieces ever written about Tolstoy – K[orney] I[vanovich] emphasises in Tolstoy that very 'negative capability', about which the poet *John Keats* once wrote[1] – and which *Renan*[2] quite wrongly attributed to Turgenev in his speech at the funeral in Paris – that fantastic ability to transpose himself into others – another – Anna, Pierre, Denisov, a horse (it was Turgenev who once said to Tolstoy that he had probably himself been a horse and can recall his 'previous life' – Oh God! What *horrible* grammatical [mistakes] I'm making in my letter to you, like some semi-literate child!) – and to transplant the reader into other bodies – each with its own centre and own atmosphere, with its personal 'melody' – and not on to some nameless pin, on to which qualities – attributes – are skewered, i.e. those gleaming but dead vignettes, so beloved of the most famous French writers, Balzac and Flaubert and even Proust. All this is subtle, and profound and brilliant and, just as everywhere in KI's case, – incredibly *fascinating* – *not* academic, not literary, but 'spontaneously' full of life and 'reality' – but sparkling as in Herzen's writing – naturally, as in Tolstoy's own case (nineteenth century) – and making it lighter and *merrier*

1 'Negative Capability, that is, when a man is capable of being in uncertainties, mysteries, doubts, without any irritable reaching after fact & reason'. Letter to George and Thomas Keats, 22 December 1817. IB here equates negative capability with empathy, but the empathiser must, as IB puts it, 'transpose himself into others', surely a further step.

2 (Joseph) Ernest Renan (1823–92), French philosopher, spoke at Turgenev's funeral in Paris on 1 October 1883.

and it does not weigh down the spirit as is the case after reading say Matthew Arnold (or Ovsyaniko-Kulikovsky) or any German whatsoever – Lukács and especially Thomas Mann.[1] What also seems interesting to me is that (although this is not mentioned for a variety of reasons) Tolstoy's attitudes are those of a land-owning nobleman. All *live* people in his work are either aristocrats or belong to that part of the world with which aristocrats – or rather landowners – maintained close ties – only peasants of a particular type (i.e. his own – not Karataev), and also cows, horses, dogs, rivers, trees, sky, earth; other creatures are sometimes extremely wooden and the peasants are stylised: holy, simple, *paysans* – while the middle class – the bourgeoisie – doesn't exist at all! The worlds of Dostoevsky or Chekhov seem to be inaccessible to him. He is God – the creator only of the world of Tolstoy's relatives and friends and acquaintances: only the nobility. Yet he creates a complete illusion: when you read him, no other world exists. Everything lives through *him*: pantheism: pan-Tolstoyism – everything is given *his* names, as in Adam's paradise – there are no other things, people, Nature, names or words. Yet I shouldn't hold forth like this – endlessly – and bore you – the totally innocent one – for giving me such real pleasure. One more thing about Tolstoy and KI: he protests at Tolstoy's philosophising, as in his day Flaubert had protested ('il moralise! et il philosophise'),[2] an oak – Nature – God, the creator of heaven and earth, shouldn't suddenly start talking – and giving lectures. That is why the late B. L. Pasternak said to me once (when I told him that Akhmatova turned on Chekhov), that Chekhov was the *only* Russian writer who *never* addresses the reader – ('he dissolved everything in art – that's *our* answer to Flaubert' – his own words) – and rightly so. Still, it seems to me – and once I even published a short book about it – ('The Hedgehog and the Fox' – which was written as an article) – that in that split – between *unquenchable* interest in *everything* ('noble'! or is that a false or vulgar accusation?), an understanding of the whole diverse, colourful, widespread universe – on the one hand, *and* the stubborn wish to subordinate *all* of that to a *single*, simple, central moral-cum-spiritual principle – to explain *everything*, to simplify *everything*, to make everything transparent, clear and brought together – a little green stick[3] – and to do this with *words* and not through art and imagination (which stems from the Devil), which *changes* everything and encourages whims, this is 'tension' – friction – this is the collision, which is so brilliantly described by KI (when he says that in many cases the didactic is presented as art, but

---

1 Matthew Arnold (1822–1888), critic and poet; Dmitry Nikolaevich Ovsyaniko-Kulikovsky (1853–1920), writer and literary critic; György Lukács (483/2); Thomas Mann (1875–1955), novelist.

2 See RT2 28. Flaubert's actual words are 'il se répète et il philosophise' ['he repeats himself and he philosophises']. Letter to Turgenev, 21 January 1880, Gustave Flaubert, *Lettres inédites à Tourguéneff*, ed. Gérard Gailly (Monaco, 1946), 218.

3 When Tolstoy was a child, his brother Nikolay told his siblings that he knew a secret that would make everyone happy. He said he had inscribed this on a green stick buried at the edge of a ravine on their ancestral estate, Yasnaya Polyana.

it is the opposite with Tolstoy – he presents the creative as didactic) – that is the actual electricity, which sparks in his work – that friction – when the scythe hits a stone – which underlies the thoughts and emotions of Tolstoy's 'heroes' ('Why do I do *this*? Live *this* life?', 'Maybe all this is fantasy and dishonest self-delusion? – *mauvaise foi*'[1] – that is what Turgenev mocked and irritated Tolstoy horribly) – it is precisely that which sets everything in motion: without it, would he have become a second Dickens (second not first) or simply a realist? Well, as Turgenev said, 'Enough'![2] I'm ageing and becoming a chatterer! But if I had known about KI's article in 1949 or 1950, when I wrote (or rather hastily dictated) my book-article about L[ev] N[ikolaevich], then I would have written it differently or wouldn't have written it at all: after all KI had already said the *key* thing: what a pity that it had remained unknown for so long! [...]

   With deep gratitude and 'Sympathie Intellectuelle'

     Isaiah Berlin

PS My God, everything has turned out *not as it should be* – illiterate and clumsy! I'm like a pianist who doesn't want to play, because he fills himself with horror – the sounds are all wrong. Forgive me for this scribble and for the whole of this 'epistle'.]

TO JEAN FLOUD

   23 August 1973 [*manuscript*]

                                                         Paraggi

Dear Jean,

   Jerusalem was full of movement: Casals, aged 96, was fêted everywhere: he plays, conducts, shouts at players, cries, but when not engaged in music, has to be wrapped in shawls (I long for that) & carried by his young Puerto Rican wife. An inconceivably vulgar American Hollywood scene – Salute to Israel or something like that – organized by a millionaire with the help of a 'party-architect' – a new profession – constructor of parties – relevant guests, décor, music, sound effects – greeted Mrs G. Meir: She was acclaimed to the strains of an aria out of *Hello Dolly*[3] with Golda in place of Dolly. Even the vulgarest Israelis were embarrassed by the hidden chorus in the Tomb of David: but she herself apparently loved it, wept, was in a state of endless bliss. I thought I shd have [a] little leisure. But as always I had to function like a dentist or psycho-analyst. Client after client – 14–15 hours a day. [...] Here

---

1 'Bad faith'.

2 'Dovol'no!', the title of a story (1864) by Turgenev.

3 *Hello, Dolly!* – hugely popular Broadway musical comedy (1964) which transferred to film (1969), Carol Channing starring in the title role of Dolly Levi on stage, and Barbra Streisand on screen, while Louis Armstrong's memorable rendition of the title song gained him a Grammy Award in 1964.

it is v.v. hot. Really you *shd* go to the Holy Land: its humours are made for a Judenkenner[1] like you: Germans, Russians, 'Anglo-Saxons' (that is Stoke Newington & Leeds) you'd be amused & horrified & touched by it all. We return on the 15th – Sorry for this non-letter. Exhausted.

Love.

I.

TO GERSHOM SCHOLEM

25 August 1973 [*manuscript*]

Paraggi

Dear Gershom,

I went to Jerusalem, and I returned; the most astonishing phenomenon was Pablo Casals at 96: his legs are weak and his appetite for food feeble, but the sounds he extracts from his cello are firm, beautiful and loud: and he conducted all those young Russian Jews with unbelievable force and clarity (he was never a good conductor, but a conductor) interspersed with speeches in broken English about what art is & what it means to him. I saw him meet Ben Gurion in a room: B.G. looks like a very well made wax-work of himself, ruddy, healthy looking, beautifully finished, but without memory or interest in what goes on. Casals congratulated him on his age (he is nine years younger than C.) & then, later, said triumphantly 'the old gentleman is rather gaga, no?' [...]

Yours,

Isaiah

TO NOEL ANNAN

31 August 1973 [*carbon*]

[Wolfson]

Dear Noel,

I have only just got your piece on Maurice[2] and your letter. You are unduly unselfconfident: it is a vivid, warm-hearted, *intensely* readable piece, and nobody else could have written about the Old Boy as you have and revealed all the things which, in my official address, I could not speak about – and anyway, which you know better and describe *brilliantly*. I read it with vast pleasure and admiration and some disagreement. [...]

Also, on p. 6, my book on Marx. This is doubtless what Maurice wrote, but it is pure fiction. Fisher[3] did not say this: and I therefore suffered no wound:

1 'Connoisseur of Jews'.
2 A draft of 'A Man I Loved', Annan's contribution to Hugh Lloyd-Jones (ed.), *Maurice Bowra: A Celebration* (London, 1974).
3 Herbert Albert Laurens Fisher (1865–1940), OM 1937, historian and politician, author of the 1918

he merely said that squeezing the book into Home University format – from its original vaster size, which I pleaded for in 1936 – 'would be the making of the book'.[1] Maurice, however, did tell me (and others) that the book read like a 'translation from the Latvian', which was mildly irritating: and I think he meant it, but I did not go by his literary opinions much, which was one of the sources of trouble, of course.[2] Fisher said nothing about the book, so far as I know: and certainly would not have said this to Maurice, whom he found entertaining but vulgar, and never said a real thing to. However, since Maurice *wrote* this, let it stand: though Fisher's daughter,[3] head of St. Hilda's – who knows the facts – will write to me and express indignant denial. Maurice thought poorly of me as a writer, and this did not worry me enough: one of the sources of trouble – indeed, the ultimate one – was my total inability to admire his later works: he dedicated a book to me: even that I *could* not read. He felt this, and it infuriated him. The same is true of Sylvester Gates, whom Maurice admired extravagantly, and loved, and who had been a friend, but thought Maurice's work worthless and avoided seeing him in his last ten years, because he said Maurice talked of *nothing* but his academic honours: hon. doctorates, etc. (he had quite a lot of these – at Harvard and Paris and so on, besides England, and you might mention those?) and he found his company intolerably boring: Maurice knew nothing of this and complained that Sylvester was always out when he telephoned: where was he all the time? Let me continue with counter-views: all our Maurices are bound to be different – like the Socrateses and Platos and the Xenophons – but I should like to make my points:

Generosity. Yes: of course: he was impulsively generous: to you, to Renée Ayer in 1939–40 – to others, poor undergraduates, Adrian Bishop[4] (who *was* all the things Maurice conveyed to you he took him to be), also *ungenerous*: to those who asked for help but who bored him: or gave him guilt: rather like his refusal to support G. E. Moore for a degree at Oxford – 'too obvious' he said: he *meant* that he was a Bloomsbury divinity and therefore hateful to him: snubbed by Bloomsbury as he had been, so brutally. In Italy, with us,

Education Act, and a distinguished Warden of New College 1925–40.

1 In November 1933 Fisher had approached IB to write a biography of Marx for the Home University Library of Modern Knowledge series; IB accepted the commission, and spent five years working on the book, which was published in September 1939 (cf. 8/5). The original contractual allowance was 50,000 words, increased in 1938 in response to Berlin's pleas to 65,000 words. Berlin wrote over 100,000 words, which he cut to the published length of 75,000 words.

2 'One could wish that Mr Berlin had a taste for shorter sentences, but on the other hand it must be said that his elaborate and almost neo-Augustan precision of style is not without charm' (R. D. Charques, 'In the name of Marx', TLS, 7 October 1939, 570).

3 Mary Letitia Somerville Bennett (1913–2005) née Fisher, civil servant; Principal, St Hilda's, 1965–80.

4 Herbert Francis ('Adrian') Bishop (1898–1942) read classics at King's, Cambridge, 1919–23; he was an impecunious and uninhibited homosexual, admired and indulged by Bowra, who likened him to Oscar Wilde, Bowra playing the part of Robbie Ross; he died in Tehran in mysterious circumstances in June/July 1942 while apparently working for British intelligence.

Maurice stood nobody any drinks, and bartered shamelessly even when we simply could *not* get enough lire to keep going: of course *this* should not be hinted at: his attitude to money was very neurotic: he could not bear to think of it and kept telling me about his forthcoming poverty – but left £130,000. The neurosis was *very* severe. But *habitually* generous he was *not*: only to some, only explosively: sporadically: like all his volcanic, eruptive gestures.

On Humphry[1] and Dunbabin.[2] You should know that while he quite liked Humphry House (my intimate friend) House *despised* him openly: yet Maurice did not mind, because he thought Humphry despised us all: as for Dunbabin, Maurice *loathed* him. So the whole thing is a piece of typical rhetorical fantasy: he just *chose* to say this, as a kind of turn: he was, as you know, capable of saying to X that Shelley was a muddled watery mess, and five minutes later to Y (D. Cecil, say) that he was the noblest poet in the English language. This cost him, apparently, nothing: it was part of a wild, impulsive, careless playing: he was easily carried away by poetry, by painting, by people, he adored the momentary crest of a wave, he hated careful, cautious calculation – all truth – but *integrity* was an empty concept to him. He lied like a trooper, to win, to enhance life, to humiliate an enemy, to do good to a friend, to get out of a corner: and was terrified of being found out ('pig's eyes' etc.): it was very disarming and warm-hearted – but not a word could be believed.

He was *not* devoted to Sparrow. Not at all. He created much of him in his youth (as with us all) but by the 1950s he *feared* John: that he might say, do *anything*: loathed his views genuinely, *liked* his company – a lot of former intimacy could be drawn on – but *not* him. All this was in part reciprocated: John loved 'the old (i.e. pre-war) Maurice' and thought the Warden a 'noisy bore'. M's *death* depressed John and brought his own condition home to him. All this I am *sure* of. So do modify your statement a little! His true friends, whom he *adored*, were (1) Dadie – could do no wrong; (2) Boothby; (3) Cyril Connolly. With these he felt entirely happy. Also, more or less, with Elizabeth Bowen. And Roy Harrod, whom he thought snobbish and ridiculous, but was bound to by deep old friendship. He was very fond of you, although, of course, he said terrible things, as about us all. He was grateful to Tony Q.[3] ('works like a s..., talks like a s..., and isn't one'), to his own junior colleagues at Wadham, liked Stuart but not really, disliked Freddie (to do with Joan Leigh Fermor,[4] with whom he was deeply in love), and, oddly enough,

---

1 (Arthur) Humphry House (1908–55), literary scholar; elected Chaplain-Fellow and Lecturer in English at Wadham in 1931, but resigned in 1932 after a crisis of faith; Senior University Lecturer in English Literature, Oxford, 1948–55; Senior Research Fellow, Wadham, 1950–5.

2 Thomas James Dunbabin (1911–55), Fellow of All Souls 1937–55; Reader in Classical Archaeology, Oxford, 1945–55.

3 Anthony Meredith Quinton (1925–2010), philosopher; Fellow of All Souls 1949–55, of New College 1955–78; later President of Trinity (1978–87) and life peer (1982).

4 Joan Elizabeth Leigh Fermor (1912–2003) née Eyres-Monsell, daughter of Bolton Meredith Eyres-

devoted to me. He *was* envious, and not of me alone. He thought I was far too lucky: too much undeserved good fortune: he was deeply irritated by my knighthood. He was against my going to Wolfson (and made a scene on Council which embarrassed everybody). But although I was an acquired taste, I was acquired for life. As of course *I* owed him a fantastic portion of my whole life. He really did form me in the 1930s, after his adoration of the aristocracy (*very* strong in the 1920s) came to a deliberate, willed, end. I really do owe him an unbelievable part of what I am, think, feel. So when the OM came ('a rich man's CH', he said to Cyril Connolly) I was *terrified* of his reaction. I thought he would hate it too much – he *did* so want it – so I wrote him a perfectly sincere hymn of praise and apology for my getting it rather than him: he rose nobly above his feeling and wrote you (and me too) as he did. It cost him a great deal, I am sure, and was very sweet and heroic. He would have minded less if K. Clark had got it, since he loved him, and was unaware of the Clarks' steps to avoid him at Christmas: efforts by some of his friends to evade him, as you know, became horrid and contemptible in the last years. I think you go on a bit too much about his envy of me (everyone testifies to it, alas: and Sparrow won't regret the appalling things he said: and Stuart made some bad blood in his day) – it should, I think, *either* be balanced by something on the basic devotion which bound us to the end – only when we were *alone* – it was *always* marvellous then – terrible in company quite often – or left out or played down as of little importance. Otherwise it singles me out as an object of horrid feelings, which seems to me embarrassing and out of focus. In this connection: do *not*, I beg you speak of my 'deprecating' tact. True, I did always pipe down, else the bile *did* rise: he was *eaten* by *envy* (not jealousy). But not 'deprecating' – just terrified – anxious to propitiate – 'propitiating' – or even 'anxious' to be more correct. I was simply afraid of unprovoked fury: and I did love him much more – towards the end – than I respected him (this was true of *all* his old friends and everyone in Oxford – including Bob Boothby and K. Clark – not Dadie perhaps?), and he knew, alas, that I had not enough regard for his love – he tried to praise mine – and that was unconvincing and went wrong too. Still, I did, somehow, become a firm fixture in his universe. He thought things came much too easily to me; and thus was offensively critical and life-diminishing, critical of him and of myself. He believed in publishing and not looking behind one – and half knew his books were not much good, and, of course, sometimes believed that, after all, there they were – the shelf of them – shored up against the Enemy: Page,[1]

Monsell (1st Viscount Monsell 1935); a society beauty – described as 'very fair, with huge myopic blue eyes' by Alan Pryce-Jones (once her fiancé) in *The Bonus of Laughter* (London, 1987), 82 – and distinguished amateur photographer, she counted among her admirers Cyril Connolly and Stephen Spender, as well as Maurice Bowra; she married (secondly) in 1968, after many years of co-habitation, the travel-writer and soldier Patrick Michael ('Paddy') Leigh Fermor (1915–2011).

1 Denys Lionel Page (1908–78), Kt 1971; Regius Professor of Greek, Cambridge, 1950–73, and Professorial Fellow, Trinity, 1950–60; Master of Jesus, Cambridge, 1959–73; President of the

Gow,[1] Lobel,[2] Fraenkel,[3] Trevor-Roper – the scholars who thought him, some of them, a charlatan and a corrupter of youth (Murray thought *that* – and *all* the Germans – and Momigliano, all but Mynors[4] and Syme[5] among the authentic). As his obsessive fever – worse than the paranoia and the terror of the blackmailer at the door which never left him[6] – was fear of death, he was preoccupied by it, and could not keep off the subject. And he was (and this *is* worth saying something about) deeply, deeply *unhappy*: after the disaster of the war – no job and all that – no real happiness. The V[ice-]C[hancellorship] had staved things off a bit – he was proud and happy of the big votes he got in elections to Council – but the poacher turned gamekeeper suffered: he longed to be with the old 'immoral front' (his phrase), and had cut that possibility off for ever. Then we went for our *à deux* journeys to Italy in 1947, and often his wounds were bared: and our real friendship was cemented then: *too* much, alas, the green-eyed goddess puts this out of proportion.

You praise him for his appointments: oh dear! You are a thousand times right: appointments are everything. The Old Boy – when *I* was on boards of electors with him – started off with one candidate. Then, if he saw the tide turning against him, swiftly switched: the Russian appointments were poor: I asked him why, e.g., he preferred some worthless British Council Greek to Steven Runciman. I got a terrible wigging: Steven was pronounced a worthless Cambridge queen whereas the Greek 'knows how to treat great men'. He stopped Wade-Gery's[7] extension, though he was a friend and admirer,

British Academy 1971–4. With Andrew Gow he edited the 2-volume *The Greek Anthology: Hellenistic Epigrams* (Cambridge, 1965): 'his tendency to see things and people in strong black and white made it hard for him to do justice to the complexity of life [...] and, after early friendship, he became estranged from Sir Maurice Bowra, for whose scholarship he had little regard' (Hugh Lloyd-Jones, ODNB).

1 Andrew Sydenham Farrar Gow (1886–1978), classical scholar, Fellow of Trinity, Cambridge, and University Lecturer in Classics 1925–51, a highly respected editor of classical texts. He could be an intimidating teacher: 'Some pupils were indeed alienated by his dryness and his caustic wit; his frequent comment on an exercise shown up to him was "Oh, death, boy!", and his highest expression of praise was "Not wholly bad!"' (Hugh Lloyd-Jones, ODNB).

2 Edgar Lobel (1888–1982), Romanian-born Greek scholar; Reader in Papyrology, Oxford, 1936–59; Senior Research Fellow, Queen's, 1938–59; from 1934 editor of the literary papyri in the Oxyrhynchus series, on which he continued to work for the rest of his life.

3 Eduard David Mortier Fraenkel (1888–1970), Berlin-born classical scholar, emigrated to England in 1934, and with the backing of A. E. Housman was elected Corpus Professor of Latin at Oxford (1935–53); found it difficult to settle in England 'and at first and for long after alienated many well-wishers by his tactlessness and insensitivity' (Hugh Lloyd-Jones, ODNB); with time he mellowed, and came to identify closely with his adoptive home.

4 Roger Aubrey Baskerville Mynors (1903–89), Kt 1963, classicist, expert on Vergil's *Georgics*; Corpus Professor of Latin, Oxford, in succession to Fraenkel 1953–70.

5 Ronald Syme (1903–89), Kt 1959, later (1976) OM, Roman historian; Camden Professor of Ancient History, Oxford, 1949–70, Fellow of Wolfson from 1970.

6 One of Bowra's nicknames, 'the Rhino', belied his acute sensitivity to criticism: 'In particular his homosexuality was always a matter of anxiety. Close friendships with Philip Ritchie, Adrian Bishop and Ernst Kantorowicz were marred by fears about exposure and blackmail' (Leslie Mitchell, ODNB).

7 Henry Theodore Wade-Gery (1888–1972), ancient historian; awarded the MC for a notable

because there was no other way of getting rid of Fraenkel, who was the greatest scholar of his time, though rude to Maurice. This is gradually turning into an indictment of M's academic role: let me say that he was a super-excellent Vice-Chancellor, and adored those years; and a splendid Warden; they all said he did no homework and cheated and deceived them and was terrible in the last year, but he doubled their size, put them on the map, and they were, rightly, intensely proud of him, and his loyalty to, and defence of, anybody at Wadham, bad, good, indifferent, was passionate, uncompromising and magnificent. Like Brendan at the MOI in the war, after Cooper, morale went up:[1] nobody could criticize *anybody* in Wadham with impunity. As an Oxford figure there was none like him: he outshone everyone, more than Sheppard[2] in Cambridge – and his mere presence made the life of dons and undergraduates more worth living – they felt it, even his detractors, even Boase, Sparrow, Hayter, all the Deans of Christ Church – than any other human being. His scholarship was *very* erratic: you quote a joke about my busyness: the Russian words, doubtless authentically his, are, alas, illiterate: it is as if one said: 'From Shakesbeard up of the Miltons'. It is a terrible giveaway and his translations have real howlers in them which a hack would avoid. Nor do I think him an intellectual: his interest in ideas – as opposed to [ ] or spiritual experience – was minimal: and, whether as a result of Joseph or not, he was made uneasy by philosophy. I think your indictment of the inhumanity of intellectuals is generalised from too narrow a Bloomsbury base [...]. But Maurice was very uncomfortable about all such; he lived by concrete images, feelings, *visions* above all, and warm blood.

Do I go too far in picking on bits here and there? Maybe. After all, your piece is of Maurice as you knew him; and if this is what *you* saw, then in the name of Tolstoy, Bloomsbury and all, this is what you must say, and there's an end on't. Three more things: (*a*) I should, in your place, leave out bits on matutinal habits (what is 'the brush'?), the call on you in your bedroom, and four-letter words. The particular readers of *this* book are liable to mild queasiness: *der grosse Publikum*[3] is used to it by now, but not *this* public, even the women whom Maurice loved best – so *I* think: it is a purely personal

action on the Somme, 1916; Fellow of Wadham 1914–39; Wykeham Professor of Ancient History, Oxford, and Fellow of New College 1939–53. Extensions proposed for both Wade-Gery and Fraenkel were turned down by the Visitatorial Board on 27 January 1953. Presumably Bowra as Vice-Chancellor opposed an extension to Wade-Gery's professorship that would have entailed similar treatment for Fraenkel.

1 Churchill's appointment of Duff Cooper as Minister of Information in May 1940 proved less than inspired, and Cooper was relieved to be relieved of that office in July 1941; his successor, Brendan Bracken, brought to bear an 'aggressive energy [that] shocked the ministry out of its malaise', and he proved brilliantly adept at handling the media and communicating with the public (Jason Tomes, ODNB).

2 John Tresidder Sheppard (1881–1968), Kt 1950, classicist; Provost, King's, Cambridge, 1933–54; a brilliantly theatrical lecturer, and a much-loved college head, whose provostship at King's was extended beyond the normal term.

3 'The general public'.

squeamishness. (*b*) The poems: the dirge to Adrian is marvellous, of course, and the bit you quote is very moving: the one about the great rogue Goronwy Rees etc. is, I think, unintelligible without elaborate footnotes. The three All Souls election songs – or the one on, say, Rowse – would be less esoteric. Maurice was, all his life, *terrified* of his poems falling into the hands of anyone outside the charmed circle.[1] (*c*) If you do want *me* in the piece, with all that truly undeserved praise, which, of course, delights me, then I would beg you to do a little more than simply to say that I was a disciple (which is absolutely true) and say something about my patient swallowing of all those insults reported by kind friends, my acceptance of it as inevitable, given his attributes – it was a price for friendship I was ready to pay – and a word or two on the fact that, despite it all, and my natural discomfort when one of these quips was repeated, a friendship, and a very deep and lifelong one, it remained – while the relationship with, e.g., Sylvester, John Sparrow, Henry Yorke,[2] was no longer such, though this you will probably not wish to say, if only because you have no direct impression of this.

One more thing: you might talk to just one neutral observer about Maurice and John, Maurice and me, Maurice and Cyril [Connolly]: say to Ann Fleming, whom Maurice *adored* to his dying day, who may not have adored him, though she gave him much pleasure, and who talks about him and his attitude to you, me, whoever it might be, with a kind of disinterested, very un-malicious penetration. She is surprisingly good on him, and on John too. M's love of her was greater than for Barbara:[3] second only, in my time, to that of Joan Eyres-Monsell, who, I suspect, was the greatest single love of his life, of either sex, and who (in some senses) loved him too.

So: I have said too much, and probably been nastier than I meant to be. I react perhaps too strongly when that central nerve of my Oxford life is touched. Discount it all, I *beg* you. Destroy this compromising document, and if you prefer this, treat it as if it was never written. Your piece is characteristically pro-life, and pro the open word, and brings out all the generous, uncalculating, liberal (the decision not to go to the Greece of the colonels was a *terrible* sacrifice for him: he asked me; I said he was right; he was very pleased indeed and grateful; I begged him to come to Italy instead), for the young, the reckless, the non-Franks (he supported him, but neither liked nor

---

1 They have now been published as *New Bats in Old Belfries* (57/2), with only moderately elaborate footnotes. The poems IB mentions are 'Old Croaker', 'A Young Man and Old' and 'Election Songs'. The former is a tribute to a man 'whom [Bowra] acknowledged as a kind of mentor [...]. It is a masterpiece of literary humour nestling on the edge of pornography': Leslie Mitchell, *Maurice Bowra: A Life* (Oxford, 2009), 129–30.

2 Henry Vincent Yorke (1905–73) novelist as 'Henry Green'; one of the group of Oxford students – others included Cyril Connolly, Evelyn Waugh and John Betjeman – who were strongly influenced by Bowra, and in Yorke's case especially by his interpretation of Symbolism.

3 Barbara Judith Hutchinson (1911–89), wife successively of Victor Rothschild, Rex Warner and Niko Ghika, 'rich, restless, predatory, with a wicked wit and a lethal sexual magnetism': Selina Hastings, *Rosamond Lehmann* (London, 2002), 267.

admired him) – the new, untried, and the reason of the heart. The Dawkins story he came back to again and again.[1] He did so die. It is a very moving and appropriate finish: both his and yours. I could not read it without unexpected tears.

Love

[Isaiah]   [...]

TO MICHAEL BROCK

4 September 1973 [*manuscript*]

Paraggi

Dear Michael,

As soon as we had ceased speaking amid (at my end) all that terrible Heathrow din, I was smitten with doubts, as I always am, about everything [...]. Yet, on reflection, it seemed to me, as the aircraft shook disagreeably over the Alps, that this *is* right. Leonard has always taken the line about the hap'worth of tar: & this is a shining example of the rule: Having refused to let drop block E – he & he alone initiated the process which culminated in the present difficulties: the tug of war must & can only be between Universal House & the firms engaged on constructing the College: the buildings are the Wolfsons' (*why* did Crossman in the *Times* call them Wolfsohn: they won't like that) memorial: we *must* keep out. [...]

As for us, we are surrounded by *fires*: the 5th in 8 days: near our house: at 1 a.m. & the like: *most* terrifying: no pumps, no extinguishers, peasants wild with hypotheses about the complicity of local police, municipal authorities, property developers: all to do with propaganda for a road & abolition of preservation: to raise prices. Exciting & disturbing. We may survive.

Isaiah

TO SHIELA SOKOLOV GRANT

24 September 1973

Wolfson

Dear Shiela,

It is really terrible about the Irish visit. The painter, Derek Hill, has asked us to the Wexford Festival, and we have accepted, but then, perhaps rashly, we agreed to go to his house in Donegal as well, because he says he wants to draw Aline. He is a very nice and gifted, but easily irritated man (just like

1 After experiencing a nursing home in the 1950s, when suffering from influenza, Bowra had a dread of a slow institutionalised end, and he envied the fate of Professor Richard MacGillivray Dawkins (1871–1955), Emeritus Professor of Byzantine and Modern Greek at Oxford, who collapsed and died in Parks Road, Oxford, at the age of 83, on 4 May 1955: 'Dear Dawkins died very nicely in front of this college. He fell down in the street and was off to eternity. [...] A nice end, and may I have one like it' (letter to Noel Annan, 12 June [1955]).

you – I am less irritable, but possibly not so nice and gifted), and since he obtained little publicity for his portrait of me, commissioned by the College, would like, I suspect, for me to circulate copies of it to the daily press which, as you may well imagine, I am not exactly anxious to do. He is now talking about the 'unveiling', which, again, I wish to avert. Anyway, I do not wish to provoke him further: he has written sharply to me saying that if all I have available is four or five days in all (and I cannot, in the middle of term, go away for longer) there can be no question of our plunging down to the South – we must return from him via Belfast. So that is another beautiful scheme blown up; I longed to come, and so did Aline, despite your uncalled-for ironies about the style of life to which we are accustomed. But it is evidently not to be this time. The slender, yet hitherto unbroken, thread which has preserved our relationship for forty years must not be allowed to grow thin; I am not afraid of it snapping, only of its wearing so thin through lapse of time and lack of effort that it could become attenuated to the point of invisibility. This must not be allowed to happen. [...]

Meanwhile, I really am desolated by the turn of events.

Yours, ⟨with fondest love –

love –⟩

   Isaiah

In the early afternoon of 6 October Egyptian and Syrian ground forces launched simultaneous attacks on Israel across the Suez Canal and in the Golan Heights. The day chosen was Yom Kippur, the holiest in the Jewish year, and a day of prayer and fasting: the Israelis were caught unprepared, and, at the points of engagement, were outnumbered, and during the next 48 hours the Egyptians and Syrians secured their greatest territorial gains of the war. After some 72 hours Israel's reservists began a counter-attack: Israeli forces eventually crossed the Suez Canal, driving a wedge 20 miles into Egypt, and recovered the Golan Heights, advancing to within 35 miles of Damascus. On 22 October a US–Soviet-brokered ceasefire was adopted at the UN, and urged on the warring parties: that it eventually came into effect owed much to the shuttle diplomacy of the American Secretary of State Henry Kissinger. Although the Israelis could claim success in the conflict, they had also sustained serious losses in bitter and prolonged fighting on two fronts, and the mood in Israel after hostilities ended was anything but triumphant. Before the war there was speculation that US policy in the Middle East was changing in response to the country's need to maintain good relations with Saudi Arabia, and also to the more aggressive stance being taken by other oil producers, notably Libya, towards US backing for Israel. The supply and cost of oil was increasingly a factor in the calculations of Western governments, a worrying development for all Jews, whether in Israel or in the Diaspora.

TO DAN SEGRE

8 October 1973 [*carbon*]

[Wolfson]

Dear Dan,

Thank you very much for your letter of 25 September. This is not a very good day on which to reply to your peaceful enquiry. Even Israel's worst enemies are unlikely to accuse her of violating the Syrian and Egyptian borders on this particular day; but that is not, alas, the point. I imagine that the Arab motives, apart from the obvious ones, are to create a situation in which the Powers will feel moved to impose a 'solution'; that whatever 'solution' is imposed will be more favourable to the Egyptians, even the Syrians, than the present borders; that the only resistance to this will come from Israel, who will thus, again, be put in the dock as the only body obstructing the peace, the free flow of oil, the security of the regimes in Saudi Arabia, Egypt, Jordan, Morocco etc: and that then Mr Kissinger and Mr Brezhnev get together, and twist the arm of Israel and, perhaps, appear to do that to the Arabs as well, which would do something to protect Arab leaders from assassination by Black September, which they would otherwise risk, if they were willing to engage on some peace initiatives themselves. Is this too fanciful? It may well be. At any rate, this is the realm of international relations, about which, as you know, I know nothing. On the assumption that life must go on, letters answered, peaceful enterprises not abandoned in the face of the most worrying and upsetting and embittered events, I will try to answer the points in your letter as if all we were looking forward to was the Feast of the Tabernacles, the Rejoicing of the Law, etc. [...]

[Isaiah]

PS I have no idea when this letter will reach you, so I had better hold it back for a day or two, until the situation is a little clearer. We are glued to our sets, so are all the Israelis in and about St Antony's. The Israel Embassy has told them not to go back – the reservists I mean, so they are frustrated, worried, profoundly sympathetic, morally, politically, to Aline and me.

TO MCGEORGE BUNDY

26 October 1973 [*carbon*]

Wolfson

Dear Mac,

In addition to the other black clouds by which the world horizon is at present so thickly covered, let me darken a tiny corner of it still further by telling you briefly the sad tale of the buildings of Wolfson College. As a college we are doing quite well – morale is high, as it always is in England under conditions of enforced collective suffering – our finest hour is going on a little too long, but it still remains moderately fine. Academically we are doing quite well, and it is, indeed, despite the inevitable eccentricity of some British academics, of whom we have our share, a far more rational body of persons, both dons and graduates, than e.g. All Souls, or New College, or City University New York, or, dare I say it, even some corners of Harvard seem to me to have been. The situation about the buildings is somewhat different.

The contractors, Messrs Shepherds of York, swore they would complete the building by about a year and a half ago. They have made several similar oaths since then; last May they were convinced that all would be finished by July – there was visible ocular evidence that this was absurd, but the formula continued to be repeated. [...]

When will it all be ready? The architects say that if the builders persist in behaving as they have done for the last year or two, there is no answer to this question. The deepest reason for all this is, I suspect, that the builders are in doubts about a satisfactory settlement from Leonard (the situation between Israel and Egypt seems very analogous). Will Mr Macmillan survive to perform the opening say a decade hence? Will the fellows?

I must now come to the official point of this letter. Leonard wonders whether the Ford Foundation would consider matching, or at any rate helping with, the additional grant which will have to be made if the building is to be paid for. I think I can guess your answer, despite Leonard's wistful memories of two million sterling in 1967 when *he* was unwilling to match that sum in full. If you would rather disregard my enquiry, I think I could interpret your silence correctly – nevertheless, I should be grateful if you could send me a letter I could forward to Leonard [...].

I don't feel as gloomy as all this sounds – perhaps that is just natural irresponsibility due to the thought that I shall retire from my office in the summer of 1975: there are conclaves and meetings of fellows all over the place to discuss the succession; the atmosphere seems friendly and gay. Do come and see us, both privately and officially. Love to Mary, and from Aline.

    Yours,
      Isaiah

TO LIONEL TRILLING

  8 November 1973

                                         Wolfson

Dear Lionel,

  [...] I saw with great pleasure your and Diana's names on that very dignified and impressive pro-Israel document printed in the *New York Times*: how much better than the rather vulgar and almost strident document that is being circulated to Oxford dons, and indeed throughout British universities. I signed an incredibly pompous document to *The Times*,[1] simply because there was nothing else to sign, and I wanted to line up. No doubt it is easier for Americans at this particular juncture; our Government is now straightforwardly pro-Arab and makes no secret of it; Mr Wilson expresses pro-Israeli views. All oppositions have always been pro-Israel, and all governments pro-Arab: but the cynicism and hypocrisy with which we surrendered to the oil interests does stir people's consciences, and has induced a sense of mild national humiliation for which both Conservatives and, I suspect, the Arabs, will ultimately pay, both politically and financially – pay not very much, but pay. As for Israel, it is bound to be carved up sooner or later: the fact that the butcher is likely to be flesh of their flesh [...] does not make this operation more palatable to them. As Felix Frankfurter's wife (still living, but in a very sad state) once said to me, 'They' (the Jews of Palestine at that time) 'haven't a friend in the world. I am *all* for them.' With South Africa and Nixon as their only friends, they really do not need all those Arabs and Africans as enemies. If they are tried too hard, they are capable of a gigantic Masada,[2] by which, in the end, the Chinese alone will profit. But I must not allow my apocalyptic imagination to run too wild.

Yours ever, ⟨with love from Aline & to Diana of course of course –⟩
Isaiah

TO AGNES HEADLAM-MORLEY[3]

26 November 1973 [*carbon*]

[Wolfson]

Dear Agnes,

I was deeply touched by your letter – both by what it said and by the fact that you wrote it at all. The moral stuff of which people are made is, in the end, all that matters. As P. G. Wodehouse said (a quotation much loved by our friend Maurice B. who brought it into many public utterances) 'The trouble about you, old boy, is that you haven't a soul, and it's the soul that delivers the goods.' All that you say is true and moving: particularly about Sir Alec [Douglas-Home], whose face alone conveys all that you attribute to him. He is much adored by many persons, but never was by me: I too have met him, but cannot talk to him, and have never much wanted to. Of course they will go on in Israel, too stubbornly perhaps, and without a thought

1 IB signed the letter as a member of the Council of the Anglo-Jewish Association: 'With our sympathy for Israel reinforced by a shared historic experience, we believe that this onslaught sustained by Soviet equipment must inevitably damage the strategic interests of Britain, the country of our allegiance' (22 October 1973, 15g).
2 i.e. mass suicide, as at Masada (278/1).
3 Agnes Headlam-Morley (1902–86), historian; Fellow and Tutor, St Hugh's, 1932–70; Montague Burton Professor of International Relations, Oxford, 1948–71.

of the outside world: but it seems to me that the only difference between Egypt and, say, Libya, is that Egypt thinks that it can destroy Israel by stages, whereas Libya wants one fell swoop; and when Israelis say that 'the full rights of the Palestinians' is a polite equivalent for a dissolution of the State of Israel, I should like to believe this to be false or exaggerated, but the evidence is all the other way. The Israelis have been and continue to be unwise in some ways, but not wicked, and their only real friends in Europe have been Adenauer[1] and Willy Brandt – he told them that he was astonished by the degree of hostility to them – quite independently of the need to keep in with the Arabs – he found in Ted Heath. They feel bitter and are desperate, and I do not blame them and feel more strongly about the whole thing than ever. Did you read Baffy Dugdale's memoirs?[2] Entertaining and moving at the same time, I found them. Meanwhile, if the Arabs go on as they are doing, there is a real danger of a huge economic recession in the West, and a vast crisis during the next five years or so before alternative fuels are developed out of solar energy, etc.: which may lead to upsets and violence, and will play into Chinese hands rather too much.

It was marvellous of you to go to the rally – more than I did myself – I feel guilt and gratitude to you. Bless you.

Yours ever,

[Isaiah]

TO NICOLAS NABOKOV

22 January 1974

Headington House

Carissimo druzhishche! Dearest Starina![3]

If you cannot read my beautifully articulated manuscript cards, I have no alternative but to have recourse to technical aids. I am glad to hear that you have left your *lazaretto*[4] and are at home. Perhaps you should not travel quite so much. Remember what Pascal said – 'Tous les maux du monde vont de ce, qu'on ne reste pas tranquillement dans une chambre.'[5] You and I are notori-

---

1 Konrad Herman Joseph Adenauer (1876–1967), German statesman; Lord Mayor of Cologne 1917–33; deposed by Nazis; co-founder of the Christian Democratic Union 1945, first Chancellor of the Federal Republic of Germany 1949–63. 'Nobody can question the absolute detestation with which he watched the Nazis' extermination of the Jews or the determination with which, when in office, he set about making what amends he could' ('Dr Adenauer's Pilgrimage', leader, *Times*, 4 May 1966, 13a); visited Israel in 1966, and was made an honorary fellow of the Weizmann Institute of Science.

2 Blanche Elizabeth Campbell ('Baffy') Dugdale (1880–1948) née Balfour, author and (non-Jewish) Zionist; niece and biographer of Prime Minister A. J. Balfour; IB refers to *Baffy: The Diaries of Blanche Dugdale, 1936–1947*, ed. N. A. Rose (London, 1973).

3 'Dearest friend! Dearest fellow!'

4 'Quarantine'.

5 'All the ills of the world stem from our failure to stay peacefully in a room.' The quotation is as usual inaccurate. In *Pensées* xxvi, 'Misère de l'homme', Pascal wrote: 'tout le malheur des

ous non-practitioners of that art. In spite of his official duties, Chip was: nevertheless, he is no more and all you say about him is entirely true. I enclose
a small tribute of my own, of which a copy, I gather, has been sent to Avis,
for whom it was principally intended.[1] I shall always mourn his passing, and
so will you: the combination of intelligence, gaiety, cosiness, and what you
rightly call his honour and total freedom from Central European characteristics, were a great asset in our lives – quite apart from America, Russia, the
world etc. [...]

I keep brooding about Israel – it cannot be denied that Kissinger has for
the moment saved them from another war with Egypt, which was not all
that remote. The entire performance is extraordinary.[2] [...] My impression
is that the relationship between the White House and our government here
has become somewhat attenuated: I cannot conceive how Kissinger and
Douglas-Home can have the faintest rapport: and I do not believe that he
and Heath are made for each other; I may be mistaken, but in the interests
of the Western world, Western values, Israel [...] etc. the Europe–American
line must not be totally snapped, even for half an hour. And I feel that this is
something to do with the influence of, if not intellectuals in the pure sense,
at any rate Kay Graham's world, which overlaps with ours very consider-
ably. The new British Ambassador, who glories in the beautiful name of
Ramsbotham (the Hon. Sir Peter),[3] who entertained us so nicely in Tehran,
is aware of this. I have warmly urged him to cultivate the intelligentsia. I have
a feeling that President Johnson was, after all, driven out of power by the universities, that the attack on Nixon, whatever its consequences, is formidable
and proceeds from the eggheads – they alone keep up the tension. This is an
unusual situation: perhaps it was so in Russia in a way in 1916–17, but people
were not conscious of it, at least, not so much [...]. Nothing like this has ever
happened in England – the Labour Government pretended it was so, but it
was not really the case – there were a few economists, statisticians etc., but
such intellectuals as there are in England (and there is no real English intelligentsia) were out of account. But in America it is a potent force. In France
there was a tornado in 1968 and that was that; in England students occupy

hommes vient de ne savoir pas se tenir en repos dans une chambre' ('All men's unhappiness
comes from not knowing how to remain peacefully in a room').

1 Chip Bohlen died on New Year's Day 1974, and IB's appreciation appeared in *The Times* the
following week: 'he studied Soviet leaders as an ornithologist studies birds: his vignettes of
Bolshevik personalities, [...] aided by considerable power of mimicry of voice and expression,
were entertaining and wholly convincing' (11 January 1974, 16g).

2 On Friday 18 January Egypt and Israel signed an agreement to disengage their forces along the
Suez Canal, a major step towards normalising relations after the Yom Kippur war, and a diplomatic achievement directly attributable to the shuttle diplomacy of Henry Kissinger.

3 Peter (Edward) Ramsbotham (1919–2010), KCMG 1972; Head of Chancery, British Embassy,
Paris, 1963–7; FO 1967–9; High Commissioner, Cyprus, 1969–71; ambassador to Iran 1971–4, to
the US 1974–7.

buildings but the ultimate effect is not decisive; in America, Kent State made a difference of a radical kind.[1] I hope someone is recording all this.

In Israel there are two really grave dangers only: one is Jerusalem, which they cannot bring themselves to let go of, intelligibly enough, and which Hussein[2] must go on demanding if he is to survive. Possibly Kissinger will do the trick again with some enormously elaborate network of a Lebanese type by which there is a complicated system whereby a Jewish Mayor is succeeded by a Muslim, succeeded by a Christian, all the Holy Places are extraterritorialised and have stamps and coins of their own, and a complicated network of little Vaticans intertwine in a semi-internationalised enclave – the Old City – governed by some mixed commission of Israelis and Jordanians. I do not suppose that this would work for long, but it might at least 'defuse' the situation for a little while. What would really be fatal to the Israelis would be a Palestinian State on the West Bank. If Hussein takes it, they can tolerate that, I should guess: an independent State would only be used by the Russians and/or the Chinese as a platform for anti-Israeli operations, and would mean the end of Israel as a state. Of that I feel convinced. If there is a referendum under the guns of the terrorists, they will surely vote for Arafat, even though all those Arab lawyers, doctors etc., of whom the towns are full, cannot want that. Still, there is at the moment some kind of gleam of light at the end of the corridor, and this is more than the Israelis hoped for when Aline and I were there and general depression reigned. [...] I do not really fear betrayal of Israel: I have a feeling that sheer indignation with the behaviour of England and France in the recent crisis is for the moment enough to buoy up support of Persia, Turkey, Israel etc. against the potentially pro-Russian Arab powers like Syria and Iraq. But I shall desist from all this idle speculation – Aline, my faithful wife, is standing over me and says that I have talked at you for something like an hour now and that it is time to stop. She sends her love to you and to Dominique, and so do I. We shall see you in March: she hopes that you have received her postcards as well as mine from Mishkenot, and that you will forgive my aimless garrulity – the idle reflections of a superfluous person. We are the last representatives of that noble class. My stepson Peter shows strong tendencies in that direction, but

1 On Monday 4 May 1970 four students at Kent State, Ohio, were shot dead, and another nine wounded, when members of the National Guard fired into a crowd protesting against the Vietnam War; the protest had been triggered by President Nixon's announcement on national television the previous Thursday, 30 April, that a major offensive against the Vietcong was under way in Cambodia. The killings at Kent State intensified opposition to the Vietnam War, and increased pressure on the Nixon administration to bring it to an end.

2 Hussein bin Talal (1935–99), King of Jordan 1953–99, sought stability and prosperity for Jordan through non-alignment amidst the maelstrom of Middle East politics; joined the 1967 Six-Day War to protect his throne, but lost the West Bank and East Jerusalem to Israel, gaining instead the unwelcome presence in his kingdom of the exiled PLO.

he has not had the benefit of the wide Russian steppe, that breadth of soul, that inability to stop.

Yours ever,

тот же старый друг[1]

IB

TO AUBREY MORGAN

4 February 1974 [*carbon*]

[Wolfson]

Dear Aubrey,

[...] I wrote that little piece about Chip Bohlen principally for his wife, Avis, since I thought that the obituary in the *Times*, although perfectly adequate so far as the public facts were concerned, did not bring out his private side at all, and I thought that she would want someone to say something about that. I thought it OK. My piece was preceded by a very proper one by Sir W. Hayter, and a slightly absurd one by Patrick Reilly,[2] who served with him both in Moscow and in Paris, and who simply talked about what a wonderful bag of birds he was able to shoot down in the company of General de Gaulle – that reminded me of *The Times* of about forty years ago – some things in England do not change much, although our present situation really is beyond words. There is a kind of lack of appetite for action and life, which worries me, as it would you, if you were here; I may be over-pessimistic but both our great parties seem vaguely paralysed by events and look upon them as external forces about which very little can be done, instead of something that can be radically modified by enough energy and imagination. Hence my admiration for Winston and other men of will and feeling, provided they are not monsters or want a form of life which one is against.

But I won't go on preaching. I am grateful also for Con's[3] manuscript note – I am not in the United States at present, although I may be coming for about one week – in and out – to deliver a lecture in Urbana, Illinois, of all places, simply as an excuse for going to the United States – as, you may imagine, I long to do from time to time – it invigorates me as nothing does, no matter how dark the situation may seem. I cannot go away too far for too long because of my mother: she is ninety-four, has ceased to recognise me, but is, nevertheless, alive, and I dare not go away to places from which I cannot return at very short notice fairly rapidly in case I am summoned by doctors to her bedside. Hence, I can only go for short flights within a narrow

1 'The same old friend'.
2 (D'Arcy) Patrick Reilly (1909–99), KCMG 1957, diplomat; ambassador to the USSR 1957–60; Deputy Under-Secretary of State, FO, 1960–4; ambassador to France 1965–8; Chairman, Banque Nationale de Paris (formerly British and French Bank), 1969–80.
3 Constance Cutter Morgan, wife of Aubrey Morgan (115/2).

radius, but seven–ten days in the United States is a risk I am prepared to take. I went to the Holy Land in December, just to see what was happening, and it really is a pathetic scene. Here is a people, quite apart from personal feelings of our own, which thought it had its fate in its own hands and was able to direct itself: indeed, they were obviously much too confident, indeed, rather cocky. Suddenly they feel that they have become the plaything of powers that they cannot control (unlike Britain, which may feel this, but is, in fact, not that, at any rate yet) and are like a boy which has got prizes all the way along until he suddenly fails in some frightfully elementary examination. It is all very well to speak of how good it is to be made to face realities, but it is hideously painful too, and they were in great disarray when I was there, and quarrelling among themselves; and yet, despite all the dangers which still face them – some of them seem convinced that there will be another war in a year or two, which they are not at all sure of winning – their desire for life is very great. It is, in the end, exhilarating to talk to them, although they are talking Hebrew more and more, and English less and less and communication is gradually, for me, becoming not as easy as it used to be.

I continue to be a liberal, as you are. It is obviously much easier to plump for one side or the other and not move along a terribly narrow causeway between extremes – between the old who hate the young, and the young who hate the old, between the pompous establishment on one side and mindless, bearded, somewhat hysterical layabouts on the other. But it cannot be helped. So one is made, and so one must continue (this noble stoicism does not exactly correspond to the inner quaking to which I am liable, but I like to think that I conceal that fairly successfully, at least from the graduates of my own college). I retire in the summer of 1975, and about enough too; at the present I have to consider such problems as what has to be done when a young man asks for married quarters with a lady not strictly his wife, and that sort of thing. I would rather be doing that than be in Heath's shoes. I do hope we shall meet soon; I look for news of you from John and Ruth.

Yours ever,

[Isaiah]

Marie Berlin died on 13 February after a long illness; she was buried the next day at Willesden Green Jewish cemetery, next to IB's father, Mendel, who had died in December 1953: 'She was not a happy or contented widow.'[1]

1 IB to Shiela Sokolov Grant, 19 February 1974.

TO JEAN FLOUD

16 February 1974 [*manuscript*]

Headington House

Dearest Jean,

Thank you for your note. My mother seems to have died peacefully: the nurse noticed, at about 3 a.m., that she seemed to be breathing less loudly (she had bronchitis of sorts) than before: & then that she had in fact stopped breathing. I was told four hours later. The funeral took place on the next day, and it was all over. In a sense, of course, I had been expecting it for a long time: and tried to imagine how it wd affect me – my mother had ceased to have any contact with [the] external world for some months before she left it – but it was different and much more painful, & slow & cumulative. Not grief: (and of course one wonders if one is a superficial brute: should I not be in deeper distress? Why do I not cry? How can I, as I obviously can, face the world? Should I not [be], am I not, ashamed?) but a sense of utter solitude: Verlassenheit:[1] gone is not only the oldest root in one's life which bound one to some infinitely solid & indestructible past on which one leant, half consciously, in all crises & moments of appalling discouragement & self contempt, but also the one & only human being of whom one knew that, no matter what, she wd always be pleased to be with one solely because one was who one was: & not for any attributes – because one was this or that, or loved her, or helped her or whatever: *this* is instinctual & irreplaceable & the snapping of that cord is final & leaves one as a kind of accidental being, without a purpose, without a divine plan, – I understand the existentialists very well: one exists: but one might just as well not have been: it makes no difference. *That* is what I feel. No doubt it will pass: time does heal: but it is an eerie sensation […].

Love

Isaiah

TO NICOLAS NABOKOV

19 February 1974

Headington House

Dearest Nicolas,

So, it has happened at last, and my mother is no more. True, at 94, and for the last three months out of all contact with the external world – she grew smaller and smaller, thinner and thinner, until she looked like an immobile waxwork – I used to dread seeing her, and understood why Plato, Christian tradition etc. looked upon the body as a mere prison of the soul,

---

1 'Abandonment', 'loneliness'.

a mere lantern not intrinsically connected with the light or darkness within it. Latterly she developed a mild bronchitis, and the nurse who looked after her reported that she was breathing somewhat heavily, the doctor pacified me and said there was no need to go to London, especially as I was having flu at the time; then the nurse, who sat in her room, telephoned to say that her breathing, which had been perfectly even, suddenly became, it seemed to her, perfectly quiet; when she went to look she saw that she was dead. I have no objection to expiring in this fashion: better than Stravinsky in hospital with a diagnosed disease; she died last Wednesday, the 13th, three days short of 94; on Thursday we buried her in Willesden Cemetery by my father, on whose tombstone there is a poem in the medieval style written by an enthusiastic but not very gifted *rifmoplyot*,[1] who performed the function of Cantor in the family synagogue. He praised his virtues in rhyming verse modelled on the 11th century Arabo-Hebrew poets of Spain. The inscription on my mother's tablet will be somewhat plainer, and will not record her one-day's apprenticeship to Rimsky-Korsakov.[2]

Although I went over this event a great many times in my mind, when it actually happened it was as if the roof of the house had lifted, and although Evelyn Waugh thinks that this opens one's gaze to the radiance of eternity, in my case it merely induced a sense of homelessness, the snapping of the last root which connected me with my origins. Dear Niouta [Kallin], and dear Wolff,[3] and dear Salome appeared at the funeral, which moved me deeply; so did Mr Edelberg, who used to sell chocolates to her, and wept in a welter of German-Russian Riga broken phraseology; Mr Edelberg used to be a fellow-traveller, but moved sharply to the right at the age of 80; he was known as Chokoladnik, and called himself that. The grocer, the greengrocer and the butcher sent representatives – not *dovol'no*,[4] as Turgenev so grandly remarked. [...]

I had always supposed that when my mother died I should experience, in addition to a sense of desolation, a certain shameful sense of relief, as people

1 'Rhymer'.

2 Marie Berlin, who possessed a good soprano voice, aspired to be a singer, and held a student identity card for the Riga section of the Imperial Russian Musical Society. Through the medium of a cousin, who was a friend of Rimsky-Korsakov (490/1), she was accepted as a pupil by the composer, but her father, Salman Izchok Volshonok (1861–1941), 'a religious bigot of the most terrible sort [who] wouldn't have a piano in the house', at once forbade the adventure (IB, *Desert Island Discs*, BBC Radio 4, 19 April 1992).

3 Mark Mikhailovich Wolff (1891–1987), Russian-born lawyer, initially called to the St Petersburg bar; left Russia with his wife in 1920, settling in London, and was called to the bar by Lincoln's Inn 1926; the Wolffs (with their daughter Tatiana) were close friends of Alexander and Salome Halpern (Wolff met Alexander in Petersburg, and was in the same chambers in London for over 40 years), the Kallins and the Angleseys; IB was in frequent contact with Wolff through their joint involvement in the Humanitarian Trust, an educational charity founded in 1946, of which Wolff was Honorary Secretary, and IB a Trustee.

4 'Enough'.

often say they do. I experience none. There is obviously something wrong with my concept of liberty.

Yours ever,

Исайя[1]

TO STUART HAMPSHIRE

23 February 1974 [*manuscript*]

Headington House

Dear Stuart,

No, not a dull blow exactly: but a sense of desolation and amputation: as if an entire world of words, symbols, allusions, reference had vanished. And of course, guilt: I shd have seen her more often when she was lonely and unhappy, shd have been more patient when I did, shd not have contradicted what seemed to me (this is always so in family relations, I know, and yet …) obstinate absurdities, or fantasies, or prevarication: and so on: all this comes lashing back at me now and will go on doing so, less persistently, I suppose, with time: but I am ashamed of the legend of what a devoted son I was: the truth is different: she irritated me too often and too easily. Having said all this, I must admit that her loss of contact with the external world did make the end easier to bear for me at least: and my debt to her is gigantic as you know too well: all the Herderian beliefs are founded on the rich & firm tradition in which I was brought up for ten years.

You once remarked that I now was closer in my opinions to those of my mother than I was in the late thirties: I cannot make up my mind about that: I doubt it: I remember you said to me on the boat to Ireland in 1936 "I thought I was talking to a socialist and a positivist: but I find you are a Zionist and a phenomenologist." I was & I am: ora e sempre:[2] and you? were & are a patriot and an intentionalist & Hume-rejecter, a Vichian & quasi-Hegelian *rerum natura*[3] ontologist: are you not? in scientific-Freudian clothing? I am convinced of it.[4]

---

1 'Isaiya'.
2 'Now and for ever'.
3 'The nature of things'.
4 IB's allusive characterisation of SNH and himself draws on a lifetime of philosophical discussion and understanding, and conveys a meaning probably fully understood only within the terms of the close friendship that inspired it. Nevertheless, some of his likely import may perhaps be roughly indicated. SNH expected IB to have firm views on the organisation of society and the distribution of goods, to eschew particularist loyalties, and to be a logical positivist committed to the most parsimonious empirical account of the furniture of the world. He discovered on further inspection that IB in fact adhered to an ancient dream of re-establishing a Jewish presence in Palestine, and believed that the pullulating contents of experience went far beyond what restrictive empiricists would countenance. For IB, SNH was a loyal Briton, and like IB held that our mental life is richer than plain empiricism allows; he favoured large-scale ideas about the development of human culture and about the contents of reality; but he felt that such ideas would seem more respectable if presented in terms of the quasi-scientific theories of Freud.

My dogmatic confidence in my own judgment, which used to irritate Maurice so, comes from my mother (she liked Maurice *very* much). I am glad you felt at ease with her: no doubt her scrutiny of basic values was sharpened by being in such absolute exile: Sir George [Weidenfeld], Goronwy, Burgess, were shot down at once; Rachmilevich[1] for lack of heart; Scholem for vanity and envy; & so on: Herbert H. she *pitied*, you passed with flying colours (Freddie too was sent spinning): she had enormous vitality, fantasies of what she might have been, passionate love of Ibsen, Hamsun,[2] D. H. Lawrence, Gorky's Lower Depths,[3] Verdi, Carmen, all forms of full blooded self asser-tion, and like Maurice, dislike of those who shush people, recoil from coarse vitality, and display refined, thin lipped disapproval. After academic relation-ships and artificial milieus, talking to her did revive me: & I shall miss that (& have missed it) quite apart from all other obvious feelings, very much indeed: & I suppose I do owe my Judaeocentricity (as you like to think of it) to her & her world & Russian-Jewish cultural roots, to her: my father had none of that. Oh dear: the disappearance of Hollycroft Avenue is a genuine trauma. It was much more real than any other home I've ever had: after it all else are *chambres meublé[e]s*.[4] I am sure you understood that better than anyone at all: I am glad you did & do: it is a source of great comfort.

yrs

    Isaiah

The Berlins spent ten days in America in March 1974; IB lectured at the University of Illinois at Urbana–Champaign on the evening of 15 March, and afterwards they spent time in Washington and New York before returning to England on Saturday 23 March.

1 Solomon Rachmilevich (1891–1953), Riga-born Jewish intellectual and Menshevik social demo-crat who lived in exile in London, where he worked as a legal adviser in the timber business of his cousin, Lionel Schalit, a partner of Mendel Berlin. He was a profound and inspiring intellectual influence on the young IB: 'the first person who gave me a taste for ideas in general, interesting ideas *telles quelles*' (MI Tape 6). See also MI 42–4.
2 Knut Hamsun (1859–1952) né Knut Pedersen, Norwegian novelist, poet and dramatist, author of the innovatory and influential *Hunger* (Copenhagen, 1890); Nobel Prize in Literature 1920; attracted notoriety by his support for Hitler during the Second World War.
3 *The Lower Depths* (premiered in 1902), drama in four acts by Maxim Gorky; describes in bleakly realistic terms the experiences and interplay of a group of down-and-outs in a lodging house in 1900s Nizhny Novgorod, the city of Gorky's birth.
4 'Furnished rooms'; 49 Hollycroft Avenue was the address proposed to English Heritage in 2009 for a blue plaque commemorating IB's intermittent residence there from 1928 to 1997. The appli-cation was deferred until 2017 on the grounds that it was 'too soon to be certain of his lasting reputation and influence' (letter from John Cattell to Henry Hardy, 22 July 2010).

TO WALTER EYTAN

26 April 1974 [*manuscript*]

Headington House

Dear Walter,

Your letter arrived while I was in America for about a week: else I shd have told you earlier how grateful for it I was and am. My mother died most peacefully: at one moment she was breathing; at the next one she ceased. I need not tell you what, no matter how often and how vividly one antici- pates it, when it comes, it is like: for you know it. My mother was indeed a very fully formed Jewish personality, and was a proud and worthy repre- sentative of a tradition and a culture: my beliefs and outlook, such as they are, derive directly from the firm & unswerving Jewish education I was given: even more from her dauntless character which I, with my hesitations, self doubt, lack of absolute values or that magnificent heart-wholeness which she exhibited, could never really measure up to. My life, at my advanced age, is cracked by this: it is as if a huge part of my heart had blown off. I loved my father, but although I felt terribly sad, his death did not sweep away my past; my mother's death has broken a vital link: I am happy to see that your father is ninety: long may he live: but when he is gathered to his fathers, you will, I think, also feel a sense of separation, a gulf to divide you, from the past: painful and eerie. My mama was a doughty fighter for all Jewish values: anima naturaliter Sionista:[1] I feel very feeble and inadequate when I think of her: but the older I get, the more I find that I return to her firm values: perhaps this is the ossification of old age: what people call becoming reac- tionary: if so, I cannot help it: beside her firm view of persons & what counts in them, & in particular the emancipation of the enslaved, colonialized, Jews, half resentful, half acquiescent, half envious of, half ashamed of longing to be accepted by, strangers – on all this I owe my views to her. She was a very shatterer of illusions: Emile Marmorstein[2] and Abie Halpern,[3] who were much given to them, quailed before her: she was not a compromiser & lacked sympathy with human weaknesses: in that respect like Weizmann, Moses, B.G., etc: no Aharonism,[4] no appeasement: she admired resolution, vitality, power: wholly unlike her sister, Ida Samunov, who succoured the halt, lame, blind, long before she became one herself. But I must not go on

1 'A naturally Zionist spirit'.
2 Emil(e) Marmorstein (1909–83), a contemporary of IB at St Paul's, worked in the European Dept of the BBC.
3 Wolf Abiram ('Abe') Halpern (1909–43), German-born contemporary of IB's at St Paul's and Oxford; naturalised July 1932; worked for Derby & Co., London metal-brokers; served with RAFVR during Second World War and was killed on active service March 1943.
4 i.e. no diplomatic dealings with the enemy like those of the biblical Aaron with the Egyptians.

so: thank you ever so much: may we soon meet again. And love from Aline
& to Beaty.[1]

Yours,

Isaiah

TO ALAN BULLOCK

30 April 1974 [*carbon*]

[Wolfson]

Dear Alan,

[...] I know nothing about Bevin before 1945[2] – at least nothing save what
was in the newspapers, etc. The Labour Party was mildly pro-Zionist while
in opposition, as all oppositions have tended to be: it is only when they are the
government that the policy, for obvious reasons, changes radically: personal
feelings probably have little to do with it. Thus, Bevin certainly must have
appeared on some Zionist platform, or signed some pro-Zionist resolutions,
and, as you say, Weizmann [...] probably did try to deal with Labour politicians, on the assumption that they would be friendly. Do I believe that Bevin
was anti-Semitic? No more so, before 1945, I daresay, than any other normal
trade unionist. I think that all horny-handed sons of toil tend to look with suspicion and some dislike on bourgeois intellectuals, Jews, diplomats, dons etc.
etc., much as, for example, say, Khrushchev did. This is instinctive, natural,
true I should think of all countries. But I suspect that when Bevin disliked,
he disliked more strongly than most; and that when he went to the Foreign
Office, the people there were at once so nervous and anxious to please – and
hard-working too – that he found ascendancy there exceedingly easy. Those
who tried to guide him – e.g. Frank Roberts – he conceived a dislike for;
those who flattered him openly, and grossly, like Bob Dixon[3] – and I saw this
in Moscow in November 1945 (the only time I ever met Bevin) – he accepted.
I have *never* seen so much butter piled so openly and hugely as was done by
Bob Dixon and Clark-Kerr,[4] who was Ambassador in Moscow. All this went
down extremely well; and Clark-Kerr very cynically told us all that that was
precisely the technique he was going to use, and my God, it worked.

1 Eytan's (second) wife, Beatrice Levinson Zion (1923–2004).
2 Bullock was then in the process of researching the third and final volume in his trilogy *The
Life and Times of Ernest Bevin* (London, 1960–83); the first two volumes were published in the
1960s but the third, entitled *Foreign Secretary, 1945–1951*, awaited the opening of the relevant British
archives.
3 Pierson John ('Bob') Dixon (1904–65), KCMG 1950, PPS to the Foreign Secretary 1943–48;
Permanent UK Representative to UN 1954–60; ambassador to France 1960–4. At a time when
Bevin's schedule was arduous, and the conferences of foreign ministers 'increasingly fraught',
Dixon had 'to act as companion, counsellor, speech-writer and administrator' for his chief (N.
Piers Ludlow, ODNB).
4 Archibald John Kerr Clark Kerr (1882–1951), KCMG 1935, 1st Baron Inverchapel 1946, diplomat;
UK ambassador to Moscow 1942–6, to Washington 1946–8.

I say all this only to underline the fact that shrewd, tough, highly intelligent and large-minded as Bevin undoubtedly was, he was endowed with a vanity which was also colossal; and those who abraded it, for example, Laski, he disliked (and so did you, and so did I); those who did not, like G. D. H. Cole, he got on with – or so Cole certainly supposed (I never saw them together) – because Cole, although he had his own vanity, was transparently simple and sincere and dedicated, and did not, apparently, irritate Bevin. So it was not just a question of left-wing intellectuals as such that Bevin disliked – only those who were awkward with him, or frightened of him, or not at all on the same wavelength, and that, I daresay, went for Zionist officials, few of whom could be described as left-wing intellectuals. He did, of course, have one or two Jewish friends – notably Montague Meyer,[1] whose son[2] is such a friend and ex-employer of Wilson. I knew Mr Montague Meyer – he owned a farm in the country in which Bevin stayed – for he was a timber-merchant and did business with my father. He was not at all a nice man. He was able, ruthless, and very clear about his values. He once said to my father, 'Remember, Mr Berlin: I am not a gentleman above £5,000.'

I think Charles Webster is probably right: I do not think that Bevin had much to do with Jews of one kind or another before 1945, but that famous phrase about 'wanting to get to the head of the queue' came tripping very naturally from his tongue. But I agree with you: I think his anti-Semitism was probably of an average kind, and would have played no part in his general attitudes and policies, if it were not for Palestine and 1945. After that, I think he conceived an image of Palestine as a country full of Laskis, clever, quick, specious, glossy, arrogant, ghastly, doing down a lot of simple, slightly brutal, but essentially decent Arab Bevins, stimulated thereto by a lot of fat, cigar-smoking Jewish capitalists in New York, who did not go themselves, but sent leaky ships in which some of the Laskis tended to be drowned, but those who landed bedevilled the British administration and the simple Arab folk who should have been unionised before now. Something like that. I do not think this is altogether a caricature.

I have no specially hostile feelings about Bevin – but when I saw him in Moscow in 1945 (as I have told you before), I had never seen anyone so xeno-phobic and so vain. There is just one remark that I remember. Someone made some critical remark about Stalin. He said, 'I don't know why you say that – he's just another fellow trying to make his way along; nothing wrong in that', which was quite funny. I have no evidence whatever for special anti-Semitism on Bevin's part before 1945, or indeed, evidence about anything to do with

---

1 Montague Levinson ('Monty') Meyer (1880–1961) né Montague Meyer Meyer, founder of Montague L. Meyer Ltd, timber merchants, 1906.

2 John Mount Montague Meyer (1915–79) joined Montague L. Meyer Ltd 1933; Chairman and Managing Director from 1961; Harold Wilson was for almost ten years (from 1951) an economic adviser to the firm, the UK's leading timber importer.

him at all; but then, a good many leaders of the Labour Party, for example, Dalton,[1] who put in a plank into the Labour platform of 1945 which went beyond the wildest dreams of the Zionists,[2] was personally distinctly anti-Semitic, as anybody who knew him will testify. So was Attlee (as Roy Jenkins could tell you), so was Herbert Morrison[3] (as John Foster could tell you). The only one who was not – in a relevant position – was Creech Jones,[4] who was terrified of Bevin, and did complain in private that Bevin's anti-Semitism went a bit too far, beyond the norm; Christopher Mayhew[5] is, in this sense, a direct descendant of all Bevin's attitudes, but would claim, I think, not to be anti-Semitic at all, though, in fact, by now he certainly is quite deeply so, unlike, say, Beeley, who is not, for all his passionate anti-Zionism. [...]

Yours,

[Isaiah]

At a meeting of the Council of the British Academy on 22 May 1974 the question of the successor to Sir Denys Page as President was considered, and a strong consensus emerged in favour of IB. He was unanimously elected at the Annual Meeting of the Academy on 10 July, there being no other nominations. Henceforth he would have to be more discreet in his comments on academic matters, in public at least. In an interview with the Dutch journalist Kornelis Poll[6] earlier that year he had indulged in a characteristic 'boutade about sociologists', denouncing 'the mumbo-jumbo that often passes for scientific terminology'.[7] He afterwards wrote to Poll:

1   (Edward) Hugh Neale Dalton (1887–1962), life peer 1960, Labour politician; Minister of Economic Warfare 1940–2; President of the Board of Trade 1942–5; Chancellor of the Exchequer 1945–7.
2   In December 1944 the Labour Party conference accepted without a vote a post-war commitment to Zionism enshrined in a policy document principally written by Dalton: 'Let the Arabs be encouraged to move out [of Palestine], as the Jews move in. [...] The Arabs have many wide territories of their own; they must not claim to exclude the Jews from this small area of Palestine, less than the size of Wales.' *Report of the 43rd Annual Conference of the Labour Party* (London, 1944), 9. Dalton's biographer Ben Pimlott notes: 'There was much in the remark of Oliver Stanley, a Tory colleague, that the Labour commitment was "Zionism plus plus".' Ben Pimlott, *Hugh Dalton* (London, 1985), 390.
3   Herbert Stanley Morrison (1888–1965), life peer 1959, Labour politician; Home Secretary and Minister of Home Security 1940–5; Deputy Prime Minister and Lord President of the Council 1945–51.
4   Arthur Creech Jones (1891–1964), conscientious objector (imprisoned 1916–19), trade unionist and Labour politician; PPS to his friend Ernest Bevin at the Ministry of Labour and National Service 1940–5; Colonial Secretary 1946–50.
5   Christopher Paget Mayhew (1915–97), later (1981) life peer; Labour MP 1945–50, Under-Secretary of State for Foreign Affairs 1946–50 under Bevin, whom he succeeded as MP for Woolwich East 1951–74; hoped to be appointed Deputy Foreign Minister under Harold Wilson 1964 but was made Minister of Defence (Royal Navy) instead, a decision he attributed to Wilson's disapproval of his prominent anti-Zionism; joined Liberal Party 1974.
6   Kornelis Lubbertus Poll (1927–90), Dutch journalist with the daily *NRC Handelsblad*; later editor of the Hague newspaper *Het Vaderland*, and a member of the editorial staff of the *Algemeen Handelsblad*.
7   IB to Poll, 13 May 1974.

I wish I thought that I had not said these things – but I fear, knowing myself
as I do, that I most probably did: for I certainly said something of the sort,
though not so sharply or offensively, more than twenty years ago in an English
periodical,[1] and I have not altogether changed my opinions since. I spoke with
vehemence because I thought that what I was saying before was becoming
a little dull, and seemed to bore you, and ended by boring myself: so I switched
to a subject on which I hold sharp, though not necessarily just or acceptable,
views. What I remember very clearly is that I did say that there was much
sociology that was extremely useful to social workers of many kinds […].
I then added that in the past there have been sociologists who made bold and
important generalisations, whether valid or not, very well worth investigating
– […] that men of this calibre have formulated generalisations which, if true,
would make a considerable difference to men's lives: what I went on to say
was that a good many academic sociologists, the vast industry that sociology
has become, do not do this; and then I made all those jokes which you, to my
distress, so faithfully report.[2] I remember asking you particularly not to mention
this, as it was a mere squib, an exaggeration, intended to provoke, and to be
made in private, but not a balanced judgement for which I am ready to accept
responsibility: any decent sociologist ('my best friends' – this was a typical piece
of irony which I hoped you would not report – indeed, you promised me not to)
would reject with justified indignation an attack upon serious specialists because
of the excesses and absurdities of their less gifted or less scrupulous colleagues.
I am ashamed, I must confess to you, to appear before Dutch, or indeed any,
readers as someone who does not recognise the genius of the nineteenth- and
early twentieth-century sociologists […], nor of the more brilliant of our own
contemporaries.[3]

*In mid-May, at around the time that he was approached about becoming the
next President of the British Academy, IB wrote again to Poll, further qualifying
his remarks.*

TO KORNELIS POLL

27 May 1974 [*carbon*]

[Wolfson]

Dear Mr Poll,

    It is I who plainly owe you an apology. I am very sorry indeed to have
moved you even to slight anger – as you may imagine, this is the last thing

1 IB's contribution to the 'Notes on the Way' column in *Time and Tide*, 12, 19 and 26 November
   1949, is printed as an appendix to L2, 'The Intellectual Life of American Universities', at 749–60:
   see especially 751.
2 One of these (as transmitted by Poll) was that sociologists reminded him of men who wear
   deep-sea diving suits to enter a room full of people in order to find out what they are doing.
   These men look unusual and impressive, but if you listen carefully to what they say, you hear
   unremarkable thoughts, whether sensible or nonsensical, of the kind that we all produce in
   ordinary conversation, but translated into quasi-scientific jargon.
3 loc. cit. (568/7).

that I should have wished to do, as it all seems to me ultimately and principally my own fault. I know that I talk much too fast, swallow my words and sentences, and cannot complain if people sometimes misunderstand – this has happened before and I ought to have learnt by past experience not to let myself be interviewed by the most sympathetic, humane and civilised persons, in their interest as much as my own. [...]

Now, as to sociology etc., believe me, I did beg you most seriously, and not half-jokingly, not to quote me on this particular topic – indeed, I told you about the awful trouble which an irresponsible statement of this nature on my part had caused me at Harvard and elsewhere. I certainly meant to draw a contrast between empirical sociology, which can certainly be useful, if nothing else, and grand generalisations which are seldom if ever arresting enough to be capable of changing our convictions or behaviour, even if they are true. If you tell me that I did not say this to you, I do, of course, believe you entirely – one sometimes remembers what one knows oneself to believe rather than what one actually said – and this must be so in this case. I am now convinced that I did not say this and you could not possibly have reported it. What worried me, of course, was the possibility that these remarks might be taken seriously: I am about to undertake a task which may involve me in activities that may make some difference to British sociologists – and the last thing I would wish them to believe is that I have a rooted prejudice against them as a body. Perhaps I have; but I certainly intend to do my very best to behave as if I had not, as fairly and impartially as I possibly can. If they read your piece, their suspicion of me (for which there may, indeed, be some basis, I fear) will be greatly strengthened, and this would certainly make my task much more painful and difficult. This, as well as concern for justice and truth, moved me to write to you as vehemently as I did. I wish I could believe that a sociologist reading the statements attributed to me would take them to be a harmless, 'half-joking' piece of deliberate caricature. If I were a sociologist, I think I might take offence, and look upon the author of these remarks as a dogmatic, prejudiced, old-fashioned Oxford obscurantist, an enemy of all true progress, which courageous pioneers and innovators are fighting for against the conservative resistance of hidebound, prejudiced, traditionalist, philistine members of the reactionary establishment. This, too, may be a caricature, but it seems to me much closer to the beliefs and emotions of most sociologists in my country than I like to believe. [...]

At the age of 65 I ought to have known myself well enough not to have allowed myself to stray into all those paths merely because I enjoyed our talk so much. It really is my fault, and a proper apology is certainly due to you.

Yours sincerely,

[Isaiah Berlin]

TO AMITZUR ILAN[1]

6 June 1974 [carbon]

[Wolfson]

Dear Amitzur,

I have read half your thesis with much enjoyment and instruction and fascination. You tell the story very vividly as a political tale of pressures and policy, and I shall write to you again when I have finished reading – I must interrupt it now in order to examine in the Politics B.Phil.

So far, I have the following comments to make: I do not believe that Weizmann or Wise were simply deceived by Roosevelt, though, of course, they were to some extent taken in by his easygoing affability. You are perfectly right when you say that until, say, 1943 or so, Roosevelt, who did not go into the matter deeply, thought that some arrangement acceptable to Zionists could be fixed up by some means or other, and that after strategic political and economic considerations began to weigh on him more heavily in mid-war, he became more cautious and secretive, and began to play seriously with the Arabs. Nevertheless, by temperament he was inclined, as you surely also think, to keep all options open and all the balls in the air, for as long as he possibly could: he jollied along the Jews and the Arabs, and everybody else, without formally making up his mind about what he would do in the end, postponing or ignoring issues if they became too awkward, and thereby irritating his own government departments and cabinet and foreign powers, who could never pin him down unless the matter became crucial. I daresay that he would, in the end, have let down the Jews, particularly after the meeting with Ibn Saud – or if there was too much produced [sic] he would have backtracked on that too. I do not think that Weizmann was unaware of this 'artful dodger' aspect of the great President: but he had poor cards to play and assumed, I still feel rightly, that given Roosevelt's immense popularity and personal power, he stood a better chance of any degree of success by negotiating with him, and the important figures in Washington, than by relying on agitation among Jews and other sympathisers, which, if it went too far, would (as in fact it sometimes did) exasperate and antagonise those who, in fact, made the policy. The part he played in getting the Negev from Truman showed that this policy of personal diplomacy sometimes worked wonders for him.[2] [...]

1 Amitzur Ilan (b. 1932), Research Fellow, Institute for Zionist Research, Tel-Aviv, Senior Associate Member of St Antony's. IB is commenting on a draft of Ilan's 1974 Oxford D.Phil. thesis *The Origin and Development of American Intervention in British Palestinian Policy, 1938–1947*.

2 On 19 November 1947 Chaim Weizmann met President Truman to argue for the inclusion of the Negev, and thus access to the Red Sea, in a prospective Jewish State. Truman subsequently strongly supported this proposal, which was included in the partition scheme (Resolution 181) of the UN General Assembly of 29 November. Weizmann also, in IB's eyes, played a decisive part in persuading Truman to recognise the State of Israel immediately on its foundation, 14 May

I did not expect you to agree with me about the fact that Israel was built in Weizmann's image: yet I still say that the State which emerged in 1948 – mixed trade-union/capitalist, politically and emotionally left of centre, a society with a mixed economy, uncommitted to any one social or political doctrine, governed by institutions inherited from and influenced by the British Mandatory [*sic*], parliamentary, loose in texture, inclined towards the West from the beginning – was much more Weizmannite in conception than anything that Berl K.[1] or BG or either socialists or Revisionists officially wanted. The later evolution of Israel is another matter: especially the history of Mapai and its right wing opponents,[2] which certainly abandoned the Lib–Lab Weizmannite non-ideology, at least in part. About that too we might argue.

Meanwhile, thank you very much for sending me your piece, which I only stopped reading with the greatest reluctance – the B.Phil. theses are terribly dreary.

Yours sincerely,

[Isaiah]

TO MCGEORGE BUNDY
22 July 1974 [*carbon*]

[Wolfson]

Dear Mac,

I was very sorry, and so was Aline, that you could not visit Oxford in June – I think you would have enjoyed it and even perhaps (who knows?) have been impressed by the Wolfsonianum. I still cannot get them to accept Romulus and Remus as the emblem – I cannot pretend not to understand why not. I have a very fine she-wolf on my walls which I conceal when Leonard W. pays me visits.

As you know, we have our formal opening on 12 November when we shall have the Chancellor, the Rt Hon. Harold Macmillan, Sir Isaac and Mr Leonard and their ladies, members of the Wolfson College Trust and the Wolfson Foundation (I wonder if Lord Z[uckerman] will honour us; we shall certainly invite him), and so on, followed by five to six hundred assorted

---

1948. See IB, 'The Biographical Facts', in Meyer W. Weisgal and Joel Carmichael (eds), *Chaim Weizmann* (London, 1962; NY, 1963), 17–56 at 54–5.

1 Berl Katznelson (1887–1944), born in Russia, emigrated to Palestine 1909 and was involved in the Zionist labour movement there; editor-in-chief of the labour newspaper *Davar*; after the promulgation of the May 1939 White Paper he became a strong advocate of illegal Jewish immigration to Palestine, and of the creation of a Jewish State.

2 Mapai (from the Hebrew acronym for the 'Workers' Party of Eretz Israel', Mifleget Poalei Eretz Yisrael): socialist Zionist party founded in 1930, and after 1948 the most important political grouping in Israel. It provided a succession of Israeli leaders, including Ben-Zvi, Ben-Gurion and Meir. Its right-wing opponents included the expansionist Herut ('Freedom') party, founded by Menachem Begin in June 1948, and which in 1973 combined to form the Likud ('Union') coalition.

figures, all of whom will have to stand while I ramble inconsequently, followed by pithy remarks by Leonard and, I hope, one of his marvellous orations by the Chancellor, who will declare the buildings open (although they will clearly have been that for some time). What about the Ford Foundation? Would you like to be represented by anyone? [...]

I ought to add that the National Union of Students have announced that there will be a nationwide series of demos in a week in November – it is sure to be our week on the principle that the worst always happens. Arab terrorists may seek to assassinate Sir Isaac, Leonard, me etc. etc. Irish terrorists collaborating with them may wish to do the same if Mr Edward Heath accepts Leonard's insistence that he be present too as his guest.[1] Some of these things are not quite as improbable as one might think – far from it, alas – I thought I would just add this, having just had a talk with the police. I shall feel some relief if I survive at 7 p.m. on 12th, when all that remains is the College dance, unlikely to be of central interest even to the students, who have started to boil just as yours have subsided.

Meanwhile, my successor, the Hon. Sir Henry Fisher, wonders if it would be a good thing for him to present himself to the Ford Foundation and meet yourself and, perhaps, some members of the Foundation. While I do not feel that this is urgent, he would rather like it, and would be prepared to go to New York for the purpose. I honestly do not think that he is doing it in the hopes of favours to come (although he may), but as an elementary courtesy. [...]

His chief rival, as you may have heard, was Michael Brock, to whom I remain deeply devoted and whose part in building up this establishment was so far ahead of anybody else's that his hopes of succession were perfectly natural and justified. All choices involve losses, and many involve acute disappointment – he has, of course, behaved beautifully, as one would expect, and will be staying on, at any rate for the time being. Fisher is being very nice to him and I am deeply grieved on his behalf, as is half the College, more than half if you include the graduates, who have no voice in these matters, but who love him greatly. The majority (technically only a recommendation to the University Council) was a perfectly clear one, and Sir Henry Fisher got nearly two thirds of the votes, and I think he will do very well if he is ready to delegate enough of his work (I was rather too good at that, but nothing disastrous seems to have happened in spite of it). The partnership with Brock was intimately happy, and I look on the whole thing with great pleasure and, probably, not enough guilt – all thanks to you, as you well know, without whom Leonard would not have budged a millimetre. There is no doubt that

---

1 The terrorist campaign waged by Irish republican paramilitaries, chiefly the Irish Republican Army (IRA), against the British State was then at its height; in December 1974 a bomb was thrown at the London home of the former Prime Minister, Edward Heath, who had not attended the opening ceremony.

there is a clear sense in which it is all your fault, although I am ready to accept some share in the blame, although so far no one has said a cross word, not even dear Lord Z. who is immensely affable when we meet.

I leave in mid-March – so that is when my successor wants to enter upon his office – and shall then be an old retired person. I look forward to that greatly – you and Mary[1] must come and stay if you can. In the spring you shall be invited to the Annual Banquet of the British Academy – that is as remarkable collection of academics as has ever been assembled under one roof – say the word and a handsome engraved invitation will be sent to you. This is the last piece of patronage I am ever likely to have. There is nobody I would so much enjoy extending it to you as yourself.

Yours ever,

[Isaiah]

WALTER EYTAN

22 July 1974

[Wolfson]

[Dear Walter,]

I was very sorry to miss you on the 18th. I knew I would have to and I wrote to your father so – I do admire his magnificent control of all his faculties and senses: even my mother was not as sound of limb and spirit as he is at that age. As for the British Academy, I was assured that if I declined there would be no President. Nobody else seemed anxious to take on the job. I pointed out all my clear shortcomings, but as I am giving up this College next March I had no real valid excuse except incompetence, which, in the past, has not proved fatal to that institute. You are quite right about the need for a sense of humour – academics are not the easiest of men, as you well know, and there is really no other way of lowering splendid outbursts of violent feeling which from time to time punctuate academic discussions about, e.g., candidates for election and distribution of grants. I hope to have something to gossip with you about in that kind of connection.

Yours ever,

[Isaiah]

TO ARTHUR LOURIE

22 July 1974 [carbon]

[Wolfson]

[Dear Arthur,]

It was characteristically kind of you to send me that very nice cable – all

---

1 McGeorge Bundy married the Radcliffe-educated teacher Mary Buckminster Lothrop (b. 1925) in 1950; they had four sons.

I can say is that the job is not at all a sinecure and involves having to make speeches, negotiate with the Government and other similar things which I dislike acutely and am not at all good at. Why then did I accept? Sheer vanity, I expect, a secret passion to go on being called President of something, and general folly. I suspect that the reason for my being chosen is that all the really formidable scholars knock each other out, and I owe this honour to my Shazar-like[1] nature, except that in his own way he was really a very good speaker and inspired quite a lot of American Rabbis – a thing I am conspicuously incapable (and not very desirous) of doing. Thank you ever so much and my love to Jeannett.

[Isaiah]

In the early hours of 17 June 1972 the offices of the Democratic National Committee in the Watergate complex in Washington, DC, were broken into. Statements by the suspects that they were working on behalf of a key member of the campaign to re-elect President Nixon were strenuously denied by the White House, and that November Nixon won a landslide victory at the polls. But two investigative reporters at the Washington Post, *Carl Bernstein and Bob Woodward, spearheaded a classic piece of investigative journalism that eventually exposed the administration's involvement in criminal activities designed to secure the President's re-election. After a protracted legal process during which Nixon further abused the privileges of his office, refusing to hand over tapes of Oval Office conversations implicating him in criminal conspiracy, the Senate prepared to vote for impeachment. To avoid this Nixon resigned on 9 August 1974. Though never indicted, he was later pardoned for all Watergate-related crimes by his successor, Gerald Ford. The pardon did not extend to members of his staff, some of whom were later tried and imprisoned for their part in 'Watergate'.*

TO ROWLAND BURDON-MULLER

11 September 1974 [*manuscript*]

Venice

Dear Rowland,

Thank you ever so much for your letter: indeed I remember telling you how unattractive I found Nixon when he came to London vice Eisenhower, to attend some solemn function – a memorial to the unknown G.I. – I think. He went on to Oxford where he won *golden* opinions: not just from the radical A. J. P. Taylor who – largely in order to swim against the stream of respectable opinion – claims he found him charming – but the Rhodes Scholars, mostly

---

1 In 1963 Shazar was a compromise candidate for the Presidency of Israel who offended neither extreme of opinion.

Democrats, who were taken with him. I argued in vain: they did remember
the dirty Californian campaign, Helen Gahagan Douglas,[1] Governor Brown[2]
and all; but it all seemed vague and past. In Italy & France, of course, all this
indignation seems bizarre: *all* politicians are crooks, mostly to line their own
pockets – Nixon at least did it to increase his power & that of his junta – *what*
is so shocking about that? At our time of life? His only crime was to have
been found out etc. Some of the more squeamish ones do rather recoil before
the gangster *argot* of the published tapes: but the rest – and my dear friend
John Sparrow, who hates high minded liberal sentiments, wrote a long letter
to the *Times* declaring that Nixon had been *hounded* by the press: how could
justice be obtained in such an atmosphere etc.?[3] But by and large the English
feel much as the Americans do: the French, Germans, Italians, do not. The
Anglo-Saxon countries think "the Continent" cynical, the accused believe
the Anglo-Americans to be deeply hypocritical. This is like the nineteenth
century. The histories of our time *will* give very *different* versions: Kissinger
will emerge as a major transformer of international relationships. His CIA
connections, Chile, etc. will be forgotten or condoned: Nixon will emerge
oddly: more intelligent than Harding,[4] a man of bold initiatives, yet evidently
blind not only to ordinary moral considerations but to the reactions of his
own people: with a deep psychological flaw, a crony of gangsters and crooks,
a great deceiver and con-man, yet also self deceived to a degree: all this quite
apart from his bad character and crimes. Now there is the row about Ford's
pardon.[5] The desire to forget if not to forgive is intelligible: people recoil from
a long trial, appeals, new trials, which block out more politically important

1 Helen Mary Gahagan Douglas (1900–80) née Gahagan appeared on the stage as Helen Gahagan
   in theatre and opera productions 1922–38. A strongly liberal supporter of FDR and the New
   Deal, she was elected Democratic Congresswoman for California 1945–51; in 1950 she ran
   against Richard Nixon for the Senate in a bitterly-fought campaign that earned Nixon the epithet
   'tricky Dick' (her coinage) for his campaign's savage denigration of her character.
2 Having lost the Presidential race in November 1960, Richard Nixon decided to contest the
   Governorship of California in 1962. The incumbent Democrat, Edmund Gerald 'Pat' Brown
   (1905–96), was urged to mount a strong campaign by President Kennedy, who said that he had
   beaten Nixon in 1960, but that Brown was to bury him. The campaign was appropriately bitter,
   and after his defeat Nixon, who had been tipped to win, told reporters: 'You don't have Nixon to
   kick around any more. This is my last press conference' (*Times*, 8 November 1962, 12e).
3 'From time to time', Sparrow wrote, 'the American people assassinate their President; never until
   today has the thing been done in slow motion before the eyes of the whole world' (21 August
   1974, 13e).
4 Warren Gamaliel Harding (1865–1923), Republican 29th President of the US 1921–3; died in
   office, his presidency overshadowed by political scandals and corruption.
5 On 8 September 1974, a month after taking office, Gerald Rudolph Ford (1913–2006), 38th
   President of the US 1974–7, extended a 'full, free and absolute' pardon to his predecessor, Richard
   Nixon, 'for all offenses against the United States' that he might have committed from the beginning of his presidency on 20 January 1969. Ford made clear how difficult the decision had been
   for him, and he was beset with criticism afterwards, but he was determined 'to firmly shut and
   seal this book': 'Remarks on Signing a Proclamation [Proclamation 4311] Granting Pardon to
   Richard Nixon. September 8, 1974', in *Public Papers of the Presidents of the United States: Gerald R.
   Ford, Containing the Public Messages, Speeches, and Statements of the President, August 9 to December 31,
   1974* (Washington, 1975), 101–3 at 102–3.

issues, & continue the nightmare: & yet reverence for law, constitution, justice is bound to be overwhelming in a nation whose bonds are not cultural or racial or religious or even linguistic or dynastic etc. but founded on a set of written principles which are evidently being flouted: Ford is behaving like a monarch, a prince who can pardon freely: I see this is painful to Americans even if they hate & despise Nixon.

Meanwhile my friend Mrs Graham emerges as the triumphant victor in this great imbroglio: I wish her well: she has behaved with much courage – but if she hadn't been rich ... I do see what the Left feel & mean.[1] Personally I wd rather they went on with the trials: amnesties are not for malefactors of great wealth or power, as T. Roosevelt used to call them.

Meanwhile here we are in Venice where I am due to deliver a lecture at the Fondazione Cini this afternoon: in English which nobody here will understand: done rapidly & nervously, as always by me, when in unfamiliar surroundings – followed by dinner with Italian Profs – a seminar tomorrow morning, God knows in what language – followed by luncheon with the Conte Cini, the founder & benefactor, an old Fascist gerarc{h}a (I suspect) no better than Nixon, if less influential. Does the statute of limitations hold after 30 years? Shd we give our moral feelings a holiday vis-à-vis all the French & Italian aristocracy, old & new, who behaved so dubiously? Are we to forget say the Duchess of Windsor's[2] pro-Nazi sentiments & not mention them before the surviving friends who paint pathetic pictures of her loneliness, deafness, isolation? Is the opposite only vindictive? Does one remain in the same room with Sir O. Mosley and his wife? I shd love to hear your views on this.

And now I must go & prepare the lecture which nobody will understand – a torture to all concerned –

with much affection –

Isaiah

1 Kay Graham's *Washington Post* had played a key role in uncovering the Watergate conspiracy, defying the Nixon administration's attempts to intimidate, and to silence, both her and her paper: 'Especially in the earlier months, when the *Post* stood almost alone against an electorally triumphant and furiously vindictive Administration – which was determined to ruin her paper's reputation – the personal pressure on Graham was formidable. But she never wavered.' 'Publisher of *The Washington Post* Who Brought Down Nixon over Watergate, and Became One of the Most Powerful Women in America', obituary of Graham, *Times*, 18 July 2001, 17a–f.

2 (Bessie) Wallis Simpson (1896–1986) née Warfield, then Spencer, Duchess of Windsor, married, June 1937, Prince Edward (1894–1972), Duke of Windsor, formerly King Edward VIII. In October 1937 the Windsors visited Germany and met Hitler, the Duke delivering the Nazi salute, and his pro-Nazism tainted her: 'it was popularly believed that she had Fascist sympathies and it has even been claimed that she worked for German intelligence, but there is no evidence that she held any considered political views, still less indulged in such activities. [...] The last fourteen years of her life were spent in increasing decrepitude; during the final five she lived in total seclusion' (Philip Ziegler, ODNB).

TO BRUCE PHILLIPS[1]

1 October 1974 [carbon]

[Wolfson]

Dear Mr Phillips,

I reply to your letter of 5 September, about the discussions between Miss Charvet[2] and Professor Freeborn about Belinsky. I must begin by making it clear that I am perhaps not a good person to consult in this connection, since my opinion of Professor Freeborn's writings is no better than his of mine: and that is certainly not at all high. [...]

Let me, despite this, try to put the matter as objectively as I can. It seems to me that the proposition that Belinsky's life and works are 'curiously separate' is the very opposite of the truth. Professor Freeborn rightly says that Belinsky has been 'frozen into the progressive pose of a piece of official Soviet statuary' by Soviet critics. But from this it does not follow that Belinsky's life is separable from his views. There is no man whose life and writings are more intimately intertwined. This is true not only of his letters – which are among the most moving written in Russian – but also of his critical essays, and entire literary work, on which his reputation and influence, both in his own lifetime and after, depended and still depend. Whether or not Belinsky was 'neurotic and ailing' is comparatively irrelevant to the intensely personal character of his tone, the fact that he transmuted the philosophical doctrines, German or French, into his own personal experience and idiom – this, whether he understood or misunderstood Kant, Fichte,[3] Schiller, Hegel, Comte, the young Hegelians and so on. Belinsky was always preaching, and it is the painfully genuine depth of feeling, the unimpeachable integrity, the moral passion which he pours into his succession of constantly changing positions that is responsible for the enormous impact that his personality and life and words made on his contemporaries, and altered the direction of Russian writing, both by direct influence and reaction against it during the century that followed his death in 1847. The fact that his life, feeling, writing are all of a piece is by now a truism, stressed by all who have written about him, so that to seek to divorce his opinions (and their philosophical sources) from his life and relationships with contemporaries seems to be astonishing – more eccentric, in his case, than it would be in that of any other writer. Contemporaries with whom his life was bound up – Bakunin, Turgenev, Katkov, Botkin, Herzen, Nekrasov – were subject to the same foreign influ-

---

1 Bruce Lovat Phillips (b. 1944), then modern languages editor at OUP.
2 (Elizabeth) Anne Victoria Charvet (b. 1943), Somerville modern languages (Russian) 1961–4; editor, Chatto & Windus, 1967–9, Oxford University Press (London office) 1969–76.
3 Johann Gottlieb Fichte (1762–1814), German philosopher, pupil of Kant; his first book was mistakenly assumed to be the work of his master, and he is regarded as the first great post-Kantian Idealist; his early works had a profound influence on the young Hegel, and on Romantic writers such as Novalis.

ences, read the same philosophical texts, and the whole life of that circle – the founding fathers of the Russian intelligentsia – is unintelligible without some knowledge and understanding of their metaphysical and moral opinions, as well as their personal circumstances and characters and histories. This needs rather more than – or at any rate something different from – efficiency in literary analysis. The standard life of Belinsky, written in the 1870s by Pypin,[1] and the essays by Ivanov-Razumnik[2] would be worth translating even now provided that they were furnished with an expert introduction.

I can only say that when I write or talk about this subject, which I have done now for more years than I can remember, I could not conceive of omitting constant references to the 'intellectual climate', which in turn presupposes some grasp of Western, and not merely Russian, intellectual history: one might perhaps write about Dostoevsky or Tolstoy without this – with far more difficulty about Dostoevsky – but in the case of Belinsky it would stultify the subject. This may sound somewhat sweeping, but I think it is no more than the obvious truth. As for psychological studies of writers in the past – say, a quasi-psychoanalytical approach – these seldom seem convincing to me, unless done by an expert at once singularly cautious, knowledgeable and imaginative, e.g. Erikson on Luther.[3]

This is my view for what it is worth, but perhaps others, better qualified than I, may think differently.

Yours sincerely,

[Isaiah Berlin]

TO NOEL ANNAN

17 October 1974

Wolfson

Dear Noel,

Thank you for 'Man of Action'[4] – it really is an idiotic title: considering that the other men of action are David Cecil, Ernst Gombrich, Stephen Spender, John Wain[5] etc., it seems marvellously ludicrous, as the BBC recognise. There is a party there that wishes to abolish it on the grounds that

1 Aleksandr Nikolaevich Pypin (1833–1904), *Belinskii: ego zhizn' i perepiska* (2 vols, St Petersburg, 1876).
2 Razumnik Vasil'evich Ivanov-Razumnik (1878–1946) né Ivanov, literary critic, wrote widely on Belinsky.
3 Erik Homburger Erikson (1902–94), *Young Man Luther: A Study in Psychoanalysis and History* (London, 1958).
4 Annan had congratulated IB on his contribution to BBC Radio 3's *Man of Action*, the thinking man's *Desert Island Discs* (but without an interviewer), a long-running series in which well-known figures recounted their life stories, interleaving reminiscence with passages from the music that meant most to them. IB's episode was first aired on 12 October 1974.
5 John Barrington Wain (1925–94), novelist and poet; 1st Fellow in Creative Arts, Brasenose, 1971–2; Professor of Poetry, Oxford, 1973–8.

the hour could be better spent in broadcasting contemporary British works
– there is no prospect that would depress me more, but do not, as Namier
used to say, spread this too far.

As for my retirement, I look forward to it more than I can say – the
burdens of the British Academy are quite enough for my back. As for the
rest, I shall spend time on some very obscure topics in the field of the history
of ideas – at once obscure and difficult without scholarly training, pedantic
without being precise, general without being of interest to anyone outside
a very narrow circle.

[...] Toscanini. Of course he altered things. I do indeed know the strange
tempo of, for example, the third movement of the *Eroica*, and he tended to
fly things through – especially in Mozart, which he was not good at [...].
What I meant was that, while he was actually conducting and one saw him as
well as heard him, the authority was such that one believed at the time that
this and only this was the truth – the intensity and the seriousness and the
sublime *terribilità* totally subdued one – not exactly pleasure, only absorption
and a kind of terror. The tautness spread to oneself, and all other interpretations seemed thin or vulgar for years afterwards. And still do: save for [Bruno]
Walter in Mozart and Schubert, Beecham one can never tell when – he was
very bad and very good depending on the mood etc. – and Klemperer in
Beethoven and, I suppose, Mahler. The rest are not fit to tie the shoelaces of
these men. All arts have their beginning, rises and peaks. Conducting was
invented in Paris in the late 1830s, rose to a great height between 1870 and
1914 – Toscanini was the greatest exponent, unless Mahler was, and then
elaboration and decline. So Vico; so, I fear, Spengler;[1] but I think this is true
of a given period of art; and (a truism) Toscanini was the actual Everest,
Karajan and Solti are mere Apennines covered with villas; the pure white ice
and snow – even the luxuriant hills and valleys (Furtwängler)[2] – are no more.

Yours,

Isaiah

---

1 Oswald Spengler (1880–1936), German philosopher of history, author of *Der Untergang des
Abendlandes: Umrisse einer Morphologie der Weltgeschichte* (2 vols, Vienna/Munich, 1918–22), trans.
Charles Francis Atkinson as *The Decline of the West* (2 vols, London, 1926–8), which argued that
civilisations advance in a cyclical progression, moving from spring through summer and autumn
towards an inevitable wintry decline, the cycle lasting around a millennium.

2 (Gustav Heinrich Ernst Martin) Wilhelm Furtwängler (1886–1954), German conductor and composer, spent most of his life with the Berlin Philharmonic Orchestra, and in 1946 was tried for
collaborating with the Nazis, but was acquitted, and resumed his career.

TO DOROTHY SHIRLEY[1]

18 October 1974 [carbon]

[Wolfson]

Dear Mrs Shirley,

I am most grateful to you, and, indeed, deeply touched by your letter about the musical programme that I was responsible for. I wish we were not called 'Men of Action' – it sounds like a hollow parody when one thinks of David Cecil, Professor Gombrich, John Wain and myself! I am glad you feel like this about 'Casta diva'[2] – it is certainly what the angels sing. I heard Callas sing it, not on that terrible occasion of which you speak in Rome, but in Covent Garden twice, and in Rome in the Teatro Argentina at least once. She sang it marvellously, with wonderful regal dignity and splendour. Nor have I heard her record of it; I daresay it is better than Ponselle's.[3] But I was introduced to it by Rosa Ponselle – and I remain loyal to her. The purity of her tone – the record is not very good – the lyrical sweetness, the touching, wistful, romantic, nostalgic quality is extraordinary and, although the 78 record[4] is not, perhaps, very good, transformed my whole conception of what Italian opera could do, and after that I never looked back. I shall certainly listen to the Callas record. I am sure you are right.

As for Toscanini, he was so authoritative that every other performance of, say, Beethoven's symphonies, and certainly the Verdi *Requiem*, sounded thin and unconvincing to me ever after [...]. If he is conducting in the heavenly sphere, the angels must be terrorised – he does not allow anyone any authority to dictate how things should be done – the inhabitants of paradise are fortunate: but the performing angels must be going through – I do not say what. Thank you ever so much for your letter: it really did give me great pleasure and I am most grateful. One never knows what anyone else feels about one's own tastes, and it sets one up tremendously.

Yours sincerely,

[Isaiah Berlin]

1 Dorothy Shirley (1895–1978) née Howard, widow of Fred(erick) Joseph John Shirley (1890–1967), headmaster, The King's School, Canterbury, 1935–62.

2 'Chaste goddess', famous aria from the opera *Norma* (1831) by the Italian composer Vincenzo Bellini (1801–35). Maria Callas sang the demanding title role triumphantly many times in her career, but at a gala performance at the Opera House in Rome on 2 January 1958, attended by the President of Italy, Giovanni Gronchi (1887–1978), she left the theatre at the end of the first act. Although she later claimed voice trouble there was widespread speculation that she was protesting at the unappreciative reaction of a section of the house: 'it is clear that Rome and Mme Callas have in the past been out of sympathy. She would, *Il Messagero* suggests, have behaved differently in Milan' (*Times*, 4 January 1958, 5c).

3 Rosa Ponselle (1897–1981) née Rosa Ponzillo, American soprano, renowned for the beauty of her voice and her technical accomplishment, made her Covent Garden debut in 1929 as Norma.

4 A shellac analogue disc played at 78 revolutions per minute, until the Second World War the standard speed for commercial music recordings (later supplanted by 33 and 45 rpm); many historic classical recordings began life as 78s.

TO STEPHEN SPENDER

4 November 1974

Headington House

Dear Stephen,

[...] The persecution of Israel is really becoming sinister: at first, all good people were for it because it was an underdog, then they turned against it because it was an overdog, now it is clearly an underdog again but I fear that won't penetrate until there is no dog at all. There is no mistake they haven't made – putting the religious party into the government again seems lunacy to me. The fact that it is the Zealots who engineered the doom of Jerusalem in 70 AD seems to me a ghastly thought.[1] The policy of the Foreign Office towards them seems to me beyond words odious: it is done with such fearful relish – disinterested malice disguised as expediency – this is practically the only thing I ever agreed with Crossman about: his disinterested malice was, at least, not disguised as anything. [...]

Yours,

Isaiah

TO HAROLD ROSENTHAL[2]

7 November 1974 [carbon]

[Wolfson]

Dear Mr Rosenthal,

I am truly flattered by your invitation to me to contribute to *Opera* for its silver jubilee.[3] I suppose I could describe my first experience of Chaliapin singing *Boris* in St Petersburg in 1916, when I was seven, or *Figaro* as performed in a cinema in Istanbul where the second act appeared to take place in a seraglio (will this compromise my Turkish visa for ever?), or the occasion during German inflation when Siegfried's horses ate Hagen's beard (alas, I did not see this myself, but Nicolas Nabokov says he did; I wonder if it is cheating to describe this as having happened to him). In short, I could probably produce a brief farcical piece which would provide hideous evidence for Peter Hall's view that people are merely patronising about opera, but whether I can get this done by, or soon after, Christmas is a problem, as I have a terrible term

1 The Israeli government formed by Yitzhak Rabin on 3 June 1974, after the resignation of Golda Meir, enjoyed a one-seat majority in the Knesset, and on 30 October Rabin augmented this number by including the National Religious Party in his coalition; when originally formed, Rabin's government had been the first since independence not to include ministers from a religious party. The Zealots were a Jewish political group in the 1st century CE fanatically opposed to Roman rule, and who played a key role in the rising of 66 CE that led to the capture and sacking of Jerusalem by the future emperor, Titus, in 70 CE.

2 Harold David Rosenthal (1917–87), lecturer, broadcaster and writer on opera, became Lord Harewood's assistant editor at *Opera* magazine on its foundation in 1950, editor 1953–86.

3 IB's contribution is 'Performances Memorable and Not So Memorable', *Opera* 26 (1975), 116–20.

before me, but I will do my best and warn you if the enterprise fails. Do not count on it! [...]

Yours sincerely,

[Isaiah Berlin]

TO IAN WILLIAMS[1]

20 November 1974 [*carbon*]

[Wolfson]

Dear Mr Williams,

Thank you for your letter of 11 November. About determinism the situation is somewhat more complicated than I think is generally supposed. I do not believe that indeterminacy – Heisenberg's Principle – is all that relevant. Even if I cannot determine the position and velocity of a given particle simultaneously, this does not seem to me to entail randomness or freedom in any intelligible sense. Popper's supposition that the act of prediction itself makes a difference to what is predicted, since it is an event in the universe with its own causal consequences, is, perhaps, more relevant, but if I were told that someone outside my system were able to predict everything that I did, the fact that such an observer could not predict his own conduct would not console me much. If someone were to come into a room and give me a sealed envelope and ask me to describe all my experiences for, let us say, a quarter of an hour, everything that I saw, heard, observed, thought etc., so far as I was able; and after I had done that, if I were to open the envelope and find a great part of this accurately described, I should certainly be shaken, wouldn't you?[2] Would you not feel that something in your belief about freedom of the will had been gravely affected? However, I daresay that, in theory, determinism can be neither proved nor disproved unless it is an empirical theory. If it is, then at least evidence for or against it can be accumulated (as I believe). [...]

Yours sincerely,

[Isaiah Berlin]

1 Ian Michael Williams (b. 1958), then a pupil at Hull Grammar School, as IB was later astonished to discover: 'His Headmaster, who is obviously a nice, humane man, rightly [...] thinks the boy ought to be encouraged'; IB duly wrote to Alan Montefiore (4 March 1975, quoted here), for advice about A-level choices, etc. Later (1977–80) Balliol PPE.

2 This thought-experiment was frequently used by IB to show how radical the effect would be of having the fine detail of one's inner life predicted by a determinist. However, as stated here (and elsewhere) the argument is surely flawed, because the knowledge that the determinist is attempting this task is bound to alter the whole stream of consciousness that is supposed to have been predicted, as would the requested description of this stream by its subject. The case needs restating so that the delivery of the envelope *follows* the sequence of experiences predicted by the description it contains, though it also needs to be the case that the compilation of the description *preceded* this sequence. Further refinements and qualifications are possible, but this is not the place to expatiate upon them.

TO MCGEORGE BUNDY

9 December 1974 [*carbon*]

[Wolfson]

[Dear Mac,]

[...] I wish you had been able to come to our opening. It went off, we can say, satisfactorily – not without previous alarms and excursions. The Wolfsons, as you know, never open buildings etc. without bringing with them an enormous train of relations, friends and clients of various sorts. The difficulty is to know how many they will actually bring. If one settles on a dozen, sometimes another dozen is announced at the last moment, and this creates appalling logistical problems. At the stone-laying by the Queen, they produced Lord Fraser of Glasgow, a Co-operative leader, whom no doubt Sir Isaac acquired twenty or thirty years ago: he was a red-faced, jolly old party, who came with quite a jolly wife. Lord Fraser reappeared on the list, but this time turned out to be head of the Conservative Central Office:[1] there is at least one other Lord Fraser, who will doubtless appear at the next festival [...]. He also invited Ted Heath, who at the last minute declined to be a mute spear-bearer in the opera.

Worse was to come: he also invited the Israeli ambassador and his wife, who of course accepted at once.[2] Michael Brock, in his innocence, explained to the General Meeting of the College, attended by graduates and everybody else,[3] about security measures which the police had to take in view of this. An Indian lady asked in what capacity the Ambassador was coming – 'as a College guest', Michael replied, correctly (all guests are College guests) but incompletely. There was apparently a moment of tense silence – I was not present, otherwise I might have explained that it was the Wolfsons' day and we did not intend to scrutinise the political attributes of their guests. In due course a very neurotic Persian, with strong pro-Arab sympathies and no love for the Shah, whipped up a certain amount of sentiment in College. Dull rumours of impending counter-measures began to circulate. The ceremony was arranged for a Tuesday. On Sunday, a letter was delivered

1 Richard Michael Fraser (1915–96), Kt 1962, life peer 1974; Director of the Conservative Research Dept 1959–64, Chairman 1970–4. We have not been able to trace the other Lord Fraser.
2 Gideon Rafael (1913–99) né Ruffer, Berlin-born Israeli diplomat, emigrated to Palestine 1934; married 1940 Nurit Weissberg; with Moshe Sharett, founded the Israeli Foreign Ministry after independence; Israel's representative at the UN during the Six-Day War; Director General of Foreign Ministry 1968–72; ambassador to UK and Ireland 1973–7.
3 'We had a thing called the College [sc. General] Meeting. That meant everybody – servants, graduate students, anybody connected. They had no executive powers, but they could make recommendations to the Governing Body. The Governing Body always accepted it, it went perfectly smoothly. During the riots, during the great student unrest, they were completely free from it. The chief leader was at Wolfson. He said that as far as this College was concerned, he had nothing against it. If everyone were like that ... Not a criticism. We were the ideal democratic college. Imagine it, under me of all people. Rather surprising, I think.' MI Tape 27.

to Michael, written by a girl whose Christian name had been changed that month from Sheila to Liam (she is a Durham miner's daughter and Liam is a man's name), a graduate of the College, to the effect that though she did not deeply love demos, there would be one, including a large number of easily procurable Arabs (who hold themselves in readiness in St Antony's for such eventualities), to block and obstruct the long street down which the Wolfsons, Macmillan, the heads of colleges, etc. would be moving. On Sunday evening I telephoned Leonard and warned him that this might take place: he reported it to his father and they both got into a most tremendous flap (kindly destroy this letter – after all, the future of the College is probably at stake). First Isaac announced he would not be coming; then Leonard desired me to communicate with the Israeli ambassador, Gideon Rafael, in case he suddenly felt that a terrible cold was coming upon him. 'Am I to tell him', I asked, 'that the publicity involving your name, which *The Times* and the *Guardian* would be sure to give, might embarrass you if he came?' I was instructed to keep their interest in the matter totally out of it, which in a sense I could understand. I then telephoned His Excellency to tell him what was impending. I asked myself whether, supposing he said something like 'Would you prefer me not to come?', I should reply 'Yes' or 'No'. It was clear that I would have to deny any such preference – too cowardly and humiliating and improper and disgusting; but then, why was I telephoning? To tell him that the Wolfsons would not care for the ensuing publicity, I suppose: would it be proper to tell him that? To say anything at all? Should one not behave with lofty dignity and take what comes as it comes? Torn by such thoughts I rang up the ambassador in a state of mounting angst: after I had informed him, he said briskly, 'Oh, we get this all the time. I'll tell my people, thank you' – and rang off. That put an end to my perplexities and I felt much better.

I then sent for Liam and addressed her for two and a half hours. I explained that we were not going to veto the Wolfsons' friends, and that her friends had got the whole thing wrong. Worn down by me she finally agreed to call it off, and all was well. Macmillan made one of his best speeches – wildly amusing and appropriate, and apart from forgetting Sir Isaac Wolfson's name for three minutes – *fou rire*[1] was only just avoided -- colleagues and honoured guests behaved with impeccable self-control while he fumbled through his mind and his notes – it was all perfectly traditional and satisfactory. Shep Stone appeared arm in arm with Alan Bullock, but Mr Heaps[2] occupied the dais:

1 'A fit of the giggles'.
2 David Heaps (1916–2000), Canadian human rights advocate; won MC serving with Canadian army in Europe during Second World War; afterwards worked for UNESCO and other organisations before joining the Ford Foundation 1959, becoming its representative in Nigeria and Tunisia during the 1960s; influential in the Foundation's decision, c.1975, to begin a large-scale international human rights programme; retired 1976.

I liked him very much; I thought he was a shrewd, amusing and intelligent man, and he displayed commendable sangfroid in view of the fact that his clothes had been stolen that morning and he appeared in curious, borrowed garments (for God's sake don't reveal to him that I told you this).

Now everything is calm again. My impending retirement is viewed without undue impatience. The press produced very reasonable accounts of the College – the buildings, persons and purposes. *The Times* did produce a headline about how little money we had[1] – true enough, but a cause of some displeasure to Leonard – my effort to persuade him that it might stimulate some unknown millionaire to give us something provoked the comment 'I would rather be envied than pitied.' I wondered afterwards which I should prefer, if these were the only alternatives: the latter, I think, but mankind, I dare say, can be divided into these two categories.

Do come and see the College: if possible while I am still here, i.e. before 15 March, but if that is impossible, after that: it really would be worth your while, if only architecturally. Rostropovich[2] is to play for us for free on the 20th, with the proceeds to found the College Musical Society. So we shall at least begin with a bang. I wish you could be there, but I suppose that is impossible. Solly Zuckerman sent us a most affable telegram to celebrate our opening. As a reward, I shall invite him to the banquet of the British Academy on 24 April – if you are in Europe, do come to it too. You will not only have the exquisite pleasure of hearing me mumble a few million well chosen words, but the PM also: can you possibly resist that?

This country is genuinely in rather a bad way. Whatever may happen in the short run, the United States has enough appetite for life, sheer vitality, apart from resources, to recover and march forward in some direction – that I do not doubt at all. This is equally true of Germany. The bright prospects of the French future seem to me exaggerated. As for this country, I would really rather not speak – for once I am in a Joe-like condition. In the end, I dare say all Cassandras turn out to be right – but our chickens are coming home to roost earlier than even Joe vaticinated (that is a good word).

Much love to you, much love to Mary,

    [Isaiah]

---

1 'New college short of money'. The story was impeccably sourced, as revealed by the paper's education correspondent, Tim Devlin: 'Sir Isaiah Berlin [...] told me before the opening ceremony: "We have not got enough money to subsidise any kind of academic research"' (13 November 1974, 18d–e).

2 Mstislav Leopol'dovich Rostropovich (1927–2007), later (1987) Hon. KBE, Russian cellist, pianist and conductor, toured the West in 1956 and was appointed Professor of Cello at Moscow Conservatory in 1957. His public support for Alexander Solzhenitsyn in 1970 led to his own proscription, and in 1975 he left the Soviet Union for the US, becoming Director of Music and Conductor of the National Symphony Orchestra in Washington, DC, 1977–94. His concert at Wolfson consisted of three solo Bach cello suites.

TO F. T. DAVIES[1]

13 December 1974 [*carbon*]

Wolfson

Dear Tommy,

[...] No head of college, I regret to say, can now get anyone into his College. The old patronage system lingered on – the President of Magdalen, for instance, used to be given three places to which he could appoint the sons of old friends, etc., but even that is gone, and admissions are done, so far as I know, in every single college, by committees on which (as in the case of, e.g., Wadham) the head of college does not even sit. Hampshire would be delighted to help, but is genuinely powerless. I should guess that great potentates like Lord Franks at Worcester, Lord Trend[2] at Lincoln, and the other Lords may preside over their admission committees, but the general rule is that the tutor for admissions is in charge, and to him one has to apply. Your Dutch friend will scarcely believe this, but it is so – I have had to write to this effect to incredulous friends of Aline's in France, and my own in America (e.g. to George Kennan, and at least one senator) in the case of graduate students. They do not believe it, but it is true, truer of Oxford than of Cambridge. There is no reason in the world why the boy should not be put down for Wadham in the normal way, although St Peter's College is probably a better bet – for anyone academically not too strong. The head of that college, Sir Alexander Kirkland [Cairncross],[3] once a Treasury knight, has a sense of international obligations, and anyone you know ex-Treasury, e.g. Lord Sherfield,[4] could probably apprise him of the case – that is the best I can do. These are the times which we live in – gone are the days when even I, a humble figure in New College, could get a young Dutch man, whose father was my father's business associate, into Wadham in Warden Bowra's golden days in the dear old 1940s.

How is your health? Portofino was sad without you last summer. Will the mosquitoes keep you away again? I hope not.

Yours,

[Isaiah]

1 Francis Thomas ('Tommy') Davies (1906–88), intelligence officer and industrialist; on board of Courtaulds from 1937; volunteered September 1938 for intelligence work, and was later assigned to the SOE, promoting intelligence liaison with its counterparts in the US.

2 Burke St John Trend (1914–87), KCB 1962, life peer 1974; Secretary of the Cabinet 1963–73; Rector, Lincoln, 1973–83.

3 Alexander Kirkland ('Alec') Cairncross (1911–98), KCMG 1967; Economic Adviser to HMG 1961–4; head of Government Economic Service 1964–9; Master of St Peter's 1969–78; Chancellor, Glasgow, 1972–96.

4 Roger Makins (233/4).

TO NOEL ANNAN

13 January 1975

Headington House

Dear Noel,

[...] I shall not be able because of these Wolfson lectures – Tuesday at 5 p.m. – to come to the Covent Garden board this month or next. There is a matter which could perhaps be taken up in my absence (or perhaps it will have been settled out of court by then, but I should be grateful if you would ask Tooley). I had booked the Box on the 21st of this month, and invited eleven guests. Today I was informed that our new Patron, the Prince of Wales, wanted to come that night, and would I yield? Of course I did – I suppose I can stuff them all into the King's Smoking Room except for one or two who will have to be laid off as they are too old and grand to be accommodated in that wagon-lit. Of course I yielded with as good a grace as possible – there was nothing else one could possibly do, and I was 'happy' to do it, in the best interests of the house, etc. But I wonder if the question of notice might be established: how long in advance do Royal personages have to say before ousting commoners, or even peers? Garrett would have had no difficulty in establishing a doctrine – Claus[1] will, I think, need a 'lead' from Lord G. and you – and in agreement with Sainsbury,[2] who, as we know, cares *deeply* about these matters. But do bring it up and say that I behaved with my usual anxiety to please but that some ruling needs to be communicated to the Palace. It is very worrying to think that our Royalty have (*a*) become musical, and (*b*) have these gratuitous gaps in their schedules. ⟨I am *not* complaining. But I am a tiny bit more republican than I was.⟩

Yours ever,
Isaiah

TO NOEL ANNAN

Thursday 16 January 1975 [*manuscript*]

Headington House

Dear Noel,

Second thought: *don't*, I beg you, raise the question of what kind of notice Royalty ought to give before booking the Box: I shd feel *acutely* embarrassed if I were thought to have made even a minor fuss about this: the Drogheda's

1 Claus Adolf Moser (b. 1922), KCB 1973, later (2001) life peer, Berlin-born British statistician and civil servant; Professor of Social Statistics, LSE, 1961–70, Visiting Professor 1970–5; Director, Central Statistical Office, and head of Government Statistical Service 1967–78; successor to Lord Drogheda as Chairman, ROH, 1974–87.
2 John Davan Sainsbury (b. 1927), later Kt (1980) and life peer (1989); Vice-Chairman, J. Sainsbury plc, 1967–9, Chairman 1969–92; Director, ROH, 1969–85, Chairman 1987–91.

were constantly displaced by the Duchess of Kent, the Q[ueen] Mother etc. – the price of involving oneself in traditional nonsense must be paid. If I am shifted towards Republicanism, it is out of personal pique: *not* a worthy motive. So *please* say nothing. […]

Isaiah

TO I. F. STONE

13 February 1975 *[carbon]*

[Wolfson]

[Dear Izzy,]

Since we last met here in Oxford I have been reading your articles in the *New York Review* with agreement and admiration: indeed, on the Nixon issue there was surely vast consensus; quite apart from all the talk about national self-purification and a new beginning, the mere fact that so many people of otherwise differing views could feel a sense of moral solidarity (and the great luxury of justified common indignation) surely has done quite a lot to restore the faith of decent persons in their own fellow citizens after the Vietnamese nightmare – and you, in particular, must have felt a strange sensation in finding yourself part of the huge majority – the United Front – of masters and men, conservatives and radicals, which normally happens only during revolutions or when a declaration of war is felt to be just (what happens next is quite a different matter, as we all know). But your latest article on the Middle East I did find disturbing, not for its theses, with which I personally agree, but for its tone and implications about what Jews may and may not do, which have taken me aback. That you should protest against the argument of Mr Robert Tucker[1] (whoever he may be) or the other man you mention, who think it possible and perhaps desirable to occupy a part of the Arabian coast and seize the oil wells, I understand well enough; and your opposition to hawks, whether in Israel or America; and your fears about a combination of the two, and a pre-emptive war, seizure of Arab territory, etc., I share; you think this stupid, dangerous and a form of the old, wicked gunboat diplomacy, and, in addition, surely counter-productive to those who try it. I see nothing to object to here. Since I agree that the proposals are dangerous and wrong and incite to aggression, I too wish that *Commentary* had not accepted the article.

But when you say they should not have published it because the journal is issued by the American Jewish Committee, that such attitudes are likely to incite anti-Semitism, in short, that it is not for Jews to advocate or even

1 Robert Charles Tucker (1918–2010), Harvard-educated US political scientist and historian; Professor of Politics and IBM Professor of International Relations, Princeton, 1962–84; founding director, Russian Studies programme, Princeton, 1963.

publish such policies – I disagree; I simply cannot believe that you mean it. For is this not precisely the same consideration that caused fears in the breasts of many highly-placed American Jews in 1939–40 about protesting too vehemently against Hitler, for fear of being thought warmongers – of being accused of dragging America into a Jewish war? I remember very well my conversation in 1941, before America entered the war, with the late Admiral Lewis L. Strauss,[1] who vigorously supported his old chief, Herbert Hoover,[2] and was inclined towards America First,[3] though he did not perhaps go so far as the Rosenwalds,[4] whose position was exceedingly undignified at that time. It was the selfsame argument as that which was used by Lindbergh[5] in the same year, when he warned the Jews against inciting America into war, a speech which justly caused his political ruin. Do you really wish to maintain that someone who thinks a given course right or expedient or worthy of discussion should not utter it because he is a Jew and this may cause hostility in some circles? You would not, I feel sure, use this argument in warning Jews, as they used to be warned by the leaders of the Jewish bourgeoisie, in Germany, in Russia, in America, against being socialists or Communists because this would identify Jews with subversion, and compromise the entire community? The reason for objecting to an invasion of a portion of the Arabian coast for the sake of the oil wells is that it is politically stupid and dangerous and morally wrong, whoever advocates it. But if someone, however wrongly in one's own view, thinks it politically expedient and/or morally right, it seems to me altogether unacceptable to order him to remain silent because he is a Jew, is suspected of having 'an interest', and this may irritate the dominant majority. You (of all people) who believe in freedom of thought and freedom of expression, cannot possibly be defending this. [...]

---

1 Lewis Lichtenstein Strauss (1896–1974) worked with Herbert Hoover's Committee for Relief in Belgium 1917–19; partner, Kuhn, Loeb & Co., bankers, 1929–41; Navy Reserve Officer assigned to Bureau of Ordnance 1941; Rear Admiral November 1945; became a leading advocate of the US nuclear weapons programme; strongly hostile to, and distrustful of, J. Robert Oppenheimer.

2 Herbert Clark Hoover (1874–1964), Republican 31st President of the US 1929–33; strongly opposed American intervention in Europe in the Second World War, but called for total victory after Pearl Harbor.

3 America First Committee: nationwide movement, 800,000 strong at its peak, dedicated to opposing US involvement in the war in Europe; formed after the fall of France, it was disbanded after Pearl Harbor.

4 Lessing Julius Rosenwald (1891–1979), businessman and art collector, married Edith Clementine Goodkind 1913; succeeded his father, Julius Rosenwald, as chairman of the retail giant Sears, Roebuck & Co., 1932–9; joined the America First national committee in September 1940 soon after its inception.

5 Charles Augustus Lindbergh (1902–74), US aviator, made the first transatlantic solo flight in May 1927. He was widely criticised for his activities on behalf of the America First Committee, and in particular for the anti-Semitic content of a speech in Des Moines, Iowa, on 11 September 1941: 'instead of agitating for war, the Jewish groups in this country should be opposing it in every possible way, for they will be among the first to feel its consequences'; tolerance 'cannot survive war and devastation' (*Washington Post*, 12 September 1941, 13).

   I realise that the chauvinism of some circles among American Jews angers you; that the refusal of, say, the religious party in Israel to recognise that they have done a wrong to the Arabs seems as intolerable to you as it does to me; and that you dread a second Holocaust, which you think Jewish and American hawks are bringing nearer. But there is justice for the Jews as well as the Arabs: mere survival on the edges of an Arab State on the West Bank, into which foreign armies are allowed to march, whether Arab or Russian, does not augur well even for survival, let alone normal development, of Israel. Yet you do not allow that this could be a terribly worrying factor, even for the mildest of Israeli doves; nor that the majority of the Jewish inhabitants of Israel would certainly settle for a return of the West bank, Gaza, etc., to the Arabs if this really did mean a high probability of peace in the foreseeable future. I think that you have a feeling that Jews or Zionists have sinned, and therefore must behave particularly well – beyond the standard required of others – suicidally, if need be[1] – in order to avoid Hobbes's maxim that anything is preferable to a violent death, and in order to live in the light of the principle that perfect justice is preferable to survival or anything else. Can this really be your view?

   [...] Israel's attitude to the Arabs leaves much to be desired, morally as well as from a utilitarian point of view. I have not forgotten Deir Yassin or Kibbiya,[2] and do not regard Arab atrocities as cancelling responsibility for that, and, indeed, have said so in print. But I detect in your argument a nervous feeling that the Jews have, as expected, gone and misbehaved again; that they need constant watching lest they get once more into the wrong company (in this case, of Gentiles who are concerned not with Israel but with oil for the USA); a desire to condemn Jews if they do not attain a moral standard which you do not really demand from others; and a feeling that you have a right to say this because you are a Jew, and therefore feel it right to be ashamed of them, and tell them so in public, before everyone. This seems to me to do them an injustice. The State of Israel, from which I have just returned, is, after all, despite everything, a far more democratic, open, human society, in which violently critical things are said in public, for which men would be jailed and sometimes done away with in the rest of the Middle East. The mood of the majority is very, very unlike that of the minority of hawks into whose hands the PLO[3] are playing; they are ready for large concessions to live in peace with Arabs who are now bent on destroying them. Nevertheless, Israel is described as 'fascist', 'criminal', deserving of

---

1 Cf. 278/1, 335/1, 555/2.
2 Cf. 486/2 & 3.
3 Palestine Liberation Organization: a union of various Palestinian Arab groups, founded in 1964, with the aim of eliminating Israel and establishing an independent Palestinian State; it came to be dominated by al-Fatah, and associated with guerrilla and terrorist attacks against Israel, launched from its bases in Jordan, and later Lebanon.

immediate destruction, by Arabs, radicals, Communists everywhere, which even Sartre and Simone de Beauvoir,[1] Jean Daniel,[2] and all but the extremist French Left, find nauseating and have at last rebelled against. In America, among Jews, only Chomsky and Miss Arendt seem to me really to think this, and this seems to me a depressing form of self-induced vanity and blindness. You are free from this, and I continue reading you, whatever you may say, because I feel deep personal affection for you and great respect, but think you – on this issue – truly mistaken. I know that you are not afflicted by the terrible lack of heart of which Scholem rightly accused Hannah Arendt. Why, then, do you say these unfair things?

Yours ever,

[Isaiah]

TO MORTON WHITE

Postmark 22[?] February 1975

[Headington House]

Dear Morty,

[…] The British Academy: I am, I fear, 'in command', and long to tell you about its inner workings – the terrible pressures put on by disgruntled members of Scottish and Northern Irish universities about lack of representation – also, of course, by the sociological world: after all, we must have something like 3,000 sociologists in England, and how many of them are members of the BA? After every effort, and immense travail, first one (a nasty but exceedingly able demographer called Glass), then, after more travail, the questionable Gellner, whom the Philosophy Section refuses to include in its ranks. Meetings are much as you must imagine them to be – slightly pompous, shot through with undertones and half-suppressed biases and hostilities both between the disciplines and their representatives; occasionally comical, but the kind of thing both you and I are perfectly used to. What terrifies me far more is the awful annual speech at the 'Banquet', at which the guest of honour is the Prime Minister – not the sort of thing I do at all well, or, indeed, at all. God! Meanwhile, the University has had its excitements:

1 Simone de Beauvoir (1908–86), French existentialist philosopher, novelist and feminist; author of *The Second Sex* (Paris, 1949) and lifelong partner of Jean-Paul Sartre; they were among a group of European intellectuals – others included Raymond Aron and Jean Daniel – who had recently declared their intention to dissociate themselves from all UNESCO activities unless that body reversed its November 1974 decision, initiated by Arab and Warsaw Pact States, effectively to expel Israel – on the pretext that its archaeological works were damaging the historic fabric of Jerusalem.

2 Jean Daniel (b. 1920) né Jean Daniel Bensaid; born in Blida, near Algiers, into a Sephardic Jewish family; fought with General Leclerc 1944–5; afterwards a journalist, covering the war in Algeria for *L'Express*; co-founded the left-wing weekly *Le Nouvel Observateur* 1964, becoming editorial director and a regular columnist.

there is the great Bhutto controversy[1] – the Council of the University, in its lunacy, offered a degree to the Prime Minister of Pakistan; my colleague Gombrich, son of Gombrich, denounced this as conferring an honour on a man he regards as a bloodstained tyrant, if not directly responsible [for] yet somehow acquiescing in the massacre in Dacca[2] which led to the deaths of various professors whom he knows personally and professionally (he is a Sanskrit scholar), at best a man under a cloud. He is ably seconded in this by Herbert Hart. On the other side is the entire establishment, plus Trevor-Roper, whose pupil Bhutto was, and disreputable characters who think that the University should not have offered him the degree, but, having done so, should not now withdraw it – plus those who denounce the University for hypocrisy – if we gave degrees to Truman (Nagasaki),[3] Selwyn Lloyd (Suez),[4] Mrs Gandhi (the Nagas),[5] why suddenly stick at Bhutto? Perhaps we should stop giving degrees to politicians altogether (which I should favour), but since we do … etc. Tremendous excitement, votes, Bhutto's degree voted down by a majority of two. Then it was discovered that two persons who had no legal right to vote were present[6] – the result, a tie: the Vice-Chancellor, had this tie been revealed at the time, could and should have broken it, but cannot legally do so retrospectively (one cannot cast one's vote backward over one's shoulder). More meetings, more excitement, more stuff in the press, more ancient friendships severed – a kind of local Munich or Suez. I cannot get excited

1 Zulfikar Ali Bhutto (1928–79), Christ Church law 1950–2, President of Pakistan 1971–3, Prime Minister 1973–7, executed 1979. A proposal to confer on him an Honorary DCL was opposed in Congregation on 21 January 1975 by Richard Gombrich, Fellow of Wolfson, and the issue was later put to a vote (note 6 below).

2 On the night of 25–6 March 1971, during an operation against the secessionist movement in East Pakistan, the Pakistan army massacred students and academic staff at the University of Dacca, a centre of the political opposition; on 26 March East Pakistan declared its independence, prompting an armed struggle that resulted in the emergence of independent Bangladesh.

3 President Truman ordered the use of the atom bomb against Nagasaki, which fell on 9 August 1945, three days after the first attack, on Hiroshima, 6 August. The ethics and necessity of the bombings have been much debated; Truman received an Honorary DCL at Oxford in 1956.

4 (John) Selwyn Brooke Lloyd (1904–78), later (1976) life peer, Conservative politician; Foreign Secretary 1955–60, Chancellor of the Exchequer 1960–2, Leader of the House of Commons 1963–4. Lloyd had favoured a negotiated settlement to the Suez Crisis, but loyally supported the military adventure hazarded by Prime Minister Anthony Eden; he was awarded an Honorary DCL at Oxford in 1960.

5 Indira Gandhi (1917–84), Indian stateswoman, only child of Jawaharlal Nehru; Prime Minister 1966–77, 1980–4. In February 1966, soon after taking office, Gandhi met with leaders of the Nagas in an attempt to bring about a permanent end to their decade-long struggle for independence (Nagaland lies in the extreme north-east of India, bordering Burma). But the talks broke down, and martial law was effectively imposed on the region. Mrs Gandhi was awarded an Honorary DCL at Oxford in 1971.

6 On 11 February 1975 Congregation voted 155 to 153 against conferring an honorary degree on Zulfikar Ali Bhutto. It was subsequently discovered that among the majority were two graduate students, unaware that they were not entitled to vote. When the vote was re-taken on 25 February, both the numbers participating and the anti-Bhutto majority (239 to 183) increased dramatically. The University later discontinued the practice of honouring serving politicians, after a proposal to award an Hon. DCL to the Prime Minister, Margaret Thatcher, in January 1985 was voted down by 738 votes to 319.

about this at all and sit comfortably on the fence contemplating the entire scene not without, I fear, intense amusement. It is the kind of thing that makes universities ridiculous, and yet a moral standard never wholly does, even if it gets itself tangled up in legal niceties, as this one has done. Then there is the appointment of Lord Goodman[1] to the Mastership of University College: he is amiable, capable, a marvellous fixer, disinterested, very funny, of a monstrous appearance – he will go down excellently with the undergraduates, fairly well with the dons, not quite so well with the heads of other colleges, and I suspect will not be too happy here himself. His world is that of the Lords, property-developers, right-wing Labour MPs, the jolly, bohemian, non-U world; whether the pedantry and pomposity and the cathedral-close, still rather Trollopian, atmosphere of Oxford, is really something he can comfortably settle into, I rather doubt – but he may. There is no doubt that we shall now get more money for music, drama, University College, and I daresay the Oxford Synagogue. He is a warm-hearted Jew of a very unconcealed kind, loves London, loves Israel, loves society, and really does make very funny jokes. An odd appointment, all the same. But not disreputable (unless, like me, you believe that all such appointments should, on principle, go to academics, or at least intellectuals; I do believe this, but I think I am in a minority – and what is reputable and disreputable in such cases I suppose depends on some kind of Humean consensus of our *Kulturkreis*).[2]

I am delighted to hear about Steve and about Nick. After all, one's children worry one more than any other single element in one's life – don't deter them from academic life. Hypocrisy is everywhere. Some people can protect themselves against involvement and pursue decent lives, addicted to subjects. Others, like you and me, respond to every tremor in the circumambient world. Your children may well belong to the former kind.

Yours,

Isaiah

TO BERNARD WILLIAMS

24 February 1975

Headington House

Dear Bernard,

By all means come to *Onegin* [...]. As for *Rosenkavalier*, of course it is a vulgar work. (The word has one sense which is pretty clear to those who think in these terms, as anybody who thinks consciously about either life or art cannot help doing [...]. Nothing that Strauss wrote wholly avoids

---

1 Arnold Abraham Goodman (1913–95), life peer 1965, founder and consultant, Goodman Derrick and Co., solicitors; director, ROH, 1972–83; Master of Univ. 1976–86.

2 'Cultural circle', a term associated with the early twentieth-century Vienna school of ethnology, which held that advances in culture and technology spread outward from innovatory centres.

vulgarity, and this applies to Mahler too, and to Rachmaninov, to the entire Mitteleuropa–Slavic world of art of that period, until the sharp, cold, neo-barbarian winds of Stravinsky, Kandinsky, the Bauhaus etc. – and Central Europe, for these purposes, includes Italy too. I fully understand the enthusiasm for the new Franco-Russian music of Virgil Thomson[1] as a 'cleansing storm' after the appallingly stuffy suffocating claustrophobia of the overblown late romanticism of Wagner's heirs. I prefer the picture postcards of Granados[2] and Rimsky-Korsakov, of the period.) [...]

Yours,

Isaiah

TO PETER GAY[3]

4 March 1975 [*carbon*]

[Wolfson]

Dear Peter,

Thank you very much for the copy of the letter to T-R. I too wrote to him, and had an answer in which, of course, he speaks of his philo-Semitism, and does not see why a sociological hypothesis about the causes of an event should not be made public, etc., and enlarges on his speculation about 'subliminal' motives. It is all very implausible, and his outburst, I think, quite ghastly – it tells us a good deal more about his subliminal condition than about that of others. I shall reply to his letter and tell him apropos of left-wing plots that the Editor of the *New Statesman*[4] is reported to have spent Christmas with Mr Bhutto. I am glad you wrote.

Yours ever,

[Isaiah]

1 (Garnett) Virgil Thomson (1896–1989), US composer. After graduating from Harvard he lived in Paris, where he came into contact with Stravinsky, Cocteau, Erik Satie and the composers known as Les Six, and formed an artistic collaboration with Gertrude Stein; Chief Music Critic for the *New York Herald Tribune* 1937–51.

2 Pantaleón Enrique Joaquín Granados Campiña (1867–1916), Spanish pianist and composer, who drew on Catalan and Spanish folk traditions to produce a distinctively nationalist style.

3 Peter Gay (b. 1923) né Peter Joachim Fröhlich, Berlin-born US historian whose family fled Nazi Germany in 1939; settled in US, becoming Professor of History, Columbia, 1962–9; Professor of Comparative and Intellectual European History, Yale, 1969–84, Sterling Professor of History 1984–93.

4 Anthony Michell Howard (1934–2010), journalist and broadcaster; political correspondent, *New Statesman*, 1961–4; Whitehall correspondent, *Sunday Times*, 1965; Washington Correspondent, *Observer*, 1966–9, political columnist 1971–2; assistant editor, *New Statesman*, 1970–2, editor 1972–8.

TO HUGH TREVOR-ROPER

4 March 1975 [*manuscript*]

Headington House

My dear Hugh,

Thank you for both your letters. I have, since writing to you, found myself defending you against charges of anti-semitism, 'racialism' and the like, which came not so much from Jews (not more than two or three of whom have talked to me about this issue) as from non-Jews: I happened to visit two (undergraduate) College S.C.R.s in turn, and the matter was discussed in both: I have no idea who most of the persons there may have been: I haven't your eye (forgive me – but I cannot resist saying this) for Jews, and defended you to these strangers on the ground that I knew you to be free from all anti-Jewish feeling, and that consequently you had used the words attributed to you without fully appreciating their likely effect. I am not sure that this last is really what I think – I cannot persuade myself that you did not know that the combination of 'left wingers' and Jews is, by now, charged with historical associations – at least from the days of *La France Juive*[1] and the Dreyfus case to Sir O. Mosley not to go any further – so that the use of this formula, even if it is a true description of a situation, can be provocative and unfair. And this indeed, is what caused me to react – not to over-react if the feelings of the indignant dons I have referred to, none of them, so far as I could tell, Jews, are any symptom – as I did and do. You say that if something is true, why shd it not be publicly stated? Many things are true – private feelings, 'subliminal' motives – which ought not to be stated publicly if decencies are to be preserved and gratuitous cruelty avoided – as I am sure you will agree. But in this case I shd be inclined to doubt or dispute your account of the facts: you say that the *majority* of those who spoke against Bhutto were Jews: Lambert? Gretton? Elvin? Do you really call Father Levi a Jew? this leaves us with only Hart and the mysterious Bentley. Nor do I believe that the Holocaust acted 'subliminally' on Jews or anyone else, but, if at all, consciously, in the sense of making people sensitive to charges of being implicated with governments or parties accused, whether rightly or wrongly, of massacres in Vietnam or Africa or wherever. But this is a matter of interpretation. Let me say again that I hold you both innocent of all racial prejudice and shd not dream of suspecting you of anything of the kind. But I wonder whether, in some moods, you do not ('subliminally' perhaps) divide men into gentlemen and the rest, and include Jews & leftists, with some clear exceptions, among "the rest": and that this influenced your (I continue to think) unfortunate analysis, and conjured up the image of a "Jew-watcher". But of course, I accept all that

---

1 *La France juive: essai d'histoire contemporaine* (2 vols, Paris, 1886), stridently anti-Semitic work by Édouard Adolphe Drumont (1844–1917), a leading anti-Dreyfusard.

you say, and let that be the end of [the] matter so far as you and I are concerned. I cannot, alas, be there on Thursday for I find that I promised to take 3 guests to Covent Garden long before all these things – so I wrote to J.C. & apologized some weeks ago. I fear the matter may go on repercussing: not so far as I am concerned.

Yrs ever
Isaiah

P.S. I am told that the editor of the *New Statesman* spent Christmas with Mr Bhutto: what would the *abbé* Barruel,[1] the plot scenter and unveiler, have made of *that*? I hope you are better.

IB retired from the Presidency of Wolfson on the Ides of March (15 March) 1975. A dinner was held in College at which speeches were made by Godfrey Lienhardt and IB, and musical entertainment provided by a Junior Research Fellow, a graduate student (who had also tried to put into words his feelings about having been at the College under IB's presidency), and IB's successor as President.

TO HENRY HARDY

15 [sc. 16] March 1975 [*manuscript*]

Wolfson

From the ⟨ex-⟩*President

Dear Henry,

To say that I was touched, even moved, by your letter would be a grave understatement. We all go about avoiding the least suspicion of sentimentality, or even a bubble of too obvious emotion, nevertheless feeling will out, and your letter means far more to me than I shall ever be able to say, even to myself; my gratitude to you is immense, not only for this expression of feeling which cannot have been altogether easy to put in words, but for everything: to you particularly, but indeed also to those in Wolfson to whom you are closest: for what they have done for the College in general & for – & to – me in particular. There is no substitute for warmth of heart, moral and intellectual spontaneity, candour, honesty, perceptiveness, unswerving nobility of purpose, public spirit, sheer human decency. I offer you this unsolicited testimonial with all my heart. And I can truthfully say that the entire Wolfson experience has been the best, happiest, and, I must admit, gayest in my long life. I *shd* have said, in my cracked-pizzicato valedictory speech

1 Abbé Augustin Barruel (1741–1820), French Jesuit priest exiled in England during the French Revolution, which he attributed to an anti-Christian conspiracy of Encyclopedists, Freemasons and Illuminists; the idea was set out in his *Mémoires pour servir à l'histoire du Jacobinisme* (translated as *Memoirs, Illustrating the History of Jacobinism*; both published in London, 1797–8).

how marvellous I thought the graduates had been: I *do* think it, odd flurries and sudden whirlpools & rapids and all: the College has genuinely, it seems to me, avoided the tensions and divisions and suspicions and factions that other establishments seem prone to: & those who nevertheless claim to find or even try to create them seem to me a minute, negligible number: & even they, when met face to face, turn out to be very nice and well meaning if (slightly) confused. Am I being unduly complacent? I expect so. If so, you must put me right. Anyway I have been terribly happy: I have worked harder, experienced more transforming events, felt stronger emotions in other contexts, but never, never have I been happier, liked and respected more people, or simply felt surrounded by a warmer & sweeter human society. I must not go on. Only to say that I (& Aline) are, & always will be infinitely grateful to you for all kinds of things: that *I* am deeply grateful for your literally unforgettable letter: & that we *must* continue to collaborate – a source of great satisfaction to

    Yours

       Isaiah

* Well after midnight.

P. S. The musical "number"[1] was a *masterpiece*: save that I was never in "intelligence" – only "information" – much less grand

1 A setting of parts of IB's entry in *Who's Who* to the Papageno/Papagena duet from Mozart's *The Magic Flute*. Ruth Padel (b. 1946; Wolfson JRF, classics, 1973–81) sung Papagena, Henry Hardy Papageno, and Harry Fisher was at the piano. One of the lines was 'War service in Intelligence', which was indeed an error, subsequently corrected to 'War Service in the MOI': ⟨http://www. wolfson .ox.ac.uk/~hardy/ dugpubs/tunes/tmr/Track18.wma⟩.

APPENDICES

TAKING SIDES ON VIETNAM

An answer to two questions:

Are you for, or against, the intervention of the United States in Vietnam?
How, in your opinion, should the conflict in Vietnam be resolved?

I am still quite clear about what I felt in the middle 1930s – I was wholly pro-Spanish Republican, and remain so still. I wish I could be equally clear about Vietnam. I do not know how that war is to be ended. I think it was probably a terrible mistake on the part of the Americans to have sent troops there in the first place. I wish the Vietnamese had originally been left to settle the issue by and for themselves; unlike the Spanish situation, Vietnam seems to me to have called for genuine non-intervention. But I do not wish American withdrawal now to lead to – as it well might – a massacre of those who are or might be found (rightly or wrongly) to be American allies. It is frightful that Vietnamese villages should be bombed and the innocent continuously killed. But it seems to me even more dreadful to abandon people to massacre by their enemies. How is one to guarantee that this will not happen? Or that a precipitate and total American withdrawal would not cause other South-East Asian governments to be intimidated into knuckling under to regimes which many of their citizens would surely hate? We are often told that their existing regimes are no better and no more popular than any communist regime would be; but I am not convinced of this. To put people in a situation where they lose their liberty or change governments under alien pressure, because they are convinced that nobody will help them – to create a kind of terrorised joining of the bandwagon like that which took place in Central Europe in the last years of the 1930s – is something that no decent person could want. I do not know whether this parallel is valid; but I need convincing that it is not. I simply do not know enough about the situation in Vietnam to know whether the various courses advocated by, say, Walter Lippmann, or Senator Fulbright, or Professor Arthur Schlesinger, Jr – phased withdrawal, for instance, or enclaves, and the like – are feasible. If such courses as these are likely to prevent the two prospects that I have mentioned, and which it seems to me to be morally indefensible for us to urge, I should be very strongly indeed for them. But I do not know how practicable such a policy in fact would be. Still, even so, if I had to vote, I should vote for it.

Thus, I find myself in the unsatisfactory position of having to qualify my answer. I wish I could answer boldly and clearly, as most of my friends seem able to do, with an unconditional yes or no. In the Spanish question I felt, whether rightly or wrongly, no doubts at all. I feel none about the policies of South Africa, Rhodesia, Spain, Portugal; or about Budapest in 1956. I felt clear about the Korean War – the United Nations seem to me to have acted rightly. I envy those who feel as certain about Vietnam. The Americans have a bear by the tail, and their position is unenviable; and that quite apart from the question of prestige and the balance of world power; yet withdrawal without a negotiated settlement could lead to even more cruelty and suffering than that which it is intended to end. I am for whatever solution is likely to cause least destruction and oppression. I am not for a ruat coelum stand on some absolute principle: least of all for an ideological crusade, or arrogant or simple-minded insistence on importing our own methods or institutions into countries which have their own, perhaps quite different, traditions and aspirations.

I am only too well aware that this is not a very clear-cut answer to your question. But I feel sure that I am not alone in experiencing the perplexities which I have done my best to describe.

After these perplexities and qualifications, which remain with me, let me add this: apart from the small group who appear to share my doubts, I cannot help finding myself far closer to those who wish the war stopped at any price than to their adversaries. If I had to choose between the two extremes, I have no doubt which I should choose.

Cecil Woolf and John Bagguley (eds), Authors Take Sides on Vietnam *(New York, 1967: Simon and Schuster), [2], 20–1*

'FREEDOM AS POLITICS': POPULAR SUMMARY

BERNARD CRICK

A poetic recapitulation of Crick's 1966 inaugural lecture at Sheffield, 'Freedom as Politics', inspired by IB's Two Concepts of Liberty. *See also 271/2.*

> Pick a big one when, with academic sagacity,
> One attacks to hide one's own inadequacy;
> So, like Peachum to Lockitt, I abuse another
> Who is my craft-master and elder brother,
> No less than Professor Sir Isaiah Berlin
> Picked not for any irredeemable sin
> But for being, like a Liberal in love,
> Reluctant to go far enough,
> Sensing an impropriety in every call
> On freedom made by rough political.
> I pick no quarrel, just a bone over tea
> With one of the *Two Concepts of Liberty*.[1]
> In his inaugural lecture, Sir Isaiah,
> Oxford but modest, said that he'd require
> Positive and negative liberty well kept apart;
> If we must choose: the virgin, not the tart.
> Positive is wanting some one thing so bad
> That it drives German and Russian sages mad;
> This view of things has come to such a pass
> That zealot sees his leader in the looking glass,
> And if I look in and still see reflected stubborn me
> Then I must be freed from error, forced to be free.
> Freedom as choosing rightly opens the college door
> To everyone else's nineteen-eighty-four.
> Negative at least preserves me as myself
> Sitting down Don-like to a well-stocked shelf,
> Choosing wines, teas and coffees not quite at random
> But knowing *de gustibus non est disputandum*.
> Now this is all quite so and very very well,
> It saves me thinking heaven hell
> But leaves me with no clear end in view
> When restless Liberty demands 'What's there to do?'

1 Published at 5s. od by the Oxford University Press, at their more fancy Clarendon address.

Makes walking *Frau Welt* and *Femme Libre* home
Almost an objection in its own.
Berlin treads so judicious, nicely and precise
That he trips up, old lady-like on ice;
Liberty is surely not just taking care
But taking care at least to get somewhere.
Sartre and Hannah Arendt complexly say
That freedom is living through the day
And acting out in public view
Some play purporting to be new;
Is shaping, through some mutual pact,
Some hand-made thing which once we lacked.
Freedom is not just avoidance of the State,
Like some computerised blind date,
Nor just an angry affirmation of 'my will',
It's more like doing something meant to fill
The social gap between the loneliness of I
And groups of demonstrators in full cry;
Something lying naked in my sheets
And donning uniform to dominate the streets.
Freedom is painting it, but not quite knowing what
Will follow from each original job-lot;
But it is painting it, not just thinking around
Projects which never quite get off the ground.
Freedom is how she always mistreats me,
But neither enduring masochistically
Nor is it just how I can kick her back,
But simply how we interact.
Berlin has little answer for the rude
Who call our freedom just 'a breakfast food' –
And so it is, but Dr Bircher-Benner's Swiss Müesli
Which can sustain most needs of life quite nicely.
But don't measure politics by the aesthete,
I've no complaint at politicians cooking good red meat,
Just let's protect ourselves from those who want it raw
And fed our heart's blood, clamour then for more.

*

Freedom was Cicero and Pericles,
Not T. D. Weldon on his knees
Picking hairs off Oxford fleas.

Freedom was Lincoln, Lilburne and William Tell,
Not Goethe's doubting gentleman from hell
With the Don-like negative soft sell.

The modern sceptic's version of the Fall
Does not involve a tempter's stirring call
But simply not doing anything at all.

So ends my anti-Berlin for this day
In which – ungrateful wretch – I roundly say
That half-truths are just a kind of play.

Does cricket mean we always field?
And get the buttered foil to wield
Till left like Peer Gynt's opinion peeled?

Life is real and life is free
To choose and make creatively,
Is wakeful coffee and not sleeping tea.

Life is you and life is me
Conceiving the community
Interindependently.

CHRONOLOGY

The events listed are divided into two columns. In the first are events of biographical significance for IB, and also those related to Oxford University; in the second, world events, with a special focus on those treated in the letters. At the end of each year is a concise listing of IB's publications: full references are at ⟨http://berlin.wolf. ox.ac.uk/lists/bibliography/⟩. The entries may give some idea of how active IB was, though they cannot do justice to the fullness of his engagements diary, except perhaps for the periods when he was in Italy.

We have tried to give a continuous record of IB's movements, but some of the dates must be regarded as tentative, if only because he was likely to have been moving between locations. And 'Oxford' may include visits to London and elsewhere in Britain.

When IB visited Princeton it was generally under the auspices of the Institute for Advanced Study. When in Oxford his home address was Headington House, Old High Street, Headington, and his base in the University, until he became President of Wolfson in July 1966, was his room in All Souls.

1960

3 February (**IB aged 50**)		Harold Macmillan's 'wind of change' speech in Cape Town
5 March	Harold Macmillan elected Chancellor, Oxford	
21 March		Sharpeville massacre, South Africa: police fire on protestors, killing 69
5 May		USSR reveals the shooting down of US U-2 spy plane
23 May		Ben-Gurion announces that Israel holds Adolf Eichmann pending trial
29 June–3 July (**IB 51**)	Venice: conference marking 50th anniversary of Tolstoy's death	
30 June		Congo gains independence but quickly descends into prolonged civil war

5 July– 13 September	Villa Cipressina, Portofino, with a week in Venice, Salzburg and Verona (1–7 August)	
13 September– March 1961	Oxford	
2 November		Penguin Books acquitted in *Lady Chatterley's Lover* obscenity trial
3 November		Gaitskell elected Labour leader
8 November		John F. Kennedy narrowly defeats Richard M. Nixon in US Presidential election
23 November	PEN Hermon Ould Memorial Lecture, 'Tolstoy and Enlightenment', at Friends' House, London, broadcast on BBC Third Programme 7 January 1961, repeated 19 March, published in *Encounter* February 1961	
December	Accepts invitation to give the 1965 Mellon Lectures in Washington	Olga Ivinskaya, Pasternak's literary assistant, imprisoned in USSR

1960 publications

Introduction to Franco Venturi, *Roots of Revolution*
'History and Theory: The Concept of Scientific History' (*History and Theory*)
'Marx', in J. O. Urmson (ed.), *Concise Encyclopedia of Western Philosophy and Philosophers*
'The Philosophical Ideas of Giambattista Vico' (*Art and Ideas in Eighteenth-Century Italy*)
'No Earthly Paradise', review of Reinhold Niebuhr, *Nations and Empires* (*Guardian*)
Review of Richard Hare, *Portraits of Russian Personalities between Reform and Revolution* (*English Historical Review*)
Review of Henry Vyverberg, *Historical Pessimism in the French Enlightenment* (*French Studies*)
(with others) 'S. A. Boycott' (letter to *Isis*)

1961

3 January		USA breaks off diplomatic relations with Cuba
9 January		French referendum approves de Gaulle's plan for Algerian independence
c.22–3 February	Meets Soviet delegation to London under auspices of GB–USSR Association	

10–*c.*17 March	Nose operation at University College Hospital, London	
16 March		South Africa withdraws from Commonwealth
30 March–10 April	Nice: with Marie Berlin	
11 April	To Villa Cipressina, Portofino	Eichmann trial begins in Jerusalem
12 April		Soviet cosmonaut Major Yuri Gagarin first man in space
17–19 April		Bay of Pigs invasion, Cuba
19–24 April	Paris: Hôtel Ritz	
22 April		'Generals' putsch' in Algeria
24 April–14 July	Oxford	
5 May		Commander Alan B. Shepard first American in space
18 May–15 June	Debate on historical inevitability with E. H. Carr in *Listener*	
6 June (**IB 52**)	Recorded panel discussion on equality, 'In Search of a Definition': BBC Third Programme, 25 November, repeated 14 December	
10 July	Recorded panel discussion, 'Equality, Education and Culture': BBC Third Programme, 29 January 1962, repeated 23 February	
15–23 July	Geneva: presides at conference on Soviet historiography	
24–7 July	Turin	
27 July–4 September	Hotel Splendido, Portofino, then Albergo Argentina, Paraggi	
10 August		Britain applies for membership of EEC
13 August		Construction of Berlin Wall begins
4–21 September	Israel (via Rome) to attend Israel Music Festival; visits BG at Sde Boker	
18 September		Dag Hammarskjöld, UN Secretary General, killed in air crash in Northern Rhodesia

21 September– 7 November	Oxford: entertains the Stravinskys at Headington House in October, and suggests biblical story of Abraham and Isaac as libretto for a composition for Israel Festival	
c.8 November– 1 December	India: lectures in Delhi (13 November) on 'Rabindranath Tagore and the Consciousness of Nationality'; joined by Aline 16 November; visits to Kathmandu, Madras, Bombay etc.	
29 November	Talk for BBC All India Radio, 'The Philosophy of History'	
1 December	Oxford (to late March 1962)	
15 December		JFK renews American commitment to preserve independence of Vietnam

1961 publications

'La théorie politique existe-t-elle?' (*Revue française de science politique*); repr. as 'Does Political Theory Still Exist?' in Peter Laslett and W. G. Runciman (eds), *Philosophy, Politics and Society*, 2nd series

(unattributed) 'Research Institutions', chapter 9 of *Research in the Humanities and the Social Sciences: Report of a Survey by the British Academy 1958–1960*

'Tolstoy and Enlightenment', PEN Hermon Ould Memorial Lecture for 1960 (*Encounter*)

Review of Elie Kedourie, *Nationalism* (*Oxford Magazine*)

'What is History?' (exchange of letters with E. H. Carr), *Listener*

(with others) telegram to Ferenc Münnich, president of the Council of Ministers, Budapest, urging the release of István Bibó (quoted in *The Times*)

1962

10 January	Interview with Bamber Gascoigne on 'Freedom of Speech' for Associated Television (ATV), broadcast 11 February, published 2008 in *Romulus* (Wolfson College)	
19 March		Évian Accords on Algerian Independence
Before 23 March	Recorded panel discussion, 'Equality between People and Nations': BBC Third Programme, 30 March, repeated 15 April	
c.24 March– 26 April	Israel: meeting of HUJ Governors (27–9 March); joined by Aline and stepsons in early April	

Late April– c.30 July	Oxford	
31 May		Eichmann hanged
10 July (**IB 53**)		Telstar, the first telecommunications satellite, launched
Late July– c.12 September	Portofino/Paraggi	
c.12–17 September	Oxford	
c.17 September– January 1963	Harvard: Ford Visiting Research Professor till January 1963; joined by Aline in first week of November	
16 October	Washington: IB meets JFK at farewell party for the Bohlens	JFK told, with photographic evidence, of Soviet missile bases on Cuba
22 October		JFK's televised address to American nation on Cuban missile crisis
28 October		Nikita Khruschev agrees to remove missiles from Cuba
Early November	Dinner at the White House	
12–15 November	Storrs Lectures at Yale: 'Three Turning Points in Political Thought'	
30 November		U Thant appointed UN Secretary General

1962 publications

'The Biographical Facts', in Meyer W. Weisgal and Joel Carmichael (eds), *Chaim Weizmann: A Biography by Several Hands*

'The Purpose of Philosophy' (*Insight* [Nigeria]; repr. in *Sunday Times*)

'Mr Carr's Big Battalions', review of E. H. Carr, *What is History?* (*New Statesman*)

(Unattributed) 'The Road to Catastrophe', review of Hans Kohn, *The Mind of Germany*, and G. P. Gooch, *French Profiles: Prophets and Pioneers* (TLS)

1963

25 January– 7 April	Oxford	
14 January		De Gaulle effectively vetoes British entry into EEC
18 January		Death of Hugh Gaitskell

14 February		Harold Wilson elected Labour leader
7–14 April	Nice: with Marie Berlin	
14 April–25 July	Oxford (with a fortnight's stay in University College Hospital, London, beginning 17 April)	
4 June		John Profumo resigns over his affair with Christine Keeler
16 June (**IB 54**)	Dines at Buckingham Palace	
26 June		JFK: 'Ich bin ein Berliner'
1 July		'Kim' Philby revealed as the 'third man'
25 July–5 August	Israel: Jerusalem and Herzlia	
5 August–13 September	Albergo Argentina, Paraggi, with a visit to Venice (21–27 August)	
28 August		'I have a dream' speech by Martin Luther King, Jr, Washington
13 September–2 December	Oxford	
18 October		Harold Macmillan resigns; Alec Douglas-Home becomes Prime Minister next day
23 October	Publication of the Robbins Report on Higher Education	
22 November		JFK assassinated in Dallas; Lyndon Johnson becomes President
2 December–c.8 January 1964	California: visiting Commonwealth Fellows at Pacific Coast universities; joined by Aline early December; Christmas and New Year in NY	

1963 publications

Contribution to Clara Urquhart (ed.), *A Matter of Life*, on civil disobedience
'Historical Note', in *Khovanshchina* (ROH opera programme)
Contribution to 'Why Are These Books Neglected?' (*Twentieth Century*)
(With others) 'Dr Ranger's Expulsion' (letter to *The Times*)

1964

9 January– 15 April	Oxford	
1 February	'The Oxford Way', conversation with Alexander Kendrick, broadcast in US on CBS TV	
7 February		Beatles arrive in NY at start of their first US tour
28–9 February	Aline visits Marie Berlin in hospital in Jerusalem	
6 March	Lecture at St Andrews	
18 March	Oliver Franks named chairman of a commission of inquiry at Oxford	
26 March	Records *Conversations for Tomorrow* with J. B. Priestley and A. J. Ayer, broadcast by BBC TV 25 April	
27 March		UN Peacekeeping Force starts work in Cyprus
15–23 April	Princeton, Washington, Baltimore, NY	
24 April–*c.*3 May	Oxford	
*c.*3 / 4–15 May	Aegean cruise: visits Istanbul, Athens, Rhodes	
15 May–5 June	Oxford	
5 June–19 August	Portofino; visits Marie Berlin in London 9–*c.*15 July	
12 June (**IB 55**)		Rivonia trial, Pretoria: Nelson Mandela and 7 others sentenced to life imprisonment for sabotage
2 July		Lyndon Johnson signs the Civil Rights Bill
27 July		Additional 5,000 US military advisers sent to South Vietnam
19–24 August	Jerusalem: for world premiere of *Abraham and Isaac* (23 August)	
24 August– 7 September	Portofino	
7 September– early October	Oxford	

c.4 October	Stanford: lecture at Hoover Library, 'Marxism and the International in the Nineteenth Century', published in SR	
c.6 October– early January 1965	Oxford	
14 October		Martin Luther King, Jr, awarded Nobel Peace Prize
15 October		Leonid Brezhnev succeeds Khrushchev as Soviet leader; Labour wins British General Election with majority of 6 – Harold Wilson becomes Prime Minister
3 November		Lyndon Johnson wins US Presidential election

1964 publications

Contribution to *Meyer W. Weisgal*
'Felix Frankfurter at Oxford', in Wallace Mendelson (ed.), *Felix Frankfurter: A Tribute*
'From Hope and Fear Set Free', Presidential Address (*Proceedings of the Aristotelian Society*)
'Hobbes, Locke and Professor Macpherson', review of C. B. Macpherson, *The Political Theory of Possessive Individualism, Hobbes to Locke* (*Political Quarterly*)
'A Note on Nationalism' (*Forethought*)
'Portrait of Ben-Gurion', review of Maurice Edelman, *Ben-Gurion: A Political Biography* (*Jewish Chronicle*)
'Rationality of Value Judgments' (*Nomos*)
(in paraphrase) Contributions to John Keep and Liliana Brisby (eds), *Contemporary History in the Soviet Mirror*
'Olga Ivinskaya' (letter to the *Observer*)
Contribution to 'The Death of Lord Marks' (*Jewish Observer and Middle East Review*)

1965

c.4 January	Rome	
Early January– early March	Oxford	
24 January		Death of Sir Winston Churchill
11 February	Representatives of All Souls give evidence to Franks Commission	
2 March		Beginning of 'Operation Rolling Thunder', US strategic bombing of North Vietnam

12 March	Oxford announces creation of two graduate colleges, St Cross and Iffley	
Early March–late April	Washington, DC: gives the A. W. Mellon Lectures at the National Gallery of Art, Washington, 'Sources of Romantic Thought', 14 March–18 April, published 1999 as *The Roots of Romanticism*	
28 March		Five-day civil rights march led by Martin Luther King, Jr, arrives in State capital of Montgomery, Alabama, from Selma
12 April	Interviewed by Arthur Schlesinger, Jr, on JFK, for the John F. Kennedy Library Oral History Project	
Late April–mid-July	Oxford	
28 April	Proposes the toast to the Royal Academy at the Academy's annual dinner; broadcast that night on BBC Home Service	
14 May	Attends unveiling of Runnymede memorial to JFK	
6 June (**IB 56**)	Anna Akhmatova receives Hon. D.Litt. from Oxford	
28 June	Opening night of *Moses and Aaron* at ROH	
7 July	'The Concert Interval', interview broadcast on BBC Third Programme (lost)	
12–14 July	Paris	
c.14 July–early September	Paraggi, with visit to Verona via Venice c.5–7 August	
28 July		Lyndon Johnson commits a further 50,000 US troops to Vietnam; Edward Heath elected Conservative Party leader
9 August	'Kits' van Heyningen named as the first master of St Cross College; later suggests IB become head of Iffley College; IB declines	
c.9–16 September	Oxford	

*c.*17 September– *c.*12 January 1966	Visiting Professor at Princeton, joined by Aline late September; lectures elsewhere, including NY, Kentucky and Toronto	
22 September		UN Security Council unanimously resolves on an unconditional ceasefire in the Indo-Pakistan war that began in April
16–17 October		Demonstrations throughout US and in London against Vietnam war
c.25–8 October	Woodbridge Lectures, Columbia, 'Two Enemies of the Enlightenment' (Hamann and Maistre)	
November	Conditionally accepts offer to become head of Iffley College; secures conditional offer of funding from McGeorge Bundy, on behalf of the Ford Foundation	
9 November		Abolition of death penalty (for murder) in the UK (made permanent 1969)
11 November		Ian Smith announces Rhodesia's Unilateral Declaration of Independence
Christmas and New Year	Barbados (as guests of Ronnie Tree)	

1965 publications

Contribution to Julian Huxley (ed.), *Aldous Huxley*
Contribution to Ian Kemp (ed.), *Michael Tippett: A Symposium on his 60th Birthday*
'Herder and the Enlightenment', in Earl R. Wasserman (ed.), *Aspects of the Eighteenth Century*
(with H. L. A. Hart) 'Postgraduate Studies in Oxford', in *University of Oxford, Commission of Inquiry* (The Franks Commission)
'Sulla teoria del Vico circa la conoscenza storica' ('On Vico's theory of historical knowledge', *Lettere italiane*)
Review of C. P. Courtney, *Montesquieu and Burke* (*Modern Language Review*)
'A Great Russian Writer', review of Osip Mandelstam, *The Prose of Osip Mandelstam* (NYRB)
'The Thought of de Tocqueville', review of Jack Lively, *The Social and Political Thought of Alexis de Tocqueville* (*History*)

1966

*c.*12 January– mid-March	Oxford: discusses possible Wolfson Foundation funding for Iffley College with Leonard Wolfson

3 February		Soviets make first controlled landing of an unmanned probe, Luna 9, on the moon
14 February		Soviet writers Yuly Daniel and Andrey Sinyavsky sentenced to the Gulag for publishing their works in the West
*c.*19–25 March	Paraggi and Portofino	
25 March–*c.*4 April	Israel: on HUJ business	
31 March		British General Election: Labour gains 96-seat majority
*c.*4 April–19 July	Oxford	
12 May	Publication of the Franks Report	
2 June		US lands space probe Surveyor 1 on moon
27 June (**IB 57**)	Hebdomadal Council indicates support for IB's plans for Wolfson College	
20 July (to early September)	Paraggi, with a visit to Venice for a congress on Verdi (30 July–4 August)	
26 July	Congregation promulgates decree creating Wolfson College, with IB as its President	
10 August–12 September	IB's 1965 Mellon Lectures broadcast on BBC Third Programme, repeated 5 October–6 November 1967	
13 August		China announces a 'Cultural Revolution' and purge of capitalist influences
5–*c.*21 September	Oxford	
22 September–28 December	NY: Professor of Humanities at CUNY; interviewed in US by Henry Brandon – the interview appears, against IB's wishes, as 'My Hopes and Fears' in *Sunday Times*, 6 November	
28 December–6 January 1967	Barbados, visiting Ronald Tree	

1966 publications

Introduction to Marc Raeff (ed.), *Russian Intellectual History*
Preface to H. G. Schenk, *The Mind of the European Romantics*
'L. B. Namier: A Personal Impression', in Martin Gilbert (ed.), *A Century of Conflict, 1850–1950: Essays for A. J. P. Taylor*
(with Mary McCarthy and others) 'The Founders' (letter to *Time*)
'The Great Blood Libel Case', review of Maurice Samuel, *Blood Accusation: The Strange History of the Beiliss Case* (*Jewish Chronicle Literary Supplement*)
'New Ways in History' (letter to the TLS)

1967

6–13 January	New York	
13 January–19 March	Oxford	
3 February	Talks for Sixth Forms, 'The Romantic Movement in Europe', in 'Four Distinguished Men' series, broadcast on BBC Home Service	
9 March		Stalin's daughter, Svetlana Allilueva, defects to the West
19 March–18 April	CUNY	
18 April–*c.*9 June	Oxford	
16 May		De Gaulle vetoes Britain's second application to join the EEC (veto formally registered in December)
*c.*5 June	Powell & Moya chosen as architects for Wolfson College buildings	
5–10 June **(IB 58)**		Six-Day War between Israel and Egypt, Syria, Jordan, Lebanon and Iraq
10–12 June	Boston and New York: awarded Hon. Doctor of Laws from Brandeis University, Massachusetts	
*c.*12 June–early July	Oxford	
6/7 July		Beginnings of the Nigeria–Biafra war
Early July–mid-September	Paraggi; Aline taken ill, nursed in Italy	

14 July		Race riots in Newark, NJ, and later in Detroit and Washington
c.13 September–24 December	Oxford	
2 October		Britain's first Polaris nuclear submarine commissioned
20 October		'Stop the Draft' demonstration in Oakland, California
Late December and New Year	Jerusalem	

1967 publications

Foreword to G. L. Seidler, *The Emergence of the Eastern World: Seven Essays on Political Ideas*
Contribution to Cecil Woolf and John Bagguley (eds), *Authors Take Sides on Vietnam*
(with others) 'Issues Behind the Oxford Fund' (letter to *The Times*)
(with others) 'Victor Gollancz' (letter to *The Times*)

1968

10 January–late February	Oxford	
30 January		Communist Tet Offensive in Vietnam: US embassy in Saigon occupied
Late February–3 March	CUNY	
4 March–4 April	Oxford	
14 March	'The Role of the Intelligentsia', talk to the Annual Conference of the University Teachers' Group, broadcast 23 April, repeated 11 August, published in *Listener* 2 May	
4–11 April	Paraggi	Martin Luther King assassinated in Memphis, Tennessee, on 4 April
11 April–5 May	Oxford	
2 May	The Queen lays foundation stone of Wolfson College	Sorbonne University closed after violent battles between student protestors and police in Paris
5–c.12 May	NY, Princeton	

13 May–early June	Oxford	
5 June		Senator Robert Kennedy fatally shot in Los Angeles
Early June	NY: Columbia University Commencement	
6 June–26 July (**IB 59**)	Oxford	
Late July– *c.*20 September	Paraggi	
20/21 August		Russian, East German and Polish forces invade Czechoslovakia, bringing an end to the 'Prague Spring'
20 September– late December	Oxford	
5 October		Civil rights march in Londonderry, Northern Ireland, ends in violence
17 October		Two black American athletes stage silent protest during medal ceremony at Mexico Olympics
*c.*23 October	Records 'Verdi and Schiller', broadcast on BBC Third Programme 11 January 1969, repeated 21 February 1969, published 1968 as 'The "Naivety" of Verdi' in *Hudson Review*	
6 November		Richard Nixon wins US presidential election
Late December– early January 1969	Jerusalem	

1968 publications

Introduction to Alexander Herzen, *My Past and Thoughts: The Memoirs of Alexander Herzen*
Comment on Richard Pipes, 'The Origins of Bolshevism: The Intellectual Evolution of Young Lenin', in Richard Pipes (ed.), *Revolutionary Russia*
'The "Naivety" of Verdi' (*Hudson Review*)
'The Role of the Intelligentsia' (*Listener*)
Contribution to 'Books of the Year: A Personal Choice' (*Observer*)

1969

Early January– mid-February	Oxford	

24 January	LSE temporarily closes after violent student protests
13 February– c.11 May	CUNY: also lectured at Harvard and in North Carolina; visited Dartmouth
17 March	Golda Meir becomes Israel's first female Prime Minister
2 May	Student sit-in at Columbia ends as authorities begin crackdown on campus protests
c.11 May–late July (**IB 60**)	Oxford
20/21 July	Apollo 11 moon landing: Neil Armstrong becomes first man to walk on moon (21 July)
Late July– c.13 Sept.	Paraggi (with 'a terrific performance' of Don Carlos in Verona)
14 August	British troops sent to Northern Ireland after sectarian violence
13–late September	Oxford
Late September	Italy: conference on Machiavelli
Late September –22 March 1970	Oxford
5 November	Anti-apartheid demonstrations at the Springboks' match against Oxford at Twickenham

1969 publications

Four Essays on Liberty

Foreword to Michael Yudkin (ed.), *General Education: A Symposium on the Teaching of Non-Specialists*

'The Hazards of Social Revolution', in Aaron W. Warner, Dean Morse and Thomas E. Cooney (eds), *The Environment of Change*

'A Note on Vico's Concept of Knowledge', in Giorgio Tagliacozzo and Hayden V. White (eds), *Giambattista Vico: An International Symposium*

'One of the Boldest Innovators in the History of Human Thought' (Vico; *New York Times Magazine*)

'Reply to Orsini' (*Journal of the History of Ideas*)

1970

22 March–c.9 April	NY, CUNY, Princeton; Columbus, Ohio; Ann Arbor, Michigan

*c.*9 April–early August	Oxford	
4 May		4 students shot dead at Kent State University, Ohio, by National Guard during anti-war demonstrations
18 June (**IB 61**)		British General Election: Conservatives returned with overall majority of 30; Edward Heath becomes Prime Minister
Early–20 August	Paraggi, with a visit to the spa at Abano Terme, Padua	
20–4 August	Oxford	
24 August– 21 September	Paraggi	
6 September		Four airliners hijacked by Palestinian terrorists; 3 planes later blown up at an airfield in Jordan
21 September– mid-February 1971	Oxford	
8 October		Nobel Prize in Literature awarded to Alexander Solzhenitsyn
9 November		Death of Charles de Gaulle
12 November	Delivers Romanes Lecture, Oxford, 'Fathers and Children: Turgenev and the Liberal Predicament', broadcast on BBC Radio 3, 14 February 1971, repeated 5 September, published 1972	

1970 publications

Foreword to R. D. Miller, *Schiller and the Ideal of Freedom: A Study of Schiller's Philosophical Works with Chapters on Kant*

'Benjamin Disraeli, Karl Marx, and the Search for Identity', in *Transactions of the Jewish Historical Society of England*

'Weizmann as Exilarch', in *Chaim Weizmann as Leader*

1971

6 February	First British soldier killed on duty in Northern Ireland 'Troubles'

17 February–early May	NY, Seattle, Vancouver	
c.7–14 April	Visits Marie Berlin in London	
14 April–early May	Returns to New York (without Aline)	
Early May–25 June	Oxford	
27 May	Order of Merit announced by Buckingham Palace	Egypt and USSR sign treaty of friendship and co-operation
25 June–1 July (**IB 62**)	Paraggi	
2–10 July	Israel	
10 July–7 September	Paraggi; returns to Oxford for Maurice Bowra's memorial service (17 July) and visits Abano Terme, Padua (14–24 August)	
8–17 September	Nicosia, Cyprus: conference on 'Human Nature and Ideology'	
c.18 September–late December	Oxford	
25 October		UN votes to admit China, which takes its seat on 15 November
late December–c.New Year	Jerusalem and Tel-Aviv	
16 December		Indo-Pakistan war ends with surrender of Pakistan's eastern command, leading to emergence of independent Bangladesh
31 December		U Thant resigns as UN Secretary General; succeeded by Kurt Waldheim

1971 publications

Sir Maurice Bowra, 1898–1971
'Georges Sorel' (TLS)
'The Question of Machiavelli' (NYRB)
'Randolph', in Kay Halle (ed.), *Randolph Churchill: The Young Unpretender*
'Tchaikovsky and Eugene Onegin', *Glyndebourne Festival Programme Book 1971*
(with others) 'George Seferis' (letter to the NYRB)
'Sir Isaiah Berlin OM replies to a letter from the Editor' (*Jewish Chronicle*)

1972

Early– c. 12 January	Paraggi via Rome	
9 January		British coal miners stage first national strike in over 40 years
12 January– 5 March	Oxford	
22 January		Edward Heath signs treaty admitting Britain to the EEC
25 January	'The Roots of Romanticism', interview for Open University course on 'The Age of Revolutions', broadcast on BBC Radio 4 (Open University) 16 October, repeated 21 October (and annually thereafter)	
30 January		'Bloody Sunday': 13 demonstrators killed by British troops in Londonderry
21 February		Richard Nixon becomes first US President to visit the People's Republic of China
5–22 March	India and Iran: gives first Humayun Kabir Memorial Lecture in Delhi, published in SR as 'Kant as an Unfamiliar Source of Nationalism'	
22 March– August	Oxford	
23 March	Attends award of Hon. DCL to Leonard Wolfson at Oxford	
13 April	Resigns from Old Pauline Club over St Paul's imposition of a quota on non-Christian admissions	
19 April	Records 'Giambattista Vico: Man of Genius', broadcast on BBC Radio 3, 25 September, repeated 29 November, published in the *Listener* 28 September	
22 May		Richard Nixon becomes first US president to visit Moscow

26 May		SALT 1 treaty on nuclear arms signed by US and USSR
17 June **(IB 63)**		Break-in at Democratic Party headquarters at Watergate complex in Washington
August–late September	Paraggi, with a week at Abano Terme, Padua, towards end of August	
5/6 September		11 members of Israeli team at Munich Olympics killed by Palestinian terrorists
Late September/ early October	Israel: delivers inaugural Yaacov Herzog Memorial Lecture, 'Zionist Politics in Wartime Washington', 2 October	
Early October– February 1973	Oxford	
6 November	Records 'The Problem of Nationalism', dialogue with Stuart Hampshire chaired by Bryan Magee, broadcast 30 November by ITV (Thames Television)	
7 November		Richard Nixon wins US Presidential election
19 December		Crew of Apollo 17, the last mission of the Apollo moon programme, return to earth

1972 publications

Fathers and Children: Turgenev and the Liberal Predicament
Zionist Politics in Wartime Washington: A Fragment of Personal Reminiscence
Foreword to Friedrich Meinecke, *Historism: The Rise of a New Historical Outlook*
'The Bent Twig: A Note on Nationalism' (*Foreign Affairs*)
'Dr Jacob Herzog' (*Jewish Chronicle*)
'Giambattista Vico' (*Listener*)
'History As We Would Like It' (*Worldview*)
'Sorel' (letter to the TLS)
(with others) 'In Memory of Cecil Roth' (letter to the *Jewish Chronicle*)
(with Kenneth Burke) 'An Exchange on Machiavelli' (letters to the NYRB)
'I Love Zionism' (letter to *Ha'aretz*)

1973

1 January	Britain, Ireland and Denmark become members of the EEC

*c.*9–25 February	Princeton: visit curtailed by Marie Berlin's ill health; gives 3 Gauss Seminars on 'The Origins of Cultural History', 19–22 February	
Late February–20 May	Oxford	
20–3 May	Switzerland	
23–30 May	Oxford	
30 May–4 June	Israel: receives honorary doctorate from University of Tel-Aviv (3 June)	
5 June– July **(IB 64)**	Oxford	
27 June		President Nixon vetoes bill to end the bombing of Cambodia
July–17 September	Paraggi	
10 August	'Tolstoy's View of Art and Morality', talk for Open University course on 'The Nineteenth-Century Novel and Its Legacy', broadcast on BBC Radio 4 (Open University), repeated 11 August (and annually thereafter)	
17 September–late December	Oxford	
6 October		Yom Kippur War begins with Egyptian and Syrian attacks on Israel
17 October		Eleven Arab States announce reduction in oil production until Israel withdraws from occupied territories, precipitating an oil crisis
22 October		UN ceasefire resolution accepted by warring parties, but fighting continues
13 November		State of emergency declared in Britain: conservation of fuel supplies, with '3-day week' 1 January–4 March 1974
14 December	Records 'The Russian Preoccupation with History', broadcast by BBC Radio 3 on 24 July 1974, repeated 17 March 1975, and by Australian Broadcasting Corporation 29 October 1975	

17 December		Government introduces further austerity measures, with cuts in public spending and increases in taxation
21 December		Middle East peace conference opens in Geneva
Late December– early January 1974	Israel	

1973 publications

'Austin and the Early Beginnings of Oxford Philosophy', in *Essays on J. L. Austin*
'The Counter-Enlightenment', in *Dictionary of the History of Ideas*
'A Nation Among Nations' (*Jewish Chronicle Colour Magazine*)
'Notes on the Foundation of Wolfson College' (*Lycidas*)
'Mr Hamilton Fish Armstrong' (*The Times*)
'Fathers and Children' (letter to the TLS)
Contribution to 'Books of the Year' (*Observer*)

1974

Early January–13 March	Oxford	
13 February	Death of Marie Berlin after long illness	Alexander Solzhenitsyn expelled from the Soviet Union
28 February		British General Election results in hung Parliament; Harold Wilson becomes Prime Minister in minority Labour government (4 March)
13–23 March	Chicago, New York, Washington	
c.23 March– 18 May	Oxford	
10 April		Golda Meir announces her resignation as Prime Minister of Israel; succeeded by Itzhak Rabin
24 April	Records 'Byron: Poet or Myth', panel discussion, broadcast by BBC Radio 3 on 5 May	
From c.18 May	Zurich	
May–July/ August	Oxford	

9 May	Records 'Equality, Liberty and Variety', dialogue with Jon Vaizey in the series 'Whatever Happened to Equality?', broadcast by BBC Radio 3 on 19 June, repeated 23 December	
July/August– 8 September (**IB 65**)	Paraggi	
10 July	Elected President of the British Academy at its Annual Meeting (served until 29 June 1978)	
9 August		Richard Nixon resigns the presidency as he faces impeachment over Watergate; succeeded by Gerald Ford
8–14 September	Venice: lecture at Fondazione Cini (10 September)	
c.14 September– late December	Oxford	
1 October	Records contribution to 'Man of Action' radio series, broadcast by BBC Radio 3 on 12 October, repeated 11 September 1976	
10 October		British General Election: Labour returned with overall majority of 3; Harold Wilson becomes Prime Minister
12 November	Official opening of Wolfson College's new buildings by the Chancellor of the University, Harold Macmillan	
21 November		Birmingham pub bombings by Irish Republican terrorists
13 December		Inflation 18.3 per cent
20 December	Rostropovich plays at Wolfson; proceeds to help found College Music Society	
Late December– New Year 1975	Israel	

1974 publications

The Divorce between the Sciences and the Humanities, 2nd Tykociner Memorial Lecture
'The Senate Foreign Relations Committee' (1943), in Thomas E. Hachey (ed.), 'American

Profiles on Capitol Hill: A Confidential Study for the British Foreign Office in
    1943' (*Wisconsin Magazine of History*)
Contribution to *Arthur Lehning in 1974*
'Mr C. E. Bohlen: Close Study of Soviet Leaders' (*The Times*)
'Mr Raimund von Hofmannsthal' (*The Times*)
Contribution to 'From Missolonghi to Apsley House – A Reappraisal of Byron' (*Listener*)
Contribution to 'I Remember, I Remember' (TLS)
Excerpt from 'The Russian Preoccupation with History', in 'Out of the Year' (*Listener*)

1975

Early January– end of April	Oxford	
11 February		Conservative Party elects Margaret Thatcher as its first woman leader
13 February		British mineworkers' leaders accept a pay offer of up to 35 per cent to end strike
15 March	Retires as President of Wolfson	

1975 publications

John Petrov Plamenatz, 1912–1975
Foreword (on Avraham Harman) to Dov Noy and Issachar Ben-Ami (eds), *Studies in the
    Cultural Life of the Jews in England*
'L'apoteosi della volontà romantica: la rivolta contro il tipo di un mondo ideale' ('The
    apotheosis of the Romantic will: the revolt against the notion of an ideal world', *Lettere
    italiane*)
'Performances Memorable and Not So Memorable' (*Opera*)
Presidential Address to the Aristotelian Society (*Proceedings of the British Academy*)
Speech at the Official Opening of Wolfson College, Oxford (*Lycidas*)
Two contributions (the first unattributed) on John Wheeler-Bennett (*The Times*)
(with others) 'Writers and the Closed Shop' (letter to the TLS)

SELECT BIOGRAPHICAL GLOSSARY

These notes on some important and/or frequently mentioned dramatis personae include rather more information than is appropriate in a footnote. The existence of these supplementary notes is flagged by asterisks attached to the relevant surnames on their first occurrence in a footnote, and in the index, thus: Isaiah *Berlin. As in the footnotes, coverage concentrates mainly on the period covered by the present volume; inclusion in the equivalent lists in earlier volumes is indicated at the end of the relevant entries.

Abramsky, Chimen (1916–2010), historian, bibliographer and book collector. Born in Minsk, the son of an internationally renowned Orthodox rabbinic scholar who left Russia for exile in Britain in 1932, Abramsky received little formal schooling, but in 1935 joined the HUJ, studying history and philosophy, and became an authority on Marx. He was a Communist Party member 1941–58. Stranded in England at the outbreak of the Second World War, he entered the book trade, but later, with the backing of IB and James Joll, pursued an academic career, becoming Senior Fellow at St Antony's 1965; he was Lecturer in Modern Jewish History, UCL, 1966–9, Reader 1969–74 and Goldsmid Professor of Hebrew and Jewish Studies 1974–83. He remained a bibilophile during his academic career, specialising in antiquarian Hebrew texts and manuscripts, and rare books on socialism and political theory, and was for many years a consultant to Sotheby's, a role which enabled him to forestall the sale by the firm on 3/4 June 1980 of some letters from famous correspondents, stolen from IB's room in All Souls: they were listed in the catalogue, but withdrawn from the sale.

Alsop, Joseph Wright ('Joe') (1910–89), newspaper columnist and commentator on foreign affairs. Alsop belonged to an old-established Connecticut family: his mother, Corinne Douglas Alsop (1886–1971) née Robinson, later Cole, was the niece of President Theodore Roosevelt, and the cousin of both Eleanor Roosevelt and Alice Longworth. Alsop wrote an influential and long-running newspaper column, 'Matter of Fact' (co-authored until 1958 by his younger brother Stewart), syndicated by the *New York Herald Tribune*, 1945–74. In spite of his family's traditional Republicanism he was an early backer of John F. Kennedy's successful 1960 presidential bid, and, in IB's phrase, was one of the devoted 'marshals' who afterwards gathered around the new Napoleon: 'not followed but very well liked – ear tweaked quite often' (to Gladwyn Gladwyn, 12 November 1962). Alsop was fiercely anti-Communist, and unwavering in his support for American intervention in Vietnam, which ultimately lost him influence. A closet homosexual subjected in 1957 to a blackmail attempt by the KGB, in 1961 he married the famed Washington political hostess Susan Mary Patten (1918–2004) née Jay, widow of Alsop's close friend the diplomat William S. Patten, Jr.; the Alsops divorced in 1973. 'As for dear Joe Alsop, those splendid bass notes pealed out more finely than ever – the sardonic laughter like Mephistopheles in the more simple-minded operas that involve him, followed by tremendous "Ah"s, which go on for two or three minutes, and end in nothing more informative than one's own Christian name' (to Gladwyn Gladwyn, 18 October 1974). L1 703, L2 786.

Annan, Noel Gilroy (1916–2000), life peer 1965; historian and college head. After wartime service in military intelligence Annan returned as a Fellow to King's, Cambridge, where he had been an undergraduate; he was Provost of King's 1956–66; Provost of UCL 1966–78; and Vice-Chancellor, London, 1978–81; he was also a director of the ROH 1967–78. Annan shared IB's interest in the history of ideas, and wrote a biography of the writer and literary critic Leslie Stephen, father of Virginia Woolf. Recommending Annan to Robert Oppenheimer for a visiting fellowship at Princeton in 1962, IB wrote: 'About him and his work I am sure you know: he was the appointed heir and Dauphin of Bloomsbury, Keynes performed some kind of laying on of hands, and the Book of Leslie Stephen was the formal offering on that particular altar. Since then he has been a most energetic Provost of his College, a university reformer, a chairman of some sort of government committee on the teaching of Russian, an appointer to vice-chancellorships in new universities, etc. etc., and is a man of great ability, and half-American to boot' (to Robert Oppenheimer, 4 December 1962).

Ayer, Alfred Jules ('Freddie') (1910–89), Kt 1970, philosopher. After reading classics at Christ Church 1928–32, Ayer lectured in philosophy at Wadham; he was Grote Professor of the Philosophy of Mind and Logic, London, 1946–59, and Wykeham Professor of Logic and Fellow of New College 1959–78; his *Language, Truth and Logic* (1936) 'scandalised established philosophy', but nevertheless permeated pre-war Oxford, principally through the discussion group of younger dons that met in IB's rooms in All Souls (Richard Wollheim, ODNB). Ayer married: (i) 1932 Renée Orde-Lees (q.v.) – they divorced in 1941; (ii) 1960 Alberta Constance ('Dee') Wells (1925–2003) née Chapman, journalist, novelist and broadcaster. L1 703, L2 786.   → Hampshire, S

Ben-Gurion, David (1886–1973) né David Gruen, statesman. Born in Płońsk in Poland, the son of a secular Zionist, he was involved in the socialist Poalei Zion party; he emigrated to Palestine 1906, taking the Hebrew name Ben-Gurion, became one of the leaders of the Jewish labour movement, and was central both to Histadrut (the General Federation of Labour) and Mapai, the Workers' Party. In 1935 he became chair of the Zionist Executive and of the Jewish Agency for Palestine, and thus effective head of the Yishuv. He led Zionist resistance to the British Mandate after the Second World War, overseeing the establishment of the State of Israel in May 1948, and securing it against the Arab attacks that ensued. He was Prime Minister of Israel 1948–53; then resigned, and retired to Sde Boker, a kibbutz in the northern Negev; returned as Prime Minister 1955–63, abruptly retiring again to Sde Boker; came out of retirement to lead the break-away RAFI (Israel Workers' List) party 1965–7, but resigned his Knesset seat in 1970. He died at Sde Boker, 1 December 1973.

Berenson, Bernard (1865–1959) né Bernhard Valvrojenski; art historian, collector, and authority on the Italian Renaissance. Born in Lithuania to Jewish parents who emigrated to the United States, Berenson converted to Christianity, becoming an Episcopalian, and later, in Italy, a Catholic. He attended Harvard and studied in Europe before settling in Italy. He acquired considerable wealth from the commissions charged on advice to collectors buying Renaissance art, and in 1907 bought the villa I Tatti in Settignano, outside Florence, where he lived until his death; there Berenson assembled an unparalleled collection of books, photographs and works of art, which he bequeathed to Harvard, along with the villa itself, as a centre for Italian Renaissance studies. L2 787.

Berlin, Aline Elisabeth Yvonne (b. 1915), daughter of Baron Pierre de Gunzbourg, a Russian-born banker who had settled in Paris, and Yvonne Deutsch de la Meurthe, the daughter of a French-Jewish industrialist. Aline married: (i) 1934 André Strauss (1903–39), son of the art collector Jules Strauss; they had one son, Michel Strauss (q.v.); (ii) 1943 Hans Halban (q.v.); they had two sons, Peter and Philippe Halban (qq.v.); they divorced in 1955; (iii) 1956 Isaiah Berlin (q.v.). Marriage to Aline provided IB with a deep sense of stability and contentment, embodied in the family home – Headington House – where the Berlins lived in Oxford. She encouraged him to accept the headship of Iffley College in November–December 1965, and took a keen interest in the evolution, design and development of Wolfson College, becoming a committed and involved 'first lady'; the College's first rowing eight was named the *Aline* in her honour. As one of the directors of the Ritz Hotel in Paris, 1948–79, she was involved in planning its renovation in 1961. L2 792 (s.v. Halban).

Berlin, Isaiah (1909–97), born in Riga on 6 June 1909; educated at St Paul's School, London, 1922–8; CCC, 1928–32, gaining first class honours in classics 1931, and in PPE 1932; Prize Fellow, All Souls, 1932–8; Lecturer in Philosophy, New College, 1932–8, Fellow 1938–50; war service with Ministry of Information in New York 1941–2, at British Embassies in Washington, 1942–6, Moscow, September 1945 to January 1946; All Souls, 1950–67 (Robertson Research Fellow 1950–7, Chichele Professor of Social and Political Theory 1957–67); President, Wolfson College, Oxford, 1966–75; Professor of Humanities, CUNY, 1966–71; Vice-President of the British Academy 1959–61, President 1974–8.

Honorary posts: Director, ROH, Covent Garden, 1954–65, 1974–87; President of the Aristotelian Society 1963–64; Academic Advisory Committee, University of Sussex, 1963–6; Committee of Awards for the Commonwealth (Harkness) Fellowships 1960–64, Kennedy Scholarships 1967–79, Trustee, Humanitarian Trust; member of editorial board, Letters and Papers of Chaim Weizmann.

Visiting professorships: Harvard 1962; Princeton 1965.

Lectures: A. W. Mellon Lectures in the Fine Arts, National Gallery of Art, Washington, DC, 1965; Danz Lectures, Washington University, 1971.

Honorary fellowships: CCC 1967; Wolfson, Cambridge, 1974; Wolfson, Oxford, 1975.

Honorary doctorates: Hull 1965; Glasgow 1967; East Anglia 1967; Brandeis 1967; Columbia 1968; Cambridge 1970; London 1971; Jerusalem 1971; Liverpool 1972; Tel Aviv 1973.

Publications include: Four Essays on Liberty (1969), *Fathers and Children: Turgenev and the Liberal Predicament* (1972), *Zionist Politics in Wartime Washington: A Fragment of Personal Reminiscence* (1972).

IB married, 1956, Aline Halban (*see* Berlin, Aline). He was knighted in 1957, appointed OM in 1971, but declined a peerage in 1979. L1 704, L2 787–8.

Berlin, (Mussa) Marie (*c.*1880–1974) née Volshonok ('Wolfson'), IB's mother, first cousin of her husband Mendel. Writing to Stuart Hampshire soon after her death in 1974 IB acknowledged her influence in shaping his character: 'I suppose I do owe my Judaeocentricity [...] & Russian-Jewish cultural roots, to her: my father had none of that' (23 February 1974). He was perhaps a more dutiful son than he then allowed – 'I am ashamed of the legend of what a devoted son I was: the truth is different' (ibid.) – but was always keenly aware that he did not visit his mother often enough, or show her enough patience when he was with her. Writing to Shirley Anglesey, in anticipation of a visit to Nice with Marie at Easter 1961, he observed: 'I am very attached to my mother whose vitality is undiminished. But the tedium of being alone with her for 10 days can be great – you know, surely, what it is like to be fond of, genuinely devoted to, delighted at the idea of being with, someone, & yet go through agonizing *ennui*?' L1 704, L2 788.

Berlin, Mendel (1884–1953), timber and bristle trader, IB's father. Depicted by IB as 'a gentle, intelligent, timid man ruled by his emotional and domineering wife' (MI 13), Mendel was not the fixture in his son's life that Marie Berlin was: 'I loved my father, but although I felt terribly sad, his death did not sweep away my past; my mother's death has broken a vital link' (to Walter Eytan, 26 April 1974). It was nevertheless through Mendel's foresight that the family escaped post-Revolutionary Russia, and through his industry that they had the means to start afresh in England; and his gifts to his son included sending him to St Paul's, even after he had failed to win the expected scholarship there. He wrote an autobiographical memoir published as 'For the Benefit of My Son' in BI. L1 704–5, L2 788.

Bohlen, Charles Eustis ('Chip') (1904–74), US diplomat and Soviet specialist. With a degree in European history from Harvard, and distant family ties linking him to the steel-producing Krupp family, Bohlen was 'much the "European" American' (*The Times*, 3 January 1974, 14e). After joining the foreign service in 1929 he was specially selected to study Russian, in advance of the official recognition of the Soviet Union by the US, and his diplomatic career was punctuated by regular spells in Moscow. From 1943 he was Roosevelt's liaison officer with the US State Dept, an arrangement extended for a time under Truman, and he later served as US ambassador to the Soviet Union 1953–7, to the Philippines 1957–9, and to France 1962–8 – the latter appointment reflecting President Kennedy's great confidence in his diplomatic skills at a time of 'almost obsessive anti-Americanism in Gaullist policies' (ibid.). In 1935 Bohlen married Avis Howard Thayer (1912–81), whom he met when she was visiting her brother, a junior diplomat, at the US Embassy in Moscow in 1934. L2 788.

Bowra, (Cecil) Maurice (1898–1971), Kt 1951; classicist, Warden of Wadham 1938–70. Bowra arrived at Oxford after serving with the Royal Field Artillery during the First World War 1917–18, and remained there for the rest of his life, much the greater part of it spent as Warden of Wadham: 'The College became the only permanent home he ever knew. It was also a community he transformed, a court he ruled, and a forum in which he established a national reputation. His ideas about the purpose of a university could not have been clearer. He saw an ongoing struggle between those who loved life and those who were interested only in undermining its wonderful possibilities. Jokingly, he declared himself "anti-prig, anti-elitist, anti-solemn, anti-Balliol" ' (L. G. Mitchell, ODNB). Bowra was a powerful and positive influence on many young lives at Oxford, notably IB's, and a 'very deep and lifelong' friendship resulted, even though towards the end – as IB put it – 'I did love him much more [...] than I respected him' (to Noel Annan, 31 August 1973). L1 705–6, L2 789.

Brock, Michael George (b. 1920), historian, educationalist and college head; Fellow and Tutor in Modern History and Politics, CCC, 1950–66, and University Lecturer 1951–70; Vice-President and Bursar, Wolfson, 1967–76; Professor of Education and Director, School of Education, Exeter, 1977–78; Warden of Nuffield College, 1978–88; author of *The Great Reform Act* (1973). In order to realise his plans for his college-in-the-making, IB sought in the summer of 1966 a 'general manager' who would run operations on the ground. This required industry, tact, an intimate knowledge of the workings of the University, and, most importantly from IB's perspective, a sense of humour, and in July 1966 he wrote to inform Leonard Wolfson that he had found his 'College builder': 'my college unanimously elected (remember, we are a democracy) a very excellent man called Michael Brock [...] a very able, tenacious, strong-willed character, conscientious and honourable and dedicated – I have great respect and liking for him. Although you may find him exaggeratedly academic, do not let his unassuming appearance deceive you!' (to Leonard Wolfson, 13 July 1966). Married 1949 Eleanor Hope Brock (b. 1921) née Morrison; LMH English 1940–3; Admiralty Secretariat, Whitehall, 1943–5; schoolteacher in Scotland 1945–9; three sons.

Bullock, Alan Louis Charles (1914–2004), Kt 1972, life peer 1976, historian, founding Master of St Catherine's 1960–80. Bullock and IB had overlapped in the senior common room of New College, where Bullock was Fellow and Tutor in Modern History 1945–52; during this time Bullock wrote his influential *Hitler: A Study in Tyranny* (1952); he left New College to become Censor (i.e. head) of the St Catherine's Society, which he transformed into a full college – complete with radical architecture and an emphasis on the sciences – and his example was one that IB kept in mind as he approached the task of building Wolfson. At IB's request, Bullock became a member of the trust that oversaw the creation and early running of the College, and in time he became one of the trustees of the Wolfson Foundation itself. He was the University's first full-time Vice-Chancellor 1969–73, a post that proved especially challenging during a period of student unrest. He relished fund-raising – the thrill of the chase – and in 1990 secured the initial funding for the editorial and publishing project of which the present volume forms the penultimate part.

Bundy, McGeorge ('Mac') (1919–96), national security adviser, academic and administrator. Bundy became dean of faculty at Harvard, where he had previously been an associate professor of government, when he was only 34, and his tenure, 1953–61, was by common consent a dramatic success. It led to his being chosen by President Kennedy as his 'Special Assistant [...] for National Security Affairs' in 1961, despite his family's traditional Republicanism. Bundy was centrally involved in all the major foreign policy episodes of the day, including the Bay of Pigs invasion and the Cuban missile crisis, but it is for his advocacy of American intervention in Vietnam that he is most remembered: although he left government relatively early in the war he was nevertheless one of its 'primary architects and defenders' (Richard Holbrooke, review of *The Doves Were Right*, *New York Times*, 28 November 2008, B12). Bundy was an 'action-intellectual' (136/4) – one of 'the best and the brightest' (the sardonic title of David Halberstam's damning 1972 indictment of the policymakers behind the Vietnam war), and his portrait adorned the cover of *Time* magazine in June 1965. In December of that year, however, he abruptly left government, following a disagreement with President Johnson, and became President of the Ford Foundation 1966–79. It was at this opportune moment that IB approached him about funding for Wolfson College, and without Bundy's personal support the venture could hardly have succeeded. They probably became acquainted some time in the first half of 1949, either at Harvard, where they were both visiting lecturers, or in Washington, where they had mutual friends.

Burdon-Muller, Rowland (1891–1980), connoisseur of the arts; educated at Eton and at Oriel, where he studied English and French. Burdon-Muller worked as a volunteer in a French military hospital during the First World War, and in 1924 moved to the US, where he established himself as an interior designer, and lived in Boston with the art collector Charles Bain Hoyt (1889–1949) (they also shared houses in Switzerland and Maine). In early 1972 Burdon-Muller moved to the luxurious Beau-Rivage Palace hotel in Lausanne, where he was given clean sheets every day. Both men made significant gifts of art to museums. While not agreeing with Burdon-Muller's radical politics, always trenchantly expressed, IB valued his commentary on current affairs: 'My letters from Burdon-Muller on the subject of [Senator] Goldwater are the most splendid philippics since the original *Philippics*, and far grander than anything Cicero or Zola ever attempted. They really are very fine' (to Arthur Schlesinger, 23 September 1964). 'I am devoted to him', he wrote to Mary McCarthy: 'he is the last witness of his age and always knew much older people than himself, even in 1910. The story of his relations with Proust is marvellous' (7 August 1964). L2 789.   *pl.* 9

Carr, Edward Hallett ('E. H.') (1892–1982), historian and diplomat. Carr entered the Foreign Office during the First World War, having been declared unfit for military service, and was appointed second secretary at HM Legation in Riga 1925–9; there he mastered Russian, and on his return to England produced biographies of Dostoevsky, Herzen and his circle, and Bakunin. His increasingly academic interests, which focused on Russian industrialisation and German politics, caused him to leave the Foreign Office for a chair at the University of Wales in Aberystwyth in 1936, and in 1939 he published his seminal *The Twenty Years' Crisis*, an influential monograph on post-Versailles international relations. Carr was Senior Research Fellow at Trinity, Cambridge, 1955–82, where he largely wrote the 14 volumes of his *A History of Soviet Russia* (1950–78), in which he was assisted by, among others, Tamara Deutscher, widow of the biographer Isaac Deutscher. His polemical Trevelyan lectures at Cambridge, published as *What Is History?* (1961), led to a debate with IB, one of his principal targets, in the pages of the *Listener*: 'harsh though the language of our controversy occasionally grows […], our personal relations happily are unaltered and continue to be affectionate and excellent' (IB to H. P. Simon, 27 May 1971).

Cecil, Lord (Edward Christian) David (Gascoyne) (1902–86), son of the 4th Marquess of Salisbury, and grandson of the 3rd Marquess (Prime Minister

1885–86, 1886–92, 1895–1902); Fellow of Wadham 1924–30, New College 1939–69; Goldsmiths' Professor of English Literature, Oxford, 1948–69. Cecil published and lectured mostly on eighteenth- and nineteenth-century English writers. On assuming the Goldsmiths' chair Cecil caused widespread anger, and jeopardised his long friendship with IB, by threatening to resign if Humphry House (1908–55), a respected literary scholar, was appointed his successor at New College. He favoured instead a gentleman amateur, John Buxton (1912–1989) – perhaps better remembered as an ornithologist than as English Literature Fellow at New College 1949–79. L1 706, L2 789.

Crossman, Richard (Howard Stafford) (1907–74), Labour politician and diarist; Fellow and Tutor in Philosophy, New College, 1930–7; leader of the Labour group, Oxford City Council, 1934–40; elected MP for Coventry East in the Labour land-slide of 1945, holding the seat until February 1974. As a member of the Anglo-American Palestine Commission in 1946, Crossman became a close friend of Chaim Weizmann, and a convert to Zionism, and, according to Lord Boothby, his efforts in support of this cause 'seriously retarded' his political career (sup-plement to obituary *The Times*, 15 April 1974, 8g). According to *The Times*, Crossman provided 'a classic illustration of the strength and limitations of the intellectual in politics, and more especially in Labour politics' (6 April 1974, 16e). Distrusted by Attlee, and suspected by the party at large for his middle-class roots – he was a Wykehamist – he spent nineteen years on the backbenches. His ministerial chance came when Harold Wilson, whose 1963 leadership campaign Crossman had effectively managed, formed his first administration in October 1964: Crossman was Minister of Housing and Local Government 1964–6; Leader of the House and Lord President of the Council 1966–8; Secretary of State for Social Services 1968–70. He was also editor of the *New Statesman* 1970–2. IB had a difficult relationship with Crossman, and wrote to Stephen Spender shortly after his death that he was 'a friend one didn't really care for' (9 April 1974). L1 707.

Drogheda, Garrett (1910–89) né (Charles) Garrett Ponsonby Moore, 11th Earl of Drogheda 1957; newspaper proprietor and opera manager; owner, and man-aging director 1945–70, of the *Financial Times*, chairman 1971–5; secretary to the board, ROH, 1951–8, chairman 1958–74. Drogheda's 'handsome looks and languid appearance concealed an iron determination to secure his ends' (Jeremy Isaacs, ODNB), and under his chairmanship Covent Garden flourished. He was legendary for dispatching pointed memoranda (the fabled 'Droghedagrams') to colleagues and employees, as well as to reviewers with whom he took issue: the unfortunate authors would receive their chastisement by motorcycle courier, early in the morning of the day that the review was due to appear: 'It was not unknown for them to be brought round, should the victim live close enough [...], by Drogheda himself, in slippers, pyjamas and dressing-gown' (ibid.). IB thought him 'a curious mixture of painstaking conscientiousness and aristo-cratic self-indulgence and impatience. But he does an excellent job and that is that' (to Jack Donaldson, 11 February 1963).

Fisher, Henry ('Harry') (Arthur Pears) (1918–2005), Kt 1968; barrister, judge and college head. The eldest son of an Archbishop of Canterbury, Fisher combined a brilliant legal practice – he was appointed QC in 1960 – with a fellowship at All

Souls 1946–73, where he also served as Estates Bursar 1961–6 and Sub-Warden 1965–7. In 1968 he became a Judge of the High Court of Justice, Queen's Bench Division, but soon found the work unsatisfying, and its social aspects uncongenial. His early resignation in 1970 proved controversial in the legal profession, not least because directly afterwards he took up a relatively lucrative City directorship (in fact legal convention forbade a direct return to the bar). He was director of J. Henry Schroder Wagg & Co. Ltd 1970–5, and of Schroder International Ltd 1973–5. However, in 1975 he left the City, returning to Oxford as IB's successor at Wolfson College, where he was President 1975–85.

Floud, Jean Esther (1915–2013), sociologist and college head; taught sociology at the University of London (LSE and Institute of Education) 1947–62; Official Fellow of Nuffield 1963–72; Commission of Inquiry into Oxford University (Franks Commission) 1964–6; UGC 1969–74; Social Science Research Council 1970–3; Principal, Newnham, Cambridge, 1972–83. She married, 1938, the civil servant Peter Floud (1911–60), who was alleged to have had connections with the Oxford spy ring to which Jenifer Hart (q.v.) had belonged. Her friend Robert Skidelsky described her in an obituary as 'one of Britain's leading educational sociologists', her career 'a triumph of brains, charm and presence over class and gender prejudice' (*Guardian*, 5 April 2013, 38). Jean Floud got to know IB through her work on the Franks Commission, had many intellectual interests in common with him, and became one of his closest friends. The present volume is dedicated to her memory.

Franks, Oliver Shewell (1905–92), Baron Franks of Headington 1962; philosopher and public servant. Franks was Fellow and Praelector in Philosophy at Queen's 1927–37, and was appointed Professor of Moral Philosophy at Glasgow in 1937. After war service in the Ministry of Supply he returned to Oxford as Provost of Queen's 1946–8, the only position 'that he ever really wanted' (Alex Danchev, ODNB), and spent a happy year there before being summoned again by the government, this time at the behest of the Foreign Secretary, Ernest Bevin, who needed him to co-ordinate the European response to the Marshall Plan. As Chairman of the Committee of European Economic Co-operation, June–September 1947, Franks melded the disparate interests of sixteen nations into a single report (with some involvement by IB: L1 35–9), and helped win Marshall's case in Washington. His reward was to be made HM Ambassador there 1948–52, a post in which he contributed to a second great feat of transatlantic bridge-building – the drafting, with Dean Acheson, of the inter-governmental accords that created NATO. Once this work was complete, Franks left the diplomatic world to become a Director of Lloyds Bank 1953–75 (Chairman 1954–62), and of Schroders 1969–84. He returned to Oxford as Provost of Worcester 1962–76, and in this capacity led the Commission of Inquiry into Oxford University 1964–6, which resulted in 'the Franks Report'. Franks was a man of immense moral authority and 'practical wisdom' (Danchev, ibid.), and IB relied heavily on his support for the Wolfson project during 1966: the following year Franks was made an Honorary Fellow of the new college. L2 791.

Graham, Katharine ('Kay') (1917–2001) née Meyer, newspaper publisher. Graham assumed the role of de facto publisher of the *Washington Post* after the suicide of her husband 'Phil' Graham in 1963; he had succeeded her father, Eugene Meyer, as publisher. Although she had a strong dynastic claim to run the *Post*, she lacked experience, in an era when very few women could expect to assume such a role; in the event she gave exceptionally strong leadership during a crucial period in the paper's history, backing her editors and reporters in their pursuit of the story that uncovered the Watergate conspiracy and led directly to the resignation of President Nixon. Later that year IB wrote to her: 'I hardly dared mention the fact that I knew you when, at a recent dinner [...], I was asked if I knew anyone of importance in Washington: it sounded like bold name-dropping' (4 November 1974). L2 791–2.

Halban, Hans Heinrich (1908–64), né von Halban, nuclear physicist. Married (1943–55) Aline Strauss née de Gunzbourg (*see* Berlin, Aline). Father of IB's stepsons, Peter and Philippe Halban. L2 792.

Halban, Peter Francis (b. 1946), publisher; Aline Berlin's second son, and IB's stepson. L2 792.

Halban, Philippe Alexandre (b. 1950), cell biologist specialising in diabetes; Aline Berlin's third and youngest son, and IB's stepson; Professor of Genetic Medicine and Development at the University of Geneva, Switzerland. L2 792.

Hampshire, (Grace Isabel) Renée (1909–80) née Orde-Lees, daughter of the explorer Colonel Thomas Orde-Lees, Royal Marines. She married (i) 1932 A. J. Ayer (q.v.) – they divorced in 1941; (ii) 1961, Stuart Hampshire (q.v.). IB considered that Renée Hampshire held her husband in thrall, and wrote to Aline on 23 October 1962, 'She *is* a monster' – a remark occasioned by his conviction that the Hampshires' move to the US, which he blamed squarely on Renée, would make his friend deeply unhappy; but on the surface, at least, relations between IB and Renée were cordial by the time that the Hampshires returned to Oxford in 1970.

Hampshire, Stuart Newton ('Hants') (1914–2004), philosopher. A Balliol classicist, Hampshire first came to know IB during the latter's fellowship at All Souls before the Second World War, and their friendship was lifelong; IB wrote, when recommending Hampshire to Teddy Kollek (q.v.): 'I think I probably like him best of anyone in England; so do be nice to him' (20 April 1959). Hampshire was Grote Professor of Mind and Logic at the University of London 1960–3, but left to take a chair at Princeton 1963–70, a move that IB firmly opposed, and subsequently did his best to reverse; Hampshire did return to England, and to Oxford, as Warden of Wadham, in succession to Maurice Bowra (q.v.), 1970–84. In 1961 Hampshire married Renée Ayer (q.v.), the former wife of his friend and colleague A. J. Ayer (q.v.), with whom he had had a long affair, which produced two children while the Ayers were still married; it was a liaison that IB never fathomed. L1 709, L2 792–3.

Hart, Herbert Lionel Adolphus (1907–92), legal philosopher and college head. Descended from nineteenth-century Polish and German Jewish immigrants, Hart read classics at New College 1926–9, and pursued a successful career at the Chancery Bar 1932–40. In 1941 he married Jenifer Williams (q.v.), and was recommended by her for work with MI5, where he served until the end of the Second World War. Influenced by her socialism, he gave up his well-paid legal practice after the war to become Fellow and Tutor in Philosophy, New College, 1945–52. He was Professor of Jurisprudence at Oxford 1952–68; Fellow of Univ. 1952–68, and Research Fellow 1969–73; Principal, Brasenose, 1973–8. Hart's dispute with Sir Patrick Devlin in the late 1950s over the extent to which criminal law should be employed to enforce a restrictive public morality – Hart opposed this notion – gave him a national prominence, and he was 'by common consent the outstanding British legal philosopher of the twentieth century' (Tony Honoré, ODNB); he declined a knighthood in 1966. Herbert and Jenifer Hart were among IB's closest, and oldest, Oxford friends. L1 710, L2 793.

Hart, Jenifer Margaret (1914–2005) née Williams, civil servant and historian. The daughter of a leading barrister, Jenifer Williams was from youth steeped in progressive principles, and before arriving at Somerville College, where she read modern history 1932–5, had already 'adopted a "humanistic hedonism" that owed much to Bloomsbury' (Margaret Howatson, *Independent*, 31 March 2005, 35). Shortly after leaving Oxford she joined the Communist Party, and was urged to join the Civil Service as a 'mole' or 'sleeper'; she was attached to the Home Office 1936–47. In 1941 she married Herbert Hart (q.v.), with whom she had lived since 1937: that she was given special dispensation to wed, in spite of the ban on women civil servants marrying, is a sign of the high regard in which she was held; she nevertheless left the Civil Service for Oxford when her husband became philosophy tutor at New College in 1945. She was Research Fellow, Nuffield, 1951–2, and Fellow and Tutor in History, St Anne's, 1952–81. An unguarded interview with the BBC in 1983 about her pre-war Communist Party associations caused aspersions to be cast on her loyalty, and, without any justification whatsoever, that of her husband, who suffered a nervous breakdown as a result; she rejected these allegations in her 1998 autobiography *Ask Me No More*. L1 722 (s.v. Williams), L2 793.

Kallin, Anna ('Niouta') (1896–1984), producer for BBC radio. Born in Moscow, and educated at Leipzig University 1912–19, Kallin arrived in England with her father in 1921, and worked as a literary freelancer until joining the BBC in June 1940. Her background and language skills were valuable assets for the newly created Monitoring Service, and she was initially based at Evesham and assigned to German broadcasts. In January 1946 she was made a producer in the Home Talks service, and was thus associated with the Third Programme from its inception; it was in this capacity that IB came to know her. 'She was an inspired producer of radio talks, a fearless exile who seemed to unite a British conception of public service with the Russian conception of the intellectual as a moral authority' (MI 204). L2 794.

Kollek, Theodor ('Teddy') (1911–2007), public administrator. Born in Hungary, and raised in a Zionist household in Vienna, Kollek emigrated to Palestine in 1935, and was centrally involved in the creation of the State of Israel, working for both the Haganah (199/4) and the Jewish Agency in Europe; after independence he was employed in the fledgling foreign ministry, and was Director-General of the Prime Minister Ben-Gurion's office 1952–64, and chair of the Government Tourist Corporation 1958–65; it was at Ben-Gurion's behest that he stood (reluctantly) for election as mayor of Jerusalem in 1965, an office that he held with distinction until 1993, presiding over the reunification of the city after the

Six-Day War in 1967. IB wrote: 'he is one of the few people in that country who behaved with warmth and understanding, real human feeling and intelligence to the Arabs in Jerusalem, and has, by this means, prevented much pain and much conflict' (to Karl Popper, 25 October 1972). L2 795.

Nabokov, Nicolas (1903–78) né Nikolay Dmitrievich, composer, teacher, writer and cultural ambassador; cousin of the novelist and poet Vladimir Nabokov. Like other members of the gentry, Nicolas Nabokov left post-Revolutionary Russia for the West, joining the exiles who gathered around Diaghilev and the Ballets russes in Paris; there he encountered Igor Stravinsky (q.v.), and his 1964 biography of the composer is in part a record of those days. Like Stravinsky, he settled in the US, becoming a naturalised citizen in 1939. He was a civilian cultural adviser to the American Military Government in Berlin 1945–7. As the Secretary General of the Congress for Cultural Freedom (CCF) 1951–63, Nabokov organised major cultural conferences and music festivals; when the CCF folded, after its covert funding from the CIA was exposed, Nabokov took a series of lectureships, notably at Princeton and CUNY. Explaining to Isaac Stern why he thought that Nabokov was not the right person to organise the 1964 Israel Music Festival, IB observed: 'If Nicolas were a masterful, ruthless Diaghilev-like genius who, by hook or crook, was able to impose his will upon his "indignant collaborators", the thing might work, although it would leave a good many corpses behind. But all the qualities for which we like him are incompatible with this kind of temperament. He is not a dictator: at the first sign of disagreement or discouragement, or obstacles whether justified or not, he falls into chronic despair and half understands the reason for them and half sympathises with them and in any case is not prepared to do enough trampling. He is not a walker over corpses' (26 April 1962). L2 795–6.

Schapiro, Meyer (1904–96), art historian, artist and polymath. From a Jewish Lithuanian background, Schapiro arrived in the US at the age of 3, and lived and worked in New York, a city with which he was closely identified. In 1928 he married the paediatrician Dr Lillian Milgram (1902–2006) – they had two children – and during the 1930s their home in Greenwich Village 'was much visited by members of the radical left' (John Russell, *New York Times*, 4 March 1996, D10). Schapiro taught art history at Columbia (from which he had graduated at the age of only 19) from 1928 until his retirement in 1973, and was, successively, professor 1952–65, University Professor 1965–73 and Emeritus Professor 1973–96. He enjoyed numerous other academic associations, and was Slade Professor of Fine Art at Oxford 1968. Schapiro was a teacher of great renown, whose special expertise lay in Romanesque sculpture and the art of the late nineteenth and the early twentieth centuries, but his approach was interconnected and inclusive: 'It was, in fact, the very essence of Schapiro that he never conceived of any aspect of art, of belief or of language in isolation' (ibid.). L1 715, L2 797.

Schlesinger, Arthur Meier, Jr (1917–2007), writer, academic and liberal political commentator; associate professor of history, Harvard, 1946–54, professor 1954–61; Albert Schweitzer Professor of the Humanities, CUNY, 1966–95, Emeritus Professor 1995–2007. Schlesinger took sabbaticals to work on the presidential campaigns of the Democratic candidate Adlai Stevenson in 1952 and 1956, but transferred his allegiance to John F. Kennedy in 1960, and left Harvard to become 'Special Assistant' to the new President 1961–3. He later campaigned on behalf of the deceased President's brother, Robert F. Kennedy, who sought the Democratic nomination in 1968. IB wrote of his old friend in 1967: 'poor Arthur has become the whipping-boy of every radical and every muckraker in America – I do not know what makes him such a target. I have just read a passionate and violent essay by a professor of linguistics and a genius in his own field [Noam Chomsky] on him in the *New York Review of Books*, which looks on him as an out-and-out scheming politician and fixer, and unfit to hold a chair, etc. I shall always defend him, for I am devoted to him, but in his own way he has made himself as unpopular as Joe – if they slew each other in mortal combat, not many would weep, even though your and my eyes would stream with genuine tears' (to Pamela Berry, 20 February 1967). L2 797–8.

Silvers, Robert Benjamin (b. 1929), founder co-editor, *New York Review of Books*. Silvers graduated from the University of Chicago in 1947 at the age of 19, and worked briefly as press secretary to the Democratic Connecticut governor Chester Bowles in 1950, before embarking on military service 1950–3. While based with the army at NATO headquarters in Paris he studied at the Sorbonne and the École polytechnique, and made the contacts that led to him becoming managing editor of the *Paris Review* 1954–8. In 1958 he returned to New York as associate editor of *Harper's Magazine*; he left *Harper's* in 1963, during a printing strike that had closed the *New York Times*, to co-found the *New York Review of Books* with Barbara Epstein (1928–2006), his co-editor until her death. IB first met Silvers in New York in 1964, and quickly came to value his friendship, not least for his reasoned objectivity: they visited Israel together at the end of 1969, when IB wrote to Edmund Wilson: 'We are here for our annual Xmas pilgrimage: accompanied this time by the sceptical and imaginative Bob Silvers: in 48 hours he has become a (perfectly reputable) authority on the entire situation despite a stern talking to by that tremendous Deborah – Mrs Golda Meir' (to Edmund Wilson, 28 December 1969).

Sparrow, John Hanbury Angus (1906–92), classicist, barrister, and Warden of All Souls 1952–77. Dominated 'to a profound degree' by his homosexuality (IB to John Lowe, 27 February 1989), Sparrow was a complex character – pugnacious, courageous, perverse, provocative, brilliant. By the early 1960s it had become clear, however, that he had no intention, as Warden, of seeking progressive solutions to the great challenges then facing higher education in Britain, and that, rather than attempt to place All Souls – one of Oxford's richest and most prestigious colleges – in the vanguard of reform, he would make of it a bastion against change. This became one of the principal reasons why IB was ready to leave the College, in spite of the many fond associations that it held for him, not least because of Sparrow himself. L1 716–17, L2 798.

Strauss, Michel Jules (b. 1936), Aline Berlin's first son, IB's stepson, and the director of the Impressionist and Modern Art Dept of Sotheby's 1961–2000, married Margery Tongway (b. 1932) in 1959 (divorced 2003). Author of *Pictures, Passions and Eye: A Life at Sotheby's* (2011).

Stravinsky, Igor Fedorovich (1882–1971), composer, conductor, pianist and writer. Born near St Petersburg in 1882, and a pupil of Rimsky-Korsakov, Stravinsky's collaborations with Diaghilev for the Ballets russes, notably *The Firebird* (1910) and *The Rite of Spring* (1913), placed him at the head of the musical avant-garde before the First World War, and he became one of the most influential and important composers of the twentieth century. After leaving Russia in 1914, he lived in Switzerland and France, before finally settling in America in 1939: he became a naturalised citizen in 1945. He married (i) 1906 his cousin Ekaterina ('Katya') Gavrilovna Nosenko (1880/1–1939); after her death he married (ii) 1940 Vera Arturovna Bosset-Shilling-Sudeikina (1888–1982) née Bosset, with whom he had begun an affair in 1921. IB greatly admired Stravinsky, and took pride in having suggested and supplied the libretto for his 'sacred ballad for baritone and orchestra' *Abraham and Isaac* (1962–3) (103).

Taylor, Alan John Percivale ('A. J. P.') (1906–90), historian; lecturer, Manchester, 1930–8; Tutor in Modern History, Magdalen, 1938–63, Fellow 1938–76. Taylor began his career researching diplomatic history in Vienna in 1928 (he could read five languages), and, in addition to a prodigious academic output, he wrote for the press, broadcast regularly on radio, and became one of the first 'telly dons'. His academic reputation was cemented with *The Struggle for Mastery in Europe, 1848–1918* (1954), but he was nevertheless passed over for the Regius Chair at Oxford in 1957 in favour of Hugh Trevor-Roper (q.v.), which embittered him, and may have contributed to the brilliantly paradoxical, and perverse, nature of some of his judgements. Satirising his style in a letter to Alan Bullock (11 January 1963), IB wrote: 'Taylor could show that Marxism had nothing to do with Lenin's wholly accidental idea that 1917 was a good time to make a revolution in Russia.' For his part, Taylor wrote to his wife Eva on 31 July 1981: 'It is strange to me how people fall for Isaiah. He is entertaining, he has an impressive manner, he implies that everything he says is profound, but what does it all amount to?' A. J. P. Taylor, *Letters to Eva: 1969–1983* (London, 1991), 438–9.

Taylor, Charles Margrave ('Chuck') (b. 1931), Canadian philosopher; graduate of Balliol; Fellow, All Souls, 1956–61; taught political theory at McGill 1961–76 (professor of philosophy 1973–6); also associated with the Département de philosophie, Montréal, 1963–71; later (1976–81) Chichele Professor of Social and Political Theory at Oxford – IB's successor but one.

Trevor-Roper, Hugh Redwald (1914–2003), later (1979) Baron Dacre of Glanton, historian; Regius Professor of Modern History at Oxford and Fellow of Oriel 1957–80; Master of Peterhouse, Cambridge, 1980–7. In 1954 he married Lady Alexandra Howard-Johnston (1907–97; 383/1), formerly the wife of Rear Admiral Clarence Howard-Johnston. IB wrote: 'I have read Edgar on Gombrich, and must say it is remorseless.[1] A real scorched earth operation. What a terrible hater he was. Reminiscent in some ways of Trevor-Roper's relentless polemics' (to Colin Hardie, 5 April 1973).

Utechin, Patricia ('Pat') (1927–2008) née Rathbone, IB's favourite and longest-serving private secretary, equally cherished by Aline Berlin. In Oxford she worked first for the economist John Hicks, then with Max Beloff at All Souls, but a falling-out

---

1 Edgar Wind had (in his victim's words) 'found it his duty to drag through the mud' Ernst Gombrich's biography of Aby Warburg (1970): see E. H. Gombrich, 'Two Minds', *LRB*, 5–18 April 1984, 4.

with Beloff in late 1961 led to her grateful acquisition by IB, who had long been 'fishing' for her (CV written by PU for Henry Hardy). IB was disconsolate when she moved to Glasgow with her husband Sergei in August 1965. In October 1970 she announced her intention to return to Oxford (IB replied that her letter 'made my day, week, month, year', 28 October 1970), and in April 1972, following an amicable separation from her husband, her happy association with IB was renewed. Pat's special skill was in managing, with great efficiency and aplomb, IB's academic and social arrangements, which were made chaotic by his frequent movements, the wide range of his interests, and his own (very readily admitted) disorganisation. Mother of the former BBC radio producer Nicholas ('Nick') Utechin, and occasional compiler of funerary Oxoniana, notably *Epitaphs from Oxfordshire* (1980).

Walicki, Andrzej (b. 1930 in Warsaw), son of the art historian Michał Walicki, studied at the universities of Łódź and Warsaw (PhD Warsaw 1957); assistant professor, Institute of Philosophy and Sociology, Polish Academy of Sciences, Warsaw, 1960–4, reader 1964–8, head, Dept of Modern Polish Philosophy and Social Thought, 1968–81, professor 1972–81; Visiting Fellow, All Souls, 1966–7; later (1986–99) first O'Neill Professor, Dept of History, Notre Dame. IB regarded Walicki as the leading authority on social and political ideas in Russia and Poland in the nineteenth and twentieth centuries, and wrote to George Weidenfeld on 5 September 1963:

> It seems to me that the country in which the most interesting ideological things are being said at present – and have been said for some time – is Poland. There is a great intellectual ferment there, and the conditions are just dangerous enough and just free enough to produce a critical mass with the resultant intellectual explosions. [...] I know Walicki, and he is a serious, fascinating, original and very brave man who goes to Moscow at regular intervals, is on the whole disapproved of there, but continues to be and to write and to influence.

Their relationship is described in Walicki's *Encounters with Isaiah Berlin: Story of an Intellectual Friendship* (Frankfurt am Main/Oxford, 2011). Six of his books were published by the Clarendon Press 1969–89.

Weizmann, Chaim (1874–1952), chemist and statesman, first President of Israel 1949–52. Born near Pinsk, Belorussia, in the Jewish pale of settlement, Weizmann was raised on Zionist principles from youth. He studied chemistry in Berlin, was awarded his doctorate at the University of Fribourg, Switzerland, and lectured at the University of Geneva, where he met his future wife Vera Chatzman (*see* Weizmann, Vera). In 1904 Weizmann took up a junior position at the University of Manchester, and was made Reader in 1913. Through his friendship with C. P. Scott, editor of the *Manchester Guardian*, he gained access to leading public figures, including A. J. Balfour, and his skilful advocacy of the Zionist cause was the driving force behind the Balfour Declaration of November 1917. This led directly to his being elected President of the Zionist Organization in 1920, a position that he held, with a hiatus (1931–5), until 1946. He played a major role in the founding of both the Hebrew University of Jerusalem and the Sieff (later Weizmann) Institute of Science at Rehovot. Weizmann, who became a naturalised British citizen in 1910, was strongly Anglophile, working for the British government during both World Wars, in the second of which he lost his son, Michael, a Flight-Lieutenant in the RAFVR. The Balfour Declaration initially appeared to justify his steadfast faith in the British government, but the subsequent vacillations in official British policy made his position untenable to a more radical generation of Zionists, and although he was elected the first President of Israel in 1949 he had for some time been effectively sidelined and denied an active role in politics. IB became an intimate friend of the Weizmanns when in Washington during the war, but although IB recognised Weizmann's genius, and defended his reputation against detractors, he also saw his limitations clearly: 'For all his anger with its shortcomings, Weizmann made the British connection the basis of his entire policy. When, in the end, he became convinced that he had been betrayed by Britain, this was the deepest wound, and, indeed, the central tragedy, of his life': IB, 'The Biographical Facts', in Meyer W. Weisgal and Joel Carmichael (eds), *Chaim Weizmann: A Biography by Several Hands* (London, 1962; New York, 1963), 26. L1 721, L2 799.

Weizmann, Vera (1881–1966) née Chatzman. Born in Russia, Vera married Chaim Weizmann – whom she had met while she was a medical student in Geneva – in England in 1906. In 1920 she was one of the co-founders of the Women's International Zionist Organization, and during the Second World War was involved in the Youth Aliyah movement. During and after Israel's war of independence she devoted herself to the rehabilitation of wounded soldiers. Some years after her death IB declined an invitation to write a conventional obituary: 'I should be ashamed of it, particularly before those who knew her as well as I did – nothing is more awful than all those references to "the gracious lady", her dignity, charm, wit, intelligence, independence of mind, humour etc. To tell the unvarnished truth will certainly not be appropriate to this occasion, even if I could bring myself to do it – at any rate the truth as it seemed to me – all that pride, snobbery, heartlessness, sentimentality, withering scorn, lack of love for the Jews, and everybody else, self-pity and false sentiment. I was very fond of her, in fact, and she was very nice to me, and we had excellent times together' (to Julian Meltzer, 19 August 1971). L2 799.

White, Morton Gabriel (b. 1917), philosopher, historian of ideas; Professor of Philosophy at Harvard 1953–70; at the Institute for Advanced Study, Princeton, 1970–87, Professor Emeritus 1987. In 1940 he married Lucia Perry (1909–96). For his long friendship with IB, which stimulated an extensive correspondence, see his autobiography, *A Philosopher's Story* (1999), especially chapter 17, 'Isaiah Berlin: A Bridge Between Philosophy and the History of Ideas'. L2 799.

Williams, Bernard Arthur Owen (1929–2003), philosopher; Fellow, All Souls, 1951–4, New College 1954–9; Lecturer in Philosophy at UCL 1959–64, Professor of Philosophy at Bedford College, London, 1964–7; Knightbridge Professor of Philosophy and Fellow of King's, Cambridge, 1967–79, Provost 1979–87. The brilliant promise of Williams's early career was realised during his Knightbridge Professorship at Cambridge, when he was closely involved in the governance of King's, and produced a series of major texts, beginning with *Morality* (1972); he was elected FBA in 1971. His philosophical outlook, in particular his rejection of all attempts to simplify the complexity of human experience, was temperamentally akin to that of IB, and they also shared a love of opera: Williams was a director of English National Opera (formerly Sadler's Wells Opera) 1968–86, and for a time chairman of its Opera Committee. He married (i) 1955 Shirley Vivienne Teresa Brittain Catlin (later Baroness Williams of Crosby), b. 1930; the marriage was dissolved in 1974; (ii) 1974 Patricia Law Skinner (b. 1942) née Dwyer, formerly senior commissioning editor in history and the social sciences at Cambridge University Press, later European editor for Harvard University Press, and publisher for the National Gallery in London. Bernard and Patricia Williams were intimate friends of the Berlins, and frequent visitors to their homes in Oxford and Italy.

Wolfson, Isaac (1897–1991), 1st Baronet 1962, businessman and philanthropist. Born and raised in a large Orthodox Jewish family in Glasgow – his impoverished parents had emigrated from Russian Poland in the 1890s – Isaac Wolfson assisted his father, a picture-framer, before setting up as a travelling salesman on his own account. In 1926 in London he married Edith (1907–81), daughter of Ralph Specterman; they had one son, Leonard (q.v.). In 1926 Wolfson was engaged as a buyer with the mail order business Universal Stores (from 1930, Great Universal Stores [GUS]), and thereafter made rapid progress in the company, becoming joint managing director in 1933, and chairman in 1946. He cleverly diversified the business, which became immensely profitable, and retained personal control by issuing only shares without voting rights. By the time of his death the stock-market value of GUS was some £3 billion; this phenomenal success 'was underpinned by the belief that the acquisition of wealth could be justified only if it contributed to the public good – a reflection of the Orthodox Jewish ethos in which he had been brought up' (Geoffrey Alderman, ODNB). In 1955 he established the Wolfson Foundation, with his wife and son as co-trustees: endowed with £6 million of GUS shares, it had as its objectives the advancement of health, education, the sciences and the humanities, and specialised in large infrastructure projects such as academic and research facilities. Isaac Wolfson was chairman of the Foundation 1963–72, president 1972–86, and honorary life president 1986–91. By 1991 its benefactions totalled some £130 million, including two sizeable endowments that made possible the foundation of postgraduate colleges – both bearing the family name – in Oxford (1966) and Cambridge (1977). In 1962 Wolfson became the first Orthodox holder of the presidency of the United Synagogue in London, his accession symbolising 'the transfer of power within Anglo-Jewry from the old, Anglicised families to the children of the Eastern-European immigrants of the late nineteenth century' (ibid.). He was created baronet in 1962 and, among numerous other honours, a Fellow of the Royal Society in 1963; a freeman of the city of Glasgow in 1971; Founder Fellow of Wolfson College, Oxford, 1967; Honorary Fellow of the Weizmann Institute of Science, Israel, 1959; he was not awarded the expected life peerage, but lived to see this honour accorded to his son in 1985.

Wolfson, Leonard Gordon (1927–2010), later (1985) life peer, businessman and philanthropist; the only child of Isaac (q.v.) and Lady (Edith) Wolfson; director of Great Universal Stores 1952–62; managing director 1962–81; joint chairman (with his father) 1981–6, sole chairman 1986–96; a founding trustee, with his parents, of the Wolfson Foundation 1955, and its chairman from 1972. Leonard Wolfson was keenly interested in history, and made prominent historians, such as J. H. Plumb and Alan Bullock (q.v.), trustees of the Wolfson Foundation. He also founded the annual Wolfson History Prize (in 1972). Inevitably compared and contrasted with his charismatic father, Leonard Wolfson had a reputation for shyness, though he was autocratic in his management style. He was knighted in 1977, and created a life peer, as Lord Wolfson of Marylebone, in 1985. He married (i) 1949 Ruth Sterling (marriage dissolved 1991); they had four daughters; (ii) 1991 Estelle (née Feldman), widow of Michael Jackson; one stepson, one stepdaughter. An observant Jew, Leonard Wolfson was president of the Jewish Welfare Board 1972–82, and supported a wide range of causes in Israel as well as in Britain. He continued his father's munificence towards Wolfson College, and a newly constructed lecture theatre there is named after him.

INDEX OF CORRESPONDENTS
AND SOURCES

Nicholas Hall

This index doubles as a reference list for those who wish to consult the originals (which are sometimes carbon copies or photocopies) of any of the letters included in this volume.

The source of a correspondent's letters is given in square brackets. The source is placed after the name, or, when there is only one letter in question, after the page number for that letter. If there is more than one source for a correspondent's letters, the main source appears after the name of the correspondent, and other sources after the relevant page number(s). If no source is given, the letter (or copy) was supplied by the relevant correspondent or his/her heir(s).

When both a top copy and a carbon of a letter were available, the source given is that of the top copy. When only a carbon was available, '[*carbon*]' is inserted in the text, after the date of the letter. In some cases, top copies are in the Isaiah Berlin Papers (in the Bodleian Library in Oxford), notably when a correspondent's letters were returned to Berlin after the death of the correspondent. Page numbers in italics show letters *to* Berlin.

Where archives have requested specific references, these are provided. Otherwise, except for the Isaiah Berlin Papers in the Bodleian, no specifics are given: these can usually be readily ascertained from the archive in question.

Abbreviations used in this index

[123/4]	Oxford, Bodleian Library, MS. Berlin (by shelfmark/folio)
Beinecke	Beinecke Library, Yale
Bodleian	Bodleian Library, Oxford
Chatto	Chatto and Windus Archive, Reading University
Codrington	Codrington Library, All Souls College, Oxford
CT	'connective tissue', i.e. editorial commentary
Ford	Ford Foundation, New York
ISA	Israel State Archives
LOC	Library of Congress
JFK	John F. Kennedy Library, Boston
NGA	National Gallery of Art, Washington
NUL	National and University Library of Israel, Jerusalem
NYPL	New York Public Library
PSF	Paul Sacher Foundation, Basel
ROH	Royal Opera House Archives, Covent Garden
WCA	Wolfson College Archive, Oxford
Weizmann	Weizmann Archives, Rehovot, Israel

GENERAL INDEX

Vicki Robinson

References in italics are to pages where a note provides basic biographical information on a person. An asterisk preceding a name indicates an entry in the Glossary. Works by IB appear under their titles, works by others under their authors' names. The Chronology is not indexed.